Western Civilization

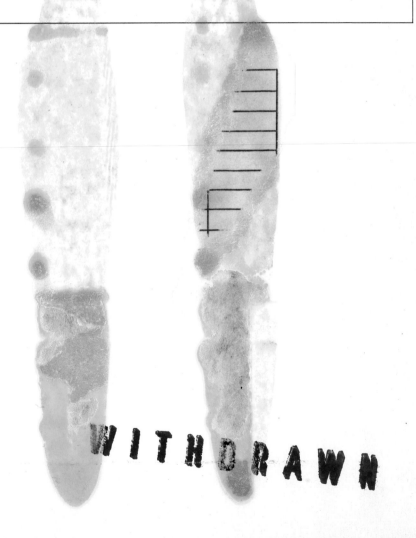

Western Civilization

Ideas, Politics & Society   Second Edition

Marvin Perry
Baruch College, City University of New York

Myrna Chase
Baruch College, City University of New York

James R. Jacob
John Jay College of Criminal Justice, City University of New York

Margaret C. Jacob
Baruch College, City University of New York

Theodore H. Von Laue
Clark University

George W. Bock, Editorial Associate

Houghton Mifflin Company   Boston

Dallas   Geneva, Illinois   Lawrenceville, New Jersey   Palo Alto

The following authors are members of The Institute for Research in History: Marvin Perry, Myrna Chase, James R. Jacob, and Margaret C. Jacob.

Copyright © 1985 by Houghton Mifflin Company. All Rights Reserved.

Printed in the U.S.A.

Library of Congress Catalog Card Number: 84-61367

ISBN: 0-395-35957-0

Credits

Cover: *Landscape with Picnic,* by L. V. Valckenborch, *Kunsthistorische Museum, Vienna*

Chapter Opening Photographs
Chapter 1: Detail, *Tomb of Nakht*; The Metropolitan Museum of Art, New York. *Chapter 2:* Arch of Titus, Rome; Ewing Galloway, New York. *Chapter 3:* Mycenaean mask; Robert Harding Picture Library. *Chapter 4:* Theater at Epidaurus; Bildarchiv Foto Marburg. *Chapter 5:* Coin of Alexander; Courtesy of The American Numismatic Society, New York. *Chapter 6:* Roman warship, relief; Vatican/Alinari/Art Resource. *Chapter 7:* Pont du Gard, Nîmes; Jean Roubier/Rapho. *Chapter 8:* Ivory panel of the crucifixion; The Granger Collection. *Chapter 9:* Coronation of Charlemagne; Scala/Art Resource. *Chapter 10:* Medieval street scene; Bibliothèque de l'Arsenal/Bibliothèque Nationale, Paris. *Chapter 11:* West doors, Chartres Cathedral; Jean Roubier. *Chapter 12:* The Jacquerie; Bibliothèque Nationale, Paris. *Chapter 13:* Palladio: Villa Rotonda; Alinari/Art Resource. *Chapter 14:* Rembrandt: *Family Portrait,* c. 1668; Herzog Anton Ulrich-Museum, Braunschweig;

photo B. P. Keiser. *Chapter 15:* Velde: *Dutch Man-of-War Saluting*; The Wallace Collection. *Chapter 16:* Versailles; French Government Tourist Office. *Chapter 17:* Louis XIV at French Academy of Sciences; Courtesy Burndy Library. *Chapter 18:* Winter Palace, St. Petersburg; William Brumfield. *Chapter 19:* Le Nain: *Peasant Family*; Louvre/Cliché des Musées Nationaux. *Chapter 20:* Retreat from Moscow; Photo Flammarion. *Chapter 21:* Anon., Pithead of coal mine; Walker Art Gallery, Liverpool. *Chapter 22:* Constable: *Salisbury Cathedral*; Copyright The Frick Collection, New York. *Chapter 23:* Daumier: *Rue Transnonain*; Philadelphia Museum of Art: Bequest of Fiske and Marie Kimball. *Chapter 24:* Courbet: *Proudhon and His Daughters*; Historical Pictures Service, Chicago. *Chapter 25:* Victor Emmanuel and Garibaldi at the Bridge of Teano, 1860; Scala/Art Resource. *Chapter 26:* Monet: *Gare St. Lazare*; Courtesy of the Fogg Art Museum, Harvard University, Bequest-Collection of Maurice Wertheim, Class of 1906. *Chapter 27:* Empress Eugénie at opening of Suez Canal; BBC Hulton Picture Library/Bettmann Archive. *Chapter 28:* Van Gogh: *Public Garden at Arles*; The Phillips Collection, Washington. *Chapter 29:* William II reviewing troops; BBC Hulton Picture Library/Bettmann Archive. *Chapter 30:* Munitions workers; Brown Brothers. *Chapter 31:* Collective farm, 1929; UPI/Bettmann Archive. *Chapter 32:* Nazi party rally, 1933; AP/Wide World Photos. *Chapter 33:* Dali: *The Persistence of Memory*; Collection, The Museum of Modern Art, New York. *Chapter 34:* St. Paul's Cathedral in London Blitz; Associated Newspapers/Pictorial Parade. *Chapter 35:* Big Three at Yalta; National Archives. *Chapter 36:* Khrushchev in Iowa, 1959; UPI/Bettmann Archive. *Chapter 37:* McDonald's, Hong Kong; Robert Harding Picture Library.

Text Credits
Page 16: Egyptian poem: From Adolf Ehrman, Editor, *The Ancient Egyptians,* by permission of Methuen & Co., publishers.
Page 19: From John A. Wilson, *The Culture of Ancient Egypt* (1951). Reprinted by permission of the publisher, The University of Chicago Press. Copyright © 1951 by The University of Chicago. *Chapter 2:* The biblical excerpts in Chapter 2 are taken from The Holy Scriptures, published in 1917

Continued after page 868.

BCDEFGHIJ-RM-898765

Contents

II The Middle Ages: The Christian Centuries 500–1450

IV An Age of Revolution: Liberal, National, Industrial 1789–1848

List of Maps

Preface

Western civilization is a grand but tragic drama. The West has forged the instruments of reason that make possible a rational comprehension of physical nature and human culture, conceived the idea of political liberty, and recognized the intrinsic worth of the individual. But the modern West, though it has unravelled nature's mysteries, has been less successful at finding rational solutions to social ills and conflicts between nations. Science, the great achievement of the Western intellect, while improving conditions of life, has also produced weapons of mass destruction. Though the West has pioneered in the protection of human rights, it has also produced totalitarian regimes that have trampled on individual freedom and human dignity. And although the West has demonstrated a commitment to human equality, it has also practiced brutal racism.

Despite the value that Westerners have given to reason and freedom, they have shown a frightening capacity for irrational behavior and a fascination for violence and irrational ideologies, and they have willingly sacrificed liberty for security or national grandeur. The world wars and totalitarian movements of the twentieth century have demonstrated that Western civilization, despite its extraordinary achievements, is fragile and perishable.

Western Civilization: Ideas, Politics, and Society examines the Western tradition—those unique patterns of thought and systems of values that constitute the Western heritage. While focusing on key ideas and important issues, the text also provides a balanced treatment of economic, political, and social history for students in Western civilization courses.

Every chapter for the second edition has been reworked to some extent. Several major structural changes have been made. The section on Byzantium and Islam in Chapter 9, "The Rise of Europe," has been enlarged. Chapter 16, "The Rise of Sovereignty," has been reorganized to give it a more straightforward chronology. Additional political and diplomatic developments have been included in Chapter 18, "The Age of Enlightenment," along with a new section on the American Revolution. Chapter 21, "The Industrial Revolution," has been resituated from later in the text. Two new chapters on intellectual history have been added: Chapter 24, "Thought and Culture in the Mid-Nineteenth Century," and Chapter 33, "Thought and Culture in an Era of World Wars." Chapter 26, "Industrial Europe," has an added section on Austria-Hungary between 1866 and 1914. Chapter 28, "Modern Consciousness," contains a new section on modernism in the arts and a rewritten and enlarged section on modern physics. The final three chapters in the text—"Western Europe Since 1945," "Eastern Europe Since 1945," and "Globalism"—have been updated to take into account new political forces in Western Europe and give some attention to the post-Brezhnev years in the Soviet Union and to recent developments in Poland and the Middle East.

The text contains several pedagogical features. Chapter introductions provide comprehensive overviews of key themes and give a sense of direction and coherence to the flow of history. Many chapters contain concluding essays that treat the larger meaning of the material. Facts have been carefully selected to illustrate key relationships and concepts and to avoid overwhelming students with unrelated and disconnected data. Appropriate quotations, many not commonly found in texts, have been integrated into the discussion. The art program has been amplified, with many new photographs and several new maps. Four essays link crucial periods in the history of art and architecture to their wider cultural setting; these essays have been revised and added to, and now incorporate color photographs. Each chapter contains an annotated bibliography and review questions that refer students to principal points. More questions have been added in this edition, with an emphasis on eliciting thoughtful answers, rather than memorized facts.

The text is written with the conviction that history is not a meaningless tale. Without a knowledge of history, men and women cannot fully know themselves, for all human beings have been shaped by institutions and values inherited from the past. Without an awareness of the historical evolution of reason and freedom, the dominant ideals of Western civilization, commitment to these ideals will diminish. Without a knowledge of history, the West cannot fully comprehend or adequately cope with the problems that burden its civilization and the world.

In attempting to make sense out of the past, the authors have been careful to avoid superficial generalizations that oversimplify historical events and forces and arrange history into too neat a structure. But we have striven to interpret and to synthesize in order to provide students with a frame of reference with which to comprehend the principal events and eras in Western history.

Western Civilization: Ideas, Politics, and Society is available in both one- and two-volume editions. Volume I of the two-volume edition treats the period from the first civilizations in the Near East through the Age of Enlightenment in the eighteenth century (18 chapters). Volume II covers the period from the growth of nation-states in the seventeenth century to the contemporary age (22 chapters). Because some instructors start the second half of their course with the period prior to the French Revolution, Volume II incorporates the last three chapters of Volume I: "The Rise of Sovereignty," "The Scientific Revolution," and "The Age of Enlightenment." Volume II also contains a compre-

hensive introduction that surveys the ancient world, the Middle Ages, and the opening centuries of the modern era; the introduction is designed particularly for students who did not take the first half of the course.

The text represents the efforts of several authors. Marvin Perry, general editor of the project, wrote Chapters 1–12, 19, 20, 22–25, 28–30, and 32–34. James R. Jacob is the author of Chapters 13 and 15. Margaret C. Jacob provided Chapters 14 and 16–18. Myrna Chase wrote Chapters 21, 26–27, and the section on reform in Britain in Chapter 23. Theodore H. Von Laue is the author of Chapters 31, 35–37, and the section on Russia in Chapter 26. The four art essays were written by Katherine Crum, and some of the material on Gothic cathedrals and modern art that she wrote for the first edition has been incorporated into the text. Marvin Perry and George Bock edited the manuscript for clarity and continuity.

The authors would like to thank the following instructors for their critical reading of sections of the manuscript:

Melvin S. Amov, *Grossmont College*
Leon Apt, *Iowa State University*
John W. Bohnstedt, *California State University, Fresno*
Werner Braatz, *University of Wisconsin, Oshkosh*
James B. Briscoe, *University of Arkansas, Fayetteville*
Ronald D. Cassell, *University of North Carolina, Greensboro*
Ron Doviak, *Borough of Manhattan Community College*
Leonard Greenspoon, *Clemson University*
Charles D. Hamilton, *San Diego State University*
Alexandra S. Korros, *Miami University, Hamilton*
Lyle E. Linville, *Prince George's Community College*
David MacDonald, *Illinois State University*
Robert Michael, *Southeastern Massachusetts University*
Algis Mickunas, *Ohio University*

Howard Negrin, *Baruch College, City University of New York*

William E. Painter, *North Texas State University*

Richard Pierard, *Indiana State University*

Paul Pinckney, *University of Tennessee, Knoxville*

Kenneth W. Rock, *Colorado State University*

Bernice Glatzer Rosenthal, *Fordham University*

Julius R. Ruff, *Marquette University*

Seymour Scheinberg, *California State University, Fullerton*

Donald J. Wilcox, *University of New Hampshire*

Many of their suggestions were incorporated into the final version. We are also grateful to the staff of Houghton Mifflin Company who lent their considerable talents to the project. I would like to express my personal gratitude to George Bock who assisted in the planning of the text from its inception and who read the manuscript with an eye for major concepts and essential relationships.

M.P.

Western Civilization

I

The Ancient World:
Foundation of the West

To A.D. 500

1

The Ancient Near East:
The First Civilizations

Civilization was not inevitable, it was an act of human creativity. The first civilizations emerged about 5,000 years ago, in the Near Eastern river valleys of Sumer and Egypt. Before that time stretched the vast ages of prehistory, when our ancestors did not dwell in cities and knew nothing of writing. Today, when civilization is threatened by a nuclear holocaust, we might reflect on humanity's long and painful climb to a civilized state.

The Rise to Civilization

The Paleolithic Age

In recent decades anthropologists and archaeologists have made important discoveries that have shed light on the prehistoric past. Richard E. Leakey speculates about one such find in East Africa:

Close to three million years ago on a campsite near the east shore of Kenya's spectacular Lake Turkana, formerly Lake Rudolf, a primitive human picked up a water-smoothed stone, and with a few skillful strikes transformed it into an implement. What was once an accident of nature was now a piece of deliberate technology, to be used to fashion a stick for digging up roots, or to slice the flesh off a dead animal. Soon discarded by its maker, the stone tool still exists, an unbreakable link with our ancestors.[1]

The period called the Paleolithic Age, or Old Stone Age, began with the earliest primitive tool-making human beings who inhabited East Africa nearly 3 million years ago. It ended 11,000 to 10,000 years ago in parts of the Near East when people discovered how to farm. Our Paleolithic ancestors lived as hunters and food gatherers. Because they had not learned how to farm, they never established permanent villages. When their food supplies ran short, they abandoned their caves or tentlike structures of branches and searched for new dwelling places.

Human social development was shaped by this 3-million-year experience of hunting and food gathering. For survival, groups of families formed bands consisting of around thirty people; members learned how to plan, organize, cooperate, trust, and share. The men hunted for meat, and the women cared for the young, tended the fires, and gathered fruits, nuts, berries, and grain. Hunters assisted each other in tracking and killing game, finding cooperative efforts more successful than individual forays. By sharing their kill and bringing some back to their camp for the rest of the group, they reinforced the social bond. Bands that did not cooperate in the hunt or distribute meat to everyone were unlikely to survive.

Hunting and food gathering also stimulated mental and physical development. Food gatherers had to know which plants were safe to eat and where to find them. Hunting required strength, speed, good eyesight and hearing, and mental ability. Hunters had to study and analyze the habits of their prey, judge weather conditions, recall the location of dens and watering places, and make better tools and weapons. The physically weak and mentally deficient, unable to track animals and to cope with new problems, did not survive long. Individuals with superior intelligence and physical qualities lived longer and had more opportunities to mate, passing on their characteristics and gradually improving the human species.

Although human progress was very slow during the long centuries of the Paleolithic Age, developments occurred that influenced the future enormously. Paleolithic people developed spoken language and learned how to make and use tools. Both accomplishments are evidence of behavior that sets human beings apart from other creatures. To be sure, primates such as apes and chimpanzees utter sounds that express emotions, but they cannot give a name to an object or describe things. And although chimpanzees use a twig as a tool to get at insects, they do not save it for future use nor progress in their toolmaking from generation to generation.

Paleolithic people, on the other hand, shaped bone, wood, and stone tools that corresponded to ideas in their minds. They preserved their creations and taught other people how to use them. Succeeding generations improved on what they had learned from their ancestors. With these simple but useful tools, Paleolithic human beings dug up roots, peeled the bark off trees, trapped, killed, and skinned animals, made clothing, and fashioned fishnets. They also discovered how to control fire, which allowed them to cook their meat, and provided warmth and protection.

Like toolmaking, language was a great human achievement. Language enabled individuals to share their knowledge, experiences, and feelings with each other. Thus, language was the decisive factor in the development of culture and its transmission from one generation to the next. Language helped parents teach their children rules of conduct and religious beliefs, as well as how to make tools and light fires.

Most likely, our Paleolithic ancestors developed mythic-religious beliefs to explain the mysteries of nature, birth, sickness, and death. To primitive peoples, the elements—sun, rain, wind, thunder, and lightning—were alive. The natural elements had spirit; they could feel and act with a purpose. To appease them, hunters and gatherers made offerings to these forces of nature. Gradually shamans, medicine men, and witch doctors emerged who, through rituals, trances, and chants, seemed able to communicate with these spirits. Also, Paleolithic people began the practice of burying their dead, sometimes with offerings, which suggests belief in life after death. Another belief is shown in the many small statues of women, made between 40,000 and 25,000 years ago, that have been found by archaeologists in Europe and Asia; fashioned from ivory, wood, and clay and often marked by huge breasts and distended stomachs, these fertility figurines represent a mother goddess who gave life, food, and protection.

Between 30,000 and 12,000 years ago, Paleolithic people sought out the dark and silent interior of caves and, with only torches for light, they painted remarkably skillful and perceptive pictures of animals on the cave walls. When these prehistoric artists drew an animal with a spear in its side, they probably believed that this act would make them successful in hunting; when they drew a herd of animals, they probably hoped that this would cause game to be plentiful.

The Neolithic Revolution

Some 10,000 to 11,000 years ago, the New Stone Age or Neolithic Age began in the Near East. During the Neolithic Age, human beings discovered farming, domesticated animals, established villages, polished stone tools, made pottery, and wove cloth. So important were these achievements that they are referred to as the Neolithic Revolution.

Agriculture—the deliberate planting and cultivation of crops—first developed in the hilly regions of the Near East, where wheat and barley grew abundantly in the wild. People there also began to domesticate the sheep and wild goats that roamed the hills. In other parts of the world, farming and the domestication of animals developed independently.

Agriculture and the domestication of animals revolutionized life. Whereas Paleolithic hunters and food gatherers had been forced to use whatever nature made available to them, Neolithic farmers altered their environment to satisfy human needs. Instead of spending their time searching for grains, roots, and berries, women and children grew crops near their homes; instead of tracking animals over great distances, men could slaughter domesticated goats or sheep nearby. Farming made possible a new kind of community. Because hunters needed to roam over large areas, hunting bands were by necessity small. If the band grew too large, some members formed a new band and moved on. In contrast, several hundred or even several thousand people might live in a farming community.

Since farmers had to live near their fields and could store food for the future, farming led to the rise of permanent settlements. Villages containing as many as 200 or 300 people had emerged in late Paleolithic times, before the discovery of agriculture. Hunter-gatherers built such villages in areas that had an abundant, stable food supply—near a river or lake well stocked with fish, or in a valley with plenty of wild wheat and barley and herds of gazelles or goats. The development of farming greatly speeded the shift to villages. It is likely that trade also impelled people to gather in village communities. Herdsmen, hunters, and food gatherers living in regions rich in salt (needed for preserving food), volcanic glass (used for mirrors, blades, and spearheads), or hematite (an iron ore that was a source of red coloring for pottery) formed trading settlements that exchanged raw materials for food.

Villages changed the patterns of life. A food surplus freed some people to devote part of their time to sharpening their skills as basket weavers or toolmakers. The demand for raw materials and the creations of skilled artisans fostered trade and the formation of trading settlements. An awareness of private property emerged. Hunters had accumulated few possessions, since belongings only presented a burden when moving from place to place. Villagers, however, acquired property that they were determined to protect from each other and from outsiders who might raid the village. Hunting bands were egalitarian; generally, no one member had more possessions or more power than another. In farming villages, a ruling elite emerged that possessed wealth and wielded power.

In recent years, archaeologists have uncovered several Neolithic villages, the oldest of which was established before 8000 B.C. Among the most famous of these sites are Çatal Hüyük in Anatolia (Turkey), Jericho in Palestine, and Jarmö in eastern Iraq. Scholars disagree on whether these communities were just highly developed villages or whether they were the first cities. The traditional view is that cities arose about 3000 B.C. in Sumer, the home of the earliest civilization. Some scholars argue that 5,000 years before the Sumerian cities, Jericho's 2,000 inhabitants had created urban life by engaging in trade and embarking on public works. Jericho's walls were 6 feet 6 inches thick at the base and in some places 20 feet high. Their construction required cooperation and a division of labor beyond the capacity of an agricultural village. Similar communities, or "primitive cities," spread throughout much of the Near East in late prehistoric times.

Neolithic people made great strides in technology. By shaping and baking clay, they made pottery containers for cooking and for storing food and water. The invention of the potter's wheel enabled them to form bowls and plates more quickly and precisely. Stone tools were sharpened by grinding them on rock. The discoveries of the wheel and the sail improved transportation and promoted trade while the development of the plow and the ox yoke made tilling the soil easier for farmers.

The Neolithic period also marks the beginning of the use of metals. First used was copper, which was easily fashioned into tools and weapons. Implements made from copper lasted longer than those made of stone and flint, and they could be recast and reshaped if broken. In time, artisans discovered how to make bronze by combining copper and tin in the proper ratio. Bronze was harder than copper, which made a sharper cutting edge possible.

During the Neolithic Age, the food supply became more reliable, village life expanded, and the population increased. Families that acquired wealth gained a higher social status and became village leaders. Religion grew more formal and structured; nature spirits evolved into deities, each with specific powers over nature or human life. Altars were erected in their honor, and ceremonies were conducted by priests, whose power and wealth increased as people gave offerings to the gods. Neolithic society was growing more organized and complex; it was on the threshold of civilization.

The First Civilizations

What we call *civilization* arose some 5,000 years ago in the Near East (in Mesopotamia and Egypt) and then later in the Far East (in India and China). The first civilizations began in cities that were larger, more populated, and more complex in their political, economic, and social structure than Neolithic villages. Because the cities depended on the inhabitants of adjacent villages for their food, farming techniques must have been developed sufficiently to produce food surpluses. Increased production provided food for urban inhabitants who engaged in nonagricultural occupations—merchants, craftsmen, bureaucrats, and priests.

The invention of writing enabled the first civilizations to preserve, organize, and expand knowledge; it allowed government officials and priests to conduct their affairs with greater efficiency. Civilized societies also possessed organized governments that issued laws and defined the boundary lines of their states. On a scale much larger than Neolithic communities, the inhabitants erected buildings and monuments, engaged in trade, and used specialized labor for different projects. Religious life grew more organized and complex, and a powerful and wealthy priesthood emerged. These developments—cities, specialization of labor, writing, organized government, monumental architecture, and a complex religious structure—differentiate the first civilizations from prehistoric cultures.

Religion was the central force in these primary civilizations. It provided satisfying explanations for the operations of nature, helped to ease the fear of death, and justified traditional rules of morality. Law was considered sacred, a commandment of the gods. Religion united people in the common enterprises needed for survival—for example, the construction and maintenance of irrigation works and the storage of food. Religion also promoted creative achievements in art, literature, and science. In addition, the power of rulers, who were regarded either as gods or as agents of the gods, derived from religion.

The emergence of civilization was a great creative act and not merely the inevitable development of agricultural societies. Many communities had learned how to farm, but only a handful made the leap into civilization. How was it possible for Sumerians and Egyptians, the creators of the earliest civilizations, to make this breakthrough? This question has intrigued and baffled historians, and no single explanation is entirely convincing. Most scholars stress the relationship between civilizations and river valleys. Rivers deposited fertile silt on adjoining fields, provided water for crops, and served as avenues for trade. But environmental factors alone do not adequately explain the emergence of civilization. What cannot be omitted is the human contribution—capacity for thought and cooperative activity.

Both the Tigris and Euphrates rivers in Mesopotamia and the Nile River in Egypt deposited fertile soil when they overflowed their banks. But before these rivers could be of any value in producing crops, swamps around them had to be drained, and dikes, reservoirs, and canals had to be built. To construct and maintain irrigation works required the cooperation of large numbers of people, a necessary condition for civilization. As anthropologist Robert J. Braidwood says:

It was not only a business of learning to control the rivers and making their waters do the farmer's work. It also meant controlling men. . . . This learning to work together for the common good was probably the real germ of the Egyptian and the Mesopotamian civilizations.[2]

In the process of constructing and maintaining irrigation networks, people learned to obey rules and developed administrative, engineering, and mathematical skills. The need to keep records stimulated the invention of writing. These creative responses to the challenges posed by nature spurred the early inhabitants of Sumer and Egypt to make the breakthrough to civilization, thereby altering the course of human destiny. By the time the Hebrews and the Greeks, the spiritual

Soundbox of Lyre from Ur. This soundbox, made of wood, gold, and lapis lazuli about 2600 B.C., suggests the artistic achievements of the Sumerians in the visual, musical, and literary realms. Animal motifs were a characteristic feature of ancient Near Eastern art. (*Reproduced by permission of The University Museum, University of Pennsylvania*)

ancestors of Western civilization, appeared on the stage of history, civilizations had been in existence for some two thousand years.

Civilization not only brought benefits, it also gave people the capacity to organize for destructive enterprises. The power generated by technology, the authority exercised by leaders, and the habits of discipline learned by the communities' inhabitants led to warfare, as well as to irrigation works. Lewis Mumford observes:

. . . War was not a mere residue of more common primitive forms of aggression. . . . In all its typical aspects, its discipline, its drill, its handling of large masses of men as units, in its destructive assaults en masse, in its heroic sacrifices, its final destructions, exterminations, seizures, enslavements, war was rather the special invention of civilization: its ultimate drama.[3]

The practice of warfare developed by the first civilizations has never been eradicated.

Mesopotamian Civilization

Mesopotamia is the Greek word for "land between the rivers." It was here, in the valleys of the Tigris and Euphrates rivers, where the first civilization began. The first to develop an urban civilization in Mesopotamia were the Sumerians, who colonized the marshlands of the lower Euphrates which, joined by the Tigris, flows into the Persian Gulf. The origin of the Sumerians is obscure; they spoke a language unrelated to the tongues of their Semitic neighbors who had migrated from Arabia into Mesopotamia and adjacent regions.

Through constant toil and imagination, the Sumerians transformed the swamps into fields of barley and groves of date palms. Their hut settlements gradually evolved into twelve independent city-states, each consisting of a city and its surrounding countryside. Among the impressive achievements of the Sumerians

were a system of symbol writing on clay tablets (cuneiform) to represent ideas; elaborate brick houses, palaces, and temples; bronze tools and weapons; irrigation works; trade with other peoples; an early form of money; religious and political institutions; schools; religious and secular literature; varied art forms; codes of law; medicinal drugs; and a lunar calendar.

Although they spoke a common language and shared the same customs and gods, the Sumerian city-states engaged in frequent warfare with each other, principally over boundaries and water rights. Weakened by warfare, the Sumerians lay open to foreign domination.

The history of Mesopotamia is marked by a succession of conquests. To the north of Sumer was a Semitic city called Akkad. About 2350 B.C., the people of Akkad, led by Sargon the Great, the warrior king, conquered the Sumerian cities. He built the world's first empire, which extended from the Persian Gulf to the Mediterranean Sea. The Akkadians adopted Sumerian cultural forms and spread them beyond the boundaries of Mesopotamia with their conquests. Mesopotamian religion became a blend of Sumerian and Akkadian elements.

Around 2180 B.C., invasions by the Guti, a semibarbaric people from Iran, along with internal dissension, caused the Akkadian empire to collapse. In the ensuing period, the Sumerian cities, though they paid tribute to the Guti, enjoyed a large measure of independence. Gutian power was short-lived, and a century later, the Sumerian city-state of Ur was able to assert its dominion over Sumer and Akkad.

From about 2135 to 2027 B.C., Sumer experienced economic expansion and cultural growth. Sumer extended its control northward into Assyria, Elam, and northwestern Mesopotamia. During this period, Sumer launched an extensive temple-building program, Sumerian literature reached its peak, and a code of laws was formed, a predecessor to the famous code of Hammurabi. But assaults by the Semitic Amorites from the

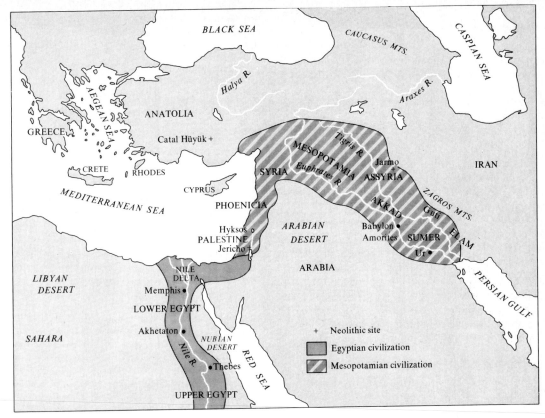

Map 1.1 Mesopotamian and Egyptian Civilizations

northeast and Elamites from Iran led to the disintegration of Sumerian power.

During the period of anarchy and war that followed, the Amorite city Babylon, northwest of Sumer on the Euphrates, became independent. Later, one of its rulers, Hammurabi (1792–1750 B.C.), launched conquests that brought Akkad and Sumer under his control.

During the centuries that followed, the Sumerian cities were incorporated into various kingdoms and empires. The Sumerian language, replaced by a Semitic tongue, became an obscure language known only to priests, and the Sumerians gradually disappeared as a distinct people. But their cultural achievements endured. Akkadians, Babylonians, Elamites, and others adopted Sumerian religious, art, legal, and literary forms. The Sumerian legacy served as the basis for a Mesopotamian civilization that maintained a distinct style for 3,000 years.

Religion: The Basis of Mesopotamian Civilization

Religion lay at the center of Mesopotamian life. Every human activity—political, military, social, legal, literary, artistic—was generally subordinated to an overriding religious purpose. Religion was the Mesopotamians' frame of reference for understanding nature, society, and themselves; it dominated and inspired all other cultural expressions. Wars between cities, for instance, were interpreted as conflicts between the gods of those cities, and victory ultimately depended on divine favor, not on human effort.

The Mesopotamians believed that people were given life so that they could execute on earth the will of the gods in heaven. No important decisions were made by kings or priests without first consulting the gods. To discover the wishes of the gods, priests sacrificed animals and then examined their livers; or the priests might find their answers in the stars or in dreams.

The cities of Mesopotamia were sacred communities dedicated to serving divine masters, and people hoped that appeasing the gods would bring security and prosperity to their cities. The Sumerians erected ziggurats—temples on huge multilevel mounds. The ziggurat in Ur measured 205 feet by 140 feet at the base and was about 70 feet high; staircases connected its levels and led to the top platform, on which stood a majestic temple.

The ziggurat was surrounded by low walls enclosing offices and houses for the priests, and shops where potters, weavers, carpenters, and tanners performed their crafts. The temple was the cultural and economic heart of the city. A particular city belonged to a god, who was the real owner of the land and the real ruler of the city; often a vast complex of temples was built for the god and the god's family. In the temple the god was offered shelter, food, clothing, and the homage of dutiful servants.

Supervised by priests, the temple was a vital part of the city's life. The temple owned land, probably most of the land in its city; temple priests collected rents, operated businesses, and received contributions for festivals. Most inhabitants of the city worked for the temple priests as tenant farmers, agricultural laborers, or servants. Priests coordinated the city's economic activity: supervising the distribution of land, overseeing the irrigation works, and storing food for emergencies. Temple scribes kept records of expenditures and receipts. By serving as stewards of the city's gods and managing their earthly estates, the priests sustained civilized life.

The gods—superhuman and immortal, invisible to human eyes but omnipresent—controlled the entire universe and everything in it. The moon, the sun, and the storm; the city, the irrigation works, and the fields—each was directed by a god. Mesopotamians saw gods and demons everywhere in nature.

There was a god in the fire and another in the river; evil demons stirred up sandstorms, caused disease, endangered women in childbirth. To protect themselves from hostile forces, Mesopotamians wore charms and begged their gods for help. Each Mesopotamian offered prayers and sacrifices to a personal god or goddess who provided protection against evil spirits.

Mesopotamians believed that they were manipulated by divine beings. When misfortune befell them, people attributed it to the gods. Even success was not due to their own efforts, but to the intervention of a god who had taken a special interest in them. Compared to the gods, an individual was an insignificant and lowly creature.

Life in Mesopotamia was filled with uncertainty and danger. Sometimes the unpredictable waters of the rivers broke through the dikes, flooding fields, ruining crops, and damaging cities. At other times an insufficient overflow deprived the land of water, causing crops to fail. Great windstorms left the countryside covered with a layer of sand, and heavy thunderstorms turned fields into a sea of mud that made travel impossible. Unlike Egypt, which was protected by vast deserts, Mesopotamia had no natural barriers to invasion. Feeling themselves surrounded by unfathomable and often hostile forces, Mesopotamians lived in an atmosphere of anxiety that permeated their civilization.

Contributing to this sense of insecurity was the belief that the gods behaved capriciously, malevolently, vindictively. What do the gods demand of me? Is it ever possible to please them? To these questions Mesopotamians had no reassuring answers, for the gods' behavior was a mystery to mere human beings:

What is good in a man's sight is evil for a god,
What is evil to a man's mind is good for his
  god.
Who can comprehend the counsel of the gods in
  heaven?
The plan of a god is deep waters, who can
  fathom it?

Where has befuddled mankind ever learned
what is a god's conduct?[4]

A Mesopotamian man or woman hoped to experience the good life by being obedient to his or her older brother, father, foreman, priest, and king and to a personal god who could influence the decisions of the other gods. The rewards for obedience were long life, health, and worldly success. But the feeling persisted that happiness was either transitory or beyond reach—a pessimism that abounded in Mesopotamian literature.

A mood of uncertainty and anxiety, an awareness of the cosmos as unfathomable and mysterious, a feeling of dread about the nature of human existence and the impermanence of human achievement—these attitudes are as old as the first civilization. The *Epic of Gilgamesh*, the finest work of Mesopotamian literature, masterfully depicts this mood of pessimism and despair: "Where is the man who can clamber to heaven? Only the gods live forever . . . but as for us men, our days are numbered, our occupations are a breath of wind."[5]

Government and Law

The government of early Sumer may have been a "primitive democracy," that is, one in which a council of elders guided everyday affairs, and an assembly of citizens appointed a temporary king when war threatened. In time, kingship became hereditary and permanent, supplanting rule by the elders. The king's chief duties were to direct the construction and maintenance of temples and irrigation canals and to wage war.

Bestowed on a man by the gods, kingship was the central institution in Mesopotamian society. Unlike Egyptian pharaohs, Mesopotamian kings did not consider themselves to be gods, but great men selected by the gods to represent them on earth. Gods governed through the kings, who reported to the gods about conditions in their land (which

was the gods' property) and petitioned the gods for advice.

The Mesopotamians viewed earthly governments as exact replicas of the government of the gods. No one Mesopotamian god was all-powerful; instead, an assembly of gods made decisions as a group. Therefore, a mortal king could not be all-powerful either. For this reason, Mesopotamian kingship usually lacked the sureness, confidence, and absolutism of Egyptian kingship. This view of kingship also contributed to the anxiety in Mesopotamian life, for there was no assurance that a king, mortal and fallible, could correctly ascertain heaven's commands.

The king administered the laws, which came from the gods. Like everyone else in the land, the king had to obey divine laws. These laws provided Mesopotamians with a measure of security. The principal collection of laws in ancient Mesopotamia was the famous code of Hammurabi, the Babylonian ruler. Unearthed by French archaeologists in 1901–1902, the code has provided invaluable insights into Mesopotamian society. In typical Mesopotamian fashion, Hammurabi claimed that his code rested on the authority of the gods; to violate it was to contravene the divine order.

The code reveals social status and mores in that area and time. Women were subservient to men, although efforts were made to protect women and children from abuse. By making death the penalty for adultery, the code sought to preserve family life. Punishments were generally severe—"an eye for an eye and a tooth for a tooth." The code prescribed death for housebreaking, kidnapping, aiding the escape of slaves, receiving stolen goods, and bearing false witness, but it also allowed consideration of extenuating circumstances. Class distinctions were expressed in the code. For example, a person received more severe punishment if he had harmed a noble than he would if he had harmed a commoner. The code's many provisions relating to business transactions show the importance of trade to Mesopotamian life.

Couple from Nippur, 2500 B.C. Large eyes and geometrical beard and hair characterize Sumerian figures. The intimacy and stability of the pose contrast with the uncertainty and pessimism found throughout Mesopotamian literature. (*Courtesy of the Oriental Institute, University of Chicago*)

Business and Trade

The economy of Mesopotamian cities depended heavily on foreign and domestic trade. Whereas trade in Egypt was conducted by the state bureaucracy, in Mesopotamia there was greater opportunity for private enterprise. In addition to merchants, temple priests engaged in trade because they possessed surplus produce collected as rents from farmers using temple land. Early in Mesopotamian history, merchants were subservient to the king and the temple priests. Over the centuries, however, merchants began to behave as professionals—not just as agents of the palace or temple, but as private entrepreneurs.

Because of trade's importance to the life of the city, governments instituted regulations to prevent fraud. Business transactions had to be recorded in writing, and severe punishments were imposed for dishonesty. A system of weights and measures facilitated trade, and efforts were made to prevent excessive interest rates for loans.

Mycerinus and Queen, C. 2525 B.C. Swelling chests and hips idealize the royal couple's humanity, but the cubic feeling of the sculpture and the rigid con-fidence of the pose proclaim their unquestioned divinity. (*Courtesy Museum of Fine Arts, Boston*)

Mesopotamians imported resources not found at home—stone, silver, and timber; in exchange they exported textiles, fine handi-crafts, and (less often because of difficulty in transporting them by donkey) agricultural products. They also imported copper from the Persian Gulf, precious metals from Af-ghanistan, ivory from Africa and the west coast of India, and cedar and cypress woods, oils, and essences from the Mediterranean coastal lands. Enterprising businessmen set up trading outposts in distant lands, making the Mesopotamians pioneers in international trade.

Writing, Mathematics, Astronomy, Medicine

The Sumerians established schools that trained the sons of the upper class in the art of cuneiform writing. Hundreds of tablets on which Sumerian students practiced their les-sons have been discovered, testifying to the years of disciplined and demanding work required to master the scribal art. To assist their pupils, teachers prepared textbooks of word lists and mathematical problems with solutions. In translating Sumerian words into the Akkadian language, they compiled what was probably the world's first dictionary. Students who completed the course of study successfully were employed by the temple, the palace, the law courts, or merchants. The Sumerian system of cuneiform writing spread to other parts of the Near East.

The Mesopotamians made some impressive achievements in mathematics. They devised multiplication and division tables, including even cubes and cube roots. They determined the area of right-angle triangles and rectangles, divided a circle into 360 degrees, and had some understanding of principles that centuries later would be developed into the Pythagorean theorem and quadratic equations. But the Babylonians, who made the chief contribution in mathematics, barely advanced to the level of making theories; they did not draw general principles or furnish proofs for their mathematical operations.

By carefully observing and accurately recording the positions of planets and constellations of stars, Babylonian sky watchers took the first steps in developing the science of astronomy, and they devised a calendar based on the cycles of the moon. As in mathematics, however, they did not form theories to coordinate and illuminate their data. They believed that the position of the stars and planets revealed the will of the gods. Astronomers did not examine the heavens because of intellectual curiosity, but rather to discover what the gods wanted. With this knowledge, people could organize their political, social, and moral lives in accordance with divine commands, and they could escape the terrible consequences that they believed resulted from ignoring the gods' wishes. Consequently, Babylonian astronomy, despite its impressive achievements, remained essentially a mythical interpretation of the universe.

Consistent with their religious world-view,

the Mesopotamians believed that disease was caused by gods or demons. To cure a patient, priest-physicians resorted to magic; through prayers and sacrifices they attempted to appease the gods and eject the demons from the sick body. Nevertheless, in identifying illnesses and prescribing appropriate remedies, Mesopotamian priest-physicians demonstrated some accurate knowledge of medicine and pharmacology.

Egyptian Civilization

During the early period of Mesopotamian civilization, the people of another river valley to the west put themselves on the path toward civilization. The Egyptians developed their civilization in the fertile valley of the Nile. For good reason, the Greek historian Herodotus called Egypt "the gift of the Nile," for without this mighty river, which flows more than 4,000 miles from central Africa northward to the Mediterranean Sea, virtually all Egypt would be a desert. When the Nile overflowed its banks, the floodwaters deposited a layer of fertile black earth that when cultivated, provided abundant food to support Egyptian civilization. The Egyptians learned how to control the river—a feat that required cooperative effort and ingenuity, as well as engineering and administrative skills.

Nature favored Egypt in a number of ways. In addition to water and fertile land, the Nile also provided an excellent transportation link between Upper (southern) and Lower (northern) Egypt. Natural barriers—mountains, deserts, cataracts in the Nile, and the Mediterranean Sea—protected Egypt from attack, allowing the inhabitants to enjoy long periods of peace and prosperity. Gold, copper, and stone were abundant, along with other natural resources. In addition, the climate of Egypt is dry and salutary. To the Egyptians, nature seemed changeless and beneficent. Thus, unlike Mesopotamians, Egyptians derived a sense of security from their environment.

Pyramids and Sphinx at Giza. In Egypt the afterlife dominated the thoughts of the living. Pharaoh's large pyramids and the lesser ones of his wives were built as monumental tombs. The colossal sphinx dates from the reign of Khafre (c. 2550 B.C.) and is a portrait of the pharaoh on the body of a lion. The sphinx continues as a royal portrait type through Egyptian history. (*Lee Boltin*)

From the Old Kingdom to the Middle Kingdom

About 2900 B.C., a ruler of Upper Egypt, known as Narmer or Menes, conquered the Nile Delta and Lower Egypt. By 2686 B.C., centralized rule had been firmly established, and great pyramids, which were tombs for the pharaohs, were being constructed. During this Pyramid Age, or Old Kingdom (2686–2181 B.C.), the essential forms of Egyptian civilization crystallized.

The Egyptians believed the pharaoh to be both a man and a god, the earthly embodiment of the deity Horus; he was an absolute ruler of the land and held his court at the city of Memphis. The Egyptians regarded the pharaoh as a benevolent protector who controlled the floodwaters of the Nile, kept the irrigation works in order, maintained justice in the land, and expressed the will of heaven. They expected that when the pharaoh died and joined his fellow gods, he would still help his living subjects.

In time, the nobles who served as district governors gained in status and wealth and gradually came to undermine the divine king's authority. The nobles' growing power and the enormous expenditure of Egypt's human and material resources on building pyramids led to the decline of the Old Kingdom. From 2181 to 2040 B.C., called the First Intermediate Period, rival families competed for the throne, thus destroying the unity of the kingdom. The civil wars and the collapse of central authority required to maintain the irrigation system cast a pall of gloom over the land, as is illustrated in this ancient Egyptian poem:

The wrongdoer is everywhere. . . .
Plunderers are everywhere. . . .
Nile is in flood, yet none plougheth for
     him. . . .
Laughter hath perished and is no longer made.
It is grief that walketh through the land,
     mingled with lamentations. . . .
The storehouse is bare.[6]

During what is called the Middle Kingdom (2040–1786 B.C.), strong kings reasserted pharaonic rule and reunited the state. With political stability restored, cultural life was reinvigorated and economic activity revived. Pharaohs extended Egyptian control south over the land of Nubia, which became a principal source of gold. A profitable trade was carried on with Palestine, Syria, and Crete.

About 1800 B.C., central authority again weakened. In the era known as the Second Intermediate Period (1786–1570 B.C.), the nobles regained some of their power, the Nubians broke away from Egyptian control, and the Hyksos (a mixture of Semites and Indo-Europeans) invaded Egypt. For centuries, desert and sea had effectively guarded Egypt from foreign invasion, but the Hyksos invaders, using horse and chariot and body armor, ended Egyptian complacency. The Hyksos succeeded in dominating Egypt for about a hundred years. Resentful of foreign rule, the Egyptians became more militant and aggressive; they learned to use the Hyksos' weapons and drove out the invaders in 1570 B.C. The period of empire building known as the New Kingdom (1570–1085 B.C.) then began.

The basic features of Egyptian civilization had been forged during the Old and Middle Kingdoms. Egyptians looked to the past, believing that the ways of their ancestors were best. For almost 3,000 years, Egyptian civilization sought to retain a harmony with that order of nature instituted at creation. Egyptians had no conception of progress. Believing that the universe was static and changeless,

the Egyptians valued the institutions, traditions, and authority that gave the appearance of permanence.

Religion: The Basis of Egyptian Civilization

Religion was omnipresent in Egyptian life and accounted for the outstanding achievements of Egyptian civilization. Religious beliefs were the basis of Egyptian art, medicine, astronomy, literature, and government. The great pyramids were tombs for the pharaohs, man-gods. Magical utterances pervaded medical practices, for disease was attributed to the gods. Astronomy evolved to determine the correct time to perform religious rites and sacrifices. The earliest examples of literature dealt wholly with religious themes. Pharaoh was a sacrosanct monarch who served as an intermediary between the gods and human beings. Justice was conceived in religious terms, something bestowed by a creator-god. The Egyptians developed an ethical code, which they believed had been approved by the gods.

Egyptian polytheism took many forms including the worship of animals, for Egyptians believed that gods manifested themselves in animal shapes. Consequently, crocodiles, cats, bulls, and other animals dwelt in temples and were mummified for burial when they died. Perhaps the Egyptians regarded animals with religious awe because an animal species continues from generation to generation without apparent change. To the Egyptian mind, says Henri Frankfort, a leading scholar in Near Eastern studies, the quality of changelessness made "animal life . . . appear superhuman . . . in that it shared directly, patently, in the static life of the universe."[7]

Certain gods were conceived by Egyptians as taking various forms. Thoth, for example, was represented as the moon, a baboon, an ibis, and an ibis-headed man. The god Amen was depicted both in human form and as a ram. To Egyptians, these different representations were not contradictory, for they did not seek logical consistency in religion. Egyptians also believed great powers in nature—sky, sun, earth, the Nile—to be gods. Thus, the universe was alive with divinities, and human lives were tied to the movements of the sun and the moon and to the rhythm of the seasons. In the heavens alive with gods, Egyptians found answers to the great problems of human existence.

A crucial feature of Egyptian religion was the afterlife. Through pyramid-tombs, mummification to preserve the dead, and funerary art, Egyptians showed their yearning for eternity and their desire to overcome death. Mortuary priests recited incantations to ensure the preservation of the dead body and the continuity of existence. Inscribed on the pyramids' interior walls were "pyramid texts" written in *hieroglyphics*—a form of picture writing in which figures, such as crocodiles, sails, eyes, and so forth, represented words, or sounds that would be combined to form words. The texts contained fragments from myths, historical annals, and magical lore and provided spells to assist the king in ascending to heaven.

At first, it was held that only the pharaoh and the royal family were immortal. In time, first the nobility and then commoners claimed that they too could share in the blessings of the "other world." Prayers hitherto reserved for the pharaoh were, for a fee, recited by priests at the burial of commoners. To Egyptians, the other world contained the same pleasures enjoyed on earth—friends, servants, fishing, hunting, paddling a canoe, picnicking with family members, entertainment by musicians and dancers, and good food. Because earthly existence was not fundamentally unhappy, however, Egyptians did not yearn for death.

Divine Kingship

"What is the king of Upper and Lower Egypt? He is a god by whose dealings one lives, the father and mother of men, alone by himself, without an equal."[8] Divine kingship was the basic institution of Egyptian civilization. Perhaps the requirements of the Egyptian environment helped to fashion the idea of the pharaoh as a living god, because a ruler with supernatural authority could hold together the large kingdom and draft the mass labor required to maintain the irrigation system.

Through the pharaoh the gods made known their wishes for the Egyptian people. As kingship was a divine, not a manmade, institution, it was expected to last for eternity. The Egyptians rejoiced in the rule of an all-powerful, all-knowing god-king. To the Egyptians, the pharaoh was "the herdsman of everyone without evil in his heart."[9] They believed that divine kingship was the only acceptable political arrangement, that it was in harmony with the order of the universe, and that it brought stability and authority to the nation.

The power of the pharaoh extended to all sectors of society. Peasants were drafted to serve in labor corps as miners or construction workers. Foreign trade was a state monopoly conducted according to the kingdom's needs. Although private ownership of land was recognized in practice, all land in theory belonged to the pharaoh. As the supreme overlord, the pharaoh oversaw an army of government officials who collected taxes, supervised construction projects, checked the irrigation works, surveyed the land, kept records, and supervised government warehouses where grain was stored as insurance against a bad harvest. Because the pharaoh's word was regarded as a divine ordinance, Egypt, unlike Mesopotamia, had no need for written laws. All Egyptians were subservient to the pharaoh, and there was no conception of political liberty. Most pharaohs took their responsibilities seriously and tried to govern as benevolent protectors of the people.

Be not evil, it is good to be kindly. . . . Do right so long as thou abidest on the earth. Calm the weeper, oppress no widow, expel no man from the possessions of his father. . . . Take heed lest thou punish wrongfully. . . . Slay not a man

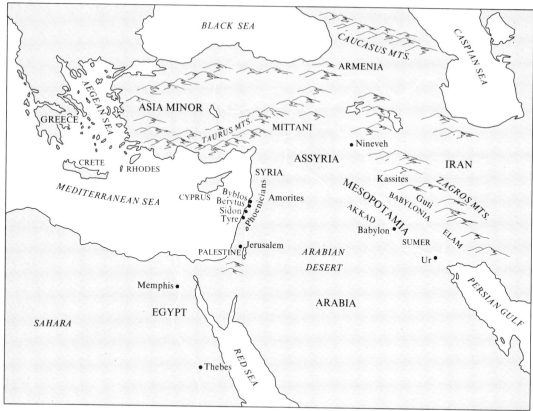

Map 1.2 Kingdoms and Peoples of the Ancient World

whose good qualities thou knowest. . . . Exalt not the son of one of high degree more than him that is of lowly birth, but take to thyself a man because of his actions.[10]

Egyptians derived a sense of security from the concept of divine kingship. It meant that earthly government and society were in harmony with the cosmic order. The Egyptians believed that the institution of kingship dated from the creation of the universe, that as part of the rhythm of the universe, kingship was necessary and beneficial to human beings, and that there was a divine order to the cosmos, which brought justice and security.

The pharaoh was seen as ruling in accordance with Ma'at which means justice, law, right, and truth. To oppose the pharaoh was to violate the order of Ma'at and to bring disorder to society. Because Egyptians regarded Ma'at as the right order of nature, they believed that its preservation must be

the object of human activity—the guiding norm of the state and the standard by which individuals conducted their lives. Those who did Ma'at and spoke Ma'at would be justly rewarded. Could anything be more reassuring than this belief that divine truth was represented in the person of the pharaoh?

Science and Mathematics

Like the Mesopotamians, the Egyptians made practical advances in the sciences. They demonstrated superb engineering skills in building pyramids and fashioned an effective system of mathematics that enabled them to solve relatively simple problems based more on experience than on reasoning. Noting that the Nile flooded after the star Sirius appeared in the sky, the Egyptians developed a calendar by which they could predict the time of the flood. The Egyptian 365-day solar calendar, based on the movements of the sun, was more accurate than the Babylonian lunar calendar.

In the area of medicine, Egyptian doctors were more capable than their Mesopotamian counterparts. They were able to identify illnesses; they recognized that uncleanliness encouraged contagion; they had some knowledge of anatomy and performed operations—circumcision and perhaps the draining of abscessed teeth. Although the progress of medicine was handicapped by the belief that gods caused illnesses, there is evidence that some Egyptian doctors examined the body in a scientific way. In a scroll, the Edwin Smith Surgical Papyrus (named after the nineteenth-century American Egyptologist who acquired it), the writer omitted all references to divine intervention in his advice for treating wounds and fractures. He described fractures in a matter-of-fact way and recommended healing them with splints and casts.

The New Kingdom and the Decline of Egyptian Civilization

The New Kingdom began in 1570 B.C. with the war of liberation against the Hyksos, which gave rise to an intense militancy and nationalism that found expression in empire building. Military-minded pharaohs conquered territory that extended as far east as the Euphrates River. From its subject states, Egypt acquired tribute and slaves. Conquests led to the expansion of the bureaucracy, the rise of a professional army, and the increased power of priests, whose temples shared in the spoils. The formation of the empire ended Egyptian isolation and accelerated commercial and cultural intercourse with other peoples. Egyptian art, for example, showed the influence of foreign forms during this period.

A growing cosmopolitanism was paralleled by a movement toward monotheism during the reign of Pharaoh Amenhotep IV (c. 1369–1353 B.C.). Amenhotep sought to replace traditional polytheism with the worship of Aton,

a single god of all men who was represented as the sun disk. Amenhotep took the name Akhenaton ("It is well with Aton"), and moved the capital from Thebes to a newly constructed holy city called Akhataten (near modern Tell el-Amarna). The city had palaces, administrative centers, and a temple complex honoring Aton. Akhenaton and his wife Nefertiti dedicated themselves to Aton—the creator of the world, the maintainer of life, and the god of love, justice, and peace. Akhenaton (or Ikhneton) also ordered his officials to chisel out the names of other gods from inscriptions on temples and monuments. With awe Akhenaton glorified Aton:

How manifold are thy works!
They are hidden from man's sight.
O sole god, like whom there is no other.
Thou hast made the earth according to thy
    desire.[11]

Akhenaton's "monotheism" had little impact on the masses of Egyptians, who retained their ancient beliefs, and was resisted by priests, who resented his changes. After Akhenaton's death the new pharaoh, Tutankhamen (1352–1344 B.C.) abandoned the capital at Amarna and returned to Thebes. Tutankhamen was succeeded by an elderly relative who reigned briefly. In 1340, Horemheb (1340–1315 B.C.), an army commander, seized power and had the monuments to Aton destroyed, along with records and inscriptions bearing Akhenaton's name.

Historians are not certain why Akhenaton made this radical break with tradition. Was he trying to strike at the priests whose wealth and prestige had increased considerably with Egypt's conquests? Did the break stem essentially from an intense religious fervor? But the most significant historical questions concerning Akhenaton are: Was his religion genuine monotheism, which pushed religious thought in a new direction? And if so, did it influence Moses, who led the Israelites out of Egypt about a century later?

These last questions have aroused controversy among historians. The principal limi-

Rosetta Stone. This ancient Egyptian stone (195 B.C.) bears the same decree in three forms—hieroglyphics in the top section, demotic (cursive Egyptian) characters next, and Greek at the bottom. The stone, which led to the deciphering of hieroglyphics, was found in August 1799 by a Frenchman serving under Napoleon; it passed into British hands with the French surrender of Egypt (1801). (*The British Museum*)

tation on the monotheistic character of Atonism is that there were really two gods in Akhenaton's religion—Aton and the pharaoh himself, who was still worshiped as a deity. Egyptologist John A. Wilson sheds light on this notion. Because Egyptians could not break with the central idea of their civilization, divine kingship, "one could say that it was the closest approach to monotheism possible within the thought of the day. That would still fall short of making it a belief in and worship of only one god."[12] Regarding the relationship of Atonism to a later Hebrew monotheism, Wilson says, "The mechanism of transmission from the faith of Akhena-

ton to the monotheism of Moses is not apparent."[13]

Late in the thirteenth century, Libyans, probably seeking to settle in the more fertile land of Egypt, attacked from the west, and the Peoples of the Sea, as unsettled raiders from the Aegean Sea area and Asia Minor were called, launched a series of strikes at Egypt. A weakened Egypt abandoned its empire. In the succeeding centuries Egypt came under the rule of Libyans, Nubians, Assyrians, Persians, and finally Greeks, to whom Egypt lost its independence in the fourth century B.C.

Egyptian civilization had flourished for almost 2,000 years before it experienced an almost 1,000-year descent into stagnation, decline, and collapse. During its long history the Egyptians tried to preserve the ancient forms of their civilization, revealed to them by their ancestors and representing for all time those unchanging values that are the way of happiness.

Empire Builders

The rise of an Egyptian empire during the New Kingdom was part of a wider development in Near Eastern history after 1500 B.C.—the emergence of international empires. Empire building led to the intermingling of peoples and cultural traditions and to the extension of civilization well beyond the river valleys.

Migration of Indo-Europeans

One reason for the growth of empires was the migration of peoples known as Indo-Europeans. Originally from a wide area ranging from southeastern Europe to the region beyond the Caspian Sea, Indo-Europeans embarked on a series of migrations around 2000 B.C. that eventually brought them into Italy, Greece, Asia Minor, Mesopotamia, Persia, and India. From a core Indo-European tongue there emerged the Greek, Latin, Germanic, Persian, and Sanskrit languages.

Several peoples established strong states in the Near East around 1500 B.C.—the Hurrians in northern Mesopotamia, the Hittites in Asia Minor, and the Kassites in southern Mesopotamia. Originally from the highlands of Armenia, the Hurrians had been infiltrating Mesopotamia for centuries. Aided by a wave of Indo-European invaders, they set up the Mitanni empire in northern Mesopotamia and adopted Mesopotamian civilization. In 1365 B.C., the Mitanni empire fell to the Hittites.

Penetrating Asia Minor, Indo-Europeans coalesced with native Hattic-speaking peoples to create the Hittite empire (1450–1200 B.C.). The Hittites ruled Asia Minor and northern Syria, raided Babylon, and challenged Egypt for control of Syria and Palestine.

The Hittites wanted to control the trade routes that ran along the Euphrates River into Syria. Mursilis I, a Hittite king, conquered part of Syria and sacked Babylon in 1595 B.C., ending the Amorite dynasty that had been established by Hammurabi four centuries earlier. Shortly after the attack, however, the Hittites withdrew from Babylon. In the 1300s, the Hittite empire reached its peak and included much of Asia Minor and northern Syria. The Hittites' success arose from their well-trained army. Mass attacks by light horse-drawn chariots demolished enemy lines, while foot soldiers made effective use of the battle axe and a short curved sword.

The Hittites borrowed several features of Mesopotamian civilization, including cuneiform, legal principles, and literary and art forms. Hittite religion blended the beliefs and practices of Indo-Europeans, native inhabitants of Asia Minor, and Mesopotamians. The Hittites were probably the first people to develop a substantial iron industry. At first, they apparently used iron only for ceremonial and ritual objects, and not for tools and weapons. However, because iron ore was more readily available than copper or tin (needed for bronze), after 1200 B.C. iron weapons and tools spread throughout the Near East, although bronze implements were

still used. Around 1200 B.C., the Hittite empire fell, most likely to Indo-European invaders from the north.

By about 1460 B.C., the Kassites, assisted by Indo-Europeans, gained control over Babylonia, giving political unity to the area. The Kassites had originated in the Zagros Mountains to the east; like the Hurrians, they adopted Mesopotamian language and culture. They ruled Babylonia for some 400 years until subdued about 1150 B.C. by Elamites from Iran.

Small Nations

During the twelfth century there was a temporary lull in empire building, which permitted a number of small nations in Syria and Palestine to assert their sovereignty. Three of these peoples—Phoenicians, Aramaeans, and Hebrews*—were originally Semitic desert nomads. The Phoenicians were descendants of the Canaanites, a Semitic people who had settled Palestine about 3000 B.C. Those Canaanites who migrated northwest into what is now Lebanon were called Phoenicians.

Settling in the coastal Mediterranean cities of Tyre, Byblos, Berytus (Beirut), and Sidon, the Phoenicians were naturally drawn to the sea. These daring explorers established towns along the coast of North Africa, on the islands of the western Mediterranean, and in Spain, and they became the greatest sea traders of the ancient world. Phoenician merchants exported lumber, glass, copper and bronze utensils, and the purple dye produced from the murex, a mollusk that was plentiful in the coastal waters. The Phoenicians (or their Canaanite forebears) devised the first alphabet, which was a monumental contribution to writing. Since all words could be represented by combinations of letters, it saved memorizing thousands of diagrams and aided

*The Hebrews will be discussed in Chapter 2.

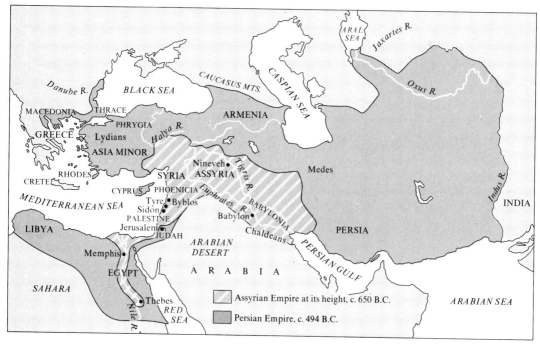

Map 1.3 The Assyrian and Persian Empires

the Phoenicians in transmitting the civilizations of the Near East to the western Mediterranean.

The Aramaeans, who settled in Syria, Palestine, and northern Mesopotamia, performed a role similar to the Phoenicians'. As great caravan traders they carried both goods and cultural patterns to various parts of the Near East. The Hebrews and the Persians, for example, acquired the Phoenician alphabet from the Aramaeans.

Assyria

In the ninth century, empire building resumed with the Assyrians, a Semitic people from the region around the upper Tigris River. Because their geographical position made them prey to other peoples in the area, the Assyrians emphasized military prowess to maintain their borders. The Assyrians care-

fully planned a military campaign and excelled in siege weapons, with which they subdued heavily fortified towns; their soldiers wore armor and wielded iron swords.

Although they had made forays of expansion in 1200 and 1100 B.C., the Assyrians began their march to "world" empire three centuries later. In the eighth and seventh centuries the Assyrians became a ruthless fighting machine that steamrolled through Mesopotamia—including Armenia and Babylonia—as well as Syria, Palestine, and Egypt. At its height, the Assyrian empire extended from the Iranian plateau in the east to the Egyptian city of Thebes.

How did the Assyrians administer such a vast empire? An Assyrian king, who was the representative and high priest of the god Ashur, governed absolutely. Nobles appointed by the king kept order in the provinces and collected tribute. The Assyrians improved roads, established messenger services, and engaged in large-scale irrigation projects to facilitate effective administration of their conquered lands and to promote prosperity. To keep their subjects obedient, the Assyrians resorted to terror and to deportation of troublesome subjects from their home territories. Assyrian kings boasted of their ruthlessness toward rebellious subjects:

13,000 of their warriors I cut down with the sword. Their blood like the water of a stream I caused to run through the squares of their city. The corpses of their soldiers I piled in heaps. . . . [The Babylonian king's] royal bed, his royal couch, the treasure of his palaces, his property, his gods and everything from his palace without number, I carried away. His captive warriors were given to the soldiers of my land like grasshoppers. The city I destroyed, I devastated, I burned with fire.[14]

Despite their harsh characteristics, the Assyrians maintained and spread the culture of the past. They copied and edited the literary works of Babylonia, adopted the old Sumerian gods, and used Mesopotamian art forms. The Assyrian king Ashurbanipal (669–626 B.C.) maintained a great library that contained thousands of clay tablets.

After a period of wars and revolts by oppressed subjects weakened Assyria, a coalition of Medes from Iran and Chaldeans, or Neo-Babylonians, sacked the Assyrian capital of Nineveh in 612 B.C. The conquerors looted and destroyed the city and the surviving Assyrians fled. Assyrian power was broken.

The Neo-Babylonian Empire

The destruction of the Assyrian empire made possible the rise of a Chaldean empire that included Babylonia, Assyria, Syria, and Palestine. Under Nebuchadnezzar, who ruled from 604 to 562 B.C., the Chaldean or Neo-Babylonian empire reached its height. A talented general and statesman, and a brilliant administrator, Nebuchadnezzar had Babylon rebuilt. The new Babylon that arose on the shore of the Euphrates had magnificent procession-ways that led to palaces and temples. On his palace grounds, Nebuchadnezzar created the famous Hanging Gardens for his Medean wife, according to legend. The 350-foot building was a series of vaulted terraces and was surrounded by a moat of flowing water. Trees, shrubs, and flowers decorated each terrace. In the interior, vaulted halls were stocked with vessels, fabrics, ornaments, and wines gathered from different regions of the empire. Here guests reclined on divans and were attended by slaves.

Persia: Unifier of the Near East

After Nebuchadnezzar's death, the Chaldean empire was torn by civil war and threatened by a new power—the Persians, an Indo-European people who had settled in southern Iran. Under Cyrus the Great and his son and successor, Cambyses, the Persians conquered all lands between the Nile in Egypt and the Indus River in India. This conquest took twenty-five years, from 550 to 525 B.C.

The Near Eastern conception of absolute monarchy justified by religion reached its culminating expression in the person of the Persian king who, with divine approval, ruled a vast empire, "the four quarters of the earth." Persian kings developed an effective system of administration—based in part on an Assyrian model—that gave stability and a degree of unity to their extensive territories. In so doing they performed a creative act of statesmanship. The Persian empire was divided into twenty provinces (*satrapies*), each one administered by a governor (*satrap*) responsible to the emperor. To guard against subversion, the king employed special agents—"the eyes and ears of the Emperor"—who supervised the activities of the governors. Persian kings allowed the provincials a large measure of self-rule. They also respected local traditions, particularly in matters of religion, as long as subjects paid their taxes, served in the royal army, and refrained from rebellion; and they deliberately tried to win the goodwill of priests in conquered lands.

Persepolis: Great Ceremonial Staircase and Audience Hall. Persepolis was the ceremonial center of the Persian empire. The repetitive geometric tribute bearers in bas relief along the staircase continue artistic traditions from distant Sumerian times. (*Courtesy of the Oriental Institute, University of Chicago*)

The empire was bound together by a uniform language, Aramaic (the language of the Aramaeans of Syria), used by government officials and merchants. Aramaic was written in letters based on the Phoenician alphabet. By making Aramaic a universal language, the Persians facilitated written and oral communication within the empire. The empire was further unified by an elaborate network of roads, an efficient postal system, a common system of weights and measures, and an empire-wide coinage based on an invention of the Lydians from western Asia Minor.

In addition to providing impressive political and administrative unity, the Persians fused and perpetuated the various cultural traditions of the Near East. Persian palaces, for example, boasted the terraces of Babylon, the colonnades of Egypt, the winged bulls that decorated Assyrian palace gates, and the craftsmanship of Median goldsmiths.

The political and cultural universalism of the Persian empire had its counterpart in the emergence of a higher religion, Zoroastrianism. Named for its founder, the Persian prophet Zoroaster, this religion taught belief in Ahura Mazda—the Wise Lord—god of light, of justice, wisdom, goodness, and immortality. But, in addition to the Wise Lord, there also existed Ahriman, the spirit of darkness, who was evil and destructive; Ahriman was in conflict with Ahura Mazda. People were free to choose whom they would follow. To serve Ahura Mazda, one had to speak the truth and be good to others; the reward for such behavior was life eternal in paradise, the realm of light and goodness. Followers of the evil spirit were cast into hell, a realm of darkness and torment. In contrast to the traditional religions of the Near East, Zoroastrianism rejected magic, polytheism, sacrifices, and temples, and instead stressed ethics.

Persia unified the nations of the Near East into a world-state, headed by a divinely appointed king, and synthesized the region's cultural traditions. Soon it would confront the city-states of Greece, whose political system and cultural orientation differed from that of the Near East.

The Religious Orientation of the Near East

All features of Near Eastern society—law, kingship, art, and science—were generally interpenetrated with, and dominated by religion. Religion was the source of the vitality and creativity of Mesopotamian and Egyptian civilizations. Near Eastern art was inspired by religion; literature and history dealt with the ways of the gods; science was permeated with religion. And priest-kings or god-kings, their power sanctioned by divine forces, furnished the necessary authority to organize large numbers of people in cooperative ventures.

A Myth-making World-View

A religious or mythopoeic (myth-making) view of the world gives Near Eastern civilization its distinctive form and allows us to see it as an organic whole. Myth-making was humanity's first way of thinking; it was the earliest attempt to make nature and life comprehensible. Appealing primarily to the imagination and emotions, not to reason, myth has been a fundamental formative element of human culture, which has expressed itself, often creatively, in language, art, poetry, and social organization.

Originating in sacred rites, ritual dances, feasts, and ceremonies, myths narrated the deeds of gods who, in some remote past, had brought forth the world and human beings. Holding that human destiny was determined by the gods, Near Eastern people interpreted their experiences through myths. Myths also enabled Mesopotamians and Egyptians to make sense out of nature, to explain the world of phenomena. Through myths the Near Eastern mind sought to give coherence to the universe, to make it intelligible. These myths gave Near Eastern peoples a framework with which to pattern their experiences into a meaningful order, justify their rules of conduct, and try to overcome the uncertainty of existence. Mythical explanations of nature and human experience made life seem less overwhelming, less filled with unbearable fears.

Religion determined the Near Eastern view of nature. Gods and demons resided within nature: the sun and stars, the rivers and mountains, the wind and lightning were either gods or the dwelling places of gods. To an Egyptian or a Mesopotamian, natural phenomena—a falling rock, a thunderclap, a rampaging river—were experienced as life facing life. They did not view nature as a physical entity, as an *it*, inanimate, impersonal, and governed by law; rather they saw every object in nature mythically, as a *thou*, suffused with life.

In other words, the ancients told myths instead of presenting an analysis or conclusions. We would explain, for instance, that certain atmospheric changes broke a drought and brought about rain. The Babylonians observed the same facts but experienced them as the intervention of the gigantic bird Imdugud which came to their rescue. It covered the sky with the black storm clouds of its wings and devoured the Bull of Heaven, whose hot breath had scorched the crops.[15]

Chronology 1.1 The Near East

3200 B.C.*	Rise of civilization in Sumeria
2900	Union of Upper and Lower Egypt
2686–2181	Old Kingdom; essential forms of Egyptian civilization take shape
2180	Downfall of Akkadian empire
1792–1750	Hammurabi of Babylon brings Akkad and Sumer under his control and fashions a code of laws
1570	Egyptians drive out Hyksos and embark upon empire building
1369–1353	Amenhotep IV; a movement toward monotheism
1200	Fall of Hittite empire
612	Fall of Assyrian empire
604–562	Reign of Nebuchadnezzar; height of Chaldean empire
550–525 B.C.	Persian conquests form a world empire

* Most dates are approximations.

The Egyptians believed that the sun rose in the morning, traveled across the sky, and set into the netherworld beyond the western horizon. After warding off the forces of chaos and disruption, the sun reappeared the next morning. For the Egyptians, the rising and setting of the sun were not natural occurrences—a celestial body obeying an impersonal law—but a religious drama.

The myth-making mind of the ancient Near East did not analyze nature systematically and rationally; it did not structure and explain reality by means of hypothesis, logical analysis, and general rules. Rather it saw the forces of nature as expressions of gods and demons; mythical relationships operated throughout the objective world.

Mesopotamians and Egyptians did not distinguish between the *subjective*—how nature appears to us through feelings, illusions, and dreams—and the *objective*, what nature really is, a system governed by laws that can be apprehended through intellectual analysis and

synthesis. Of course, Near Eastern people did engage in rational forms of thought and behavior. They certainly employed reason in building irrigation works, in preparing a calendar, and in performing mathematical operations. But, because rational or logical thought remained subordinate to a mythic-religious world-view, Near Eastern people did not arrive at a *consistently* and *self-consciously* rational method of inquiring into physical nature and human culture. They did not fashion a body of philosophic and scientific ideas that were logically structured, discussed, and debated.

Near Eastern civilization reached the first level in the development of science—observing nature, recording data, and improving technology in mining, metallurgy, and architecture. But it did not advance to the level of self-conscious philosophic and scientific thought—that is, logically deduced abstractions, hypotheses, and generalizations. These later developments were the singular achievement of Greek philosophy, which gave a "rational interpretation to natural occurrences which had previously been explained by ancient mythologies. . . . With the study of nature set free from the control of mythological fancy, the way was opened for the development of science as an intellectual system."[16]

Near Eastern Achievements

Sumerians and Egyptians demonstrated enormous creativity and intelligence. They built irrigation works and cities, organized governments, charted the course of heavenly bodies, performed mathematical operations, constructed large-scale monuments, engaged in international trade, established bureaucracies and schools, and advanced the level of technology considerably. And without the Sumerian invention of writing—one of the great creative acts in history—what we mean by *civilization* could not have emerged.

Many elements of ancient Near Eastern civilization were passed on to the West. The wheeled vehicle, the plow, and the phonetic alphabet—all important to the development of civilization—derive from the Near East. In the realm of medicine, the Egyptians knew the value of certain drugs, such as castor oil; they also knew how to use splints and bandages. The innovative divisions that gave 360 degrees to a circle and 60 minutes to an hour originated in Mesopotamia. Egyptian geometry and Babylonian astronomy were utilized by the Greeks and became a part of Western knowledge. In Christian art, too, one finds connections to the Mesopotamian art forms—for example, the Assyrians depicted winged angel-like beings.

In addition to concrete facts and artifacts, ideas and stories entered Western civilization from the Near East. One such idea was the belief that a king's power comes from a heavenly source. Mesopotamian literary themes were also borrowed, by both the Hebrews and the Greeks. For example, some biblical stories—the Flood, the quarrel between Cain and Abel, and the Tower of Babel—stem from Mesopotamian antecedents. A similar link exists between the Greek and the earlier Mesopotamian mythologies.

Thus, many achievements of Egyptians and Mesopotamians were inherited and assimilated by both Greeks and Hebrews. Even more important for an understanding of the essential meaning of Western civilization are the ways in which Greeks and Hebrews rejected or transformed elements of the older Near Eastern traditions to create new points of departure for the human mind.

Notes

1. Richard E. Leakey and Roger Lewin, *Origins* (New York: E. P. Dutton, 1977), p. 8.

2. Robert J. Braidwood, *Prehistoric Man* (Glenview, Ill.: Scott, Foresman, 1967), p. 141.

3. Lewis Mumford, *Transformation of Man* (New York: Harper Torchbooks, 1972), pp. 46–47.

4. Quoted in Sabatino Moscati, *The Face of the Ancient Orient* (Garden City, N.J.: Doubleday Anchor Books, 1962), p. 87.

5. *The Epic of Gilgamesh*, with an introduction by N. K. Senders (Baltimore: Penguin Books, 1965), pp. 69, 104.

6. Adolf Ehrman, ed., *The Ancient Egyptians* (New York: Harper Torchbooks, 1966), pp. 94, 97, 99.

7. Henri Frankfort, *Ancient Egyptian Religion* (New York: Harper Torchbooks, 1961), p. 14.

8. Quoted in ibid., p. 43.

9. John A. Wilson, "Egypt," in Henri Frankfort, et al., *Before Philosophy* (Baltimore: Penguin Books, 1949), p. 88.

10. Erhman, *The Ancient Egyptians*, pp. 76–78.

11. Quoted in John A. Wilson, *The Culture of Ancient Egypt* (Chicago: University of Chicago Press, Phoenix Books, 1951), p. 227.

12. Ibid., p. 225.

13. Ibid., p. 226.

14. Quoted in John Oates, *Babylon* (London: Thames and Hudson, 1979), pp. 110–111.

15. Frankfort, et al., *Before Philosophy*, p. 15.

16. S. Sambursky, *The Physical World of the Greeks* (New York: Collier Books, 1962), pp. 18–19.

Suggested Reading

Cook, J. M., *The Persian Empire* (1983). An up-to-date history of ancient Persia.

David, Rosalie A., *The Ancient Egyptians* (1982). Focuses on religious beliefs and practices.

Fagan, Brian M., *People of the Earth* (1980). A survey of world prehistory.

Frankfort, Henri, *Ancient Egyptian Religion* (1948). An interpretation of the origins and nature of Egyptian religion.

Frankfort, Henri, et al., *Before Philosophy* (1949). Brilliant discussions of the role of myth in the ancient Near East by distinguished scholars.

Gowlett, John, *Ascent to Civilization* (1984). An up-to-date study with excellent graphics.

Hallo, W. W., and Simpson, W. K., *The Ancient Near East* (1971). An authoritative survey of the political history of the Near East.

Leakey, Richard E. *Origins* (1977). What new discoveries reveal about the emergence of the human species.

Mertz, Barbara, *Red Land, Black Land* (1966). A social history of the people of Egypt.

Moscati, Sabatino, *The Face of the Ancient Orient* (1962). An illuminating survey of the various peoples of the ancient Near East.

Oates, John. *Babylon* (1979). A survey of the history of Babylon from its origin to Hellenistic times; includes a discussion of the legacy of Babylon.

Oppenheim, A. L., *Ancient Mesopotamia* (1964). Stresses social and economic history.

Roux, Georges, *Ancient Iraq* (1964). A balanced survey of Mesopotamian history and society.

Saggs, H. W. F., *The Greatness That Was Babylon* (1962). Strong on social and cultural history.

Wilson, John A., *The Culture of Ancient Egypt* (1951). An interpretation by a distinguished Egyptologist.

Review Questions

1. What progress did human beings make during the Paleolithic age?

2. Why is the development of the Neolithic Age referred to as the Neolithic Revolution?

3. What is meant by civilization? Under what conditions did it emerge?

4. The Sumerian achievement served as the basis for Mesopotamian civilization. Discuss.

5. How did religion influence Mesopotamian civilization?

6. What achievements did the Mesopotamians make in trade, mathematics, and science?

7. Define Old Kingdom, Middle Kingdom, and New Kingdom.

8. What role did the pharaoh play in Egyptian life? Do you think the pharaoh really believed that he was divine? Explain.

9. How did the Egyptians' religious beliefs affect their civilization?

10. What is the significance of Akhenaton?

11. The Egyptians would not have comprehended our concept of progress. Discuss.

12. What were the achievements of the Phoenicians and Aramaeans?

13. How did the Persians give unity to the Near East?

14. What advances in science were made by Near Eastern civilization? How was science limited by a myth-making view of nature?

15. Why has religion played such an important role in world history?

16. What were the accomplishments of the civilizations of the Near East? What elements of Near Eastern civilization were passed on to Western civilization?

2

The Hebrews: A New View
of God and the Individual

*A*ncient Mesopotamia and Egypt, the birthplace of the first civilizations, are not the spiritual ancestors of the West; for the origins of the Western tradition, we must turn to the Hebrews and the Greeks. As Egyptologist John A. Wilson says:

> *The Children of Israel built a nation and a religion on the rejection of things Egyptian. Not only did they see God as one, but they ascribed to him consistency of concern for man and consistency of justice to man. . . . Like the Greeks, the Hebrews took forms from their great neighbors; like the Greeks, they used those forms for very different purposes.*[1]

In this chapter we examine one source of the Western tradition, the Hebrews, whose conception of God broke with the outlook of the Near East and whose ethical teachings helped to fashion the Western idea of the dignity of the individual.

Outline of Hebrew History

The Hebrews originated in Mesopotamia and migrated to Canaan, a portion of which was later called Palestine. The Hebrew patriarchs—Abraham, Isaac, and Jacob, so prominently depicted in the Old Testament—were chieftains of seminomadic clans that roamed Palestine and occasionally journeyed to Mesopotamia and Egypt. The early Hebrews absorbed some features of Mesopotamian civilization. For example, there are parallels between biblical law and the Mesopotamian legal tradition. Several biblical stories—the Creation, the Flood, the Garden of Eden—derive from Mesopotamian sources.

Some Hebrews journeyed from Canaan to Egypt to be herdsmen and farmers, but they eventually became forced laborers for the Egyptians. Fearful of becoming permanent slaves of pharaoh, the Hebrews yearned for an opportunity to escape. An extraordinary leader rose among them called Moses, who

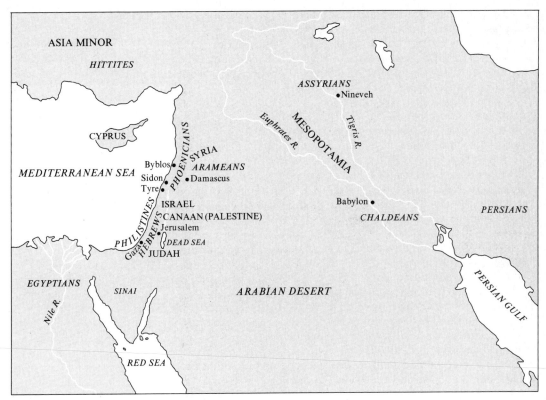

Map 2.1 Hebrews and Other Peoples of the Ancient Middle East

came to his people as a messenger of God. Leading the Hebrews in their exodus from Egypt in the thirteenth century B.C., Moses transformed them during their wanderings in the wilderness of Sinai into a nation, welded together and uplifted by a belief in Yahweh, the one God.

The Israelite Kingdom

The wandering Hebrews returned to Canaan to rejoin other Hebrew tribes that had not migrated to Egypt. The conquest of the Canaanites, who possessed a material culture superior to the Hebrews', took many generations. Settling in Canaan, the Israelites became an agricultural nation.

After the conquest, the Israelites did not form a state with a central government, but were loosely organized into a tribal confederation bound by a commitment to Yahweh. When enemies threatened, the elders of each of the twelve tribes would decide whether to engage in joint action. During emergencies, judges, who were leaders distinguished by their courage and empowered by "the spirit of Yahweh," rallied the clans against the common enemy. The tribal confederation lasted for about 200 years, until a threat by the Philistines in the late eleventh century B.C. led the Israelites to draw closer together under a king.

Originally from the islands of the Aegean Sea and the coast of Asia Minor, the Philistines (from whom the name Palestine derives) had invaded Canaan in the early part of the twelfth century B.C. From the coastal regions they expanded into the interior, extending their dominion over much Israelite territory. During this time of crisis, the twelve tribes united under the leadership of Saul, a charismatic hero whom they acclaimed as their first king. Under Saul's successor, David, a gifted warrior and a poet, the Hebrews (or Israelites) broke the back of Philistine power and subdued neighboring peoples.

The creation of an Israelite kingdom under David and his son Solomon in the tenth century B.C. was made possible by the declining power of other states in the Near East—Babylonia, Assyria, the Hittite Kingdom, and Egypt. Solomon's kingdom engaged in active trade with neighboring states, particularly Tyre (located along the Phoenician coast). Solomon's merchant fleet, built and manned by Phoenicians, traded with southerly lands bordering the Red Sea. Another sign of economic progress was extensive construction, especially in Jerusalem, the Hebrew spiritual center, where Solomon built a royal palace and beside it a magnificent temple honoring God.

New cities were built, and Jerusalem grew larger. The use of the iron-tipped plow improved agricultural productivity which, in turn, contributed to a significant population increase. Under Solomon, Israel also experienced a cultural flowering—some magnificent sections of the Old Testament were written and music flourished.

Old tribal patterns weakened as urban life expanded and some grew wealthy. Tribal society had been distinguished by a large measure of economic equality, but disparity between the rich and the poor grew, between those who considered themselves aristocrats and the common people.

Under Solomon, ancient Israel was at the height of its power and prosperity, but opposition to Solomon's tax policies and his favored treatment of the region of Judah in the south led to the division of the kingdom after his death in 922 B.C. The tribes loyal to Solomon's son belonged to the Kingdom of Judah, while the other tribes organized the northern Kingdom of Israel. Both second-rate powers, neither Judah nor Israel could hold on to earlier conquests.

Conquest, Captivity, Restoration, and Rebellion

In 722 B.C., Israel fell to the Assyrians, who deported many Hebrews to other parts of the Assyrian empire. These transported Hebrews merged with neighboring peoples and lost their identity as the people of God. In 586 B.C., the Chaldeans conquered Judah, destroyed the temple, devastated the land, and deported several thousand Hebrews to Babylon. The prophets Isaiah, Ezekiel, and Jeremiah declared that the destruction of Judah was a punishment that the Hebrews had brought upon themselves by violating God's laws. This time was the darkest moment in the history of the Hebrews. Their state was gone, and neighboring peoples had overrun their land; their holy temple, built during the reign of King Solomon, was in ruins; thousands had died in battle or had been executed; others had fled to Egypt and other lands, and thousands more were in exile in Babylon. This exile is known as the Babylonian Captivity.

Still the Hebrews, in what is a marvel of history, survived as a people. Although many of the exiles in Babylon assimilated Babylonian ways, some remained faithful to their God Yahweh and the Law of Moses and longed to return to their homeland. Thus, their faith enabled them to endure conquest and exile. In Babylon another prophet, known as Second Isaiah, comforted the uprooted Hebrews. Isaiah declared that soon Yahweh, who controlled the course of history, would restore the erring but repentant Hebrews to their land in a second Exodus. When the Persians conquered Babylon, King Cyrus, in 538 B.C., permitted the exiles to return to Judah, now a Persian province, and to rebuild the temple.

The majority of Judeans preferred to remain in prosperous and cosmopolitan Babylon, but some of them did return to Judah, and in 515 B.C. the Hebrews, now commonly called Jews, dedicated the second temple at Jerusalem.

During the first half of the fifth century B.C. the restored Jewish community seemed on the verge of disintegration. Exploitation of the poor created internal tensions; intermarriage with non-Jews grew more frequent; and there was spiritual backsliding, including neglect of the Sabbath. Under the leadership of Nehemiah and Ezra in the second half of the fifth century B.C., administrative reforms were introduced and spiritual life was invigorated. Once again the Jews had overcome threats to their communal existence.

In the late fourth century B.C., Alexander the Great, commander of a Macedonian and Greek army, conquered the Near East, including Palestine. After Alexander's death his generals seized different parts of his empire. One general, Ptolemy, became ruler of Egypt; a second, Seleucus, became ruler of Syria. Palestine was seized by the Ptolemies, but in 198 B.C., Antiochus III the Great, a Seleucid king, defeated the Egyptians and annexed Palestine. His son Antiochus IV (175–163 B.C.) was insensitive to the religious feelings of the Jews; he suspended observance of the Sabbath, forbade the circumcision of children, destroyed copies of the Law, erected pagan temples, and forced the Jews, under penalty of death, to eat the flesh of pigs. In the most grievous insult to the Jews, he set an altar to the god Zeus in the holy temple. Under the leadership of Mattathias and his five sons, the Jews waged a patriotic religious struggle. When Mattathias died in 166 B.C., his third son Judas, called Maccabeus (which may mean "the hammer") assumed leadership of the revolt. Under Judas' brilliant generalship, the Jews retook control of Jerusalem and cleansed the temple of pagan symbols. The Feast of Hanukkah, in commemoration of the rededication of the temple, has been celebrated by Jews ever since.

Judaea Capta S(enatus) C(onsulto). With a commander's baton in hand and his foot upon a helmet, a victorious centurion proclaims Rome's victory over Judea, personified weeping at the foot of the palm tree. The destruction of the city of Jerusalem under Titus was complete, but the ethics of Old Testament writing would become part of the foundation of Western European culture. (*Courtesy of The American Numismatic Society, New York*)

The Old Testament

In the following centuries, the Jews would lose their independence to Rome and become a dispersed people. But they never relinquished their commitment to God and his Law as recorded in the Old Testament. Called Tanak by Jews, the Old Testament consists of thirty-nine books* by several authors who lived in different centuries. Jews call the first five books of the Old Testament—Genesis,

---

* In ancient times, the number of books was usually given as twenty-four. Certain books are now divided into two parts and the twelve works by the minor prophets are now counted as individual books.

Exodus, Leviticus, Numbers, and Deuteronomy—the Torah. Often the Torah is referred to as the Pentateuch, a Greek word meaning "five books."

The Old Testament represents Hebrew literary and oral tradition dating from about 1250 to 150 B.C. Compiled by religious devotees, not research historians, it understandably contains factual errors, imprecisions, and discrepancies. However, there are also passages that contain reliable history, and historians find the Old Testament an indispensable source for studying the ancient Near East. Students of literature study it for its poetry, legends, and themes, all of which are an integral part of the Western literary tradition. But it is as a work of religious inspiration that the Old Testament attains its profoundest importance.

The Old Testament is the record of more than 1,000 years of ancient Jewish history; containing Jewish laws, wisdom, hopes, legends, and literary expressions, it describes an ancient people's efforts to comprehend the ways of God. The Old Testament emphasizes and values the human experience; its heroes are not demigods, but human beings. Human strength as well as weakness is depicted. Some passages exhibit cruelty and unseemly revenge, while others express the highest ethical values. As set forth in the Old Testament, the Hebrew idea of God and his relationship to human beings is one of the foundations of the Western tradition.

God: One, Sovereign, Transcendent, Good

The Hebrew view of God evolved through the history and experiences of the Hebrew people. In the days of the patriarchs, before the sojourn in Egypt, the Hebrews most likely were not monotheists. They probably devoted themselves to the god of their particular clan and expressed no hatred for the idolatrous beliefs of neighboring peoples. The chief of each clan established a special attachment to the god of his fathers, hoping that the deity would protect and assist the clan. It is likely that the patriarchs' religion contained spiritual elements that later would aid in the transition to monotheism. But this probability cannot be documented with certainty, for much of patriarchal religion still remains a mystery.

Some historians say that Moses' religion was not pure monotheism because it did not rule out the existence of other gods. According to this view, not until the prophets, centuries later, did the Hebrews explicitly deny that other gods existed and that Yahweh stood alone. Other scholars believe that Moses proclaimed a monotheistic idea, that this idea became the central force in the life of the Hebrews at the time of the Exodus from Egypt, and that it continues to be central today. John Bright, an American biblical scholar, suggests a judicious balance. The religion of Moses did not deny the existence of other gods, says Bright, but it "effectively denied them status as gods."[2] The Hebrews could serve only Yahweh and "accorded all power and authority to Him." Consequently Israel was:

. . . forbidden to approach [other deities] as gods. . . . The gods were thus rendered irrelevant, driven from the field. . . . To Israel only the one God was God. . . . The other gods, allowed neither part in creation, nor function in the cosmos, nor power over events . . . were robbed of all that made them gods and rendered non-entities, in short, were "undeified." Though the full implications of monotheism were centuries in being drawn, in the functional sense Israel believed in but one God from the beginning.[3]

The Hebrew view of the one God marked a profound break with Near Eastern religious thought. Pagan gods were not truly free; their power was not without limits. Unlike Yahweh, Near Eastern gods were not eternal, but were born or created; they issued from some prior realm. They were also subject to biological conditions requiring food, drink, sleep, and sexual gratification. Sometimes they became ill, or grew old, or died. When they behaved wickedly, they had to answer to fate, which demanded punishment as retribution; even the gods were subject to fate's power.

The Hebrews regarded God as *fully sovereign*. He ruled all and was subject to nothing. Yahweh's existence and power did not derive from a preexisting realm as pagan gods' did. The Hebrews believed that no realm of being preceded God in time or surpassed him in power. They saw God as eternal, the source of all in the universe, and having a supreme will. He created and governed the natural world and shaped the moral laws that govern human beings. He was not subservient to fate but determined what happened.

Whereas Near Eastern divinities dwelt within nature, the Hebrew God was *transcendent*, above nature and not a part of it. Yahweh was not identified with any natural force and did not dwell in a particular place in heaven or on earth. Since God was the creator and ruler of nature, there was no place for a sun-god, a moon-god, a god in the river, or a demon in the storm. Nature was God's creation but was not itself divine. Therefore, when the Hebrews confronted natural phenomena, they experienced God's magnificent handiwork, not objects with wills of their own. The stars and the planets were creations of Yahweh, not divinities or the abodes of divinities. The Hebrews neither regarded them with awe nor worshiped them.

The Hebrews demythicized nature, but concerned with religion and morality, they did not create theoretical science. As testimony to God's greatness, nature inspired people to sing the praises of the Lord; it invoked worship of God, not scientific curiosity. When Hebrews gazed at the heavens, they did not seek to discover mathematical relationships, but admired God's handiwork. The Hebrews did not view nature as a system governed by natural law. Rather, they saw the rising sun, spring rain, summer heat, and winter cold as God intervening in an orderly manner in his creation. The Hebrews, unlike the Greeks, were not philosophers. They were concerned with God's will, not

Temple Floor Mosaic. Images in Hebrew art are extremely rare because of the biblical injunction against graven images. This floor mosaic from Beth Alpha synagogue in Israel is a zodiacal calendar, with the chariot of the sun in the middle. (*Consulate General of Israel*)

the human intellect; with the feelings of the heart, not the power of the mind; with righteous behavior, not abstract thought. Human mistakes stemmed not from ignorance but from disobedience and stubbornness.

Unlike the Greeks, the Hebrews did not speculate about the origins of all things and the operations of nature; they knew that God had created everything. For the Hebrews, God's existence was based on religious conviction, not on rational inquiry; on revelation, not reason. It was the Greeks, not the Hebrews, who originated rational thought. But Christianity, born of Judaism, retained the Hebrew view of a transcendent God and the orderliness of his creation—concepts that could accommodate Greek science.

The Hebrews also did not speculate about God's nature. They knew only that he was *good* and that he made ethical demands on his people. Unlike Near Eastern gods, Yahweh was not driven by lust or motivated by evil, but was "merciful and gracious, long-suffering, and abundant in goodness and truth . . . forgiving iniquity and transgression and sin" (Psalm 145:8).[4]* In contrast to pagan gods who were indifferent to human beings, Yahweh was attentive to human needs.

By asserting that God was *one, sovereign, transcendent*, and *good*, the Hebrews effected a religious revolution that separated them forever from the world-view held by the peoples of the Near East.

The Individual and Moral Autonomy

This new conception of God made possible a new awareness of the individual. In confronting God, the Hebrews developed an awareness of *self* or *I*. Each individual became conscious of his or her own person, moral autonomy, and personal worth. The Hebrews believed that God, who possessed total freedom himself, had bestowed on his people moral freedom—the capacity to choose between good and evil.

Fundamental to Hebrew belief was the insistence that God did not create people to be his slaves. The Hebrews regarded God with awe and humility, with respect and fear, but they did not believe that God wanted people to grovel before him; rather he wanted them to fulfill their moral potential by freely making the choice to follow or not to follow God's Law. Thus, in creating men and women in his own image, God granted them autonomy and sovereignty. In God's plan for the universe, human beings are the highest creation, subordinate only to God. Of all his creations, only they have been given the freedom to choose between righteousness and wickedness, between "life and good, and death and evil" (Deuteronomy 30:15).

God demanded that the Hebrews have no other gods and that they make no images

"nor any manner of likeness, or any thing that is in heaven above, or that is in the earth beneath, . . . thou shalt not bow down unto them nor serve them" (Exodus 20: 4–5). The Hebrews believed that the worship of idols deprived people of their freedom and dignity; people cannot be fully human if they surrender themselves to a lifeless idol. Hence the Hebrews had to destroy images and all other forms of idolatry. A crucial element of Near Eastern religion was the use of images—art forms that depicted divinities—but the Hebrews believed God, the Supreme Being, could not be represented by pictures or sculpture fashioned by human beings. The Hebrews rejected entirely the belief that an image possessed divine powers that could be manipulated for human advantage. Ethical considerations, not myth or magic, were central to Hebrew religious life.

By making God the center of life, Hebrews could become free moral agents; no person, no human institution, no human tradition could claim their souls. Because God alone was the supreme value in the universe, only he was worthy of worship. Thus, to give *ultimate* loyalty to a king or a general violated God's stern warning against the worship of false gods. The first concern of the Hebrews was supposed to be righteousness, not power, fame, or riches, which were only idols and would impoverish a person spiritually and morally.

There was, however, a condition to freedom. For the Hebrews, people were not free to create their own moral precepts or their own standards of right and wrong; freedom meant the voluntary acceptance of commands that originated with God. Evil and suffering were not caused by blind fate, malevolent demons, or arbitrary gods, but they resulted from people's disregard of God's commandments. The dilemma is that in possessing freedom of choice, human beings are also free to disobey God, to commit a sin, which leads to suffering and death. Thus, in the Genesis story Adam and Eve were punished for disobeying God in the Garden of Eden.

For Hebrews, to know God was not to

*The Bible passages in this chapter are quoted from *The Holy Scriptures*.

comprehend him intellectually, to define him, or to prove his existence; to know God was to be righteous and loving, merciful and just. When men and women loved God, the Hebrews believed, they were uplifted and improved. Gradually they learned to overcome the worst elements of human nature and to treat people with respect and compassion.

By giving devotion to God, the Hebrews asserted the value and the autonomy of human beings. Thus, the Hebrews conceived the idea of moral freedom, that each individual is responsible for his or her own actions. Also inherited by Christianity, this idea of moral autonomy is central to the Western tradition.

The Covenant and the Law

Central to Hebrew religious thought and decisive in Hebrew history was the covenant—God's special agreement with the Hebrew people:

And Moses went up unto God, and the Lord called unto him out of the mountain saying: "Thus shalt thou say to the house of Jacob and tell the children of Israel: Ye have seen what I did unto the Egyptians, and how I bore you on eagles' wings, and brought you unto Myself. Now therefore, if ye will hearken unto My voice indeed, and keep My covenant, then ye shall be Mine own treasure from all peoples; for all the earth is Mine; and ye shall be unto Me a kingdom of priests and a holy nation." [Exodus 19:3–6]

By this act the Israelites as a nation accepted God's lordship.

The Hebrews became conscious of themselves as a unique nation, as a "chosen people," for God had given them a special honor, a profound opportunity, and (as they could never forget) an awesome responsibility. The Hebrews did not claim that God had selected them because they were better than other peoples or because they had done anything special to deserve God's election. They believed that God, in a remarkable manner,

had rescued them from bondage in Egypt and had selected them to receive the Law so that their nation would set an example of righteous behavior and ultimately make God and the Law known to the other nations.

This responsibility to be the moral teachers of humanity weighed heavily on the Hebrews. They believed that God had revealed his Law—including the moral code known as the Ten Commandments—to the Hebrew people as a whole, and obedience to the Law became the overriding obligation of each Hebrew. Violating the Law meant breaking the sacred covenant—an act that could lead to national disaster. As the Law originated with the one God, the necessary prerequisite for understanding and obeying it was surrendering belief in other gods forever, for they were barriers to comprehending and carrying out God's universal Law.

Ethical concerns resulted in decrees dealing with economic, social, and political relationships, which were designed to give practical expression to God's universal norms of morality. And because the covenant was made with the entire Hebrew nation, society as a whole had a religious obligation to root out evil and to make justice prevail. Thus, there were laws to protect the poor, widows, orphans, resident aliens, hired laborers, and slaves. Israelite law incorporated many elements from Near Eastern legal codes and oral traditions. But by making people more important than property, by expressing mercy toward the oppressed, and by rejecting the idea that law should treat the poor and the rich differently, Israelite law demonstrated a greater ethical awareness and a more humane spirit than other legal codes of the Near East:

And a stranger shalt thou not wrong, neither shalt thou oppress him; for ye were strangers in the land of Egypt. Ye shall not afflict any widow or fatherless child. [Exodus 22:20–21]

If thy brother, a Hebrew man, or a Hebrew woman, be sold unto thee, he shall serve thee six years; and in the seventh year thou shalt let him go free from thee. And when thou lettest him go free from thee, thou shalt not let him go empty;

Masada. For four years the defenders of the hilltop fortress of Masada resisted the Roman forces that had earlier captured Jerusalem in A.D. 70. In the end, they preferred suicide to submission. The constancy of Jewish beliefs remained, in spite of internal political divisions, defeats, and dispersion. (*Consulate General of Israel*)

thou shalt furnish him liberally. . . . [Deuteronomy 15:12–14]

Thou shalt not curse the deaf, nor put a stumbling-block before the blind, but thou shalt fear thy God: I am the Lord. . . . thou shalt love thy neighbor as thyself. [Leviticus 19:14,18]

Hebrew law regulated all aspects of daily life including family relationships. The father had supreme authority in the family, extending to his married sons and their wives if they remained in his household. Although polygamy was permitted, monogamy was the general rule; adultery was punishable by death.

Like other Near Eastern societies, the Jews placed women in a subordinate position. The husband was considered his wife's master, and she often addressed him as a servant or subject would speak to a superior. A husband could divorce his wife, but she could not divorce him. Only when there was no male heir could a wife inherit property from her husband or a daughter inherit from her father. Outside the home, women were not regarded as competent witnesses in court and played a lesser role in organized worship.

On the other hand, the Jews also showed respect for women. Wise women and prophetesses like Judith and Esther were respected by the community and were consulted by its leaders. Prophets compared God's love for the Hebrews with a husband's love for his wife. The Book of Proverbs describes a woman of valor:

Strength and dignity are her clothing;
And she laugheth at the time to come.

She openeth her mouth with wisdom;
And the law of kindness is on her tongue.
She looketh well to the ways of her household,
And eateth not the bread of idleness.
Her children rise up and call her blessed;
Her husband also, and he praiseth her. . . .
    [Proverbs 31:25–28]

Jewish law regarded the woman as a person, not as property. Even female captives taken in war were not to be abused or humiliated. The law required a husband to respect and support his wife and never to strike her. One of the Ten Commandments called for honoring both father and mother.

The Hebrew Idea of History

Their idea of God made the Hebrews aware of the crucial importance of historical time. Holidays commemorating such specific historical events as the Exodus from Egypt and the receiving of the Ten Commandments on Mount Sinai kept the past alive and vital. Egyptians and Mesopotamians did not have a similar awareness of the uniqueness of a given event: to them today's incident merely reproduced events experienced by their ancestors. To the Jews, the Exodus and the covenant were singular, nonrepetitive occurrences, decisive in shaping their national history. This historical uniqueness and importance of events derived from the idea of a universal God profoundly involved in human affairs—a God who cares, teaches, and punishes.

The Jews valued the future as well as the past. They envisioned a great day when God would establish on earth a glorious age of peace, prosperity, happiness, and human brotherhood. This utopian notion has become deeply embedded in Western thought. Two thousand years later when Karl Marx claimed that a golden age would be ushered in after the destruction of capitalism and the creation of a classless society, he was echoing an ancient Hebrew longing for utopia.

The Jews saw history as a divine drama filled with sacred meaning and moral significance. Historical events revealed the clash of human will with God's commands. Through history's specific events, God's presence was disclosed and his purpose made known. When the Hebrews suffered conquest and exile, they interpreted these events as retribution for violating God's Law and as punishments for their stubbornness, sinfulness, and rebelliousness. The ancient Hebrews, says historian Millar Burrows, were convinced that history was "the work of a personal divine will, contending with the foolish, stubborn wills of men, promising and warning, judging and punishing and destroying, yet sifting, saving, and abundantly blessing those found amenable to disipline and instruction."[5] Because historical events revealed God's attitude toward human beings, these events possessed spiritual meaning, and therefore were worth recording, evaluating, and remembering.

The Prophets

Jewish history was marked by the emergence of spiritually inspired persons called *prophets*, who felt compelled to act as God's messengers. The prophets cared nothing for money or possessions, feared no one, and preached without invitation. Often emerging in times of social distress and moral confusion, the prophets pleaded for a return to the covenant and the Law. They exhorted the people and taught that when his people forgot God and made themselves the center of all things, they would bring disaster on themselves and their community.

The prophets saw national misfortune as an opportunity for penitence and reform. They were remarkably courageous men who did not quake before the powerful. In the late eighth century an angry Isaiah warned:

The Lord will enter into judgment
With the elders of His people, and the princes
    thereof:
"It is ye that have eaten up the vineyard;

The spoil of the poor is in your houses;
What mean ye that ye crush my *people,*
And grind the face of the poor?" [Isaiah
    3:14–15]

Social Justice

The flowering of the prophetic movement—
the age of classical or literary prophecy—
began in the eighth century B.C. In attacking
oppression, cruelty, greed, and exploitation,
the classical prophets added a new dimension
to Israel's religious development. These
prophets were responding to problems emanating from Israel's changed social structure.
The general lack of class distinctions char-
acterizing a tribal society had been altered
by the rise of Hebrew kings, the expansion
of commerce, and the growth of cities. By
the eighth century, there was a significant
disparity between the wealthy and the poor.
Small farmers in debt to moneylenders faced
the loss of their land or even bondage; the
poor were often dispossessed by the greedy
wealthy. To the prophets, these social evils
were religious sins. Amos, a mid-eighth-cen-
tury prophet, felt a tremendous compulsion
to speak out against these injustices. In the
name of God, he denounced the heartless
rich, protested against the pursuit of luxury,
and warned that Israel would be punished
for its sins:

I hate, I despise your feasts,
And I will take no delight in your solemn
    assemblies.
Yea, though ye offer me burnt-offerings and
    your meal-offerings,
I will not accept them;
Neither will I regard the peace offerings of your
    fat beasts.
Take thou away from Me the noise of thy
    songs;
And let Me not hear the melody of the
    psalteries.
But let justice well up as waters,
And righteousness as a mighty stream. [Amos
    5:21–24]

God is compassionate, insisted the prophets. He cares for all, especially the poor, the

unfortunate, the sufferer, and the defenseless.
God's injunctions, declared Isaiah, were to:

Seek justice, relieve the oppressed,
Judge the fatherless, plead for the widow.
    [Isaiah *1:17*]

Prophets de-emphasized sacrifices and rituals and stressed the direct spiritual-ethical
encounter between the individual and God.
It was the inner person more than the outer
forms of religious activity that concerned the
prophets. Holding that the essence of the
covenant was universal righteousness, the
prophets criticized priests whose commitment
to rites and rituals was not supported by a
deeper spiritual insight nor matched by a
zeal for morality in daily life. To the prophets,
an ethical sin was far worse than a ritual
omission. Above all, said the prophets, God
demands righteousness. To live unjustly, to
mistreat one's neighbors, to act without compassion—these actions violated God's law and
endangered the entire social order.

The prophets thus created a social conscience that has become part of the Western
tradition. This revolutionary social doctrine
states that everyone has a God-given right
to social justice and fair treatment; that each
person has a religious obligation to denounce
evil and oppose mistreatment of others; and
that the community has a moral responsibility
to assist the unfortunate. The prophets held
out the hope that life on earth could be improved, that poverty and injustice need not
be accepted as part of an unalterable natural
order, and that the individual was capable
of elevating himself or herself morally and
could respect the dignity of others.

Universalism

Two tendencies were present in Hebrew
thought: parochialism and universalism. Parochial-mindedness stressed the special nature, destiny, and needs of the chosen people,
a nation set apart from others. This outlook
was offset by universalism, a concern for all
humanity, which found expression in those
prophets who envisioned the unity of all

Dead Sea Scroll. The sacredness of the biblical text and the authority of the recorded word of God remain a theme and a unifying factor in ancient as well as modern Jewish history. Found in caves at Khirbet Qumran the Dead Sea Scrolls contained a version of an almost complete text of Isaiah that differed insignificantly from the modern version, yet the scroll dated from the second century B.C. and is the earliest version extant. (© *John C. Trever, 1970*)

people—a brotherhood of man under the fatherhood of God. All people were equally precious to God.

In that day shall there be a highway out of Egypt to Assyria, and the Assyrian shall come into Egypt, and the Egyptian into Assyria; and the Egyptians shall worship with the Assyrians. In that day shall Israel be the third with Egypt and with Assyria, . . . for that the Lord of hosts hath blessed him saying: "Blessed be Egypt My people and Assyria the work of My hands, and Israel Mine inheritance." [Isaiah 19:23–24]

Israel was charged with a sacred mission: to lead in the struggle against idolatry and to set an example of righteous behavior for all humanity.

The prophets were not pacifists, particularly if a war were being waged against the enemies of Yahweh. But some prophets denounced war as obscene and looked forward to its elimination. In a world where virtually everyone glorified the warrior, the prophets of universalism envisioned the day when peace would reign over the earth, when nations:

. . . shall beat their swords into plowshares,
And their spears into pruning-hooks;
Nation shall not lift up sword against nation,
Neither shall they learn war any more. [Isaiah 2:4]

These prophets maintained that when people glorify force, they dehumanize their oppo-

Chronology 2.1 The Hebrews

1250 B.C.*	Hebrew Exodus from Egypt
1024–1000	The reign of Saul, Israel's first king
1000–961	The creation of a united monarchy under David
961–922	The reign of Solomon; construction of the First Temple
750–430	The Age of Classical Prophecy
722	Kingdom of Israel falls to Assyrians
586	Kingdom of Judah falls to Chaldeans; the temple is destroyed
586–539	Babylonian Exile
538	Cyrus of Persia allows exiles to return to Judah
515 B.C.	Second Temple is dedicated

* Most dates are approximations.

responsibility of their religious inspiration and conviction.

Prophets emphasized the individual's responsibility for his or her own actions. In coming to regard God's law as a *command to conscience, an appeal to the inner person,* the prophets heightened the awareness of the human personality. They indicated that the individual could not know God only by following edicts and by performing rituals; the individual must experience God. Precisely this I-Thou relationship could make the individual fully conscious of self and could deepen and enrich his or her own personality. At Mount Sinai, God gave the Law to a tribal people who obeyed largely out of fear and compulsion; by the prophets' time, the Jews appeared to be autonomous individuals who heeded the Law because of a deliberate, conscious, and inner commitment.

Monotheism had initiated a process of self-realization and self-discovery unmatched by other peoples of the Near East. The prophets' ideals helped sustain the Jews throughout their long and often painful historical odyssey, and they remain a vital force for Jews today. Incorporated into the teachings of Jesus, these ideals, as part of Christianity, are embedded in the Western tradition.

nents, brutalize themselves, and dishonor God. When violence rules, there can be no love of god and no regard for the individual.

Individualism

The prophets' universalism was accompanied by an equally profound awareness of the individual and his worth to God. Before the prophets, virtually all religious tradition had been produced communally and anonymously. The prophets, however, spoke as fearless individuals who, by affixing their signatures to their thoughts, fully bore the

Notes

1. John A. Wilson, "Egypt—the Kingdom of the 'Two Lands'," in E. A. Speiser, *At the Dawn of Civilization* (New Brunswick, N.J.: Rutgers University Press, 1964), pp. 267–268. Volume I in *The World History of the Jewish People.*

2. John Bright, *A History of Israel* (Philadelphia: The Westminster Press, 1972), p. 154.

3. Ibid.

4. From *The Holy Scriptures* (Philadelphia: The Jewish Publication Society of America, 1917). The scriptural quotations are used in this chapter with the permission of the Jewish Publication Society of America.

5. Millar Burrows, "Ancient Israel," in Robert C. Dentan, ed., *The Idea of History in the Ancient Near East* (New Haven: Yale University Press, 1955), p. 128.

Suggested Reading

Albright, W. F., *The Biblical Period from Abraham to Ezra* (1963). Analyzes the culture and history of ancient Israel and explains the growing spiritual nature of the Hebrew conception of God.

Anderson, Bernhard, *Understanding the Old Testament*, 2nd ed. (1966) An excellent survey of the Old Testament in its historical setting.

Bright, John, *A History of Israel* (1972). A thoughtful, clearly written survey; the best of its kind.

de Vaux, Roland, *Ancient Israel*, vol. I, *Social Institutions* (1965). All phases of Israelite society—family, monarchy, law, war, and so on.

Ehrlich, E. L., *A Concise History of Israel* (1965). An interpretive essay covering the period from the Patriarchs to the destruction of the Jerusalem Temple in A.D. 70.

Heschel, Abraham, *The Prophets*, 2 vols. (1962). A penetrating analysis of the nature of prophetic inspiration.

Kaufmann, Yehezkel, *The Religion of Israel* (1960). An abridgment and translation of Kaufmann's classic multivolume work.

Kuntz, Kenneth J., *The People of Ancient Israel* (1974). An up-to-date introduction to Old Testament literature, history, and thought.

Muilenburg, James, *The Way of Israel* (1961). A discussion of biblical faith and ethics.

Scott, R. B. Y., *The Relevance of the Prophets* (1968). An introduction to the Old Testament prophetic tradition.

Snaith, N. H., *The Distinctive Ideas of the Old Testament* (1964). Discusses those central ideas that distinguish Hebrew religion from other religions of the Near East.

Review Questions

1. What role did each of the following play in Jewish history: Moses, Saul, David, Solomon, Babylonian Captivity, Judas Maccabeus?

2. How did the Hebrew view of God mark a revolutionary break with Near Eastern religious thought?

3. How did Hebrew religious thought promote the idea of moral autonomy?

4. How did the Hebrews interpret the covenant?

5. What was the Hebrew view of women? What was the significance of this view for Western history?

6. Provide examples showing that Hebrew law expressed a concern for human dignity.

7. Why did the Hebrews consider history to be important, and how did they demonstrate its importance?

8. Both parochialism and universalism were evident in ancient Hebrew thought and history. Discuss. Are both traditions also evident in modern Jewish history? Explain.

9. What role did the prophets play in Hebrew history? What is the enduring significance of their achievement?

10. Why are the Hebrews regarded as one source of Western civilization?

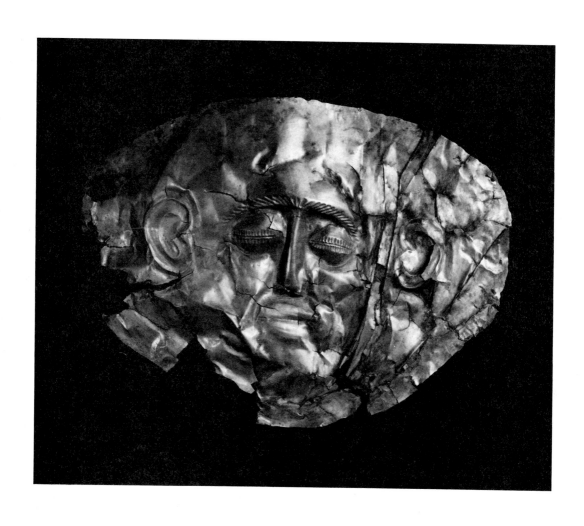

3

*The Greek City-State:
Democratic Politics*

*T*he Hebrew conception of ethical monotheism, with its stress on human dignity, is one source of the Western tradition. The other source derives from ancient Greece. Both Hebrews and Greeks absorbed the achievements of Near Eastern civilizations, but they also developed their own distinctive viewpoints and styles of thought that set them apart from the Mesopotamians and Egyptians. The great achievements of the Hebrews lay in the sphere of religious-ethical thought; those of the Greeks lay in the development of rational thought. As Greek society evolved, says British historian James Shiel, there

was a growing reliance on independent reason, a devotion to logical precision, progressing from myth to logos [reason]. Rationalism permeated the whole social and cultural development. . . . Architecture . . . developed from primitive cultic considerations to sophisticated mathematical norms; sculpture escaped from temple image to a new love of naturalism and proportion; political life proceeded from tyranny to rational experiments in democracy. From practical rules of thumb, geometry moved forward in the direction of the impressive Euclidian synthesis. So too philosophy made its way from "sayings of the wise" to the Aristotelian logic, and made men rely on their own observation and reflection in facing the unexplained vastness of the cosmos.[1]

The Greeks conceived of nature as following general rules, not acting according to the whims of gods or demons. They saw human beings as having a capacity for rational thought, a need for freedom, and a worth as individuals. Although the Greeks never dispensed with the gods, they increasingly stressed the importance of human reason and human decisions; they came to assert that reason is the avenue to knowledge and that people—not the gods—are responsible for their own behavior. In this shift of attention from the gods to the individual, the Greeks broke with the myth-making orientation of the Near East and created the rational outlook that is a distinctive feature of Western civilization.

Early Aegean Civilizations

Minoan Statuette of a Snake Goddess, Sixteenth Century B.C. Early Aegean religion still maintained elaborate ritual. In Crete, the female goddess was prominent. The exact meaning of the snakes is unknown, except for their link with ancient fertility cults. (*Courtesy Museum of Fine Arts, Boston*)

Until the latter part of the nineteenth century, historians placed the beginning of Greek history in the eighth century B.C. Although the ancient Greek poet Homer had spoken of an earlier Greek civilization in his works, historians believed that Homer's epics dealt with myths and legends, not with a historical past. In 1871, however, a successful German businessman, Heinrich Schliemann, began a search for earliest Greece. Having been enthralled by Homer's epics as a youth, Schliemann was convinced that they referred to an actual civilization. In excavating several sites mentioned by Homer, Schliemann discovered tombs, pottery, ornaments, and the remains of palaces of what hitherto had been a lost Greek civilization. The ancient civilization was named after Mycenae, the most important city of the time. Mycenaean civilization pervaded the Greek mainland and the islands of the Aegean Sea for much of the second millennium B.C.

In 1900, Arthur Evans, a British archaeologist, made an equally extraordinary discovery; excavating on the island of Crete southeast of the Greek mainland, he unearthed a civilization even older than that of the Mycenaean Greeks. The Cretans, or Minoans, were not Greeks and did not speak a Greek language, but their influence on mainland Greece was considerable and enduring. Minoan civilization lasted about 1350 years (2600 B.C. to 1250 B.C.) and reached its height during the period from 1700 to 1450 B.C.

Religion and life were closely integrated in Minoan times, as they were in all the early civilizations. The king performed priestly functions, and sacred symbols were placed in palaces and homes. Cretan art expressed religious themes, and the worship of a mother goddess as well as other deities was common.

The centers of Minoan civilization were magnificent palace complexes, whose construction was evidence of the wealth and power of Minoan kings. That the palaces' architects and the artists who decorated the walls were sensitive to beauty is shown in the ruins that have been uncovered at various Cretan sites. The palaces housed royal families, priests, and government officials, and contained workshops that produced decorated silver vessels, daggers, and pottery for local use and for export. In Egypt, Syria, Asia Minor, and Greece, numerous Cretan artifacts have been found that attest to a substantial export trade.

Minoan creativity survived many disasters. Successive waves of destruction caused by earthquakes and accompanying fires shook the island. The palaces were probably all but destroyed three times during the late nineteenth and eighteenth centuries B.C. The last earthquake necessitated a complete reconstruction of the palaces. Cultural life, too, had to be renewed, along with economic life, for the palaces were central to Cretan civilization.

Despite these disasters, Minoan civilization recovered and progressed, aided by peaceful conditions. The palaces, swiftly rebuilt, were grander than ever—the palace at Knossos had more than 1,500 rooms. Cretan ships dominated the Aegean Sea. Economic and cultural contacts with the advanced civilizations of the Near East expanded, and art flourished. Cretan civilization had entered its golden age.

Judging by the archaeological evidence, the Minoans seemed peaceful. Minoan art did not generally depict military scenes, and Minoan palaces, unlike the Mycenaean, had no defensive walls or fortifications. Thus the Minoans were vulnerable to the warlike Mycenaean Greeks, who invaded and conquered Knossos. The Minoans never recovered from this blow, and within two centuries Minoan civilization faded away.

Who were these Mycenaeans? About 2000 B.C., Greek-speaking tribes moved southward into the Greek peninsula where, together with the pre-Greek population, they fashioned the Mycenaean civilization. In the Peloponnesus, the Mycenaeans built palaces that were based in part on Cretan models. In these palaces, Mycenaean kings conducted affairs of state and priests and priestesses carried out religious ceremonies; potters, smiths, tailors, and chariot builders practiced their crafts in the numerous workshops, much like their Minoan counterparts. Mycenaean arts and crafts owed a considerable debt to Crete. A script that permitted record keeping also probably came from Crete. The Mycenaeans were traders, too, exchanging goods with the peoples of Egypt, Phoenicia, Sicily, southern Italy, Macedon, and the western coast of Asia Minor.

At the apex of Mycenaean society was the king, who headed the armed forces, controlled production and trade, and was the highest judicial authority. Assisting the king were aristocrats who were officers in the army and held key positions in the administration. Also in the upper echelons of the society were the priestesses and priests, who supervised sanctuaries and other properties of the gods. Farmers, stockbreeders, and craftsmen constituted the bulk of the free population. Slaves, principally foreign prisoners of war, were at the bottom of the social pyramid.

Mycenaean civilization reached its height in the period from 1400 to 1230 B.C. Following that, constant warfare between the Mycenaean kingdoms (and perhaps foreign invasions) led to destruction of the palaces and abrupt disintegration of the Mycenaean civilization about 1100 B.C. But to the later Greek civilization the Mycenaeans left a legacy of religious forms, pottery making, metallurgy, agriculture, language, a code of honor immortalized in the Homeric epics, and myths and legends that offered themes for Greek drama.

The Rise of Hellenic Civilization

From 1100 to 800 B.C., the Greek world passed through the Dark Age, an era of transition between a dead Mycenaean civilization and a still unborn Hellenic civilization. The Dark Age saw the migration of Greek tribes from the barren mountainous regions of Greece to more fertile plains, and from the mainland to Aegean islands and the coast of Asia Minor. One group of invaders, the Dorians, penetrated the Peloponnesian peninsula in the south and later founded Sparta. Another group, called the Ionians, settled in Attica, where Athens is located, and later crossed to Asia Minor. During this period the Greeks experienced insecurity, warfare, poverty, and isolation. The bureaucratic system of Mycenaean government had disappeared, extensive trade had ceased, the art of writing had been forgotten, the palace workshops no longer existed, and art had reverted to primitive forms.

After 800 B.C., however, town life revived. Writing again became part of the Greek culture, this time with the more efficient Phoenician script. The population increased dramatically, there was a spectacular increase in the use of metals, and overseas trade expanded. Gradually Greek cities founded settlements on the islands of the Aegean, along the coast of Asia Minor and the Black Sea, and to the west in Sicily and southern Italy. These colonies, established to relieve overpopulation and land hunger, were independent, self-governing city-states, not possessions of the homeland city-states. During these two hundred years of colonization (750–550 B.C.), trade and industry expanded, the pace of urbanization quickened, and a new class emerged—the merchants, whose wealth derived from goods and money rather than from the land. In time, this middle class would challenge the landholding aristocracy.

Homer, Shaper of the Greek Spirit

The poet Homer lived during the eighth century B.C., just after the Dark Age. His great epics, the *Iliad* and the *Odyssey*,* helped to

---

* Many scholars hold that while Homer composed the *Iliad*, the *Odyssey* was probably the work of an unknown poet who lived sometime after Homer; some say that Homer composed both epics in their earliest forms and that others altered them.

shape the Greek spirit and Greek religion. Homer was the earliest molder of the Greek outlook and character.

For centuries Greek youngsters grew up reciting the Homeric epics and admiring the Homeric heroes. The *Iliad* deals in poetic form with a small segment of the last year of the Trojan War, which had taken place centuries before Homer's time during the Mycenaean period. At the very beginning, Homer states his theme:

The Wrath of Achilles is my theme, that fatal wrath which, in fulfillment of the will of Zeus, brought the Achaeans [Greeks] so much suffering and sent the gallant souls of many noblemen to Hades, leaving their bodies as carrion for the dogs and passing birds. Let us begin, goddess of song, with the angry parting that took place between Agamemnon King of Men and the great Achilles Son of Peleus.[2]

The story goes on to reveal the cause for this wrath. In depriving "the swift and excellent" Achilles of his rightful prize (the captive girl, Briseis), King Agamemnon has gravely insulted Achilles' honor and has violated the solemn rule that warrior heroes treat each other with respect. Achilles, his pride wounded by this offense to his honor, refuses to rejoin Agamemnon in battle against Troy. Achilles plans to retain his honor by demonstrating that the Achaeans need his valor and military prowess. Not until many brave men have been slain, including his dearest friend Patroclus, does Achilles set aside his quarrel with Agamemnon and enter the battle.

Homer employs a *particular* event, the quarrel between an arrogant Agamemnon and a revengeful Achilles, to demonstrate a *universal* principle—that "wicked arrogance" and "ruinous wrath" will cause much suffering and death. Homer grasps that there is an internal logic to existence, a significant order to human affairs. For Homer, says British classicist H. D. F. Kitto, "actions must have their consequences; ill-judged actions must have uncomfortable results."[3] People, even

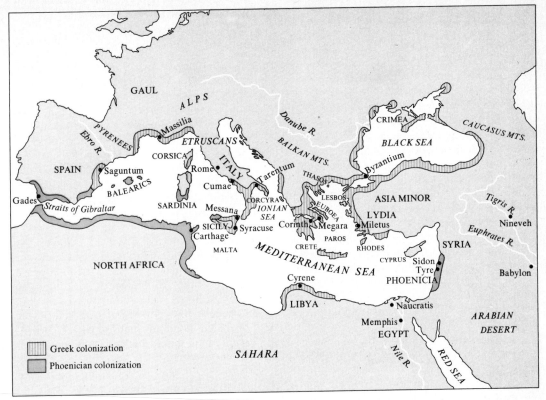

Map 3.1 Greek Colonization of the Mediterranean Basin

the gods, operate within a certain unalterable framework; their deeds are subject to the demands of fate, or necessity. With a poet's insight, Homer sensed what would become a fundamental attitude of the Greek mind: there is a universal order to things. Later Greeks would formulate it in philosophical terms.

Although human life is governed by laws of necessity, the Homeric warrior expresses a passionate desire to assert himself, to demonstrate his worth, to gain the glory that poets would immortalize in their songs—that is, to achieve *arete*, excellence. In the *Iliad*, Hector, prince of Troy, does battle with Achilles, even though defeat and death seem certain. He fights not because he is a fool rushing madly into a fray nor because he relishes combat, but because he is a prince bound by a code of honor and conscious of his reputation. In the code of the warrior aristocrats, honor meant more than life itself.

In the warrior-aristocrat world of Homer, *excellence* was principally interpreted as bravery and skill in battle. Homer's portrayal also bears the embryo of a larger conception of human excellence, one that combines thought with action. A man of true worth, says the wise Phoenix to a stubborn Achilles, is both "a speaker of words and a doer of deeds." In this passage, we find the earliest statement of the Greek educational ideal—the molding of a man who, says classicist Werner Jaeger, "united nobility of action with nobility of mind," who realized "the whole of human potentialities."[4] Thus, in Homer we find the beginnings of Greek humanism—a concern with man and his achievements.

To Mesopotamian and Egyptian minds, the gods were primarily responsible for the good or evil that befell human beings. To Homer, the gods are still very much involved in human affairs, but he also makes the individual a decisive actor in the drama of life. Human actions and human personality are very important. Homer's men demonstrate a considerable independence of will. Men pay respect to the gods but do not live in perpetual fear of them; they choose their own way, at times even defying the gods. As British classicist C. M. Bowra says, "the human actors . . . pursue their own aims and deal their own blows; the gods may help or obstruct them, but success or failure remains their own. The gods have the last word, but in the interval men do their utmost and win glory for it."[5]

Homer's works are essentially an expression of the poetic imagination and mythical thought. But his view of the eternal order of nature and his conception of the individual striving for excellence form the foundations of the Greek outlook.

Greek Religion

During the Dark Age, Greek religion was a mixture of beliefs and cults inherited from the Mycenaean past and from an even older Indo-European past imported from Asia Minor. The Greeks had no prophets or works of scripture in the manner of the Hebrews, but Homer's epics gave some clarity and structure to Greek religion. He did not intend his poetry to have any theological significance, but his treatment of the gods had important religious implications for the Greeks. In time, Homer's epics formed the basis of the Olympian religion accepted thoughout Greece. The principal gods were said to reside on Mount Olympus and on its highest peak was the palace of Zeus, the chief deity. The Olympian gods were recognized by all Greeks, but each city retained local gods and rituals that had been transmitted through generations by folk memory.

Many Greeks found an outlet for their religious feelings in the sacred ceremonies of mystic cults. Devotees of the cult of Dionysus, the god of wine and agricultural fertility, engaged in ecstatic dances and frenzied prayers for abundant harvests. Participants in the Eleusinian cult felt purified and reborn

through their rituals and believed in a happy life after death. The Orphic cult, which was popular in the sixth century B.C., taught the unimportance of earthly life and the need to prepare for life after the grave. The Orphics believed that the soul, which once enjoyed a happy existence in another world, was imprisoned in the body for an unknown fault, and that if the individual controlled his or her bodily desires, the soul would be liberated after death.

In the early stages of Greek history, most people sought to live in accordance with the wishes of the gods. Through prayer, offerings, and ritual purification, they tried to appease the gods and consulted oracles to divine the future. Although religion pervaded daily life, the Greeks had no official body of priests who ruled religious matters and could intervene in politics. Instead, religious ceremonies were conducted by citizens chosen to serve as priests. But in time, traditional religion would be challenged and undermined by a growing secular and rational spirit.

Evolution of the City-State

The Break with Theocratic Politics

Greek society from 750 B.C. to the death of Alexander the Great in 323 B.C. comprised small independent city-states. The city-state based on tribal allegiances was generally the first political association during the early stages of civilization. Moreover, Greece's many mountains, bays, and islands—natural barriers to political unity—favored this type of political arrangement.

The scale of the city-state, or *polis*, was small; most city-states had less than 5,000 male citizens. Athens, which was a large city-state, had some 35,000 male citizens; the rest of its population of 350,000 consisted of women, children, resident aliens, and slaves, none of whom could participate in lawmaking. The citizens of the polis, many of whom were related by blood, knew each other well, and together they engaged in athletic contests and religious rituals. The polis gave individuals a sense of belonging, for its citizens were intimately involved in the political and cultural life of the community.

In the fifth century B.C., at its maturity, the Greeks viewed their polis as the only avenue to the good life—"the only framework within which man could realize his spiritual, moral, and intellectual capacities," in the words of Kitto.[6] The mature polis was a self-governing community that expressed the will of free citizens, not the desires of gods, hereditary kings, or priests. In the Near East, religion dominated political activity, and to abide by the mandates of the gods was the ruler's first responsibility. The Greek polis also had begun as a religious institution in which the citizens sought to maintain an alliance with their deities. But gradually the citizens de-emphasized the gods' role in political life and based government not on the magic powers of divine rulers, but on human intelligence as expressed through the community. The great innovation introduced by the Greeks into politics and social theory, says classicist Mason Hammond, was "the view that law did not emanate from gods, or divine rulers, but from the human community."[7]

The evolution of the Greek polis from a tribal-religious institution to a secular-rational institution was only a part of the general transition of the Greek mind from myth to reason. The emergence of rational attitudes did not, of course, spell the end of religion, particularly for the peasants, who remained devoted to their ancient cults, gods, and shrines. Greek commanders and statesmen, at times, were not beyond consulting omens and oracles before making decisions, and a considerable part of Athenian revenue went to the construction of temples and the observance of religious festivals. The Greeks were careful to show respect for the gods, for it was believed that these deities could aid or harm a city. Worshipping the god of the city was a required act of patriotism to which Greeks unfailingly adhered.

Thus, the religious-mythical tradition never died in Greece, but existed side by side with a growing rationalism. As Greek rationalism gained in influence, traditional religious beliefs and restrictions either were made to comply more with the demands of reason, or grew weaker through neglect and disuse. When Athenian democracy reached its height in the middle of the fifth century B.C., religion was no longer the dominant factor in politics. For many Athenians, religion had become largely ceremonial, a way of expressing loyalty to the city; they had actually come to rely on human reason, not divine guidance, in their political and intellectual life.

Greek political life was marred by violent party conflicts, demagoguery, intercity warfare, and the exploitation of weak states by stronger ones. Nevertheless, the Greek political achievement was extraordinary. What made Greek political life different from that of earlier Near Eastern civilizations, as well as of enduring significance, was the Greeks' gradual realization that community problems are caused by human beings and require human solutions. Thus the Greeks came to understand law as an achievement of the rational mind rather than as an edict imposed by the gods; law was valued because it expressed the will and needs of the community, not out of fear of the divine. The Greeks also valued free citizenship. An absolute king who ruled arbitrarily and by decree, who was above the law, was abhorrent to them.

The ideals of political freedom are best exemplified by Athens. But before turning to Athens, let us examine another Greek city, which followed a different political course.

Sparta: A Garrison State

Situated on the Peloponnesian peninsula, further inland than most Greek cities, Sparta had been settled by Dorian Greeks. While the other Greek city-states dealt with overpopulation and land hunger by establishing colonies, Sparta conquered its neighbors, including Messenia, in the eighth century B.C.

Instead of selling the Messenians abroad, the traditional Greek way of treating a defeated foe, the Spartans kept them as state serfs, or *helots*. Helots were owned by the state rather than by individual Spartans. Enraged by their enforced servitude, the Messenians, also a Greek people, desperately tried to regain their freedom. After a bloody struggle, the Spartans suppressed the uprising, but the fear of a helot revolt became indelibly stamped on Spartan consciousness.

To maintain their dominion over the Messenians who outnumbered them ten to one, the Spartans—with extraordinary single-mindedness, discipline, and loyalty—transformed their own society into an armed camp. Agricultural labor was performed by helots; trade and crafts were left to the *perioikoi*, conquered Greeks who were free but who had no political rights; and the Spartans learned only one craft, soldiering.

The Spartans were trained in the arts of war and indoctrinated to serve the state. Military training for Spartan boys began at age seven; they exercised, drilled, competed, and endured physical hardships. Other Greeks admired the Spartans for their courage, obedience to law, and achievement in molding themselves according to an ideal. Spartan soldiers were better trained and disciplined and were more physically fit than other Greeks. But the Spartans were also criticized for having a limited conception of arete.

Before converting itself into a military state, Sparta's cultural development had paralleled that of the other Greek cities. By isolating itself economically and culturally from the rest of Greece, however, Sparta became a closed provincial town and did not share in the cultural enlightenment that pervaded the Greek world. A culturally retarded Sparta paid a heavy price for military strength.

By 500 B.C., Sparta had emerged as the leader of the Peloponnesian League, an alliance of southern Greek city-states whose land forces were superior to those of any other combination of Greek cities. Sparta, though, was concerned with controlling its conquests, not with further imperialism.

Cautious by temperament and always fearful of a helot uprising, Spartans viewed the Peloponnesian League as an instrument for defense, not for aggression.

Athens: The Rise of Democracy

The contrast between the city-states of Athens and Sparta is striking. Whereas Sparta was a land power and exclusively agricultural, Athens was located on the peninsula of Attica near the coast, possessed a great navy, and was the commercial leader among the Greeks. Sparta's leaders were reluctant to send soldiers far from home, where they were needed to control the helots, so they pursued an isolationist foreign policy. The Athenians, daring and ambitious, endeavored to extend their hegemony over other Greek cities. Finally, Athenians and Spartans held different conceptions of freedom. To the Spartans, freedom meant preserving the independence of their fatherland; this overriding consideration demanded order, discipline, and regimentation. The Athenians also wanted to protect their city from enemies, but unlike the Spartans, they valued political freedom and sought the full development and enrichment of the human personality. Thus, while authoritarian Sparta became culturally sterile, the relatively free and open society of Athens became the cultural leader of Hellenic civilization.

Greek city-states generally moved through four stages: rule by a king (monarchy), rule by landowning aristocrats (oligarchy), rule by one man who seized power (tyranny), and rule by the people (democracy). In a monarchy, the first stage, the king, who derived his power from the gods, commanded the army and judged civil cases.

The second stage, an oligarchy, was instituted in Athens during the eighth century B.C. when aristocrats usurped power from hereditary kings. In the next century, aristocratic regimes experienced a social crisis. First, there was tension between the landholding nobility that dominated the govern-

Acropolis. On top of the rocky Acropolis stood Athens's most impressive structures, including the Temple of Athena Nike, and the majestic Parthenon. These monuments were a symbol of Athenian civic pride and creative genius. (*Greek National Tourist Organization*)

ment and the newly rich and ambitious merchants who wanted a share in governing Athens. Second, peasants who borrowed from the aristocracy, pledging their lands as security, lost their property and even became enslaved for nonpayment of their debts. In Athens the embittered and restless peasants demanded and were granted one concession. In 621 B.C., the aristocrats appointed Draco to draw up a code of law. Although Draco's code let the poor know what the law was and reduced the possibilities of aristocratic judges behaving arbitrarily, penalties were extremely severe, and the code provided no relief for the peasants' economic woes. Athens was moving toward civil war as the poor began to organize and press for the cancellation of their debts and the redistribution of land.

Solon, the Reformer In 594 B.C. Solon, a traveler and poet with a reputation for being wise, was elected chief executive. Two years later, the aristocrats, to avert open warfare, gave Solon the power to work out a solution to Athens's problems. Solon maintained that a principle of justice, *Dike*, underlies the human community, and that when people violate this standard of justice, they bring ruin upon the city. Thus, he held that the wealthy landowners, through their greed, had disrupted community life and brought Athens to the brink of civil war. A distinguishing feature of Greek intellectual life was the belief in the orderliness of the universe. For Solon (c. 640–559 B.C.), universal law also operated in the sphere of social life.

Originally, justice had been conceived in religious terms as the will of Zeus; in regarding justice as a principle operating within society, Solon withdrew justice from the province of religion and gave it a secular foundation. He initiated a rational approach to the problems of society by reducing the gods' role in human affairs: he attributed the city's ills to the specific behavior of individuals; he sought worldly remedies for these ills; and he held that written law should be in harmony with the natural order of things. In Solon's career can be detected the embryo of political thought and reform based on reason.

Underlying Solon's reforms was a concern for the interests of the community as a whole, a commitment to moderation, and an avoidance of radical extremes. Solon aimed at restoring a sick Athenian society to health by restraining the nobles and improving the lot of the poor. To achieve this goal, he canceled debts, freed Athenians enslaved for debt, and brought back to Athens those who had been sold abroad; but he refused to confiscate and redistribute the nobles' land as the extremists demanded.

Solon recognized that the aristocrats had abused their political power, but he did not believe that the common people were prepared for self-government. His political reforms rested on the assumption that aristocrats would continue to exercise a guiding role in government. He permitted all classes of free men, even the poorest, to sit in the Assembly, which elected magistrates and accepted or rejected legislation proposed by a new Council of Four Hundred, and opened the highest offices in the state to wealthy commoners, who had previously been excluded from these positions because they lacked noble birth. Thus, Solon undermined the traditional rights of the hereditary aristocracy and initiated the transformation of Athens from an aristocratic oligarchy into a democracy.

Solon also instituted ingenious economic reforms. Recognizing that the poor soil of Attica was not conducive to growing grain, he urged the cultivation of grapes for wine and the growing of olives, whose oil could be exported. To encourage industrial expansion, he ordered that all fathers teach their sons a trade and granted citizenship to foreign craftsmen willing to migrate to Athens. These measures and the fine quality of the native reddish-brown clay allowed Athens to become the leading producer and exporter of pottery. Solon's economic policies had transformed Athens into a great commercial center.

With imagination and intelligence, Solon had reformed Athenian society. His reforms completed, Solon retired from office. In refusing to use his prestige to become a tyrant, a one-man ruler, Solon demonstrated that his statesmanship rested on the highest moral principles—on a conception of justice. Believing that only the rule of law can hold the community together, Solon refused to act outside the law; wanting to imbue his fellow Athenians with a sense of responsibility, he refused to act irresponsibly. However, Solon's reforms did not eliminate factional disputes among the aristocratic clans nor relieve all the discontent of the poor.

Pisistratus, the Tyrant Pisistratus (c. 605–527 B.C.), another aristocrat, endeavored to take advantage of the general instability to become a one-man ruler. After two abortive efforts, he secured power in 546 B.C. and drove into exile those fellow aristocrats who had opposed him. Tyranny thus had replaced oligarchy.

Tyranny occurred frequently in the Greek city-states. Almost always aristocrats themselves, tyrants generally posed as champions of the poor in their struggle against the aristocracy, another indication that the government had to reckon with the needs of the entire community. To increase their own base of support, some tyrants extended citizenship to the landless and even to foreigners.

Pisistratus sought popular support by having conduits constructed to increase Athens's water supply; like tyrants in other city-states he gave to peasants land confiscated from exiled aristocrats, and granted state loans to small farmers. By concerning himself with the problems of the masses, Pisistratus continued the trend initiated by Solon. In a deliberate attempt to pacify the population, Pisistratus exercised personal power without abolishing the existing constitution.

Pisistratus' great achievement was the promotion of cultural life. He initiated grand architectural projects, encouraged sculptors and painters, arranged for public recitals of the Homeric epics, and founded festivals that included dramatic performances. In all these ways he made culture, formerly the province of the aristocracy, available to commoners. Pisistratus thus launched a policy that eventually led Athens to emerge as the cultural capital of the Greeks. In further weakening the power of the landed aristocracy, Pisistratus made the establishment of democracy under Cleisthenes possible.

Cleisthenes, the Democrat   After Pisistratus' death in 527 B.C., his power passed to his two sons. One was assassinated and the other driven from Athens by Spartans, whose intervention had been urged by exiled Athenian aristocrats who opposed one-man rule. In the power vacuum that ensued, a faction headed by Cleisthenes, an aristocrat sympathetic to democracy, assumed leadership.

By an ingenious method of redistricting the city, Cleisthenes ended the aristocratic clans' traditional jockeying for the chief state positions, which had caused so much divisiveness and bitterness in Athens. Cleisthenes replaced this practice, rooted in tradition and authority, with a new system devised by reason to ensure that historic allegiance to tribe or clan would be superseded by loyalty to the city.

Cleisthenes hoped to make democracy the permanent form of government for Athens. To safeguard the city against tyranny, he introduced the practice of *ostracism*. Once a year Athenians were given the opportunity to inscribe on a potsherd *(ostracon)* the name of anyone who they felt endangered the state.

An individual against whom sufficient votes were cast was ostracized, that is, forced to leave Athens for ten years.

Although some aristocratic features still existed in the government (notably the Council of the Areopagus, consisting of retired high officials), Cleisthenes had firmly secured democratic government in Athens. The Assembly, which Solon had opened to all male citizens, was in the process of becoming the supreme authority in the state. But the period of Athenian greatness lay in the future; the Athenians first had to fight a war of survival against the Persian Empire.

Athenian Greatness

The Persian Wars

In 499 B.C., the Ionian Greeks of Asia Minor rebelled against their Persian overlord. Sympathetic to the Ionian cause, Athens sent twenty ships to aid the revolt, an act that the Greek historian Herodotus said "was the beginning of trouble not only for Greece, but for the rest of the world as well." Bent on revenge, Darius I, king of Persia, sent a small detachment to Attica. In 490 B.C., on the plains of Marathon, the citizen army of Athens defeated the Persians—for the Athenians, one of the finest moments in their history. Ten years later, Xerxes, Darius' son, organized a huge invasion force of some 250,000 men and over 500 ships with the aim of reducing Greece to a Persian province. Setting aside their separatist instincts, most of the city-states united to defend their independence and their liberty. Herodotus viewed the conflict as a struggle for freedom.

The Persians crossed the waters of the Hellespont (Dardanelles) and made their way into northern Greece. Herodotus describes their encounter at the mountain pass of Thermopylae with 300 Spartans, who were true to their training and ideal of arete and "resisted to the last with their swords if they had them, and if not, with their hands and teeth, until the Persians, coming on from the front over the ruins of the wall and closing in from behind, finally overwhelmed them."[8] Northern Greece fell to the Persians, who continued south, burning a deserted Athens.

When it appeared that the Greeks' spirit had been broken, the Athenian statesman and general Themistocles (c. 527–460 B.C.) demonstrating in military affairs the same rationality that Cleisthenes had shown in political life, lured the Persian fleet into the narrows of the Bay of Salamis. Unable to deploy their more numerous ships in this cramped space, the Persian armada was destroyed by Greek ships manned by crews who understood what was at stake. In 479 B.C., a year after the Athenian naval victory at Salamis, the Spartans defeated the Persians in the land battle of Plataea. The inventive intelligence with which the Greeks had planned their military operations and a fierce desire to preserve their freedom had enabled them to defeat the greatest military power the Mediterranean world had yet seen.

The Persian Wars were decisive in the history of the West. Had the Greeks been defeated, it is very likely that their cultural and political vitality would have been crushed. The confidence and pride that came with victory, however, propelled Athens into a golden age, which became marred by the Athenian urge for dominance in Greece.

The Delian League

The Persian Wars ushered in an era of Athenian imperialism that had drastic consequences for the future. Immediately after the wars, more than 150 city-states organized a confederation, the Delian League, to protect themselves against a renewed confrontation with Persia. Because of its wealth, its powerful fleet, and the restless energy of its citizens, Athens assumed leadership of the Delian League. Largely because of the Athenian fleet, the league was able to drive both pirates and Persians from the Aegean Sea. Conceived as a voluntary association of independent Greek states seeking protection against Persia, the league gradually came under the domination of Athens.

Athenians consciously and rapaciously manipulated the league for their own economic advantage, seeing no conflict between imperialism and democracy. They coveted the empire that gave them wealth, power, and glory, and they considered it natural for strong states to increase their might at the expense of weaker ones. Moreover, the Athenians claimed that the other city-states benefited from Athenian hegemony. Athens forbade member states to withdraw, crushed revolts, and stationed garrisons on the territory of confederate states. It used both tribute from members and the League's treasury to finance public works in Athens.

Although member states did receive protection, were not overtaxed, and enjoyed increased trade, they resented Athenian domination. As the Persian threat subsided, hatred for Athenian imperialism grew. In converting the Delian League into an instrument of Athenian imperialism, Athens may have lost an opportunity to perform a great creative act, as historian Arnold Toynbee suggests:

If the Athenians had resisted the temptation to abuse their trust, as the leading power in the confederacy, for their own narrow national advantage, the economic tide making for closer political union would probably have kept the confederacy of Delos in existence on a voluntary footing; and this might have led on, in time, to some kind of voluntary political unification of the Hellenic World as a whole. The course taken at this critical time, by Athenian policy under Pericles' leadership, led to a renewal of fratricidal warfare [and] the breakdown of Hellenic Civilization.[9]

The Mature Athenian Democracy

Athenian imperialism was one consequence of the Persian Wars; another was the flowering of Athenian democracy and culture. Democracy became more firmly entrenched when in 462 B.C. the aristocratic Council of the Areopagus was stripped of its political powers.

Map 3.2 The Aegean Basin

The Athenian state was a direct democracy, in which the citizens themselves, not elected representatives, made the laws. In the Assembly, which was open to all adult male citizens and which met some forty times a year, Athenians debated and voted on key issues of state—they declared war, signed treaties, and spent public funds. The lowliest cobbler, as well as the wealthiest aristocrat, had the opportunity to express his opinion in the Assembly, to vote, and to hold office. By the middle of the fifth century, the will of the people as expressed in the Assembly was supreme.

The Council of Five Hundred (which had been established by Cleisthenes to replace Solon's Council of Four Hundred) managed the ports, military installations, and other state properties and prepared the agenda for the Assembly. Because its members were chosen annually by lot and could not serve more than twice in a lifetime, the Council could never supersede the Assembly. Some

350 magistrates, also chosen by lot, performed administrative tasks. The ten generals, because of the special competence their posts required, were not chosen by lot, but were elected by the Assembly.

Athens has been aptly described as a government of amateurs; there were no professional civil servants, no professional soldiers and sailors, no state judges, no elected lawmakers. The duties of government were performed by ordinary citizens. Such a system rested on the assumption that the average citizen was capable of participating intelligently in the affairs of state; that he would, in a spirit of civic patriotism, carry out his responsibilities to his city. In fifth-century Athens, excellence was equated with good citizenship.

The introduction of pay for government officials marked a great democratic advance. It meant that a poor person could afford to leave his job for a year in order to serve on the Council of 500, on a commission overseeing the administration of the city, or in the law courts.

Although Athens was a democracy in form, in practice aristocrats continued to dominate political life for most of the fifth century. The generals elected by the people came from noble houses as did the leading politicians in the Assembly. This situation was not surprising, for aristocrats took for granted a responsibility to exercise leadership and acquired the education needed to perform this role. The economic expansion after the Persian Wars produced a wealthy class of tradesmen who eventually challenged aristocratic dominance in the Assembly during the last third of the fifth century B.C.

Athenian democracy undoubtedly had its limitations and weaknesses. Modern critics point out that resident aliens were almost totally barred from citizenship and therefore from political participation. Slaves, who constituted about one-fourth of the Athenian population, enjoyed none of the freedoms that Athenians considered so precious. The Greeks regarded slavery as a necessary precondition for civilized life; for some to be free and prosperous, they believed, others had to be enslaved. Whereas people today regard slavery and freedom as contradictory, to the Greeks they were complementary.

Slaves usually did the same work as Athenian citizens—farming, commerce, manufacturing, domestic chores. Some slaves—the 300 Scythian archers who made up the police force and those sufficiently educated to serve the state as clerks—enjoyed a privileged position. However, slaves who toiled in the mines suffered a grim fate. In Athens, some slaves were Greeks, but most were foreigners. Slaves were generally prisoners of war and captives of pirates.

Athenian women were another group denied legal or political rights. They were barred from attending the Assembly and holding public office, and generally they could not appear in court without a male representative. Like the Near Eastern societies, Greek society was male-dominated. Since it was believed that a woman could not act

independently, she was required to have a guardian—normally her father or husband—who controlled her property and supervised her behavior.

Ancient critics also attacked Athenian democracy. Having no confidence in the ability of the common people to govern, these aristocratic critics equated democracy with mob rule. The Assembly did at times make rash and foolish decisions and was swayed by the oratory of demagogues. For the most part, however, concludes British historian A. H. M. Jones,

the Assembly seems to have kept its head, and very rarely to have broken its rules of procedure. . . . Moreover, the people demanded high standards of its advisors. . . . It was informed advice, and not mere eloquence, that the people expected from rising politicians, and they saw to it that they got it.[10]

That the Athenians found democracy an indispensable form of government is proved by the paucity of revolts. In the almost two hundred years after Cleisthenes, there were only two attempts to undo the democracy. Both occurred under the stress of the Peloponnesian War, and both were short-lived.

The flaws in Athenian democracy should not cause us to undervalue its extraordinary achievement. The idea that the state represented a community of free citizens remains a crucial principle of Western civilization. Athenian democracy embodied the principle of the legal state—a government based on laws debated, devised, altered, and obeyed by free citizens.

This idea of the legal state could only have arisen in a society that had an awareness of and a respect for the rational mind. In the same way that the Greeks demythicized nature, they also removed myth from the sphere of politics. Holding that government was something that people create to satisfy human needs, the Athenians regarded their leaders neither as gods nor as priests, but as men who had demonstrated a capacity for statesmanship. Athens was unique, says Italian historian Mario Attilio Levi, for Athenians "had the audacity to maintain that human reason is itself the source of legitimacy and therefore of the right to govern and command, in a world in which the only recognized source of legitimacy was the gods."[11]

Both systematic political thought and democratic politics originated in Greece. There, people first asked questions about the nature and purpose of the state, rationally analyzed political institutions, speculated about human nature and justice, and discussed the merits of various forms of government. It is to Greece that we ultimately trace the idea of democracy and all that accompanies it—citizenship, constitutions, equality before the law, government by law, reasoned debate, respect for the individual, and confidence in human intelligence.

But there is a fundamental difference between the Greek concept of liberty and our own. We are concerned with protecting the individual from the state, which we often see as a threat to personal freedom and a hindrance to the pursuit of our personal lives. Identifying the good of the individual with the good of the community, the Greeks were not concerned with erecting safeguards against the state; they did not see the state as an alien force to be feared or to be protected against. To the Greeks, the state was a moral association, a second family that taught proper conduct and enabled them to fulfill their human potential.

Pericles: Symbol of Athenian Democracy

Pericles (c. 495–429 B.C.), a gifted statesman, orator, and military commander, was the central figure in Athenian life during the middle of the fifth century B.C. So impressive was his leadership that this period is called the Age of Pericles. The Athenians achieved greatness in politics, drama, sculpture, architecture, and thought during these decades.

In the opening stage of the monumental clash with Sparta, the Peloponnesian War

(431–404 B.C.), Pericles delivered an oration in honor of the Athenian war casualties. The oration contains a glowing description of the Athenian democratic ideal:

We are called a democracy, for the administration is in the hands of the many and not of the few. But while the law secures equal justice to all alike in their private disputes, the claim of excellence is also recognized; and when a citizen is in any way distinguished, he is preferred to the public service . . . as the reward of merit. Neither is poverty a bar. . . . a spirit of reverence pervades our public acts; we are prevented from doing wrong by respect for authority and for the laws. . . .[12]

Throughout the speech, Pericles contrasted the narrow Spartan concept of excellence with the Athenian ideal of the full development of the human personality. Unlike Sparta, Athens valued both political freedom and cultural creativity; indeed, as Pericles recognized, freedom released an enormous amount of creative energy, making possible Athens's extraordinary cultural accomplishments. "Our love of what is beautiful does not lead to extravagance, our love of the things of the mind does not make us soft," continued Pericles in praise of Athenian society.[13]

The Decline of the City-States

Although the Greeks shared a common language and culture, they remained divided politically. A determination to preserve city-state sovereignty prevented the Greeks from forming a larger political grouping, which might have contained the intercity warfare that ultimately cost the city-state its vitality and independence. But the creation of a Pan-Hellenic union would have required a radical transformation of the Greek character that for hundreds of years had regarded the city-state as the only suitable political system.

Youth Singing and Playing the Kithara (detail). This young man's figure presents an impressive picture of how ancient music was performed. The making of vases, ordinarily a craft, became high art in the archaic and classical periods of Greek civilization. Hundreds of examples of signed works allow us to talk of individual artists for the first time in history. This red-figured vase is by the "Berlin painter." (Attic, c. 490 B.C.) (*The Metropolitan Museum of Art, Fletcher Fund, 1956*)

The Peloponnesian War

Athens's control of the Delian League engendered fear in the Spartans and their allies in the Peloponnesian League. Sparta and the Peloponnesian states decided on war because they felt that their independence was threatened by a dynamic and imperialistic Athens. At stake for Athens was hegemony over the Delian League, which gave Athens political power and contributed to its economic prosperity. Neither Athens nor Sparta anticipated the catastrophic consequences the war would have for Greek civilization.

The war began in 431 B.C. and ended in 404 B.C., with a temporary and uneasy interlude of peace from 421 to 414 B.C. Possessing superior land forces, the Peloponnesian League invaded Attica and set fire to the countryside. In 430 B.C., a plague, probably coming from Ethiopia by way of Egypt, ravaged Athens, killing about one-third of the population, including its leader, Pericles (in 429 B.C.). Because of Athenian sea power and Spartan inability to inflict a crushing defeat on Athenian ground troops, the first stage of the war ended in stalemate. In 421 B.C., the war-weary combatants concluded a peace treaty.

What led to the resumption of the war and the eventual defeat of Athens was the Athenian expedition against Sicily and its largest city, Syracuse. Athenians were intoxicated by an imperialist urge to extend the empire in the west and by prospects of riches. Swayed by speeches that stirred the emotions, the Athenian populace, believing disaster to be impossible and forsaking caution and reason, approved the Sicilian venture. In the words of Thucydides, the great fifth-century B.C. Athenian historian,

There was a passion for the enterprise which affected everyone alike. . . . The result of this excessive enthusiasm of the majority was that the few who actually were opposed to the expedition were afraid of being thought unpatriotic if they voted against it, and therefore kept quiet.[14]

In 415 B.C. the largest army ever assembled by a Greek city departed for distant Sicily. Unable to overcome the Syracusans, Nicias, the Athenian commander, appealed for reinforcements. Repeating their previous recklessness, the Athenians voted to send a second large expedition to Syracuse. Failure continued. Finally, as his army grew more dispirited and the Syracusans were reinforced by other Sicilian cities, Nicias consented to withdraw.

Then occurred an event that demonstrates

the persistence of the nonrational in Greek life. Just when the Athenians were ready to depart, there was an eclipse of the full moon, and Nicias took it as an omen. Heeding the advice of seers, Nicias postponed the evacuation for twenty-seven days, during which time the Syracusans blocked the mouth of the harbor. After failing in a desperate attempt to break out by sea, the Athenians tried to escape by land. It was a death march. Harassed on all sides by the Syracusans, the Athenians retreated in panic, leaving their wounded behind. They were trapped and were forced to surrender. Imprisoned in Sicilian rock quarries, they perished of hunger, thirst, and disease. Athens and its allies lost 50,000 men and 200 ships in the venture.

Launched with extravagant expectations, the Sicilian expedition ended in dismal failure and cost Athens all hope of victory in the struggle with Sparta. Fearful that victory in Sicily would increase Athenian manpower and wealth, Sparta had again taken up the sword. Strengthened by financial support from Persia and by the defection of some Athenian allies, Sparta moved to end the war. Finally, a besieged Athens, with a decimated navy and a dwindling food supply, surrendered. Sparta dissolved the Delian League, left Athens with only a handful of ships, and forced the city to pull down its long walls— ramparts designed to protect it against siege weapons; but the Spartans refused to massacre Athenian men and enslave the women and children as some allies had urged.

The Peloponnesian War shattered the spiritual foundations of Hellenic society. During the course of the long war, men became brutalized, selfish individualism triumphed over civic duty, moderation gave way to extremism, and politics degenerated into revolution. The moral basis of Hellenic society was wrecked. In the words of Thucydides:

Love of power, operating through greed and through personal ambition, was the cause of all these evils. To this must be added the violent fanaticism which came into play once the struggle had broken out. Leaders of parties . . . in professing to serve the

public interest . . . were seeking to win the prizes for themselves. In their struggle for ascendancy nothing was barred; terrible indeed were the actions to which they committed themselves, and in taking revenge they went further still. Here they were deterred neither by the claims of justice nor by the interests of the state. . . . Thus neither side had any use for conscientious motives; more interest was shown in those who could produce attractive arguments to justify some disgraceful action. As for the citizens who held moderate views, they were destroyed by both the extreme parties. . . . As the result of these revolutions, there was a general deterioration of character throughout the Greek World.[15]

Athens shared the political problems of the Greek world during the war. Pericles had provided Athenians with effective leadership in the three decades prior to the war; when the Assembly seemed to support unwise policies, he had won it over with sound arguments. After his death in 429 B.C., the quality of leadership deteriorated. Succeeding statesmen were motivated more by personal ambition than by civic devotion; rather than soberly examining issues, they supported policies that would gain them popularity. Without Pericles' wise statesmanship, the Assembly at times acted rashly, as it did in the case of the Sicilian expedition.

The deterioration of Greek political life was exemplified by conflicts between oligarchs and democrats. Oligarchs, generally from the wealthier segments of Athenian society, wanted to concentrate power in their own hands by depriving the lower classes of political rights. Democrats, generally from the poorer segment of society, sought to preserve the political rights of adult male citizens. Strife between oligarchs and democrats was quite common in the Greek city-states even before the Peloponnesian War. Both sides sought to dominate the Assembly and to manipulate the courts; both resorted to bribery and at times even assassinated opponents. During the Peloponnesian War these party conflicts erupted into civil war in a number of cities, including Athens.

Taking advantage of the decline in morale following the failure of the Sicilian expedition, oligarchs gained control of Athens in 411 B.C.; a body of Four Hundred citizens wielded power. Seeking to deprive the lower classes of political influence, the Four Hundred restricted citizenship to 4,000 men. But the crews of Athenian ships, loyal to democracy, challenged the authority of the Four Hundred, who were forced to flee.

After Athens's defeat in 404 B.C., oligarchs again gained control, this time with the support of Spart . A ruling council of thirty men, the so-called Thirty Tyrants, held power. Led by Critias, an extreme antidemocrat, the Thirty trampled on Athenian rights, confiscating property and condemning many people to death. In the winter of 404–403, returned exiles led an uprising against the Thirty, who were unseated.

The Fourth Century

The Peloponnesian War was the great crisis of Hellenic history. The city-states never recovered from their self-inflicted spiritual wounds. The civic loyalty and confidence that had marked the fifth century waned and the fourth century was dominated by a new mentality that the leaders of the Age of Pericles would have abhorred. A concern for private affairs superseded devotion to the general good of the polis. Increasingly, the tasks of government were administered by professionals instead of by ordinary citizens, and mercenaries began to replace citizen soldiers.

The political history of the fourth century can be summed up briefly. Athens, the only state that might have conceivably imposed unity on the Greek world, had lost its chance. A culturally sterile, provincial-minded, and heavy-handed Spartan government lacked the talent to govern the Greeks. In many cities, Sparta replaced democratic governments with pro-Spartan oligarchies under the supervision of a Spartan governor. But Spartan hegemony was short-lived; before long the Greek city-

states had thrown off the Spartan yoke. The quarrelsome city-states formed new systems of alliances and peristed in their ruinous conflicts. Some Greek thinkers, recognizing the futility of constant war, argued that peace should be the goal of Greek politics. But their efforts were in vain.

In addition to wars between city-states, fourth-century Greece experienced a new outbreak of civil wars between rich and poor. Athens largely escaped these ruinous conflicts, but they engulfed many other cities. With good reason, Greek thinkers regarded social discord as the greatest of evils.

While the Greek cities battered each other in fratricidal warfare, a new power was rising in the north—Macedonia. To the Greeks, the Macedonians, a wild mountain people who had acquired a sprinkling of Hellenic culture, differed little from other non-Greeks whom they called barbarians. In 359 B.C., twenty-three-year-old Philip (382–336 B.C.) became Philip II, king of Macedonia. Having spent three years as a hostage in Thebes, Philip had learned the latest military tactics and had witnessed firsthand the weaknesses of the warring Greek states. He converted Macedonia into a first-rate military power and began a drive to become master of the Greeks.

Patient, deceitful, clever, and unscrupulous, Philip gradually extended his power over the Greek city-states. Not correctly assessing Philip's strength, the Greeks were slow to organize a coalition against Macedonia. In 338 B.C. at Chaeronea, Philip's forces inflicted a decisive defeat on the Greeks and all of Greece was his. The city-states still existed, but they had lost their independence. The world of the small, independent, and self-sufficient polis drew to a close and Greek civilization took a different shape.

The Dilemma of Greek Politics

There were deeper reasons why the Greek cities declined and fell victim to Macedonian

Chronology 3.1 The Greek City-State

1700–1450 B.C.*	Height of Minoan civilization
1400–1230	Height of Mycenaean civilization
1100–800	Dark Age
c. 700	Homer
750–550	Age of Colonization
621	Draco's code of law
594	Solon is given power to institute reforms
546–527	Under Pisistratus tyranny replaces oligarchy
507	Cleisthenes broadens democratic institutions
499	Ionians revolt against Persian rule
490	Athenians defeat Persians at Battle of Marathon
480	Xerxes of Persia invades Greece; Greek naval victory at Salamis
479	Spartans defeat Persians at Plataea, ending Persian Wars
478–477	Formation of Delian League
431	Start of Peloponnesian War
429	Death of Pericles
413	Athenian defeat at Syracuse
404	Athens surrenders to Sparta, ending Peloponnesian War
399	Execution of Socrates
387	Plato founds a school at Athens
359	Philip II becomes king of Macedonia
338 B.C.	Battle of Chaeronea; Greek city-states fall under dominion of Macedonia

* Some dates are approximations.

imperialism. Despite internal crisis and persistent warfare, the Greeks were unable to fashion any other political framework than the polis. The city-state was fast becoming an anachronism, but the Greeks were unable to see that in a world moving toward larger states and empires, the small city-state could not compete. An unallied city-state with its small citizen army could not withstand the powerful military machine that Philip had created. A challenge confronted the city-states—the need to shape some form of political union, a Pan-Hellenic federation, that would end the suicidal internecine warfare, promote economic well-being, and protect the Greek world from hostile states. Because they could not respond creatively to this challenge, the city-states ultimately lost their independence to foreign conquerors.

The waning of civic responsibility among the citizens was another reason for the decline of the city-states. The vitality of the city-state depended on the willingness of its citizens to put aside private concerns for the good of the community. Although Athens had recovered commercially from the Peloponnesian War, for example, its citizens had suffered a permanent change in character; the abiding devotion to the polis that had distinguished the Age of Pericles greatly diminished during the fourth century. The factional strife, the degeneration of politics into personal ambition, the demagoguery, and the fanaticism that Thucydides had described persisted into the fourth century and was aggravated by the economic discontent of the poor. The Periclean ideal of citizenship dissipated as Athenians neglected the community to concentrate on private affairs, or sought to derive personal profit from public office. The decline in civic responsibility could be seen in the hiring of mercenaries to replace citizen soldiers and in the indifference and hesitancy with which Athenians confronted Philip. The Greeks did not respond to the Macedonian threat as they had earlier rallied to fight off the Persian menace, because the quality of citizenship had deteriorated.

Greek political life evidenced both the best and the worst features of freedom, both the capabilities and limitations of reason. On the one hand, as Pericles boasted, freedom encouraged active citizenship, reasoned debate, and government by law. On the other hand, as Thucydides lamented, freedom could degenerate into factionalism, demagoguery, unbridled self-interest, and civil war.

Rationalism also presented problems. Originally the polis was conceived as a divine institution in which the citizen had a religious obligation to obey the law. As the rational and secular outlook became more pervasive, the gods lost their authority. When law was no longer conceived as an expression of sacred traditions ordained by the gods, but as a merely human contrivance, respect for the law diminished, weakening the foundations of the society. The results were party conflicts, politicians who scrambled for personal power, and moral uncertainty. Recognizing the danger, conservatives insisted that law must again be regarded as issuing from the gods; the city must again treat with reverence its ancient traditions. Although the Greeks originated the lofty ideal that human beings could regulate their political life according to reason, their history, marred by intercity warfare and internal violence, demonstrates the extreme difficulties involved in creating and maintaining a rational society.

Notes

1. James Shiel, *Greek Thought and the Rise of Christianity* (New York: Barnes & Noble, 1968), pp. 5–6.

2. Homer, *The Iliad*, trans. by E. V. Rieu (Baltimore: Penguin Books, 1950), p. 23.

3. H. D. F. Kitto, *The Greeks* (Baltimore: Penguin Books, 1957), p. 60.

4. Werner Jaeger, *Paideia: The Ideals of Greek Culture* (New York: Oxford University Press, 1945), 1:8.

5. C. M. Bowra, *Homer* (London: Gerald Buckworth, 1972), p. 72.

6. Kitto, *The Greeks*, p. 78.

7. Mason Hammond, *The City in the Ancient World* (Cambridge, Mass.: Harvard University Press, 1972), p. 189.

8. Herodotus, *The Histories*, trans. by Aubrey de Sélincourt (Baltimore: Penguin Books, 1954), p. 493.

9. Arnold Toynbee, *Hellenism* (New York: Oxford University Press, 1959), pp. 109–110.

10. A. H. M. Jones, *Athenian Democracy* (Oxford, England: Basil Blackwell, 1969), pp. 132–133.

11. Mario Attilio Levi, *Political Power in the Ancient World* (New York: Mentor Books, 1968), pp. 122–123.

12. Thucydides, *The Peloponnesian War*, trans. by B. Jowett (Oxford, England: Clarendon Press, 1881), bk. II, ch. 37.

13. Thucydides, *The Peloponnesian War*, trans. by Rex Warner (Baltimore: Penguin Books, 1954), p. 118.

14. Ibid., p. 382.

15. Ibid., p. 210.

Suggested Reading

Bowra, C. M., *The Greek Experience* (1957). An excellent introduction to Greek culture and society.

———, *Periclean Athens* (1971). A discussion of Athens at its height.

Claster, J. N., *Athenian Democracy* (1967). A useful collection of readings on the triumphs and failures of Athenian democracy.

Fine, John, V. A., *The Ancient Greeks* (1983). An up-to-date, reliable analysis of Greek history.

Finley, M. I., *The Ancient Greeks* (1964). An excellent popular account of Greek civilization.

———, *Early Greece* (1970). A survey of Minoan and Mycenaean civilizations and early Greek history.

Hammond, N. G. L., *The Classical Age of Greece* (1975). An interpretation of major developments in Greek history.

History of the Hellenic World (1974–). A multivolume history prepared by leading Greek scholars. It has been translated from the Greek and published by the Pennsylvania State University Press. The first volume, *Prehistory and Protohistory*, is excellent for Minoan and Mycenaean civilizations.

Hooper, Finley, *Greek Realities* (1978). A literate and sensitive presentation of Greek society and culture.

Kitto, H. D. F., *The Greeks* (1957). A stimulating survey of Greek life and thought.

Nilsson, M. P., *A History of Greek Religion* (1964). A highly regarded work on Greek religion.

Robinson, C. E., *Hellas* (1948). A useful short survey.

Taylour, William Lord, *The Mycenaeans* (1983). An account of all phases of Mycenaean life.

Webster, T. B. L., *Athenian Culture and Society* (1973). Discusses Athenian religion, crafts, art, drama, education, and so on.

Willetts, R. F., *The Civilization of Ancient Crete* (1977). An account of all phases of Minoan civilization.

Review Questions

1. Describe the main features of Minoan and Mycenaean civilizations.

2. What was the legacy of the Mycenaeans to Hellenic civilization?

3. Why is Homer called "the shaper of Greek civilization"?

4. How did the Greek polis break with the theocratic politics of the Near East?

5. Contrast Spartan society with Athenian society.

6. What were the accomplishments of Solon? Pisistratus? Cleisthenes?

7. What was the significance of the Persian Wars?

8. What contradictions do you see between Athenian democratic ideals and Athenian imperialism? Why did no such contradiction exist for the Athenians?

9. Describe the basic features and the limitations of Athenian democracy.

10. Compare and contrast Athenian democracy with American democracy.

11. What were the causes and the results of the Peloponnesian War?

12. Give reasons for the decline of the polis.

13. What were the causes of the Peloponnesian War? What was the significance of the expedition to Sicily? What was the impact of the Peloponnesian War on the Greek world?

14. What problems did the city-states face in the fourth century B.C.?

15. Explain how Greek political life evidenced both the best and the worst features of freedom, both the capabilities and the limitations of reason.

4

*Greek Thought: From Myth
to Reason*

Philosophy

Cosmologists: Rational Inquiry
into Nature

The Sophists: A Rational Investigation
of Human Culture

Socrates: The Rational Individual

Plato: The Rational Society

Aristotle: Creative Synthesis

Drama

Aeschylus

Sophocles

Euripides

Aristophanes

History

Herodotus

Thucydides

The Greek Achievement:
Reason, Freedom, Humanism

The Greeks broke with the mythopoeic outlook of the Near East and conceived a new way of viewing nature and human society that is the basis of the Western scientific and philosophic tradition. After an initial period of mythical thinking, by the fifth century B.C. the Greek mind had gradually applied reason to the physical world and to all human activities. This emphasis on reason marks a turning point for human civilization.

The development of rational thought in Greece is a process, a trend, not a finished achievement. The process began when some advanced intellects became skeptical of Homer's gods and went beyond mythical explanations for natural phenomena. The non-philosophic majority did not, however, totally eliminate the language, attitudes, and beliefs of myth from its life and thought. Even in the mature philosophy of Plato and Aristotle, mythical modes of thought persisted. What is of immense historical importance is not the degree to which the Greeks successfully integrated the norm of reason, but that they originated this norm, defined it, and applied it to their intellectual development and social life.

Philosophy

The first theoretical philosophers in human history emerged in the sixth century B.C. in the Greek cities of Ionia in Asia Minor. Curious about the essential composition of nature and dissatisfied with earlier creation legends, the Ionians sought physical, rather than mythic-religious, explanations for natural occurrences. In the process, they arrived at a new concept of nature and a new method of inquiry. They maintained that nature was not manipulated by arbitrary and willful gods and that it was not governed by blind chance. The Ionians said that underlying the seeming chaos of nature were principles of order—general laws ascertainable by the human mind. This discovery marks the beginning of scientific thought.

What conditions enabled the Greeks to make this breakthrough? Perhaps their familiarity with Near Eastern achievements in mathematics and science stimulated their ideas. But this influence should not be exaggerated, says Greek student of philosophy John N. Theodorakopoulos, for Egyptians and Mesopotamians "had only mythological systems of belief and a knowledge of practical matters. They did not possess those pure and crystal-clear products of the intellect which we call science and philosophy. Nor did they have any terminology to describe them."[1] Perhaps the poets' conception of human behavior being subject to universal destiny was extended into the philosophers' belief that nature was governed by law. Perhaps the breakthrough was fostered by the Greeks' freedom from a priesthood and rigid religious doctrines that limit thought. Perhaps Greek speculative thought was an offspring of the city, because if law governed human affairs, providing balance and order, should not the universe also be regulated by principles of order?

Cosmologists: Rational Inquiry into Nature

Ionian philosophy began with Thales (c. 624–c. 548 B.C.) of Miletus, a city in Ionia. He was a contemporary of Solon of Athens, and concerned himself with how nature came to be the way it was. Thales said that water was the basic element, the underlying substratum of nature, and that through some natural process—similar to the formation of ice or steam—water gave rise to everything else in the world.

Thales revolutionized thought because he omitted the gods from his account of the origins of nature and searched for a natural explanation of how all things came to be. Thales also broke with the commonly held belief that earthquakes were caused by Poseidon, god of the sea, and offered instead a naturalistic explanation for these disturbances: he thought that the earth floated on

water, and that when the water experienced turbulent waves, the earth was rocked by earthquakes.

Anaximander (c. 611–547 B.C.), another sixth-century Ionian, rejected Thales' theory that water was the original substance. He rejected any specific substance and suggested that an indefinite substance, which he called the Boundless, was the source of all things. From this primary mass, which contained the powers of heat and cold, he believed that there gradually emerged a nucleus, the seed of the world. He said that the cold and wet condensed to form the earth and its cloud cover, while the hot and dry formed the rings of fire that we see as the moon, the sun, and the stars. The heat from the fire in the sky dried the earth and shrank the seas. From the warm slime on earth arose life, and from the first sea creatures there evolved land animals, including human beings. Anaximander's account of the origins of the universe and nature understandably contained fantastic elements. Nevertheless, by offering a natural explanation for the origin of nature and life, it surpassed the creation myths.

Like his fellow Ionians, Anaximenes, who died about 525 B.C., made the transition from myth to reason. He also maintained that a primary substance—air—underlay reality and accounted for the orderliness of nature. Air that was rarefied became fire, while wind, clouds, and water were formed from condensed air. When condensed still further, water turned to earth, and when condensed even more, water turned to stone. Anaximenes also rejected the old belief that a rainbow was the goddess Iris; instead, he said that the rainbow was caused by the sun's rays falling on dense air.

The Ionians have been called "matter philosophers" because they held that everything issued from a particular material substance. Other sixth-century B.C. thinkers tried a different approach. Pythagoras (c. 580–c. 507 B.C.) and his followers, who lived in the Greek cities in southern Italy, did not find the nature of things in a particular substance but in mathematical relationships. The Pythagoreans discovered that the intervals in the musical scale can be expressed mathematically. Extending this principle of proportion found in sound to the universe at large, they concluded that the cosmos also contained an inherent mathematical order. Thus the Pythagoreans shifted the emphasis from matter to form, from the world of sense perception to the logic of mathematics. The Pythagoreans were also religious mystics who believed in the immortality and transmigration of souls. Consequently, they refused to eat animal flesh, fearing that it contained former human souls.

Parmenides (c. 515–450 B.C.), a native of the Greek city of Elea in southern Italy, challenged the fundamental view of the Ionians that all things emerged from one original substance. In developing his position, Parmenides applied to philosophic argument the logic used by the Pythagoreans for mathematical thinking. In putting forth the proposition that an argument must be consistent and contain no contradictions, Parmenides became the founder of formal logic. Reality is one, eternal, and unchanging, asserted Parmenides; it is made known not through the senses, which are misleading, but through the mind—not through experience, but through reason. Truth could be reached through abstract thought alone.

Democritus (c. 460–370 B.C.), from the Greek mainland, renewed the Ionians' concern with the world of matter and reaffirmed their confidence in knowledge derived from sense perception. But he also retained Parmenides' reverence for reason. His model of the universe consisted of two fundamental realities— empty space and an infinite number of atoms. Eternal, indivisible, and imperceptible, these atoms moved in the void. All things consisted of atoms, and combinations of atoms accounted for all change in nature. In a world of colliding atoms, everything behaved according to mechanical principles.

Concepts essential to scientific thought thus emerged in embryonic form with Greek philosophers: the mathematical order of nature (Pythagoras), logical proof (Parmenides), and

the mechanical structure of the universe (Democritus). By giving to nature a rational, rather than a mythical, foundation and by holding that theories should be grounded in evidence and be capable of being defended logically, the early Greek philosophers pushed thought in a new direction. Their achievement made possible theoretical thought and the systematization of knowledge—as distinct from the mere observation and collection of data.

This systematization of knowledge extended into several areas. Greek mathematicians, for example, organized the Egyptians' practical experience with land measurements into the logical and coherent science of geometry. Both Babylonians and Egyptians had performed fairly complex mathematical operations, but unlike the Greeks, they made no attempt to prove mathematical principles. In another area, Babylonian priests had observed the heavens for religious reasons, believing that the stars revealed the wishes of the gods. The Greeks used the data collected by the Babylonians, but not in religion; they sought to discover the geometrical laws that underlie the motions of heavenly bodies.

A parallel development occurred in medicine. No Near Eastern medical text explicitly attacked magical beliefs and practices. In contrast, Greek doctors, because of the philosophers' work, were able to distinguish between magic and medicine. The school of the Greek physician Hippocrates (c. 460–377 B.C.), located on the island of Cos off the Asia Minor coast, was influenced by the thought of the early Greek cosmologists. The following tract from the school of Hippocrates is on epilepsy, considered a sacred disease, and illustrates this growth of a scientific spirit in medicine:

I am about to discuss the disease called "sacred." It is not, in my opinion, any more divine or sacred than any other diseases, but has a natural cause, and its supposed divine origin is due to men's inexperience, and to their wonder at its peculiar character. Now . . . men continue to believe in its divine origin because they are at a loss to understand it. . . . My own view is that those who first attributed a sacred character to this malady were like the magicians, purifiers, charlatans, and quacks of our own day; men who claim great piety and superior knowledge. Being at a loss, and having no treatment which would help, they concealed and sheltered themselves behind superstition, and called this illness sacred, in order that their utter ignorance might not be manifest.[2]

The Sophists: A Rational Investigation of Human Culture

In their effort to understand the external world, the cosmologists had created the tools of reason. Greek thinkers then turned away from the world of nature and attempted a rational investigation of people and society. Exemplifying this shift in focus were the Sophists, professional teachers who wandered from city to city teaching rhetoric, grammar, poetry, gymnastics, mathematics, and music. The Sophists insisted that it was futile to speculate about the first principles of the universe, for such knowledge was beyond the grasp of the human mind; they urged instead that individuals improve themselves and their cities by applying reason to the tasks of citizenship and statesmanship.

The Sophists answered a practical need in Athens, which had been transformed into a wealthy and dynamic imperial state after the Persian Wars. Because the Sophists claimed that they could teach *political arete*—the ability to formulate the right laws and policies for cities and the art of eloquence and persuasion—they were sought as tutors by politically ambitious young men, especially in Athens. The Western humanist tradition owes much to the Sophists, who examined political and ethical problems, cultivated the minds of their students, and invented formal secular education.

Traditionally the Greeks had drawn a sharp distinction between Greeks and non-Greeks, and held that some people were slaves by nature. Some Sophists in the fourth century

Black-figured Athenian Vase. The black-figured vase style used a red background to outline form. Musculature could then be incised or painted in red on the light-colored bodies. Physical fitness and athletics were highly prized by the Greeks. Poets sang the praise of Olympic champions, and sculptors and vase painters captured the beauty of athletic physiques for an admiring public. (*The Metropolitan Museum of Art, Rogers Fund, 1914*)

B.C. arrived at a broader conception of humanity. They asserted that slavery was based on force or chance, that people were not slaves nor masters by nature, and they also held that all people, Greek and non-Greek, were fundamentally alike.

The Sophists were philosophical relativists; that is, they held that no truth is universally valid. Protagoras, a fifth-century Sophist, said that "man is the measure of all things." By this he meant that good and evil, truth and falsehood, are matters of individual judgment—there are no universal standards that apply to all people at all times.

In applying reason to human affairs, the Sophists attacked the traditional religious and moral values of Athenian society. Some Sophists taught that speculation about the divine was useless; others went further and asserted that religion was just a human invention to ensure obedience to traditions and laws.

The Sophists also applied reason to law with the same effect—the undermining of traditional authority. The laws of a given city, they asserted, did not derive from the gods; nor were they based on any objective and universal standards of justice and good, for such standards did not exist. Each community determined for itself what was good or bad, just or unjust. Beginning with this premise, some Sophists simply urged changing laws to meet new circumstances. More radical Sophists argued that law was merely something made by the most powerful citizens for their own benefit. This principle had dangerous implications: first, law did not need to be obeyed since it rested on no higher principle than might; second, the strong should do what they have the power to do, and the weak must accept what they cannot resist. Both interpretations were disruptive of community life, for they stressed the selfish interests of the individual over the general welfare of the city.

Some Sophists combined this assault on law with an attack on the ancient Athenian idea of *sophrosyne*—moderation and self-discipline—because it denied human instincts. Instead of moderation, they urged that people should maximize pleasure and trample underfoot those traditions that restricted them from fully expressing their desires. To these radical Sophists, traditions were only invented by the weak to enslave nobler natures.

In subjecting traditions to the critique of reason, the radical Sophists triggered an intellectual and spiritual crisis. Their doctrines encouraged disobedience to law, neglect of

civic duty, and selfish individualism. These attitudes became widespread during and after the Peloponnesian War, dangerously weakening community bonds.

Socrates: The Rational Individual

In attempting to comprehend nature, the cosmologists had discovered theoretical reason. The Sophists then applied theoretical reason to society. In the process they created a profound problem for Athens and other city-states—the need to restore the authority of law and a respect for moral values. Conservatives argued that this restoration could only be accomplished by renewing allegiance to those sacred traditions undermined by the Sophists.

Socrates, one of the most extraordinary figures in the history of Western civilization, took a different position. Socrates was born in Athens, probably in 469 B.C., about ten years after the Persian Wars, and was executed in 399 B.C., five years after the end of the Peloponnesian War. His life spanned the glory years of Greece, when Athenian culture and democracy were at their height, as well as the tragic years of the lengthy and shattering war with Sparta.

Both the Sophists and Socrates continued the tradition of reason initiated by the cosmologists, but unlike the cosmologists, both felt that knowledge of the individual and society was more important than knowledge of nature. Socrates and the Sophists endeavored to improve the individual and thought that this could be accomplished through education. Despite these similarities, Socrates' teaching marks a profound break with the Sophist movement.

Socrates felt that the Sophists taught skills, but that they had no insights into questions that really mattered: What is the purpose of life? What are the values by which man should live? How does man perfect his character? Here the Sophists failed, said Socrates; they taught the ambitious to succeed in politics, but persuasive oratory and clever reasoning do not instruct a man in the art of living. He felt that the Sophists had attacked the old system of beliefs, but had not provided the individual with a constructive replacement.

Socrates' central concern was the perfection of individual human character, the achievement of moral excellence. Moral values, for Socrates, did not derive from a transcendent God as they did for the Hebrews. They were attained when the individual regulated his life according to objective standards arrived at through rational reflection, that is, when reason became the formative, guiding, and ruling agency of the soul. For Socrates, true education meant the shaping of character according to values discovered through the active and critical use of reason.

Socrates wanted to subject all human beliefs and behavior to the clear light of reason, and in this way to remove ethics from the realm of authority, tradition, dogma, superstition, and myth. Socrates believed that reason was the only proper guide to the most crucial problem of human existence—the question of good and evil. Socrates taught that rational inquiry was a priceless tool that allowed one to test opinions, weigh the merit of ideas, and alter beliefs on the basis of knowledge. To Socrates, when humans engaged in critical self-examination and strove tirelessly to perfect their nature, they liberated themselves from accumulated opinions and traditions and based their conduct on convictions that they could rationally defend. Socrates believed that people with critical minds could not be swayed by sophistic eloquence, nor delude themselves into thinking that they knew something when they really did not.

Dialectics   In urging Athenians to think rationally about the problems of human existence, Socrates offered no systematic ethical theory, no list of ethical precepts. What he did supply was a method of inquiry called *dialectics*, or logical discussion. As Socrates used it, a dialectical exchange between individuals, a *dialogue*, was the essential source of knowledge. It forced people out of their apathy and smugness and compelled them to examine their thoughts critically, to confront illogical, inconsistent, dogmatic, and imprecise assertions, and to express their ideas in clearly defined terms.

Dialectics affirmed that the acquisition of knowledge was a creative act. The human mind could not be coerced into knowing; it was not a passive vessel into which a teacher poured knowledge. The dialogue compelled the individual to play an active role in acquiring the values by which he was to live. In a dialogue, individuals became thinking participants in a search for knowledge. Through relentless cross-examination, Socrates induced his partner to explain and justify his opinions through reason, for only thus did knowledge become a part of one's being.

Dialogue implied that reason was meant to be used in relations between human beings, and that they could learn from each other, help each other, teach each other, and improve each other. It implied further that the human mind could and should make rational choices. To deal rationally with oneself and others is the distinctive mark of being human. Through the dialectical method, people could make ethical choices, impose rules on themselves, and give form to their existence.

For Socrates, the ethical way of life required conscious choice as a prerequisite. The highest form of excellence was taking control of one's life and shaping it according to ethical values reached through reflection. Doing what was right either by accident or imitation was insufficient. Morality did not originate in the decrees of gods or in traditions, but within the individual. Through self-examination and self-discipline, a person could acquire moral values. The good life is attained by the exercise of reason, the development of intelligence— this precept is the essence of Socratic teaching. Socrates made the individual the center of the universe, reason the center of the individual, and moral worth the central aim of human life. In Socrates, Greek humanism found its highest expression.

The Execution of Socrates   Socrates devoted much of his life to his mission—persuading

Porch of the Maidens, Attic Sculpture. The architect has incorporated the human form as a functional element in a rationally organized structure. The balance and harmony of the Porch of the Maidens weds humanity with art. (*Brown Brothers*)

For many years, Socrates challenged Athenians without suffering harm, for Athens was generally distinguished by its freedom of speech and thought. In the uncertain times during and immediately after the Peloponnesian War, though, Socrates made enemies. When he was seventy, he was accused of corrupting the youth of the city, and of not believing in the city's gods but in other new divinities. Underlying these accusations was the fear that Socrates was a troublemaker, a subversive, a Sophist who threatened the state by subjecting its ancient and sacred values to the critique of thought.

Socrates denied the charges and conducted himself with great dignity at his trial, refusing to grovel and beg forgiveness. Instead he defined his creed:

If you think that a man of any worth at all ought to . . . think of anything but whether he is acting justly or unjustly, and as a good or a bad man would act, you are mistaken. . . . If you were therefore to say to me, "Socrates, . . . We will let you go, but on the condition that you give up this investigation of yours, and philosophy. If you are found following these pursuits again you shall die." I say, if you offered to let me go on these terms, I should reply: . . . As long as I have breath and strength I will not give up philosophy and exhorting you and declaring the truth to every one of you whom I meet, saying, as I am accustomed, "My good friend, you are a citizen of Athens . . . are you not ashamed of caring so much for making of money and for fame and prestige, when you neither think nor care about wisdom and truth and the improvement of your soul?"[4]

his fellow Athenians to think critically about how they lived their lives. "No greater good can happen to a man than to discuss human excellence every day,"[3] he said. Always self-controlled and never raising his voice in anger, Socrates engaged any willing Athenian in conversation about his values. Through probing questions, he tried to make people realize how directionless and purposeless their lives were.

Convicted by an Athenian court, Socrates was ordered to drink poison. Had he attempted to appease the jurors, he probably would have been given a light punishment, but he would not alter his principles even under threat of death.

Socrates did not write down his philosophy and beliefs. We are able to construct a coherent account of his life and ideals largely through the works of his most important disciple, Plato.

Plato: The Rational Society

Plato (c. 429–347 B.C.) used his master's teachings to create a comprehensive system of philosophy that embraced both the world of nature and the social world. But Plato had a more ambitious goal than Socrates' moral reformation of the individual. Plato tried to arrange political life according to rational rules, and he held that Socrates' quest for personal morality could not succeed unless the community also was transformed on the basis of reason. Virtually all the problems discussed by Western philosophers for the past two millenniums were raised by Plato. We shall focus on two of his principal concerns, the theory of Ideas and that of the just state.

Theory of Ideas Socrates had taught that universal standards of right and justice exist and that these are arrived at through thought. Building on the insights of his teacher Socrates and of Parmenides, who said that reality is known only through the mind, Plato insisted on the existence of a higher world of reality, independent of the world of things that we experience every day. This higher reality, he said, is the realm of Ideas or Forms—unchanging, eternal, absolute, and universal standards of beauty, goodness, justice, and truth. To live in accordance with these standards constitutes the good life; to know these forms is to grasp truth.

Truth resides in this world of Forms and not in the world made known through the senses. For example, a person can never draw a perfect square, but the properties of a perfect square exist in the world of Forms. Also, a sculptor observes many bodies, and they all possess some flaw; in his mind's eye he tries to penetrate the world of Ideas and to reproduce with art a perfect body. Again, the ordinary person only forms an opinion of what beauty is from observing beautiful things; the philosopher, aspiring to true knowledge, goes beyond what he sees and tries to grasp with his mind the Idea of beauty. Similarly, the ordinary individual lacks a true conception of justice or goodness; such knowledge is available only to the philosopher whose mind can leap from worldly particulars to an ideal world beyond space and time.

Plato saw the world of phenomena as unstable, transitory, and imperfect, while his realm of Ideas was eternal and universally valid. An individual man partakes in an imperfect and limited way in the Idea of man; men may come and go, but the Idea of man persists eternally. Thus true wisdom is obtained through knowledge of the Ideas, not the imperfect reflections of the Ideas that are perceived with the senses.

Plato was a champion of reason who aspired to study and to arrange human life according to universally valid standards. In contrast to sophistic relativism, he maintained that objective and eternal standards do exist. Although Plato advocated the life of reason and wanted to organize society according to rational rules, his writing also includes a religious-mystical side. At times Plato seems like a mystic seeking to escape from this world into a higher reality, a realm that is without earth's evil and injustice.

Because Platonism is a two-world philosophy, it has had an important effect on religious thought. In future chapters we will examine the influence of Platonic otherworldliness on later philosopher-mystics and Christian thinkers.

The Just State In adapting the rational legacy of Greek philosophy to politics, Plato constructed a comprehensive political theory. What the Greeks had achieved in practice—the movement away from mythic and theocratic politics—Plato accomplished on the level of thought: the fashioning of a rational model of the state.

Like Socrates, Plato attempted to resolve the problem caused by the radical Sophists—the undermining of traditional values. Socrates tried to dispel this spiritual crisis through a moral transformation of the individual, while Plato wanted the entire community to conform to rational principles. Plato said that if human beings are to live an ethical life, they must do it as citizens of a just and rational state.

In an unjust state, people cannot achieve Socratic wisdom, for their souls will mirror the state's wickedness.

Plato had experienced the ruinous Peloponnesian War and the accompanying political turmoil. He saw Athens undergo one political crisis after another; most shocking of all, he had witnessed Socrates' trial and execution. Disillusioned by the corruption of Athenian morality and politics, Plato refused to participate in political life. He came to believe that under the Athenian constitution neither the morality of the individual Athenian nor the good of the state could be enhanced, and that Athens required moral and political reform founded on Socrates' philosophy.

In his great dialogue, *The Republic*, Plato devised an ideal state based on standards that would rescue his native Athens from the evils that had befallen it. *The Republic* attempted to analyze society rationally and to reshape the state so that individuals could fulfill the best within them—to attain the Socratic goal of moral excellence. For Plato, the just state could not be founded on tradition (for inherited attitudes did not derive from rational standards), nor on the doctrine of might being right (a principle taught by radical Sophists and practiced by Athenian statesmen). A just state for Plato conformed to universally valid principles and aimed at the moral improvement of its citizens, not at increasing its power and material possessions. Such a state required leaders distinguished by their wisdom and virtue, rather than by sophistic cleverness and eloquence.

Fundamental to Plato's political theory as formulated in *The Republic* was his criticism of Athenian democracy. An aristocrat by birth and temperament, Plato believed that it was foolish to expect the common man to think intelligently about foreign policy, economics, or other vital matters of state. Yet the common man was permitted to speak in the Assembly, to vote, and, by lot, to be selected for executive office. A second weakness of democracy was that leaders were chosen and followed for nonessential reasons like persuasive speech, good looks, wealth, and family background.

A third danger of democracy was that it could degenerate into anarchy, said Plato. Intoxicated by liberty, the citizens of a democracy could lose all sense of balance, self-discipline, and respect for law:

The citizens become so sensitive that they resent the slightest application of control as intolerable tyranny, and in their resolve to have no master they end up by disregarding even the law, written or unwritten.[5]

As liberty leads to license, continued Plato, then the democratic society will deteriorate morally.

The parent falls into the habit of behaving like the child, and the child like the parent: the father is afraid of his sons, and they show no fear or respect for their parents, in order to assert their freedom. . . . To descend to smaller matters, the schoolmaster timidly flatters his pupils, and the pupils make light of their masters. . . . Generally speaking, the young . . . argue with . . . [their elders] and will not do as they are told; while the old, anxious not to be thought disagreeable tyrants, imitate the young and condescend to enter into their jokes and amusements.[6]

As the democratic city falls into disorder, a fourth weakness of democracy will become evident. A demagogue will be able to gain power by promising to plunder the rich to benefit the poor. To retain his hold over the state, the tyrant

begins by stirring up one war after another, in order that the people may feel their need of a leader, and also be so impoverished by taxation that they will be forced to think of nothing but winning their daily bread, instead of plotting against him.[7]

Because of these inherent weaknesses of democracy, Plato insisted that Athens could not be saved by more doses of liberty. He believed that Athens would be governed properly only when the wisest men, the philosophers, attained power.

Unless either philosophers become kings in their countries or those who are now called kings and rulers come to be sufficiently inspired with a genuine desire for wisdom; unless, that is to say, political power and philosophy meet together . . . there can be no rest from troubles . . . for states, nor yet, as I believe, for all mankind.[8]

Plato rejected the fundamental principle of Athenian democracy: that the average person is capable of participating sensibly in public affairs. People would not entrust the care of a sick person to just anyone, said Plato, nor would they allow a novice to guide a ship during a storm. Yet, in a democracy, amateurs were permitted to run the government and to supervise the education of the young— no wonder Athenian society was disintegrating. Plato felt that these duties should be performed only by the best people in the city, the philosophers who would approach human problems with reason and wisdom derived from knowledge of the world of unchanging and perfect Ideas. Only these possessors of truth would be competent to rule, said Plato. Whereas Socrates believed that all people could base their actions on reason and acquire virtue, Plato maintained that only a few were capable of philosophic wisdom, and these few were the state's natural rulers.

The organization of the state, as formulated in *The Republic*, corresponded to Plato's conception of the individual soul, of human nature. Plato held that the soul had three major capacities: reason (the pursuit of knowledge), spiritedness (self-assertion, courage, ambition), and desire (the "savage many-headed monster" that relishes food, sex, and possessions). In the well-governed soul, spiritedness and desire are guided by reason and knowledge—standards derived from the world of Ideas.

Plato divided people into three groups; those who demonstrated philosophic ability should be rulers; those whose natural bent revealed exceptional courage should be soldiers; those driven by desire, the great masses, should be producers (tradesmen, artisans, or farmers). In what was a radical departure from the general attitudes of the times, Plato held that men and women should receive the same education and have equal access to all occupations and public positions, including philosopher-ruler.

Plato felt that the entire community must recognize the primacy of the intellect, and sought to create a harmonious state in which each individual performed what he or she was best qualified to do and preferred to do. This would be a just state, said Plato, for it would recognize human inequalities and diversities and make the best possible use of them for the entire community. Clearly this conception of justice was Plato's response to the radical Sophists who taught that justice consisted of the right of the strong to rule in their own interest, or that justice was doing whatever one desired.

In *The Republic*, philosophers were selected by a rigorous system of education open to all children. Those not demonstrating sufficient intelligence or strength of character were to be weeded out to become workers or warriors, depending on their natural aptitudes. After many years of education and practical military and administrative experience, the philosophers were to be entrusted with political power. If they had been properly educated, the philosopher-rulers would not seek personal wealth or personal power; they would be concerned with pursuing justice and serving the community. The philosophers were to be absolute rulers. Although the people would have lost their right to participate in political decisions, they would have gained a well-governed state whose leaders, distinguished by their wisdom, integrity, and sense of responsibility, sought only the common good. Only thus could the individual and the community achieve well-being.

Plato repudiated the fundamental principles of a free community: the right to participate in government, equality before the law, and checks on leaders' power. Even freedom of thought was denied the great mass of people in Plato's state. Philosopher-rulers would search for truth, but the people were to be told clever stories—"noble lies," Plato called them—to keep them obedient. But the philosopher-rulers, said Plato, would not be seekers of power or wealth; as wise and virtuous people, the best products of polis education, it would not be in their character to behave like ruthless tyrants.

The purpose of *The Republic* was to warn Athenians that without respect for law, wise leadership, and proper education for the young, their city would continue to degenerate. Plato wanted to rescue the city-state from disintegration by re-creating the community spirit that had vitalized the polis—and he wanted to re-create it based not on mere tradition but on a higher level with knowledge and philosophy. The social and political institutions of Athens, Plato felt, must be reshaped according to permanent and unalterable ideals of justice.

Aristotle: Creative Synthesis

Aristotle (384–322 B.C.) stands at the apex of Greek thought because he achieved a creative synthesis of the knowledge and theories of earlier thinkers. Aristotle studied at Plato's Academy for twenty years. Later he became tutor to young Alexander, the son of Philip of Macedonia. Returning to Athens after Alexander had inherited his father's throne, Aristotle founded a school called the Lyceum.

The range of Aristotle's interests and intellect is extraordinary. He was the leading expert of his time in every field of knowledge, with the possible exception of mathematics. Even a partial listing of his works shows the universal character of his mind and his all-consuming passion to understand the worlds of nature and of humankind: *Logic, Physics, On the Heavens, On the Soul, On the Parts of Animals, Metaphysics, Nicomachean Ethics, Politics, Rhetoric,* and *Poetics.*

Aristotle undertook the monumental task of organizing and systematizing the thought of the Pre-Socratics, Socrates, and Plato. He shared with the natural philosophers a desire to understand the physical universe; he shared with Socrates and Plato the belief that

reason was a person's highest faculty and that the polis was the primary formative institution of Greek life. Out of the myriad of Aristotle's achievements, we shall discuss only three: his critique of Plato's theory of Ideas, his ethical thought, and his political thought.

Critique of Plato's Theory of Ideas   Like Democritus before him, Aristotle renewed confidence in sense perception; he wanted to swing the pendulum back from Plato's higher world to the material world. Possessing a scientist's curiosity to understand the facts of nature, Aristotle appreciated the world of phenomena, of concrete things. He respected knowledge obtained through the senses, as the following selection from his observations of the animal kingdom shows:

With the common hen after three days and three nights there is the first indication of the embryo. . . . Meanwhile the yolk comes into being . . . and, the heart appears, like a speck of blood, in the white of the egg. This point beats and moves as though endowed with life.[9]

Aristotle retained Plato's stress on universal principles. But he wanted these standards to derive from human experience with the material world; in this way they could be adapted to the requirements of the natural sciences. To the practical and empirically minded Aristotle, the Platonic notion of an independent and separate world of Forms beyond space and time seemed contrary to common sense. To comprehend reality, said Aristotle, one should not escape into another world. For him, Plato's two-world philosophy suffered from too much mystery, mysticism, and poetic fancy; moreover, Plato undervalued the world of facts and objects revealed through sight, hearing, and touch, a world that Aristotle valued. Like Plato, Aristotle desired to comprehend the essence of things and held that understanding universal principles is the ultimate aim of knowledge. But unlike Plato, he did not turn away from the world of things to obtain such knowledge.

For Aristotle, the Forms were not located

in a higher world outside and beyond phenomena, but existed in things themselves. He said that through human experience with such things as men, horses, and white objects, the essence of man, horse, and whiteness can be discovered through reason; the Form of Man, the Form of Horse, and the Form of Whiteness can be determined. These universals, which apply to all men, all horses, and all white things, were for both Aristotle and Plato the true objects of knowledge. For Plato, these Forms existed independently of particular objects, so the Forms for men or horses or whiteness or triangles or temples existed, whether or not representations of these Ideas in the form of material objects were made known to the senses. For Aristotle, however, without examination of particular things, universal Ideas could not be determined. Whereas Plato's use of reason tended to stress otherworldliness, Aristotle tried to bring philosophy back to earth.

By holding that certainty in knowledge comes from reason alone and not from the senses, Plato was predisposed toward mathematics and metaphysics—pure thought that transcends the world of change and material objects. By stressing the importance of knowledge acquired through the rational examination of sense experience, Aristotle favored the development of empirical sciences—physics, biology, zoology, botany, and other disciplines based on the observation and investigation of nature and the recording of data. Aristotle maintained that theory must not conflict with facts and must make them more intelligible, and that it was the task of science to arrange facts into a system of knowledge.

Ethical Thought   Like Socrates and Plato, Aristotle believed that a knowledge of ethics was possible and that it must be based on reason. Aristotle's ethical thought derived from a realistic appraisal of human nature and a common-sense attitude toward life. For him, the good life was the examined life; it meant making intelligent decisions when confronted with specific problems. Persons

Philosopher (Statuette), c. 280 B.C. Greek artists were the first to excel in realistic portraiture. The philosopher is neither a divinely inspired seer nor a divine king, but a person in quest of knowledge. (*The Metropolitan Museum of Art, Rogers Fund, 1910*)

could achieve happiness when they exercised the distinctively human trait of reasoning, when they applied their knowledge relevantly to life, and when their behavior was governed by intelligence and not by whim, tradition, or authority.

Aristotle recognized that people are not entirely rational, that there is a passionate element of the human personality that can never be eradicated or ignored. Aristotle held that surrendering completely to desire was to descend to the level of beasts, but that denying the passions and living as an ascetic was a foolish and unreasonable rejection of human nature. Aristotle maintained that by proper training, people could learn to regulate their desires. They could achieve moral well-being, or virtue, when they avoided extremes of behavior and rationally chose the way of moderation. "Nothing in excess" is the key to Aristotle's ethics.

Aristotle believed that the contemplative life of the philosopher would yield perfect happiness. The pursuit of philosophic wisdom and beauty, he stated, offered "pleasures marvellous for their purity and their enduringness."[10] But Aristotle did not demand more from an individual than human nature would allow; he did not set impossible standards for behavior, but recognized that all persons cannot pursue the life of contemplation, for some lack sufficient leisure or intelligence. But by applying reason to human affairs, all individuals could experience a good life.

Political Thought   Aristotle's *Politics* complements his *Ethics*. To live the good life, he said, a person must do it as a member of a political community. Only the polis would provide people with an opportunity to lead a rational and moral existence. With this assertion, Aristotle demonstrated a typically Greek attitude. At the very moment when his pupil Alexander the Great was constructing a world-state that unified Greece and Persia, Aristotle defended the traditional system of independent city-states. Indeed, his *Politics* summed up the polis-centered orientation of Hellenic civilization.

Like Plato, Aristotle presumed that human affairs could be rationally understood and intelligently directed. In *Politics*, as in *Ethics*, he adopted a common-sense, practical attitude. He did not aim at utopia, but wanted to find the most effective form of government for most men in typical circumstances.

Aristotle emphasized the importance of the rule of law. He placed his trust in law rather than in individuals, for they are subject to passions. Aristotle recognized that at times laws should be altered but recommended great caution; otherwise, people would lose respect for law and legal procedure.

. . . For the law has no power to command obedience except that of habit, which can only be given by time, so that a readiness to change from old to new laws enfeebles the power of the law.[11]

Tyranny and revolution, Aristotle said, can threaten the rule of law and the well-being of the citizen. To prevent revolution, the state must maintain

the spirit of obedience to law, more especially in small matters; for transgression creeps in unperceived and at last ruins the state. [This cannot be done] unless the young are trained by habit and education in the spirit of the constitution. [To live as one pleases] is contradictory to the true interests of the state. . . .

Men should not think it slavery to live according to the rule of the constitution, for it is their salvation.[12]

Drama

In the sixth century B.C., lawgivers, tyrants, and artists demonstrated their individuality by announcing their names. Seventh- and sixth-century lyric poets and dramatists also gave expression to this rise of the individual through their awareness of human personality.

One of the earliest and best of the Greek poets was Sappho, who lived about 600 B.C.

on the island of Lesbos. Sappho established a school to teach music and singing to well-to-do girls and to prepare them for marriage. With great tenderness, Sappho wrote poems of friendship and love: "Some say the fairest thing on earth is a troop of horsemen, others a band of foot-soldiers, others a squadron of ships. But I say the fairest thing is the beloved."[13] And of her daughter Cleïs, she wrote:

I have a child; so fair
As golden flowers is she,
My Cleïs, all my care.
I'd not give her away
For Lydia's* wide sway
Nor lands men long to see.[14]

Pindar (c. 518–438 B.C.) was another Greek lyric poet. In his poem of praise for a victorious athlete, Pindar expressed the aristocratic view of excellence. Life is essentially tragic—triumphs are short-lived, misfortunes are many, and ultimately death overtakes all; still man must demonstrate his worth by striving for excellence.

He who wins of a sudden, some noble prize
In the rich years of youth
Is raised high with hope; his manhood takes
*   wings;*
He has in his heart what is better than wealth
But brief is the season of man's delight.
Soon it falls to the ground;
Some dire decision uproots it.
—Thing of a day! such is man; a shadow in a
*   dream.*
Yet when god-given splendour visits him
A bright radiance plays over him, and how
*   sweet is life!*[15]

The high point of Greek poetry is the drama, an art form that originated in Greece. The Greek dramatist portrayed the sufferings, weaknesses, and triumphs of individuals. Just as a Greek sculptor shaped a clear visual image of the human form, a Greek dramatist

brought the inner life of a human being into sharp focus and tried to find the deeper meaning of human experience. Thus, in both art and drama, the growing self-awareness of the individual was evident.

Drama originated in the religious festivals honoring Dionysus, the god of wine and agricultural fertility. A profound innovation in these sacred performances, which included choral songs and dances, occurred in the last part of the sixth century B.C. Thespis, the first actor known to history, stepped out of the chorus and engaged it in dialogue. By separating himself from the choral group, Thespis demonstrated a new awareness of the individual.

With only one actor and a chorus, however, the possibilities for dramatic action and human conflicts were limited. Then Aeschylus introduced a second actor in his dramas, and Sophocles a third. Dialogue between individuals thus became possible. The Greek actors wore masks, and by changing them, each actor could play several roles in the same performance. This flexibility allowed the dramatists to depict the clash and interplay of human wills and passions on a greater scale.

Because of the grandeur of the dramatists' themes, the eminence of their heroes, and the loftiness of their language, Greek spectators felt intensely involved in the tragedies of the lives portrayed. What they were witnessing went beyond anything in their ordinary lives, and they experienced the full range of human emotions.

A parallel development to Socratic dialectics—dialogue between thinking individuals—occurred in Greek drama. Greek tragedy evolved as a continuous striving toward humanization and individualization. Through the technique of dialogue, early dramatists first pitted human beings against the gods and destiny. Later, by setting characters in conflict against each other, dramatists arrived at the idea of individuals as active subjects responsible for their behavior and decisions, which were based on their own feelings and thoughts.

*Ancient country in Asia Minor.

Aphrodite. One of the oldest of the gods, Aphrodite has come down through the centuries as the goddess of beauty. The Greeks humanized their gods, and in this graceful figure, the qualities of human beauty are evident. The pose dates this work to late Hellenistic times (mid-second century B.C.). On the other hand, the head and face recall prototypes of the fourth century B.C. (*Veroia Museum/TAP Service, Athens*)

Like the natural philosophers, Greek dramatists saw an inner logic to the universe, which they called Fate or Destiny; both physical and social worlds obeyed laws. When people were stubborn, narrow-minded, arrogant, or immoderate, they were punished. The order in the universe required it, said Sophocles:

The man who goes his way
Overbearing in the word and deed,
Who fears no justice,
Honors no temples of the gods—
May an evil destiny seize him.
And punish his ill-starred pride.[16]

In being free to make decisions, the dramatist says, individuals have the potential for greatness, but in choosing wrongly, unintelligently, they bring disaster to themselves and others.

Also like philosophy, Greek tragedy entailed rational reflection. The tragic hero was not a passive victim of fate. He was a thinking human being who felt a need to comprehend his position, to explain the reasons for his actions, and to analyze his feelings.

The essence of Greek tragedy lies in the tragic hero's struggle against cosmic forces and insurmountable obstacles that eventually crush him. But what impressed the Greek spectators (and today's readers of Greek drama) was not the vulnerability nor weaknesses of human beings but their courage and determination in the face of these forces.

Aeschylus

Aeschylus (525–456 B.C.), an Athenian nobleman, had fought in the battle of Marathon. He wrote over eighty plays, of which only seven survive. In these plays, there are common themes. As an Athenian patriot, he urged adherence to traditional religious beliefs and moral values. Like Solon, the statesman, Aeschylus believed that the world was governed by divine justice that could not be violated with impunity, and that when individuals evinced *hubris* (overweening pride or arrogance), which led them to overstep the bounds of moderation, they must be punished. Another principal theme was that through suffering, persons acquired knowledge: the terrible consequences of sins against the divine order should remind all to think and act with moderation and caution.

Aeschylus' play *The Persians* dealt with an actual event, the defeat of Xerxes, the Persian emperor, by the Greeks. Xerxes' intemperate ambition to become master of Asia and Greece was in conflict with the divine order of the universe. For this *hubris*, Xerxes must pay:

A single stroke has brought about the ruin of great
Prosperity, the flower of Persia fallen and gone.[17]

The suffering of Xerxes should make man aware of what he can and cannot do:

And heaps of corpses even in generations hence
Will signify in silence to the eyes of men
That mortal man should not think more than mortal thoughts.
For hubris blossomed forth and grew a crop of ruin,
And from it gathered in a harvest full of tears.
. . . .
In face of this, when Xerxes, who lacks good sense, returns,
Counsel him with reasoning and good advice,
To cease from wounding God with overboastful rashness.[18]

Whereas Aeschylean drama dealt principally with the cosmic theme of the individual in conflict with the moral universe, later dramatists, while continuing to use patterns fashioned by Aeschylus, gave greater attention to the psychology of the individual.

Sophocles

Another outstanding Athenian dramatist was Sophocles (c. 496–406 B.C.). His greatness as

a playwright lay in both the excellence of his dramatic technique and the skill with which he portrayed character. The people that he created possessed violent passions and tender emotions; they were human in their actions but noble in their nature. Sophocles consciously formulated a standard of human excellence: individuals should shape their character in the way a sculptor shapes a form—according to laws of proportion. Sophocles felt that when these principles of harmony were violated by immoderate behavior, a person's character would be thrown off balance and misfortune would strike. The physical world and the sphere of human activities obey laws, said Sophocles, and human beings cannot violate these laws with impunity.

Whereas Aeschylus concentrated on religious matters and Euripides dealt with social issues, Sophocles wrote about the perennial problem of well-intentioned human beings struggling valiantly but unwisely and vainly against the tide of fate. His characters, who were determined on some action fraught with danger, would resist all appeals to caution and unknowingly but inescapably meet with disaster.

In *Oedipus Rex*, Oedipus is warned not to pursue the mystery of his birth. But he refuses to give up the search: "Nothing will move me. I will find the whole truth." (He had unsuspectingly killed his father and married his mother.) For this determination, born more of innocence than arrogance, he will suffer. Events do not turn out, as Oedipus discovers, the way a person thinks and desires that they should; the individual is impotent before the relentless universal laws of human existence. It seems beyond imagining that Oedipus, whom all envied for his intelligence and good works, would meet with such a dreadful revelation.

But tragedy also gives Oedipus the strength to assert his moral independence. Although struck down by fate, Oedipus remains an impressive figure. In choosing his own punishment—self-inflicted blindness—Oedipus demonstrates that he still possesses the distinctly human qualities of choosing and acting, that he still remains a free man responsible for his actions. Despite his misery, Oedipus is able to confront a brutal fate with courage and to demonstrate nobility of character.

Euripides

The rationalist spirit of Greek philosophy permeated the tragedies of another Athenian, Euripides (c. 485–406 B.C.). Like the Sophists, Euripides subjected the problems of human life to critical analysis and challenged human conventions. It was this critical spirit that prompted the traditionalist Aristophanes to attack Euripides for introducing the art of reasoning into tragedy. Women's conflicts, the moral implications of adultery, the role of the gods, the rearing of children, and the meaning of war were carefully scrutinized in Euripides' plays. Euripides blends a poet's insight with the psychologist's probing to reveal the tangled world of human passions and souls in torment.

Euripides recognized the power of irrational, demonic forces that seethe within people—what he called "the bloody Fury raised by fiends of Hell."[19] A scorned Medea, seeking revenge against her husband by murdering their children, says:

I know indeed what evil I intend to do,
But stronger than all my afterthoughts is my
  fury,
Fury that brings upon mortals the greatest
  evils.[20]

In his plays, Euripides showed that the great tragedy of human existence is that reason can offer only feeble resistance against these compelling, relentless, and consuming passions. The forces that destroy erupt from the volcanic nature of human beings.

A second distinctive feature of Euripidean tragedy is its humanitarianism. No other Greek thinker expressed such concern for a fellow human being, such compassion for human suffering. In *The Trojan Women*, Euripides depicted war as agony and not glory, and the warrior as brutish and not noble. He described the torments of women for whom war meant the loss of homes, husbands, children, and freedom. In 416 B.C., Athens massacred the men of the small island of Melos, sold its women and children into slavery, and sacked the city. *The Trojan Women*, performed a year later, warned Athenians:

How are ye blind,
Ye treaders down of cities, ye that cast
Temples to desolation, and lay waste
Tombs, the untrodden sanctuaries where lie
The ancient dead; yourselves so soon to die![21]

By exposing war as barbaric, Euripides was expressing his hostility to the Athenian leaders who persisted in continuing the disastrous Peloponnesian War.

Aristophanes

Aristophanes (c. 448–c. 380 B.C.) was the greatest of the Greek comic playwrights. He lampooned Athenian statesmen and intellectuals, censured government policies, and protested against the decay of traditional Athenian values. Behind Aristophanes' sharp wit lay a deadly seriousness, for there was much in Athens during the Peloponnesian War that angered him. As an aristocrat, he was repelled by Cleon, the common tanner who succeeded Pericles. As an admirer of the ancient values of honor, duty, and moderation, he was infuriated by the corruption resulting from the Sophists' teachings. As a man of common sense, he recognized that the Peloponnesian War must end. In the process of serving as a social critic, Aristophanes wrote some of the most hilarious lines in world literature.

In *Lysistrata*, an antiwar comedy, the women of Greece agree to abstain from having sexual relations with their husbands and lovers to compel the men to make peace. Lysistrata reveals the plan:

For if we women will but sit at home,
Powdered and trimmed, clad in our daintiest
lawn,
Employing all our charms, and all our arts
To win men's love, and when we've won it,
then
Repel them firmly, till they end the war,
We'll soon get Peace again, be sure of that.[22]

After the plan has been implemented, many women become "husband-sick" and seek to desert the temple where they have gathered. But the men also suffer:

Oh me! these pangs and paroxysms of love,
Riving my heart, keen as a torturer's wheel![23]

Through these unorthodox methods, the women achieve their goal, peace. Performed during the darkest days of the war, this play reminded its audiences to concentrate their efforts in the real world on securing peace.

In *The Clouds*, Aristophanes ridiculed the Sophist method of education both for turning the youth away from their parents' values and for engaging the youth in useless, hair-splitting logic. To Aristophanes, the worst of the Sophists was Socrates, who is depicted in *The Clouds* as a fuzzy-minded thinker with both feet planted firmly in the clouds. Socrates is made to look ridiculous, a man who walks on air, contemplates the sun, and teaches such absurd things as "Heaven is one vast fire extinguisher" or "How many feet of its own a flea could jump." The Sophists in the play teach only how "to succeed just enough for my need and to slip through the clutches of the law." A student of these Sophists becomes a "concocter of lies . . . a supple, unprincipled, troublesome cheat."[24]

To Aristophanes, Socrates was a subversive who caused Athenians to repudiate civil morality and to speculate about nonsense questions. Clearly, Aristophanes admired the Athens of the battle of Marathon and feared the rationalism that Euripides, the Sophists, and Socrates had injected into Athenian intellectual life.

History

The Mesopotamians and the Egyptians kept annals that purported to narrate the deeds of gods and their human agents, the priest-kings or god-kings. The Hebrews valued history, but believing that God acted in human events, they did not remove history entirely from the realm of myth. The Greeks initiated a different approach to the study of history. As the gods were eliminated from the nature philosophers' explanations for the origins of things in the natural world, mythical elements also were removed from the writing of history.

Greek historians asked themselves questions about the deeds of people, based their answers on available evidence, and wrote in prose, the language of rational thought. They not only narrated events but also examined causes. British philosopher and historian R. G. Collingwood states:

The Greeks quite clearly and consciously recognized both that history is, or can be, a science, and that it has to do with human actions. Greek history is not legend, it is research; it is an attempt to get answers to definite questions about matters of which one recognizes oneself as ignorant. It is not theocratic, it is humanistic; the matters inquired into are not of gods, they are of men. Moreover, it is not mythical. The events inquired into are not events in a dateless past, at the beginning of things; they are events in a dated past, a certain number of years ago. This is not to say that legend, either in the form of theocratic history or in the form of myth, was a thing foreign to the Greek mind. . . . But what is remarkable about the Greeks was not the fact that their historical thought contained a certain residue of elements which we should call non-historical, but the fact that side by side with these, it contained elements of what we call history.[25]

In several respects, however, the Greeks were unhistorical. To them history moved in cycles; events and periods constantly repeated themselves. Unlike the Hebrews, they had little awareness of historical uniqueness and progression. Nor was history as vital to the Greeks as it was to the Hebrews. Greek philosophers, fixing their minds on eternal truths, were largely indifferent to history.

Herodotus

Often called the "father of history," Herodotus (c. 484–c. 424 B.C.) wrote a history of the Persian Wars. Herodotus valued the present and recognized that it is not timeless but has been shaped by earlier happenings. To understand the conflict between Persia and Greece, the most important event in his world during his lifetime, he first inquired into the histories of these societies. Much of his information was derived from posing questions to natives of the lands he visited. Interested in everything, Herodotus frequently interlaced his historical narrative with a marvelous assortment of stories and anecdotes.

The central theme of Herodotus' *Histories* is the contrast between Near Eastern despotism and Greek freedom and the subsequent clash of these two world-views in the Persian Wars. Certain of their superiority, the Greeks considered the non-Hellenic world to be steeped in ignorance and darkness. But Herodotus was generally free of this arrogance. A fair-minded and sympathetic observer, tolerant of differences, he took joy in examining the wide range of human character and experience.

Though Herodotus found much to praise in the Persian Empire, he was struck by a lack of freedom and what he considered barbarity. Herodotus emphasized that the mentality of the free citizen was foreign to the East, where men were trained to obey the ruler's commands absolutely. Not the rule of law but the whim of despots prevailed in the East. When a Persian official urged some Greeks to submit to Xerxes, Herodotus wrote that the Greeks said: "You understand well enough what slavery is, but freedom you have never experienced, so you do not know if it tastes sweet or bitter. If you ever did come to experience it, you would advise us

to fight for it not with spears only, but with axes too."[26] Of all the Greek city-states, Herodotus admired Athens most. Freedom had enabled Athens to achieve greatness, said Herodotus, and it was this illustrious city that had rescued the Greek world from Persia.

Another theme evident in Herodotus' work was punishment for hubris. In seeking to become king of both Asia and Europe, Xerxes had acted arrogantly; although he behaved as if he was superhuman, "he too was human, and was sure to be disappointed of his great expectations."[27] Like the Greek tragedians, Herodotus drew universal moral principles from human behavior.

In several ways Herodotus was a historian rather than a teller of tales. First, he asked questions about the past, instead of merely repeating ancient legends; he tried to discover what had happened and the motivations behind the actions. Second, Herodotus at times demonstrated a cautious and critical attitude toward his sources of information:

The course of my story now leads me to Cyrus: who was this man who destroyed the empire of Croesus, and how did the Persians win their predominant position in Asia? I could, if I wished, give three versions of Cyrus' history, all different from what follows; but I propose to base my account on those Persian authorities who seem to tell the simple truth about him without trying to exaggerate his exploits.[28]

Third, while the gods appeared in Herodotus' narrative, they played a far less important role than they did in Greek popular mythology. Nevertheless, by retaining a belief in the significance of dreams, omens, and oracles, and by allowing for divine intervention, Herodotus fell short of being a thoroughgoing rationalist. Herodotus' writings contain the embryo of rational history; Thucydides brought it to maturity.

Thucydides

Thucydides (c. 460–c. 400 B.C.) also concentrated on a great political crisis confronting the Hellenic world—the Peloponnesian War.

Living in Periclean Athens, whose life blood was politics, Thucydides regarded the motives of statesmen and the acts of government as the essence of history. He did not just catalogue facts, but sought those general concepts and principles that the facts illustrated. His history was the work of an intelligent mind trying to make sense out of his times.

Thucydides applied a rationalist empiricism worthy of the Ionian natural philosophers to the sphere of political history. He searched for the truth underlying historical events and attempted to present it objectively.

Of the events of the war I have not ventured to speak from any chance information, nor according to any notion of my own; I have described nothing but what I either saw myself, or learned from others of whom I made the most careful and particular inquiry. The task was a laborious one, because eyewitnesses of the same occurrences gave different accounts of them, as they remembered or were [partial to] one side or the other. And very likely the strictly historical character of my narrative may be disappointing to the ear. But if he who desires to have before his eyes a true picture of the events which have happened, and of the like events which may be expected to happen hereafter in the order of human things, then I shall be satisfied.[29]

In Thucydides' history, there was no place for myths, for legends, for the fabulous—all hindrances to historical truth. He recognized that a work of history was a creation of the rational mind and not an expression of the poetic imagination. The historian seeks to learn and to enlighten, not to entertain.

Rejecting the notion that the gods interfere in history, Thucydides looked for the social forces and human decisions behind events. Undoubtedly, he was influenced by Hippocratic doctors who frowned on divine explanations for disease and distinguished between the symptoms of a disease and its causes. Where Herodotus occasionally lapsed into supernatural explanations, Thucydides wrote history in which the gods were absent, and he denied their intervention in human affairs.

In addition to being a historian, Thucydides was also a political philosopher with a specific view of governments and statesmen. He warned against the dangers of extremism unleashed by the strains of war, and he believed that when reason was forsaken, the state's plight would worsen. He had contempt for statesmen who waged war lightly, acting from impulse, reckless daring, and an insatiable appetite for territory. For this reason, he regarded the decision to attack Syracuse in Sicily as a gross political blunder. Although Thucydides admired Athens for its democratic institutions, rule of law, sense of civic duty, and cultural achievements, he recognized an inherent danger in democracy—the emergence of demagogues who rise to power by stirring up the populace.

Political scientists, historians, and statesmen still turn to Thucydides for insights into the realities of power politics, the dangers of political fanaticism, the nature of imperialism, the methods of demagogues, and the effects of war on democratic politics.

The Greek Achievement: Reason, Freedom, Humanism

Like other ancient peoples, the Greeks warred, massacred, and enslaved; they could be cruel, arrogant, contentious, and superstitious; and they often violated their ideals. But their achievement was unquestionably of profound historical significance. Western thought begins with the Greeks who first defined the individual by his capacity to reason. It was the great achievement of the Greek spirit to rise above magic, miracles, mystery, authority, and custom and to discover the means of giving rational order to nature and society. Every aspect of Greek civilization—science, philosophy, art, literature, politics, historical writing—showed a growing reliance on human reason and a diminishing dependence on the gods.

In Mesopotamia and Egypt, people had no clear conception of their individual worth and no understanding of political liberty. They were not citizens, but subjects who marched to the command of a ruler whose power originated with the gods; such royal power was not imposed on an unwilling population, but was religiously accepted and obeyed.

In contrast, the Greeks created political freedom. They saw the state as a community of free citizens who made laws in their own interest. The Greeks held that men are capable of governing themselves and valued active citizenship. For the Greeks, the state was a civilizing agent that permitted people to live the good life. Greek political thinkers arrived at a conception of the rational or legal state in which law was an expression of reason, not of whim or divine commands; of justice, not of might; of the general good of the community, not of self-interest.

The Greeks also gave to Western civilization a conception of inner, or ethical, freedom. People were free to choose between shame and honor, cowardice and duty, moderation and excess. The heroes of Greek tragedy suffered, not because they were puppets being manipulated by higher powers, but because they possessed the freedom of decision. The idea of ethical freedom reached its highest point with Socrates. To shape oneself according to ideals known to the mind, to become an autonomous and self-directed person, became for the Greeks the highest form of freedom.

Underlying everything accomplished by the Greeks was a humanist attitude toward life. The Greeks expressed a belief in the worth, significance, and dignity of the individual; they called for the maximum cultivation of human talent, the full development of human personality, and the deliberate pursuit of excellence. In valuing the human personality, the Greek humanists did not approve of living without restraints; they aimed at creating a higher type of man. Such a man would mold himself according to worthy standards; he would make his life as harmonious and flawless as a work of art. This aspiration required effort, discipline, and intelligence. Fundamental to the Greek humanist outlook was the belief that man could master himself. Although people could not alter the course of

nature, for there was an order to the universe over which neither human beings nor gods had control, the humanist believed that people could control their own lives.

By discovering theoretical reason, by defining political freedom, and by affirming the worth and potential of human personality, the Greeks broke with the past and founded the rational and humanist tradition of the West. "Had Greek civilization never existed," says poet W. H. Auden, "we would never have become fully conscious, which is to say that we would never have become, for better or worse, fully human."[30]

Notes

1. John N. Theodorakopoulos, "The Origins of Science and Philosophy," in *History of the Hellenic World: The Archaic Period* (University Park: Pennsylvania University Press, 1975), p. 438.

2. Quoted in George Sarton, *A History of Science,* vol. 1 (Cambridge, Mass.: Harvard University Press, 1952), pp. 355–356.

3. Plato, *Apology,* trans. by F. J. Church and rev. by R. D. Cummings (Indianapolis: Bobbs-Merrill, 1956), Section 28.

4. Ibid., Sections 16–17.

5. Plato, *The Republic,* trans. by F. M. Cornford (New York: Oxford University Press, 1945), p. 289.

6. Ibid.

7. Ibid., p. 293.

8. Ibid., pp. 178–179.

9. *Historia Animalium* in *Works of Aristotle,* vol. 4, trans. by D'Arcy Wentworth Thompson (New York: Oxford University Press, 1962), p. 561.

10. *Nicomachean Ethics* in Richard McKeon, ed., *Basic Works of Aristotle* (New York: Random House, 1941), p. 1104.

11. *Politics,* in McKeon, *Basic Works of Aristotle,* p. 1164.

12. Ibid., pp. 1246, 1251.

13. Cited in Werner Jaeger, *Paideia: The Ideals of Greek Culture* (New York: Oxford University Press, 1945), 1:135.

14. "A Girl," in *The Oxford Book of Greek Verse in Translation,* T. F. Higham and C. M. Bowra, eds. (Oxford, England: Clarendon Press, 1938), p. 211.

15. Cited in H. D. F. Kitto, *The Greeks* (Baltimore: Penguin Books, 1957), pp. 174–175.

16. Sophocles, *Oedipus the King,* trans. by Bernard M. W. Knox (New York: Washington Square Press, 1959), p. 61.

17. Aeschylus, *The Persians,* trans. by Anthony J. Podlecki (Englewood Cliffs, N.J.: Prentice-Hall, 1970), p. 49, lines 250–251.

18. Ibid., pp. 96–97, lines 818–822, 829–831.

19. *The Medea,* trans. by Rex Warner in David Grene and Richard Lattimore, *The Complete Greek Tragedies, Euripides,* vol. 1 (Chicago: University of Chicago Press, 1955), p. 101.

20. Ibid., p. 96, lines 1078–1080.

21. Euripides, *The Trojan Women,* trans. by Gilbert Murray (New York: Oxford University Press, 1915), lines 95–97, p. 16.

22. *Lysistrata,* in *Five Comedies of Aristophanes,* trans. by Benjamin Bickley Rogers (Garden City, N.Y.: Doubleday Anchor Books, 1955), p. 292.

23. Ibid., p. 320.

24. *The Clouds,* in ibid., pp. 156–157, 169–170.

25. R. G. Collingwood, *The Idea of History* (New York: Oxford University Press, 1956), pp. 17–18.

26. Herodotus, *The Histories,* trans. by Aubrey de Sélincourt (Baltimore: Penguin Books, 1954), p. 458.

27. Ibid., p. 485.

28. Ibid., p. 53.

29. Thucydides, *The Peloponnesian War,* trans. by B. Jowett (Oxford, England: Clarendon Press, 1881), bk. I, ch. 22.

30. W. H. Auden, ed., *The Portable Greek Reader* (New York: Viking, 1952), p. 38.

Suggested Reading

Copleston, Frederick, *A History of Philosophy,* I (1962). An excellent analysis of Greek philosophy.

Cornford, F. M., *Before and After Socrates* (1968). The essential meaning of Greek philosophy clearly presented.

Dodds, E. R., *The Greeks and the Irrational* (1957). Analyzes the role of primitive and irrational forces in Greek culture.

Guthrie, W. K. C., *The Greek Philosophers from Thales to Aristotle* (1960). A short reliable survey of Greek philosophy.

Jaeger, Werner, *Paideia: The Ideals of Greek Culture* (1939–1944). A three-volume work on Greek culture by a distinguished classicist. The treatment of Homer, the early Greek philosophers, and the Sophists in volume I is masterful.

Jones, W. T., *A History of Western Philosophy,* I (1962). Clearly written; contains useful passages from original sources.

Kitto, H. D. F., *Greek Tragedy* (1954). A valuable introduction to Greek drama.

Lloyd, G. E. R., *Early Greek Science* (1970). A survey of Greek science from Thales to Aristotle.

Robinson, J. M., *An Introduction to Early Greek Philosophy* (1968). Combines original sources with lucid discussion.

Snell, Bruno, *The Discovery of the Mind* (1953). A collection of essays focusing on the Greek origins of European thought.

Taylor, A. E., *Socrates.* A discussion of the man and his thought.

Review Questions

1. What was the achievement of the Ionian natural philosophers?

2. How did Pythagoras, Parmenides, and Democritus contribute to the development of science?

3. How did the Sophists advance the tradition of reason initiated by the natural philosophers? How did they contribute to a spiritual crisis in Athens?

4. What was Socrates' answer to the problems posed by the Sophists?

5. What is the educational value of the Socratic dialogue?

6. How did Plato make use of Socrates'

thought? What does Plato mean by the realm of Ideas or Forms?

7. Describe the essential features of Plato's *Republic* and the reasons that led him to write it.

8. Discuss whether Plato's political thought has any value for us today.

9. How did Aristotle both criticize and accept Plato's theory of Ideas? What do Aristotle's political and ethical thought have in common?

10. Do you agree with Aristotle that "men should not think it slavery to live according to the rule of the constitution, for it is their salvation"?

11. What did the Greek dramatists have in common with Socrates?

12. Greek dramatists explored the inner life of the individual. Discuss this statement and give examples to support it.

13. The rationalist spirit of Greek philosophy permeated the tragedies of Euripides. Discuss.

14. Why do the Greek plays have perennial appeal?

15. Why is Herodotus called the "father of history"? How did Thucydides surpass Herodotus as a historian? Why is Thucydides still worth reading today?

16. The Greeks broke with the mythopoeic outlook of the ancient Near East and conceived a world-view that is the foundation of Western civilization. Discuss.

5

The Hellenistic Age:
Cultural Diffusion

*G*reek civilization, or Hellenism, passed through three distinct stages—the Hellenic Age, the Hellenistic Age, and the Greco-Roman Age. The Hellenic Age began in 800 B.C. with the early city-states, reached its height in the fifth century B.C., and endured until the death of Alexander the Great in 323 B.C. From that date the ancient world entered the Hellenistic Age, which ended in 30 B.C. when Egypt, the last major Hellenistic state, fell to Rome. The Greco-Roman Age lasted 500 years, encompassing the period of the Roman Empire up to the collapse of the Empire's western half in the last part of the fifth century A.D.

Although the Hellenistic Age had absorbed the heritage of classical (Hellenic) Greece, its style of civilization changed. During the first phase of Hellenism, the polis had been the center of political life. The polis had given the individual identity, and only within the polis could a Greek live a good and civilized life. With the coming of the Hellenistic Age, this situation changed. The city-state was eclipsed in power and importance by kingdoms. While cities retained a large measure of autonomy in domestic affairs, they had lost their freedom of action in foreign affairs. No longer were they the self-sufficient and independent communities of the Hellenic period.

Unable to stand up to kingdoms, the city-state had become an outmoded institution. The bonds between the individual and the city loosened. People had to deal with the feelings of isolation and insecurity produced by the decline of the polis.

As a result of Alexander the Great's conquests of the lands between Greece and India, tens of thousands of Greek soldiers, merchants, and administrators settled in eastern lands. Their encounters with the different peoples and cultures of the Near East widened the Greeks' horizon and weakened their ties to their native cities. Because of these changes, the individual had to define a relationship not to the narrow, parochial society of the polis, but to the larger world. The Greeks had to examine their place in a world more complex, more foreign, more threatening than the polis. They had to fashion a conception of a community that would be more comprehensive than the parochial city-state had been.

Hellenistic philosophers struggled with these problems of alienation and community. They sought to give people the inner strength to endure in a world where the polis no longer provided security. In this new situation, philosophers no longer assumed that the good life was tied to the affairs of the city; freedom from emotional stress—not active citizenship and social responsibility—was the avenue to the good life. This pronounced tendency of people to withdraw into themselves and seek emotional comfort helped shape a cultural environment that contributed to the spread and triumph of Christianity in the Greco-Roman Age.

In the Hellenic Age, Greek philosophers had a limited conception of humanity, dividing the world into Greek and barbarian. In the Hellenistic Age, the intermingling of peoples caused a shift in focus from the city to the *oikoumene* (the inhabited world); parochialism gave way to universalism and cosmopolitanism, as people began to think of themselves as members of a world community. Philosophers came to regard the civilized world as one city, the city of man. This was their response to the decline of the city-state and the quest for an alternate form of community.

By uniting the diverse nationalities of the Mediterranean world under one rule, Rome gave political expression to the Hellenistic philosophers' longing for a world community. But the vast and impersonal Roman Empire could not rekindle that sense of belonging, that certainty of identity, that came with being a citizen of a small polis. In time, a resurgence of the religious spirit, particularly in the form of Christianity, helped to overcome the feeling of alienation by offering an image of community that stirred the heart.

Alexander the Great

After the assassination of Philip of Macedon in 336 B.C., his twenty-year-old son, Alexander, succeeded to the throne. Alexander inherited a proud and fiery temperament from his mother. From his tutor Aristotle, Alexander acquired an appreciation for Greek culture, particularly the Homeric epics. Undoubtedly, the young Alexander was aroused by these stories of legendary heroes, particularly of Achilles, and their striving for personal glory. Alexander acquired military skills and qualities of leadership from his father.

Alexander also inherited from Philip an overriding policy of state—the invasion of Persia. Such an exploit attracted the adventurous spirit of the young Alexander; a war of revenge against the Persians, who were masters of the Greek city-states of Asia Minor, also appealed to Alexander's Pan-Hellenic sentiments. Alexander was heir to the teachings of the fourth-century orator, Isocrates, who urged a crusade against Persia to unite the Greeks in a common cause. Philip had intended to protect his hold on Greece by driving the Persians from Asia Minor. But Alexander, whose ambition knew no bounds, aspired to conquer the entire Persian Empire. Daring, brave, and intelligent, Alexander possessed the irrepressible energy of a romantic adventurer.

With an army of 35,000 men, Alexander crossed into Asia Minor in 334 B.C. After capturing the coast of Asia Minor, Alexander marched into Syria and defeated the Persian army at the battle of Issus. Rather than pursuing the fleeing Persian king, Darius III, Alexander stayed with his master plan, which included the capture of coastal ports to crush the Persian navy. He captured Tyre, thought to be an impregnable city, and advanced into Egypt. Grateful to Alexander for having liberated them from Persian rule, the Egyptians made him pharaoh. Alexander appointed officials to administer the country and founded a new city, Alexandria.

Having destroyed or captured the Persian

Mosaic of a Lion Hunt. This pebble mosaic floor may be an illustration of a rescue of Alexander by his friend Krateros; it was found at the Macedonian capital, Pella. The lion hunt as a theme in art appears in Egyptian, Assyrian, and Mycenaean cultures; the king is the guardian of his flock and must protect it from predators. Subduing lions may also be an allusion to one of the labors of Hercules. (*Pella Museum/TAPService, Athens*)

fleet, Alexander in 331 B.C. moved into Mesopotamia in pursuit of Darius and his army. The Macedonians defeated the numerically superior Persians at Gaugamela, just east of the Tigris River, but Darius escaped. After a stopover at Babylon and at Persepolis, which he burned (in revenge for Xerxes' destruction of Athens more than 150 years earlier), Alexander resumed the chase. When he finally caught up with Darius, the Persian king was dead, killed by Persian conspirators.

Alexander relentlessly pushed deeper into Asia, crossing from Afghanistan into north India where he defeated the king of Pontus in a costly battle. When Alexander announced plans to push deeper into India, his troops, exhausted and far from home in a strange land, resisted. Alexander yielded to their wishes, and returned to Babylon in 324 B.C. In these campaigns, Alexander proved himself to be a superb strategist and leader of men.

Winning every battle, Alexander's army had carved an empire that stretched from Greece to India. Future conquerors, including Caesar and Napoleon, would read of Alexander's career with fascination and longing.

The world after Alexander differed sharply from that existing before he took up the sword. Alexander's conquests brought West and East closer together, marking a new epoch. Alexander himself helped implement this transformation. He took a Persian bride, arranged for 80 of his officers and 10,000 of his soldiers to marry oriental women, and planned to incorporate 30,000 Persian youths in his army. Alexander founded Greek-style cities in Asia, where Greek settlers mixed with orientals.

As Greeks acquired greater knowledge of the Near East, the parochial-mindedness of the polis gave way in many ways to a world outlook. As trade and travel between West

Greek Art and Roman Reflections

Figure 1 The Parthenon, Athens, 447–432 B.C (*Art Resource*)

Figure 2 Procession of Horsemen, from the Parthenon Frieze. (*The British Museum*)

The concept of beauty formulated by Greek artists of the fifth century B.C. has challenged and inspired the Western world for over two thousand years. Around 450 B.C., the architects, painters, and sculptors of Athens created the new classic style. As the everyday use of the term suggests, *classic style* is idealized, calm, measured, and free of superfluous detail. All these adjectives fit the prototypical Greek classical temple, the Parthenon.

Built in Athens between 447 and 432 B.C., the Parthenon brought to perfection the architectural form that the Greeks had developed during the sixth century B.C. It replaced an unfinished temple, destroyed by the Persians when they sacked the city in 479 B.C. At the very first glimpse of the Parthenon, one can see that its proportions and placement fit the site perfectly. The temple seems sus-

pended before the distant hills, crowning the high plateau of the Acropolis (Figure 1).

Although the Parthenon's majestic site can still be seen, it takes imagination to picture the original appearance of the building. It once housed an immense statue of the goddess Athena made of ivory and gold. The temple front was painted, and the triangular spaces above the colonnades (called *pediments*) were filled with colored life-size sculptures.

Behind the temple colonnade, high above the temple floor, ran a continuous sculptured frieze depicting the great Panathenaic procession (Figure 2). Every four years, all the citizens of Athens re-affirmed their dedication to Athena, the patron goddess of the city, by participating in a procession that led from the city up through the single entrance gate to the Acropolis and around the temple.

The ceremony culminated in the presentation to Athena of a sacred robe. The long frieze, a portion of which is shown here, forms an ideal image of the Athenian city-state. Citizens of all ages are shown moving along in the procession, some on foot, some on horseback, some moving quickly, others waiting. All of them show a calm, measured grace that befits Athena, the model of self-restraint and wisdom.

Greek craftsmanship and taste appear in the production of pottery vessels, as well as in the "high art" of the Parthenon. Although commonly called *vases* in modern times, Greek pottery vessels were intended for everyday use. A *lekythos* held olive oil; its narrow neck prevented the oil's flowing rapidly (Figure 3). A *krater* was used for mixing water with wine (Figure 4). The manufacture and export of pottery was an important source of income for Athens.

Decoration on the pottery provides much information about everyday life in ancient Greece. In the black-figured lekythos, women are depicted spinning wool and folding the finished cloth. On the krater is a sculptor's workshop, where a marble statue of Herakles is receiving a finishing coat of colored wax. The artist is applying a coat of pigment and wax to the hero's lion skin, while a shop assistant is heating a metal burnisher to melt the wax and cause the paint to penetrate the stone. Behind the artist, Herakles himself observes the work in progress, along with two other deities.

The Greeks left an enduring legacy in the classical figure style. Approximately one hundred fifty years separate the Metropolitan Museum's *Kouros* figure (Figure 5) of about

600 B.C. from Polykleitos' *Doryphoros* (Figure 6) of about 450 B.C. The obvious difference between the two nude male figures is that the later one looks more like a real human being. But increased naturalism is only one component of the change in style. It is more accurate to think of this development as a shift from a simple pattern to a more subtle and complex pattern.

Around 600 B.C., Greek sculptors began carving life-sized figures, borrowing a pose favored by the Egyptians. In this pose, the figure faces directly forward. Both legs are extended, one foot in front of the other; the arms are held close to the sides, fists clenched. Early Greek sculptures in this pose are called *kouros* figures from the ancient Greek word for *young man*.

Throughout the sixth and early fifth centuries, Greek sculptors adapted and refined the kouros figures. They retained the original pose, adding more and more observed detail. Then another pattern emerged, the classical figure style. Greek sculpture made between about 480 and 450 B.C. shows a new sense of individuality. In looking at such works as

Figure 5 Youth of the "Apollo type." Athenian marble statue, 615–600 B.C. (*The Metropolitan Museum of Art, Fletcher Fund, 1932*)

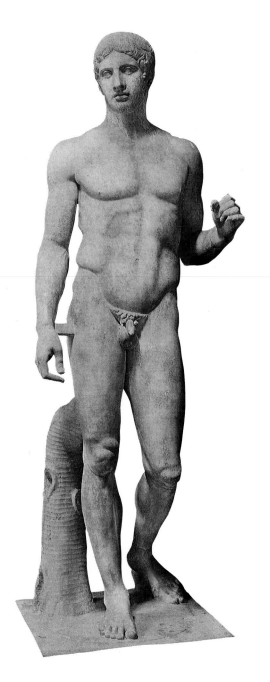

the famous *Doryphoros*, one is made aware of the vulnerability and sensitivity of an individual human being. The pathos and complexity of life, so profoundly revealed in Greek poetry and drama, is expressed in classical art as well. Such an attitude toward life and art stands in marked contrast to the chiseled, abstract formality of work produced in the Near East at the same time.

The *Doryphoros*, meaning *spear-carrier*, was probably made in Athens by Polykleitos around 450 B.C. The original was a bronze statue, which no longer exists. Its pose and structure are known only from Roman copies. In the *Doryphoros*, Polykleitos demonstrates the idealization that is such an important element of classical style. Although the statue looks lifelike, it resembles no one specific individual. Its features are naturalistic, but they are perfected and refined. The figure has no idiosyncratic details, no warts or wrinkles. Its beauty is distilled from many examples, a beauty transcending that of any single earthly individual.

Another important element of Greek classical style is the subtle balance of forces expressed through the pose. The pose of the

Figure 6 Polykleitos' Doryphoros. Roman marble copy. (*Alinari/Art Resource*)

Figure 7 Mosaic of Swan. Roman, fourth century A.D.; restored c. 1200. (*Robert Harding Associates*)

Doryphoros, and of many other fifth-century sculptures, describes a pattern that was copied and recopied for centuries afterward. The figure stands with one knee bent, one knee straight, so that an S-shaped axis curves through the body. One arm is flexed, while the other is extended; the shoulders and hips tilt; and the head is turned. The figure seems to stand in perfect balance—alert yet relaxed, still yet filled with potential movement. This impression of action and repose, of tension and relaxation, does not result from a "snapshot" pose. Standing in the pose of the *Doryphoros* is neither natural nor comfortable. The figure communicates the sense of ideal beauty not through strictly realistic representation, but through the use of a highly formalized pattern.

According to literary sources, Polykleitos consciously worked from a mathematical model. He wrote a book on ideal proportions,

now lost, that was based on the Pythagorean theory of beauty. This theory held that ideal beauty could be revealed by re-creating in art the perfect mathematical ratios upon which the universe itself is structured.

When the Romans sought to develop culture, they looked to Greek models in the visual arts, just as they did in many other fields. Much of our knowledge about ancient Greek art stems from the enthusiasm of Roman connoisseurs. How did archaeologists know that the sculpture they unearthed at Pompeii was a copy of Polykleitos' *Doryphoros*? It bore no inscription, but it did accord with a description of Polykleitos' spear-carrier, mentioned by the Roman Pliny in his *Natural History* (first century A.D.).

Well-to-do Romans built villas in the countryside as retreats from the pressures of metropolitan life (Figure 9). One villa at Boscoreale, about a mile north of Pompeii, was

Figure 8 The Pantheon, Rome, c. A.D. 125. (*Anderson/Art Resource*)

preserved by ash from the eruption of Mount Vesuvius in 79 A.D. Its elaborate wall decoration interweaves reality and illusion. The walls are divided by fictive (painted) columns, so that one seems to be looking out from the interior through an open colonnade. The scenes beyond the columns include landscapes and complex architectural views, all rendered with illusionism that seems to recreate the effects of spatial perception. The mosaic floor combines geometric patterns with illusionistic scenes (*emblemata*). Many elegant mosaic floors have survived since Roman times. Among the most colorful is the swan in Figure 7.

The Pantheon, the most complete surviving building of Roman antiquity (Figure 8), was built by the Emperor Hadrian in the second century A.D. He was an educated man with a thorough appreciation of Greek culture. In the temple, Greek forms of ornamentation are combined with Roman building techniques. The vast hemispherical dome was constructed by pouring concrete into great wooden forms; then the interior was faced with marble. In contrast to a Greek temple, where the exterior is paramount, the Roman temple emphasizes interior space.

—KATHERINE CRUM

Figure 9 Cubiculum from Boscoreale. Roman, 40–30 B.C. (*The Metropolitan Museum of Art, Rogers Fund, 1903*)

and East expanded, as Greek merchants and soldiers settled in Asiatic lands, and as Greek culture spread to non-Greeks, the distinctions between barbarian and Greek lessened. Although Alexander never united all the peoples in a world-state, his career pushed the world in a new direction toward a fusion of disparate peoples and the intermingling of cultural traditions.

Hellenistic Society

The Competing Dynasties

In 323 B.C., Alexander, not yet thirty-three years of age, died of a fever. Alexander had built an empire that stretched from Greece to the Punjab of India, but he was denied the time needed to organize effective institutions to govern these vast territories. After Alexander's premature death, his generals engaged in a long and bitter struggle to see who would succeed the conqueror. Since none of the generals or their heirs had enough power to hold together Alexander's vast empire, the wars of succession ended in a stalemate. By 275 B.C., the empire was fractured into three dynasties: the Ptolemies in Egypt, the Seleucids in Asia, and the Antigonids in Macedonia. Macedonia—Alexander's native country—continued to dominate the Greek cities, which periodically tried to break its hold. Later, the kingdom of Pergamum in western Asia Minor emerged as the fourth Hellenistic monarchy. These Hellenistic kings were not native rulers enjoying local support (except in Macedonia), but were foreign conquerors. Consequently, they had to depend on mercenary armies and loyal administrators.

In the third century B.C., Ptolemaic Egypt—which ruled Cyprus, islands in the Aegean Sea, cities on the coast of Asia Minor, and southern Syria including Palestine—was the foremost power in the Hellenistic world. Its great fleet ensured access to its far-flung provinces and protected its trade. Internal revolts, court intrigues, and wars with the

kingdom of Seleucia weakened Ptolemaic power in the second century B.C.

The Seleucid Empire, like that of the Ptolemies, was an absolute monarchy in which the king was worshiped as a god. But the Seleucid Empire stretched from the Mediterranean to the frontiers of India and encompassed many different peoples, among them several warlike groups; thus this empire was more difficult to control. Attempts by the Seleucids to extend their power in the west were resisted by the Ptolemies. In the third century, these two Hellenistic kingdoms waged five long wars. Finally, the Seleucid ruler Antiochus III (201–198 B.C.) defeated the Ptolemaic forces and established Seleucid control over Phoenicia and Palestine. Taking advantage of Egypt's defeat, Macedonia seized several of Egypt's territories.

In 169–168 B.C., Seleucid Syria invaded Egypt with the intention of annexing it to the Seleucid Empire. This aim would likely have been realized except for the intervention of a new power to the west, Rome. Rome became increasingly drawn into the affairs of the quarrelsome Hellenistic kingdoms; by the middle of the second century B.C., Rome had imposed its will upon them. From this time on, the political fortunes of the western and eastern Mediterranean were inextricably linked.

Cosmopolitanism

Hellenistic society was characterized by a mingling of peoples and an interchange of cultures. Greek traditions spread to the Near East, while Mesopotamian, Egyptian, Hebrew, and Persian traditions—particularly religious beliefs—moved westward. The parochialism of the city-state was replaced by a growing cosmopolitanism. Although the rulers of the Hellenistic kingdoms were Macedonians and their high officials and generals were Greeks, the style of government was modeled after that of the ancient oriental kingdoms. In the Hellenic Age, the law had expressed the will of the community, but in

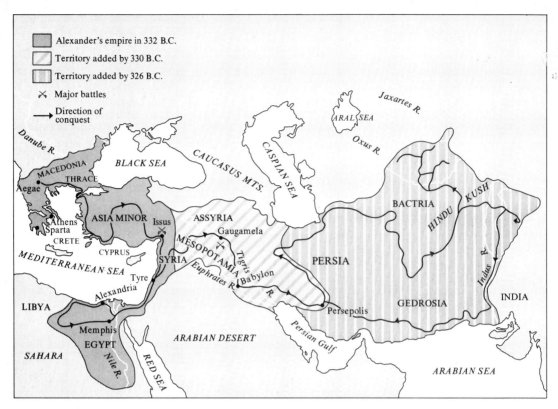

Map 5.1 Alexander's Conquests

this new age of monarchy, the kings were the law. The Macedonian rulers encouraged the oriental practice of worshiping the king as a god or as a representative of the gods. In Egypt, for example, the priests conferred on the Macedonian king the same divine powers and titles traditionally held by Egyptian pharaohs. Also, in accord with ancient tradition, statues of the divine king were installed in Egyptian temples.

The Seleucids, following Alexander's lead, founded cities in the east patterned after the city-states of Greece. Thousands of Greeks settled in these cities, which were Greek in architecture and contained Greek schools, temples, theaters, and gymnasia. Hellenistic kings brought books, paintings, and statues to their cities from Greece. Hellenistic cities, inhabited by tens of thousands of people from many lands and dominated by a Hellenized upper class, served as centers and agents of Hellenism, which non-Greeks adopted. The ruling class in each Hellenistic city was united

by a common Hellenism which overcame national, linguistic, and racial distinctions. *Koine*, a form of Greek, came to be spoken throughout much of the Mediterranean world.

Hellenistic cities engaged in economic activity on a much greater scale than the classical Greek city-states had. Increased trade integrated the Near East and Greece into a market economy, and business methods became more sophisticated. The middle and upper classes enjoyed homes, furniture, and jewelry more elegant than those of Periclean Athenians, and some people amassed great fortunes. In contrast to the ideal of citizenship that distinguished the fifth-century polis, many Greeks who settled in Egypt, Syria, and other eastern lands ran roughshod over civil law and moral values, and engaged in competitive struggles for wealth and power.

The greatest city of the time and the one most representative of the Hellenistic Age was Alexandria. Strategically located at one of the mouths of the Nile, Alexandria became a center of commerce and culture. The most populous city of the Mediterranean world, Alexandria at the beginning of the Christian era contained perhaps a million people— Egyptians, Persians, Macedonians, Greeks, Jews, Syrians, and Arabs. The city was an unrivaled commercial center; goods from the Mediterranean world, east Africa, Arabia, and India circulated in its marketplaces. This cosmopolitan center also attracted poets, philosophers, physicians, astronomers, and mathematicians.

In addition to the proliferation of Greek urban institutions and ideas, Hellenistic cosmopolitanism was expressed by an increased movement of peoples, the adoption of common currency standards, and an expansion of trade. International trade was facilitated by improvements in navigation techniques, better port facilities, the extension of the monetary economy at the expense of barter, and the rapid development of banking. The makeup of Hellenistic armies also reflected the cosmopolitanism of the age. Serving the Hellenistic kings were men from lands stretching from India to the little-known areas north of the Danube. The cities in Egypt and Syria saw the emergence of a native elite who spoke Greek, wore Greek-style clothing, and adopted Greek customs.

All phases of cultural life were permeated by cultural exchange. Sculpture showed the influence of many lands. Historians wrote world histories, not just local histories. Greek astronomers worked with data collected over the centuries by the Babylonians. The Hebrew Scriptures were translated into Greek for use by Greek-speaking Jews, and Jewish thinkers began to take note of Greek philosophy. Greeks increasingly demonstrated a fascination for oriental religious cults. Philosophers helped to break down the barriers between peoples by asserting that all inhabit a single fatherland. As the philosopher Crates said, "My fatherland has no single tower, no single roof. The whole earth is my citadel, a home ready for us all to live in."[1]

The spread of Greek civilization from the Aegean to the Indus River gave the Hellenistic world a cultural common denominator, but Hellenization did not transform the East and make it one with the West. Hellenization was limited almost entirely to the cities, and in many urban centers it was often only a thin veneer. In Alexandria, for example, conflicting customs often led to riots between different nationalities. Many Egyptians in Alexandria learned Greek, and some assumed Greek names, but for most, Hellenization did not go much deeper. In the countryside, there was not even the veneer of Greek culture. Retaining traditional attitudes, the countryside in the East resisted Greek ways. In the villages, local and traditional law, local languages, and family customs remained unchanged; and religion, the most important ingredient of the civilizations of the Near East, also kept its traditional character.

Hellenistic Culture

Literature and History

There was a great outpouring of literary works during the Hellenistic Age. Callimachus (c. 305–240 B.C.), an Alexandrian scholar-poet, felt that no one could duplicate the great epics of Homer or the plays of the fifth-century B.C. dramatists. He urged poets to write short, finely crafted poems, instead of composing on a grand scale.

Apollonius of Rhodes (third–second century B.C.) took issue with Callimachus and wrote the *Argonautica*. This Homeric-style epic tells the story of Jason's search for the Golden Fleece. Apollonius was a gifted poet, although the epic was not the best genre for expressing his talent. His poetic talent and psychological insight are shown in this description of how love for Jason takes possession of Medea:

Time and again she darted a bright glance at Jason. All else was forgotten. Her heart, brimful of this new agony, throbbed within her and overflowed with the sweetness of the pain. A working woman, rising before dawn to spin and needing

Nike and Two-Horse Chariot: Hellenistic Gold Earring. The Hellenistic Age broadened the outlook of Hellenic Greece. In cosmopolitan Hellenistic society, life became more complex. This elaborate earring is vastly different from the simple ornaments of the Periclean Age and mirrors the new complexities. (*Courtesy Museum of Fine Arts, Boston*)

light in her cottage room, piles brushwood on a
smouldering log, and the whole heap kindled by
the little brand goes up in a mighty blaze. Such
was the fire of Love, stealthy but all-consuming,
that swept through Medea's heart. In the turmoil
of her soul, her soft cheeks turned from rose to
white and white to rose.[2]

Theocritus (c. 315–250 B.C.), who lived on the island of Sicily, wrote pastorals that showed great sensitivity to natural beauty. With uncommon feeling, Theocritus responded to the sky and wind, to the hills, trees, and flowers, and to the wildlife of the countryside:

Amid the shadowing foliage the brown cicalas
chirped

And chattered busily without pause; and far
away was heard
From the dense bramble-thicket the tree-frog's
fluted note.[3]

The Athenian playwright Menander (c. 342–291 B.C.) depicted Athenian life at the end of the fourth century. Menander's plays, unlike Aristophanes' lampoons of inept politicians, dealt little with politics. Apparently Menander reflected the attitude of his fellow Athenians who, bored with public affairs, had accepted their loss of freedom to Macedonia and were preoccupied with their own private lives. Menander dealt sympathetically with human weakness and wrote about stock characters: the clever slave, the young playboy, the elderly seducer, the heroine in trouble.

The leading historian of the Hellenistic Age was Polybius (c. 200–118 B.C.), whose history of the rise of Rome is one of the great works of historical literature. Reflecting the universal tendencies of the Hellenistic Age, Polybius endeavored to explain how Rome had progressed from a city-state to a world conqueror. As a disciple of Thucydides, Polybius sought rational explanations for human events. Also like Thucydides, he relied on eyewitness accounts (including his own personal experiences), checked sources, and strove for objectivity.

Science

During the Hellenistic Age, Greek scientific achievement reached its height. When Alexander invaded Asia Minor, the former student of Aristotle brought along surveyors, engineers, scientists, and historians, who continued with him into Asia. The vast amount of data in botany, zoology, geography, and astronomy collected by Alexander's staff stimulated an outburst of activity. To integrate so much information, scientists had to specialize in the various disciplines. Hellenistic scientists attempted a rational analysis of nature; they engaged in research, organized

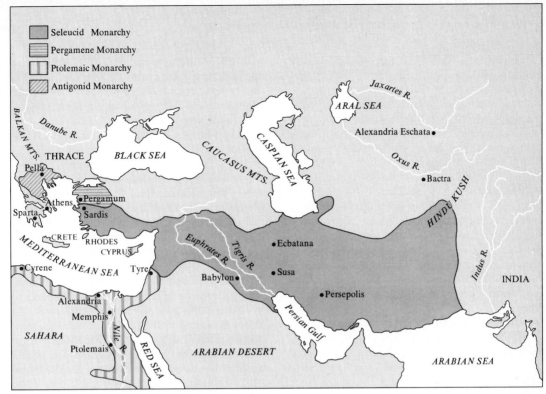

Map 5.2 The Division of Alexander's Empire and the Spread of Hellenism

knowledge in logical fashion, devised procedures for mathematical proof, separated medicine from magic, grasped the theory of experiment, and applied scientific principles to mechanical devices. Hellenistic science, says historian Benjamin Farrington, stood "on the threshold of the modern world. When modern science began in the sixteenth century, it took up where the Greeks left off."[4]

Alexandria was the principal center of scientific research, but Athens still retained some of its former luster in this area. After Aristotle's death in 322 B.C., he was succeeded as head of the Lyceum by Theophrastus and then Strato. Both wrote treatises on many themes—logic, ethics, politics, physics, and botany. Theophrastus systematized knowledge of botany in a manner similar to Aristotle's treatment of animals. Strato is most famous for his study of physics. It is likely that Strato, in his investigation of physical problems, did not rely on logic alone but

performed a series of experiments to test his investigations.

Because of its state-supported museum, Alexandria attracted leading scholars and superseded Athens in scientific investigation. The museum contained a library of more than half a million volumes, as well as botanical gardens and an observatory. It was really a research institute in which some of the best minds of the day studied and worked.

Alexandrian doctors advanced medical skills. They improved surgical instruments and techniques, and through dissecting bodies, they added to anatomical knowledge. Through their research, they uncovered organs of the body not known heretofore, made the distinction between arteries and veins, divided nerves into those comprising the motor and sensory systems, and identified the brain as the source of intelligence. Their investigations advanced knowledge of anatomy and physiology to a level that was not significantly improved until the sixteenth century A.D.

Knowledge in the fields of astronomy and mathematics also increased. Eighteen centuries before Copernicus, Alexandrian astronomer Aristarchus (310–230 B.C.) said that the sun was the center of the universe, that the planets revolved around it, and that the stars are situated at great distances from the earth. But these revolutionary ideas were not accepted, and the belief in an earth-centered universe persisted. In geometry, Euclid, an Alexandrian mathematician who lived around 300 B.C., creatively synthesized earlier developments. Euclid's hundreds of geometrical proofs, derived from reasoning alone, are a profound witness to the power of the rational mind.

Alexander's expeditions had opened the eyes of Mediterranean peoples to the breadth of the earth and had stimulated explorations and geographical research. Eratosthenes (c. 275–195 B.C.), an Alexandrian geographer, sought a scientific understanding of this enlarged world. He divided the planet into climatic zones, declared that the oceans are joined, and with extraordinary ingenuity and accuracy measured the earth's circumference.

Archimedes of Syracuse, who studied at Alexandria, was a mathematician, a physicist, and an ingenious inventor. His mechanical inventions, including war engines, dazzled his contemporaries. However, Archimedes dismissed his practical inventions, preferring to be remembered as a theoretician. In one treatise, he established the general principles of hydrostatics—a branch of physics that treats the pressure and equilibrium of liquids at rest.

Philosophy

Hellenistic thinkers preserved the rational tradition of Greek philosophy. Like their Hellenic predecessors, they regarded the cosmos as governed by universal principles intelligible to the rational mind. For the philosophers of both ages, a crucial problem was the achievement of the good life. And both Hellenic and Hellenistic thinkers sought rules for human conduct that accorded with rational standards; both believed that individuals attain happiness through their own efforts, unaided by the gods. In the tradition of Socrates, Hellenistic thinkers taught a morality of self-mastery. But although they retained the inheritance of the classical age, they also transformed it, for they had to adapt thought to the requirements of a cosmopolitan society.

In the Hellenic Age, the starting point of philosophy was the citizen's relationship to the city; in the Hellenistic Age, the point of departure was the solitary individual's relationship to humanity, his personal destiny in a complex world. Philosophy tried to deal with the feeling of alienation resulting from the weakening of the individual's attachment to the polis and to arrive at a conception of community that corresponded to the social realities of a world grown larger. Unlike Plato and Aristotle, Hellenistic philosophers were moralists, not great speculators and theorists. The Hellenistic schools of philosophy, in contrast to their predecessors, were far less concerned with the scientific understanding of nature. Philosophy was now primarily preoccupied with understanding the human condition, and it tried to alleviate spiritual uneasiness and loss of security; it aspired to make persons ethically independent so that they could achieve happiness in a hostile and competitive world.

In striving for tranquillity of mind and relief from conflict, Hellenistic thinkers reflected the general anxiety that pervaded their society. They retained respect for reason and aspired to the rational life, but by stressing peace of mind and the effort to overcome anxiety they were performing a quasi-religious function. Philosophy was trying to provide comfort for the individual suffering from feelings of loneliness and insignificance, and this attempt was an indication that Greek civilization was undergoing a spiritual transformation (the full meaning of which we will examine in Chapters 7 and 8). This gravitation toward religiosity in an effort to relieve despair gathered momentum in the centuries that followed. Thus Hellenistic philosophies helped prepare people to accept Christianity, which promised personal salvation. Ultimately the Christian answer to the problems of alienation and the need for community would predominate over the Greco-Roman attempt at resolution.

Epicureanism   Four principal schools of philosophy arose in the Hellenistic world: Epicureanism, Stoicism, Skepticism, and Cynicism. In the tradition of Plato and Aristotle, Epicurus (342–270 B.C.) founded a school at Athens at the end of the fourth century B.C. In significant ways Epicurus broke with the attitude of the Hellenic Age. Unlike classical Greek philosophers, Epicurus, reflecting the Greek's changing relationship to the city, taught the value of passivity and withdrawal from civic life. To him, citizenship was not a prerequisite for individual happiness. Wise persons, said Epicurus, would refrain from engaging in public affairs, for politics could deprive them of their self-sufficiency, their freedom to choose and to act. Nor would wise individuals pursue wealth, power, or fame, for the pursuit would only provoke anxiety. For the same reason, wise persons would not surrender to hate or love, desires that distress the soul. Nor could there be happiness when they worried about dying or pleasing the gods.

To Epicurus, fear that the gods interfered in human life and could inflict suffering after death was the principal cause of anxiety. To remove this source of human anguish, he favored a theory of nature that had no place for the activity of gods. Therefore he adopted the physics of Democritus, which taught that all things consist of atoms in motion. In a universe of colliding atoms, there could be no higher intelligence ordering things; there was no room for divine activity. Epicurus taught that the gods probably did exist, but that they were not involved in human affairs, so individuals could order their own lives. Epicurus embraced atomism, not as a disinterested scientist aspiring to truth, but as

Epicurus. The direct gaze of this marble head of Epicurus shows an inner calm, which was the goal of Epicurean philosophy. In the tradition of Greek philosophy, Epicurus maintained that happiness came from a rationally ordered life. But unlike fifth-century Greeks, Epicurus urged his followers not to engage in public affairs. (*The Metropolitan Museum of Art, Rogers Fund, 1911*)

a moral philosopher seeking to liberate emotional life from fear of the gods.

People could achieve happiness, said Epicurus, when their bodies were "free from pain" and minds "released from worry and fear." Although Epicurus wanted to increase pleasure for the individual, he rejected unbridled hedonism. Because happiness must be pursued rationally, he believed, those merely sensuous pleasures that have unpleasant aftereffects (such as overeating and overdrinking) are to be avoided. In general, Epicurus espoused the traditional Greek view of moderation and prudence.

By opening his philosophy to men and women, slave and free, Greek and barbarian, and by separating ethics from politics, Epicurus fashioned a philosophy adapted to the post-Alexandrian world of kingdoms and universal culture.

Stoicism About the same time as the founding of Epicurus' school, Zeno (335–263 B.C.) also opened a school in Athens. Zeno's teachings, called Stoicism, became the most important philosophy in the Hellenistic world. By teaching that the world constituted a single society, Stoicism gave theoretical expression to the world-mindedness of the age. By arriving at the concept of a world-state, the city of humanity, Stoicism offered an answer to the problem of community and alienation posed by the decline of the city-state. By stressing inner strength in dealing with life's misfortunes, Stoicism offered an avenue to individual happiness in a world fraught with uncertainty.

At the core of Stoicism was the belief that the universe contained a principle of order, variously called the Divine Fire, God, and Divine Reason (*Logos*). This ruling principle underlay reality and permeated all things; it accounted for the orderliness of nature. The Stoics reasoned that because people are part of the universe, they too shared in the logos that operated throughout the cosmos. The logos was implanted in every human soul; it enabled people to act intelligently, and to comprehend the principles of order that governed nature. Since reason was common to all, human beings were essentially brothers and fundamentally equal. Reason gave individuals dignity and enabled them to recognize and respect the dignity of others. To the Stoics, all people, Greek and barbarian, free and slave, rich and poor, were fellow human beings, and one law, the law of nature, applied to all human beings. Thus the Stoics, like the Hebrews, arrived at the idea of the oneness of humanity.

Pericles had spoken of the Athenian's obligation to abide by the laws and traditions of his city; Stoics, viewing people as citizens of the world, emphasized the individual's duty to understand and obey the natural law that governed the cosmos and applied to all. Socrates had taught a morality of self-mastery based on knowledge; the Stoics spread Socrates' philosophy beyond Athens, beyond Greece, and enlarged it, offering it as a way of life for all. Like Socrates, the Stoics believed that a person's distinctive quality was the ability to reason and that happiness came from the disciplining of emotions by the rational part of the soul. Also like Socrates, the Stoics maintained that individuals should progress morally, should perfect themselves.

In the Stoic view, wise persons ordered their lives according to the natural law—the law of reason—that underlay the cosmos. This harmony with the logos would give them the inner strength to resist the torments inflicted by others, by fate, and by their own passionate natures. Self-mastery and inner peace, or happiness, would follow. Such individuals remain undisturbed by life's misfortunes, for their souls are their own. Even slaves were not denied this inner freedom; although their bodies were subjected to the power of their masters, their minds still remained independent and free.

Stoicism had an enduring impact upon the Western mind. To some Roman political theorists the Empire fulfilled the Stoic ideal of a world community in which people of different nationalities held citizenship and were governed by a worldwide law that accorded with the law of reason, or natural law that operated throughout the universe. Stoic beliefs—by nature we are all members of one family, each person is significant, distinctions of rank and race are of no account, and human law should not conflict with natural law—were incorporated into Roman jurisprudence, Christian thought, and modern liberalism. There is continuity between Stoic thought and the principle of inalienable rights stated in the Declaration of Independence.

Skepticism The Epicureans tried to withdraw from the evils of this world and to attain personal happiness by reducing physical pain and mental anguish. The Stoics sought happiness by actively entering into harmony with universal reason. Both philosophies sought peace of mind, but the Stoics did not disengage themselves from political life and often exerted influence over Hellenistic rulers. Skepticism, another school of philosophy, attacked the Epicurean and Stoic belief that there is a definite avenue to happiness. Skeptics held that one could achieve spiritual comfort by recognizing that none of the beliefs by which people lived was true or could bring happiness.

Some Skeptics taught indifference to all theory and urged conformity to accepted views whether or not they were true. This attitude would avoid arguments and explanations. Gods might not exist, said the Skeptics, but to refuse to worship or to deny their existence would only cause trouble—therefore individuals should follow the crowd. The life of the mind did not bring truth or happiness; so why should one bother with it? Suspend judgment, recognize the inability to understand, do not commit oneself to a system of belief—by these means one could achieve peace of mind.

Metaphysical speculation, inquiring into the origin of things, and clever reasoning would bring neither assurance nor happiness. Instead of embracing doctrines, said the Greek writer Lucian, individuals should go their way "with ever a smile and never a passion."[5] This was the position of those Skeptics who were suspicious of ideas and hostile to intellectuals.

The more sophisticated Skeptics did not run away from ideas, but pointed out their limitations and weaknesses: they did not avoid theories, but disputed and refuted them. In doing so, they did not reject reason, but focused on a problem of reason—whether indeed it could arrive at truth. Thus, Carneades of Cyrene (213–129 B.C.) insisted that all ideas, even mathematical principles, must be regarded as hypotheses and assumptions, not as absolutes. Just because the universe showed signs of order, Carneades argued, one could not assume that it had been created

Veiled Dancer, Alexandrian, Third Century B.C. The twisting movement and the profusion of angles characterize Hellenistic art, which abandoned the simplicity, balance, and repose of classical Greek art. (*Metropolitan Museum of Art, bequest of Walter C. Baker, 1972*)

by God. The principles of religion rested on faith; they could not be rationally defended. Since there was never any certainty, only probability, morality should not derive from dogma, but from practical experience.

Cynicism   The Cynics were not theoretical philosophers but supreme individualists who rebelled against established values and conventions—against every barrier of society that restrained individuals from following their own natures. Cynics regarded laws and public opinion, private property and employment, and wives and children as hindrances to the free life. Extreme individualists, the Cynics had no loyalty to family, city, or kingdom and ridiculed religion, philosophy, and literature.

Cynics put their philosophy into practice. They cultivated idleness, indifference, and apathy. To harden themselves against life's misfortunes, they engaged in strenuous exercise, endured cold and hunger, and lived ascetically. Not tied down by property or employment, Cynics wandered shoeless from place to place, wearing dirty and ragged clothes and carrying staffs. To show their disdain for society's customs, Cynics grew long scraggly beards, used foul language, and cultivated bad manners. Diogenes, a fourth-century B.C. Greek Cynic, supposedly said: "Look at me, . . . I am without a home, without a city, without property, without a slave; I sleep on the ground; I have neither wife nor children, no miserable governor's mansion, but only earth, and sky, and one rough cloak. Yet what do I lack? Am I not free from pain and fear, am I not free?"[6]

In their attack on inherited conventions, Cynics strove for self-sufficiency and spiritual security. Theirs was the most radical philosophical quest for meaning and peace of soul during the Hellenistic Age.

The Hellenistic Age encompassed the period from the death of Alexander to the formation of the Roman Empire. During these three centuries, Greek civilization spread eastward as far as India, and westward to Rome. Peoples began to conceive of themselves as members of a world community, speaking a common Greek language and sharing a common Greek civilization. It was Rome, conqueror of the Mediterranean world and transmitter of Hellenism, that inherited the universalist tendencies of the Hellenistic Age and embodied them in law and institutions.

Notes

1. Quoted in John Ferguson, *The Heritage of Hellenism* (New York: Science History Publications, 1973), p. 30.

2. Apollonius of Rhodes, *The Voyage of Argo*, trans. by E. V. Rieu (Baltimore: Penguin Books, 1959), p. 117.

3. *The Idylls of Theocritus*, trans. by R. C. Trevelyan (London: The Casanova Society, 1925), p. 28.

4. Benjamin Farrington, *Greek Science* (Baltimore: Penguin Books, 1961), p. 301.

5. Quoted in J. H. Randall, Jr., *Hellenistic Ways of Deliverance and the Making of the Christian Synthesis* (New York: Columbia University Press, 1970), p. 74.

6. Epictetus, *The Discourses as Reported by Arrian, the Manual and Fragments*, trans. by W. A. Oldfather (Cambridge, Mass.: Harvard University Press, 1966), II:147.

Suggested Reading

Bonnard, Andre, *Greek Civilization*, III (1961). Self-contained chapters on various phases of late classical and Hellenistic periods.

Bury, J. B., et al., *The Hellenistic Age* (1970). First published in 1923; contains valuable essays by leading classicists.

Cary, M., *A History of the Greek World 323–146 B.C.* (1972). A standard survey of the Hellenistic world.

Ferguson, John, *The Heritage of Hellenism* (1973). A good introduction to Hellenistic culture.

Grant, Michael, *From Alexander to Cleopatra* (1982). A fine survey of all phases of Hellenistic society and culture.

Green, Peter, *Alexander the Great* (1970). A lavishly illustrated study.

Hadas, Moses, *Hellenistic Culture* (1972). Focuses on the cultural exchanges between East and West.

Peters, F. E., *The Harvest of Hellenism* (1970). A comprehensive treatment of Hellenistic history and culture.

Randall, J. H., Jr., *Hellenistic Ways of Deliverance*

and the Making of the Christian Synthesis (1970). An astute discussion of Hellenistic and early Christian thought.

Tarn, W. W., *Alexander the Great* (1956). A controversial interpretation.

Wallbank, F. W. *The Hellenistic World* (1982). A survey of the Hellenistic world that makes judicious use of quotations from original sources.

Review Questions

1. What were the basic differences between the Hellenic and Hellenistic Ages?

2. How did Alexander the Great contribute to the shaping of the Hellenistic Age?

3. Provide examples of Hellenistic cosmopolitanism.

4. In what ways is New York closer to Hellenistic Alexandria than to Hellenic Athens?

5. What was the significance of the Museum at Alexandria?

6. Hellenistic science stood on the threshold of the modern world. Explain.

7. What problems concerned Hellenistic philosophers?

8. What were the Epicurean, Stoic, Skeptic, and Cynic prescriptions for achieving happiness?

9. What was the enduring significance of Stoicism?

10. Which of the Hellenistic philosophies has the most appeal for you?

6

The Roman Republic:
City-State to World Empire

*R*ome's great achievement was to transcend the narrow political orientation of the city-state and to create a world-state that unified the different nations of the Mediterranean world. Regarding the polis as the only means to the good life, the Greeks had not desired a larger political unit and had almost totally excluded foreigners from citizenship. Although Hellenistic philosophers had conceived the possibility of a world community, Hellenistic politics could not shape one. But Rome overcame the limitations of the city-state mentality and developed an empirewide system of law and citizenship. The Hebrews were distinguished by their prophets, and the Greeks by their philosophers; Rome's genius found expression in law and government.

Roman history falls into two periods: the Republic began in 509 B.C. with the overthrow of the Etruscan monarchy; and the Empire started in 27 B.C. when Octavian (Augustus) became in effect the first Roman emperor, ending almost five hundred years of republican self-government. By conquering the Mediterranean world and extending its law and, in some instances, citizenship to different nationalities, the Roman Republic transcended the parochialism typical of the city-state. The Republic initiated the trend toward political and legal universalism, which reached fruition in the second phase of Roman history, the Empire.

Evolution of the Roman Constitution

By the eighth century B.C., peasant communities existed on some of Rome's seven hills near the Tiber River in central Italy. To the north and south stood Etruscan and Greek cities whose higher civilizations were gradually absorbed by the Romans. The origin of the Etruscans remains a mystery, although some scholars believe that they came from Asia Minor and settled in northern Italy. From them, Romans acquired architectural styles and skills in road construction, sanitation, hydraulic engineering including underground conduits, metallurgy, ceramics, and portrait sculpture. Symbols of authority and rule were also borrowed from the Etruscans—purple robes, ivory-veneer chariots, thrones for state officials, and a bundle of rods and an ax held by attendants. Etruscan words and names entered into the Latin language, and Etruscan gods were absorbed by Roman religion.

The Etruscans had expanded their territory in Italy during the seventh and sixth centuries B.C., and they controlled the monarchy in Rome. But the Etruscan city-states failed to establish a federal union with a centralized government. Defeated by Celts, Greeks, and finally Romans, by the third century B.C. the Etruscans had ceased to exercise any political power in Italy.

Rome became a republic at the end of the sixth century B.C. when the landowning aristocrats, or patricians, overthrew the Etruscan king. As in the Greek cities, the transition from theocratic monarchy to republic offered possibilities for political and legal growth. In the opening phase of republican history, religion governed the people, dictated the law, and legitimized the rule of the patricians, who regarded themselves as the preservers of sacred traditions. Gradually the Romans loosened the ties between religion and politics and hammered out a constitutional system that paralleled the Greek achievement of rationalizing and secularizing politics and law. In time the Romans, like the Greeks, came to view law as an expression of the public will and not as the creation of god-kings, priest-kings, or a priestly caste.

The impetus for the growth of the Roman constitution came from a conflict—known as the Struggle of the Orders—between the patricians and the commoners, or plebeians. At the beginning of the fifth century B.C., the patrician-dominated government was composed of two consuls together with the Centuriate Assembly and the Senate. Patricians owned most of the land and controlled the army. The executive heads of government were the two annually elected consuls who came from the nobility; they commanded the army, served as judges, and initiated legislation. To prevent either consul from becoming an autocrat, decisions had to be approved by both of them. In times of crisis the consuls were authorized by the Senate to nominate a dictator; he would possess absolute powers during the emergency, but these powers would expire after six months. The consuls were aided by other annually elected magistrates and administrators. The Centuriate Assembly was a popular assembly but, because of voting procedures, was controlled by the nobility. The assembly elected consuls and other magistrates and made the laws, which also needed Senate approval. The Senate advised the assembly but did not itself enact laws; it controlled public finances and foreign policy. Senators either were appointed for life terms by the consuls or were former magistrates. The Senate was the principal organ of patrician power.

The tension between patricians and commoners stemmed from plebeian grievances, which included enslavement for debt, discrimination in the courts, prevention of intermarriage with patricians, lack of political representation, and the absence of a written code of laws. Resentful of their inferior status, the plebeians organized and waged a struggle for political, legal, and social equality. They were resisted every step of the way by patricians, who wanted to preserve their own dominance. The plebeians had one decisive weapon: their threat to secede from Rome, that is, not to pay taxes, work, or serve in the army. Realizing that Rome, which was constantly involved in warfare on the Italian peninsula, could not endure without plebeian help, the pragmatic patricians begrudgingly made concessions. Thus the plebeians slowly gained legal equality.

Early in the fifth century the plebeians won the right to form their own assembly (the Plebeian Assembly when later enlarged was called the Tribal Assembly). This Assembly could elect officials called tribunes, who were empowered to protect plebeian rights. As a result of plebeian pressure, about 450 B.C. the first Roman code of laws was written; called the Twelve Tables, the code gave plebeians some degree of protection against unfair and oppressive patrician officials. Other concessions gained later by the plebeians included the right to intermarry with patricians, access to the highest political, judicial, and religious offices in the state, and the elimination of slavery as payment for debt. In 287 B.C., a date generally recognized as the termination of the plebeian-patrician struggle, the acts of the Tribal Assembly became binding on all and did not need Senate approval.

Although the plebeians had gained legal equality and the right to sit in the Senate and to hold high offices, Rome was still ruled by an upper class. True, the Tribal Assembly and the tribunes constituted democratic elements and, in theory, seemed to balance the power of the patrician-dominated Senate. In actual fact, however, power was concentrated in a ruling oligarchy consisting of patricians and influential plebeians who had joined forces with the old nobility. Marriages between patricians and politically powerful plebeians strengthened this alliance. As wealthy plebeians generally became tribunes, they tended to side with the old nobility rather than to defend the interests of poor plebeians. By using bribes, the ruling oligarchy maintained control over the Assembly, and the Senate remained a bastion of aristocratic power. In the Greek cities, tyrants had succeeded in breaking aristocratic dominance, thereby clearing a pathway for democratic government. But in the Roman Republic, the nobility maintained its tight grip on the reins of power until the civil wars of the first century B.C.

Regarding themselves as Rome's finest citizens, the ruling oligarchy led Rome during its period of expansion and demonstrated a sense of responsiblity and a talent for statesmanship. In noble families, parents and elders prepared the young for public service. They recounted the glorious deeds of ancestors and reminded youngsters of their responsibility to bring additional honors to the family.

During their two-hundred-year class struggle, the Romans forged a constitutional system based on civic needs rather than on religious mystery. The essential duty of government ceased to be the regular performance of religious rituals and became the maintenance of order at home and the preservation of Roman might and dignity in international relations. Although the Romans retained the ceremonies and practices of their ancestral religion, public interest, not religious tradition, determined the content of law and was the standard by which all the important acts of the city were judged. In the opening stage of republican history, law was priestly and sacred, spoken only by priests and known only to men of religious families. Gradually, as law was written, debated, and altered, it became disentangled from religion. Another step in this process of secularization and rationalization occurred when the study and interpretation of law passed from the hands of priests to a class of professional jurists, who analyzed, classified, systematized, and sought common-sense solutions to legal problems.

The Roman constitution was not a product of abstract thought, nor was it the gift of a great lawmaker like the Athenian Solon. Rather, like the British constitution, the Roman constitution evolved gradually and empirically in response to specific needs. The Romans, unlike the Greeks, were distinguished by practicality and common sense, not by a love of abstract thought. In their pragmatic and empirical fashion, they gradually developed the procedures of public politics and the legal state.

Undoubtedly, the commoners' struggle for rights and power did arouse bitter hatred on both sides. But unlike the domestic strife in Greek cities, Rome's conflict did not end in civil war. This peaceful solution testifies to the political good sense of the Romans. Fear of foreign powers and the tradition of civic patriotism prevented the patrician-plebeian conflict from turning into a fight to the death. At the time of the class struggle, Rome was also engaged in the extension of its power

Cinerary Urn, Etruscan, C. 160–140 B.C. The Etruscan influence on the Romans extended to portrait sculpture. The Etruscans had adopted the Greek style in portraiture to commemorate their ancestors. (*Worcester Art Museum, Massachusetts*)

over the Italian peninsula. Without civic harmony and stability, Rome could not have achieved expansion.

Roman Expansion to 146 B.C.

By 146 B.C., Rome had become the dominant power in the Mediterranean world. Roman expansion had occurred in three main stages: the uniting of the Italian peninsula, which gave Rome the manpower that transformed it from a city-state into a great power; the collision with Carthage, from which Rome emerged as ruler of the western Mediterranean; and the subjugation of the Hellenistic states, which brought Romans in close contact with Greek civilization. As Rome expanded territorially, its leaders enlarged their vision. Instead of restricting citizenship to people having racial kinship, Rome assimilated other peoples into its political community. As law had grown to cope with the earlier grievances of the plebeians, it adjusted to the new situations resulting from the creation of a multinational empire. The city of Rome was evolving into the city of humanity—the cosmopolis envisioned by the Stoics.

The Uniting of Italy

Frequent conflicts with hostile neighbors had forced Romans to develop militarily and to strengthen their commitment to Rome. These developments fostered expansion. During the first stage, Rome extended its hegemony over Italy, subduing in the process neighboring Latin kinsmen, semicivilized Italian tribes, the once dominant Etruscans, and Greek city-states in southern Italy. At the beginning, Roman warfare was principally motivated by the peasants' land hunger. As Rome grew stronger and its territory and responsibilities increased, it was often drawn into conflict to protect its expanded boundaries and its allies.

Rome's conquest of Italy stemmed in part from superior military organization and discipline. Copying the Greeks, the Romans organized their soldiers into battle formations; in contrast, their opponents often fought as disorganized hordes that were prone to panic and flight. Fighting as part of a unit strengthened the courage and confidence of the Roman soldier, for he knew that his comrades would stand with him. (Roman soldiers who deserted their post or fled from battle were punished and disgraced, an ordeal more terrible than facing up to the enemy.) Also, the promise of glory and rewards impelled the Roman soldier to distinguish himself in battle.

Ultimately, Rome's success was due to the character of its people and the quality of its statesmanship. The Roman farmer-soldier was dedicated, rugged, persevering, and self-reliant. He could march thirty miles a day laden with arms, armor, and equipment weighing sixty pounds. In the face of danger he remained resolute and tenacious, obedient to the poet Virgil's maxim: "Yield you not to ill fortune, but go against it with more daring." Romans willingly made sacrifices so that Rome might endure. In conquering Italy, they were united by a moral and religious devotion to their city strong enough to overcome social conflict, factional disputes, and personal ambition.

Despite its army's strength, Rome could not have mastered Italy without the cooperation of other Italian peoples. Instead of reducing adversaries to slavery and taking all their land—a not uncommon method of warfare in the ancient world—Rome endeavored, through generous treatment, to gain the loyalty of conquered people. Some defeated communities retained a measure of self-government but turned the conduct of foreign affairs over to Rome and contributed contingents to the army when Rome went to war. Other conquered people received partial or full citizenship. In extending its dominion over Italy, Rome displayed a remarkable talent for converting former enemies into allies and eventually into Roman citizens. No Greek city had ever envisaged integrating nonnatives into its political community.

The Italian Confederation formed by Rome was a unique and creative organization that conferred on Italians a measure of security and order previously unknown. Rome prevented internecine wars within the peninsula, suppressed internal revolutions within city-states, and protected the Italians from barbarians (Gallic invaders from the north). In the wars of conquest outside Italy, a share of the glory and plunder fell to all Italians, another benefit of the confederation.

By 264 B.C., Rome had achieved two striking successes. First, it had secured social cohesion by redressing the grievances of the plebeians. Second, Rome had increased its military might by conquering Italy, obtaining the human resources with which it would conquer the Mediterranean world.

The Conquest of the Western Mediterranean: The Punic Wars

When Rome finished unifying Italy, there were five great powers in the Mediterranean area: the Seleucid monarchy in the Near East, the Ptolemaic monarchy in Egypt, the kingdom of Macedonia, Carthage in the western Mediterranean, and the Roman-dominated Italian Confederation. One hundred and twenty years later—146 B.C.—Rome had subjected these states to its dominion, "an event for which the past affords no precedent," said the contemporary Greek historian Polybius.

Roman expansion beyond Italy did not proceed according to predetermined design. Indeed, some Roman leaders considered involvement in foreign adventures a threat to both Rome's security and its traditional way of life. But it is difficult for a great power not to get drawn into conflicts as its interests grow, and without planning it, Rome acquired an overseas empire.

Shortly after asserting supremacy in Italy, Rome engaged Carthage, the other great power in the western Mediterranean, in a prolonged conflict. Founded about 800 B.C. by Phoenicians, the North African city of Carthage had become a prosperous commercial center. Its wealth was derived from a virtual monopoly of trade in the western Mediterranean and along the west coasts of Africa and Europe. The Carthaginians had acquired an empire comprising North Africa and coastal regions of southern Spain, Sardinia, Corsica, and western Sicily. Carthaginians pursued a cautious foreign policy, preferring diplomacy to conflict and avoiding wars offering no promise of commercial gain.

War between the two great powers began because Rome feared Carthage's designs on the northern Sicilian city of Messana, whose ruling oligarchy had appealed to Rome for protection. Although it had no territorial or commercial interests in Sicily, Rome was apprehensive about the southern Italian city-states that were its allies, fearing that Carthage would use Messana either to attack them or to interfere with their trade. In 264 B.C., after much uncertainty and debate, Rome decided that the security of its allies required intervention in Sicily. Since Carthage would not surrender its claim to Messana, the two powers stumbled into a collision that neither had deliberately sought. As the war progressed, Rome's objectives amplified. No longer satisfied with driving Carthage from Messana, Rome wanted to expel Carthaginians from Sicily altogether, a decision that lengthened

the war by twenty years and turned it into a war of exhaustion.

Although Rome suffered severe losses—including the annihilation of an army that had invaded North Africa and the destruction of hundreds of ships in battle and storms—the Romans never considered anything but a victor's peace. Drawing manpower from loyal allies throughout Italy, Rome finally prevailed over Carthage, which had relied principally on a mercenary army and could not recoup its sea losses. Without the means of continuing the war, Carthage made peace in 241 B.C., surrendering Sicily to Rome. Three years later, Rome seized the islands of Corsica and Sardinia from a weakened Carthage. With the acquisition of these territories beyond Italy, which were made into provinces, Rome had the beginnings of an empire.

Carthaginian expansion in Spain precipitated the Second Punic War (218–201 B.C.). The Carthaginian army was commanded by Hannibal (247–183 B.C.), whose military genius astounded the ancients. Hannibal led a seasoned army, complete with war elephants for charging enemy lines, across mountain passes so steep and icy that men and animals sometimes lost their footing and fell to their deaths. Some 26,000 men survived the crossing into Italy; 15,000 more were recruited from Gallic tribesmen of the Po Valley. At the battle of Cannae (216 B.C.), Hannibal's army completely destroyed a Roman army of 60,000 soldiers, the largest single force Rome had ever put into the field.

Romans were in a state of shock. Mixed with grief for the dead was the fear that Hannibal would crown his victory with an attack on Rome itself. To prevent panic, the Senate ordered women and children indoors, limited mourning to thirty days, and prepared to raise a new army. Adding to Rome's distress was the defection of many southern Italian allies to Hannibal.

These were the Republic's worst days. Nevertheless, says the Roman historian Livy, the Romans did not breathe a word of peace.

Map 6.1 Roman Conquests During the Republic ▶

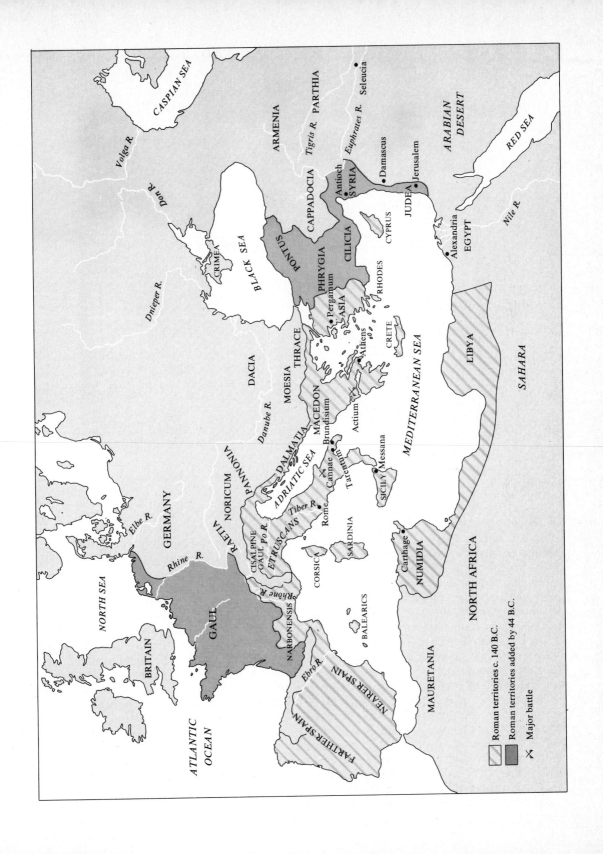

CASPIAN SEA

Volga R.

Don R.

ARMENIA

PARTHIA

Tigris R.

Euphrates R.

Seleucia

Damascus

ARABIAN DESERT

RED SEA

CAPPADOCIA

Antioch

SYRIA

Jerusalem

JUDEA

Nile R.

Alexandria

EGYPT

CYPRUS

Dnieper R.

CRIMEA

BLACK SEA

PONTUS

PHRYGIA

CILICIA

RHODES

Pergamum

ASIA

CRETE

Athens

MEDITERRANEAN SEA

LIBYA

SAHARA

DACIA

Danube R.

MOESIA

THRACE

MACEDON

Actium

Brundisium

PANNONIA

NORICUM

RAETIA

DALMATIA

ADRIATIC SEA

Cannae

Tarentum

Messana

SICILY

GERMANY

Elbe R.

Rhine R.

Tiber R.

Rome

ETRUSCANS

CISALPINE GAUL Po R.

Rhône R.

SARDINIA

CORSICA

Carthage

NUMIDIA

NORTH AFRICA

NORTH SEA

BRITAIN

GAUL

NARBONENSIS

BALEARICS

ATLANTIC OCEAN

Ebro R.

NEARER SPAIN

FARTHER SPAIN

MAURETANIA

Roman territories c. 140 B.C.

Roman territories added by 44 B.C.

X   Major battle

Roman Forum, House of the Vestals, and the Capitol. The Forum was the center of Roman government and administration under both the Republic and the Empire. Here the *curia* (Senate house) and important basilicas were located. (*ENIT/Italian Government Travel Office*)

Hannibal could not follow up his victory at Cannae with a finishing blow, for Rome wisely would not allow its army to be lured into another major engagement. Nor did Hannibal possess the manpower to capture the city itself, particularly since the central cities remained loyal to Rome. But for nearly fifteen years, Hannibal's army ravaged Italy.

At the same time that Hannibal was devastating Italy, his brother Hasdrubal was engaging Roman forces in Spain, commanded by the brothers Publius and Cnaeus Scipio. Reinforced by troops from Carthage, Hasdrubal destroyed the divided armies of the Scipios, both of whom perished in battle. In 210 B.C., Publius Scipio's son, who bore the same name, was dispatched to Spain to redeem the defeat.

The younger Scipio possessed superior self-confidence, a trait that he conveyed to his troops. After completing the conquest of Spain by 206 B.C., Scipio invaded North Africa, threatening Carthage and forcing Hannibal to withdraw his troops from Italy in order to defend his homeland. Hannibal, who had won every battle in Italy, was defeated by Scipio at the battle of Zama in North Africa in 202 B.C.; this battle marked the end of the Second Punic War. Thus Rome's superior reserves of manpower, determination, and willingness to make sacrifices had overcome Hannibal's military feats. Carthage was compelled to surrender Spain and to give up its elephants and its navy.

The Conquest of the Hellenistic World

The Second Punic War left Rome the sole great power in the western Mediterranean;

it also hastened Rome's entry into the politics of the Hellenistic world. As in Rome's uniting of Italy and conquest of the western Mediterranean, its expansion in the East followed no predetermined plan. Rome did not deliberately seek territorial aggrandizement. As a great power, Rome was drawn into Greek affairs, fearing political disorder. Intervention in Greece then led to Roman involvement in the Hellenistic kingdoms of the Near East and Asia Minor—Seleucia, Egypt, and Pergamum. The inability of the Hellenistic states to settle their own disputes prompted Rome to attempt to impose its dominion over them; their failure to present unified resistance simplified Rome's military effort. Overcome by superior power, the Hellenistic states became client kingdoms of Rome and, they consequently lost their freedom of action in foreign affairs.

Roman imperialism is a classic example of a great power being snared into overseas adventures. To achieve security, Rome protected its allies, prevented endemic warfare, and thwarted any would-be conquerors of Italy. In the course of these actions came considerable spoils of war, but Rome's principal motives for expansion were strategic and political, not economic.

In 146 B.C., the same year that Rome's hegemony over the Hellenistic world was assured, Rome concluded the Third Punic War with Carthage. Although Carthage was a second-rate power and no longer a threat to Rome's security, Rome had launched this war of annihilation against Carthage in 149 B.C. The Romans were driven by old hatreds and the traumatic memory of Hannibal's near-conquest. Rome sold Carthaginian survivors into slavery, obliterated the city, and turned the land into the Roman province of Africa. Rome's savage and irrational behavior toward a helpless Carthage was an early sign of the failure of senatorial leadership; there would be others.

Rome had not yet reached the limits of its expansion, but there was no doubt that by 146 B.C. the Mediterranean world had been subjected to its will.

The Consequences of Expansion

Thousands of Greeks came to Rome; many were educated persons who had been enslaved as a result of Rome's eastern conquests. This influx accelerated the process of Hellenization begun earlier with Rome's contact with the Greek cities of southern Italy.

A crucial consequence of expansion was Roman contact with the legal experience of other peoples, including the Greeks. Roman jurists, demonstrating the Roman virtues of pragmatism and common sense, selectively incorporated into Roman law elements of the legal codes and traditions of these nations. Thus Roman jurists gradually and empirically fashioned the *jus gentium,* the law of nations or peoples.

Roman jurists then identified the *jus gentium* with the natural law (*jus naturale*) of the Stoics. The jurists said that law should accord with rational principles inherent in nature—universal norms that are capable of being discerned by rational people. As the Roman statesman Cicero said,

True law is right reason in agreement with nature; it is of universal application, unchanging and everlasting. . . . And there will not be different laws at Rome and at Athens, or different laws now and in the future, but one eternal and unchangeable law will be valid for all nations and all times.[1]

The law of nations combined Roman civil law—the law of the Roman state—with principles drawn from Greek and other sources, and it eventually replaced much of the local law in the empire. This evolution of a universal code of law that gave expression to the Stoic principles of common rationality and humanity was the great achievement of Roman rule.

Rome's conquests also contributed to the rise of a middle class of commoners. Their wealth was derived from contracts to supply the army, to construct public buildings, and to collect taxes in the provinces. Rome had no professional civil service, and the collection of public revenues was open to bidding—the highest bidder receiving a contract to collect customs' duties, rents on public lands, and tribute in the provinces. The collector's profit came from milking as much tax money as he could from the provincials. These financiers belonged to a group called the Equites, which also included prosperous landowners. Generally, the interests of the Equites paralleled those of the ruling oligarchy. At times, however, they did support generals—notably Julius Caesar—who challenged senatorial rule.

The immense wealth brought to Rome from the East gave the upper classes a taste for luxury. The rich built elaborate homes, which they decorated with fine furniture and works of art and staffed with servants, cooks, and tutors. They delighted in sumptuous banquets that contained all types of delicacies. Wealthy matrons wore fancy gowns and coiffures to match. These excesses prompted Roman moralists to castigate the people for violating traditional values.

Roman conquerors had transported to Italy hundreds of thousands of war captives, including Greeks, from all over their empire. The more fortunate slaves worked as craftsmen and servants; the luckless and more numerous toiled on the growing number of plantations or died early laboring in mines. Roman masters often treated their slaves brutally. Although slave uprisings were not common, their ferocity terrified the Romans. In 135 B.C., slaves in Sicily revolted and captured some key towns, defeating Roman forces before being subdued. In 73 B.C., gladiators led by Spartacus broke out of their barracks. Proclaiming a war for the liberation of all slaves, Spartacus was joined by tens of thousands of runaways. The slave army defeated Roman armies and devastated southern Italy before the superior might of Rome prevailed. Some 6,000 of the defeated slaves were crucified.

Republican Rome treated the people in overseas lands differently from its Italian allies. Italians were drafted into the Roman army, but provincials as a rule served only in emergencies, for Rome was not certain of their loyalty nor of their readiness to meet

Roman standards of discipline. Whereas Rome had been somewhat generous in extending citizenship to Italians, provincials were granted citizenship only in exceptional cases. All but some favored communities were required to pay taxes to Rome. Roman governors, lesser officials, and businessmen found the provinces a source of quick wealth; they were generally unrestrained by the Senate, which was responsible for administering the overseas territories. Exploitation, corruption, and extortion soon ran rampant. The Roman nobility proved unfit to manage a world empire.

Despite numerous examples of misrule in the provinces, there were many positive features of Roman administration. Rome generally allowed its subjects a large measure of self-government and did not interfere with religion and local customs. Usually the Roman taxes worked out to be no higher than, and in some instances were lower than those under previous regimes. And most important, Rome reduced the endemic warfare that had plagued these regions.

Rome used its power essentially for constructive ends—to establish order; to build roads, aqueducts, and public buildings; and to promote Hellenism. When Rome destroyed, it rebuilt creatively; when it conquered, it spread civilization and maintained peace. But no doubt its hundreds of thousands of prisoners of war, uprooted, enslaved, and degraded, would not have viewed Roman conquest as beneficial; nor would the butchered Spanish tribesmen or the massacred Carthaginians. To these hapless victims, Rome appeared as an evil oppressor, not as the creator of a cosmopolis that brought order and security.

Culture in the Republic

A chief consequence of expansion was increased contact with Greek culture. During the third century B.C., Greek civilization started to exercise an increasing and fruitful influence upon the Roman mind. Greek teachers, both slave and free, came to Rome and introduced Romans to Hellenic cultural achievements. As they conquered the eastern Mediterranean, Roman generals began to ship libraries and works of art from Greek cities to Rome. In time, Romans acquired from Greece knowledge of scientific thought, philosophy, medicine, and geography. Roman writers and orators used Greek history, poetry, and oratory as models. Adopting the humanist outlook of the Greeks, the Romans came to value human intelligence and eloquent and graceful prose and poetry. Wealthy Romans retained Greek tutors, poets, and philosophers in their households and sent their sons to Athens to study. Thus, Rome creatively assimilated the Greek achievement and transmitted it to others, thereby extending the orbit of Hellenism. To be sure, some conservative Romans were hostile to the Greek influence, which they felt threatened traditional Roman values, but the tide of Hellenism could not be stemmed.

Plautus (c. 254–184 B.C.), Rome's greatest playwright, adopted features of fourth- and third-century Greek comedy. His plays had Greek characters and took place in Greek settings; the actors wore the Greek style of dress. But the plays also contained familiar elements that appealed to Roman audiences—scenes of gluttony, drunkenness, womanizing, and the pains of love.

Not the throes of all mankind
Equal my distracted mind.
I strain and I toss
On a passionate cross;
Love's goad makes me reel,
I whirl on Love's wheel,
In a swoon of despair
Hurried here, hurried there—
Torn asunder, I am blind
With a cloud upon my mind.[2]

Another playwright, Terence (c. 190–159 B.C.), was originally from North Africa, and was brought to Rome as a slave. His owner, a Roman senator, provided the talented youth

with an education and freed him. Like Plautus, Terence was influenced by Menander, the fourth-century Athenian comic playwright. Terence's Latin style, graceful and polished, was technically superior to that of Plautus. But Terence's humor, restrained and refined, lacked the boisterousness of Plautus' writing that appealed to the Roman audience. For this reason, Terence's plays were less popular. Terence demonstrated more humaneness than Plautus did, a quality that is depicted in his attitude toward child rearing:

I give—I overlook; I do not judge it necessary to exert my authority in everything. . . . I think it better to restrain children through a sense of shame and liberal treatment than through fear. . . . This is the duty of a parent to accustom a son to do what is right rather of his own choice, than through fear of another.[3]

Catullus (87–54 B.C.) is generally regarded as one of the greatest lyric poets in world literature. He was a native of northern Italy whose father had provided him with a gentleman's education. In his early twenties, Catullus came to Rome and fell in love with Clodia; she was the wife of the governor of Cisalpine Gaul, who was away at the time. For the older Clodia, Catullus was a refreshing diversion from her many other lovers. Tormented by Clodia's numerous affairs with other men, Catullus struggled to break away from passion's grip:

I look no more for her to be my lover
As I love her. That thing could never be.
Nor pray I for her purity—that's over.
Only this much I pray, that I be free.

Free from insane desire myself, and guarded
In peace at last. O heaven, grant that yet
The faith by which I've lived may be
    rewarded.
Let me forget.[4]

The historian Sallust (c. 86–35 B.C.) sided with Caesar against the senatorial oligarchy. After Caesar's death, Sallust withdrew from public life, devoting himself to writing history.

His works contain brilliant character sketches. With a high moral tone, Sallust condemned the breakdown of republican values.

Growing love of money, and the lust for power which followed it, engendered every kind of evil. Avarice destroyed honor, integrity, and every other virtue, and instead taught men to be proud and cruel, to neglect religion, and to hold nothing too sacred to sell. Ambition tempted many to be false . . . At first these vices grew slowly and sometimes met with punishments; later on, when the disease had spread like a plague, Rome changed: her government, once so just and admirable, became harsh and unendurable.[5]

Lucretius (c. 94–c. 55 B.C.), the leading Roman Epicurean philosopher, was influenced by the conflict fostered by two generals, Marius and Sulla, which is discussed later in this chapter. Distraught by the seemingly endless strife, Lucretius yearned for philosophic tranquillity. Like Epicurus, he believed that religion prompted people to perform evil deeds and caused them to experience terrible anxiety about death and eternal punishment. In his work, *On the Nature of Things,* Lucretius expressed his appreciation of Epicurus. Like his mentor, Lucretius advanced a materialistic conception of nature and denounced superstition and religion for fostering psychological distress. He proposed that the simple life, devoid of political involvement and excessive passion, was the highest good and the path that would lead from emotional turmoil to peace of mind. Epicurus' hostility to traditional religion, disparagement of politics and public service, and rejection of the goals of power and glory ran counter to the accepted Roman ideal of virtue. On the other hand, his glorification of the quiet life amid a community of friends had great appeal to first-century Romans, who were disgusted with civil strife.

Cicero (106–43 B.C.), a leading Roman statesman, was also a distinguished orator, an unsurpassed Latin stylist, and a student of Greek philosophy. His letters, more than eight hundred of which have survived, provide modern historians with valuable insights into late republican politics. Dedicated to republicanism, Cicero sought to prevent one-man rule. He adopted the Stoic belief that natural law governs the universe and applies to all, and that all belong to a common humanity.

. . . there is no difference in kind between man and man; for . . . Reason, which alone raises us above the level of the beasts and enables us to draw inferences, to prove and disprove, to discuss and solve problems, and to come to conclusions, is certainly common to us all, and though varying in what it learns, at least in the capacity to learn it is invariable. . . . In fact, there is no human being of any race who, if he finds a guide, cannot attain virtue.[6]

Stoicism was the most influential philosophy in Rome. Its stress on virtuous conduct and performance of duty coincided with Roman ideals, and its doctrine of natural law that applies to all nations harmonized with the requirements of a world empire.

The Collapse of the Republic

In 146 B.C., Roman might spanned the Mediterranean world. After that year the principal concerns of the Republic no longer were foreign invasions, but adjusting city-state institutions to the demands of empire and overcoming critical social and political problems at home. In both instances the Republic was unequal to the challenge. Instead of developing a professional civil service to administer the conquered lands, Roman leaders attempted to govern an empire with city-state institutions that had evolved for a different purpose. In addition, the Republic showed little concern for the welfare of its subjects, and provincial rule worsened as governors, tax collectors, and soldiers shamelessly exploited the provincials.

During Rome's march to empire, all its classes had demonstrated a magnificent civic spirit in fighting foreign wars. With Carthage and Macedonia no longer threats to Rome, this cooperation deteriorated. Internal dissension tore Rome apart as the ferocity and drive for domination formerly directed against foreign enemies turned inward against fellow Romans. Civil war replaced foreign war.

The Romans had prevailed over their opponents partly because of their traditional virtues—resoluteness, simplicity of manners, and willingness to sacrifice personal interests for the good of Rome. But the riches flowing into Rome from the plundered provinces caused these virtues to decay, and rivalry for status and wealth overrode civic patriotism. The masses, landless and afflicted with poverty and idleness, withdrew their allegiance from the state.

In this time of agony, both great and self-seeking individuals emerged. Some struggled to restore the social harmony and political unity that had prevailed in the period of expansion. Others, political adventurers, attacked the authority of the Senate to gain personal power. And the Senate, which had previously exercised leadership creatively and responsibly, degenerated into a self-serving oligarchy that resisted reform and fought to preserve its power and privilege.

Neither the Senate nor its opponents could rejuvenate the Republic. Eventually it collapsed, a victim of class tensions, poor leadership, power-hungry demagogues, and civil war. Underlying all these conditions was the breakdown of social harmony and the deterioration of civic patriotism. The Republic had conquered an empire only to see the spiritual qualities of its citizens decay.

The Crisis in Agriculture

The downhill slide of the Republic was triggered by an agricultural crisis. In the long war with Hannibal in Italy, each side had tried to deprive the other of food supplies; in the process, they ruined farmlands, destroyed farmhouses and farm equipment, and slaughtered animals. With many Roman sol-

Detail of Wall Painting, Villa at Boscoreale, First Century B.C. The painter's illusionism draws the viewer into the crowded architecture of the city. The Romans built single-family dwellings (the *domus*), as well as apartment dwellings several stories in height. (*The Metropolitan Museum of Art; Rogers Fund, 1903*)

dier-farmers serving long periods in the army, fields lay neglected. Returning veterans with small holdings lacked the money to restore their land; they were forced to sell their farms to wealthy landowners at low prices.

Another factor that helped to squeeze out the small farmowners was the importation of hundreds of thousands of slaves to work on large plantations called *latifundia*. Farmers who had formerly increased meager incomes by working for wages on neighboring large estates no longer were needed. Sinking ever deeper into poverty and debt, farmers gave up their lands and went to Rome seeking work. The dispossessed peasantry found little to do in Rome, where there was not enough industry to provide them with employment and where much of the work was done by slaves. The once-sturdy and independent Roman farmer, who had done all that his country had asked of him, was becoming part of a vast urban underclass—poor, embittered, and alienated. The uprooting of a formerly self-reliant peasantry was Hannibal's "posthumous revenge" on Rome; it would prove more deadly than Cannae.

The Gracchi Revolution

In 133 B.C., Tiberius Gracchus (163–133 B.C.), who came from one of Rome's most honored families, was elected tribune. Distressed by the injustice done to the peasantry and recognizing that the Roman army depended on the loyalty of small landowners, Tiberius made himself the spokesman for land reform. He proposed a simple and moderate solution for the problem of the landless peasants: he would re-enact an old law barring any Roman from using more than 312 acres of the state-owned land obtained in the process of uniting Italy. For many years the upper class had ignored this law, occupying vast tracts of public land as squatters and treating this land as their own. By enforcing the law, Tiberius hoped to free land for distribution to landless citizens.

Rome's leading families viewed Tiberius as a revolutionary who threatened their property and political authority. They thought him a democrat who would undermine the Senate, the seat of aristocratic power, in favor of the Assembly, which represented the commoners. For one thing, Tiberius had proposed that the Assembly settle the affairs of Pergamum, Rome's newest province and dispose of its treasury. Surely that would violate the Senate's right to control the purse and to administer provinces, the senators said. When Tiberius sought re-election as a tribune, a violation of constitutional tradition, the senators were convinced that he was a rabble-rouser who aimed to destroy the republican constitution and become a one-man ruler. To preserve the status quo, with wealth and power concentrated in the hands of a few hundred families, senatorial extremists killed Tiberius and some three hundred of his followers, dumping their bodies into the Tiber.

The cause of land reform was next taken up by Gaius Gracchus (153–121 B.C.), a younger brother of Tiberius. An emotional and gifted speaker, Gaius won the support of the city poor and was elected tribune in 123 B.C. A more astute politician than his brother, Gaius increased his following by favoring the Equites, the new class of plebeian businessmen, and by promising full citizenship to all Italians. He aided the poor by reintroducing his brother's plan for land distribution and by enabling them to buy grain from the state at less than half the market price. But like his brother, Gaius aroused the anger of the senatorial class. A brief civil war raged in Rome during which Gaius Gracchus (who may have committed suicide) and 3,000 of his followers perished.

By killing the Gracchi, the Senate had substituted violence for reason and made murder a means of coping with troublesome opposition. A governing class cannot behave like hoodlums with impunity. Soon the club and the dagger became common weapons in Roman politics, thereby hurling Rome into an era of political violence that ended with the destruction of the Republic. Though the Senate considered itself the guardian of republican liberty, in reality it was expressing the determination of a few hundred families to retain their control over the state. It is a classic example of a once-creative minority clinging tenaciously to power long after it had ceased to govern effectively, or to inspire allegiance. The Senate that had led Rome to empire had become a self-seeking, unimaginative, entrenched oligarchy that was leading the Republic and the Mediterranean world into disaster.

Rome in the first century B.C. was very different from the Rome that had defeated

Hannibal. Entranced by eastern luxuries and determined to retain oligarchic rule, the senatorial families neglected their responsibility to the state. Many upper-class Romans, burning to achieve the dignity that would mark them as great men, tried to climb onto the crowded stage of Roman politics, but the best roles were already reserved for members of the senatorial families. With so few opportunities, aspirants to political power stopped at nothing.

Roman politics in the century after the Gracchi was bedeviled by intrigues, rivalries, personal ambition, and political violence. Political adventurers exploited the issue of cheap grain and free land in order to benefit their careers. Whereas the Gracchi were sincere reformers, these later champions of social reform were unscrupulous demagogues, who cleverly charmed and manipulated the city poor with bread and circuses—low-cost food and free admission to games. These demagogues aspired to the tribunate of the plebes, an office possessing powers formidable enough to challenge the Senate and yet not too difficult to obtain, since ten tribunes were elected each year. By riding a wave of popular enthusiasm, these political adventurers hoped to sweep aside the Senate and concentrate power in their own hands. The poor, denied land and employment, demoralized, alienated and lulled into political ignorance by decades of idleness, food handouts, and free entertainment, were ready to back whoever made the most glittering promises. The Senate behaved like a decadent oligarchy, and the Tribal Assembly, which had become the voice of the urban mob, demonstrated a weakness for demagogues, an openness to bribery, and an abundance of deceit and incompetence. The Roman Republic had passed the peak of its greatness.

Rival Generals

Marius (157–86 B.C.), who became consul in 107 B.C., adopted a military policy that eventually contributed to the wrecking of the Republic. Short of troops for a campaign in Numidia in North Africa, Marius disposed of the traditional property requirement for entrance into the army and filled his legions with volunteers from the urban poor, a dangerous precedent. These new soldiers, disillusioned with Rome, served only because Marius held out the promise of pay, loot, and land grants after discharge. Their loyalty was given not to Rome but to Marius, and they remained loyal to their commander only as long as he fulfilled his promises.

Marius had set an example that other ambitious commanders followed. They saw that a general could use his army to advance his political career, that by retaining the confidence of his soldiers, he could cow the Senate and dictate Roman policy. The army, no longer an instrument of government, became a private possession of generals. Seeing its authority undermined by generals appointed by the Assembly, the Senate was forced to seek army commanders who would champion the cause of senatorial rule. In time, Rome would be engulfed in civil wars, as rival generals used their troops to further their own ambitions or political affiliations.

Meanwhile, the Senate continued to deal ineffectively with Rome's problems. When Rome's Italian allies pressed for citizenship, the Senate refused to make concessions. The Senate's shortsightedness plunged Italy into a terrible war, known as the Social War. As war ravaged the peninsula, the Romans reversed their policy and conferred citizenship on the Italians. The unnecessary and ruinous rebellion petered out.

While Rome was fighting its Italian allies, Mithridates, king of Pontus in northern Asia Minor, invaded the Roman province of Asia. In 88 B.C., he aroused the local population to massacre 80,000 Italian residents of the province. Mithridates and his forces crossed into Greece and occupied Athens and other cities. Faced with this crisis, the Senate entrusted command to Sulla (138–78 B.C.), who had distinguished himself in the Social War. But supporters of Marius, through intrigue and violence, had the order rescinded and the command given to Marius.

Sulla refused to accept his loss of command

and with his loyal troops proceeded to the capital. This was a fateful moment in Roman history: the first march on Rome, the first prolonged civil war, and the first time a commander and his troops defied the government. Sulla won the first round. But when Sulla left Rome to fight Mithridates in Greece, Marius and his troops retook the city and in a frenzy lashed out at Sulla's supporters. The killing lasted for five days and nights.

Marius died shortly afterwards. Then Sulla quickly subdued Marius' supporters on his return and became dictator of Rome. Sulla instituted a terror that far surpassed Marius' violence. Without legal sanction and with frightening and cold-blooded cruelty, Sulla marked his opponents for death; the state seized their property and declared their children and grandchildren ineligible for public office.

Sulla resolved to use his absolute power to revive and make permanent the overriding rule of the Senate. He believed that only rule by an aristocratic oligarchy could protect Rome from future military adventurers and assure domestic peace. He therefore restored the Senate's right to veto acts of the Assembly, limited the power of the tribunes and the Assembly, and reduced the military authority of provincial governors to prevent any march on Rome. To make the Senate less oligarchical, he increased its membership to six hundred. Having put through these reforms, Sulla retired.

Julius Caesar

But the Senate failed to wield its restored authority effectively. The Republic was still menaced by military commanders who used their troops for their own political advantage, and underlying problems remained unsolved. In 60 B.C., a triumvirate consisting of Julius Caesar (c. 100–44 B.C.), a politician, Pompey, a general, and Crassus, a wealthy banker, conspired to take over Rome. The ablest of the three was Caesar.

Recognizing the importance of a military command as a prerequisite for political prominence, Caesar gained command of the legions in Gaul in 59 B.C. The following year he began the conquest of that part of Gaul outside of Roman control. The successful Gallic campaigns and invasion of Britain revealed Caesar's exceptional talent for generalship. Indeed, his victories alarmed the Senate, which feared that Caesar would use his devoted troops and soaring reputation to seize control of the state.

Meanwhile the triumvirate had fallen apart. In 53 B.C., Crassus had perished with his army in a disastrous campaign against the Parthians in the East. The bonds between Pompey and Caesar were weak, consisting essentially of Pompey's marriage to Caesar's daughter Julia. After her death in 54 B.C., Pompey and Caesar grew apart. Pompey, who was jealous of Caesar's success and eager to expand his own power, drew closer to the Senate. Supported by Pompey, the Senate ordered Caesar to relinquish his command. Without his troops, Caesar realized that he would be defenseless; he decided instead to march on Rome. After Caesar crossed the Rubicon River into Italy in 49 B.C., civil war again ravaged the Republic. Pompey proved no match for so talented a general; the Senate acknowledged Caesar's victory and appointed him to be dictator for ten years.

Caesar realized that republican institutions no longer operated effectively and that only strong and enlightened leadership could permanently end the civil warfare destroying Rome. His reforms were designed to create order out of chaos. Caesar fought the corruption that had so angered provincial subjects by lowering taxes, making the governors responsible to him, preventing capitalists from exploiting the regions, and generously extending citizenship to more provincials. To aid the poor in Rome, he began a public works program that provided employment and beautified the city. He also relocated over 100,000 veterans and members of Rome's lower class to the provinces, where he gave them land. To improve administration, he reorganized town governments in Italy and reformed the courts.

In February of 44 B.C., Rome's ruling class—

jealous of Caesar's success and power and afraid of his ambition—became thoroughly alarmed when his temporary dictatorship was converted into a lifelong office. The aristocracy saw this event as the end of senatorial government and their rule, which they equated with liberty, and as the beginnings of a Hellenistic type of monarchy. A group of aristocrats, regarding themselves as defenders of republican traditions more than four and a half centuries old, assassinated Caesar on March 15 in the year 44 B.C. Cicero expressed the general feeling of the conspirators:

Our tyrant deserves his death, [for his] was the blackest crime of all. [Caesar was] a man who was ambitious to be king of the Roman people and master of the whole world. . . . The man who maintains that such an ambition is morally right is a madman, for he justifies the destruction of law and liberty.[7]

There was also a strong element of jealousy in the conspirators' motivation.

The Republic's Last Years

The assassination of Julius Caesar did not restore republican liberty, but plunged Rome into renewed civil war. Two of Caesar's trusted lieutenants, Mark Antony and Lepidus, joined with Octavian, Caesar's adopted son, and defeated the armies of Brutus and Cassius, two instigators of Caesar's death. After Lepidus was forced into political obscurity, Antony and Octavian fought each other with the empire as the prize. In 31 B.C., at the naval battle of Actium in western Greece, Octavian crushed the forces of Antony and his wife, Egypt's Queen Cleopatra. Octavian emerged as master of Rome and four years later became, in effect, the first Roman emperor. The Roman Republic, whose death throes had lasted for decades and kept the Mediterranean world in turmoil, had finally perished.

The Roman Republic, which had amassed power to a degree hitherto unknown in the ancient world, was not wrecked by foreign

Bust of Caesar. Julius Caesar tried to rescue a dying Roman world by imposing strong rule. He paved the way for the transition from Republic to imperial rule. (*Ewing Galloway*)

invasion, but by internal weaknesses: the personal ambitions of power seekers, the degeneration of senatorial leadership, and the willingness of politicians to use violence; the formation of private armies in which soldiers gave their loyalty to their commander rather than to Rome; the transformation of a self-reliant peasantry into an impoverished and demoralized city rabble; and the deterioration of those ancient virtues that had been the source of the state's vitality. Before 146 B.C., the threat posed by foreign enemies, particularly Carthage, forced Romans to work together for the benefit of the state, and the

Chronology 6.1 The Roman Republic

509 B.C.	Expulsion of the Etruscan monarch
449	Law of Twelve Tables
287	The end of the struggle of the orders
264–241	First Punic War; Rome acquires provinces
218–201	Second Punic War; Hannibal is defeated
149–146	Third Punic War; destruction of Carthage
133–122	Land reforms by the Gracchi brothers; they are murdered by the Senate
88–83	Conflict between Sulla and the forces of Marius; Sulla emerges as dictator
79	Sulla retires
73–71	Slave revolt is led by Spartacus
58–51	Caesar campaigns in Gaul
49–44	Caesar is dictator of Rome
31 B.C.	Antony and Cleopatra are defeated at Actium by Octavian

equilibrium achieved during the patrician-plebeian struggle was maintained. This social cohesion broke down when foreign danger had been reduced, and in the ensuing century of turmoil, the apparatus of city-state government failed to function effectively.

Thus, the high point of Roman rule was not achieved under the Republic. The city-state constitution of the Republic was too limited to govern an immense empire. Rome first had to surpass the narrow framework of city-state government before it could unite the Mediterranean world in peace and law. The genius of Augustus (Octavian), the first emperor, made this development possible.

Notes

1. Cicero, *De Re Publica*, trans. by C. W. Keyes (Cambridge, Mass.: Harvard University Press, Loeb Classical Library, 1928), 3. 22 (p. 211).

2. Quoted in J. Wright Duff, *A Literary History of Rome* (New York: Barnes & Noble, 1960), pp. 136–137.

3. Terence, *The Brothers*, trans. by H. T. Riley (London: Henry G. Bohn, 1853), pp. 202–203.

4. Catullus, quoted in E. A. Havelock, *The Lyric Genius of Catullus* (New York: Russell & Russell, 1929), p. 63.

5. Sallust, *The Conspiracy of Catiline*, trans. by S. A. Handford (Baltimore: Penguin Books, 1963), pp. 181–182.

6. Cicero, *De Legibus*, trans. by C. W. Keyes (Cambridge, Mass.: Harvard University Press, Loeb Classical Library, 1928), 1. 10 (pp. 329–330).

7. Cicero, *De Officiis*, trans. by Walter Miller (Cambridge, Mass.: Harvard University Press, Loeb Classical Library, 1913), 3. 21 (p. 357).

Suggested Reading

Badian, E., *Roman Imperialism in the Late Roman Republic* (1968). An interpretive essay on the interaction between Roman domestic politics and foreign policy.

Boren, H. C., *Roman Society* (1977). A social, economic, and cultural history of the Republic and the Empire; written with the student in mind.

Brunt, P. A., *Social Conflicts in the Roman Republic* (1971). Concerned with the discontents of the rural and urban poor and internal struggles within the propertied classes.

Crawford, M., *The Roman Republic* (1982). A recent and reliable survey, with many quotations from original sources.

Errington, R. M., *The Dawn of Empire: Rome's Rise to World Power* (1972). A study of Rome the reluctant imperialist.

Gelzer, Matthias, *Caesar: Politician and Statesman* (1968). A revised edition of a classic work first published in 1921.

Grant, Michael, *A History of Rome* (1978). A recent synthesis of Roman history by a leading classical scholar; valuable for both the Republic and the Empire.

Gruen, E., *The Last Generation of the Roman Republic* (1974). An account of the Roman Republic from Sulla to Caesar; stresses social history.

Homo, Leon, *Roman Political Institutions* (1962). Reprint of the 1929 classic study of the Roman constitution down to the fall of the Empire in the West.

Lewis, N., and M. Reinhold, eds., *Roman Civilization* (1966). A two-volume collection of source readings. Volume I covers the Republic.

Lintott, A. W., *Violence in Republican Rome* (1968). Deals with the corruption of politics through violence.

Mazzolani, L. S., *The Idea of the City in Roman Thought* (1970). How Roman philosophers, poets, and statesmen view the polis and the cosmopolis.

Scullard, H. H., *From the Gracchi to Nero* (1963). A reliable history of the death of the Roman Republic and the rise of the Roman Empire.

Starr, C. G., *The Emergence of Rome* (1953). A short, clearly written introduction to the emergence of Roman power in Italy and the Mediterranean.

Review Questions

1. What were the complaints of the Roman plebeians at the beginning of the fifth century B.C.? What was the outcome of the patrician-plebeian conflict?

2. The Romans forged a constitutional system based on civic needs, not on religious mystery. Discuss this statement.

3. What factors enabled Rome to conquer Italy?

4. Without planning it, Rome acquired an overseas empire. Explain.

5. What did the first two Punic Wars reveal about the character of the Roman people?

6. What were the consequences of Roman expansion?

7. How was Roman cultural life influenced by Greek civilization?

8. What were the causes of the agricultural crisis faced by Rome in the second century B.C.?

9. How did the Gracchi brothers try to deal with the agricultural crisis? Why were they opposed by Rome's leading families?

10. What was the significance of the struggle between Marius and Sulla?

11. How did Caesar try to cope with the problems afflicting Rome? Why was he assassinated?

12. Analyze the reasons for the collapse of the Roman Republic.

13. Discuss what the parallels are between the collapse of the Roman Republic and the downfall of Athens.

14. The institutions of the Roman Republic were not suited to governing a world empire. Discuss this statement.

7

The Roman Empire:
A World-State

Rome's republican institutions, designed for a city-state, proved incapable of coping with the problems created by the conquest of a world empire. Invincible against foreign enemies, the Republic collapsed from within. But after Octavian's brilliant statesmanship brought order out of chaos, Rome entered its golden age under the rule of emperors. For almost two hundred years, from 27 B.C. to A.D. 180, the Mediterranean world enjoyed unparalleled peace and stability. The Roman world-state—erected on a Hellenic cultural foundation and cemented with empirewide civil service, laws, and citizenship—gave practical expression to Stoic cosmopolitanism and universalism. But even this impressive monument had structural defects, and in the third century A.D., the Empire was wracked by crises from which it never fully recovered. In the fifth century, German tribesmen overran the western half of the Empire, which had by then become a shadow of its former self.

During its time of trouble, Rome also experienced an intellectual crisis; forsaking the rational and secular values of classical humanism, many Romans sought spiritual comfort in oriental religions. One of these religions, Christianity, won out over its competitors, and was made the official religion of the Empire. With the triumph of Christianity in the Late Roman Empire, Western civilization took a new direction. Christianity would become the principal shaper of the European civilization that emerged from the ruins of Rome.

Augustus and the Foundations of the Roman Empire

After Octavian's forces defeated those of Antony and Cleopatra at the battle of Actium in 31 B.C., no opponents could stand up to him. The century of civil war, political murder, corruption, and mismanagement had exhausted the Mediterranean world, which longed for order. Like Caesar before him, Octavian recognized that only a strong monarchy could rescue Rome from civil war and anarchy. But learning from Caesar's assassination, he also knew that republican ideals were far from dead. To exercise autocratic power openly like a Hellenistic monarch would have aroused the hostility of the Roman ruling class, whose assistance and good will Octavian desired.

Octavian demonstrated his political genius by reconciling his military monarchy with republican institutions—he held absolute power without abruptly breaking with a republican past. Magistrates were still elected and assemblies still met; the Senate administered certain provinces, retained its treasury, and was invited to advise Octavian. With some truth, Octavian could claim that he ruled in partnership with the Senate. By maintaining the façade of the Republic, Octavian camouflaged his absolute power and contained senatorial opposition, which had already been weakened by the deaths of leading nobles in battle or in the purges that Octavian had instituted against his enemies. Moreover, Octavian's control over the armed forces made resistance futile, and the terrible violence that had followed Caesar's assassination made senators amenable to change.

In 27 B.C., Octavian shrewdly offered to surrender his power, knowing that the Senate, purged of opposition, would demand that he continue to lead the state. By this act, Octavian could claim to be a legitimate constitutional ruler leading a government of law, not one of a lawless despotism so hateful to the Roman mentality. In keeping with his policy of maintaining the appearance of traditional republican government, Octavian refused to be called king or even, like Caesar, dictator; instead, he cleverly disguised his autocratic rule by taking the inoffensive title *Princeps* (First Citizen). The Senate also conferred upon him the semireligious and revered name of *Augustus*.

Augustus' reign signified the end of the Roman Republic and the beginning of the Roman Empire, the termination of aristocratic politics and the emergence of one-man rule. As the historian Tacitus recognized, Augustus had accomplished a profound revolution in Roman political life: "The country had been transformed, and there was nothing left of the fine old Roman character. Political equality was a thing of the past; all eyes watched for imperial commands."[1] Under Augustus the power of the ruler was disguised; in ensuing generations, however, emperors would wield absolute power openly. As Rome became more autocratic and centralized, it took on the appearance of an oriental monarchy.

Augustus introduced the practice of emperor worship. In the eastern provinces, where oriental and Hellenistic monarchs had been regarded as divine, the person of Augustus was worshiped as a god. In Italy, where the deification of leaders was alien to the republican spirit, divine honors were granted to Augustus's genius or spirit of leadership; once deceased, Augustus and his successors were deified. By the third century, Italians and other peoples in the western territories viewed the living emperor as a god-king.

Despite his introduction of autocratic rule, Augustus was by no means a self-seeking tyrant, but a creative statesman. Heir to the Roman tradition of civic duty, he regarded his power as a public trust delegated to him by the Roman people. He was faithful to the classical ideal that the state should promote the good life by protecting civilization from barbarism and ignorance, and he sought to rescue a dying Roman world.

To prevent a renewal of civil war and to safeguard the borders of the Empire, Augustus reformed the army. As commander-in-chief, he could guard against the reemergence of ambitious generals like those whose rivalries and private armies had wrecked the Republic. Augustus maintained the loyalty of his soldiers by assuring that veterans, on discharge, would receive substantial bonuses and land in Italy or in the provinces. By organizing a professional

Imperial Family in Procession. This relief is no procession of timeless gods as in the Greek Parthenon. Children tug at their parents' togas, and the imperial family fulfills its civic duties as visible embodiments of the state. The relief is from the altar of peace, which honors Augustus. (*Alinari/Art Resource*)

standing army made up principally of volunteers who generally served for twenty-five years, Augustus was assured of a well-trained and loyal force capable of maintaining internal order, extending Roman territory, and securing the frontier.

For the city of Rome, Augustus had aqueducts and water mains built that brought water to most Roman homes. He created a fire brigade that reduced the danger of great conflagrations in crowded tenement districts, and he organized a police force to contain violence. He improved the distribution of free grain to the impoverished proletariat, and financed out of his own funds the popular gladiatorial combats.

In Italy, Augustus had roads repaired, and fostered public works. He arranged for Italians to play a more important role in the administration of the Empire. For the Italians' security, his army suppressed the brigandage that had proliferated in the countryside during the preceding century of agony, and guarded the northern borders from barbarian incursions.

By ending the civil wars and their accompanying devastation and by ruling out forced requisition of supplies and extortion of money, Augustus earned the gratitude of the provincials. Also contributing to his empirewide popularity were his efforts to correct tax abuse and to end corruption through improving the quality of governors and enabling aggrieved provincials to bring charges against

Roman officials. Augustus also continued the sensible practice of not interfering with the traditional customs and religions of the provinces. During his forty-year reign, Rome overcame the chaos of the years of revolution. The praise bestowed on him by grateful provincials was not undeserved. One decree from the province of Asia called Augustus

the savior of all mankind in common whose prov-
ident care has not only fulfilled but even surpassed
the hopes of all: for both land and sea are at peace,
the cities are teeming with the blessings of concord,
plenty, and respect for law, and the culmination
and harvest of all good things bring fair hopes for
the future and contentment with the present.[2]

The Pax Romana

The brilliant statesmanship of Augustus inaugurated Rome's greatest age. For the next two hundred years the Mediterranean world enjoyed the blessings of the *pax Romana*, the Roman Peace. The ancient world had never experienced such a long period of peace, order, efficient administration, and prosperity. Although both proficient and inept rulers succeeded Augustus, the essential features of the pax Romana persisted.

The Successors of Augustus

The first four emperors who succeeded Augustus were related either to him or to his third wife, Livia. They constituted the Julio-Claudian dynasty, which ruled from A.D. 14 to A.D. 68. Although their reigns were marked by conspiracies, summary executions, and assassinations, the great achievements of Augustus were preserved and strengthened. The Senate did not seek to restore republicanism, and continued to assist the Princeps; the imperial bureaucracy grew larger and more professional; the army, with some exceptions, remained a loyal and disciplined force.

The Julio-Claudian dynasty came to an end in A.D. 68 when Emperor Nero committed suicide. Nero had grown increasingly tyrannical and had lost the confidence of the people, the senatorial class, and the generals, who rose in revolt. In the year following his death, anarchy reigned as military leaders competed for the throne. After a bloody civil war, the execution of two emperors, and the suicide of another, Vespasian gained the Principate. Vespasian's reign (A.D. 69–79) marked the beginning of the Flavian dynasty. By rotating commanding officers and stationing native troops far from their homelands, Vespasian improved discipline and discouraged mutiny. By having the great Colosseum of Rome constructed for gladiatorial contests, he earned the gratitude of the city's inhabitants. Vespasian also had nationalist uprisings put down in Gaul and Judea.

In Judea, Roman rule clashed with Jewish religious-national sentiments. Recognizing the tenaciousness with which Jews clung to their faith, the Roman leaders deliberately refrained from interfering with Hebraic religious beliefs and practices. Numerous privileges, such as exemption from emperor worship because it conflicted with the requirements of strict monotheism, were extended to Jews not only in Judea but throughout the Empire. But sometimes the Romans engaged in activities that outraged the Jews. For example, Pontius Pilate, the Roman procurator in Judea from A.D. 26 to 36, at one point ordered a Roman army unit into Jerusalem with banners bearing the image of the emperor. The entire Jewish nation was aroused. To the Jews, this display of a pagan idol in their holy city was an abomination. Realizing that the Jews would die rather than permit this act of sacrilege, Pilate ordered the banners removed. Another explosive situation emerged when the Emperor Caligula (A.D. 37–41) ordered that a

Map 7.1 The Roman Empire under Augustus and Hadrian ▶

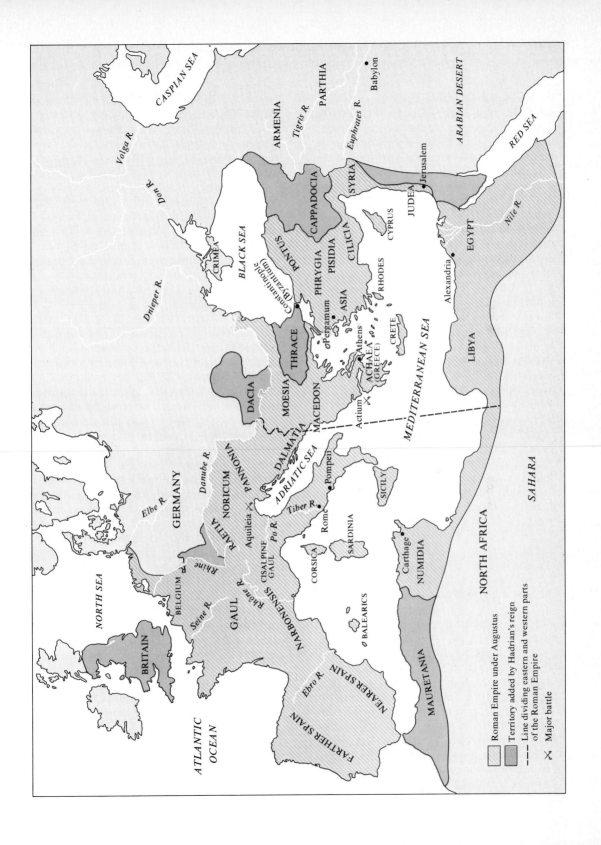

CASPIAN SEA

Volga R.

Don R.

Dnieper R.

CRIMEA

BLACK SEA

Constantinople (Byzantium)

PONTUS

ARMENIA

Tigris R.

PARTHIA

Euphrates R.

CAPPADOCIA

PHRYGIA

PISIDIA

ASIA

Pergamum

CILICIA

SYRIA

Jerusalem

JUDEA

CYPRUS

RHODES

CRETE

Babylon

ARABIAN DESERT

RED SEA

EGYPT

Alexandria

Nile R.

LIBYA

MEDITERRANEAN SEA

Athens

ACHAEA (GREECE)

Actium

MACEDON

THRACE

DACIA

MOESIA

DALMATIA

ADRIATIC SEA

PANNONIA

NORICUM

RAETIA

Danube R.

GERMANY

Elbe R.

NORTH SEA

Aquileia

CISALPINE GAUL

Po R.

Pompeii

Tiber R.

Rome

SARDINIA

CORSICA

SICILY

Carthage

NUMIDIA

BALEARICS

MAURETANIA

NORTH AFRICA

SAHARA

Rhine R.

BELGIUM

GAUL

Seine R.

Rhône R.

NARBONENSIS

Ebro R.

NEARER SPAIN

FARTHER SPAIN

ATLANTIC OCEAN

BRITAIN

Roman Empire under Augustus

Territory added by Hadrian's reign

Line dividing eastern and western parts of the Roman Empire

Major battle

golden statue of himself be placed in Jerusalem's temple. Again the order was rescinded when the Jews demonstrated their readiness to resist. Relations between the Jews of Judea and the Roman authorities deteriorated progressively in succeeding decades. Militant Jews who rejected Roman rule as a threat to the purity of Jewish life urged their people to take up arms. Feeling a religious obligation to re-establish an independent kingdom in their ancient homeland and unable to reconcile themselves to Roman rule, the Jews launched a full-scale war of liberation in A.D. 66. In A.D. 70, after a five-month siege had inflicted terrible punishment on the Jews, Roman armies captured Jerusalem and destroyed the temple. After the conquest of Jerusalem, some fortresses, including the Masada on the western side of the Dead Sea, continued to resist. The defenders of the Masada withstood a Roman siege until A.D. 73; refusing to become Roman captives, they took their own lives.

Vespasian was succeeded by his sons Titus (A.D. 79–81) and Domitian (A.D. 81–96). The reign of Titus was made memorable by the eruption of Vesuvius, which devastated the towns of Pompeii and Herculaneum. After Titus' brief time as Emperor, his younger brother Domitian became ruler. After crushing a revolt led by the Roman commander in Upper Germany, a frightened Domitian executed many leading Romans. These actions led to his assassination in A.D. 96, ending the Flavian dynasty. The Flavians, however, had succeeded in preserving internal peace and in consolidating and extending the borders of the Empire.

The Senate selected one of its own, Nerva, to succeed the murdered Domitian. Nerva's reign (A.D. 96–98) was brief and uneventful. But he introducd a practice that would endure until A.D. 180: he adopted as his son and designated as his heir a man with proven ability, Trajan, the governor of Upper Germany. This adoptive system assured a succession of competent rulers.

Trajan (ruled A.D. 98–117) eased the burden of taxation in the provinces, provided for the needs of poor children, and had public works built. With his enlarged army he conquered Dacia (parts of Rumania and Hungary), where he seized vast quantities of gold and silver, and made the territory into a Roman province, adding to the large frontier Rome had to protect. Trajan also made war against Parthia (a kingdom southeast of the Caspian Sea that had once been part of the Hellenistic kingdom of Seleucia), capturing Armenia and advancing to the Persian Gulf. Overextended lines of communication, revolts by Jews in several eastern provinces, and counterattacks by the Parthians, however, forced his armies to return to Rome.

Trajan's successor, Hadrian (A.D. 117–138) abandoned what remained of Trajan's eastern conquests. He strengthened border defenses in Britain, and fought the second Hebrew revolt in Judea (A.D. 132–135). After initial successes, including the capture of Jerusalem, the Jews were again defeated by superior Roman might. The majority of Palestinian Jews were killed, sold as slaves, or forced to seek refuge in other lands. The Romans renamed the province Syria Palestina; they forbade Jews to enter Jerusalem, except once a year, and encouraged non-Jews to settle the land. Although the Jews continued to maintain a presence in Palestine, they had become a dispossessed and dispersed people.

After Hadrian came another ruler who had a long reign, Antoninus Pius (A.D. 138–161). He introduced humane and just reforms, in particular, limits on the right of masters to torture their slaves to obtain evidence, and the establishment of the principle that an accused person be considered innocent until proven guilty. During Antoninus' reign the Empire remained peaceful and prosperous.

Marcus Aurelius (A.D. 161–180), the next emperor, was also a philosopher whose *Meditations* was an eloquent expression of Stoic thought. His reign was marked by strife. Roman forces had to fight Parthians, who had seized Armenia, a traditional bone of contention between Rome and Parthia. The Roman legions were victorious in this campaign but brought back from the East an epidemic that decimated the population of the Empire. Marcus Aurelius also had to deal with German incursions into Italy and the Balkan peninsula that were far more serious than any faced by previous emperors. Roman legions gradually repulsed the Germans, but the wars forced Marcus Aurelius to resort to a desperate financial measure—devaluation of the coinage.

From the accession of Nerva in A.D. 96 to the death of Marcus Aurelius in A.D. 180 the Roman Empire was ruled by the "Five Good Emperors." During this period the Empire was at the height of its power and prosperity, and nearly all its peoples benefited. The four emperors preceding Marcus Aurelius had no living sons, so they had resorted to the adoptive system in selecting successors, which served Rome effectively. But Marcus Aurelius chose his own son Commodus to succeed him. With the accession of Commodus, a misfit and a megalomaniac, in A.D. 180, the pax Romana came to an end.

The Time of Happiness

The Romans called the pax Romana the "Time of Happiness." This period was the fulfillment of Rome's mission—the creation of a world-state that provided peace, security, ordered civilization, and the rule of law. Roman legions defended the Rhine-Danube river frontiers from incursions by German tribesmen, held the Parthians at bay in the East, and subdued the few uprisings that occurred. Nerva's adoptive system of selecting emperors provided Rome with internal stability and a succession of emperors with exceptional ability. These Roman emperors did not use military force needlessly, but fought for sensible political goals; generals did not wage war recklessly, but tried to limit casualties, avoid risks, and deter conflicts by a show of force.

Constructive Rule   Roman rule was constructive. The Romans built roads, improved harbors, cleared forests, drained swamps, irrigated deserts, and cultivated undeveloped lands. Goods were transported over roads made safe by Roman soldiers and across a Mediterranean Sea swept clear of pirates. A wide variety of goods circulated throughout the Empire: gold, silver, copper, tin, fruit, and salt from Spain; wool, cheese, ham, and glass products from Gaul; iron, hides, and tin from Britain; wine, honey, and marble from Greece and Macedonia; textiles, olive oil, carpets, and jewels from Asia Minor; leather goods, perfume, drugs, and timber from Syria, Judea, and Arabia, and grain from Egypt. From Parthia, China, and India—lands beyond the eastern borders of the Empire—came silk, spices, pearls, cotton, jewels, perfumes, and drugs; from African lands south of the Sahara came gold, ivory, and wild animals. A stable currency, generally not subject to depreciation, contributed to the economic well-being of the Mediterranean world.

Scores of new cities sprang up, and old ones grew larger and wealthier. Although these municipalities had lost their power to wage war and had to bow to the will of the emperors, they retained considerable freedom of action in local matters. Imperial troops guarded against civil wars within the cities and prevented warfare between cities—two traditional weaknesses of city life in the ancient world. The municipalities served as centers of Greco-Roman civilization, which spread to the farthest reaches of the Mediterranean, continuing a process initiated during the Hellenistic Age. Regions of North Africa, Gaul, Britain, and South Germany, hitherto untouched by Hellenism, were brought into the orbit of Greco-Roman civilization. Barriers between Italians and provincials broke down, as Spaniards, Gauls, Africans, and other provincials rose to high positions in the army and in the imperial administration, and even became emperors. Citizenship, generously granted, was finally extended to virtually all free men by an edict of A.D. 212.

Improved Conditions for Both Slaves and Women   Conditions improved for those at

The Colosseum. The amphitheatrum Flavianum, which we call the Colosseum, was built during the reign of Vespasian (A.D. 69–79). It could seat some 50,000 spectators who came to watch the gladiator contests and the beast-hunts. (*Anderson/Art Resource*)

the bottom of society, the slaves. At the time of Augustus, slaves may have accounted for a quarter of the population of Italy. But their numbers declined as Rome engaged in fewer wars of conquest. The freeing of slaves also became more common during the Empire. Freed slaves became citizens, with most of the rights and privileges of other citizens; their children suffered no legal disabilities whatsoever.

During the Republic, slaves had been terribly abused; they were often mutilated, thrown to wild beasts, crucified, or burned alive. Several emperors issued decrees protecting slaves from cruel masters. Claudius forbade masters to kill sick slaves; Vespasian forbade masters to sell slaves into prostitution. Domitian prohibited the castration of slaves, and Hadrian barred the execution of slaves without a judicial sentence. The Stoic philosopher Seneca (c. 4 B.C.–A.D. 65) told Romans that slaves were not beasts of burden, but fellow humans: "Kindly remember that he whom you call your slave sprang from the same stock, is smiled upon by the same skies, and like yourself breathes, lives, and dies."[3]

The status of women had been gradually improving during the Republic. In the early days of the Republic, a woman had lived under the absolute authority of her husband. By the time of the Empire, a woman could own property and, if divorced, keep her dowry. A father no longer forced his daughter to marry against her will. Women could make business arrangements and draw up wills without the consent of their husbands. Roman women, unlike their Greek counterparts, were not secluded in their homes, but could come and go as they pleased. Upper-class women of Rome had far greater opportunities for education than did those of Greece.

The history of the Empire, indeed Roman history in general, was filled with talented and influential women. The historian Sallust said that Sempronia, the wife of a consul and the mother of Brutus, one of the assassins of Julius Caesar, was "well-educated in Greek and Latin literature. . . . She could write poetry, crack a joke, and converse at will . . . she was in fact a woman of ready wit and considerable charm."[4] Some wives and mothers became deeply involved in political life. Livia, the dynamic wife of Augustus, was often consulted on important government matters, and during the third century there were times when women controlled the throne.

Law and Order   From Britain to the Arabian Desert, from the Danube River to the sands of the Sahara, some seventy million people with differing native languages, customs, and histories were united by Roman rule into a world community. Unlike those of the Republic, when corruption and exploitation in the provinces were notorious, officials of the Empire felt a high sense of responsibility to preserve the Roman peace, institute Roman justice, and spread Roman civilization.

The achievement of the pax Romana found expression in law. Evolving gradually since the republican conquests, the law of nations (*jus gentium*) came to be applied throughout the Empire, although it never entirely supplanted local law. In the eyes of the law, a citizen was not a Syrian, or a Briton, or a Spaniard, but a Roman. Based on principles thought to be rational, just, and common to all humanity, jus gentium gave recognition to the Stoic conception of natural law.

In creating a stable and orderly political community with an expansive conception of citizenship, Rome resolved the problems posed by the limitations of the city-state—civil war, intercity warfare, and a parochial attitude that divided men into Greek and non-Greek. Rome also brought to fruition an ideal of the Greek city-state—the rational state that protected and promoted civilized life. By constructing a world community that broke down barriers between nations, by preserving and spreading Greco-Roman civilization, and by developing a rational system of law that applied to all humanity, Rome completed the trend toward universalism and cosmopolitanism that had emerged in the Hellenistic Age. The Roman world-state was the classical mind's response to the problem of community posed by the decline of the city-state in the era of Alexander the Great. Aelius Aristides, a second-century rhetorician, glowingly extolled the Roman achievement:

Neither sea nor any intervening distance on land excludes one from citizenship. No distinction is made between Asia and Europe in this respect. Everything lies open to everybody; and no one fit for office or a position of trust is an alien. . . . You have made the word "Roman" apply not to a city but to a universal people. . . . You no longer classify peoples as Greek or barbarian. . . . You have redivided mankind into Romans and non-Romans. . . . Under this classification there are many in each city who are no less fellow citizens of yours than those of their own stock, though some of them have never seen this city.[5]

Roman Culture During the Pax Romana

During the late Roman Republic, Rome had creatively assimilated the Greek achievement (see pages 87–88) and transmitted it to others, thereby extending the orbit of Hellenism. Rome had acquired Greek scientific thought, philosophy, medicine, and geography. Roman writers used Greek models; sharing in the humanist outlook of the Greeks, they valued human intelligence and achievement and expressed themselves in a graceful and eloquent style. Roman cultural life reached its high point during the reign of Augustus, when Rome experienced the golden age of Latin literature.

At the request of Augustus, who wanted a literary epic to glorify the Empire and his role in founding it, Virgil wrote the *Aeneid,* a masterpiece in world literature. The *Aeneid* is a long poem that recounts the tale of Aeneas and the founding of Rome. The first six books describing the wanderings of Aeneas show the influence of Homer's *Odyssey;* the last six books relating the wars in Italy show the *Iliad's* imprint. Intensely patriotic, Virgil ascribed to Rome a divine mission to bring peace and civilized life to the world, and he praised Augustus as a divinely appointed ruler who had fulfilled Rome's mission. The Greeks might be better sculptors, orators, and thinkers, said Virgil, but only the Romans knew how to govern an empire.

For other peoples will, I do not doubt,
still cast their bronze to breathe with softer
*   features,*
or draw out of the marble living lines,
plead causes better, trace the ways of heaven
with wands and tell the rising constellations;
but yours will be the rulership of nations,
remember, Roman, these will be your arts:
to teach the ways of peace to those you
*   conquer,*
to spare defeated peoples, to tame the proud.[6]

In his *History of Rome,* the historian Livy (59 B.C.–A.D. 17) also glorified the Roman character, customs, and deeds. He praised Augustus for attempting to revive traditional Roman morality, to which Livy felt a strong attachment. Modern historians criticize Livy for failing to utilize important sources of information in this work, for relying on biased authorities, and for allowing a fierce patriotism to warp his judgment. Although Livy was a lesser historian than Thucydides or Polybius, his work was still a major achievement, particularly in its depiction of the Roman character that helped make Rome great.

Horace (65–8 B.C.) was the son of a freed slave. An outstanding poet, he broadened his education by studying literature and philosophy in Athens, and Greek ideals are reflected in his writings. Horace enjoyed the luxury of country estates, banquets, fine clothes, and courtesans along with the simple pleasures of mountain streams and clear skies. His poetry touched on many themes—the joy of good wine, the value of moderation, and the beauty of friendship. Desiring to blend reason and emotion, Horace urged men to seek pleasurable experiences, but to avoid extremes and to keep desire under rational control.

Unlike Virgil, Livy, or Horace, Ovid (43 B.C.–A.D. 17) did not experience the civil wars during his adult years. Consequently he was less inspired to praise the Augustan peace. His poetry showed a preference for romance and humor, and he is best remembered for his advice to lovers. To the man who wants to win a woman, Ovid advised:

First of all, be quite sure that there isn't a woman who cannot be won, and make up your mind that you will win her. Only you must prepare the ground.

You must play the lover for all you're worth. Tell her how you are pining for her.

Never cease to sing the praises of her face, her hair, her taper fingers, and her dainty foot.

Tears too are a mighty useful resource in the matter of love. They would melt a diamond. Make a point, therefore, of letting your mistress see your face all wet with tears.

Women are things of many moods. You must adapt your treatment to the special case.[7]

The writers who lived after the Augustan age were of a lesser quality than the preceding men, although the historian Tacitus (A.D. 55–c. 118) was an exception. Sympathetic to republican institutions, Tacitus denounced Roman emperors and the imperial system in his *Histories* and *Annals.* In *Germania,* he turned his sights on the habits of the Germanic peoples. He describes the Germans as undisciplined but heroic and brave, with a strong love of freedom.

The satirist Juvenal (A.D. c. 55–138) attacked evils of Roman society, such as the misconduct of emperors, the haughtiness of the wealthy, the barbaric tastes of commoners, the failures of parents, and the noise, congestion, and poverty of the capital.

. . .

a piece of pot
Falls down on my head, how often a
  broken vessel is shot
From the upper windows, with what
  force it strikes and dints
The cobblestones! . . .

. . .

But these aren't your only terrors.
  For you can never restrain
The criminal element. Lock up your
  house, put bolt and chain
On your shop, but when all's quiet,
  someone will rob you or he'll
Be a cutthroat perhaps and do you
  in quickly with cold steel.[8]

The two most prominent scientists during the Greco-Roman age were Ptolemy, the mathematician, geographer, and astronomer who worked at Alexandria in the second century A.D., and Galen (A.D. c. 130–c. 201), who investigated medicine and anatomy. Ptolemy's thirteen-volume work, *Mathematical Composition*—more commonly known as the *Almagest*, a Greek-Arabic term meaning the *greatest*—summed up antiquity's knowledge of astronomy and became the authoritative text during the Middle Ages. In the Ptolemaic system, a motionless, round earth stood in the center of the universe; the moon, sun, and planets moved about the earth in circles, or in combinations of circles. The Ptolemaic system was built on a faulty premise, as modern astronomy eventually showed; however, it did work, that is, it did provide a model of the universe that adequately accounted for most observed phenomena.

As Ptolemy's system dominated astronomy,

so the theories of Galen dominated medicine down to modern times. By dissecting both dead and living animals, Galen attempted a rational investigation of the body's working parts. Although his work contains many errors, he made essential contributions to a knowledge of anatomy.

Romans borrowed art forms from other peoples, particularly the Greeks, but they borrowed creatively, transforming and enhancing their inheritance. Roman portraiture continued trends initiated during the Hellenistic Age. Hellenistic art, like Hellenistic philosophy, expressed a heightened awareness of the individual. Whereas Hellenic sculpture aimed to depict ideal beauty—the perfect body and face—Hellenistic sculpture captured individual character and expression, often of ordinary people. This movement from idealism to realism was carried forward by Roman sculptors who realistically carved every detail of a subject's face—unruly hair, prominent nose, lines and wrinkles, a jaw that showed weakness or strength. Sculpture also gave expression to the imperial ideal. Statues of emperors conveyed nobility and authority; reliefs commemorating victories glorified Roman might and grandeur.

In architecture, the Romans most creatively transformed the Greek inheritance. The Greek temple was intended to be viewed from the outside; the focus was exclusively on the superbly balanced exterior. By using arches, vaults, and domes, the Romans built structures with large, magnificent interiors. The vast interior, massive walls, and overarching dome of the famous Pantheon, a temple built in the early second century during the reign of Hadrian, symbolizes the power and majesty of the Roman world-state.

Despite its many achievements, Roman culture presents a paradox. On the one hand, Roman law and literature evidence high standards of civilization; on the other hand, the Romans institutionalized barbaric practices. The major forms of entertainment both in the Republic and the Empire were chariot races, wild-animal shows, and gladiatorial combat. Chariot races were gala events in

Hadrian's Wall. Between A.D. 122 and 127, the Romans constructed an elaborate defensive system in Britain consisting of a wall of solid masonry and a series of forts. Built on high ground, Hadrian's Wall extended from the estuary of the Solway to that of the Tyne, a distance of 73 miles. (*Photograph by The British Tourist Authority*)

which the most skillful riders and the finest and best-trained stallions raced in an atmosphere of incredible excitement. The charioteers, many of them slaves hoping that victory would bring them freedom, became popular heroes. The rich staked fortunes on the races, and the poor bet their last coins.

The Romans craved brutal spectacles. One form of entertainment pitted wild beasts against each other or against men armed with spears. Another consisted of battles, sometimes to the death, between highly trained gladiators. The gladiators, mainly slaves and condemned criminals, learned their craft at schools run by professional trainers. Some gladiators entered the arena armed with a sword, others with a trident and a net. If the spectators were displeased with a losing gladiator's performance, they would call for his execution.

Over the centuries, these spectacles grew more bizarre and brutal. Hundreds of tigers were set against elephants and bulls; wild bulls tore apart men dressed in animal skins; women battled in the arena; dwarfs fought each other. During the reign of Emperor Titus, five thousand beasts were slaughtered in one day. In fact, much of the African trade was devoted to supplying the animals for these contests.

Signs of Trouble

The pax Romana was one of the finest periods in world history. But even during the Time of Happiness, signs of trouble appeared that would grow to crisis proportions in the third century.

Internal Unrest

The Empire's internal stability was always subject to question. Were the economic foundations of the Empire strong and elastic enough to endure hard blows? Could the Roman Empire retain the loyalty of so many diverse nationalities, each with its own religious and cultural traditions? And were the mass of people committed to the values of Greco-Roman civilization, or would they withdraw their allegiance and revert to their native traditions if imperial authority weakened?

During the pax Romana, dissident elements did come forth, particularly in Gaul, Judea, and Egypt. The Jews fought two terrible and futile wars to try to liberate their land from Roman rule. Separatist movements in Gaul were also crushed by Roman forces. To provide free bread for Rome's poor, Roman emperors exploited the Egyptian peasantry. Weighed down by forced labor, heavy taxes, requisitions, and confiscations, Egyptian peasants frequently sought to escape from farmwork.

The unrest in Egypt, Gaul, and Judea demonstrated that not all people at all times welcomed the grand majesty of the Roman peace, that localist and separatist tendencies persisted in a universal empire. In the centuries that followed, as Rome staggered under the weight of economic, political, and military difficulties, these native loyalties reasserted themselves. Increasingly the masses and even the Romanized elite of the cities withdrew their support from the Roman world-state.

Social and Economic Weaknesses

A healthy world-state required empirewide trade to serve as an economic base for political unity, expanding agricultural production to feed the cities, and growing internal mass markets to stimulate industrial production. But the economy of the Empire during the pax Romana had serious defects. The means of communication and transportation were slow, which hindered long-distance commerce. Roman roads, built for military rather than commercial purposes, were often too narrow for large carts and in places were too steep for any vehicles. Many nobles, considering it unworthy for a gentleman to engage in business, chose to squander their wealth rather than invest it in commercial or industrial enterprises. Thus deprived of the stimulus of capital investment, the economy could not expand.

Limited employment opportunities resulted from the Greco-Roman civilization's failure to improve its technology substantially. Scarce employment left the masses with little purchasing power; this, in turn, adversely affected business and industry. Many unemployed inhabitants of Italian towns lived on free or cheap grain provided by the state. To feed this unemployed proletariat, the government kept the price of grain artificially low, discouraging farmers from expanding grain production and forcing many of them to seek other livelihoods. As more farmers left the countryside, the towns became swollen with an impoverished proletariat, and rural areas eventually faced a serious shortage of laborers.

Ultimately, only a small portion of the population—the middle and upper classes of the cities: landlords, merchants, and administrators—reaped the benefits of the Roman peace. They basked in luxury, leisure, and culture. The urban poor, on the other hand, shared little in the political and cultural life of the city and derived none of the economic gains. The privileged class bought off the urban poor with bread and circuses, but occasionally mass discontent expressed itself in mob violence. Outside the cities, the peasantry, still the great bulk of the population, was exploited to provide cheap food for the city dwellers. Between town and countryside, an enormous cultural gap existed. In reality, the cities were small islands of high culture surrounded by a sea of peasant barbarism.

Such a parasitical, exploitative, and elitist social system might function in periods of peace and tranquility, but could it survive crises? Would the impoverished people of town and country—the overwhelming majority of the population—remain loyal to a state whose benefits barely extended to them and whose sophisticated culture, which they hardly comprehended, virtually excluded them?

Cultural Stagnation and Transformation

Perhaps the most dangerous sign for the future was the spiritual paralysis that crept over the ordered world of pax Romana. A weary and sterile Hellenism underlay the Roman peace. The ancient world was undergoing a transformation of values that foreshadowed the end of Greco-Roman civilization.

During the second century A.D., Greco-Roman civilization lost its creative energies, and the values of classical humanism were challenged by mythic-religious movements. No longer regarding reason as a satisfying guide to life, the educated elite subordinated their intellect to feelings and imagination. People no longer found the affairs of this world to have purpose; they placed their hope in life after death. The Roman world was undergoing a religious revolution and was seeking a new vision of the divine.

The application of reason to nature and society, as we have seen, was the great achievement of the Greek mind. But, despite its many triumphs, Greek rationalism never entirely subdued the mythic-religious mentality, which draws its strength from human emotion. The masses of peasants and slaves remained attracted to religious forms. Ritual, mystery, magic, and ecstasy never lost their hold on the ancient world—nor, indeed, have they in our own scientific and technological society. During the Hellenistic Age the tide of rationalism gradually receded, and the nonrational, an ever-present undercurrent, showed renewed vigor. This resurgence of the mythical mentality could be seen in the popularity of the occult, magic, alchemy, and astrology. Feeling themselves controlled by heavenly powers, burdened by danger and emotional stress, and fearing fate as fixed in the stars, people turned for deliverance to magicians, astrologers, and exorcists.

They also became devotees of the many Eastern religious cults that promised personal salvation. More and more people felt that the good life could not be achieved by individuals through their own efforts; they needed outside help. Philosophers eventually sought escape from this world through union with a divine presence greater than human power. Increasingly the masses, and then even the educated elite, came to believe that the good life could not be found on earth but only in a world beyond the grave. Believing themselves to be isolated souls wandering aimlessly in a social desert, people sought refuge in religion. Reason had been found wanting; the time for faith and salvation was at hand.

What brought about the resurgence of the mythical mentality? We have seen that the city-state provided individuals with a sense of belonging and purpose. They found self-fulfillment and self-realization as citizens. The decline of the city-state and its absorption first into Hellenistic kingdoms and later into the Roman Empire left something vital missing in people's lives. Gone were the exhilaration of city-state politics and the sense of community that the city-state had provided. The Roman Empire had imposed peace and stability, but it could not alleviate the feelings of loneliness, anxiety, impotence, alienation, and boredom that had been gaining ground in the Mediterranean world since the fourth century B.C.

As Roman emperors became increasingly autocratic, opportunities for political activity decreased precipitously, and interest in public affairs waned. More than ever before, individuals felt that they had no personal control over their own lives. Their political significance lost, the psychological security provided by the city gone, individuals felt abandoned and isolated. The Roman world-state, vast, remote, and autocratic, could never provide that sense of community, that air of excitement, that feeling of belonging to something larger than oneself, that had derived from an individual's attachment to a city. Nothing replaced the old ideal of civic liberty and civic participation that had generated cultural creativity.

A spiritual malaise had descended upon the Greco-Roman world. Among the upper classes, the philosophic and scientific spirit withered; rational and secular values were in retreat. Deprived of the excitement of politics and bored by idleness and pleasure, the best minds, says historian M. I. Rostovtzeff,

lost faith in the power of reason. . . . Creative genius dwindled; science repeated its previous results. The textbook took the place of research; no new artistic discoveries were made, but echoes of the past were heard . . . [writers] amuse[d] the mind but [were] incapable of elevating and inspiring it.[9]

The Spread of Mystery Religions

The proliferation of oriental mystery religions was a clear expression of this transformation of classical values. During the Hellenistic era, slaves, merchants, and soldiers brought many

Sacred Relief: Mithras Sacrifices a Bull. The spread and popularity of mystery religions during the Empire was one sign of spiritual malaise. Mithras, god of the soldiers, and his cult were widespread. Of all the mystery religions, Mithraism was Christianity's most serious rival. (*Cincinnati Art Museum, Gift of Mr. and Mrs. Fletcher E. Nyce, 1968*)

religious cults westward from Persia, Babylon, Syria, Egypt, and Asia Minor. The various mystery cults possessed many common features. Their rites were secret, revealed only to members. Converts underwent initiation rites and were bound by oath to secrecy. The initiates, in a state of rapture, attempted to unite with the deity after first purifying themselves through baptism (sometimes with the blood of a bull), fasting, having their heads shaved, or drinking from a sacred vessel. Communion was achieved by donning the god's robe, eating a sacred meal, or visiting the god's sanctuary. This sacramental drama propelled initiates through an intense mystical experience of exaltation and rebirth; cultists were certain that their particular savior-god would protect them from misfortune and ensure their soul's immortality.

Of special significance was the cult of Mithras, which had certain parallels with early Christianity and was its principal competi-tor. Originating in Persia, Mithraism spread westward into the Roman Empire. Because it stressed respect for the masculine virtues of bravery and camaraderie, it became particularly popular with the army. The god Mithras, whose birthdate was celebrated on December 25, had as his mission the rescuing of humanity from evil. He was said to demand high standards of morality, to judge souls after death, and to grant eternal life to his faithful followers.

The popularity of magic and mystery demonstrates that many people in Roman society either did not comprehend or had lost faith in the rational and secular values of classical humanism. Religion proved more comforting to the spirit. People felt that the gods could provide what reason, natural law, and world affairs could not: a sure way of overcoming life's misfortunes and discouragements, a guarantee of immortality, a sense of belonging to a community of brethren who cared, an exciting outlet for bottled-up emotions, and a sedative for anxiety at a time when dissatisfaction with the human condition showed itself in all phases of society and life.

Spiritualization of Philosophy

The religious orientation also found expression in philosophy, which demonstrated attitudes markedly at odds with classical humanism. These attitudes, commonly associated with religion, included indifference to the world, withdrawal, and pessimism about the earthly state. From trying to understand nature and individuals' relationships to one another, the philosophers more and more aspired for communion with a higher reality. Like the mystery religions, philosophy reached for something beyond this world in order to comfort the individual.

Stoicism was the principal philosophy of the pax Romana, and its leading exponents were Seneca, Epictetus (A.D. c. 60–c. 117), and Marcus Aurelius. Perpetuating the rational tradition of Greek philosophy, Rome's early Stoics saw the universe as governed by reason and esteemed the human intellect. Like Socrates, they sought the highest good in this world, not in an afterlife, and envisioned no power above human reason. Moral values were obtained from reason alone. The individual was self-sufficient, and depended entirely on rational faculties for knowing and doing good.

But with time, Roman Stoics increasingly viewed philosophy as a means of gaining spiritual consolation and inner strength to endure life's misfortunes. Their thought revealed a sense of weariness with the world and of the sadness of life. Many such tired souls would be attracted by Christianity. In urging compassion, mercy, and forgiveness, Seneca revealed a Christian-like concern for his fellows.

The Stoic conception of God underwent a gradual transformation that reflected the religious yearnings of the times. For the early Stoics, God was an intellectual necessity, an impersonal principle that gave order to the universe. For later Roman Stoics, God had become a moral necessity that comforted and reassured people. While maintaining the traditional Stoic belief that the individual can attain virtue through unaided reason, Epictetus and Marcus Aurelius came close to seeking God's help to live properly. The gap between Greek philosophy and Christianity was narrowing. Marcus Aurelius, the last of the great Stoics, maintained that reason, the noblest part of human nature, came from universal Reason or God; that by heeding the promptings of reason, by directing one's actions according to right reason, one obeyed God. This religious turn in Stoicism was clearly reflected in the thought of Epictetus, who wrote concerning the person who has recognized God in and through reason,

. . . why should not such a man call himself a citizen of the universe? Why should he not call himself a son of God? And why shall he fear anything that happens among men? . . . but to have God as our maker, and father, and guardian— shall this not suffice to deliver us from griefs and fears?[10]

Despite its spiritual leanings, Stoicism did not seek refuge in life after death, did not conceive of God as a personal savior with whom a person enters into communion, and did not turn to revelation as a guide to life. But in Neo-Platonism, which replaced Stoicism as the dominant school of philosophy in the Late Roman Empire, religious yearnings were transformed into a religious system that transcended reason.

Plotinus (A.D. c. 205–c. 270), the most influential spokesman of Neo-Platonism, went far beyond Marcus Aurelius' natural religion; in aspiring to the ecstatic union of the soul with God, he subordinated philosophy to mysticism. Plato's philosophy, we have seen, contained both a major and a minor key. The major key stressed a rational interpretation of the human community and called for reforming the polis on the basis of knowledge, whereas the minor key urged the soul to rise to a higher world of reality. Although Plotinus retained Platonic rationalism (he viewed the individual as a reasoning being and used rational argument to explain his religious orientation), he was intrigued by Plato's otherworldliness.

What Plotinus desired was union with the One or the Good, sometimes called God—the source of all existence. Plotinus felt that the intellect could neither describe nor understand the One, which transcended all knowing, and that joining with the One required a mystical leap, a purification of the soul so that it could return to its true eternal home. For Plotinus, philosophy became a religious experience, a contemplation of the eternal. In comparison to this union with the divine One, of what value was knowledge of the sensible world or a concern for human affairs? For Plotinus this world was a sea of tears and troubles from which the individual yearned to escape. Reality was not in this world, but beyond it, and the principal goal of life was not comprehension of the natural world nor the fulfillment of human potential nor the betterment of the human community, but knowledge of the One. Thus, his philosophy broke with the essential meaning of classical humanism.

Plotinus' philosophy, concludes historian of philosophy W. T. Stace, "is founded upon . . . the despair of reason." It seeks to reach the Absolute not through reason but through "spiritual intoxication." This marks the end of philosophy in the ancient world.

For philosophy is founded upon reason. It is the effort to comprehend, to understand, to grasp the reality of things intellectually. Therefore it cannot admit anything higher than reason. To exalt intuition, ecstasy, or rapture, above thought—this is the death of philosophy. . . . In Neo-Platonism, therefore, ancient philosophy commits suicide. This is the end. The place of philosophy is taken henceforth by religion.[11]

By the Late Roman Empire, mystery religions intoxicated the masses, and mystical philosophy beguiled the educated elite. Clas-

sical civilization was undergoing a transformation. Philosophy had become subordinate to religious belief; secular values seemed inferior to religious experience. The earthly city had raised its eyes toward heaven. The culture of the Roman world was moving in a direction in which the quest for the divine was to predominate over all human enterprises.

The Decline of Rome

Third-Century Crisis

At the death of Marcus Aurelius in A.D. 180 the Empire was politically stable, economically prosperous, and militarily secure. In the third century, the ordered civilization of the pax Romana ended. Several elements caused this disruption. The Roman Empire was plunged into military anarchy, was raided by Germanic tribes, and was burdened by economic dislocations. In addition, Eastern religions that undermined the rational foundations of Greco-Roman civilization pervaded the Roman world.

The degeneration of the army was a prime reason for the third-century crisis. During the great peace, the army had remained an excellent fighting force, renowned for its discipline, organization, and loyalty. In the third century A.D., however, there was a marked deterioration in the quality of Roman soldiers. Lacking loyalty to Rome and greedy for spoils, soldiers used their weapons to prey on civilians and to make and unmake emperors. From A.D. 235 to 285, military mutiny and civil war raged, and many emperors were assassinated. The once stalwart army neglected its duty of defending the borders and disrupted the internal life of the Empire.

Perhaps this change in attitude can be explained by liberal granting of citizenship. In A.D. 212, citizenship was extended to virtually all freeborn inhabitants of the Empire. Previously, army recruits had been drawn from provincials who were attracted by the promise of citizenship and its advantages. These recruits generally were men of a high caliber

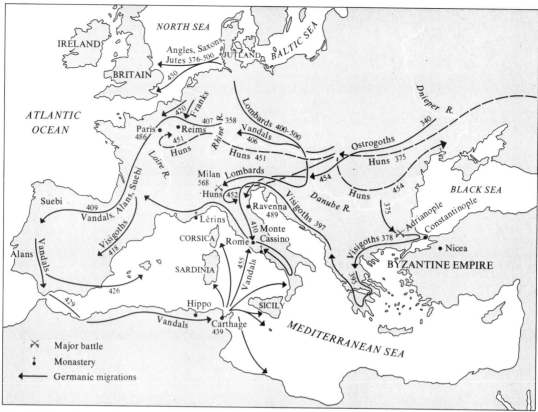

Map 7.2 Incursions and Migrations, c. A.D. 300–500

who were interested in bettering themselves and their families' lot. With citizenship no longer an inducement for enlistment, says Edward T. Salmon,

recruits were now only too likely to be drawn from the lowest and most primitive elements . . . men of the rough and reckless type, who were joining the army chiefly in order to get weapons in their hands with which they would be able to extort for themselves an even greater share of the Empire's collective wealth . . . men who knew little and cared less about Rome's mission and who, when not preying upon the civilians, had not the slightest compunction about preying upon one another.[12]

Taking advantage of the military anarchy, Germanic tribesmen crossed the Rhine-Danube frontier to loot and destroy. The Goths raided coastal cities of Asia Minor and Greece and even burned much of Athens.

In the west, other Germanic tribes penetrated Gaul, Spain, and Italy, and engaged the Romans in a full-scale battle near Milan. At the same time that the European defense lines were being breached, a reborn Persian Empire, led by the Sassanid Dynasty, attacked and for a while conquered Roman lands in the east. Some sections of the Empire, notably in Gaul, attempted to break away; these moves reflected an assertion of local patriotism over Roman universalism. The "city of mankind" was crumbling.

These eruptions had severe economic repercussions. Cities were pillaged and destroyed, farmlands ruined, and trade disrupted. To obtain funds and supplies for the military, emperors confiscated goods, exacted forced labor, and debased the coinage by minting more currency without an increase in the supply of precious metal. These measures led many citizens to withdraw their loyalty from Rome and brought ruin to the middle class. As inflation and devaluation cheapened the value of money, some parts of the Empire turned to barter as a medium of exchange.

Invasions, civil war, rising prices, a debased coinage, declining agricultural production, disrupted transportation, and the excessive demands of the state caused economic havoc and famine in the cities. The urban centers of the ancient world, creators and disseminators of high civilization, were caught in a rhythm of breakdown. As cities decayed, the center of life gravitated back to the countryside. Large, fortified estates owned by the emperor or wealthy aristocrats provided refuge for the uprooted and destitute of town and country.

The majority of citizens had no deep investment in urban life. The Roman army, consisting principally of peasants and barbarian volunteers, felt no deep commitment to the cities and their culture either. In the countryside, people were not much affected by classical civilization, which had made little headway against native languages, religions, and manners. Even the emperors, traditional guardians of the cities, began to seek their support in the food-producing countryside and in the peasant-dominated army.

During the third century A.D., the spiritual crisis intensified as the rational foundations of Greco-Roman civilization eroded further. People turned increasingly to the mystery cults, which offered relief from earthly misery, a sense of belonging, and a promise of immortality. In philosophy, creative energies were directed not toward a greater understanding of nature or society, but toward a knowledge of God, which philosophers were teaching to be the path to happiness. Hellenism was breaking down.

Diocletian and Constantine: The Regimented State

The emperors Diocletian (A.D. 285–305) and Constantine (A.D. 306–337) tried to contain the awesome forces of disintegration. At a time when agricultural production was steadily declining, they had to feed the city poor and an army of 400,000 strung out over the Empire. They also had to prevent renewed outbreaks of military anarchy and to defend the borders against barbarian attacks. Their solution was to tighten the reins of government and to squeeze more taxes and requisitions out of the citizens. In the process they transformed Rome into a bureaucratic, regimented, and militarized state.

Ruling like an oriental despot, Diocletian completed a trend that had been developing for generations. He imitated the pomp of the East and wore magnificent robes and jewels; he demanded that subjects prostrate themselves in his presence. Cities lost their traditional right of local self-government, which consolidated a trend started earlier. To ensure continuous production of food and goods, as well as the collection of taxes, the state forced unskilled workers and artisans to hold their jobs for life and to pass them on to their children. For the same reasons, peasants were turned into virtual serfs, bound to the land that they cultivated. An army of government agents was formed to hunt down peasants who fled the land to escape crushing taxes and poverty.

Also frozen into their positions were city officials (*curiales*). They often found it necessary to furnish from their own pockets the difference between the state's tax demands and the amount that they could collect from an already overtaxed population. This system of a hereditary class of tax collectors and of crippling taxes to pay for a vastly expanded bureaucracy and military establishment enfeebled urban trade and industry. These conditions killed the civic spirit of townsmen, who desperately sought escape. By overburdening urban dwellers with taxes and regulations, Diocletian and Constantine shattered the vitality of city life on which Roman prosperity and civilization depended.

Rome was governed by an oriental despotism, a highly centralized monarchy regimenting the lives of its subjects. Whereas Augustus had upheld the classical ideal that the commonwealth was a means of fostering the good life for the individual, Diocletian adopted the oriental attitude that the individual lives for the state. The absolutism inherent in the concept of the Principate had completely and irrevocably asserted its ascendancy over the republican elements that had endured in Augustus's settlement.

To guard against military insurrection, Diocletian appointed a loyal general to govern the western provinces of the Empire, while he ruled the East; although both emperors bore the title Augustus, Diocletian remained superior. By building a new imperial capital, Constantinople, at the Bosporus, a strait where Asia meets Europe, Constantine furthered this trend of dividing the Empire into eastern and western halves.

Barbarian Invasions

By imposing some order on what had been approaching chaos, Diocletian and Constantine prevented the Empire from collapsing. Rome had been given a reprieve. A long period of peace might have brought economic recovery, but misfortune continued to burden Rome and the process of breakdown and disintegration resumed. In the last part of the fourth century the problem of guarding the frontier grew more acute.

The Huns, a savage Mongol people from central Asia, swept across the plains of Russia and put pressure on the Visigoths, a Germanic tribe that had migrated into southeastern Europe. Terrified of the Huns, the Goths sought refuge within the Roman Empire. Hoping to increase his manpower and unable to stop the panic-stricken Germans, Emperor Valens permitted them to cross the Danube frontier. But two years later, in 378, the Goths and the Romans fought each other in a historic battle at Adrianople. The barbarian calvary defeated the Roman legions, an indication that Rome could no longer defend its borders. The Goths were in the Empire to stay.

Other Germanic tribes increased their pressure on the Empire's borders. Attracted by the warmer climate, riches, and advanced civilization of the Roman Empire, they also were looking for new lands to farm and were frightened by the advent of the Huns. The borders finally collapsed at the end of 406, as Vandals, Alans, Suebi, and other tribes joined the Goths in devastating and overrunning the Empire's western provinces. In 410, the Visigoths sacked Rome.

Economic conditions continued to deteriorate. Cities in Britain, Gaul, Germany, and Spain lay abandoned. Other metropolises saw their populations dwindle and production stagnate. The great network of Roman roads was not maintained, and trade in the West almost disappeared or passed into the hands of Greeks, Syrians, and Jews from the east.

In 451 Attila (c. 406–453), called "the Scourge of God," led his Huns into Gaul, where he was defeated by a coalition of Germans and the remnants of the Roman army. He died two years later, having come within a hairsbreadth of turning Europe into a province of a Mongolian empire. But Rome's misfortunes persisted. In 455, Rome was again sacked, this time by the Vandals. Additional regions fell under the control of Germanic chieftains. Germanic soldiers in the pay of Rome gained control of the government and dictated the choice of emperor. In 476, German officers overthrew the Roman Emperor Romulus and placed a German on the throne. This act is traditionally regarded as the end of the Roman Empire in the west.

The Underlying Reasons for Decline

What were the underlying causes for the decline and fall of the Roman Empire in the west? Surely no other question has intrigued the historical imagination more than this one. Implicit in the answers suggested by historians and philosophers is a concern for their own civilization. Will it suffer the same fate as Rome?

To analyze so monumental a development as the fall of Rome, some preliminary observations are necessary. First, the fall of Rome

Arch of Constantine. Constantine managed to bring the Empire under his control for almost a quarter of a century. He tightened the screws of regimentation and built a capital at Constantinople (Byzantium); he tolerated and later was converted to Christianity. (*ENIT/Italian Government Travel Office*)

was a process lasting hundreds of years; it was not a single event that occurred in A.D. 476. Second, only the western half of the Empire fell. The eastern half—wealthier, more populous, less afflicted with civil wars, and less exposed to barbarian invasions—survived as the Byzantine Empire until the middle of the fifteenth century. Third, no single explanation suffices to account for Rome's decline; multiple forces operated concurrently to bring about the fall.

The Role of the Barbarians Was Rome's fall suicide or murder? Did the barbarians walk over a corpse, or did they contribute sub-stantially to Rome's decline and fall? Undoubtedly an Empire enfeebled by internal rot succumbed to the barbarian invasions. Perhaps a stronger Rome might have secured its borders, as it had done during the pax Romana. But the barbarian attacks occurred mainly in the west, and the western Empire, poorer and less populated than the eastern portion, reeled under these increasingly more numerous and more severe barbarian on-slaughts. Also, the pressures exerted by the barbarians along an immense frontier aggra-vated Rome's internal problems. The barbarian attacks left border regions impover-ished and depopulated. The Empire imposed high taxes and labor services on its citizens in order to strengthen the armed forces, causing the overburdened middle and lower classes to hate the imperial government that took so much from them.

Spiritual Considerations   The classical mentality, once brimming with confidence about the potentialities of the individual and the power of the intellect, suffered a failure of nerve. The urban upper class, upon whom the responsibility for preserving cosmopolitan Greco-Roman culture traditionally rested, became dissolute and apathetic, no longer taking an interest in public life. The aristocrats secluded themselves behind the walls of their fortified country estates; many did not lift a finger to help the Empire. The townsmen demonstrated their disenchantment by avoiding public service and by rarely organizing resistance forces against the barbarian invaders. The great bulk of the Roman citizenry, apathetic and indifferent, simply gave up, despite the fact that they overwhelmingly outnumbered the barbarian hordes.

Political and Military Considerations   The Roman government itself contributed to this spiritual malaise through its increasingly autocratic tendencies, which culminated in the regimented rule of Diocletian and Constantine. The insatiable demands and regulations of the state in the Late Roman Empire sapped the initiative and civic spirit of its citizens. The ruined middle and lower classes withdrew their loyalty. For many the state had become the enemy, and its administration was hated and feared more than the barbarians.

Related to the political decline was the inability of the government to control ambitious military commanders who used their troops to seize the throne and its immense power. The internal security and stability of the Empire was thus constantly imperiled by army leaders more concerned with grandiose personal dreams than with defending the Empire's borders. These civil wars imposed ter-

rible financial burdens on the Empire and gravely weakened the frontier defenses—an invitation to the Germans to increase their pressure.

The deteriorated quality of Roman soldiers was another reason why Rome failed to defend its borders, even though the German invaders were fewer numerically. During the third century the army consisted predominantly of the provincial peasantry. These nonurban, non-Italian, semicivilized soldiers, often the dregs of society, were not committed to Greco-Roman civilization. They had little comprehension of Rome's mission, and at times used their power to attack the cities and towns. The emperors also recruited large numbers of barbarians into the army to fill depleted ranks. Ultimately, the army consisted predominantly of barbarians, as both legionnaires and officers. Although these Germans made brave soldiers, they too had little loyalty to Greco-Roman civilization and to the Roman state. This deterioration of the Roman army occurred because many young citizens evaded conscription. No longer imbued with patriotism, they considered military service a servitude to be shunned.

Economic Considerations   Among the economic causes contributing to the decline of the Roman Empire in the west were population decline, the failure to achieve a breakthrough in technology, the heavy burden of taxation, and the economic decentralization that abetted political decentralization.

The population of the Empire may have shrunk from 70 million during the pax Romana to 50 million in the Late Roman Empire. The epidemic during the reign of Marcus Aurelius, which might have been the bubonic plague, lasted fifteen years. A second plague struck the Empire during the reign of Commodus, Marcus Aurelius' son. Other plagues in the middle of the third century and constant warfare further reduced the population. The birthrate did not rise to compensate for these losses. Worsening economic conditions and a lack of hope in the future apparently discouraged people from increasing the sizes of their families.

The decline in population adversely affected the Empire in at least three important ways. At the same time that the population was declining, the costs of running the Empire were spiraling, which created a terrible burden for taxpayers. Second, fewer workers were available for agriculture, the most important industry of the Empire. Third, population decline reduced the manpower available for the army, forcing emperors to permit the establishment of Germanic colonies within the Empire's borders to serve as feeders for the army. This situation led to the barbarization of the army.

The Roman peace brought stability but it failed to discover new and better ways of producing goods and agricultural products. To be sure, some advances in technology did take place during the Hellenistic Age and the pax Romana: rotary mills for grain, screwpresses, and improvements in glass-blowing and field-drainage methods. But the high intellectual culture of Greece and Rome rested on a meager economic and technological foundation. The widespread use of slave labor probably precluded a breakthrough in technology, for slaves had little incentive to invent more efficient ways of producing. The upper classes, identifying manual labor with slavery, would not condescend to engage in the mechanical arts. This failure to improve the level of technology limited employment opportunities for the masses. Because the masses could not increase their purchasing power, business and industry were without a mass internal market that might have acted as a continual stimulus for the accumulation of capital and for economic expansion.

Instead of expanding industry and trade, towns maintained their wealth by exploiting the countryside. The Roman cities were centers of civilized life and opulence, but they lacked industries. They spent, but they did not produce. The towns were dominated by landlords whose estates lay beyond the city and whose income derived from corn, oil, and wine. Manufacturing was rudimentary, confined essentially to textiles, pottery, furniture, and glassware. The methods of production were simple, the market limited, the cost of transportation high, and agricultural productivity low—the labor of perhaps nineteen peasants was required to support one townsman. Such a fundamentally unhealthy economy could not weather the dislocations caused by uninterrupted warfare and the demands of a mushrooming bureaucracy and military.

With the barbarians pressing on the borders, the increased military expenditures overstrained the Empire's resources. To pay for the food, uniforms, arms, and armor of the soldiers, taxes rose, growing too heavy for peasants and townsmen. The state also requisitioned wood and grain and demanded that citizens maintain roads and bridges. The government often resorted to force to collect taxes and exact services. Crushed by these demands, many peasants simply abandoned their farms and sought the protection of large landowners, or turned to banditry.

Making the situation worse was the administrative separation of the Empire into east and west undertaken by Diocletian and Constantine. As a result, western emperors could no longer rely on financial aid from the wealthier east to finance the defense of the borders. Slow communications and costly transport continued to hamper the economic unity—an empirewide trade that was required for Roman political unity. Meanwhile, industries gravitated outward to search for new markets in the frontier army camps and for new sources of slaves in border regions. This dispersion further weakened the bonds of economic unity. Gradually, trade became less international and more local, and provincial regions grew more self-sufficient. The strife of the third century intensified the drift toward economic self-sufficiency in the provinces, a condition that promoted localism and separatism.

Contributing to the economic decentralization was the growth of industries on lat-

---

Chronology 7.1 The Roman Empire

27 B.C.	Octavian assumes the title *Augustus* and becomes, in effect, the first Roman emperor; start of the pax Romana
14 B.C.	The death of Augustus; Tiberius gains the throne
A.D. 66–70	The Jewish revolt; Romans capture Jerusalem and destroy the Second Temple
79	Eruption of Mount Vesuvius and destruction of Pompeii and Herculaneum
132–135	Hadrian crushes another revolt by the Hebrews
180	Marcus Aurelius dies; the end of the pax Romana
212	Roman citizenship is granted to virtually all free inhabitants of Roman provinces
235–285	Military anarchy; attacks by barbarians
285–305	Diocletian tries to deal with the crisis by creating a regimented state
378	Battle of Adrianople; the Goths defeat the Roman legions
406	Borders collapse, and barbarians pour into the Empire
410	Rome is sacked by Visigoths
455	Rome is sacked by Vandals
476	The end of the Roman Empire in the West

---

ifundia, the large fortified estates owned by wealthy aristocrats. Producing exclusively for the local market, these estates contributed to the impoverishment of urban centers by reducing the number of customers available to buy goods made in the cities. As life grew more desperate, urban craftsmen and small farmers sought the protection of these large landlords, whose estates grew in size and importance. The growth of latifundia was accompanied by the decline of cities and the transformation of independent peasants into virtual serfs.

These great estates were also new centers of political power that the imperial government could not curb. A new society was tak-

ing shape in the Late Roman Empire. The center of gravity had shifted from the city to the landed estate, from the imperial bureaucrats to the local aristocrats. These developments epitomized the decay of ancient civilization and presaged the Middle Ages.

Notes

1. Tacitus, *The Annals of Imperial Rome*, trans. by Michael Grant (Baltimore: Penguin Books, 1959), I. 3, p. 31.

2. Cited in David Magie, *Roman Rule in Asia Minor* (Princeton, N.J.: Princeton University Press, 1950), p. 490.

3. Seneca, *Epistles*, trans. by Richard M. Grummere (Cambridge, Mass.: Harvard University Press, Loeb Classical Library, 1917), Epistle 47, p. 307.

4. Sallust, *The Conspiracy of Cataline*, trans. by S. A. Handford (Baltimore: Penguin Books, 1963), p. 193.

5. Excerpted in Naphtali Lewis and Meyer Reinhold, eds., *Roman Civilization Sourcebook*, vol. 2, *The Empire* (New York: Harper Torch Books, 1966), p. 136.

6. *The Aeneid of Virgil*, trans. by Allen Mandelbaum (Berkeley: University of California Press, 1971), pp. 160–161.

7. *The Art of Love and Other Love Books of Ovid* (New York: Grosset & Dunlap, The Universal Library, 1959), pp. 117–118, 130–132, 135.

8. *The Satires of Juvenal*, trans. by Hubert Creekmore (New York: Mentor Books, 1963), ll. 242–248, 269–272, 302–305, pp. 58–61.

9. M. I. Rostovtzeff, *Rome* (New York: Oxford University Press, 1960), p. 322.

10. Epictetus, *The Discourses*, trans. by W. A. Oldfather (Cambridge, Mass.: Harvard University Press, Loeb Classical Library, 1925), p. 65.

11. W. T. Stace, *A Critical History of Greek Philosophy* (London: Macmillan, 1924), p. 377.

12. Excerpted in Mortimer Chambers, ed., *The Fall of Rome* (New York: Holt, Rinehart & Winston, 1963), pp. 45–46.

Suggested Reading

Carcopino, Jerome, *Daily Life in Ancient Rome* (1940). All phases of Roman society during the second century.

Chambers, Mortimer, ed., *The Fall of Rome* (1963). A valuable collection of readings.

Clarke, M. L., *The Roman Mind* (1968). Studies in the history of thought from Cicero to Marcus Aurelius.

Jones, A. H. M., *Augustus* (1970). An authoritative discussion of the Augustan settlement.

Katz, Solomon, *The Decline of Rome* (1955). A helpful introduction.

Lewis, Naphtali, and Meyer Reinhold, *Roman Civilization*, vol. 2 (1966). Primary sources.

MacMullen, Ramsay, *Constantine* (1969). An account of the man and his times.

Mazzarino, Santo, *The End of the Ancient World* (1966). Describes how many thinkers have viewed the idea of the death of Rome and offers a modern interpretation.

Paoli, R. E., *Rome: Its People, Life and Customs* (1963). Surveys all phases of Roman society—women, slavery, clothing, industry, law, medicine, and so on.

Rostovtzeff, Michael, *Rome* (1960). The concluding chapters offer a stimulating and controversial interpretation for the fall of the Empire.

Rowell, H. T., *Rome in the Augustan Age* (1962). The city and its people in the era of Augustus.

Starr, C. G., *Civilization and the Caesars* (1965). A fine interpretive essay on the collapse of classical humanism and the spread of religion in the four centuries from Cicero to Augustine.

Wheeler, Mortimer, Sir, *Roman Art and Architecture* (1964). An interpretive study, filled with insight.

White, Lynn, ed., *The Transformation of the Roman World* (1973). A useful collection of essays on the transformation of the ancient world and the emergence of the Middle Ages.

Review Questions

1. In what ways was Augustus a creative statesman?

2. The Roman world state completed the trend toward cosmopolitanism and universalism that had emerged during the Hellenistic Age. Discuss this statement.

3. Why is the pax Romana regarded as one of the finest periods in world history?

4. Describe the achievements of some Roman writers and scientists during the pax Romana.

5. What signs of trouble existed during the pax Romana?

6. Why were people attracted to mystery religions?

7. How was classical humanism in retreat in the second and third centuries A.D.?

8. Describe the crisis that afflicted Rome in the third century.

9. How did Diocletian and Constantine try to deal with the Empire's crisis?

10. What was the significance of the westward movement of the Huns? What effect did the Battle of Adrianople have on the Empire?

11. What role did the barbarians play in the decline of Rome?

12. Analyze the spiritual, military, political, and economic reasons for the decline of the Roman Empire.

13. Could creative statesmanship have saved the Roman Empire? Explain why it might or might not have saved the Empire.

8

Early Christianity:
A World Religion

*A*s confidence in human reason and hope for happiness in this world waned in the last centuries of the Roman Empire, a new outlook began to take hold. Evident in philosophy and in the popularity of oriental religions, this viewpoint stressed escape from an oppressive world and communion with a higher reality. Christianity evolved and expanded within this setting of declining classicism and heightening otherworldliness. As one response to a declining Hellenism, Christianity offered a spiritually disillusioned Greco-Roman world a reason for living—the hope of personal immortality. The triumph of Christianity marked a break with classical antiquity and a new stage in the evolution of the West, for there was a fundamental difference between the Hellenic and the Christian concepts of God, the individual, and the purpose of life.

Origins of Christianity

Judaism in the First Century B.C.

A Palestinian Jew named Jesus was executed by the Roman authorities during the reign of Tiberius (A.D. 14–37), who was Augustus' successor. At the time, few people paid much attention to what proved to be one of the most pivotal events in world history. In the quest for the historical Jesus, scholars have stressed the importance of both his Jewishness and the religious ferment that prevailed in Palestine in the first century B.C. Jesus' ethical teachings are rooted in the moral outlook of Old Testament prophets and, says Andrew M. Greeley, a student of religion, must be viewed as

a logical extension of the Hebrew Scriptures . . . a product of the whole religious environment of which Jesus was a part. Jesus defined himself as a Jew, was highly conscious of the Jewishness of his message and would have found it impossible to conceive of himself as anything but Jewish. . . . The teachings of Jesus, then, must be placed

154

squarely in the Jewish religious context of the time.[1]

In the first century B.C., four principal social-religious parties or sects existed among the Palestinian Jews: Sadducees, Pharisees, Essenes, and Zealots. Composed of the upper stratum of Jewish society—influential landed gentry and hereditary priests who controlled the temple in Jerusalem—the Sadducees insisted on a strict interpretation of Mosaic Law and the perpetuation of temple ceremonies. Challenging the Sadducees, the Pharisees adopted a more flexible attitude toward Mosaic Law; the Pharisees allowed for discussion and varying interpretations of the Law and granted authority to oral tradition as well as to written Scripture. Unlike the Sadducees, the Pharisees believed in life after death; the concept of personal immortality, a later addition to Hebrew religious thought probably acquired from Persia, had gained wide acceptance by the time of Jesus. The Pharisees had the support of the bulk of the Jewish nation. The third religious party, the Essenes, established a semimonastic community near the Dead Sea. Like the Pharisees, they believed in the physical resurrection of the body, but gave this doctrine a more compelling meaning by tying it to the immediate coming of God's kingdom. Another sect, the Zealots, demanded that the Jews neither pay taxes to Rome nor acknowledge the authority of the Roman emperor. Devoted patriots, the Zealots engaged in acts of resistance to Rome.

In addition to the afterlife, another widely recognized idea in the first century B.C. was the belief in a Messiah, a redeemer chosen by God to liberate Israel from foreign rule. In the days of the Messiah, it was predicted, Israel would be free, the exiles would return, and the Jews would be blessed with peace, unity, and prosperity. Jesus (c. 4 B.C.–c. A.D. 29) performed his ministry within this context of Jewish religious-national expectations and longings. The hopes of Jesus' early followers encompassed a lower-class dissatisfaction with the aristocratic Sadducees, a Pharisee emphasis on prophetic ideals and the afterlife, an Essene preoccupation with the end-of-days, a belief in the nearness of God and the need for repentance, and a conquered people's yearning for a Messiah who would liberate their land from Roman rule and establish God's reign.

Jesus: The Inner Man

Historians are able to speak with greater certainty about social-religious developments in Judea at the time of Jesus than they can about Jesus himself. In reconstructing what Jesus did and believed, the historian labors under a handicap, for the sources are few. Jesus himself wrote nothing, and nothing was written about him during his lifetime. In the generations following Jesus' death, both Roman and Jewish historians paid him scant attention. Consequently, virtually everything we know about Jesus derives from the Bible's New Testament, which was written decades after Jesus' death by devotees seeking to convey a religious truth and to propagate a faith.

Modern historians in quest of the historical Jesus have rigorously and critically analyzed the New Testament; their analyses have provided some insights into Jesus and his beliefs. Nevertheless, much about Jesus remains obscure. Very little is known about his childhood. Like other Jewish youths he was taught Hebrew religious-ethical thought and the many rules that governed daily life. At about the age of thirty, no doubt influenced by John the Baptist, Jesus felt called upon by God to preach the imminent coming of the reign of God and the need for repentance—a moral transformation so that a person could gain entrance into God's kingdom. "Now after John was arrested, Jesus came into Galilee, preaching the gospel of God, and saying, 'The time is fulfilled, and the kingdom of God is at hand; repent, and believe in the gospel.' " (Mark 1:14–15)[2]*

---

*The biblical quotations in this chapter are taken from the Revised Standard Version of the Holy Bible.

For Jesus, the coming of the kingdom was imminent; the process leading to the establishment of God's kingdom on earth had already begun. A new order would soon be established in which God would govern his people righteously and mercifully. Hence the present became critical for him—a time for spiritual preparedness and penitence—because an individual's thoughts, goals, and actions would determine whether he or she would gain entrance into the kingdom. People must change their attitudes, he said. They must eliminate base, lustful, hostile, and selfish feelings; they must stop pursuing wealth and power; they must purify their hearts and show their love for God and their fellow human beings.

Like the Hebrew prophets, Jesus saw ethics as the core of Mosaic Law: "So whatever you wish that men would do to you, do so to them; for this is the law and the prophets." (Matthew 7:12) Jesus did not intend to lead his fellow Jews away from their ancestral religion: " 'Think not that I have come to abolish the law and the prophets; I have come not to abolish them but to fulfil them.' " (Matthew 5:17)

Although Jesus did not seek to break with his past, he was distressed with the Judaism of his day. The rabbis taught the Golden Rule, as well as God's love and mercy for his children, but it seemed to Jesus that these ethical considerations were being undermined by an exaggerated rabbinical concern with ritual, restrictions, and the fine points of the Law, and that the center of Judaism had shifted from prophetic values to obedience to rules and prohibitions regulating the smallest details of daily life. Such legalism and ritualism, Jesus held, distorted the meaning of prophetic teachings. The proliferation of rules, Jesus felt, dealt only with an individual's visible behavior; rules did not penetrate to the person's inner being and lead to a moral transformation. Observing the Lord's command to rest on the Sabbath—for example, by not eating an egg laid on Saturday or by not lifting a chair on that day—did not purify a person's soul.

The inner person concerned Jesus, and it was an inward change that he sought. " 'For from within, out of the heart of man, come evil thoughts, fornication, theft, murder, adultery, coveting, wickedness, deceit, licentiousness, envy, slander, pride, foolishness. All these evil things come from within, and they defile a man.' " (Mark 7:21–23) Individuals must feel again that God is at hand; they must choose God's way by conquering their sinful selfishness and pride and by demonstrating compassion for their neighbors. To Jesus, the spirit of Mosaic Law was more important than the letter of the Law, and right living and a pure loving heart were more important than legal quibbling. With the fervor of a prophet, he urged a moral transformation of human character through a direct encounter between the individual and God.

By preaching active love for one's fellows and by stressing a personal and intimate connection between the individual and God, Jesus associated himself more with the Hebrew prophetic tradition than with the Hebrew rituals, rules, and prohibitions that served to perpetuate a national and cultural tradition of a distinct people. We have seen that Hebrew history reveals both universal and parochial components; Jesus' teachings are more indicative of the universalism inherent in the concept of the one God and in the prophets' teachings.

It was inevitable that Jewish scribes and priests, guardians of the faith, would regard Jesus as a threat to ancient traditions. To Jewish leaders, Jesus was a troublemaker, a subversive who was undermining respect for the Sabbath and religious rites, an arrogant man who claimed that he above all other men was favored by God, another in a long line of messiahs who had been condemned and executed. To the Romans who ruled Palestine, Jesus was a political agitator who could ignite Jewish messianic expectations into a revolt against Rome. (It is likely that several of Jesus' early followers were Zealots, and the Romans may have viewed Jesus as a Zealot leader.) After Jewish leaders turned

Jesus over to the Roman authorities, the Roman procurator, Pontius Pilate, sentenced him to death by crucifixion.

Some Jews, believing that Jesus was an inspired prophet or even the long-awaited Messiah, had become his followers—the chief of these were the Twelve Disciples. At the time of Jesus' death, Christianity was not a separate religion, but a small Hebrew sect with dim prospects for survival. What established the Christian movement and gave it strength was the belief of Jesus' followers that he was raised from the dead on the third day after he was buried. The doctrine of the resurrection enabled people to regard Jesus as more than a superb ethical soul, more than a prophet, more than the Messiah; it made possible belief in Jesus as a divine savior-god, who had come to earth to show people the way to heaven.

In the years immediately following the crucifixion, the religion of Jesus was confined almost exclusively to Jews, who could more appropriately be called Jewish-Christians. The word *Christian* came from a name given Jesus: *Christ* (the Lord's Anointed, the Messiah). Missionaries of this dissenting Christian movement within Judaism were called Apostles—those sent out to preach the gospel, or good news, about Christ. They addressed themselves to Jews and to converts to Judaism who, because they did not adhere fully to Mosaic Law, were not wholly accepted by the Jewish community. Before Christianity could realize the universal implications of Jesus' teachings and become a world religion, as distinct from a Jewish sect, it had to extricate itself from Jewish ritual, politics, and culture. This achievement was the work of a Hellenized Jew named Saul, known to the world as Saint Paul.

Saint Paul: From a Jewish Sect to a World Religion

Saint Paul (A.D. c. 5–c. 67) came from the Greek city of Tarsus in southeastern Asia Minor. He belonged to the Diaspora, or the

Saint Paul. Early Christian art brought to an end the classical concern with the visible real world. Mosaics such as this of Saint Paul of translucent glass transformed the interiors of churches into heavenly abodes. Bodies assumed unnatural poses and became spiritualized. (*Scala/Art Resource*)

"Dispersion"—the millions of Jews living outside Palestine. Though the Jews of the Diaspora retained their ancient faith, they also were influenced by Greek culture. An example is the Alexandrian Jew, Philo (c. 30 B.C.–c. A.D. 40), who tried to demonstrate that Hebrew Scripture could be explained and justified in terms of Greek philosophy. The Jews of the Diaspora were more receptive to foreign ideas, and had a broader conception of humanity than did the Palestinian Jews, who were noted for their intense nationalism and religious exclusiveness. Non-Jews, or *Gentiles*, coming into contact with Jews of the Diaspora, were often favorably impressed with Hebrew monotheism, ethics, and family life. Some Gentiles embraced Hebrew monotheism, but refused to adhere to provisions of the Law requiring circumcision and dietary regulations. Among these Gentiles and non-Palestinian Jews who were greatly influenced by the Greco-Roman milieu, Jesus' Apostles would find receptive listeners.

Reared in Tarsus, a stronghold of Greek culture, Saul knew Greek well, but it is unlikely that he had great familiarity with Greek literature and philosophy. Trained in the outlook of the Pharisees, the young Saul went to Jerusalem to study with Rabban Gamaliel, an outstanding Pharisee teacher. In Jerusalem, Saul persecuted the followers of Jesus, but then he underwent a spiritual transformation and became a convert to Jesus. Serving as a zealous missionary of Jewish Christianity in the Diaspora, Saint Paul preached to his fellow Jews in synagogues. Recognizing that the Christian message applied to non-Jews as well, Paul urged spreading it to the Gentiles.

Although neither the first nor the only missionary to the Gentiles, Saint Paul was without doubt the most important. In the process of his missionary activity—and he traveled extensively through the Roman Empire—he formulated doctrines that represented a fundamental break with Judaism and became the heart of this new religion. Paul taught that all people, both Jew and Gentile, were sinners, as a consequence of Adam's original defiance of God; that Jesus had come to earth to save all people from sin; that by dying on the cross, he had atoned for the sins of all and made it possible for all to have eternal life in heaven; and that by believing in Jesus, people could gain this salvation. Alone, the individual was helpless, possessed by sin, unable to overcome his or her wicked nature. Jesus was the only hope, said Paul. "Wretched man that I am! Who will deliver me from this body of death? Thanks be to God through Jesus Christ our Lord!" (Romans 7:24–25) Through the ritual of baptism—purification by water—individuals could enter into a personal union with Christ.

Christ: A Savior-God To the first members of the Christian movement, Jesus was both a prophet who proclaimed the power and purpose of God and the Messiah whose coming heralded a new age. To Saint Paul, Jesus was a resurrected redeemer who held out the promise of salvation to the entire world, a savior-god who took on human flesh to atone for the sins of humanity by suffering death on the cross.

The idea of a slain savior-god was well known in the mystery religions of the eastern Mediterranean and in Gnosticism, a pre-Christian religious movement that synthesized many mythological and philosophical traditions. Like these religions, Christianity initiated converts into the mysteries of the faith, featured a sacramental meal, and developed a priesthood. But the similarities between Christianity and the mystery cults should not be overstressed, since the differences are more profound.

Unlike the cultic gods, Jesus had actually lived in history. Hence people could identify with him in a more personal way, which enormously increased the appeal of this new religion. Also, the deities of the mystery religions were killed against their will by evil powers. In Jesus, it was said, God had become a man and suffered pain and death out of compassion and pity to show a floundering humanity the way that would lead from sin to eternal life. This suffering savior evoked from a distressed humanity deep feelings of love and loyalty. Finally, Christianity, with its Hebraic heritage, would tolerate no other divinity but God. Pagans, on the other hand, often belonged to more than one cult, or at least recognized the divinity of the gods of other cults.

The Break with Judaism   In attempting to reach the Gentiles, Saint Paul had to disentangle Christianity from a Jewish sociocultural context. Thus, he held that neither Gentile nor Jewish followers of Jesus were bound by the hundreds of rituals and rules that constitute Mosaic Law. For Saint Paul, there was no distinctive difference between Jew and Gentile; in his view, the ministry of Jesus was intended for all. In the wake of Jesus' coming, Paul insisted, Mosaic regulations were obsolete and a hindrance to missionary activity among the Gentiles.

To Paul, the new Christian community was the true fulfillment of Judaism; it was granted the promise that God had earlier bestowed on Israel; it was the means for moral transformation and eternal life. The Jews regarded their faith as a national religion, bound organically with the history of their people. For Paul, the new Christian community was not a nation but an *oikoumene*, a world community. To this extent, Christianity shared in the universalism of the Hellenistic Age. Jesus not only fulfilled the messianic aspirations of the Jews, but he also fulfilled the spiritual needs and expectations of all peoples.

In preaching the doctrine of a risen Savior and insisting that Mosaic Law had been superseded Paul, whatever his intentions, was breaking with his Jewish roots and transforming a Jewish sect into a new religion. Separating Christianity from Judaism enormously increased its appeal for non-Jews who were attracted to Hebrew ethical monotheism but repelled by circumcision, dietary regulations, and other strict requirements of Mosaic Law. Paul built on the personalism and universalism implicit in the teachings of Jesus (and the Hebrew prophets) to create a religion intended not for a people with its own particular history, culture, and land, but for all humanity.

Spread and Triumph of Christianity

By de-Judaizing Christianity, Saint Paul made the new religion fit for export to the Greco-Roman world. But its growth was slow. Originating in the first century, Christianity took firm root in the second, grew extensively in the third, and became the official religion of the Roman Empire at the end of the fourth century.

The Appeal of Christianity

The triumph of Christianity was related to a corresponding decline in the vitality of Hellenism and a shift in cultural emphasis—a movement from reason to emotion and revelation. Offering comforting solutions to the existential problems of life and death, religion demonstrated a greater capacity to stir human hearts than reason did. Hellenism had invented the tools of rational thought, but the power of mythical thought was never entirely subdued. By the Late Roman Empire, science and philosophy were unable to compete with mysticism and myth.

This deterioration of the classical outlook was demonstrated by the growing popularity of Eastern religions and the transformation of philosophy. Although the Greco-Roman world had conquered the East militarily, the oriental world, through its religions, waged a counteroffensive that eventually overwhelmed a decaying Greco-Roman civilization. Mystery cults, which promised personal salvation, were spreading and gaining followers. Stoicism and Epicureanism were performing a religious function by trying to help individuals overcome emotional stress, while Neo-Platonists yearned for a mystical union with the One. Astrology and magic, which offered supernatural explanations for the op-

Map 8.1 The Journeys of Saint Paul

erations of nature, were also popular. This drift away from rational and worldly values helped prepare the way for Christianity. In a culturally stagnating and spiritually troubled Greco-Roman world, Christianity gave to life a new meaning and offered to disillusioned men and women a new hope.

During the Hellenistic Age, the individual had struggled with the problems of alienation and community. With the decline of the independent city-state, the individual searched for a new frame of reference, a new form of attachment. The Roman Empire represented one possible allegiance. But for many people, it was not a satisfying relationship—the individual found it difficult to be devoted to so vast, remote, and impersonal a political organization. The Christian message of a divine Savior, a concerned Father, and brotherly love inspired men and women who were dissatisfied with the world of here-and-now, who felt no attachment to city or empire, who derived no inspiration from philosophy, and who suffered from a profound sense of loneliness. Christianity offered the individual

what the city and the Roman world-state could not: a profoundly personal relationship with God, an intimate connection with a higher world, and membership in a community of the faithful who cared for each other.

Stressing the intellect and self-reliance, Greco-Roman thought did not provide for the emotional needs of the ordinary person. Christianity addressed itself to this defect in the Greco-Roman outlook. The poor, the oppressed, and the slaves were attracted to the personality, life, death, and resurrection of Jesus, his love for all, and his concern for suffering humanity. They found spiritual sustenance in a religion that stretched out a hand of love, that taught that a person of worth need not be well-born, rich, educated, or talented. To people burdened with misfortune and terrified by death, Christianity held the promise of eternal life, a kingdom of heaven where they would be comforted by God the Father. Thus, Christianity gave to the common person what the aristocratic values of Greco-Roman civilization generally did not—a sense of dignity. Hellenic philosophy offered little compassion for the sufferer, but the cardinal principle of Christianity held that Jesus had endured earthly torments because of his love for all human beings.

Christianity's success was due not only to the appeal of its message but to the power of an institution. To retain the devotion of the faithful, to win new converts, to protect itself from opponents, and to administer its services, Christianity needed an organized body of followers. This body became the Christian church, which grew into a strong organization uniting the faithful. To city-dwellers—lonely, alienated, disillusioned with public affairs, stranded mortals groping for a sense of community—the church that called its members brother and sister filled an elemental need of human beings to belong. Another attraction for converts was the lack of painful or expensive initiation rites, which were standard requirements for entrance into Mithraism, a leading rival (see page 141 Chapter 7). Also, unlike Mithraism, the church welcomed women converts, who were often the first to join and brought their menfolk after them. Among other reasons, the church attracted women because it commanded that husbands treat their wives kindly, remain faithful, and provide for the children. The church won new converts and retained the loyalty of the old ones by providing social services for the poor and infirm, welcoming slaves, criminals, sinners, and other outcasts, and extending a hand of brotherhood and comfort during difficult times.

The ability of an evolving Christianity to assimilate elements from Greek philosophy and even from the mystery religions also contributed in no small measure to its growth. By becoming infused with Greek philosophy, Christianity was able to present itself in terms intelligible to those versed in Greek learning, and was thus able to attract some educated people. Because some Christian doctrines (a risen Savior-God, a Virgin and her child, life after death), practices (baptism), and holy days (December 25) either paralleled or were adopted from the mystery religions, it became relatively easy to win converts from these rivals.

Christianity and Rome

Generally tolerant of religions, the Roman government at first did not significantly interfere with Christianity. Indeed, Christianity benefited in many ways from its association with the Roman Empire. Christian missionaries, among them some of the Twelve Apostles who were the original followers of Christ, traveled throughout the Empire, over roads and across seas made safe by Roman arms. The common Greek dialect, the *koine,* spoken in most parts of the Empire, facilitated the task of missionaries. Had the Mediterranean world been fractured into separate and competing states, the spread of Christianity might well have faced an insurmountable obstacle. The universalism of the Roman Empire, which made citizenship available to peoples of many nationalities, prepared the way for the universalism of Christianity, which welcomed membership from all nations.

As the number of Christians increased, Roman officials started to pay the Christians more mind; they began to fear the Christians as subversives, preaching allegiance to God and not to Rome. To many Romans, Christians were enemies of the social order—strange people who would not accept the state gods, would not engage in Roman festivals, scorned gladiator contests, stayed away from public baths, glorified pacifism, refused to honor deceased emperors as gods, and worshiped a crucified criminal as Lord. Romans ultimately found in Christians a universal scapegoat for the ills burdening the Empire, such as famines, plagues, and military reverses. In an effort to stamp out Christianity, emperors resorted to persecution. Christians were imprisoned, beaten, starved, burned alive, torn apart by wild beasts in the arena for the amusement of the Romans, and crucified.

The persecutions fell into two main categories. The early persecutions, beginning with those incited under Emperor Nero in A.D.

64, were local and did not cause much loss of life; they were too sporadic to impede the growth of Christianity. But two centuries later, in A.D. 250, Emperor Decius unleashed a brief but brutal terror against the Christians that extended throughout much of the Empire. Decius' successors, Gallus (251–253) and Valerian (253–260), also issued anti-Christian edicts and had Christians murdered.

Christians lived in relative peace from 260 to 303, but then Diocletian (284–305) instituted the most severe persecution they had yet faced, lasting for three years in the west and longer in the east. The persecutions under the mid-third-century emperors and Diocletian caused the brutal deaths of many Christians. Some, fearful of torture and death, abandoned their faith. However, the persecutions did not last long enough to extirpate the new religion. Actually, they strengthened the determination of most of the faithful and won new converts who were awed by the extraordinary courage of the martyrs, who willingly died for their faith.

Unable to crush Christianity by persecution, Roman emperors decided to gain the support of the growing number of Christians within the Empire. In A.D. 313, Constantine, genuinely attracted to Christianity, issued the Edict of Milan granting toleration to Christians. By allowing for the free flow of Christian teachings and by instituting legislation favorable to the Church, Constantine and his successors accelerated the growth of Christianity and the Christianization of the Empire. By A.D. 392, Theodosius I had made Christianity the state religion of the Empire and declared the worship of pagan gods illegal. Persecution did not end, but its target had shifted from Christians to heretics.

Christianity and Greek Philosophy

Christianity synthesized both the Hebrew and the Greco-Roman traditions. Having emerged from Judaism, Christianity assimilated Hebrew monotheism and prophetic morality and retained the Old Testament as the Word of God. Without this Hebraic foundation,

Christianity cannot be understood. As the new religion evolved, it also assimilated elements of Greek philosophy. But there was a struggle between conservatives who wanted no dealings with pagan philosophy and those believers who recognized the value of Greek thought to Christianity.

To conservative church fathers, classical philosophy was all in error because it did not derive from divine revelation. They believed that whereas philosophers merely battled over words, Christianity possessed *the Word*, true wisdom revealed by God. As the final statement of God's truth, Christianity superseded both pagan philosophy and pagan religions. These conservatives feared that studying classical authors would contaminate Christian morality (did not Plato propose a community of wives and did not the dramatists treat violent passions?) and promote heresy (was not classical literature replete with references to pagan gods?). For these church fathers there could be no compromise between Greek philosophy and Christian revelation. They regarded their life's mission to be preaching the gospel of Jesus, which required no reinforcement from pagan ideas. "What indeed has Athens to do with Jerusalem?" asked Tertullian (A.D. 150–225). "With our faith, we desire no further belief. For this is our [first] faith that there is nothing which we ought to believe besides."[3]

Some early church fathers, however, defended the value of studying classical literature. Properly taught, such literature could aid in the moral development of children because it contained many examples of virtuous deeds. Some church fathers maintained that Greek philosophy contained a dim glimmer of God's truth, a pre-Christian insight into divine wisdom. Christ had corrected and fulfilled an insight reached by the philosophic mind. Knowledge of Greek philosophy, they argued, helped a Christian to explain his beliefs logically and to argue intelligently with pagan critics of Christian teachings.

Utilizing the language and categories of Greek philosophy, Christian intellectuals transformed Christianity from a simple ethical creed into a theoretical system, a theology.

This effort to express Christian beliefs in terms of Greek rationalism is referred to as the Hellenization of Christianity. Greek philosophy enabled Christians to explain in rational terms God's existence and revelation. Using philosophical concepts, church fathers attempted to show that the Trinity, although a mystery, did not violate the law of contradiction; that God the Father, God the Son, and God the Holy Spirit did not conflict with monotheism. They attributed the order and regularity of nature and the natural law, standing above human law—two cardinal principles of Stoic thought—to God the designer of the universe.

Christ was depicted as the divine *logos* (reason) in human form. The Stoic teaching that all people are fundamentally equal because they share in universal reason could be formulated in Christian terms—that all are united in Christ. Stoic ethics that stressed moderation, self-control, and brotherhood could be assimilated by Christian revelation. Particularly in Platonism, which drew a distinction between a world perceived by the senses and a higher order open to the intellect, Christian thinkers found a congenial medium for expressing Christian beliefs. The perfect and universal Forms, or Ideas, which Plato maintained were the true goal of knowledge and the source of ethical standards, were held by Christians to exist in God's mind.

That Greek philosophy exercised a hold over church doctrine is of immense importance; it meant that rational thought, the priceless achievement of the Greek mind, was not lost. But this Hellenization of Christianity was not a triumph of classicism over Christianity. The reverse is the essential truth: Christianity triumphed over Hellenism; Greek philosophy had to sacrifice its essential autonomy to the requirements of Christian revelation. Although Christianity made use of Greek philosophy, Christian truth rested on faith, not reason. As Tertullian stated, "And the Son of God died; it is by all means to be believed, because it is absurd. And He was buried, and rose again; the fact is certain because it is impossible."[4]

The Antioch Chalice. From the fourth century A.D., this cup is the earliest surviving Christian chalice. The transformation of the wine of the mass into the very blood of Christ was central to Christian worship. In later medieval times, historical kings and knights in literature would search for the original chalice of the Last Supper, the Holy Grail. (*The Metropolitan Museum of Art, The Cloisters Collection, 1950*)

Growth of Christian Organization, Doctrine, and Attitudes

Early in its history the church developed along hierarchical lines. Those members of the Christian community who had the authority to preside over the celebration of the Mass—breaking bread and offering wine as Christ had done in the Last Supper—were called either priests or bishops. Gradually the designation *bishop* was reserved for the one clergyman in the community with the authority to resolve disputes over doctrines and practices. Regarded as the successors to Christ's Twelve Apostles, bishops supervised religious activities within their regions. The most influential bishops ministered to the leading cities of the Empire—Rome, Alexandria, Antioch, and Milan.

The Primacy of the Bishop of Rome

The bishop of Rome, later to be called the pope, claimed primacy over the other bishops, maintaining that the Apostle Peter founded the Roman see (official seat of authority), and that both Peter and Paul were martyred in Rome. Moreover, as the traditional capital of the Empire, Rome seemed the logical choice to serve as the center of the church.

In developing the case for their supremacy over the church organization, bishops of Rome increasingly referred to the famous New Testament passage in which Jesus says to his Disciple Simon (also called Peter): " 'And I tell you, you are Peter, and on this rock I will build my church.' " (Matthew 16:18) Because *Peter* in Greek means *rock (petra)*, it was argued that Christ had chosen Peter to succeed him as ruler of the universal church. It was commonly accepted that Saint Peter had established a church in Rome and was martyred there, so it was argued further that the Roman bishop inherited the power that Christ had passed on to Peter. Thus, the argument continued, the bishop of Rome held a unique office: of all the bishops, only he had inherited the powers originally granted by Christ to Peter. Because the Apostles had been subordinate to Peter, so too must the bishops defer to Peter's successor. In the fourth and fifth centuries, popes took a leading part in doctrinal disputes that threatened to divide the church. More and more Christians came to esteem Rome as the champion of true Christianity.

The Rise of Monasticism

Not all Christians welcomed the growing wealth and power of the church. Inspired by Jesus' example of self-denial and seeking to escape from the agonies and corruptions of this world, some ardent Christians withdrew to deserts and mountains in search of spiritual renewal. In their zeal for holiness they sometimes practiced extreme forms of asceticism—self-flogging, wearing spiked corsets, eating only herbs, or living for years on a column thirty feet above the ground.

Gradually, colonies of these hermits sprang up, particularly in Egypt; in time, the leaders of these monastic communities drew up written rules for prayer and work. In the first half of the fourth century, Saint Pachomius set up several regulated monasteries in Egypt, and the first convent was founded about 320 in the Egyptian desert by Mary, Pachomius' sister. Saint Basil (c. 329–c. 379), a Greek who was bishop of Caesarea in Palestine, established the rule that became the standard of monasteries in the East. Basil required monks to refrain from bodily abuses and to engage in manual labor. Through farming, weaving, and construction, monks could make a monastery self-supporting and have the means to assist the needy. Basil forbade his monks to own personal property other than clothing and insisted that they spend much of their time in silence.

The monastic ideal spread from east to west. Saint Martin of Tours established a monastery in Gaul, which actively converted the pagan peasants. But the principal figure in the shaping of monasticism in the West was Saint Benedict, who founded a monastery at Monte Cassino, Italy, in 529. The rule of Saint Benedict called for the monks to live in poverty and to study, labor, and obey the abbot, the head of the monastery. Monks were required to pray often, work hard, talk little, and surrender private property. In imposing discipline and regulations, Benedict eliminated the excessive and eccentric individualism of the early monks; he socialized and institutionalized the spiritual impulse that led monks

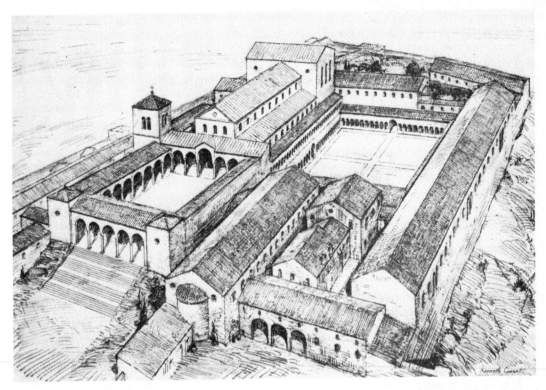

Plan of Monte Cassino Abbey. Founded by Saint Benedict in 529, Monte Cassino Abbey still serves as a religious community today, although the buildings have had to be rebuilt several times after the ravages of war. Benedict's rule instructed monks to live in poverty, to labor, to study, and to aid the sick and the poor. (*From Kenneth John Conant,* The Pelican History of Art: Carolingian and Romanesque Architecture, 800–1200 [*Penguin Books, 1959*], *Reprinted by permission of Penguin Books Ltd.*)

to withdraw from the world. Benedict demonstrated the same genius for administration that Romans had shown in organizing and governing their Empire. Benedict's rule became the standard for monasteries in Western Europe.

Doctrinal Disputes

Christ's sayings and actions were preserved by word of mouth. Sometime around A.D. 66–70, Saint Mark formulated the Christian message from this oral tradition and perhaps from some material that had been put in writing earlier. Later Saint Matthew and Saint Luke, relying heavily on Mark's account, wrote somewhat longer Gospels. The Gospels of Mark, Matthew, and Luke are called *synoptic* because their approach to Jesus is very similar. The remaining Gospel, written by Saint John, varies significantly from the Synoptic Gospels. The Synoptic Gospels, The Gospel According to Saint John, Acts of the Apostles, the twenty-one Epistles, including those written by Saint Paul, and Revelation constitute the twenty-seven Books of the Christian New Testament. Christians also accepted the Old Testament of the Hebrews as God's Word.

The early Christians had a Bible and a clergy to teach it. But Holy Writ could be interpreted differently by equally sincere believers, and controversies over doctrine threatened the unity of the early church. The most important controversy concerned how people viewed the relationship between God and Christ. Arius (A.D. 250–336), a Greek priest in Alexandria, led one faction; he denied the complete divinity of Christ—one of the basic tenets of the church. To Arius, Christ was more than man but less than God; the Father and the Son did not possess the same nature or essence. Arius said that there was no permanent union between God and Christ; the Father alone is eternal and truly God.

The Council of Nicaea (325 A.D.), the first assembly of bishops from all parts of the Roman world, was called to settle the controversy. The Council condemned Arius and ruled that God and Christ were of the same substance, coequal and coeternal. The position adopted at Nicaea became the basis of the Nicene Creed, which remains the official doctrine of the church. Although Arianism, the name given Arius' heresy, won converts for a time, it eventually lost supporters.

Another controversy arose over the relationship between Christ's divine and human natures. Some theologians, viewing Christ as a great ethical soul, tended to emphasize his human nature at the expense of his divine nature. Other theologians argued that Christ's human nature had been absorbed by his divine nature—in effect, that Christ possessed a single divine nature. The Council of Chalcedon in A.D. 451 formulated the orthodox position that Christ is truly God and truly man, and that two distinct natures, one divine and the other human, are joined and preserved in his person. The other views were declared heretical but continued to persist in the eastern part of the Empire.

The controversies over Christ's nature and his relationship to God were by no means theological hairsplitting. What was at stake was the central message of Christianity: Christ had descended to earth to show men and women the path to heaven, and they could achieve salvation by following the Son who was one with the Father.

Christianity and Society

While salvation was their ultimate aim, Christians still had to dwell within the world and deal with its imperfections. In the process, Christian thinkers challenged some of the mores of Greco-Roman society and formulated attitudes that would endure for centuries.

The first Christians condemned warfare, regarding acts of revenge and the shedding of blood as a violation of Christ's precepts. But after Roman emperors professed Christianity, Christians began to serve the government with greater frequency. With the barbarians menacing the borders, these officials could not advocate pacifism. Christian theorists began to argue that under certain circumstances—to punish injustice or to restore peace—war was just. But even such wars must not entail unnecessary violence.

Christians denounced the gladiator combats and contests between men and beasts as bloodlust and murder. Nevertheless, these spectacles persisted even after the majority of the population had converted to Christianity. When the games finally ended, it was probably due more to the growing poverty of the Western Empire than to the Christian conscience.

Sharing in the patriarchal tradition of Jewish society, Saint Paul subjected the wife to her husband's authority. "Wives, be subject to your husbands, as to the Lord. For the husband is the head of the wife as Christ is the head of the church." (Ephesians 5:22–23) Paul wanted women to remain quiet at church meetings. "If there is anything they desire to know, let them ask their husbands at home. For it is shameful for a woman to speak in church." (I Corinthians 14:35) But Paul also held that all are baptized in Christ: "There is neither Jew nor Greek, there is neither slave nor free, there is neither male nor female; for you are all one in Christ Jesus." (Galatians 3:28) Consequently, both men and women possessed moral autonomy. The early church held to strict standards on sexual matters. It condemned adultery and held virginity for spiritual reasons in high esteem.

Christians waged no war against slavery, which was widely practiced and universally accepted in the ancient world. Saint Paul commanded slaves to obey their masters, and many Christians were themselves slave owners. However, Christians taught that slaves too were children of God, sought their conversion, and urged owners not to treat them harshly.

Saint Augustine: The Christian World-View

During the early history of Christianity, many learned men, "fathers of the church," explained and defended church teachings. Most of the leading early fathers wrote in Greek, but in the middle of the fourth century, three great Latin writers—Saint Jerome, Saint Ambrose, and Saint Augustine—profoundly influenced the course of Christianity in the West.

As a youth, Saint Jerome (A.D. c. 340–420) studied Latin literature in Rome. Throughout his life, he remained an admirer of Cicero, Virgil, Lucretius, and other great Latin writers, and he defended the study of classical literature by Christians. Baptized in his mid-twenties, Jerome became attracted to the ascetic life and lived for a while as a hermit in the desert of Chalcis near Antioch. After becoming a priest, he visited holy places in Palestine and intensely studied the Scriptures in Constantinople. Returning to Rome, Jerome became secretary to Pope Damasus and spiritual adviser to a group of wealthy women attracted to the ascetic life. Facing criticism for his attacks on the luxurious living and laxness of the clergy, Jerome left Rome. He established a monastery near Bethlehem, where he devoted himself to prayer and study.

Saint Jerome wrote about the lives of the saints and promoted the spread of monasticism. But his greatest achievement was the translation of the Old and New Testaments from Greek and Hebrew into Latin. Jerome's text, the common or Vulgate version of the Bible, became the official edition of the Bible for the western church.

Saint Ambrose (A.D. 340–397), bishop of Milan, Italy, composed religious hymns and wrote books on Scripture, dogma, and morality. In his work on the duties of the clergy, Ambrose provided humane rules for dealing with the poor, the old, the sick, and the orphaned. He urged clerics not to pursue wealth, but to exercise humility and to avoid favoring the rich over the poor. Ambrose sought to defend the autonomy of the church against the power of the state. Emperors are not the judges of bishops, he wrote. His dictum that "The Emperor is within the church, not above it" became a cardinal principle of the medieval church.

The most important Christian theoretician in the Late Roman Empire was Saint Augustine (A.D. 354–430), bishop of Hippo in North Africa. Born in the North African province of Numidia, Augustine attended school at Carthage where he studied the Latin classics. During his student days, Augustine took a concubine, by whom he had a son. Struggling to find meaning in a world that abounded with evil, Augustine turned to Manichaeism, an oriental sect whose central doctrine was the struggle of the universal forces of light and good against those of darkness and evil. But still Augustine, now a professor of rhetoric, felt spiritually restless. In Milan, Augustine, inspired by the sermons of Ambrose, abandoned Manichaeism, and devoted his life to following Christ's teachings. After serving as a priest, he was appointed bishop of Hippo in 395.

In his autobiography, the *Confessions*, Augustine described his spiritual quest and appealed to devotees of Manichaeism and to adherents of pagan philosophy to embrace Christianity. Augustine wrote *The City of God* at the turn of the fifth century when the Greco-Roman world-view was disintegrating and the Roman world-state was collapsing. Augustine became the principal architect of the Christian outlook that succeeded a dying classicism.

In 410, when Augustine was in his fifties, Visigoths sacked Rome—a disaster for which the classical consciousness was unprepared. Throughout the Empire people panicked. Pagans blamed the tragedy on Christianity. The Christians had predicted the end of the world, they said, and by refusing to offer sacrifices to ancient gods, Christians had turned these deities against Rome. Pagans also accused Christians of undermining the empire by refusing to serve in the army. Even Christians expressed anxiety. Why were the righteous also suffering? Where was the kingdom of God on earth that had been prophesied?

Augustine's *The City of God* was a response to the crisis of the Roman Empire in the same manner that Plato's *Republic* was a reaction to the crisis of the Athenian polis. But whereas Plato expressed hope that a state founded on rational principles could remedy the abuses of Athenian society, Augustine maintained that the worldly city could never be the central concern of a Christian. He said that the ideal state could not be realized on earth, that it belonged only to heaven. The misfortunes of Rome, therefore, should not distress a Christian unduly, for Christianity belonged to the realm of the spirit and could not be identified with any state. The collapse of Rome did not diminish the greatness of Christianity, for the true Christian was a citizen of a heavenly city that could not possibly be pillaged by ungodly barbarians, but would endure forever. Compared to God's heavenly city, the decline of Rome was unimportant. The welfare of Christianity was not to be identified with Rome's material progress or even its existence.

Augustine provided comfort to Christians anguished by Rome's misfortunes. They were assured that the decay or prosperity of Rome was ultimately meaningless compared to the bliss that awaited them in the heavenly city. They were told that Christianity was measured neither by Rome's successes nor by its failures. What really mattered in history, said Augustine, was not the coming to be or the passing away of cities and empires, but the individual's entrance into heaven or hell.

Yet Augustine was still a man of this world. He stipulated that although the earthly city was the very opposite of the heavenly city, it was a reality that people must face. Christians could not reject their city entirely, but must bend it to fit a Christian pattern. The city that someday would rise from the ruins of Rome must be based upon Christian principles. Warfare, economic activity, education, and the rearing of children should all be conducted in a Christian spirit. Although the City of Man was ever evil, imperfect, and of no consequence in comparison to the City of God, it was not about to disappear and be replaced by the Kingdom of God on earth. The church could not neglect the state, but must guide it to protect human beings from their own sinful natures. The state must employ repression and punishment to restrain people, who were inherently sinful, from destroying each other and the few good men and women that God had elected to save from hell. But the earthly city would always be inhabited predominantly by sinners, said Augustine. People should be under no illusion that it could be transformed into the City of God, for everywhere in human society we see

love for all those things that prove so vain and . . . breed so many heartaches, troubles, griefs, and fears; such insane joys in discord, strife, and war; such wrath and plots of enemies . . . such fraud and theft and robbery; such perfidy . . . homicide and murder, cruelty and savagery, lawlessness and lust; all the shameless passions of the impure—fornication and adultery . . . and countless other uncleanness too nasty to be mentioned; the sins against religion—sacrilege and heresy . . . the iniquities against our neighbors—calumnies and cheating, lies and false witness, violence to persons and property . . . and the innumerable other miseries and maladies that fill the world, yet escape attention.[5]

Yet, God, infinitely compassionate, still cared for his creation, said Augustine. By coming to earth as man in the person of Jesus Christ and by enduring punishment and suffering,

God had emancipated human beings from the bondage of original sin.

But Augustine did not hold that by his death Christ had opened the door to heaven for all. The majority of humanity remained condemned to eternal punishment, said Augustine; only a handful had the gift of faith and the promise of heaven. People could not by their own efforts overcome a sinful nature; a moral and spiritual regeneration stemmed not from human will power but from God's grace. And God determined who would be saved and who would be damned.

Whereas the vast majority of people, said Augustine, were citizens of a doomed earthly city, the small number endowed with God's grace constituted the City of God. These people lived on earth as visitors only, for they awaited deliverance to the Kingdom of Christ, where together with the good angels and God they would know perfect happiness. But the permanent inhabitants of the earthly city were destined for eternal punishment in hell. A perpetual conflict existed between the two cities and between their inhabitants; one city stood for sin and corruption, the other for God's truth and perfection.

For Augustine, the highest good was not of this world but consisted of eternal life with God. Augustine's distinction between this higher world of perfection and a lower world of corruption remained influential throughout the Middle Ages. However, the church, rejecting Augustine's doctrine that only a limited number of people are predestined for heaven or hell, emphasized that Christ had made possible the salvation of all who would embrace the opportunity.

Augustine repudiated the distinguishing feature of classical humanism—the autonomy of reason. For him, ultimate wisdom could not be achieved through rational thought alone; reason had to be guided by faith. Without faith there could be no true knowledge, no understanding. Philosophy had no validity if it did not first accept as absolutely true the existence of God and the authority of his revelation. Valid ethical standards could not be formulated by reason alone, but were

revealed to people by the living God. Christian truth did not rest on theoretical excellence or logical consistency; it was true because its source was God.

Augustine's belief contrasts with that of Socrates, who insisted that through rational reflection each individual could arrive at standards of good and evil. For the humanist Socrates, ultimate values were something that the individual could grasp through thought alone and could defend rationally. Augustine insisted that individuals, without divine guidance, lacked the capacity to comprehend ultimate truth or to regenerate themselves morally, and that without God they could not attain wisdom nor liberate themselves from sin.

Thus, against the classical view that asserted the primacy of reason, Augustine opposed the primacy of faith. But he did not necessarily regard reason as an enemy of faith, and he did not call for an end to rational speculation. Augustine possessed rare intelligence; a student of the classics and an admirer of Platonism, he respected the power of thought. What he denied of the classical view was that reason *alone* could attain wisdom. The wisdom that Augustine sought was Christian wisdom, knowledge of God and God's expectations for humanity. The starting point for this knowledge, he said, was belief in God and the Scriptures. For Augustine, secular knowledge for its own sake was of little value; the true significance of knowledge lay in its role as a tool for comprehending God's will. Augustine adapted the classical intellectual tradition to the requirements of Christian revelation.

With Augustine, the human-centered outlook of classical humanism—which for centuries had been undergoing transformation—gave way to a God-centered world-view. The fulfillment of God's will, not the full development of human talent, became the central concern of life.

Augustinian Christianity is a living philosophy because it still has something vital to say about the human condition. To those who believe that people have the intelligence and good will to transform their earthly city into a rational and just community that promotes human betterment, Augustine warns of human sinfulness, weakness, and failure. He reminds the optimist that progress is not certain, that people, weak and ever prone to wickedness, are their own worst enemies, that success is illusory, and that misery is the essential human reality.

Christianity and Classical Humanism: Alternate World-Views

Christianity and classical humanism are the two principal components of the Western tradition. The value that modern Western civilization places on the individual derives ultimately from classical humanism and the Judeo-Christian tradition. Classical humanists believed that individual worth came from the individual's capacity to reason, to shape his character and his life according to rational standards. Christianity also places great stress on the individual. In the Christian view, God cares for each person; he wants people to behave righteously and to enter heaven; Christ died for all because he loves humanity. Christianity espouses active love and genuine concern for fellow human beings. Without God, people are as Augustine described them—"foul, crooked, sordid, bespotted, vicious"; with God, the human personality can undergo a moral transformation and become loving, good, and ethically free.

But Christianity and classical humanism also represent two essentially different world-views. The triumph of the Christian outlook signified a break with the essential meaning of classical humanism; it pointed to the end of the world of antiquity and the beginning of an age of faith, the Middle Ages. With the victory of Christianity, the ultimate goal of life shifted. Life's purpose was no longer to achieve excellence in this world through the full and creative development of human talent, but to attain salvation in a heavenly city. A person's worldly accomplishments amounted to very little if he or she did not accept God and his revelation.

In the classical view, history had no ultimate end, no ultimate meaning; periods of happiness and misery repeated themselves endlessly. In the Christian view, history is filled with spiritual meaning. It is the profound drama of individuals struggling to overcome their original sin in order to gain eternal happiness in heaven. History began with Adam and Eve's defiance of God and would end when Christ returns to earth, when evil is eradicated, when God's will prevails.

Classicism held that there was no authority higher than reason; Christianity teaches that without God as the starting point, knowledge is formless, purposeless, and prone to error. Classicism held that ethical standards were laws of nature that reason could discover. Through reason, individuals could arrive at those values by which they should regulate their lives. Reason would enable them to govern desires and will; it would show them where their behavior was wrong and teach them how to correct it. Because individuals sought what was best for themselves, they would obey the voice of reason. Early Christianity, on the other hand, maintained that ethical standards emanated from the personal will of God. Without obedience to God's commands, people would remain wicked forever; the human will, essentially sinful, could not be transformed by the promptings of reason. Only when individuals turned to God for forgiveness and guidance—only then would they find the inner strength to overcome their sinful nature. People cannot perfect themselves through scientific knowledge; it is spiritual insight and belief in God that they require and that must serve as the first principle of their lives. For classicism, the ultimate good was sought through thought and action; for Christianity, ultimate good comes through knowing and loving God.

But Christian thinkers respected Greek philosophy and did not seek to eradicate the intellectual heritage of Greece. Rather, they sought to fit it into a Christian framework. By preserving the Greek philosophical tra-

Chronology 8.1 Early Christianity

A.D. 29	The crucifixion of Jesus
c. 34–64	Missionary activity of Saint Paul
c. 66–70	The Gospel According to Mark is written
250–260	A decade of brutal persecution of Christians by the Romans
313	Constantine grants toleration of Christianity
320	The first convent is founded
325	The Council of Nicaea rules that God and Christ are of the same substance, coequal and coeternal
392	Theodosius I makes Christianity the state religion
430	Death of Saint Augustine
451	The Council of Chalcedon rules that Christ is truly God and truly man
529	Monte Cassino is founded by Saint Benedict

dition, Christian thinkers performed a task of immense historical significance.

Christianity inherited the Hebrew view of the overriding importance of God for humanity: God makes life intelligible and purposeful. For the Christian, God is a living being, loving and compassionate, in whose company one seeks to spend eternity; one knows God essentially through faith and feeling. Although the Greek philosophers had a conception of God, it was not comparable to the God of Hebrews and Christians. For the Greek, God was a logical abstraction, a principle of order, the supreme good, the highest truth; God was a concept, impersonal, unfeeling, and uninvolved with human concerns. The Greeks approached God through the intellect, not the heart; they neither loved nor worshiped God. In addition, because religion was at the periphery, not the center, of classical humanism, the idea of God did not carry the same significance that it did for Christianity.

In the classical world, the political community was the avenue to justice, happiness, and self-realization. In early Christianity, the good life was not identified with worldly achievement but with life eternal, and the ideal commonwealth could only be one that was founded and ruled by Christ. It was entrance into God's kingdom that each person must make the central aim of life. For the next thousand years, this distinction between heaven and earth, this otherworldly, theocentric outlook would define the Western mentality.

In the Late Roman Empire, when classical values were in decay, Christianity was a dynamic and creative movement. Possessing both institutional and spiritual strength, Christianity survived the fall of Rome. Because it retained elements of Greco-Roman civilization and taught a high morality, Christianity served as a civilizing agent in the centuries that followed Rome's collapse. Indeed, Christianity was the essential shaper of the European civilization that emerged in the Middle Ages.

Notes

1. Andrew M. Greeley, "Hippie Hero? Superpatriot? Superstar? A Christmas Biography,"

New York Times Magazine (December 23, 1973), p. 28.

2. The biblical quotations are used with permission from The Holy Bible, Revised Standard Version (New York: Thomas Nelson & Sons, 1952). The Revised Standard Version is the text used for biblical quotations throughout, except when noted otherwise.

3. Tertullian, "On Prescription Against Heretics," Ch. 7, in Alexander Roberts and James Donaldson, *The Anti-Nicene Fathers* (New York: Charles Scribners Sons, 1918), III, p. 246.

4. Tertullian, "On the Flesh of Christ," in ibid., p. 525.

5. Saint Augustine, *The City of God.* An abridged version from the translation by Gerald G. Walsh, et al. (Garden City, N.Y.: Doubleday Image Books, 1958), p. 519.

Suggested Reading

Armstrong, A. H., and R. A. Markus, *Christian Faith and Greek Philosophy* (1960). A presentation of the dialogue between Christianity and Greek philosophy.

Chadwick, Henry, *The Early Church* (1967). A survey of early Christianity in its social and ideological context.

Cochrane, C. N., *Christianity and Classical Culture* (1957). A study of thought from Augustus to Augustine; difficult, but worth the effort.

Davies, J. G., *The Early Christian Church* (1967). A splendid introduction to the first five centuries of Christianity.

Dodds, E. R., *Pagan and Christian in an Age of Anxiety* (1965). Examines the philosophical and spiritual climate from the accession of Marcus Aurelius to the conversion of Constantine.

Enslin, M. S., *Christian Beginnings* (1956). Strong on the Jewish background to Jesus.

Grant, Michael, *Jesus* (1977). A recent examination of the Gospels.

Jaeger, Werner, *Early Christianity and Greek Paideia* (1961). How the church fathers perpetuated and transformed Greek ideas.

Latourette, K. S., *A History of Christianity* (1953). Clearly written and eminently readable.

Mattingly, Harold, *Christianity in the Roman Empire* (1967). A brief, well-informed survey.

Nock, A. D., *Early Christianity and Its Hellenistic Background* (1964). A superb scholarly treatment of the relationship of Christianity to the wider cultural setting.

Nock, A. D., *St. Paul* (1963). A highly respected account of the principal Christian Apostle to the Greco-Roman world.

Pelikan, Jaroslav, *The Christian Tradition* (1971), vol. 1, *The Emergence of the Catholic Tradition.* The first of a five-volume series on the history of Christian doctrine.

Review Questions

1. Why does the life of Jesus present a problem to the historian?

2. What were Jesus' basic teachings?

3. What is the relationship of early Christianity to Judaism?

4. What was the historical significance of the belief in Jesus' resurrection?

5. How did Saint Paul transform a Jewish sect into a world religion?

6. What factors contributed to the triumph of Christianity in the Roman Empire?

7. Why did some early Christian thinkers object to the study of classical literature? What arguments were advanced by the defenders of classical learning? What was the outcome of this debate? Why was it significant?

8. What arguments were advanced by the bishop of Rome to support his supremacy over the church organization?

9. What is the historical significance of Saint Basil, Saint Martin of Tours, and Saint Benedict?

10. What is the signficance of the controversy over Christ's nature and his relationship to God?

11. What were Saint Augustine's attitudes toward the fall of Rome, the worldly city, humanity, and Greek philosophy?

12. Compare and contrast the world-views of early Christianity and classical humanism.

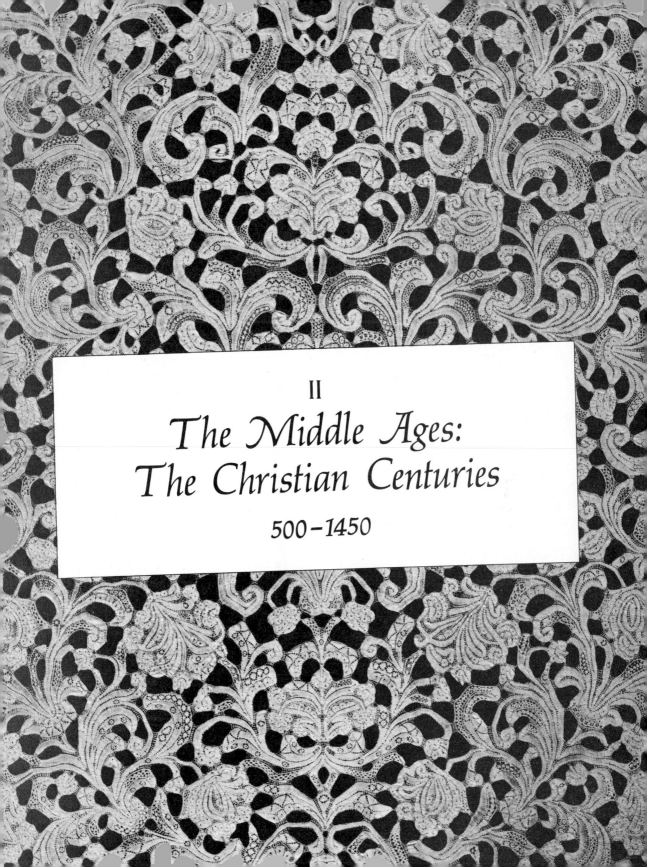

II
The Middle Ages:
The Christian Centuries
500–1450

9

The Rise of Europe: Fusion of Classical, Christian, and German Traditions

*T*he triumph of Christianity and the establishment of Germanic Kingdoms on once-Roman lands constituted a new phase in Western history: the end of the ancient world and the beginning of the Middle Ages, a period that spanned a thousand years. In the ancient world the locus of Greco-Roman civilization was the Mediterranean Sea; the heartland of medieval civilization shifted to the north, to regions of Europe that Greco-Roman civilization had barely penetrated. During the Middle Ages, a common European civilization evolved that integrated Christian, Greco-Roman, and Germanic elements. Christianity was at the center of medieval civilization; Rome was the spiritual capital, and Latin the language of intellectual life; Germanic customs pervaded social and legal relationships.

An Age of Transition

The Medieval East: Byzantium and Islam, an Overview

Three new civilizations based on religion emerged on the ruins of the Roman Empire: Byzantium, Islam, and Latin Christendom (western and central Europe). Although the Roman Empire in the west fell to the German tribes, the eastern provinces survived. They did so because they were richer and more populous and because the main thrust of the Germanic and Hunnish invaders had been directed at the west. In the eastern regions, Byzantine civilization took shape. Its religion was Christianity, its culture Greek, and its machinery of administration Roman. The capital, Constantinople, was built on the site of the ancient Greek city of Byzantium, on a peninsula in the Straits of the Bosporus, the dividing line between Asia and Europe. Constantinople was a fortress city perfectly situated to resist attacks from land and sea.

Hagia Sophia. The extensive interior mosaics that once transformed the vaults of Hagia Sophia into the golden sky of heaven linked this Byzantine structure with Early Christian architecture. But the heights and vast domed interior were new and the hallmark of the First Golden Age of Byzantine art. The emperors strongly identified themselves with Christ, and elaborate church ceremonies necessitated the presence of the emperor. Hagia Sophia provided the dramatic setting. © *Bruno Barbey/Magnum)*

Byzantium During the Early Middle Ages (500–1050), Byzantine civilization was economically and culturally far more advanced than the Latin West. At a time when few Westerners (Latin Christians) could read or write, Byzantine scholars studied the literature, philosophy, science, and law of ancient Greece and Rome. Whereas trade and urban life had greatly declined in the West, Con-stantinople was a magnificent Byzantine city of schools, libraries, open squares, and bustling markets.

Over the centuries, many differences developed between the Byzantine church and the Roman church. The pope resisted domination by the Byzantine emperor, and the Byzantines would not accept the pope as head of all Christians. The two churches quarreled over ceremonies, holy days, the display of images, and the rights of the clergy. The final break came in 1054; the Christian church split into the Roman Catholic in the West and the Eastern (Greek) Orthodox in the East, a division that still persists.

Political and cultural differences widened the rift between Latin Christendom and Byzantium. Latin Christians refused to recognize that the Byzantine emperors were, as they claimed, successors to the Roman emperors. In the Byzantine empire, Greek was the language of religion and intellectual life; in the West it was Latin.

Byzantine emperors were absolute rulers who held that God had chosen them to rule and to institute the Lord's will on earth. As successors to the Roman emperors, they claimed to rule all the lands once part of the Roman Empire. Emperor Justinian, who reigned from 527 to 565, sought to regain the lands in the western Mediterranean that had been conquered by Germanic invaders. During his reign, Byzantine forces retook North Africa from the Vandals, part of southern Spain from the Visigoths, and Italy from the Ostrogoths, establishing a western capital at Ravenna.

The long and costly wars drained the treasury, however, and led to the neglect of defenses in the Near East and the Balkan Peninsula. The Balkans were invaded by Slavic tribes from the Black Sea region and by Avars and Bulgars originally from Central Asia; Syria was ravaged by the Persians. Nor were the conquered territories in the west secure. The Germanic Lombards, who had moved into northern Italy in the late sixth century, conquered much Byzantine territory that had been recently recovered from the Ostrogoths, and by 629 the Visigoths had driven the Byzantines from Spain.

In the early seventh century, the Byzantines faced a renewed threat from the Persians, who seized the Byzantine provinces of Syria, Palestine, and Egypt. In an all-out effort, however, Emperor Heraclius (ruled 610–641) regained the provinces and in 627 crushed the Persians near the ruins of the ancient

Ivory of Romanos II. Sculpture survived during the Byzantine period in the form of religious ivory panels. The figures of the emperor and empress exhibit the favored style: the bodies are elongated, stiff, and weightless. (*Cabinet des Médailles, Paris/Hirmer Fotoarchiv*)

city of Nineveh. But an exhausted Byzantine Empire had become vulnerable to the Muslim Arabs, who had burst out of the Arabian Desert seeking to propagate their new faith (see page 181). By 642 the Arabs had stripped the Byzantine Empire of Syria, Palestine, and Egypt, and by the beginning of the eighth century, they had taken North Africa. Near the end of the seventh century and again in

Islamic Astrolabe. The astrolabe, which measured latitude, served both an astronomical and an astrological purpose; it was used to tell the time of day, to locate the position of the planets, and to prepare horoscopes. (*Mas, Barcelona*)

717, the Muslims besieged Constantinople. But the Byzantine fleet was armed with a new weapon, "Greek fire"—a fiery explosive liquid shot from tubes, which set enemy ships afire and made blazing pools of flame on the water's surface. Thus, the light Byzantine ships were able to repulse the better-built Arab ships.

The Arabs' failure to take Constantinople was crucial not only for the Byzantine Empire, but also for the history of Christianity. Had this Christian fortress fallen in the eighth century, the Arabs would have been able to overrun the Balkan Peninsula and sail up the Danube River into the European heartland. After this defeat, however, Islamic armies largely concentrated their conquests outside Europe.

From the late ninth to the early eleventh

centuries, the Byzantine forces grew stronger and even took the offensive against the Muslims. But soon new enemies threatened. By 1071 the Normans from France had driven the Byzantines from Italy; in the same year, the Seljuk Turks defeated the Byzantines in Asia Minor and subjugated most of the peninsula, the heart of the Byzantine Empire. Internal dissensions, however, led to the breakup of the Seljuk Empire.

Seeking to exploit Seljuk weakness and to regain lost territories, the Byzantines appealed to Latin Christians for help. Although European Christians had little love for the Byzantines, they did want to free Christian holy places from the Muslims. For this purpose, they undertook a series of Crusades beginning in the late eleventh century (see Chapter 10). In 1204, during the Fourth Crusade, Latin Christian knights (greedy for wealth) and Venetian merchants (eager to gain control of the rich Byzantine trade) decided to take Constantinople rather than to fight the Muslims.

The Latin Christians looted the city, destroying sacred books, vandalizing churches, and carrying huge amounts of gold, jewels, and works of art back to western Europe. They also seized islands along Constantinople's major trade routes, set up kingdoms on Byzantine lands, and tried to force Latin forms of Christianity upon the Byzantine Greeks. The Orthodox Greeks resisted, and for nearly sixty years Latin and Greek Christians fought one another. Not until 1261 were the Westerners driven from Constantinople. The Byzantine Empire regained its independence, but its power was disastrously weakened. Crushing taxes, decreasing agricultural production, declining trade, and civil war continued to weaken the tottering empire.

The deathblow to the empire was dealt by another group of Turks. The Ottoman Turks had accepted Islam and had begun to build an empire. They drove the Byzantines from Asia Minor and conquered much of the Balkans. By the beginning of the fifteenth century, the Byzantine Empire consisted of only two small territories in Greece and the city

Mosque of Cordoba. The richness of Islamic culture and architecture is evident in Spain where Muslim rule lingered until the conquest of Granada in 1492. The arch of alternating stone would find its way into Christian churches, most memorably at Vezelay in southern France. (*Mas, Barcelona*)

of Constantinople. In 1453 the Ottoman Turks broke through Constantinople's great walls, looted the city, and slaughtered thousands of its inhabitants. After more than a thousand years, the Byzantine Empire had come to an end.

During its thousand-year history, Byzantium made a significant impact on world history. First, it prevented the Muslim Arabs from advancing into eastern Europe. Had the Arabs broken through Byzantine defenses, much of Europe might have been converted to the new faith of Islam. Another far-reaching effect arose under Justinian when the laws of ancient Rome were codified. This monumental achievement preserved Roman law's principles of reason and justice. Today's legal codes in much of Europe and Latin America

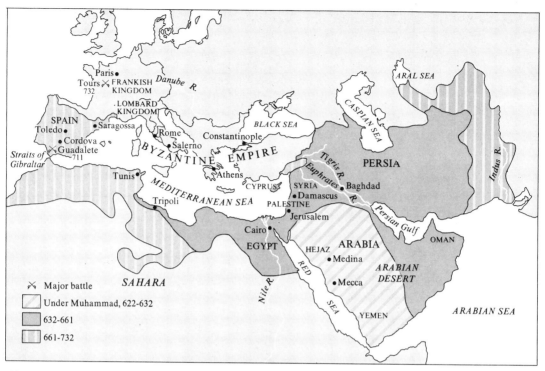

Map 9.1 The Expansion of Islam, 622–732

trace their roots to the Roman law recorded by Justinian's lawyers. The Byzantines also preserved the philosophy, science, mathematics, and literature of ancient Greece. Contacts with Byzantine civilization stimulated learning in both the Islamic world to the east and Latin Christendom to the west. Speros Vryonis, a student of Byzantine civilization, states: "The Byzantines carried the torch of civilization unextinguished at a time when the barbarous Germanic and Slav tribes had reduced much of Europe to near chaos: and they maintained this high degree of civilization until Western Europe gradually emerged and began to take form."[1] Byzantium also carried a higher civilization and Orthodox Christianity to the Slavic peoples, including the Russians, of eastern Europe. Byzantium gave the Slavs legal principles, art forms, and an alphabet—the Cyrillic, based on the Greek—that enabled them to write in their own languages.

Islam A second civilization to arise after Rome's fall was based on the vital new religion of Islam, which emerged in the seventh century among the Arabs of Arabia. Its founder was Muhammad (c. 570–632), a prosperous merchant in the trading city of Mecca. When Muhammad was about forty, he believed that he was visited by the Angel Gabriel, who ordered him to "recite in the name of the Lord!" Transformed by this vision, Muhammad was convinced that he had been chosen to serve as a prophet.

Although most desert Arabs worshipped tribal gods, in the towns and trading centers many Arabs were familiar with Judaism and Christianity, and some had accepted the idea of one God. Rejecting the many deities of the tribal religions, Muhammad offered the Arabs a new monotheistic faith, *Islam,* which means "surrender to Allah" (God).

Islam standards of morality and rules governing daily life are set by the Koran, which Muslims believe contains the words of Allah as revealed to Muhammad. Muslims believe that their religion is the completion and perfection of Judaism and Christianity. They regard the ancient Hebrew prophets as messengers of God and value their message of compassion and the oneness of humanity. Muslims also regard Jesus as a great prophet, but do not believe that he was divine.

The merchants of Mecca would not accept this new faith, and to escape persecution, Muhammad and his small band of followers left Mecca in 622 for Medina, a town about 200 miles away. Their flight, known as the *Hegira*, or "breaking of former ties," is one of the most important events in Muslim history and is commemorated by yearly pilgrimages. The date of the Hegira became year one of the Muslim calendar.

In Medina, Muhammad gained converts and won respect as a judge, rendering decisions on such matters as family relations, property inheritance, and criminal behavior. Preaching a holy war against unbelievers, Muhammad urged followers to raid the trading caravans from Mecca and to subdue unfriendly Bedouin tribes. He tried to convert the Jews of Medina, but they would not accept him as a prophet, and mocked his unfamiliarity with the Old Testament and the learned writings of the rabbis. For a time, Muhammad actively persecuted Arabian Jews, expelling several thousand from Medina, seizing Jewish property, beheading some 600 Jewish men, and enslaving women and children. Later, Muhammad permitted the Arabian Jews the free exercise of their religion and guaranteed the security of their property. In 630, Mecca surrendered to a Muslim army without a fight. Soon Bedouin tribes all over Arabia had embraced Islam and recognized the authority of the Prophet Muhammad.

In a little more than two decades, Muhammad had united the often feuding Arabian tribes into a powerful force dedicated to Allah and the spreading of the Islamic faith. After Muhammad's death in 632, his friend Abu Bakr became his successor, or caliph; regarded as the defender of the faith, whose power derived from Allah, the caliph governed in accordance with Muslim law as defined in the Koran. Islam gave the many Arab tribes the unity, discipline, and organization to succeed in their wars of conquest. Under the

first four caliphs, who ruled from 632 to 661, the Arabs with breathtaking speed overran the Persian Empire, stripped Byzantium of some of its provinces, and invaded Europe. Muslim warriors believed that they were engaged in a holy war (*jihad*) to spread Islam to nonbelievers and that those who died in the jihad were assured a place in paradise. A desire to escape from the barren Arabian desert and to exploit the rich Byzantine and Persian lands was another compelling reason for expansion. In the east, Islam's territory eventually extended into India and to the borders of China; in the west, it encompassed North Africa and most of Spain but the Muslims' northward push lost momentum and was halted in 732 at the battle of Tours in southern France.

In the eighth and ninth centuries under the Abbasid caliphs, Muslim civilization entered its golden age. Islamic civilization creatively synthesized Arabic, Byzantine, Persian, and Indian cultural traditions. During the Early Middle Ages, when learning was at a low point in western Europe, the Muslims had forged a high civilization.

Muslim science, philosophy, and mathematics rested largely on the achievements of the ancient Greeks. The Muslims acquired Greek learning from the older Persian and Byzantine civilizations, which had kept alive the Greek inheritance. By translating Greek works into Arabic and commenting on them, Muslim scholars performed the great historical task of preserving the philosophic and scientific heritage of ancient Greece. Greek learning, supplemented by original contributions of Muslim scholars and scientists, was then passed on to Christian Europe.

There are numerous examples of Muslim brilliance in mathematics, science, and philosophy. Muslim mathematicians did original work in algebra and trigonometry; Muslim astronomers corrected the observations made by ancient astronomers, particularly Ptolemy. Building on the medical knowledge of the Greeks, Muslim physicians became the best-trained and most skillful doctors of the time. Surgeons performed amputations, removed cancerous tissue, devised new medicines, and used anesthetics in performing operations. The best Muslim hospitals had separate wards for fevers, surgical cases, eye diseases, and dysentery. Well ahead of their time were those Muslim doctors who recommended humane treatment for the mentally ill.

Muslim thinkers employed the categories of Greek philosophy to explain Islamic doctrine. Al-Farabi (c. 870–950), who wrote commentaries on Aristotle, offered proofs for God's existence based on Aristotelian logic that were later studied by medieval Christian philosophers. The most eminent Muslim thinker, Ibn-Sina, known to the West as Avicenna (980–1037), was a poet, doctor, scientist, and philosopher who wrote on every field of knowledge. His philosophic works, which relied heavily on Aristotle, had an important influence on medieval Christian thinkers. Another giant of Muslim learning was Ibn-Rushd, whom westerners call Averroës (1126–1198). Averroës insisted that the Koran did not oppose the study of philosophy and held that the ancient Greeks— even though they were not Muslims—had discovered truth. His commentaries on Aristotle were studied in western universities, where they sparked an important controversy (see Chapter 11).

The Arab Empire, stretching from Spain to India, was unified by a common language (Arabic), a common faith, and a common culture. By the eleventh century, however, the Arabs began losing their dominance in the Islamic world. The Seljuk Turks, who had taken Asia Minor from the Byzantines, also conquered the Arabic lands of Syria, Palestine, and much of Persia. Although the Abbasid caliphs remained the religious and cultural leaders of Islam, political power was exercised by Seljuk sultans. In the eleventh and twelfth centuries, the Muslims lost Sicily and most of Spain to Christian knights, and European Crusaders carved out kingdoms in the Near East.

In the thirteenth century came a new wave of invaders, the Mongols from Central Asia. Led by Genghis Khan, Mongolian archers, mounted on fast-moving ponies, poured across Asia into Muslim lands. By 1227, when Genghis Khan died, the eastern part of the Muslim world had fallen to the Mongols. After the death of Genghis Khan, some Mongol forces swept across Russia and threatened Central Europe; others continued to advance on Muslim lands in the Near East. Storming Baghdad in 1258, the Mongols burned, plundered, and killed with savage fury; among the 50,000 people slaughtered was the last Abbasid caliph. The Mongols devastated the palaces, libraries, and schools that had made Baghdad the cultural capital of the Islamic world. A year later they marched into Syria, again killing and looting. Their brutal advance westward was finally stopped in 1260 in Palestine by Egyptian forces.

By the beginning of the fourteenth century, the Muslim world seemed less threatened. In the Near East, the Muslims had recaptured the last Christian state founded by the Crusaders, while the Mongols, who had by this time converted to Islam, remained in Persia and were unable to advance westward. In the late fourteenth century, however, the Mongols under Tamerlane again menaced the Near East. Another bloody conqueror, Tamerlane cowed opposition with huge pyramids built from the skulls of thousands of slaughtered victims. After Tamerlane's death in 1404, his empire disintegrated and its collapse left the way open for the Ottoman Turks.

The Ottoman Empire reached its height in the sixteenth century with the conquest of Egypt, North Africa, Syria, and the Arabian coast. The Ottomans developed an effective system of administration, but their empire lacked the vitality that had kept the Muslim world more advanced than western Europe for most of the Middle Ages. Thus, the Ottomans did not restore the cultural brilliance, the thriving trade, or the prosperity that the Muslim world had known under the Abbasid Caliphs of Baghdad.

Although they experienced centuries of cultural greatness, neither Byzantium nor Islam made the breakthroughs in science, technology, philosophy, economics, and political thought that gave rise to the modern world. This process would be the singular achievement of Europe. During the Early Middle Ages, Latin Christendom was culturally far behind the two Eastern civilizations, but by the twelfth century it had caught up. In succeeding centuries it produced the movements that ushered in the modern age: Renaissance, Reformation, Scientific Revolution, Age of Enlightenment, French Revolution, and Industrial Revolution.

Western Europe: Political and Economic Transformation

From the sixth to the eighth centuries, Europe was struggling to overcome the disorders created by the breakup of the Roman Empire and the deterioration of Greco-Roman civilization. A new civilization with its own distinctive style was taking root. It consisted of elements from the Greco-Roman past, the traditions of the Germans, and the Christian outlook. But it would take centuries for this new civilization to bear fruit.

In the fifth century, German invaders founded kingdoms in North Africa, Italy, Spain, Gaul, and Britain—lands formerly belonging to Rome. Even before the invasions, the Germans had acquired some knowledge of, and attraction for Roman culture. Therefore, the new Germanic rulers did not seek to destroy Roman civilization, but to share in its advantages. For example, Theodoric the Great, the Ostrogoth ruler of Italy, retained the Roman senate, government officials, civil service, and schools; the Burgundians in Gaul and the Visigoths in Spain maintained Roman law for their conquered subjects; and Clovis, a Frankish ruler, wore Roman imperial colors and took Roman titles.

But the Germanic kingdoms, often torn by warfare, internal rebellion, and assassination, provided a poor political base on which to revive a decadent and dying classical civilization. Most of the kingdoms survived for only a short time and had no enduring impact.

In 533–534, Byzantium destroyed the Vandal kingdom in North Africa and the Vandals disappeared as a people; a similar fate befell the Ostrogoth kingdom in Italy two decades later. In the early eighth century, Muslim Arabs destroyed the Visigoth kingdom in Spain. An exception to this trend occurred in Gaul, where the most successful of the Germanic kingdoms was established by the Franks—the founders of the new Europe.

The Roman world was probably too far gone to be rescued, but even if this were not so, the Germans were culturally unprepared to play the role of rescuer. By the end of the seventh century the old Roman lands in the West showed a marked decline in central government, town life, commerce, and learning. The German invaders, while vigorous and brave, were essentially a rural and warrior people who were tribal in organization and outlook. Their native culture, without cities or written literature, was primitive in comparison to the literary, philosophic, scientific, and artistic achievements of the Greco-Roman world. The Germans were not equipped to reform the decaying Roman system of administration and taxation, to cope with the economic problems that had burdened the Empire, or to breathe new life into the dying humanist culture.

Roman ideas of citizenship and the legal state were totally alien to Germanic tradition. The Germans gave loyalty to their kindred and to a tribal chief, not to an impersonal state that governed citizens of many nationalities. The king viewed the land he controlled as a private possession that could be divided among his sons after his death—a custom that produced numerous and devastating civil wars and partitions. Unlike the Romans, the Germanic invaders had no trained civil servants to administer the state and no system of taxation to provide a secure financial base for government. Barbarian kings subdivided their kingdoms into districts and chose members of the great noble families to administer each district. These noble counts dispensed justice, maintained order, and collected taxes in their districts. The danger always existed that the counts would usurp the monarch's authority.

The Germans also found Roman law strange. Roman law incorporated elements of Greek philosophy and was written, whereas German law at the time of the invasions consisted of unwritten tribal customs. Roman law applied to all people throughout the Empire regardless of nationality; a German could be judged only by the law of his own tribe. Roman judges investigated evidence and demanded proof; German courts relied on trial by ordeal. In a typical ordeal, a bound defendant was thrown into a river. If he sank, he was innocent; floating was interpreted as divine proof of guilt, as the pure water had "rejected" the evildoer. Although primitive by Roman standards, Germanic law did help to lessen blood feuds between families. Before long the Germanic kingdoms began to put customary tribal law, which had absorbed and continued to absorb elements from Roman law, into writing. Replacing Roman law and spreading throughout Europe, Germanic law became an essential element of medieval society.

The distinguishing feature of classical civilization, the vitality of its urban institutions, had deteriorated in the Late Roman Empire. This shift from an urban to a rural economy accelerated under the kingdoms created by Germanic chieftains. While the German kings retained Roman cities as capitals, they did not halt the process of decay that had overtaken urban centers. These rulers settled their people in the countryside, not in towns; they did not significantly utilize cities as instruments of local government; and they failed to maintain Roman roads. Although towns did not vanish altogether, they continued to lose control over their surrounding countryside and to decline in wealth and importance. They were the headquarters of bishops, rather than centers of commerce and intellectual life. Italy remained an exception to this general trend. There Roman urban institutions persisted, even during the crudest period of the Early Middle Ages. Italian cities kept some metal currency in circulation and traded with each other and with Byzantium.

Shrinking commerce during the Early Middle Ages was part of the process of decline begun in the Late Roman Empire. Although commerce never wholly disappeared—and indeed experienced temporary periods of renewed activity—it was predominantly localized and was controlled by colonies of Jews, Syrians, and Greeks, a sign of the economic inertia of Latin Christians. From the last decade of the fifth century to the middle of the seventh century, Byzantine merchants established themselves in the West and exchanged papyrus, spices, and textiles for European slaves. However, this trade dropped off greatly in the second half of the seventh century because as Muslim power expanded to control the Mediterranean, Byzantine merchants had to turn eastward for markets. Thus the bonds between East and West weakened, and Europe shifted its axis northward away from the Mediterranean. Few goods exchanged hands and few coins circulated; people produced for themselves what they needed.

The Waning of Classical Culture

Greco-Roman humanism, which had been in retreat since the Late Roman Empire, continued its decline in the centuries immediately following Rome's demise. The old Roman upper classes abandoned their heritage and absorbed the ways of their Germanic conquerors; the Roman schools closed and Roman law faded into disuse. The human figure, which had been the subject for Greco-Roman artists, was supplanted by primitive, geometric shapes. Few people other than clerics could read and write Latin, and even learned clerics were rare. Knowledge of the Greek language in Europe was almost totally lost, and the Latin rhetorical style deteriorated. Many literary works of classical antiquity were either lost or neglected. European culture seemed much poorer than the high civilizations of Byzantium, Islam, and ancient Rome.

During this period of cultural poverty, the few persons who were learned generally did not engage in original thought, but salvaged and transmitted remnants of classical civilization. Given the context of the times, this was a considerable achievement. These individuals retained respect for the inheritance of Greece and Rome at the same time that they remained devoted to Christianity. In a rudimentary way, they were struggling to create a Christian culture that combined the intellectual tradition of Greece and Rome with the religious teachings of the Christian church.

An important figure in the intellectual life of this transitional period was Boethius (480–c. 525), a descendant of a noble family. Boethius had received a classical education at the Platonic Academy at Athens before Emperor Justinian closed it in 529. Later Boethius served the Ostrogothic king Theodoric I (c. 489–526), who ruled Italy. Recognizing that Greco-Roman civilization was dying, Boethius tried to rescue the intellectual heritage of antiquity. Boethius translated into Latin some of Aristotle's treatises on logic. In addition, Boethius wrote commentaries on Aristotle, Cicero, and Porphyry, a Neo-Platonist philosopher, as well as treatises on theology and textbooks on arithmetic, astronomy, and music. But his life was cut short when Theodoric had him executed in 524 or 525 for allegedly participating in a plot against the throne.

While in prison awaiting execution, Boethius wrote *The Consolation of Philosophy*, which is regarded as one of the masterpieces of world literature. After a sudden turn of fortune had deprived him of power, prestige, and possessions and had confronted him with the imminence of death, Boethius pondered the meaning of life: "Think you that there is any certainty in the affairs of mankind when you know that often one swift hour can utterly destroy a man?"[2] Alone in his dungeon, he turned not to Christ, but to the philosophical training of his youth for guidance and consolation. He derived comfort from Lady Philosophy, who reassured him, in the tradition of Socrates and the Stoics, that "if then you are master of yourself, you will be in possession of that which you will never wish to lose, and which Fortune will never be able to take from you."[3] No tyrant

can "ever disturb the peculiar restfulness which is the property of a mind that hangs together upon the firm basis of its reason."[4] In the life and thought of Boethius the classical tradition lived on. He was a bridge between a classical civilization too far gone to be revived and a Christian civilization still in embryo.

Until the twelfth century virtually all that Latin Christendom knew of Aristotle came from Boethius's translations and commentaries. Similarly, his work in mathematics, which contains fragments from Euclid, was the principal source for the study of that discipline in the Early Middle Ages. He also bequeathed to future generations basic philosophic definitions and terms. In his theological writings he attempted to demonstrate that reason did not conflict with orthodoxy, an early attempt to attain a rational comprehension of belief—to join faith to reason, as he expressed it. Boethius's effort to examine Christian doctrines rationally, a principal feature of medieval philosophy, would grow to maturity in the twelfth and thirteenth centuries. Writing in the sixth century, Boethius was a forerunner of this movement.

Cassiodorus (c. 490–575), a contemporary of Boethius, was born in southern Italy of a good family; he served three Ostrogoth kings. Although Cassiodorus wrote the twelve-volume *History of the Goths* and some theological treatises, his principal importance was as a collector of Greek and Latin manuscripts and as an advocate of higher education to improve the clergy's quality. In his educational writings he justified the importance of studying secular literature as an aid to understanding sacred writings. Even though his works were not original, they did rescue some ideas of the ancients from oblivion; these ideas would bear fruit again in later centuries. Cassiodorus's plans for founding a university in Rome modeled after the one in Alexandria did not materialize; in fact, six hundred years would elapse before universities would arise in Latin Christendom. Leaving political office, Cassiodorus retired to a monastery where he initiated the monastic practice of copying classical texts. Without this tradition, many key Christian and pagan works would undoubtedly have perished.

In Spain, Isidore of Seville (c. 576–636) compiled an encyclopedia, *Etymologiae*, covering a diversity of topics from arithmetic to God to furniture. Isidore derived his information from many secular and religious sources. Quite understandably his work contained many errors, particularly in its references to nature. For centuries, though, the *Etymologiae* served as a standard reference work and was found in every monastic library of note.

The translations and compilations made by Boethius, Cassiodorus, and Isidore, the books collected and copied by monks, and schools established in monasteries (particularly those in Ireland, England, and Italy) kept intellectual life from dying out completely in the Early Middle Ages. Amid the deterioration of political authority, the stagnation of economic life, and the decline in learning, a new civilization was emerging. German and Roman peoples intermarried, and Roman, German, and Christian traditions intermingled. But it was the church more than anything else that gave form and direction to the emerging civilization.

The Church: The Shaper of Medieval Civilization

The Church as Unifier

Christianity was the integrating principle, and the church was the dominant institution of the Middle Ages. During the Late Roman Empire, as the Roman state and its institutions decayed, the church gained in power and importance; its organization grew stronger and its membership increased. Unlike the Roman state, the church was a healthy and vital organism. The elite of the Roman Empire had severed their commitment to the values of classical civilization, whereas the church leaders were intensely devoted to their faith.

During the invasions of the fifth and sixth centuries, the church assumed many political functions formerly performed by the Roman state, and continued to convert the Germanic tribes. By teaching a higher morality, the church tamed the warrior habits of the German peoples. By preserving some of the high culture of Greece and Rome, it opened German minds to new ideas. When the Empire collapsed, the church retained its administrative system and preserved elements of Greco-Roman civilization. The church served as a unifying and civilizing agent and provided people with an intelligible and purposeful conception of life and death. In a dying world, the church was the only institution capable of reconstructing civilized life.

Thus, the Christian outlook was the foundation of medieval civilization, not the traditions of the German barbarians. People saw themselves as participants in a great drama of salvation. There was only one truth—God's revelation to humanity. There was only one avenue to heaven, and it passed through the church. God had established the church to administer the rites through which his love and protection (grace) was bestowed on people. Without the church, people would remain doomed sinners. To the medieval mind, society without the church was as inconceivable as life without the Christian view of God and the purpose of life. Membership in a universal church replaced citizenship in a universal empire. Across Europe, from Italy to Ireland, a new society centered on Christianity was forming.

Monks and the Papacy

Monks were instrumental in constructing the foundations of medieval civilization. During the seventh century, intellectual life on the Continent continued its steady decline. In the monasteries of England and Ireland, however, a tradition of learning persisted. In the early fifth century, Saint Patrick had converted the Irish to Christianity. In Ireland, Latin became firmly entrenched as the lan-

Monastery of Mont St. Michel. The monastic institutions throughout western Europe stood firm amid the intellectual and cultural confusion of the early Middle Ages. By copying ancient manuscripts and studying Latin, monks preserved elements of classical civilization. (*French Government Tourist Office*)

guage of both the church and scholars at a time when it was in danger of disappearing in many parts of the Continent. Irish clergymen preserved and cultivated both Greek and Latin and revived Latin's use during their missionary activities on the Continent. Irish scholars engaged in Biblical analysis, and in addition to copying manuscripts, they decorated them with an exquisite eye for detail. In England, the Anglo-Saxons, who converted to Christianity mainly in the seventh century, also established monasteries that kept learning alive. The Venerable Bede (673–735) wrote commentaries on Scripture and translated the fourth Gospel (Saint John's) into Anglo-Saxon. Bede is best known for his *Ecclesiastical History of the English People*, one of the finest historical works in the Middle Ages.

In the sixth and seventh centuries, Irish monks practiced their Christian missionary activities from monasteries on the Continent. Once converted, many Anglo-Saxons embraced Benedictine monasticism and, continuing the efforts of Irish monks, became the chief agents for the conversion of the people in Northern Europe. By converting pagans to Christianity, monks made possible a unitary European civilization based on a Christian foundation. By copying and preserving ancient texts, monks and nuns also kept alive elements of ancient civilization.

During the Early Middle Ages, when cities were in decay, monasteries were the principal cultural centers; they would remain so until the rebirth of towns in the High Middle Ages. By instructing peasants in superior methods of farming, monks were partly responsible for the reclamation of lands that had been neglected or devastated during the great invasions. Monasteries also offered succor to the sick and the destitute and served as places of refuge for travelers. To the medieval mind, the monk's selfless devotion to God, his adoption of poverty, and his dedication to prayer and contemplation represented the highest expression of the Christian way of life; it was the finest and most certain path to salvation. Regarding the monks as soldiers in the war against paganism, unorthodoxy, and heresy, the papacy protected monasteries and encouraged their spread.

The Early Middle Ages was a formative period for the papacy, as it was for society in general. The status of the papacy was closely tied to events in Italy. In the sixth century, the Byzantine Emperor Justinian, who viewed the breakup of Rome as only temporary, sought to regain western lands lost to the Germanic invaders. In 533–534, a Byzantine force led by Belisarius destroyed the Vandal kingdom in North Africa. The Byzantines then invaded Italy, breaking the power of the Ostrogoths. The destruction of the Ostrogoth kingdom opened the way for the Lombards, the last Germanic people to settle in once Roman lands. In the last part of the sixth century the Lombards invaded Italy and seized much of the territory that the Byzantines had regained from the Ostrogoths.

The Lombard invasion provided the papacy with an opportunity to free itself from Byzantine domination. Increasingly, popes assumed control over the city of Rome and the surrounding territory, while at the same time seeking to protect these lands from the Lombards. At this critical stage, Gregory I, the Great (590–604), became pope. A descendant of a prominent and wealthy Roman senatorial family and a monk, Gregory turned out to be one of the ablest of the medieval popes. He used Roman methods of administration to organize and administer effectively papal property in Italy, Sicily, Sardinia, Gaul, and other regions. The papacy owned huge estates worked by serfs, timberlands, and mines, which provided the income for maintaining

the clergy, churches, monasteries, hospitals, and orphanages in Rome and other places. Because of Gregory's efforts, the papacy became the leading financial institution of the day.

Gregory tried to strengthen the pope's authority within the church, insisting that all bishops and the Byzantine church in Constantinople were subject to papal authority. Establishing monasteries, he tightened the bonds between the monks and the papacy, and it was he who dispatched Benedictine monks to England to win over the Anglo-Saxons. The newly established Anglo-Saxon church looked to Rome for leadership. Gregory realized that if the papacy were to lead Christendom effectively, it must exercise authority over churches outside of Italy—a policy adopted by popes who succeeded him.

In addition to providing the papacy with a sound financial base and strengthening its ties with monasteries and non-Italian churches, Gregory engaged in other activities. Gregory wrote commentaries on the books of the Bible and authored many works dealing with Christian themes—the duties of bishops, the lives of saints and monks, miracles, and purgatory. Because of his many writings, Gregory is regarded as a father of the Latin church. Gregory was also an astute diplomat, and he knew that the papacy required the political and military support of a powerful kingdom to protect it from its enemies, especially the Lombards. Accordingly he set his sights on an alliance with the Franks; finally materializing 150 years later, this alliance between the papacy and Frankish kings was instrumental in the shaping of medieval history.

The Kingdom of the Franks

From their homeland in the Rhine River Valley, the Frankish tribes had expanded into Roman territory during the fourth and fifth centuries. The ruler Clovis united the various Frankish tribes and conquered most of Gaul.

In 496, he converted to Roman Christianity. Clovis's conversion to Catholicism was an event of great significance. A number of other German kings had adopted the Arian form of Christianity, which the church had declared heretical. By embracing Roman Christianity, the Franks became a potential ally of the papacy.

After Clovis's death in 511, the Frankish lands suffered hard times. His kingdom was divided, and the Merovingian rulers (so named after Merovech, a semilegendary ancestor of Clovis) engaged in fratricidal warfare and brutal murder. In the seventh century the various Merovingian rulers had become ineffective and lost much of their power to great landowners. The real ruler of each Frankish realm was the Mayor of the Palace, the king's chief officer. One of these, Pepin II of Heristal (687–714), triumphed over his rival mayors and became ruler of Frankland. Pepin was the founder of the Carolingian dynasty (so named after Charlemagne, the greatest of the Carolingians).

Succeeding Pepin was his son Charles Martel, who served as Mayor of the Palace from 717 to 741. Charles Martel subjected all Frankland to Carolingian rule and repulsed the Muslims in southern Gaul. But Muslim Arabs and Berbers from North Africa, who had conquered Visigoth Spain in the early eighth century, crossed the Pyrenees into Frankish Gaul and advanced northward along the old Roman road. At the Battle of Tours in 732, the Franks defeated the Muslims. Although the Muslims continued to occupy the Iberian Peninsula, they would advance no farther north into Europe. Charles Martel was succeeded by his son Pepin the Short, who in 751 deposed the last Merovingian king. With the approval of the papacy and his nobles, Pepin was crowned king by Boniface, a prominent bishop.

In approving Pepin's royal accession, the papacy was continuing Gregory's earlier efforts to gain an ally in its struggle against the Lombards, who still had designs on papal territory. In 753, Pope Stephen II journeyed across the Alps to confer with Pepin, who

Book of Kells. The beauty of the Book of Kells lies in the intricate richness of its interlacing and abstract design. The Virgin and Child on this manuscript page illustrate a more primitive representation of the human form than that found in classical art; the barbarian kingdoms had brought artistic activity to a virtual standstill. (*The Board of Trinity College, Dublin*)

welcomed the pontiff with respect. The pope anointed Pepin again as king of the Franks and appealed to him to protect the papacy from the Lombards. Pepin invaded Italy, defeated the Lombards, and turned over captured lands to the papacy. Pepin's donation made the pope ruler of the territory between

Rome and Ravenna, which became known as the Papal States.

The Era of Charlemagne

The alliance between the Franks and the papacy was continued by Pepin's successor, Charlemagne (Charles the Great), who ruled from 768 to 814. Charlemagne continued the Carolingian policy of expanding the Frankish kingdom. He destroyed the Lombard kingdom and declared himself king of the Lombards. He added Bavaria to his kingdom, and after long, terrible wars, he forced the Saxons to submit to his rule and to convert to Christianity. He conquered a region in northern Spain, the Spanish March, that served as a buffer between the Christian Franks and the Muslims in Spain.

Immense difficulties arose in governing the expanded territories. Size seemed an insuperable obstacle to effective government, particularly since Charlemagne's administrative structure, lacking in trained personnel, was primitive by Islamic, Byzantine, or Roman standards. The empire was divided into about 250 counties administered by counts—nobles personally loyal to the ruler. Men from powerful families, the counts served as generals, judges, and administrators, implementing the king's decisions. To supervise the counts, Charlemagne created *missi dominici* (royal messengers)—generally two laymen and a bishop or abbot—who made annual journeys to the different counties. The purpose of the missi dominici was to prevent counts and their subordinates from abusing their power and from undermining Charlemagne's authority.

On Christmas Day in Rome in the year 800, Pope Leo crowned Charlemagne Emperor of the Romans. The initiative for the coronation probably came from the papacy, not from Charlemagne. The meaning of this event has aroused conflicting opinions among historians, but certain conclusions seem justified. The title signified that the tradition of a world empire still survived, despite the demise of the western Roman Empire three hundred years earlier. But because it was the pope who crowned Charlemagne, this meant that the emperor had a spiritual responsibility to spread and defend the faith. Thus Roman universalism was fused with Christian universalism.

The Frankish empire, of course, was only a dim shadow of the Roman Empire. The Franks had no Roman law nor Roman legions; there were no cities that were centers of economic and cultural activity; officials were not trained civil servants with a world outlook, but were uneducated war chieftains with a tribal viewpoint. Yet Charlemagne's empire did embody the idea of a universal Christian empire, an ideal that would endure throughout the Middle Ages.

The crowning of a German ruler as Emperor of the Romans by the head of the church represented the merging of German, Christian, and Roman elements, which is the essential characteristic of medieval civilization. This blending of traditions was also evident on a cultural plane, for Charlemagne, a German warrior-king, showed respect for classical learning and Christianity, both non-Germanic traditions.

Carolingian Renaissance

Charlemagne felt that it was his religious duty to raise the educational level of the clergy so that they understood and could properly teach the faith. To do so, it was necessary to overcome the illiteracy or semiliteracy of clergymen and to prepare sacred Scriptures that were uniform, complete, and free of errors. Charlemagne also fostered education to train administrators who would be capable of overseeing his kingdoms and royal estates; such men had to be literate.

To achieve his purpose, Charlemagne gathered some of the finest scholars in Europe. Alcuin of Northumbria, England (735–804), was given charge of the Palace School attended by Charlemagne and his family, high lords, and youths training to serve the em-

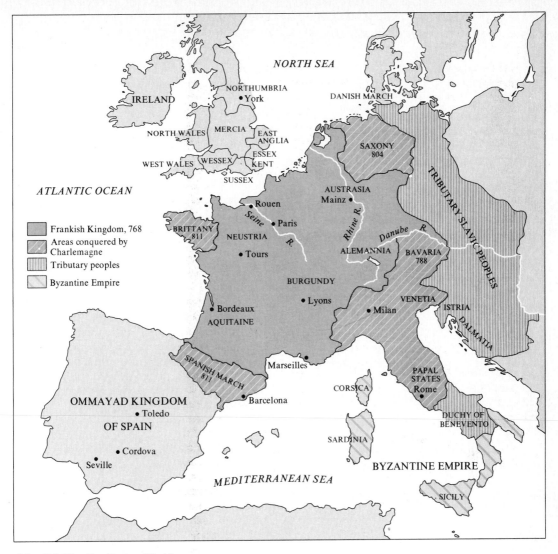

Map 9.2 The Carolingian World

peror. Alcuin was assigned the task of preparing a definitive text of the Bible from the various versions then in use. His text was an important achievement, for it was generally accepted, with modifications and corrections, as the standard version of the Bible throughout the Middle Ages.

The focus of the Carolingian Renaissance was predominantly Christian—an effort to train clergymen and improve their understanding of the Bible and the writings of the church fathers. This process raised the level of literacy and improved the Latin style. Most important, monastic copyists continued to preserve ancient texts, which otherwise might never have survived—the oldest surviving manuscripts of many ancient works are Carolingian copies. Carolingian scholars thus helped to fertilize the cultural flowering known as the Twelfth-Century Awakening—the high point of medieval civilization.

Compared to the Greco-Roman past, to the cultural explosion of the twelfth and thirteenth centuries, or to the great Italian Renaissance of the fifteenth century, the Carolingian Renaissance seems slight indeed. Although the

Viking memorial stone. A migratory people, the Vikings did not produce monumental art. Viking art was simple but vital in its design and bold carving, as is illustrated in this memorial stone, which depicts a horseman and sailors. (*Antikvarisk-Topografiska Arkivet [ATA], Stockholm*)

vailed before the era of Charlemagne. The Carolingian Renaissance reversed the process of cultural decay that characterized much of the Early Middle Ages. Learning would never again fall to the low level it had reached in the centuries following the decline of Rome.

During the era of Charlemagne, a distinct European civilization had taken root. It blended the Roman heritage of a world empire, the intellectual achievement of the Greco-Roman mind, Christian otherworldliness, and the customs of the Germanic peoples. This nascent western European civilization differed from Byzantine and Islamic civilizations, and Europeans were growing conscious of the difference. But the new civilization was still centuries away from fruition.

Charlemagne's empire also engendered the ideal of a unified Latin Christendom—a single Christian community under one government. The ideal of a Christian world-state, Christendom, inspired many people, both clergy and laity, and would reach its peak from the eleventh to the thirteenth centuries.

The Breakup of Charlemagne's Empire

After Charlemagne's death in 814, his son Louis the Pious inherited the throne. Louis aimed to preserve the empire, but the task was virtually impossible. The empire's strength rested more on the personal qualities of Charlemagne than on any firm economic or political foundation. Moreover, the empire was simply too large and consisted of too many diverse peoples to be governed effectively. Along with facing Frankish nobles who sought to increase their own power at the emperor's expense, Louis had to deal with his own rebellious sons. After Louis died in 840, the empire was divided among the three sons who survived.

The Treaty of Verdun in 843 gave Louis the German the eastern part of the empire, which marked the beginning of Germany; to Charles the Bald went the western part, which was the start of France; and Lothair received the Middle Kingdom, which extended from

Carolingian Renaissance did rediscover and revive ancient works, it did not recapture the spirit of Greece and Rome. Carolingian scholars did not engage in independent philosophical speculation or search for new knowledge, nor did they achieve that synthesis of faith and reason that would be constructed by the great theologians of the twelfth and thirteenth centuries. But we must bear in mind the cultural poverty that had pre-

Rome to the North Sea. This Middle Kingdom would become a source of conflict between France and Germany into the twentieth century. As central authority waned, large landowners increasingly came to exercise authority in their own regions. Simultaneous invasions from all directions furthered this movement toward localism and decentralization.

In the ninth and tenth centuries, Latin Christendom was attacked on all sides. From bases in North Africa, Spain, and southern Gaul, Muslims ravaged coastal regions of southern Europe. The Magyars, Mongolian nomads, had crossed the steppes of Russia and established themselves on the plains of the Danube; their horsemen launched lightning raids into northern Italy, western Germany, and parts of France. Defeated in Germany in 933 and again in 955, the Magyars withdrew to what is now Hungary; they ceased their raids and adopted Christianity.

Still another group of invaders, the Northmen, or Vikings, sailed south from Scandinavia on their long wooden ships to plunder the coasts and river valleys of western Europe. These ferocious warriors spread terror wherever they landed. Superb seamen, the Vikings crossed the North Atlantic and settled in Iceland and Greenland; from there, they almost certainly travelled and landed on the coast of North America.

In pursuit of slaves, jewels, and precious metals hoarded in monasteries, these invaders plundered, destroyed, and murdered. Villages were devastated, ports were destroyed, and the population was decimated. Trade was at a standstill, coins no longer circulated, and farms were turned into wastelands. The European economy collapsed, the political authority of kings disappeared, and cultural life and learning withered.

These terrible attacks heightened political insecurity and accelerated anew the process of decentralization that had begun with the decline of Rome. During these chaotic times counts came to regard as their own the land that they administered and defended for their king. Similarly, the inhabitants of a district looked on the count or local lord as their ruler, for his men and fortresses protected them. In their regions, nobles exercised public power formerly held by kings, an arrangement later designated as feudalism.

In instances where great lords failed to protect their territories from neighboring counts or from invaders, political power was further fragmented. In other areas local nobles chipped away at a count's authority in his county. In many regions the political unit shrank from the county to the *castellany*, the land close to a lord's castle. In such areas the local lord exercised virtually supreme authority; people turned to him for protection and for the administration of justice. Europe had entered an age of feudalism in which the essential unit of government was not a kingdom but a county or castellany, and political power was the private possession of local lords.

Feudal Society

Arising during a period of collapsing central authority, invasion, scanty public revenues, and declining commerce and town life, feudalism attempted to provide some order and security. Feudalism was not an organized system deduced logically from abstract principles, but an improvised response to the challenge posed by ineffectual central authority. Feudal practices were not uniform; they differed from locality to locality, and in some regions had barely taken root. Feudalism was a stopgap system of government that provided some order, justice, and law during an era of breakdown, localism, and transition. Feudalism would remain the predominant political arrangement until kings reasserted their authority.

Vassalage

Feudal relationships enabled lords to increase their military strength. The need for military support was the principal reason for the practice of vassalage, in which a man, in a solemn ceremony, pledged loyalty to a lord.

This feature of feudalism derived from an ancient German ceremony during which warriors swore personal allegiance to the head of the war-band. Among other things, the vassal gave military service to his lord, and received in return a *fief*, which was usually land. This fief was inhabited by peasants, and the crops that they raised provided the vassal with his means of support.

In return for the fief and the lords's protection, the vassal owed several obligations to his lord. These duties included rendering military assistance and supplying knights for his lord; sitting in the lord's court and judging cases, such as the breach of feudal agreements between the lord and his other vassals; providing lodgings when the lord traveled through the vassal's territory; giving a gift when the lord's son was knighted or when his eldest daughter married; and raising a ransom if the lord were captured by an enemy.

Generally, both lord and vassal felt honor-bound to abide by the oath of loyalty. It became an accepted custom for a vassal to renounce his loyalty to his lord if the latter failed to protect him from enemies, mistreated him, or increased the vassal's obligations as fixed by the feudal contract. Similarly, if a vassal did not live up to his obligations, the lord would summon him to his court where he would be tried for treachery. If found guilty, the vassal could lose his fief and perhaps his life. Sometimes disputes between vassals and lords erupted into warfare. Because a vassal often held land from more than one lord and sometimes was himself a lord to vassals, situations frequently became awkward, complex, and confusing. On occasion, a vassal had to decide to which lord he owed *liege homage* (prime loyalty).

As feudalism evolved, the king came to be regarded as the chief lord, who had granted fiefs to the great lords, who in turn had divided them into smaller units and regranted them to vassals. Thus all members of the ruling class, from the lowliest knights to the king, occupied a place in the feudal hierarchy. In theory the king was the highest political authority and the source of land tenure, but in actual fact he was often less powerful than other nobles of the realm. Feudalism would decline when kings converted their theoretical powers into actual powers.

Feudal Law

Feudal law, which incorporated many features of traditional German law, differed markedly from Roman law. Roman law was universal, for it was enacted by a central government for a world empire; it was rational, for it sought to be in accord with natural law that applied to all; it was systematic, for it offered a framework of standards that applied to individual cases. Feudal law, on the other hand, was local, covering only a small region. And it was personal; in the Roman view the individual as a citizen owed obligations to the state, whereas under feudalism, a vassal owed loyalty and service to a lord according to the terms of a personal agreement made between them.

In the feudal view, lords and kings did not make law; rather, they discovered and confirmed it by examining ancient customs. Therefore, feudal patterns of landownership, military service, and wardship came to be regarded as an expression of ancient, unchanging, and inviolable custom. Consequently, if the vassal believed that his lord had violated the feudal agreement, that is, had broken faith with him and had transgressed upon traditions, the vassal would demand restoration of customary rights before an audience of his fellow vassals. Often lords battled each other, believing that they were defending their rights. Similarly, lords claimed the right to resist kings who did not honor their feudal agreements.

Feudal Warriors

Feudal lords viewed manual labor and commerce as degrading for men of their rank. They considered only one vocation worthy—

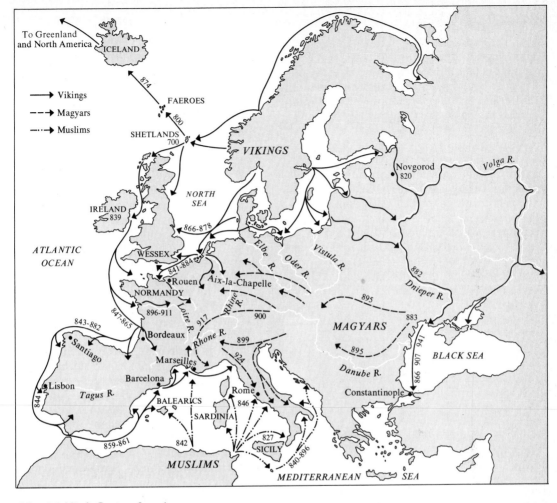

Map 9.3 Ninth-Century Invasions

that of warrior. Through combat, the lord demonstrated his valor, earned his reputation, measured his individual worth, derived excitement, added to his wealth, and defended his rights. Warfare was his whole purpose in life. During the twelfth century, to relieve the boredom of peacetime, nobles staged gala tournaments in which knights, fighting singly or in teams, engaged each other in battle to prove their skill and courage. The victors in these pageants not only gained honor from fellow nobles and admiring ladies, but also received prizes—falcons, crowns, and substantial amounts of money. The feudal glorification of combat became deeply ingrained in Western society, and has endured into the twentieth century. Over the centuries a code

of behavior, called *chivalry*, evolved for the feudal nobility. A true knight was expected to fight bravely, to demonstrate loyalty to his lord, and to treat other knights with respect and courtesy.

The church, in time, interjected a religious element into the warrior culture of the feudal knight. It sought to use the fighting spirit of the feudal class for Christian ends—knights could assist the clergy in enforcing God's will. To the Germanic tradition of loyalty and courage was added a Christian component; as a Christian gentleman, a knight was expected to honor the laws of the church and to wield his sword in the service of God. A knight was supposed to protect women, children, and the weak, and defend the church against heretics and infidels. The very ceremony of knighthood was placed within a Christian framework. A priest blessed the future knight's arms and prayed that the knight would always "defend the Just and Right."

Regarding the private warfare of lords as a lawless violence that menaced social life, the church in the eleventh century imposed strictures called "the Peace of God" and "the Truce of God." These restrictions limited feudal warfare to certain days of the week and certain times of the year. Thus the church tried to regulate warfare according to moral principles. Although only relatively effective, the Peace of God did offer Christian society some respite from plundering and incessant warfare.

Noblewomen

Feudal society was very much a man's world. In theory, women were held to be inferior to men; in practice, they were subjected to male authority. Fathers arranged the marriages of their daughters. Girls from aristocratic families were generally married at age sixteen or younger to men often twice their age; aristocratic girls who did not marry often had to enter a convent. The wife of the lord was at the mercy of her husband; if she annoyed him, she might expect a beating. But as the lady of the castle, she performed important duties. She assigned tasks to the servants, made medicines, preserved food, taught young girls how to sew, spin, and weave, and despite her subordinate position, took charge of the castle when her husband was away. Although the church taught that both men and women were precious to God and that marriage was a sacred rite, some clergymen viewed women as agents of the Devil—evil temptresses who, like the Biblical Eve, lured men into sin.

Feudalism had an enduring impact on Western civilization. It contributed to Western notions about honor, gentlemen, and romantic love (see Chapter 11). And most importantly, the principle of limiting a king's power and the practice of parliamentary government also derived from feudal traditions (see Chapters 10 and 12).

Agrarian Society

Feudalism was built on an economic foundation known as *manorialism*. Although pockets of free peasantry remained, a village community (manor) consisting of serfs bound to the land became the essential agricultural arrangement in medieval society. The manorial village was the means of organizing an agricultural society with limited markets and money. Neither the lords who warred nor the clergymen who prayed performed economically productive work. Their ways of life were made possible by the toil of serfs.

The origins of manorialism can be traced in part to the Late Roman Empire, when peasants depended on the owners of large estates for protection and security. This practice developed further during the Early Middle Ages, especially during the invasions of Northmen, Magyars, and Muslims in the ninth and tenth centuries. Peasants continued to sacrifice their freedom in exchange for protection, or in some cases, they were too weak to resist the encroachments of local magnates. Like feudalism, manorialism was not a neat system, but consisted of improvised relationships and practices that varied from region to region.

A lord controlled at least one manorial village; great lords might possess hundreds. A small manor had a dozen families; a large one had as many as fifty or sixty. The manorial village was never completely self-sufficient, because salt, millstones, and metalware were generally obtained from outside sources; it did, though, constitute a balanced economic setting. Peasants grew grain and raised cattle, sheep, goats, and hogs; blacksmiths, carpenters, and stonemasons did the building and repairing; the village priest cared for the souls of the inhabitants; and the lord defended

Chronology 9.1 The Rise of Europe

496	Clovis adopts Roman Christianity
523	Boethius writes *Consolation of Philosophy*
540	Cassiodorus establishes a monastic library at Vivarium
596	Pope Gregory sends missionaries to convert the Anglo-Saxons
717	Charles Martel becomes Mayor of the Palace under a weak Merovingian king
732	Charles Martel defeats the Muslims at Tours
751	Pepin the Short, with the support of the papacy, deposes the Merovingian ruler and becomes king of the Franks
755	Pepin donates lands taken from Lombards to the papacy
768	Charlemagne becomes king of the Franks
774	Charlemagne defeats the Lombards
782	Alcuin of York heads Charlemagne's Palace School
c. 799	Charlemagne subdues the Saxons
800	Charlemagne is crowned Emperor of the Romans by Pope Leo III
814	Charlemagne dies and is succeeded by his son Louis the Pious
840	Death of Louis the Pious; the empire is divided among his sons
c. 840s	The height of Viking attacks
c. 890	Magyars invade central Europe

the manor and administered the customary law.

When a manor was attacked by another lord, the peasants found protection inside the walls of their lord's house. By the twelfth century, this building had in many places become a well-fortified stone castle. Poor roads, few bridges, and dense forests made travel difficult; thieves and warring knights made it unsafe. Peasants generally lived, worked, and died on the lord's estate and were buried in the village churchyard. Few persons had any contact with the world beyond the village of their birth.

In return for protection and the right to cultivate fields and to pass these holdings on to their children, the serf owed obligations to his lord, and his personal freedom was restricted in a variety of ways. Bound to the land, he could not leave the manor without the lord's consent. Before a serf could marry, he had to obtain the lord's permission and pay a fee. The lord could select a wife for his serf and force him to marry her. Sometimes a serf, objecting to the lord's choice, preferred to pay a fine: "Thomas of Oldbury came on summons and was commanded to take Agatha of Halesowen to wife; he said he would rather be fined."[5] These rules also applied to the serf's children, who inherited their parents' obligations. In addition to working his allotted land, the serf had to tend the fields reserved for the lord. Other services exacted by the lord included digging ditches, gathering firewood, building fences, repairing roads and bridges, and sewing clothes. Probably somewhat more than half the serf's workweek was devoted to fulfilling these labor obligations. Serfs also paid a variety of dues to the lord. These included the annual *capitation*, a tax considered a sign of servitude; the *taille*, a tax upon the serf's property; and the *heriot*, an inheritance tax imposed when a deceased serf's sons acquired the right to their father's lands. In addition, serfs paid *banalities* for using the lord's mill, bake-oven, and winepress—fees the serfs viewed as particularly odious.

Serfs derived some benefits from manorial relationships. They received protection during a chaotic era, and they possessed customary rights, which the lord often respected, to cottages and farmlands. If a lord demanded more services or dues than was customary, or if he interfered with their right to cottages or strips of farmland, the peasants might demonstrate their discontent by refusing to labor for the lord. Up to the fourteenth century, however, open rebellion was rare because lords possessed considerable military and legal power. The manorial system promoted attitudes of dependency and servility among the serfs; their hopes for a better life were directed toward heaven.

Medieval agriculture suffered from several deficiencies. Among them was the short supply of fertilizer; farmers depended solely on animal manure. Inadequate wood ploughs and primitive methods of harnessing draft animals resulted in low yields. Yet as the Middle Ages progressed, important improvements in agriculture (discussed in Chapter 10) did take place that had wide ramifications for medieval economic and social life.

Manorialism and feudalism presupposed an unchanging social order—clergy who prayed, lords who fought, and peasants who toiled. People believed that society functioned smoothly when each person accepted his or her status and performed his or her proper role. Consequently, a person's rights, duties, and relationship to law depended on one's ranking in the social order. To change position was to upset the organic unity of society. And no one, serfs included, should be deprived of the traditional rights associated with his or her rank. This arrangement was justified by the clergy:

God himself has willed that among men, some must be lords and some serfs, in such a fashion that the lords venerate and love God, and that the serfs love and venerate their lord following the word of the Apostle; serfs obey your temporal lords with fear and trembling; lords treat your serfs according to justice and equity.[6]

The revival of an urban economy and the reemergence of central authority in the High Middle Ages would undermine feudal and manorial relationships.

Notes

1. Speros Vryonis, Jr., *Byzantium and Europe* (New York: Harcourt, Brace & World, 1967), p. 193.

2. Boethius, *The Consolation of Philosophy*, trans. by W. V. Cooper (New York: Modern Library, 1943), p. 26.

3. Ibid., p. 29.

4. Ibid., p. 34.

5. Quoted in G. G. Coulton, *Medieval Village, Manor, and Monastery* (New York: Harper Torchbooks, 1960), p. 82.

6. Quoted in V. H. H. Green, *Medieval Civilization in Western Europe* (New York: St. Martin's Press, 1971), p. 35.

Suggested Reading

Barber, Richard, *The Knight and Chivalry* (1982). The world of the feudal warrior.

Bark, W. C., *Origins of the Medieval World* (1960). The Early Middle Ages as a fresh beginning.

Dawson, Christopher, *The Making of Europe* (1957). Stresses the role of Christianity in shaping European civilization.

Duby, Georges, *The Early Growth of the European Economy* (1974). By a leading French medievalist.

Focillon, Henri, *The Year 1000* (1971). Conditions of life toward the end of the Early Middle Ages.

Ganshof, F. L., *Feudalism* (1964). A concise treatment of feudal institutions.

Keen, Maurice, *The Pelican History of Medieval Europe* (1969). A brief survey.

Laistner, M. L. W., *Thought and Letters in Western Europe* A.D. *500 to 900* (1957). A comprehensive survey of European thought in the Early Middle Ages.

Latouche, Robert, *The Birth of Western Economy* (1966). Economic decline during the Early Middle Ages.

Lewis, A. R., *Emerging Medieval Europe* (1967). Good discussions of economic and social changes.

Lot, Ferdinand, *The End of the Ancient World* (1961). The transition from the ancient world to the Middle Ages.

Morrall, John B., *The Medieval Imprint* (1971). A brief survey.

Rowling, Marjorie, *Life in Medieval Times* (1973). All phases of medieval daily life.

Southern, R. W., *The Making of the Middle Ages* (1953). A brief survey.

Thompson, J. W., and Johnson, E. N., *An Introduction to Medieval Europe* (1937). Still a valuable text.

Tierney, Brian, *Western Europe in the Middle Ages* (1970). An outstanding text.

Zacour, Norman, *An Introduction to Medieval Institutions* (1969). Comprehensive essays on all phases of medieval society.

Review Questions

1. In what ways were Greco-Roman ideas and institutions alien to Germanic traditions?

2. How was the Roman world in the West transformed by the seventh century?

3. The civilization of Latin Christendom was a blending of Christian, Greco-Roman, and Germanic traditions. Explain this statement.

4. What was the significance of monks to medieval civilization?

5. Explain the significance of the following Frankish rulers: Clovis, Charles Martel, and Pepin the Short.

6. What crucial developments occurred during the reign of Charlemagne? Why were they significant?

7. What were the causes and effects of the breakup of Charlemagne's empire?

8. What conditions led to the rise of feudalism? How did feudal law differ from Roman law?

9. What conditions led to the rise of manorialism? What obligations did a serf have to the lord? What did the serf derive in return?

10

The High Middle Ages: Vitality and Renewal

By the end of the eleventh century, Europe showed many signs of recovery and vitality. The invasions of Magyars and Vikings had ended, and powerful lords and kings imposed greater order in their territories. Improvements in technology and the clearing of new lands increased agricultural production. More food, the fortunate absence of plagues, and the limited nature of feudal warfare contributed to a population increase. The revival of long-distance trade and the emergence of towns were other visible signs of economic expansion. Offensives against the Muslims—in Spain, in Sicily, and (at the end of the century) in the Holy Land—demonstrated Europe's growing might and self-confidence. So too did the German conquest and colonization of lands on the northeastern frontier of Latin Christendom.

Reform movements strengthened the bonds between the church and the people and increased the power of the papacy. During the High Middle Ages (1050–1270) the pope, as vice regent of Christ, sought to direct, if not to rule, all Christendom. European economic and religious vitality was paralleled by a cultural flowering in philosophy, literature, and the visual arts. The civilization of Latin Christendom had entered its golden age.

Economic Expansion

The High Middle Ages was a period of economic vitality. It witnessed an agricultural revolution, a commercial revolution, the rebirth of towns, and the rise of an enterprising and dynamic middle class.

An Agricultural Revolution

During the Middle Ages, important advances were made in agriculture. Many of these innovations occurred in the early Middle Ages, but were only gradually adopted and were

Eleventh-Century Calendar: Almanac Illustration of January. The innovation of the heavy plow helped spark an agricultural revolution. Increased produc-tivity, in turn, contributed to the growth of towns and trade. (*The Bettmann Archive*)

not used everywhere; however, in time, they markedly increased production. By the end of the thirteenth century, medieval agriculture had reached a technical level far superior to that of the ancient world.

One innovation was a heavy plow that cut deeply into the soil. This new plow enabled farmers to work more quickly and effectively. As a result, they could cultivate more land, including the heavy moist soils of northern Europe that had offered too much resistance to the light plow. Another important advance in agricultural technology was the invention of the collar harness. The old yoke harness worked well with oxen, but it tended to choke horses which, because they move faster and have greater stamina than oxen, are more valuable for agricultural work. The intro-duction of the horseshoe to protect the soft hoofs of horses added to their ability to work on difficult terrain.

Two other developments were the widening use of the watermill by the tenth century and the introduction of windmills, which came into use in the twelfth century. Both inven-tions saved labor in grinding grain, and they replaced ancient hand-worked mills.

The gradual emergence of the three-field system of managing agricultural land, par-ticularly in northern Europe, increased pro-duction. In the old, widely used two-field system, half the land was planted in autumn with winter wheat, while the other half was left fallow to restore its fertility. In the new three-field system, one third of the land was planted in autumn with winter wheat, a sec-ond third was planted the following spring with oats and vegetables, and the last third remained fallow. The advantage of the three-field system was, first, that two thirds of the land was farmed and only one third was not in use. Second, the diversification of crops made more vegetable protein available.

Increased agricultural production reduced the number of deaths by starvation and di-etary disease and thus contributed to a pop-ulation increase. Grain surpluses also meant that draft animals and livestock could survive the winter. The growing number of animals provided a steady source of fresh meat and milk and increased the quantity of manure for fertilizer.

Soon the farmlands of a manorial village could not support its growing population. Consequently, peasants had to look beyond their immediate surroundings and colonize trackless wastelands. Lords vigorously pro-moted this conversion of uncultivated soil into agricultural land because it increased their incomes. Monastic communities also actively engaged in this enterprise. Almost every-where, peasants were draining swamps, clearing forests, and establishing new villages. Their endeavors during the eleventh and twelfth centuries brought vast areas of Europe under cultivation for the first time. New agricultural land was also acquired through expansion, the most notable example being the organized settlement of lands to the east by German colonists.

The colonizing and cultivation of virgin lands contributed to the decline of serfdom. Lords owned vast tracts of forests and swamps that would substantially increase their incomes if cleared, drained, and farmed. But serfs were often unwilling to move from their customary homes and fields to do the hard labor needed to cultivate these new lands. To lure serfs away from their villages, lords promised them freedom from most or all personal services. In many cases the settlers fulfilled their obligations to the lord by paying rent rather than by performing services or providing foodstuffs, thus making the transition from serfs to freemen. In time, they came to regard the land as their own. As a result of these changing economic conditions, the percentage of French peasants who were serfs had fallen from 90 percent in 1050 to about 10 percent in 1350.

The improvement in agricultural technology and the colonization of new lands altered the conditions of life in Europe. Surplus food and the increase in population freed people to work at nonfarming occupations, making possible the expansion of trade and the revival of town life.

The Revival of Trade

Expanding agricultural production, the termination of Viking attacks, greater political stability, and an increasing population produced a revival of commerce. During the Early Middle Ages, Italians and Jews kept alive a small amount of long-distance trade between Catholic Europe and the Byzantine and Islamic worlds. In the eleventh century, sea forces of Italian trading cities cleared the Mediterranean of Muslim fleets. As in Roman times, goods could circulate once again from one end of the sea to the other. The cities of Venice, Amalfi, Genoa, and Pisa grew prosperous from the lucrative Mediterranean

trade. The expanding population of northern Europe provided a market for Eastern silks, sugar, spices, and dyes, and Italian merchants were quick to exploit this demand.

By the beginning of the eleventh century the European economy showed unmistakable signs of recovery from the disorders of the previous century. During the next two centuries, local, regional, and long-distance trade gained such a momentum that some historians describe the period as a commercial revolution that surpassed the commercial activity of the Roman Empire during the pax Romana. A class of traders emerged that had business contacts in other lands, know-how, and ambition.

Crucial to the growth of trade were international fairs, where merchants and craftsmen set up stalls and booths to display their wares—swords, leather saddles, tools, rugs, shoes, silks, spices, furs, fine furniture, and other goods. Because of ever-present robbers, lords provided protection for merchants carrying their wares to and from fairs. Each fair lasted about three to six weeks; then the merchants would move on to another site. The Champagne region in northeastern France was the great center for fairs.

The principal arteries of trade flowed between the eastern Mediterranean and the Italian cities, between Scandinavia and the Atlantic coast, between northern France, Flanders, and England, and from the Baltic Sea in the north to the Black Sea and Constantinople via Russian rivers. The fine woolen cloth manufactured in Flanders provided the principal stimulus for commerce along the Atlantic coast, and Flemish merchants prospered. In exchange for Flemish cloth, Scandinavians traded hunting hawks and fur; the English traded raw wools; and the Germans traded iron and timber. A wine trade also flourished between French vineyards and English wine merchants.

Because of their strategic position, Italian towns acted as middlemen between the trade centers of the eastern Mediterranean and those of Latin Christendom. Luxury goods from as far away as India and China were transported to Italy by Italian ships, and then taken overland to parts of Germany and France. In addition, the Italians extended their trade and increased their profits by sailing westward into the Atlantic Ocean and then north to the markets of Spain, the Netherlands, and England. On return voyages they brought back wool and unfinished cloth, which in turn stimulated the Italian textile industry. Since individual businessmen often lacked sufficient capital for these large-scale enterprises, groups of merchants formed partnerships. By enabling merchants to pool their capital, reduce their risks, and expand their knowledge of profit-making opportunities, these arrangements furthered commerce.

Increased economic activity led to other advances in business techniques. Underwriters insured cargoes; the development of banking and credit instruments made it unnecessary for merchants to carry large amounts of cash. The international fairs not only were centers of international trade, but also served as capital markets for international credit transactions. The arrangements made by fair-going merchants to settle their debts held the origin of the bill of exchange. The development of systematic bookkeeping, without which no large-scale commercial activity can be conducted on a continuous basis, was another improvement in business techniques. So too was the formation of a body of commercial law that defined the rules of conduct for debts and contracts.

The Rise of Towns

In the eleventh century, towns emerged anew throughout Europe, and in the next century they became active centers of commercial and intellectual life. Towns were a new and revolutionary force—socially, economically, and culturally. Towns contributed to the decline of manorialism because they provided new opportunities, other than food producing, for commoners. A new class of merchants and

craftsmen came into being. This new class—the middle class—was made up of people who unlike the lords and serfs, were not affiliated with the land. The townsman was a new man with a different value system from that of the lord, the serf, or the clergyman.

One reason for town growth was the increased food supply arising from advances in agricultural technology. Surplus farm production meant that the countryside could support an urban population of artisans and professionals. Another reason for the rise of urban centers was the expansion of trade. Towns emerged in locations that were natural for trade—sea coasts, riverbanks, crossroads, and market sites; they also sprang up outside fortified castles and monasteries and on surviving Roman sites. The colonies of merchants who gathered at these places were joined by peasants skilled in crafts or willing to work as laborers. From a medieval record comes this description of the emergence of a town.

After this castle was built, certain traders began to flock to the place in front of the gate to the bridge of the castle, that is merchants, tavernkeepers, then other outsiders drifted in for the sake of food and shelter of those who might have business transactions with the count, who often came there. Houses and inns were erected for their accommodation, since there was not room for them within the chateau. These habitations increased so rapidly that soon a large ville came into being.[1]

Medieval towns were protected from outside attack by thick high walls, towers, and drawbridges. Most towns had a small population; the largest ones—Florence, Ghent, and Paris—had between 50,000 and 100,000 inhabitants. Covering only small areas, these walled towns were crowded with people. The narrow and crooked streets were lined with the booths and wares of merchants and artisans and were strewn with refuse. During the day the streets were jammed with mer-

Map 10.1 Medieval Trade Routes ▶

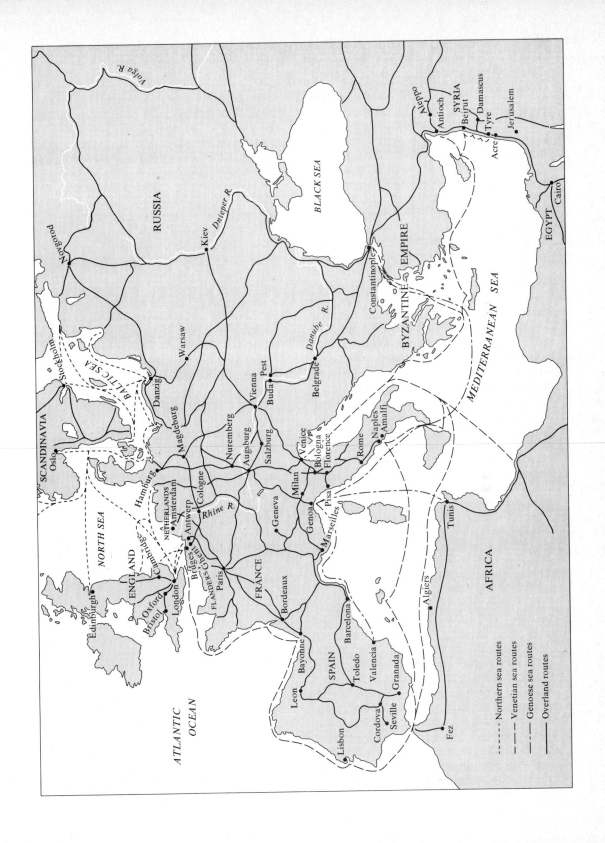

ATLANTIC
OCEAN

NORTH SEA

BALTIC SEA

Volga R.

Dnieper R.

Danube R.

BLACK SEA

MEDITERRANEAN SEA

Rhine R.

SCANDINAVIA

RUSSIA

ENGLAND

FRANCE

NETHERLANDS

FLANDERS

SPAIN

AFRICA

BYZANTINE EMPIRE

SYRIA

EGYPT

Novgorod

Oslo

Stockholm

Edinburgh

Oxford
Cambridge
Bristol
London
Bruges Ghent
Antwerp
Amsterdam
Hamburg
Cologne
Paris
Bordeaux
Bayonne

Leon
Lisbon
Toledo
Valencia
Barcelona
Cordova
Seville
Granada

Fez

Algiers

Tunis

Danzig
Warsaw
Magdeburg
Nuremberg
Augsburg
Salzburg
Vienna
Buda
Pest
Belgrade

Kiev

Geneva
Milan
Genoa
Marseilles
Pisa
Venice
Bologna
Florence
Rome
Naples
Amalfi

Constantinople

Aleppo
Antioch
Beirut
Damascus
Tyre
Acre
Jerusalem

Cairo

- - - - - Northern sea routes
————— Venetian sea routes
— · — · — Genoese sea routes
————— Overland routes

chants hawking their goods, women carrying baskets, men carting produce and merchandise, beggars pleading, and children playing. A festive occasion such as a procession honoring a patron saint sometimes brought traffic to a standstill; a hanging or a beheading was looked on as another festive occasion and always attracted a huge crowd. At night, the streets were deserted; few people ventured forth because the few elderly watchmen were no match for the numerous thieves.

Merchants and craftsmen organized guilds to protect their members from outside competition. The merchant guild in a town prevented outsiders from doing much business. A craftsman new to a town had to be admitted to the guild of his trade before he could open a shop. Competition between members of the same guild was discouraged. To prevent any guild member from making significantly more money than another member, a guild required that its members work the same number of hours, pay employees the same wages, produce goods of equal quality, and charge customers a just price. These rules were strictly enforced. Guilds also performed social and religious functions. Guildsmen attended meetings in the guildhall, celebrated holidays together, and marched in processions. The guilds cared for members who were ill or poor and extended help to widows and children of deceased members.

Because many towns were situated on land belonging to lords or on the sites of old Roman towns ruled by bishops, these communities at first came under feudal authority. In some instances, lords encouraged the founding of towns, for urban industry and commerce brought wealth to the region. However, tensions soon developed between merchants who sought freedom from feudal restrictions and lords and bishops who wanted to preserve their authority over the towns. Townsmen, or burghers, refused to be treated as serfs bound to a lord and liable for personal services and customary dues. The burghers wanted to travel, trade, marry, and dispose of their property as they pleased; they wanted

to make their own laws and levy their own taxes. Sometimes by fighting, but more often by payments of money, the townsmen obtained charters from the lords giving them the right to set up their own councils. These assemblies passed laws, collected taxes, and formed courts that enforced the laws. Towns became more or less self-governing city-states, the first since Greco-Roman days.

The leading citizens of the towns were the merchant-bankers, called patricians. Some patricians in the prosperous Italian towns enjoyed great wealth, owned considerable real estate, and engaged in business transactions involving large sums. These people generally dominated town politics; often the patricians obtained country estates and merged with the feudal aristocracy. Successful doctors and lawyers, in many instances the sons of patricians, also belonged to the urban elite. Below them on the social scale were master craftsmen in the more lucrative crafts (goldsmiths, for example) and large retailers. Then came small retailers, masters in the less profitable crafts, and journeymen training to be masters. At the bottom were the laboring poor—the bulk of the population—who were unprotected by guilds, had no special skills, and were subject to unemployment.

In a number of ways, towns loosened the hold of lords on serfs. Seeking freedom and fortune, serfs fled to the new towns where, according to custom, lords could no longer reclaim them after a year and a day. Enterprising serfs earned money by selling food to townsmen. When they acquired a sufficient sum, they bought their freedom from lords, who needed cash to pay for goods bought from merchants. Lords increasingly began to accept fixed cash payments from serfs in place of labor services or foodstuffs. As serfs met their obligations to lords with money, they gradually became rent-paying tenants and, in time, were no longer bound to the lord's land. The manorial system of personal relations and mutual obligations was disintegrating.

The activities of townsmen made them a

new breed; they engaged in business and had money and freedom. Their world was the market rather than the church, the castle, or the manor. Townsmen were freeing themselves from the prejudices both of feudal aristocrats who considered trade and manual work degrading and of the clergy who cursed the pursuit of riches as an obstacle to salvation. The townsmen were critical, dynamic, and progressive—a force for change. Medieval towns nurtured the origins of the bourgeoisie, the urban middle class, which would play a crucial role in modern European history.

The Rise of States

The revival of trade and the growth of towns were signs of a growing vitality in Latin Christendom. Another sign of strength was the greater order and security provided by the emergence of states. While feudalism fostered a Europe that was split into many local regions, each ruled by a lord, the church envisioned a vast Christian commonwealth, *Respublica Christiana,* governed by an emperor who was guided by the pope. During the High Middle Ages, the ideal of a universal Christian community seemed close to fruition. Never again would Europe possess such spiritual unity.

But there were forces at work propelling Europe in a different direction. Aided by educated and trained officials who enforced royal law, tried people in royal courts, and collected royal taxes, kings expanded their territory and slowly fashioned strong central governments. Gradually, subjects began to transfer their prime loyalty away from the church and lords to the person of the king. These developments laid the foundations of European states. Not all areas followed the same pattern. While England and France achieved a large measure of unity during the Middle Ages, Germany and Italy remained divided into numerous independent territories.

England

After the Roman legions abandoned England in the fifth century, the Germanic Angles and Saxons invaded the island and established several small kingdoms. In the ninth century, the Danes, one group of the Northmen who raided western Europe, conquered most of Anglo-Saxon England. But the Saxon kingdom of Wessex, ruled by Alfred the Great (871–899), survived. To resist the Danes, Alfred strengthened his army and built a fleet; to stem the decline in learning that accompanied the Danish invasions, Alfred, like Charlemagne, founded a palace school to which he brought scholars from other areas. Alfred himself studied Latin and translated a work of Pope Gregory I into Anglo-Saxon. He also had other works translated into Anglo-Saxon, including Boethius' *Consolation of Philosophy.* Alfred's descendants gradually regained land from the Danes and re-established Anglo-Saxon control over the island.

In 1066 the Normans—those Northmen who had first raided and then settled in France—conquered Anglo-Saxon England. Determined to establish effective control over his new kingdom, William the Conqueror, duke of Normandy, kept a sixth of conquered England for himself. In accordance with feudal practice, he distributed the rest among his Norman nobles, who swore an oath of loyalty to William and provided him with military assistance. But William made certain that no feudal baron had enough land or soldiers to threaten his power. The Norman conquest had led to the replacement of an Anglo-Saxon aristocracy with a Norman one.

To strengthen royal control, William retained Anglo-Saxon administrative practices. The land remained divided into *shires* (counties) administered by *sheriffs* (royal agents). This structure gave the king control over local government. To determine how much money he could demand, William ordered a vast census taken of people and property in every village. This data, compiled in the *Domesday Book,* listed the quantities of tenants, cattle,

Battle of Hastings from the Bayeux Tapestry. The Battle of Hastings (1066) resulted in the conquest of England by William, duke of Normandy. As a result of the Norman Conquest, England was unified at a stroke. William's victory also led to the introduction of the French language to England. This fused with Anglo-Saxon to produce Middle English. Otherwise, English would have remained a Germanic dialect. (*Anderson/Art Resource*)

sheep, pigs, and farm equipment throughout the realm. Thus, better than any other monarch of his day, William knew what the assets of his kingdom were. Because William had conquered England in one stroke, his successors did not have to travel the long, painful road to national unity followed by French monarchs.

A crucial development in shaping national unity was the emergence of *common law*. When Henry I became king in 1100, England had conflicting baronial claims and legal traditions that were a barrier to unity. There was the old Anglo-Saxon law, the feudal law introduced by the Normans from France, the church law, and the commercial law emerging among the town businessmen. During the reigns of Henry I (1100–1135) and Henry II (1154–1189), royal judges traveled to different parts of the kingdom. Throughout England, important cases began to be tried in the king's court rather than in local courts, thereby increasing royal power. The decisions of royal judges were recorded and used as guides for future cases. In this way, a law common to

the whole land gradually came to prevail over the customary law of a specific locality. Because common law applied to all England, it served as a force for unity. It also provided a fairer system of justice. The common law remains the foundation of the English legal system.

Henry II made trial by jury a regular judicial procedure for many cases heard in the king's court, laying the foundations of the modern system. Henry II also ordered representatives of a given locality to report under oath to visiting royal judges any local persons who were suspected of murder or robbery. This indictment jury was the ancestor of the modern grand jury system.

Paralleling the development of a strong judicial system was the growth of an efficient financial administration. The Exchequer, the royal accounting office, was formed during the early years of Henry I's reign. Its officials saw to the collection of all revenues owed the king. These officials, like the judges, formed a class of professional administrators personally loyal to the king.

King John (1199–1216) inadvertently precipitated a situation that led to another step in the political development of England. Fighting a costly and losing war with the king of France, John had coerced his vassals into giving him more and more revenue; also he had punished some vassals without a proper trial. In 1215, the angry barons rebelled and compelled John to fix his seal to a document called the Great Charter, or *Magna Carta*. The Magna Carta is celebrated as the root of the unique English respect for basic rights and liberties. Although essentially a feudal document directed against a king who had violated feudal practices, the Magna Carta stated certain principles that could be interpreted more widely.

Over the centuries, these principles were expanded to protect the liberties of Englishmen against governmental oppression. The Magna Carta stated that no unusual taxes "shall be imposed in our kingdom except by the common consent of our kingdom." In time, this right came to mean that the king could not levy taxes without the consent of Parliament, the governmental body that represents the English people. The Magna Carta also provided that "no freeman shall be taken or imprisoned . . . save by the lawful judgment of his peers or by the law of the land." The barons who drew up the document had intended it to mean that they must be tried by fellow barons. As time passed, these words were regarded as a guarantee of trial by jury for all men, a prohibition against arbitrary arrest, and a command to dispense justice fully, freely, and equally. Implied in the Magna Carta is the idea that the king cannot rule as he pleases, but must govern according to the law, and that not even the king can violate the law of the nation. Centuries afterward, when Englishmen sought to limit the king's power, they would interpret the Magna Carta in this way.

In Anglo-Saxon England the tradition had emerged that the king should consider the advice of the leading men in the land. Later, William the Conqueror continued this practice by seeking the opinions of leading nobles and bishops. In the thirteenth century it became accepted custom that the king should not decide major issues without consulting these advisors as assembled in the Great Council. Lesser landowners and townsmen also began to be summoned to meet with the king. These two groups were eventually called the House of Lords (bishops and nobles) and the House of Commons (knights and burghers). Thus the English Parliament had evolved, and by the mid–fourteenth century it had become a permanent institution of government.

Frequently in need of money but unable to levy new taxes without the approval of Parliament, the king had to turn to that body for help. Parliament used this control over money matters to increase its power. The tradition grew that the power to govern rested not with the king alone, but with the king and Parliament together.

During the Middle Ages, England became a centralized and unified state. But the king did not have unlimited power; he was not above the law. The rights of the people were protected by certain principles implicit in the common law and the Magna Carta, and by the power of Parliament.

France

In the 150 years following Charlemagne's death, the western part of his empire, which was destined to become France, faced terrible ordeals. Charlemagne's heirs fought each other for the crown; the Vikings raided everywhere their ships would carry them; Muslims from Spain plundered the southern coast; and strong lords usurped power for themselves. With the Carolingian family unable to maintain the throne, the great lords elected the king. In 987, they chose Hugh Capet (987–996), the count of Paris. Because many great lords held territories far larger than those of Hugh, the French king did not seem a threat to noble power. But Hugh strengthened the French monarchy by having the lords also elect his son as his co-ruler. This practice endured until it became understood that the crown would remain with the Capetian family.

With the accession of Louis VI (1108–1137), a two-hundred-year period of steadily increasing royal power began. Louis started this trend by successfully subduing the barons in his own duchy. A decisive figure in the expansion of royal power was Philip Augustus (1180–1223). Philip struck successfully at King John of England (of Magna Carta fame), who held more territory in France than Philip did. When William, duke of Normandy in western France, had conquered England in 1066, he became ruler of England and Normandy; William's great-grandson Henry II had acquired much of southern France through marriage to Eleanor of Aquitaine in 1152. By stripping King John of most of his French territory (Normandy, Anjou, and much of Aquitaine), Philip trebled the size of his kingdom and became stronger than any French lord.

Louis IX (1226–1270)—pious, compassionate, conscientious, and a genuine lover of peace—was perhaps the best-loved French monarch of the Middle Ages. Departing from feudal precedent, Louis issued ordinances for the entire realm without seeking the consent of his vassals. One ordinance prohibited private warfare among the nobility. Another promoted the nationwide circulation of coins produced by royal mints. These ordinances furthered royal power and promoted order.

Under Louis IX and his successors, the power of the French monarch continued to grow. Kings added to their lands by warfare and marriage; they devised new ways of raising money, including taxing the clergy. A particularly effective way of increasing the monarch's power was by extending royal justice. In the thirteenth century, the king's court, *Parlement*, became the highest court in France. Quarrels between the king and his vassals were resolved in the Parlement, and many cases previously tried in lords' courts were transferred to the king's court. Moreover, since the decision of feudal courts could be appealed to the Parlement, lords no longer had the last say on legal questions.

In the beginning of the fourteenth century, Philip IV (the Fair) engaged in a struggle with the papacy (see pages 255–256). Seeking to demonstrate that he had the support of his subjects, Philip convened a national assembly called the *Estates General*, representing clergy, nobility, and townsmen. It would be called again to vote funds for the crown. But unlike the English Parliament, the Estates General never became an important body in French political life, and it never succeeded in controlling the monarch. While the basis for limited monarchy had been established in England, no comparable checks on the king's power developed in France. By the end of the Middle Ages, French kings had succeeded in creating a unified state. But regional and local loyalties remained strong and persisted for centuries.

Germany

After the destruction of Charlemagne's empire, its German territories were broken into large duchies. Following an ancient German practice, the ruling dukes elected one of their own as king. The German king, however, had little authority outside his own duchy. Some German kings tried not to antagonize the dukes, but Otto the Great (936–973) was determined to control them. He entered into an alliance with German bishops and archbishops who could provide him with fighting men and trained administrators—a policy continued by his successors.

In 951, Otto marched into northern Italy in an attempt to assert his influence. Ten years later, he returned to protect the pope from his Italian enemies. In 962, in emulation of the coronation of Charlemagne, the pope crowned Otto "Emperor of the Romans." (Later the title would be changed to Holy Roman emperor.)

The revival of the empire meant that the history of medieval Germany was closely tied to that of Italy and the papacy. Otto and his successors wanted to dominate Italy and the pope—an ambition that embroiled the Holy Roman emperor in a life-and-death struggle

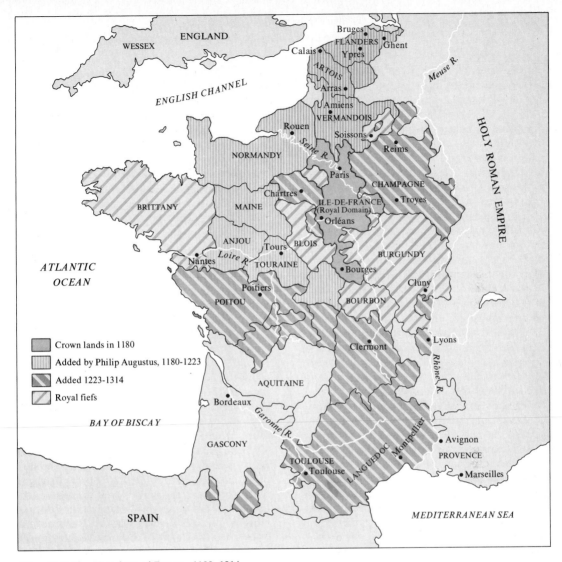

Map 10.2 The Kingdom of France, 1180–1314

Crown lands in 1180

Added by Philip Augustus, 1180-1223

Added 1223-1314

Royal fiefs

with the papacy. The papacy allied itself with the German dukes and the Italian cities, enemies of the emperor. The intervention in papal and Italian politics was the principal reason why German territories did not achieve unity in the Middle Ages.

The Emergence of Representative Institutions

One great contribution of the Middle Ages to the modern world was the representative institution. Representative assemblies, or parliaments, had their beginnings at the end of the twelfth century in the Spanish kingdom of León. In the thirteenth century, they had developed in other Spanish kingdoms—Castile, Aragon, Catalonia, Valencia—and in Portugal, England, and the Holy Roman Empire. In the fourteenth century, parliaments arose in France and the Netherlands.

Kings generally came to accept the principles that parliamentary consent was required for levying taxes and that the king should consult parliament about important laws and obtain its approval. The parliaments had usually grown out of royal dependence on the nobility for military support. Because of this dependence, monarchs considered it wise to listen to the opinions of the lords. Consequently, it became customary for the king to summon councils to discuss matters of war and peace and other vital questions. As the high clergy also constituted an important group in the realm, they too were consulted. And as towns gained in wealth and significance, townsmen also were asked to royal councils. Leading nobles came to represent the nobility as an order of society; members of the upper clergy—archbishops, bishops, and abbots—represented the entire clergy; and deputies from the towns represented their fellow townsmen. An important tradition had been established: the duty of the monarch to seek advice and consent on issues of concern to his subjects. Perhaps the practice of representative government was influenced by those church lawyers who held that the pope should seek the guidance of the Christian community as expressed in church councils— meetings of representatives of the secular and regular clergy.

To be sure, in succeeding centuries parliaments would either be ignored or dominated by kings. Nevertheless, the principle of constitutional government—government by consent—was woven into the fabric of Western society. The representative parliament is unique to Western civilization; it has no parallel in the political systems of the non-European world. Originating in the Middle Ages, the representative assembly is a distinct achievement and contribution of Western civilization.

The Growth of Papal Power

Accompanying economic recovery and increased political stability in the High Middle Ages was a growing spiritual vitality marked by several developments. The common people were showing greater devotion to the church.

Within the church, reform movements were attacking clerical abuses, and the papacy was growing more powerful. A holy war against the Muslims was drawing the Christian community closer together. During this period, the church tried with great determination to make society follow divine standards; that is, it tried to shape all institutions and expressions of the intellect according to a comprehensive Christian outlook.

The Sacraments

As the sole interpreters of God's revelation and the sole ministers of his sacraments, the clergy imposed and supervised the moral outlook of Christendom. Divine grace was channeled through the sacraments, which could be administered only by the church, the indispensable intermediary between the individual and God. For those persons who resisted its authority, the church could impose the penalty of excommunication (expulsion from the church and denial of the sacraments, without which there could be no salvation).

Through the seven sacraments, the community of the church encompassed the individual from birth to death. The rite of baptism cleansed the individual—usually an infant—of the stain of original sin. Confirmation granted the young adult additional grace to that received at baptism. Matrimony made marriage a holy union. Extreme unction was administered to the dying in an effort to remove the remains of sin. The sacrament of the Eucharist, derived from the Gospel accounts of Christ's Last Supper, took place within a liturgical service, the Mass; in a solemn ceremony, the bread and wine were miraculously transformed into the substance of the body and blood of Christ, which the priest administered, allowing the faithful to partake of Christ's saving grace. The sacrament of penance required a sinner to show sorrow for his sin, to confess it to a priest,

Map 10.3 The Holy Roman Empire, c. 1200 ▶

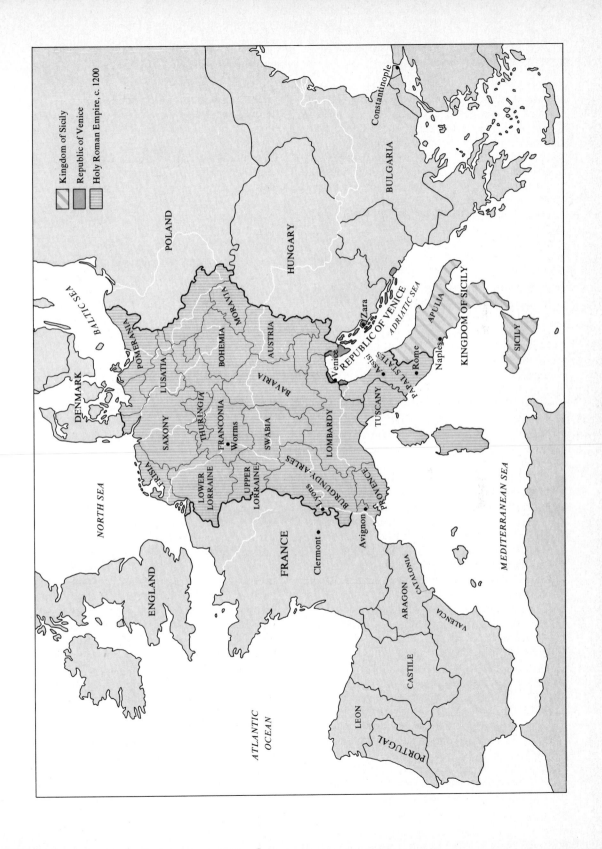

Kingdom of Sicily
Republic of Venice
Holy Roman Empire, c. 1200

BALTIC SEA

NORTH SEA

ATLANTIC
OCEAN

ENGLAND

DENMARK

POMERANIA

POLAND

FRISIA

SAXONY

LUSATIA

THURINGIA

BOHEMIA

MORAVIA

HUNGARY

LOWER
LORRAINE

FRANCONIA

Worms

UPPER
LORRAINE

SWABIA

BAVARIA

AUSTRIA

FRANCE

Clermont

BURGUNDY-ARLES

Lyons

LOMBARDY

PROVENCE

Avignon

TUSCANY

REPUBLIC OF VENICE

Venice

Zara

ADRIATIC SEA

BULGARIA

Constantinople

ASSISI

PAPAL STATES

Rome

Naples

KINGDOM OF SICILY

APULIA

SICILY

MEDITERRANEAN SEA

PORTUGAL

LEON

CASTILE

ARAGON

CATALONIA

VALENCIA

and to perform an act of penance—prayer, fasting, almsgiving, or a pilgrimage to a holy shrine; through the priest the sinner could receive absolution and be rescued from spending eternity in hell. This sacrament enabled the church to enforce its moral standards throughout Latin Christendom. The final sacrament, ordination, was used in consecrating men in holy orders.

The Gregorian Reform

By the tenth century, the church was Western Europe's leading landowner, owning much of Italy and vast properties in other lands. However, the papacy was in no position to exercise commanding leadership over Latin Christendom. The office of pope had fallen under the domination of aristocractic families; they conspired and on occasion murdered in order to place one of their own on the wealthy and powerful throne of Saint Peter. As the papacy became a prize for Rome's leading families, it was not at all unusual for popes themselves to be involved in conspiracies and assassinations. Also weakening the authority of the papacy were local lords, who dominated churches and monasteries by appointing bishops and abbots and by collecting the income from church taxes. These bishops and abbots, appointed by lords for political reasons, lacked the spiritual devotion to maintain high standards of discipline among the priests and monks.

What raised the power of the papacy to unprecedented heights was the emergence of a reform movement, particularly in French and German monasteries. High-minded monks called for a reawakening of spiritual fervor and the elimination of moral laxity among the clergy, especially a concern for worldly goods, the taking of mistresses, and a diminishing commitment to the Benedictine rule. Of the many monasteries that participated in this reform movement, the Benedictine monks of Cluny in Burgundy, France, were the most influential.

Founded in 910, Cluny soon established daughter houses in France, Germany, England, and Italy, which were supervised by the mother monastery. Cluniac monks attempted to impose Christian ideas on society. The monks demanded that clergymen should not take wives or mistresses, and that they should not purchase their offices in the church. The monks tried to liberate their monasteries from the control of lords and commanded them to use their arms not for personal advantage but for Christian ends—the protection of the church and the unfortunate.

In the middle of the eleventh century, popes came under the influence of the monastic reformers. In 1059, a special synod convened by the reform-minded Pope Nicholas II moved to end the interference of Roman nobles and German Holy Roman emperors in the selection of the pope. Henceforth, a select group of clergymen called *cardinals* would essentially be responsible for choosing the pontiff.

The reform movement found its most zealous exponent in the person of Hildebrand, who became Pope Gregory VII in 1073. For Gregory, human society was part of a divinely ordered universe governed by God's universal law. As the supreme spiritual leader of Christendom, the pope was charged with the mission of establishing a Christian society on earth. As successor to Saint Peter, the pope had the final word on matters of faith and doctrine. All bishops came under his authority; so did kings, whose powers should be used for Christian ends. The pope was responsible for instructing rulers in the proper use of their God-given powers, and kings had the solemn duty to obey these instructions. If the king failed in his Christian duty, the pope could deny him his right to rule. Responsible for implementing God's law, the pope could never take a subordinate position to kings.

Like no other pope before him, Gregory VII made a determined effort to assert the pre-eminence of the papacy over both the church hierarchy and secular rulers. This determination led to a bitter struggle between the papacy and German monarch and future

Holy Roman emperor Henry IV. The dispute was a dramatic confrontation between two competing versions of the relationship between secular and spiritual authority.

Through his reforms, Gregory VII intended to improve the moral quality of the clergy and to liberate the church from all control by secular authorities. He forbade priests who had wives or concubines to celebrate mass, deposed clergy who had bought their offices, excommunicated bishops and abbots who received their estates from a lay lord, and expelled from the church lay lords who invested bishops with their office. The appointment of bishops, Pope Gregory insisted, should be controlled entirely by the church.

This last point touched off the conflict, called the *Investiture Controversy*, between Henry and Pope Gregory. Bishops served a dual function. On the one hand, they belonged to the spiritual community of the church; on the other, as members of the nobility and holders of estates, they were also integrated into the feudal order. Traditionally, emperors had both granted bishops their feudal authority and invested them with their spiritual authority. In maintaining that no lay rulers could confer ecclesiastical offices on their appointees, Pope Gregory threatened Henry's authority.

Seeking allies in the conflict with feudal nobility in earlier times, German kings had made vassals of the upper clergy. In return for a fief, bishops had agreed to provide troops for a monarch in his struggle against the lords. But if kings had no control over the appointment of bishops—in accordance with Pope Gregory's view—they would lose the allegiance, military support, and financial assistance of their most important allies. To German monarchs, bishops were officers of the state who served the throne. Moreover, by agreeing to Gregory's demands, German kings would lose their freedom of action and be dominated by the Roman pontiff. Henry IV regarded Gregory VII as a fanatic who trampled on custom, meddled in German state affairs, and threatened to subordinate kingship to the papacy.

Emperor Henry IV and His Anti-Pope, Clement III, Expelling Pope Gregory VII, Twelfth Century. Papal intervention in political matters led to violent opposition from monarchs in England, France, and Germany. None was as bitter as the conflict between Henry IV and Gregory VII. The *Republica Christiana* foundered. (*The Granger Collection*)

With the approval of the German bishops, Henry called for Pope Gregory to descend from the throne of Saint Peter. Gregory in turn excommunicated Henry and deposed him as king. German lands were soon embroiled in a civil war, as German lords used the quarrel to strike at Henry's power. The princes declared that they would not recognize Henry as king if the ban of excommunication were not lifted, and they invited Gregory to meet with them in Germany. Henry, who did not want Gregory to come to Germany and stir up his rebellious subjects, shrewdly planned to journey to Italy and appeal to Gregory to remove the stigma of excommunication. As Christ's vicar, Gregory was obligated to forgive a humble penitent. In midwinter, the German monarch crossed the Alps into northern Italy and headed for the castle of Canossa, where Gregory was staying. After three days the pope forgave Henry. This act of humility was, in a way, a victory for Henry, because with the ban of excommunication removed, he was able to deal more effectively with his rebellious lords. The image of the German emperor pleading for forgiveness, however, had the effect of increasing the prestige of the papacy enormously.

But the civil war persisted. The lords declared Henry deposed and elected Rudolf as his successor. Gregory, again disillusioned with Henry, recognized Rudolf as the new king. Not to be outdone, Henry, with the support of his warrior-bishops, declared Pope Gregory deposed. Finally Henry's troops crossed the Alps, successfully attacked Rome, and installed a new pope who, in turn, crowned Henry Emperor of the Romans. Gregory died in exile.

The papacy had resiliency, however. Gregory's successors were energetic men who skillfully promoted papal interests. Finally in 1122, the church and Emperor Henry V reached a compromise. Bishops were to be elected exclusively by the church and to be invested with the staff and the ring—symbols of spiritual power—by the archbishop, not the king. This change signified that the bishop owed his role as spiritual leader to the church only. But the king would grant the bishop the scepter, an act that would indicate that the bishop was also the recipient of a fief and the king's vassal, owing feudal obligations to the crown. This compromise, called the *Concordat of Worms,* recognized the dual function of the bishop as a spiritual leader in the church and a feudal landowner. Similar settlements were reached with the kings of France and England.

The Investiture Controversy had important consequences both for German territories and for the papacy. As a result of the civil war, the great German lords strengthened their control over their lands, thereby thwarting the unifying and centralizing efforts of the monarchy. The conflict with the papacy kept Germany, unlike England and France, from emerging from the Middle Ages as a unified state. Despite the exile of Gregory VII and the appointment of a new pope by Henry IV, the Investiture Controversy was no defeat for the papacy. The Concordat of Worms recognized that the church was an independent body headed by the papacy, over which rulers had no authority. Moreover, Gregory's vision of a Christendom guided by the pope, and of the state subordinate to and in the service of the papacy, persisted. Future popes, sharing his vision, would raise the papacy to new heights of power.

The conflict between the papacy and the German rulers continued after the Concordat of Worms—a contest for supremacy between the heir of Saint Peter and the heir of Charlemagne. German monarchs aimed at controlling the papacy and the prosperous north Italian cities. When Frederick I (1152–1190), known as Frederick Barbarossa ("Red Beard"), tried to assert authority over these cities, they resisted. In 1176, the armies of an alliance of Italian cities supported by the pope decisively defeated Frederick's forces. The Italian infantry showed that it could defeat knights on horseback, and Frederick was compelled to recognize the independence of the Italian cities. His numerous expeditions to Italy weakened his authority; German princes strengthened themselves at the expense of the monarchy, thereby continuing to preclude German unity.

Frederick did, however, achieve a diplomatic triumph. He arranged for his son, Henry VI, to marry the heiress to the kingdom of Sicily. Consisting of the island of Sicily and most of the Italian mainland south of Rome, the kingdom was well run and economically advanced. The papacy waged a relentless struggle to separate Sicily from the Holy Roman Empire. In attempting to join Sicily to Germany, Henry and his successors severely strained German resources. Taking advantage of the emperor's difficulties in Sicily, German princes continued to consolidate their power at home.

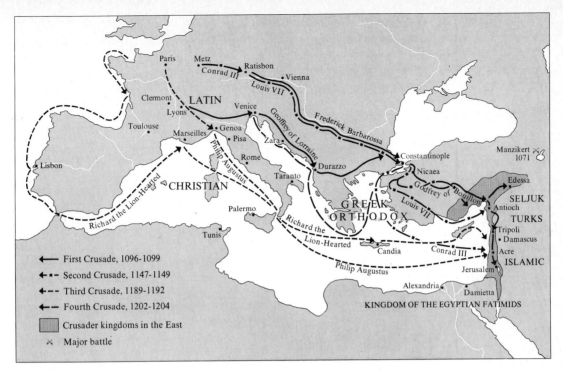

Map 10.4 The Routes of the Crusades

The Crusades

Like the movement for spiritual renewal associated with the Cluniac reformers, the Crusades—wars to regain the Holy Land from the Muslims—were an outpouring of Christian zeal and an attempt by the papacy to assert its pre-eminence. The Crusades were another sign—like the renewal of commerce and the growth of towns—of growing vitality and self-confidence. The victims of earlier Muslim attacks, Latin Christians now took the offensive.

The Crusades were also part of a general movement of expansion that took place in Europe during the High Middle Ages. Latin Christians were venturing forth as pioneers to open new lands to cultivation and as conquerors to expand the borders of Christendom.

By the middle of the eleventh century, Genoans and Pisans had driven the Muslims from Sardinia. In 1087, they successfully attacked the North African port of Tunis, a leading base for Muslim pirates, and forced the Emir of Tunis to free Christian captives and to favor Genoese and Pisan merchants. By 1091, Normans had taken Sicily from the Muslims and southern Italy from Byzantium. With the support of the papacy, Christian knights engaged in the long struggle to drive the Muslims from Spain; by 1248, after more than two centuries of conflict, only the small southern kingdom of Granada remained in Muslim hands. Germans conquered and colonized lands south of the Baltic coast inhabited by non-Christian Slavs, Balts, and Prussians. German settlers brought with them Christianity and German language and culture. They cleared vast tracts of virgin land for farming and established towns in a region where urban life had virtually been unknown.

In the eleventh century the Seljuk Turks, who had earlier embraced Islam, conquered vast regions of the Near East, including Anatolia, a province of the Byzantine Empire. With the death of the Turkish sultan in 1092, the Seljuk Empire broke up, which reduced the pressure on Byzantium. Seeking to strengthen his army in preparation for the reconquest of Anatolia, Byzantine Emperor Alexius appealed to the West for mercenaries.

Pope Urban II, at the Council of Clermont (in France) in 1095, exaggerated the danger confronting Eastern Christianity. He called for a holy crusade against the heathen Turks, whom he accused of defiling and destroying Christian churches. Several months later he expanded his objectives to include the conquest of Jerusalem. A Christian army, mobilized by the papacy to defend the faith and to regain the Holy Land from nonbelievers, accorded with the papal concept of a just war; it would channel the energies of Europe's warrior class in a Christian direction. A crusade against the Muslims also held the promise of bringing the Eastern church, which had formally broken with Rome in 1054, under papal leadership. In organizing a crusade for Christian ends, Urban II, like Pope Gregory in his struggle with Henry IV, sought to demonstrate the supremacy of the papacy.

What motivated the knights and others who responded to Urban's appeal? No doubt the Crusaders regarded themselves as armed pilgrims dedicated to rescuing holy places from the hated Muslims. Through the years Christian pilgrims had made the journey to Jerusalem to do penance for crimes against the church and to demonstrate their piety. These pilgrims and other devout Christians found it deplorable that Christian holy places were controlled by heathen Muslims. Moreover, Urban declared that participation in a crusade was itself an act of penance, an acceptable way of demonstrating sorrow for sin. In their enthusiasm to recruit warriors, popular preachers went even further; they promised cancellation of penalties for sin. To a knight, a crusade was no doubt a great adventure that promised glory and plunder, but it was also an opportunity to remit sins by engaging in a holy war. The enthusiasm with which knights became Christian warriors demonstrated the extent to which the warrior mentality of the nobles had become penetrated by Christian principles.

Stirred by popular preachers, the common people also became gripped by the crusading spirit. The most remarkable of the evangelists was Peter the Hermit. Small and thin, with a long gray beard caked with mud, Peter rode his donkey through the French countryside arousing the religious zeal of plain folk. Swayed by the old man's eloquence, thousands of poor people abandoned their villages and joined Peter's march to Jerusalem. As this army of the poor crossed Germany, the credulous peasants expected to find Jerusalem just beyond the horizon; some thought that Peter was leading them straight to heaven. While Peter's army made its way to Constantinople, another army of commoners recruited in Germany began their crusade by massacring the Jews of the Rhineland, despite the efforts of bishops to protect them. Unlike Peter's army, these commoners never reached Constantinople; after plundering Hungary, they were slaughtered by Hungarians (Magyars). Camped in the suburbs of Constantinople, Peter's restless recruits crossed into Turkish territory where they also were massacred. Faith alone could not win Jerusalem.

Departing later than the commoners, an army of knights assembled in Constantinople in the spring of 1097. After enduring the long march through Anatolia, the Christian army arrived at Antioch in Syria, which they captured after a long siege. In June 1099, three years after leaving Europe, the Crusaders stood outside the walls of Jerusalem. Using siege weapons, they broke into the city and slaughtered the Muslim and Jewish inhabitants.

Weakened by local rivalries and religious quarrels, the Muslim world failed to unite against the Christian invaders who, in addition to capturing Jerusalem, carved out four principalities in the Near East. But how long could these Christian states, islands in a Muslim sea, endure against a Muslim counteroffensive?

Never resigned to the establishment of Christian states in their midst, Muslim leaders called for a *jihad,* or holy war. In 1144, one

Capture of Jerusalem. "Mad with joy, we reached the city of Jerusalem on the Tuesday, eight days before the Ides of June, and laid seige to it," wrote one crusader. Two months later, the crusaders broke into the city and massacred its inhabitants. (*Bibliothèque Nationale, Paris*)

of the Crusader states, the County of Edessa, fell to the resurgent forces of Islam. Alarmed by the loss of Edessa, Pope Eugenius II called for a second crusade. In 1147, King Louis VII of France and Emperor Conrad III of Germany led their forces across the Balkans into Asia Minor. Both armies, traveling independently, were decimated by Seljuk Turks, and only a fraction of the Christian forces reached their destination. The Second Crusade was a complete failure.

After 1174, Saladin, a brilliant commander, became the most powerful leader in the Muslim Near East, and in 1187 he invaded Pal-estine. Saladin annihilated a Christian army near Nazareth and captured Jerusalem in 1189. In contrast to Christian knights of the First Crusade, who filled Jerusalem with blood and corpses, Saladin permitted no slaughter. The capture of Jerusalem led to the Third Crusade, in which some of Europe's most prominent rulers participated—Richard I, the Lion Hearted, of England, Philip Augustus of France, and Frederick Barbarossa of Germany. The Crusaders captured Acre and Jaffa, but Jerusalem remained in Muslim hands.

Other crusades followed, but the position of the Christian states in the Near East continued to deteriorate. In 1291, almost two centuries after Pope Urban's appeal, the last Christian strongholds in the Near East had fallen.

The Crusades had some immediate effects on Latin Christendom. They increased the wealth of the Italian cities that had furnished transportation for the Crusaders and had benefited from the increased trade with the East. They may have contributed to the decline of feudalism and the strengthening of monarchy, because many lords were killed in battle or squandered their wealth financing expeditions to the Holy Land. Although the call for the Crusades demonstrated the growing power of the papacy, in the long run the crusading movement may have diminished the papacy in the eyes of Christendom. In time, popes corrupted the crusading ideal, employing it for political reasons as a weapon against European rulers.

The two centuries of conflict between Christendom and Islam did not produce many significant results. The Crusades did foster trade between Latin Christendom and the East, but the revival of trade had already begun and would have proceeded without the Crusades. The Crusades stimulated an interest in geography and travel and became a theme in literature, but they did not significantly influence European cultural progress. The Crusaders had no contact with Muslim centers of learning in the Near East; it was through Spain and Sicily that Muslim learning penetrated Latin Christendom and helped stimulate the cultural awakening of the twelfth and thirteenth centuries. Over the centuries, people have praised the Crusades for inspiring idealism and heroism; others have castigated the movement for corrupting the Christian spirit, for unleashing religious intolerance and fanaticism that would lead to strife in future centuries.

Dissenters and Reformers

Freedom of religion is a modern concept; it was totally alien to the medieval outlook.

Regarding itself as the possessor and guardian of divine truth, the church felt a profound obligation to purge Christendom of heresy—beliefs that challenged Christian orthodoxy. To the church, heretics had committed treason against God and were carriers of a deadly infection. Heresy was the work of Satan; lured by false ideas, people might abandon the true faith and deny themselves salvation. The church could never create a Christian world community if heretics rebelled against clerical authority and created divisions among the faithful. In the eyes of the church, heretics not only obstructed individual salvation, but also undermined the foundations of society.

To compel obedience, the church used its power of excommunication. An excommunicated person could not receive the sacraments or attend church services—fearful punishments in an age of faith. In dealing with a recalcitrant ruler, the church could declare an interdict on his territory, which in effect denied the ruler's subjects the sacraments (although exceptions could be made). The church hoped that the pressure exerted by an aroused populace would compel the offending ruler to mend his ways.

The church also conducted heresy trials. Before the thirteenth century, local bishops were responsible for locating heretics and putting them on trial. In 1233 the papacy established the Inquisition, a court specially designed to fight heresy. Accused heretics were presumed guilty until proven innocent, were not told the names of their accusers, and were not permitted lawyers. To wrest a confession from the accused, torture was permitted. Accused persons who persisted in their beliefs were turned over to the civil authorities to be burned at the stake.

The Waldensians　　Dissent in the Middle Ages was often reformist in character. Inspired by the Gospels, reformers criticized the church for its wealth and involvement in worldly affairs; they called for a return to the simpler, purer life of Jesus and the Apostles. Reform movements drew support from the new class of town dwellers; the church often rebuked the way of life in towns and only slowly adjusted to the townsmen's spiritual needs.

In their zeal to emulate the moral purity and material poverty of the first followers of Jesus, these reform-minded dissenters attacked ecclesiastical authority. The Waldensians, followers of Peter Waldo, a rich merchant of Lyon, were a case in point. In the 1170s, Peter distributed his property to the poor and attracted both male and female supporters. Like their leader, they committed themselves to poverty and to preaching the Gospel in the *vernacular,* or native tongue, rather than in the church's Latin, which many Christians did not understand. The Waldensians considered themselves true Christians, faithful to the spirit of the apostolic church. Repelled by Waldensian attacks against the immorality of the clergy and by the fact that these laymen were preaching the Gospel, ecclesiastical authorities condemned the movement as heretical. Despite persecution, however, the Waldensians continued to survive as a group in northern Italy.

The Cathari Catharism was the most radical heresy to confront the medieval church. This belief represented a curious mixture of Gnosticism and Manichaeism—Eastern religious movements that had competed with Christianity in the days of the Roman Empire—and of doctrines condemned as heretical by the early church. Carried to Italy and southern France by Bulgarian missionaries, Catharism gained followers in regions where opposition to the worldliness and wealth of the clergy was already strong.

Cathari tenets differed considerably from those of the church. The Cathari believed in an eternal conflict between the forces of the god of good and those of the god of evil. Because the evil god, whom they identified with the God of the Old Testament, created the world, this earthly home was evil. The soul, spiritual in nature, was good, but it was trapped in wicked flesh. Because sexual activity was responsible for imprisoning the spirit in the flesh, the Cathari urged abstinence to avoid the birth of still another wicked human. They also abstained from eggs, cheese, milk, and meat because these foods were the products of sexual activity. The Cathari taught that since the flesh is evil, Christ would not have taken a human form; hence he could not have suffered on the cross nor have been resurrected. Nor could God have issued forth from the evil flesh of the Virgin. According to Catharism, Jesus was not God but an angel. In order to enslave people, the evil god created the church, which demonstrated its wickedness by pursuing power and wealth. Repudiating the church, the Cathari organized their own ecclesiastical hierarchy.

The center for the Catharist heresy was southern France, where a strong tradition of protest existed against the moral laxity and materialism of the clergy. When the Cathari did not submit to peaceful persuasion, Innocent III called on kings and lords to exterminate Catharism with the sword. Lasting from 1208 to 1229, the war against the Cathari was marked by brutality and fanaticism.

The Franciscans and the Dominicans Driven by a zeal for reform, devout laymen condemned the clergy for moral abuses. Sometimes their piety and resentment exploded into heresy; other times it was channeled into movements that served the church. Such was the case with the two great orders of friars, Franciscans and Dominicans.

Like Peter Waldo, Saint Francis of Assisi (c. 1181–1226) came from a wealthy merchant family. After undergoing an intense religious experience, Francis abandoned his possessions and devoted his life to imitating Christ. Dressed as a beggar, he wandered into villages and towns preaching, healing, and befriending. Unlike the monks who withdrew into walled fortresses, Francis proclaimed Christ's message to the poor of the towns. Like Peter Waldo, he preached a religion of personal feeling; like Jesus, he stretched out a hand of love to the poor, to the helpless, to the sick, and even to lepers whom everyone feared to approach. The saintly Francis soon attracted disciples called *Little Brothers,* who followed in the footsteps of their leader.

To suspicious churchmen the Little Brothers seemed another heretical movement protesting against a wealthy and worldly church. However, Francis respected the authority of the priesthood and the validity of the sacraments. Recognizing that such a popular movement could be useful to the church, Innocent III allowed Francis to continue his mission. Innocent hoped that the Franciscans would help keep within the church those laymen who had deep religious feelings but were dissatisfied with the leadership of the traditional hierarchy.

As the Franciscans grew in popularity, the papacy exercised greater control over their activities; in time the order was transformed from a spontaneous movement of inspired laymen into an organized agent of papal policy. The Franciscans served the church as teachers and missionaries in eastern Europe, North Africa, the Near East, and China. The papacy set aside Francis's prohibition against the Brothers owning churches, houses, and lands corporately. His desire to keep the movement a lay order was abandoned when the papacy granted the Brothers the right to hear confession. Francis's opposition to formal learning as irrelevant to preaching Gospel love was rejected when the movement began to urge university education for its members. Those who protested against these changes as a repudiation of Francis's spirit were persecuted, and a few were even burned at the stake as heretics.

The Dominican order was founded by Saint Dominic (c. 1170–1221), a Spanish nobleman who had preached against the Cathari in southern France. Believing that those well-versed in Christian teaching could best combat heresy, Dominic, unlike Francis, insisted that his followers engage in study. In time, the Dominicans became some of the leading theologians in the universities. Like the Franciscans they went out into the world to preach the Gospel and to proselytize. Dominican friars became the chief operators of the Inquisition. For their zeal in fighting heresy, they were known as the watchdogs of the Lord.

Innocent III: The Apex of Papal Power

During the pontificate of Innocent III (1198–1216), papal theocracy reached its zenith. More than any earlier pope, Innocent made the papacy the center of European political life; in the tradition of Gregory VII, he forcefully asserted the theory of papal monarchy. As head of the church, Vicar of Christ, and successor of Saint Peter, Innocent claimed the authority to intervene in the internal affairs of secular rulers when they threatened the good order of Christendom. According to Innocent, the pope, "lower than God but higher than man . . . judges all and is judged by no one."[2] And again: "Princes have power in earth, priests over the soul. As much as the soul is worthier than the body, so much worthier is the priesthood than the monarchy. . . . No king can reign rightly unless he devoutly serve Christ's vicar."[3]

Innocent applied these principles of papal supremacy in his dealings with the princes of Europe. When King Philip Augustus of France repudiated Ingeborg of Denmark the day after their wedding and later divorced her to marry someone else, Innocent placed an interdict on France to compel Philip to take Ingeborg back. For two decades, Innocent III championed Ingeborg's cause until she finally became the French queen. When King John of England rejected the papal candidate for archbishop of Canterbury, Stephen Langton, Innocent first laid an interdict on the country. Then he excommunicated John, who expressed his defiance by confiscating church property and by forcing many bishops into exile. However, when Innocent urged Philip Augustus of France to invade England, John backed down. He accepted Innocent's nominee for archbishop, returned the property to the church, welcomed the exiles back, and as a sign of complete capitulation, turned his kingdom over to Innocent to receive it back as a fief. Thus, as vassals of the papacy, John and his successors were obligated to do homage to the pope and to pay him a feudal

Chronology 10.1 The High Middle Ages

910	The founding of Abbey of Cluny
962	Otto I crowned Emperor of the West, beginning the Holy Roman Empire
987	Hugh Capet becomes king of France
1054	The split between the Byzantine and the Roman churches
1061–1091	The Norman conquest of Sicily
1066	The Norman conquest of England
1075	Start of the Investiture Controversy
1096	Start of the First Crusade
c. 1100	Revival of the study of Roman law at Bologna
1163	Start of the construction of the Cathedral of Notre Dame
1198–1216	Pontificate of Innocent III; the height of the church's power
1267–1273	Saint Thomas Aquinas writes *Summa Theologica*
c. 1321	Dante completes the *Divine Comedy*

tribute. Innocent also laid interdicts on the Spanish kingdoms of Castile and León and on Norway.

Pope Innocent also sought to separate Sicily from the Holy Roman Empire. When the candidacy for Holy Roman emperor was disputed, Innocent backed young Frederick II, king of Sicily and grandson of Frederick Barbarossa. In return for Innocent's backing, Frederick agreed to give up Sicily. When Frederick (1215–1250) emerged victorious over his rival, Otto of Brunswick, Innocent thought that the Holy Roman emperor would finally be subservient to the papacy. But Frederick, breaking his promise, refused to renounce Sicily. Subsequently, a furious struggle was waged between Frederick II (and his heirs) and the successors of Innocent III. The outcome was a disaster for the Holy Roman emperor who lost Sicily and saw his authority over the German princes evaporate. Once again, because of the Italian adventures of the emperors, Germany stayed fragmented; it would remain broken into separate and

independent territories until the last part of the nineteenth century.

Innocent called the Fourth Crusade to demonstrate anew that the papacy was the shepherd of Christendom. In 1202, ten thousand Crusaders gathered in Venice prepared to depart for the East. But the Venetians who had agreed to provide transport and food would not set sail because the Crusaders produced less money than the agreement had called for. The wily Venetians then proposed a new deal. They would allow the Crusaders to postpone payment in exchange for their cooperation in capturing the trading port of Zara, a rival of Venice controlled by the king of Hungary. Infuriated by this attack against a Christian city, Innocent excommunicated the Crusaders and the Venetians. But anxious to save the Crusade, he quickly lifted the sentence on the soldiers.

Again the Crusade was diverted. Alexius IV, pretender to the throne of Byzantium, offered the Venetians and the Christian army a huge sum in exchange for their aid in restoring his throne. While some Crusaders rejected the bribe and sailed to Syria to fight the Muslims, the bulk of the crusading army attacked Constantinople in 1204. In a contradictory display of barbarism, they looted and defiled churches and massacred citizens. This shameful behavior, along with the belief that the papacy was exploiting the crusading ideal to extend its own power, weakened both the papacy and the crusading zeal of Christendom.

After the disastrous Fourth Crusade, Innocent's attention turned to the Cathari. Unable to eliminate the Catharist heresy in southern France through preaching, Innocent decided on force. An army of crusading knights headed by a papal legate assembled in northern France; it headed south, massacring heretics. Soon command of the crusading army passed to Simon de Montfort, a minor baron with great ambition. De Montfort slaughtered suspected heretics throughout the county of Toulouse and for a short time he held the title of count of Toulouse. The crusading knights had effectively broken the power of the nobles who had protected the heretics. Innocent III sent legates to the region to arrest and try the Cathari. Under his successor, Dominican and Franciscan inquisitors completed the task of exterminating them.

The culminating expression of Innocent's supremacy was the Fourth Lateran Council, called in 1215. Composed of about twelve hundred clergy and representatives of secular rulers, the council issued several far-reaching orders. It maintained that the Eastern Orthodox church was subordinate to the Roman Catholic church; it prohibited the state from taxing the clergy, and declared laws detrimental to the church null and void. The council made bishops responsible for ferreting out heretics in their dioceses and ordered secular authorities to punish convicted heretics. It insisted on high standards of behavior for the clergy and required that each Catholic confess his or her sins to a priest at least once a year.

Christians and Jews

Latin Christendom's growing self-consciousness, which found expression in hostility to Muslims and condemnation of heresy, also sparked a hatred of Jews—a visibly alien group in a society dominated by the Christian world-view. In 1096, bands of Crusaders massacred Jews in French and German towns. One contemporary wrote:

I know not whether by a judgment of the Lord, or by some error of mind, they rose in a spirit of cruelty against the Jewish people scattered throughout these cities and slaughtered them without mercy, . . . asserting it to be their duty against the enemies of the Christian faith. . . . The Jews of [Mainz], knowing of the slaughter of their brethren, . . . fled in hope of safety to Bishop Rothard. . . . He placed the Jews in the very spacious hall of his own house, . . . [but the crusaders] attacked the Jews in the hall with arrows and lances. Breaking the bolts and doors, they killed the Jews, about seven hundred in number, who in vain resisted the force and attack of so many thousands. They killed the women, also, and with their swords pierced tender children of whatever age and sex.[4]

In 1290, Jews were expelled from England, and in 1306 from France. Between 1290 and 1293, expulsions, massacres, and forced conversions led to the virtual disappearance of a centuries-old Jewish community life in southern Italy. In Germany, savage riots periodically led to the torture and murder of Jews.

Several factors contributed to anti-Jewish feelings during the Middle Ages. To medieval Christians, the refusal of the Jews to embrace Christianity was an act of wickedness, particularly since the church taught that the coming of Christ had been prophesied by the Old Testament. Related to this prejudice was the depiction of the crucifixion in the Gospels. In the minds of medieval Christians, the crime of deicide—the killing of God—eternally stained the Jews as a people. The flames of hatred were fanned by the false allegation that Jews, made bloodthirsty by the spilling of Christ's blood, tortured and murdered Christians, particularly children, to obtain blood for ritual purposes. This blood libel was widely believed by the credulous masses and incited numerous riots that led to the murder, torture, and expulsion of countless Jews, despite the fact that popes condemned the charge as groundless.

The role of Jews as money lenders also contributed to animosity toward them. As Jews were increasingly excluded from international trade and were barred from the guilds, and in some areas from landholding, virtually the only means of livelihood open to them was money lending. This activity, which was forbidden to Christians, aroused the hatred of individual peasants, clergy, lords, and kings who did the borrowing.

The policy of the church toward the Jews was that they should not be harmed, but that they should live in humiliation. Hence the Fourth Lateran Council barred Jews from public office, required them to wear a distinguishing badge on their clothing, and ordered them to remain off the streets during Christian festivals. Christian art, literature, and religious instruction depicted the Jews in a derogatory manner. Deeply etched into the minds and hearts of Christians, the distorted image of the Jew as a contemptuous creature persisted in the popular mentality into the twentieth century.

Despite their precarious position, medieval Jews maintained their faith, expanded their tradition of biblical and legal scholarship, and developed a flourishing Hebrew literature. The work of Jewish translators, doctors, and philosophers would contribute substantially to the flowering of medieval culture in the High Middle Ages.

Europe in the High Middle Ages showed considerable vitality. The population increased, long-distance trade revived, new towns emerged, states started to take shape, and papal power increased. The culminating expression of this recovery and resurgence was the cultural awakening of the twelfth and thirteenth centuries, the high point of medieval civilization and a great creative period in Western history.

Notes

1. Quoted in J. W. Thompson, *Social and Economic History of the Middle Ages* (New York: Frederick Ungar, 1959), 2:772.

2. Excerpted in Brian Tierney, ed., *The Crisis of Church and State, 1050–1300* (Englewood Cliffs, N.J.: Prentice-Hall, 1964), p. 132.

3. Quoted in James Westfall Thompson and Edgar Nathaniel Johnson, *An Introduction to Medieval Europe* (New York: W. W. Norton, 1937), p. 645.

4. A. C. Krey, ed., *The First Crusade: The Accounts of Eye-Witnesses and Participants* (Princeton, N.J.: Princeton University Press, 1921), pp. 54–55.

Suggested Reading

Gimpel, Jean, *The Medieval Machine* (1977). Technological advances in the Middle Ages.

Lopez, R. S., *The Commerical Revolution of the Middle Ages* (1976). Commercial and industrial expansion in the High Middle Ages.

Mayer, H. E., *The Crusades* (1972). A short scholarly treatment.

Mundy, J. H., *Europe in the High Middle Ages 1150–1309* (1973). All phases of society in the High Middle Ages.

Pernoud, Regine, ed., *The Crusades* (1964). A compilation of original sources.

Petit-Dutaillis, Charles, *The Feudal Monarchy in France and England* (1964). A comparative study of the development of French and English medieval institutions.

Pounds, N. J. G., *An Economic History of Medieval Europe* (1974). A lucid survey.

Rorig, Fritz, *The Medieval Town* (1971). A study of medieval urban life.

Schafer, William, ed., *The Gregorian Epoch* (1964).
A useful collection of readings on the Cluniac
Movement, Gregory VII, and the Investiture
Controversy.

Strayer, J. R., *On the Medieval Origins of the
Modern State* (1970). Characteristics of medieval
state-building.

Synan, Edward A., *The Popes and the Jews in the
Middle Ages* (1965). An exploration of Jewish-
Christian relations in the Middle Ages.

Tierney, Brian, ed., *The Crisis of Church and State,
1050–1300* (1964). Contains many documents
illustrating this crucial medieval development.

Trachtenberg, Joshua, *The Devil and the Jews*
(1961). The medieval conception of the Jew
and its relationship to modern anti-Semitism.

White, Lynn, Jr., *Medieval Technology and Social
Change* (1964). A study of medieval advances
in technology.

Review Questions

1. What advances in agriculture occurred during the Middle Ages? What was the effect of these advances?

2. What factors contributed to the rise of towns? What was the significance of the medieval town?

3. Identify and explain the importance of the following: William the Conqueror, common law, Magna Carta, and Parliament.

4. Identify and explain the significance of the following: Hugh Capet, Philip Augustus, Louis IX, and Estates General.

5. Why did Germany not achieve unity during the Middle Ages?

6. What is the significance of the medieval representative institution?

7. What were the goals of Cluniac reformers?

8. What was Gregory VII's view of the papacy? How was the Investiture Controversy resolved? What was the significance of this controversy?

9. What prompted Urban II to call a crusade against the Turks? What prompted lords and commoners to go on a crusade? What was the final importance and outcome of the Crusades?

10. Why did the church regard Waldensians and Cathari as heretics?

11. What were the achievements of Saint Francis and Saint Dominic?

12. Papal power reached its height under Innocent III. Discuss this statement.

13. What factors contributed to the rise of anti-Semitism during the Middle Ages? How does anti-Semitism demonstrate the power of mythical thinking?

14. The High Middle Ages showed many signs of recovery and vitality. Discuss this statement.

11

The Flowering of Medieval Culture:
The Christian Synthesis

*T*he high point of papal power in the Middle Ages coincided with a cultural flowering in philosophy, the visual arts, and literature. Creative intellects achieved on a cultural level what the papacy accomplished on an institutional level—the integration of society around a Christian viewpoint. The High Middle Ages saw the restoration of some of the learning of the ancient world, the rise of universities, the emergence of an original form of architecture (the Gothic), and the erection of an imposing system of thought called *scholasticism*. Medieval theologian-philosophers fashioned Christian teachings into an all-embracing philosophy that represented the spiritual essence, the distinctive style of medieval civilization. They achieved what Christian thinkers in the Roman Empire had initiated and what the learned men of the Early Middle Ages were groping for—a synthesis of Greek philosophy and Christian revelation.

Revival of Learning

In the late eleventh century, Latin Christendom began to experience a cultural revival; all areas of life showed vitality and creativeness. In the twelfth and thirteenth centuries, a rich civilization with a distinctive style united an educated elite in the lands from Britain to Sicily. Gothic cathedrals, an enduring testament to the creativeness of the religious impulse, were erected throughout Europe. Universities sprang up in scores of cities. Roman authors were again read and their style imitated; the quality of written Latin—the language of the church, learning, and education—improved, and secular and religious poetry, both in Latin and in the vernacular, abounded. Roman law emerged anew in Italy, spread to northern Europe, and regained its importance (lost since Roman times) as worthy of intellectual scholarship. Some key works of ancient Greece were translated into Latin and studied in universities. Pursuing the ra-

Map 11.1 Medieval Centers of Learning

tional tradition of Greece, men of genius harmonized Christian doctrines and Greek philosophy.

Several conditions contributed to this cultural explosion known as the Twelfth-Century Awakening. As attacks of Vikings, Muslims, and Magyars ended and kings and great lords imposed more order and stability, people found greater opportunities for travel and communication. The revival of trade and the growth of towns created a need for literacy and provided the wealth required to support learning. Growing contact with Islamic and Byzantine cultures led to the translation into Latin of ancient Greek works preserved by these Eastern civilizations. The Twelfth-Century Awakening was also kindled by the legacy of the Carolingian Renaissance, whose cultural lights had dimmed but never wholly vanished in the period of disorder following the dissolution of Charlemagne's empire.

In the Early Middle Ages the principal educational centers were the monastic schools. During the twelfth century, cathedral schools in towns grew in importance. Their teachers, paid a stipend by a local church, taught grammar, rhetoric, and logic. But the chief expression of expanding intellectual life was the university, a distinct creation of the Middle Ages.

The origins of the medieval university are obscure and varied. The first universities were not planned but grew up spontaneously. They arose as students eager for knowledge gathered around prominent teachers. The renewed importance of Roman law for business and politics, for example, drew students to Bologna to study with acknowledged masters.

The university was really a guild or corporation of masters or students who joined together to defend their interests against episcopal or town authorities or the townspeople. A university might emerge when students united because of common needs, such as protection against townspeople who overcharged them for rooms and necessities. Organized into a body, students could also make demands on their instructors. At Bologna, professors faced fines for being absent or for giving lectures that drew fewer than five students; they were required to leave behind a deposit as security to ensure their return if they took a journey. A corporation of students formed the University at Bologna. The University of Paris, which evolved from the Cathedral School of Notre Dame, was the creation of a corporation of masters.

University students attended lectures, studied for examinations, and earned degrees. They studied grammar, rhetoric, logic, arithmetic, geometry, astronomy, music, and, when prepared, church law and theology, which was considered the queen of the sciences. The curriculum relied heavily on Latin translations of ancient texts, principally the works of Aristotle. In mathematics and astronomy, students read Latin translations of Euclid and Ptolemy, while students of med-

icine studied the works of two great medical men of the ancient world, Hippocrates and Galen.

But sometimes students followed other pursuits. They turned to drinking, gambling, and fighting, instead of studying. At Oxford University, it was reported that students "went through the streets with swords and bows and arrows . . . and assaulted all who passed by."[1] Fathers complained that their sons preferred "play to work and strumming a guitar while the others are at their studies."[2] Students often faced financial problems, and they knew whom to ask for help: "Well-beloved father, to ease my debts . . . at the tavern, at the baker's, with the doctor . . . and to pay . . . the laundress and the barber, I send you word of greetings and of money."[3]

Universities performed a vital function in the Middle Ages. Students learned the habit of reasoned argument. Universities trained professional secretaries and lawyers, who administered the affairs of church and state; these institutions of learning also produced theologians and philosophers, who shaped the climate of public opinion. The learning disseminated by universities tightened the cultural bonds that united Christian Europe, and established in the West a tradition of learning that has never died; there is direct continuity between the universities of our own day and medieval universities.

The Medieval World-View

A distinctive world-view based essentially on Christianity evolved during the Middle Ages. This outlook differed from both the Greco-Roman and the modern scientific and secular views of the world. In the Christian view, not the individual but the Creator determined what constituted the good life. Thus, reason that was not illuminated by revelation was either wrong or inadequate, for God had revealed to his children the proper rules for the regulation of individual and social life. Ultimately, the good life was not of this world but came from a union with God in a higher

College of Henricus Allemagna, School of Bologna, Second Half of Fourteenth Century. The core of the medieval curriculum included the *trivium* and the *quadrivium*. Students mastered grammar, rhetoric, and dialectic—the "three ways" (trivium)—and then pro- ceeded to mathematics, geometry, astronomy, and music (the quadrivium). The technique of teaching was the *disputatio,* or oral disputation between master and student. (*Bildarchiv Preussischer Kulturbesitz*)

world. This Christian belief as formulated by the church made life and death purposeful and intelligible. It was the outlook that dominated the thought of the Middle Ages.

The Universe: Higher and Lower Worlds

Medieval thinkers sharply differentiated between spirit and matter, between a realm of grace and an earthly realm, between a higher world of perfection and a lower world of imperfection. Moral values were derived from the higher world, which was also the final destination for the faithful. Two sets of laws operated in the physical universe, one for the heavens and one for the earth. The cosmos was a giant ladder with God at the summit; earth, composed of base matter, stood just above hell.

From Aristotle and Ptolemy, medieval thinkers inherited the theory of an earth-centered universe—the geocentric theory—which they impregnated with Christian symbolism. The geocentric theory held that revolving around the motionless earth at uniform speeds were seven transparent spheres in which were embedded each of the seven "planets"—the moon, Mercury, Venus, the sun, Mars, Jupiter, and Saturn. A sphere of fixed stars enclosed this planetary system. Above the firmament of the stars were the three heavenly spheres: the outermost, the Empyrean Heaven, was the abode of God and the Elect; through the Prime Mover—the sphere below—God transmitted motion to the planetary spheres; the first heavenly sphere was the invisible Crystalline Heaven. (See illustration on page 235.)

An earth-centered universe accorded with the Christian idea that God created the universe for men and women and that salvation was the essential aim of life. Because God had created people in his image, they deserved this central position in the universe. Although they might be living at the bottom rung of the cosmic ladder, only they, of all living things, had the capacity to ascend to heaven, the realm of perfection. Everything depended on how well they played their role in the drama of salvation.

Also acceptable to the Christian mentality was the sharp distinction drawn by Aristotle between the world above the moon and the one below it. Aristotle held that terrestrial bodies on earth were made of four elements—earth, water, air, fire. Celestial bodies that occupied the region beyond the moon were composed of a fifth element, the ether, too clear, too pure, too perfect to be found on earth. The planets and stars existed in a world apart; they were made of the divine ether and followed laws of nature that did not apply to earthly objects. Whereas earthly bodies underwent change—ice converting to water, a burning log converting to ashes—heavenly objects were incorruptible, immune to all change. Unlike earthly objects, they were indestructible.

Heavenly bodies also followed different laws of motion than earthly objects did. Aristotle said that it was natural for celestial bodies to move eternally in uniform circles, such motion being considered a sign of perfection. According to Aristotle, it was also natural for heavy bodies (stone) to fall downward and for light objects (fire, smoke) to move upward toward the celestial world; the falling stone and the rising smoke were finding their natural place in the universe.

This view of the universe would be shat-tered by the Scientific Revolution of the sixteenth and seventeenth centuries. The Scientific Revolution removed earth from its central position in the universe and made it just another planet that revolves about the sun. It dispensed with the medieval division of the universe into higher and lower worlds and postulated the *uniformity* of nature and of nature's laws: the cosmos knows no privilege of rank; heavenly bodies follow the same laws of nature as earthly objects do. Space is geometric and homogeneous, not hierarchic, heterogeneous, and qualitative. The universe was no longer conceived as finite and closed but as infinite, and the operations of nature were explained mathematically.

The Individual: Sinful but Redeemable

At the center of medieval belief was the image of a perfect God and a wretched and sinful human being. God had given Adam and Eve freedom to choose; rebellious and presumptuous, they had used their freedom to defy God. In doing so, they made evil an intrinsic part of the human personality. But God, who has not stopped loving human beings, has shown them the way out of sin. God became man and died so that human beings might be saved. Men and women are weak, egocentric, and sinful. With God's grace they can overcome their sinful nature and gain salvation; without grace, they are utterly helpless.

The medieval individual's understanding of self related to a comprehension of the universe as a hierarchy culminating in God. On earth, the basest objects were stones devoid of souls; higher than stones were plants, which possessed a primitive type of soul that allowed for reproduction and growth. Still higher were animals that had the capacity to move. The highest of the animals were human beings who, unlike other animals, could grasp some part of universal truth. Far superior to them were the angels who, without difficulty, apprehended God's truth. At the summit of this graduated universe was God, who was pure Being, without limitation, and the source of all existence. God's revelation reached down to humanity through the hierarchic order. From God, revelation passed to the angels, who were also arranged hierarchically. From the angels, the truth reached men and women, grasped first by prophets and apostles and then by the multitudes. Thus, all things in the universe, from angels to men and women to the lowest earthly objects, occupied a place peculiar to their nature and were linked by God in a great, unbroken chain.

Medieval individuals derived a sense of security from this hierarchical universe in which the human position was clearly defined. True, they were sinners who dwelt on a corruptible earth at the bottom of the cosmic hierarchy. But they *could* ascend to the higher world of perfection beyond the moon. As children of God, they enjoyed the unique privilege that each human soul was precious; all individuals commanded respect insofar as they were not formal heretics. (A heretic forfeited dignity and could be justly executed.) Medieval thinkers also arranged knowledge in a hierarchic order: knowledge of spiritual things surpassed all worldly knowledge, all human sciences. Therefore, the true Christian understood that the study of the individual and society cannot proceed properly unless guided by the Creator's teachings. To know what God wanted of the individual was the summit of self-knowledge and led to entrance into heaven. Thus, God was both the source and the end of knowledge; by God alone it exists, and only through God can it be perfected. The human capacity to think and to act freely constituted the image of God within each individual; it ennobled man and woman and offered them the promise of associating with God in heaven. As the only creatures to possess these traits, human beings had been granted " 'dominion over the fish of the sea, and over the birds of the air, and over the cattle, and over all the earth, and over every creeping thing that creeps upon the earth.' " (Genesis 1: 26–27) But the ultimate end of knowledge was always to gain salvation.

True, human nobility derived from intelligence and free will. But if individuals used these attributes without recognizing their debt to God, if they forgot that they were never his equal—in short, if they committed the sin of pride—they brought misery on themselves. To challenge the divine will with human will constituted contempt for God and a violation of the divine order. Such sinful behavior invited self-destruction. To save themselves from damnation, people must demonstrate the purity of their intentions in obeying God's moral laws. They must appeal to God for forgiveness and for the strength to do right.

In the medieval view, neither nature nor man could be understood apart from God and his revelation. All of reality emanated from God and was purposefully arranged in a spiritual hierarchy. Three great expressions of this view of life were scholastic philosophy, the *Divine Comedy* of Dante, and the Gothic cathedral.

Philosophy-Theology

Medieval philosophy, or *scholasticism*, attempted to apply reason to revelation. It was an attempt to explain and clarify Christian teachings by means of concepts and principles of logic derived from Greek philosophy. Scholastics tried to show that the teachings of faith, although not derived from reason, were not contrary to reason. They tried to prove through reason what they already held to be true through faith. For example, the existence of God and the immortality of the soul, which every Christian accepted as articles of faith, could also, they thought, be demonstrated by reason. In struggling to harmonize faith with reason, medieval thinkers constructed an extraordinary synthesis of Christian and Greek thought.

The scholastic masters used reason not to challenge faith but to serve faith—to elucidate, clarify, and buttress it. They did not break with the central concern of Christianity, that of earning God's grace and achieving salvation. Although this goal could be realized solely by faith, scholastic thinkers insisted that a science of nature did not obstruct the pursuit of grace and that philosophy could assist the devout in the contemplation of God. They did not reject Christian beliefs that were beyond the grasp of human reason and therefore could not be deduced by rational argument. Instead, they held that such truths rested entirely on revelation and were to be accepted on faith. To medieval thinkers, reason did not have an independent existence, but ultimately had to acknowledge a suprarational, superhuman standard of truth. They wanted rational thought to be directed by faith for Christian ends and guided by scriptural and ecclesiastical authority. Ultimately, faith had the final word.

Not all Christian thinkers welcomed the use of reason. Regarding Greek philosophy as an enemy of faith, a fabricator of heresies, and an obstacle to achieving communion of the soul with God, conservative theologians opposed the application of reason to Christian revelation. In a sense the conservatives were right. By giving renewed vitality to Greek thought, medieval philosophy nurtured a powerful force that would eventually shatter the medieval concepts of nature and society and weaken Christianity. Modern Western thought was created by philosophers' refusal to subordinate reason to Christian orthodoxy. Reason proved a double-edged sword: it both ennobled and undermined the medieval world-view.

Saint Anselm and Abelard

An early scholastic, Saint Anselm (1033–1109) was abbot of the Benedictine monastery of Le Bec in Normandy. He used rational argument to serve the interests of faith. Like Augustine before him and other thinkers who followed him, Anselm said that faith was a precondition for understanding. Without belief there could be no proper knowledge. He developed philosophical proof for the exis-

tence of God. Anselm argued as follows: We can conceive of no being greater than God. But if God were to exist only in thought and not in actuality, his greatness would be limited; he would be less than perfect. Hence he exists. Anselm's motive and method reveal something about the essence of medieval philosophy. He does not begin as a modern might: "If it can be proven that God exists, I will adopt the creed of Christianity; if not, I will either deny God's existence (atheism) or reserve judgment (agnosticism)." Rather, Anselm accepts God's existence as an established fact because he believes what Holy Scripture says and what the church teaches. He then proceeds to employ logical argument to demonstrate that God can be known not only through faith but also through reason. He would never use reason to subvert what he knows to be true by faith. In general, this attitude would characterize later medieval thinkers, who also applied reason to faith.

As a young teacher of theology at the Cathedral School of Notre Dame, Peter Abelard (1079–1142) acquired a reputation for brilliance and combativeness. His tragic affair with Héloise, whom he tutored, has become one of the geat romances in Western literature. Héloise had a child and entered a nunnery; Abelard was castrated on orders of Canon Fulbert, Héloise's guardian, and sought temporary refuge in a monastery. After resuming his career as a teacher in Paris, Abelard again had to seek refuge, this time for writing an essay on the Trinity that church officials found offensive. After further difficulties and flights, he again returned to Paris to teach dialectics. Not long afterward, his most determined opponent, Bernard of Clairvaux, accused Abelard of using the method of dialectical argument to attack faith. To Bernard, a monk and mystic, subjecting revealed truth to critical analysis was fraught with danger:

. . . *the deepest matters become the subject of undignified wrangling. . . . Virtues and vices are discussed with no trace of moral feelings, the sacraments of the Church with no evidence of faith, the mystery of the Holy Trinity with no spirit of humility or sobriety: all is presented in a distorted form, introduced in a way different from the one we learned and are used to.*[4]

Hearkening to Bernard's powerful voice, the church condemned Abelard and confined him to a monastery for the rest of his days.

Abelard believed that it was important to apply reason to faith and that careful and constant questioning led to wisdom. In *Sic et Non* (Yes and No), he took 150 theological issues and, by presenting passages from the Bible and the church fathers, showed that there were conflicting opinions. He suggested that the divergent opinions of authorities could be reconciled through proper use of dialectics. But like Anselm before him, Abelard did not intend to refute traditional church doctrines. Reason would buttress, not weaken, the authority of faith. He wrote after his condemnation in 1141:

I will never be a philosopher, if this is to speak against St. Paul; I would not be an Aristotle if this were to separate me from Christ. . . . I have set my building on the cornerstone on which Christ has built his Church. . . . I rest upon the rock that cannot be moved.[5]

Saint Thomas Aquinas: The Synthesis of Reason and Christianity

The introduction into Latin Christendom of the major works of Aristotle created a dilemma for religious authorities. Aristotle's comprehensive philosophy of nature and man, a product of human reason alone, conflicted in many instances with essential Christian doctrine. For Aristotle, God was an impersonal principle that accounted for order and motion in the universe. For Christianity, not only was God responsible for order in the physical universe, but he was also a personal being—a loving Father concerned about the deeds of his children. Whereas Christianity taught that God created the universe at a specific point in time, Aristotle held that the universe was eternal. Nor did Aristotle believe

God as Architect of the Universe, French Old Testament Miniature, Thirteenth Century. To the medieval mind, God was the origin of all. The universe was a known hierarchical system, and a "chain of being" extended downward to the lowest forms. Human beings, because of their immortal souls, could ascend toward God or, as a result of sinning, could descend into hell. (*Österreichische Nationalbibliothek, Vienna*)

in the personal immortality of the soul, another cardinal principle of Christianity. Church officials feared that the dissemination of Aristotle's ideas and the use of Aristotelian logic would endanger faith. At various times in the first half of the thirteenth century they forbade teaching the scientific works of Aristotle at the University of Paris. Because the ban did not apply throughout Christendom and was not consistently enforced in Paris, Aristotle's philosophy continued to be studied.

Rejecting the position of conservatives who insisted that philosophy would contaminate faith, Saint Thomas Aquinas (c. 1225–1274) upheld the value of human reason and natural knowledge. He set about to reconcile Aristotelianism with Christianity. Aquinas taught at Paris and organized the Dominican school of theology in Naples. His greatest work, *Summa Theologica,* is a systematic exposition of Christian thought. As a devout Catholic and member of the Dominican order, he of course accepted the truth of revelation. Belief in God and the fulfillment of his commands, Aquinas always maintained, are necessary for achieving salvation. He would not use reason to refute revelation.

Aquinas divided revealed truth into two categories: beliefs whose truth can be demonstrated by reason, and beliefs that reason cannot prove to be either true or false. For example, he believed that philosophical speculation could prove the existence of God and the immortality of the human soul, but that it could not prove or disprove the doctrines of the Trinity, the Incarnation, and the Redemption; these articles of faith wholly surpassed the capacity of human reason. But this fact did not detract from their certainty. Doctrines of faith did not require rational proof to be valid. They were true because they originated with God, whose authority is unshakable.

Can the teachings of faith conflict with the evidence of reason? For Aquinas, the answer was emphatically no. He said that revelation could not be the enemy of reason because revelation did not contradict reason, and reason did not corrupt the purity of faith. Revelation supplemented and perfected reason. If there appeared to be a conflict between philosophy and faith, it was certain that reason had erred somewhere, for the doctrines of faith were infallible. Since *both* faith and reason came from God, they were not in competition with each other but, properly understood, supported each other and formed an organic unity. Consequently, reason should not be feared, for it was another avenue to God. Because there was an inherent

agreement between true faith and correct reason—they both ultimately stemmed from God—contradictions between the two were only a misleading appearance. Although philosophy had not yet been able to resolve the dilemma, for God no such contradictions existed. In heaven, human beings would attain complete knowledge as well as complete happiness. While on earth, however, they must allow faith to guide reason; they must not permit reason to oppose or undermine faith.

Because reason was no enemy of faith, its application to revelation should not be feared. As human reasoning became more proficient, said Aquinas, it also became more Christian, and apparent incompatibilities between faith and reason disappeared. Recognizing that both faith and reason point to the same truth, the wise person accepts the guidance of religion in all questions that relate directly to knowledge needed for salvation. There also existed a wide range of knowledge that God had not revealed and that was not required for salvation. Into this category fell much knowledge about the natural world of things and creatures, which human beings had perfect liberty to explore.

Thus, in exalting God, Aquinas also paid homage to human intelligence, proclaimed the value of rational activity, and asserted the importance of physical reality revealed through human senses. Therefore, he valued the natural philosophy of Aristotle. Correctly used, Aristotelian thought would provide faith with valuable assistance. To synthesize Aristotelianism with the divine revelation of Christianity was Aquinas's great effort. That the two could be harmonized he had no doubt. He made use of Aristotelian categories in his five proofs of God's existence. In his first proof, for example, Aquinas argued that a thing cannot move itself. Whatever is moved must be moved by something else, and that by something else again. "Therefore, it is necessary to arrive at a first mover, moved by no other; and this everyone understands to be God."[6]

Aquinas also found a place for Aristotle's

conception of man. Aristotle, said Aquinas, was correct to regard man as a natural being and to devise for man a natural system of ethics and politics. Aristotle, however, did not go far enough. Aquinas said that, in addition, human beings are also special children of God. Consequently, they must define their lives according to the standards God has set. Aquinas insisted that much of what Aristotle had to say about man is accurate and valuable, for he was a gifted philosopher; but he possessed no knowledge of God. The higher insight provided by revelation did not disqualify what natural reason had to say about human beings, but improved upon it.

Aquinas upheld the value of reason. To love the intellect was to honor God and not to diminish the truth of faith. He had confidence in the power of the rational mind to comprehend most of the truths of revelation, and he insisted that in nontheological questions about specific things in nature—those questions not affecting salvation—people should trust only to reason and experience.

Aquinas gave new importance to the empirical world and to scientific speculation and human knowledge. The traditional medieval view based largely on Saint Augustine drew a sharp distinction between the higher world of grace and the lower world of nature, between the world of spirit and the world of sense experience. Knowledge derived from the natural world was often seen as an obstacle to true knowledge. Aquinas altered this tradition by affirming the importance of knowledge of the social order and the physical world. He gave to human reason and to worldly knowledge a new dignity. Thus, the City of Man was not merely a sinful place from which people tried to escape in order to enter God's city; it was worthy of investigation and understanding. But Aquinas remained a medieval and not a modern thinker, as historian Steven Ozment explains:

Aquinas brought reason and revelation together, but strictly as unequals. . . . In this union, reason, philosophy, nature, secular man and the state ultimately had value only in subservience to the *higher goals of revelation, theology, grace, religious man, and the church. . . . Thomist theology was the most sophisticated statement of the medieval belief in the secondary significance of the lay and secular world, a congenial ideology for a church besieged by independent and aggressive secular political powers.*[7]

Strict Aristotelianism: The Challenge to Orthodoxy

Some teachers in the Faculty of Arts at Paris found Aquinas's approach of Christianizing or explaining away Aristotle unacceptable. Unlike Aquinas, they did not seek to reconcile Aristotle's philosophy with Christian dogma. They held that certain Aristotelian propositions contradicting faith were philosophically true, or at least could not be proven false. These teachers maintained that it was impossible to refute these propositions by natural reason alone—that is, without recourse to faith. For example, by reason alone Aristotle had demonstrated that the world was eternal and that the processes of nature were unalterable. The first doctrine conflicted with the Christian belief that God created the universe at a point in time; the second conflicted with the belief that God could work miracles.

But these teachers did not take the next step and argue that Aristotle was correct and faith wrong. They only maintained that Aristotle's arguments could not be refuted by natural reason, and that the philosopher— as a philosopher, not as a Christian—based his judgments on rational arguments only, not on miracles and revelation. These strict Aristotelians did not deny the truths of faith, but they did assert that natural reason could construct conclusive proofs for propositions that the church had explicitly stated to be false.

In 1277, the Bishop of Paris condemned 219 propositions, many of them taught by these expositors of Aristotle at the University of Paris. Included in the condemnation were some propositions held by Aquinas. This move attempted to prevent Aristotle's philosophical naturalism from undermining Christian beliefs. Consequently, the condemnation was a triumph for conservative theologians who had grown increasingly worried about the inroads made by Aristotelianism. To them, even the Christian Aristotelianism of Aquinas was suspect.

Condemnations generally hinder the pursuit of knowledge, but ironically the condemnation of 1277 may have had the opposite effect. It led some thinkers to examine critically and reject elements of Aristotle's natural philosophy. This development may have served as a prelude to modern science, which, born in the sixteenth and seventeenth centuries, grew out of a rejection of Aristotelian physics.

Science

During the Early Middle Ages, few scientific works from the ancient world were available to western Europeans. Scientific thought was at its lowest ebb since it had originated more than a thousand years earlier in Greece. In contrast, both Islamic and Byzantine civilizations preserved and in some instances added to the legacy of Greek science. In the High Middle Ages, however, many ancient texts were translated from Greek and Arabic into Latin, and entered Latin Christendom for the first time. The principal centers of translation were Spain, where Christian and Muslim civilizations met, and Sicily, which had been controlled by Byzantium up to the last part of the ninth century and then by Islam until Christian Normans completed conquest of the island by 1091.

In the thirteenth and fourteenth centuries, a genuine scientific movement did occur. Impressed with the naturalistic and empirical approach of Aristotle, some medieval schoolmen spent time examining physical nature. Among them was the Dominican Albert the Great (Albertus Magnus). Albert (c. 1206–1280) was born in Germany, studied at Padua, and taught at the University of Paris, where Thomas Aquinas was his student. To Albert, philosophy meant more than employing

Greek reason to contemplate divine wisdom: it also meant making sense of nature. Albert devoted himself to editing and commenting on the vast body of Aristotle's works.

While retaining the Christian stress on God, revelation, the supernatural, and the afterlife, Albert (unlike many earlier Christian thinkers) considered nature a valid field for investigation. In his writings on geology, chemistry, botany, and zoology, Albert, like Aristotle, displayed a respect for the concrete details of nature by using them for empirical evidence:

I have examined the anatomy of different species of bees. In the rear, i.e. behind the waist, I discovered a transparent, shining bladder. If you test this with your tongue, you find that it has a slight taste of honey. In the body there is only an insignificant spiral-shaped intestine and nerve fibers which are connected with the sting. All this is surrounded with a sticky fluid.[8]

Showing a modern-day approach, Albert approved of inquiry into the material world, stressed the value of knowledge derived from experience with nature, sought rational explanations for natural occurrences, and held that theological debates should not stop scientific investigations. He pointed to a new direction in medieval thought.

Another scholar of the scientific movement was Robert Grosseteste (c. 1175–1253), chancellor of Oxford University. He declared that the roundness of the earth could be demonstrated by reason. In addition, he insisted that mathematics was necessary in order to understand the physical world, and he carried out experiments on the refraction of light.

Another Englishman, the monk and philosopher Roger Bacon (c. 1214–1294), foreshadowed the modern attitude of using science to gain mastery over nature. He recognized the practical advantages that might come from science and prophesied:

Machines for navigation can be made without rowers so that the largest ships on rivers or seas will be moved by a single man in charge with

greater velocity than if they were full of men. Also oars can be made so that without animals they will move with unbelievable rapidity. . . . Also flying machines can be constructed so that a man sits in the midst of the machine revolving some engine by which artificial wings are made to beat the air like a flying bird. Also a machine small in size can be made for walking in the sea and rivers, even to the bottom without danger.[9]

Bacon valued the study of mathematics and read Arabic works on the reflection and refraction of light. Among his achievements were experiments in optics and the observation that light travels much faster than sound. In searching for the cause of the rainbow, he demonstrated some understanding of the inductive method of reasoning. His description of the anatomy of the vertebrate eye and optic nerves was the finest of that era, and he recommended dissecting the eyes of pigs and cows to obtain greater knowledge of the subject.

The study of the ancient texts of Hippocrates and Galen and their Islamic commentators, particularly Avicenna's *The Canon of Medicine*, which synthesized Greek and Arabic medicine, elevated medicine to a formal discipline. Although these texts contained numerous errors and contradictions, they had to be mastered, if only to be challenged, before modern medicine could emerge. In addition, medieval doctors dissected animals and, in the late fourteenth century, human bodies. From practical experience, medieval doctors, monks, and laypersons added to the list of plants and herbs that would ease pain and hasten healing.

Medieval scholars did not make the breakthrough to modern science. They kept the belief that the earth was at the center of the universe and that different sets of laws operated on earth and in the heavens. They did not invent analytic geometry or calculus or arrive at the modern concept of inertia (see Chapter 17). Medieval science was never wholly removed from a theological setting. Modern science self-consciously seeks the advancement of specifically scientific knowledge, but in the Middle Ages, many questions involving nature were raised merely to clarify a religious problem.

Medieval scholars and philosophers did, however, advance knowledge about optics, the tides, and mechanics. They saw the importance of mathematics for interpreting nature, and they performed experiments. By translating and commenting on ancient Greek and Arabic works, medieval scholars provided future ages with ideas to reflect on and to reject, a necessary precondition for the emergence of modern science.

Medieval thinkers also developed an anti-Aristotelian physics that some historians of science believe influenced Galileo, the creator of modern mechanics, more than two centuries later. To explain why heavy objects do not always fall downward—why an arrow released by a bow moves in a straight line before it falls—Aristotle said that when the arrow leaves the bow, it separates the air, which then moves behind the arrow and pushes it along. Aristotle, of course, had no comprehension of the law of *inertia* which, as formulated by Isaac Newton in the seventeenth century, states that a body in motion will continue in a straight line unless interfered with. Unable to imagine that a body in motion is as natural a condition as a body at rest, Aristotle maintained that an outside force must maintain continual contact with the moving object. Hence, the flying arrow requires the "air-engine" to keep it in motion.

In the fourteenth century, Jean Buridan, a professor at Paris, rejected Aristotle's theory. Buridan argued that the bowstring transmits to the arrow a force called *impetus*, which keeps the arrow in motion. Whereas Aristotle attributed the arrow's motion to the air, which was external to the arrow, Buridan found the motive force to be an agent imparted to the arrow by the bowstring. Although still far from the modern theory of inertia, Buridan's impetus theory was an advance over Aristotle's air-engine. In the impetus theory, a moving body requires a cause to keep it in motion. In the theory of inertia, once a body is in motion, no force is required to keep it moving in a straight line. The state of motion is as natural as the state of rest.

In other ways, late medieval physics went beyond Aristotle, particularly in the importance given to expressing motion mathematically. The extent to which late medieval thinkers influenced the thinkers of the Scientific Revolution is a matter of debate. Some historians regard modern science as the child of the Middle Ages. Other historians believe that the achievements of medieval science were slim and that modern science is very little indebted to the Middle Ages.

Recovery of Roman Law

During the Early Middle Ages, western European law essentially consisted of Germanic customs, some of which had been put into writing. Some elements of Roman law endured as custom and practice, but the formal study of Roman law had disappeared. The late eleventh and twelfth centuries saw the revival of Roman law, particularly in Bologna, Italy. Irnerius lectured on the *Corpus Juris Civilis*, codified by Byzantine jurists in the sixth century. He made Bologna the leading center for the study of Roman law. Irnerius and his students employed the methods of organization and logical analysis that scholastic theologians used in studying philosophical texts.

Unlike traditional Germanic law, Roman law assumed the existence of universal principles that could be grasped by the human intellect and expressed in the law of the state. Roman jurists had systematically and rationally structured the legal experience of the Roman people. The example of Roman law stimulated medieval jurists to organize their own legal tradition. Intellectuals increasingly came to insist upon both a rational analysis of evidence and judicial decisions based upon rational procedures. Law codes compiled in parts of France and Germany and in the kingdom of Castile were influenced by the recovery of Roman law.

Roman legal experience contained political principles that differed markedly from feudal practices. According to feudal tradition lords, by virtue of their large estates, were empowered to exercise political authority. Roman jurists, on the other hand, had attributed governmental powers to the state and had granted wide powers to the emperor. The *Corpus Juris Civilis* stated that the power to make laws had originally resided with the Roman people, but that they had surrendered this power to the emperor. Medieval lawyers in the service of kings used this concept to justify royal absolutism, holding that the monarch possessed the absolute powers that the Roman legal tradition had granted to the Roman emperor. This strong defense of the monarch's power helped kings to maintain their independence from the papacy.

Roman law also influenced the law of the church (canon law), which was derived from the Bible, the church fathers, church councils, and the decisions of popes. In the last part of the eleventh century, church scholars began to codify church law and were helped by the Roman legal tradition.

Literature

Medieval literature was written both in Latin and in the vernacular. Much of medieval Latin literature consisted of religious hymns and dramas depicting the life of Christ and saints. A typical hymn by Saint Thomas Aquinas follows.

Sing, my tongue, the Savior's glory
Of his Flesh the mystery sing;
Of the Blood, all price exceeding,
Shed by our immortal King,
Destined for the world's redemption,
From a noble womb to spring.[10]

Medieval university students, like their modern counterparts, lampooned their elders and social conventions, engaged in drinking bouts, and rebelled against the rigors of study.

French Tapestry of a Courtier and His Lady. The courtly love tradition, in which women were worshipped and untouchable, inspired poetry. By inviting poets to their courts and writing poetry themselves, noblewomen actively influenced the rituals and literature of courtly love. (*Musée de Cluny/Lauros-Giraudon/ Art Resource*)

And they put their feelings into poetry written in Latin.

We in our wandering,
Blithesome and squandering;
Tara, tantara, teino!

Eat to satiety,
Drink with propriety;
tara, tantara, teino!

Laugh till our sides we split,
Rags on our hides we fit;
Tara, tantara, teino!

Jesting eternally,
Quaffing infernally;
Tara, tantara, teino![11]

The High Middle Ages saw the emergence of a vernacular literature. The French *chansons de geste*—epic poems of heroic deeds that had first been told orally—were written in the vernacular of northern France. These poems dealt with Charlemagne's battles against the Muslims, with rebellious nobles, and with feudal warfare. The finest of these epic poems, *The Song of Roland*, expressed the vassal's loyalty to his lord and the Christian's devotion to his faith. Roland, Charlemagne's nephew, was killed in a battle with the Muslims.

The *Nibelungenlied*, the best expression of the heroic epic in Germany, is often called "the *Iliad* of the Germans." Like its French counterpart, it dealt with heroic feats.

In stories of our fathers, high marvels we are
told
Of champions well-approved in perils manifold.
Of feasts and merry meetings, of weeping and
of wail,
And deeds of gallant daring I'll tell you in my
tale.[12]

Pisa Cathedral and Tower. Italian Gothic architecture remained very conservative. The basilican style, which had emerged in the Early Christian era, prevailed. The flying buttresses and extensive use of stained glass never took firm root in Italy. (*Alinari/Art Resource*)

The *roman*—a blending of old legends, chivalric ideals, and Christian concepts—combined love with adventure, war, and the miraculous. Among the romans were the tales of King Arthur and his Round Table. Circulating by word of mouth for centuries, these tales spread from the British Isles to France and Germany. In the twelfth century, they were put into French verse.

Another form of medieval poetry, which flourished particularly in Provence in southern France, dealt with the romanic glorification of women. Sung by *troubadours,* many of them nobles, the courtly love poetry expressed a changing attitude toward women. Although medieval men generally regarded women as inferior and subordinate, courtly love poetry ascribed to noble ladies superior qualities of virtue. To the nobleman, the lady became a goddess worthy of all devotion, loyalty, and worship. He would honor her and serve her as he did his lord; for her love he would undergo any sacrifice. Troubadours sang love songs that praised ladies for their beauty and charm and expressed both the joys and pains of love:

I sing of her, yet her beauty
is greater than I can tell,
with her fresh color, lively eyes,
and white skin, untanned
and untainted by rouge.
She is so pure and noble
that no one can speak ill of her.

But above all, one must praise,
it seems to me, her truthfulness,
her manners and her gracious speech
for she never would betray a friend. . . .[13]

Noblewomen actively influenced the rituals and literature of courtly love. They often invited poets to their courts and wrote poetry

Reims façade. In Reims Cathedral, the High Gothic style makes a complete statement: the portals are deeply recessed with rich sculpture. The towers are symmetrical with an elaborate, heavily sculpted, con- necting screen, and the rose window facing the front is so large that it serves as a translucent wall. (*Jean Roubier*)

themselves. They demanded that knights treat them with gentleness and consideration, and that knights dress neatly, bathe often, play instruments, and compose (or at least recite) poetry. To prove worthy of his lady's love, a knight had to demonstrate patience, charm, bravery, and loyalty. By devoting himself to a lady, it was believed, a knight would ennoble his character.

Courtly love did not involve a husband-wife relationship, but a noble's admiration and yearning for another woman of his class. Among nobles, marriages were arranged for political and economic reasons. The rituals of courtly love, it has been suggested, provided an expanded outlet for erotic feelings condemned by the church. They also expanded the skills and refined the tastes of the noble. The rough warrior acquired wit, manners, charm, and skill with words. He was becoming a courtier and a gentleman.

Written in the vernacular, *The Canterbury*

Tales of Geoffrey Chaucer (c. 1340–1400) is a masterpiece of English literature. Chaucer chose as his theme twenty-nine pilgrims en route from London to the religious shrine at Canterbury. In describing the pilgrims, Chaucer displayed humor, charm, an understanding of human nature, and a superb grasp of the attitudes of the English. Few writers have pictured their times better.

An Oxford Cleric, still a student though,
One who had taken logic long ago,
Was there; his horse was thinner than a rake,
And he was not too fat, I undertake,
But had a hollow look, a sober stare;
The thread upon his overcoat was bare.
He had found no preferment in the church
And he was too unworldly to make search
For secular employment. By his bed
He preferred having twenty books in red
And black, of Aristotle's philosophy,
To having fine clothes, fiddle or psaltery. . . .
The thought of moral virtue filled his speech
And he would gladly learn, and gladly teach.
· · · · · · · · · · · · · · · · · · ·
A worthy woman *from beside* Bath *city*
Was with us, somewhat deaf, which was a
pity.
In making cloth she showed so great a bent
She bettered those of Ypres and of Ghent. . . .
A worthy woman all her life, what's more
She'd have five husbands, all at the church
door,
Apart from other company in youth;
No need just now to speak of that, forsooth.[14]

The greatest literary figure of the Middle Ages was Dante Alighieri (1265–1321) of Florence. Dante appreciated the Roman classics and wrote not just in Latin, the traditional language of intellectual life, but also in Italian, his native tongue. In this respect he anticipated the Renaissance. In the tradition of the troubadours, Dante wrote poems to his beloved Beatrice:

My lady carries love within her eyes:
All that she looks on is made pleasanter;
Upon her path men turn to gaze at her;
He whom she greeteth feels his heart to rise,
And droops his troubled visage, full of
sighs,
And of his evil heart is then aware:
Hate loves, and Pride becomes a wor-
shipper.
O women, help to praise her in somewise.
Humbleness, and the hope that hopeth well,
By speech of hers into the mind are
brought,
And who beholds is blessed often-
whiles.
The look she hath when she smiles
Cannot be said, nor holden in the thought;
'Tis such a new and gracious miracle.[15]

In the *Divine Comedy*, Dante synthesized the various elements of the medieval outlook and summed up, with immense feeling, the medieval understanding of the purpose of life. Written while Dante was in exile, the *Divine Comedy* describes the poet's journey through hell, purgatory, and paradise. Dante arranges hell into nine concentric circles; in each region, sinners are punished in proportion to their earthly sins. The poet experiences all of hell's torments—burning sand, violent storms, darkness, and fearful monsters who whip, claw, bite, and tear sinners apart. The ninth circle, the lowest, is reserved for Lucifer and traitors. Lucifer has three faces, each a different color, and two batlike wings. In each mouth he gnaws on the greatest traitors in history—Judas Iscariot, who betrayed Jesus, and Brutus and Cassius, who assassinated Caesar. Those condemned to hell are told: "All hope abandon, ye who enter in."

In purgatory, Dante meets sinners who, although they undergo punishment, will eventually enter paradise. In paradise, an abode of light, music, and gentleness, the poet, guided by Beatrice, meets the great saints and the Virgin Mary. For an instant, he glimpses the Vision of God. In this indescribable mystical experience, the aim of life is realized.

Architecture

Two styles of architecture evolved during the Middle Ages: Romanesque and Gothic. The Romanesque style predominated in the eleventh and greater part of the twelfth centuries. Romanesque buildings—many of them monasteries as well as churches—contained massive walls supporting stone barrel vaults, rounded arches, and small windows. A construction of thick walls with few gaps for windows was necessary to hold up the great weight of the roofs. The interiors of Romanesque churches were dark, with an air of mystery, and the columns and walls were decorated with sculptured religious scenes. The development of the pointed arch allowed for supports that lessened the bearing pressure of the roof on the walls. This new style, the Gothic, allowed buildings to have lofty, vaulted ceilings, and huge windows, which made the interior lighter than Romanesque churches. The Romanesque church produced an impression of massive solidity; the Gothic cathedral, one of soaring grace.

Although Gothic cathedrals displayed a new style, they retained many architectural features that had been traditional in Christian churches for nearly a millennium. For instance, their floor plans are cruciform—in the shape of a cross. The head of the cross, where the altar is located, almost always faces east, the direction of the rising sun, itself a symbol of resurrection and rebirth.

The Gothic cathedral gave a visual expression of the medieval view of a hierarchical universe. Historian Joan Gadol concludes: "Inside and out, the Gothic cathedral is one great movement upward through a mounting series of grades, one ascent through horizontal levels marked by arches, galleries, niches, and towers. . . . the material ascends to the spiritual, the natural is assumed into the supernatural—all in a gradated rise."[16]

Magnificently designed stained-glass windows depicted scenes from the Bible and the lives of saints for the edification of the people, many of whom were illiterate. The subtle

Rose Window, Amiens Cathedral. Inseparable from the quest for height was the new aesthetic of light. The stained glass window became a signature of the Gothic style; it transformed the quality of light admitted, infusing the interior with a spiritual atmosphere. (*Bildarchiv Foto Marburg*)

light of the stained glass windows evokes a religious experience. Light was a principal medieval metaphor for God. Although light itself is usually invisible, it enables human beings to see; similarly, God is invisible, but his existence makes possible the world of space and time.

Reims Smiling Angel. This angel of the Annunciation is more lifelike than the elongated jamb statues of the earliest Gothic sculpture. Its head turns in a natural way. Pathos, shared suffering, would soon appear in sculpture, but only the Renaissance would see statues divorced from their architectural setting. (*Jean Roubier*)

The space of a Gothic cathedral is symbolic, too. The complex interior space seems to thrust upward at the same time it seems to surge forward. The sense of weightless upward thrust implies the immanence and energy of God. Much of the impression of upward movement is created by the springing pointed arches, which are more dynamic than the earlier round-headed ones. The proportions throughout the interior are tall and narrow. Long, thin vertical colonnettes extend, almost unbroken, from the floor to the vaults of the ceiling.

Soaring height seems effortless in a Gothic cathedral because the individual parts of the interior look light. Walls that are actually ten feet thick or more appear thin because of the slim, crisp colonnettes that articulate them. Walls are opened up by delicate carved decoration, called *tracery,* and the upper reaches of the walls are filled with large stained-glass windows. There is so much tracery and such large windows that scarcely any wall space is left visible.

The reduction in wall space is made possible by the flying buttresses on the building's exterior. These great arcs of masonry distribute the weight and thrust of the stone vaults out to the exterior walls. Esthetically, the light cage of buttresses surrounding the cathedral keeps the exterior silhouette looking as airy and diffuse as the interior space.

Some Gothic cathedrals took more than fifty years to complete. Only in an age of intense religious faith could such energy have been spent to glorify God. These vast building projects, many of them in northern France, were made possible by unprecedented economic prosperity. Cathedrals, which acted as headquarters for all the surrounding churches serving the laity, raised funds from a variety of sources. Cathedrals owned income-producing properties, such as farmland, mills, and forests; they received donations from pilgrims visiting the relics of famous saints; clerics also collected tolls and taxes on goods shipped to fairs through their region.

The Gothic style was to remain vigorous until the fifteenth century, spreading from France to England, Germany, Spain, and beyond. Revived from time to time thereafter, it has proved to be one of the most enduring styles in Western art and architecture.

Not too long ago some intellectuals viewed the Middle Ages as a period of ignorance and superstition, an era of cultural sterility that stood between the high civilizations of ancient Greece and Rome and the modern West. This view of the Middle Ages as a dark age has been abandoned, and quite properly so, for the High Middle Ages saw the crystallization of a rich and creative civilization. To be sure, its religious orientation set it apart both from classical civilization and from our own modern secular and scientific civilization. But the *Summa Theologica* of Aquinas, the *Divine Comedy* of Dante, and the Gothic cathedral all attest to the creativeness of the medieval religious spirit.

Notes

1. Quoted in G. G. Coulton, *Life in the Middle Ages* (New York: Macmillan, 1928), 1:74.

2. Quoted in Charles Homer Haskins, *The Rise of Universities* (Ithaca, N.Y.: Cornell University Press, 1957), p. 79.

3. Quoted in Coulton, *Life in the Middle Ages*, 3:113.

4. Quoted in Anders Piltz, *The World of Medieval Learning* (Oxford, England: Blackwell, 1981), p. 83.

5. Quoted in David Knowles, *The Evolution of Medieval Thought* (New York: Vintage Books, 1964), p. 123.

6. *Summa Theologica*, Part I, Question 2, Art. 3.

7. Steven Ozment, *The Age of Reform* (New Haven, Conn.: Yale University Press, 1980), p. 20.

8. Quoted in Piltz, *The World of Medieval Learning*, p. 176.

9. Quoted in A. C. Crombie, *Medieval and Early Modern Science* (Garden City, N.Y.: Doubleday Anchor Books, 1959), 1:55–56.

10. Excerpted in Charles W. Jones, ed., *Medieval Literature in Translation* (New York: Longmans, Green, 1950), p. 903.

11. Quoted in Haskins, *The Rise of Universities*, pp. 86–87.

12. *The Fall of the Nibelungers*, trans. by William Nanson Lettsom (London: Williams & Norgate, 1890), p. 1.

13. Excerpted in Anthony Bonner, ed., *Songs of the Troubadours* (New York: Schocken Books, 1972), pp. 42–43.

14. Geoffrey Chaucer, *The Canterbury Tales*, trans. Neville Coghill (Baltimore: Penguin Books, 1958), pp. 27, 31.

15. Dante Alighieri, *The New Life*, trans. Dante Gabriel Rossetti (London: Elis & Elvey, 1899), pp. 82–83.

16. Joan Gadol, *Leon Battista Alberti, Universal Man of the Early Renaissance* (Chicago: The University of Chicago Press, 1969), pp. 149–150.

Suggested Reading

Baldwin, John W., *The Scholastic Culture of the Middle Ages* (1971). A useful survey for the introductory student.

Brooke, Christopher, *The Twelfth-Century Renaissance* (1969). Surveys schools, learning, theology, literature, and leading figures.

Copleston, F. C., *Aquinas* (1955). A study of Aquinas's thought.

——, *A History of Medieval Philosophy* (1974). A lucid, comprehensive survey of medieval philosophy.

Crombie, A. C., *Medieval and Early Modern Science*, 2 vols. (1959). All phases of medieval science.

Dales, R. C., ed. *The Scientific Achievement of the Middle Ages* (1973). A collection of readings from original sources.

Gilson, Etienne, *Reason and Revelation in the Middle Ages* (1966). A superb, brief exposition of the medieval philosophic tradition.

Haskins, C. H., *The Renaissance of the 12th Century* (1957). Reprint of a still-useful work.

Knowles, David, *The Evolution of Medieval Thought* (1964). One of the best of its kind.

Mâle, Emile, *The Gothic Image* (1958). A valuable study of medieval art.

Pieper, Josef, *Scholasticism* (1964). Written with intelligence and grace.

Piltz, Anders, *The World of Medieval Learning* (1981). A clearly written, informative survey of medieval education and learning.

Wieruszowski, Helene, *The Medieval University* (1966). A good survey, followed by documents.

Review Questions

1. What factors contributed to the revival of learning in the late eleventh and twelfth centuries?

2. What was the significance of medieval universities?

3. Compare and contrast medieval universities with universities today.

4. Describe the essential features of the medieval view of the universe. How does it differ from the modern view of the universe?

5. The medieval individual's understanding of himself or herself was related to a comprehension of the universe as a hierarchy culminating in God. Explain this statement.

6. What were scholastic philosophers trying to accomplish?

7. Does the scholastic goal have any relevance for us today?

8. Aquinas did not consider reason to be an enemy of faith. Explain this statement.

9. What was the significance of Aquinas's thought?

10. What would Socrates have thought of Aquinas?

11. What did the Middle Ages contribute to the growth of science?

12. What was the significance of the revival of Roman law?

13. Describe what each of the following tells about the attitudes and interests of medieval people: troubadour poetry, *The Canterbury Tales, Divine Comedy,* and Gothic cathedrals.

12

The Late Middle Ages:
Crisis and Dissolution

By the opening of the fourteenth century, Latin Christendom had experienced more than 250 years of growth. On an economic level, agricultural production had expanded, commerce and town life had revived, and the population had increased. On a political level, kings had become more powerful, bringing greater order and security over large areas. On a religious level, the papacy had demonstrated its strength as the spiritual leader of Christendom, and the clergy had been reformed. On a cultural level, a unified world-view blending faith and reason had been forged.

During the Late Middle Ages, roughly the fourteenth and early fifteenth centuries, medieval civilization was in decline. The fourteenth century, an age of adversity, was marked by crop failures, famine, population decline, plagues, stagnating production, unemployment, inflation, devastating warfare, and abandoned villages. Violent rebellions by the disadvantaged of towns and countryside were ruthlessly suppressed by the upper classes. This century witnessed flights into mysticism, outbreaks of mass hysteria, and massacres of Jews; it was an age of pessimism and general insecurity. The papacy declined in power, heresy proliferated, and the synthesis of faith and reason, erected by Christian thinkers during the High Middle Ages, began to disintegrate. All these developments were signs the stable and coherent civilization of the thirteenth century was drawing to a close.

But all was not decline and gloom. On the positive side, representative institutions developed and thinkers showed a greater interest in the world of nature. And in Italy, the dynamic forces of urbanism and secularism were producing a period of cultural and humanistic flowering known as the *Renaissance.*

An Age of Adversity

In the Late Middle Ages, Latin Christendom was afflicted with severe economic problems.

The earlier increases in agricultural production did not continue. Limited use of fertilizers and limited knowledge of conservation exhausted the topsoil. As more grazing lands were converted to the cultivation of cereals, animal husbandry decreased, causing a serious shortage of manure needed for arable land. Intermittent bouts of prolonged heavy rains and frost also hampered agriculture. From 1301 to 1314, there was a general shortage of food, and from 1315 to 1317, famine struck Europe. Throughout the century, starvation and malnutrition were widespread.

Other economic problems abounded. A silver shortage, caused by technical problems in sinking deeper shafts in mines, led to the debasement of coins and a spiraling inflation, which hurt the feudal nobility in particular. Prices for manufactured luxury goods, which the nobility craved, rose rapidly. At the same time, the dues that the nobility collected from peasants diminished. To replace their revenues, lords and knights turned to plunder and warfare.

Compounding the economic crisis was the Black Death, or bubonic plague. This disease was carried by fleas on black rats and probably first struck Mongolia in 1331–1332. From there it crossed into Russia. Carried back from Black Sea ports, the plague reached Sicily in 1347. Spreading swiftly throughout much of Europe, the plague attacked an already declining and undernourished population. The first crisis lasted until 1351, and other serious outbreaks occurred in later decades. The crowded cities and towns had the highest mortalities. Perhaps twenty million people—about one-quarter to one-third of the European population—perished in the worst human disaster in recorded history.

Deprived of many of their intellectual and spiritual leaders, the panic-stricken masses drifted into immorality and frenzied forms of religious life. Hysteria and popular superstition abounded. Flagellants marched from region to region beating each other with sticks and whips in a desperate effort to appease God, who they believed had cursed them with the plague. Black magic, witchcraft, and sexual license found eager supporters.

Great Plague. The Black Death, or bubonic plague, devastated Europe, carrying off entire villages. A new piety swept through European art in the plague's aftermath. The elegant French courtly love style was replaced by tightly swaddled infants and suffering saints. (*Bibliothèque Royale Albert I, Brussels*)

Dress became increasingly ostentatious and bizarre; art forms concentrated on morbid scenes of decaying flesh, dances of death, and the torments of Hell. Sometimes this hysteria was directed against Jews, who were accused of causing the plague by poisoning wells. Terrible massacres of Jews occurred despite the pleas of the papacy.

The millions of deaths caused production of food and goods to plummet and some prices to soar. Nobles tried to make peasants bear the brunt of the crisis, as the value of land decreased and agricultural income lessened. A law decreed in England in 1349 required peasants to work for lords at fixed wages. Similar regulations of wages in German, Spanish, and Portuguese principalities aggravated tensions between peasants and nobles.

Economic and social tensions, some of them antedating the Black Death, escalated into rebellions. Each rebellion had its own specific causes, but a general pattern characterized the uprisings in the countryside. When kings and lords, breaking with customary social relationships, imposed new and onerous regulations, the peasants rose in defense of their traditional rights. In 1323, the lords' attempt to reimpose old manorial obligations infuriated the free peasants of Flanders, whose condition had improved in earlier decades. The peasants' revolt lasted five bloody years. In 1358, French peasants took up arms in protest against the plundering of the countryside by soldiers. Perhaps 20,000 peasants died in the uprising known as the *Jacquerie*. In 1381, English peasants revolted, angered over legislation that tied them to the land and imposed new taxes. John Ball, who claimed to be a priest, expressed egalitarian sentiments:

My good friends, things cannot go on well in England, nor ever will until everything shall be in common; when there shall neither be vassal nor lord, and all distinctions leveled; when the lords shall be no more masters than ourselves. But ill have they used us! and for what reason do they thus hold us in bondage? Are we not all descended from the same parents, Adam and Eve? and what can they show, or what reasons give, why they should be more the masters than ourselves? except, perhaps, in making us labor and work, for them to spend. . . . They have handsome manors, when we must brave the wind and rain in our labors in the field; but it is from our labor they have wherewith to support their pomp.[1]

Like the revolts in Flanders and France, the uprising in England failed. To the landed aristocracy, the peasants were sinners attacking a social system ordained by God. Possessing superior might, the nobility suppressed the peasants, sometimes with savage cruelty.

Social unrest afflicted the towns as well as the countryside. The wage earners of Florence (1378), the weavers of Ghent (1382), and the poor of Paris (1382) rose up against the ruling oligarchy. These revolts were generally initiated not by the poorest and most downtrodden, but by those who had made some gains and were eager for more. The rebellions of the urban poor were crushed just as the peasant uprisings were.

Fourteenth-century Europeans suffered because of the numerous long wars that devastated towns and farmlands and seriously hampered economic life. To deprive an invading army of food, fields were laid waste. The invaders also decimated farmlands in order to destroy the enemy's morale, and bands of discharged soldiers plundered the countryside.

In earlier centuries, wars had generally been short and small in scale, sparing noncombatants from the worst effects. In the fourteenth century this trend changed. The most destructive war was the series of conflicts between France and England known as the Hundred Years' War (1337–1453). Because English kings had ruled parts of France, conflicts between the two monarchies had been common. By 1214 the French monarchy had succeeded in acquiring most English territories in France. In 1328 the Capetian dynasty came to an end with the death of Charles IV, the son of Philip IV, the Fair. An assembly of French barons gave the crown to Philip VI of Valois, nephew of Philip the Fair. Edward III, king of England, insisted that he had a superior claim to the throne because his mother was Philip the Fair's daughter. Edward's attempt to gain the French throne was one reason for a new conflict. Another was the effort of the French monarch to squeeze taxes from Flemish towns, like Bruges, which had grown rich as trade and cloth-making centers. Dependent on English wool and resentful of the French monarchy's demands, the Flemish towns threw their support behind Edward III.

In the opening phase of the war, the English inflicted terrible defeats on French knights at the battles of Crécy (1346) and Poitiers (1356). Using longbows, which allowed them to shoot arrows rapidly, English archers cut down wave after wave of charging French cavalry. The war continued on and off

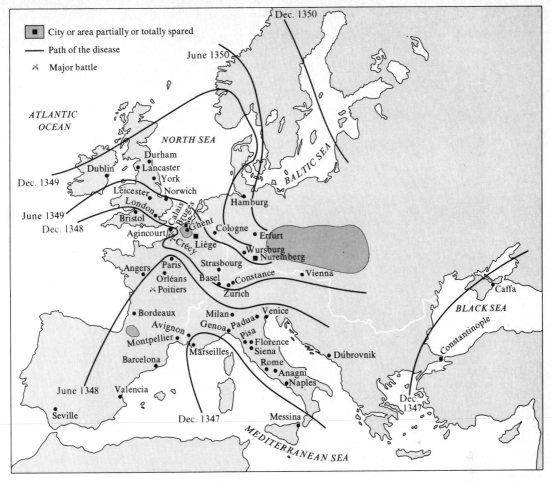

Map 12.1 Path of the Black Death, 1347–1350

throughout the fourteenth century. During periods of truce, gangs of unemployed soldiers roamed the French countryside killing and stealing, actions that precipitated the Jacquerie.

After the battle of Agincourt (1415), won by the English under Henry V, the English controlled most of northern France. It appeared that England would shortly conquer France and join the two lands under one crown. At this crucial moment in French history, a young and illiterate peasant girl, Joan of Arc (1412–1431), helped to rescue France. Believing that God commanded her to drive the English out of France, Joan rallied the demoralized French troops, leading them in battle. In 1429, she liberated the besieged city

of Orléans. Imprisoned by the English, Joan was condemned as a heretic and a witch in 1431 by a hand-picked church court. She was burned at the stake. The English intended to undermine the French cause by demonstrating that Joan was not divinely chosen. But Joan's life and death inspired the French people with a sense of devotion to their country. The reorganized and aroused French army recaptured Paris. By 1453, the English were driven from all French territory except for the port of Calais.

During the Hundred Years' War, French kings introduced new taxes that added substantially to their incomes. These monies furnished them with the means to organize a professional army of well-paid and loyal

Charles d'Orléans in the Tower of London. The battle of Agincourt gave the English control over much of northern France: Although relatively short-lived, the English victory became a source of high patriotism; Shakespeare would immortalize it in *Henry V.* In contrast, the French nobleman Charles d'Orléans captured there and imprisoned in the Tower for the next twenty-five years wrote melancholy poems. (*The British Library, Royal Ms. 16, F. II, folio 73*)

troops. By evoking a sense of pride and oneness in the French people, the war also contributed to a growing, but still incomplete, national unity. The English too emerged from the war with a greater sense of solidarity.

However, the war had terrible consequences for the French peasants. Thousands of farmers were killed and valuable farmland was destroyed by English armies and marauding bands of mercenaries. In another portentous development, the later stages of the Hundred Years' War saw the use of gunpowder and heavy artillery.

The Decline of the Church

The principal sign of fragmentation in the Late Middle Ages was the waning authority and prestige of the papacy. In the High Middle Ages, the papacy had been the dominant institution in Christendom, but in the Late Middle Ages, its power disintegrated. The medieval ideal of a unified Christian commonwealth guided by the papacy shattered. Papal authority declined in the face of the growing power of kings who championed the parochial interests of states. Papal prestige and its capacity to command waned as it became more embroiled in European politics. Many pious Christians felt that the pope behaved more like a secular ruler than like an Apostle of Christ. Political theorists and church reformers further undermined papal authority.

Conflict with France

Pope Boniface VIII (1294–1303) vigorously upheld papal claims to supremacy over secular rulers. In the famous bull *Unam Sanctam,* he declared:

. . . if the earthly power errs, it shall be judged by the the spiritual power, . . . but [the pope] can be judged only by God not by man. . . . Whoever therefore resists this power so ordained by God resists the ordinance of God. . . . Therefore, we declare, state, define, and pronounce that it is altogether necessary to salvation for every human creature to be subject to the Roman Pontiff.[2]

But in trying to enforce this idea of papal supremacy on proud and increasingly more powerful kings, Boniface suffered defeat and humiliation.

Philip IV of France (1285–1314) and Edward I of England (1272–1307) taxed the churches in their lands to raise revenue for the war they planned to wage. In doing so, they disregarded the church prohibition against the taxing of its property by the state without papal permission. In the bull *Clericis laicos,* Boniface decreed that kings and lords who impose taxes on the clergy, and clergy who pay them, would incur the sentence of excommunication. Boniface badly miscalculated. Far from bowing to the pope's threat, both Edward and Philip acted forcefully to assert their authority over the churches in their kingdoms. Boniface backed down from his position, declaring that the French king could tax the clergy in times of national emergency. Thus the matter was resolved to the advantage of the state.

A second dispute had more disastrous

Portrait of Joan of Arc. A witch to the English and a heroine to the French, this simple, illiterate peasant girl rallied French forces to reverse the tide of English supremacy in France. She was burned at the stake in 1431 by the English. Her life and death became the impetus France needed to reorganize and finally to drive the English by 1453 from all French territory except Calais. Joan was made a saint by the Roman Catholic church in the twentieth century. (*Archives Nationales, Paris*)

consequences for Boniface. Philip tried and imprisoned a French bishop despite Boniface's warning that this was an illegal act and a violation of church law and tradition, which held that the church, not the state, must judge the clergy. Philip summoned the first meeting of the Estates General to gain the backing of the nation. Shortly afterwards, Boniface issued the bull *Unam Sanctam,* previously quoted, and threatened to excommunicate Philip. The outraged monarch decided to seize Boniface and to replace him with a new pope. Aided by Italian mercenaries and enemies of Boniface, French conspirators attacked the papal summer palace at Anagni in September 1303 and captured the pope. Although Boniface was released, this terrible event proved too much for him, and a month later he died.

Boniface's successors, Benedict XI (1303–1304) and Clement V (1305–1314) tried to conciliate Philip. In particular, Clement agreed to suppress the Templars, a wealthy religious-military order to whom the French crown was in debt. Another victory for Philip was Clement's decision to remain at Avignon, a town on the southeastern French frontier, where he had set up a temporary residence.

From 1309 to 1377, a period known as the *Babylonian Captivity*, the popes were all French. During this time, the papacy, removed from Rome and deprived of revenues from the Papal States in Italy, was often forced to pursue policies favorable to France. Worsening the papal image was growing anti-papalism among laymen, who were repelled by the luxurious style of living at Avignon and by the appointment of high churchmen to lands where they did not know the language and where they demonstrated little concern for the local population. Under these circumstances, more and more people questioned the value and necessity of the papacy.

Critique of Papal Power

The conflict between Boniface and Philip provoked a battle of words between proponents of papal supremacy and defenders of royal rights. In his treatise, *On Ecclesiastical Power*, Giles of Rome (c. 1245–1316) vigorously supported the doctrine of papal power. Because the spiritual is inherently superior to the temporal, he argued, the pope has the authority to judge temporal rulers. All temporal lords ought to be governed by spiritual and ecclesiastical authority, and especially by the pope, who heads the church.

Defenders of royal prerogatives challenged the pope's claim to primacy over both secular rulers and the clergy. In taking this position, they weakened the medieval church. *On Kingly and Papal Power* (1302) by John of Paris (c. 1241–1306) attacked the theory of papal monarchy championed by Giles of Rome and

asserted the independence of the French monarchy. For John, the church was primarily a spiritual body charged with administering the sacraments; as such, its authority did not extend to temporal affairs. Indeed, clerical interference in secular affairs threatened the state's stability. While granting that "the priest is superior to the ruler in dignity," John maintained that "it is not necessary to be superior to him in all things." Since both rulers and priests derive their power from God, said John, they are each superior in their own spheres. "The priest is, therefore, superior in spiritual matters and conversely, the ruler is superior in temporal matters."[3]

The most important critique of clerical intrusion into worldly affairs was *The Defender of the Peace* (1324) by Marsiglio of Padua (c. 1290–c. 1343). Marsiglio held that the state ran according to its principles, which had nothing to do with religious commands originating in a higher realm. Religion dealt with a supernatural world and with principles of faith that could not be proved by reason, said Marsiglio. Politics, on the other hand, dealt with a natural world and with the affairs of the human community. And political thinkers should not try to make the earthly realm conform to articles of faith. For Marsiglio, the state was self-sufficient; it needed no instruction from a higher authority. Thus Marsiglio denied the essential premises of medieval papal political theory: that kings received their power from God; that the pope, as God's vicar, was empowered to guide kings; that the state, as part of a divinely ordered world, must conform to and fulfill supernatural ends; and that the clergy were above the laws of the state. Marsiglio felt that the church should be a spiritual institution with no temporal power.

The Great Schism

The Avignon popes were often competent men who, despite the hard times that had overtaken the papacy, tried to bolster papal power. They tightened their hold over church administration by reserving for themselves certain appointments and collections of fees formerly handled by local bishops. Through a deliberate effort at financial centralization, including the imposition of new taxes and the more efficient collection of old ones, the Avignon popes increased papal income substantially.

Pope Gregory XI returned the papacy to Rome in 1377, ending the Babylonian Captivity. But the papacy was to endure an even greater humiliation—the Great Schism. Elected pope in 1378, Urban VI immediately displayed tactlessness, if not mental imbalance, by abusing and even imprisoning cardinals. Fleeing from Rome, the cardinals declared that the election of Urban had been invalid and elected Clement VII as the new pope. Refusing to step down, Urban excommunicated Clement who responded in kind. To the utter confusion and anguish of Christians throughout Europe, there were now two popes—Urban ruling from Rome and Clement from Avignon.

Prominent churchmen urged the convening of a general council—the Council of Pisa— to end the disgraceful schism. Held in 1409 and attended by hundreds of churchmen, the Council of Pisa deposed both Urban and Clement and elected a new pope. Neither deposed pope recognized the council's decision, so that Christendom then had three popes! A new council was called at Constance in 1414. In the struggle that ensued, each of the three popes either abdicated or was deposed in favor of an appointment by the council. In 1417, the Great Schism ended.

During the first half of the fifteenth century, church councils met at Pisa (1409), Constance (1414–1418), and Basel (1431–1449) in order to end the schism, combat heresy, and reform the church. The Conciliar movement attempted to transform the papal monarchy into a constitutional system in which the pope's power would be regulated by a general council. Supporters of the movement held that the papacy could not reform the church as effectively as a general council representing the clergy. But the Conciliar movement ended

in failure. As the Holy Roman emperor and then the French monarch withdrew support from the councils, the papacy regained its authority over the higher clergy. In 1460, Pope Pius II condemned the Conciliar movement as heretical.

The papacy was deeply embroiled in European power politics and the worldly life of Renaissance Italy and often neglected its spiritual and moral responsibilities. Many devout Christians longed for a religious renewal, a return to simple piety; the papacy barely heard this cry for reform. The papacy's failure to provide creative leadership for reform made possible the Protestant Reformation of the sixteenth century. The Reformation, by splitting Christendom into Catholic and Protestant, destroyed forever the vision of a Christian world commonwealth guided by Christ's vicar, the pope.

Fourteenth-Century Heresies

Another threat to the medieval ideal of a universal Christian community came from radical reformers questioning the function and authority of the entire church hierarchy. These heretics in the Late Middle Ages were forerunners of the Protestant Reformation.

The two principal dissenters were the Englishman John Wycliffe (c. 1320–1384) and the Czech John Huss (c. 1369–1415). By stressing a personal relationship between the individual and God and by claiming the Bible itself, rather than church teachings, to be the ultimate Christian authority, they challenged the fundamental position of the medieval church: that the avenue to salvation passed through the church alone. They attacked the wealth of the higher clergy and sought a return to the spiritual purity and material poverty of the early church. To Wycliffe, the wealthy, elaborately organized hierarchy of the church was unnecessary and wrong. The splendidly dressed and propertied bishops had no resemblance to the simple people who first followed Christ. Indeed, these worldly bishops headed by a princely and tyrannical

pope were really anti-Christians, the "fiends of Hell." Wycliffe wanted the state to confiscate church property and the clergy to embrace poverty. By denying that priests changed the bread and wine of communion into the substance of the body and blood of Christ, Wycliffe and Huss rejected the sacerdotal power of the clergy. Although both movements were declared heretical and Huss was burned at the stake, the church could not crush the dissenters' followers or eradicate their teachings. The doctrines of the Reformation would parallel the teachings of Wycliffe and Huss to some extent.

Breakup of the Thomistic Synthesis

In the Late Middle Ages, the papacy lost power, as kings, political theorists, and religious dissenters effectively challenged papal claims to supreme leadership. Also breaking down was the great theological synthesis constructed by philosophers. The process of fragmentation seen in the history of the church also took place in philosophy.

Saint Thomas Aquinas's system culminated the scholastic attempt to show the basic agreement of philosophy and religion. In the fourteenth century, a number of thinkers cast doubt on the possibility of synthesizing Aristotelianism and Christianity, that is, reason and faith. Consequently, philosophy grew more analytical and critical. Denying that reason could demonstrate the truth of Christian doctrines with certainty, philosophers tried to separate reason from faith. Whereas

Left: **Hubert and/or Jan van Eyck: The Last Judgment,** c. **1420.** The major concern of medieval people was the salvation of their souls. At the Last Judgment, the good would be drawn to heaven for an eternity of bliss, while the damned would be sealed in hell. The Flemish artist depicts in graphic detail this final division. (*The Metropolitan Museum of Art, Fletcher Fund, 1933*)

Aquinas had said that reason proved or clarified much of revelation, fourteenth-century thinkers asserted that the basic propositions of Christianity were not open to rational proof. Whereas Aquinas had held that faith supplements and perfects reason, some philosophers were now proclaiming that reason often contradicts faith.

Duns Scotus (1265–1308), an English Franciscan, held that human reason cannot prove that God is omnipotent, that he forgives sins, that he rewards the righteous and punishes the wicked, or that the soul is immortal. These Christian doctrines, which scholastic philosophers believed could be proven by reason, were for Scotus the province of revelation and faith, not reason.

To be sure, this new outlook did not urge abandoning faith in favor of reason. Faith had to prevail in any conflict with reason because faith rested on God, the highest authority in the universe. But the relationship between reason and revelation was altered. Articles of faith, it was now held, had nothing to do with reason; they were to be believed, not proved. Reason was not an aid to theology, but a separate sphere of activity. This new attitude snapped the link between reason and faith that Aquinas had so skillfully forged. The scholastic synthesis was disintegrating.

A principal proponent of this new outlook was William of Ockham (c. 1280–1349). In contrast to Aquinas, Ockham insisted that natural reason could not prove God's existence, the soul's immortality, or any other essential Christian doctrine. Reason could only say that God probably exists and that he probably endowed man with an immortal soul. But it could not prove these propositions with *certainty.* The tenets of faith were beyond the reach of reason, said Ockham; there was no rational foundation to Christianity. For Ockham, reason and faith were different ways of proceeding; it was neither possible nor helpful to join reason to faith. He did not, however, seek to undermine faith—only to disengage it from reason.

In the process of proclaiming the authority of theology, Ockham also furthered using reason to comprehend nature. Ockham's approach, separating natural knowledge from religious dogma, made it easier to explore the natural world empirically without fitting it into a religious framework. With Ockham, then, we see a forerunner of the modern mentality: a separation of reason from religion, and a growing interest in the empirical investigation of nature.

Medieval civilization began to decline in the fourteenth century, but no new dark age descended on Europe; its economic and political institutions and technological skills had grown too strong. Instead, the waning of the Middle Ages opened up possibilities for another stage in Western civilization—the modern age.

The Middle Ages and the Modern World: Continuity and Discontinuity

In innumerable ways the modern world is linked to the Middle Ages. European cities, the middle class, the state system, English common law, universities—all had their origins in the Middle Ages. During that period, important advances were made in business practices. By translating and commenting on the writings of Greek and Arabic thinkers, medieval scholars preserved a priceless intellectual heritage, without which the modern mind could never have evolved. And between the thought of the scholastics and that of early modern philosophers there are numerous connecting strands.

During the Middle Ages, Europeans began to take the lead over the Muslims, the Byzantines, the Chinese, and all the other peoples in the use of technology. Medieval technology and inventiveness stemmed in part from Christianity, which taught that God had created the world specifically for human beings to subdue and utilize. Consequently, medieval people tried to employ animal power and laborsaving machinery to relieve human drudgery. Moreover, Christianity taught that God was above nature, not within it, so for the Christian there was no spiritual obstacle to exploiting nature as there was, for example, for the Hindu. Unlike classical humanism, the Christian outlook did not consider manual work degrading—even monks combined study with manual labor.

Believing that God's law was superior to state or national decrees, medieval philosophers provided a theoretical basis for opposing tyrannical kings who violated Christian principles. The idea that both the ruler and the ruled are bound by a higher law would, in a secularized form, become a principal element of modern liberal thought.

The Christian stress on the sacred worth of the individual and on the higher law of God has never ceased to influence Western civilization. Although in modern times the various Christian churches have not often taken the lead in political and social reform, the ideals identified with the Judeo-Christian tradition have become part of the common Western heritage. As such, they have inspired social reformers who may no longer identify with their ancestral religion.

Feudal traditions lasted long after the Middle Ages. Up to the French Revolution, for instance, French aristocrats enjoyed special privileges and exercised power over local government. In England, the aristocracy controlled local government until the Industrial Revolution transformed English society in the nineteenth century. Retaining the medieval ideal of the noble warrior, aristocrats continued to dominate the officer corps of European armies through the nineteenth century and even into the twentieth. Aristocratic notions of duty, honor, loyalty, and courtly love have also endured into the twentieth century.

Feudalism also contributed to the history of liberty. According to feudal theory the king, as a member of the feudal community, was duty-bound to honor agreements made by his vassals. Lords possessed personal rights that the king was obliged to respect. Resentful of a king who ran roughshod over customary

feudal rights, lords also negotiated contracts with the crown, such as the famous Magna Carta, to define and guard their customary liberties. To protect themselves from the arbitrary behavior of a king, feudal lords initiated what came to be called *government by consent* and the *rule of law*.

Thus, in the Middle Ages there gradually emerged the ideas that law was not imposed on inferiors by an absolute monarch, but required the collaboration of the king and his subjects; that the king, too, was bound by the law; and that lords had the right to resist a monarch who violated agreements. Related to these ideas, representative institutions also emerged with which the king was expected to consult on the realm's affairs. The most notable was the British Parliament which, although it was subordinate to the king, became a permanent part of the state. Later, in the seventeenth century, Parliament would successfully challenge royal authority. Continuity, therefore, exists between the feudal tradition of a king bound by law and the modern practice of limiting the authority of the head of state.

Although the elements of continuity are concrete, the characteristic outlook of the Middle Ages is as different from that of the modern age as it was from that of the ancient world. Religion was the integrating feature of the Middle Ages, whereas science and secularism determine the modern outlook. The period from the Italian Renaissance of the fifteenth century through the eighteenth-century Age of Enlightenment constituted a breaking away from the medieval worldview—a rejection of the medieval conception of nature, the individual, and the purpose of life.

Medieval thought began with the existence of God and the truth of his revelation as interpreted by the church, which set the standards and defined the purposes for human endeavor. The medieval mind rejected the fundamental principle of Greek philosophy—the autonomy of reason. Without the guidance of revealed truth, reason was seen as feeble.

The Polos Embarking from Venice. The journey of the Polos to the court of the great Khan sees the medieval world almost at an end. The exploration of the East would soon be followed by voyages to Africa and the discovery of the New World. Commerce and trade would transform the western economy. The role of the individual would change from that of a functioning member in an ordered political and spiritual realm to that of an explorer of new worlds: physical, intellectual, and artistic. (*Bodleian Library, Oxford, Ms. Bodley 264, fol. 218R*)

Scholastics reasoned closely and carefully, drew fine distinctions, and at times demonstrated a critical attitude. They engaged in genuine philosophical speculation, but they did not allow philosophy to challenge the basic premises of their faith. Unlike either ancient or modern thinkers, medieval schoolmen believed ultimately that reason alone could not provide a unified view of nature or society. A rational soul had to be guided by a divine light. For all medieval philosophers, the natural order depended on a supernatural order for its origin and purpose. To understand the natural world properly it was necessary to know its relationship to the higher world.

In the modern view, both nature and the human intellect are self-sufficient. Nature is a mathematical system that operates without miracles or any other form of divine intervention. To comprehend nature and society, the mind needs no divine assistance; it accepts no authority above reason. The modern mentality finds it unacceptable to reject the conclusions of science on the basis of clerical authority and revelation, or to base politics, law, or economics on religion; it refuses to accept dogma uncritically and insists on scientific proof.

The medieval philosopher arranged both nature and society into a hierarchic order. Heaven was the source of moral values, and the church was responsible for teaching and upholding these ethical norms. Kings acquired their right to rule from God. The entire social structure constituted a hierarchy: the clergy guided society according to Christian standards; lords defended Christian society from its enemies; serfs, at the bottom of the social order, toiled for the good of all. There was also a hierarchy of knowledge. A lower form of knowledge derived from the senses, and the highest type of knowledge, theology, dealt with God's revelation. To the medieval mind this hierarchic ordering of nature, society, and knowledge had a divine sanction.

Rejecting the medieval division of the universe into higher and lower realms and superior and inferior substances, the modern view came to regard the universe as one and nature as uniform; the modern thinker studies mathematical law and chemical composition, not grades of perfection. Spiritual meaning is not sought in an examination of the material world. Roger Bacon, for example, described seven coverings of the eye and then concluded that God had fashioned the eye in this manner in order to express the seven gifts of the Spirit. This way of thinking is alien to the modern outlook.

The modern West also broke with the rigid division of medieval society into three orders: clergy, nobles, and commoners. Opposing the feudal principle that an individual's obligations and rights are a function of his or her rank in society, the modern West stressed equality of opportunity and equal treatment under the law. It rejected the idea that society should be guided by clergymen who possess a special wisdom, by nobles who were entitled to special privileges, and by a king who received his power from God.

The modern West also rejected the personal and customary character of feudal law. As the modern state developed, law assumed an impersonal and objective character. For example, if the lord demanded more than the customary forty days of military service,

the vassal might refuse to comply, seeing the lord's request as an unpardonable violation of custom and agreement and an infringement on his liberties. In the modern state with a constitution and a representative government, if a new law increasing the length of military service is passed, it merely replaces the old law. People do not refuse to obey it because the government has broken faith or violated custom.

In the modern world, the individual's relationship to the universe has been radically transformed. To medieval thinkers, human beings ranked below angels, but were superior to inanimate objects, plants, and animals. People in the Middle Ages knew why they were on earth and what was expected of them; they never doubted that heaven would be their reward for living a Christian life. J. H. Randall, Jr., a historian of philosophy, eloquently sums up the medieval world-view:

The world was governed throughout by the omnipotent will and omniscient mind of God, whose sole interests were centered in man, his trial, his fall, his suffering and his glory. Worm of the dust as he was, man was yet the central object in the whole universe. . . . And when his destiny was completed, the heavens would be rolled up as a scroll and he would dwell with the Lord forever. Only those who rejected God's freely offered grace and with hardened hearts refused repentance would be cut off from this eternal life.[4]

This comforting medieval vision is alien to the modern outlook. Today, in a universe fifteen billion years old in which the earth is a tiny speck floating in an endless cosmic ocean, where life evolved over tens of millions of years, many Westerners no longer are certain that human beings are special children of God; that heaven is their ultimate goal; that under their feet is Hell; that God is an active agent in human history. To many intellectuals the universe seems unresponsive to the religious supplications of people, and life's purpose is sought within the limits of earthly existence. Almost ruthlessly, science and secularism have driven Christianity and

Chronology 12.1   The Late Middle Ages

September 1303	The French attack the papal summer place at Anagni
1309–1377	The "Babylonian Captivity"; the popes are all French and influenced by the French monarchy
1323–1328	The peasants revolt in Flanders
1328	The end of France's Capetian dynasty; Edward III of England tries to gain the French throne
1337–1453	The Hundred Years' War between England and France
1346	The battle of Crécy—the French are defeated by the British
1347–1351	The Black Death reaches Italian ports and ravages Europe
1356	The battle of Poitiers—the French are defeated by the English
1358	The Jacquerie, the French peasants' revolt
1377	Pope Gregory XI returns the papacy to Rome
1378	The Florentine laborers revolt
1378–1417	The Great Schism; Christendom has two and then three popes
1381	The English peasants revolt
1382	The weavers revolt in Ghent
1415	The battle of Agincourt—the French are defeated by Henry V of England; John Huss, Bohemian religious reformer, is burned at the stake
1429	Joan of Arc liberates Orléans
1431	Joan of Arc is condemned as a witch
1453	The English are driven from France, except Calais; the end of the Hundred Years' War
1460	Pope Pius II condemns the Conciliar movement as heretical

faith from their central position to the periphery of human concerns.

The modern outlook emerged gradually in the period from the Renaissance to the eighteenth-century Age of Enlightenment. Mathematics rendered the universe comprehensible. Economic and political thought broke free of the religious frame of reference. Science became the great hope of the future. The thinkers of the Enlightenment wanted to liberate humanity from superstition, ignorance, and traditions that could not pass the test of reason. Rejecting the Christian idea of a person's inherent sinfulness, they held that the individual was basically good, and that evil resulted from faulty institutions, poor education, and bad leadership. Thus the concept of a rational and free society in which individuals could realize their potential slowly emerged.

In the following chapters, we will examine how the medieval conception of the cosmos, society, and the individual gradually crumbled before the onset of science and secularism. Western thinkers abandoned religious interpretations of nature and sought to transform institutions so that they followed rational norms. This effort kindled enormous enthusiasm and hope, for it held the promise of emancipating men and women from abuses of the past. But the path to a rational and free society became choked with obstacles— some created by the very success of reason and freedom. People began to lose confidence in reason and weakened their commitment to freedom; this change engulfed Western civilization in a spiritual crisis that still persists.

Notes

1. Jean Froissart, *Chronicles of England, France, Spain* (London: Henry G. Bohn, 1849), p. 653.

2. Excerpted in Brian Tierney, ed., *The Crisis of Church and State 1050–1300* (Englewood Cliffs, N.J.: Prentice Hall, 1964), p. 189.

3. Excerpted in Ralph Lerner and Muhsin Mahdi, *Medieval Political Philosophy* (New York: The Free Press, 1963), pp. 413–414.

4. J. H. Randall, Jr., *The Making of the Modern Mind* (Boston: Houghton Mifflin, 1940), p. 34.

Suggested Reading

Bowsky, W. M., ed., *The Black Death* (1971). A collection of readings on the impact of the plague.

Ferguson, W. K., *Europe in Transition 1300–1520* (1962). The transition from Middle Ages to Renaissance.

Hay, Denys, *Europe in the Fourteenth and Fifteenth Centuries* (1966). A good survey of the Late Middle Ages.

Hilton, Rodney, *Bond Men Made Free* (1977). An analysis of medieval peasant movements.

Holmes, George, *Europe: Hierarchy and Revolt, 1320–1450* (1975). A good survey of the period.

Huizinga, Johan, *The Waning of the Middle Ages* (1924). An old but still valuable discussion of late medieval culture.

Lerner, Robert E., *The Age of Adversity* (1968). A short, readable survey of the fourteenth century.

McFarlane, K. B., *John Wycliffe and the Beginnings of English Nonconformity* (1952). The man and his influence.

Mollat, Guillaume, *The Popes at Avignon* (1963). The papacy in the fourteenth century.

Ozment, Steven, *The Age of Reform, 1250–1550* (1980). An intellectual and religious history of Late Medieval and Reformation Europe.

Perroy, Edouard, *The Hundred Years' War* (1965). The best treatment of the conflict.

Spinka, M., *John Hus and the Czech Reform* (1941). A reliable work on Huss and the Hussite wars.

Review Questions

1. What economic problems made the fourteenth century an age of adversity?

2. What were the principal reasons for peasant uprisings in the fourteenth century?

3. What was the fundamental issue at stake in the conflict between Boniface VIII and Philip IV?

4. How did John of Paris and Marsiglio of Padua challenge the pope's claim to primacy over secular authority?

5. Identify and explain the historical significance of the Babylonian Captivity, Great Schism, and Conciliar movement.

6. Why did the church regard Wycliffe and Huss as heretics?

7. What was the significance of Ockham's philosophy?

8. What is the legacy of the Middle Ages to the modern world?

9. How does the characteristic outlook of the Middle Ages differ from that of the modern age?

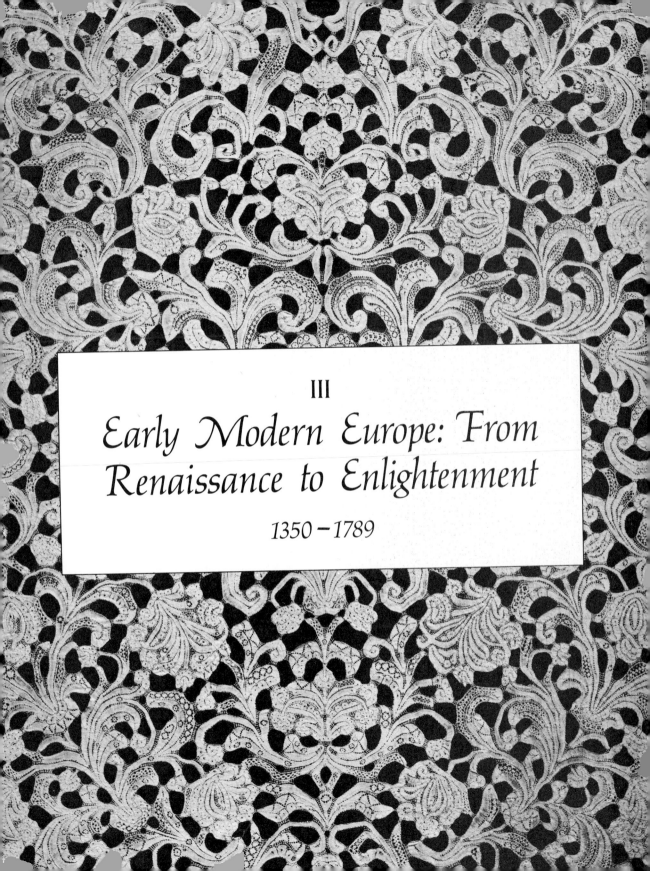

III

Early Modern Europe: From Renaissance to Enlightenment

1350 – 1789

13

The Renaissance: Transition
to the Modern Age

*F*rom the Italian Renaissance of the fifteenth century through the Age of Enlightenment of the eighteenth century, the outlook and institutions of the Middle Ages disintegrated and distinctly modern forms emerged. The radical change in European civilization could be seen on every level of society. On the economic level, commerce and industry expanded greatly, and capitalism largely replaced medieval forms of economic organization. On the political level, central government grew stronger at the expense of feudalism. On the religious level, the rise of Protestantism fragmented the unity of Christendom. On the social level, the prosperous people in both city and country gained in numbers and strength and were preparing for political and cultural leadership. On the cultural level, the clergy lost its monopoly over learning, and the otherworldly orientation of the Middle Ages gave way to a secular outlook in literature and the arts. Theology, the queen of knowledge in the Middle Ages, surrendered its crown to science. Reason, which in the Middle Ages had been subordinate to revelation, asserted its independence.

Many of these tendencies manifested themselves dramatically during the Renaissance. The word *renaissance* means rebirth and it is used to refer to the attempt by artists and thinkers to recover and apply the ancient learning and standards of Greece and Rome. In historical terms, the Renaissance is both a cultural movement and a period. As a movement it was born in the city-states of northern Italy and spread to the rest of Europe. As a period it runs from about 1350 to 1600. Until the late fifteenth century the Renaissance was restricted to Italy. What happened there in the fourteenth and fifteenth centuries sharply contrasts with civilization in the rest of Europe, which until the end of the fifteenth century still belonged to the Late Middle Ages.

The nineteenth-century historian Jacob Burckhardt in his classic study, *The Civilization of the Renaissance in Italy* (1860), held that the Renaissance is the point of departure for the modern world. During the Renaissance, said Burckhardt, individuals showed an increasing concern for worldly life and self-consciously aspired to shape their destinies, an attitude that is the key to modernity.

Burckhardt's thesis has been challenged, particularly by medievalists who view the Renaissance as an extension of the Middle Ages, not as a sudden break with the past. These critics argue that Burckhardt neglected important links between medieval and Renaissance culture. A distinguishing feature of the Renaissance, the revival of classical learning, had already emerged in the High Middle Ages to such an extent that historians speak of "the renaissance of the twelfth century." The Renaissance owes much to the legal and scholastic studies that flourished in the Italian universities of Padua and Bologna before 1300. Town life and trade, hallmarks of Renaissance society, were also a heritage from the Middle Ages.

To be sure, the Renaissance was not a complete and sudden break with the Middle Ages. Many medieval ways and attitudes persisted. Nevertheless, Burckhardt's thesis that the Renaissance represents the birth of modernity has much to recommend it. Renaissance writers and artists themselves were aware of their age's novelty. They looked back on the medieval centuries as a "Dark Age" that followed the grandeur of ancient Greece and Rome, and they believed that they were experiencing a rebirth of cultural greatness. Renaissance artists and writers were fascinated with the cultural forms of Greece and Rome; they sought to imitate classical style and to capture the secular spirit of antiquity. In the process they broke with medieval artistic and literary forms. They valued the full development of human talent and expressed a new excitement about the possibilities of life in this world. This outlook represents a new trend in European civilization.

The Renaissance, then, was an age of transition that saw the rejection of certain elements of the medieval outlook, the revival of classical

cultural forms, and the emergence of distinctly modern attitudes. This rebirth began in Italy during the fourteenth century and gradually spread north and west to Germany, France, England, and Spain during the late fifteenth and the sixteenth centuries.

Italy: Birthplace of the Renaissance

The city-states of northern Italy that spawned the Renaissance were developed urban centers where people had the wealth, freedom, and inclination to cultivate the arts and to enjoy the fruits of worldly life. In Italy, moreover, reminders of ancient Rome's grandeur were visible everywhere. Roman roads, monuments, and manuscripts intensified the Italians' links to their Roman past.

Political Evolution of the City-States

During the Middle Ages the feudal states of northern Italy had been absorbed into the Holy Roman Empire. They continued to owe nominal allegiance to the German emperor during the early Renaissance. But its protracted wars with the papacy had sapped the empire of vitality. Its subsequent weakness meant that the states of northern Italy were able to develop as autonomous political entities. Also promoting this development was the weakening of the papacy in the fourteenth century (see pages 254–258).

The city-states that developed in northern Italy were similar in their size and their varied types of governments to those of ancient Greece. Among the more important city-states were Rome, Milan, Florence, Venice, Mantua, Ferrara, Padua, Bologna, and Genoa. These city-states markedly differed from most of Europe in two fundamental respects. First, by the late eleventh and twelfth centuries

Map 13.1 Italian City-States, C. 1494 ▶

DUCHY OF SAVOY

DUCHY OF MILAN

Milan

Pavia • Lodi

Turin

SALUZZO

REP. OF GENOA

Genoa

Po R.

M. OF MANTUA

Mantua

D. OF MODENA

Padua

Venice

REPUBLIC OF VENICE

Ferrara

D. OF FERRARA

Bologna • Ravenna

OTTOMAN EMPIRE

DALMATIA

REP. OF LUCCA

Arno R.

Pisa

REP. OF FLORENCE

Florence

FLORENCE

Siena

REP. OF SIENA

Urbino

Tiber R.

Assisi

PAPAL STATES

ADRIATIC SEA

CORSICA

Rome

SARDINIA

KINGDOM OF NAPLES

Naples • Bari

Salerno

Palermo

KINGDOM OF SICILY

M E D I T E R R A N E A N   S E A

the city-states had developed as flourishing commercial and banking centers and had monopolized the trade in Mediterranean areas, which included trade between the Orient and the West. So the merchant fleets, especially those of Venice and Genoa, carried goods from ports in the eastern Mediterranean westward into the Atlantic and from there north to the Baltic Sea. Unlike that of the rest of Europe, the wealth of these cities lay not in land, but in commerce and industry. When popes, monarchs, and feudal magnates of Europe needed money, they borrowed it from Italian, especially Florentine, merchant-bankers.

Second, the predominance of business and commerce within these city-states meant that the feudal nobility, who held the land beyond the city walls, played a much less important part in government than they did elsewhere in Europe. By the end of the twelfth century the city-states had ceased to be dominated by the feudal nobility, or landed aristocracy. The aristocracy and the rich merchants had to share power, and when their alliances broke down, as they often did, the two groups struggled for power based on their opposing interests and outlooks. The interests of the smaller merchants and the artisans in the towns also had to be catered to. When they were not, these groups rioted and rebelled, as they did, for instance, in 1378 during the revolt of the *Ciompi* (the wool-workers) in Florence.

Politically these city-states were inherently unstable. They managed to keep both papacy and Empire at bay, sometimes by playing one giant against the other in the manner of Third World nations today. But the price of this continued independence was that the city-states, without any externally imposed power structure, had to seek solutions to their own instability. This instability arose from two sources—the internal conflict between merchants and nobles and the external rivalry between the city-states themselves. Out of this situation came experiments in the form and technique of government. The origins of modern political thought and practice can be

discerned in this experimentation, thus forging an important connection between the Renaissance and the modern age.

The political experimentation that went on in the northern Italian city-states can usefully, if only roughly, be divided into two periods—the first (1300–1450) marked by the defense of republicanism and the second (1450–1550) by the triumph of despotism. By the end of the twelfth century the city-states had adopted a fairly uniform pattern of republican self-government built around the office of a chief magistrate. He was elected by the citizens on the basis of a broad franchise, and he ruled with the advice of two councils—a large public one and a small secret one. His powers were tightly circumscribed by the constitution; with his term of office restricted ordinarily to six months, he could be removed from government or punished at the end of his tenure.

The city-states not only developed republican institutions; they self-consciously devised important theories to defend and justify their liberty and self-government in the face of their external enemies, the papacy and the Empire. To the emperor they argued that their customary feudal subjection to his authority must be radically adjusted to fit the changed reality that they were in fact self-governing. To the papacy they argued that Christ had denied all political jurisdiction to the clergy, including the pope, and so undercut the papal claim to political control in Italy and elsewhere.

However, the republicanism of the city-states, with their internal instability and their rivalry, proved precarious. During the fourteenth and early fifteenth centuries the republican institutions in one city after another toppled in favor of rule by despots. Three conditions were responsible for this development. First, class war between rich merchants and nobles caused one group or the other, or both, to seek a resolution of the crisis by turning to one-man rule. Second, the economic disasters, famine, and disease of the period from 1350 to 1450 encouraged the drift toward despotism. Northern Italy

Presentation of the Infant Jesus in the Temple, attributed to Giotto (c. 1266/76–1337). The monumentality of Giotto's figures and their dramatic glances and gestures were received with awe in Florence. Renaissance artists were strongly influenced by Giotto's work. (*Isabella Stewart Gardner Museum, Boston*)

was particularly hard hit by the bubonic plague. The citizenry lost faith in the ability of short-term republican governments to cope with such emergencies and put their trust in long-term, one-man rule. Third, and perhaps most important, the city-states had come to rely on mercenary troops, whose leaders, the notorious *condottieri*—unschooled in and owing no loyalty to the republican tradition—simply seized power during emergencies.

Some city-states held out against the trend toward despotism for a long time; among those that did, Florence was by far the most successful. In the process, the Florentines developed new arguments and theories for the maintenance of republicanism and liberty

(see pages 279–281). But by the mid-fifteenth century, even Florentine republicanism was giving way before the intrigues of a rich banking family—the Medici. They had installed themselves in power in the 1430s with the return of Cosimo de' Medici from exile. Cosimo's grandson, Lorenzo the Magnificent, completed the destruction of the republican constitution in 1480, when he managed to set up a government staffed by his own supporters.

The one city-state where republicanism survived until the advent of Napoleon was Venice. Protected from the rest of Italy by lagoons, Venice during the Middle Ages controlled a far-flung and exceptionally lucrative seagoing trade and a maritime empire stretching along the Adriatic and the eastern Mediterranean seas. Venice's maritime commercial successes were matched by political ones at home. For centuries, Venice managed to govern itself without major upheaval; its republican constitution made this stability possible. Its chief executive offices, the Council of Ten, were elective, but after 1297, both these offices and the electorate were narrowly restricted by law to old patrician families. Venice was an aristocratic republic. The government proved remarkably effective because the ruling elite was able to engender a sense of public duty in its young that passed on from one generation—and one century— to the next. Venetian government, because it was at once stable and republican, served as a powerful model to republican theorists in seventeenth- and eighteenth-century Europe.

The city-states, excepting Venice, were not only internally unstable, but they were also constantly at war with one another. By the middle of the fifteenth century, however, five major powers had emerged from the fighting: the kingdom of Naples and Sicily in the south; the Papal States, where the popes had built up, bit by bit, a territory running across the center of the Italian peninsula; and in the north the city-states of Florence, Venice, and Milan. In 1454 these five powers, largely through the efforts of Cosimo de' Medici, concluded the Peace of Lodi. For the next forty years they were relatively peaceful, until the French king Charles VIII invaded northern Italy in 1494.

The Peace of Lodi endured so long because of diplomacy. The essential techniques of modern diplomacy were worked out and applied in the second half of the fifteenth century in Italy. The practices of establishing embassies with ambassadors, sending and analyzing intelligence reports, consulting and negotiating during emergencies, and forming alliances all developed during this period. Some historians also see this time in Italian history as the seedbed for the notion of balance of power—a pattern that eventually became fundamental to the diplomacy of all

Europe. Later, in the early modern period, European governments formed alliances so that no single state or group of allied states could dominate the Continent. Some elements of this balance of power were anticipated in the struggles among the Italian city-states.

Renaissance Society

Paralleling the new developments in relations among city-states was the new way of life emerging within the city-states. Prosperous merchants played a leading role in the political and cultural life of the city. With the expansion of commerce and industry, the feudal values of birth, military prowess, and a fixed hierarchy decayed in favor of ambition and individual achievement, whether at court, in the counting house, or inside the artist's studio. Not that the old feudal, chivalric code was destroyed—rather, it was transformed to serve different purposes.

The new urban, commercial oligarchies could not justify their power in the old way, through heredity. Moreover, they had to function within the inherently unstable political climate of the city-states. Faced with this dual problem, the oligarchs fell back on the feudal idea of honor and developed elaborate codes. These codes differed in significant ways from their medieval antecedents. First came a depreciation (although never a complete elimination) of birth as a basis of merit, with a corresponding emphasis on effort, talent, and (in the case of the artist) creative genius. Second, honor was no longer defined in narrow, largely military terms, but was expanded to include both the civic and courtly virtues of the worthy citizen and courtier and the artistic achievement of the painter, sculptor, architect, and poet.

The new code, however, remained elitist and even aristocratic. Indeed, because of their very newness and insecurity, the new oligarchs of the Renaissance were all the more anxious to adopt the aristocratic outlook of the old nobility. The *nouveaux riches* (new rich) aped the feudal aristocracy in dress and manners, even as they accommodated the code of knightly chivalry to the demands of a new urban and commercial culture. Renaissance society was a highly unstable compound of old and new.

Marriage and Family Life   City life profoundly altered family structure, marriage patterns, and relations between the sexes. Elsewhere in Europe most people still lived on the land and tended to marry early in order to produce large families to work the fields. But in cities, early marriage could be a liability for a man who was attempting to make his fortune. The results were that older men married young brides, which meant that wives usually outlived their husbands. Because a widow inherited her husband's property, she was not pressed to remarry and she brought up her children in a single-parent household.

The large number of single, relatively prosperous, and leisured adults probably explains why Renaissance cities were notorious for sodomy, prostitution, and triangles involving an older husband, a young wife, and a young lover. Such sexual behavior was encouraged by the relative anonymity of the large cities and by the constant influx of young men of talent from the country districts.

Single-parent households might also account for the high incidence of homosexuality during the Renaissance. Historian David Herlihy maintains that sons became attached to their mothers in the absence of their fathers and their heterosexual development was stifled. Whether one accepts this Freudian interpretation or not, Herlihy's other conclusion has much to recommend it: that so many women were responsible for nurturing their children may have encouraged the development of the Renaissance idea of a gentleman, which emphasized civility, courtliness, and an appreciation of art, literature, and the feminine graces.

Whatever the effect on their sons, upper-class women enjoyed greater freedom in greater numbers than they had since the Fall of Rome. If they were married, they had the income to pursue pleasure in the form of clothes, conversation, and romance. If a well-to-do husband died while his wife was still young, she had no financial reasons to remarry. She was then free, to a degree previously unknown, to go her own way.

Patronage of the Arts   Members of the urban upper class became patrons of the arts, providing funds to support promising artists and writers. Urban patricians whose wealth was based upon commerce and banking, not land, had become dominant in both republican Florence and despotic Milan. Unable to claim power by birth or to rely on traditional loyalties, they looked to culture to provide the trappings and justification of power.

For the newly rich, art could serve a political function. In its sheer magnificence, art could manifest power and cast that spell over subjects or citizens that all governments must depend on to some extent. Art could also serve as a focus of civic pride and patriotism, just as literature could (see page 277). Just as they contended on the battlefield, insecure rulers competed for art and artists to bolster their egos. Art became a desirable political investment, especially when in the fifteenth century, economic investments were not offering as much return as they had a century or two before. The popes, too, invested in art. Having lost the battle for temporal dominion in Europe, the papacy concentrated on increasing its direct dominion in Italy by consolidating and expanding the Papal States. As an adjunct to this policy, the popes heaped wealth on artists to enhance their own papal prestige and perhaps to recover some of their shattered self-esteem. So the popes became the most lavish patrons of all, as the works of Michelangelo and Raphael testify.

The result of this new patronage by popes and patricians was an explosion of artistic creativity. The amount and especially the nature of this patronage also helped to shape both art and the artist. Portraiture became a separate genre for the first time since antiquity and was developed much further than ever

Michelangelo Buonarroti (1475–1564): The Dying Slave. The human figure inspired the greatest works of Michelangelo. As a Neo-Platonist, he saw a constant struggle between the soul of the individual and the body that entrapped it. *The Dying Slave* was part of a monument for Pope Julius. (*Louvre/Cliché des Musées Nationaux*)

before. Patrician rivalry and insecurity of status, fed by the Renaissance ethic of achievement and reward, produced a scramble for honor and reputation. This pursuit fostered the desire to be memorialized in a painting, if not in a sculpture. A painter like Titian was in great demand.

The great artists emerged as famous men by virtue of their exercise of brush and chisel. In the Middle Ages, artists had been regarded as craftsmen who did lowly (manual) labor and who, as a result, were to be accorded little if any status. Indeed, they remained anonymous for the most part. But the unparalleled Renaissance demand for art brought artists public recognition for the first time. They enjoyed this status until the Industrial Revolution, when art once more depreciated in value. Artistic fame did not come without effort, and the drive for it, stimulated again by the Renaissance ethos of competition and by the humanist ethic, may have spurred artists to greater creative achievements than might otherwise have developed.

Secularism   Renaissance society was marked by a growing secular outlook. Intrigued by the active life of the city and eager to enjoy worldly pleasures that their money could obtain, wealthy merchants and bankers moved away from the medieval preoccupation with salvation. To be sure, they were neither nonbelievers nor atheists, but increasingly religion had to compete with worldly concerns. Consequently, members of the urban upper class paid religion less heed, or at least did not allow it to interfere with their quest for the full life. The challenge and pleasure of living well in this world seemed more exciting than the promise of heaven. This outlook found concrete expression in Renaissance art and literature.

Individualism   Individualism was another hallmark of Renaissance society. Urban life released people of wealth and talent from the old constraints of manor and church. The urban elite sought to assert their own personalities, to discover and to express their own peculiar feelings, to demonstrate their unique talents, to win fame and glory, and to fulfill their ambitions. This Renaissance ideal was explicitly elitist. It applied only to the few, entirely disregarding the masses; it valued what was distinctive and superior in an individual, not what was common to all men; it was concerned with the distinctions of the few, not the needs or rights of the many. Individualism became deeply embedded in the Western soul, and was expressed in artists who sought to capture individual character, in explorers who ventured into uncharted seas, in conquerors who carved out empires in the New World, and in merchant-capitalists who amassed fortunes.

The Renaissance Outlook: Humanism and Secular Politics

Humanism

The most characteristic intellectual movement of the Renaissance was *humanism*, an educational and cultural program based on the study of ancient Greek and Roman literature. The humanist attitude toward antiquity differed from that of medieval scholars. Medieval scholars sought to fit classical learning into a Christian world-view. Renaissance humanists, in contrast, did not subordinate the classics to the requirements of Christian doctrines; rather, they valued ancient literature for its own sake—for its clear and graceful style, for its insights into human nature. From the ancient classics, humanists expected to learn much that could not be provided by medieval writings—how to live well in this world and how to perform one's civic duties, for example. For the humanists the classics were a guide to the good life, the active life. To achieve self-cultivation, to write well, to speak well, and to live well, it was necessary to know the classics. In contrast to scholastic philosophers who used Greek philosophy to prove the truth of Christian doctrines, Italian humanists used classical learning to nourish their new interest in a worldly life.

Whereas medieval scholars were familiar with only some ancient Latin writers, Renaissance humanists restored to circulation every Roman work that could be found. Similarly, whereas knowledge of Greek was very rare in Latin Christendom during the Middle Ages, Renaissance humanists increasingly cultivated the study of Greek in order to read Homer, Demosthenes, Plato, and other ancients in the original.

Although predominantly a secular movement, Italian humanism was not un-Christian. True, humanists often treated moral problems in a purely secular manner, but when they did deal with religious and theological questions, they did not challenge Christian belief or question the validity of the Bible. They did, however, attack scholasticism for its hairsplitting arguments and preoccupation with trivial questions. They stressed instead a purer form of Christianity based on the direct study of the Bible and writings by the church fathers.

A principal source of humanism was the study of law that flourished in the thirteenth and fourteenth centuries in Bologna, Padua, and Ravenna. Not only did students learn the law; they also learned rhetoric—how to argue and how to speak. In these adjuncts to legal study lie some origins of humanism. Using classical Roman models for their arguments, teachers and students went beyond their textbook exercises to make comments on contemporary political issues. Here was the earliest regular use of classical sources to make a judgment or to point to a moral for the present. The Roman classics in the hands of the legists and rhetoricians became source books for the defense of liberty and independence, first against emperors and popes and later against the threat of home-grown despots. So well developed did this tradition become that it eventually outgrew the bounds of the legal studies where it was first nurtured and took the form of a separate enterprise. Men of letters, prehumanists, wrote chronicles of their cities, glorifying the historical struggle against tyranny. Political advice books, based on classical Roman wisdom that instructed rulers and citizens in how to oppose tyranny, also appeared rather steadily starting in the fourteenth century.

An early humanist, sometimes called the father of humanism, was Petrarch (1304–1374). Petrarch and his followers carried the recovery of the classics further by making a systematic attempt to discover the classical roots of medieval Italian rhetoric. Petrarch's own efforts to learn Greek were largely unsuccessful, but by encouraging his students to master the ancient tongue, he advanced humanist learning. Petrarch was particularly drawn to Cicero, the ancient Roman orator. Following the example of Cicero, Petrarch insisted that education should consist not only of learning and knowing things, but also of learning how to communicate one's knowledge and how to use it for the public good. Therefore, the emphasis in education should be on rhetoric and moral philosophy, wisdom combined with eloquence. This was the key to virtue in the ruler, the citizen and the republic. Petrarch helped to make Ciceronian values dominant among the humanists. His followers set up schools to inculcate the new Ciceronian educational ideal.

Implicit in the humanist educational ideal was a radical transformation of the Christian idea of men and women. According to the medieval (Augustinian) view, men and women were not only incapable of attaining excellence through their own efforts and talents, but it was wrong and sinful for them even to try. Human beings were completely subject to divine will. In contrast, the humanists, recalling the classical Greek concept of *arete*, made the achievement of excellence through individual striving the end not only of education, but of life itself. Because individuals were capable of this goal, moreover, it was their duty to pursue it as the end of life. The pursuit was not effortless; indeed, it took extraordinary energy and skill.

People, then, were capable of excellence in every sphere and duty-bound to make the effort. This emphasis on human creative powers was one of the most characteristic and influential doctrines of the Renaissance. A classic expression of it is found in *Oration on the Dignity of Man* (1486) by Giovanni Pico della Mirandola (1463–1494). Man, said Pico, has the freedom to shape his own life. Pico has God say to man: "We have made you a creature" such that "you may, as the free and proud shaper of your own being, fashion yourself in the form you may prefer."[1]

Pico also spells out another implication of man's duty to realize his potential: through his own exertions, man can come to understand and control nature. One of the new and powerful Renaissance images of man was as the *magus*, the magician. The vision of the mastery of nature continued to inspire experimentalists, like Francis Bacon, and natural philosophers, like Robert Boyle and Isaac Newton, until at least the early eighteenth century. A major psychological driving force of the scientific revolution, this vision stemmed in large part from the philosophy of Italian humanists like Pico.

The attack on the medieval scholastics was implicit in the humanist educational ideal. From the humanist perspective, scholasticism failed not only because its terms and Latin usage were barbarous, but also because it did not provide useful knowledge. This humanist emphasis on the uses of knowledge also offered a stimulus to science and art.

So hostile were the humanists to all things scholastic and medieval that they reversed the prevailing view of history. The Christian view saw history as a simple unfolding of God's will and providence. The humanists stressed the importance of human actions and human wills in history—of people as active participants in the shaping of events. The humanists rejected the providentialist scheme in favor of a cyclical view deriving from the ancients, particularly Aristotle, Polybius, and Cicero. History alternated between times of darkness and times of light, of ignorance and illumination, of decline and rebirth.

This cyclical view allowed the humanists

to characterize the epoch preceding their own as a period of declension from classical heights. Equally, it allowed them to see themselves and their own time as representing a period of rebirth, the recovery of classical wisdom and ideals. On the basis of this cyclical view, the humanists invented the notion of the Middle Ages as that period separating the ancient world from their own by a gulf of darkness. To the humanists, then, we owe the current periodization of history into ancient, medieval, and modern. There was also an element in the humanist view of today's idea of progress: they dared to think that they, "the moderns," might even surpass the ancient glories of Greece and Rome.

The humanist emphasis on historical scholarship yielded a method of critical inquiry that in the right hands could help to undermine traditional loyalties and institutions. The work of Lorenzo Valla (c. 1407–1457) provides the clearest example of this trend. Educated as a classicist, Valla trained the guns of critical scholarship on the papacy in his most famous work, *Declamation Concerning the False Decretals of Constantine.* The papal claim to temporal authority rested on a document that purported to verify the so-called Donation of Constantine, whereby when the Emperor Constantine moved the capital to Constantinople in the fourth century, he had bestowed on the pope dominion over the entire western Empire. But Valla proved that the document was based on an eighth-century forgery because the language at certain points was unknown in Constantine's own time and did not come into use until much later.

Also embedded in the humanist re-evaluation of individual potential was a new appreciation of the moral significance of work. For the humanist the honor, fame, and even glory bestowed by one's city or patron for meritorious deeds was the ultimate reward for effort. The humanist pursuit of praise and reputation became something of a Renaissance cult.

In fourteenth- and fifteenth-century republican Florence, at least until the Medici took control, Petrarchan humanism was not

Lorenzo de' Medici. The Medici preferred to wield power behind the scenes through secret alliances and intrigue. Lorenzo, who became head of the family in his teens, fostered the fiction of the good citizen; this portrait of him is by Agnolo Bronzino. (*Scala/Art Resource*)

meant for a court elite. Humanism was meant rather as a civic idea—to educate and inform citizens so that they could contribute to the common good to the greatest possible extent. In this sense, humanism was put in the service of republican values and the republican cause, and the mixture of the two is what has come to be called *civic humanism* by recent historians. This civic ideal developed furthest in the Florentine republic.

By the second half of the fifteenth century, as the Medici gained increasing control, the civic ideal was being replaced by another that was more fitting to the times, the ideal of princely rule. This princely ideal borrowed much from civic humanism, even though it was directed toward princes and courtiers and not toward citizens. The emphasis on the pursuit of virtue and honor was still there. Like the ideal gentleman, the ideal prince evolved through a humanistic education that would prepare him for the struggle between virtue and fortune so that virtue would prove victorious.

But the similarities between the civic and princely ideals were not as important as the differences. The aim of princely rule was no longer liberty, but peace and security. The best means to this end was no longer a republic, but hereditary monarchy. This new princely ideal was reflected in a new spate of advice books; the most influential of these was *The Book of the Courtier*, written between 1513 and 1518 by Baldassare Castiglione (1478–1529). These books promoted the notion that the ideal ruler should be universally talented and skillful, equally commanding on the battlefield, at court, and in the state, and virtuous throughout. These advice books, especially Castiglione's, were to serve as indispensable handbooks for courtiers and would-be gentlemen not only in Renaissance Italy, but throughout Europe. This ideal held sway until well into the seventeenth century, when the type finally began to give way before a new idea of virtue and virtuosity.

A Revolution in Political Thought

One advice book transcended the class of these works: *The Prince*, written in 1513 by the Florentine Niccolò Machiavelli (1469–1527). Machiavelli's book offered a critique of the humanist ideal of princely rule and in so doing made some fundamental contributions to political theory. Indeed, Machiavelli may be called the first major modern political thinker. To Machiavelli the humanist ideal is naive in its insistence on the prince's virtues and eloquence to the exclusion of all other considerations. He attacks the medieval and humanist tradition of theoretical politics:

Since my intention is to say something that will prove of practical use to the inquirer, I have thought it proper to represent things as they are in real truth, rather than as they are imagined. Many have dreamed up republics and principalities which have never in truth been known to exist; the gulf between how one should live and how one does live is so wide that a man who neglects what is actually done for what should be done learns the way to self-destruction.[2]

Politics, Machiavelli argues, requires the rational deployment of force as well as, and even prior to, the exercise of virtue.

On this point, Machiavelli's advice is quite specific. He wrote *The Prince* in part as a plea. Since 1494, Italy had fallen prey to France and Spain. Their great royal armies overpowered the mercenary armies of the city-states and went on to lay waste to Italy in their struggle for domination of the peninsula. To prevent this, Machiavelli says, the Italians must relinquish humanistic Christian utopianism and unite behind a leader—the prince—whose first act would be to disband the mercenaries and forge a new citizen army, worthy of the glorious Roman past and capable of repelling the "barbarian" invasion. "Mercenaries," Machiavelli claims, "are useless and dangerous." They are "useless" because "there is no . . . inducement to keep them on the field apart from the little they are paid, and this is not enough to make them want to die for you." And they are "dangerous" because their leaders, the infamous *condottieri*, "are anxious to advance their own greatness" at the expense of the city-state. Reliance on mercenaries is the sole cause of "the present ruin of Italy,"[3] and the cure lies in the creation of a national militia, led by a prince.

This prince must be both wily and virtuous—not (as humanists had said) virtuous alone: "The fact is that a man who wants to act virtuously in every way necessarily comes to grief among so many who are not virtuous." So Machiavelli scandalized Christian Europe by asserting that "if a prince wants to maintain his rule he must learn how not to be virtuous, and to make use of this or not according to his need."[4] Even more shocking, the prince must know how to dissemble, that is, to make all his actions appear virtuous, whether they are so or not. In ironic parody of conventional advice-book wisdom, Machiavelli argues that a ruler must cultivate a *reputation* for virtue rather than virtue itself. In this connection Machiavelli arrived at a fundamental political truth—that politics (and especially the relationship between ruler and ruled) being what it is, the road to success for the prince lies in dissimulation. "Everyone sees what you appear to be, few experience what you really are. And those few dare not gainsay the many who are backed by the majesty of the state."[5] Here again the Renaissance arrived at modernity.

Machiavelli broke with both the scholastic and the humanist traditions of political thought. He was a secularist who tried to understand and explain the state without recourse to Christian teachings. Influenced by classical thought and especially the works of Livy, he rejected the prevailing view that the state is God's creation and that the ruler should base his policies on Christian moral principles. For Machiavelli, religion was not the foundation for politics but merely a useful tool in the prince's struggle for success. The prince might even dissemble, if he thought he had to, in matters of the faith, by appearing pious, whether or not he was, and by playing on and exploiting the piety of his subjects.

Renaissance Art

The most graphic image of the Renaissance is conveyed through its art, particularly architecture, sculpture, and painting. Renaissance examples of all three art forms reflect a style that stressed proportion, balance, and harmony. These artistic values were achieved through a new, revolutionary conceptualization of space and spatial relations. Renaissance art also reflects to a considerable extent the values of Renaissance humanism, a return to classical models in architecture, to the rendering of the nude human figure, and to a heroic vision of human beings.

Medieval art sought to represent spiritual aspiration; the world was a veil merely hinting at the other perfect and eternal world. Renaissance art did not stop expressing spiritual aspiration, but its setting and character differ altogether. This world is no longer a shroud, but becomes the *place* where people live, act, and worship. The reference is less to the other world and more to this world, and people are treated as creatures who find their spiritual destiny as they fulfill their human one.

The Middle Ages had produced a distinctive art known as the Gothic. By the fourteenth and fifteenth centuries, Gothic art had evolved into what is known as the International Style, characterized by careful drawing, flowing and delicate lines, harmonious composition, and delightful naturalistic detail.

Renaissance art at its most distinctive represents a conscious revolt against this late Gothic trend. This revolt produced revolutionary discoveries that served as the foundation of Western art up to this century. In art, as in philosophy, the Florentines played a leading role in this esthetic transformation. They, more than anyone else, were responsible for the way artists saw and drew for centuries and for the way most Western people still see or want to see.

Early Renaissance Art

The first major contributor to Renaissance painting was the Florentine painter Giotto (c. 1266/76–1337). Borrowing from Byzantine painting, he created figures modeled by alterations in light and shade. He also developed several techniques of perspective, representing three-dimensional figures and objects in two-dimensional surfaces, so that they appear to stand in space. Giotto's figures also look remarkably alive (see page 273). They are drawn and arranged in space to tell a story, and the expressions they wear and the illusion of movement they convey heighten the dramatic effect. Giotto's best works were *frescoes*, wall paintings painted

Botticelli (1444–1510): The Birth of Venus. Botticelli was a member of the Florentine group of Neo-Platonists. They tried to harmonize Greco-Roman ideals with those of Christianity. The nude goddess is Venus, but the modest tilt of the head is the traditional pose of the Virgin Mary. To Botticelli the beauty of Venus and the purity of Mary were identical. (*Alinari-Scala/Art Resource*)

while the plaster was still wet or *fresh*. Lionized in his own day, Giotto had no immediate successors, and his ideas were not taken up and developed further for almost a century.

By the early fifteenth century the revival of classical learning had begun in earnest. In Florence it had its artistic counterpart among a circle of architects, painters, and sculptors who sought to revive classical art. The leader of this group was an architect, Filippo Brunelleschi (1377–1446). He abandoned Gothic prescriptions altogether and designed churches (Florence Cathedral, for instance) reflecting classical models. To him, we also owe a scientific discovery of the first importance in the history of art: the rules of perspective. Giotto had revived the ancient technique of foreshortening; Brunelleschi completed the discovery by rendering perspective in mathematical terms. Brunelleschi's

devotion to ancient models and his new tool of mathematical perspective set the stage for the further development of Renaissance painting.

Brunelleschi's young Florentine friend Masaccio (1401–1428) took up the challenge. Faithful to the new rules of perspective, Masaccio was also concerned with painting statuesque figures and endowing his paintings with a grandeur and simplicity whose inspiration is classical. Perspective came with all the force of religious revelation.

Early Renaissance artists were dedicated to representing things as they are, or at least as they are seen to be. Part of the inspiration for this was also classical. The ancient ideal of beauty was the beautiful nude. Renaissance admiration for ancient art meant that artists for the first time since the Fall of Rome studied anatomy; they learned to draw the human form by having models pose for them, a practice fundamental to artistic training to this day. Another member of Brunelleschi's circle, the Florentine sculptor Donatello (1386–1466), also showed renewed interest in the human form and conscious rejection of Gothic taste.

Another approach to the observation of nature—besides the imitation of the ancients—developed in northern Europe, principally in the Netherlands. Its original exponent was Jan van Eyck (c. 1390–1441), who worked mostly in what is now Belgium. Van Eyck's art developed out of the International Style. Within that style there was an interest in the faithful depiction of objects and creatures in the natural world. Van Eyck carried this tendency so far that it became the principal aim of his art: his pictures are like photographs in their infinitely scrupulous attention to the way things look. Unlike his contemporaries in Florence, van Eyck subordinated anatomy and perspective to appearance and showed no interest in classical models. In his concern to paint what he saw, he also developed oil painting. At that time, most paints were egg-based, but oil-based paints allowed him to obtain more lifelike and virtuoso effects (see page 258). The technique spread quickly to Italy, with astonishing results.

Late Renaissance Art

The use of perspective posed a fundamental problem for Renaissance painters: how to reconcile perspective with composition and the search for harmony. A chief interest of later fifteenth-century Italian painting lay in the various ways in which artists tackled this problem.

Among the Florentine artists of the second half of the fifteenth century who strove for a solution of this question was the painter Sandro Botticelli (c. 1444–1510). One of his most famous pictures depicts not a Christian legend, but a classical myth—*The Birth of Venus*. Representing, as it does, the way that

beauty came into the world, this painting is another expression of the Renaissance desire to recover the lost wisdom of the ancients. Botticelli has succeeded in rendering a perfectly harmonious pattern—but at the cost of sacrificing solidity and anatomical correctness. In *The Birth of Venus*, what the viewer notices are the graceful, flowing lines that unify and vivify the painting. Even the liberties that Botticelli took with nature—for example, the unnatural proportions of Venus's neck and shoulders—enhance the esthetic outcome.

New approaches to this problem of perspective and composition were developed by the three greatest artists of the Renaissance—Leonardo da Vinci (1452–1519), Michelangelo Buonarroti (1475–1564), and Raphael Santi (1483–1520). All of them were closely associated with Florence, and all of them were contemporaries.

Leonardo was a scientist and engineer, as well as a great artist. He was an expert at fortifications and gunnery, an inventor, an anatomist, and a naturalist. He brought this close observation of nature to his paintings and combined it with powerful psychological insight to produce works that although few in number, were of unsurpassed genius. Among the most important of these are *The Last Supper* and *La Gioconda* (the Mona Lisa). The Mona Lisa is an example of an artistic invention of Leonardo's—what the Italians call *sfumato*. Leonardo left the outlines of the face a little vague and shadowy; this freed it of any wooden quality, which more exact drawing would impart, and thus made it more lifelike and mysterious. Here was a major breakthrough in solving the problem of perspective. The artist must not be too exact and rigid in adhering to the rules; he must introduce a correcting softness and atmosphere to achieve a reconciliation between perspective and the demands of design.

Michelangelo's route to artistic harmony was through a mastery of anatomy and drawing. His model in painting came from sculpture; his paintings are sculpted drawings. He was of course a sculptor of the highest genius whose approach to his art was poetic

Leonardo da Vinci (1452–1519): Mona Lisa. Leonardo da Vinci's paintings are few in number and difficult to interpret. Psychological mystery characterizes the *Mona Lisa*. Poets, essayists, and art historians have not fully explained her smile. Like most of his paintings, it is in an unfinished state. (*Louvre/Cliché des Musées Nationaux*)

and visionary. Instead of trying to impose form on marble, he thought of sculpting as releasing the form from the rock. Among his greatest sculptures are *David, Moses,* and *The Dying Slave* (page 276). Michelangelo was also an architect and, patronized by the pope, he designed the dome of the new St. Peter's basilica in Rome. But perhaps his most stupendous work was the ceiling of the Sistine Chapel in the Vatican, commissioned by Pope Julius II. In four years, working with little assistance, Michelangelo covered the empty

space with the most monumental sculpted pictures ever painted, pictures that summarize the Old Testament story. The Creation of Adam is the most famous of these superlative *frescoes.*

Raphael, the last of these three artistic giants, was the complete master of design in painting. His balanced compositions sacrifice nothing to perspective. Rather, perspective becomes just another tool, along with *sfumato* and mathematical proportion, for achieving harmony. Raphael is especially famous for the sweetness of his Madonnas. But he was capable of painting other subjects and of conveying other moods as well, as his portrait of his patron, *Pope Leo X with Two Cardinals,* reveals.

Renaissance painting came late to Venice, but when it arrived in the late fifteenth and early sixteenth centuries, it produced a tradition of sustained inventiveness whose keynote was the handling of color. Giovanni Bellini (c. 1431–1516) may be said to have discovered color as a tool of composition. He borrowed perspective from Florentine painting, but he used color too as a principal means of achieving unity and harmony.

This use of color was extended in a revolutionary direction by another Venetian, Giorgione (c. 1478–1510), to whom only five paintings can be ascribed with absolute certainty. Until Giorgione, landscape had functioned primarily as decorative and sometimes imaginative background, as in the Mona Lisa. But Giorgione made landscape a part of the subject of his paintings and, through his handling of light and color, used it to unify and integrate his canvases. According to art historian E. H. Gombrich, "This was almost as big a step forward . . . as the invention of perspective had been."[6] Perhaps Giorgione's greatest experiment in this respect was *The Tempest.*

The bewitching effects of color were carried to their fullest development by Titian (c. 1477–1576), a leading Venetian painter. He was a complete professional for whom the brushstroke was all. His portraits were magical in their ability to capture both features and personality. Titian also defied artistic convention by deliberately using unbalanced groups of figures and by achieving harmony not through positioning, but by means of light and color.

The Spread of the Renaissance

The Renaissance spread to Germany, France, England, and Spain in the late fifteenth and the sixteenth centuries. In its migration northward, Renaissance culture adapted itself to conditions unknown in Italy, such as the growth of the monarchical state and the strength of lay piety. In England, France, and Spain, Renaissance culture tended to be court-centered and hence antirepublican, as it was, for instance, under Francis I in France and Elizabeth I in England. In Germany and the Rhineland, no monarchical state existed, but a vital tradition of lay piety was present in the Low Countries. For example, the Brethren of the Common Life was a lay movement emphasizing education and practical piety. Intensely Christian and at the same time anticlerical, the people in such lay movements found in Renaissance culture tools for sharpening their wits against the clergy—not to undermine the faith, but rather to restore it to its Apostolic purity.

Thus, northern humanists were profoundly devoted to ancient learning, just as the humanists in Italy had been. But nothing in northern humanism compares to the paganizing trend associated with the Italian Renaissance. The northerners were chiefly interested in the problem of the ancient church and, in particular, the question of what constituted original Christianity. They sought a model in light of which they might reform the corrupted church of their own time.

Everywhere, two factors operated to accelerate the spread of Renaissance culture after 1450: growing prosperity and the printing press. Prosperity, brought on by peace and

Raphael (1483–1520): Pope Leo X. Raphael is often called the great synthesizer because he emulated Michelangelo in *The School of Athens* and Leonardo da Vinci in many paintings of the Madonna and Christ child. His portraits of individual statesmen, like this one of Pope Leo X with Cardinals Giulio de' Medici and Luigi de' Rossi, are among his most perceptive works psychologically. (*Alinari-Scala/Art Resource*)

the decline of famine and plague, led to the founding of schools and colleges. The sons (women were excluded) of gentlemen and merchants were sent to school to receive a humanistic education imported from Italy. The purpose of such education was to prepare men for a career in the church or the civil service of the expanding state and for acceptance into higher social spheres.

Printing with movable type, which was invented in the middle of the fifteenth century, quickened the spread of Renaissance ideas. Back in the Late Middle Ages the West had learned, through the Muslims from the Chinese, of printing, paper, and ink. However, in this block printing process, a new block had to be carved from wood for each new impression, and the block was discarded as unusable as soon as a slightly different impression was needed. About 1445, Johann Gutenberg (c. 1398–1468) and other printers in Mainz in the Rhineland invented movable metal type to replace the cumbersome blocks. It was possible to use and reuse the separate pieces of type, as long as the metal in which they were cast did not wear down, simply by arranging them in the desired order. This invention made books, and hence ideas, more quickly available, cheaper, and more numerous than ever before; it also made literacy easier to achieve. Printing provided a surer basis for scholarship and prevented the further corruption of texts through handcopying. By giving all scholars the same text to work from, it made progress in critical scholarship and science faster and more reliable.

Humanism outside Italy was less concerned with the revival of classical values than with the reform of Christianity and society through a program of Christian humanism. The Christian humanists cultivated the new arts of rhetoric and history, as well as the classical languages—Latin, Greek, and Hebrew. But the ultimate purpose of these pursuits was more religious than it had been in Italy, where secular interests predominated.

Erasmian Humanism

To Erasmus (c. 1466–1536) belongs the credit for making Renaissance humanism an international movement. He was educated in the Netherlands by the Brethren of the Common Life, which was one of the most advanced religious movements of the age, combining mystical piety with rigorous humanist pedagogy. Erasmus traveled throughout Europe as a humanist educator and Biblical scholar. Like other Christian humanists, Erasmus trusted the power of words and used his pen to attack scholastic theology and clerical

abuses and to promote his philosophy of Christ. His weapon was satire, and his *Praise of Folly* and *Colloquies* won him a reputation for acid wit vented at the expense of conventional religion.

True religion, Erasmus argued, does not depend on dogma, ritual, or clerical power. Rather it is revealed clearly and simply in the Bible and therefore is directly accessible to all people, from the wise and great to the poor and humble. Nor is true religion opposed to nature. Rather, people are naturally capable of both apprehending and living according to the good as set out in the Scriptures. A perfect harmony between human nature and true religion allows humanity to attain, if not perfection, at least the next best thing, peace and happiness in this life.

This clear but quiet voice was drowned out by the storms of the Reformation, and the Erasmian emphasis on the individual's natural capacities fell down before a renewed emphasis on human sinfulness and dogmatic theology. Erasmus was caught in the middle and condemned on all sides; for him, the Reformation was both a personal and historical tragedy. He had worked for peace and unity and was treated to a spectacle of war and fragmentation. Erasmian humanism, however, survived these horrors as an ideal, and during the next two centuries, whenever thinkers sought toleration and rational religion (Rabelais and Montaigne, for instance), they looked back to Erasmus for inspiration.

Germany and France

German and French humanists pursued Christian humanist aims. They used humanist scholarship and language to satirize and vilify medieval scholastic Christianity and to build a purer, more Scriptural Christianity. These northern humanists had great faith in the power of words. The discovery of accurate Biblical texts, it was hoped, would lead to a great religious awakening. Protestant reformers, including Martin Luther, relied on humanist scholarship.

Medieval and Renaissance Art

Figure 1 Rose Window, Chartres Cathedral. (*Robert Harding Associates*)

Figure 2 *May* from *Les Très Riches Heures* of Jean, Duke of Berry, 1413–1416. (*Chantilly, Musée Condé/Giraudon/Art Resource*)

Figure 3 Master of the Prayer Books: *Dance of Mirth*, c. 1500. In Guillaume de Lorris and Jean de Meun, *Roman de la Rose*. (*The British Library, Harley MS. 4425, fol. 14v*)

Figure 4 Jan van Eyck: *St. Barbara*, 1437. (*Koninklijk Museum, Antwerp*)

Medieval sources tell us that the builders of Gothic cathedrals consciously intended their churches to symbolize heavenly realms. Much of the uplifting experience in viewing the churches' interiors comes from the luminous light of their stained-glass windows (Figure 1). Their colored atmosphere seems as tangible as the massive stone buildings themselves. Light was one of the main metaphors that medieval people used for God. The interior space of a Gothic cathedral (Figure 6) is symbolic too, with its soaring height implying the indwelling presence and energy of God. (See a discussion of Gothic architecture on pages 245–246.)

The Gothic style, which originated in the twelfth century, remained vigorous for the next three hundred years in some parts of Europe. In Italy, however, the style was replaced earlier with a new, humanist style in the early fifteenth century. In Florence, Filippo Brunelleschi (c. 1377–1446) designed San Lorenzo (Figure 5), the parish church of Cosimo de' Medici, in 1418. Although the interior retained many traditional features of Christian churches, such as a cross-shaped floor plan, its ornamentation was radically new. Brunelleschi introduced "correct" classical ornaments: coffered ceilings, rounded arches and Greek Corinthian capitals (the tops of columns decorated with carved acanthus leaves)—all found in such ancient buildings as the Pantheon (Figure 8 in the first art essay, "Greek Art and Roman Reflections"). In an attempt analogous to that of his contemporaries who were philosophers and writers, Brunelleschi sought to create a synthesis between antique forms and the Christian architectural heritage.

Painters also developed a new style during the fifteenth century. Representations of God, Jesus, angels, and saints gained a new immediacy as artists placed them in recognizable,

Figure 5 *Top:* Filippo Brunelleschi: San Lorenzo, Florence, 1421. (*Scala/Art Resource*)

Figure 6 *Bottom:* Nave and Choir, Notre Dame Cathedral, Paris, Built 1163–c. 1200. (*Jean Roubier*)

everyday settings and attempted to re-create in painting many of the effects of perceiving forms in light and space. Artists of the Northern Renaissance, such as Jan van Eyck (active 1422–1441), worked in an area now encompassed by Belgium, primarily in Bruges. Van Eyck's work is distinguished for his acute study of the effects of encompassing light, which influenced later Italian artists, especially those of the Venetian school. He also adapted traditional symbols to include concrete contemporary detail. For example, *St. Barbara* (Figure 4) is traditionally designated by the presence of a tower, the site of her martyrdom. Van Eyck's representation has a tower under construction and shows technology of his time, including scaffolding and the great wheels designed to hoist stone blocks.

Italian artists of the early fifteenth century, like Fra Angelico (1387–1455), tended to reduce detail and emphasize consistent, believable space. The loggia (roofed, open gallery) of his *Annunciation* (Figure 7), is constructed in accordance with the new perspective system so that the figures of Mary and the Angel Gabriel seem to inhabit a space similar to the one that our eyes and mind would perceive in viewing such a scene. Raphael (1483–1520), who worked a half-century later, shows further development of Renaissance illusionism in his *Annunciation* (Figure 8). The figures are also set in a consistent, measurable space, but the interior space is larger in relation to the figures and their poses are somewhat more complex and animated. Raphael's treatment of light, color, and landscape owes much to the innovations of van Eyck.

Many changes in monumental painting were reflected in book illumination. Illustrated manuscripts produced during the Late Middle Ages and the Renaissance, such as the *Très Riches Heures* (Figure 2) and the *Roman de la Rose* (Figure 3), are magnificent miniature works of art. These exquisite book illuminations show the new naturalistic mode of representation. Painted in part by the Limbourg brothers for the Duke of Berry during

Figure 7 *Left:* Fra Angelico: *The Annunciation,* c. 1440–1450. Fresco, San Marco, Florence. (*Scala/Art Resource*)

Figure 8 *Above:* Raphael: *The Annunciation.* The Vatican, Rome. (*Scala/Art Resource*)

the years 1413–1416, then completed seventy years later by another artist, the *Très Riches Heures* is an exceptional example of a Book of Hours, or personal prayers for each liturgical hour of the day; these books often contained other texts, such as Psalms and masses.

Figure 2 represents a month from the calendar at the beginning of the manuscript, and depicts the members of the Duke's court celebrating the first of May. The figures lie in the space beyond the "window" of the simple border. In the background, the artist has included in accurate and minute architectural detail a view of one of the Duke's residences.

Almost a century later, the Flemish Master of the Prayer Books (c. 1500) illustrated a copy of the *Roman de la Rose,* of which the *Dance of Mirth* is a page; the manuscript was commissioned by Count Engelbert II of Nassau, a governor of the Netherlands. Both manuscripts contain rich colors and fine detail, but the later *Dance of Mirth* shows the more natural and animated poses of contemporary Renaissance paintings. The border framing the scene with true renditions of iris, moth, and snail represents a Flemish revolution in

manuscript style; it forms a space independent from the rest of the page. The flowers and the other subjects contrast with the more formalized trees in the *May* scene, just as the faces and figures in their dance evidence more expression than the sober, less individualistic faces in *May.*

In contrast to the fine detail of manuscripts are the massive sculptures by Michelangelo (1475–1564), who flourished during the Italian High Renaissance. His works were commissioned by Popes, including Julius II for whom he painted the Sistine Chapel ceiling. Michelangelo's *Moses* (Figure 9) was made for Pope Julius's tomb. This project, like many other grandiose High Renaissance schemes, was too costly and elaborate to complete; the original plans called for about forty figures arranged upon an immense pyramid. Michelangelo designed the *Moses* to occupy one corner, which explains the prominence of the right angle formed by the figure's knee. In the final form of the tomb, completed in 1547, forty-two years after its conception, there are only six figures, and *Moses* appears in the center.

—KATHERINE CRUM

Figure 9 Michelangelo: *Moses*, 1513–1516. Marble, 100 1/2 in. high. San Pietro in Vincoli, Rome, in the mausoleum of Pope Julius II (*Alinari/Art Resource*)

French thinkers of the next generation exploited and carried the humanist legacy in more radical directions. Among them, two were outstanding: Michel de Montaigne (1533–1592) and François Rabelais (c. 1494–1553). Both thought and wrote in reaction to the religious wars resulting from the Reformation. In the face of competing religious dogmatisms—Catholic, Protestant, and sectarian—Montaigne advanced a skepticism in which he maintained that one can know little or nothing with certainty. He therefore advocated political quietism and acceptance of Christianity on faith. This skepticism also entailed tolerance. An individual was not fully responsible for his or her beliefs, since they were the product of frail reason and force of circumstance. Thus, people should not be punished for their beliefs. The only ones who deserved to be severely dealt with were the dogmatists in religion, because their certainty and self-righteousness flew in the face of a fundamental epistemological fact—that "reason does nothing but go astray in everything, and especially when it meddles with divine things."

Montaigne was not a systematic philosopher but devoted himself to what he could learn by Socratic self-examination, the results of which he set down in his *Essays*. In their urbane and caustic wit and their intense self-absorption, the *Essays* betray a crucial shift in humanist thought that became more pronounced in the next century. Gone is the optimism and emphasis on civic virtue of the High Renaissance. In their place come skepticism and introspection, the attempt to found morality on the self rather than on public values. This shift represented a retreat from the idealism of Renaissance humanism, no doubt produced by the increasing scale and violence of religious war.

Rabelais took a different route from Montaigne's. In response to religious dogmatism, Rabelais asserted the essential goodness of the individual and the right to be free to enjoy the world rather than being bound down, as Calvin later would have it, by fear of a vengeful God. Rabelais's folk-epic,

Erasmus by Hans Holbein the Younger (c. 1497–1543). The brilliance and honesty of Erasmus's philosophical treatises endeared him to both conservative Catholic and Protestant reformers. He travelled freely throughout Europe in his pursuit of truth. (*The Metropolitan Museum of Art, Robert Lehman Collection, 1975* [1975.1.138])

Gargantua and Pantagruel, in which he celebrates earthly and earthy life, is the greatest French work of its kind and perhaps the greatest in any literature. Rabelais said that once freed from religion, people could, by virtue of their native goodness, build a paradise on earth and disregard the one dreamed up by theologians. In *Gargantua and Pantagruel,* Rabelais imagined a monastery where men and women spend their lives "not in laws, statutes, or rules, but according to their own free will and pleasure." They slept and ate when they desired and learned to "read, write, sing, play upon several musical instruments, and speak five or six . . . languages and compose in them all very quaintly." Only one rule did they observe: "DO WHAT THOU WILT."[7]

Spanish Humanism

Spanish humanism represents a special case. The church hierarchy gained such a tight grip in Spain during the late fifteenth and early sixteenth centuries that it monopolized humanist learning and exploited it for its own repressive purposes. There was little or no room for a dissenting humanist voice such as there was in Germany, France, or England. The mastermind behind this authoritarian Spanish humanism was Cardinal Francisco Jiménez de Cisneros (1436–1517). Jiménez founded the University of Alcalá not far from Madrid for the instruction of the clergy. He also sponsored and published the Complutensian Polyglot Bible with Hebrew, Latin, and Greek texts in parallel columns. Jiménez, like Christian humanists elsewhere, sought the enlightenment of the clergy through a return to the pure sources of religion, and he saw his Polyglot Bible as furnishing a principal means of realizing that goal.

A century after Jiménez, Miguel de Cervantes Saavedra (1547–1616) produced his great novel, *Don Quixote,* in which he satirizes the ideals of knighthood and chivalry. Don Quixote, the victim of his own illusions, roams the countryside looking for romance and the chance to prove his knightly worth. To Quixote's servant, Sancho Panza, Cervantes assigns the role of pointing up the inanity of his master's quest by always acting prudently and judging according to common sense. Despite his earthy realism, however, Panza must share his master's misfortunes—so much for realism in a world run by men full of illusions. Cervantes's satire is very gentle. That knightly valor was still a valid subject for satire indicates how wedded Spain was even in the early seventeenth century to the conservative values of its crusading past.

English Humanism

Christian humanism in England sharply contrasted to that in Spain. It was developed by secular men in government as much as by clerics, and its objectives were often opposed to authority and tradition. Various Italian humanists came to England during the fifteenth century as bishops, merchants, court physicians, or artists. Englishmen also studied in Italy, especially in Florence, and introduced the serious humanistic study of the classics at Oxford University toward the end of the century.

The most influential humanist of the early English Renaissance was Sir Thomas More (1478–1535), who studied at Oxford. His impact arose from both his writing and his career. Trained as a lawyer, he became a successful civil servant and member of Parliament. His most famous book is *Utopia,* the major utopian treatise to be written in the West since Plato's *Republic* and one of the most original works of the entire Renaissance.

Many humanists had attacked private wealth as the principal source of pride, greed, and human cruelty. But More was the only one to carry this insight to its logical conclusion: in *Utopia,* he called for the elimination of private property. He had too keen a sense of human weakness to think that people could become perfect, but he used *Utopia* to call attention to contemporary abuses and to suggest radical reforms. He exploited the satirical and ironical potential of recent overseas discoveries by setting *Utopia* among a non-Christian people, which made his criticism more caustic and pointed. More succeeded Cardinal Wolsey as Lord Chancellor under Henry VIII. But when the king broke with the Roman Catholic church, More resigned, unable to reconcile his conscience with the king's rejection of papal supremacy. Three years later, in July 1535, More was executed for treason for refusing to swear an oath acknowledging the king's ecclesiastical supremacy.

William Shakespeare (1564–1616), widely

Chronology 13.1 The Renaissance

1200–1300	Bologna, Padua, and Ravenna become centers of legal studies
1300–1450	Republicanism reigns in northern Italian city-states
1304–1374	Petrarch, "Father of humanism"
1378	The Ciompi revolt in Florence
1407–1457	Lorenzo Valla issues the *Declamation Concerning the False Decretals of Constantine*
c. 1445	Johann Gutenberg invents movable metal type
1454	The Peace of Lodi is signed
1494	Charles VIII of France invades northern Italy; Pope Julius II commissions frescoes by Michelangelo in the Vatican's Sistine Chapel
1513	Machiavelli writes *The Prince*
1528	*The Courtier*, by Baldassare Castiglione, is published
1535	Sir Thomas More, English humanist and author of *Utopia*, is executed for treason

considered the greatest playwright the world has ever produced, gave expression to Renaissance values—honor, heroism, and the struggle against fate and fortune. But there is nothing conventional about Shakespeare's treatment of characters possessed of these virtues. His greatest plays, the tragedies (*King Lear, Julius Caesar,* and others), explore a common theme: men, even heroic men, despite virtue, are able only with the greatest difficulty, if at all, to overcome their human weaknesses. What fascinates Shakespeare is the contradiction between the Renaissance image of nobility, which is often the self-image of Shakespeare's heroes, and man's capacity for evil and self-destruction. Thus Ophelia says of Hamlet, her lover, in the play of the same name:

O, what a noble mind is here o'erthrown!
The courtier's, soldier's, scholar's, eye, tongue, sword;
The expectancy and rose of the fair state,
The glass of fashion and the mould of form,
The observ'd of all observers, quite, quite down!
[And] I, of ladies most deject and wretched,

That suck'd the honey of his music vows,
Now see that noble and most sovereign reason,
Like sweet bells jangled, out of tune and harsh;
That unmatch'd form and feature of blown youth
Blasted with ecstasy. O, woe is me,
T' have seen what I have seen, see what I see![8]

The plays are thus intensely human, but so much so that humanism fades into the background. Thus, art transcends doctrine to represent life itself.

The Renaissance and the Modern Age

The Renaissance, then, marks the birth of modernity—in art, in the idea of the individual's role in history and in nature, and in society, politics, war, and diplomacy. Central to this birth is a bold new view of human nature: individuals in all endeavors are free of a given destiny imposed by God from the outside—free to make their own destiny guided only by the example of the past, the force of present circumstances, and the drives of their own inner nature. Individuals, set free from theology, are seen to be the products, and in turn the shapers, of history. Their future is not wholly determined by providence, but is partly the work of their own free will.

Within the Italian city-states where the Renaissance was born, rich merchants were at least as important as the church hierarchy and the old nobility. The city-states were almost completely independent because of the weakness of church and empire. So the northern Italians were left free to invent new forms of government in which merchant oligarchs, humanists, and *condottieri* played a more important part than the priests and nobles who dominated politics in the rest of Europe. Of course this newness and lack of tradition produced, along with the inventiveness, disorder and violence. Condottieri grabbed power from hapless citizens, and republics gave way to despotism.

But the problems created by novelty and instability demanded solutions, and the wealth of the cities called forth the talent to find them. Commercial wealth and a new politics produced a new culture: Renaissance art and humanism. Talented individuals—scholars, poets, artists, and government officials—returned to classical antiquity, which in any case lay near to hand in Italy and Greece. Ancient models in art, architecture, literature, and philosophy provided the answers to their questions. This return to antiquity also entailed a rejection of the Middle Ages as dark, barbarous, and rude. The humanists clearly preferred the secular learning of ancient Greece and Rome to the clerical learning of the more recent past. The reason for this was obvious: the ancients addressed the same problems faced by the humanists; the scholastics did not.

The revival of antiquity by the humanists did not mean, however, that they identified completely with it. The revival itself was done too self-consciously for that. In the very act

of looking back, the humanists differentiated themselves from the past and recognized that they were different. They were in this sense the first modern historians, because they could study and appreciate the past for its own sake and to some degree on its own terms.

In the works of Renaissance artists and thinkers the world was, to a large extent, depicted and explained without reference to a higher supernatural realm of meaning and authority. This is clearly seen in Machiavelli's analysis of politics. Closely associated with this secular element in Renaissance culture was a new realism that beckoned toward the modern outlook. What else is Machiavelli's new politics but a politics of realism, dealing with the world as he finds it rather than as it ought to be? This realism also manifests itself in the realm of art, where mathematical perspective renders the world in its spatial dimension and gives it a solidity and drama that constitute a modern visual and esthetic realism. The sources for both the esthetic and the political realism were the cultural forms of ancient Greece and Rome.

Renaissance humanism exuded a deep confidence in the capacities of able people, instructed in the wisdom of the ancients, to understand and change the world. Renaissance realism, then, was mixed with idealism, and this potent combination departed sharply from the medieval outlook. In place of Christian resignation there grew a willingness to confront life directly and a belief that able humans can succeed even against great odds.

This new confidence is closely related to another distinctive feature of the Renaissance—the cult of the individual. Both prince and painter were motivated in part by the desire to display their talents and to satisfy their ambitions. This individual striving was rewarded and encouraged by the larger society of rich patrons and calculating princes who valued ability. Gone was the medieval Christian emphasis upon the virtue of self-denial and the sin of vainglory. Instead, the Renaissance placed the highest value upon self-expression and self-fulfillment, upon the realization of individual potential, especially of the gifted few. The Renaissance fostered an atmosphere in which talent, even genius, was allowed to flourish. The ideal, at least, was meritocracy.

To be sure, the Renaissance image of the individual and the world, bold and novel, was the exclusive prerogative of a small, well-educated urban elite and did not reach down to include the masses. Nevertheless, the Renaissance set an example of what people might achieve in art and architecture, taste and refinement, education and urban culture. In many fields the Renaissance set the cultural standards of the modern age.

Notes

1. Giovanni Pico della Mirandola, *Oration on the Dignity of Man,* trans. by A. Robert Caponigri (Chicago: Henry Regnery, 1956), p. 7.

2. Niccolò Machiavelli, *The Prince,* trans. by George Bull (Harmondsworth, England: Penguin Books, 1961), pp. 90–91.

3. Ibid., pp. 77–78.

4. Ibid., p. 91.

5. Ibid., p. 101.

6. E. H. Gombrich, *The Story of Art,* 12th ed. (London: Phaidon, 1972), p. 250.

7. François Rabelais, *Gargantua and Pantagruel,* trans. by Sir Thomas Urquhart (1883), Bk. I, Ch. 57.

8. From *Hamlet, Prince of Denmark,* in *The Complete Plays and Poems of William Shakespeare,* ed. by William Allan Neilson and Charles Jarvis Hill (Boston: Houghton Mifflin, 1942), p. 1067.

Suggested Reading

Baron, Hans, *The Crisis of the Early Italian Renaissance* (1966). Influential interpretation of the origins of civic humanism.

Bouwsma, William J., *Venice and the Defense of Republican Liberty* (1968). The Venetian origins of Western republicanism.

Brucker, Gene A., *Renaissance Florence* (rev. ed., 1983). An excellent reader.

Burckhardt, Jacob, *The Civilization of the Renaissance in Italy* (1860). 2 vols. (1958). The first major interpretative synthesis of the Renaissance; still an essential resource.

Burke, Peter, *Popular Culture in Early Modern Europe* (1978). A fascinating account of the social underside from the Renaissance to the French Revolution.

Caspari, Fritz, *Humanism and the Social Order in Tudor England* (1968). Relations between thought and society.

Eisenstein, Elizabeth, *The Printing Press as an Agent of Change,* 2 vols. (1978). The definitive treatment—informative, argumentative, and suggestive.

Gilbert, Felix, *Machiavelli and Guicciardini* (1965). Florentine political and historical writing in the fifteenth and early sixteenth centuries.

Ginzburg, Carlo, *The Cheese and the Worms* (1982). A lively, penetrating account of the cosmos as seen from the point of view of a sixteenth-century Italian miller.

Harbison, E. Harris, *The Christian Scholar in the Age of Reformation* (1956). Relations between humanism and Protestantism.

Huizinga, Johan, *Erasmus and the Age of Reformation* (1957). A readable study of the greatest northern European humanist.

Maclean, Ian, *The Renaissance Notion of Woman* (1980). The birth of modern ideas and attitudes regarding women.

Pocock, J. G. A., *The Machiavellian Moment* (1975). A heady adventure in the history of ideas, tracing republicanism from its Italian Renaissance origins through the English and American revolutions.

Pullen, B., *A History of Early Renaissance Italy* (1973). A solid, brief account.

Skinner, Quentin, *The Foundations of Modern Political Thought,* 2 vols. (1978). The first volume covers the Renaissance; highly informed.

Wittkower, R., *Architectural Principles in the Age of Humanism* (1952). Architecture as the expression of Renaissance values and ideas.

Review Questions

1. What does the word *renaissance* mean, and where and when did it first occur?

2. What is the connection between the Renaissance and the Middle Ages? What special conditions gave rise to the Italian Renaissance?

3. Which forms of government predominated among the Italian city-states? In the end, which was the most successful? Why?

4. In what ways did the social patterns of Renaissance Italy depart from those of the rest of Europe?

5. What are some connections between Renaissance society and Renaissance art and culture?

6. What is *humanism* and how did it begin? What did the humanists contribute to education and history?

7. What is the difference between civic humanism and the princely ideal of government, and from what does this difference come?

8. How can it be said that Machiavelli invented a new politics by standing the ideal of princely rule on its head?

9. What is *perspective*? To whom do we owe the discovery of its rules?

10. What is the basic difference between Early and Late Renaissance painting?

11. What factors encouraged the spread of the Renaissance into the western European monarchies and the Rhineland?

12. To what key invention do we owe the rise of the printing press? What were the effects of the printing press on European civilization?

13. Why is the Renaissance considered the departure from the Middle Ages and the beginning of modernity?

14

The Reformation: Shattering of Christendom

*B*y the early sixteenth century the one European institution that alone transcended geographic, ethnic, linguistic, and national boundaries was under severe attack from reformers. For centuries the Catholic church, with its center in Rome, had extended its influence into every aspect of European society and culture. As a result, however, the church's massive wealth and power appeared to take predominance over its commitment to the search for holiness in this world and salvation in the next. Encumbered by wealth, addicted to international power, and desiring to protect their own interests, the clergy, from the pope on down, became the center of a storm of criticism. Humanists, made self-confident by the new learning of the Renaissance, called for the reform and renewal of the church, setting the stage for the Protestant Reformation. Eventually, though, that movement came to deviate quite significantly from what the Renaissance humanists had in mind.

Schooled in the techniques of criticism developed during the Renaissance, humanists first used those techniques on the documents that supposedly justified papal authority. Thus did they refute the Donation of Constantine (see page 279). But the fraud that especially vexed the humanists lay not on parchments, but in the very practices by which the church governed the faithful.

However, the Protestant Reformation did not originate in elite circles of humanistic scholars. Rather, it began in the mind of Martin Luther (1483–1546), an obscure German monk and a brilliant theologian. Luther rejected the church's claim to be the only vehicle for human salvation and defied the pope's right to silence, reprimand, and excommunicate any Christian who rejected papal authority or denied the truth of certain of the church's teachings. In a public defiance, undertaken after much soul-searching, Luther instituted a rebellion against the church's authority that in less than one decade shattered irrevocably the religious unity of Christendom. The Reformation, begun in 1517, dominated European history throughout much of the sixteenth century.

The Renaissance breathed new energy into European intellectual life and in the process discarded the medieval preoccupation with theology. Similarly, the Reformation marked the beginning of a new religious outlook. Personal faith, rather than adherence to the practices of the church, became central to the religious life of European Protestants. Local congregations and national churches came to replace the international church, which survived the Reformation but had vast areas of its wealth and power dismantled. Like the Renaissance humanists, some Protestant leaders were trained in ancient learning, but they gave humanism a religious meaning. Renaissance humanists had sought to reinstitute the wisdom of ancient times; Protestant reformers wanted to restore the spirit of early Christianity, in which faith seemed purer, believers more sincere, and clergy uncorrupted by luxury and power. By the 1540s the church initiated its own internal reformation, but it came too late to stop the movement toward Protestantism in some parts of northern and western Europe.

During the Late Middle Ages various attempts were made to reform the church from within. These movements were generated by bishops, monks, and scholars who assumed that the church's difficulties stemmed from the inefficiency and corruption of the papacy. These reformers sought to wrest power from the popes and to place it in the hands of a general council of the church's hierarchy. This was indeed one of the aims, in addition to ending the Great Schism and combatting heresy, of the Conciliar movement in the first half of the fifteenth century. However, the councils of Constance and of Basel (see page 257) failed to leave a meaningful inheritance to the church, largely because the special interests of kings and nations undercut their authority. The defeat of the Conciliar movement prevented the church from reforming itself from within and made possible a more general reformation.

Background to the Reformation: The Medieval Church in Crisis

During the Early Middle Ages the church had served as the great unifying and civilizing force in Latin Christendom. Culturally, and even administratively, it performed functions formerly carried out by the Roman Empire. By the fourteenth century, however, the usefulness and authority of its popes and bishops, as well as the vitality of its teachings, were being doubted. As kings increased their power and as urban centers with their sophisticated laity grew in size and numbers, people began to question the authority and independence of the international church and its clergy.

Several areas of the church's power were being closely examined. In theory, both popes and kings derived their authority from God. But where did one authority begin and the other leave off? According to Christian teachings, popes could instruct monarchs in the proper use of their authority: lay kings must serve and not challenge the church. But increasingly, monarchs did challenge the church's supremacy in worldly matters. The church also taught that new ideas must bend to the primacy of theology. But new learning in the hands of laymen endangered the supremacy of the monasteries and clergy-dominated universities as centers of learning. Lay scholarship also threatened the church's teachings on matters of authority. As national economies and local elites grew stronger, trouble brewed over the issue of paying taxes to a distant spiritual ruler in Rome whose wealth seemed more than sufficient. The manner in which church officials were appointed, with greater emphasis on their social place than their piety, also led to widespread attacks on the church's leadership.

By the Late Middle Ages the church had entered a time of crisis. During this period, political theorists rejected the pope's claim to supremacy over kings. The central idea of medieval Christendom—a Christian commonwealth led by the papacy—increasingly

The Sacred Heart of Jesus, Hand-colored Woodcut Sold as an Indulgence, Nuremberg, 1480s. The practice of selling indulgences to erase purgatory time disgusted Martin Luther. The veneration of relics—objects associated with the life of Christ or his saints, even bones or hair—was also condemned. Rival churches would often claim to have the "only authentic" head of a certain saint. (*The Metropolitan Museum of Art, New York; bequest of James Clarck McGuire, 1931*)

of European society. Towns and cities contributed to the growth of an indigenous culture that focused on vernacular languages and regional dialects, rather than on the Latin of the monks and their schools. The townspeople had achieved a new wealth and a new self-confidence that made them resent any interference by bishops in their economic affairs. Urban centers also challenged the role of monasteries as economic innovators and centers of commercial life. By the early fourteenth century the church no longer held the initiative in worldly matters. When economic and social crises enveloped Europe in the second half of the fourteenth century, new reformers, despairing of the church's traditional privileges and even of its teachings, cast doubt on its authority.

For all these social and economic reasons, Latin Christendom during the late fourteenth century witnessed the first systematic attacks ever launched against the church. Church corruption—such as the selling of indulgences, nepotism (the practice of appointing one's relatives to offices), the holding of many bishoprics, and the sexual indulgence of the clergy—was nothing new. What was new and startling was the willingness of educated and uneducated Christians to attack these practices publicly. In *The Canterbury Tales*, Chaucer singles out two of his characters, who held clerical offices, for special scorn: the pardoner, who sold indulgences, that is, the remission of time spent in purgatory for one's sins; and the summoner, who served writs to appear in church courts. Chaucer paints a black picture of their arrogance and corruption. Less corrupt figures, such as his prioress, are let off with only mild caricatures. But in this first major English poem, Chaucer made the point that the church was corrupt.

fell into disrepute. Theorists were arguing that the church was only a spiritual body, and therefore its power did not extend to the political realm. They said that the pope had no authority over kings, that the state needed no guidance from the papacy, and that the clergy were not above secular law.

Political theories were aimed at the educated elite, but the common people of town and countryside also expressed dissatisfaction with the church. By the Late Middle Ages, new material forces were affecting large segments

Millenarianism

The peasant revolts of the Late Middle Ages frequently assumed a heretical cast. These movements foreshadowed the popular unrest so characteristic of the German Reformation.

In many instances, they combined heretical beliefs with hatred for church officials and protest against social and economic inequities and injustices. These popular heretical protest movements often took a doctrine accepted by the offical church and reinterpreted it to express their vision of a society where religion ensures justice for the poor and oppressed. For instance, the church preached that at some time in the future the world would end and Christ would come again to finally judge all men. Those whom Christ chose to be with him would be called saints, and they would reign with him in heaven. But medieval reformers, many drawn from, and followed by the poorer segments of European society, interpreted that doctrine to mean that Christ would condemn the rich and propertied and would establish a new society where the poor would inherit the earth. For a thousand years, a millennium, the poor would rule in Christ's kingdom.

Millenarianism, as this radical interpretation of the Last Judgment is called, gave its believers religious justification for attacking established institutions and institutional corruption. That Christ would rule with the poor in a future paradise meant that the society of their own day must be ruled by Antichrist. For many later medieval reformers, the concept of Antichrist, or the image of the "whore of Babylon" taken from the Bible, became a shorthand for the corruption of the church. When in the early sixteenth century Luther and other reformers called the pope himself the Antichrist, or the whore of Babylon, they were appealing to a tradition of reform and protest that had existed in the West for centuries.

Wycliffe and Huss

The two most serious attempts to reform the church, prior to Luther, occurred in the late fourteenth century in England and Bohemia. In both cases the leaders of these movements, John Wycliffe in England and John Huss in Bohemia, were learned theologians who attacked some church doctrines and practices (see Chapter 12). By expressing their ideas in learned and precise language, Wycliffe and Huss made heresy intellectually respectable. By incorporating popularly held beliefs, they appealed to the common people and sought and found mass support.

John Wycliffe (c. 1320–1384), a master at Oxford University, attacked the church's authority at its root by arguing simply that the church did not control the individual's eternal destiny. He said that salvation came only to those who possess faith, a gift freely given by God and not contingent on participating in the church's rituals or on receiving its sacraments. From this position, which in effect made the clergy far less important, Wycliffe attacked the church's wealth and argued that all true believers in Christ were equal and were, in effect, Christ's priests. To make faith accessible to them, Wycliffe translated portions of the Bible into English.

Wycliffe received powerful support from members of the English nobility, who hated the church's economic and secular power. However, when his ideas were taken up by articulate peasants and spoken during the abortive Peasants' Revolt of 1381, Wycliffe lost many powerful backers. In the end his attempt to reform the church by bringing it under secular control failed. But partly because he retained strong supporters and because he was more interested in scholarship than leadership, Wycliffe survived the failure of his movement and died a natural death. His ideas remained alive in popular religious beliefs, and his movement, the Lollards, helped foster Protestantism in England during the sixteenth century.

A harsher fate awaited the Bohemian (Czech) reformer, John Huss, who was burned at the stake in 1415. Partly under the influence of Wycliffe's writings Huss, in his native Prague, attacked the church for its wealth and power. After his execution, his followers broke with Rome and for a brief time nationalized the Bohemian church. This movement, like the Lollards in England, prepared the ground for the success of the Protestant Reformation. Until well into the seventeenth century, Bohemia remained a battleground of popular Protestantism against the official church.

Mysticism and Humanism

Wycliffe's and Huss's intensely practical attempts to initiate reform coincided with a powerful new religiosity that also made its appearance in the fourteenth century. All religions can inspire mystical experience, although in Western Christianity it often appears at times of acute institutional crisis. Late medieval mystics sought an immediate and personal communication with God; such experiences inspired them to advocate concrete reforms for the purpose of renewing the church's spirituality. Interesting from the viewpoint of the Protestant Reformation's later appeal to women, many late medieval mystics were women who, by virtue of their sex, had been deprived of an active role in governing the church. First mysticism and then Protestantism offered women a way of expressing their independence in religious matters.

The church hierarchy inevitably regarded this form of intense religiosity with some suspicion. For if individuals can experience God directly, they would seemingly have little need for the church and its rituals. In the fourteenth century, these mystical movements seldom became heretical. But in the sixteenth and seventeenth centuries, radical reformers often found in Christian mysticism a powerful alternative to institutional control and even to the necessity of a priesthood.

The Brethren of the Common Life, in the Low Countries, propounded a religious movement known as the *devotio moderna*, which was inspired by mysticism. A semi-monastic order of laity and clergy, the Brethren expressed their practical piety by dedicating their lives to the service of the entire community. With their teaching, they trained a new generation of scholars and humanists who became, during the late fifteenth century, some of the church's severest critics. Signif-

icantly, the Brethren's new schools flourished in the most heavily urbanized part of western Europe. For the linen merchants of Antwerp or the drapers of Amsterdam, a new religiosity was all too welcome by the late fifteenth century. They had grown increasingly disillusioned not only with the church taxes but also with the inefficiency of the church when compared to their own strenuous economic life.

Both mysticism and humanistic Christianity seemed for a time to offer sufficient alternatives to the scholasticism of the clergy. Certainly Erasmus thought that the critical gaze of the humanist would be sufficient to show the clergy the folly of their ways, which he ridiculed in *The Praise of Folly* (1510). Yet mysticism, with its emphasis on inner spirituality, and humanism, with its emphasis on classical learning, could not in themselves capture the attention of thousands of ordinary Europeans. A successful reform movement required leaders of an active and aggressive temperament who could do battle with political realities and win lay support against the local and international power of the church.

The Lutheran Revolt

Only an attack on papal and clerical authority could alter the power and practices of the church. Such an attack would have to involve winning over the multitudes, appealing to princes, and making heresy respectable. This feat required someone who had experienced the personal agony of doubting the church's power to give salvation and who could translate that agony into language understandable to all Christians. Martin Luther had experienced just such a personal crisis, and he possessed the will and the talent to offer it as an example for other Christians. Luther wrote voluminously and talked freely to his friends and students. Using this mass of recorded material, historians have been able to reconstruct the life and personality of this Augustinian monk who began the Reformation.

Luther's father, born a peasant, apparently was unusually ambitious. Hans Luther left the land, became a miner, and finally a manager and lessee of several mines, in an industry that was booming in late-fifteenth-century Germany. Like many newly successful individuals, Hans Luther had ambitious plans for his son; he wanted Martin to study law at the university in order to attain the status of an educated man. Luther's mother came from a burgher family and displayed an intense piety, thus putting him in closer touch with German popular religion and piety than was common among his contemporary scholars.

At the prestigious University of Erfurt, Luther embarked on an intellectual career that was to make him one of the foremost theologians and Biblical scholars of his day. As a young student, Luther fulfilled his father's wish and studied law. His earlier education gave him a fine grounding in classical learning, which served him throughout his life. At the university, Luther developed an interest in theology and philosophy, particularly the teachings of the fourteenth-century philosopher William of Ockham (see Chapter 12). Ockham had stressed the difference between faith and reason; he had insisted that truth learned through revelation was a matter of faith that might not be capable of demonstration by human reason; thus church teachings, and consequently salvation, rested entirely on faith. Since the church supported the synthesis of faith and reason achieved by the scholastics, notably Thomas Aquinas, it regarded Ockham's notions with suspicion.

At the age of twenty-one, Luther suddenly abandoned his legal studies to enter the Augustinian monastery at Erfurt. All the steps that led to this rebellion against parental authority are not known, but the actual decision was made swiftly. In later life, Luther recounted that the decision had been made in fear, as a vow to Saint Anne in the midst of a fierce lightning storm, by a young man convinced that his death at that moment would bring him eternal damnation. Why Luther presumed his damnation is not

Portrait of Martin Luther, 1546: School of Lucas Cranach (1472–1553). Martin Luther's personal struggle to attain spiritual peace through faith led to the fragmentation of Christendom. For him, the time was right for reform. The church was worldly and corrupt, and a nationalistic temper made many European monarchs and aristocrats hostile toward Roman authority. (*Busch Reisinger Museum, Harvard University, Gift, Paul J. Sachs and Meta Sachs*)

known, but his guilt conspired with his vivid imagination to kindle what must have been a growing resentment against his father's domination. Luther began his search for spiritual and personal identity, and therefore for salvation, within the strict confinement and discipline of the monastery. He pursued his theological studies there and prepared for ordination into the priesthood.

The Break with Catholicism

As he studied and prayed, Luther grew increasingly terrified about the possibility o his damnation. As a monk he sought union with God, and he understood the church's teaching that salvation depended upon faith, works, and grace. He participated in the sacraments of the church, which according to its teaching were intended to give grace. Indeed, after his ordination, Luther administered the sacraments. Yet he felt the weight of his sins, and nothing the church could offer seemed to relieve that burden.

Seeking solace and salvation, Luther increasingly turned to reading the Bible. Two passages seemed to speak directly to him: "For in it the righteousness of God is revealed through faith for faith: as it is written, 'He who through faith is righteous shall live.' " (Romans 1:17); and "They are justified by his grace as a gift, through the redemption which is in Christ Jesus." (Romans 3:24). In these two passages, Luther found, for the first time in his adult life, some hope for his own salvation. Faith, freely given by God through Christ, entitles the recipient to salvation.

The emphasis on faith alone in the Scriptural passages conformed to Luther's earlier interest in Ockham's teachings. But more important, the concept of salvation by faith alone seemed to provide an answer to his spritual quest. Practicing good works, along with prayer, fasting, pilgrimages, the Mass, and the other sacraments—had never brought Luther peace of mind. He concluded that no amount of good works, however necessary for maintaining the Christian community, would bring salvation. Through reading the Bible and through faith alone, the Christian could find the meaning of earthly existence. For Luther, the true Christian was a courageous figure who faced the terrifying quest for salvation armed only with the hope that God had granted the gift of faith. The new Christian served others not to trade good works for salvation, but solely to respond to the demands of Christian love.

During his personal struggle over the possibility of salvation, Luther had not lived as a cloistered monk. Pursuing his theological studies, he became a professor at the nearby university at Wittenberg and a preacher in that city's church. From approximately 1513 onward, Luther shared his personal and intellectual struggle with his students and his congregations. At the University of Wittenberg and in the province of Saxony in general, Luther found an audience receptive to his views, and his popularity and reputation grew as a result. Before 1517, he was considered a dynamic and controversial preacher whose passionate interest lay in turning Christians away from their worldly interests and from reliance on good works, while focusing their attention on Christ and the truth contained within Scripture. After 1517, he became a figure of international reputation and eventually a publicly condemned heretic in the eyes of the church.

The starting point for the Reformation was Luther's attack in 1517 on the church's practice of selling indulgences. The church taught that some individuals go directly to heaven or hell, while others go to heaven only after spending time in purgatory; this waiting period is necessary for those who have sinned excessively in this life but who have had the good fortune to repent before death. To die in a state of mortal sin meant to suffer in hell eternally. Naturally people worried about how long they might have to spend in purgatory. Indulgences were intended to remit portions of that time and were granted to individuals by the church for their prayers, attendance at Mass, and almost any good works—including monetary offerings to the church. This last good work was the most controversial, since it could easily appear that people were buying their way into heaven.

In the autumn of 1517 a monk named Tetzel was selling indulgences in the area near Wittenberg. Some of the money he obtained was for rebuilding St. Peter's Basilica in Rome, but the rest was for paying off debts incurred by a local archbishop in purchasing his office from the pope. Although Luther did not know about this second purpose, he was incensed both by Tetzel's crude manner and by his flagrant exploitation of the people's ignorance and money. Luther launched his attack on

Tetzel and the selling of indulgences by tacking on the door of the Wittenberg castle church his ninety-five theses.* Luther's theses (propositions) challenged the entire notion of selling indulgences, not only as a corrupt practice but also as a theologically unsound assumption—namely, that salvation can be earned by good works. In the ninety-five theses the outline of Luther's later theology is already evident, and his reliance on faith as the only means to salvation is implicitly stated.

At the heart of Luther's argument in the ninety-five theses and in his later writings was the belief that the individual achieves salvation through personal religiosity, a sense of contrition for sins, and trust in God's mercy. He also believed that church attendance, fasting, pilgrimages, charity, and other good works did not earn salvation. The church, on the other hand, held that *both* faith and good works were necessary for salvation. Luther further insisted that every individual could discover the meaning of the Bible unaided by the clergy, although the church maintained that only the clergy could read and interpret the Bible properly. Luther argued that in matters of faith there was no difference between the clergy and the laity. Each person could receive faith directly and freely from God. But the church held that the clergy were intermediaries between individuals and God and that in effect Christians reached eternal salvation through the clergy. For Luther, no priest, no ceremony, no sacrament could bridge the gulf between the Creator and his creatures, and the possibility of personal damnation remained a distinct reality. Hope lay only in a personal relationship between the individual and God, as expressed through faith in God's righteousness. No church could mediate that faith for the individual, and to that extent Luther's theology destroyed the foundations of the church's spiritual power.

---

* Some scholars debate whether this public display ever occurred. If it did not, the document was nevertheless widely circulated almost immediately.

But if faith alone, freely given by God, brings salvation to the believer, how can a person know if he or she has faith? Luther seemed content to assert that the search itself was a sign that God had favored a pious and penitent supplicant. Yet in Luther's doctrine of faith the notion of predestination is barely beneath the surface. The predestination argument continues today. God, of course, is all-knowing and eternal and his will is absolute. Not only does he give faith to whomever he chooses, but he does so for his own inscrutable reasons. Since God's existence, and therefore his will, is timeless, he knows the fate of each individual even as he or she is searching for salvation. In that sense every person is predestined either for heaven or for hell. But the problem remains, how can one know if one has been chosen? Luther said simply that no one could ever really know. Subsequent reformers would make much of the doctrine of predestination in their struggle to systematize Protestant doctrine and to create an identifying experience for all true Christians.

Although Luther did not realize it in 1517, the Reformation had begun. Quickly translating the theses from Latin into German, his students printed and distributed them, first in Saxony and eventually throughout Germany. Local church authorities recognized in Luther a serious threat and prepared to silence him. But Luther was tenacious; he began to write and preach his theology with increasing vigor.

At this point, politics intervened. Recognizing that his life might be in danger if he continued to preach without a protector, Luther appealed for support to the prince of his district, Frederick, the elector of Saxony. The elector was a powerful man in international politics—one of seven lay and ecclesiastical princes who chose the Holy Roman emperor. Frederick's support convinced church officials, including the pope, that this monk would have to be dealt with cautiously.

The years 1518–1519 were momentous ones for the Holy Roman Empire. Before his death in 1519, the Holy Roman Emperor Maximilian

Print Shop, Sixteenth-Century Print. Neither the Renaissance nor the Reformation would have been so widespread without printing, which was invented in Nuremberg in the 1450s. The printed word was the medium for the rapid transmission of Luther's and Calvin's revolutionary treatises, first in Germany and Switzerland and then elsewhere in Europe. (*BBC Hulton Picture Library/Bettmann Archive*)

I wanted to see his grandson, Charles, king of Spain, elected to succeed him. The papacy at first opposed Charles's candidacy, even looking to Frederick of Saxony as a possible alternative. Frederick wisely declined to be a candidate; as one of the seven electors, his vote was courted by the contenders—Charles, Francis I of France, and Henry VIII of England. Charles bribed his way onto the throne. But during this crucial election period and for some years afterward, he had to proceed cautiously on issues that might offend powerful German princes.

These political considerations explain the delay in Luther's official condemnation and excommunication by the pope. When in 1520 the pope finally acted against him, it was too late; Luther had been given the needed time to promote his views. He proclaimed that the pope was Antichrist and that the church was the "most lawless den of robbers, the most shameless of all brothels, the very kingdom of sin, death and Hell."[2] When the papal bull excommunicating him was delivered, Luther burned it.

No longer members of the church, Luther and his followers established congregations for the purpose of Christian worship. Christians without the church needed protection, and in 1520 Luther published the *Address to the Christian Nobility of the German Nation*. In it, he appealed to the emperor and the German princes to reform the church and to cast off their allegiance to the pope, who he argued had used taxes and political power to exploit them for centuries. His appeal produced some success; the Reformation flourished on the resentment against foreign papal intervention that had long festered in Germany. Luther also wrote to the German people and conveyed the meaning of his personal experience as a Christian. In *The Freedom of the Christian Man* (1520), Luther called on his followers to strive for true spiritual freedom through faith in Christ, to discipline themselves to live as law-abiding members of society, to obey legitimate political authority, and to perform good works according to the dictates of Christian love. In these treatises Luther made it clear that he wanted to present no threat to legitimate political authority, that is, to the power of the German princes.

In 1521, Charles V, the Holy Roman emperor, who was a devout Catholic, summoned Luther to Worms, giving him a pass of safe conduct. There Luther was to answer to the charge of heresy, both an ecclesiastical and a civil offense. On his journey, Luther received a warm public response from great crowds of people. But the emperor and his officials coldly demanded that he recant. Luther's reply, delivered after some deliberation, is undoubtedly his most famous statement: "Unless I am convinced of error by the testimony of Scripture or by clear reason . . . I cannot and will not recant anything, for it is neither safe nor honest to act against one's conscience. God help me. Amen." Shortly after this confrontation with the emperor, Luther went into hiding to escape arrest. During that one-year period he translated the New Testament into German. With this work he offered his compatriots the opportunity to take the same arduous spiritual odyssey that he had and to join him as a new type of Christian. These people were eventually called *Protestants*, those who protested against the established church, or in the case of the nobility, actually took up arms against it.

The Appeal and Spread of Lutheranism

Once Luther recognized the need for followers, he appealed to every level of German society for support. And he was successful. His brilliance as a theologian was matched by his ability to bridge the gap between his sophisticated version of Christianity and the beliefs and aspirations of all Christians. Spread rapidly by the new printing press, the tenets of Protestantism offered the hope of revitalization and renewal not only for true religion but for society and government.

Lutheranism appealed to the devout, who resented the worldliness and lack of piety of many clergy. But the movement found its greatest following among German townspeople who objected to money flowing from their country to Rome in the form of church taxes and payment for church offices. In addition, the Reformation provided the nobility with the unprecedented opportunity to confiscate church lands, to eliminate church taxes, and to gain the support of their subjects by serving as leaders of a popular and dynamic religious movement. The Reformation also gave the nobles a way of resisting the Catholic Holy Roman emperor, Charles V, who wanted to extend his authority over the German princes. Resenting the Italian domination of the church, many other Germans who supported Martin Luther believed that they were freeing German Christians from foreign control.

Lutheranism also drew support from the peasantry, who saw Luther as their champion against their oppressors—feudal lay and ecclesiastical lords and the townspeople. Indeed, in his writings and sermons Luther often attacked the greed of the princes and bemoaned the plight of the poor. Nevertheless, Luther was a political conservative who hesitated to challenge secular authority. To him, the good Christian was an obedient citizen.

Although Luther had spoken forcefully about the discontent of Christians with their church, he never understood that in the minds of the poor and socially oppressed, the church's abuses were visible signs of the exploitation encountered in their daily lives. Wealthy and powerful feudal lords who governed them and prosperous townspeople who bought their labor for the lowest possible wages were no different from the venal clergy; indeed, in some cases the lord was a local bishop.

In the early sixteenth century, a rapid population explosion throughout Europe had produced severe inflation coupled with high unemployment and low wages. These conditions seriously affected the poor. The peasantry in Germany was probably worse off than in England and the Low Countries; and in the German states, the feudal power of lords over every feature of peasant life remained unbroken. In 1524, the long-suffering peasants openly rebelled against their lords. The Peasants' Revolt spread to over one-third of Germany; some 300,000 people took up arms against their masters.

Undoubtedly, Luther's successful confrontation with the authorities had served to inspire the peasants, and he had at one time chastised the nobles for failing to care for the poor as commanded in the Gospel. But he had no intention of associating his movement with a peasant uprising at the risk of alienating the nobility who supported him. Luther virulently attacked the rebellious peasants, urging the nobility to become "both judge and executioner" and to "knock down, strangle, and stab . . . and think nothing so venomous, pernicious, Satanic as an insurgent . . . Such wonderful times are these that a prince can merit heaven better with bloodshed than another with prayer."[3] By 1525 the peasants had been put down by the sword. Thousands died or were left homeless, and many were permanently alienated from the Lutheran Reformation.

The Peasants' Revolt was not the last violent confrontation for the German Reformation. Catholic power also threatened. Initially, the Holy Roman emperor hesitated to intervene militarily, a delay that proved crucial. His involvement in international power politics at first precluded him from acting in Germany: he was at war with France over control of portions of Italy, and Turkey threatened his territories in the east, particularly Austria. Soon, however, Catholic and Protestant princes in various territories of the empire were waging intermittent warfare over its religious fate.

Religious strife was only settled, and then in a piecemeal fashion, by the Peace of Augsburg (1555). It decreed by the famous dictum *cuius regio, eius religio* ("whoever rules, his religion") that each territorial prince should determine the religion of his subjects. Broadly speaking, northern Germany became largely Protestant, while Bavaria, Baden-Württemberg, and other southern territories remained in the church. The victors were the local princes. Toward the end of his life, Charles V expressed his bitter regret for not having intervened more forcefully in those early years. The decentralization of the empire and its division into Catholic and Protestant areas would block German unity until the last part of the nineteenth century.

The Spread of the Reformation

Nothing better illustrates people's dissatisfaction with the church in the early sixteenth century than the rapid spread of Protestantism. There was a pattern to this phenomenon. Protestantism grew strong in northern Europe—northern Germany, Scandinavia, the Netherlands, and England; it failed in the Romance countries, although not without a struggle in France. In general, Protestantism was an urban phenomenon, and it prospered where local magistrates supported it and where the distance from Rome was greatest.

Protestantism also appeared simultaneously in different places—a sure indication of its popular roots. For example, in the Swiss city of Zurich, the priest and reformer Ulrich Zwingli (1484–1531) preached a form of Christianity very close to that of Luther and claimed that he developed his ideas independently of Luther. Zwingli and Luther both

Map 14.1 The Protestant and the Catholic Reformations ▶

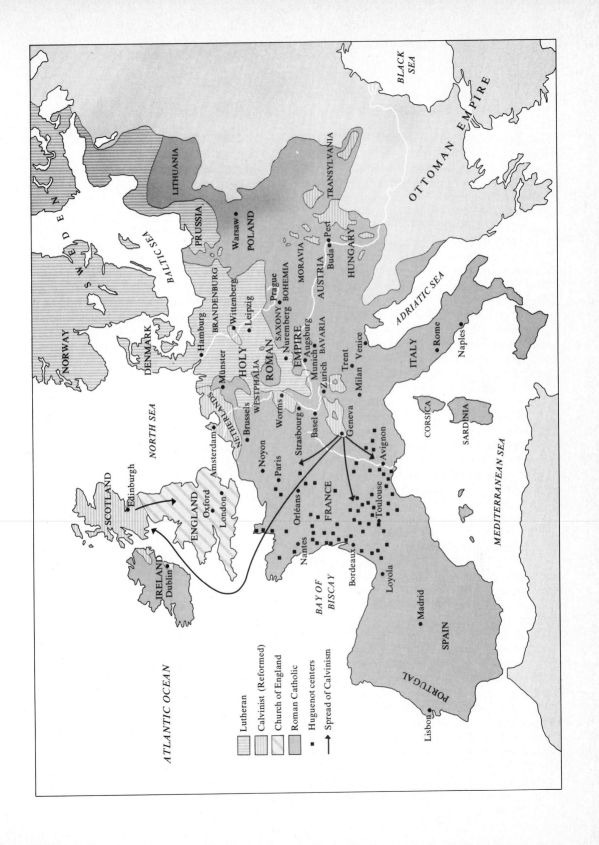

ATLANTIC OCEAN

NORWAY

SWEDEN

NORTH SEA

BALTIC SEA

DENMARK

• Hamburg

SCOTLAND
• Edinburgh

IRELAND
• Dublin

ENGLAND
Oxford •
London •

NETHERLANDS
Amsterdam •
Brussels •
WESTPHALIA
Münster •

HOLY
ROMAN
EMPIRE

BRANDENBURG
Wittenberg •
• Leipzig

PRUSSIA

LITHUANIA

POLAND
Warsaw •

SAXONY
Prague •
Nuremberg
BOHEMIA
Augsburg •
Munich •
BAVARIA
Zürich •

MORAVIA

AUSTRIA

HUNGARY
Buda •• Pest

TRANSYLVANIA

Worms •
Strasbourg •
Basel •
Geneva •

Trent •
Milan •• Venice

ADRIATIC SEA

ITALY
Rome •

Naples •

OTTOMAN EMPIRE

BLACK SEA

• Noyon
Paris •

FRANCE
Orléans •

Avignon •
Toulouse •

CORSICA

SARDINIA

MEDITERRANEAN SEA

Nantes •
Bordeaux •

BAY OF
BISCAY

Loyola •

SPAIN
• Madrid

PORTUGAL

Lisbon •

Lutheran

Calvinist (Reformed)

Church of England

Roman Catholic

■ Huguenot centers

→ Spread of Calvinism

sought a ceremonial alternative to the doctrine of transubstantiation—the priest's transformation of communion bread and wine into the substance of Christ's body and blood—and the enormous power it gave to the priesthood. But the two reformers came to differ bitterly over the exact form of the ceremonial. Zwingli turned the communion service into a feast of commemoration. In their quarrel we see the fate that awaited many reformers. Once free to read and interpret the Bible for themselves, they could not agree on its meaning, or on the ritual expressions they would give to their new versions of Christianity.

Zwingli died on the battlefield defending the Reformation. His teachings laid the foundation for a strong reformation in Switzerland, and the major reform movement of the next generation, Calvinism, benefitted from Zwingli's reforms.

Calvinism

The Reformation's success outside Germany derived largely from the work of John Calvin (1509–1564), a French scholar and theologian. For decades, French humanists had attacked the corruption of the church. Their views found sympathy at the court of the French king, Francis I. His sister, Margaret of Navarre, had helped foster this critical humanism, and her intellectual circle looked favorably on Luther's writings. By the 1530s, Lutheran treatises circulated widely in Paris. Some university students, including the young John Calvin, were impressed by the reformer's ideas.

Calvin was born into a French family of substantial bourgeois status, although his father, somewhat like Luther's, was self-made and ambitious. A lawyer and administrator, the elder Calvin had served the civil and ecclesiastical authorities of the city of Noyon until a dispute over finances led to his excommunication. He desired prosperous careers for his sons. John first studied to be a priest and then, at his father's insistence, took up the study of law at the University

of Orléans. Unlike the rebellious Luther, Calvin waited until his father's death to return to Paris and resume his theological studies.

Sometime in 1533 or 1534, Calvin met French followers of Luther and became convinced of the new theology's truth. He began to spread its beliefs immediately after his conversion, and within a year he and his friends were in trouble with the civil and ecclesiastical authorities. Calvin was arrested, but was released because of insufficient evidence.

King Francis I, a bitter rival of the Holy Roman emperor, could countenance Protestantism in Germany, but he had no intention of permitting disruptive religious divisions in his own France. Riots had already broken out in Paris between Catholics and supporters of the Reformation. In 1534 the French church, supported by royal decree, declared the Protestants heretics and subjected them to arrest and execution.

Within a year, young Calvin had abandoned his humanistic and literary studies to become a preacher of Reformation. Calvin explained his sudden conversion as an act of God—"He subdued and reduced my heart to docility, which, for my age, was over-much hardened in such matters."[4] From early in his religious experience, Calvin emphasized the power of God over sinful and corrupt humanity. Calvin's God thundered and demanded obedience, and the terrible distance between God and the individual was mediated only by Christ.

Calvin's understanding of God's relationship to the individual stressed its legal rather than its personal nature. Calvin said that God's laws must be rigorously obeyed; that social and moral righteousness must be earnestly pursued; that political life must be carefully regulated; and that human emotions must be strictly controlled. What psychological forces induced Calvin to embrace such a stern theology are not known, but they were not unique to him. The compelling force of Calvinist belief is an extraordinary aspect of the Protestant Reformation, and its historical consequences were great.

Like Luther, Calvin explained salvation in terms of uncertain predestination. He argued that although people are predestined to salvation or damnation, they can never know their fate in advance. This terrible decree could and did lead some to despair. For others—in a paradox difficult for the modern mind to comprehend—Calvinism gave a sense of self-assurance and righteousness that made *the saint*, that is, the truly predestined man or woman, into a new kind of European. Most of Calvin's followers seemed to believe that in having comprehended the fact of predestination, they had received a bold insight into their unique relationship with God.

The social and political implications of that insight were immediate: Calvinists became militant Protestants capable of ruling their town or city with the same iron will used to control their unruly passions. Again like Luther, Calvin always stressed that Christians should obey legitimate political authority. But Calvinists were individuals who assumed that only unfailing dedication to God's law could be seen as a sign of salvation; their obedience to human laws would always be contingent on their inner sense of righteousness. Thus, Calvinism made for stern men and women, active in their congregations and willing to suppress vice in themselves and others. Calvinism could also produce revolutionaries willing to defy any temporal authorities that were perceived to be in violation of God's laws. For Calvin, obedience to Christian law became the dominating principle of his life. Rigorous enforcement of the law ensured obedience to God's law; it also served as an alternative to the decrees and obligations formerly imposed by the Catholic church.

The political situation in France forced Calvin to leave. After his flight from Paris, he finally sought safety in Geneva, a small, prosperous Swiss city near the French border. There Calvin eventually established a Protestant church that did not hesitate to dominate the lives of many others less committed to the Reformation. Switzerland was a logical choice; its cities had long been in the vanguard of the Reformation. Before Calvin's arrival,

Geneva's citizens were in revolt against their Catholic bishops. The French-born reformer Guillaume Farel led a small Protestant congregation there and implored Calvin to stay with him to continue the work of the Reformation. Together they became the leaders of the Protestant movement in Geneva. After many setbacks, Calvin emerged as the most dynamic agent of reform in the city. Until his death in 1564, his beliefs and actions dominated Geneva's religious and social life.

Calvin established a kind of theocracy—a society where the church regulates the political and social lives of its citizens. The older and more pious male members of the community governed the city. These elders of the Calvinist church imposed strict discipline in dress, sexual mores, church attendance, and business affairs; they severely punished irreligious or sinful behavior. This rigid discipline contributed to Geneva's prosperity; indeed, Calvin had instituted the kind of social discipline that the ruling merchants had always wanted. At every turn prosperous merchants, as well as small shopkeepers, saw in Calvinism a series of doctrines that justified the self-discipline they already exercised in their own lives and wished to impose on the unruly masses. They particularly approved of his economic views, for Calvin saw nothing sinful about commercial activities and even gave his assent to the practice of charging interest.

Geneva became the center of international Protestantism. Calvin trained a new generation of Protestant reformers of many nationalities, who carried his message back to their homelands. Calvin's *Institutes of the Christian Religion* (1536), in its many editions, became (after the Bible) the leading textbook of the new theology. In the second half of the sixteenth century, Calvin's theology of uncertain predestination spread into France, England, the Netherlands, and parts of the Holy Roman Empire.

Calvin always opposed any recourse to violence. Yet when monarchy became their persecutor, his followers felt compelled to respond. Calvinist theologians became the first political theoreticians of modern times to publish cogent arguments for opposition to monarchy, and eventually for political revolution. In France and later in the Netherlands, Calvinism became a revolutionary ideology, complete with an underground organization composed of dedicated followers who challenged monarchical authority. (In the seventeenth century, the English version of Calvinism—Puritanism—performed the same function.) In certain circumstances, Calvinism possessed the moral force to undermine the claims of the monarchical state over the individual.

France

Although Protestantism was illegal in France after 1534, its persecution was half-hearted and never systematic. The Protestant minority in France, the Huguenots, grew and became a well-organized underground movement that attracted nobles, urban dwellers, some peasants, and women especially. Huguenot churches, often under the protection of powerful nobles, assumed an increasingly political character in response to monarchy-sponsored persecution. By 1559, French Protestants were sufficiently organized and militant to challenge their persecutors, King Henry II and the Guise—one of the foremost Catholic families in Europe, tied by marriage and conviction to the Spanish monarchy and its rigorous form of Catholicism. Guise power in the French court meant that all Protestant appeals for more lenient treatment went unheeded, and in 1562 civil war erupted between Catholics and Protestants. What followed was one of the most brutal religious wars in the history of Europe. In 1572, an effort at conciliation through the marriage of a Protestant leader into the royal family failed when the Catholics, urged on by the queen mother, Catherine de' Medici, murdered the assembled Protestant wedding guests. Over the next week, a popular uprising against Protestants left thousands of them dead; the streets, according to eyewitness accounts, were stained red with blood. This slaughter,

known as the Saint Bartholomew's Day Massacre, inspired the pope to have a mass said in thanksgiving for a Catholic "victory." Such was the extent of religious hatred in Europe by the late sixteenth century.

After nearly thirty years of brutal fighting throughout France, victory went to the Catholic side—but only barely. Henry of Navarre, the Protestant bridegroom who in 1572 had managed to escape the fate of his supporters, became king, but only after he had reconverted to Catholicism. He established a tentative peace by granting Protestants limited toleration. In 1598 he issued the Edict of Nantes, the first document in any nation-state that attempted to institutionalize a degree of religious toleration. In the seventeenth century the successors of Henry IV (assassinated in 1610) gradually revoked the edict. The theoretical foundations of toleration, as well as its practice, remained weak in early modern Europe.

England

The Reformation was initiated in England not by religious reformers, but by the king himself. Henry VIII (1509–1547) removed the English church from the jurisdiction of the papacy because the pope had refused to grant him an annulment of his marriage to his first wife. The English Reformation began as a political act on the part of a self-confident Renaissance king. But its origins stretched back into the Middle Ages, and its character, once it got underway, became intensely religious and increasingly Protestant.

Unlike the French and Spanish kings, the English Tudors had never frightened the papacy. The Tudors had enjoyed a good measure of control over the English church, but they had never played a major role in European and papal politics. When Henry VIII decided that he wanted a divorce from the Spanish princess Catherine of Aragon, in 1527–1528, the pope in effect ignored his request. Henry had a shaky case from a theological point of view and not enough international political power to force his will on the papacy. As the pope stalled, Henry grew more desperate—he needed a male heir and presumed that the failure to produce one lay with his wife. At the same time, he desired the shrewd and tempting Anne Boleyn. But Spain's power over the papacy, symbolized by the Spanish army that had sacked Rome in 1525, ensured that Henry's pleas for an annulment would go unheeded.

Although anticlericalism and resentment toward the papacy was rife throughout Europe at this time, the English also possessed a tradition of popular opposition to the church that stretched back to Wycliffe in the fourteenth century. Aware of that tradition, Henry VIII arranged to grant himself a divorce by severing England from the church. To do so, he had to call Parliament, which in turn passed a series of statutes drawn up at his initiative and guided through Parliament by his minister, Thomas Cromwell. Beginning in 1529, Henry convinced both houses of Parliament to accept his Reformation, and so began an administrative and religious revolution. In 1534 he had himself declared supreme head of the Church of England. In 1536 he dissolved the monasteries and seized their property, which was distributed or sold to his loyal supporters. In most cases, it went to the lesser nobility and landed gentry.

In the eleven years following Henry's death in 1547, there were four monarchs. Henry VIII was succeeded by his son, Edward VI, who reigned from 1547 to 1553 and was a Protestant. On his death, he was succeeded by Mary (1553–1558), the daughter of Henry VIII and Catherine of Aragon. A devout Catholic, Mary persecuted Protestants in England. By the 1558 succession of Elizabeth I, Henry's second daughter (by Anne Boleyn), England was a Protestant country again.

The English, or Anglican, church as it developed in the sixteenth century differed little in its customs and ceremonies from the Roman Catholicism it replaced. And large sections of the English population, including aristocratic families, remained Catholic and even used their homes as centers for Catholic

Henry VIII. Henry VIII initiated the break with Rome. Ironically, earlier as a youthful monarch, he received from a grateful papacy the title "Defender of the Faith" for a published treatise against Martin Luther. (*National Portrait Gallery, London*)

rituals performed by clandestine priests. These divisions boded ill for the future.

In addition, the exact nature of England's Protestantism was a subject of growing dispute. Was the Anglican church to be truly Protestant? Was its hierarchy to be responsive to, and possibly even appointed by, the laity? Were its services and churches to be simple, lacking in "popish" rites and rituals and centered only around Scripture and sermon? Was Anglicanism to conform to Protestantism as practiced in Switzerland, either in Calvinist Geneva or Zwinglian Zurich? Clearly the clergy, especially the English bishops, would accept no form of Protestantism that might

Elizabeth I. The genius of Elizabeth I confounded her countrymen and the Catholic Church alike. Parliament wanted her to marry and give over power to her husband. The Catholic Church long held hopes for the English monarchy to reconcile with Rome. Elizabeth capitulated to no one and carefully charted a course that consolidated her personal power and allowed England to gain strength as a Protestant nation. Her portrait is by Nicholas Hilliard. (*Walker Art Gallery, Liverpool*)

limit their ancient privileges, ceremonial functions, and power.

Despite these religious issues, raised in large measure by the growing number of English Calvinists, or *Puritans* as they were called, Elizabeth's reign was characterized by a heightened sense of national identity. The English Reformation enhanced that sense, as did the increasing fear of invasion by Spain, a Catholic power with twice England's population and a vast colonial empire that was intent on returning England to the papacy.

Spain and Italy

In Spain, Protestantism met with no success. In the Middle Ages, church and state had successfully allied in a religious and nationalist crusade to drive out the Muslims, forging strong links between the Spanish monarchy and the church. The church augmented and justified the power and authority of the monarchy and at the same time retained its economic and political power. About one-quarter of the Spanish population held clerical office of one kind or another, and the church owned one-half of Spain's land. Furthermore, the church possessed judicial authority sanctioned by the state; its judicial arm, the Inquisition, enforced public and private morality.

Luther's works circulated in Spain for a brief time, but the Spanish authorities quickly and thoroughly stamped out Protestantism. After 1560, even the Inquisition was hardpressed to find Protestants. The Spanish church was efficient, self-confident, and undoubtedly the most repressive in Europe. The absence of civil liberty and freedom of thought until very recently in modern Spain has historical roots in the Inquisition of the sixteenth century. Late in that century, Spain became the main defender of Catholicism on the Continent, and that imperial mission gradually sapped its vast military power. Yet Protestant antagonism toward Spain remained vital until well into the eighteenth century.

A similar pattern developed in Italy, where Luther's ideas were discussed in Italian humanist circles but gained no popular audience. The Italian humanists distrusted Luther's emphasis on human sinfulness, and church authorities persecuted the few converts. Attempts to reform the Italian church were largely unsuccessful, and even reform-minded popes in the 1520s and 1530s had little support among the Vatican's Italian bureaucracy.

The Radical Reformation

The mainstream of the Protestant Reformation can be described as *magisterial;* that is, the leading reformers generally supported established political authorities, whether they were territorial princes or urban magistrates. For the reformers, human freedom was a spiritual, not a social, concept. Yet the Reformation did help trigger revolts among the artisan and peasant classes of central and then western Europe. Indications are that church doctrine had not made great inroads into the folk beliefs of large segments of the European masses. Late medieval records of church interrogations, usually in towns and villages where heresy or witchcraft was suspected, show the people to have deviated to an extraordinary degree from official doctrines and beliefs. For example, some peasants held the very unchristian beliefs that Nature was God or that witches had as much spiritual power as priests did. By the 1520s, several radical reformers arose, often from the lower classes of European society, and attempted to channel popular religion and folk beliefs into a new version of reformed Christianity that spoke directly to the temporal and spiritual needs of the oppressed.

The proliferation of many radical groups throughout the Continent makes them difficult to classify. Nevertheless, some beliefs were common to the Radical Reformation. Like Lutherans and Calvinists, the radicals struggled with the problem of salvation. Luther argued that faith alone, freely given by God, provides salvation for the believer. Radical reformers proclaimed that God's will was known by his saints—those predestined for salvation. In a world where survival itself was often precarious for the poor and oppressed, the radicals argued that even ordinary men and women have certain knowledge of their salvation through the *inner light*— a direct and immediate communication from God to his chosen saints. That knowledge makes the saint free. For the radicals, such spiritual freedom justified their demands for social and economic freedom and equality. Protestantism, radically interpreted, proclaimed the righteousness and the priesthood of all believers. It said that all people can have faith if God wills it, and that God would

not abandon the wretched and humble of the earth.

The radicals said that the poor shall inherit an earth that at present is ruled by Antichrist, and that the end of the world has been proclaimed by Scripture. The saints' task is to purge this earth of evil to make it ready for Christ's Second Coming. For the radicals the faith-alone doctrine came to mean certain salvation for the poor and lowly, and the Scriptures became an inspiration for social revolution. Luther, Calvin, and the other reformers vigorously condemned the social doctrines that were preached by the radical reformers.

The largest group in the Radical Reformation prior to 1550 has the general name of *Anabaptists*. Having received the inner light—the message of salvation—the Anabaptist felt born anew and yearned to be rebaptized. This notion had a revolutionary implication: the first baptism—one's first Christian allegiance to an established church (Protestant or Catholic)—does not count. The Anabaptist is a new Christian, a new person led by the light of conscience to seek reform and renewal of all institutions in preparation for the Second Coming of Christ. Millenarian doctrines about the end of the world provided a sense of time, of urgency.

In 1534 the Anabaptists captured the city of Münster in Westphalia near the western border of Germany. They seized the property of nonbelievers, burned all books except the Bible, and in a mood of jubilation and sexual excess, openly practiced a repressive (as far as women were concerned) polygamy. All the while the Anabaptists proclaimed that the Day of Judgment was close at hand. The leaders at Münster were men totally unprepared for power, and their actions led to a universal condemnation of the radicals. Their defeat was achieved by an army led by the Lutheran prince, Philip of Hesse.

In early modern Europe, *Münster* became a byword for dangerous revolution. Determined to prevent these wild enthusiasts from gaining strength in their own territories, princes attacked them with ferocity. In Münster today, the cages still hang from the church steeple where the Anabaptist leaders were tortured and left to die as a warning to all would-be imitators.

By the late sixteenth century, many radical movements had either gone underground or grown quiet. But a century later, during the English Revolution (1640–1660), the beliefs and political goals of the Radical Reformation again surfaced, threatening to push the revolution in a direction that its gentry leaders desperately feared. Although the radicals failed in England too, they left a tradition of democratic and antihierarchical thought. The radical assertion that saints, who have received the inner light, are the equal of anyone, regardless of social status, helped shape modern democratic thought.

The Catholic Response

The church could never have predicted the force of the Protestant Reformation, especially the number of powerful noblemen attracted to it. When it developed, the papacy seemed incapable of responding with needed reforms of its own, perhaps because it feared the forces that would be unleashed within the church and might challenge its own power. In the first instance, the energy for reform came from ordinary clergy as well as lay people such as Ignatius Loyola (1491–1556). Trained as a soldier, this pious Spanish reformer sought to create a new religious order fusing the intellectual excellence of humanism with a reformed Catholicism that would appeal to powerful economic and political groups. Founded in 1534, the Society of Jesus, more commonly known as the Jesuits, became the backbone of the Catholic Reformation in southern and western Europe. The Jesuits combined traditional monastic discipline with a dedication to teaching and an emphasis on the power of preaching, and they sought to use both to win converts back to the Church.

The Jesuits sought to bypass local corruption and appealed to the papacy to lead a truly international movement to revive Christian universalism. The Jesuits saw most clearly the power of the bitter fragmentation produced by the Reformation, and they also saw one of the central flaws in Protestant theology. Predestination offered salvation especially to the literate and prosperous laity and also, at least in theory, to the poor.

But equally, it included the possibility of despair for the individual or of a life tormented by a fear of damnation. In response, the Jesuits offered hope—a religious revival based upon ceremony, tradition, and the power of the priest to offer forgiveness. In addition, they opened some of the finest schools in Europe. Just as the Lutherans in Germany sought to bring literacy to the masses so that they might read the Bible, the Jesuits sought to bring intellectual sophistication to the laity, especially to the rich and powerful. The Jesuits pursued positions as confessors to princes and urged them to press their efforts to strengthen the church in their territories. They even sought to develop a theology that permitted "small sins" in the service of an ultimately just cause. In this way the Jesuits, by the seventeenth century, became the greatest teachers in Europe, and also the most controversial religious group within the church—were they the true voice of a reformed church, or did they use religion simply as a disguise to seek political power of their own, to make themselves the Machiavellian servants of princes? It was a controversy that neither their contemporaries nor historians have been able to solve.

The Jesuits built schools and universities throughout Europe, designed churches, and even fostered a distinct style of art and architecture: cherubic angels grace the ornate decor of Jesuit churches; heaven-bound virgins beckon the penitent. This baroque style, so lavish and emotive, was intended to move the heart, just as the skilled preacher sought to move the intellect. The Protestant message had been heard: religion is ultimately a private, psychological matter that is not always satisfied by scholastic argumentation.

By the 1540s the Counter Reformation was well underway. This attempt to reform the church from within combined several elements that had always stood for renewal within traditional Catholicism. For example, the Jesuits were imitating such preaching orders of the Middle Ages as the Dominicans and the Franciscans, and Catholic reformers looked to Renaissance humanism like that of Erasmus as the key to the church's total reformation. The leaders of this Catholic movement attacked many of the same abuses that had impelled Luther to speak out, but they avoided a break with the doctrinal and spiritual authority of the clergy.

The Counter Reformation also took aggressive and hostile measures against Protestantism. The church tried to counter the popular appeal of Protestantism by offering dramatic, emotional, even sentimental piety to the faithful. For individuals who were unmoved by this appeal to sentiment or by the church's more traditional spirituality and who allied with Protestant heresy, the church resorted to sterner measures. The Inquisition expanded its activities, and wherever Catholic jurisdiction prevailed, unrepentant heretics were subject to death or imprisonment. Catholics did not hold a monopoly on persecution: wherever Protestantism obtained official status—in England, Scotland, and Geneva, for instance—Catholics or religious radicals also sometimes faced persecution. But the church possessed greater national power in certain countries, and hence its power to persecute was greater. This was an age when only skeptics or freethinkers valued religious toleration.

The censorship of printed literature was an inherent part of European intellectual life, lasting until well into the nineteenth century. By the 1520s the impulse to censor and burn dangerous books had surfaced dramatically. In the rush to eliminate heretical literature, the church condemned the works of reforming Catholic humanists as well as those by Protestants. Indeed not only books were burnt; Calvin executed by fire the naturalist and skeptic Michael Servetus, who opposed the doctrine of the Trinity; in 1600 the church burned Giordano Bruno for similar reasons.

El Greco (1541–1614): Portrait of a Cardinal (probably Don Fernando Niño de Guevara). The Spanish church fiercely opposed the Reformation. The Inquisition persecuted Protestants relentlessly. The tenseness of the sitter captures the wary militancy of Spanish Catholicism. The Cardinal's cool glance is belied by his claw-like hand. *(The Metropolitan Museum of Art, New York; bequest of Mrs. H. O. Havemeyer, 1929. The H. O. Havemeyer Collection)*

These victims were merely two famous men who fell in an age of persecution; thousands were imprisoned or executed. The Index of Prohibited Books became an institutional part of the church's life; it was finally abolished in 1966.

Much of the Catholic response to the Reformation entailed hostility and rejection. Yet within the church itself, reformers succeeded in putting through concrete changes. In 1545 the Council of Trent met to reform the church and to strengthen it to face the Protestant challenge. Over the many years that it was convened (until 1563), the Council modified and unified church doctrine; abolished many corrupt practices, such as the selling of indulgences; and vested final authority in the papacy, thereby ending the long and bitter struggle within the church over papal authority. The Council of Trent purged the church and gave it doctrinal clarity on such matters as the roles of faith and good works in attaining salvation. It passed a decree that the church shall be the final arbiter of the Bible and demanded that texts be taken literally wherever possible. Galileo was to experience great difficulties in the next century because that decree made the motion of the earth into a contradiction of Scripture (see pages 386–387). But the intention of the decree was to offer the church as a clear voice amid the babble of Protestant tongues. All compromise with Protestantism was rejected (not that Protestants were anxious for it). The Reformation had split western Christendom irrevocably.

The Reformation and the Modern Age

At first glance, the Reformation seems to have renewed the medieval stress on otherworldliness and reversed the direction toward a secularized humanism taken by the Renaissance. Yet a careful analysis shows decisively modern elements in Reformation thought, as well as antifeudal tendencies in its political history. The Reformation shattered the religious unity of Europe, the chief characteristic of the Middle Ages, and further weakened the church, the principal institution of medieval society, whose moral authority, rejected by millions, and political power waned considerably. Yet by the early seventeenth century, the policies of enlightened education, vigorous preaching, church building, cen-

sorship and persecution, had brought thousands of Germans and Bohemians, in particular, back to the church. To this day Europe remains a continent of Catholic and Protestant. Although doctrinal rigidity (and in some places church attendance) has largely disappeared, the split between the southern Catholic countries and the Protestant north is still alive in various customs and traditions.

By strengthening the power of monarchs and magistrates at the expense of religious bodies, the Reformation furthered the growth of the modern state. Protestant rulers totally repudiated the pope's claim to temporal power and extended their authority over Protestant churches in their lands. In Catholic lands, the church reacted to the onslaught of Protestantism by supporting the monarchies, but at the same time it preserved a significant degree of political independence. Protestantism did not create the modern secular state; it did, however, help to free the state from subordination to religious authority; such autonomy is an essential feature of modern political life.

Very indirectly, Protestantism contributed to the growth of political liberty—another ideal, although not always a reality, in the modern West. To be sure, neither Luther nor Calvin championed political freedom. Luther said that subjects should obey the commands of their rulers, and Calvinists created a theocracy in Geneva that closely regulated its citizens. Nevertheless, the Reformation provided a basis for challenging monarchical authority. During the religious wars, some Protestant theorists supported resistance to monarchs whose edicts, they believed, defied God's law. Moreover, the Protestant view that all believers—laity, clergy, lords, kings—were masters of their own spiritual destiny eroded hierarchical authority and accorded with emerging constitutional government.

The Reformation also contributed to the creation of an individualistic ethic. Protestants sought a direct and personal relationship with God and interpreted the Bible for themselves. Facing the prospect of salvation or damnation entirely on their own, without the church to

Chronology 14.1 The Reformation

1381	English peasants revolt; support John Wycliffe, early reformer
1414–1418	The Council of Constance
1431–1449	The Council of Basel
1517	Martin Luther writes his ninety-five theses and the Reformation begins
1520	Pope Leo X excommunicates Luther
1524–1526	The German peasants revolt
1529	The English Parliament accepts Henry VIII's Reformation
1534	Henry VIII is declared head of Church of England; King Francis I of France declares Protestants heretics; Ignatius Loyola founds the Society of Jesus; Anabaptists, radical reformers, capture Münster in Westphalia
1536	Henry VIII dissolves monasteries and seizes their properties; Calvin publishes *Institutes of the Christian Religion*
1536–1564	John Calvin leads the Reformation in Geneva with Guillaume (William) Farel
1545–1563	The Council of Trent
1553–1558	Mary, Catholic Queen of England, persecutes Protestants
1555	The Peace of Augsburg
1562–1598	French wars of religion between Catholics and Protestants are settled by the Edict of Nantes in 1598
1640–1660	The English Revolution

provide aid and security, and believing that God had chosen them to be saved, Protestants developed an inner confidence and assertiveness. This religious individualism was the counterpart of the intellectual individualism of the Renaissance humanists.

The Protestant ethic of the Reformation developed concurrently with a new economic system. Theorists have argued ever since about whether the new individualism of the Protestants brought on the growth of capitalism or whether the capitalistic values of the middle class gave rise to the Protestant ethic. In the middle of the nineteenth century, Karl Marx theorized that Protestantism gave expression to the new capitalistic values of the bourgeois: thrift, hard work, self-reliance, and rationality. Hence, Marx argued, the success of Protestantism can be explained by reference to the emergence of Western cap-

italism. In 1904, German sociologist Max Weber argued that Marx had got it backwards, that Protestantism encouraged the growth of capitalism, not vice versa.[5] Weber began with the assumption that religious beliefs do in fact have relevance to the way individuals act in the world. Religion is not primarily a series of doctrines, said Weber, but an ethic that possesses a spirit. Weber saw in the Protestant ethic of the reformation, as it evolved through the life experiences of its followers, the spirit of a nascent capitalism.

Weber acknowledged that capitalism existed in Europe before the Reformation—for example, the merchant-bankers in Italian and German towns. But, argued Weber, not all capitalism is the same, and in the West it has been a particular type of capitalism that has proved most dynamic. Weber saw the spirit of capitalism embodied in the entrepreneur, the *parvenu*, the self-made man. He strives for business success and brings to his enterprise self-discipline and self-restraint. He makes profit not for pleasure, but for more profit. He brings to his enterprise moral virtues of frugality and honesty. And he strives to render work and business efficient and planned, with profits carefully accumulated over time.

For Weber, Protestants made the best capitalists because predestination made them *worldly ascetics*—Christans forced to find salvation without assistance and through activity in this world. The reformers had condemned the monastery as an unnatural life, and their concomitant emphasis on human sinfulness established a psychology of striving that could only be channeled into worldly activity. So Protestants fulfilled their vocation, or calling, by service to the community or state and by dedication to this daily work. Commerce could become, if Weber is right, sanctified. But this ethic did little to alleviate the condition of the poor, which had worsened by the end of the sixteenth century.

By the late seventeenth century in Europe, the center of economic growth was shifting away from Mediterranean and Catholic countries toward northern Atlantic areas: England, the Netherlands, and parts of northern France. Protestant cities, with their freer printing presses, were also becoming centers of intellectual creativity. The characteristics of the modern world—individual expression, economic exploitation, and scientific learning—were to become most visibly present in western European Protestant cities like London, Amsterdam, and Geneva. Both the Protestant entrepreneur and the Protestant intellectual began to symbolize the most advanced forms of economic and creative life.

The tradition of individual striving for material gain, so much a part of Western culture today, developed out of what had once been a religious quest for salvation, made urgent in this world by the theology of the Protestant Reformation. Sixteenth-century Protestantism created a new, highly individual, spirituality. Survival in this world and salvation in the

next came to depend on inner faith and self-discipline; for the prosperous, both eventually became useful in a highly competitive world where individuals rule their own lives and the labor of others and represent themselves and others in government.

Notes

1. John Dillenberger, Ed., *Martin Luther: Selections from His Writings* (New York: Doubleday, 1961), p. 46, taken from *The Freedom of a Christian* (1520).

2. Martin Luther, *Luther's Works*, Robert Schultz, ed. (Philadelphia: Fortress Press, 1967), 46:50–52.

3. François Wendel, *Calvin* (Paris: Presses Universitaires de France, 1950), p. 20.

4. See Max Weber, *Protestant Ethic and the Spirit of Capitalism*, trans. by Talcott Parsons (New York: Scribners, 1958).

Suggested Reading

Elton, G. R., *Reformation Europe, 1517–1559* (1966). A good, though very conservative, account.

Erikson, Erik H., *Young Man Luther* (1958). A psychological interpretation of Luther.

Grimm, Harold J., *The Reformation Era, 1500–1650,* 2nd ed. (1973). The best and most complete narrative available.

Huizinga, Johan, *Erasmus and the Age of Reformation* (1957). The best available survey.

Koenigsberger, H. G., and Mosse, George L., *Europe in the Sixteenth Century* (1968). Some very good chapters on the Reformation.

Neale, J. E., *The Age of Catherine de Medici* (1960). This book manages to make sense out of a complex period.

Scarisbrick, J. J., *Henry VIII* (1968). A very fair and balanced account of a most complex and willful monarch.

Spitz, Lewis William, *The Religious Renaissance of the German Humanists* (1963). Good coverage of the German humanists.

Tawney, R. H., *Religion and the Rise of Capitalism* (1962; reprint of 1926 ed.). Should be read by all students of Protestantism.

Weber, Max, *The Protestant Ethic and the Spirit of Capitalism,* trans. by Talcott Parsons (rev. ed. 1977). This classic essay argues the case for Protestantism as a force encouraging the development of capitalism. Written before World War I, it has never been surpassed.

Wendel, François, *Calvin* (1950). This is the standard biography.

Review Questions

1. Why did the Reformation begin in the early sixteenth century rather than in the fourteenth century at the time of Huss and Wycliffe? Describe the conditions and personalities responsible for starting the Reformation.

2. What personality traits did Martin Luther possess? Which traits seemed responsible for his role and actions in the Reformation? How did Luther's theology mark a break with the church? Why did many Germans become followers of Luther?

3. What role did the printing press play in the Reformation?

4. What were Calvin's major achievements?

5. In what ways did the radical reformers differ from the other Protestants?

6. What did *Münster* symbolize in early modern Europe?

7. Which features in Protestantism were likely to have made its followers more successful capitalists than their Catholic contemporaries?

8. How did the Reformation in England differ from that in Germany?

9. Why did France not become a Protestant country? Give the reasons and describe the circumstances.

10. What role did the Jesuits and the Inquisition play in the Counter Reformation? What did the Counter Reformation accomplish?

11. How did the Reformation weaken medieval institutions and traditions?

15

European Expansion:
Colonization, Commerce,
and Capitalism

*D*uring the period from 1450 to 1750, western Europe entered an era of overseas exploration and economic expansion that transformed society. By 1450, Europe had recovered from the severe contraction of the fourteenth century, produced by plague and marginal agriculture, and was resuming the economic growth that had been the pattern in the twelfth and early thirteenth centuries. This new period of growth, however, was no mere extension of the earlier one, but a radical departure from medieval economic forms.

Overseas exploration changed the patterns of economic growth and society. European adventurers discovered a new way to reach the rich trading centers of India by sailing around Africa. They also conquered, colonized, and exploited a new world across the Atlantic. These discoveries and conquests brought about an extraordinary increase in business activity and the supply of money, which stimulated the growth of capitalism. People's values were transformed into shapes that were alien and hostile to the medieval outlook. By 1750 the model Christian in northwestern Europe was no longer the selfless saint, but the enterprising businessman. The era of secluded manors and walled towns was drawing to a close. A world economy was emerging in which European economic life depended on the market in Eastern spices, African slaves, and American silver. During this age of exploration and commercial expansion, Europe generated a peculiar dynamism unmatched by any other civilization. A process was initiated that, by 1900, would give Europe mastery over most of the globe and wide-ranging influence over other civilizations.

The economic expansion from 1450 to 1650 or 1700 did not, however, raise the living standards of the masses. The vast majority of the people, 80 to 90 percent, lived on the land, and their main business was the production of primary goods—food, especially cereals, and wool. For most of these people, life hovered around the subsistence level, sometimes falling below subsistence during times of famine and disease. Whenever the standard of living improved, any surplus resources would soon be taken up by the survival of more children and hence more mouths to feed. The beneficiaries of the commercial expansion, those whose income rose, were the rich, especially the *nouveaux riches.*

In these respects, then, early modern Europe was comparable to an underdeveloped country today whose society consists of two main economic groups—a small, wealthy elite and a large and growing population that exists on the margin of subsistence and is wracked by recurrent hunger and disease. Developments during overseas exploration and economic expansion should be viewed in the context of these social conditions.

European Expansion

During the Middle Ages the frontiers of Europe had expanded, even if only temporarily in some instances. The Crusaders carved out feudal kingdoms in the Near East. Christian knights pushed back the Muslims on the Iberian Peninsula and drove them from Mediterranean islands. Germans expanded in the Baltic region at the expense of non-Christian Balts, Prussians, and Slavs. Genoa and Venice established commercial ports in the Adriatic Sea, the Black Sea, and the eastern Mediterranean. In the fifteenth and sixteenth centuries, western Europeans embarked on a second and more lasting movement of expansion that led them into the uncharted waters of the Atlantic, Indian, and Pacific oceans. Combined forces propelled Europeans outward and enabled them to dominate Asians, Africans, and American Indians.

Forces Behind Expansion

The population of western Europe increased rapidly between 1450 and 1600. This increase occurred at all levels of society, and among the gentry it was translated into land hunger. As the numbers of the landed classes exceeded the supply of available land, the sons of the aristocracy looked beyond Europe for the lands and fortunes denied them at home. Nor was it unnatural for them to do so by plunder and conquest—their ancestors had done the same thing for centuries. Exploits undertaken and accomplished in the name of family, church, and king were legitimate, perhaps the most legitimate, ways of earning merit and fame, as well as fortune. So the gentry provided the leadership—Cortés is an example—for the expeditions to the New World.

Merchants and shippers, as well as the sons of the aristocracy, also had reason to look abroad. Trade between Europe, Africa, and the Orient had gone on for centuries, but always through intermediaries who increased the costs and decreased the profits on the European end. Gold had been transported by Arab nomads across the Sahara from the riverbeds of West Africa. Spices had been shipped from India and the East Indies by way of Muslim and Venetian merchants. Western European merchants now sought to break those monopolies by going directly to the source—to West Africa for gold, slaves, and pepper, and to India for pepper, spices, and silks. Moreover, incentive grew for such commercial enterprise because between 1450 and 1600 the wealth of prosperous Europeans increased dramatically. This wealth was translated into new purchasing power and the capacity to invest in foreign ventures that would meet the rising demand among the prosperous for luxury goods.

The centralizing monarchical state also played its part in expansion. Monarchs, like Ferdinand and Isabella of Spain, who had successfully established royal hegemony at home looked for opportunities to extend their control overseas. The Spanish rulers looked over their shoulders at their neighbors, the Portuguese, and this competition spurred the efforts of both countries in their drive to the East. Later the Dutch, English, and French engaged in a century-long rivalry. From overseas empires came gold, silver, and commerce that paid for ever-more expensive royal government at home and for war against rival dynasties abroad.

Finally, religion helped in expansion. The crusading tradition was well established, especially on the Iberian Peninsula, where a five-hundred-year struggle known as the Reconquest had taken place to drive out the Muslims. Cortés, for example, saw himself as following in the footsteps of Paladin Roland, the great medieval military hero who had fought to drive back Muslim and pagan. The Portuguese too were imbued with the crusading mission. Prince Henry the Navigator hoped that the Portuguese expansion into Africa would serve two purposes: the discovery of gold and the extension of Christianity at the expense of Islam. In this second aim, his imagination was fired by the legend of Prester John, which told of an ancient Christian kingdom of fabled wealth in the heart of Africa. If the Portuguese could reach that land, Prince Henry reckoned, the two kingdoms would join in a crusade against Islam.

Thus, expansion involved a mixture of economic, political, and religious forces and motives. The West possessed a crusading faith; divided into a handful of competing, warlike states, it expanded by virtue of forces built into its structure and culture. Not only did the West have the will to expand, it also possessed the technology needed for successful expansion. This factor also distinguished the West from China and Islam and helps to explain why the West, not the Oriental civilizations, launched an age of conquest resulting in global mastery.

Not since the Early Middle Ages had there been such a rapid technological revolution as that which began in the fifteenth century. Europeans learned about gunpowder from the Chinese as early as the late thirteenth century, and by the fifteenth century its military application had become widespread. The earliest guns were big cannons meant to knock holes in the walled defenses characteristic of

The New World, Engraving by G. Mercator. The development of the sailing ship and the gunship allowed Spain and Portugal to roam the seas with impunity. Spain had hoped that the New World would provide an abundance of costly spices. However, the land and precious metals there more than made up for the lack of spices. *(The Hispanic Society of America, New York)*

the Middle Ages. In the sixteenth and seventeenth centuries, handheld firearms (particularly the musket) and smaller, more mobile field artillery were perfected. Dynastic and religious wars and overseas expansion kept demand for armaments high, and the armament industry was, as a result, important to the growth of trade and manufacturing.

Another technological development during the period from 1400 to 1650 was the sailing ship. The vessels of the ancient world had been driven principally by oars and human energy. Such vessels, called galleys, were suitable for the shorter distances, calmer waters, and less variable conditions of the Mediterranean, the Black, and the Red seas. But galleys were unsuitable for the Atlantic and other great oceans that Europeans began to ply in the early sixteenth century. In western Europe by the fifteenth century, moreover, labor was in short supply, making it difficult to recruit or condemn men to the galleys. For these reasons the Portuguese, the Dutch, and the English abandoned the galley in favor of the sailing ship.

The sail and the gun were crucially important in allowing Europeans to overcome non-Europeans and penetrate and exploit their worlds. Western Europeans combined these devices in the form of the gunned ship. Not only was the sailing vessel more maneuverable and faster in the open seas than the galley, but the addition of guns gave it another tactical advantage over its rivals. The galleys of the Arabs in the Indian Ocean and the junks of the Chinese were not armed with guns below deck for firing at a distance to cripple or sink the enemy. In battle they relied instead on the ancient tactic of coming up alongside the enemy vessel, shearing off its oars, and boarding to fight on deck.

The gunned ship gave the West naval superiority from the beginning. The Portuguese, for example, made short work of the Muslim fleet sent to drive them out of the Indian Ocean in 1509. That victory at Diu, off the western coast of India, indicated that the West not only had found an all-water route to the Orient but was there to stay. Material and religious motives led Europeans to explore and conquer; superior technology ensured the success of their enterprises.

The Portuguese Empire

Several reasons account for Portugal's overseas success. Portugal's long Atlantic coastline ensured that its people would look to the sea—initially for fishing and trade and then for exploration. A sunny climate also spurred seafaring and commercial expansion. Portugal was Northern Europe's closest supplier of

subtropical products—olive oil, cork, wine, and fruit. The feudal nobility, typically antagonistic to trade and industry, was not as powerful in Portugal as elsewhere in Europe. Although feudal warriors had carved Portugal out of Moorish Iberia in the twelfth century, their descendants were blocked from further interior expansion by the presence of the strong Christian Kingdom of Castile in the east. The only other outlet for expansion was the sea.

Royal policy also favored expansion. The central government promoted trading interests, especially after 1385 when the merchants of Lisbon and the lesser ports helped establish a new dynasty in opposition to the feudal aristocracy. In the first half of the fifteenth century a younger son of the king, named Prince Henry the Navigator (1394–1460) by English writers, sponsored voyages of exploration and the nautical studies needed to undertake them. In these endeavors he spent his own fortune and the wealth of the church's crusading order that he headed. Prince Henry sought to revive the anti-Muslim crusade to which Portugal owed its existence as a Christian state. This connection between the medieval crusades and the early modern expansion of Europe ran through Portuguese and Spanish history.

As early as the fifteenth century the Portuguese expanded into islands in the Atlantic Ocean. In 1420 they began to settle Madeira and raise corn there, and in the 1430s they pushed into the Canaries and the Azores in search of new farmlands and slaves for their colonies. In the middle decades of the century they moved down the West African coast to the mouth of the Congo River and beyond, establishing trading posts as they went.

By the last quarter of the century they had developed a viable imperial economy among the ports of West Africa, their Atlantic islands, and Western Europe—an economy based on sugar, black slaves, and gold. Africans panned the gold in the riverbeds of central and west-

Map 15.1 Overseas Exploration and Conquest, c. 1400–1600 ▶

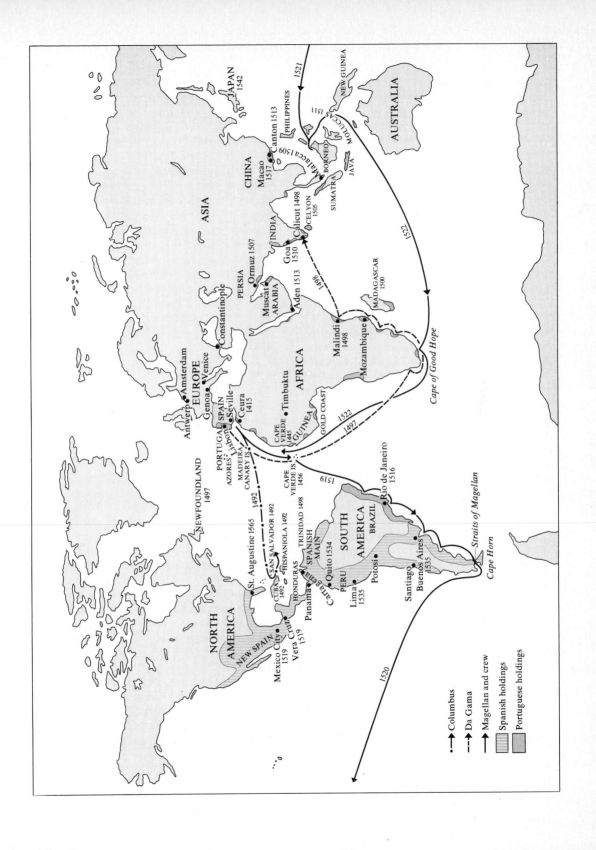

NORTH AMERICA

NEW SPAIN

Mexico City 1519
Vera Cruz 1519
HONDURAS
Panama
Cartagena
SPANISH MAIN
PERU
Quito 1534
Lima 1535
Potosí
Santiago
Buenos Aires 1535

SOUTH AMERICA
BRAZIL
Rio de Janeiro 1516

St. Augustine 1565
CUBA 1492
SAN SALVADOR 1492
HISPANIOLA 1492
TRINIDAD 1498

NEWFOUNDLAND 1497

1492

Straits of Magellan
Cape Horn

1519
1520
1522
1497

AZORES
MADEIRA
CANARY IS.
CAPE VERDE IS. 1456

PORTUGAL
Lisbon
SPAIN
Seville
Ceuta 1415
Genoa
Venice
Amsterdam
Antwerp
EUROPE
Constantinople

CAPE VERDE 1445
GUINEA
GOLD COAST
Timbuktu
AFRICA
Cape of Good Hope
1522
1497
1498

MADAGASCAR 1500
Mozambique
Malindi 1498

PERSIA
Muscat
ARABIA
Aden 1513
Ormuz 1507

ASIA

INDIA
Goa 1510
Calicut 1498
CEYLON 1505

CHINA
Macao 1517
Canton 1513

JAPAN 1542

MALACCA 1509
SUMATRA
BORNEO
JAVA
MOLUCCAS 1511
PHILIPPINES
NEW GUINEA

AUSTRALIA

1521

→ Columbus
→ Da Gama
→ Magellan and crew
   Spanish holdings
   Portuguese holdings

ern Africa, and the Portuguese purchased it at its source. They paid in cloth and slaves at a profit of at least 500 percent. Then the Portuguese transported the gold to Europe where they sold it for even more profit. Slaves figured not only in the purchase of gold but also in the production of sugar. In their Atlantic islands the Portuguese grew sugar cane, and little else by the end of the century, as a cash crop for European consumption, and slaves were imported from West Africa to do the work. There was also a lively trade in slaves to Portugal itself and elsewhere in southern Europe.

The Portuguese did not stop in western Africa. By 1488, Bartholomeu Dias had reached the southern tip of the African continent; a decade later Vasco da Gama sailed around the Cape of Good Hope and across the Indian Ocean to India. By discovering an all-water route to the Orient, Portugal broke the commercial monopoly of Eastern goods that Genoa and Venice had enjoyed.

In search of spices, the Portuguese went directly to the source, to India and the East Indies. As along the African coast, they established fortified trading posts—most notably at Goa on the western coast of India (Malabar) and at Malacca (now Singapore) in the Malay Peninsula.

Demand for spices was insatiable. Pepper and other spices are relatively unimportant items in the modern diet, but in the era before refrigeration, fresh meat was available only at slaughtering time, customarily twice a year. The rest of the year the only meat available, for those who could afford it at all, was dried, stringy, and tough; spices made meat and other foods palatable.

The infusion of Italian, particularly Genoese, investment and talent contributed to Portuguese expansion. As Genoese trade with the Near East, especially the Black Sea, shrank due to the Ottoman Turkish expansion, Genoese merchants shifted more and more of their capital and mercantile activities from the eastern to the western Mediterranean and the Atlantic, that is, to Spain and Portugal and their possessions overseas. This shift is evident in the life of Christopher Columbus (1451–1506), a Genoese sailor, who worked in Portugal before finally winning acceptance for his scheme to find a westward route to the spices of the East at the court of Castile in Spain. Initially, much of the Genoese investment was in the sugar plantations in Portuguese colonies in the Atlantic. The Portuguese gained not only Genoese capital, but also the expertise to put it to use. The Genoese had established their own sugar colonies in Cyprus and Crete two centuries before, and they knew from long experience what would work. The plantation system based on slave labor was an Italian import; only now the slaves were black Africans instead of Slavs, as they had often been in the eastern Mediterranean.

The Spanish Empire

Spain stumbled onto its overseas empire, which nonetheless proved to be the biggest and richest of any until the eighteenth century. Columbus won the support of Isabella, queen of Castile. But on his first voyage (1492) he landed on the large Caribbean island that he named *Española* (Little Spain). To the end of his life, even after subsequent voyages, Columbus believed that the West Indies were part of the East. Two forthcoming events would reveal that Columbus had discovered not a new route to the East, but new continents: Vasco Nuñez de Balboa's discovery of the Pacific Ocean at the Isthmus of Panama in 1513 and Ferdinand Magellan's circumnavigation of the globe (1520–1521) through the strait at the tip of South America bearing his name.

The Spanish found no spices in the New World, but they were more than compensated by the abundant land and the large quantities of precious metals. Stories of the existence of larger quantities of gold and silver to the west lured the Spaniards from their initial settlements in the Caribbean to Mexico. In 1519, Hernando Cortés landed on the Mexican coast with a small army; during two years

Isabella and Ferdinand. With the marriage of Ferdinand of Aragon to Isabella of Castile, Spain came into being as a nation. At the Battle of Granada, they defeated the last of the Islamic forces on the Spanish mainland. Columbus courted and won the patronage of Isabella. Monies that had previously been used to fight Islam were diverted to exploration. The wealth of the New World would repay her patronage beyond all expectation. *(Copyright reserved to H.M. The Queen)*

of campaigning he managed to defeat the native rulers, the Aztecs, and to conquer Mexico for the Spanish crown. A decade later, Francisco Pizarro achieved a similar victory over the mountain empire of the Incas in Peru. Both Cortés and Pizarro exploited the hostility that the subject tribes of Mexico and Peru felt toward their Aztec and Incan overlords, a strategy that accounts in large part for the Spaniards' success.

For good reasons, the Mexican and Peruvian conquests became the centers of the Spanish overseas empire. First, there were the gold hoards accumulated over the centuries by the rulers for religious and ceremonial purposes. And when these supplies were exhausted, the Spanish discovered silver at Potosí in Upper Peru in 1545 and at Za-

catecas in Mexico a few years later. From the middle of the century, the annual treasure fleets sailing to Spain became the financial bedrock of Philip II's war against the Muslim Turks and the Protestant Dutch and English.

Not only gold and silver lured Spaniards to the New World. The crusading tradition also acted as a spur. Cortés, Pizarro, and many of their followers were *hidalgos*—lesser gentry whose status depended on the possession of landed estates and whose training and experience taught that holy war was a legitimate avenue to wealth and power. Their fathers had conquered Granada, the last Muslim kingdom in Spain, in 1492; they had expelled the Jews the same year and had carried the Christian crusade across to North Africa. The conquest and conversion of the

Silver mines at Potosí, Sixteenth Century. The Spanish conquest of the Incas and the Aztecs filled the coffers of Spain with gold and silver. The native population was decimated, and most native art and artifacts were destroyed, regarded as heathen work beneath the Europeans' consideration. *(In the Library of the Hispanic Society of America, New York)*

pagan peoples of the New World was an extension of the crusading spirit that marked the five previous centuries of Spanish history. The rewards were what they had always been: the propagation of the true faith, service to the crown, handsome land grants, and control over the inhabitants, who would work the fields. The land was especially attractive in the sixteenth century because the number of hidalgos was increasing with the general rise in population, and the amount of land available to them at home was as a result shrinking.

The conquerors initially obtained two kinds of grants from the crown, *encomiendas* and *estancias*. The latter were land grants, either of land formerly belonging to the native priestly and noble castes, or of land in remoter and less fertile regions. Encomiendas were royal grants of authority over the natives. Those who received such authority, the *encomenderos*, promised to give protection and instruction in the Christian religion to their charges. In return they gained the power to extract labor and tribute from the peasant masses, who were worked beyond their capacity.

The royal grants of encomiendas during the first generation of Spanish settlement were partially responsible for the decimation within a century of European occupation of the native population in the New World. Between 1500 and 1600 the number of natives shrank from about twenty million to little more than two million. The major cause of this catastrophe, however, was not forced labor but the diseases introduced from Europe—dysentery, malaria, hookworm, smallpox—against which the natives had little or no natural resistance. Beginning in the 1540s the position of the natives gradually improved as the crown withdrew grants that gave authority over the natives and took increasing responsibility for controlling the Indians.

Power and wealth gradually concentrated in fewer and fewer hands. As the Spanish landholders lost authority over the native population to royal officials and their associates, the latter gained substantially in power and privilege. As recurrent depressions ruined smaller landowners, they were forced to sell out to their bigger neighbors. On their conversion to Christianity, the Indians were persuaded to give more and more land to the church. Thus, Spanish America became permanently divided between the privileged elite and the impoverished masses.

One group suffered even more than the Indians: the blacks. The natives at least escaped the degradation of slavery. But blacks were imported from Africa in increasing numbers, especially as the Indian population declined, to work as slaves in the fields and the mines. The Portuguese and, in the eighteenth century, the British were the most important slave traders. Africans were captured by rival black tribes in western Africa, then enslaved and sold to Europeans in ports along the West African coast. The Africans were then herded onto ships for passage to the New World under such brutal conditions that only about half of them survived. Those who did were sold at auction in the ports of the Caribbean and North America; sellers and buyers considered the age and physical condition of the slaves, with little or no regard for any other aspects of their well-being—family ties for instance.

The Price Revolution

Linked to overseas expansion was another phenomenon—an unprecedented inflation during the sixteenth century, known as the *price revolution*. Evidence is insufficient on the general rise in prices. However, cereal prices multiplied by as much as eight times or more in certain regions in the course of the sixteenth century, and they continued to rise, although more slowly, during the first half of the next century. After 1650 prices leveled off or fell in most places; this pattern continued throughout the eighteenth century in England and off and on in France up to the Revolution. Economic historians have generally assumed that the prices of goods other than cereals increased by half as much as grain prices. Since people at that time did not understand why prices rose so rapidly, inflation was not subject to control. On the contrary, the remedies governments applied, like currency debasement, often worsened the problem.

Like colonization, the price revolution played an enormous role in the commercial revolution and did, in fact, partially result from the silver mining conducted in New Spain. The main cause of the price revolution, however, was the population growth during the late fifteenth and sixteenth centuries.

The population of Europe almost doubled between 1460 and 1620, and then it leveled off and decreased in some places. The patterns of population growth and of cereal prices thus match in the sixteenth and seventeenth centuries. Until the middle of the seventeenth century the number of mouths to feed outran the capacity of agriculture to supply basic foodstuffs, causing the vast majority of people to live close to subsistence. Until food production could catch up with the increasing population, prices, especially those of the staple food, bread, would continue to rise.

Why population grew so rapidly in the fifteenth and sixteenth centuries is not known, but the reasons why the population declined in the seventeenth century are. By then, the population had so outgrown the food supply that scarcity began to take its toll. Malnourishment, starvation, and disease pushed the death rate higher than the birth rate. With time, of course, prices lowered as population and hence demand declined in the 1600s.

The other principal cause of the price revolution was *probably* the silver that, beginning in 1552, flowed into Europe from the New World via Spain. But as a cause, the influx of silver lies on shakier ground than the inflationary effects of an expanding population. The increases in production and consumption following the growth in population would, to some degree, have necessitated an increase in the money supply to accommodate the greater number of commercial transactions. At some point it is assumed that the influx of silver exceeded the necessary expansion of the money supply and itself began contributing to the inflation. The most that can now be said is that the price revolution was caused by *too many people with too much money chasing too few goods.* The effects of the price revolution were momentous.

The Expansion of Agriculture

The greatest effects of the price revolution were on the land. Food prices, rising roughly twice as much as the prices of other goods, spurred ambitious farmers to take advantage of the situation and to produce for the expanding market. The opportunity for profit drove some farmers to work harder and manage their land better. The impact of the price revolution follows from that incentive.

The Old Pattern of Farming

The effects of the price revolution on farming were governed by the general social and po-

litical conditions operating in any given region or country. The effects in England were one sort; among the Dutch, another; in France, Spain, and the Mediterranean, still another; and in the Holy Roman Empire east of the Elbe River, in Poland, and in Russia, yet a fourth type. These differences must be compared against a background of European agriculture as it was practiced before the price revolution.

All over Europe, landlords held their properties in the form of manors. A particular type of rural society and economy had evolved on these manors in the Late Middle Ages. By the fifteenth century, much manor land was held by peasant-tenants according to the terms of a tenure known in England as *copyhold.* The tenants had certain hereditary rights in the land in return for the performance of certain services and the payment of certain fees to the landlord. Principal among these rights was the use of the commons—the pasture, woods, and pond. For the copyholder, access to the commons often made the difference between subsistence and real want, because the land tilled on the manor might not produce enough to keep a family.

Arable land was worked according to ancient custom. The land was divided into strips, and each peasant of the manor was assigned a certain number of strips. This whole pattern of peasant tillage and rights in the commons was known as the *open-field system.* After changing little for centuries, it was met head-on by the incentives generated by the price revolution.

Enclosure

In England, landlords aggressively pursued the possibilities for profit resulting from the inflation of farm prices. This pursuit required far-reaching changes in ancient manorial agriculture, changes that are called *enclosure.* The open-field system was geared to providing subsistence for the local village and, as such, prevented large-scale farming for a distant market. In the open-field system, the commons could not be diverted to the production of crops for sale. Moreover, the division of the arable land into strips made it difficult to engage in profitable commercial agriculture.

English landlords in the sixteenth century fought a two-pronged attack against the open-field system in their attempts to transform their holdings into market-oriented, commercial ventures. First they deprived their tenant peasantry of the use of the commons; then they changed the conditions of tenure from copyhold to leasehold. Whereas copyhold was heritable and fixed, leasehold was not. When a lease came up for renewal, the landlord could raise the rent beyond the tenant's capacity to pay. Restriction of rights to the commons deprived the poor tenant of critically needed produce. Both acts of the landlord forced peasants off the manor or into the landlord's employ as farm laborers.

With tenants gone, fields could be incorporated into larger, more productive units. Subsistence farming gave way to commercial agriculture—the growing of a surplus for the marketplace. Landlords would either hire laborers to work recently enclosed fields or rent these fields to prosperous farmers in the neighborhood. Either way, landlords stood to gain. They could hire labor at bargain prices because of the swelling population and the large supply of peasants forced off the land by enclosure. If the landlords chose to rent out their fields, they also profited. Prosperous farmers who themselves grew for the market could afford to pay higher rents than the previous tenants, the subsistence farmers; and they were willing to pay more because farm prices tended to rise even faster than rents.

The Yeomanry in England

The existence of prosperous farmers, sometimes called *yeomen,* in English rural society was crucial to the commercialization of farming. Yeomen were men who may not have owned much land themselves, but who rented enough to produce a marketable surplus,

sometimes a substantial one. They emerged as a discernible rural group in the High Middle Ages and were a product of the unique English inheritance custom, observed by peasantry and gentry alike, of *primogeniture.* The eldest son inherited the land, and the younger sons had to fend for themselves. Thus the land remained undivided, and the heirs among the peasantry often had enough land to produce a surplus for market. Many a gentleman landowner enclosed his fields not to work them himself, but to rent them to neighboring yeomen at rates allowing him to keep abreast of spiraling prices. Yeomen were better suited to work the land than the landlord, depending on it as they did for their livelihood.

One other process growing out of the price revolution promoted the commercialization of farming. Rising prices forced less businesslike landlords, who did not take advantage of the profit to be made from farming, to sell property in order to meet current expenses. The conditions of the price revolution thus tended to put an increasing amount of land into more productive hands. But rural poverty and violence increased because of the mass evictions of tenant farmers.

Convertible Husbandry

The effects of the price revolution on agriculture in the Netherlands were as dramatic and important as those in England. The Dutch population had soared and the majority of people had moved to the cities by the seventeenth century. As a result, a situation unique in all Europe—the problem of land use—became vitally important, especially as there was so little land to start with. The Dutch continued their efforts to reclaim land from the sea, which began in the Middle Ages. More significant, however, was their development in the fifteenth and sixteenth centuries, of a new kind of farming, known as *convertible husbandry.* This farming system employed a series of innovations that replaced the old three-field system of crop rotation,

Peter Brueghel the Younger (1564–1638): Harvesting Scene. England and the Netherlands underwent major agricultural changes in the sixteenth and seventeenth centuries. The enclosure system in England intensified land use and led to commercialization of agriculture. Convertible husbandry in the Netherlands ensured that the land was engaged for diversified agriculture, with no plots of land remaining unused. *(Nelson Gallery-Atkins Museum, Kansas City, Mo.; Nelson Fund)*

which had left one-third of the land unused at any given time. The new techniques used all the land every year and provided a more diversified agriculture.

The techniques combined soil-depleting cereals with soil-restoring legumes and grazing. For a couple of years, a field would be planted in cereals; in the third year, peas or beans would be sown to return essential nitrogen to the soil; for the next four or five years, the field became pasture for grazing animals, whose manure would further restore the soil for replanting cereals to restart the cycle. Land thus returned to grain would produce much more than land used in the three-field system. These devices for increasing productivity, when exported from the Netherlands and applied in England and France between 1650 and 1750, were essential in the complicated process by which these countries eventually became industrialized. For industrialization requires an agriculture productive enough to feed large, nonfarming urban populations.

Agricultural Change in Eastern Europe

In the Europe that stretches from the Elbe River across the Baltic plain to Russia, the effects of the price revolution were as dramatic as they were in England. The Baltic plain played an essential role in the European economy in the fifteenth, sixteenth, and early seventeenth centuries. Because western Europeans continued to outrun their food supply (in some places until the middle of the seventeenth century), they turned to the Baltic for regular shipments of grain.

Thus the landlords in the Baltic plain became commercial farmers producing for an international market. This trade led to a reorganization in the region south and east of the Baltic. There, as in England, enclosure to produce an agricultural surplus took place on a vast scale. But in contrast to the English experience, the peasant-tenants who had engaged in subsistence farming on these lands for generations were not evicted; nor did they become farm laborers working for low wages. Instead they remained on the land, and the terms of their tenure gradually shifted toward serfdom. As in Spain, a two-caste society emerged, a world of noble landlords and serfs. But unlike Spain's, this society produced for the marketplace.

The Expansion of Trade and Industry

The conditions of the price revolution also caused trade and industry to expand. Population growth exceeding the capacity of local food supplies stimulated commerce in basic foodstuffs, for example the Baltic trade with western Europe. Equally important as a stimulus to trade and industry was the growing income of landlords, merchants, and in some instances, peasants. This income created a rising demand for consumer goods, which helps explain several activities already mentioned. For example, the Portuguese spice trade with the East and the sugar industry in the Portuguese islands developed because prosperous people wanted such products. Rising income also created a demand for farm products other than cereals—meat, cheese, fruit, wine, and vegetables. The resulting land use reduced the area available for grain production and contributed to the rise in bread prices, which meant even larger profits.

Another factor in the commercial and industrial expansion was the growth of the state. With increasing amounts of tax revenue to spend, the expanding monarchies of the sixteenth and seventeenth centuries bought more and more supplies—ships, weapons, uniforms, paper—and so spurred economic expansion.

The Putting-Out System

Along with commercial and industrial expansion came a change in the nature of the productive enterprise. Just as the price revolution produced, in the enclosure movement, a reorganization of agriculture and agrarian society, it similarly affected trade and manufacturing. The reorganization there took place especially in the faster-growing industries—woolen and linen textiles—where an increasingly large mass market outpaced supply and thus made prices rise. This basic condition of the price revolution operated, just as it did in food production, to produce expansion. In the textile industries, increasing demand promoted specialization. For example, eastern and southwestern England made woolens, and northwestern France and the Netherlands produced linen.

Markets tended to shift from local to regional or even to international, a condition that gave rise to the merchant-capitalist. Unlike local producers, the merchant-capitalists' operations extended across local and national boundaries. This mobility allowed these capitalists to buy or produce goods where costs were lowest and to sell where prices and volume were highest. Because of the size and range of a business, an individual capitalist could control the traditional local producers, who increasingly depended on him for the widespread marketing of their expanded production.

This procedure, which was well developed by the seventeenth century, gave rise to what is known as the *putting-out system* of production. The manufacture of woolen textiles is a good example of how the system worked. The merchant-capitalist would buy the raw wool from English landlords who had enclosed their manors to take advantage of the rising price of wool. The merchant's agents collected the wool and took it (put it out) to nearby villages for spinning, dyeing, and weaving. The work was done in the cottages of peasants, many of whom had been evicted from the surrounding manors as a result of enclosure and therefore had to take what work they could get at the lowest possible wages. When the wool was processed into cloth, it was picked up and shipped to market.

The putting-out system represents an important step in the evolution of capitalism. It was not industrial capitalism, because there were no factories and the work was done by hand rather than by power machinery; nevertheless, the putting-out system significantly breaks with the medieval guild system. The new merchant-capitalists saw that the work was performed in the countryside, rather than in the cities and towns, to avoid guild restrictions (on output, quality, pay, and working conditions). The distinction between a master and an apprentice who will someday replace the master, which is assumed in the guild framework, had given place to the distinction between the merchant-owner (the person who provided the capital) and the worker (the one who provided the labor in return for wages and would probably never be an owner).

Enclosure also served to capitalize industry. Mass evictions lowered the wages of cottage workers because labor was plentiful. This condition provided additonal incentive on the part of the merchant-capitalist to invest in cottage industry. But the changes in farming were much more important in the economic development of Europe than the changes in industry, because agriculture represented a much larger share of total wealth than industry did.

Innovations in Business

Accompanying the emergence of the merchant-capitalist and the putting-out system was a cluster of other innovations in business life. Banking operations grew more sophisticated, making it possible for depositors to pay their debts by issuing written orders to their banks to make transfers to their creditors' accounts—the origins of the modern check. Accounting methods also improved. The widespread use of double-entry bookkeeping made errors immediately evident and gave a clear picture of the financial position of a commercial enterprise. Although known in the ancient world, double-entry bookkeeping was not widely practiced in the West until the fourteenth century. In this and other business practices the lands of southern Europe, especially Italy, were the forerunners; their accounting techniques spread to the rest of Europe in the sixteenth century.

The fourteenth century also saw the development of business practices related to shipping. A system of maritime insurance, without which investors would have been highly reluctant to risk their money on expensive vessels, evolved in Florence. By 1400, maritime insurance had become a regular item of the shipping business, and it was destined to play a major role in the opening of Atlantic trade. At least equally important to overseas expansion was the form of business enterprise known as the joint-stock company, which allowed small investors to buy shares in a venture. These companies made possible the accumulation of the large amounts of capital needed for large-scale operations, like the building and deployment of merchant fleets, which were quite beyond the resources of one person.

Map 15.2 Industrial Centers in the Sixteenth Century ▶

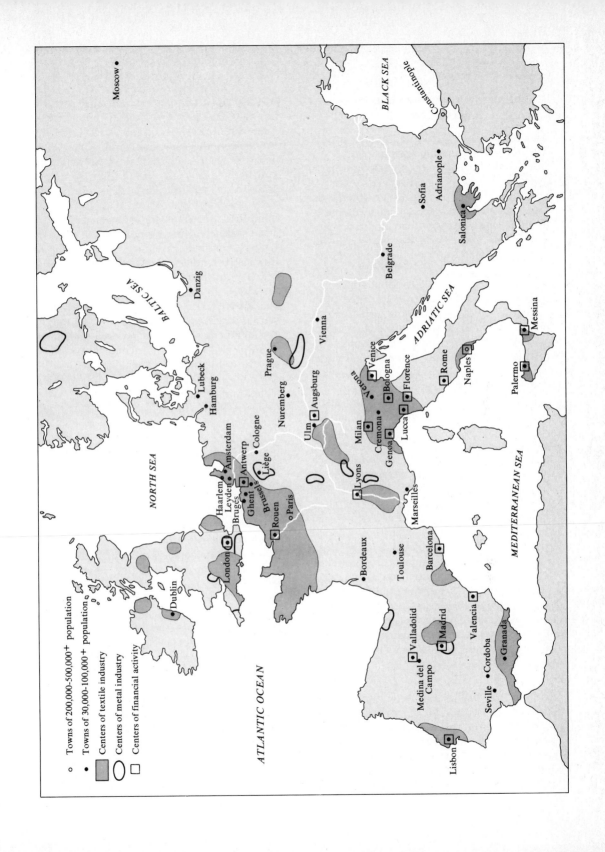

MEDITERRANEAN SEA

ATLANTIC OCEAN

NORTH SEA

BALTIC SEA

BLACK SEA

ADRIATIC SEA

Moscow

Danzig

Lübeck

Hamburg

Dublin

London

Amsterdam

Haarlem

Leyden

Bruges

Ghent

Brussels

Antwerp

Cologne

Liège

Paris

Rouen

Nuremberg

Prague

Vienna

Ulm

Augsburg

Lyons

Milan

Verona

Cremona

Genoa

Venice

Bologna

Florence

Lucca

Rome

Naples

Palermo

Messina

Marseilles

Bordeaux

Toulouse

Barcelona

Valencia

Madrid

Valladolid

Medina del Campo

Cordoba

Seville

Granada

Lisbon

Belgrade

Sofia

Adrianople

Salonica

Constantinople

o Towns of 200,000-500,000+ population
• Towns of 30,000-100,000+ population
   Centers of textile industry
   Centers of metal industry
   Centers of financial activity

Different Patterns of Commercial Development

The response to the price revolution in trade and industry differed in various parts of Europe—and the different responses hinged again on social and political conditions. In both the United Provinces (the Netherlands) and England there were far fewer strictures on trade and industry than in France and Spain. Thus, in the sixteenth and seventeenth centuries England and the United Provinces were better placed than France and Spain to take advantage of the favorable conditions for business expansion. In the United Provinces, this favorable position resulted from the weakness of feudal culture and values in comparison to commercial ones; other factors were its small land area and a far larger percentage of urban population than elsewhere in western Europe.

England's advantage derived from a different source: not the weakness of the landed gentry, but its habits. Primogeniture operated among those who owned large estates just as it did among the yeomanry, with much the same effect. Younger sons were forced to make their fortunes elsewhere. Those who did so by going into business would often benefit from an infusion of venture capital that came from their elder brothers' landed estates. And of course capital was forthcoming from such quarters because of the profitable nature of English farming. In a reverse process, those who made fortunes in trade would typically invest money in land and rise gradually into landed society. Those skills that had brought wealth in commerce would then be applied to new estates, usually with equal success.

England and the Netherlands In both England and the United Provinces the favorable conditions led to large-scale commercial expansion. In the 1590s the Dutch devised a new ship, the *fluit* or flyboat, to handle bulky grain shipments at the lowest possible cost. This innovation allowed them to capture the Baltic trade, which became a principal source

of their phenomenal commercial expansion between 1560 and 1660. Equally dramatic was their commercial penetration of the Orient. Profits from the European carrying trade built ships that allowed them first to challenge and then to displace the Portuguese in the spice trade with the East Indies during the early seventeenth century. The Dutch chartered the United East India Company in 1602 and established trading posts in the islands, which were the beginnings of a Dutch empire that lasted until World War II.

The English traded throughout Europe in the sixteenth and seventeenth centuries, especially with Spain and the Netherlands. The staples of this trade were raw wool and woolens, but increasingly they included such items as ships and guns. The seventeenth century saw the foundation of a British colonial empire along the Atlantic seaboard in North America from Maine to the Carolinas and in the West Indies, where the English managed to dislodge the Spanish in some places.

In both England and the United Provinces, government promoted the interests of business. In the late sixteenth and early seventeenth centuries the northern provinces of the Spanish Netherlands, centered around Holland, won their independence from Spain in a protracted struggle. Political power in these so-called United Provinces passed increasingly into the hands of an urban patriciate of merchants and manufacturers based in cities like Delft, Haarlem, and especially Amsterdam. These urban interests pursued public policies that served their pocketbooks. The southern provinces of the Netherlands (Flanders) and Antwerp, their commercial capital, remained under Spanish domination. From the 1590s the Dutch, as the inhabitants of the United Provinces were called, sent ships to close the Scheldt (the river linking Antwerp to the North Sea) to commercial traffic. This act dealt a fatal blow to the economic fortunes of the city that had dominated trade between northern and southern Europe and between England and the Continent in the late fifteenth and much of the sixteenth centuries. Antwerp's position of leadership as a trading

Frans Hals (c. 1580–1666): Banquet of the Officers of the St. George Civic Guard Company. Hals's painting captures the new merchant "princes" of the Netherlands. They lived the good life surrounded by worldly products of the best quality. They did not concern themselves with theories of "divine right." Instead, as merchants, they were most interested in profits. *(Frans Halsmuseum, Haarlem, The Netherlands)*

center passed to Amsterdam, and later to London and Hamburg. The founding of the Dutch East India Company and the Bank of Amsterdam in the first decade of the seventeenth century also stemmed from an alliance between business and government for their mutual interests. The Bank of Amsterdam expanded credit, lowered interest rates, and increased confidence. The Dutch East India Company regulated trade, reduced wasteful competition between formerly independent traders, and hence consolidated investment.

In seventeenth-century England the central government increasingly took the side of the capitalist producer. At the beginning of the century the king had imposed feudal fees on landed property, acted against enclosures, and granted monopolies in trade and manufacture to court favorites, which restricted opportunities for investment. Also the king spent revenues on maintaining an unproductive aristocracy. But by the end of the century, due to the revolutionary transfer of power from the king to Parliament, economic policy more closely reflected the interests of big business, whether agricultural or commercial. Landowners no longer paid feudal dues to the king. Enclosure went on unimpeded, in fact abetted, by parliamentary enactment. The Bank of England, founded in 1694, brought the same benefits to English investors that the Bank of Amsterdam had been offering the Dutch for almost a century.

The Navigation Act, first passed in 1651, allowed all English shippers to carry goods anywhere, replacing the old system that had restricted trade with certain areas to specific traders. The Act also required that all goods be carried in English ships, allowing merchants, as Christopher Hill writes, "to buy English and colonial exports cheap and sell them dear abroad, to buy foreign goods cheap and sell them dear in England."[1] English shippers also gained the profits of the carrying trade, one factor leading to the displacement of the Dutch by the English as the leading power in international commerce after 1660.

France and Spain France benefited from commercial and industrial expansion, but not to the same degree as England. A principal reason for this was the aristocratic structure of French society. Family ties and social intercourse between gentry and merchants, such as existed in England, were largely absent in France. Consequently, the French aristocracy remained contemptuous of commerce. Also inhibiting economic expansion were the guilds—remnants of the Middle Ages that restricted competition and production. In France there was relatively less room than in England for the merchant capitalist operating outside the guild structures.

Spain presents an even clearer example of failure to grasp the opportunities afforded by the price revolution. By the third quarter of the sixteenth century, Spain possessed the makings of economic expansion: unrivaled amounts of capital in the form of silver, a large and growing population, rising consumer demand, and a vast overseas empire. These factors did not bear fruit because the Spanish value system regarded business as a form of social heresy. The Spanish held in high esteem those gentlemen who possessed land gained through military service and crusading ardor, which enabled them to live on rents and privileges. So commerce and industry remained contemptible pursuits.

Numerous wars in the sixteenth century (with France, the Lutheran princes, the Ottoman Turks, the Dutch, and the English)

put an increasing strain on the Spanish treasury, even with the annual shipments of silver from the New World. Spain spent its resources on maintaining and extending its imperial power and Catholicism, rather than on investing in economic expansion. In the end, the wars cost even more than Spain could handle. The Dutch, for a time, and the English and the French, more permanently, displaced Spain as the great power. The English and the Dutch had taken advantage of the opportunities presented by the price revolution; the Spanish had not.

The Growth of Capitalism

What Is Capitalism?

The changes described—especially in England and the Netherlands—represent a crucial stage in the development of the modern economic system known as *capitalism*. This is a system of *private enterprise*: the main economic decisions (what, how much, where, and at what price to produce, buy, and sell) are made by private individuals in their capacity as either owners, workers, or consumers. Capitalism is also said to be a system of *free enterprise*: the basic decisions are not left to individuals only; these decisions are also made in response to market forces. People are free, in other words, to obey the law of supply and demand. When goods and labor are scarce, prices and wages rise; when they are plentiful, prices and wages fall.

In the Middle Ages, capitalistic enterprise had not been widespread because the market, and therefore the operation of market forces, were severely restricted. The vast majority of people lived as self-sufficient subsistence farmers (peasants or serfs) on the land. There was some trade and a few small cities, especially in Italy, where capitalistic enterprise was conducted, but this commerce accounted for only a tiny fraction of total economic activity. Even in the cities, capitalistic forms of enterprise were hampered by guild restrictions, which set limits on production, wages, and prices without regard for market forces. In addition, the economic decay of the fourteenth and early fifteenth centuries did not predispose those who had surplus money to gamble on the future.

But conditions changed in certain quarters beginning in the fifteenth and sixteenth centuries, generating the incentive to invest—to take risks for future profit rather than to consume. This process was due, more than anything else, to the economic situation prevailing in Europe between 1450 and 1600.

The Fostering of Mercantile Capitalism

Several conditions fostered a sustained incentive to invest and reinvest—a basic factor in the emergence of modern capitalism. One was the price revolution stemming from a supply of basic commodities that could not keep pace with rising demand. Prices continued to climb, creating the most powerful incentive of all to invest rather than to consume. Why spend now, those with surplus wealth must have asked, when investment in commercial farming, mining, shipping, and publishing (to name a few important outlets) is almost certain to yield greater wealth in the future? The price revolution reduced the risk involved in investment, thus helping to overcome the wealthy's resistance to engaging in capitalistic enterprise.

Another condition that encouraged investment was that wealth was distributed in a way that promoted investment. Three distinct patterns of distribution worked to this effect. First, inflation widened the gap between rich and poor during the sixteenth century; the rich who chose to invest garnered increasing amounts of wealth, which probably added to their incentive to go on investing. Because of the growing population and the resulting shortage of jobs, employers could pay lower and lower wages; thus, again, their profits increased, encouraging reinvestment. Merchant capitalists were an important group of investors who gained from these factors.

As they grew, they were able to exercise a controlling influence in the marketplace because they operated on a large scale, from regional to international; thus they were able to dictate terms of production and employment, displacing the local guilds. This displacement represents another factor in the pattern of wealth distribution (and redistribution) favorable to investment and growth. Mercantile capitalism did not benefit all alike; in fact it produced increasing inequities between rich and poor, owners and workers, independent merchant-capitalists and local guildsmen.

The second pattern of wealth distribution that encouraged investment grew out of the practice of primogeniture wherever (as in England) it was the unwritten custom. The concentration of inherited property in the hands of the eldest child (usually the oldest son) meant that he had sufficient wealth to be persuaded to invest at least part of it. Any younger sons were left to make their own way in the world and often turned their drive and ambition into profits.

Finally, a pattern of international distribution of wealth promoted investment in some lands. The classic example is that of Spain in relation, say, to England. Spain in the sixteenth century devoted its wealth and energies to religious war and empire and relied on producers elsewhere for many of its supplies. So Spanish treasure was exported to England to pay for imports, stimulating investment there rather than in Spain. Capitalism did not develop everywhere at the same pace, and as the Spanish case shows, the very conditions that discouraged it in one place encouraged it somewhere else.

Another stimulus for investment came from government—and this occurred in two ways. First, governments acted as giant consumers whose appetites throughout the early modern period were expanding. Merchants who supplied governments with everything from guns to frescoes not only prospered, but were led to reinvest because of the constancy and growth of government demand. Governments also sponsored new forms of investment, whether to supply the debauched taste for new luxuries at the king's court or to meet the requirements of the military. Private investors also reaped incalculable advantages from overseas empires. Colonies supplied cheap raw materials and cheap (slave) labor and served as markets for exports. They greatly stimulated the construction of both ships and harbor facilities and the sale of insurance.

The second government stimulus was state policies meant to increase investment, which they no doubt sometimes, although not always, did. Collectively, these policies constitute what is known as *mercantilism:* the conscious pursuit by governments of those courses supposed to augment national wealth and power. One characteristic expression of mercantilism was the pursuit of a favorable balance of international payments. According to conventional wisdom, wealth from trade was measured in gold and silver, of which there was believed to be a more or less fixed quantity. The state's goal in international trade became to sell more abroad than it bought, that is, to establish a favorable balance of payments. When the amount received for sales abroad was greater than that spent for purchases, the difference would be an influx of precious metal into the state. By this logic, mercantilists were led to argue for the goal of national sufficiency: a country should try to supply most of its own needs to keep imports to a minimum. This argument, of course, ignored the fact that in international trade, the more a country buys, the more it can sell. The English were the first to see this fact and relinquish mercantilistic thinking, if only for a time, during the second half of the seventeenth century.

Mercantilism did have a positive side. Governments increased economic activity by employing the poor, subsidizing new industries, and chartering companies to engage in overseas trade. Particularly valuable were the steps taken by states to break down local trade barriers, such as guild regulations and internal tariffs, in an attempt to create national markets and internal economic unity.

The English also saw that mercantilistic calculations of national wealth should be made over the long run. For example, Thomas Mun (1571–1641) argued that a country might import more than it exported in the short run and still come out ahead in the end, because raw materials that are imported and then reprocessed for export will eventually yield a handsome profit.

In addition, Thomas Mun was one of the first to see the virtues of *consumerism,* a phenomenon that is still extremely important for achieving sustained economic growth. Speaking of foreign trade, he maintained that the more English merchants did to advertise English goods to potential customers, the greater the overseas market for those goods would be. In other words, demand can be *created.* Just as there is an urge to invest and make profits, so there is an appetite to consume and enjoy the products of industry, and both inclinations have played their part in the growth of capitalism. Nor was the message restricted to the foreign market. Between 1660 and 1750 England became the world's first consumer society: more and more people had more and more money to spend, and they acquired a taste for conspicuous consumption (which had always before been confined to the aristocracy). Discretionary goods were available—lace, tobacco, housewares, flowers—and consumers wanted them. Concomitantly, just as today, the more stimulus there was to buy, the harder the consumer worked, which induced further growth.

The price revolution, the concentration of wealth in private hands, and government activity combined to provide the foundation for sustained investment and for the emergence of mercantile capitalism. This new force in the world should not be confused with industrial capitalism. The latter evolved with the first industrial revolution in eighteenth-century England, but mercantile capitalism paved the way for it.

Chronology 15.1 The Commercial Revolution

1394–1460	Henry the Navigator, prince of Portugal, encourages expansion into Africa for gold and his anti-Muslim crusade
1430	The Portuguese expand into the Canaries and the Azores
1488	Bartholomeu Dias reaches the tip of Africa
1492	Christopher Columbus reaches the Caribbean island of Española on his first voyage; the Jews are expelled from Spain; Granada, the last Muslim kingdom in Spain, is conquered, ending the reconquest
1497	Vasco da Gama sails around Cape of Good Hope (Africa) to India
1509	The Portuguese defeat the Muslim fleet at Diu in the Indian Ocean
1513	Balboa discovers the Pacific Ocean at the Isthmus of Panama
1519–1521	Hernando Cortés conquers the Aztecs in Mexico
1520–1521	Magellan's soldiers circumnavigate the globe
1531–1533	Francisco Pizarro conquers the Incas in Peru
1545	Silver is discovered by the Spaniards at Potosí, Peru
1552	Silver from the New World flows into Europe via Spain, contributing to a price revolution
1590s	The Dutch develop shipping carriers for grain
1602–1609	The Dutch East India Company is founded; the Bank of Amsterdam is founded, expanding credit
1651	The Navigation Act is passed in England to accomplish the goals of mercantilism
1694	The Bank of England is founded

Seventeenth-Century Decline and Renewal

Population began to decline in Spain as early as the 1590s, and by the second quarter of the seventeenth century, it was declining throughout Europe. The decline resulted because during the price revolution demand continued to outrun supply, prices rose, and real wages fell. The diet of the masses deteriorated because they could not earn enough to buy sufficient bread. Bad harvests produced massive famines, and cities were overgrown and increasingly unsanitary. When plague struck, as it continued to do periodically, it did so among a weakened populace and took more lives. Finally, there was the Thirty Years' War (1618–1648) which ravaged the Holy Roman Empire and reduced its population by at least one-third.

The economic consequences of these factors were quick to follow. Prices fell and there was general economic dislocation. The new Atlantic powers, however, responded in a way that would lead to their recovery—England by the last quarter of the century and France by the 1730s. English and French farmers turned increasingly to enclosure and the application of the Dutch technique of convertible husbandry. Initially, these efforts attempted to make up for falling prices by increasing productivity. But over the long run they had the effect of increasing production and of sustaining a growing population.

By the second quarter of the eighteenth century, the population of western Europe was once more growing—but with significant differences from the earlier increase. The food supply tended to keep pace with rising demand, so the prices of basic foodstuffs stabilized and even declined. This achievement had enormous impact on the subsequent history of France and England. At last, enough was produced to feed a growing population without a rise in prices. Less income would have to be spent on food at a time when national income was rising because of expanded production for the needs of a growing population.

Given these developments, who benefited, why, and to what effect? First of all, many peasants could for the first time produce a surplus for market. This increased production meant a rise in income. The largest farmers, curiously enough, probably did not benefit, unless they were also landlords; they had long been producing for the market, sometimes for generations, and their increased production did not make up for the falling off of farm prices.

Second, the landlords' income increased. They had land to rent to the growing number of farmers who engaged in commercial farming and whose growing profits enabled them to pay even higher rents. This tendency was especially prevalent in France. There, enclosure was not widespread, and inherited land was divided among all the children in a family, a practice called *partible inheritance*. As a result, more and more peasants, because of population growth, sought a livelihood from the soil.

Third, there was a growth in the incomes of everyone whose earnings were in excess of the price of bread. This group would have included at least a majority of the urban population because, of course, bread prices were falling.

Thus the new agronomy produced a situation in which *more and more people had more and more money to spend on, or to invest in, things other than food*—namely, industry and its products. This increasing income manifested itself in rising demand for goods and services. This demand was one of the basic preconditions for the Industrial Revolution in the eighteenth and early nineteenth centuries, particularly in England. Before large-scale industry could come into being, a market for its products was necessary.

In the process of industrialization, England gained the advantage over France largely because of the different patterns that agriculture took in the two countries. Beginning in the 1780s, French agriculture could not sustain the pattern that it had shared with England from the 1730s. By the 1780s, too many people were living on the land in France to allow adequate surpluses in years of poor harvest. At such times, peasants produced only enough to feed themselves, if that, and shortages caused bread prices to soar. Peasant incomes shrank from the lack of a marketable surplus. And higher bread prices reduced consumer spending power. The momentum for industrialization weakened or dissolved, a situation prevailing until the next century. Partible inheritance in France slowed industrial development. Primogeniture and enclosure in England speeded it up.

Toward a Global Economy

The transformations considered in this chapter were among the most momentous in the world's history. In an unprecedented development that may never be repeated, one small part of the world, western Europe, had become lord of the sea-lanes, master of many lands throughout the globe, and the banker and profit-taker in an emerging world economy. Western Europe's global hegemony was to last well into this century. In conquering and settling new lands, Europeans exported Western culture around the globe, a process that accelerated in the twentieth century.

The effects of overseas expansion were profound. The native populations of the New World were decimated. As a result of the labor shortage, millions of blacks were imported from Africa to work as slaves on plantations and in mines. Black slavery would produce large-scale effects on culture, politics, and society to the present day.

The widespread circulation of plant and animal life had great consequences. Horses and cattle were introduced to the New World. (So amazed were the Aztecs to see man on horseback that at first they thought horse and rider were one demonic creature.) In return the Old World was introduced to corn, the tomato, and most important, the potato, which was to become a staple of the northern European diet. Manioc, from which tapioca is made, was transplanted from the New World to Africa where it helped sustain the population.

Western Europe was wrenched out of the subsistence economy of the Middle Ages and launched on a course of sustained economic growth. This transformation resulted from the grafting of traditional forms, like primogeniture and holy war, onto new forces, like global exploration, price revolution, and convertible husbandry. Out of this change emerged the beginnings of a new economic system, mercantile capitalism, which in large measure provided the economic thrust for European world predominance and paved the way for the Industrial Revolution of the eighteenth and nineteenth centuries.

Notes

1. Christopher Hill, *Reformation to Industrial Revolution* (Baltimore: Penguin, 1969), pp. 159–160.

Suggested Reading

Appleby, Joyce, *Economic Thought and Ideology in Seventeenth-Century England* (1978). The invention of a science of economics in the context of an emerging capitalist society.

Boxer, C. R., *The Portuguese Seaborne Empire 1415–1825* (1969). A comprehensive treatment.

Cipolla, Carlo M., *Guns, Sails and Empires* (1965). Connections between technological innovation and overseas expansion, 1400 to 1700.

Davis, David Brion, *The Problem of Slavery in Western Culture* (1966). Authoritative and highly suggestive.

Davis, Ralph, *The Rise of the Atlantic Economies* (1973). A reliable recent survey of early modern economic history.

Elliott, J. H., *The Old World and the New 1492–1650* (1972). The impact of America on early modern Europe.

Haley, K. H. D., *The Dutch in the Seventeenth Century* (1972). A very readable, informative survey.

Hanke, Lewis, *The Spanish Struggle for Justice in the Conquest of America* (1949). A treatment of the priestly view of Indian rights under Spanish rule.

Hill, Christopher, *Reformation to Industrial Revolution* (1969). A concise Marxist interpretation of English economic development.

Kamen, H., *The Iron Century* (1971). Insight into the social and class basis of economic change.

Parry, J. H., *The Age of Reconnaissance* (1963). A short survey of exploration.

Wilson, C., *England's Apprenticeship, 1600–1763* (1965). Authoritative account.

Review Questions

1. What are the links between the Middle Ages and early modern overseas expansion? What were the new forces for expansion operating in early modern Europe?

2. Compare Spanish and Portuguese overseas expansion in terms of their motives, their areas of expansion, and the character of the two empires.

3. What is the connection between the price revolution and overseas expansion? What was the principal cause of the price revolution? Why?

4. What was *enclosure*? How did the price revolution encourage it?

5. Compare open-field farming and enclosure in terms of who worked the land, how the land was worked, and what the results of each method were.

6. What was *convertible husbandry*, where did it originate, and why was it such an important innovation?

7. What factors favored Spanish agricultural and commercial development, and why, nevertheless, did it stall later?

8. Compare farming in England with that in France and Spain. Why did the English method yield the most?

9. What was the *putting-out system*? What were its advantages over the guilds and its long-term effects?

10. What is *mercantile capitalism*? What three patterns of the distribution of wealth fostered its development?

11. How did economic decline in the seventeenth century provide conditions for the subsequent economic recovery and progress? Where was this progress greatest, and why?

12. How did the commercial revolution produce a global economy? What were its effects?

16

The Rise of Sovereignty: Transition to the Modern State

*F*rom the thirteenth to the seventeenth century a new and unique form of political organization emerged in the West: the dynastic or national state, which harnessed the power of its nobility and the material resources of its territory. Neither capitalism nor technology could have enabled the West to dominate other lands and peoples had it not been for the power of the European states. They channeled and organized violence into the service of national power by directing the energies of the ruling elite into national service and international competition. A degree of domestic stability ensued, and the states encouraged commerce and industry, which could in turn be taxed. Although they nurtured the aristocracy, many states also required that both lord and peasant serve in national armies for the purpose of foreign conquest as well as for defense.

At every turn the pivotal figures in the development of states were the kings. Europeans, whether landed or urban, grudgingly gave allegiance to these ambitious, and at times ruthless, authority figures. In general, a single monarch seemed the only alternative to the even more brutal pattern of war and disorder so basic to the governing habits of the feudal aristocracy. In the process of increasing their own power, the kings of Europe not only subordinated the aristocracy to their needs and interests but also gained firm control over the Christian churches in their territories. Gradually, religious zeal was made compatible with and largely supportive of the state's goals, rather than papal dictates or even universal Christian aspirations.

Various components characterized the dynastic states of the early modern period. All states required a language that was dominant enough to be used for government. Moreover, states maintained standing armies as soon as the system of tax collection gave them a sufficient economic foundation to do so. If kings were to subdue local aristocrats and terrify other kings, armies were essential, and they were established by the seventeenth century in Spain, France, and finally late in the century in England. These domestic armies, often used in conjunction with foreign mercenaries, were crucial to the maintenance and extension of state power. In many early modern states a vast bureaucracy coordinated and administered the activities of the central government and its army. Another characteristic was that the creation of a strong central government required a struggle between the monarch and localized systems of power, feudal aristocrats, bishops, and even occasionally representative assemblies.

Where early modern European monarchs succeeded in subduing, destroying, or reconstituting local aristocratic and ecclesiastical power systems, dynastic states were formed. Where the monarchs failed, as they did in the Holy Roman Empire and Italy, no viable states evolved until well into the nineteenth century. Those failures derived from the independent authority of local princes or city-states, and in the case of Italy, from the decentralizing influence of papal authority. In the Holy Roman Empire, feudal princes found allies in the newly formed Protestant communities, and in such a situation, religion worked as a decentralizing force. Successful early modern kings had to bring the churches under their authority and subordinate religion to the needs of the state. They did so not by separating church and state (as was later done in the United States), but rather by linking their subjects' religious identity with the national identity. For example, in England by the late seventeenth century, to be a true Protestant was to be a true English subject, while in Spain the same equation operated for the Catholic (as opposed to the Muslim or the Jew, who came to be regarded as non-Spanish).

The elements that made up the early modern state evolved slowly and at first haltingly. In the thirteenth century, most Europeans still identified themselves with their localities: their villages, manors, or towns. They gave political allegiance to their local lord or bishop. They knew little, and probably cared less, about the activities of the king and his court, except when the monarch called on them for taxes or military service. By the late seven-

teenth century, in extreme contrast, aristocrats in many European countries defined the extent of their political power in terms of their relationship to king and court. By then the lives of very ordinary people were being affected by national systems of tax collection, by the doctrines and practices of national churches, and by conscription.

Increasingly prosperous town dwellers, the bourgeoisie, realized also that their prosperity hinged, in part, on court-supported foreign and domestic policies. If the king assisted their commercial ventures, the bourgeoisie gave their support to the growth of a strong central state. Only in two states, England and the Netherlands, did the strikingly successful bourgeoisie manage to redistribute political power so that by the late seventeenth century, it could be shared by a monarchy (or a social oligarchy) and a powerful representative assembly.

The Rise of Hapsburg Spain

The Spanish political experience of the sixteenth century stands as one of the most extraordinary in the history of modern Europe. Spanish kings built a dynastic state that burst through its frontiers and encompassed Portugal, part of Italy, the Netherlands, and enormous areas in the New World. Spain became an intercontinental empire—the first in the West since Roman times.

In the eighth and ninth centuries, the Muslims controlled all Spain except for some tiny Christian kingdoms in the far north. Beginning in the ninth century, the Christian states began a 500-year struggle—the Reconquest—to drive the Muslims from the Iberian Peninsula. By the middle of the thirteenth century, Granada in the south was all that remained of Muslim lands in Spain.

Hispania as a concept and geographical area existed in Roman times, and citizens of Portugal, Castile, Aragon, Catalonia, and Andalusia, to name only the larger and more important areas of the peninsula, recognized a certain common identity—no more, no less.

Until 1469, Spain had not existed as a political entity. In that year, Ferdinand, heir to the throne of Aragon, married his more powerful and prosperous cousin, Isabella, heiress of Castile. Yet even after the unification of Castile and the Crown of Aragon, relations among the various and fiercely independent provinces of Spain were often tense.

Rich from the wool trade and more populous than other provinces, Castile became the heart of Spain. But the Crown of Aragon (Catalonia, Aragon, and Valencia) supplied commercial expertise to the union, as well as control over the western Mediterranean. Ferdinand's Aragon also contributed a vibrant tradition of constitutional government characterized by a concern for individual and class rights, as distinct from the rights of kings. Perhaps no territory in Europe possessed a more vital set of representative and judicial institutions. Aragonese independence is best summed up in the famous oath said to be taken by its nobility to the king: "We who are as good as you swear to you who are no better than we to accept you as our king and sovereign lord, provided you observe all our liberties and laws; but, if not, not."[1] Obviously any monarch set upon increasing royal authority in Aragon would have to proceed cautiously.

Ferdinand and Isabella

Ferdinand and Isabella displayed extraordinary statecraft in managing the various areas within their newly formed land. The success of their rule (1479–1516) laid the foundations for Spanish empire and Spanish domination of European affairs throughout the sixteenth century. They used Castile as their power base and set about ridding it of its military caste—those aristocrats who, in effect, operated from their fortified castles like private kings waging at will their private wars. In contrast, Ferdinand and Isabella rationalized and modernized the Spanish state's government.

Beginning in the late fifteenth century, Castilian dominance over government and administration was recognized and continually preserved, yet Aragonese rights were left more or less intact. Ferdinand and Isabella never established a unified state: there was no common currency and no single legal or tax system. Commonality of interests, rather than of administration and law, united Spain; and certain policies of Ferdinand and Isabella contributed decisively to this unity. They sought the reconquest of Spanish territory still held by the Muslims, and concomitantly they sought to assert the uniquely Christian character of the peninsula, to bring the Spanish church into alliance with the state.

Given the territorial and legal divisions within Spain, it is understandable why the church became the only universal institution in Spain, and why its legal arm, the Inquisition, played such an important role in the intellectual and religious life of this most disparate of kingdoms. It was most important for the development of strong monarchy that the Spanish rulers bring the church's interests in line with their own. Ferdinand and Isabella's alliance with the church and their war against the Muslims in the southern portion of the peninsula were interrelated. A crusade against the Muslim infidel presupposed an energetic church and a deep and militant Catholicism with the rulers committed to the aims of the church, and the church to the aims of the rulers. While other Europeans, partly under the impact of the Renaissance, questioned the church's leadership and attacked its corruption, the Catholic Kings (as Ferdinand and Isabella were called) reformed the church, making it responsive to their needs and also invulnerable to criticism. Popular piety and royal policy led in 1492 to a victory over Granada, the last Muslim-ruled territory in Spain.

The five-hundred-year struggle for Christian hegemony in the Iberian Peninsula left the Spanish fiercely religious and strongly suspicious of foreigners. Despite centuries of intermarriage with non-Christians, by the early sixteenth century, purity of blood and

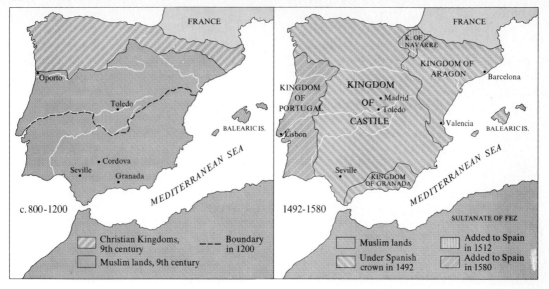

FRANCE

Oporto

Toledo

BALEARIC IS.

MEDITERRANEAN SEA

Cordova

Seville
Granada

c. 800-1200

▨ Christian Kingdoms,   ---- Boundary
   9th century   in 1200
☐ Muslim lands, 9th century

FRANCE

K. OF NAVARRE

KINGDOM OF ARAGON   Barcelona

KINGDOM OF PORTUGAL

KINGDOM OF CASTILE

Madrid
Toledo

Valencia

BALEARIC IS.

Lisbon

MEDITERRANEAN SEA

Seville

KINGDOM OF GRANADA

1492-1580

SULTANATE OF FEZ

☐ Muslim lands   ▨ Added to Spain
                            in 1512
▨ Under Spanish   ▨ Added to Spain
   crown in 1492   in 1580

Map 16.1 Spain during the Ninth to Sixteenth Centuries

orthodoxy of faith became necessary for, and synonymous with Spanish identity. In 1492 the Jews and the Muslims were physically expelled from Spain or forced to convert. This process of detection and conversion was supervised by the church, or more precisely, by the Inquisition. Run by clerics but responsive to state policies, the Inquisition existed to enforce religious uniformity and to ferret out the increasing numbers of Muslims and Jews who ostensibly converted to Catholicism but who remained secretly loyal to their own religions. The Inquisition developed extremely sophisticated systems of interrogation, used its legal right to torture as well as burn heretics, and eventually extended its authority to Christians as well. It represented the dark side of Spanish genius at conquest and administration, and its shadow stretched down through the centuries well into the twentieth.

The wars against the Muslims gave the Spanish invaluable military experience and rendered their army one of the finest in Europe. The wars also created a pattern in the growth of the Spanish empire: it victories always lay in the south—in Italy, in Latin America, and against the Turks—while its defeats and setbacks occurred in the north—

in the Netherlands, in opposition to the Lutheran Reformation in the Holy Roman Empire, and against England.

With a superior army, with the great magnates pacified, and with the church and the Inquisition under monarchical control, the Catholic Kings expanded their interests and embarked on an imperialist foreign policy in Europe and abroad that had extraordinary consequences. Ultimately it made Spain dominant in the New World.

Ferdinand and Isabella gambled on Columbus's voyage and they won. Then, beginning in 1519, the conquistador Cortés defeated the Aztec nation with 600 foot soldiers and 16 horses, a feat that cannot be explained simply by citing the superior technology of the Spanish. This conquest rested primarily on the character and achievements of Spain's lesser gentry—the hidalgos. The willingness of the hidalgos to serve crown and church was equaled or surpassed only by their desire to get rich. Lured by gold and land, they made excellent soldiers and explorers in foreign lands; while at home they entered the governmental and ecclesiastical bureaucracies. They formed the core of a loyal civil service that was responsive to the needs of the monarchy and distrustful of and resentful toward

Titian (1477–1576): Portrait of the Emperor Charles V, 1548. With the wealth of the New World and the Hapsburg domination of the Holy Roman Empire, Charles V was the greatest ruler of his age. Titian's portraits revealed the characters of his subjects. (*Bayerischen Staatsgemäldesammlungen, Munich*)

The Reign of Charles V: King of Spain and Holy Roman Emperor

Dynastic marriage constituted another crucial part of Ferdinand and Isabella's foreign policy. They strengthened their ties with the Austrian and Flemish (or Burgundian) kings by marrying one of their children, Juana (called *the Mad* for her insanity) to Philip the Fair, son of Maximilian of Austria, the head of the ruling Hapsburg family. Philip and Juana's son Charles (1516–1556) inherited the kingdom of Ferdinand and Isabella; through his other grandparents, he also inherited the Netherlands, Austria, Sardinia, Sicily, the kingdom of Naples, and Franche Comté. In 1519 he was also elected Charles V, Holy Roman Emperor. Charles became the most powerful ruler in Europe, but his reign also saw the emergence of political, economic, and social problems that eventually led to Spain's decline.

Charles's inheritance was simply too vast to be governed effectively, but that was only dimly perceived at the time. The Lutheran Reformation proved to be the first successful challenge to Hapsburg power. It was the first phase of a religious and political struggle between Catholic Spain and Protestant Europe that would dominate the last half of the sixteenth century.

Charles established a court filled with foreigners and spent much of his time in the northern provinces, while still collecting taxes in Castile. These policies produced a full-scale revolt in the Castilian towns in 1520 and 1521. Led by artisans and merchants, the revolt took on elements of a class war against the landed nobility. The nobles, in turn, rallied around Charles's royal army, and eventually the revolt was crushed. But the event and its outcome reveals much about the nature of Spanish absolutism. It relied on its aristocracy (unlike the French kings who tried to suppress their aristocrats), and it never encouraged the growth of a bourgeoisie.

The achievements of Charles V's reign rested on the twin instruments of army and

the great nobles, or *grandees*. Spanish bureaucracy in the sixteenth century became a primary vehicle for social mobility, and the foreign and domestic policies initiated by Ferdinand and Isabella and continued by their successors received their greatest support from the gentry.

bureaucracy. The Hapsburg empire in the New World was vastly extended and, on the whole, effectively administered and policed. Out of this sprawling empire with its newly enslaved native populations came the greatest flow of gold and silver ever witnessed by Europeans. Constant warfare in Europe, coupled with the immensity of the Spanish administrative network, required a steady intake of capital. However, this easy access to capital appears to have been detrimental in the long run to the Spanish economy (see Chapter 15). There was no incentive for the development of domestic industry, bourgeois entrepreneurship, or international commerce. Moreover, constant war engendered and perpetuated a social order geared to the aggrandizement of a military class, rather than to the development of a commercial class. And while war expanded Spain's power, it also increased the national debt. The weak economic foundation of Spanish power in the sixteenth century, combined with numerous expensive wars, sowed the seeds for the financial crises of the 1590s and beyond, and for the eventual decline of Spain as a world power. But also setting the stage for Spain's troubles were events in the two emerging powers to the north.

The Growth of French Power

Two states in the early modern period succeeded most effectively in consolidating the power of their central governments: France and England. Each became a model of a very different form of statehood. The French model emphasized, at every turn, the glory of the king and, by implication, the sovereignty of the state and its right to stand above the interests of its subjects. France's monarchy became *absolute*. Yet this evolution of the French state was a very gradual process, one not completed until the late seventeenth century.

When Hugh Capet became king of France in 987 he was, in relation to France's other great feudal lords, merely first among equals. He could demand military service from his vassals (only forty days a year) and was regarded as the protector of the church. But he only ruled over a small area around Paris, and the succession of his heirs to the kingship was by no means secure. Yet even at this early date, his title and his person were regarded as sacred. He was God's anointed, and his power, such as it was, rested on divine authority.

From this small power base, more symbolic than real, Hugh Capet's successors extended their territory and dominion at the expense of feudal lords' power. By 1328, when the Capetian family became extinct and the crown passed to the Valois family, the Capetians had made the French monarch the ruler of areas as distant from Paris as Languedoc in the south and Flanders in the north. To administer their territories, the Capetians established an efficient bureaucracy composed of townsmen and trustworthy lesser nobles who unlike the great feudal lords, owed their wealth and status directly to the king. These royal officials, an essential element of monarchical power, collected the king's feudal dues and administered justice. At the same time, French kings emphasized that they had been selected by God to rule, a theory known as the divine right of kings. This theory gave monarchy a sanctity that various French kings used to enforce their commands over rebellious feudal lords and to defend themselves against papal claims of dominance over the French church.

Yet medieval French kings never sought absolute power. Not until the seventeenth century was the power base of the French monarchy consolidated to the extent that kings and their courts could attempt to rule without formal consultations with their subjects. In the Middle Ages the French monarchs recognized the rights of, and consulted with, representative assemblies called *Estates*. These assemblies (whether regional or national) were composed of deputies drawn from the various elites: the clergy, the nobility, and significantly, the leadership of cities and towns in a given region. The Estates met as circumstance—wars, taxes, local disputes—warranted, and the nationally representative assembly, the *Estates General*, was always summoned by the king. In general, medieval French kings consulted these assemblies to give legitimacy to their demands and credibility to their administration. They also recognized that the courts—especially the highest court, the Parlement of Paris—had the right to administer the king's justice with a minimum of royal interference. Medieval kings did not see themselves as originators of law; they were its guarantors and administrators.

War came to serve the interests of a monarchy bent on consolidating its power and authority. As a result of the Hundred Years' War (1338–1453), the English were eventually driven from France and their claims to the French throne dashed. In the process of war and taxation to meet its burden, the French monarchy grew richer. The necessities of war enabled the French kings to levy new taxes, often enacted without the consent of the Estates General, and to maintain a large standing army under royal command. The Hundred Years' War also provoked allegiance to the king as the visible symbol of France. The war heightened the French sense of national identity; the English were a common enemy, discernibly different in manners, language, dress, and appearance.

With revenue and an army at their disposal, the French kings subsequently embarked on territorial aggrandizement. Charles VIII (1483–1498) invaded Italy in 1494. Machiavelli, a shrewd assessor of the implications of power, observed that while Italy's weakness derived from its lack of unity, the power of this new cohesive state of France derived in large measure from the strength of its prince and his huge and mostly native-born army. Although the French gained little territory from the Italian campaign, they did effectively challenge Spanish power in Italy and intimidate an already weakened papacy.

Religion and the French State

In every emergent state, tension existed between the monarch and the papacy. At issue was control over the church within that territory—over its personnel, wealth, and, of course, its pulpits, from which an illiterate majority learned what their leaders believed they should know, not only in matters of religious belief but also about questions of obedience to civil authority. The monarch's power to make church appointments could ensure a complacent church. A church that was willing to preach about the king's divine right and was tractable on matters of taxes was especially important in France because legally the church had to pay no taxes and only had to give donations to the crown. Centuries of tough bargaining with the papacy paid off when in 1516 Francis I concluded the Concordat of Bologna; Pope Leo X permitted the French king to nominate, and therefore effectively to appoint, men of his choice to all the highest offices in the French church.

The Concordat of Bologna laid the foundation for what became known as the *Gallican church*—a term signifying the immense power and authority of the Catholic church in France—which was sanctioned and overseen by the French kings. By the early sixteenth century, religious homogeneity had strengthened the central government at the expense of papal authority and of traditional privileges enjoyed by local aristocracy. This ecclesiastical and religious settlement lay at the heart of monarchical authority. Consequently, the Protestant Reformation threatened the very survival of France as a unified state. Throughout the early modern period the French kings had assumed that their states must be governed by one king, one faith, and one set of laws. Any alternative to that unity offered local power elites, whether aristocratic or cleric, the opportunity to channel religious dissent into their service. Once linked, religious and political opposition to any central government could be extremely dangerous.

Francis I (1515–1547) perceived that Protestantism in France would undermine the sacredness of his office, challenge his authority, and diminish his control over church officials. In 1534 the king, in conjunction with the court of Paris (the Parlement), declared Protestant beliefs and practices illegal and punishable by fine, imprisonment, and even execution. The Protestant reformer Calvin and his friends fled from Paris and eventually to Geneva (see Chapter 14), but they never abandoned the hope of converting Francis and France to the Protestant cause.

During the decades that followed, partly through the efforts of the Huguenot underground and partly because the French king and his ministers vacillated in their efforts at persecution, the Protestant minority grew in strength and dedication. By challenging the authority of the Catholic church, Protestants were also inadvertently challenging royal authority, for the French church and the French monarchy supported each other. Protestantism became the basis for a political movement of an increasingly revolutionary nature.

From 1562 to 1598, France experienced waves of religious wars that cost the king control over vast areas of the kingdom. Protestantism became for some adherents a vehicle for expressing their rage against the French church and the increasing power of the Valois kings. The great aristocratic families, the Guise for the Catholics and the Bourbons for the Protestants, drew up armies that scourged the land, killing and maiming their religious opponents. When entwined with religion, local grievances for a time proved capable of dismantling the authority of the central government. In Protestant urban centers, townsmen asserted their right to control local government, as well as to worship publicly in the Protestant manner. They allied with those aristocrats who would convert to the Reformation, for whatever reasons. The French Catholics, on the other hand, turned to the House of Guise for protection—a vivid reminder of the strength of feudal elites centuries after feudalism as an institution had

Francis I of France, by Joos Van Cleve (1485–1540). Francis I was a true Renaissance prince, power-hungry yet a patron of the arts. The aged Leonardo da Vinci ended his days at Francis's court at Amboise as guest of the French king. Francis was also a brilliant politician who helped found the Gallican Church through his Concordat of Bologna with Pope Leo X. Henceforth, the French monarchs alone were to appoint men of their choice to church offices in France. (*Cincinnati Art Museum; Bequest of Mary M. Emery*)

ceased to be the main expression of political authority.

In 1579, extreme Huguenot theorists published the *Vindiciae contra Tyrannos*. This theoretical statement combined with a call to action was the first of its kind in early modern times. It justified rebellion against, and even the execution of, an unjust king. European monarchs might claim power and divinely sanctioned authority, but by the late sixteenth century, their subjects had available the moral justification to oppose by force, if necessary, their monarch's will, and this justification rested on Scripture and religious conviction. Significantly, this same treatise was translated into English in 1648, a year before Parliament publicly executed Charles I, king of England.

The Valois kings floundered in the face of this kind of politico-religious opposition. The era of royal supremacy instituted by Francis I came to an abrupt end during the reign of his successor Henry II (1547–1559). Wed to Catherine de Medici, a member of the powerful Italian banking family, Henry occupied himself not with the concerns of government, but with the pleasures of the hunt. The sons who succeeded Henry—Francis II (1559–1560), Charles IX (1560–1574), and Henry III (1574–1589)—were uniformly weak. In this power vacuum, their mother Catherine emerged as virtual ruler—a queen despised for her foreign and nonaristocratic lineage, for the fact that she was a woman, and for her propensity for dangerous intrigue. One of the most hated figures of her day, Catherine de Medici defies dispassionate assessment. She ordered the execution of thousands of Protestants by royal troops in Paris—the infamous St. Bartholomew's Day Massacre (1572) which, with the blood bath that followed, became both a symbol and a legend in subsequent European history: a symbol of the excesses of religious zeal and a legend of Protestant martyrdom that gave renewed zeal to the cause of international Protestantism.

The civil wars begun in 1562 were renewed in the massacre's aftermath. They dragged on until the death of the last Valois king in 1589. The Valois failure to produce a male heir to the throne placed Henry, duke of Bourbon and a Protestant, in line to succeed to the French throne. Realizing that the overwhelmingly Catholic population would not accept a Protestant king, Henry (apparently without much regret) renounced his adopted religion and embraced the church. His private religious beliefs may never be known, but outward conformity to the religion of the Catholic majority was the only means to effect peace and re-establish political stability. Under the reign of Henry IV (1589–1610) the French

throne acquired its central position in national politics. Henry granted to his Protestant subjects and former followers a degree of religious toleration through the Edict of Nantes (1598), but they were never welcomed in significant numbers into the royal bureaucracy. Throughout the seventeenth century, every French king attempted to undermine the Protestants' regional power bases and ultimately to destroy their religious liberties.

The Consolidation of French Monarchical Power

The defeat of Protestantism as a national force set the stage for the final consolidation of the French state in the seventeenth century under the great Bourbon kings, Louis XIII and Louis XIV. Louis XIII (1610–1643) realized that his rule depended on an efficient and trustworthy bureaucracy, an ever-replenishable treasury, and constant vigilance against the localized claims to power by the great aristocracy and by the Protestant cities and towns. Many of the latter were capable of taking military action against the central government or even of forming alliances with foreign princes. Cardinal Richelieu, who served as Louis XIII's chief minister from 1624 to 1642, became the great architect of French absolutism.

Richelieu was the king's loyal servant; in this way he served the state. His morality rested on one sacred principle embodied in the phrase he invented: *raison d'état,* "reason of state." For Richelieu the state's necessities and the king's absolute authority were synonymous; one was inconceivable without the other. In accordance with his political philosophy, Richelieu brought under control the disruptive and antimonarchical elements within French society. He increased the power of the central bureaucracy, attacked the power of independent, and often Protestant, towns and cities, and persecuted the Huguenots. Above all, he humbled the great nobles by limiting their effectiveness as councilors to

Map 16.2 Europe, 1648 ▶

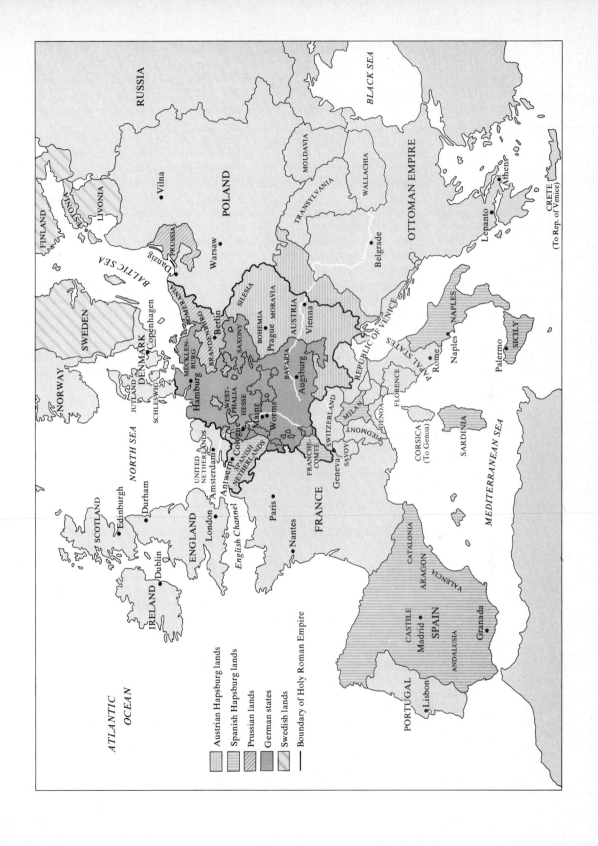

ATLANTIC
OCEAN

RUSSIA

BLACK SEA

FINLAND

NORWAY

SWEDEN

DENMARK

BALTIC SEA

POLAND

Vilna

Warsaw

Danzig

PRUSSIA

POMERANIA

OTTOMAN EMPIRE

MOLDAVIA

TRANSYLVANIA

WALLACHIA

Belgrade

CRETE
(To Rep. of Venice)

Athens

Lepanto

NORTH SEA

SCOTLAND

Edinburgh

Durham

IRELAND

Dublin

ENGLAND

London

English Channel

UNITED
NETHERLANDS

Amsterdam

Antwerp

SPANISH
NETHERLANDS

Cologne

Hamburg

SCHLESWIG

JUTLAND

Copenhagen

Berlin

BRANDENBURG

MECKLEN-
BURG

SILESIA

SAXONY

WEST-
PHALIA

HESSE

Mainz

Worms

BOHEMIA

MORAVIA

Prague

BAVARIA

Augsburg

AUSTRIA

Vienna

REPUBLIC OF VENICE

SWITZERLAND

Geneva

FRANCHE-
COMTÉ

SAVOY

PIEDMONT

MILAN

GENOA

FLORENCE

PAPAL STATES

Rome

NAPLES

Naples

Palermo

SICILY

CORSICA
(To Genoa)

SARDINIA

MEDITERRANEAN SEA

FRANCE

Paris

Nantes

PORTUGAL

Lisbon

SPAIN

Madrid

CASTILE

ARAGON

VALENCIA

CATALONIA

ANDALUSIA

Granada

Austrian Hapsburg lands

Spanish Hapsburg lands

Prussian lands

German states

Swedish lands

Boundary of Holy Roman Empire

ESTONIA

LIVONIA

the king and by prohibiting their traditional privileges, like using a duel rather than court action to settle grievances.

Reason of state also guided Richelieu's foreign policy. Since the treaty of Cateau-Cambrésis (1559) that ended nearly a century of French-Spanish rivalry, both countries had ceased their armed hostilities to concentrate on the threat posed to internal order by the Protestant Reformation. This relative peace had enhanced Spanish power at the expense of the French, yet both countries were Catholic powers, interrelated by aristocratic marriages. When Richelieu came to power at the French court in 1624, the king and his mother were pursuing a policy of appeasement toward the Spanish. But reason of state, as Richelieu saw it, necessitated that France turn against Spain and enter on the Protestant and hence anti-Spanish side the war that was raging at the time in the Holy Roman Empire. The outcome of France's entry into the Thirty Years' War (1618–1648) produced a decided victory for French power on the Continent.

By the time of his death in 1642, Richelieu had established certain practices and policies that were continued by his successors to great effect. First, the avaricious and unprincipled Cardinal Mazarin, who took charge during the minority of Louis XIV (who was five years old when Louis XIII died) continued Richelieu's policies. Then Louis XIV (1643–1715) himself continued the work of his father's minister. The growth of royal absolutism produced a severe reaction among its victims: peasants who paid the burden of the state's taxes; aristocrats who bitterly resented their loss of power; and judges in the royal courts, the parlements, who resented attempts by the king and his ministers to bypass their authority.

Richelieu's policies, as administered by his corrupt successor Mazarin, produced a rebellious reaction, the *Fronde*—a series of street riots that eventually cost the government control over Paris and lasted from 1648 to 1653. Centered in Paris and supported by the great aristocracy, the courts, and Paris's poorer classes, the Fronde threatened to de-velop into a full-scale uprising. And it might have but for one crucial factor: its leadership was fundamentally divided. Court judges (lesser nobility who had often just risen from the ranks of the bourgeoisie) deeply distrusted the great nobility and refused in the end to make common cause with them. And both groups feared disorder among the urban masses. The discontented elites could not unite, and as a result they could offer no viable alternative except disorder to the rule of absolute kings and their ministers.

When Louis XIV finally assumed responsibility for governing in 1661, he vowed that the events he witnessed as a child during the Fronde would never be repeated. In the course of his reign, he achieved the greatest degree of monarchical power ever witnessed during the early modern period. Indeed, no absolute monarch in Western Europe, before or possibly since, held so much personal authority or commanded such a vast and effective military and administrative machine. Louis XIV's reign represents the culmination of a process of increasing monarchical authority that had been underway for centuries. Yet Louis himself possessed such qualities of intelligence and cunning, coupled with a unique understanding of the capacities of his office, that some attention must be paid to this man who became the envy of his age.

Louis XIV's education had been practical, rather than theoretical. He knew that a hardworking monarch could dispense with chief ministers while still maintaining the effectiveness of his administration. Louis XIV worked long hours at being king, and he never undertook a venture without an eye to his personal grandeur. The sumptuous royal palace at Versailles was built for that reason; similarly, etiquette and style were cultivated there on a scale never before seen in any European court. A lengthy visit to Versailles, a necessity for any aristocrat who wanted his views and needs attended to, could bankrupt the less well-to-do.

Perhaps the most brilliant of Louis XIV's many policies was his treatment of the aristocracy. He simply dispensed with their services as influential advisers; indeed, Louis XIV would not have any minister assume the power that his father had accorded to Richelieu. He treated the aristocrats to elaborate rituals, feasts, processions, displays, and banquets; but amid all the clamor, their political power dwindled. The wiser members of the aristocracy stayed home and managed their estates; others made their way at court as minor functionaries and basked in the glory of the "Sun King."

Louis XIV's domestic policies centered around his incessant search for new revenues. Not only the building of Versailles, but also wars cost money, and Louis XIV waged them to excess. To raise capital, he used the services of Jean Baptiste Colbert, a brilliant administrator who improved methods of tax collecting, promoted new industries, and encouraged international trade. Such ambitious national policies were possible because Louis XIV had inherited an efficient system of administration introduced by Richelieu. Instead of relying on the local aristocracy to collect royal taxes and to administer royal policies, Richelieu had appointed the king's own men as *intendants*, functionaries dispatched with wide powers into the provinces. At first, their missions had been temporary and their success minimal, but gradually they became a permanent feature of royal administration. During the reign of Louis XIV, the country was divided into thirty-two districts controlled by intendants. Operating with a total bureaucracy of about a thousand officials and no longer bothering even to consult the parlements or Estates, Louis XIV ruled absolutely.

Why did such a system of absolute authority work? Did the peasants not revolt? Why did the old aristocracy not rise in rebellion? For the aristocrats, the loss of political authority was not accompanied by a comparable loss in wealth and social position; indeed, quite the contrary was true. During the seventeenth century, the French nobility—2 percent of the population—controlled approximately 20 to 30 percent of the total national income. The church, too, fared well under Louis, re-

Louis XIV by Lorenzo Bernini (1598–1680). The French king called in Italian Baroque architect and sculptor Bernini to redesign the Louvre. Louis rejected his designs for the palace and turned to the more solidly neoclassical work of Perrault. Bernini's bust would also not receive sanction as the official style, but it captures the Sun King and his grandiose ambitions. (*Château de Versailles/Alinari-Scala/Art Resource*)

ceiving good tax arrangements provided it preached about the king's divinely given rights. While there were peasant upheavals throughout the century, the sheer size of the royal army and police—over 300,000 by the end of Louis's reign—made successful revolt nearly impossible. When in the early 1700s a popular religious rebellion led by Protestant visionaries broke out in the south, royal troops crushed it. Thus, absolutism rested on the complicity of the old aristocracy, the self-aggrandizement of government officials, the church's doctrines, the revenues squeezed out of the peasantry, and the power of a huge military machine.

Yet Louis XIV's system was fatally flawed. Without any effective check on his power and dreams of international conquest, there was no limit imposed on the state's capacity to make war or on the ensuing national debt. Louis XIV coveted vast sections of the Holy Roman Empire; he also sought to check Dutch commercial prosperity and had designs on the Spanish Netherlands. By the 1680s, his domestic and foreign policies took on a violently aggressive posture. In 1685, he revoked the Edict of Nantes, forcing many of the country's remaining Protestants to flee. In 1689, he embarked upon a military campaign to secure territory from the Holy Roman Empire. And in 1701, he tried to bring Spain under the control of the Bourbon dynasty. Yet Louis XIV had underestimated the power of his northern rivals, England and the Netherlands. He viewed the apparent chaos of English politics during much of the seventeenth century as an inherent weakness of the English state. The combined power of England and the Netherlands in alliance with the Holy Roman Empire and the Austrians brought defeat to Louis XIV's ambitions.

Louis XIV's long wars emptied the royal treasury. By the late seventeenth century taxes had risen intolerably, and they were essentially levied on those least able to pay—the peasants. In the 1690s, the combination of taxes, bad harvests, and plague led to widespread poverty, misery, and starvation in large areas of France. Thus, for the great majority of French people, absolutism meant a decline in living standards and a significant increase in mortality rates. Absolutism also meant increased surveillance over the population: royal authorities censored books; spied on heretics, Protestants, and freethinkers; and even tortured and executed opponents of state policy.

By 1715, France was a tightly governed society whose treasury was bankrupt. Protestants had been driven into exile or forced to convert. Strict censorship laws closely governed publishing, causing a brisk trade in clandestine books and manuscripts. Direct taxes burdened the poor and were legally evaded by the aristocracy. Critics of state policy within the church had been effectively silenced. And over the long run, foreign wars had brought no significant gains.

In the France of Louis XIV, the dynastic state had reached maturity and had begun to display some of its classic characteristics: centralized bureaucracy; royal patronage to enforce allegiance; a system of taxation universally, but inequitably applied; and suppression of political opposition either through the use of patronage or, if necessary, through force. Another important feature was the state's cultivation of the arts and sciences as a means of increasing national power and prestige. Together, these policies enabled France and its monarchs to achieve political stability, to enforce a uniform system of law, and to channel the country's wealth and resources into the service of the state as a whole.

Yet at his death in 1715, Louis XIV left his successors a system of bureaucracy and taxation that was vastly in need of overhaul but was still locked into the traditional social privileges of the church and nobility to an extent that made reform virtually impossible. The pattern of war, excessive taxation of the lower classes, and expenditure in excess of revenues had severely damaged French finances. Failure to reform the system led to the French Revolution of 1789.

The Growth of Limited Monarchy and Constitutionalism in England

England achieved national unity earlier than any other major European state. Its fortunate geography freed it from the border disputes that plagued emerging states on the Continent. By an accident of fate, its administrative structure also developed in such a way as to encourage centralization. In 1066, William, duke of Normandy and vassal to the French king, had invaded and conquered England, acquiring at a stroke the entire kingdom. In contrast, the French kings took centuries to bring the territory of France under their domain.

The conquering Norman kings and their followers represented a distinct minority in England. Eventually they intermarried and merged with the larger population. In the first century of their rule, the Norman kings frequently lived in France for long periods and depended therefore on an efficient bureaucracy and on their own knowledge of the English kingdom to maintain their power.

Out of necessity, therefore, these medieval Norman kings consulted with their powerful subjects—archbishops, bishops, earls, and barons. By the middle of the thirteenth century, these consultations, or *parlays*, came to be called *parliaments*. Gradually the practice grew of inviting to these parliaments representatives from the shires—knights and burgesses. These lesser-than-noble but often wealthy and prominent representatives of the counties grew to see Parliament as a means of self-expression for redressing their grievances. In turn, the later medieval kings saw Parliament as an effective means of exercising control and of raising taxes. By 1297 the Lords and Commons (as the lower house was called) had obtained the king's agreement that no direct taxes could be levied without their consent. By the fourteenth century, Parliament had become a permanent institution of government. Its power was entirely subservient to the crown, but its right to question royal decisions had been established.

The medieval Parliament possessed two characteristics that distinguished it from its many Continental counterparts, such as the various French Estates. The English Parliament was national and not provincial, and more important, its representatives were elected across caste lines, with voting rights dependent on property and not on noble birth or status. These representatives voted as individuals, not collectively as clergy, nobles, or commoners, that is, as Estates. In the Middle Ages, Parliament and monarchy were in-terdependent; they were seen not as rivals but as complementary forms of centralized government. Yet that very interdependence would ultimately lead to conflict.

Also emerging during the Middle Ages in England was the constitution—a set of precedents, laws, and royal acts that came to embody the basic principles of government. And in contrast to the French model, England grew to be a *constitutional* monarchy. This theoretical foundation—up to this time not written as a single constitution—grew out of legal practices and customs described under the generic title *common law*. As opposed to feudal law, which applied only to a local region, the common law extended throughout the realm and served as a force for unity.

The strength of the monarchy during the later Middle Ages received dramatic expression in English victories against France during the Hundred Years' War. The power of the English kings enabled them to rally the nobility, who in turn benefited enormously from pillaging France. Only after the revitalization of the French monarchy and its subsequent victories were the English aristocrats forced to take their skills and taste for war back home. The consequences of their return were devastating. Civil war ensued—the Wars of the Roses (1453–1485)—and the medieval war machine turned inward. Gangs of noblemen with retainers roamed the English countryside, and lawlessness prevailed for a generation. Only in 1485 did the Tudor family emerge triumphant.

The Tudor Achievement

Victory in the civil wars allowed Henry VII (1485–1509) to begin the Tudor dynasty. Henry and his successors strove to secure their power by remaking and revitalizing the institutions of government. Henry VII's goal was to bring an unruly nobility into check. Toward this end, he brought commoners into the government; these commoners, unlike the great magnates, could be channeled into royal service because they craved what the

King offered—financial rewards and elevated social status. Although they did not fully displace the aristocracy, commoners were brought into Henry VII's inner circle, into the Privy Council, into the courts, and eventually into all the highest offices of the government. The strength and efficiency of Tudor government was shown during the Reformation when Henry VIII (1509–1547) made himself head of the English church. He was only able to take this giant step toward increasing royal power because his father had restored order and stability. But Henry VIII's step still entailed a struggle (see Chapter 14).

The Protestant Reformation in England was a revolution in royal, as well as ecclesiastical government. It attacked and defeated a main obstacle to monarchical authority—the power of the papacy. At the same time, the Reformation greatly enhanced the power of Parliament. Henry used Parliament to make the Reformation because he knew that he needed the support of the lords, the country gentry, and the merchants. No change in religious practice could be instituted by the monarchy alone. Parliament's participation in the Reformation gave it a greater role and sense of importance than it had ever possessed in the past. Yet the final outcome of this administrative revolution enhanced monarchical power. By the end of his reign, Henry VIII easily possessed as much power as his French rival, Francis I. Indeed, up to the early seventeenth century the history of monarchical power in England, with its absolutist tendencies, was remarkably similar to the Continental pattern.

At Henry's death, the Tudor bureaucracy and centralized government was strained to its utmost, and it survived. The government weathered the reign of Henry's sickly son, Edward VI (1547–1553), with the extreme Protestantism of some of his advisers, and it survived the brief and deeply troubled reign of Henry's first daughter, Mary (1553–1558), who attempted to return England to Catholicism. At Mary's death, England had come dangerously close to the religious instability that undermined the French kings during the final decades of the sixteenth century.

Henry's second daughter, Elizabeth I (whose mother was Anne Boleyn), became queen in 1558. The Elizabethan period was characterized by a heightened sense of national identity. The English Reformation enhanced that sense, as did the increasing fear of foreign invasion by a Catholic power intent on returning England to the papacy. Such was the threat posed by Spain, possessor of twice England's population and of a vast colonial empire. The fear was real enough and was only abated by the defeat—more psychologically than militarily crippling—of the Spanish Armada in 1588. In the seventeenth century, the English would look back on Elizabeth's reign as a golden age. It was the calm before the storm, a time when a new commercial class was formed that, in the seventeenth century, would demand a greater say in government operations.

The Elizabethan age's capitalistic social and economic changes can be seen, in microcosm, by looking at the Durham region in northern England. From 1580 to 1640, a new coal-mining industry developed there through the efforts of entrepreneurs—gentlemen with minor lands whose industry and skill enabled them to exploit their mineral resources. The wool trade also prospered in Durham. By 1600 social and political tensions had developed. The wool merchants and the entrepreneurial gentry were demanding a greater say in governing the region. They were opposed by the traditional leaders of Durham society—the bishops and the dozen or so aristocratic families with major lands and access to the court in London.

This split is described as one between court and country. *Court* refers to the traditional aristocratic magnates, the hierarchy of the church, and royal officialdom. *Country* denotes a loose coalition of merchants and rising agricultural and industrial entrepreneurs from the prosperous gentry class, whose economic worth far exceeded their political power. The pattern found in Durham was repeated in other parts of the country, generally where industry and commerce grew and prospered. The agricultural and industrial gentry grew in social status and wealth. In the seventeenth century, these social and economic tensions would help foster revolution.

By the early seventeenth century in England the descendants of the old feudal aristocracy differed markedly from their Continental counterparts. Their insular isolation from the great wars of the Reformation had produced an aristocracy less military and more commercial in orientation. Furthermore, the lesser ranks of the land-owning aristocracy, gentlemen without titles (the gentry), had prospered significantly in Tudor times. In commercial matters they were often no shrewder than the great landed magnates, but they had in Parliament, as well as in their counties, an effective and institutionalized means of expressing their political interests. The great nobles, on the other hand, had largely abandoned the sword as the primary expression of their political authority without putting anything comparable in its place. Gradually, political initiative was slipping away from the great lords into the hands of a gentry that was commercially and agriculturally innovative, as well as fiercely protective of its local base of political power.

Religion played a vital role in this realignment of political interests and forces. Many of the old aristocracy clung to the Anglicanism of the Henrican Reformation, and in some cases to Catholicism. The newly risen gentry found in the Protestant Reformation of Switzerland and Germany a form of religious worship more suited to their independent and entrepreneurial spirit. They felt that it was their right to appoint their own preachers and that the church should reflect local tastes and beliefs, rather than a series of doctrines and ceremonies inherited from a discredited Catholicism. In late Tudor times gentry and merchant interests fused with Puritanism to produce a political-religious vision with ominous potential.

The English Revolution, 1640–1689

The forces threatening established authority were dealt with ineffectively by the first two Stuart kings—James I (1603—1625), and Charles I (1625–1649). Both believed, as did their Continental counterparts, in royal absolutism. Essentially, these Stuart kings tried to do in England what Louis XIII and later Louis XIV were to do in France: to establish court and crown as the sole governing bodies within the state. What the Stuarts lacked, however, was an adequate social and institutional base for absolutism. They did not possess the vast independent wealth of their French counterparts.

These kings had preached, through the established church, the doctrine of the divine right of kings. James I conducted foreign policy without consulting Parliament. Both tried to revitalize the old aristocracy and to create new peers to re-establish the feudal base of monarchical authority. After 1629, Charles brought his hand-picked advisers into government in the hope that they would purge the church of Puritans and the nation of his opponents. Charles disbanded Parliament and attempted to collect taxes without its consent. These policies ended in disaster.

The English Revolution broke out in 1640 because Charles I needed new taxes to defend the realm against a Scottish invasion. Parliament, finally called after an eleven-year absence, refused his request unless he granted certain basic rights: Parliament to be consulted in matters of taxation, trial by jury, *habeas corpus*, and a truly Protestant church responsive to the beliefs and interests of its laity. Charles refused, for he saw these demands as an assault on royal authority. The ensuing civil war was directed by Parliament, financed by taxes and the merchants, and fought by the New Model Army led by Oliver Cromwell (1599–1658), a Puritan squire who gradually realized his potential for leadership.

The New Model Army was unmatched by any ever seen before in Europe. Parliament's rich supporters financed it, gentleman farmers led it, and religious zealots filled its ranks along with the usual cross section of poor artisans and day laborers. This army brought defeat to the king, his aristocratic followers, and the Anglican church's hierarchy.

In January 1649, Charles I was publicly executed by order of Parliament. During the

Sir Christopher Wren (1632–1723): The Royal Hospital at Greenwich. The classical design of the Royal Hospital derives ultimately from Palladio and Michelangelo, but its blend of grave monumentality and simplicity reflect the taste of late-seventeenth-century England. The buildings are now part of the Royal Naval College: left, the Chapel; right, the Painted Hall. In the middle distance is the Queen's House, designed by Inigo Jones. (*A. F. Kersting*)

Interregnum of the next eleven years, one Parliament after another joined with the army to govern the country as a republic. In the distribution of power between the army and the Parliament, Cromwell proved to be a key element. He had the support of the army's officers and some of its rank and file, and he had been a member of Parliament for many years. His control over the army had only been secured, however, after its rank and file had been purged not of royalists, but of radical groups. Some of these radicals wanted to level society, that is, to redistribute property by ending monopolies and to give the vote to all male citizens. In the context of the 1650s, Cromwell was a moderate republican who also believed in religious toleration; yet history has painted him, somewhat unjustly, as a military dictator.

The English Revolution was begun by an agricultural and commercial bourgeoisie, urban merchants as well as landed gentry, who were imbued with the strict Protestantism of the Continental Reformation. But in the 1650s the success of their revolution was jeopardized by growing discontent from the poor or less prosperous who had made up the rank and file of the army and who demanded that their economic and social grievances be rectified. The radicals of the English Revolution—men like Gerrard Winstanley, the first theoretician of social democracy in modern times, and John Lilburne, the Leveller—demanded a redistribution of property, voting rights for the vast majority of the male population, and the abolition of religious and intellectual elites whose power and ideology supported the interests of the ruling classes. The radicals rejected Anglicanism, moderate Puritanism, and even, in a few cases, the lifestyle of the middle class; they opted instead for libertine and communistic beliefs and practices. The radicals terrified even devoted Puritans like Cromwell. By 1660 the country was adrift without effective leadership.

Parliament, having secured the economic interests of its constituency (gentry, merchants, and some small landowners), chose to return to court and crown and invited the exiled son of the executed king to return to the kingship. Having learned the lesson his father had spurned, Charles II (1660–1685) never instituted royal absolutism, although he did try to minimize Parliament's role in the government. His court was a far more open institution than his father's had been, for Charles II feared a similar death.

But Charles's brother James II (1685–1688) was a foolishly fearless Catholic and admirer of French absolutism. James gathered at his court a coterie of Catholic advisers and supporters of royal prerogative and attempted to bend Parliament and local government to the royal will. James's Catholicism was the crucial element in his failure. The Anglican church would not back him, and political forces similar to those that had gathered against his father, Charles I, in 1640 descended on him. The ruling elites, however, had learned their lesson back in the 1650s: civil war would produce social discontent among the masses. The upper classes wanted to avoid open warfare and preserve the monarchy as a constitutional authority, but not as an absolute one. Puritanism, with its sectarian fer-

vor and its dangerous association with republicanism, was allowed to play no part in this second and last phase of the English Revolution.

In early 1688, Anglicans, some aristocrats, and opponents of royal prerogative (Whigs) formed a conspiracy against James II. Their purpose was to invite his son-in-law, William of Orange, *stadholder* of the Netherlands and husband of James's Protestant daughter Mary, to invade England and rescue its government from James's control. It was hoped that the final outcome of this invasion would be determined by William and his conspirators, in conjunction with a freely elected Parliament. This dangerous plan succeeded for three main reasons: William and the Dutch desperately needed English support against the threat of a French invasion; James had lost the loyalty of key men in the army, powerful gentlemen in the counties, and the Anglican church; and the political elite was committed and united in its intentions. James II fled the country, and William and Mary were declared king and queen by act of Parliament.

This bloodless revolution—sometimes called the Glorious Revolution—created a new political and constitutional reality. Parliament secured its rights to assemble regularly and to vote on all matters of taxation; the rights of *habeas corpus* and trial by jury (for men of property and social status) were also secured. These rights were in turn legitimated in a constitutionally binding document, the Bill of Rights (1689). All Protestants, regardless of their sectarian bias, were granted toleration. The Revolution Settlement of 1688–1689 resolved the profound constitutional and social tensions of the seventeenth century and laid the foundations of English government until well into the nineteenth century. The revolution, says historian J. H. Plumb, established "the authority of certain men of property, particularly those of high social standing either aristocrats or linked with aristocracy, whose tap root was in land but whose side roots reached out to commerce, industry and finance."[2] Throughout the eighteenth century, England was ruled by kings and Parliaments

William and Mary in Triumph. This detail of the ceiling painting by Sir James Thornhill in the Painted Hall of the Royal Hospital (see page 360) shows William III and Mary II being received triumphantly after the ouster of James II in the Glorious Revolution of 1688–89. (*Royal Naval College, Greenwich*)

that represented the interests of an oligarchy whose cohesiveness and prosperity ensured social and political stability.

The English Revolution, in both its 1640 and its 1688 phases, secured English parliamentary government and the rule of law, and it also provided a degree of freedom for the propertied. In retrospect, we can see that absolutism according to the French model probably never had a chance in England. There were simply too many gentlemen there who possessed enough land to be independent of the crown, and yet not so much that they could control whole sections of the

kingdom. But to contemporaries, the issues seemed different: the English opponents of absolutism spoke of their rights, as granted by their ancient constitution and the feudal law, of the need to make the English church truly Protestant, and among the radicals, of the right of lesser men to secure their property. These opponents possessed an institution—Parliament—where they could express their grievances; eventually, they also acquired an army that waged war to secure the demands of the propertied classes. The result was limited monarchy as established in 1689 and a constitutional system based upon the laws made by Parliament and sanctioned by the king. Very gradually the monarchical element in that system would yield to the power and authority of parliamentary ministers and state officials.

The Revolution of 1688–1689 was England's last revolution. In the nineteenth and twentieth centuries, parliamentary institutions would be gradually and peacefully reformed to express a more democratic social reality. The events of 1688–1689 have rightly been described as "the year one," in that they fashioned a system of government that was not only resilient in Britain, but also capable of being adopted with modification elsewhere. The British system became a model for other forms of bourgeois representative government that were adopted in France and former British colonies, beginning with the United States.

The Netherlands: A Bourgeois Republic

One other area in Europe developed a system of representative government that also survived for centuries. The Netherlands, or Low Countries (Holland and Belgium), had been part of Hapsburg territory since the fifteenth century. When Charles V ascended to the Spanish throne in 1516, the Netherlands grew into an economic linchpin of the Spanish empire. Spain exported wool and bullion to the Low Countries in return for manufactured textiles, hardware, grain, and naval stores. Flanders, with Antwerp as its capital, was the manufacturing and banking center of the Spanish empire.

The Spanish monarchy exploited its colonies in both the old and new worlds to finance wars against the Turks and the Italian city-states, and by the 1540s, its crusade against Protestant Germany. In the northern Low Countries especially, this tax burden joined with administrative inefficiency, unemployment, and religious repression to create the conditions that sparked the first successful bourgeois revolution in history.

During the reign of Charles V's successor, Philip II, a tightly organized Calvinist minority, with its popular base in the cities and its military strategy founded on sea raids, at first harassed and then aggressively challenged Spanish power. In the 1560s the Spanish responded by trying to export the Inquisition into the Netherlands and by sending an enormous standing army there under the Duke of Alva. It was a classic example of overkill; thousands of once-loyal Flemish and Dutch subjects turned against the Spanish Crown. The people either converted secretly to Calvinism or aided the revolutionaries. Led by William the Silent (1533–1584), head of the Orange Dynasty, the seven northern provinces (Holland, Zeeland, Utrecht, Gelderland, Overijssel, Friesland, and Groningen) joined in the Union of Utrecht (1579) to protect themselves against Spanish aggression. Their determined resistance, coupled with the serious economic weaknesses of the overextended Spanish empire, eventually produced unexpected success for the northern colonies.

By 1609 the seven northern provinces were effectively free of Spanish control and loosely tied together under a republican form of government. Seventeenth-century Netherlands became a prosperous bourgeois state. Rich from the fruits of manufacture and trade in everything from flower bulbs to ships, the Dutch merchants ruled their cities and provinces with a fierce pride. By the early seventeenth century, this new nation of only one and a half million practiced the most innovative commercial and financial techniques in Europe.

In this fascinating instance, capitalism and Protestantism fused to do the work of princes; the Dutch state emerged without absolute monarchy, and indeed in opposition to it. From that experience, the ruling Dutch oligarchy retained a deep distrust of hereditary monarchy. The exact position of the House of Orange remained a vexing constitutional question until well into the eighteenth century. The oligarchs and their party, the Patriots, favored a republic without a single head, ruled by them through the Estates

Jan Vermeer (1632–1675): Young Woman with a Water Jug. Vermeer used many of the same objects in his light-filled, balanced interiors. The wall map is a reminder of Dutch trade. The rich oriental carpet, the stained glass, and the solid pitcher reflect a society that valued possessions having both beauty and utility (*The Metropolitan Museum of Art, Gift of Henry G. Marquand, 1889 (89.15.21)*

General. The Calvinist clergy, old aristocrats, and a vast section of the populace—all for very different reasons—wanted the head of the House of Orange to govern as stadholder (head) of the provinces, in effect as a limited monarch in a republican state. These unresolved political tensions prevented the Netherlands from developing a form of republican government that might have rivaled the stability of the British system of limited monarchy. The Dutch achievement came in other areas.

Calvinism had provided the ideology of revolution and national identity. Capital, in turn, created a unique cultural milieu in the Dutch urban centers of Amsterdam, Rotterdam, Utrecht, and The Hague. Wide toleration without a centralized system of censorship made the Dutch book trade, which often disseminated works by refugees from the Spanish Inquisition and later by French Protestants, the most vital in Europe right up to the French Revolution. And the sights and sounds of an active and prosperous population, coupled with a politically engaged and rich bourgeoisie, fed the imagination as well as the purses of various artistic schools. Rembrandt van Rijn, Jan Steen, Frans Hals, Jan Vermeer, and Jan van del Velde are at the top of a long list of great Dutch artists—many of them also refugees. They left timeless images portraying the people of the only republican national state to endure throughout the seventeenth century.

The Failure of Spanish Power

The revolt in the Netherlands dealt a devastating blow to the Spanish economy, as well as to its northern defenses against France. Spain's most psychologically upsetting defeat of the century, however, was the destruction of the Armada in 1588 in an unsuccessful attempt to invade England. During the reign of Philip II, Spanish self-confidence was shaken and a long decline in political power began.

Philip II

In 1556, Charles V abdicated the Spanish throne in favor of his son, Philip, to whom he bequeathed an empire that was governed effectively, yet burdened by the specters of bankruptcy and heresy. Philip II (1556–1598) dedicated himself to the imposition of orthodoxy in Spain. He bided his time with foreign infidels and heretics, awaiting the day when the crown would possess the revenue necessary to launch an offensive against the Turks and against international Protestantism.

To Philip II, being truly Spanish meant

being Christian in faith and blood; the racist tendencies, already evident in the later fifteenth century, gained full expression during his reign. Increasingly, the country came to be ruled by an exclusive class of old Christians who claimed to be untainted because for centuries they had refused to marry Muslims or Jews. Traditional in their thinking and in their control over the church, the religious orders, and the Inquisition, the Old Christians tried to preserve an imperial system badly in need of reform.

Melancholic and standoffish by temperament, Philip II worked arduously and declined most of life's enjoyments. He pored over his ministers' reports, editing and commenting, yet in the end he was strangely indecisive. Some problems remained unsolved for years, as frustrated advisers begged in vain for the king to take action. A zeal for Catholicism ruled his private conduct and infused his foreign policy.

By the 1580s, Philip's foreign policy was overextended in every direction: the campaign against England was matched by unsuccessful attempts to intervene on the side of the Guise in the French wars of religion. Meanwhile, the military campaign in the Netherlands wrought a catastrophe. In 1576 the Spanish themselves were forced to flood and sack Antwerp, their leading commercial and banking city in northern Europe. Antwerp's trade gradually moved to Amsterdam, a Protestant stronghold, which replaced its southern rival as an international capital and as the center of the new Dutch national state.

At every turn in northern Europe, Philip II's policies proved futile. One dramatic event came to symbolize this malaise in the Spanish mind: the defeat of the powerful Armada by England, widely believed to be an inferior power. Spain had regarded an assault on England as a holy crusade against the "heretic and bastard" Queen Elizabeth. Some Spanish officials had reasoned that a successful invasion would ignite a Catholic uprising by (vastly overestimated) numbers of English Catholics. Philip II had longed for the opportunity to conquer England; it was the main

Protestant power in Europe, and Philip particularly resented its assistance to Dutch rebels.

Outfitted in Lisbon harbor and constantly delayed by shortages of equipment, the Armada was composed of 130 ships, only a fourth of the originally planned fleet. These main ships and numerous smaller vessels carried 22,000 seamen and soldiers. The English fleet numbered less than 75. Sailing from Lisbon in May 1588, the Armada was poorly equipped. Its ships were too large and cumbersome to negotiate the treacherous English Channel, where the English sailing ships easily outmaneuvered them. The English sent fire ships against the Armada, which broke its formation; a Spanish army to be launched from Flanders failed to make its rendezvous; and perhaps most decisively, strong winds drove the Armada out of striking position. The victory went to the English, and both sides believed it to be a sign from God.

This defeat had an enormous psychological effect on the Spanish. They openly pondered what they had done to incur divine displeasure. Protestant Europe, on the other hand, hailed this victory as a sign of its election, and the "Protestant wind" stirred by divine intervention entered the mythology of many a proud Englishman. In the rise and fall of nations, self-confidence has played a crucial, if inexplicable, role.

The End of the Spanish Hapsburgs

After the defeat of the Armada, Spain gradually and reluctantly abandoned its imperial ambitions in northern Europe. The administrative structure built by Charles V and Philip II did remain strong throughout the seventeenth century; nevertheless, by the first quarter of the century enormous weaknesses had surfaced in Spanish economic and social life. In 1596, Philip II was bankrupt, his vast wealth overextended by the cost of foreign wars. Bankruptcy reappeared at various times in the seventeenth century, while the agricultural economy, at the heart of any early modern nation, stagnated. The Spanish in their golden age had never devoted enough attention to increasing domestic production.

Although Spain retained vast portions of its empire during the seventeenth century, important pieces broke away. First, the northern Netherlands secured its virtual independence. Then, in 1640, Portugal successfully revolted, as did Catalonia, although Catalonia was eventually brought back into the empire. And from 1606 to 1650, Spanish trade with the Americas dropped by 60 percent.

Despite these setbacks, Spain was still capable of taking a very aggressive posture during the Thirty Years' War (1618–1648). The Austrian branch of the Hapsburg family joined forces with their Spanish cousins, and neither the Swedes and Germans nor the Dutch could stop them. Only French participation in the Thirty Years' War on the Protestant side tipped the balance decisively against the Hapsburgs. Spanish aggression brought no victories, and with the Peace of Westphalia (1648), Spain officially recognized the independence of the Netherlands and severed its diplomatic ties with the Austrian branch of the family. The latter signed a separate treaty with the French. Austria itself would develop under this central European branch of the Hapsburg dynasty as a dynamic state, but not until the eighteenth century.

Spain had only one great statesman in the seventeenth century—Gaspar de Guzmán, count of Olivares (d. 1645), whose skill and efficiency matched his craving to restore Spain's imperial glory. He served Philip IV for over twenty years until his aggressive foreign and domestic policies brought ruin. One strength of the Spanish monarchy had been its ability to favor Castile while respecting the liberties and privileges of the provinces, Aragon and Catalonia in particular. Olivares attempted to bring the provincial laws into conformity with those of Castile and to force greater provincial participation in Spanish affairs. Clearly neither the provincial assemblies, the *Cortes,* nor the provincial aristocrats wished to undo the status

quo, and Olivares's policies led to revolt in Catalonia.

By 1660 the imperial age of the Spanish Hapsburgs had come to an end. The rule of the Protestant princes had been secured in the Holy Roman Empire; the Protestant and Dutch Republic flourished; Portugal and its colony of Brazil were independent of Spain; and dominance over European affairs had passed to France. The quality of material life in Spain deteriorated rapidly, and the ever-present gap between rich and poor widened even more drastically. The traditional aristocracy and the church retained their land and power, but failed conspicuously to produce effective leadership.

In the second half of the seventeenth century, Spanish leadership grew markedly worse. Palace intrigue replaced diplomacy and statesmanship. The reign of Charles II (1665–1700), whose Hapsburg parents were related as uncle and niece, witnessed the total administrative and economic collapse of Castile. What vitality remained in Spain could be found in its periphery, in Catalonia and Andalusia. At his death in 1700, Charles II (whose marriages had been childless) declared in favor of a French successor, Philip of Anjou, Louis XIV's grandson.

Charles's act, coupled with Louis XIV's designs on the kingdom of Spain, provoked another European war. The War of the Spanish Succession (1701–1713) pitted the Holy Roman Empire, England, and the Netherlands against France. Its outcome defeated Louis's desire to unite Spain and France under the Bourbons. Philip V, although king of Spain, was forced to renounce his claim to the French throne. Spain retained its political independence, but the Hapsburg dynasty in Spain had come to an end. From 1700 until very recently the Spanish state has been ruled by either dictators or Bourbons.

Of all the sovereign states of Europe to emerge in the early modern period, Spain presents the greatest set of paradoxes. It was the least centralized of all the states of the sixteenth and seventeenth centuries. In that lay its strength and its weakness. In the six-

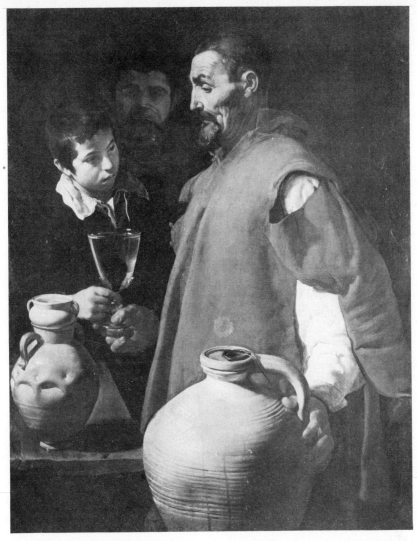

Diego Velázquez (1599–1660): The Water-Seller of Seville. The dramatic use of light makes Velázquez a Baroque artist, but his subject matter drawn from the lower classes shows the influence of Dutch genre scenes of everyday life. (*Victoria and Albert Museum*)

teenth century, Castile led the nation without crippling it. Spanish achievements in that century are nothing short of extraordinary in art, literature, navigation, exploration, administration, and even religious zeal. Then came the gradual and almost inexplicably precipitous decline in the seventeenth century, from which Spain has yet to recover.

The Spanish experience illustrates two observations in the history of the European state. First, the state as empire could only survive and prosper if the domestic economic base remained sound. The Spanish reliance on bullion from its colonies and its failure to cultivate industry and to reform the taxation system spelled disaster. Second, states with a vital and aggressive bourgeoisie flourished at the expense of societies where aristocracy and church dominated and controlled society and its mores—Spain's situation. The latter social groups tended to despise manual labor, profit taking, and technological progress. Although kings and dynastic families originally created them, after 1700 the major dynastic states were increasingly nurtured by the economic activities of the bourgeoisie. Bureaucracies drawn from the lesser aristocracy, however, still governed the states.

The Holy Roman Empire: The Failure to Unify Germany

In contrast to the French, English, Spanish, and Dutch experiences in the early modern period, the Germans failed to achieve national unity, which produced a legacy of frustration and antagonism toward the other powerful European states. The German failure to unify is tied to the history of the Holy Roman Empire. That union of various distinct central European territories was created in the tenth century when Otto I, in a deliberate attempt to revive Charlemagne's empire, was crowned Emperor of the Romans. Later the title was changed to Holy Roman emperor, with the kingdom consisting of mostly German-speaking principalities.

Most medieval emperors busied themselves not with administering their territories, but with attempting to secure control over the rich Italian peninsula and with challenging the rival authority of various popes. In the meantime, the German nobility extended and consolidated their rule over their peasants and over various towns and cities. Their aristocratic power remained a constant obstacle to German unity. Only by incorporating the nobility into the fabric of the state's power, into the court and the army, and by sanctioning their oppressive control over the peasants, would German rulers manage to create a unified German state. But that process of assimilation only commenced (first in Prussia) during the eighteenth century.

In the medieval and early modern periods the Holy Roman emperors were dependent on their most powerful noble lords—including an archbishop or two—because the office of emperor was an elected one, not the result of hereditary succession. German noble princes—some of whom were electors—such as the archbishops of Cologne and Mainz, the Hohenzollern elector of Brandenburg, the landgrave of Hesse, and the duke of Saxony—were fiercely independent. All belonged to the empire, yet all regarded themselves as autonomous powers. These decentralizing tendencies were highly developed by the fifteenth century, when the emperors gradually realized that the outer frontiers of their empire were slipping away. The French had conducted a successful military incursion into northern Italy and on the western frontier of the empire. Hungary had fallen to the Turks, while the Swiss were hard to govern and, given their terrain, impossible to beat into submission. At the same time, the Hapsburgs maneuvered themselves into a position from which they could monopolize the imperial elections. The empire became increasingly German and Hapsburg, with Worms as the seat of imperial power.

The Holy Roman Empire in the reigns of the Hapsburg emperors Maximilian I (1493–1519) and Charles V (1519–1556) might have achieved a degree of cohesion comparable to that in France and Spain. Certainly the impetus of war—against France and against the Turks—required the creation of a large standing army and the taxation to maintain it. Both additions could have worked to the benefit of a centralized, imperial power. But the Protestant Reformation, begun in 1517, meshed in with the already well-developed tendencies toward local independence. As a result, it destroyed the last hope of Hapsburg domination and German unity. The German nobility were all too ready to use the Reformation as a vindication of their local power, and indeed Luther made just such an appeal to their interests.

At precisely the moment, in the 1520s, when Charles V had to act with great determination to stop the spread of Lutheranism, he was at war with France over its claims to Italian territory. Charles had no sooner won his Italian territories, in particular the rich city-state of Milan, when he had to make war against the Turks, who in 1529 besieged Vienna. Not until the 1540s was Charles V in the position to attack the Lutheran princes. By then they had had considerable time to solidify their position and had united for mutual protection in the Schmalkaldic League.

War raged in Germany between the Protestant princes and the imperial army led by Charles V. In 1551, Catholic France entered the war on the Protestant side, and Charles V had to flee for his life. Defeated and exhausted, Charles abdicated and retired to a Spanish monastery. The Treaty of Augsburg (1555) conferred on every German prince the right to determine the religion of his subjects. The princes had won their territories, and a unified German state was never constructed by the Hapsburgs.

When Emperor Charles V abdicated in 1556, he gave his kingdom to his son Philip and his brother. Philip inherited Spain and its colonies and Ferdinand acquired the Austrian territories. Two branches of the Hapsburg family were thus created, and well into the late seventeenth century they defined their interests in common and often waged war accordingly. The enormous international power of the Hapsburgs was checked only by their uncertain authority over the Holy Roman Empire. Throughout the sixteenth century the Austrian Hapsburgs barely managed to control these sprawling and deeply divided German territories. Protestantism, as protected by the Treaty of Augsburg, and the particularism and provinciality of the German nobility continued to prevent the creation of a German state.

The Austrian Hapsburg emperors, however, never missed an opportunity to further the cause of the Counter Reformation and to court the favor of local interests opposed to the nobility. No Hapsburg was ever more fervid in that regard than the Jesuit-trained Archduke Ferdinand II, who ascended to the throne in Vienna in 1619. He immediately embarked on a policy of religious intolerance and used Spanish officials as his administrators. His policies provoked a war within the empire that engulfed the whole of Europe.

The Thirty Years' War (1618–1648) began when the Bohemians, whose anti-Catholic tendencies can be traced back to the Hussite reformation, attempted to put a Protestant king on their throne. The Austrian and Spanish Hapsburgs reacted by sending an army into the kingdom of Bohemia, and suddenly the whole empire was forced to take sides along religious lines. The Bohemian nobility, after centuries of enforcing serfdom, failed to rally the rural masses behind them, and victory went to the emperor. Indeed, Bohemia suffered an almost unimaginable devastation; the ravaging Catholic army sacked and burned three-fourths of the kingdom's towns and practically exterminated its aristocracy.

Until the 1630s, it looked as if the Hapsburgs would be able to use the war to enhance their power and to promote centralization. But the intervention of Protestant Sweden, led by Gustavus Adolphus and encouraged by France, wrecked Hapsburg ambitions. The ensuing military conflict devastated vast areas of northern and central Europe. The civilian population suffered untold hardships: soldiers raped women and pillaged the land, and thousands of refugees took to the roads and forests. Partly because the French finally intervened directly, the Spanish Hapsburgs emerged from the Thirty Years' War with no benefits. At the Treaty of Westphalia (1648), their Austrian cousins reaffirmed their right to govern the eastern states of the kingdom with Vienna as their capital. Austria took shape as a dynastic state, while the German territories in the empire remained fragmented by the independent interests of their largely unreformed feudal nobility.

The Emergence of Austria and Prussia

Austria

As a result of the settlement at Westphalia, the Austrian Hapsburgs gained firm control over Hungary and Bohemia, where they installed a virtually new and foreign nobility. At the same time, they strengthened their rule in Vienna. In one of the few spectacular

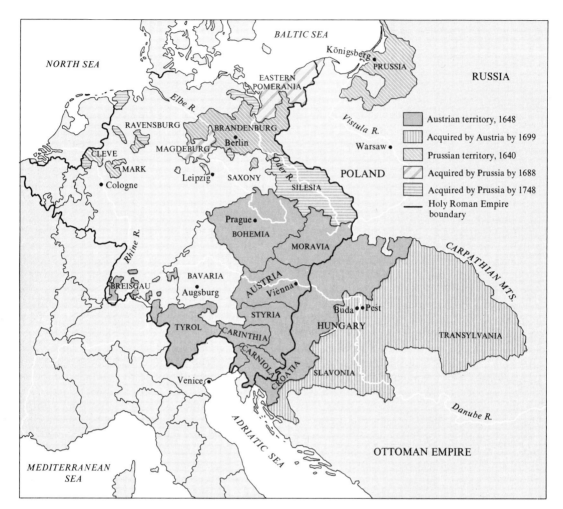

Map 16.3 The Growth of Austria and Brandenburg-Prussia, c. 1650–1750

successes achieved by the Counter Reformation, the ruling elites in all three territories were forcibly, or in many cases willingly, converted back to Catholicism. At long last, religious predominance could be used as a force—long delayed in eastern Europe because of the Protestant Reformation—for the creation of the Austrian dynastic state.

One severe obstacle to territorial hegemony remained: the military threat posed by the Turks, who sought to control much of Hungary. During the reign of Austrian Emperor

Leopold I (1658–1705), warfare against the Ottoman Empire—a recurrent theme in Hapsburg history beginning with Charles V— once again erupted, and in 1683 the Turks besieged the gates of Vienna. However, the Ottoman Empire no longer possessed its former strength and cohesiveness. A Catholic and unified Austrian army, composed of a variety of peoples from that kingdom and assisted by the Poles, managed to defeat the Turks and recapture the whole of Hungary and Transylvania and part of Croatia. Austria's right to govern was firmly accepted by the Turks at the Treaty of Karlowitz (1699).

The Austrian Hapsburgs and their victorious army had now entered the larger arena of European power politics. In 1700, at the death of the last Spanish Hapsburg, Leopold I sought to place his second son, Archduke Charles, on the Spanish throne. But this brought Leopold into a violent clash with Louis XIV. Once again Bourbon and Hapsburg rivalry, a dominant theme in early modern history, provoked a major European war.

In the War of the Spanish Succession the Austrians, with their army led by the brilliant Prince Eugene of Savoy, joined forces with the English and the Dutch. This war brought rewards in western Europe to the Austrian Hapsburgs, who acquired the Spanish Netherlands (Belgium today), as well as Milan and small holdings in Italy. But the Hapsburgs did not succeed in capturing the Spanish throne.

In the reign of Emperor Charles VI (1711–1740) Austria emerged as a major European power. Vienna became a cultural center in its own right. Austria's vast but loosely governed territories in the east, however, were not matched by territories in western and southern Europe.

Up to the early eighteenth century the Austrian Hapsburgs had struggled to achieve territorial hegemony and to subdue the dissident religious groups (Protestant and Turkish Muslim) that in very different ways threatened to undermine their authority. Warfare and the maintenance of a standing army had taken precedence over adminstrative reform and commercial growth. Yet military victory created the conditions within which centralization could occur.

The Austrian achievement of the eighteenth century, which made Austria a major force in European affairs, derived in large measure from the administrative reforms and cultural revival initiated by Charles VI (assisted militarily by Eugene of Savoy) and continued by his successors, Maria Theresa and Joseph II. These eighteenth-century monarchs embraced a style of government sometimes described as *enlightened* (see pages 421–423). They sought through education and liberal policies to catch up with the more established and older dynastic states of Europe.

Prussia

By the seventeenth century in northern Europe, the cohesive state governed by an absolute monarch (or by bourgeois oligarchs as in the Netherlands) had replaced feudalism as a system of government. Serfdom had disappeared in western Europe by the late sixteenth century, although it remained in parts of central and eastern Europe. The feudal aristocracy recouped their losses, however. No longer free to play at war or to control the lives of their peasants, progressive aristocrats improved their agricultural systems or sought offices and military commands in the service of the absolutist state. On the whole, western European aristocrats did not fare too badly under absolutism, but in the course of the early modern period, the state decisively checked their independent power.

Prussia was different. Prussia was a state, within the Holy Roman Empire, that had emerged very late in northern Europe (in the late seventeenth century). Like Austria, Prussia displayed certain unique characteristics. Although it did develop an absolute monarchy like France, its powerful aristocracy only acquiesced to monarchical power in exchange for guarantees of their feudal power over the peasantry. In 1653 the Prussian nobility granted the elector power to collect taxes for the maintenance of a powerful army, but only after he issued decrees rendering serfdom permanent.

The ruling dynasty of Prussia, the Hohenzollerns, had a most inauspicious beginning in the later Middle Ages. These rulers were little more than dukes in the Holy Roman Empire until 1415, when the Emperor Sigismund made one of them an imperial elector with the right to choose imperial successors. For centuries, the Hohenzollerns had made weak claims to territory in northern

Germany. They finally achieved control over Prussia and certain other smaller principalities by claiming the inheritance of one wife (1608) and by single-minded, ruthless aggression.

The most aggressive of these Hohenzollerns was the Elector Frederick William (1640–1688), who played a key role in forging the new Prussian state. Frederick William had inherited the territories of the beleaguered Hohenzollern dynasty, whose main holding, Brandenburg in Prussia, was very poor in natural resources. Indeed, Prussia had barely survived the devastation wrought by the Thirty Years' War, especially the Swedish army's occupation of the electorate.

A distaste for foreign intervention in Prussia, and for the accompanying humiliation and excessive taxes, prompted the *Junker* class (the landed Prussian nobility) to support national unity and strong central government. But they would brook no threat to their economic power over their lands and peasants. By 1672 the Prussian army, led by Junker officers, was strong enough to enter the Franco-Dutch war on the Dutch side. The war brought no territorial gains, but it allowed the elector to raise taxes. Once again the pattern of foreign war, taxes, and military conscription led to an increase in the power of the central government. But in Prussia, in contrast to western lands, the bureaucracy was entirely military. No clerics or rich bourgeois shared power with this Junker class. The pattern initiated by the Great Elector (Frederick William) would be continued in the reigns of his successors: Frederick I (d. 1713), Frederick William I, and Frederick the Great.

The alliance between aristocracy and monarchy was especially strengthened in the reign of Frederick William I (1713–1740). In the older dynastic states, absolute monarchs in every case tried to dispense with representative institutions once the monarchy's power could stand on its own. So, too, did Frederick William undercut the Prussian provincial assemblies, the *Landtage,* which still had power over taxation and army recruitment. Gradually, he rendered the Landtage superfluous.

But he was only able to do so by incorporating the landowning Junker class into the machinery of government—especially into the army—and by keeping the tax-paying peasants in the status of serfs.

In a nation where representative institutions in the twentieth century have struggled, often unsuccessfully, for survival, it is interesting that such institutions did exercise considerable influence in Prussia up to the early eighteenth century. Like the Austrians during the eighteenth century, the Prussians also embarked on a program of modernization, which has occasionally been described as enlightened.

Russia

Although remote from developments in western Europe, Russia in the early modern period took on some characteristics remarkably similar to those of western European states. Russia, also, relied on absolute monarchy reinforced by a feudal aristocracy. As in Europe, the latter's power to wreak havoc had to be checked and its energies channeled into the state's service. But the Russian pattern of absolutism breaks with the Western model and resembles that adopted in Prussia, where serfdom increased as the power of centralized monarchy grew. The award of peasants was the bribe by which the monarchy secured the aristocrats' cooperation in the state's growth.

Russian absolutism experienced a false start under Ivan IV, "The Terrible" (1547–1584). Late in the sixteenth century Ivan sought to impose a tsarist autocracy. He waged a futile war against Sweden and created an internal police force that was entrusted with the administration of central Russia. His failure in war and an irrational policy of repression (fueled in part by Ivan's mental instability) doomed his premature attempt to impose absolutism. Much of Ivan's state-building was

Map 16.4 The Expansion of Russia, 1300–1725 ▶

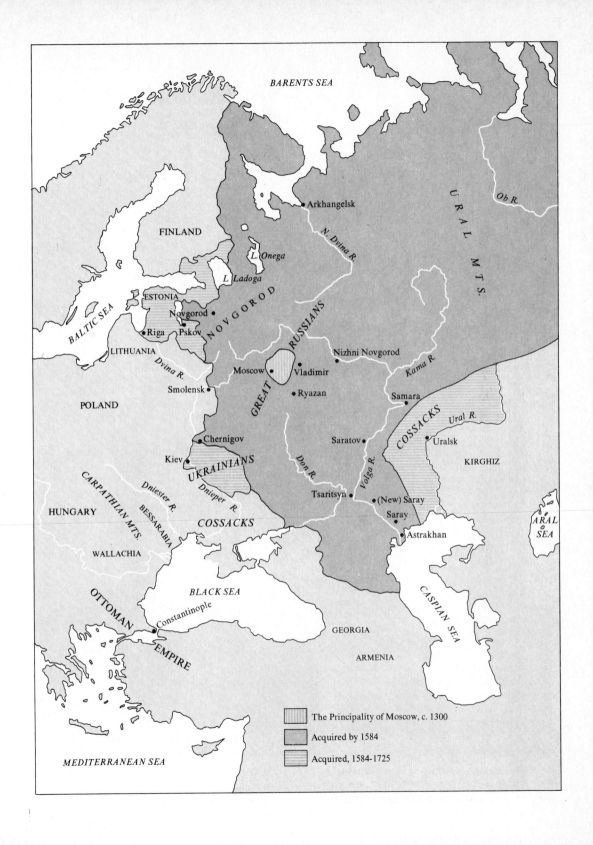

BARENTS SEA

FINLAND

• Arkhangelsk

N. Dvina R.

URAL MTS.

Ob R.

L. Onega

L. Ladoga

ESTONIA

Novgorod •

Riga •

• Pskov

N O V G O R O D

BALTIC SEA

LITHUANIA

Dvina R.

POLAND

Smolensk •

Moscow •

Vladimír •

G R E A T

R U S S I A N S

Nizhni Novgorod •

Kama R.

Ryazan •

Samara •

COSSACKS

Ural R.

Uralsk •

KIRGHIZ

Chernigov •

Kiev •

U K R A I N I A N S

Dniester R.

Dnieper R.

Don R.

Saratov •

Saratov •

Volga R.

CARPATHIAN MTS.

HUNGARY

BESSARABIA

COSSACKS

Tsaritsyn •

• (New) Saray

• Saray

ARAL SEA

WALLACHIA

• Astrakhan

OTTOMAN

BLACK SEA

CASPIAN SEA

Constantinople •

GEORGIA

EMPIRE

ARMENIA

MEDITERRANEAN SEA

The Principality of Moscow, c. 1300

Acquired by 1584

Acquired, 1584–1725

St. Basil's Cathedral, Moscow. The cathedral of St. Basil is a fusion of native folk art and late Byzantine architecture. Russia in the seventeenth century had strong roots in its medieval past. Peter the Great forcefully rejected many traditions and made Russia turn to the West for inspiration. (*William Brumfield*)

undone with his death, which launched a "Time of Troubles"—a period of foreign invasion and civil warfare—that endured for years.

Order was restored in the country only in 1613 when the Romanov dynasty gained the support of the aristocracy. The accession of Michael Romanov as tsar marks the emergence of a unified Russian state. Of that dynasty, by far the most important ruler was Peter the Great (1689–1725). He ruthlessly suppressed the independent aristocrats, while inventing new titles and ranks for those loyal to the court. Both nobility and gentry were brought into the army by universal service obligations. The peasants were made the personal property of their lords, to be sold at will; thus, the distinction between serf and slave was obliterated. Finally, Peter brought the church under the control of the state by establishing a new office called the Holy Synod; its head was a government official.

From 1700 to 1707, taxes on the peasants multiplied five times over. Predictably, the money went toward the creation of a professional army along European lines and to making war. The preparation led this time to victory over the Swedes.

Peter succeeded in wedding the aristocracy to the absolutist state, and the union was so successful that strong Russian monarchs in the eighteenth century, like Catherine the Great, could embrace enlightened reforms without jeopardizing the stability of their regimes. Once again, repression and violence in the form of taxation, serfdom, and war led to the creation of a dynastic state—one that proved the least susceptible to reform, eventually to be dismantled in 1917 by the Russian Revolution.

The State and Modern Political Development

By the early seventeenth century, Europeans had developed the concept of a *state*—a distinctive political entity to which its subjects owed duties and obligations. That concept would become the foundation of the modern science of politics. The one essential ingredient of the Western concept of the state, as it emerged in the early modern period, was the notion of *sovereignty;* that is, within its borders the state was supreme, and all corporations and organizations—by implication even the church—were allowed to exist only by the state's permission.

The modern concept of the state first developed not in Renaissance Italy, as might be expected, but in France and England in the mid-1500s. In every instance where early modern theorists—with the exception of Calvinist revolutionaries—discussed a state, it was to instruct the prince in its governance. These theorists were responding to a new political reality: princes had become significantly more powerful than any other single group within a country. But simultaneously an entity larger than its component parts and even more important than its rulers had emerged; the state seemed increasingly to possess its own reason for existence. The art of government entailed molding the ambitions and strength of the powerful into their state's service. The state, its power growing through war and taxation, had become the basic unit of political authority in the West.

Significantly, the concept of human liberty, now so basic to Western thought, was not articulated first in the sovereign states of Europe. Rather, it was largely an Italian creation, discussed with great vehemence by the Italian theorists of the later Middle Ages and the Renaissance. These humanists lived and wrote in the independent city-states, and they often aimed their treatises against the encroachments of the Holy Roman emperor—in short, against princes and their search for absolute power. In the sixteenth and seventeenth centuries, the idea of liberty was generally found only in the writings of Calvinist opponents of absolutism. Not until the mid-seventeenth century in England was there a body of political thought arguing that human liberty could be ensured within the confines of a

Chronology 16.1 The Rise of Sovereignty

1453	The Hundred Years' War ends
1453–1485	The War of Roses in England between rival nobles
1469	Ferdinand and Isabella begin rule of Castile and Aragon
1485	Henry VII begins the reign of the Tudor dynasty in England
1517	The Protestant Reformation begins in Germany
1519	Charles V of Spain becomes Hapsburg emperor of the Holy Roman Empire
1553–1558	Queen Mary attempts to return England to Catholicism
1556–1598	Philip II of Spain persecutes Jews and Muslims
1559	The Treaty of Cateau-Cambrésis between France and Spain
1560s–1609	The Netherlands revolts from Spanish rule
1562–1598	Religious wars in France
1572	The St. Bartholomew's Day Massacre—Queen Catherine of France orders thousands of Protestants executed
1579	*Vindiciae contra Tyrannos*, published by Huguenots, justifies regicide
1588	The Spanish Armada is defeated by the English fleet
1590s	Boris Gudonov leads a reaction in Russia against Ivan IV, "The Terrible"
1593	Henry IV of France renounces his Protestantism to restore peace in France

powerful national state—one governed by mere mortals and not by divinely sanctioned and absolute kings. In general, despite the English and Dutch developments, absolutism in its varied forms (Spanish, French, Prussian) dominated the political development of early modern Europe.

Although first articulated in the Italian republics and then enacted briefly in England and more durably in the Netherlands, the republican ideal did not gain acceptance as a viable critique of absolutism until the European Enlightenment of the eighteenth century. In the democratic and republican revolutions of the late eighteenth century, western Europeans and Americans repudiated monarchical systems of government in response to the republican ideal. By then, princes and the aristocratic and military elites had outlived their usefulness in many parts of Europe. The states they had created, in large measure to further their own interests, had indeed become larger than their creators. Eventually the national states of western Europe, as well as of the Americas, proved able to survive and prosper without kings or aristocrats, while they retained the administrative and military mechanisms so skilfully and relentlessly developed by early modern kings and their court officials.

Chronology 16.1 continued

1598	The French Protestants are granted religious toleration by the Edict of Nantes
1624–1642	Cardinal Richelieu, Louis XIII's chief minister, determines royal policies
1640	The Portuguese revolt successfully against Spain
1640–1660	The English Revolution
1648	The Peace of Westphalia ends the Thirty Years' War
1648–1653	The Fronde, a rebellious reaction centered in Paris
1649	Charles I, Stuart king of England, is executed by an act of Parliament
1649–1660	England is co-ruled by Parliament and the army under Oliver Cromwell
1660	Charles II returns from exile and becomes king of England
1681	The Turks attack Vienna and are defeated; the Austrians recapture Hungary, Transylvania, and parts of Croatia
1685	Louis XIV of France revokes the Edict of Nantes
1688–1689	Revolution in England; end of absolutism
1701	Louis XIV tries to bring Spain under French control
1702–1713	The War of the Spanish Succession
1740	Frederick the Great of Prussia invades Silesia, starting war with Austria
1789	The French Revolution begins

Notes

1. J. H. Elliott, *Imperial Spain, 1469–1716* (New York: St. Martin's Press, 1963), p. 18.

2. J. H. Plumb, *The Growth of Political Stability in England: 1675–1725* (London: Macmillan, 1967), p. 69.

Suggested Reading

Anderson, Perry, *Lineages of the Abolutist State* (1974). An excellent survey, written from a Marxist perspective.

Elliott, J. H., *Imperial Spain, 1469–1716* (1963). An excellent survey of the major European power of the early modern period.

Goubert, Pierre, *Louis XIV and Twenty Million Frenchmen* (1966). An important reappraisal of the "Sun King," emphasizing the effects of his policies on ordinary French people.

Hill, Christopher, *God's Englishman* (1970). A biography of Oliver Cromwell.

Koenigsberger, H. G., and Mosse, G. L., *Europe in the Sixteenth Century* (1968). Some excellent chapters on the monarchies, the Dutch revolt, and the Hapsburgs.

Parker, Geoffrey, *Spain and The Netherlands, 1559–1659* (1979). A good survey of a complex relationship.

Plumb, J. H., *The Growth of Political Stability in England, 1675–1725* (1967). A basic book, clear and readable.

Shennan, J. H., *The Origins of the Modern European State* (1974). An excellent brief introduction.

Smith, Lacey Baldwin, *This Realm of England, 1399 to 1688* (revised ed., 1983). Still the best survey of England during this period.

Wedgwood, C. V., *William the Silent* (1944). A good biography of one of the founders of the Dutch republic.

Zagorin, Perez, *Rebels and Rulers, 1500–1660*, 2 vols. (1982). A good general survey of recent scholarship.

Review Questions

1. What role did the aristocracy play in the formation of the European states?

2. In what ways did early modern kings increase their power, and what relationship did they have to the commercial bourgeoisie in their countries?

3. What is meant by *raison d'état* and by the divine right of kings?

4. What role did religion and national churches play in creating the state?

5. Why did England move in the direction of parliamentary government, while most countries on the Continent embraced absolutism? Describe the main factors.

6. What made the Dutch state so different from its neighbors? Describe the differences.

7. What were the strengths and weaknesses of the Spanish state?

8. What makes the Prussian, Russian, and Austrian experiences of statehood roughly comparable?

9. Discuss the differences between the treatment of the peasants in eastern Europe and the treatment of those in western Europe.

10. Government has sometimes been described as being, in the final analysis, organized violence. Is that an adequate description of early modern European governments?

17

The Scientific Revolution:
The Mechanical Universe

Starting in the late fourteenth century, the cohesive medieval world began to disintegrate, a process lasting to the late seventeenth century. Not only did the basic medieval institutions like feudalism weaken, but also the medieval view of the universe became transformed into the modern and scientific understanding of nature.

Three historical movements during the early modern period made this intellectual transformation, called the *Scientific Revolution,* possible. The Italian Renaissance created new literary and artistic styles that sought to portray people and nature as they are, and this effort aroused a curiosity that fostered investigation into physical phenomena. Then the Reformation shattered the unity of Christendom, and a different religious person, one intent on finding personal salvation without the assistance of priests or sacraments, came into existence. Protestant cities and countries inevitably found themselves in opposition to the Roman church and its teaching authority; very gradually the practitioners of the new science found a more congenial atmosphere for work in those Protestant centers. Both the Renaissance and the Reformation encouraged a sense of confidence in human ability to arrive at new truths about the physical environment. Finally, feudalism and manorialism were replaced by sovereign states and commercial capitalism. And by the late seventeenth century the leaders of those states actively encouraged science as a key to increasing human control over the environment. They saw that such control, particularly through agricultural experiments, might increase prosperity.

The unique contribution of the Scientific Revolution to the making of the modern world lay in its new mechanical conception of nature, which enabled Westerners to discover and to explain the laws of nature mathematically. They came to see nature as composed solely of matter whose motion, occurring in space and measurable by time, was governed by laws of force. This philosophically elegant construction renders the physical world knowable, and even possibly manageable.

The Scientific Revolution also entailed the discovery of a new, scientific methodology. Because of the successful experiments performed by scientists and natural philosophers such as Galileo Galilei (1564–1642), William Harvey (1578–1657), Robert Boyle (1627–1691), and Isaac Newton (1642–1727), Western science acquired its still-characteristic methodology of observation and experimentation. By the late seventeenth century, no one could entertain a serious interest in any aspect of the physical order without actually doing experiments or without observing, in a rigorous and systematic way, the behavior of physical phenomena. The mechanical concept of nature coupled with a rigorous methodology gave modern scientists the means to unlock and explain the secrets of nature.

Mathematics increasingly became the language of the new science. For centuries, Europeans had used algebra and geometry to explain certain physical phenomena. With the Scientific Revolution came a new mathematics, the calculus; but even more important, philosophers became increasingly convinced that all nature—physical objects as well as invisible forces—could be expressed mathematically. By the late seventeenth century, even geometry had become so complex that a gifted philosopher like John Locke (1632–1704), a friend and contemporary of Isaac Newton, could not understand the sophisticated mathematics used by Newton in the *Principia*. A new scientific culture had been born that during the eighteenth-century Enlightenment (see Chapter 18), achieved great importance as a model for progress in both the natural and human sciences.

Medieval Cosmology

The unique character of the modern scientific outlook is most understandable in contrast with what went before it—the medieval understanding of the natural world and its physical properties. That understanding rested on a blend of Christian thought with theories derived from ancient Greek writers like Aristotle and Ptolemy. The explanations given by Aristotle (384–322 B.C.) for the motion of heavy bodies permeated medieval scientific literature. In trying to understand motion, Aristotle had argued simply that it was in the nature of things to move in certain ways. A stone falls because it is absolutely heavy; fire rises because it is absolutely light. Weight is an absolute property of a physical thing; therefore, motion results from the properties of bodies, and not from the forces or laws of motion at work in nature. It follows (logically but incorrectly) that if the medium through which a body falls is taken as a constant, then the speed of its fall could be doubled if its weight were doubled. Only rigorous experimentation could refute this erroneous concept of motion; it was many centuries before such experimentation was undertaken.

Aristotle's physics fitted neatly into his cosmology, or world picture. The earth, being the heaviest object, lay stationary and suspended at the center of the universe. The sun, the planets, and the moon revolved in circles, or in combinations of circles, around the earth. Aristotle presumed that since the planets were round themselves, always in motion and seemingly never altered, the most "natural" motion for them should be circular.

Aristotle's physics and cosmology were unified. He could put the earth stationary at the center of the universe because he presumed its absolute heaviness; all other heavy bodies that he had observed do fall toward it. He presumed that the planets were made of a kind of luminous ether and were held in their circular orbits by luminous spheres, or "tracks." These spheres possessed a certain reality, although invisible to human beings, and hence they came to be known as the crystalline spheres.

Aristotle believed that everything in motion had been moved by another object that was itself in motion—a continuing chain of movers and moved. By inference, this belief led back

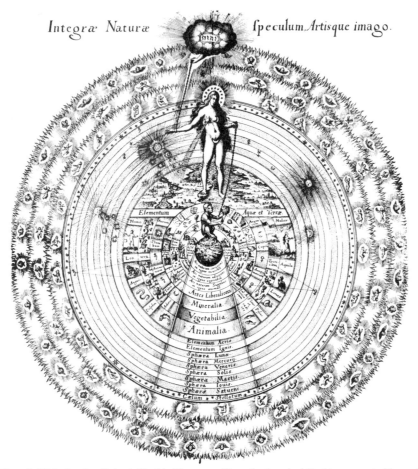

Integræ Naturæ   *Speculum, Artisque imago.*

Utriusque Cosmi Historia, by Robert Fludd: The Universe. This engraving from the early seventeenth century illustrates the persistence of the medieval view of the universe. Christian theology had reinterpreted classical models from Aristotle and Ptolemy. Here the hand of God is connected by a chain to the goddess Nature, who stands upon the earth, the center of the universe. (*By permission of the Houghton Library, Harvard University*)

to some object or being that began the motion. Christian philosophers of the Middle Ages argued that Aristotle's Unmoved Mover must be the God of Christianity. For Aristotle, who had no conception of a personal God or an afterlife, and who believed that the universe was eternal rather than created at a specific point in time, such an identification would have been meaningless.

Although Aristotle's cosmology never obtained the stature of orthodoxy among the ancient Greeks, by the second century A.D. in Alexandria, Greek astronomy became codified and then rigid. Ptolemy of Alexandria produced the *Almagest* (A.D. 150), a handbook of Greek astronomy based on the theories of

Aristotle. Central to that work was the assumption that a motionless earth stood at the center of the universe (although some Greeks had disputed the notion) and that the planets move about it in a series of circular orbits interrupted by epicycles. By the Late Middle Ages, Ptolemy's handbook, because of the support it lent to Aristotelian cosmology, had come to embody standard astronomical wisdom. As late as the middle of the seventeenth century, over one hundred years after Polish astronomer Nicolaus Copernicus had argued mathematically that the sun was the center of the universe, educated Europeans in most universities still believed the earth had that central position.

In the thirteenth century, mainly through the philosophical efforts of Thomas Aquinas (1225–1274), Aristotle's thought was adapted to Christian beliefs, often in tortured ways. Aquinas emphasized that order pervaded nature and that every physical effect had a physical cause. The tendency in Aquinas's thought and that of his followers, the scholastics, was to search for these causes—again to ask why things move, rather than how they move. But Aquinas denied that these causes stretched back to infinity. Instead, he insisted that nature proves God's existence; God is the First Cause of all physical phenomena. Despite the scholastic adaptations of Aristotle, the church still regarded Christian Aristotelianism with some suspicion, and in 1277 many of Aristotle's theories were condemned. That condemnation indirectly served to keep medieval science from falling totally under the influence of scholastic teachings.

Medieval thinkers integrated the cosmology of Aristotle and Ptolemy into a Christian framework that drew a sharp distinction between the world beyond the moon and an earthly realm. Celestial bodies were composed of the divine ether, a substance too pure, too spiritual to be found on earth; heavenly bodies, unlike those on earth, were immune to all change and obeyed different laws of motion than earthly bodies did. The universe was not homogeneous but was divided into a higher world of the heavens and a lower world of earth. Earth could not compare with the heavens in spiritual dignity, but God had nevertheless situated it in the center of the universe. Earth deserved this position of importance, for only here was the drama of salvation performed. This vision of the universe was to be shattered by the Scientific Revolution.

A New View of Nature

Renaissance Background

With the advent of the Renaissance, which began in Italy in the late fourteenth century, a new breed of intellectuals began to challenge medieval assumptions about human beings and nature. These thinkers were armed with a collection of newly discovered ancient Greek and Roman texts (see Chapter 13). The philosophy of Plato was seized on as an alternative to medieval scholasticism.

The great strength of Plato's philosophy lay in his belief that one must look beyond the appearance of things to an invisible reality that is simple, rational, and given to coherent, mathematical explanation. Plato's search for this fundamental reality would influence thinkers of the Scientific Revolution.

Renaissance Platonists interpreted Plato from a Christian perspective, and they believed that the Platonic search for truth about nature, about God's work, was but another aspect of the search for knowledge about God. The universities of Italy, as well as the independent academies founded in Italian cities, became centers where the Platonists taught, translated, and wrote commentaries about Plato's philosophy. These humanists tried to study the invisible world of Ideas and Forms that Plato claimed to be the essence of reality. Music and mathematics, they believed, provided contact with this universal, eternal, and unchanging higher reality. The leading thinkers of the Scientific Revolution found inspiration in the Platonic tradition that nature's truths apply universally and possess the elegance and simplicity of mathematics.

The thinkers of the Scientific Revolution also drew on a tradition of magic that reached back to the ancient world. In the first and second centuries A.D., various practitioners and writers elaborated on the mystical and magical approach to nature. Many of these anonymous students of magic were in contact with the Hermetic tradition. They believed that there had once been an ancient Egyptian priest, Hermes Trismegistus, who had possessed secret knowledge about nature's processes and the ultimate forces at work in the universe. In the second century A.D., this magical tradition was written down in a series of mystical dialogues about the universe. When Renaissance Europeans rediscovered these second-century writings, they erroneously assumed the author to be Hermes and his followers. Hence the writings seemed to be even older than the Bible.

This Hermetic literature glorified both the mystical and the magical. It prescribed that true knowledge comes from a contemplation of the One, or the Whole—a spiritual reality higher than, yet significantly for the development of science, embedded in nature. Some of these ancient writings argued that the sun was the natural symbol of this Oneness, and such an argument seemed to give weight to a heliocentric picture of the universe. The Renaissance followers of Hermes indulged in both what would now be called magic and what would be called science without seeing any fundamental distinction between them. The route that the searcher for nature's wisdom took did not matter as much as the quest did. As a result, in early modern Europe the practitioners of alchemy and astrology could also be mathematicians and astronomers, and the distinction we draw today between magic and science—between the irrational and the rational—would not have been understood by leading natural philosophers of the sixteenth and seventeenth centuries.

The Hermetic approach to nature also resembled Platonism in certain important ways. Both strove for perfection and a higher, spiritual reality, but the *magus,* or Hermetic magician, took certain shortcuts. The magus presumed that study and mental discipline were important, but that ultimate wisdom could come to its seeker through *gnosis,* an immediate, overpowering insight into the One, or God, or Nature. Important contributors to the Scientific Revolution, notably Johannes Kepler and Isaac Newton, grasped at the promise of such wisdom. Kepler believed in astrology, and Newton was profoundly interested in alchemy.

The Renaissance revival of ancient learning contributed a new approach to nature, one that was simultaneously mathematical, experimental, and magical. While the achievements of modern science depend on experimentation and mathematical logic, the compelling impulse to search for nature's secrets presumes a degree of self-confidence best exemplified and symbolized by the magician. Eventually, in one of the important by-products of the Scientific Revolution, the main practitioners of the new science would repudiate magic, largely because of its secretive quality and because of its associations with popular culture and religion. But the demise of magic should not obscure its initial role, among many other factors, as a stimulus for scientific inquiry and enthusiasm.

The Copernican Revolution

Nicolaus Copernicus was born in Poland in 1473. As a young man, he enrolled in the University of Cracow, where he may have come under the influence of Renaissance Platonism, which was spreading outward from the Italian city-states. Copernicus also journeyed to Italy, and in Bologna and Padua he may have been exposed to ancient Greek texts containing arguments for the sun being the center of the universe.

Copernicus' interest in mathematics and astronomy was stimulated by contemporary discussions of the need for calendar reform, and this topic required a thorough understanding of Ptolemaic astronomy. But the latter's mathematical complexity troubled Copernicus, trained, as he had been, in the new humanism. Copernicus believed that truth was the product of elegance and simplicity, and those qualities were lacking in Ptolemaic astronomy. In addition, Copernicus knew that Ptolemy had predecessors among the ancients who philosophized about a heliocentric universe or who held Aristotle in little regard. His Renaissance education gave Copernicus not a body of new scientific truth, but rather the courage to break with traditional truth taught in the universities.

Toward the end of his stay in Italy, Copernicus became convinced that the sun lay at the center of the universe. So he set out on a lifelong task to work out mathematical explanations of how the heliocentric universe operated. Because he did not want to engage in controversy with the followers of Aristotle, Copernicus published his findings only in 1543 in a work entitled *On the Revolutions of the Heavenly Spheres*. Legend says his book, which in effect began the Scientific Revolution, was brought to him on his deathbed.

The treatise retained some elements of the Aristotelian-Ptolemaic system. Copernicus never doubted Aristotle's basic notion of the perfect circular motion of the planets, or the existence of crystalline spheres within which the stars revolved, and he retained many of Ptolemy's epicycles. But Copernicus was trying to propose a heliocentric model of the universe that was mathematically simpler than Ptolemy's earth-centered universe. In this effort, Copernicus partially succeeded, for his system eliminated a significant number of Ptolemy's epicycles and cleared up some problems that had troubled astronomers.

Copernicus' genius was expressed in his ability to pursue an idea—a sun-centered universe—and to bring to that pursuit lifelong dedication and brilliance in mathematics. By removing the earth from its central position and by giving it motion—that is, by making the earth just another planet—Copernicus undermined the system of medieval cosmology and made the birth of modern astronomy possible.

But because they were committed to the Aristotelian-Ptolemaic system and to Biblical statements that supported it, most thinkers rejected Copernicus' conclusions. They also raised specific objections. The earth, they said, is too heavy to move. How, they asked, can an object falling from a high tower land directly below the point from which it was dropped if the earth is moving so rapidly?

Tycho and Kepler: The Laws of Planetary Motion

The most gifted astronomer in the generation after Copernicus, Tycho Brahe (1546–1601),

Tycho Brahe and His Observatory's Interior. Although Tycho Brahe remained a staunch Aristotelian, his observation of a new star in 1572 and a comet in 1577 challenged these traditional views. His precise scientific approach to astronomy and careful mathematical calculations were to be his greatest legacy. (*The British Library*)

never accepted the Copernican system. He did, however, realize more fully than any contemporaries the necessity for new observations. Aided by the king of Denmark, Tycho built the finest observatory in Europe to use in his work.

In 1572 he observed a new star in the heavens—a discovery that offered a direct and serious challenge to the Aristotelian assumption that the heavens are unalterable, fixed, and perfect. To this discovery of what eventually proved to be an exploding star, Tycho added his observations on the comet of 1577. He demonstrated that it moved unimpeded through the areas between the planets, that it passed right through the crystalline spheres. This discovery raised the question of whether such spheres existed, but Tycho himself remained an Aristotelian. Although his devotion to a literal reading of the Bible led Tycho to reject the Copernican sun-centered universe, he did propose an alternative system in which the planets revolved around the sun, but the sun moved about a motionless earth.

Tycho's fame ultimately rests on his skill as a practicing astronomer. He bequeathed to future generations precise calculations about the movements of heavenly bodies, which proved invaluable. These calculations were put to greatest use by Johannes Kepler (1571–1630), a German who collaborated with Tycho during the latter's final years. Tycho bequeathed his astronomical papers to Kepler, who brought to this data a scientific vision that was both experimental and mystical.

Kepler searched persistently for harmonious laws of planetary motion. He did so because he believed profoundly in the Platonic ideal: a spiritual force infuses the physical order; beneath appearances are harmony and unity; and the human mind can begin to comprehend that unity only through gnosis—a direct and mystical realization of unity—and through mathematics. Kepler believed that both approaches were compatible, and he managed to combine them. He believed in and practiced astrology (as did Tycho), and throughout his lifetime, Kepler tried to contact an ancient but lost and secret wisdom.

In the course of his studies and observations of the heavens, Kepler discovered the three basic laws of planetary motion. First, the orbits of the planets are elliptical, not circular as Aristotle and Ptolemy had assumed, and the sun is one focus of the ellipse. Unlike Tycho,

Kepler accepted Copernicus' theory and provided proof for it. Kepler's second law demonstrated that the velocity of a planet is not uniform, as had been believed, but increases as its distance from the sun decreases. Kepler's third law—that the squares of the times taken by any two planets in their revolutions around the sun are in the same ratio as the cubes of their average distances from the sun—brought the planets together into a unified mathematical system.

The significance of Kepler's work was immense. He gave sound mathematical proof to Copernicus' theory, eliminated forever the use of epicycles that had saved the appearance of circular motion, and demonstrated that mathematical relationships can describe the planetary system. But Kepler left a significant question unresolved: what kept the planets in their orbits? Why did they not fly out into space or crash into the sun? The answer would be supplied by Isaac Newton, who synthesized the astronomy of Copernicus and Kepler with the new physics developed by Galileo.

Galileo: Experimental Physics

At the same time that Kepler was developing a new astronomy, his contemporary Galileo Galilei (1564–1642) was breaking with the older physics of Aristotle. A Pisan by birth, Galileo lived for many years in Padua, where he conducted some of his first experiments on the motion of bodies. Guided by the dominant philosophy of the Italian Renaissance—the revived doctrines of Plato—Galileo believed that beyond the visible world lay universal truths, subject to mathematical verification. Galileo insisted that the study of motion entails not only the use of logic (as Aristotle had believed) but also the application of mathematics. For this Late Renaissance natural philosopher, mathematics became the language of nature. Galileo also believed that only after experimenting with the operations of nature can the philosopher formulate the harmonious laws of the universe and give them mathematical expression.

In his mechanical experiments, Galileo discovered that uniform force applied to bodies of unequal weights would produce, all other things being equal, a uniform acceleration. He demonstrated that bodies fall with arithmetic regularity. Motion could, therefore, be treated mathematically.

Galileo came very close to perceiving that inertia governs the motion of bodies, but his concept of inertia was flawed. He believed that inertial force was circular. He did not grasp what Newton would later proclaim, that bodies move in a straight line at a uniform velocity unless impeded. But Galileo's effect was enormous; he had suggested that terrestrial objects could in theory stay in motion forever.

Galileo established a fundamental principle of modern science—the order and uniformity of nature. There are no distinctions in rank or quality between the heavens and earth; heavenly bodies are not perfect and changeless as Aristotle had believed. In 1609, Galileo built a telescope through which he viewed the surface of the moon. The next year, in a treatise called *The Starry Messenger*, he proclaimed to the world that the moon "is not smooth, uniform, and precisely spherical as a great number of philosophers believe it and the other heavenly bodies to be, but is uneven, rough, and full of cavities . . . being not unlike the face of the earth, relieved by chains of mountains and deep valleys."[1] In addition, Galileo observed spots on the sun, providing further evidence that heavenly objects, like earthly objects, undergo change. There are no higher and lower worlds; nature is the same throughout.

Through his telescope Galileo also saw moons around Jupiter—a discovery that served to support the Copernican hypothesis. If Jupiter had moons, then all heavenly bodies did not orbit the earth. The moons of Jupiter removed a fundamental criticism leveled against Copernicus and opened up the possibility that indeed the earth, with its own moon, might be just like the planet Jupiter, and both might in turn revolve around a central point—the sun.

With Galileo, the science of Copernicus and the assault on Aristotle entered a new phase. Priests began to attack Galileo from their pulpits in Florence, and they were backed by teachers within the academic community who routinely taught the old astronomy. These teachers saw a threat to their own power in Galileo's public notoriety and following among the laity. A secret group of priests and academics, named the "Liga," formed with the express purpose of silencing Galileo, and they used Aristotle and the Bible to attack him. Galileo had boldly defied this old elite and championed a new scientific learning for the laity; he proclaimed the new science as a new body of learning that required a new elite freed from the chains of tradition, knowledgeable in mathematics, and committed to experimentation. But in the early sixteenth century the Catholic church saw danger on every front: Protestants in Germany, recalcitrant people in nearly every state, laity demanding new schools offering practical education for their children. Now Galileo was supporting a view of the universe that conflicted with certain scriptural texts.

In 1632, Galileo's teachings were condemned and he was placed under house arrest. In this confrontation between the old clerical elite and the new secular elite, the old won out. But the price paid was high indeed. Science as preached by Galileo was not, as he knew perfectly well, inherently dangerous to Catholicism. But the clergy and their academic allies saw it as a challenge to their power, and they could enlist the papacy and the Inquisition in their support. As a result, students of the new science in Catholic countries looked to Protestant countries as places to live or publish their books. Censorship worked to stifle intellectual inquiry, and by the middle of the seventeenth century science had become, because of historical circumstance, an increasingly Protestant and northern European phenomenon.

The Newtonian Achievement

By the middle of the seventeenth century, largely because of the work of Copernicus, Kepler, and Galileo, Aristotle and Ptolemy had been dethroned. A new philosophy of nature and a new science had come into being whose essence lay in the mathematical expression of physical laws that describe matter in motion. Yet what was missing was an overriding law that could explain the motion observed in the heavens and on earth. This law was supplied by Isaac Newton.

Newton was born in 1642 in Lincolnshire, England, the son of a modest yeoman. He acquired a place at Trinity College, Cambridge, because of his intellectual promise, and there he devoted himself to natural philosophy and mathematics. His native talents were cultivated by tutors who gave him the latest works in philosophy to read; some of these works, in a form of Christian Platonism, emphasized the workings in the universe of spiritual forces derived from God. Newton's student notebooks survive and show him mastering these texts while also trying to understand the fundamental truths of Protestant Christianity as taught at Cambridge. Combining a Christian Platonism with a genius for mathematics, Newton produced an elegant synthesis of the science of Kepler and Galileo that eventually captured the imagination of European intellectuals.

In 1666, Newton formulated the mathematics for the universal law of gravitation, and in the same year, after rigorous experimentation, he determined the nature of light. The sciences of physics and optics were transformed. However, for many years, Newton did not publish his discoveries, partly because even he did not see the immense significance of his work. Finally, another mathematician and friend, Edmund Halley, persuaded him to publish under the sponsorship of the Royal Society. The result was the *Principia Mathematica* of 1687. In 1704, Newton published his *Opticks* and revealed his theory that light was corpuscular in nature and that it emanated from luminous bodies in a way that scientists later described as waves.

Of the two books, both monumental achievements in the history of science, the *Principia* made the greater impact on contemporaries. Newton not only formulated universal mathematical laws, but offered a philosophy of nature that sought to explain the essential structure of the universe: matter is always the same; it is atomic in structure, and in its essential nature it is dead or lifeless; and it is acted upon by immaterial forces that are placed in the universe by God. Newton said that the motion of matter could be explained by three laws: inertia, that a body remains in a state of rest or continues its motion in a straight line unless impelled to change by forces impressed upon it; acceleration, that the change in the motion of a body is proportional to the force acting upon it; and that for every action there is an equal and opposite reaction.

Newton argued that these laws apply not only to observable matter on earth but also to the motion of planets in their orbits. He showed that planets did not remain in their orbits because circular motion was "natural" or because crystalline spheres kept them in place. Rather, said Newton, planets keep to their orbits because every body in the universe exercises a force on every other body, a force that he called *universal gravitation*. Gravity is proportional to the product of the masses of two bodies and inversely proportional to the square of the distance between them. It is operative throughout the universe, whether on earth or in the heavens, and it is capable of mathematical expression. Newton was building his theory on the work of other scientific giants, notably Kepler and Galileo; yet no one before him possessed the breadth of vision, mathematical skill, and dedication to rigorous observation to combine this knowledge into one grand synthesis.

With Newton's discovery of universal gravitation, the Scientific Revolution reached its culmination. The universe could now be described as matter in motion; it was governed by invisible forces that operated everywhere, both on earth and in the heavens, and these forces could be expressed mathematically. The medieval picture of the world as closed, earth-bound, and earth-centered had been replaced by a universe seen to be infinite, governed by universal laws, and containing the earth as simply another planet.

But what was God's role in this new universe? Newton and his circle labored to create a mechanical world-picture dependent on the will of God, and in those efforts they were largely successful. Newton retained a central place for a providential deity who operates constantly in the universe; at one time he believed that gravity was simply the will of God operating on the universe. As Newton said in the *Opticks*, the physical order "can be the effect of nothing else than the wisdom and skill of a powerful ever-living agent."[2] Because of his deeply held religious convictions, Newton allowed his science to be used in the service of the established Anglican church. Newton, a scientific genius, was also a deeply religious thinker, who was committed to Protestant government.

Biology, Medicine, and Chemistry

The spectacular advances made in physics and astronomy in the sixteenth and seventeenth centuries were not matched in the biological sciences. Indeed, the day-to-day practice of medicine throughout western Europe changed little in the period from 1600 to 1700, for much of medical practice relied frequently on astrology.

Doctors clung to the teachings of the ancient practitioners Galen and Hippocrates. In general, Galenic medicine paid little attention to the discovery of specific cures for particular diseases. As a follower of Aristotle, Galen emphasized the elements that make up the body—he called their manifestations *humors.* A person with an excess of blood was sanguine; a person with too much bile was cho-

Sir Isaac Newton by Sir Godfrey Kneller (1646–1723). Newton's discovery of universal gravitation, a process that could be expressed mathematically, capped the Scientific Revolution. Pope's epitaph for him proclaimed, "Nature, and Nature's Laws lay hid in Night./ God said, 'Let Newton be!' and All was Light." (*National Portrait Gallery, London*)

leric. Health consisted of a restoration of balances among these various elements, so Galenic doctors often prescribed purges of one sort or another. The most famous of these was bloodletting, but sweating was also a favorite remedy. These methods were often as dangerous as the diseases they sought to cure, but they were taught religiously in the medical schools of Europe.

Despite the tenacity of Galenic medicine, innovators and reformers attempted during the sixteenth and seventeenth centuries to challenge and overturn medical orthodoxy. With an almost missionary zeal, Paracelsus (1493–1541), a Swiss-German physician and

Hermeticist, introduced the concept of diagnostic medicine. He argued that particular diseases can be differentiated and are related to chemical imbalances. His treatments relied on chemicals and not on bloodletting or the positions of the stars (although he did not discount such influences), and he proclaimed an almost ecstatic vision of human vitality and longevity. In most universities the faculties of medicine bitterly opposed his views, but by the mid-seventeenth century in England, and later in that century in France, Paracelsian ideas had many advocates. Support for Paracelsian medicine invariably accompanied an attack on the traditional medical establishment and its professional monopoly, and it often indicated support for the new science in general. The struggle between Galenists and Paracelsians quickly took on a social dimension; the innovators saw themselves pitted against a medical elite that, in their opinion, had lost its commitment to medical research and existed solely to perpetuate itself.

Victory came very slowly to the Paracelsians. In late-seventeenth-century France, the king himself intervened to allow medical students at the Sorbonne to read the writings of the medical reformers. But Paracelsian medicine was not really accepted until the eighteenth century. Universities like Leiden in The Netherlands adopted a new chemical approach to medicine and spawned a new generation of doctors who were capable of advancing daily medical practice beyond a slavish following of the ancient texts. Simultaneously, there was an upgrading in the social position of surgeons, who had been seen until then as lowly handworkers quite separate from and beneath medical practitioners. Gradually during the eighteenth century, enlightened doctors developed skill in both chemistry and surgery.

The medical reforms of the eighteenth century did not rest solely on the Paracelsian approach; they also relied heavily on the experimental breakthroughs made in the science of anatomy. A pioneer in this field was the Belgian surgeon Andreas Vesalius (1514–

1564), who published *The Structure of the Human Body* in 1543. Opposing Galenic practice, Vesalius argued for observation and anatomical dissection as the keys to knowing how the human body works. By the late seventeenth century, doctors had learned a great deal about the human body, its structure, and its chemistry.

The study of anatomy yielded dramatic results. In 1628, William Harvey (1578–1657) announced that he had discovered the circulation of the blood. Harvey compared the functioning of the heart to that of a mechanical pump, and once again this tendency to mechanize nature, so basic to the Scientific Revolution in physics, led to a significant discovery. Yet the acceptance of Harvey's work was very slow, and the practical uses of his discovery were not readily apparent.

The mechanization of the world-picture entailed more than the destruction of the cosmology advanced by Aristotle and Ptolemy. What was also at stake were the explanations offered for everyday physical events. In the Aristotelian and medieval outlook, bodies moved because it was in their nature to do so. Aristotle had postulated "forms" at work in nature; Latin translations and scholastic commentaries identified these forms as spirits, invisible forces inherent in nature that produced changes as diverse as the growth in plants, the fall of heavy objects to the earth, or even (according to Catholic theologians) the transformation of bread and wine into the body and blood of Christ. The dethroning of Aristotelian explanations for physical phenomena assaulted whole systems of knowledge, often of a theological nature, that went to the heart of medieval belief about the nature of creation and God's relation to it.

Predictably, the final assault on the Aristotelian world view came from Protestant England. By the seventeenth century, English scientific reformers had begun to equate Aristotle with Catholic teachings. Robert Boyle (1627–1691), the father of modern chemistry, believed that Aristotle's physics amounted to little more than magic. Boyle wanted to abolish the spirits on which Catholic theology rested; he advocated that scientists adopt the zeal of the magicians without their secretive practices and their conjuring with spirits. As an alternative to spirits, Boyle adopted the atomic explanation that matter is made up of small, hard, indestructible particles that behave with regularity and explain changes in gases, fluids, and solids.

Boyle pioneered in the experimental method with such exciting and accurate results that by the time of his death, no serious scientist could attempt chemical experiments without following his guidelines. Thus the science of chemistry acquired its characteristic experimentalism; it was also based on an atomic theory of matter. But not until late in the eighteenth century was this new discipline applied to medical research.

Prophets and Proponents of the New Science

The spectacular scientific discoveries of the early modern period necessitated a complete rethinking of the social and intellectual role of scientific inquiry. Science needed prophets and social theorists to give it direction and to assess its implications. During the early modern period, three major reformers attempted, in disparate ways, to channel science into the service of specific social programs: Giordano Bruno (1548–1600), Francis Bacon (1561–1626), and René Descartes (1596–1650).

Bruno

Giordano Bruno's life is one of the most fascinating and tragic to be found in the turbulent world of the Reformation and Counter Reformation. Born in Italy, Bruno began his mature years as a monk and was burned at the stake by the church. What led him to this cruel fate was his espousal of new religious ideas, which were in fact as old as the second century A.D., but which threatened the beliefs of the church. Bruno found in Hermetic philosophy, which he believed to be confirmed by Copernicus' heliocentric theory, the foundation of a new universal religion. He proposed that religion should be based on the laws found in nature and not on supernaturally inspired doctrines taught by the clergy.

Bruno was one of those Late Renaissance reformers who believed that the Hermetic philosophy, with its mystical approach to God and nature, held the key to true wisdom. The Hermetic philosophy accords the sun a special symbolic role because it infuses life into nature. On the basis of his belief, Bruno accepted Copernicus' sun-centered concept of the universe and began to write and preach about it all over Europe. Indeed, Bruno's fertile imagination, fired by Hermetic mysticism and the new science, led him to be one of the first Europeans to proclaim that the universe is infinite, filled with innumerable worlds. He also speculated that there might be life on other planets.

All of these notions were regarded by the church as dangerous. Bruno was in effect posing the Hermetic philosophy coupled with the new science as an alternative religious vision to either Protestantism or Catholicism. His sense of awe and enchantment with the natural order is similar to that found later among eighteenth-century freethinkers, who saw the scientific study and contemplation of nature, along with a vague sense of the Creator's majesty, as an alternative to organized religious worship. Bruno was a prophet of the new science to the extent that he saw its discoveries as confirming his belief in the wonders of creation. Creation was indeed so wondrous that it could be worshiped—the natural world could replace the supernatural as a fitting object for human curiosity and glorification.

Bacon

In contrast to Bruno's mysticism, the decidedly practical and empirical Francis Bacon stands as the most important English proponent of the new science, although not its most important practitioner. Unlike Bruno, Bacon became profoundly suspicious of magic and the magical arts, not because they might not work, but because he saw secrecy and arrogance as characteristic of their practitioners. Bacon was Lord Chancellor of England under James I, and he wrote about the usefulness of science partly in an effort to convince the crown of its advantages.

No philosopher of modern science has surpassed Bacon in elevating the study of nature into a humanistic discipline. In the *Advancement of Learning* (1605), Bacon argued that science must be open and free and all ideas must be allowed a hearing. Science must have human goals: the improvement of humanity's material condition and the advancement of trade and industry, but not the making of war or the taking of lives. Bacon also preached the necessity that science possess an inductive methodology grounded on experience; the scientist should first of all be a collector of facts.

Although Bacon was rather vague about how the scientist as a theorist actually works, he knew that preconceived ideas imposed on nature seldom yield positive results. An opponent of Aristotle, Bacon argued that university education should move away from the ancient texts and toward the new learning. As a powerful civil servant, Bacon was not afraid to attack the guardians of tradition. The Baconian vision of progress in science leading to an improvement of the human condition inspired much scientific activity in the seventeenth century, particularly in England.

Descartes

René Descartes, a French philosopher of the first half of the seventeenth century, went to the best French schools and was trained by the Jesuits in mathematics and scholastic philosophy. Yet in his early twenties, he experienced a crisis in confidence. He felt that everything he had been taught was irrelevant and meaningless.

Descartes began to search within himself for what he could be sure was clear and distinct knowledge. All he could know with certainty was the fact of his existence, and even that he knew only because he experienced not his body, but his mind: "I think, therefore I am." From this point of certitude, Descartes deduced God's existence. God exists because Descartes had in his mind an idea of a supreme, perfect being which, he reasoned, could only have been put there by such a being, not by any ordinary mortal. Therefore, God's existence means that the physical world must be real, for no Creator would play such a cruel trick and invent a vast hoax.

Descartes thus found confidence in the fact of his own existence and in the reality of the physical world, which he thought could best be understood through reason and mathematics. Scientific thought for Descartes meant an alternative to the chaos of conflicting opinions and the tyranny of truths learned, but not experienced, for oneself. Descartes, possibly as a result of knowing Bacon's ideas, also believed that "it is possible to attain knowledge which is very useful in life, and that, instead of that speculative philosophy which is taught in the schools, we may find a practical philosophy by means of which . . . we can . . . thus render ourselves the masters and possessors of nature"[3] (*Discourse on Method*).

Descartes has rightly been called the father of modern philosophy and one of the first prophets of modern science. He recognized the power that can come to individuals who ground knowledge not on the fact of God's existence, but on a willful assertion of their own ability as thinkers and investigators. Solely by applying their human minds to the world around them, human beings can achieve scientific knowledge that will make them the masters and possessors of nature. Descartes believed so fully in the power of unaided human reason that his practical science was largely deductive and not sufficiently based on rigorous experimentation. He thought that the scientist, aided by mathematics, could arrive at correct theories without necessarily testing them against experience.

The prophetic visions of Bruno, Bacon, and Descartes brought for the first time in the West the realization of the potential importance of scientific knowledge. Science could become the foundation of a new religiosity grounded on the practical study of nature—one that was eventually used by Enlightenment reformers to displace the authority of traditional religion. At the same time, science could also serve the needs of humanity. It could give to its practitioners a sense of power and self-confidence unimagined even by Renaissance proponents of individualism.

The Social Context of the Scientific Revolution

The Scientific Revolution reached its culmination during the second half of the seventeenth century in England at a time when that society was torn by revolution and civil war. That revolutionary context profoundly affected the direction of modern science. In the society that produced Boyle and Newton, the dreams of Bacon and Descartes were never actualized in ways they would have recognized, because social and political events intervened to shape science in ways they could not have expected.

By the 1640s, the influence of the writings of Kepler, Galileo, Bacon, and Descartes, had created in England a new science, with mechanical principles, mathematical theorems, and universal forces replacing the old world view. Just as the new science was developing as a recognized body of learning, political revolution erupted. In opposition to absolute monarchy and the established church, the Puritans sought social and political reform, the rule of Parliament, and a church governed by true Calvinists rather than by bishops. This Puritan Revolution played a crucial role in the formation of modern science.

René Descartes by Franz Hals (c. 1580–1666). Descartes is both the father of modern philosophy and the prophet of modern science. He placed his faith above all in the human intellect and its ability to achieve scientific knowledge, and made significant practical contributions in algebra. (*Royal Museum of Fine Arts, Copenhagen*)

The Puritan reformers championed the new science and encouraged young experimentalists to follow Bacon's call to put science in the service of humanity. The Puritan encouragement of science made it socially respectable, as well as religiously wholesome; the fear that mechanical notions might separate Creator from Creation seemed irrelevant. The Puritan promoters of science encouraged young gentlemen like Robert Boyle and his circle at Oxford to experiment and to use science to reform the university and improve the human condition, both material and spiritual.

As victory came to the Puritan side with the execution of Charles I in 1649, the revolution began to take a turn never intended by the Puritan reformers. The victorious army was dangerously close to becoming an independent force, and its ranks were made up of religious and political radicals. As representatives of the lower classes, they demanded a share in the reforms initiated by the Puritan landowners. They also questioned the social uses of the new science and advocated in its place the introduction of scientific learning closer to the folk practices and needs of the poor. Boyle and his scientific associates grew increasingly alarmed by these demands, and they in turn advocated their science as an alternative to the science and magic proposed by the radicals. Suddenly, the new science assumed a social and political meaning never imagined by its earliest proponents, yet similar to its role in modern industrial society.

Science, Boyle argued, must be conducted by cautious experimentation, and its benefits should be determined by scientists who are supported by the state. Despite Bacon's dreams, Boyle and his circle argued that science should focus on unraveling the mysteries of the universe and that the practical application of these theoretical insights, although desirable, should not be given highest priority. When science was applied practically, they said, it should not be primarily a means of redressing human ills, but should serve the interests of commerce and industry. Finally, natural philosophy, the understanding of nature underlying scientific research, should be compatible with the truths of Christianity. Boyle and his associates reacted violently against versions of the mechanical philosophy, as found in Descartes, that threatened to divorce science from religion.

The English Revolution anticipated a development that would become common: the channeling of science in the interest of the state and existing social arrangements. The Puritan reformers gave England a lead over much of Europe in scientific innovation. By the second half of the seventeenth century, many major scientific discoveries of the Scientific Revolution, particularly Newton's work, occurred within the intellectual milieu created by the English Revolution.

Newton adopted the experimental techniques first advocated by Boyle and his associates. He also embraced a highly spiritualized version of God's relationship to material creation—one taught in reaction to the reforming and democratizing tendencies within the English Revolution. As a result of his experimental rigor, his mathematical genius, and the philosophy of nature he learned as a young man at Cambridge, Newton articulated universal laws that became the foundation for the next century or more of European scientific inquiry.

The Newtonian synthesis came to mean more than simply a program for further scientific research. With his encouragement, Newton's followers preached the meaning of his science from their Anglican pulpits and also in countless books translated into every European language. They argued that Newtonian science should be used as a model for all human learning and, further, that the order and harmony of the Newtonian universe stood for the order and harmony that legally bound kings may impose on their subjects. The Newtonian universe would be constitutional at the same time that it was monarchical, and therein lay its appeal to Continental Europeans disillusioned with the excesses of absolute monarchy. What impressed them was the way in which the advocates of English science also accepted the principle of religious toleration and supported the rule of law binding both king and parliament. It was a model that thinkers we now describe as enlightened eagerly embraced.

According to this Newtonian model, just as God controls matter, people should control natural resources, trade, and industry—all for the purpose of serving their own interests. Order will result from the pursuit of self-interest, because order is inherent in the universe, which also means that society and government must be firmly controlled by legitimate authority. To challenge the existing social and political order, provided it operates according to constitutional law, would be, in effect, to challenge the harmony intended by God for both the human and the natural worlds.

The version of human progress suggested by the Newtonian synthesis laid great emphasis on the application of mechanical science to practical problems such as mining, hydrostatics, and the invention of mechanical devices. The Newtonians of the eighteenth century encouraged in their scientific lectures an approach to nature that made early industrialization possible, first in England and then gradually on the Continent.

Newtonian ideas, however, also encouraged European reformers to use the new science as an alternative to the doctrinal rigidity of established churches. The earliest supporters of Newtonian science in Europe before 1730 were committed to establishing learned journals or editing new encyclopedias intended to make learning accessible to as wide an audience as possible. In their eagerness to embrace the order, constitutional harmony, and progress promised by the Newtonian vision, however, European reformers of the eighteenth century were in one sense blind. Generally they failed to notice the dangers inherent in ruthlessly exploiting nature through the application of mechanical devices. The results of that exploitation only became apparent during the first decades of the nineteenth century in the industrialized areas of England and Scotland. By then, however, the Newtonian faith in the benefits offered by science, and the assumption that these benefits could be reaped without destroying the human and natural resources upon which they rested, had become nearly universal.

The Meaning of the Scientific Revolution

The Scientific Revolution was decisive in shaping the modern mentality; it shattered the medieval view of the universe and replaced it with a wholly different world-view. Gone was the belief that a motionless earth was at the center of a universe that was finite and enclosed by a ring of stars. Gone too was the belief that the universe was divided into higher and lower worlds and that different laws of motion operated in the heavens than operated on earth. The universe was now viewed as a giant machine operating according to universal laws that could be expressed mathematically; nature could be mastered.

The methodology that produced this new view of nature—the new science—played a crucial historical role in reorienting Western thought away from medieval theology and metaphysics and toward the study of physical and human problems. In the later Middle Ages, most men of learning were Aristotelians and theologians. But by the mid-eighteenth century, knowledge of Newtonian science and the dissemination of useful learning had become the goal of the educated classes. All knowledge, it was believed, could emulate scientific knowledge; it could be based on observation, experimentation, and rational deduction; it could be systematic, verifiable, progressive, and useful. At every turn the advocates of this new approach to learning hailed the scientists of the sixteenth and seventeenth centuries as proof that no institution or dogma had a monopoly on truth—the scientific approach would yield knowledge that might, if properly applied for the good of all people, produce a new and better age. Such an outlook gave thinkers new confidence in the power of the human mind to master nature and led them to examine European institutions and traditions with an inquiring, critical, and skeptical spirit. Thus inspired, the reformers of the eighteenth century would seek to create an Age of Enlightenment.

The Scientific Revolution ultimately weakened traditional Christianity. God's role in a mechanical universe was not clear. Newton had argued that God not only set the universe in motion but still intervened in its operations, thus leaving room for miracles. Others retained a place for God as Creator but regarded miracles as limitations on nature's mechanical perfection. Soon other Christian teachings came under attack as contrary to the standards of verification postulated by the new science. Applied to religious doctrines, Descartes's reliance on methodical doubt and clarity of thought and Bacon's insistence on careful observation led thinkers to question the validity of Christian teachings. Theology came to be regarded as a separate and somewhat irrelevant area of intellectual inquiry that was not fit for the interests of practical, well-informed people. Not only Christian doctrines but also various widespread and popular beliefs came under attack. Magic, witchcraft, and astrology, still widespread among the European masses, were regarded with disdain by elite culture. The Scientific Revolution widened the gap between the elite culture of the rich and landed and popular culture. The masses of people remained devoted to some form of traditional Christianity, while the uncertainty of a universe governed by devils, witches, or the stars continued to make sense to peasants and laborers who remained powerless in the face of nature or the domination of the rich and landed.

In Catholic countries, where the Scientific Revolution began, there was, by the early seventeenth century, a growing hostility toward scientific ideas. The mentality of the Counter Reformation enabled lesser minds to exercise their fears and arrogance against any idea they regarded as suspicious. Galileo was caught in this hostile environment, and

the Copernican system was condemned by the church in 1616.

As a result, by the second half of the seventeenth century science had become an increasingly Protestant phenomenon. The major Protestant countries like England and the Netherlands accorded greater intellectual freedom and their presses were relatively free. Eventually, science also proved to be more compatible with the Protestant mind's emphasis on individual striving and the mercantile exploitation of nature for material gain.

Gradually the science of Newton became the science of western Europe: nature mechanized, analyzed, regulated, and mathematicized. As a result of the Scientific Revolution, learned Westerners came to believe more strongly than ever that nature could be mastered. Mechanical science—applied to canals, engines, pumps, and levers—had become the science of industry. Thus the Scientific Revolution, operating on both the intellectual and commercial levels, laid the groundwork for two major developments of the modern West—the Industrial Revolution and the Age of Enlightenment.

Notes

1. Excerpted in Stillman Drake, ed., *Discoveries and Opinions of Galileo* (New York: Doubleday, 1957), p. 28.

2. Excerpted in *Newton's Philosophy of Nature,* H. S. Thayer, ed. (New York: Hafner, 1953), p. 177.

3. Excerpted in Norman Kemp Smith, ed., *Descartes' Philosophical Writings* (New York: Modern Library, 1958), pp. 130–131.

Suggested Reading

Bernal, J. D., *Science in History* (1969). A learned classic on the meaning of science in history.
Briggs, Robin, *The Scientific Revolution of the Seventeenth Century* (1969). A clearly written survey with documents.

Butterfield, Herbert, *The Origins of Modern Science* (1957). A highly regarded analysis of the emergence of modern science.

Clark, G. N., *Science and Social Welfare in the Age of Newton* (1949). A standard work on the social uses of the new science.

Cohen, I. B., *The Birth of a New Physics* (1960). Authoritative, but difficult for the novice.

Drake, Stillman, ed., *Discoveries and Opinions of Galileo* (1957). A good place to start to learn Galileo's most important ideas.

Jacob, James R., *Robert Boyle and the English Revolution* (1977). Deals with the relationship between Boyle's science and the English Revolution.

Jacob, Margaret C., *The Newtonians and the English Revolution* (1976). Deals with the social meaning of Newton's science.

Kearney, Hugh, *Science and Social Change, 1500–1700* (1971). Includes a discussion of the social setting of the Scientific Revolution.

Koestler, Arthur, *The Watershed: A Biography of Johannes Kepler* (1960). A fascinating biography of a founder of modern science and a practitioner of magic.

Kuhn, Thomas, *The Structure of Scientific Revolutions* (1962). One of the first non-Marxist attempts to show that science has social implications.

Whitehead, Alfred North, *Science and the Modern World* (1960). An early and important meditation on the meaning of modern science.

Review Questions

1. What was the difference between the scientific understanding of the universe and the medieval understanding of it?

2. Describe the major achievements of Copernicus, Kepler, Galileo, and Newton.

3. How did the practice of medicine change during the Scientific Revolution? Describe the changes.

4. What were Bruno's differences with the church? Describe what happened.

5. Does modern science conform to Francis Bacon's ideals? List these ideals and discuss why each does/does not conform.

6. In what ways did the English Revolution shape modern science?

7. How did early modern Europeans perceive the new science as it was developing?

18

The Age of Enlightenment:
Reason and Reform

The eighteenth century is called the Age of Enlightenment or Age of Reason, for during this period an educated elite, expressing supreme confidence in the power of reason, attempted a rational analysis of European institutions and beliefs. The Enlightenment was heavily indebted to the discoveries of the seventeenth-century Scientific Revolution—to the experimental method pioneered by Galileo, Boyle, and Newton and to the mechanical picture of the universe formed by Newton. The Scientific Revolution seemed to show that order and mathematically demonstrable laws were at work in the physical universe. The thinkers of the Enlightenment, called *philosophes*, argued that it should be possible to examine *human* institutions with the intention of imposing a comparable order and rationality.

Late in the eighteenth century Immanuel Kant (1724–1804), a moderate German leader of the Enlightenment, was asked to define it. Kant argued that it was the bringing of "light into the dark corners of the mind," the dispelling of ignorance and superstition. Kant went to the heart of one aspect of the Enlightenment, that is, its insistence that each individual should reason independently without recourse to the authority of the schools, churches, and universities.[1]

Kant believed that this call for self-education meant no revolutionary disruption of the political order. In general, modern liberal and enlightened culture aimed at a gradual evolutionary transformation of the human condition; only a few radical thinkers during the eighteenth century were prepared to envision an immediate political disruption of the traditional authority of monarchy, aristocracy, and church. The mainstream of the Enlightenment was politically moderate, worshipful of the new science, critical of the clergy and all rigid dogma, tolerant in religious matters, and even loyal to enlightened monarchs who were prepared to keep the clerical censors away from the new books.

Philosophes were found most commonly in the major European cities, with Paris during the 1770s becoming the center of the Enlightenment. These embattled reformers developed a new style of writing philosophy, one that tried to make it understandable and even simple, sometimes entertaining. In the process the philosophes became journalists, propagandists, and in some cases brilliant literary stylists who made their various languages more readable for literate laymen and also the growing number of literate women.

Enlightenment culture relied heavily on the printing press as an agent of propaganda. Through it, reformers could address the increasingly large audiences found in the major European cities—London, Amsterdam, and Paris, in particular. Thanks to the power of the printed word, the Enlightenment was able to agitate for reform by addressing an educated and urban lay audience directly. In essays, monthly journals, works of fiction, and even mildly pornographic and anonymous tales, the philosophes attacked many of the abuses of eighteenth-century society—religious fanaticism and intolerance, the idleness and corruption of the aristocracy, the use of torture, terrible prison conditions, slavery, and violations of natural rights.

Although not profoundly original, the philosophes were bold in their criticism of existing institutions, especially the churches and the clergy. In essence, the philosophes were condemning all vestiges of medieval culture. Inevitably, modern liberal thought, as initiated by the Enlightenment, emerged as hostile to scholastic learning, priests, and eventually in some quarters, to Christianity itself. The philosophes expressed confidence in science and reason, espoused humanitarianism, and struggled for religious liberty and freedom of thought and person. Combining these values with a secular orientation and a belief in future progress, the philosophes helped to shape, if not to define, the modern outlook.

The Science of Religion

Christianity Under Attack

No single thread had united Western culture more powerfully than Christianity. Until the eighteenth century, educated people, especially rulers and servants of the state—however un-Christian their actions—had to give allegiance to one or another of the Christian churches. The Enlightenment's importance lies in the fact that it produced the first widely read and systematic assault on Christianity launched from within the ranks of the educated. The leaders of the Enlightenment sought to repudiate traditional Christianity and to put in its place a rational system of ethics and philosophy based on scientific truths.

The philosophes offered several approaches to the problem posed by religion. Moderates like Kant wanted simply to put a basic belief in God's existence and his providence in place of the formal dogmas of the Christian churches. *Deists* wanted God to be so removed from his creation as to be irrelevant to everyday human concerns. *Pantheists* or *materialists* wanted people to acknowledge Nature as if it were God; they wished to eliminate at a single stroke any form of religious belief and worship that remotely resembled Christianity. Members of this last group were labeled atheists by their enemies.

Most philosophes were deists who tried to make religion compatible with a scientific understanding of nature. Deists believed only those Christian doctrines that could meet the test of reason. For example, they considered it reasonable to believe in God, for only with a creator, they said, could such a superbly organized universe have come into being. But after God set the universe in motion, said the deists, he took no further part in its operations. Thus, while deists retained belief in God the Creator, they rejected clerical authority, revelation, original sin, and miracles. They held that Biblical accounts of the resurrection and of Jesus walking on water or waking the dead could not be reconciled with natural law. Deists viewed Jesus as a great moral teacher, not the son of God, and they regarded ethics, not faith, as the essence of religion; rational people, they said, served God best by treating their fellow human beings justly.

Whatever the remedy proposed to address the problem of religion, the effect was the same: the clergy of every denomination conducted a counteroffensive against the philosophes that went on throughout the eighteenth century. Nevertheless, in the last decade of the seventeenth century, the Enlightenment was well underway in England and in the Netherlands. Two factors were crucial in creating this new intellectual milieu: the Revolution of 1688–89 (see Chapter 16) and the relative freedom of the press in both countries. The Revolution of 1688–89 weakened the power of the established church in England. The church lost the right to prosecute heretics and to control the licensing of books. The Revolution also united England and the Netherlands in a war against French aggression and the absolutist regime of the French king, Louis XIV (d. 1715). Suddenly it seemed to educated people on both sides of the English Channel that the unchecked power of kings, supported as they were in European countries by established churches firmly in their control, was the most serious abuse of all time. It appeared as though only in those countries where the power of the clergy had been weakened, would true intellectual inquiry occur.

Skeptics and Freethinkers

The earliest examples of enlightened thinking show the importance of both the Revolution of 1688–89 and the war being waged against France. During the 1690s, the intellectual response to the unbridled power of Louis XIV joined with an assault on the power of the clergy; skeptics like Pierre Bayle (1647–1706) came to distrust all dogmas and to see su-

perstition as a social evil far more dangerous than atheism. Bayle was a French Protestant forced to flee to the Netherlands as a result of Louis XIV's campaign against his coreligionists. Although a Calvinist himself, Bayle also ran into opposition from the strict Calvinist clergy, who regarded him as lax on doctrinal matters. He attacked his critics and persecutors in a new and brilliant form of journalism: his *Historical and Critical Dictionary* (1697), which was more an encyclopedia than a dictionary. Under alphabetically arranged subjects and in copious footnotes, Bayle gave the most recent learning of the day on various matters and never missed an opportunity to ridicule the dogmatic, the superstitious, or the just plain arrogant. In Bayle's hands, skepticism became a tool; rigorous questioning of accepted ideas became a method for arriving at new truths. As Bayle noted in his *Dictionary:* "it is therefore only religion that has anything to fear from Pyrrhonism [i.e., skepticism]."[2] In this same critical spirit, Bayle, in his dictionary article entitled "David," compared Louis XIV to Goliath. The message was clear enough: great tyrants and the clergy who prop them up should beware of self-confident, independently minded citizens who are skeptical of the claims of authority made by kings and churches and are eager to use their own minds to search for truth.

Bayle's *Dictionary*, which was in effect the first encyclopedia, had an enormous impact throughout Europe. Its very format captured the imagination of the philosophes. Here was a way of simply, even scientifically, classifying and ordering knowledge. In Paris during the 1740s, a group of publishers decided to produce a bigger and better encyclopedia than any of the others that had yet been published. They hired a young and impoverished hack writer named Denis Diderot to compile it, and thus began the rise to fame of one of the most important philosophes of the Enlightenment. Encyclopedias not only created an easy way of acquiring the most recent learning; they sometimes also established the literary careers of their editors.

Partly through Bayle's writings, *skepticism* became an integral part of the Enlightenment's approach to religion. In the middle of the eighteenth century, Scottish philosopher and historian David Hume (1711–1776) used skepticism to reject revealed religion and to arrive at a universal religion based on reason and common sense. In *An Enquiry Concerning Human Understanding* (1748), Hume argued that what is called *cause and effect* is not that at all. He said that the human mind associates events or ideas; they have no inherent association, and they were not designed by some outside force to be causes and effects.

The implications of skepticism as articulated by Bayle and Hume were clear: randomness, not the providential design argued by the clergy, governs human events, and it is the individual's job to impose order where none exists. All should be skeptical of assertions that "God ordains" certain human actions. Skepticism dealt a serious blow to revealed religion and seemed to point in the direction of "natural" religion, that is, toward a system of beliefs and ethics designed by rational people on the basis of their own needs.

The idea of natural religion had already been championed during the 1690s by the English freethinkers. These early representatives of the Enlightenment used the term *freethinking* to signal their hostility to established church dogmas and their ability to think for themselves.

They looked back to the English Revolution of mid-century for their ideas about government; many of the English freethinkers were republicans in the tradition established by important figures of the Interregnum. Indeed, the English freethinkers of the 1690s and beyond helped to popularize English republican ideas at home and in the American colonies, where in 1776 they would figure prominently in the thinking of American revolutionaries.

The freethinkers had little use for organized religion, or even for Christianity itself. For example, in 1696 the freethinker John Toland (1670–1722) published a tract called *Christianity Not Mysterious*, in which he argued that any religious doctrine that seemed to contradict reason or common sense—for example, Jesus' resurrection or the miracles of the Bible—ought to be discarded. Toland also attacked the clergy's power; in his opinion the Revolution of 1688–89 had not gone far enough in undermining the power of the established church and the king. Toland and his freethinking associates Anthony Collins and Matthew Tindal wanted England to be a republic governed by "reasonable" people who worshiped, as Toland proposed, not a mysterious God but intelligible Nature.

In science combined with skepticism and anticlericalism, thoughtful critics could find ample reason for abandoning all traditional authority. By 1700 a general crisis of confidence in established authority had been provoked by the works of Bayle and the freethinkers and of some seventeenth-century philosophers, such as Descartes. Once started in England and the Netherlands and broadcast via Dutch printers, the Enlightenment almost immediately became international.

Freemasons

As the Enlightenment's search for a new foundation of religious belief went on, some seekers inevitably attempted to found new clubs or societies. These groups tried to fulfill social and intellectual needs no longer being met by the traditional churches. In 1717 a group of London gentlemen, many of them very interested in the new science and in the spread of learning in general, founded the Grand Lodge, a collection of various Masonic lodges that had met in pubs around the city. From that date can be traced the origins of European Freemasonry and its spread into almost every European country.

Freemasonry was not originally intended to rival the churches. Nevertheless, the lodges became, especially on the Continent, alternative meeting places for men interested in the Enlightenment. Some French philosophes joined lodges in Paris, as did some clergy. In Vienna at the time of Mozart, who was a Freemason, and in Berlin during the reign of Frederick the Great, Masonic membership came to denote support for enlightened and centralized government, often in opposition to the local power of the clergy and the old aristocracy. For a few extreme rationalists bent on destroying the Christian churches, the Masonic lodges also seemed to function as a commendable alternative form of religion, complete with ritual, charitable funds, and sense of community. By the middle of the eighteenth century, perhaps as many as 50,000 men belonged to Masonic lodges in just about every major European city and in many towns as well. These lodges became places where men could gather and openly discuss their beliefs and the writings of the philosophes if they cared to do so. The ideals of equality and liberty took on meaning in these private gatherings, where the participants could reflect on the inequality they perceived in the world around them. Eventually some lodges admitted women as members.

Voltaire the Philosophe

The French possessed a vital tradition of intellectual skepticism going back to the late sixteenth century, as well as a tradition of scientific rationalism easily identified with Descartes. In the early eighteenth century, however, the French found it difficult to gain access to the new literature of Enlightenment because the French printing presses were among the most tightly controlled and censored in Europe. As a result a brisk but risky traffic developed in clandestine books and manuscripts subversive of authority, and French-language journals poured from Dutch presses.

As a poet and writer struggling for recognition in Paris, the young François Marie Arouet, known to the world as Voltaire (1694–1778), encountered some of the new ideas that were being discussed in private gatherings (called *salons*) in Paris. Care had to be taken in the French capital by those educated people who wanted to read books and discuss ideas hostile to the church or to the Sorbonne,

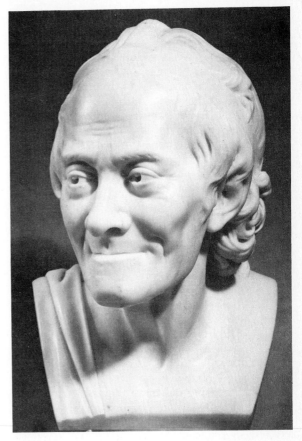

Bust of Voltaire by Jean-Antoine Houdon, (1741–1828). Voltaire (born François Marie Arouet) was the internationally famous supporter of the Enlightenment. He was poet, journalist, essayist, and utopian thinker. Superstition, the Catholic church, and arbitrary government were the constant targets of his critical pen. (*The Fine Arts Museums of San Francisco, Mr. and Mrs. E. John Magnin Gift*)

the clerically controlled university. Individuals had been imprisoned for writing, publishing, or owning books hostile to Catholic doctrine. Although Voltaire learned something of the new enlightened culture in Paris, it was in 1726, when he journeyed to London, that Voltaire the poet became Voltaire the philosophe.

In England, Voltaire became acquainted with the ideas of John Locke (1632–1704) and

Isaac Newton. From Newton, Voltaire learned the mathematical laws that govern the universe; he witnessed the power of human reason to establish general rules that seem to explain the behavior of physical objects. From Locke, Voltaire learned that people should believe only those ideas received from the senses. Locke's theory of learning, his epistemology, impressed many of the proponents of the Enlightenment. Again the implications for religion were most serious: if people believe only those things that they experience, they will be unable to accept mysteries and doctrines simply because they are taught by churches and the clergy. Voltaire experienced considerable freedom of thought in England and saw a religious toleration that stood in stark contrast to the absolutism of the French kings and the power of the French clergy. He also witnessed a freer mixing of bourgeois and aristocratic social groups than was permitted in France at this time.

Throughout his life Voltaire was a fierce supporter of the Enlightenment and a bitter critic of churches and the Inquisition. Although his own books were banned in France, he probably did more there than any other philosophe to popularize the Enlightenment and to mock the authority of the clergy. In *Letters Concerning the English Nation* (1733), Voltaire wrote about his experiences in England. He offered constitutional monarchy, new science, and religious toleration as models to be followed by all of Europe. In the *Letters* he praised English society for its encouragement of these ideals.

Voltaire never ceased to mock the purveyors of superstition and blind obedience to religious authority. In such works as *Candide* (1759) and *Micromegas* (1752), Voltaire castigated the clergy, as well as other philosophical supporters of the status quo who would have people believe that this was the best of all possible worlds.

Voltaire was a practical reformer who campaigned for the rule of law, a freer press, religious toleration, humane treatment of criminals, and a more effective system of government administration. His writings

constituted a radical attack on aspects of eighteenth-century French society. Yet like so many of the philosophes, Voltaire feared the power of the people, especially if goaded by the clergy. He was happiest in the company of the rich and powerful, provided they tolerated his ideas and supported reform. Not surprisingly, Voltaire was frequently disappointed by eighteenth-century monarchs, like Frederick the Great in Prussia, who promised enlightenment but sought mainly to increase their own power and that of their armies.

Political Thought

With the exception of Machiavelli in the Renaissance and Thomas Hobbes and the republicans during the English Revolution, the Enlightenment produced the greatest originality in political thought witnessed in the West up to that time. Three major European thinkers and a host of minor ones wrote treatises on politics that remain relevant to this day: John Locke, *Two Treatises of Government* (1690), Montesquieu, *The Spirit of the Laws* (1748), and Jean Jacques Rousseau, *The Social Contract* (1762). All repudiated the divine right of kings and were concerned with checking the power of monarchy; each offered different formulas for achieving that goal. These major political theorists of the Enlightenment were also aware of the writings of Machiavelli and Hobbes and, although often disagreeing with them, borrowed some of their ideas.

Machiavelli had analyzed politics in terms of power, fortune, and the ability of the individual ruler; he did not call in God to justify the power of princes or to explain their demise. Machiavelli had also preferred a republican form of government to monarchy, and his republican vision never lost its appeal during the Enlightenment. Very late in the century, most liberal theorists recognized that the republican form of government, or at the least the virtues practiced by citizens in a

Map 18.1 Europe, 1715 ▶

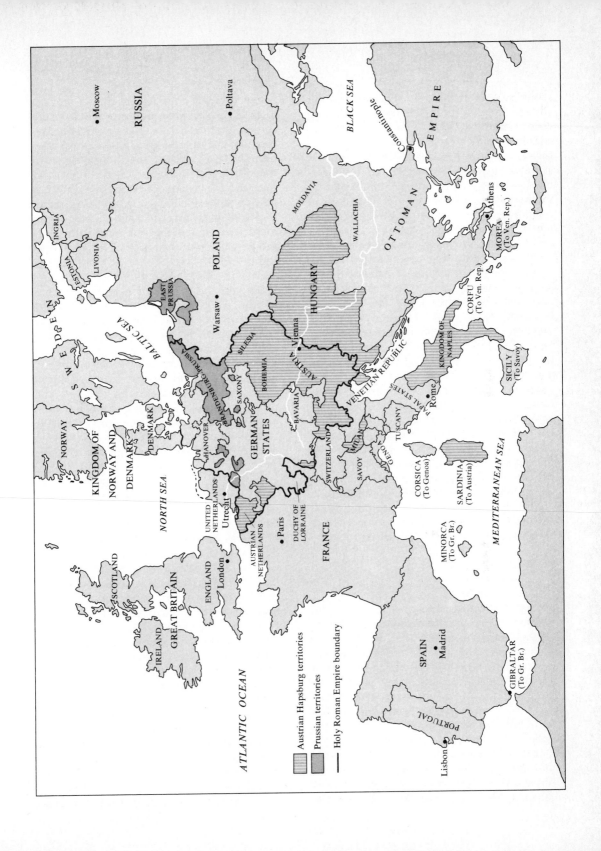

ATLANTIC OCEAN

RUSSIA
Moscow
Poltava

SWEDEN

BLACK SEA

Constantinople

OTTOMAN EMPIRE

MOREA
(To Ven. Rep.)

Athens

POLAND
Warsaw

MOLDAVIA

WALLACHIA

HUNGARY

INGRIA

LIVONIA

ESTONIA

BALTIC SEA

EAST PRUSSIA

BRANDENBURG-PRUSSIA

SILESIA

Vienna

AUSTRIA

BOHEMIA

SAXONY

BAVARIA

CORFU
(To Ven. Rep.)

KINGDOM OF NAPLES

SICILY
(To Savoy)

VENETIAN REPUBLIC

MILAN

PAPAL STATES

Rome

TUSCANY

GENOA

NORWAY

KINGDOM OF NORWAY AND DENMARK

DENMARK

HANOVER

GERMAN STATES

SWITZERLAND

SAVOY

NORTH SEA

UNITED NETHERLANDS

Utrecht

AUSTRIAN NETHERLANDS

Paris

DUCHY OF LORRAINE

FRANCE

CORSICA
(To Genoa)

SARDINIA
(To Austria)

MINORCA
(To Gr. Br.)

MEDITERRANEAN SEA

SCOTLAND

IRELAND

GREAT BRITAIN

ENGLAND

London

SPAIN

Madrid

GIBRALTAR
(To Gr. Br.)

PORTUGAL

Lisbon

Austrian Hapsburg territories

Prussian territories

Holy Roman Empire boundary

republic, offered the only alternative to the corruption and repression associated with absolutist monarchy.

Enlightenment political thinkers were ambivalent toward much of the writing of Thomas Hobbes (1588–1679). All, however, liked the fact that Hobbes championed self-interest as a valid reason for engaging in political activity and that he produced a secular theory of politics, refusing to bring God into his system to justify the power of kings. Hobbes said that their power rested not on divine right but on a contract made with their subjects. Hobbes made that contract unbreakable—once established, the power of the government, whether king or parliament, was absolute. But Hobbes published his major work, *Leviathan,* in 1651, soon after England had been torn by civil war; as a result he was obsessed with the issue of political stability. He feared that left to their own devices, men would kill one another; the "war of all against all"[3] would prevail without the firm hand of a sovereign to stop it. Enlightenment theorists, beginning with John Locke, denied that governments possessed absolute power over their subjects, and to that extent they repudiated Hobbes. Many European thinkers of the eighteenth century, including Rousseau, also rejected his gloomy view that human nature is greedy and warlike.

Locke

Probably the most widely read political philosopher during the first half of the eighteenth century was John Locke. His *Two Treatises of Government* were seen as a justification for the Revolution of 1688–89 and the notion of government by consent of the people. Although they were published in 1690, Locke had written his treatises before the Revolution, but that was not known during the Enlightenment.

Locke's theory, in its broad outlines, stated that the right to govern derived from the consent of the governed and was a form of contract. When people gave their consent to

a government, they expected it to govern justly, to protect their property, and to ensure certain liberties for the propertied. If a government attempted to rule absolutely and arbitrarily—if it violated the natural rights of the individual—it reneged on its contract and forfeited the loyalty of its subjects. Such a government could be legitimately overthrown. Locke believed that a constitutional government that limited the power of rulers was the best defense of property and individual rights.

Late in the eighteenth century, Locke's ideas were used to justify liberal revolutions both in Europe and in America. Indeed, the importance of Locke's political philosophy was not simply his recourse to contract theory as a justification of constitutional government; it was also his assertion that the community may take up arms against its sovereign in the name of the natural rights of liberty and property. Locke's ideas about the foundation of government had greater impact on the Continent and in America in the eighteenth century than they did in England.

Montesquieu

Baron de la Brède et de Montesquieu (1689–1755) was a French aristocrat who, like Voltaire, visited England late in the 1720s and who knew the writings of Locke. Montesquieu had little sympathy for revolutions, but he did approve of constitutional monarchy. His primary concern was to check the unbridled authority of the French kings. In opposition to the Old Regime, Montesquieu proposed a balanced system of government with an executive branch offset by a legislature whose members were drawn from the landed and educated elements in society. Montesquieu genuinely believed that the aristocracy possessed a natural and sacred obligation to rule and that their honor called them to serve the community. He also aimed to fashion a government that channeled the interests and energies of its people, a government that was not bogged down in corruption and inefficiency. His writings, particularly *The Spirit of the Laws*, established Montesquieu as a major philosophe whose philosophy possessed republican tendencies and as a critic of the Old Regime in France. Once again, innovative political thinking highlighted the failures of absolutist government and pointed to the need for some kind of representative assembly in every European country.

Rousseau

Not until the 1760s did democracy find its champion in Jean Jacques Rousseau (1712–1778). Rousseau based his politics on contract theory—the people choose their government and, in so doing, they effectively give birth to civil society. But Rousseau further demanded that the contract be constantly renewed, and that government be made immediately and directly responsible to the will of the people. *The Social Contract* opened with this stirring cry for reform: "Man is born free; and everywhere he is in chains," and it went on to ask how that can be changed. Freedom is in the very nature of man; "to renounce liberty is to renounce being a man, to surrender the rights of humanity and even its duties."[4]

Rousseau's political ideal was the small Greek city-state, for in these ancient communities people participated actively and directly in politics and were willing to sacrifice self-interest to the needs of the community. To the ancient Greek, said Rousseau, the state was a moral association that made him a better person, and good citizenship was the highest form of excellence. In contrast, modern society, said Rousseau, was prey to many conflicting interests; the rich and powerful used the state to preserve their interests and power, and the poor and powerless viewed it as an oppressor. Consequently, the obedience to law, the devotion to the state, and the freedom that had characterized the Greek city-state had been lost.

In the *Social Contract*, Rousseau tried to resolve the conflict between individual freedom and the demands of the state. His solution was a small state, modeled after the Greek city-state. Such a state, said Rousseau, should be based on the *general will*—that which is best for the community, which expresses the community's common interests. Rousseau wanted laws of the state to coincide with the general will; people would have the wisdom to arrive at law that served the common good, but to do so they would have to set aside selfish interests for the good of the community. For Rousseau freedom consisted of obeying laws prescribed by citizens inspired by the general will. Citizens themselves must constitute the lawmaking body; lawmaking cannot be entrusted to a single person or a small group.

For Rousseau, those who disobey laws—who act according to their private wills rather than in accordance with the general will as expressed in law—degrade themselves and undermine the community. Therefore government has the right to force citizens to be obedient—to compel them to exercise their individual wills in the proper way. Rousseau believed that government has the right to enforce freedom, but he did leave the problem of minority rights unresolved.

No philosopher of the Enlightenment was more dangerous to the Old Regime than Rousseau. His ideas were perceived as truly revolutionary—as a direct challenge to the power of kings, churches, and aristocrats. Although Rousseau thought that many leaders of the Enlightenment had been corrupted by easy living and the life of the salons, with their attendant elegant ladies and dandies, he nevertheless earned an uneasy place in the ranks of the philosophes. In the French Revolution, his name would be invoked to justify democracy, and of all the philosophes, Rousseau would probably have been least horrified by the early phase of that revolutionary upheaval.

Rousseau also saw society as the corrupter of human beings who, left to their own devices, were inherently virtuous and freedom loving. A wide spectrum of opinion in the Enlightenment also saw society if not as corrupting, then at least as needing constant reform. Some enlightened critics were prepared to work with those in power in an effort to bring about concrete social reforms. Other philosophes believed that the key to reform lay not in social and political institutions, but in a change in mentality brought about by education and propaganda.

Social Thought

Psychology and Education

Just as Locke's *Two Treatises of Government* was instrumental in shaping the political thought of the Enlightenment, his *Essay Concerning Human Understanding* (1689) provided the theoretical foundations for an unprecedented interest in education. Locke's view that at birth the mind is blank, a clean slate or *tabula rasa*, held two important implications. First, if human beings were not born with innate ideas, then they were not, as Christianity taught, inherently sinful as a result of Adam and Eve's defiance of God. Second, a person's environment was the decisive force in shaping that person's character and intelligence. Nine of every ten men, wrote Locke, "are good or evil, useful or not, [because of] their education." Such a theory was eagerly received by the reform-minded philosophes, who preferred attributing wickedness to faulty institutions, improper rearing, and poor education—which could be remedied—rather than to a defective human nature.

"Locke has unfolded to man the nature of human reason," Voltaire wrote in his *Letters.* For the Enlightenment, the proper study of humanity addressed the process by which people can and do know. Locke had said that individuals take the data produced by their senses and reflect on it; in that way they arrive at complex ideas. Education obviously requires, in addition to an environment that promotes learning, the active participation of students. Merely receiving knowledge not tested by their own sense experience is inadequate.

More treatises were written on education during the eighteenth century than in all previous centuries combined. On the Continent where the clergy controlled many schools and all universities, the educated laity began to demand state regulation and inspection of all educational facilities. This insistence was one practical expression of the growing discontent with the clergy and their independent authority. By the second half of the century, new schools and universities in Prussia, Belgium, Austria, and Russia attempted to teach practical subjects suited to the interests of the laity. Predictably, science was given a special place in these new institutions. Yet in 1762, one French author estimated that fewer than one-tenth of all school-age boys in France received a proper education. France was one of the more advanced European countries; by 1789 probably about half of the men and about 20 percent of the women were literate.

Prussia and Scotland excelled in the field of education, but for very different reasons. In Prussia, Frederick the Great decreed universal public education for boys as part of his effort to surpass the level of technical expertise found in other countries. His educational policy was another example of his using the Enlightenment to increase the power of the central government. In Scotland the improvements in education were largely sponsored by the established Calvinist church. The heirs of the Protestant Reformation, with its emphasis on the Bible and hence on the printed word, were fully capable of sponsoring progressive educational policies without the help of the Enlightenment.

In the teaching of medicine, the University of Leiden in the Netherlands became the most advanced institution in Europe in the eighteenth century. Indeed, its scientific faculty presented Newtonian physics and the latest chemistry to a generation of doctors and engineers assembled from all over Europe. A new medical school was also founded in Vienna. Many Scottish students, often trained in Leiden, brought their knowledge home to make Edinburgh University a major center for medical students.

Locke's doctrine that knowledge comes primarily through experience found its most extreme expression in the writings of Rousseau on education. In *Émile* (1762), Rousseau argued that individuals learn from nature, from people, or from things. Indeed Rousseau wanted the early years of a child's education to be centered on developing the senses, not spent chained to a schoolroom desk. Later, attention would be paid to intellectual pursuits, then finally to morality. Rousseau grasped a fundamental principle of modern psychology—the child is not a small adult, and childhood is not merely preparation for adulthood but a particular stage, with its own distinguishing characteristics, in human development. Children, said Rousseau astutely, should be permitted to behave like children.

Rousseau appealed especially to women to protect their children from social convention, that is, to teach their children about life. There were problems with Rousseau's educational system. He would render the family into the major educational force and he wanted its products to be cosmopolitan and enlightened, singularly free from superstition and prejudice. In the process, women (whom Rousseau would confine to the home) would bear the burden of instilling enlightenment, although they had little experience of the world beyond the family. Rousseau's contradictions sprang in large measure from his desperate search for an alternative to the formal educational systems that existed in his day. In the field of education, the reality of most European schools fell far below the ideal put forward by the philosophes.

Humanitarianism

Crime and Punishment   No society founded on the principles of the Enlightenment could condone the torture of prisoners and the inhumanity of a corrupt legal system. On that all the philosophes were clear, and they had plenty of evidence from their own societies on which to base their condemnation of torture and the inhumanity of the criminal justice system.

If education of children in the eighteenth century was poor, the treatment of criminals was appalling. Conditions differed little whether an individual was imprisoned because of unpaid debts or for being a bandit or murderer. Prisoners were often starved or exposed to disease, or both. On the Continent, where torture was still legal, prisoners could be subjected to brutal interrogation or to random punishment—treatment comparable to anything found today in many dictatorships. In 1777 an English reformer, John Howard, published a report on the state of the prisons in England and Wales: "the want of food is to be found in many country gaols. In about half these, debtors have no bread; although it is granted to the highwayman, the housebreaker, and the murderer; and medical assistance, which is provided for the latter, is withheld from the former." Torture was illegal in England, except in cases of treason, but the prison conditions were often as harmful to the physical and mental health of their inmates as torture was.

Although there is something particularly reprehensible about the torturer, his skills were consciously applauded in many countries during the eighteenth century. Fittingly, the most powerful critique of the European system of punishment came from Italy, where the Inquisition and its torture chambers had reigned with little opposition for centuries. In Milan during the early 1760s, the Enlightenment had made very gradual inroads, and in a small circle of reformers the practices of the Inquisition and the relationship between church and state in the matter of criminal justice were avidly discussed.

Out of that intellectual ferment came one of the most important books of the Enlightenment, *Of Crime and Punishment* (1764) by the Milanese reformer Cesare Beccaria (1738–1794). For centuries, sin and crime had been wedded in the eyes of the church; the function of the state was to punish the second because it was a manifestation of the first. Beccaria cut through that thicket of moralizing and argued that the church should concern itself with sin; it should abandon its prisons and courts. The state should concern itself with crimes against society, and the purpose of punishment should be to reintegrate the individual into society.

Beccaria also went further and inquired into the causes of crime. Abandoning the concept of sin Beccaria, rather like Rousseau, who saw injustice and corruption in the very fabric of society, regarded private property as the root of social injustice and hence the root of crime. Pointedly he asked: "What are these laws I must respect, that they leave such a huge gap between me and the rich? Who made these laws? Rich and powerful men. . . . Let us break these fatal connections. . . . let us attack injustice at its source."[5]

Beccaria's attackers labeled him a *socialist*— the first time (1765) that that term was used— by which they meant that Beccaria paid attention only to people as social creatures and that he wanted a society of free and equal citizens. In contrast, the defenders of the use of torture and capital punishment, and of the necessity of social inequality, argued that Beccaria's teachings would lead to chaos and to the loss of all property rights and legitimate authority. These critics sensed the utopian aspect of Beccaria's thought. His humanitarianism was not directed toward the reform of the criminal justice system alone; he sought to restructure society in such a way as to render crime far less prevalent and, whenever possible, to re-educate its perpetrators.

When Beccaria's book and then the author himself turned up in Paris, the philosophes greeted them with universal acclaim. By the 1760s, Paris had become the center of the Enlightenment, and that period is commonly called the High Enlightenment. All the leaders of the period—Voltaire, Rousseau, Diderot, and the atheist d'Holbach—embraced one or another of Beccaria's views. But if the criminal justice system as well as the schools were subject to scrutiny by enlightened critics, what did the philosophes have to say about

slavery, the most pernicious of all Western institutions?

Slavery   On both sides of the Atlantic during the eighteenth century there was growing criticism of slavery. At first it came from religious thinkers like the Quakers, whose own religious version of enlightenment predated the European-wide phenomenon by several decades. The Quakers were born out of the turmoil of the English Revolution, and their strong adherence to democratic ideas grew out of their conviction that the light of God's truth works in every man and woman. Many philosophes on both sides of the Atlantic knew Quaker thought, and Voltaire, who had mixed feelings about slavery, and Benjamin Franklin, who condemned it, admired the Quakers and their principles.

On the problem of slavery the Enlightenment was strangely ambivalent. In an ideal world—just about all philosophes agreed— slavery would not exist. But such was not the world, and given human wickedness, greed, and lust for power, Voltaire thought that slavery as well as exploitation might be inevitable: "the human race," Voltaire wrote in his *Philosophical Dictionary* (1764), "constituted as it is, cannot subsist unless there be an infinite number of useful individuals possessed of no property at all."[6] Denis Diderot thought that slavery was probably immoral, but given that the French empire subsisted in part on its slaves, their rights could not be discussed, he argued, in a monarchy. Indeed, not until 1794 after the first years of the French Revolution and only after agonized debate, did the French government, no longer a monarchy, finally abolish slavery.

It must be remembered that Enlightenment political thinkers, among them Locke (who condoned slavery) and Montesquieu (whose ideas were used to condone it), rejected God-given political authority and argued for the rights of property-holders and for social utility as the foundations of good government. Those criteria, property and utility, played right into the hands of the proslavery apologists. They particularly cited Montesquieu, who had said

Slaves Processing Sugar in a Colonial Plantation. This diagram shows slaves running machinery to grind sugar cane into pulp. In the colonies of European countries in the New World and other lands, subjected peoples were used to perform hard labor in the plan-tations and mines. The immorality of slavery was raised initially by religious thinkers and then taken up by Diderot in his *Encyclopédie*. (*Courtesy of the University of Minnesota Libraries*)

that in tropical countries where sloth was "natural," slavery might be useful and even necessary to force people to work. Montesquieu was uncertain about the morality of slavery, but he had also argued that in despotisms the individual would lose little by willingly choosing enslavement. Proslavery propagandists argued, as well, that since most African tribes were despotic, the slaves in European colonies were in effect better off.

Yet the Enlightenment must also be credited with bringing the problem of slavery into the forefront of public discussion in Europe and in the American colonies. The utility argument cut both ways. If the principle held, as so many philosophes argued, that human hap-piness was the greatest good, how could slavery be justified? In his short novel *Candide*, Voltaire has his main character, Candide, confront the spectacle of a young Negro who has had his leg and arm cut off merely because it is the custom of a country. Candide's philosophical optimism is shattered as he reflects on the human price paid by this slave who harvested the sugar that Europeans enjoyed so abundantly. Throughout the eighteenth century the emphasis placed by the Enlightenment on moral sensibility produced a literature that used shock to emphasize over and over again, and with genuine revulsion, the inhumanity of slavery.

By the second half of the century, again

in that ferment of intellectual creativity described as the High Enlightenment, strongly worded attacks on slavery were issued by a new generation of philosophes. With Rousseau in the vanguard, they condemned slavery as a violation of the natural rights of man. In a volume issued in 1755, the great *Encyclopedia* of the Enlightenment, edited by Diderot, condemned slavery in no uncertain terms: "There is not a single one of these hapless souls . . . who does not have the right to be declared free . . . since neither his ruler nor his father nor anyone else had the right to dispose of his freedom."[7] That statement made its way into thousands of copies and various editions of an encyclopedia that was probably the most influential publication resulting from the French Enlightenment.

The *Encyclopedia*'s wide circulation (about 25,000 copies were sold before 1789), often despite the vigorous efforts of censors to stop it, probably tipped the scales to put the followers of the Enlightenment in the antislavery camp. But that victory for humanitarian principles must be seen as clouded by much ambiguous language, coming straight from the pens of some of Europe's supposedly most enlightened thinkers, and downright prejudice against the Negro as a non-European.

Women   The men of the Enlightenment also had some ambiguous things to say about women. Not entirely unlike slaves, women had few property rights within marriage, and their physical abuse by husbands was widely regarded as beyond the purview of the law. Women's education was slighted, and social theorists had for centuries regarded them as inferior. The origins of that sexual inequality intrigued the earliest political theorists, Hobbes and Locke. Both saw that neither nature nor Scripture gave the father dominion in the household. As Hobbes said in *Leviathan,* "in the state of nature, if a man and woman contract so, as neither is subject to the command of the other, the children are the mother's."[8] Yet this perception was never taken up by any of the major philosophes, and indeed neither Hobbes nor Locke concerned

himself with correcting the legal inferiority of women.

Yet by the middle of the eighteenth century, many French philosophes had begun to think about the condition of women and, in the cases of Voltaire and Diderot, had taken up with women, outside of marriage, who were in several areas their intellectual equals. Diderot fretted, as a result, about the poor education accorded to women; yet he also distrusted their apparent commitment to the old religiosity. By the 1750s in Paris, rich women had become the organizers of fashionable salons where writers and enlightened reformers gathered for free and open conversation; Diderot attended such a salon. But Baron d'Holbach, who led the most famous gathering of the 1770s, specifically excluded women because he believed that they lowered the tone and seriousness of the discussion. Rousseau, who had little use for Paris and its fashionable salons, also disdained the elegant women of the drawing rooms.

Rousseau's own conception of women specifically excluded them from the social contract, in that he saw nature as having given men dominion over women and children. Outside the family, in civil society, that dominion is never absolute; it rests on the will of the majority (presumably of men, because in *The Social Contract* Rousseau never mentions women as a part of civil society). In *A Discourse on Political Economy* (1755), Rousseau insists that the patriarchal structure of the family is natural; the primary function of the family is to "preserve and increase the patrimony of the father."[9] Yet Rousseau does allot to women the education of children, and at the end of the eighteenth century, many women saw Rousseau as an ally because his views would lead to an improvement in their domestic status and conceivably in their educational benefits.

With his characteristic skepticism, Hume saw all this ambiguity about women as resulting from men's desire to preserve their power and patrimony. Since men had no guarantees that the children their wives bore were in fact fathered by them, the only re-

Mme. Geoffrin's Salon. The High Enlightenment in the 1740s had Paris as its capital. The new thinking concentrated on social inequalities, especially those that stiffled talented human beings. The salons of exclusive Parisian society, such as that of Mme. Geoffrin, became the forum for the next generation of philosophers after Voltaire and Diderot. (*Lauros-Giraudon/Art Resource*)

course was to try to repress women sexually. According to Hume the necessity "to impose a due restraint on the female sex"[10] led to sexual inequality. But Hume was never troubled sufficiently by that inequality to discuss the point in any detail. And Kant, who defined the Enlightenment so eloquently, argued that the differences between men and women were simply natural. In *Observations on the Feeling of the Beautiful and Sublime* (1764), Kant argued with characteristic idealism that "women have a strong inborn feeling for all that is beautiful, elegant, and decorated . . . they love pleasantry and can be entertained by trivialities." Predictably, Kant concluded that "laborious learning or painful pondering, even if a woman should greatly succeed to it, destroys the merits that are proper to her sex." In that treatise, Kant came dangerously close to denying women any need to know the new science or to speculate: "her philosophy is not to reason, but to sense."[11] This major philosophe almost denied women a right to enlightenment.

Only late in the century, after the French Revolution had begun, did any thinker representative of the Enlightenment challenge Rousseau's views on women. Educated in enlightened circles and familiar with radical philosophies like the American revolutionary Thomas Paine, the English feminist Mary Wollstonecraft (1759–1797) extended the principles of the Enlightenment to the position and status of women. With devastating logic, her *Vindication of the Rights of Woman* (1792) called for "a revolution in female manners— time to restore to them their lost dignity— and make them, as part of the human species, labor by reforming themselves, to reform the world." She mocked the notion of sexual virtues, such as the beauty and modesty of which Kant had written. She believed, somewhat in the manner of Rousseau, only without his one-sex conclusions, that society had corrupted women: "from the tyranny of man the greater part of female follies proceed." Wollstonecraft viewed this corruption as analogous to the evils stemming from property rights and the vast inequalities in privilege and opportunity between the rich and the poor. True to Enlightenment ideals, Wollstonecraft did not attack property rights as such, but she did urge a significant reduction in the gap between the wealthy and the poor. Again in keeping with enlightened prescriptions, she urged that equal public education be made available to both men and women. For Wollstonecraft, feminism brought with it a commitment to universal human values, to excellence in learning—which she had never had the opportunity to pursue—and to "the power of generalizing ideas, of drawing comprehensive conclusions from individual observations."[12] Although she explicitly wrote for middle- and upper-class women and her work had little impact during her lifetime, Wollstonecraft's *Vindication* became a text on which nineteenth-century reformers and socialists could and did build.

Economic Thought

The Enlightenment's emphasis on property as the foundation for individual rights and its search for uniform laws inspired by Newton's scientific achievement led to the development of the science of economics. Appropriately, that intellectual achievement occurred in the most advanced capitalistic nation in Europe, Great Britain. Not only were the British in the vanguard of capitalist expansion; by the third quarter of the eighteenth century that expansion had brought on the start of the Industrial Revolution. Its new factories and markets for the manufacture and distribution of goods provided a natural laboratory where theorists, schooled in the Enlightenment's insistence on observation and experimentation, could observe the ebb and flow of capitalist production and distribution. In contrast to its harsh criticisms leveled against existing institutions and old elites, the Enlightenment on the whole approved of the independent businessman—the entrepreneur. And there was no one more approving than Adam Smith (1732–1790), whose *Wealth of Nations* (1776) became a kind of bible for those who would have capitalist activity stand as uniformly worthwhile, never to be inhibited by outside regulation.

Throughout the seventeenth century in England there had been a long tradition of economic thought. The resulting ideology stressed independent initiative and the freedom of market forces to determine the value of money and the goods it can buy. By 1700 English economic thought was already well ahead of what could be found on the Continent, with the exception of some Dutch writings. That sophistication undoubtedly reflected the complexity of market life in cities like London and Amsterdam.

One important element in seventeenth-century economic thought, as well as in the most advanced thinking on ethics, was the role of self-interest. Far from being viewed as crude or socially dangerous, it was seen as a good thing, to be accepted and even encouraged. In the mid-seventeenth century, Hobbes took the view that self-interest lay

Map 18.2 European Expansion, 1715 ▶

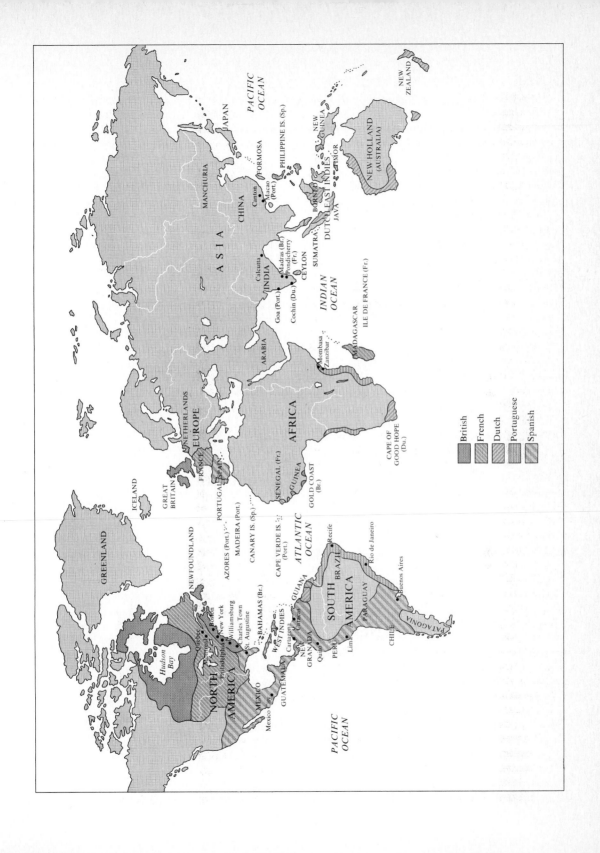

at the root of political action, and by the end of the century, Locke argued that government, rather than primarily restraining the extremes of human greed and the search for power, should first reflect the interests of its citizens. By the middle of the eighteenth century, enlightened theorists all over Europe—especially in England, Scotland, and France—had decided that self-interest was the foundation of all human actions and that at every turn government should assist people in expressing their interests and thus in finding true happiness.

Of course in the area of economic life, government had for centuries regulated most aspects of the market. The classic economic theory behind such regulation was mercantilism. Mercantilists believed that a constant shortage of riches—bullion, goods, whatever—existed, and that governments must so direct economic activity in their states as to compete successfully with other nations for a share of the world's scarce resources. There was also another assumption implicit in mercantilist theory: that money has a "real" value, which governments must protect. Its value is not to be determined solely by market forces.

It required enormous faith in the inherent usefulness of self-interest to assert that government should cease regulating economic activity, that the market should be allowed to be free. That doctrine of *laissez faire*—to leave the market to its own devices—was made the centerpiece of Adam Smith's massive economic study on the origins of the wealth of nations.

As a professor in Glasgow, Scotland, Smith actually went out and observed factories at work; he was one of the first theorists to see the importance of the division of labor in making possible the manufacture of more and cheaper consumer goods. Smith viewed labor as the critical factor in a capitalist economy: the value of money, or of an individual for that matter, rested on the ability to buy labor or the by-products of labor, namely goods and services. According to *The Wealth of Nations*, "Labor is the real measure of the ex-

changeable value of all commodities."[13] The value of labor is in turn determined by market forces, by supply and demand. Before the invention of money or capital, labor belonged to the laborer, but in the money and market society that had evolved since the Middle Ages, labor belonged to the highest bidder.

Smith was not distressed by the apparent randomness of market forces. Beneath this superficial chaos he saw order—the same order he saw in physical nature through his understanding of the new science. He used the metaphor of "the invisible hand" to explain the source of this order; by that he probably meant Newton's regulatory God, made very distant by Smith, who was a deist. That hand would invisibly reconcile self-interest to the common or public interest. With the image of the invisible hand, Smith expressed his faith in the rationality of commercial society and laid the first principle for the modern science of capitalist economics. He did not mean to license the oppression of the poor and the laborer. Statements in *The Wealth of Nations* such as: "Landlords, like all other men, love to reap where they never sowed," or "Whenever there is great property, there is great inequality,"[14] reveal Smith to be a moralist. Yet he knew of no means to stop the exploitation of labor. He believed that its purchase at market value ensured the working of commercial society, and he assumed that the supply of cheap labor was inexhaustible.

The thought of Adam Smith includes extreme versions of two tendencies within Enlightenment thought. The first was the search for laws of society that would imitate the laws postulated by the new science. The second, which was not shared by all philosophes, was an unshakable belief in progress: "In the progress of society . . . each individual becomes more expert in his own peculiar branch, more work is done upon the whole, and the quantity of science is considerably increased by it."[15] Knowledge is progressive, and by implication, the human condition also yields to constant improvement. Smith ignored the appallingly low life-expectancy rates in the new factory towns, and in the process bequeathed a vision of progress wedded to capitalism that remains powerful in some quarters to this day.

The High Enlightenment

More than any other political system in western Europe, the Old Regime in France was directly threatened by the doctrines and reforming impulse of the Enlightenment. The Catholic church was deeply entrenched in every aspect of life—landownership, control over universities and presses, and access to both the court and, through the pulpit, the people. For decades the church had brought its influence to bear against the philosophes, yet by 1750 the Enlightenment had penetrated learned circles and academies in Paris and the provinces. After 1750, censorship of the press was relaxed by a new censor deeply influenced by Enlightenment ideals. In fact, censorship had produced the opposite of the desired effect: the more irreligious and atheistic the book or manuscript was, the more attractive and sought-after it became.

By the 1740s, the fashion among proponents of the Enlightenment was to seek an encyclopedic format for presenting their ideas. This form of writing was the natural byproduct of the Enlightenment's desire to encompass all learning. After Bayle's *Dictionary,* the first successful encyclopedia was published in England by Ephraim Chambers in 1728, and before too long a plan was underway for its translation into French. A leading Freemason in France, the Chevalier Ramsay, even advocated that all the Masonic lodges in Europe should make a financial contribution to this effort, but few, if any, responded to the call.

Four aggressive Parisian publishers took up the task of producing the encyclopedia. One of them had had some shady dealings in clandestine literature that had acquainted him with the more irreligious and daring philosophes in Paris, which is how he knew the young Denis Diderot (1713–1784). Out of that consortium of publishers and philosophes came the most important book of the Enlightenment, Diderot's *Encyclopedia.* Published in 1751 and in succeeding years and editions, the *Encyclopedia* initiated a new stage in the history of Enlightenment publishing. In the process it brought to the forefront pantheistic and materialistic ideas that until that time, only the most radical freethinkers in England and the Netherlands had openly written about. The new era thus ushered in is called the *High Enlightenment.* It permeated exclusive Parisian society, and it was characterized by a violent attack on the church's privileges and the very foundations of Christian belief. From the 1750s to the 1780s, Paris became the capital of the Enlightenment. The philosophes were no longer a persecuted minority (Diderot had spent six months in jail for his philosophical and libertine writings). Instead, they became cultural heroes. The *Encyclopedia* had to be read by anyone claiming to be educated.

In his preface to the *Encyclopedia,* Diderot's collaborator, Jean d'Alembert (c. 1717–1783), summed up the principles on which it had been compiled. In effect, he wrote a powerful summation of the Enlightenment's highest ideals. He also extolled Newton's science and gave a short description of its universal laws. The progress of geometry and mechanics in combination, d'Alembert wrote in his preface, "may be considered the most incontestable monument of the success to which the human mind can rise by its efforts."[16] In turn, he urged that revealed religion should be reduced to a few precepts to be practiced; religion should, he implied, be made scientific and rational. The *Encyclopedia* itself was self-consciously modeled on Bacon's admonition that the scientist should first of all be a collector of facts; in addition, it gave dozens of examples of useful new mechanical devices.

D'Alembert's preface also praised the psychology of Locke: all that is known, is known through the senses. He added that all learning should be catalogued and made easily and readily available, that the printing press should serve the needs of enlightenment, and that literary societies should be set up that would encourage men of talent. D'Alembert added that "they should banish all inequalities that might exclude or discourage men who are endowed with talents that will enlighten others."[17]

During the High Enlightenment, reformers dwelt increasingly on the Old Regime's inequalities that seemed to stifle men of talent. The aristocracy and the clergy were not always talented and seldom were they agitators for enlightenment and reform. Their privileges seemed increasingly less rational. By the 1780s, Paris had spawned a new generation of philosophes for whom Voltaire, Diderot, and Rousseau were aged or dead heroes. But these young authors found the life of the propagandist to be poor and solitary, and they looked at society's ills as victims rather than reformers. They gained firsthand knowledge of the injustices catalogued so brilliantly by Rousseau in *The Social Contract*.

The High Enlightenment's systematic, sustained, and occasionally violent attacks on the clergy and the irrationality of privilege link that movement with the French Revolution. The link did not lie in the comfortable heresies of the great philosophes, ensconced as they were in the fashionable Parisian salons. Rather, it lay in the way those heresies were interpreted by a new generation of reformers, Marat and Robespierre among them, who in the early days of the Revolution used the Enlightenment as a mirror against which they reflected the evils of the old order.

European Political and Diplomatic Developments

Warfare

The dreams of the philosophes, articulated in almost every area of human experience, seemed unable to forestall troublesome developments in power politics, war, and diplomacy. The century was dominated by two areas of extreme conflict: Anglo-French rivalry over control of territory in the New World and hegemony in northern Europe; and intense rivalry between Austria and Prussia over control of central Europe. These major powers, with their imperialistic ambitions, were led by cadres of aristocratic ministers or generals; the Enlightenment did little to displace the war-making role that had belonged to the aristocracy since the Middle Ages.

Yet even in international affairs there was a growing realization, not unrelated to the propaganda of the philosophes, that extreme power held by one state would threaten the order and stability of the whole of Europe. By the early eighteenth century, every European state identified France, by virtue of its sheer wealth and size, as the major threat to European stability.

By this time, France and England were the great rivals in the New World, although colonization had been well underway since the early sixteenth century. Spain had been the first sovereign state to establish an empire in America; located principally in South America and Central America, this empire was based on mining, trade, and slaves. The English and Dutch had followed, first as settlers and then also as slave traders, but their colonies lay to the north—in Virginia, New Amsterdam (later to become New York), and New England. Further north, the French explored and exploited Canada and the region now known as the Midwestern United States. By the early eighteenth century, the Dutch and the Spanish had largely dropped out of the race for colonies in North America, leaving the field to the French and the English.

By the middle of the eighteenth century, the rivalry of these two powers for territory in the New World infected European rivalry in the Old World. Earlier the British had sought to contain the French colossus and to ensure their historic trading interests in

Map 18.3 Europe, 1789 ▶

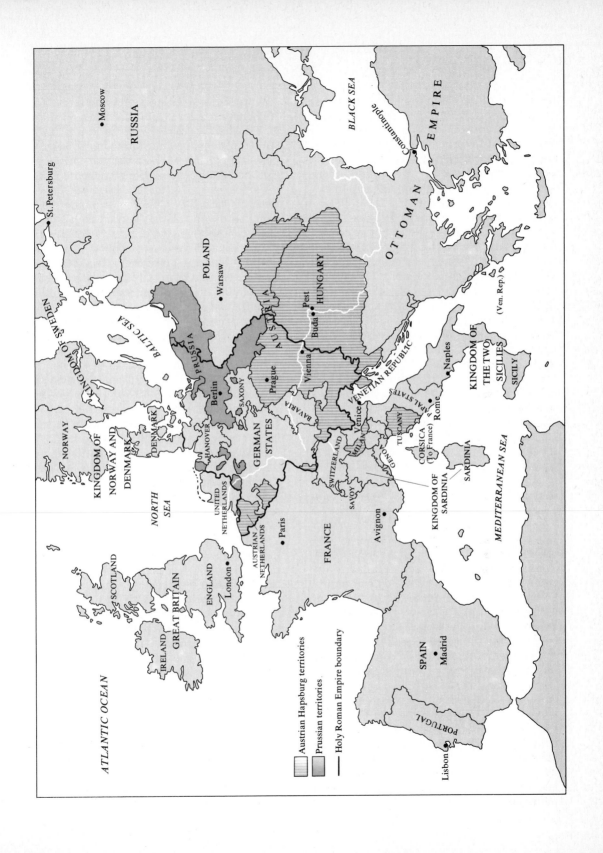

ATLANTIC OCEAN

IRELAND

GREAT BRITAIN

SCOTLAND

ENGLAND

London

NORTH SEA

KINGDOM OF NORWAY AND DENMARK

NORWAY

DENMARK

KINGDOM OF SWEDEN

BALTIC SEA

St. Petersburg

Moscow

RUSSIA

POLAND

Warsaw

PRUSSIA

Berlin

HANOVER

SAXONY

GERMAN STATES

Prague

AUSTRIA

Vienna

Buda

Pest

HUNGARY

BLACK SEA

Constantinople

OTTOMAN   EMPIRE

BAVARIA

SWITZERLAND

SAVOY

AUSTRIAN NETHERLANDS

UNITED NETHERLANDS

FRANCE

Paris

Avignon

GENOA

MILAN

Venice

VENETIAN REPUBLIC

(Ven. Rep.)

PAPAL STATES

Rome

Naples

TUSCANY

CORSICA (To France)

KINGDOM OF SARDINIA

SARDINIA

MEDITERRANEAN SEA

KINGDOM OF THE TWO SICILIES

SICILY

SPAIN

Madrid

PORTUGAL

Lisbon

Austrian Hapsburg territories

Prussian territories.

Holy Roman Empire boundary

the Low Countries and the Rhineland by allying with the Dutch Republic and the Austrians, who controlled what is today called Belgium. This alliance of the Maritime Powers (Britain and the Netherlands) with Austria provided the balance of power against France for the entire first half of the eighteenth century.

The English obsession with the security of the Low Countries and with the protection of the market there for English grain and wool led Britain to intervene in Dutch internal affairs. The French were given to invading the Netherlands; they actually did so during the War of the Spanish Succession (1701–1713) and during the War of the Austrian Succession (1740–1748). As a result of the constant French threats, England sought to secure a government in The Hague that would be favorable to British interests, and in 1747 assisted in the restoration of the Dutch stadtholderate to William IV for that purpose. From that time on, the central government in the Netherlands remained cordial to British interests, although Dutch merchants were frequently hostile to that relationship.

The other major European rivalries broke out into hostilities in the 1740s. Wars between Prussia and Austria and between Austria and France were fought because these major powers wanted to secure their areas of domination both in Europe and in the New World. The wars signaled the rise of Prussia to the status of a major power but left the control of northern Europe open to negotiation. If any power could be described as the loser in that decade, it was the French. The wars exposed weaknesses in the French military system, without resolving the larger question of hegemony in Europe and the New World.

The wars also had an unexpected result. In the 1740s it became clear to the English and their Austrian allies that the Dutch did not possess the will or the resources to guard their southern borders adequately. No longer viewed as the centerpiece in the anti-French alliance, the Dutch Republic appeared to be best suited to a weak and ineffectual neutrality.

With the weakening of this tie with the Netherlands, Austria grew discontented with its old allies, while realizing that it was mortally threatened by the growing power of Prussia. In 1740, Frederick the Great of Prussia launched an aggressive foreign policy against neighboring states—the Austrian state of Silesia, in particular. The forces of the new Austrian queen, Maria Theresa, were powerless to resist this kind of military onslaught. In two years, Prussia had acquired what was probably the largest territory captured by any Continental European state in that era. Silesia augmented the Prussian population by 50 percent, and Frederick also acquired a relatively advanced textile manufacturing area. The Austrians never forgave his transgression.

In 1756, Maria Theresa formed an alliance with France against Prussia; the ensuing Seven Years' War (1756–1763) involved every major European power. Austria's alliance with France in 1756, which ended the historic rivalry between France and the house of Hapsburg, is known as the "diplomatic revolution." The Austrians had grown to fear Prussia in the north more than they feared the French. From the Austrian point of view, Prussia had stolen Silesia in 1740, and its restoration was more important than preserving historic rivalries with France. On the French side, King Louis XV longed for an alliance with a Roman Catholic power and for peace in Europe so that France would be better able to wage war against Britain in the New World.

For their part, the British had long since grown disaffected with the Austrians, and they sought and won a new ally in Frederick the Great. He stood at the head of a new state that was highly belligerent yet insecure, for all the European powers had reasons to want to keep Prussia weak and small. The Seven Years' War—which seesawed back and forth, with French, Austrian, and Russian forces ranged against Frederick's Prussians— changed things little in Europe, but it did reveal the extraordinary power of the Prussian war machine. Prussia joined the ranks of the Great Powers.

Hostilities in North America tipped the

balance of power there in favor of the English. From 1754 to 1763 the French and the English fought over their claims in the New World. England's victory in this conflict—known in American history as the French and Indian War—led ultimately to the American Revolution. England secured its claim to control the colonies of the eastern seaboard, a market that would enrich the English industrialists of the next generation enormously—although, from the colonists' viewpoint, unjustly.

The Dutch Revolution of 1747–1748—the only one to occur in western Europe outside of a city-state or colony in the period from 1689 to 1787—was the only indication to be seen there that the Great Powers or the merchant capitalists had anything to fear from their home populations (or from their slave populations), or that the ideas advanced by the philosophes might be put into practice. Unrest began in Amsterdam in 1747 when minor philosophes, freemasons, journalists, and devotees of English ideas shared in leading an artisan-based democratic uprising that failed utterly to achieve its goals. That minor ripple went unnoticed by the many kings, aristocrats, and oligarchs who ruled so comfortably elsewhere. A generation later, their complacency would wither as democratic revolutions swept first through the American colonies and then through every western European state on the Continent. The wars in the mid-1700s, though destructive in many ways, seemed to confirm the internal security and stability of the ruling elites that controlled their respective states.

Enlightened Despotism

Although some of the enlightened prescriptions for the operation of modern society, such as laissez faire, remain current, one ideal commonly discussed and occasionally advocated by the philosophes has long since fallen by the wayside. It was extinguished in large measure by the democratic revolutions of the late eighteenth century.

Enlightened despotism, although apparently a contradiction in terms, was used as a phrase by the French philosophe Diderot as early as the 1760s. Wherever this phrase is used by the philosophes, it refers to an ideal shared by many of them: the strong monarch who would implement rational reforms, who would remove obstacles to freedom and allow the laws of nature to work, particularly in trade, commerce, and book censorship. When historians use the term *enlightened despotism*, they generally are describing the reigns of specific European monarchs and their ministers—Frederick the Great in Prussia; Catherine the Great in Russia; Charles III of Spain; Maria Theresa and, to a greater extent, her son Joseph II in Austria; and Louis XV of France.

These eighteenth-century monarchs listed above instituted specific reforms in education, trade, and commerce and against the clergy. This type of enlightened government must be understood in context: these countries developed late relative to the older states of Europe. Prussia, Austria, and Russia had to move very quickly if they were to catch up to the degree of centralization achieved in England and France. And when monarchies in France and Spain also occasionally adopted techniques associated with enlightened despotism, they generally did so to compete against a more advanced rival—for example, France against England and Spain against France.

Austria   In the course of the eighteenth century, Austria became a major centralized state as a result of the reforms of Charles VI and his successors (see Chapter 16). Although Catholic and devout at home, Charles allied abroad with Protestant Europe against France. In the newly acquired Austrian Netherlands, he supported the progressive and reforming elements in the nobility that opposed the old aristocracy and clergy.

His daughter Maria Theresa (1740–1780) continued this pattern, and the Austrian administration became one of the most innovative and progressive on the Continent.

Maria Theresa, Empress of Austria, by Martin Van Meytens (detail). *Enlightened despot* is used to describe European rulers like Maria Theresa. The philosophes hoped that such monarchs would initiate reforms to guarantee basic freedoms and allow the laws of nature to work. Maria Theresa continued reforms and cultural revivals begun by Charles VI, but always with the purpose of increasing her own power. (*Collection of the John and Mabel Ringling Museum of Art, Sarasota, Florida*)

Many of its leading ministers, like the Comte du Cobenzl in the Netherlands or Gerard van Swieten, Joseph II's great reforming minister, were Freemasons. This movement often attracted progressive Catholics (as well as Protestants and freethinkers) who despised what they regarded as the medieval outlook of the traditional clergy.

Dynastic consolidation and warfare did contribute decisively to the creation of the

Austrian state. But in the eighteenth century, the intellectual and cultural forces known as the Enlightenment enabled the state to establish an efficient system of government and a European breadth of vision. With these attributes, Austria came to rival (and in Spain's case to surpass) the older, more established states in Europe. Frustrated in their German territories, the Austrian Hapsburgs concentrated their attention increasingly on their eastern states. Vienna gave them a natural power base, while Catholic religiosity gradually united the ruling elites in Bohemia and Hungary with their Hapsburg kings. Hapsburg power created a dynastic state in Austria, yet all efforts to consolidate the western Empire and to establish effective imperial rule met with failure. The unification of Germany would proceed very slowly and come from somewhat unexpected quarters.

Prussia Under the most famous and enlightened Hohenzollern of the eighteenth century, Prussian absolutism (see Chapter 16) acquired some unique and resilient features. Frederick II, the Great, (1740–1786) pursued a policy of religious toleration and, in so doing, attracted French Protestant refugees, who had manufacturing and commercial skills. Intellectual dissidents, such as Voltaire, were also attracted to Prussia. Voltaire eventually went home disillusioned with this new Prussian "enlightened despotism," but not before Frederick had used him and in the process acquired a reputation for learning. By inviting various refugees from French clerical oppression, Frederick gave Berlin a minor reputation as a center for Enlightenment culture. But along with Frederick's courtship of the French philosophes with their enlightened ideals, there was the reality of Prussian militarism and the servitude of its peasants.

Yet the Hohenzollern dynasty succeeded in creating a viable state built by the labor of its serfs and the power of its Junker-controlled army; and this state would manage to survive as a monarchy until the First World War. By the middle of the eighteenth century, this small nation of no more than 2.5 million inhabitants exercised inordinate influence in European affairs because of its military prowess.

Prussian absolutism rested on the army and the Junker class, and its economy was state directed and financed. Its court expenses were held to a minimum—most state expenditures went into maintaining an army of 200,000 troops—the largest in relation to population for all Europe.

Russia   Russia during the eighteenth century made significant strides, under various monarchs, toward joining the European state system. During the reign of Peter the Great (1682–1725), the Russians established strong diplomatic ties in almost every European capital. In addition, the Russian metal industry became vital to European development. The English, who lacked the forest lands and wood necessary to fire smelting furnaces, grew dependent on Russian-produced iron.

Catherine the Great (1762–1796) consciously pursued policies intended to reflect her understanding of the Enlightenment. These presented contradictions. She entered into respectful correspondence with philosophes, but at the same time she extended serfdom to the entire Ukraine. She promulgated a new, more secular, educational system and sought at every turn to improve Russian industry, but her policies rested on the aggrandizement of the agriculturally based aristocracy. The Charter of Nobility in 1785 forever guaranteed the aristocracy's right to hold the peasants in servitude. The Enlightenment, as interpreted by this shrewd monarch, completed the tendency to monarchical absolutism that had been well underway since the sixteenth century.

The Effects of Enlightened Despotism

Enlightened despotism was, in reality, the use of Enlightenment principles by enlightened monarchs to enhance the central government's power and thereby their own.

These eighteenth-century monarchs knew, in ways their predecessors had not, that knowledge is power; they saw that application of learned theories to policy can produce useful results.

But did these enlightened despots try to create more humanitarian societies in which individual freedom flourished on all levels? In this area, enlightened despotism must be pronounced a shallow deployment of Enlightenment ideals. For example, Frederick the Great decreed the abolition of serfdom in Prussia, but had no means to force the aristocracy to conform because he desperately needed their support. And in the 1780s, Joseph II instituted liberalized publishing laws in Austria, until he heard of artisans reading pamphlets about the French Revolution. He quickly retreated and reimposed censorship. In the 1750s, Frederick the Great had also loosened the censorship laws, and writers were free to attack traditional religion, but they never were allowed to criticize the army, the key to Frederick's aggressive foreign policy. Catherine the Great gave Diderot a pension, but she would hear of nothing that compromised her political power, and her ministers were expected to give her unquestioning service.

Finally, if the Enlightenment means the endorsement of reason over force, peace and cosmopolitan unity over ruthless competition, then the foreign policies of these enlightened despots were uniformly despotic. The evidence lies in a long series of aggressions, including Frederick's invasion of Silesia in 1740, Austria's secret betrayal of its alliance with the English and Dutch and the ensuing Seven Years' War, and Austria's attempt in the 1770s to claim Bavaria. In short, the Enlightenment provided a theory around which central and eastern European states that were only recently unified could organize their policies. The theory also justified centralization over the power of local elites grown comfortable through centuries of unopposed authority. There were no major philosophes who did not grow disillusioned with enlightened monarchs on the rare occasions when their actions could be observed at close range. The Enlightenment did provide new principles for the organization of centralized monarchical power, but centralization with economic rationalization and management did not make their practitioners or beneficiaries any more enlightened. Enlightened despotism was extinguished largely by the democratic revolutions of the late eighteenth century.

The American Revolution

England's victory over France in the French and Indian War (1754–1763) set in motion a train of events that culminated in the American Revolution. The war had drained the British treasury, and now Britain had the additional expense of paying for troops to guard the new North American territories that it had gained in the war. As strapped British taxpayers could not shoulder the whole burden, Parliament members thought it quite reasonable that American colonists help pay the bill; they reasoned that Britain had protected the colonists from the French and was still protecting them in their conflicts with Indians. New colonial taxes and import duties were imposed by Parliament. Particularly galling to the colonists were the Stamp Act (which placed a tax on newspapers, playing cards, liquor licenses, and legal documents) and the Quartering Act (which required colonists to provide living quarters and supplies to English troops stationed in America).

Vigorous colonial protest compelled the British Parliament to repeal the Stamp Act, yet new taxes were imposed that raised the price of many everyday articles, including tea. The stationing of British troops in Boston, the center of rebelliousness, worsened tensions. In March 1770, a crisis ensued after a squad of British soldiers fired into a crowd of Bostonians who had been taunting them and pelting them with rocks and snowballs. Five Bostonians died, and six were wounded. A greater crisis occurred in 1773 when Par-

liament granted the East India Company exclusive rights to sell tea in America. The colonists regarded this as yet another example of British tyranny. When a crowd of Bostonians dressed as Indians climbed aboard East Indian ships and dumped about 90,000 pounds of tea overboard, the British responded with a series of repressive measures, including suppressing self-government in Massachusetts and closing the port of Boston.

The quarrel turned to bloodshed in April and June 1775. On July 4, 1776, delegates from the various colonies adopted the Declaration of Independence, written mainly by Thomas Jefferson. Applying Locke's theory of natural rights, this document declared that government derives its power from the consent of the governed, that it is the duty of a government to protect the rights of its citizens, and that people have the right to "alter or abolish" a government that deprives them of their "unalienable rights."

Why were the American colonists so ready to revolt? For one thing, they had brought with them a highly idealized understanding of English liberties; long before 1776 they had extended representative institutions to include small property owners who probably could not have voted in England. The colonists had come to expect representative government, trial by jury, and protection from unlawful imprisonment. Each of the thirteen colonies had an elected assembly that acted like a miniature parliament; in these assemblies, Americans gained political experience and quickly learned to be self-governing.

Familiarity with the thought of the Enlightenment and the republican writers of the English Revolution also contributed to the Americans' awareness of liberty. The ideas of the philosophes traversed the Atlantic and influenced educated Americans, particularly Thomas Jefferson and Benjamin Franklin. Like the philosophes, American thinkers expressed a growing confidence in reason, valued freedom of religion and of thought, and championed the principle of natural rights.

Another source of hostility toward estab-

The Signing of the Declaration of Independence, July 4, 1776 (detail) by John Trumbull. The success of the American Revolutionary War was hailed as a victory of liberty over tyranny. Jefferson and Franklin were intimately familiar with the thinking of the Enlightenment and stressed a confidence in reason, freedom of religion and thought, and the existence of natural rights. (*Copyright Yale University Art Gallery*)

lished authority among the American colonists was their religious traditions, particularly that of the Puritans, who believed that the Bible was infallible and its teachings a higher law than the law of the state. Like their counterparts in England, American Puritans challenged political and religious authorities who, in their view, contravened God's law. Thus Puritans acquired two habits that were crucial to the development of political liberty—dissent and resistance. When transferred to the realm of politics, these Puritan tendencies would lead Americans to resist authority that they considered unjust.

American victory came in 1783 as a result of several factors. George Washington proved a superior leader, able to organize and retain the loyalty of his troops. France, seeking to avenge its defeat in the Seven Years' War, helped the Americans with money and provisions and then in 1778 entered the conflict. Britain had difficulty shipping supplies across three thousand miles of ocean, was fighting the French in the West Indies and elsewhere

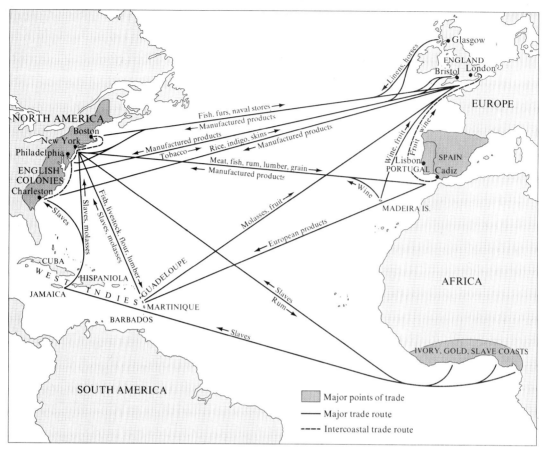

Map 18.4 Trade Routes Between the Old and New Worlds

at the same time, and ultimately lacked commitment to the struggle.

Reformers in other lands quickly interpreted the American victory as a successful struggle of liberty against tyranny. During the Revolution the various states drew up constitutions based on the principle of popular sovereignty and included bills of rights that protected individual liberty. Rejecting both monarchy and hereditary aristocracy, the Constitution of the United States created a republic in which power derived from the people. A system of separation of powers and checks and balances set safeguards against the abuse of power, and the Bill of Rights provided for protection of individual rights. To be sure, the ideals of liberty and equality were not extended to all people— slaves knew nothing of the freedom that white

Americans cherished, and women were denied the vote and equal opportunity. But to reform-minded Europeans, it seemed that Americans were fulfilling the promise of the Enlightenment; they were creating a freer and better society.

The Enlightenment and the Modern World

Enlightenment thought was the culmination of a trend instituted by Renaissance artists and humanists who attacked medieval otherworldliness and gave value to individual achievement and the worldly life. It was a direct outgrowth of the Scientific Revolution, which provided a new method of inquiry and verification and demonstrated the power and self-sufficiency of the human intellect. If nature were autonomous—that is, if it operated according to natural laws that did not require divine intervention—then the human intellect could also be autonomous. Through its own powers, it could uncover those general principles that operate in the social world as well as in nature.

The philosophes sought to analyze nature, government, religion, law, economics, and education through reason alone, without any reference to Christian teachings, and they rejected completely the claims of clerics to a special wisdom. The philosophes broke decisively with the medieval view that the individual is naturally depraved, that heaven is the true end of life, and that human values and norms derive from a higher reality and are made known through revelation. Instead, they upheld the potential goodness of the individual, regarded the good life on earth as the true end of life, and insisted that solely by the light of reason, individuals could improve themselves and their society. The outlook of the philosophes, as expressed by the French materialist, the Baron d'Holbach, demonstrates that the passage from medieval to modern, if not complete, was irreversible:

[In the past, the] human mind, confused with its theological opinions, forgot itself, doubted its own powers, mistrusted experience, feared truth, disdained its reason, and abandoned her direction, blindly to follow authority. Man was a mere machine in the hands of his tyrants and priests, who alone had the right of directing his actions; always led like a slave, he ever had his vices and character. These are the true causes of the corruption of morals, to which religion ever opposes only ideal barriers, and that without effect. Ignorance and servitude are calculated to make men wicked and unhappy. Knowledge, reason, and liberty can alone reform them, and make them happier; but every thing conspires to blind them, and confirm their errors. Priests cheat them, tyrants corrupt, the better to enslave them. . . . To learn the true principles of morality, men have no need of theology, of revelation, or gods: They have need only of reason.[18]

The political philosophies of Locke, Montesquieu, and Rousseau held an entirely new and modern concept of the relationship between the state and the individual: states should exist not simply to accumulate power unto themselves, but also to enhance human happiness. From that perspective, monarchy and even oligarchy not based upon merit began to seem increasingly less useful. And if happiness be a goal, then it must be assumed that some sort of progress is possible in history.

The philosophes were generally optimistic about the future, believing that advances in science, a growing concern for natural rights, and an enlightened attitude toward torture, intolerance, and other injustices would usher in an age of human betterment. The philosophes insisted that people plan for the future victory of enlightenment by fostering education, judicial reform, political maturity, and even the creation of new religions that would be more civil than godly and more interested in humanity and nature than in heaven and sectarian dogma.

The philosophes wanted a freer, more humane, and more rational society, but they feared the people and their potential for revolutionary action. As an alternative to revolution, most philosophes offered science as the universal improver of the human condition. Faith in reform without the necessity of revolution proved to be a doctrine for the elite of the salons. In that sense the French Revolution can be said to have repudiated the essential moderation of philosophes like Voltaire, d'Alembert, and Kant. Yet the Enlightenment established a vision of humanity so independent of Christianity and so focused on the needs and abuses of present society that no established institution, once grown corrupt and ineffectual, could long withstand its penetrating critique. To that extent the writings of the philosophes point toward the democratic revolutions of the late eighteenth century.

Chronology 18.1 The Enlightenment

1685	Revocation of the Edict of Nantes; persecution of Protestants in France
1687	Publication of Newton's *Principia*
1688–89	Revolution in England; weakening of the clergy's power and loosening of censorship
1690	Publication of Locke's *Second Treatise of Civil Government*
1717	Founding of the Grand Lodge, London; the beginning of organized Freemasonry
1733	Voltaire publishes *Letters Concerning the English Nation*
1740	Frederick the Great invades Silesia; the War of Austrian Succession ensues
1748	Hume publishes *An Enquiry Concerning Human Understanding;* Montesquieu publishes *The Spirit of the Laws*
1749–50	French advocates of the Enlightenment become increasingly critical of their government
1751	Publication of Diderot's *Encyclopedia* in Paris
1762	Rousseau publishes *Émile*
1768–1774	The Russo-Turkish War
1775	The American Revolution begins
1776	Adam Smith publishes *Wealth of Nations*
1785	The Russian Charter of Nobility; the servitude of the peasants is guaranteed
1789	The French Revolution begins

Notes

1. "An Answer to the Question: 'What Is Enlightenment?' " in Hans Reiss, ed., *Kant's Political Writings* (Cambridge, England: Cambridge University Press, 1970), pp. 54–60.

2. Pierre Bayle, *Historical and Critical Dictionary*, Richard H. Popkin, ed. (New York: Bobbs-Merrill, 1965), p. 195.

3. Thomas Hobbes, *Leviathan*, C. B. Macpherson, ed. (Harmondsworth, England: Penguin Books, 1977), p. 189.

4. Jean Jacques Rousseau, *The Social Contract and Discourses* (New York: Dutton, 1950), pp. 3, 9.

5. Quoted in Franco Venturi, *Utopia and Reform in the Enlightenment* (Cambridge, England: Cambridge University Press, 1971), p. 101.

6. Voltaire, *Philosophical Dictionary*, Theodore Besterman, ed. (Harmondsworth, England: Penguin, 1974), p. 183.

7. Quoted in David B. Davis, *The Problem of Slavery in Western Culture* (Harmondsworth, England: Penguin, 1970), p. 449.

8. Quoted in Rosemary Agonito, ed., *History of Ideas on Women: A Source Book* (New York: G. P. Putnam's Sons, 1977), p. 101.

9. Ibid., p. 118.

10. Ibid., p. 124.

11. Ibid., p. 130.

12. Ibid., pp. 154–155.

13. Excerpted from Adam Smith, *The Wealth of Nations*, George Stigler, ed. (New York: Appleton, 1957), p. 3.

14. Ibid., p. 98.

15. Ibid., p. 7.

16. Jean Le Rond d'Alembert, *Preliminary Discourse to the Encyclopedia of Diderot*, trans. by Richard N. Schwab (New York: Bobbs-Merrill, 1963), p. 22.

17. Ibid., pp. 101–102.

18. Excerpted in Frank E. Manuel, ed., *The Enlightenment* (Englewood Cliffs, N.J.: Prentice-Hall, 1965), 60–61.

Suggested Reading

Anderson, M. S., *Europe in the Eighteenth Century, 1713–1783* (1961). A good general survey of the century with excellent chapters on cultural and intellectual life.

Becker, Carl, *The Heavenly City of the Eighteenth-Century Philosophers* (1932). Still a provocative assessment of the Enlightenment's relation to Christianity.

Cassirer, Ernst, *The Philosophy of the Enlightenment* (1951). A classic and basic account of Enlightenment philosophy; difficult reading.

Goldmann, Lucien, *The Philosophy of the Enlightenment: The Christian Burgess and the Enlightenment* (1968). Intended as a corrective to Cassirer, by a prominent European Marxist historian.

Hazard, Paul, *The European Mind, 1680–1715* (1963). Indispensable for the early period of the Enlightenment.

The Institute for Research in History, ed., *Women and the Enlightenment* (1984). A collection of essays asking the question: "Did women have an Enlightenment?"

Jacob, Margaret, *The Radical Enlightenment: Pantheists, Freemasons and Republicans* (1981). A study of the radical materialists and their contribution to the Enlightenment, especially in the first half of the century.

Venturi, Franco, *Utopia and Reform in the Enlightenment* (1971). A difficult but rewarding book, focussed on the more extreme reformers of the age.

Wangermann, Ernst, *The Austrian Achievement, 1700–1800* (1973). An excellent case study of the strengths and weaknesses of the most enlightened of European monarchies.

Review Questions

1. What is meant by the Age of Enlightenment? Where did the Enlightenment begin, and what contributed to its spread?

2. How did Christianity come under attack by deists, skeptics, freethinkers, and materialists?

3. In what ways does Voltaire exemplify the philosophes?

4. Why was Freemasonry important in the eighteenth century? Did its secrecy violate the ideals of the Enlightenment?

5. Describe the essential characteristics of the political thought of each of the following: Hobbes, Locke, Montesquieu, and Rousseau. Make relevant comparisons and contrasts.

6. Describe Locke's theory of learning. What was its significance for the Enlightenment?

7. How did the philosophes come to terms with the status of slaves and criminals?

8. Compare the views of Rousseau and Wollstonecraft on the position of women in society.

9. The philosophes approved of capitalism. Defend or refute this statement.

10. What made the High Enlightenment different from what went before it? Describe how it differed. How did the *Encyclopedia* exemplify the High Enlightenment?

11. List the major military conflicts of the eighteenth century. Discuss the significance of each.

12. Enlightened despotism was in reality the use of Enlightenment principles by monarchs to enhance the central government's power and thereby their own. Discuss this statement.

13. In what ways was the American Revolution based on Enlightenment principles?

14. The Enlightenment was a pivotal period in the shaping of the modern mentality. Discuss this statement.

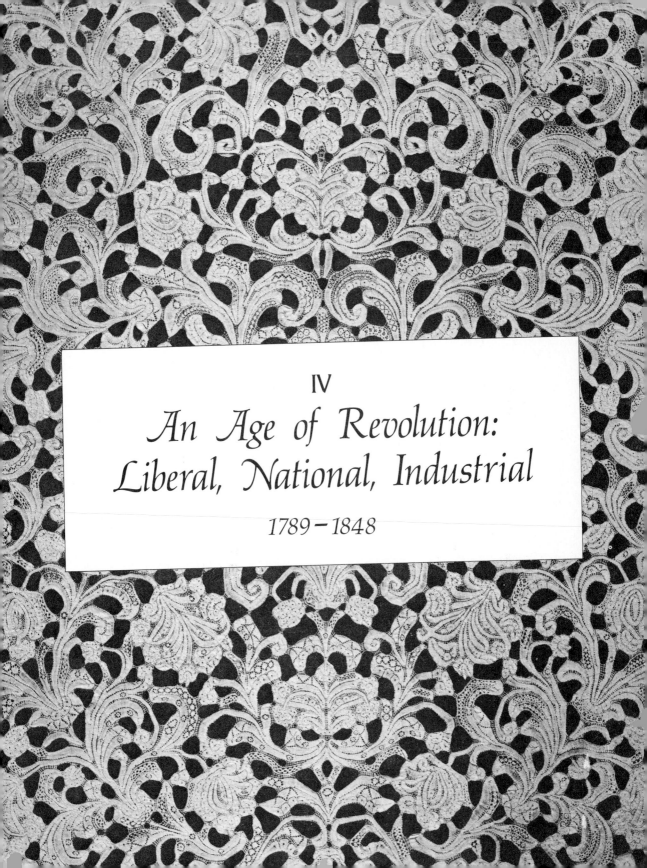

IV
An Age of Revolution:
Liberal, National, Industrial

1789 – 1848

19

The French Revolution: Affirmation of Liberty and Equality

*T*he outbreak of the French Revolution in 1789 stirred the imagination of Europeans. Both participants and observers sensed that they were living in a pivotal age. On the ruins of the Old Order founded on privilege and despotism, a new era was forming that promised to realize the ideals of the Enlightenment. These ideals included the emancipation of the human personality from superstition and tradition, the triumph of liberty over tyranny, the refashioning of institutions in accordance with reason and justice, and the tearing down of barriers to equality. It seemed that the natural rights of the individual, hitherto a distant ideal, would now reign on earth, ending centuries of oppression and misery. Never before had people shown such confidence in the power of human intelligence to shape the conditions of existence. Never before had the future seemed so full of hope.

This lofty vision kindled emotions akin to religious enthusiasm and attracted converts throughout the Western world. "If we succeed," wrote the French poet André Chénier, "the destiny of Europe will be changed. Men will regain their rights and the people their sovereignty."[1] The editor of the Viennese publication *Wiener Zeitung* wrote to a friend: "In France a light is beginning to shine which will benefit the whole of humanity."[2] British reformer John Cartwright expressed the hopes of reformers everywhere: "Degenerate must be that heart which expands not with sentiments of delight at what is now transacting in . . . France. The French . . . are not only asserting their own rights, but they are asserting and advancing the general liberties of mankind."[3]

The Old Regime

The causes of the French Revolution reach back into the aristocratic structure of society in the Old Regime. Eighteenth-century French

433

society was divided into three orders, or Estates: the clergy constituted the First Estate; the nobility the Second Estate; and everyone else (about 96 percent of the population) belonged to the Third Estate. The clergy and nobility, totaling about 400,000 out of a population of 26 million, enjoyed special privileges. The semifeudal social structure of the Old Regime, based on inequalities sanctioned by law, produced the tensions that precipitated the Revolution.

The First Estate

The powers and privileges of the French Catholic church made it a state within a state. As it had done for centuries, the church registered births, marriages, and deaths; collected tithes (a tax on products from the soil); censored books considered dangerous to religion and morals; operated schools; and distributed relief to the poor. Since it was illegal for Protestants to assemble together for prayer, the Catholic church enjoyed a monopoly on public worship. Although it owned an estimated 10 percent of the land, which brought in an immense revenue, the church paid no taxes. Instead it made a "free gift" to the state— the church determined the amount—which was always smaller than direct taxes would have been. Critics denounced the church for promoting superstition and obscurantism, for impeding reforms, and for being more concerned with wealth and power than with the spiritual message of Jesus.

The clergy reflected the social divisions in France. The upper clergy shared the attitudes and way of life of the nobility from which they sprang. The parish priests, commoners by birth, resented the haughtiness and luxurious living of the upper clergy. In 1789, when the Revolution began, many priests sympathized with the reform-minded people of the Third Estate.

The Second Estate

Like the clergy, the nobility was a privileged order. Nobles held the highest positions in the church, army, and government. They were exempt from most taxes, collected manorial dues from peasants, and owned approximately 20 percent of the land. And in addition to the income that they drew from their estates, nobles were becoming increasingly involved in such nonaristocratic enterprises as banking and finance. All nobles were not equal, however; there were gradations of dignity among the 200,000 to 250,000 members of the nobility.

Enjoying the most prestige were *nobles of the race*—families who could trace their aristocratic status back to time immemorial. (Of these, many were officers in the king's army and were called *nobles of the sword.*) The highest of the ancient nobles were engaged in the social whirl at Versailles and Paris, receiving pensions and sinecures from the king but performing few useful services for the state. Most nobles of the race, unable to afford the gilded life at court, remained on their provincial estates, the poorest of them barely distinguishable from prosperous peasants.

Alongside this ancient nobility, a new nobility had arisen, created by the monarchy. To obtain money, reward favorites, and weaken the old nobility, French kings had sold titles of nobility to members of the bourgeoisie and had conferred noble status on certain government offices bought by wealthy members of the bourgeoisie. Particularly significant were the *nobles of the robe,* whose ranks included many former bourgeois who had purchased judicial offices in the parlements, the high law courts. In the late eighteenth century the nobles of the robe championed the cause of aristocratic privilege.

In the seventeenth century, Louis XIII's minister Richelieu had humbled the great nobles. Determined not to share his power and fearful of threats to the throne, Louis XIV (1643–1715) had allowed the nobility social prestige, but denied it a voice in formulating high policy. In the eighteenth century, nobles sought to regain the power that they had lost under Louis XIV. This resurgence of the nobility was led not by regenerated ancient aristocrats, but by the new nobility, the nobles of the robe. The parlements became obstreperous critics of royal policy and opponents of any reform that threatened aristocratic and provincial privileges. This "feudal reaction" triggered the Revolution.

However, all nobles did not think alike. A minority, influenced by the liberal ideals of the philosophes, sought to reform France; they wanted to end royal despotism and establish a constitutional government. To this extent, the liberal nobility had a great deal in common with the bourgeoisie. These liberal nobles saw the king's difficulties in 1788 as an opportunity to regenerate the nation under enlightened leadership. But the majority of nobles, hostile to liberal ideals, resisted enlightened reforms. In doing so, they contributed to the destruction of the aristocracy in 1789.

The Third Estate

The Third Estate was composed of the bourgeoisie, peasants, and urban laborers. While the bourgeoisie provided the leadership for the Revolution, its success depended on the support given by the rest of the Third Estate.

The Bourgeoisie   The bourgeoisie consisted of merchant-manufacturers, wholesale merchants, bankers, master craftsmen, doctors, lawyers, intellectuals, and government officials below the top ranks. Although the bourgeois had wealth, they lacked social prestige. A merchant, despite his worldly success, felt that his occupation denied him the dignity enjoyed by the nobility. "There are few rich people who at times do not feel humiliated at being nothing but wealthy," observed an eighteenth-century Frenchman.[4]

Influenced by the aristocratic values of the day, the bourgeoisie sought to erase the stigma of common birth by obtaining the most esteemed positions in the nation and by entering the ranks of the nobility, whose style of life they envied. Traditionally, some bourgeoisie had risen socially either by purchasing a judicial or political office that carried with it a title of nobility, or by gaining ad-

mission to the upper clergy and the officer ranks of the army. As long as these avenues of upward social mobility remained open, the bourgeoisie did not challenge the existing social structure, including the special privileges of the nobility.

But in the last part of the eighteenth century it became increasingly difficult for the bourgeois to gain the most honored offices in the land. Finding the road to social dignity blocked in every direction, the bourgeois came to resent a social system that valued birth more than talent. Envy of the nobility turned to hatred; instead of aspiring to acquire noble status, the bourgeois, by 1789, sought to abolish the privileges of birth and to open careers to talent.

Practical considerations of social prestige and economic gain, however, do not alone explain the revolutionary mentality of the bourgeoisie. When they challenged the Old Regime, the bourgeois felt that they were fulfilling the ideals of the philosophes and serving all humanity. This idealism would inspire sacrifice and heroism.

By 1789 the bourgeois had many grievances. They wanted all positions in church, army, and state open to men of talent regardless of birth. They sought a parliament; a constitution that would limit the king's power and guarantee freedom of thought, a fair trial, and religious toleration; and administrative reforms that would eliminate waste, inefficiency, and interference with business. In effect, the bourgeois aspired to political power and social prestige in proportion to their economic power. Because the bourgeois were the principal leaders and chief beneficiaries of the French Revolution, many historians view it, along with the English revolutions of the seventeenth century and the growth of capitalism, as "an episode in the general rise of the bourgeoisie."[5]

The Peasantry   The condition of the more than 21 million French peasants was a paradox. On the one hand, they were better off than peasants in Austria, Prussia, Poland, and Russia, where serfdom still predominated. In France, serfdom had largely dis-

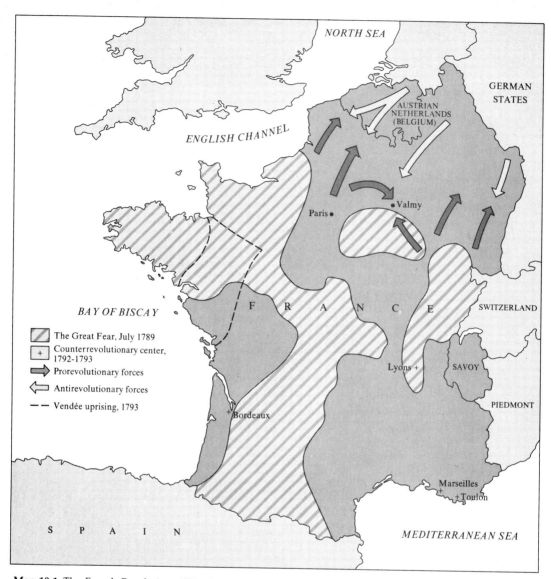

Map 19.1 The French Revolution, 1789–1793

appeared; many peasants owned their own land, and some were even prosperous. On the other hand, most French peasants lived in poverty, which worsened in the closing years of the Old Regime.

Peasants owned between 30 and 40 percent of the land, but the typical holding was barely large enough to eke out a living. The rising birthrate (between 1715 and 1789 the population may have increased from 18 million to 26 million) led to the continual subdivision of farms among heirs. Moreover, many peasants did not own their own land but rented

it from a nobleman or a prosperous neighbor. Others worked as sharecroppers, turning over to their creditors a considerable share of the harvest.

Unable to survive on their small holdings, many peasants tried to supplement their incomes. They hired themselves out for whatever employment was available in their region—as agricultural day laborers, charcoal burners, transporters of wine, or textile workers in their own homes. Landless peasants tried to earn a living in such ways. The increasing birthrate resulted in an overabundance of rural wage earners. This worsened the plight of small landowners and reduced the landless to beggary. "The number of our children reduces us to desperation,"[6] was a common complaint of the peasants by 1789.

An unjust and corrupt system of taxation weighed heavily on the peasantry. Louis XIV had maintained his grandeur and financed his wars by milking ever more taxes from the peasants, a practice that continued throughout the eighteenth century. An army of tax collectors victimized the peasantry. In addition to royal taxes, peasants paid the tithe to the church and manorial dues to lords.

Although serfdom had ended in most parts of France, lords continued to demand obligations from peasants as they had done in the Middle Ages. In addition to performing labor services on the lord's estate, peasants still had to grind their corn in the lord's mill, bake their bread in his oven, press their grapes in his winepress, and give him part of their produce in payment. In addition, the lord collected a land rent from peasant proprietors, levied dues on goods at markets and fairs, and exercised exclusive hunting rights on lands tilled by peasants. The last was a particularly onerous right, for the lord's hunting parties damaged crops. Lords were determined to hold on to these privileges not only because of the income they brought, but because they were symbols of authority and social esteem. The peasants, on the other hand, regarded these obligations as odious medieval anachronisms from which they derived no benefit.

In the last part of the eighteenth century, lords sought to exact more income from their lands by reviving manorial dues that had not been collected for generations, by increasing the rates on existing dues, and by contracting businessmen to collect payments from the peasants. These capitalists naturally tried to squeeze as much income as possible from the peasants, making them hate the whole system of manorial obligations even more.

Inefficient farming methods also contributed to the poverty of the French peasants. In the eighteenth century, France did not

experience a series of agricultural improvements comparable to those in England. Failure to invest capital in modernizing agricultural methods meant low yields per acre and a shortage of farm animals.

A rise in the price of necessities during the closing years of the Old Regime worked hardship on those peasants who depended on wages for survival. With prices rising faster than wages, only the more prosperous peasants with produce to sell benefited. The great majority of peasants were driven deeper into poverty, and the number of beggars roaming the countryside increased.

A poor harvest in 1788–89 aggravated peasant misery and produced an atmosphere of crisis. The granaries were empty; the price of bread, the staple food of the French, soared; and starvation threatened. Hatred of the manorial order and worsening poverty sparked a spontaneous and autonomous peasant revolution in 1789.

Urban Laborers   The urban laboring class in this preindustrial age consisted of journeymen working for master craftsmen, factory workers in small-scale industries, and wage earners such as day laborers, gardeners, handymen, and deliverymen, who were paid by those they served. The poverty of the urban poor, like that of the peasant wage earners, had worsened in the late eighteenth century. From 1785 to 1789 the cost of living increased by 62 percent, while wages rose only 22 percent. For virtually the entire decade of the Revolution, urban workers struggled to keep body and soul together in the face of food shortages and rising prices, particularly that of their staple food, bread. Material want drove the urban poor to acts of violence that affected the course of the Revolution.

Inefficient Administration and Financial Disorder

The administration of France was complex, confusing, and ineffective. The practice of buying state offices from the king, introduced as a means of raising money, resulted in many incompetent officeholders. "When his Majesty created an office," stated one administrator, "Providence called into being an imbecile to buy it."[7] Tariffs on goods shipped from one province to another and differing systems of weights and measures hampered trade. No single law code applied to all the provinces; instead, there were overlapping and conflicting law systems based on old Roman law or customary feudal law, which made the administration of justice slow, arbitrary, and unjust. To admirers of the philosophes, the administrative system was an insult to reason. The Revolution would sweep the system away.

Financial disorders also contributed to the weakness of the Old Regime. In the last years of the Old Regime the government could not raise sufficient funds to cover expenses. By 1787, it still had not paid off the enormous debt incurred during the wars of Louis XIV, let alone the costs of succeeding wars during the eighteenth century, particularly France's aid to the colonists in the American Revolution. The king's gifts and pensions to court nobles and the extravagant court life further drained the treasury.

Finances were in a shambles not because France was impoverished, but because of an inefficient and unjust tax system. Few wealthy Frenchmen, including the bourgeois, paid their fair share of taxes. Because tax revenue came chiefly from the peasants, it was bound to be inadequate. Excise duties and indirect taxes on consumer goods yielded much-needed revenue in the last decades of the Old Regime. However, instead of replenishing the royal treasury, these additional funds were pocketed by rich tax collectors who, for a fixed payment to the state, had obtained the right to collect these indirect taxes. The financial crisis, although serious, was solvable if the clergy, nobility, and bourgeoisie would pay their fair share of taxes. King Louis XVI (1774–1792) recognized the need for tax reform, but his efforts were resisted by nobles who clung tenaciously to their ancient privileges.

Mainly through the parlements, the nobles were able to thwart royal will. Many parlementaires were originally wealthy bourgeois who had purchased their offices from the state (nobles of the robe). Both the office and status of nobility remained within the family. The Paris parlement and twelve provincial parlements reviewed the judgments of lower courts and registered royal edicts. The parlements had the right to *remonstrate,* that is, to pass judgment on the legality of royal edicts before registering them. If the courts considered the king's new laws at variance with previous legislation or ancient traditions, they would refuse to register them. The king could revise the edicts in accordance with the parlements' instructions, or force their registration by means of a *lit de justice*—a solemn ceremony in which the monarch appeared before the court. If the parlementaires persisted in their resistance, the king might order the arrest of their leaders. While the king could force his will on the parlements, their bold opposition embarrassed royal prestige.

With France on the brink of bankruptcy, the king's ministers proposed that the nobility and church surrender some of their tax privileges. The parlements, steadfast defenders of noble prerogative, protested and remonstrated, and the church insisted on the immunity of its property from taxation. Throughout the nation, members of the privileged orders united in their determination to preserve their social exclusiveness.

The resistance of the nobility forced the government, in July 1788, to call for a meeting of the Estates General—a medieval representative assembly that had last met in 1614—to deal with the financial crisis. The body was to convene in May 1789. Certain that they would dominate the Estates General, the nobles intended to weaken the power of the throne and to regain power that they had lost under Louis XIV. Once in control of the government, they would introduce financial reforms. But the revolt of the nobility against the crown had unexpected consequences; it opened the way for revolutions by the Third Estate that destroyed the Old Regime and with it the aristocracy and its privileges.

The Moderate Stage, 1789–1791

The Clash Between the Nobility and the Third Estate

Frenchmen in great numbers met in electoral assemblies to elect deputies to the Estates General. Churchmen and nobles voted directly for their representatives. Most deputies of the clergy were parish priests, many of them sympathetic to reform. Although the majority of deputies of the Second Estate were conservative country nobles, there was a sizable liberal minority, including some who had fought in the American Revolution, that favored reform; political liberalism was not a monopoly of the bourgeoisie. The representatives from the Third Estate were elected indirectly with virtually all taxpaying males over age twenty-five eligible to vote. The delegates of the Third Estate consisted predominantly of bourgeois drawn from government service and the professions, including many articulate lawyers.

Each Estate drew up lists of grievances and suggestions (*cahiers de doléances*). The *cahiers* from all three orders expressed loyalty to monarchy and church, recognized the sanctity of property rights, and called for a written constitution and an elected assembly. The cahiers drawn up by the bourgeoisie stressed guarantees of personal liberty; the cahiers of the nobility predictably insisted on the preservation of manorial rights and honorific privileges.

As the Estates General prepared to meet, reform-minded Frenchmen held great hopes for the regeneration of France and the advancement of liberty. But immediately it became clear that the hopes of reformers clashed with the intentions of the aristocracy. What had started as a struggle between the crown and the aristocracy was turning into something far more significant—a conflict between the two privileged orders on one side and the Third Estate on the other. One pamphleteer, Abbé Sieyès (1748–1836), expressed the hatred the bourgeoisie held for the ar-istocracy. "The privileged order has said to the Third Estate: 'Whatever be your services, whatever be your talents, you shall go thus far and no farther. It is not fitting that you be honored.' " The higher positions in the land, said Sieyès, should be the "reward for talents," not the prerogative of birth. Without the Third Estate, "nothing can progress"; without the nobility, "everything would proceed infinitely better."[8]

Formation of the National Assembly

The Estates General convened at Versailles on May 5, 1789, but was stalemated by the question of procedure. Seeking to control the assembly, the nobility insisted that the three Estates follow the traditional practice of meeting separately and voting as individual bodies. Since the two privileged orders were likely to stand together, the Third Estate would always be outvoted, two to one. But the delegates from the Third Estate, unwilling to allow the nobility and the higher clergy to dominate the Estates General, proposed instead that the three Estates meet as one body and vote by head. There were some 610 delegates from the Third Estate; the nobility and clergy together had an equivalent number. Since the Third Estate could rely on the support of sympathetic parish priests and liberal nobles, it would be assured a majority if all orders met together.

On June 10, the Third Estate broke the stalemate. It invited the clergy and nobility to join with it in a common assembly; if they refused, the Third Estate would go ahead without them. A handful of priests answered the roll call, but not one noble. On June 17, the Third Estate made a revolutionary move. It declared itself the National Assembly. On June 20, locked out of their customary meeting hall (apparently by accident), the Third Estate delegates moved to a nearby tennis court and took a solemn oath not to disband until a constitution had been drawn up for France. By these acts the bourgeois delegates had demonstrated their desire and determination to reform the state.

Approval of the Tennis Court Oath (detail). On June 17, 1789, the Third Estate declared itself the National Assembly. On June 20, they met on a nearby tennis court when they found their customary meeting hall locked. They vowed not to disband until a constitution had been drawn up for the entire nation. In this painting by Jacques Louis David, aristocrat, clergyman, and commoner embrace before a cheering National Assembly. (*Versailles/Cliché des Musées Nationaux*)

Louis XVI commanded the National Assembly to separate into orders, but the Third Estate held firm. The steadfastness of the delegates and the menacing actions of Parisians who supported the National Assembly forced Louis XVI to yield. On June 27 he ordered the nobility (some had already done so) and the clergy (a majority had already done so) to join with the Third Estate in the National Assembly. The Third Estate had successfully challenged the nobility and defied the king. It would use the National Assembly to institute reforms, including the drawing up of a constitution that limited the king's power.

But the victory of the bourgeoisie was not yet secure, for most nobles had not resigned themselves to a bourgeois-dominated National Assembly. Recognizing that France was on the threshold of a social revolution that threatened their status, the nobles reversed their position of previous years; they joined with the king in an effort to crush the National Assembly. Louis XVI, influenced by his wife Queen Marie Antoinette, his brother Comte d'Artois, and court aristocrats, ordered special foreign regiments to the outskirts of Paris and Versailles. He also replaced Necker, a reform-minded minister, with a nominee of the queen. It appeared that Louis XVI, overcoming his usual hesitancy and vacillation, had resolved to use force against the National Assembly and to stop the incipient revolution. At this point, uprisings by the common people of Paris and peasants in the countryside saved the National Assembly and ensured the victory of the forces of reform.

Storming of the Bastille

In July 1789, the level of tension in Paris was high for three reasons. First, the calling of the Estates General had aroused hopes for reform. Second, the price of bread was soaring: in August 1788, a Parisian laborer had spent 50 percent of his income on bread; by July 1789 he was spending 80 percent. A third element in the tension was the fear of an aristocratic plot to crush the National Assembly. Fearful that royal troops would bombard and pillage the city, Parisians searched for weapons.

On July 14, eight hundred to nine hundred Parisians gathered in front of the Bastille, a fortress used as a prison and a despised symbol of royal despotism. They gathered primarily to obtain gunpowder and to remove the cannon that threatened a heavily populated working-class district. Fearing an attack, the governor of the Bastille, de Launay, ordered his men to fire into the crowd; they killed ninety-eight and wounded seventy-three of the people. When the tables were turned and five cannons were aimed on the main gate of the Bastille, de Launay surrendered. Although promised that no harm would come to him, de Launay and five of his men were killed, and their heads were paraded on pikes through the city.

Historians hostile to the French Revolution have long depicted the besiegers of the Bastille as a destructive mob composed of the dregs of society—smugglers, beggars, bandits, degenerates. However, more contemporary scholarship[9] reveals that the Bastille crowd was not drawn from the criminal elements, but consisted almost entirely of small tradesmen, artisans, and wage earners—concerned

citizens driven by hunger, fear of an aristocratic conspiracy, and hopes for reform.

The fall of the Bastille had far-reaching consequences: a symbol of the Old Regime had fallen; some court nobles hostile to the Revolution decided to flee the country; the frightened king told the National Assembly that he would withdraw the troops ringing Paris. The revolutionary act of the Parisians had indirectly saved the National Assembly and with it the bourgeois revolution.

The Great Fear

The uprising of the Parisians strengthened the hand of the National Assembly. Revolution in the countryside also served the interests of the reformers. The economic crisis of 1788–89 had worsened conditions for the peasantry; the price of bread soared and the number of hungry beggars wandering the roads spreading terror multiplied. Also contributing to this revolutionary mentality were the great expectations unleashed by the summoning of the Estates General, for like the urban poor, the peasants hoped that their grievances would be remedied. In the spring of 1789, peasants were attacking food convoys and refusing to pay royal taxes, tithes, and manorial dues. These revolutionary outbreaks intensified at the end of July 1789, as rumors spread that aristocrats were organizing bands of brigands to attack the peasants and steal their crops. Inflamed by hunger and fear, stimulated by the uprising of the Parisians, and suspicious of an aristocratic plot to thwart efforts at reform, the peasants in some regions panicked. When the mythical army of brigands did not materialize, the peasants let loose centuries of stored-up hatred against the nobles, raiding the chateaux and burning manorial registers on which were inscribed their obligations to the lords.

Known as the Great Fear, this peasant upheaval in late July 1789, like the insurrection in Paris, worked to the advantage of the reformers. It provided the National Assembly with an opportunity to strike at noble priv-

Engraving of Bastille Day. About 900 Parisians gathered on July 14, 1789, in front of the Bastille to obtain gunpowder and remove a cannon threatening a populated working-class district. When fired upon, they attacked the ancient fortress and put its commander and five of his men to death. A hated symbol of absolutism had fallen to the Revolution. (*Brown Brothers*)

ileges by putting into law what the peasants had accomplished with the torch—the destruction of feudal remnants. On the night of August 4, 1789, aristocrats, seeking to restore calm in the countryside, surrendered their special privileges—exclusive hunting rights, tax exemptions, monopoly of highest offices, manorial courts, and the right to demand labor services from peasants. The assembly maintained that "the feudal regime had been utterly destroyed."*

In the decrees of August 5 and 11, the National Assembly implemented the resolutions of August 4. The assembly also declared that the planned constitution should be prefaced by a declaration of rights. On August 26, it adopted the Declaration of the Rights of Man and the Citizen. The August Decrees and the Declaration of Rights marked the death of the Old Regime.

October Days

Louis XVI, cool to these reforms, postponed his approval of the August Decrees. It would require a second uprising by the Parisians to force the king to agree to the reforms and to nail down the victory of the reformers.

On October 5, 1789, Parisian housewives marched twelve miles to Versailles to protest the lack of bread to the National Assembly and the king. A few hours later, 20,000 Paris Guards, a citizen militia sympathetic to the Revolution, also set out for Versailles in support of the women protesters. The king had

*This was not entirely true. Some peasant obligations were abolished outright. However, for being released from other specified obligations, peasants were required to compensate their former lords. The peasants simply refused to pay, and in 1793 the Jacobins, recognizing reality, declared the remaining debt null and void.

no choice but to promise bread and to return with the demonstrators to Paris. Two weeks later the National Assembly abandoned Versailles for Paris.

Once again the "little people" had aided the bourgeoisie. Louis XVI, aware that he had no control over the Parisians and fearful of further violence, approved the August Decrees and the Declaration of the Rights of Man and the Citizen. Nobles who had urged the king to use force against the assembly and had tried to block reforms fled the country in large numbers.

Reforms of the National Assembly

With resistance enfeebled, the National Assembly continued the work of reform begun in the summer of 1789. By abolishing the special privileges of the nobility and the clergy and promoting the interests of the bourgeoisie, the reforms of the National Assembly destroyed the Old Regime:

1. *Abolition of special privileges.* By ending the special privileges of the nobility and the clergy in the August Decrees, the National Assembly pronounced the equality that the bourgeoisie had demanded. The aristocratic structure of the Old Regime, a remnant of the Middle Ages that had hindered the progressive bourgeoisie, had been eliminated.

2. *Statement of human rights.* The Declaration of the Rights of Man and the Citizen expressed the liberal and universal goals of the philosophes and the particular interests of the bourgeoisie. To contemporaries it was a refutation of the Old Regime, a statement of ideals that, if realized, would end longstanding abuses and usher in a new society. In proclaiming the inalienable right to liberty of person and thought and to equal treatment under the law, the Declaration affirmed the dignity of human personality; it asserted that government belonged not to any ruler but to the people as a whole, and that its aim was the preservation of the natural rights of the individual. Because the Declaration stood

in sharp contrast to the principles espoused by an intolerant clergy, a privileged aristocracy, and a despotic monarch, it has been called the death warrant of the Old Regime.

The declaration expressed the view of the philosophes that people need not resign themselves to the abuses and misfortunes of human existence: through reason, they could improve society. But in 1789 the declaration was only a statement of intent; it remained to be seen whether its principles would be achieved.

3. *Subordination of church to state.* The National Assembly also struck at the privileges of the Roman Catholic church. The August Decrees declared the end of tithes. To obtain badly needed funds, the Assembly in November 1789 confiscated church lands and put them up for sale. In 1790 the Assembly passed the Civil Constitution of the Clergy, which altered the boundaries of the dioceses, reducing the number of bishops and priests, and transformed the clergy into government officials elected by the people and paid by the state.

Almost all bishops and many priests opposed the Civil Constitution. One reason was that reorganization deprived a sizable number of clergymen of their positions. Moreover, Protestants and nonbelievers could, in theory, participate in the election of Catholic clergy. In addition, the assembly had issued the decree without consulting the pope or the French clergy as a body. When the Assembly required the clergy to take an oath that they would uphold the Civil Constitution, only about one-half would do so, and many believing Catholics supported the dissenting clergy. The Civil Constitution divided the French and gave opponents of the Revolution an emotional issue around which to rally supporters.

4. *Constitution for France.* In September 1791 the National Assembly achieved the goal at which it had been aiming since June 1789: a constitution limiting the power of the king and guaranteeing all French citizens equal treatment under the law. Citizens paying less than a specified amount in taxes could not

vote. Probably about 30 percent of the males over age twenty-five were excluded by this stipulation, and only the more well-to-do citizens qualified to sit in the Legislative Assembly, a unicameral parliament that would succeed the National Assembly. Despite this restriction, suffrage requirements under the Constitution of 1791 were far more generous than in Britain.

5. *Administrative and judicial reforms.* The National Assembly aimed to reform the chaotic administrative system of France. It replaced the patchwork of provincial units with eighty-three new administrative units, or departments, approximately equal in size. The departments and their subdivisions were allowed a large measure of self-government.

Judicial reforms complemented the administrative changes. A standardized system of courts replaced the innumerable jurisdictions of the Old Regime, and the sale of judicial offices was ended. All judges were selected from graduate lawyers, and citizen juries were introduced in criminal cases. In the penal code completed by the National Assembly, torture and barbarous punishments were abolished.

6. *Aid for business.* The National Assembly abolished all tolls and duties on goods transported within the country, maintained a tariff to protect French manufacturers, and insisted that French colonies trade only with the mother country. The Assembly also established a uniform system of weights and measures, eliminated the guilds (medieval survivals that blocked business expansion), and forbade workingmen to form unions or to strike.

By ending absolutism, striking at the privileges of the nobility, and preventing the mass of people from gaining control over the government, the National Assembly consolidated the rule of the bourgeoisie. With one arm, it broke the power of aristocracy and throne; with the other, it held back the common people. While the reforms benefited the bourgeoisie, it would be a mistake to view them merely as a selfish expression of bour-

geois interests. The Declaration of the Rights of Man was addressed to all; it proclaimed liberty and equality as the right of all and called for citizens to treat each other with respect. Both French and foreign intellectuals believed that the Revolution would lead ultimately to the emancipation of humanity. "The men of 1789," says Lefebvre, "thought of liberty and equality as the common birthright of mankind."[10] These ideals became the core of the liberal-democratic credo that spread throughout much of the West in the nineteenth century.

The Radical Stage, 1792–1794

The Sans-Culottes

Pleased with their accomplishments—equality before the law, careers open to talent, a written constitution, parliamentary government—the men of 1789 wished the Revolution to go no further. But revolutionary times are unpredictable. Soon the Revolution moved in a direction neither anticipated nor desired by the reformers. A counterrevolution was led by irreconcilable nobles and alienated churchmen; supported by socially unprogressive and strongly Catholic peasants, it began to threaten the changes made by the Revolution, forcing the revolutionary leadership to resort to extreme measures.

Also propelling the Revolution in the direction of radicalism was the discontent of the *sans-culottes*—small shopkeepers, artisans, and wage earners. Although they had played a significant role in the Revolution, particularly in the storming of the Bastille and the October Days, they had gained little. The sans-culottes, says French historian Albert Soboul, "began to realize that a privilege of wealth was taking the place of a privilege of birth. They foresaw that the bourgeoisie would succeed the fallen aristocracy as the ruling class."[11] Inflamed by poverty and their hatred of the rich, the sans-culottes insisted that it was the government's duty to guarantee them the "right of existence," a policy that ran counter to the economic individualism of the bourgeoisie. They also demanded that the government increase wages, set price controls on food supplies, end food shortages, punish food speculators and profiteers, and deal severely with counterrevolutionaries.

Although most sans-culottes upheld the principle of private property, they wanted laws to prevent extremes of wealth and poverty. Socially, their ideal was a nation of small shopkeepers and small farmers. "No one should own more than one workshop or one store," read a sans-culotte petition.[12] Whereas the men of 1789 sought equality of rights, liberties, and opportunities, the sans-culottes expanded the principle of equality to include narrowing the gap between rich and poor. To reduce economic inequality, the sans-culottes called for higher taxes for the wealthy and the redistribution of land. Politically, they favored a democratic republic in which the common man had a voice.

In 1789 the bourgeoisie had demanded equality with the aristocrats—the right to hold the most honored position in the nation and an end to the special privileges of the nobility. By the end of 1792 the sans-culottes were demanding equality with the bourgeois—political reforms that would give the poor a voice in the government and social reforms that would improve their lot.

Despite the pressures exerted by reactionary nobles and clergy on the one hand and discontented sans-culottes on the other, the Revolution might not have taken a radical turn had France remained at peace. The war that broke out with Austria and Prussia in April 1792 exacerbated internal dissensions, worsened economic conditions, and threatened to undo the reforms of the Revolution. It was under these circumstances that the Revolution moved from its moderate stage into a radical one that historians refer to as the Second French Revolution.

Foreign Invasion

In June 1791, Louis XVI and the royal family, traveling in disguise, fled Paris for the north-

Jacques Louis David (1748–1825): A Woman of the Revolution. Although David portrayed royalty and would go on to glorify Napoleon, he captured here the obdurate woman of the Revolution. Driven by hunger, she would demand bread and march twelve miles to Versailles to state her case before National Assembly and king on October 5, 1789. She would favor social reforms and condone terror in order to achieve the goals of the Revolution. (*Museé des Beaux-Arts, Lyons*)

east of France to join with *émigrés* (nobles who had left revolutionary France and were organizing a counterrevolutionary army) and to rally foreign support against the Revolution. Discovered at Varennes by a village postmaster, they were brought back to Paris as virtual prisoners. The flight of the king turned many French people against the monarchy, strengthening the position of radicals who wanted to do away with kingship altogether and establish a republic. But it was foreign invasion that led ultimately to the destruction of the monarchy.

In the Legislative Assembly, the lawmaking body that had succeeded the National Assembly in October 1791, one group, called the *Girondins,* urged an immediate war against Austria, which was harboring and supporting the émigrés. The Girondins believed that a successful war would unite France under their leadership, and they were convinced that Austria was already preparing to invade France and destroy the Revolution. Moreover, regarding themselves as crusaders in the struggle of liberty against tyranny, the Girondins hoped to spread revolutionary reforms to other lands to provoke a war of the people against kings.

On April 20, 1792, the Legislative Assembly declared war on Austria. Commanded by the Duke of Brunswick, a combined Austrian and Prussian army crossed into France. French forces, short of arms and poorly led (about 6,000 of some 9,000 officers had abandoned their command), could not halt the enemy's advance. Food shortages and a counterrevolution in the south increased the unrest. Into an atmosphere already charged with tension, the Duke of Brunswick issued a manifesto declaring that if the royal family were harmed he would exact a terrible vengeance on the Parisians. On August 10, 1792, enraged Parisians and militia from other cities attacked the king's palace, killing several hundred Swiss guards.

In early September, as foreign troops advanced deeper into France, there occurred an event analogous to the Great Fear of 1789. As rumors spread that jailed priests and aristocrats were planning to break out of their cells to support the Duke of Brunswick, the Parisians panicked. Driven by fear, patriotism, and murderous impulses, they raided the prisons and massacred 1,100 to 1,200 prisoners. Most of the victims were not political prisoners but ordinary criminals.

On September 21–22, 1792, the National Convention (the successor to the Legislative Assembly) abolished the monarchy and established a republic. In December 1792, Louis XVI was placed on trial, and in January 1793, he was executed for conspiring against the liberty of the French people. The execution of Louis XVI intensified tensions between the revolutionaries and the crowned heads of Europe. The uprising of August 10, the September Massacres, the creation of a republic, and the execution of Louis XVI all confirmed that the Revolution was falling into radicalism.

Meanwhile the war continued. Short of supplies, hampered by bad weather, and possessing insufficient manpower, the Duke of Brunswick never did reach Paris. Outmaneuvered at Valmy on September 20, 1792, the foreign forces retreated to the frontier, and the armies of the Republic took the offensive. By the beginning of 1793, French forces had overrun Belgium (then a part of the Austrian Empire), the German Rhineland, and the Sardinian provinces of Nice and Savoy. To the peoples of Europe the National Convention had solemnly announced that it was waging a popular crusade against privilege and tyranny, against aristocrats and princes.

Frightened by these revolutionary social ideas, by the execution of Louis XVI, and most importantly by French expansion that threatened the balance of power, the rulers of Europe, urged on by Britain, had formed an anti-French alliance by the spring of 1793. The allies' forces pressed toward the French borders. The Republic was endangered.

Counterrevolutionary insurrections further undermined the fledgling Republic. In the Vendée in western France, peasants who were protesting against taxation and conscription and were still loyal to their priests took up arms against the Republic. Led by local nobles, the peasants of Vendée waged a guerrilla war for religion, royalism, and their traditional way of life. In other quarters, federalists revolted in the provinces, objecting to the power wielded by the centralized government in Paris. The Republic was unable to exercise control over much of the country.

The Jacobins

As the Republic tottered under the weight of foreign invasion, internal insurrection, and economic crisis, the revolutionary leadership grew still more radical. In June 1793, the Jacobins replaced the Girondins as the dominant group in the National Convention. Whereas the Girondins favored a government in which the departments would exercise control over their own affairs, the Jacobins wanted a strong central government with Paris as the center of power. Whereas the Girondins opposed government interference with business, the Jacobins would support temporary government controls to deal with the needs of war and economic crisis. This last point was crucial; it won the Jacobins the support of the sans-culottes.

Both Girondins and Jacobins came from the bourgeoisie, but some Jacobin leaders were more willing to listen to the economic and political demands of the hard-pressed sans-culottes. The Jacobins also sought an alliance with the sans-culottes in order to defend the Revolution against foreign and domestic enemies. The Jacobins had a further advantage in the power struggle: they were tightly organized, well-disciplined, and convinced that only they could save the Republic. On June 2, 1793, some 80,000 armed sans-culottes surrounded the Convention and demanded the arrest of Girondin delegates— an act that enabled the Jacobins to gain control of the government.

The problems confronting the Jacobins were staggering. They had to cope with civil war, particularly in the Vendée, economic distress, blockaded ports, and foreign invasion. They lived with the terrible dread that if they failed, the Revolution for liberty and equality would perish. Only strong leadership could save the Republic; it was provided by the Committee of Public Safety. Serving as a cabinet for the convention, the Committee of Public Safety organized the nation's defenses, formulated foreign policy, supervised ministers, ordered arrests, and imposed the central government's authority throughout the na-

tion. The twelve members of the committee, all ardent patriots and veterans of revolutionary politics, constituted "a government of perhaps the ablest and most determined men who have ever held power in France."[13]

Jacobin Achievements

The Jacobins continued the work of reform. A new constitution, in 1793, expressed Jacobin enthusiasm for political democracy. It contained a new Declaration of Rights that affirmed and amplified the principles of 1789. By giving all adult males the right to vote, it overcame sans-culotte objections to the Constitution of 1791. However, due to the threat of invasion and the revolts, implementation of the Constitution of 1793 was postponed, and it never was put into effect. By abolishing both slavery in the French colonies and imprisonment for debt and by making plans for free public education, the Jacobins revealed their humanitarianism and their debt to the philosophes.

Jacobin economic policies derived from the exigencies of war. To halt inflation and gain the support of the poor—both necessary for the war effort—the Jacobins decreed the *law of the maximum*, which fixed prices on bread and other essential goods and raised wages. To win over the peasants, the Jacobins made it easier for them to buy the property of émigré nobles. To equip the Army of the Republic, the Committee of Public Safety requisitioned grain, wool, arms, shoes, and other items from individual citizens, required factories and mines to produce at full capacity, and established state-operated armament and munition plants.

The Nation in Arms

To fight the war against foreign invaders, the Jacobins, in an act that anticipated modern conscription, drafted unmarried men between eighteen and twenty-five years of age. They mobilized all the resources of the nation, infused the army with a love for *la patrie* (the nation), and in a remarkable demonstration of administrative skill, equipped an army of more than 800,000 men. In creating the nation in arms, the Jacobins heralded the emergence of modern warfare. The citizen-soldiers of the Republic, commanded by officers who had proved their skill on the battlefield and inspired by the ideals of Liberty, Equality, and Fraternity, won decisive victories. In May and June of 1794, the French routed the allied forces on the vital northern frontier, and by the end of July, France had become the triumphant master of Belgium.

In demanding complete devotion to the nation, the Jacobin phase of the Revolution also heralded the rise of modern nationalism. In the schools; in newspapers, speeches, and poems; on the stage; and at rallies and meetings of patriotic societies, the French people were told of the glory won by Republican soldiers on the battlefield and were reminded of their duties to la patrie. "The citizen is born, lives and dies for the fatherland."[14] These words were written in public places for all citizens to read and ponder. The soldiers of the Revolution fought not for money or for a king, but for the nation. "When *la patrie* calls us for her defense," wrote a young soldier to his mother, "we should rush to her. . . . Our life, our goods, and our talents do not belong to us. It is to the nation, to *la patrie*, to which everything belongs."[15] Could this heightened sense of nationality that concentrated on the special interests of the French people be reconciled with the Declaration of the Rights of Man, whose principles were addressed to all humanity? The revolutionaries themselves did not understand the implications of the new force that they had unleashed.

The Republic of Virtue and the Reign of Terror

Robespierre   At the same time that the Committee of Public Safety was forging a revolutionary army to deal with external enemies,

it was also waging war against internal opposition. The pivotal personality in this struggle was Maximilien Robespierre (1758–1794). Robespierre had served in the National Assembly and was an active Jacobin. Although neither a brilliant orator nor a hero in appearance, he was distinguished by a fervent faith in the rightness of his beliefs, a total commitment to republican democracy, and a pure integrity that earned him the name *the Incorruptible.*

Robespierre wanted to create a better society founded on reason, good citizenship, and patriotism. In his Republic of Virtue, there would be no kings or nobles; men would be free, equal, and educated; reason would be glorified and superstition ridiculed; there would be no extremes of wealth or poverty; man's natural goodness would prevail over vice and greed; laws would preserve, not violate, inalienable rights. In this utopian vision, an individual's duties would be "to detest bad faith and despotism, to punish tyrants and traitors, to assist the unfortunate, to respect the weak, to defend the oppressed, to do all the good one can to one's neighbor, and to behave with justice towards all men."[16]

A disciple of Rousseau, Robespierre conceived the national general will as ultimate and infallible. Its realization meant the establishment of a Republic of Virtue; its denial meant the death of an ideal and a return to despotism. Robespierre felt certain that he and his colleagues in the Committee of Public Safety had correctly ascertained the needs of the French people. He was sure the committee members were the genuine interpreters of the general will, and he felt duty-bound to ensure its realization. He pursued his ideal society with religious zeal. Knowing that the Republic of Virtue could not be established while France was threatened by foreign and civil war, Robespierre urged harsh treatment for enemies of the Republic, who "must be prosecuted by all not as ordinary enemies, but as rebels, brigands, and assassins."[17]

The Jacobin leadership, with Robespierre playing a key role, defined the enemies of the Republic: Girondins who challenged Jacobin authority, federalists who opposed a strong central government emanating from Paris, counterrevolutionary priests and nobles and their peasant supporters, and profiteers who hoarded food. The Robespierrists also executed Danton, a hero of the Revolution, who wished to end the terror and negotiate peace with the enemy. The Jacobins even sought to discipline the ardor of the sans-culottes who had given them power. Fearful that sans-culotte spontaneity would undermine central authority and promote anarchy, Robespierrists brought about the dissolution of sans-culotte societies. Robespierrists also executed sans-culotte leaders known as *enragés*, who threatened insurrection against Jacobin rule and pushed for more social reforms than the Jacobins would allow. The enragés wanted to set limits on incomes and on the size of farms and businesses and preached the deChristianization of France—policies considered far too extreme by the supporters of Robespierre.

To preserve republican liberty, the Jacobins made terror a deliberate government policy. Said Robespierre:

Does not liberty, that inestimable blessing . . . have the . . . right to sacrifice lives, fortunes, and even, for a time, individual liberties? . . . Is not the French Revolution . . . a war to the death between those who want to be free and those content to be slaves? . . . There is no middle ground; France must be entirely free or perish in the attempt, and any means are justifiable in fighting for so fine a cause.[18]

Perhaps as many as 40,000 people perished during the Reign of Terror.

Robespierre and his fellow Jacobins did not resort to the guillotine because they were bloodthirsty or power mad. Instead, they sought to establish a temporary dictatorship in a desperate attempt to save the Republic and the Revolution. Deeply devoted to republican democracy, the Jacobins viewed themselves as bearers of a higher faith. Like all visionaries, Robespierre was convinced that he knew the right way, that the new society

Robespierre: A Contemporary Cartoon Wherein Robespierre Executes the Executioner After All of France Had Been Executed by the Jacobin Leader's Orders. To create a Republic of Virtue where men would be free and equal, Maximilien Robespierre considered terror necessary. Robespierre lost favor with his own party and was himself guillotined. (*University of Rochester Library, Rochester, New York*)

he envisaged would benefit all humanity, and that those who impeded its implementation were not just opponents, but sinners who had to be liquidated for the good of humanity.

The Jacobins did save the Republic. Their regime expelled foreign armies, crushed the federalist uprisings, contained the counterrevolutionaries in the Vendée, and prevented anarchy. Without the discipline, order, and unity imposed on France by the Robespierrists, it is likely that the Republic would have collapsed under the twin blows of foreign invasion and domestic anarchy.

The Significance of the Terror The Reign of Terror poses fundamental questions about the meaning of the French Revolution and the validity of the Enlightenment conception of man. To what extent was the Terror a reversal of the ideals of the Revolution as formulated in the Declaration of the Rights of Man? To what extent did the feverish passions and fascination for violence demonstrated in the mass executions in the provinces and in the public spectacles in Paris indicate a darker side of human nature beyond control of reason? Did Robespierre's religion of humanity revive the fanaticism and cruelty of the wars of religion that had so disgusted the philosophes? Did the Robespierrists, who considered themselves the staunchest defenders of the Revolution's ideals soil and subvert these ideals by their zeal? By mobilizing the might of the nation, by creating the mystique of la patrie, by imposing temporary dictatorial rule in defense of liberty and equality, and by legalizing and justifying terror committed in the people's name, were the Jacobins unwittingly unleashing new forces that, in later years, would be harnessed by totalitarian ideologies consciously resolved to stamp out the liberal heritage of the Revolution? Did 1793 mark a change in the direction of Western civilization: a movement away from the ideals of the philosophes, and the opening of an age of violence and irrationalism that would culminate in the cataclysms of the twentieth century?

The Fall of Robespierre

The Terror had been instituted during a time of crisis and keyed-up emotions. By the summer of 1794, with the victory of the Republic seemingly assured, the fear of an aristocratic conspiracy had subsided, the will to punish "traitors" had slackened, and popular fervor for the Terror had diminished. As the need and enthusiasm for the Terror abated, Robespierre's political position weakened.

Opponents of Robespierre in the convention, feeling the chill of the guillotine blade on their own necks, ordered the arrest of Robespierre and some of his supporters. On July 27, 1794, the ninth of Thermidor according to the new republican calendar, Robespierre was guillotined. Parisian sans-culottes might have saved him, but they made no attempt. With their political clubs dissolved, the organization needed for an armed uprising was lacking. Moreover, the sans-culottes' ardor for Jacobinism had waned. They resented Robespierre for having executed their leaders, and apparently the social legislation instituted by the Robespierrist leadership had not been sufficiently carried out to soothe sans-culotte discontent.

After the fall of Robespierre, the machinery of the Jacobin Republic was dismantled. Leadership passed to the property-owning bourgeois who had endorsed the constitutional ideas of 1789–1791, the moderate stage of the Revolution. The new leadership, known as *Thermidoreans* until the end of 1795, wanted no more of the Jacobins or of Robespierre's society. They had considered Robespierre a threat to their political power because he would have allowed the common people a considerable voice in the government, and a threat to their property because he would have introduced some state regulation of the economy to aid the poor.

The Thermidorean reaction was a counterrevolution. The new government purged the army of officers who were suspected of Jacobin leanings, abolished the law of the maximum, and declared void the Constitution of 1793. A new constitution, approved in 1795, re-established property requirements for voting. The counterrevolution also produced a counterterror, as royalists and Catholics massacred Jacobins in the provinces.

At the end of 1795, the new republican government, called the *Directory*, was burdened by war, a sagging economy, and internal unrest. The Directory crushed uprisings by royalists seeking to restore the monarchy and by Parisian sans-culottes maddened by hunger and hatred of the rich. As military and domestic pressures worsened, power began to pass into the hands of generals. One of them, Napoleon Bonaparte, seized control of the government in November 1799, pushing the Revolution into yet another stage.

The Meaning of the French Revolution

The French Revolution has been described as a series of concurrent revolutions. In addition to the revolution of the bourgeoisie, there occurred an autonomous peasant revolution precipitated by increasing poverty, hatred of the manorial order, and rising hopes aroused by the calling of the Estates General. There also occurred a third uprising, that of urban journeymen, wage earners, and lesser bourgeois shopkeepers and craftsmen hard hit by food shortages and rising prices.

But bad economic conditions alone need not lead to revolution. "No great event in history," states Henri Peyre, a twentieth-century student of French culture, "has been due to causes chiefly economic in nature, and certainly not the French Revolution."[19] For centuries, Indian untouchables and Egyptian fellahin lived under the most wretched of conditions, bearing their misery without raising a voice in protest. In the eighteenth century, the peoples of eastern and central Europe were far worse off than the average French citizen. Yet it was in France that the great revolution broke out.

Revolutions are born in the realm of the spirit. Revolutionary movements, says George Rudé, a historian of the French Revolution, require "some unifying body of ideas, a common vocabulary of hope and protest, something, in short, like a common 'revolutionary psychology.' "[20] The philosophes were them-

selves not revolutionaries, asserts Peyre, but their ideas helped to create a revolutionary psychology.

Eighteenth-century philosophy taught the Frenchman to find his condition wretched, or in any case, unjust and illogical and made him disinclined to the patient resignation to his troubles that had long characterized his ancestors. . . . The propaganda of the "Philosophes" perhaps more than any other factor accounted for the fulfillment of the preliminary condition of the French Revolution, namely discontent with the existing state of things.[21]

The American Revolution, which gave practical expression to the liberal philosophy of the philosophes, helped to pave the way for the French Revolution. The Declaration of Independence proclaimed the natural rights of man and approved resistance against a government that deprived men of these rights. The Americans set an example of social equality unparalleled in Europe. In the United States there was no hereditary aristocracy, no serfdom, and no state church. Liberal French aristocrats, such as the Marquis de Lafayette, who had fought in the American Revolution returned to France more optimistic about the possibilities of reforming French society.

The French Revolution was a decisive period in the shaping of the modern West. It implemented the thought of the philosophes, destroyed the hierarchic and corporate society of the Old Regime, promoted the interests of the bourgeoisie, and speeded the growth of the modern state.

The French Revolution weakened the aristocracy. With their feudal rights and privileges eliminated, the nobles became simply ordinary citizens. Throughout the nineteenth century, France would be governed by both the aristocracy and the bourgeoisie; property, not noble birth, determined the composition of the new ruling elite.

The principle of careers open to talent gave the bourgeoisie access to the highest positions in the state. The destruction of feudal remnants, internal tolls, and the guilds speeded up the expansion of a competitive market economy. Possessing wealth, talent, ambition, and now opportunity, the bourgeoisie would play an ever more important role in French political life. Throughout the continent, the reforms of the French Revolution served as a model for progressive bourgeois who, sooner or later, would challenge the Old Regime in their own lands.

The French Revolution transformed the dynastic state of the Old Regime into the modern state: national, liberal, secular, and rational. When the Declaration of the Rights of Man and the Citizen stated that "the source of all sovereignty resides essentially in the nation," the concept of the state took on a new meaning. The state was no longer merely a territory or a federation of provinces; it was not the private possession of the king claiming to be God's lieutenant on earth. In the new conception, the state belonged to the people as a whole, and the individual, formerly a subject, was now a citizen with both rights and duties and was governed by laws that drew no distinction on the basis of birth.

The liberal thought of the Enlightenment found practical expression in the reforms of the Revolution. Absolutism and divine right of monarchy, repudiated in theory by the philosophes, were invalidated by constitutions that set limits to the powers of government and by elected parliaments that represented the governed. By providing for equality before the law and the protection of human rights— habeas corpus, trial by jury, freedom of religion, speech, and the press—the Revolution struck at the abuses of the Old Regime. These gains seemed at times more theoretical than actual, because of violations and interruptions; nevertheless, these liberal ideals reverberated throughout the Continent. During the nineteenth century the pace of reform would quicken. And with the demands of the sans-culottes for equality with the bourgeois, for political democracy and social reform, the voice of the people in politics began to be heard. This phenomenon would intensify increasingly with growing industrialization.

By disavowing any divine justification for the monarch's power and by depriving the church of its special position, the Revolution accelerated the secularization of European political life. Sweeping aside the administrative chaos of the Old Regime, the Revolution attempted to impose rational norms on the state. The sale of public offices that produced ineffective and corrupt administrators was eliminated, and the highest positions in the land were opened to men of talent, regardless of birth. The Revolution abolished the peasantry's manorial obligations that hampered agriculture and swept away barriers to economic expansion. It based taxes on income and streamlined their collection. In the nineteenth century, reformers in the rest of Europe would follow the lead set by France.

The French Revolution also unleashed two potentially destructive forces identified with the modern state: total war and nationalism. These contradicted the rational and universal aims of the reformers as stated in the Declaration of the Rights of Man. Whereas eighteenth-century wars were fought by professional soldiers for limited aims, the French Revolution, says British historian Herbert Butterfield,

brings conscription, the nation in arms, the mobilization of all the resources of the state for unrelenting conflict. It heralds the age when peoples, woefully ignorant of one another, bitterly uncomprehending, lie in uneasy juxtaposition watching one another's sins with hysteria and indignation. It heralds Armageddon, the giant conflict for justice and right between angered populations each of which thinks it is the righteous one. So a new kind of warfare is born—the modern counterpart to the old conflicts of religions.[22]

The world wars of the twentieth century are the terrible fulfillment of this new development in warfare.

The French Revolution also gave birth to modern nationalism. During the Revolution, loyalty was directed to the entire nation, not to a village or province or to the person of the king. The whole of France became the

Chronology 19.1 The French Revolution

July 1788	Calling of the Estates-General
May 5, 1789	Convening of the Estates-General
June 17, 1789	The Third Estate declares itself the National Assembly
July 14, 1789	The storming of the Bastille
Late July 1789	The Great Fear
August 4, 1789	Nobles surrender their special privileges
June 1791	Flight of Louis XVI
October 1791	The Legislative Assembly succeeds the National Assembly
April 20, 1792	The Legislative Assembly declares war on Austria
August 10, 1792	Parisians attack the king's palace
September 1792	The September Massacres
September 20, 1792	The Battle of Valmy
September 21–22, 1792	Abolition of the monarchy
June 1793	Jacobins replace the Girondins as the dominant group in the National Convention
July 27, 1794	Robespierre is guillotined

fatherland. Under the Jacobins, the French became converts to a secular faith preaching total reverence for the nation. "In 1794 we believed in no supernatural religion; our serious interior sentiments were all summed up in the one idea, how to be useful to the fatherland. Everything else . . . was, in our eyes, only trivial. . . . It was our only religion."[23] Few suspected that the new religion of nationalism was fraught with danger. Saint-Just, a young, ardent Robespierrist, was gazing into our own century when he declared: "There is something terrible in the sacred love of the fatherland. This love is so exclusive that it sacrifices everything to the public interest, without pity, without fear, with no respect for the human individual."[24]

The Revolution attempted to reconstruct society on the basis of Enlightenment thought. The Declaration of the Rights of Man, whose spirit permeated the reforms of the Revolution, upheld the dignity of the individual, demanded respect for the individual, attributed to each person natural rights, and barred the state from denying these rights. It insisted that society and state have no higher duty than to promote the freedom and autonomy of the individual. "It is not enough to have overturned the throne," said Robespierre; "our concern is to erect upon its remains holy Equality and the sacred Rights of Man."[25] The tragedy of the Western experience is that this humanist vision, brilliantly expressed by the Enlightenment and given recognition in the reforms of the French Revolution, would weaken in later generations. And, ironically, by spawning total war, nationalism, terror as government policy, and a revolutionary mentality that sought to change the world through violence, the French Revolution itself contributed to the shattering of this vision.

Notes

1. Quoted in G. P. Gooch, *Germany and the French Revolution* (New York: Russell & Russell, 1966), p. 39.

2. Quoted in Ernst Wangermann, *From Joseph II to the Jacobin Trials* (New York: Oxford University Press, 1959), p. 24.

3. In Alfred Cobban, ed., *The Debate on the French Revolution* (London: Adam & Charles Black, 1960), p. 41.

4. Quoted in Elinor G. Barber, *The Bourgeoisie in Eighteenth-Century France* (Princeton, N.J.: Princeton University Press, 1967), p. 57.

5. Georges Lefebvre, *The French Revolution from 1793 to 1799* (New York: Columbia University Press, 1964), 2: 360.

6. Quoted in C. B. A. Behrens, *The Ancien Regime* (New York: Harcourt, Brace and World, 1967), p. 43.

7. Quoted in Leo Gershoy, *The French Revolution and Napoleon* (New York: Appleton-Century-Crofts, 1933), p. 18.

8. John Hall Stewart, ed., *A Documentary Survey of the French Revolution* (New York: Macmillan, 1951), pp. 43–44.

9. See George Rudé, *The Crowd in the French Revolution* (New York: Oxford University Press, 1959).

10. Georges Lefebvre, *The Coming of the French Revolution* (Princeton, N.J.: Princeton University Press, 1967), p. 210.

11. Albert Soboul, *The Parisian Sans-Culottes and the French Revolution, 1793–94*, trans. by Gwynne Lewis (London: Oxford University Press, 1964), pp. 28–29.

12. Ibid., p. 64.

13. Alfred Cobban, *A History of Modern France* (Baltimore: Penguin, 1961), 1: 213.

14. Quoted in Hans Kohn, *Nationalism: Its Meaning and History* (Princeton, N.J.: D. Van Nostrand, 1965), p. 25.

15. Quoted in Carlton J. H. Hayes, *The Historical Evolution of Modern Nationalism* (New York: Richard R. Smith, 1931), p. 55.

16. George Rudé, ed., *Robespierre* (Englewood Cliffs, N.J.: Prentice-Hall, 1976), p. 72.

17. Ibid., p. 57.

18. E. L. Higgins, ed., *The French Revolution* (Boston: Houghton Mifflin, 1938), pp. 306–307.

19. Henri Peyre, "The Influence of Eighteenth-Century Ideas on the French Revolution," *Journal of the History of Ideas,* 10(1949): 72.

20. George Rudé, *Revolutionary Europe, 1783–1815* (New York: Harper Torchbooks, 1966), p. 74.

21. Peyre, "The Influence of Eighteenth-Century Ideas," p. 73.

22. Herbert Butterfield, *Napoleon* (New York: Collier Books, 1962), p. 18.

23. Quoted in Carlton J. H. Hayes, *The Historical Evolution of Modern Nationalism* (New York: Russell & Russell, 1931), p. 55.

24. Quoted in Hans Kohn, *Making of the Modern French Mind* (New York: D. Van Nostrand, 1955), p. 17.

25. Quoted in Christopher Dawson, *The Gods of Revolution* (New York: New York University Press, 1972), p. 83.

Suggested Reading

Doyle, William, *Origins of the French Revolution* (1980). In recent decades, several historians have challenged the traditional view that the French Revolution was an attempt by the bourgeoisie to overthrow the remnants of aristocratic power and privilege, that it was a victory of a capitalist bourgeois order over feudalism. This book summarizes the new scholarship and argues that the nobility and bourgeoisie had much in common prior to the Revolution.

Gershoy, Leo, *The Era of the French Revolution* (1957). A brief survey with useful documents.

Higgins, E. L., ed. *The French Revolution* (1938). Excerpts from contemporaries.

Kafker, F. A., and Laux, J. M., *The French Revolution: Conflicting Interpretations* (1976). Excerpts from leading historians.

Lefebvre, Georges, *The French Revolution*, 2 vols. (1962, 1964). A detailed analysis by a master historian.

———, *The Coming of the French Revolution* (1967). A brilliant analysis of the social structure of the Old Regime and the opening phase of the Revolution.

Palmer, R. R., *The Age of the Democratic Revolution*, 2 vols. (1959, 1964). The French Revolution as part of a revolutionary movement that spread on both sides of the Atlantic.

———, *Twelve Who Ruled* (1965). An admirable treatment of the Terror.

Rudé, George, *The Crowd in the French Revolution* (1959). An analysis of the composition of the crowds that stormed the Bastille, marched to Versailles, and attacked the king's palace.

———, *Robespierre: Portrait of a Revolutionary Democrat* (1976). A recent biography of the revolutionary leader.

Soboul, Albert, *The Sans-Culottes* (1972). An abridgment of the classic study of the popular movement of 1793–94.

Stewart, J. H., *A Documentary Survey of the French Revolution* (1951). A valuable collection of documents.

Review Questions

1. What privileges were enjoyed by clergy and nobility in the Old Regime?

2. What were the grievances of the bourgeoisie, the peasantry and the urban laborers?

3. Why was France in financial difficulty?

4. Analyze the causes of the French Revolution.

5. Identify and explain the significance of the following: formation of the National Assembly, storming of the Bastille, the Great Fear, and the October Days.

6. Analyze the nature and significance of the reforms of the National Assembly.

7. What were the grievances of the sans-culottes?

8. Identify and explain the significance of the following: Flight of the King, the Brunswick Manifesto, and the September Massacres.

9. What were the principal differences between the Jacobins and the Girondins?

10. What were the accomplishments of the Jacobins?

11. Analyze Robespierre's basic philosophy.

12. Why was the French Revolution a decisive period in the shaping of the West?

20

Napoleon: Destroyer and Preserver of the Revolution

*T*he loosening of the bonds of authority in a revolutionary age offers opportunities for popular and ambitious military commanders to seize power. History affords numerous examples of revolutions culminating in military dictatorships. The upheavals of the French Revolution made possible the extraordinary career of Napoleon Bonaparte. This popular general combined a passion for power with a genius for leadership. Under Napoleon's military dictatorship, the constitutional government for which the people of 1789 had fought and the republican democracy for which the Jacobins had rallied the nation seemed lost. Nevertheless, during the Napoleonic era, many achievements of the Revolution were preserved, strengthened, and carried to other lands.

Rise to Power

Napoleon was born on August 15, 1769, on the island of Corsica, the son of a petty noble. After finishing military school in France, he became an artillery officer; the wars of the French Revolution afforded him an opportunity to advance his career. In December 1793, Napoleon's brilliant handling of artillery forced the British to lift their siege of the city of Toulon. Two years later he saved the Thermidorean Convention from a royalist insurrection by ordering his troops to fire into the riotous mob—the famous "whiff of grapeshot." In 1796 he was given command of the French Army of Italy. His star was rising.

In Italy, against the Austrians, Napoleon demonstrated a dazzling talent for military planning and leadership that earned him an instant reputation. Having tasted glory, he could never do without it; having experienced only success, nothing seemed impossible. He sensed that he was headed for greatness. Years later he recalled: "[In Italy] I realized I was a superior being and conceived the ambition of performing great things, which hitherto had filled my thoughts only as a fantastic dream."[1]

In November 1797, Napoleon was ordered to plan an invasion of England. Aware of the weakness of the French navy, he recommended postponement of the invasion, urging instead an expedition to the Near East to strike at British power in the Mediterranean and British commerce with India, and perhaps to carve out a French empire in the Near East. With more than 35,000 troops, Napoleon set out for Egypt, then a part of the Turkish empire. Although he captured Cairo, the Egyptian campaign was far from a success. At the Battle of the Nile (1798), the British, commanded by Admiral Nelson, annihilated Napoleon's fleet. Deprived of reinforcements and supplies, with his manpower reduced by battle and plague, Napoleon was compelled to abandon whatever dreams he might have had of threatening India. Although the Egyptian expedition was a failure, Napoleon, always seeking to improve his image, sent home glowing bulletins about French victories. To people in France, he was seen as the conqueror of Egypt as well as of Italy.

Meanwhile, political unrest, financial disorder, and military reversals produced an atmosphere of crisis in France. Napoleon knew that in such times people seek out a savior. A man of destiny must act. Without informing his men, he slipped out of Egypt, avoided British cruisers, and landed in France in October 1799.

Coup d'État

When Napoleon arrived in France, a conspiracy was already underway against the government of the Directory. Convinced that only firm leadership could solve France's problems, some politicians plotted to seize power and establish a strong executive. Needing the assistance of a popular general, they turned to Napoleon, whom they thought they could control. Although the hastily prepared coup d'état was almost bungled, the government of the Directory was overthrown. The French Revolution entered a new stage, that of military dictatorship.

Portrait of Napoleon. This engraving idealizes the features of Napoleon. He is here reminiscent of Roman imperial busts and coinage. (*Brown Brothers*)

Demoralized by a decade of political instability, economic distress, domestic violence, and war, most of the French welcomed the leadership of a strong man. The bourgeois, in particular, expected Napoleon to protect their wealth and the influence they had gained during the Revolution.

The new constitution (1799) created a strong executive. Although three Consuls shared the executive, the First Consul, Napoleon, monopolized power. Whereas Napoleon's fellow conspirators, who were political moderates, sought only to strengthen the executive, Napoleon aspired to personal rule. He captured the reins of power after the coup, and his authority continued to expand. In 1802 he was made First Consul for life with the right to name his successor. And on December 2, 1804, in a magnificent ceremony at the Cathedral of Notre Dame in Paris, Napoleon crowned himself Emperor of the French. General, First Consul, and then Emperor— it was a breathless climb to the heights of power. And Napoleon, who once said he loved "power as a musician loves his violin,"[2] was determined never to lose it.

The Character of Napoleon

What sort of man was it upon whom the fate of France and Europe depended? Napoleon's personality, complex and mysterious, continues to baffle biographers. However, certain distinctive characteristics are evident. Napoleon's intellectual ability was impressive. His mind swiftly absorbed details that his photographic memory classified and stored. With surgical precision he could probe his way to the heart of a problem while still retaining a grasp over peripheral considerations. Ideas forever danced in his head, and his imagination was illuminated by sudden flashes of insight. He could work for eighteen or twenty hours at a stretch, deep in concentration, ruling out boredom or tiredness by an act of will. Napoleon, man of action, warrior par excellence, was in many ways, says Georges Lefebvre, "a typical man of the eighteenth century, a rationalist, a *philosophe* . . . [who] placed his trust in reason, in knowledge, and in methodical effort."[3]

Rationalism was only one part of his personality. There was also that elemental, irresistible urge for action, "the romantic Napoleon, a force seeking to expand and for which the world was no more than an occasion for acting dangerously."[4] This love of action fused with his boundless ambition. Continues Lefebvre:

His greatest ambition was glory. "I live only for posterity," he exclaimed, "death is nothing, but to live defeated and without glory is to die every day." His eyes were fixed on the world's great leaders: Alexander who conquered the East and dreamed of conquering the world; Caesar, Augustus, Charlemagne. . . . They were for him examples, which stimulated his imagination and lent *an unalterable charm to action. He was an artist, a poet of action, for whom France and mankind were but instruments.*[5]

He also exuded an indefinable quality of personality, a charismatic force that made people feel they were in the presence of a superior man. Contemporaries remarked that his large gray eyes, penetrating, knowing, yet strangely expressionless, seemed to possess a hypnotic power. He was capable of moving men to obedience, to loyalty, to heroism.

The rationalist's clarity of mind and the romantic's impassioned soul, the adventurer's love of glory and the hero's personal magnetism—these were the components of Napoleon's personality. There was also an aloofness, some would say callousness, that led him to regard people as pawns to be manipulated in the pursuit of his destiny. "A man like me," he once said, "troubles himself little about the lives of a million men."[6]

Napoleon's genius might have gone unheralded, his destiny unfulfilled, had it not been for the opportunities created by the French Revolution. By opening careers to talent, the Revolution enabled a young Corsican of undistinguished birth to achieve fame and popularity. By creating the nation in arms and embroiling France in war, it provided a military commander with enormous sources of power. By plunging France into one crisis after another, it opened up extraordinary possibilities for a man with a gift of leadership and an ambition "so intimately linked with my very being that it is like the blood that circulates in my veins."[7] It was the Revolution that made Napoleon conscious of his genius and certain of his destiny.

Napoleon and France

Living in a revolutionary age, Napoleon had observed firsthand the precariousness of power and the fleetingness of popularity. A superb realist, he knew that his past reputation would not sustain him. If he could not solve the problems caused by a decade of revolution and war and bind together the different classes of French people, his prestige would diminish and his power collapse. The general must become a statesman, and when necessary, a tyrant. His domestic policies, showing the influence of both eighteenth-century enlightened despotism and the Revolution, affected every aspect of society and had an enduring impact on French history. They continued the work of the Revolution in destroying the institutions of the Old Regime.

Government: Centralization and Repression

In providing France with a strong central government, Napoleon continued a policy initiated centuries earlier by Bourbon monarchs. Although the Bourbons had not been able completely to overcome the barriers presented by provinces, local traditions, feudal remnants, and corporate institutions, Napoleon succeeded in giving France administrative uniformity. An army of officials, subject to the emperor's will, reached into every village, linking together the entire nation. This centralized state suited Napoleon's desire for orderly government and rational administration, enabled him to concentrate power in his own hands, and provided him with the taxes and soldiers needed to fight his wars. To suppress irreconcilable opponents, primarily die-hard royalists and republicans, Napoleon used the instruments of the police state—secret agents, arbitrary arrest, summary trials, executions.

Napoleon also shaped public opinion to prevent hostile criticism of his rule and to promote popular support for his policies and person. In these actions, he was a precursor of twentieth-century dictators. Liberty of the press came to an end. Printers swore an oath of obedience to the Emperor, and newspapers were converted into government mouthpieces. Printers were forbidden to print, and booksellers to sell or circulate, "anything

which may involve injury to the duties of subjects toward the sovereign or the interests of the state."[8] When Napoleon's secretary read him the morning newspapers, Napoleon would interrupt: "Skip it, skip it. I know what is in them. They only say what I tell them to."[9] These efforts at indoctrination even reached schoolchildren, who were required to memorize a catechism glorifying the ruler, which ran, in part,

. . . because God, who creates emperors and distributes them according to his will, in loading our Emperor with gifts, both in peace and in war, has established him as our sovereign. . . . To honor and to serve our Emperor is then to honor and to serve God himself. . . .

. . . those who may be lacking in their duty towards our Emperor . . . would be resisting the order established by God himself and would make themselves worthy of eternal damnation.[10]

By repressing liberty, subverting republicanism, and restoring absolutism, Napoleon reversed some of the liberal gains of the Revolution. Although favoring equality before the law and equality of opportunity as necessary for a well-run state, Napoleon believed that political liberty impeded efficiency and threatened the state with anarchy. He would govern in the interest of the people as an enlightened but absolute ruler.

Religion: Reconciliation with the Church

For Napoleon, who was a deist if not an atheist, the value of religion was not salvation, but social and political cohesion. It promoted national unity and prevented class war. He stated:

Society cannot exist without inequality of fortunes, and inequality of fortunes cannot exist without religion. When a man is dying of hunger alongside another who stuffs himself, it is impossible to make him accede to the difference unless there is an

authority which says to him God wishes it thus; there must be some poor and some rich in the world, but hereafter and for all eternity the division will be made differently.[11]

This is what Napoleon probably had in mind when he said: "Men who do not believe in God—one does not govern them, one shoots them."[12]

With the Catholic church, Napoleon attempted to close the breach that had emerged during the Revolution. Such a reconciliation would gain the approval of the mass of the French people, who still remained devoted to their faith, and would reassure those peasants and bourgeois who had bought confiscated church lands. For these reasons, Napoleon negotiated an agreement with the pope. The Concordat of 1801 recognized Catholicism as the religion of the great majority of the French, rather than as the official state religion (the proposal that the pope desired). The clergy were to be paid and nominated by the state, but consecrated by the pope.

In effect, the Concordat guaranteed the reforms of the Revolution. The church did not regain its confiscated lands nor its right to collect the tithe. The French clergy remained largely subject to state control. And by not establishing Catholicism as the state religion, the Concordat did not jeopardize the newly won toleration of Jews and Protestants. Napoleon had achieved his aim. The Concordat made his regime acceptable to Catholics and to owners of former church lands.

Law: The Code Napoléon

Under the Old Regime, France was plagued with numerous and conflicting law codes. Reflecting local interests and feudal traditions, these codes obstructed national unity and administrative efficiency. Efforts by the revolutionaries to draw up a unified code of laws bogged down. Recognizing the value of such a code in promoting effective administration throughout France, Napoleon pressed for the completion of the project.

The Code Napoléon incorporated many principles of the Revolution: equality before the law, the right to choose one's profession, freedom of conscience, protection of property rights, the abolition of serfdom, and the secular character of the state.

The Code also had its less liberal side, denying equal treatment to workers in their dealings with employers, to women in their relations with their husbands, to children in their relations with their fathers. In making wives inferior to their husbands in matters of property, adultery, and divorce, the Code reflected both Napoleon's personal attitude and the general view of the times toward women and family stability. Of women, he once said that "the husband must possess the absolute power and right to say to his wife: 'Madam, you shall not go out, you shall not go to the theater, you shall not receive such and such a person: for the children you shall bear shall be mine!'"[13]

Adopted in lands conquered by France, the Code Napoléon helped to weaken feudal privileges and institutions and clerical interference with the secular state. With justice, Napoleon could say: "My true glory is not to have won forty battles. . . . Waterloo will erase the memory of so many victories. . . . But what nothing will destroy, what will live forever, is my Civil Code."[14]

Education: The Imperial University

Napoleon's educational policy was in many ways an elaboration of the school reforms initiated during the Revolution. Like the revolutionaries, Napoleon favored a system of public education with a secular curriculum and a minimum of church involvement. For Napoleon, education served a dual purpose: it would provide him with capable officials to administer his laws and trained officers to lead his armies; and it would indoctrinate the young in obedience and loyalty. He established the University of France, a giant board of education that placed education under state control. To this day the French school system, unlike that in the United States, is strictly centralized, with curriculum and standards set for the entire state.

The emperor did not consider education for girls important, holding that "marriage is their whole destination."[15] Whatever education girls did receive, he believed, should stress religion. "What we ask of education is not that girls should think but that they should believe. The weakness of woman's brains, the instability of their ideas, the place they fill in society, their need for perpetual resignation . . . all this can only be met by religion."[16]

Economy: Strengthening the State

Napoleon's financial and economic policies were designed to strengthen France and enhance his popularity. To stimulate the economy and to retain the favor of the bourgeois who supported his seizure of power, Napoleon aided industry through tariffs and loans and fostered commerce (while also speeding up troop movements) by building or repairing roads, bridges, and canals. To protect the currency from inflation, he established the Bank of France, which was controlled by the nation's leading financiers. By keeping careers open to talent, he endorsed one of the key demands of the bourgeoisie during the Revolution. Fearing a revolution based on lack of bread, he provided food at low prices and stimulated employment for the laboring poor. He endeared himself to the peasants by not restoring feudal privileges and by allowing them to keep the land they had obtained during the Revolution.

Napoleon did not identify with the republicanism and democracy of the Jacobins, but rather he belonged to the tradition of eighteenth-century enlightened despotism. Like the reforming despots, Napoleon admired administrative uniformity and efficiency, hated feudalism, religious persecution, and civil inequality, and favored government regulation of trade and industry. He saw in enlightened despotism a means of ensuring political stability, overcoming the confusion presented by feudal and corporative institutions, avoiding the dangers of democracy, which he equated with mob rule, and strengthening the state militarily. By preserving many social gains of the Revolution while suppressing political liberty, Napoleon showed himself an heir of the enlightened despots.

While Napoleon's domestic policies gained him wide support, it was his victories on the battlefield that mesmerized the French people and gratified their national vanity. Ultimately his popularity and his power rested on the sword.

Napoleon and Europe

Napoleon, the Corsican adventurer, realized Louis XIV's dream of French mastery of Europe. Between 1805 and 1807, Napoleon inflicted decisive defeats on Austria, Prussia, and Russia, to become the virtual ruler of Europe. In these campaigns, as in his earlier successes in Italy, Napoleon demonstrated his greatness as a military commander.

Napoleon's Art of War

While foregoing a set battle plan in favor of flexibility, Napoleon was guided by certain general principles that comprised his art of war. He stressed the advantage of "a rapid and audacious attack" in preference to waging defensive war from a fixed position. "Make war offensively; it is the sole means to become a great captain and to fathom the secrets of the art."[17] Warfare could not be left to chance, but required mastering every detail and anticipating every contingency. "I am accustomed to thinking out what I shall do three or four months in advance, and I base my calculations on the worst of conceivable

Map 20.1 Napoleon's Europe, 1810 ▶

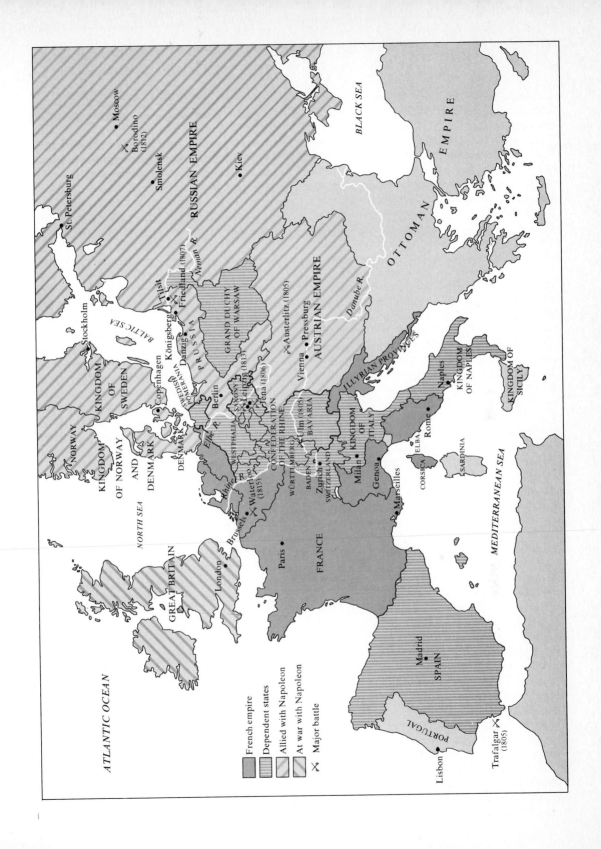

ATLANTIC OCEAN

GREAT BRITAIN

London

NORTH SEA

KINGDOM OF NORWAY AND DENMARK

NORWAY

DENMARK

KINGDOM OF SWEDEN

Stockholm

BALTIC SEA

St. Petersburg

Moscow

Borodino (1812)

Smolensk

Kiev

RUSSIAN EMPIRE

BLACK SEA

OTTOMAN EMPIRE

Copenhagen

SWEDISH POMERANIA

Königsberg

Danzig

Tilsit

Friedland (1807)

Neman R.

PRUSSIA

GRAND DUCHY OF WARSAW

Berlin

Elbe R.

WESTPHALIA

SAXONY

LEIPZIG (1813)

Jena (1806)

CONFEDERATION OF THE RHINE

WÜRTTEMBERG

Rhine R.

Waterloo (1815)

Brussels

Ulm (1805)

BADEN

BAVARIA

Zurich

SWITZERLAND

Austerlitz (1805)

Vienna

Pressburg

AUSTRIAN EMPIRE

Danube R.

ILLYRIAN PROVINCES

KINGDOM OF ITALY

Milan

Genoa

Marseilles

Rome

ELBA

CORSICA

SARDINIA

Naples

KINGDOM OF NAPLES

KINGDOM OF SICILY

MEDITERRANEAN SEA

FRANCE

Paris

SPAIN

Madrid

PORTUGAL

Lisbon

Trafalgar (1805)

French empire

Dependent states

Allied with Napoleon

At war with Napoleon

✕ Major battle

circumstances."[18] Every master plan contained numerous alternatives to cover all contingencies.

Surprise and speed were essential ingredients of Napoleonic warfare. Relying heavily on surprise, Napoleon employed various stratagems to confuse and deceive his opponents: providing newspapers with misleading information, launching secondary offensives, and placing a dense screen of cavalry ahead of marching columns to prevent penetration by enemy patrols. Determined to surprise and consequently demoralize the enemy by arriving at a battlefield ahead of schedule, he carefully selected the best routes to the chosen destination, eliminated slow-moving supply convoys by living off the countryside, and inspired his men to incredible feats of marching as they drew closer to the opposing army. In the first Italian campaign, his men drove 50 miles in thirty-six hours; in 1805, against Austria, they marched 275 miles in twenty-three days.

His campaigns anticipated the blitzkrieg, or lightning warfare, of the twentieth century. As the moment of battle neared, Napoleon would disperse his troops over a wide area; the enemy would counter by dividing its forces. Then, by rapid marches, Napoleon would concentrate a superior force against a segment of the enemy's strung-out forces. Here the hammerblow would fall. Employing some troops to pin down the opposing force, he moved his main army to the enemy's rear or flank, cutting off the enemy supply line. Conducted with speed and deception, these moves broke the spirit of the opposing troops. Heavy barrages by concentrated artillery opened a hole in the enemy lines that was penetrated first by heavy columns of infantry and then by shock waves of cavalry. Unlike the typical eighteenth-century commander, who maneuvered for position and was satisfied with his opponent's retreat, Napoleon sought to annihilate the enemy army, thereby destroying its source of power.

The emperor thoroughly understood the importance of morale in warfare. "Moral force rather than numbers decides victory," he once said.[19] He deliberately sought to shatter his opponent's confidence by surprise moves and lightning thrusts. Similarly, he recognized that he must maintain a high level of morale among his own troops. By sharing danger with his men, he gained their affection and admiration. He inspired his men by appealing to their honor, vanity, credulity, and love of France. "A man does not have himself killed for a few halfpence a day or for a petty distinction," he declared. "You must speak to the soul in order to electrify the man."[20] This Napoleon could do. It was Napoleon's charisma that led the duke of Wellington to remark: "I used to say of him that his presence on the field made a difference of 40,000 men."[21]

Despite his reputation, Napoleon was not essentially an original military thinker. His greatness lay rather in his ability to implement and coordinate the theories of earlier strategists. Eighteenth-century military planners had stressed the importance of massed artillery, rapid movement, deception, living off the countryside, and the annihilation of the enemy army. Napoleon alone had the will and ingenuity to convert these theories into battle-field victories.

Similarly, Napoleon harnessed the military energies generated during a decade of revolutionary war. The Revolution had created a mass army, had instilled in the republican soldier a love for la patrie, and had enabled promising young soldiers to gain promotions on the basis of talent rather than birth. Napoleon took this inheritance and perfected it.

The Grand Empire: Diffusion of Revolutionary Institutions

In 1802, Napoleon had made peace with Austria and Great Britain. But when the French ruler expanded his interests in Italy and the Rhineland, Britain organized another coalition against France. In 1805, Britain signed an alliance with both Austria and Russia, and in the summer, Austrian and Russian armies advanced westward.

Napoleon acted swiftly. He outmaneuvered

an Austrian army at Ulm in Bavaria (October 1805), forcing its surrender, and occupied Vienna. At Austerlitz (December 1805), he decimated a Russo-Austrian force. In the peace of Pressburg, Austria surrendered its Italian possessions to the Kingdom of Italy, a French satellite in northern Italy.

In October 1806, Napoleon decisively defeated the Prussians at Jena and entered Berlin. Another French victory at Friedland (June 1807) compelled the Russian tsar Alexander I to request an armistice. In 1807, peace treaties were concluded at Tilsit with Prussia and with Russia. Prussia's Polish territories became the duchy of Warsaw, a French protectorate ruled by the King of Saxony. Prussian territories west of the Elbe River became the Kingdom of Westphalia, ruled by Napoleon's youngest brother Jerome. These territorial losses reduced the number of subjects controlled by Prussia from ten to five million. Russia's territorial losses were slight. More important was the tsar's promise to side with France if Britain refused to make peace with Napoleon. In an incredibly short period of time, the terrible Corsican had routed the three leading Continental powers and established his domination over Europe.

By 1810, Napoleon dominated the Continent, except for the Balkan Peninsula. The *Grand Empire* comprised lands annexed to France, vassal states, and cowed allies. The French Republic had already annexed Belgium and the German Left Bank of the Rhine. Napoleon incorporated several other areas into France: German coastal regions as far as the western Baltic and large areas of Italy, including Rome, Geneva and its environs, Trieste, and the Dalmatian Coast.

Vassal states in the Grand Empire included five kingdoms ruled by Napoleon's relatives, two of them in Italy. In 1796 Napoleon, then a young general, had defeated the Austrians in Italy, and the following year he organized northern Italy into the Cisalpine Republic. The leaders of the republic, imbued with the reforming spirit of the Enlightenment and the French Revolution, attacked the privileges of the nobility and the church, granted Jews equal rights, did away with guilds and internal tolls, and established a free press. However, in 1799 the Austrians drove the French from northern Italy and imprisoned or executed supporters of the republic. After his successful coup d'état, Napoleon crossed into Italy, crushed the Austrians at Marengo (1800), and restored republican government to northern Italy. In 1805 he transformed the republic into the Kingdom of Italy, with himself as king and Eugène de Beauharnais as viceroy. Eugène, a twenty-three-year-old cavalry officer, was the son, by her first marriage, of Josephine, Napoleon's wife. In 1806 Napoleon seized Naples in southern Italy to deny Britain a Mediterranean port. The Bourbon rulers fled, and Napoleon installed his brother Joseph as King of Naples.

In 1794–95 the French Republic had overrun the United Provinces (Holland), converting it into the Batavian Republic. In 1806 Napoleon renamed the Batavian Republic the Kingdom of Holland and placed his brother Louis on the throne. But in 1810 Louis was forced to abdicate and Holland was annexed to France. The Kingdom of Westphalia, ruled by Jerome Bonaparte, was formed in 1807 from Prussian lands. In 1808 Napoleon turned his Spanish ally into still another satellite kingdom, giving the Spanish throne to his brother Joseph who was transferred from Naples.

Besides the five satellite kingdoms in Italy, Holland, Westphalia, and Spain, there were several other vassal states within the Grand Empire. Napoleon formed the Confederation of the Rhine in 1806. Its members, a loose association of sixteen (later eighteen) German states, were subservient to the Emperor, as were the nineteen cantons of the Swiss confederation. The Grand Duchy of Warsaw, formed in 1807 from Prussia's Polish lands, was placed under the rule of the German King of Saxony, one of Napoleon's vassals.

Finally, the Grand Empire included states compelled to be French allies—Austria, Prussia, and Russia, as well as Sweden and Denmark. Napoleon required these "allies" not to import goods from Britain, his resolute opponent.

With varying degrees of determination and

success, Napoleon extended the reforms of the Revolution to other lands. His officials instituted the Code Napoléon, organized an effective civil service, opened careers to talent, and equalized the tax burden. They abolished serfdom, manorial payments, and the courts of the nobility. They did away with clerical courts, promoted freedom of religion, permitted civil marriage, pressed for civil rights for Jews, and fought clerical interference with secular authority. They abolished guilds, introduced a uniform system of weights and measures, did away with internal tolls, and built roads, bridges, and canals. They promoted secular education and improved public health. Napoleon had launched a European-wide social revolution that attacked the privileges of the aristocracy and the clergy—who regarded him as that "crowned Jacobin"—and worked to the advantage of the bourgeoisie. This diffusion of revolutionary institutions weakened the Old Regime irreparably in much of Europe and speeded up the modernization of nineteenth-century Europe.

Napoleon's purpose in implementing these reforms was twofold: he wished to promote administrative efficiency and to win the support of conquered peoples.

What the people of Germany desire with impatience is that the individuals who are not nobles and who have talents have an equal right to your consideration and to positions; it is that every kind of serfdom and intermediary bonds between the sovereign and the lowest class of people be entirely abolished.[22]

Pleased by the overhaul of feudal practices and the reduction of clerical power, many Europeans, particularly the progressive bourgeoisie, welcomed Napoleon as a liberator.

But there was another side to Napoleon's rule. Napoleon, the tyrant of Europe, turned conquered lands into satellite kingdoms and exploited them for the benefit of France. The following, from a letter to Prince Eugène, Viceroy of Italy, reveals Napoleon's policy:

All the raw silk from the Kingdom of Italy goes to England. I wish to divert it from this route to the advantage of my French manufacturers: otherwise my silk factories, one of the chief supports of French commerce, will suffer substantial losses. My principle is France first. You must never lose sight of the fact that . . . France should claim commercial supremacy on the continent.[23]

The satellite states and annexed territories were compelled to provide recruits for Napoleon's army and taxes for his war treasury. Opponents of Napoleon faced confiscation of property, the galleys, and execution.

These methods of exploitation and repression increased hatred against Napoleon and French rule. Subject peoples, including bourgeois liberals who felt that he had betrayed the ideals of the Revolution, came to view Napoleon as a tyrant ready for his downfall.

The Fall of Napoleon

In addition to the hostility of subject nationals, Napoleon had to cope with the determined opposition of Great Britain. Its subsidies and encouragement kept resistance to the emperor alive. But perhaps Napoleon's greatest obstacle was his own boundless ambition, which warped his judgment; from its short-lived peak, the emperor's career slid downhill from defeat to dethronement to deportation.

Failure to Subdue England

Britain was Napoleon's most resolute opponent. It could not be otherwise, for any power that dominated the Continent could organize sufficient naval might to threaten British commerce, challenge its sea power, and invade the island kingdom. Britain would not make peace with any state that sought European hegemony, and Napoleon's ambition would settle for nothing less.

Unable to make peace with Britain, Napoleon resolved to crush it. Between 1803

Death of Nelson by Daniel Maclise. Although Admiral Horatio Nelson died during the Battle of Trafalgar, England was victorious. Napoleon could not destroy British seapower, and he had to abandon his plans for invasion. The dying Nelson is pictured in the traditional pose of a "Lamentation" of Christ. (*Walker Art Gallery, Liverpool*)

and 1805 he assembled an invasion flotilla on the English Channel. But there could be no invasion of Britain while British warships commanded the channel. In 1805 the battle of Trafalgar demonstrated British naval power when Admiral Nelson devastated a combined French and Spanish fleet. Napoleon was forced to postpone his invasion scheme indefinitely.

Unable to conquer Britain by arms, Napoleon decided to bring what he called "the nation of shopkeepers" to its knees by damaging the British economy. His plan, called the *Continental System*, was to bar all countries under France's control from buying British goods. However, by smuggling goods onto the Continent and increasing trade with the New World, Britain, although hurt, escaped economic ruin. Moreover, the Continental System punished European lands dependent on British imports. Hundreds of ships lay idle in European ports. Industries closed down. The bourgeoisie, generally supportive of Napoleon's social and administrative reforms, turned against him because of the economic distress caused by the Continental System. Furthermore, Napoleon's efforts to enforce the system enmeshed him in two catastrophic blunders: the occupation of Spain and the invasion of Russia.

The Spanish Ulcer

An ally of France since 1796, Spain proved a disappointment to Napoleon. It failed to prevent the Portuguese from trading with Britain and contributed little military or financial aid to France's war effort. Napoleon decided to incorporate Spain into his empire. In 1808, while a French army moved toward Madrid, Charles IV, the aged and mentally feeble Spanish ruler, was forced to abdicate by his son, who proclaimed himself Ferdinand VII. The change in rulers pleased the Spanish people, but Napoleon had other plans. De-

And There Is No Remedy—Etching by Francisco Goya (1746–1828). Napoleon could not understand the resistance of Spain to his grand plan. Spaniards rejected Napoleon's gentle brother as their new monarch. Their revolt was a "war to the knife." Executions and repression followed. Napoleon would state, "that miserable Spanish affair killed me." (*Philadelphia Museum of Art: Smithkline Corporation Collection*)

termined to control Spain, he forced both Charles and Ferdinand to surrender their rights to the throne and designated his brother Joseph as king of Spain.

Napoleon believed the Spanish would rally round the gentle Joseph and welcome his liberal reforms. This confidence was a fatal illusion and perhaps Napoleon's worst blunder, for what appeared to be another French victory and the establishment of another satellite kingdom became, in Napoleon's words, "that miserable Spanish affair . . . [that] killed me."[24] Spanish nobles and clergy feared French liberalism; the overwhelmingly peasant population, illiterate and credulous, intensely proud, fanatically religious, and easily aroused by the clergy, viewed Napoleon as the Devil's agent. Loyal to the Spanish monarchy and faithful to the church, the Spanish fought a "War to the Knife" against the invaders.

The Peninsular War was fought with a special cruelty. Wrote one shocked French officer: "At La Carolina we established a hospital and left 167 of our sick and wounded men. That hospital was set afire . . . all were burned alive or horribly massacred. The barbarians believed they had done a glorious thing for God and religion!"[25] Guerrilla bands, aided and encouraged by priests preaching holy war, congregated in mountain hideouts. Striking from ambush, they raided French convoys and outposts, preventing the French from consolidating their occupation and keeping the French forces in a permanent state of anxiety. An invisible army had spread itself over Spain. The war waged by Spanish partisans foreshadowed a twentieth-century phenomenon—the inability of a great power, using trained soldiers and modern weapons, to subdue peasant guerrillas.

Seeking to keep alive the struggle against Napoleon, Britain came to the aid of the Spanish insurgents. The intervention of British troops commanded by Sir Arthur Wellesley, the future duke of Wellington, led to the ultimate defeat of Joseph in 1813. The "Spanish ulcer" drained Napoleon's treasury, tied down hundreds of thousands of French troops, enabled Britain to gain a foothold on the Continent from which to invade southern France, and inspired patriots in other lands to resist the French emperor.

The German War of Liberation

Anti-French feeling also broke out in the German states. Hatred of the French invaders evoked a feeling of national outrage among some Germans, who up to this time had thought only in terms of their own particular state and prince.

The humiliation of defeat, combined with a flourishing national culture fashioned by talented writers using a common literary language, imbued some German intellectuals with a sense of national identity and national purpose. Using the emotional language of nationalism, these intellectuals called for a war of liberation against Napoleon and, in some instances, for the creation of a unified Germany. In urging Germans to seek vengeance against the conqueror, Ernst Moritz Arndt insisted that it was "the highest religion to love the Fatherland more dearly than lords and princes, fathers and mothers, wives and children."[26]

Other than this handful of intellectuals, however, few Germans were aroused by a desire for political unification. Nor did there occur anything like the general uprising that took place in Spain. Nevertheless, during the Napoleonic wars, German nationalism took shape and would continue to grow in intensity, for students, professors, and poets had found a cause worthy of their idealism.

In addition to arousing a desire for national independence and unity, French domination of Germany stimulated a movement for reform and revitalization. The impact of revolutionary ideals, armies, and administration reached into Prussia, giving rise to a reform movement among members of the Prussian high bureaucracy and officer corps. The disastrous defeat of the Prussians at Jena (1806), the oppressive Peace of Tilsit (1807), the presence of a French army of occupation, and the weakening of the Prussian economy by Napoleon's policy of "France first" spurred the reform party to act. If Prussia were to survive in a world altered by the French Revolution, it would have to learn the principal lessons of the Revolution—that aroused citizens fighting for a cause make better soldiers than mercenaries and oppressed serfs, and that officers selected for daring and intelligence command better than nobles possessing only a gilded birthright.

To drive the French out of Prussia, it would be necessary to overcome the apathy of the Prussian people—so painfully demonstrated at Jena and in their passive responses to French occupation—and to bind the Prussians to the monarchy in a spirit of cooperation and loyalty. The heart of the Prussian nation must beat with that same national energy that spurred the armies of the Jacobin Republic against foreign invaders. This strengthening of the state, it was felt, could be accomplished only through immediate and far-reaching social and political reforms.

The reforms were largely the achievement of Baron vom Stein, who served for a while as first minister to King Frederick William III. Stein believed that the elimination of social abuses would overcome defeatism and apathy and encourage Prussians to serve the state willingly and to fight bravely for national honor. A revitalized Prussia could then deal with the French. "The chief idea," said Stein, "was to arouse a moral, religious, and patriotic spirit in the nation, to instill into it again courage, confidence, readiness for every sacrifice in behalf of independence from foreigners and for the national honor, and to seize the first favorable opportunity to begin the bloody and hazardous struggle."[27]

Among the important reforms introduced in Prussia between 1807 and 1813 were the abolition of serfdom, the granting to towns of a large measure of self-administration, the awarding of army commissions on the basis of merit instead of birth, the elimination of cruel punishment in the ranks, and the establishment of national conscription. In 1813 the reform party forced King Frederick William III to declare war on France. The military reforms did improve the quality of the Prussian army. In the War of Liberation (1813), Prussian soldiers demonstrated far more enthusiasm and patriotism than they had at Jena in 1806, and the French were driven from Germany. The German War of Liberation came on the heels of Napoleon's disastrous Russian campaign.

Disaster in Russia

The unsuccessful invasion of Russia in 1812 diminished Napoleon's glory and hastened the collapse of his empire. Deteriorating relations between Russia and France led Napoleon to his fatal decision to attack the Eastern giant. Unwilling to permit Russia to become a Mediterranean power, the emperor resisted the tsar's attempts to acquire Constantinople. Napoleon's creation of the Grand Duchy of Warsaw irritated the tsar, who feared a revival of Polish power and resented French influence on Russia's border. Another source of friction between the tsar and Napoleon was Russia's illicit trade with Britain in violation of the Continental System. If the tsar were permitted to violate the trade regulations, Napoleon reasoned, other lands would soon follow and England would never be subdued. No doubt Napoleon's inex-

haustible craving for power also compelled him to strike at Russia.

Napoleon assembled one of the largest armies in history—some 614,000 men, 200,000 animals, and 20,000 vehicles. Frenchmen comprised about half the *Grande Armée de la Russie;* the other soldiers, many serving under compulsion, were drawn from a score of nationalities. The emperor intended to deal the Russians a crushing blow, compelling Tsar Alexander I to sue for peace. But the Russians had other plans—to avoid pitched battles, retreat eastward, and refuse to make peace with the invader. Napoleon would be drawn ever deeper into Russia in pursuit of the enemy.

In June 1812, the Grand Army crossed the Nieman River into Russia. Fighting only rear-guard battles and retreating according to plan, the tsar's forces lured the invaders into the vastness of Russia far from their lines of supply. In September the Russians made a stand at Borodino, some seventy miles west of Moscow. Although the French won, opening the road to Moscow, they lost 40,000 men and failed to destroy the Russian army, which withdrew in order. Napoleon still did not have the decisive victory with which he hoped to force the tsar to make peace. At midnight on September 14, the Grand Army, its numbers greatly reduced by disease, hunger, exhaustion, desertion, and battle, entered Moscow. Expecting to be greeted by a deputation of nobles, Napoleon found instead that the Muscovites had virtually evacuated their holy city.

Taking up headquarters in Moscow, Napoleon waited for Alexander I to admit defeat and come to terms. But the tsar remained intransigent. Napoleon was in a dilemma: to penetrate deeper into Russia was certain death; to stay in Moscow with winter approaching meant possible starvation. Faced with these alternatives, Napoleon decided to retreat westward to his sources of supply in Poland. On October 19, 1812, 95,000 troops and thousands of wagons loaded with loot left Moscow for the long trek back.

In early November came the first snow and

frost. Army stragglers were slaughtered by Russian Cossacks and peasant partisans. Hungry soldiers pounced on fallen horses, carving them up alive. The wounded were left to lie where they dropped. Some wretches, wrote a French officer, "dragged themselves along, shivering . . . until the snow packed under the soles of their boots, a bit of debris, a branch, or the body of a fallen comrade tripped them and threw them down. Then their moans for help went unheeded. The snow soon covered them up and only low white mounds showed where they lay. Our road was strewn with these hummocks, like a cemetery."[28]

In the middle of December, with the Russians in pursuit, the remnants of the Grand Army staggered across the Nieman River into East Prussia. Napoleon had left his men earlier in the month and, traveling in disguise, reached Paris on December 18. Napoleon had lost his army; he would soon lose his throne.

Final Defeat

After the destruction of the Grand Army, the empire crumbled. Although Napoleon raised a new army, he could not replace the equipment, cavalry horses, and experienced soldiers squandered in Russia. Now he had to rely on schoolboys and overage veterans.

Most of Europe joined in a final coalition against France. In October 1813, allied forces from Austria, Prussia, Russia, and Sweden defeated Napoleon at Leipzig; in November, Anglo-Spanish forces crossed the Pyrenees into France. Finally, in the spring of 1814, the allies captured Paris. Napoleon abdicated and was exiled to the tiny island of Elba off the coast of Italy. The Bourbon dynasty was restored to the throne of France in the person of Louis XVIII, younger brother of the executed Louis XVI and the acknowledged leader of the émigrés.

Only forty-four years of age, Napoleon did not believe that it was his destiny to die on Elba. On March 1, 1815, he landed on the French coast with a thousand soldiers. Louis

XVIII ordered his troops to stop Napoleon's advance. When Napoleon's small force approached the king's troops, Napoleon walked up to the soldiers who blocked the road. "If there is one soldier among you who wishes to kill his Emperor, here I am." It was a brilliant move by a man who thoroughly understood the French soldier. The king's troops shouted, "Long live the Emperor!" and joined Napoleon. On March 20, 1815, Napoleon entered Paris to a hero's welcome. He had not lost his charisma.

Raising a new army, Napoleon moved against the allied forces in Belgium. There the Prussians, led by Field Marshal Gebhard von Blücher, and the British, led by the duke of Wellington, defeated Napoleon at Waterloo in June 1815. Napoleon's desperate gamble to regain power—the famous "hundred days"—had failed. This time the allies sent Napoleon to St. Helena, a lonely island in the South Atlantic a thousand miles off the coast of southern Africa. On this gloomy and rugged rock, Napoleon Bonaparte, emperor of France and would-be conqueror of Europe, spent the last six years of his life.

The Legend and the Achievement

"Is there anyone whose decisions have had a greater consequence for the whole of Europe?" asks Dutch historian Pieter Geyl about Napoleon.[29] It might also be asked: Is there anyone about whom there has been such a wide range of conflicting interpretations? Both Napoleon's contemporaries and later analysts have seen Napoleon in many different lights.

Napoleon himself contributed to the historical debate. Concerned as ever with his reputation, he reconstructed his career while on St. Helena. His reminiscences are the chief source of the Napoleonic legend. According to this account, Napoleon's principal aim was to defend the Revolution and consolidate its gains. He emerges as a champion of equality,

Chronology 20.1 Napoleon's Career

1796	Napoleon gets command of French Army of Italy
1798	Battle of the Nile; the British annihilate Napoleon's fleet
November 10, 1799	He helps overthrow the Directory's rule, establishing a strong executive in France
1802	He becomes First Consul for life; peace is made with Austria and Britain
March 21, 1804	The Civil Code (called Code Napoléon in 1807)
December 2, 1804	He crowns himself Emperor of the French
October 1805	French forces occupy Vienna
October 21, 1805	The battle of Trafalgar—French and Spanish fleets are defeated by the British
December 1805	The battle of Austerlitz—Napoleon defeats Russo-Austrian force
1806	War against Prussia and Russia
October 1806	He defeats the Prussians at Jena and French forces occupy Berlin
June 1807	French victory over the Russians at Friedland
July 1807	The treaties of Tilsit
1808–1813	The Peninsular War—Spaniards, aided by the British, war against French occupation
September 14, 1812	The Grand Army reaches Moscow
October–December 1812	The Grand Army retreats from Russia
October 1813	Allied forces defeat Napoleon at Leipzig
1814	Paris is captured and Napoleon is exiled to Elba
March 20, 1815	Escaping, he enters Paris and begins a 100 days' rule
June 1815	Defeated at Waterloo, he is exiled to St. Helena

a supporter of popular sovereignty, a destroyer of feudalism, a restorer of order, an opponent of religious intolerance, and a lover of peace forced to take up the sword because of the implacable hatred of Europe's reactionary rulers. According to this reconstruction, it was Napoleon's intention to spread the blessings of the Revolution to Germans, Dutch, Spanish, Poles, and Italians, and to create a United States of Europe, a federation of free and enlightened nations living in peace.

Had Napoleon realized this vision of a socially modernized, economically integrated, rationally ruled, and politically unified western Europe, which already shared a common cultural tradition, he would have performed one of the great creative acts in human history.

Undoubtedly, Napoleon did disseminate many gains of the Revolution. Nevertheless, say his critics, this account overlooks much. It ignores the repression of liberty, the subverting of republicanism, the oppression of conquered peoples, and the terrible suffering resulting from his pursuit of glory. The reminiscences were another example of Napoleonic propaganda.

While the debate over Napoleon continues, historians agree on two points. First, his was no ordinary life. A self-made man who had harnessed the revolutionary forces of the age and imposed his will on history, Napoleon was right to call his life a romance. His drive, military genius, and charisma propelled him to the peak of power; his inability to moderate his ambition bled Europe, distorted his judgment, and caused his downfall. His overweening pride, the hubris of the Greek tragedians, would have awed Sophocles; the dimensions of his mind and the intricacies of his personality would have intrigued Shakespeare; his cynicism and utter unscrupulousness would have impressed Machiavelli. Second, historians agree that by spreading revolutionary ideals and institutions, Napoleon made it impossible for the traditional rulers to restore the Old Regime intact after the emperor's downfall. The destruction of feudal remnants, the secularization of society, the transformation of the dynastic state into the modern national state, and the prominence of the bourgeoisie were assured.

The new concept of warfare and the new spirit of nationalism also became an indelible part of the European scene. In the course of succeeding generations, the methods of total warfare in the service of a belligerent nationalism would shatter Napoleon's grandiose vision of a united Europe and subvert the liberal humanism that was the essential heritage of the Enlightenment and the French Revolution.

Notes

1. Quoted in Felix Markham, *Napoleon and the Awakening of Europe* (New York: Collier Books, 1965), p. 27.

2. J. Christopher Herold, ed., *The Mind of Napoleon* (New York: Columbia University Press, 1965), p. 260.

3. Georges Lefebvre, *Napoleon* (New York: Columbia University Press, 1969), 2: 65.

4. Ibid., 2: 67.

5. Ibid., 2: 66.

6. Quoted in David Chandler, *The Campaigns of Napoleon* (New York: Macmillan, 1966), p. 157.

7. Maurice Hutt, ed., *Napoleon* (Englewood Cliffs, N.J.: Prentice-Hall, 1972), p. 3.

8. David L. Dowd, ed., *Napoleon: Was He the Heir of the Revolution?* (New York: Holt, Rinehart, and Winston, 1966), p. 42.

9. Quoted in Feilx Markham, *Napoleon* (New York: Mentor Books, 1963), p. 100.

10. Frank Malloy Anderson, ed., *The Constitution and Other Select Documents Illustrative of the History of France* (Minneapolis: H. W. Wilson, 1908), pp. 312–313.

11. Quoted in Robert B. Holtman, *The Napoleonic Revolution* (Philadelphia: J. B. Lippincott, 1967), pp. 123–124.

12. Quoted in ibid., p. 121.

13. Quoted in Markham, *Napoleon,* p. 97.

14. Dowd, *Napoleon,* p. 27.

15. Quoted in Holtman, *The Napoleonic Revolution,* p. 143.

16. Hutt, *Napoleon,* pp. 49–50.

17. Quoted in Chandler, *The Campaigns of Napoleon,* p. 145.

18. Ibid.

19. Ibid., p. 155.

20. Ibid.

21. Ibid., p. 157.

22. Quoted in Jacques Godechot, Beatrice F. Hyslop, and David L. Dowd, *The Napoleonic Era in Europe* (New York: Holt, Rinehart, and Winston, 1971), pp. 170, 172.

23. Dowd, *Napoleon,* p. 57.

24. Quoted in Owen Connelly, *Napoleon's Satellite Kingdoms* (New York: The Free Press, 1965), p. 223.

25. Quoted in Owen Connelly, *The Gentle Bonaparte* (New York: Macmillan, 1968), pp. 110–111.

26. Quoted in Boyd C. Shafer, *Nationalism: Myth and Reality* (New York: Harcourt, Brace, 1955), p. 139.

27. Quoted in Gordon A. Craig, *The Politics of the Prussian Army, 1640–1945* (New York: Oxford University Press, 1964), p. 40.

28. Quoted in J. Christopher Herold, *The Age of Napoleon* (New York: Dell, 1963), p. 320.

29. Pieter Geyl, *Napoleon For and Against* (New Haven: Yale University Press, 1964), p. 16.

Suggested Reading

Chandler, David, *The Campaigns of Napoleon* (1966). An exhaustive analysis of Napoleon's art of war.

Connelly, Owen, *Napoleon's Satellite Kingdoms* (1965). Focuses on the kingdoms in Naples, Italy, Holland, Spain, and Westphalia that were created by Napoleon and ruled by his relatives.

Cronin, Vincent, *Napoleon Bonaparte* (1972). A recent highly acclaimed biography.

Geyl, Pieter, *Napoleon For and Against* (1949). A critical evaluation of French writers' views of Napoleon.

Herold, J. C., ed., *The Mind of Napoleon* (1961). A valuable selection from the written and spoken words of Napoleon.

———, *The Horizon Book of the Age of Napoleon* (1965). Napoleon and his times.

Holtman, R. B., *The Napoleonic Revolution* (1967). Napoleon as revolutionary innovator who influenced every aspect of European life; particularly good on Napoleon the propagandist.

Hutt, Maurice, ed., *Napoleon* (1972). Excerpts from Napoleon's words and the views of contemporaries and later historians.

Lefebvre, Georges, *Napoleon*, 2 vols. (1969). An authoritative biography.

Markham, Felix, *Napoleon* (1963). A first-rate short biography.

———, *Napoleon and the Awakening of Europe* (1965). Napoleon's influence on other lands.

Review Questions

1. What made it possible for Napoleon to gain power?

2. What personality traits did Napoleon possess?

3. What principles underlay Napoleon's domestic reforms?

4. What was Napoleon's "art of war"? Describe his tactics.

5. Napoleon both preserved and destroyed the ideals of the French Revolution. Discuss this statement.

6. Why did England feel compelled to resist Napoleon? What were the intent and significance of the Continental System?

7. What was the significance of the Peninsular War?

8. Why did Prussian officials urge reforms? Describe the nature and significance of these reforms.

9. Account for Napoleon's defeat in Russia.

10. Identify and explain the historical significance of the Battle of Leipzig and the "hundred days."

11. What were Napoleon's greatest achievements? What were his greatest failures?

12. Why do some people regret that Napoleon did not establish a "United States of Europe"?

21

The Industrial Revolution: The Transformation of Society

*F*orces at work in the European economy and society in the second half of the eighteenth century were destined to have greater significance for humanity than the French Revolution. Experimentation with agriculture and with new forms of organizing labor and capital had so startling an impact that French observers of the English economy in the 1820s gave these developments a name—*industrialism*, or the *Industrial Revolution.* These changes took place first in England, but within a short time, the "English system" spread to Europe and the United States, and by the twentieth century it had affected the entire world.

The term *Industrial Revolution* refers to the shift from an agrarian, handicraft economy to one dominated by machine manufacture, division of labor, factories, and greater concentrations of population in urban areas. For contemporaries of the Industrial Revolution, applying inventions to human tasks seemed the most significant change taking place in England. Many contemporaries were impressed by the promise that technological change might alleviate poverty, want, and harsh labor. Other contemporaries knew industrialization and urbanization were destroying a way of life and creating immense problems for the individual and the state. Today, we are less impressed by the early inventions, many of which were simple alterations of existing tools, than we are by the new and more efficient ways of organizing tasks, by the increase in agricultural productivity, and by the harnessing of plentiful labor to stretch limited resources and capital, making the expansion of production possible. More goods could be produced faster and, therefore, cheaper than ever before.

Industrial progress did not proceed everywhere at the same pace. The changes that began in England in the middle of the eighteenth century did not start in France until the French Revolution. From the 1780s to

1850, French social and political turmoil both advanced and hindered economic development. In central Europe industrial growth began as late as the 1840s, lagging because the German states were not united under one government. The central European social disruption of that era originated in the hardships that the rapid expansion of industry, once it began, brought to artisans and craftsmen in a very short period of time. That rapidity of development may have worsened the plight of the artisan class, although their travails were comparable to those faced by their class in England a generation earlier. Industry grew phenomenally after German unification in 1870 but traditional economic forms and customs persisted alongside revolutionary industrial changes, which some historians say characterize a second industrial revolution after the 1850s (see Chapter 26). Industrialization proceeded slowly in Italy, too, where it was hampered by the sharp economic divisions between north and south, the comparative dearth of natural resources, and the late unification of the peninsula. In eastern Europe, the beginnings of industrialization were delayed to the very last decade of the nineteenth century, long after western Europe and the United States had industrialized.

In the first half of the century, then, Britain stepped out ahead of Belgium, the United States, and France, while the states in the west of Germany took the first steps of industrialization. By the second half of the century, Germany, France, and the United States had moved into genuine competition with Britain as industrial powers; Italy, Russia, and Austria-Hungary had been drawn into transportation and production revolutions. Almost irresistibly, Western states, and eventually lands around the globe, were driven to adopt the revolutionary changes in agriculture and industry that had begun in England. Everywhere that it penetrated, the Industrial Revolution transformed conditions of labor and life.

The Rise of the Industrial Age

Western European Expansion

The Industrial Revolution began in western Europe for a number of reasons. On the eve of industrialization, western Europe was wealthier than most of the world, and its wealth was spread across more classes of people. Wealth had slowly accumulated over centuries, despite the devastations of famine, plague, and war. Then came the rapid expansion of trade, both overseas and on the Continent, during the Commercial Revolution of the sixteenth and seventeenth centuries. This expansion, which was an aggressive search for new markets rather than for new methods of production, built on the capitalist practices of medieval and Renaissance bankers and merchants. The resources of the New World and of Africa, both human and material, had fueled Europe's accumulation of wealth.

Western agriculture, which differed from that of the Orient in many ways, also contributed greatly to the coming of the industrial age in Europe. Western agriculture was comparatively thrifty of land, capital, and human labor. Grain crops could grow on lands varying in fertility and contour and did not require the costly irrigation ditches, dams, and canals of rice cultivation. In western Europe no development of state power comparable to that in China or Russia kept labor tied to the land; over the centuries, the decline of serfdom and manorial obligations and the increasing efficiency of agriculture freed people for new forms of labor. (The era of the Commercial Revolution did not free labor everywhere, of course; in eastern Europe, serf labor was bound tighter to the land than it had been in previous centuries and held there more effectively by the steadily increasing power of the state; and in the Americas, native Indians and Africans were captive laborers.)

Against this background, in the early modern period the states that had centralized power in the hands of a strong monarch—England, Spain, Portugal, and France—competed for markets, for territory, and for prestige in ways that contributed to economic expansion. Engaged in fierce military and commercial rivalries, the states, with varying degrees of success, actively promoted industries to manufacture weaponry, uniforms, and ships and encouraged commerce for tax revenues. Thus aided, the growth in commerce nurtured a greatly expanded economy in which many levels of society participated—great estate owners, merchant princes, innovative entrepreneurs, the sugar plantation colonials, slave traders, sailors, and peasants (see Chapter 15).

The Population Explosion

The Commercial Revolution laid the economic and social foundation for industrialization; population growth provided industry with both consumers and labor. Europe's population expanded enormously in the eighteenth century. Most of this growth took place after the middle of the century and continued into the nineteenth century. In the Europe of 1800, there were about 190 million people; by 1914 there were 460 million people with about 200 million other Europeans scattered throughout the world. Most contemporaries did not know of the great population explosion taking place because records were poorly kept and because rural areas were actually losing population.

The population expanded rapidly for several reasons. First, the number of deaths from war, famine, and disease declined during the eighteenth century. More efficient agriculture and better food distribution reduced malnutrition, which meant better health, more births, and fewer deaths. The signs of better nutrition and better health included height—the average European man was 5 feet 6 inches tall in 1900, compared to 5 feet a century earlier—and a drop in the age at which girls began to menstruate. The number of births actually increased; and with better nutrition,

more children survived, grew stronger and taller, could work harder and longer, and were intellectually more able.

The Agricultural Revolution

Population growth might have brought famine, disease, and misery to Europe once again, as it had so many times before. The signs of rural destitution were apparent at the end of the eighteenth century and contributed to social unrest. But major changes in agriculture—a "green revolution"—not only increased productivity enough to feed the growing population but also improved the diet of many Europeans.

By the eighteenth century traditional patterns of farming were breaking up in western Europe. Agriculture became more and more a capitalist enterprise; production was undertaken for the market, not for family or village consumption. Land freed from traditional obligations became just another commodity to be bought, sold, and traded. Many people, aristocrats as well as peasants, persisted in their traditional obligations to one another, but powerful market forces gradually influenced most farm production, first in western European lands, then in central and finally in eastern Europe. After 1750 the British and Dutch practice of selective breeding of animals became more widespread, and land use grew more efficient. Through convertible husbandry, which cycled land from grain or root-crop production through soil-restoring crops of legumes and then pasturage, farmers could keep all fields in production, rather than leaving some lands fallow, as had been the practice in Europe for centuries. The improved methods gradually extended to the peasantry. However, in some areas within every country, particularly in central and eastern Europe, the old practices continued well into the nineteenth century.

Peasants freed from manorial obligations joined the ranks of entrepreneurs, tenants, or wage laborers, all farming for the market.

Land formerly used in common by villagers for grazing animals was claimed for private use. Usually the great landowners took advantage of their power, or of the law, and laid claim to common lands. This took place over much of Europe. In England the greatest acreage of enclosure actually took place in the sixteenth and seventeenth centuries. At the end of the eighteenth century, however, people were overwhelmed by the social disruption caused by the new agriculture. They thought the *last* portioning of land by enclosure was the cause rather than the result of the rural revolution. Some large landowners applied the latest and most efficient agricultural techniques to enclosed lands. But grasping landlords who wanted to maximize their profits immediately with little investment, rather than build a future of greater profits, were often as much the enemy of experimentation as the peasantry who held on to traditional ways. Such landlords maximized their profits merely by raising rents, which drove poor peasants off the land altogether.

By the middle of the nineteenth century, the application of technical ingenuity to farming brought improved plows, reapers, horse-drawn rakes, and threshers. These innovations greatly increased efficiency and production, although peasants did not usually own even these simple machines until the end of the century. Overall, though, the changes in agriculture meant that fewer men and women could produce more food and raw materials, leaving greater numbers to work in industry.

Britain First

Great Britain was the first country to industrialize, although it was not the only country with many of the prerequisites for industrialization. In the eighteenth century, England had serious economic competition from France, which was wealthier, more populous, and an empire equal to England's in trading

importance. The French had a skilled populace; their government, if anything, was more responsive than Britain's to the need for transportation and communication. The French had established schools for technicians and fostered civil engineers for public works such as water works, canals, roads, and bridges. (Some of the French monarch's attempts to encourage industry, such as establishing royal monopolies to provide luxuries for the court, may have done more harm than good, however.)

The French, though, seemed less willing than the British to change traditional ways—methods of agriculture, for example. Moreover, much of the French economy produced luxury items rather than goods for mass consumption. Although the French generally lived less well than the English, they had enough wealth to make an effective demand for products at home. Well into the nineteenth century, however, the French economy continued to produce fine goods by hand for the few, rather than cheap goods by machine for the many. A more serious obstacle to French industrialization, which German and Italian states faced later, was the existence of internal tariffs until the French Revolution abolished them. England did not have these obstacles to the free flow of goods within the country, and after the union of Scotland with England in 1707, trade flowed freely throughout all Britain as well.

In some ways, the French Revolution perpetuated traditional agricultural and commercial practices. Peasants who acquired land in the Revolution often gained small plots where the new methods of farming were difficult to apply. Thus, the new landholders continued to use the old practices, trying to restrict their needs and even the sizes of their families to hold on to their land and feed themselves. Under such circumstances, it was hard to grow a surplus for the market.

Like France, the Dutch Republic had sufficient wealth to support industrialization. For almost a century, the Dutch had developed techniques of finance and commerce that

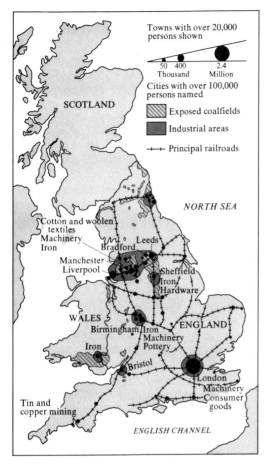

Map 21.1 Industrial Growth in England, Mid–1800s

Towns with over 20,000 persons shown

50   400   2.4
Thousand   Million

Cities with over 100,000 persons named

Exposed coalfields

Industrial areas

+—+—+ Principal railroads

SCOTLAND

NORTH SEA

Cotton and woolen textiles
Machinery
Iron
Leeds
Bradford
Manchester
Liverpool
Sheffield
Iron
Hardware

WALES
Birmingham Iron
Machinery
Pottery
Iron
Bristol

ENGLAND

London
Machinery
Consumer goods

Tin and copper mining

ENGLISH CHANNEL

every nation tried to imitate. They also had a good transportation system. They lacked natural resources, however, and rather than expanding manufacturing and trade, they put their efforts into finance throughout the eighteenth century.

Britain possessed several advantages that enabled it to take the lead. A large and easily developed supply of coal and iron had given the British a long tradition of metallurgy and mining. In the early stages of industrialization, Britain's river-transportation system was supplemented by canals and toll roads (turnpikes) that private entrepreneurs had financed and built for profit. In addition, Britain had a labor pool in Scotland, England, and Ireland of farmers who could no longer earn a living

for themselves and their families on the land. Parliament enclosed the common lands, pushing poor farmers out. It chartered businesses, such as toll bridge and canal builders, which expanded the economy. The state aided industrialization by providing law, order, and protection of private property. The freedom of entry into economic activity was truly remarkable, far less restricted by monopolies, charters, and guilds than it had been in England in the seventeenth century and still was in other European countries.

Changes in Technology

The Industrial Revolution brought a change from hand to machine manufacture and from human or animal power to other forms of energy such as steam or, later, the internal combustion engine. The first stages of industrialization in any particular trade, however, often resulted from simple changes made, sometimes without altering the power source, by workers as they plied their craft.

Long the home of an important wool trade, Britain in the late eighteenth century jumped ahead in the production of cotton, the industry that first showed the possibility of unprecedented growth rates. British cotton production expanded tenfold between 1760 and 1785, and another tenfold between 1785 and 1825. A series of inventions revolutionized the industry and drastically altered the social conditions of the work. In 1733, long before expansion started, a simple invention—John Kay's flying shuttle—made it possible for weavers to double their output. This shuttle, which could be used in the home, was an adaptation of machinery that had been used in the wool trade for generations. Weavers produced faster than spinners could spin until James Hargreaves's spinning jenny, perfected by 1768, allowed an operator to work several spindles at once; Hargreaves's jenny still used only human power, however. Within five years Richard Arkwright's water frame spinning machine could be powered by water or animal energy, and Samuel Crompton's spinning mule (1779) at first powered many spindles by human power, then by animal and water energy. These changes improved spinning productivity so much that bottle-necks in weaving developed until Edmund Cartwright developed a power loom in 1787.

Arkwright's water frame made it more efficient to bring many workers together, rather than putting work out to individuals in their own homes. This development was the beginning of the factory system, which, within a generation, would revolutionize the conditions of labor. To the end of the century there was a race to speed up the process by applying water power to looms or new, larger devices to the jenny. Because water power drove these early machines, mills were located near rivers and streams. There towns grew up as workers took up residence; the factory system urbanized labor.*

Weavers and spinners—not technicians, engineers, or scientists—invented these simple devices, which were modeled after machines already in use. The inventions did not begin the cotton industry's explosive expansion—that resulted from social and economic demand—but once begun, the expansion was so great and the demand so urgent that more and more complicated technology was called for. A role emerged for the engineer, an expert in building and adapting machines.

James Watt developed the steam engine in the 1760s, but it was too expensive to be adapted to production for some time. Although women and children, who earned less than men, could easily tend steam-powered machinery, male labor was so cheap that entrepreneurs were reluctant to make the shift. Over the long run, though, as en-

gines and fuel became cheaper, they did shift, and then expansion became even more rapid. Because they ran on coal or wood, not water power, steam engines allowed greater flexibility in locating textile mills. No longer restricted to the power supplied by a river or a stream or to the space available beside flowing water, factories could be built anywhere. Cities grew larger, congregating more people and workplaces in one area than ever before seen.

Once steam power was applied, particularly to transportation, it produced the incredible rate of change and progress that most people identify with the Industrial Revolution. But most of the steam-generated transformation took place in the middle of the nineteenth century. The two previous centuries of slower development powered by people, by animals, and by water were a heroic achievement, but one that did not alter the worker's role to the extent that steam power did. With steam, the whole pattern of work changed because weaker, younger, and less skilled workers could be taught the few simple tasks necessary to mind the machine. The shift from male to female and child labor was a major social change. Moreover, as steam took hold, human participation in the process of manufacture diminished; engines replaced people, and workers began to be referred to as "hands" or "hired hands" that drove machines.

Although steam power made it possible to hire weaker people to operate machinery, it also required machines made of stronger metal to withstand the forces generated by a stronger power source. The history of the search for better iron illustrates how developments in one industry necessitated change in related industries; it is also a good example of trial and error as a method of invention.

Before the eighteenth century, iron was produced by much the same methods as in the Middle Ages. The first step in increasing the production of high-quality iron came when Abraham Darby produced coke-smelted cast iron in 1709. His son and grandson tried improving the quality of coke and making a better bellows to heat the furnaces. Their

---

*Developments in America were keeping pace to meet the demand for raw cotton. Eli Whitney's cotton gin removed the seeds from raw cotton quickly and cheaply, leading American farmers and plantation owners to turn much land to cotton cultivation. More laborers were required for the fields and less to process the cotton, which increased the demand for slave labor, bringing about far-reaching changes in the American labor system.

A Cotton Mill. The movement from cottage to factory as the place of manufacture occurred during the late eighteenth and early nineteenth centuries. Until reform acts protected workers from exploitation, women and children worked long hours for extremely low wages. (*The Mansell Collection*)

methods worked, and by the mid-eighteenth century the quality of cast iron was so high that it began to replace wood in construction. Another major advance was turning cast iron into wrought iron. High quality wrought iron was expensive because the cost of wood to fire the furnaces was so high. Thus, English smelters tried ways to use coal, which was cheap but contained impurities that made a poor, brittle metal. Henry Cort borrowed a French idea of making a furnace with two separate compartments, one for coal and one for iron, but he altered the process by puddling (stirring) the molten iron and then rolling it as it cooled. His methods reduced the impurities and made the process much faster. By the 1780s, wrought iron had become the most widely used metal and would remain so until steel was cheaply produced in the 1860s.

The iron industry made great demands on the coal mines to fuel its furnaces. Because steam engines enabled miners to pump water from the mines more efficiently and at a much deeper level, rich veins in existing mines became accessible for the first time. Steam engines also lifted the coal up the main shaft to the surface. Britain's production of coal kept pace with the industrial growth it powered and rose from 16 million tons at the end of the Napoleonic Wars to 30 million in 1836 and to 65 million in 1856.

The greater productivity in coal allowed the continued improvement of iron smelting. Then in 1856, Henry Bessemer developed a process for converting pig iron into steel by removing the impurities in the iron. In the 1860s, William Siemens and the Martin brothers developed the open hearth process, which could handle much greater amounts of metal than Bessemer's converter could. Steel became so cheap to produce that it quickly replaced iron in industry because of its greater tensile strength and durability.

Changes in mining, metallurgy, textiles, pottery, and farming speeded change in other industries and, above all, in transportation and communications. Transportation was revolutionized, providing a network that could support expansion in many other areas of the economy. Major road building took place in the eighteenth century in England and in France, and later in the rest of Europe. Canals were constructed in Britain and the United States between 1760 and 1820 only to be quickly outmoded by railroads, which although more expensive, were more flexible and were immensely popular as they caught the public imagination. Steam-powered engines replaced horses as the power source for railroads in the 1820s. Continental governments regarded railroads as essential to their power and unity, and expended major efforts to develop railroad networks. Governments licensed and encouraged the early railroads, hoping that they would fill in the transportation network where canals or roads were inadequate. Railroads were so successful that in England by midcentury, roads were mere auxiliaries to the railroads—just paths leading to the station. It would not be until the turn of the twentieth century that a complete network of roads was thought essential to public transport in Britain.

Britain was not first in every new mode of transportation. Steamboats could not be widely used for internal navigation because Britain's rivers were small, but in the United States many steamboats plied the broad rivers in the first part of the nineteenth century. However, for long journeys, such as transatlantic crossings, steamboats could not compete with the tall-masted clipper ships of the 1850s. These sailing ships were faster and did not have to carry coal for an engine, so their cargo holds could be filled entirely with profitable goods.

Unprecedented amounts of private British capital built Britain's system of roads, canals, and railways. Continental states were slower to adopt steam transport because they lacked capital and skilled civil engineering. Only France invested a great percentage of private capital in transportation (although not until after the 1830s). It took various failures of management and finance before the French government assumed control of its railroads, but state control was widespread in the rest of Europe. In central and eastern Europe railroads were built with direct government intervention. In the United States, Congress gave enormous grants of land to railroad companies to encourage the laying of tracks. Everywhere during the railroad-building boom that extended through the nineteenth century, financiers thought investment in railroads to be sound, and the flow of capital from western Europe, particularly Britain and France, to other lands was an awesome achievement.

Communications changed as spectacularly as transportation did. Britain inaugurated the penny post in 1840, making it possible to send a letter to any part of the kingdom for one cent. But the cost of postage was so high elsewhere that letters were rarely written; many letters of the time fill every space on a single sheet of paper because the postage rate was cheapest for one sheet. Business, particularly across distant markets, needed cheaper and faster communication, and the telegraph was the first astonishing breakthrough. The first telegraphic message was sent from Baltimore to Washington, D.C., in 1844. Within seven years the first submarine cable was laid under the English Channel, and by 1866 transatlantic cable was operating. Although certainly not inexpensive until the last quarter of the nineteenth century, the telegraph was quickly employed by business.

Changes in Finance

The first steps of industrialization—the use of new crop mixes and tools in agriculture, and the first changes in spinning and weaving—did not require much capital. Subsequent

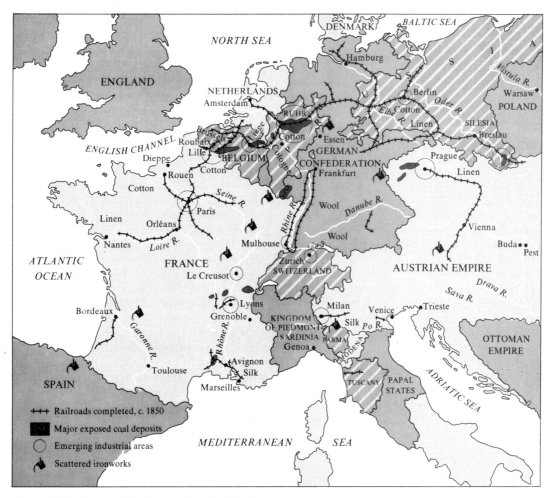

Map 21.2 Industrial Growth on the Continent, Mid–1800s

growth—from the growth of factories to the extensive application of machinery to agriculture, the expansion of mining, and construction in the cities—required the investment of enormous capital. Railroads and steamship lines were often, but not always, so expensive that only governments could finance them; even in Belgium, where they were privately financed at first, the king was the major investor. Funding the steel industry also required large investments.

In the earliest stages of industrialization, the owning family was the source of a company's finance, its management, and even its technical innovation. Family firms dominated industry. But outside investment grew

with the demand for capital, which rose steadily from 1760 to the end of the First World War (1918). In Britain, for example, wealthy merchants and landlords provided investment capital, and low interest rates encouraged borrowing. On the Continent the supply of capital was limited, and the British became international investors of the first rank, furnishing much of the capital for the industrialization of other nations. French investors, who were sometimes reluctant to invest at home because they feared political instability, financed railroads in Austria and were the major investors in the great Suez Canal and in the first canal project in Panama, which failed. Among banking families—including the Barings of London and the Rothschilds of France, England, and Germany—kinship ties joined together large amounts of investment capital. These investor groups were very important to European industrialization. People of the same religion or region would often band together to gather capital for development, as the Protestant and Jewish bankers of France did.

Banking, however, was risky business in the nineteenth century; dozens of banks failed in every financial crisis. Lacking insurance for deposits and possessing only limited resources, banks could not protect their investors. They tended to pursue cautious policies because they were vulnerable. To avoid the risk of losing everything in the failure of a single industry, banks diversified their investments. Thus, in any given country the number of industries able to borrow substantial amounts of capital was limited in the early stages of industrialization. In some countries, bankers preferred the safety of investing in government debt, which slowed down the development of industry.

One major difficulty in financing industry was the lack of a formal organization that would enable a number of people to pool their capital safely. In the existing joint-stock companies, individuals could be held responsible for all the debts of the enterprise. Although joint-stock companies were thought risky, more and more individuals were joining together in this manner, keeping the right to transfer their shares without the consent of other stockholders. England finally repealed the laws against this practice in 1825 and permitted incorporation in 1844. By incorporating, an organization would be treated as an individual before the law, although it actually was comprised of a number of individuals joined together for commerce. The practice created firms that could live long after all the founders had died or sold their shares. More importantly, investors were liable for a corporation's debts only in proportion to the number of shares they owned. In 1844, after nearly a century of industrial progress, England had almost 1,000 such

companies , with a stock value of 345 million pounds, ready to legally incorporate, compared to 260 similar companies in France. In the 1850s, limited liability was applied to the stock of most English businesses, and a little later it was extended to banking and insurance companies. This change meant that investors endangered only the actual amount they paid for their stock, not all the funds they possessed. By the 1860s the French, the Germans, and all the American states permitted limited liability, which released such a flow of savings that it sparked a surge of industrial energy.

Society Transformed

The changes in agricultural production, business organization, technology, and the uses of power had revolutionary consequences for society and politics. People were drawn from the countryside into cities and from one country to another. Traditional ways of life changed for Europeans, and eventually for non-Westerners too. Industrialism made the world smaller; the whole world was drawn into commerce and manufacturing at a dizzying speed.

European society before the Industrial Revolution was based on kinship. Property in the form of land was the basis of social class and social power, which was usually exercised on a local or provincial level. Industrialization brought a new world in which there were many forms of property and several kinds of power, and the nation became more important than the province, region, or local area. In this new world, individuals were increasingly important—before the law, in trade, and in political thought—but in trying to make their way through day-to-day adversity, they came to feel small, powerless, and isolated—cut adrift from families and villages. In a sense, individuals were made freer by the breakdown of family and town controls, but it was also true that in time of need, such as unemployment or illness, towns and families had offered irreplaceable support.

Jean François Millet (1814–1875): Planting Potatoes (detail). For the romantic, the peasant and his lowly occupation became fit subjects for literature and painting. The emotions of a beggar were now seen as important as those of an emperor. (*Courtesy, Museum of Fine Arts, Boston*)

While the foundations of new socioeconomic patterns were being laid, much of the old life persisted, particularly for the first half of the nineteenth century. Landed property was still the principal form of wealth, and landowners with large holdings continued to exercise political power. From England to Russia, families of landed wealth (they were often the old noble families) continued to constitute the social elite. European society remained overwhelmingly rural. As late as the middle of the century, only England was half urban.

Still, contemporaries were so overwhelmed by industrialization that they saw it as a sudden and complete break with the past—the shattering of traditional moral and social patterns. Some people could remember the past, others idealized it as a golden age in which the relations between classes, between master and servant, had been based on values other than wages and hours. Historians, on the other hand, view the Industrial Revolution as a process of gradual but sustained growth over 150 years and see the industrial development in the first half of the nineteenth century as laying the foundation for the rapid changes of the next hundred years.

Urbanization

Cities grew in number, size, and population as a result of industrialization. No longer just seats of government and commerce, they became places of manufacture and industry.

Before 1800, about 10 percent of the European population lived in cities (in Great Britain and the Netherlands, the leading areas of urban living, 20 percent did). A mere forty-five cities in the world had more than 100,000 people. Halfway through the nineteenth century, when 52 percent of the British lived in cities, only 25 percent of the French did, 36 percent of the Germans, 7 percent of the Russians, and only 10 percent of the inhabitants of the United States. Most of the shift from rural to urban living in Europe and the United States has taken place in the twentieth century. But the increase in Europe's urban population during the 1800s was nonetheless acute in its influence. And in some regions, it was particularly concentrated; industrial areas grew up in each country almost overnight—the Midlands in England, the Lowlands in Scotland, the northern plains in France, the German Rhineland, the northeastern United States, and parts of northern Italy.

Industrial cities in the nineteenth century, particularly in England, grew rapidly without planning or, at first, much regulation by local or national governments. Government and business were often reluctant to use taxation to finance remedies for the resulting poor living conditions. Civic pride and private patronage were the only forces—and they were too weak—to combat the effects of unregulated private enterprise. On the European continent where industrialization came later, states were more willing to regulate both industrial and urban development, but planning efforts were still inadequate.

So much growth with so little planning or control led to cities with little sanitation, no lighting, wretched housing, poor transportation, and little security. Cities had grown without planning before, but they had not been home and workplace for such large numbers of people, many of them new arrivals. Rich and poor alike suffered in this environment of disease, crime, and ugliness, although the poor obviously bore the brunt of these evils.

Major cities showed traits in common, so they appeared to result from a single plan.

These developments, however, grew from the wide disparity in economic and social power between the classes. By the mid-nineteenth century, the wealthiest inhabitants' homes circled the city's edge and were close to the country, in "suburbs" that were roomier and cleaner than the city proper. The general rule was the farther one lived from the central city, the wealthier one was, and the houses in that area were detached and usually had gardens. The outer ring of the city was the location most preferred by the middle class and shared many characteristics of the wealthier suburbs. In the inner ring were the artisans' dwellings, which ranged from those resembling middle-class residences to small attached row houses perhaps with a small garden. Further down the social scale, artisans' housing verged on workers' row houses in the center of industrial towns. Long rows, several stories high, were jammed together as near the factories as possible, separated one from the next by a courtyard. Usually this comprised a strip of mud or cobblestones containing a pump in the middle for water and for washing, serving all the residents adjoining the courtyard. When public transportation developed in the second half of the century, workers' districts dispersed, sometimes to circle great governmental cities, such as London and Paris, where the wealthy monopolized the central city. In industrial cities the earlier pattern remained, although new workers' housing might be scattered.

Almost universally, those who wrote about industrial cities—Manchester, Leeds, Liverpool, and Lyons—described the stench, the filth, the inhuman crowding, the poverty, and the immorality. Novelists Charles Dickens, George Sand, and Émile Zola captured the horrors of urban industrial life and the plight of the poor. Factual parliamentary reports equalled the novelists when describing a London row:

In the centre of this street there is a gutter into which potato parings, the refuse of vegetable and animal matter of all kinds, the dirty water from the washing of clothes and of the houses are all poured, and where they stagnate and putrefy . . .

all the lanes and alleys of the neighbourhood pour their contents into the centre of the main street. . . . Families live in the cellars and kitchens of these undrained houses.

An 1842 government report from Leeds depicted:

. . . walls unwhitewashed for years, black with the smoke of foul chimneys, without water . . . and sacking for bedclothing, with floors unwashed from year to year, without out-offices [lavatories]. Outside there are streets, raised a foot, sometimes two above the level of the causeway, by the accumulation of years . . . stagnant puddles here and there . . . and excrementitious deposits on all sides as a consequence, undrained, unpaved, unventilated, uncared-for by any authority but the landlord, who weekly collects his miserable rents from his miserable tenants.

Changes in Social Structure

From the eighteenth century, as industry and commerce developed, the middle class grew in number and in power, first in England and then throughout western Europe. Industrial and financial capitalism had grown up inside a preindustrial agrarian society with traditional political organizations and social classes. Throughout the eighteenth century—and the nineteenth as well for most of Europe—the middle class struggled with the aristocracy to remove political, economic, and social discrimination; they forced radical changes, but they still had to function in a political and social world that had been made before they had gained influence. Although industrialization reduced barriers between the elite of the Old Regime and the middle class, it sharpened the distinctions between the middle class (bourgeoisie) and the laboring class (proletariat).

During the nineteenth century the social changes resulting from the Industrial Revolution brought the middle class greater political power and social respectability. By the end of the century, bourgeois politicians held

the highest offices in much of western Europe and shared authority with aristocrats, whose birth no longer guaranteed them the only political and social power in their nations. As industrial wealth became more important in the modern world, the middle class became more influential, but it was common throughout Europe for wealthy bourgeois to spend fortunes buying great estates and emulating aristocratic manners and pleasures. Conscious of their social position, the middle class valued respectability. In this and many other ways, they copied the aristocracy, more than they competed with it, for most of the century.

Defining the middle class presents problems. Contemporaries often referred to the bourgeoisie as a plural unit—the middle classes. The middle class was made up of people of common birth, rather than noble, but they were not laboring people as they engaged in trade and other capitalist ventures. The wealthiest were bankers, factory and mine owners, and merchants. The middle class also included shopkeepers, managers, doctors, and lawyers. The virtues of work, thrift, ambition, and caution characterized the middle class, as did the perversion of these virtues into materialism, selfishness, callousness, harsh individualism, and cultural philistinism.

Defining the laboring classes is equally difficult. Aristocrats often referred to all who labored as "the poor," but there were rural laborers, miners, and city workers. And in the cities there were many gradations of workers. Artisans practiced various crafts; factory workers were the newest and most rapidly growing social group, but at mid-century they did not constitute the majority of laboring people in any major city (as late as 1890 they were only one-sixth the population of London, for example). A third group of urban workers were the servants, especially numerous in capital cities such as London and Paris.

The artisans were the largest group in the cities for the first half of the nineteenth century, and in some places for much longer than that. They worked in construction, in printing, in small tailoring or dress-making establishments, in food preparation and processing, and in crafts producing luxury items such as furniture, jewelry, lace, and velvet. Artisans as a group were distinct from factory workers; their technical skills were difficult to learn, and traditionally their crafts were acquired in guilds, which still functioned as both social and economic organizations. Artisans were usually educated (they could read and write), lived in one city or village for generations, and maintained stable families, often securing places for their children in their craft.

As the Industrial Revolution progressed, however, artisans were threatened by the increased numbers of factory workers and the use of machinery in their crafts. To compete with cheap factory-produced goods, artisans began to downgrade their skills by dropping apprenticeship training or by forcing journeymen to work longer hours with shoddy materials. By the nineteenth century in Britain and in France, the guilds had lost their special economic role in regulating the hours and conditions of labor, the ages of workers, and similar concerns. In central Europe, guilds fared better; in 1848, artisans were at the forefront of the revolutionary movement as they tried to save themselves from the effects of the Industrial Revolution (pages 530–534). Artisans, rather than factory workers, seem to have been the center of political and economic protest decrying industrialization and favoring political representation. Their guild organizations were models for many early socialists, and artisans were generally in the front ranks of supporters of utopian movements.

Together with the artisans among city workers, there was a substantial group of servants. In the first half of the nineteenth century in cities like Paris and London, where the number of factories was not great, there were more servants than factory workers. The great increase in domestic labor in the nineteenth century freed middle-class women from household chores so that they could spend more time with their husbands and children or pursuing interests in the outside world if they chose to do so.

Working in a middle- or upper-class household, servants lived in a world apart from factory workers and artisans. They were often women who had come to the city from the country, where they might also have been servants. They were completely at the command of their employers; they might be exploited or they might be treated decently, but they had little recourse when they were abused. Some worked their entire lives as servants; others left service to marry working-class men. Servants usually had some education. If they married and had a family, they taught their children to read and write and sometimes to observe the manners and values of the household in which the parent had worked. Many historians believe that these servants passed on to their children their own deference to authority and their aspiration to bourgeois status, which may have limited social discontent and radical political activity.

The Condition of Industrial Workers

Industrialization created a new class, which did not have a place in traditional society, as artisans and servants did. Factory workers differed from artisans in many ways. In general, they were recent arrivals from agricultural areas where they had been driven off the land; they had no special skills or traditions of working with others in a craft. Frequently, factory workers had moved to the city without their families, leaving them behind until they could afford to support them in town; other workers were single men or women who could find no jobs as servants or farm laborers in their villages. These people entered rapidly growing industries where long hours—sometimes fifteen a day—were not unusual; farming had meant long hours, too, but the pace of the machine and the routine made factory work more oppressive.

Although the Industrial Revolution arose from technological advances in machinery, the machines demanded highly regulated human labor—generally menial, often dangerous. In Britain's mercurially productive coal mines, for example, steam engines did not chop the coal from the veins; they did not even haul the coal wagons to the main shaft. Human beings—men, women, and small children—hacked the coal out and sorted it, while horses and mules pulled coal wagons on rails to the central or main shaft where (by the middle of the nineteenth century) steam-powered engines lifted tons of coal to the surface. The workers in Britain's mines labored under the hazards of cave-ins, explosions, and deadly gas fumes. In the dark, deep under the earth's surface, life was cold, wet, and tenuous. Their bodies stunted and twisted, their lungs wrecked, miners labored their lives away in "the pits."

Factory workers fared a little better than the miners. Sometimes, compared to their lives in the country, the workers' standard of living rose, particularly if they were part of a whole family that found work. The pay for a family might be better than they could have earned for agricultural labor. But working conditions were terrible, as were living conditions, and frequently dangerous. The factories were dirty, hot, unventilated. Workers often lived in overcrowded and dirty housing. If they were unmarried or had left their family in the country, they often lived in a barracks with other members of their sex. If they lost their jobs, they also lost their shelter.

Factory workers' lives were depressing. They had very little connection with their surroundings, and like immigrants to a new country, they lived with hardship and deprivation. In the villages they had left, they had been poor, but were socially connected to family, church, and even to local landlords. But in the cities, factory workers labored in plants with twenty to a hundred workers and had little contact with their employers; instead, hired foremen pushed them to work hard and efficiently, to keep up with the machines. Unlike journeymen, factory workers possessed no tools and had only their labor to sell. In all, they had few of the ar-

tisans' advantages for withstanding the adversities of industrialization. Torn from their traditions, lacking organization and a sense of comradeship, uneducated, with no experience of city living, they found little succor when times were bad.

But factory workers did make lives for themselves. They married or entered into some relationship at a younger age than artisans did, and they had more children on the average than other classes did. Children were actually an economic asset, because they worked to help the family; when workers grew old or were disabled, their children were their only pension. Many workers developed a life around the pub, the cafe, or some similar gathering place where there were drinks and games and the gossip and news of the day. On Sundays, their one day off, workers drank and danced; absenteeism was so great on Monday that the day was called *holy Monday*. In Manchester, England, in the 1830s a population of almost 200,000 supported more than 1,500 alehouses and inns, about seven times as many as the same population would frequent today. Gin drinking, however, was denounced on all sides; workers and reformers alike urged temperance. Factory workers attended churches that reached out to them. These were not usually the established church, which seemed to them to be only for the wealthy. In England the Methodists and Dissenters welcomed workers, and the Catholic Church sought out Irish workers; revivalists also attracted the working classes. Many workers played sports, and some social organizations grew up around their sporting games. In these and other ways, factory workers developed a culture of their own—a culture that was misunderstood and often deplored by middle-class reformers.

For the most part, factory workers and miners did not protest their conditions violently, although sometimes they did—and in some countries more than others. In general, factory workers just endured. They worked long hours, were fined for mistakes or tardiness, were fired at the will of their employer or foreman, and suffered from work insecurity. Yet, they rarely broke machines, which country laborers did to protest the mechanization of agriculture. Factory workers had few organizations and no political rights. They lacked the traditions and organizations of the craftsmen, but they did join with artisans in movements for political rights—the Chartists in England and the republicans in France. But even a peaceful demonstration, during which they sang hymns and prayed, might be disrupted by soldiers and gunfire. Workers who protested lost their jobs and were "blackballed" (employers circulated their names so that other employers would not hire them). Workers were neither wealthy enough nor organized enough to take offending employers to court for violations of the law.

Many workers and radicals believed that the only hope for their class was in unified action through trade unions, mutual-aid societies, cooperatives, or political organizations. After the middle of the nineteenth century in England and western Europe, trade unions appeared despite the fact that they were illegal. Unions made some headway in protecting their members from unemployment and dangerous working conditions. But strikes were rarely successful; they were usually misunderstood by the general public, imbued with individualist principles, and often suppressed by force. Not until the 1870s and 1880s was widespread discontent expressed by militant trade unions (see Chapter 26).

Deterioration in the quality of life among the working classes seemed greatest among the artisans, especially the handweavers who tried to hold on to their craft. Artisans and farm laborers were sometimes violent; they were called Luddites, and broke machinery. They were suppressed when they protested, if they were caught. Many could find no work at all in their craft because of factory products. Unsteady work was perhaps worse, because an artisan did not know whether to abandon the trade and seek other work, or to hang on in the hope of a better day. There was widespread discontent—strongest among the

Gustave Doré (1833–1883): Bluegate Fields in Nineteenth-Century London. A population explosion took place between 1700 and 1850, as well as a population shift that peopled industrial cities. Contemporaries were dimly aware of the total increase in population, and there was inadequate planning for urban expansion. Rich and poor alike suffered from disease, crime, and squalor in the cities. (*Courtesy of the Boston Athenaeum*)

better-educated and better-organized artisans. The Chartists in England and the strikes and violence in France in the 1830s reflect the social tension; the Chartists were harassed, repressed, and ignored, and their strikes were violently suppressed.

Although workers' political agitation was not effective in the first half of the nineteenth century, they made some progress in economic actions. Workers formed "friendly societies" or "mutual-aid" and cooperative organizations to help themselves if they were out of work or sick. They paid some dues or took up special collections when one of their members was killed on the job. They also created clubs where they could learn to read and write or where someone could read to them and write their letters. Self-help organizations often grew into unions; sometimes they were unions in disguise because the law prohibited unions.

In England, unions became legal in 1825. But they were forbidden to strike, and if a union's officer ran away with its treasury, English law did not protect the workers' dues. Unions developed despite these obstacles. Small unions were powerless, so in 1834 there was an attempt in England to join all unions together in a Grand National Consolidated Trade Union—but what would help one trade would not necessarily help another. Repression scared many workers away from the unions, and when unions finally surfaced again in the 1850s after the repression, highly skilled workers joined together in a single craft union. If a mechanic, or a metallurgist, or a miner refused to work, it was difficult to find a replacement; in industrial countries, these craft unions were more successful than other unions. Still the vast majority of workers was not organized during much of the nineteenth century.

Relief and Reform

Poverty became an issue with the onset of industrialization. There had always been poor people—society was enjoined by religion and by custom to care for the poor in times of need—but with industrialization the economic and psychological hardships borne by the work force seemed to be worse than ever before. There were strong feelings that the poor—those who were so unfortunate that they needed the assistance of others—were growing in number, that their condition was deplorable, and that it had actually deteriorated in the midst of increased wealth. If machines could produce so much wealth and so many products, many wondered why there were so many poor people.

The new developments caused by industrial growth overwhelmed local and national authorities. Britain was first to face the worsening condition of the poor. In the eighteenth century, English agricultural laborers had a higher standard of living than their counterparts on the Continent. As Britain rapidly industrialized, the appalling conditions convinced observers, foreign and English, that both rural and urban workers' lives worsened. More and more people turned to local government authorities for relief under the poor law; this had been devised three centuries earlier to provide seasonal relief for agricultural labor, but not assistance against unemployment for great numbers of workers.

Many government leaders (and classical economists) despaired of legislative relief because they believed that only free enterprise would speed industrialization and only increasing economic capacity would end distress. But would the economy expand and benefit the lowliest workers by itself, or did it need direction from the state? Others believed relief would come through better organization of industry and government. The latter group included utilitarians, early socialists, and practical reformers (see pages 511–513).

Parliamentary reports and investigations of civic-minded citizens documented the suffering for all to read. These parliamentary "blue books" aimed to make reforms, and they did—for example, the Factory Acts tried to control the employment of women and children. At first, legislation remained almost unenforceable because it did not provide inspection.

The Factory Acts also required children to spend time in school. It was felt that one way to protect working-class children—to hold them responsible for their lives and yet to give them the opportunity to change—was to educate them. England was much slower than France or Germany to provide schools; British private enterprise and charities, rather than the government, took the initiative. France had mandated compulsory education by the nineteenth century, as some German states had, but penurious governments often failed to provide adequate funds for schools. Sometimes there were schools for boys and not for girls, and it was often argued that for moral reasons the sexes should not mix in the same classroom, even though they worked side by side in the factory. Under the first compulsory-education provisions of English law (which did not provide for the schools), children often worked ten or twelve hours and then attended rudimentary schools.

Other legislation was passed in 1834: a reform of the poor law, the relief system; this tried to differentiate between the "deserving" poor and the "undeserving" poor by requiring any recipient of assistance to enter a workhouse. The legislators thought that only those who were truly needy—those who were unable to labor because they were disabled, or too old or too young—would submit to the terrible conditions of the workhouse just to receive a meal and shelter. Generally, they were right. The poor and the unemployed working class hated and feared the workhouse and "pauperization." Humanitarians railed against these harsh and inadequate reforms.

In general, Parliament's reforms lifted existing regulations, rather than created new ones. Some legislation protected women and children from the worst evils of factories and mines. But legislators usually held the poor responsible for their plight, an attitude evident in the New Poor Law.

In much of Europe, people accepted more readily than they did in Britain the idea that the state could interfere with the market; further, most states in Europe had larger bureaucracies to enforce regulations and carry out relief measures. However, statesmen on the Continent worried about their nation's handicaps in the marketplace due to late industrialization. Therefore, they were vulnerable to arguments against the protection of labor, because it would make the price of goods uncompetitive with Britain's. Governments in Germany, France, and Belgium did not always follow the logic of these arguments for a policy of unrestricted industry, but sometimes they did. Such policies deepened class bitterness.

Historians still debate just how bad workers' conditions were in the early stages of in-

dustrialization. Although most workers experienced periods of acute distress, particularly during and immediately after the French Revolution and Napoleonic Wars, historians generally conclude that the standard of living improved over the eighteenth and nineteenth centuries. Although they may take an optimistic view about the long-range effects of industrialization, it is nonetheless true that the rapidity of change itself worked great hardships on the workers of all countries. They faced cruel conditions in factories and slums; craft workers faced competition from machines and displacement; and Irish farm laborers and their families faced starvation during the midcentury Great Famine that decimated their population. Emigration to England, Britain's colonies, or to the United States might mean that Irish workers might escape starvation, but they lived desperately hard lives. And for those workers in Europe who did not emigrate, statistical evidence showing an increase in the quantity of goods they received does not reveal much about the deprivations in the quality of life that men, women, and children experienced as they moved from rural communities to urban factories, slums, and daily insecurity.

Industrialization in Perspective

In 1851 the people who attended the great Crystal Palace exhibition in London knew they were on the threshold of a new age of industrialization. The Crystal Palace was a gigantic temple of glass and cast iron—an exhibition hall in which a modern version of the medieval fair was housed to glorify the industrial greatness of the nations that entered exhibits and sent delegates. The spectators marveled at the displays of inventions like the sewing machine and the McCormick reaper, and they gazed at the quality of goods from many nations (many of which were still made by artisans rather than factory workers). For a century, the process of industrialization

Chemical Lectures, 1810, by Thomas Rowlandson (1756–1827). The reaction of polite society to advances in science and industry is captured in this cartoon by Rowlandson. (*The British Museum*)

had been going on, but it was new and startling to those—including princes, princesses, and potentates—who visited the Crystal Palace. The circus atmosphere, with its 1,500 exhibits, celebrated the Industrial Revolution that was transforming Europe and the United States.

In 1851 the whole legacy of industrialization was undreamed of by even the most enthusiastic spectator viewing the new inventions. In the long run the Industrial Revolution was a great force for the democratization of human life, but democratization would take place slowly over the nineteenth and twentieth centuries. The French working class, which won the right to vote in 1848, did so because of the political tradition of their nation, not because of their economic role in industrialization. Economic power would not come for more than a generation after midcentury. In

no other country had workers won the suffrage. The middle class, however, had won representation in France, Britain, and parts of central Europe at midcentury, which indicated that the social power of landowners was slowly losing ground to forces arising from industrialization. Gradually across the century, first the middle class and then the working class gained the right to participate in the political life of their countries. The secularization of society—that is, the movement away from belonging to a community of families united by religious belief and customary ceremony—had begun in some places, but by the mid-nineteenth century in most of Europe, the priest, the village, and the family were still the dominant social forces.

The urbanization of Europe and America had barely begun, but people were aware of the problems that would follow greater industrialization and were trying, within their respective political frameworks, to adopt reform measures. The growth of state power and its influence on everyone's life, which would take place in the second half of the nineteenth century and drastically alter political life in this century, hardly seemed inevitable in 1851. Far-flung Europeanization, which would be forced on the world in the last half of the century, was scarcely foreseen by those who attended the Crystal Palace exhibition.

The social thought of liberals, conservatives, and radicals, was sometimes brilliantly prescient with regard to the problems that faced modern industrial society. But the institutions with which the best-intentioned reformers had to work were survivals of the old regime—although adapted and modified, they were still tools for governing another society, not an industrialized one. Sometimes, social thought was romantically nostalgic for "the good old days," when master knew his man and both had obligations to one another. Sometimes even the most ardently revolutionary "realists" incorporated in their vision of the future a romantic nostalgia for conditions of work that had not existed for more than a century, if they had ever existed. Yet the social thought of the first half of the nineteenth century supplied the ideas and analysis with which, until deep into our century, men and women tried to understand and to mold their industrializing world.

Suggested Reading

The Cambridge Economic History of Europe, vol. 6 (1965). Includes several fine essays on industrialization, all by specialists in central and eastern Europe.

Cameron, Rondo, *France and the Economic Development of Europe, 1800–1914* (1975). Puts emphasis on France's role as investor in the development of the rest of Europe.

Clapham, J. H., *Economic Development in France and Germany, 1815–1914*, 4th ed. (1935). A classic work.

Deane, Phyllis, *The First Industrial Revolution, 1750–1850* (1965). An excellent introduction.

Halévy, Elie, *A History of the English People in the Nineteenth Century*, Vols. 1–3, rev. ed. (1949). A classic work.

Hamerow, Theodore, *Restoration, Revolution, Reaction: Economics and Politics in Germany, 1815–1871* (1958). Traces the economic and social developments that contributed to the failure to establish a liberal Germany.

Himmelfarb, Gertrude, *The Idea of Poverty: England in the Early Industrial Age* (1983). A brilliant history of English social thought focused on the condition of the poor.

Hobsbawm, Eric, *The Age of Revolution 1789–1848* (1964). A general survey from a Marxist viewpoint of the political and economic history of the period.

———, *Labouring Men* (1964). A number of controversial essays on labor and social history.

Landes, David, *The Unbound Prometheus: Technological Change and Industrial Development in Western Europe from 1750 to the Present* (1969). A classic treatment of a complex subject, beautifully and intelligently written.

Langer, William L., *Political and Social Upheaval 1832–1852* (1969). An excellent source with good references and bibliography.

Thompson, Edward P., *Making of the English Working Class* (1966). A very readable, dramatic, enormously influential, and controversial book.

Webb, R. K., *Modern England from the Eighteenth Century* (1967 and 1980). A text that is balanced, well-written, well-informed, and up-to-date on historical controversies.

Novels of special note:

Balzac, Honoré de, *Eugenie Grandet; Père Goriot*. A great novelist's studies of the decay of human character under social and economic pressures.

Dickens, Charles, *Hard Times; Our Mutual Friend; Oliver Twist*. The great humanitarian's social protest novels.

Disraeli, Benjamin, *Sybil*. A politician's program in novel form.

Zola, Émile, *Germinal*. Published in 1885, the condition of miners described is drawn from the 1850s and 1860s. Very interesting to compare with Richard Llewellyn's novel of Welsh miners *How Green Was My Valley.*

Review Questions

1. Why did England experience industrialization before the rest of Europe? How did political and social factors influence industrialization in England?

2. How did political and social factors influence industrialization, or the lack of it, in France, in the German states, in the Netherlands?

3. How did changes in European agriculture in the early nineteenth century reflect the impact of capitalism and of industrialization?

4. What factors promoted the growth of cities between 1800 and 1860?

5. Historians argue about the relative importance of labor, capital, government, technological invention, and natural resources and geography in the process of industrialization. Construct arguments for the primacy of each of these factors on the basis of the experience of the first industrial revolution.

6. Historians argue for and against the concept of Industrial Revolution. What are the arguments that they would make that industrialization is a slow process? What are the arguments that they would make that industrialization as experienced by 1850 was rapid?

7. What groups were designated middle class in nineteenth-century Europe? What groups were designated working class, or lower orders, in nineteenth-century Europe? Why did contemporaries and some historians make the terms plural?

8. Why did organized religion play a decreasing role in the lives of working-class people in the middle of the nineteenth century?

9. What aspects of working-class culture did the middle class try to change or reform in the nineteenth century?

10. How did the law discriminate against and punish the working class during the early stages of industrialization? How did it try to protect it?

22

Ferment of Ideas: Romanticism,
Conservatism, Liberalism, Radicalism,
Early Socialism, Nationalism

Romanticism: A New Cultural Orientation
Exalting Imagination and Feelings
Nature, God, History
The Impact of the Romantic Movement

Conservatism: The Value of Tradition
Hostility to the French Revolution
The Quest for Social Stability

Liberalism: The Value of the Individual
The Sources of Liberalism
Individual Liberty
Liberal Economic Theory
Liberalism and Democracy

Radicalism and Democracy: The Expansion of Liberalism

Early Socialism: New Possibilities for Society
Saint-Simon: Technocratic Socialism
Fourier: Psychological Socialism
Owen: Industrial Socialism

Nationalism: The Sacredness of the Nation
The Emergence of Modern Nationalism
Nationalism and Liberalism

*I*n 1815 the armies of France no longer marched across the Continent, and Napoleon was imprisoned on an island a thousand miles off the coast of Africa. The traditional rulers of Europe, some of them just restored to power, were determined to protect themselves and society from future Robespierres who organized reigns of terror and Napoleons who obliterated traditional states. As defenders of the status quo, they attacked the reformist spirit of the philosophes that had produced the Revolution. In *conservatism*, which championed tradition over reason, hierarchy over equality, and the community over the individual, they found a philosophy to justify their assault on the Enlightenment and the French Revolution.

But the forces unleashed by the French Revolution had penetrated European consciousness too deeply to be eradicated. One force for revolution was *liberalism*, which aimed to secure the liberty and equality proclaimed by the French Revolution. Another was *nationalism*, which called for the liberation of subject peoples and the unification of broken nations.

The postrevolutionary period also saw a new cultural orientation. *Romanticism*, with its plea for the liberation of human emotions and the free expression of personality, challenged the Enlightenment stress on rationalism. Although primarily a literary and artistic movement, Romanticism also permeated philosophy and political thought, particularly conservatism.

Still another force emerging in the post-Napoleonic period was socialism. Reacting to the problems created by the Industrial Revolution, socialists called for creating a new society based on cooperation rather than on capitalist competition. A minor movement in the era from 1815 to 1848, socialism in its Marxist version became a major intellectual and social force in the last part of the century.

Romanticism: A New Cultural Orientation

The Romantic Movement, which began in the closing decades of the eighteenth century, dominated European cultural life in the first half of the nineteenth century. Historians recognize the prominence of romanticism in nineteenth-century cultural life, but the movement was so complex, and the differences so innumerable among the various romantic writers, artists, and musicians that historians cannot agree on a definition of romanticism. Romantics were both liberals and conservatives, revolutionaries and reactionaries; some were preoccupied with religion and God, while others paid little attention to faith.

Most of Europe's leading cultural figures came under the influence of the Romantic Movement. Among the exponents of romanticism were the poets Shelley, Wordsworth, Keats, and Byron in England; the novelist Victor Hugo and the Catholic philosopher Chateaubriand in France; the writers A. W. and Friedrich Schlegel and philosophers Schiller and Schelling in Germany. Caspar David Friedrich in Germany and John Constable in England expressed the romantic mood in art, and the later Beethoven, Schubert, Chopin, and Wagner expressed it in music.

Exalting Imagination and Feelings

Perhaps the central message of the romantics was that the imagination of the individual should determine the form and content of an artistic creation. This outlook ran counter to the rationalism of the Enlightenment, which itself had been a reaction against the otherworldly Christian orientation of the Middle Ages. The philosophes had attacked faith because it thwarted and distorted reason; romantic poets, philosophers, and artists now denounced the rationalism of the philosophes because it crushed the emotions and impeded creativity. The philosophes, said the romantics, had turned flesh-and-blood human beings into soulless thinking machines, and vibrant nature into lifeless wheels, cogs, and pulleys. The reign of reason had separated individuals from their feelings; it had prevented them from realizing their human nature; it had deadened their hearts and paralyzed their wills. To restore human beings to their true nature, to make them whole again, they must be emancipated from the tyranny of excessive intellectualizing; the feelings must be nourished and expressed. Taking up one of Rousseau's ideas, romantics yearned to rediscover a pristine freedom and creativity in the human soul that had been squashed by habits, values, rules, and standards imposed by civilization.

The philosophes had concentrated on people in general—those elements of human nature shared by all people. Romantics, on the other hand, emphasized human uniqueness—those distinctive traits that set one human being apart from others. Each person yearns to discover and to express his or her true self. Each plays his or her own music; each writes his or her own poetry; each paints his or her own personal vision of nature. Each experiences love and suffering in his or her own way. In the opening lines of his autobiography, *Confessions,* Jean Jacques Rousseau, a romantic in an age of reason, expressed the intense subjectivism that characterized the Romantic Movement:

I am commencing an undertaking, hitherto without precedent and which will never find an imitator. I desire to set before my fellows the likeness of a man in all the truth of nature, and that man myself. Myself alone! I know the feelings of my heart, and I know men. I am not made like any of those I have seen. I venture to believe that I am not made like any of those who are in existence. If I am not better, at least I am different.[1]

Whereas the philosophes had regarded the feelings as an obstacle to clear thinking, to the romantics they were the human essence. People could not live by reason alone, said the romantics. They agreed with Rousseau, who wrote: "For us, to exist is to feel and our sensibility is incontestably prior to our reason."[2] For the romantics, reason was cold and dreary, its understanding of people and life meager and inadequate. Reason could not comprehend or express the complexities of human nature nor the richness of human experience. By always dissecting and analyzing, by imposing deadening structure and form, and by demanding adherence to strict rules, reason crushed inspiration and creativity and barred true understanding. "The Reasoning Power in Man," said William Blake, the British poet, artist, and mystic, is "an incrustation over my immortal Spirit."[3]

For the romantics, the avenue to truth was not the intellect, but spontaneous human emotions. By cultivating instincts and imagination, individuals could experience reality and discover their authentic selves. The romantics wanted people to feel and to experience—to "bathe in the waters of life," said Blake.[4] Or as Johann Goethe, Germany's great poet, wrote in *Faust:* "My worthy friend, gray are all theories,/And green alone Life's golden tree."[5]

For this reason, the romantics insisted that imaginative poets had a greater insight into life than analytical philosphers did. Poetry is a true philosophy, the romantics said; it can do what rational analysis and geometric calculations cannot—clarify life's deepest mysteries, participate in the eternal, and penetrate to the depths of human nature. "I am certain of nothing but of the holiness of the Heart's affections and the truth of Imagination," wrote John Keats. "O for a Life of Sensations rather than of Thoughts,"[6] For reason to function best, it must be nourished by the poetic imagination.

The Enlightenment mind had been clear, critical, and controlled. It had adhered to standards of aesthetics thought to be universal that had dominated European cultural life since the Renaissance. That mind stressed technique and form and tended to reduce the imagination to mechanical relationships. "Analysis and calculation make the poet, as they make the mathematician," wrote Étienne

Condillac, a prominent French philosophe. "Once the material of a play is given, the invention of the plot, the characters, the verse, is only a series of algebraic problems to be worked out."[7] Following in this tradition, Népomucène Lemercier determined that there were twenty-six rules for tragedy, twenty-three for comedy, and twenty-four for the epic; he proceeded to manufacture plays and epics according to this formula.

Romantic poets, artists, and musicians broke with the traditional styles and austere rules and created new cultural forms and techniques. "We do not want either Greek or Roman Models," said Blake, but should be "just and true to our own Imaginations."[8] For the romantics, one did not learn how to write poetry or paint pictures by following textbook rules; one could not comprehend the poet's or artist's intent by judging works according to fixed standards. "It is the beginning of poetry," wrote Friedrich Schlegel, "to abolish the law and the method of the rationally proceeding reason and to plunge us once more into the ravishing confusion of fantasy, the original chaos of human nature."[9] Only by trusting to their own feelings could individuals fulfill their creative potential and achieve self-realization. The most beautiful works of art, for example, were not photographic imitations of nature, but authentic and spontaneous expressions of the artist's feelings, fantasies, and dreams. Similarly, the romantics were less impressed by Beethoven's constructions than by the intensity and fury that this music embodied.

The romantics explored the inner life of the mind that Freud would later call *the unconscious.* It was this layer of the mind—mysterious, primitive, more elemental and more powerful than reason, the wellspring of creativity—that the romantics yearned to revitalize and release.

Nature, God, History

The philosophes had viewed nature as a lifeless machine—a giant clock, all of whose parts worked together in perfect precision and har-

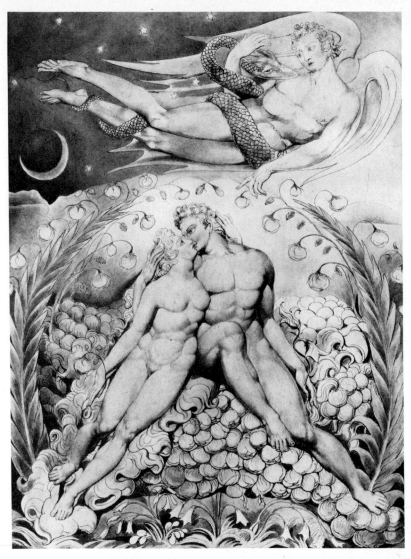

William Blake (1757–1827): Satan Watching the Caresses of Adam and Eve, 1808. An early romantic poet and artist, William Blake was also a mystic who believed that heavenly messengers dictated his poetry to him. He held that reason was destructive to the imagination, expressed admiration for the Middle Ages, and had visions of angels and devils. (*Courtesy, Museum of Fine Arts, Boston*)

mony. Nature's laws, operating with mathematical certainty, were uncovered by the methodology of science. To the romantics, nature was alive and suffused with God's presence. Nature stimulated the creative energies of the imagination; it taught human beings a higher form of knowledge, as William Wordsworth wrote:

One impulse from a vernal wood
May teach you more of man,
Of moral evil and of good,
Than all the sages can.[10]

For the romantics, nature did not consist of mechanical parts, but of trees, lakes, mountains, clouds, and stars; one experienced nature in an emotional way seeking mystical union. Not the mathematician's logic, but the poet's imagination unlocked nature's most important secrets. In perhaps the most vigorous application of this principle, English romantics reacted against their country's drab factories—the "dark satanic mills" that deprived life of its joy and separated people from nature.

The philosophes had seen God as a great watchmaker—an idle observer of a self-operating mechanical universe—and they tried to reduce religion to a series of scientific propositions. Many romantics viewed God as a spiritual force that inspired people, and they deplored the decline of Christianity. The cathedrals and ceremonies, poetic and mysterious, satisfied the aesthetic impulse; Christian moral commands, compassionate and just, elevated human behavior to a higher level. The romantics condemned the philosophes for weakening Christianity by submitting its dogmas to the test of reason. For the romantics, religion was not science and syllogism, but a passionate and authentic expression of human nature.

The philosophes had viewed the Middle Ages as an era of darkness, superstition, and fanaticism and regarded surviving medieval institutions and traditions as barriers to progress. The romantics, on the other hand, revered the Middle Ages. The wars of the French Revolution, Napoleon, and the breakdown of political equilibrium had produced a sense of foreboding about the future. Some sought spiritual security by looking back to the Middle Ages when Europe was united by a single faith. Then, said romantics, no rationalist's blade dissected and slashed Christian mysteries; no wild-eyed revolutionaries tore apart the fabric of society. To the romantic imagination, the Middle Ages abounded with heroic deeds, noble sentiments, and social harmony.

Romantics and philosophes held differing conceptions of history. For the philosophes, history served a didactic purpose by providing examples of human folly. Such knowledge assisted people in preparing for a better fu-

ture, and for that reason alone history should be studied. To the romantics, a historical period, like an individual, was a unique entity with its own soul. They wanted the historian to portray and analyze the bewildering variety of nations, traditions, and institutions that constituted the historical experience. The command of the romantics to study the specific details of history and culture and to comprehend them within the context of their times is the foundation of modern historical scholarship.

Searching for universal principles, the philosophes had dismissed folk traditions as peasant superstitions and impediments to progress. The romantics, on the other hand, rebelling against the standardization of culture, saw native languages, songs, and legends as the unique creations of a people and the deepest expression of national feeling. The romantics regarded the legends, myths, and folk traditions of a people as the wellspring of poetry and art, the spiritual source of a people's cultural vitality and creativity. Hence they examined these earliest cultural expressions with awe and reverence. In this way, romanticism was instrumental in the shaping of modern nationalism.

The Impact of the Romantic Movement

The romantic revolt against the Enlightenment had an important and enduring impact on European history. By focusing on the creative capacities inherent in the emotions—intuition, instinct, passion, will, empathy—the romantics shed light on a side of human nature that the philosophes had often overlooked or undervalued. By encouraging personal freedom and flexibility in art, music, and literature, they greatly enriched European cultural life. Future artists, writers, and musicians would proceed along the path paved by the romantics. Modern art, for example, owes much to the Romantic Movement's emphasis on the legitimacy of human feeling and its exploration of the hidden world of dreams and fantasies. The romantic emphasis on feeling sometimes found expression in humanitarian movements that fought slavery, child labor, and poverty. By recognizing the distinctive qualities of historical periods, peoples, and cultures, the romantics helped to create the modern historical outlook. By valuing the nation's past, romanticism contributed to modern nationalism and conservatism.

But there was a potentially dangerous side to the Romantic Movement. By waging their attack on reason with excessive zeal, the romantics undermined the rational foundations of the West. The romantic idealization of the past and glorification of ancient folkways, native soil, and native language introduced a highly charged, nonrational component into political life. In the decades to come, romanticism, particularly in Germany, fused with political nationalism and "created a general climate of inexact thinking, an intellectual . . . dream world and an emotional approach to problems of political action to which sober reasoning should have been applied."[11]

The philosophes would have regarded the romantics' veneration of a people's history and traditions, their search for a nation's soul in an archaic culture, as barbarous—a regression to superstition, the triumph of myth over philosophy. Indeed, when transferred to the realm of politics, the romantics' idolization of the past did reawaken a mythic way of thinking about the world, which rested more on feeling than on reason. In the process, people became committed to ideas that were fraught with danger.

Conservatism: The Value of Tradition

To the traditional rulers of Europe—kings, aristocrats, clergy—the French Revolution was a great evil that had inflicted a near-fatal wound on civilization. As far as they were concerned, the revolutionaries heralded chaos

Lord Byron (1788–1824). One of the leading romantic poets, Byron created the "Byronic hero," a lonely and mysterious figure. His own short life exalted the emotions and the senses. He went to Greece in 1824 to aid the revolutionaries and died there from poor health. (*Historical Pictures Service, Chicago*)

when they executed Louis XVI, confiscated the land of the church, destroyed the special privileges of the aristocracy, and instituted the Reign of Terror. Then the Revolution gave rise to Napoleon, who deposed kings, continued the assault on the aristocracy, and sought to dominate Europe. Disgusted and frightened by the revolutionary violence, terror, and warfare, the traditional rulers sought to refute the philosophes' world-view that had spawned the Revolution. To them, natural rights, equality, the goodness of man, and perpetual progress were perverse doctrines that had produced the Jacobin "assassins." In conservatism they found a political philosophy to counter the Enlightenment ideology.

Edmund Burke's *Reflections on the French Revolution* (1790) was instrumental in shaping conservative thought. Burke (1729–1797), a British philosopher and statesman, wanted to warn his countrymen of the dangers inherent in the ideology of the revolutionaries. Although writing in 1790, Burke astutely predicted that the Revolution would lead to terror and military dictatorship. To Burke, fanatics armed with pernicious principles—abstract ideas divorced from historical experience—had dragged France through the mire of revolution. Burke developed a coherent political philosophy that served as a counterweight to the ideology of the Enlightenment and the Revolution.

Hostility to the French Revolution

The philosophes and French reformers, entranced by the great discoveries in science, had believed that the human mind could also transform social institutions and ancient traditions according to rational models. Progress through reason became their faith. Dedicated to creating a new future, the revolutionaries abruptly dispensed with old habits, traditional authority, and familiar ways of thought.

To conservatives, who like the romantics venerated the past, this was supreme arrogance and wickedness. They regarded the revolutionaries as presumptuous men who recklessly severed society's links with ancient institutions and traditions and condemned venerable religious and moral beliefs as ignorance. Moreover, the revolutionaries forgot—or never knew—that the traditions and institutions they wanted to destroy did not belong solely to them. Past generations and indeed future generations had a claim to these creations of French genius. By attacking time-honored ways, the revolutionaries had deprived French society of moral leadership and had opened the door to anarchy and terror. "You began ill," said Burke of the revolutionaries, "because you began by despising everything that belonged to you. . . . When ancient opinions and rules of life are taken away, the loss cannot possibly be estimated. From that moment we have no compass to govern us; nor can we know distinctly to what port we steer."[12]

The philosophes and French reformers had expressed unlimited confidence in the power of the human intellect to understand and to change society. While appreciating human rational capacities, conservatives also recognized the limitations of reason. They saw the Revolution as a natural outgrowth of an arrogant Enlightenment philosophy that overvalued reason and sought to reshape society in accordance with abstract principles.

For conservatives, human beings were not by nature good. Human wickedness was not due to a faulty environment, as the philosophes had proclaimed, but was at the core of human nature, as Christianity taught. Evil was held in check not by reason, but by tried and tested institutions, traditions, and beliefs. Without these habits inherited from ancestors, said conservatives, the social order was threatened by sinful human nature.

Because monarchy, aristocracy, and the church had endured for centuries, argued the conservatives, they had worth. The clergy taught proper moral values; monarchs preserved order and property; aristocrats guarded against despotic kings and the tyranny of the common people. All protected and spread civilized ways. By despising and uprooting these ancient institutions, the revolutionaries had hardened the people's hearts, perverted their morals, and caused them to commit terrible outrages upon each other and society.

Conservatives detested attempts to transform society according to a theoretical model. They felt that human nature was too intricate and that social relations were too complex for such social engineering. For conservatives, the revolutionaries had reduced people and society to abstractions divorced from their historical settings; consequently, they had destroyed ancient patterns that seemed inconvenient and had drawn up constitutions based on the unacceptable principle that government derives its power from the consent of the governed.

For conservatives, God and history were the only legitimate sources of political authority; states were not made, but were an expression of the nation's moral, religious, and historical experience. No legitimate or sound constitution could be drawn up by a group assembled for that purpose. Scraps of paper with legal terminology and philosophic visions could not produce an effective government; instead, a sound political system evolved gradually and inexplicably in response to circumstances. For this reason, conservatives admired the English constitution. It was not a product of abstract thought; no assembly had convened to fashion it. Because it grew imperceptibly out of the historical experience and needs of the English people, it was durable and effective.

For conservatives, society was not a machine with replaceable parts, but a complex and delicate organism. Tamper with its vital organs, as the revolutionaries had done, and it would die.

The Quest for Social Stability

The liberal philosophy of the Enlightenment and the French Revolution started with the individual. The philosophes and the revolutionaries envisioned a society in which the individual was free and autonomous. Conservatives believed that society was not a mechanical arrangement of disconnected individuals, but a living organism held together by centuries-old bonds. Alone, a person would be selfish, unreliable, frail; it was only as a member of a social group—family, church, or state—that one acquired the ways of cooperation and the manners of civilization. By exalting the individual, the revolutionaries had threatened to dissolve society into disconnected parts. Individualism would imperil social stability, destroy obedience to law, and fragment society into self-seeking isolated atoms.

Holding that the community was more important than the individual, conservatives rejected the philosophy of natural rights. Rights were not abstractions that preceded an individual's entrance into society and pertained to all people everywhere. Rather, the state,

always remembering the needs of the entire community and its links to past generations, determined what rights and privileges its citizens might possess. There were no "rights of man," only rights of the French, the English, and so forth, as determined and allocated by the particular state.

Conservatives viewed equality as another pernicious abstraction that contradicted all historical experience. For conservatives, society was naturally hierarchical, and they believed that some men by virtue of their intelligence, education, wealth, and birth were best qualified to rule and instruct the less able. They said that by denying the existence of a natural elite and uprooting a long-established ruling elite that had learned its art though experience, the revolutionaries had deprived society of effective leaders, brought internal disorder, and prepared the way for a military dictatorship.

Whereas the philosophes had attacked Christianity for promoting superstition and fanaticism, conservatives saw religion as the basis of civil society. Excess liberty and the weakening of religion had brutalized people and shattered the foundations of society. Catholic conservatives, in particular, held that God had constituted the church and monarchy to check sinful human nature. "Christian monarchs are the final creation of the development of political society and of religious society," said Louis de Bonald, a French émigré. "The proof of this lies in the fact that when monarchy and Christianity are both abolished society returns to savagery."[13]

Conservatism pointed to a limitation of the Enlightenment. It showed that human beings and social relationships are far more complex than the philosophes had imagined. People do not always respond to the rigorous logic of the philosopher and are not eager to break with ancient ways, however illogical they appear to the intellect. They often find familiar customs and ancestral religions more satisfying guides to life than the blueprints of philosophers. The granite might of tradition remains an obstacle to all the visions of reformers.

Liberalism: The Value of the Individual

The decades after 1815 saw a spectacular rise of the bourgeoisie. Talented and ambitious bankers, merchants, manufacturers, professionals, and officeholders wanted to break the stranglehold that the landed nobility, the traditional elite, held on political power and social prestige; they also wanted to eliminate restrictions on the free pursuit of profits.

The political philosophy of the bourgeoisie was most commonly liberalism. While conservatives sought to strengthen the foundations of traditional society, which had been severely shaken in the period of the French Revolution and Napoleon, liberals wanted to alter the status quo and to carry out the promise of the Enlightenment and the French Revolution. Conservatives concentrated on the community, but liberals gave central concern to individual freedom. Conservatives tried to preserve a social hierarchy based on inherited aristocracy, but liberals insisted that a person's value was measured not by birth but by achievement. Conservatives held that the state rests on tradition, but liberals sought the rational state in which political institutions and procedures were based on intelligible principles. Conservatives wanted individuals, inherently evil, to obey their betters. Liberals, on the other hand, had confidence in the capacity of individuals to control their own lives.

The Sources of Liberalism

In the long view of Western civilization, liberalism is an extension and development of the democratic practices and rational outlook that originated in ancient Greece. Also flowing into the liberal tradition is Judeo-Christian respect for the individual. But the immediate historical roots of nineteenth-century liberalism extended back to seventeenth-century England. At that time, the struggle for religious toleration by English Protestant dissenters established the principle of freedom of conscience, which is easily transferred into freedom of opinion and expression in all matters. The Glorious Revolution of 1688 set limits on the power of the English monarchy. In that same century John Locke's natural-rights philosophy declared that the individual was by nature entitled to freedom, and it justified revolutions against rulers who deprived citizens of their lives, liberty, or property.

The French philosophes were instrumental in the shaping of liberalism. From Montesquieu, liberals derived the theory of the separation of powers and of checks and balances—principles intended to guard against autocratic government. The philosophes had supported religious toleration and freedom of thought, expressed confidence in the capacity of the human mind to reform society, maintained that human beings are essentially good, and believed in the future progress of humanity—all fundamental principles of liberalism.

The American and French revolutions were crucial phases in the history of liberalism. The Declaration of Independence gave expression to Locke's theory of natural rights; the Constitution of the United States incorporated Montesquieu's principles and demonstrated that people could create an effective government; the Bill of Rights protected the person and rights of the individual. In destroying the special privileges of the aristocracy and opening careers to talent, the French National Assembly of 1789 had implemented the liberal ideal of equality under the law. They also drew up the Declaration of the Rights of Man and the Citizen, which affirmed the dignity and rights of the individual, and a constitution that limited the king's power. Both the American and French revolutions explicitly called for the protection of property rights, another basic premise of liberalism.

Individual Liberty

The liberals' central concern was the enhancement of individual liberty. They agreed with German philosopher Immanuel Kant that every person exists as an end in himself or herself and not as an object to be used arbitrarily by others. If uncoerced by government and churches and properly educated, a person could develop into a good, creative, and self-directed human being. Every individual could make his or her own decisions, base actions on universal moral laws, and respect others' rights.

Liberals rejected a legacy of the Middle Ages, the classification of the individual as a commoner or aristocrat on the basis of birth. They held that a man was not born into a certain station in life, but made his way through his own efforts. Taking their cue from the French Revolution, liberals called for an end to all privileges of the aristocracy.

In the tradition of the philosophes, liberals stressed the pre-eminence of reason as the basis of political life. Unfettered by ignorance and tyranny, the mind could eradicate evils that had burdened people for centuries and begin an age of free institutions and responsible citizens. For this reason, liberals supported the advancement of education. They believed that educated people apply reason to their political and social life, and thus they act in ways beneficial to themselves and society and are less likely to submit to tyrants.

Liberals attacked the state and other authorities that prevented the individual from exercising the right of free choice, that interfered with the right of free expression, and that prevented the individual from self-determination and self-development. They agreed with John Stuart Mill, the British philosopher, who declared that "over his own body and mind, the individual is sovereign. . . . that the only purpose for which power can be rightfully exercised over any member of a civilized community, against his will, is to prevent harm to others."[14]

The great question that confronted nineteenth-century liberals was the relationship between state authority and individual liberty. To guard against the absolute and arbitrary authority of kings, liberals demanded written constitutions that granted freedom of speech, the press, and religion; freedom from arbitrary arrest; and the protection of property rights. To prevent the abuse of political authority, liberals called for a freely elected parliament and the distribution of power among the various branches of government. Liberals held that a government that derived its authority from the consent of the governed, as given in free elections, was least likely to violate individual freedom. A corollary of this principle was that the best government is one that governs least—that is, one that interferes as little as possible with the economic activities of its citizens and does not involve itself in their private lives or their beliefs.

Liberal Economic Theory

Liberals held that the economy, like the state, should proceed according to natural laws rather than the arbitrary fiat of rulers. Adopting the laissez-faire theory of Adam Smith, they maintained that a free economy, in which private enterprise would be unimpeded by government regulations, was as important as political freedom to the well-being of the individual and the community. When people acted from self-interest, the liberals said, they worked harder and achieved more; self-interest and natural competitive impulses spurred economic activity and ensured the production of more and better goods at the lowest possible price, thereby benefiting the entire nation. For this reason, the government must neither block free competition nor deprive individuals of their property, which was their incentive to work hard and efficiently. The state contributed to the nation's prosperity when it maintained domestic order; it endangered economic development when it tampered with the free pursuit of profits. Believing that individuals were responsible for their own misfortunes, liberals were often unmoved by the misery of the poor and considered social reforms to alleviate poverty as unwarranted and dangerous meddling with the natural laws of supply and demand.

Nicolò Paganini (1782–1840), by Jean Auguste Dominique Ingres (1780–1867). The structure and order of classical music gave way to sweeping melodies and rich harmonies. Paganini, the composer-performer, stunned audiences with his virtuosity. Paganini's name became synonymous with the violin, as Franz Liszt's was with the piano. (*Louvre/Cliché des Musées Nationaux*)

Two attitudes emerged from liberal economic principles—one optimistic, hoping for the expansion of human productive capacities and the end of want; and the other pessimistic, predicting a cycle of increasing pressure on scarce resources and deepening competition among workers for the necessities of life. For the first half of the nineteenth century, Thomas Malthus (1766–1834), author of the *Essay on the Principle of Population,* had an impact as great as Adam Smith's on the lives of workers and the thought of reformers. Malthus argued that population increase would outstrip increases in food production, which suggested that the poverty of the

working class was permanent. Malthus reasoned that if wages were raised, workers' families would grow and the extra wages would be used to support the added members. This doctrine was called Malthusianism and seemed to supply "scientific" justification for opposing governmental action to aid the poor; for poverty was an iron law of nature, the result of population pressure on resources.

Fellow economist David Ricardo (1772–1823) used Malthus' idea to form another theory that also made poverty seem inevitable and irremediable. Wages, he said, tended to remain at the minimum needed to maintain workers. An increase in wages encouraged laborers to increase their families. As the supply of workers increased, competition for jobs also increased, causing wages to decline. Ricardo's disciples made his law inflexible—an "Iron Law of Wages," which offered dismal prospects. Further, Ricardo reasoned that the scarcity of goods and well-located land drew more of society's resources to the landowning class, rather than to the capitalists who invested in machinery and other products that would steadily increase productivity. Thus, land scarcity would tend to put a brake on possible growth, and in Ricardo's view, without growth there could be no increase in the standard of living.

Many workers felt the new science of economics offered little hope for them. They argued that the liberals were only concerned with their class and national interests, that they were hard, callous, and apathetic toward the sufferings of the poor. The liberals responded that the cure for the evils of industrialization was more industrialization.

Early in the nineteenth century, liberals feared that state interference in the economy to redress social ills would threaten individual rights and the free market that they thought was essential to personal liberty. They also feared privileged groups and preferred a weak state to a powerful one in the hands of the elite. In time, the liberals modified their position, first supporting government action to provide education or opportunity for all and then accepting the principle of state aid to the poor. They came to believe that justice required some protection against the economy's ravages for those who were powerless. They thought reform was possible without losing the advantages of capitalism and without sacrificing personal liberty.

Liberalism and Democracy

The French Revolution presented a dilemma for liberals. They supported the reforms of the moderate stage: the destruction of the special privileges of the aristocracy, the drawing up of a declaration of rights and a constitution, the establishment of a parliament, the opening of careers to talent; but they repudiated Jacobin radicalism. Liberals were frightened by the excesses of the Jacobin regime: its tampering with the economy, which liberals felt violated the rights of private property; its appeal to the "little people," which they felt invited mob rule; its subjection of the individual to the state, which they regarded as the denial of individual rights; its use of the guillotine, which awakened the basest human feelings.

Although many liberals still adhered to the philosophy of natural rights, some who were disturbed by the Jacobin experience discarded the theory underlying the reforms of the Revolution. These liberals, fearing social disorder as much as conservatives did, did not want to ignite revolutions by the masses. In the hands of the lower classes, the natural-rights philosophy was too easily translated into the democratic creed that all people should share in political power, a prospect that the bourgeois regarded with horror. To them, the participation of commoners in politics meant a vulgar form of despotism and the end to individual liberty. The masses—uneducated, unpropertied, inexperienced, and impatient—had neither the ability nor the temperament to maintain liberty and protect property.

In this new age, said Alexis de Tocqueville, a French political theorist, the masses had a passion for equality, not liberty. They de-

manded that the avenue to social, economic, and political advancement be opened to all; they no longer accepted disparity in wealth and position as part of the natural order. They would willingly sacrifice political liberty to improve their material well-being. Looking to the state as the guarantor of equality, said de Tocqueville, the people would grant it ever more power. The state then would regulate its citizens' lives, crush local institutions impeding centralized control, and impose the beliefs of the majority on the minority. Liberty would be lost not to the despotism of kings, but to the tyranny of the majority.

Because bourgeois liberals feared that democracy could crush personal freedom as ruthlessly as any absolute monarch could, they called for property requirements for voting and officeholding. They wanted political power to be concentrated in the hands of a safe and reliable—that is, a propertied and educated—middle class. Such a government would prevent revolution from below, a prospect that caused anxiety among bourgeois liberals.

Early nineteenth-century liberals engaged in revolutions, to be sure, but their aims were always limited. Once they had destroyed absolute monarchy and gained a constitution and a parliament or a change of government, they quickly tried to terminate the revolution. When the fever of revolution spread to the masses, liberals either withdrew or turned counterrevolutionary, for they feared the stirrings of the multitude.

Although liberalism was the political philosophy of a middle class generally hostile to democracy, the essential ideals of democracy flowed logically from liberalism. Eventually, democracy became a later stage in the evolution of liberalism, because the masses, their political power enhanced by the Industrial Revolution, would press for greater social, political, and economic equality. Thus, by the early twentieth century, many European states had introduced universal suffrage, abandoned property requirements for officeholding, and improved conditions for workers.

But the fears of nineteenth-century liberals were not without foundation. In the twentieth century, the participation of common people in politics has indeed threatened freedom. Impatient with parliamentary procedures, the masses, particularly when troubled by economic problems, have in some instances turned their support to demagogues who promised swift and decisive action. The granting of political participation to the masses has not always made people more free. The confidence of democrats has been shaken in the twentieth century by the seeming willingness of common people to trade freedom for authority, order, economic security, and national power.

Radicalism and Democracy: The Expansion of Liberalism

In the early nineteenth century democratic ideals were advanced by thinkers and activists called radicals. Inspired by the democratic principles expressed in Rousseau's *Social Contract* and by the republican stage of the French Revolution, French radicals championed popular sovereignty—rule by the people. In contrast to liberals, who feared the masses, French radicals trusted the common person. Advocating universal suffrage and a republic, radicalism gained the support of French workers in the 1830s and 1840s.

English radicals, like their liberal cousins, inherited the Enlightenment's confidence in reason and its belief in the essential goodness of the individual. In the first half of the nineteenth century, English radicals sought parliamentary reforms, because some heavily populated districts were barely represented in Parliament, while lightly populated districts were overrepresented; they demanded payment for members of Parliament to permit the nonwealthy to hold office; they sought universal manhood suffrage to give the masses representation in Parliament; and they insisted on the secret ballot to prevent intim-

idation. Radicals attacked the aristocracy and the privileged, and many supported the working-class struggle for reform.

British radicalism was inspired by Tom Paine (1737–1809) and Jeremy Bentham (1748–1832). Responding to Burke's *Reflections on the French Revolution,* Paine, in the *Rights of Man* (published in two parts in 1791 and 1792), denounced reverence for tradition, defended the principle of natural rights, and praised as progress the destruction of the Old Regime. From Paine, the English radical tradition acquired a faith in reason and human goodness, a skeptical attitude toward established institutions, a dislike of organized religion, the belief that the goal of government was the greater happiness of ordinary people, and the conviction that the exclusion of common people from political participation was an injustice.

In contrast to Paine, Jeremy Bentham rejected the doctrine of natural rights as an abstraction that had no basis in reality, and he regarded the French Revolution as an absurd attempt to reconstruct society on the basis of principles as misguided as those that had supported the Old Regime. Bentham's importance to the English radical tradition derives from his principle of *utility,* which he offered as a guide to reformers. The central fact of human existence, said Bentham, is that human beings seek to gratify their desires, that they prefer pleasure to pain. Consequently any political, economic, judicial, or social institution and any legislation should be judged according to a simple standard: does it bring about the greatest happiness for the greatest number? If not, it should be swept away. By focusing on the need for reform on every level of society and by urging a careful and objective analysis of social issues, Bentham contributed substantially to the shaping of British radicalism.

Bentham said that those in power had always used what they considered the highest principles—God's teachings, universal standards, honored traditions—to justify their political and social systems, their moral codes, and their laws. On the highest grounds, they

Art in a Revolutionary Era: Rococo, Neoclassical & Romantic

Figure 1 Pierre Vignon: Church of the Madeleine, Paris. (*Ciccione/Rapho*)

Figure 2 *Left:* Francois Boucher: *The Toilet of Venus,* 1751. Oil on canvas. H. 42 5/8 in. W. 33 1/2 in. (*The Metropolitan Museum of Art, Bequest of William K. Vanderbilt, 1920*)

Figure 3 *Below:* Antonio Canova: *Pauline Borghese as Venus,* 1808. Marble, life-size. (*Borghese Gallery, Rome/Scala/Art Resource*)

Figure 4 *Opposite:* Jacques Louis David: *Le Sacre.* (*Louvre/Scala/Art Resource*)

In mid-eighteenth century France, François Boucher (1703–1770) epitomized the style known as Rococo (Figure 2). In *The Toilet of Venus*, as in his other works, his palette is light, his brushwork quick and feathery. In this prerevolutionary era, he presents the gods and goddesses of the ancients as gay, amorous playmates relaxing in fanciful bucolic settings. Almost all of Boucher's works were intended to decorate specific rooms and were embedded in elaborate, gilded wood panelling. *The Toilet of Venus* and a companion piece were originally installed as overdoors of the dressing room of the Marquise de Pompadour, mistress of Louis XV.

As one might expect, in this Enlightenment period the philosophes reacted against the uses and meanings of Rococo style and advocated a very different function for art. They argued that the artist's role should be to inspire people to work for noble causes, such as justice and the honor of one's country.

The most appropriate models, they believed, could be derived from ancient history, so young men were encouraged to study in Italy where examples of classical art were to be found.

The new values of the Enlightenment spread and influenced many countries and their art. Across the channel in England, the idea of marriage based upon affection, rather than on financial convenience, may have influenced Thomas Gainsborough (1727–1788). The pose of the couple in *The Morning Walk* (Figure 5) conveys the couple's mutual respect and dignity. The well-to-do English couples who sat for Gainsborough portraits were often the same patrons who commissioned interiors like the library at Kenwood House (Figure 6) by designer Robert Adam (1728–1792). The exteriors of many contemporary buildings were designed in neoclassical style, but Adam was the first to use Greek and Roman motifs in interiors.

Figure 5 Sir Thomas Gainsborough: *Mr. and Mrs. William Hallett* (*The Morning Walk*), 1785. (*National Gallery, London*)

Figure 6 Robert Adam: The Adam Library, Kenwood House, Hampstead, 1767–1769. (*A. F. Kersting*)

Figure 7 *Above:* John Constable: *The Haywain,* 1821. (*National Gallery, London*)

Figure 8 *Opposite:* J. M. W. Turner: *Burning of the Houses of Parliament,* c. 1835. Oil on canvas. H. 36 1/4 in. W. 48 1/2 in. (*Philadelphia Museum of Art: The John H. McFadden Collection*)

The English played an important role in conducting archaeological excavations, particularly at Pompeii, and artists, Adam among them, went to Rome to study ancient ruins and artifacts. Although the classical elements he used at Kenwood are light enough not to overburden a private interior, many details are archaeologically correct. The niche cut behind the colonnade recalls the Pantheon in Rome (Figure 8 in the first art essay, "Greek Art and Roman Reflections").

In the 1780s, two artists working in Rome produced revolutionary works that met the philosophes' criteria for art and defined the neoclassical style. The new style developed by France's Jacques Louis David (1748–1825) and Italy's Antonio Canova (1757–1822) explored themes of self-sacrifice, valor, and honor in austere compositions, which were stripped of the gaiety and detail of the Rococo. Although one of David's first major neoclassical works was commissioned by Louis XVI, he subsequently became the principal artist of the Jacobin government. For these patrons he produced portraits of martyrs of the French Revolution, such as Marat, murdered by Charlotte Corday.

Later, Napoleon adopted the neoclassical style in a somewhat different form. Clearly structured compositions and references to classical art remained, but they were used to impress the viewer with the ruler's power, as well as with his virtue. For example, David, now in the service of Napoleon, used his gifts for composition to produce a great ceremonial painting (19 by 39 feet) of Napoleon's coronation (Figure 4), called *Le Sacre.*

Wherever members of Napoleon's family

ruled, they patronized the arts. In Canova's grandiloquent portrait of Napoleon's sister Pauline Borghese, she is shown as *Venus Victrix,* the victorious goddess awarded the golden apple for her beauty. The pose recalls classical sculpture, but the colored marbles and gilding of the bed bespeak imperial splendor, rather than republican austerity (Figure 3).

Several famous Paris landmarks link Napoleon with imperial Rome: the column in the Place Vendôme, the Arc de Triomphe, and the Church of the Madeleine (Figure 1). Imitating a Roman temple—which, in turn, imitated the Greeks' Parthenon—the Madeleine was first intended as a temple of glory for the French army. Napoleon himself awarded the commission to Pierre Vignon (1768–1828). The neoclassical building was not completed until long after the fall of Napoleon; it was consecrated as a Christian church in 1842.

Protests against Napoleon—and against totalitarianism and modern war—appear in *The Third of May, 1808* (Figure 9) by Francisco Goya (1746–1828). The painting commemorates French retaliation against thousands of Spanish civilians for the resistance of a few to Napoleon's occupying forces. Painted in 1814, soon after the French had withdrawn, Goya has distilled from the years of brutal occupation an instant of terror, as his helpless countrymen are shot to death. Goya did not portray a massacre by re-creating a work of ancient literature in the neoclassical style. He sought, rather, to explore the emotions and sensibilities of people.

The focus on emotion and sensibility is

Figure 9 Francisco Goya: *The Third of May, 1808,* c. 1814. (*Museo del Prado, Madrid*)

also evident in the work of two English artists of the Romantic period: J. M. W. Turner (1775–1851) and John Constable (1776–1837). Turner often observed nature in its most violent moments, as in *The Burning of the Houses of Parliament* (Figure 8). This fire in October 1834 inspired a series of pictures. Turner re-creates in his painting the turbulent flames, steam, and smoke with brilliant color and bold brushstrokes.

A quieter side of nature was portrayed by John Constable in his works recording the peaceful English countryside. *The Haywain* (a wagon used to carry harvested hay) captures what Constable called "the feeling of country life," which, he maintained, was the essence of landscape (Figure 7). *The Haywain* was exhibited at the Paris salon of 1825, where it became a major influence on the French artists of the Romantic period.

—Katherine Crum

persecuted and abused people, instituted practices rooted in ignorance and superstition, and imposed values that made people miserable because they conflicted with human nature and the essential needs of men and women.

The principle of utility, said Bentham, permits the reforming of society in accordance with people's true nature and needs. It does not impose upon men and women unrealistic standards, but accepts people as they are. Utilitarianism, he declared, bases institutions and laws on an objective study of human behavior rather than on unsubstantiated religious beliefs, unreliable traditions, and philosophical abstractions. Bentham's utilitarianism led him to support both extending the suffrage and the secret ballot and to attack political corruption and clerical control of education. In contrast to laissez-faire liberals, Bentham and his followers argued for some legislation to protect women and children in the factories and for sanitation reform to improve the conditions in the cities. The utilitarians also championed prison reform and demanded that the archaic English system be reformed.

Early Socialism: New Possibilities for Society

A new group called socialists went further than either the liberals or the radicals, demanding the creation of a new society based on the spirit of cooperation, rather than on competition. Reflecting the spirit of the Enlightenment and the French Revolution, they were convinced that people could create a better world according to the principles of reason, and that they could do it in a relatively short time. The socialists' thought was romantic as well, in that they dreamed of a new social order in which each individual could fulfill his or her own nature. The most important early socialist thinkers—Saint-Simon, Fourier, and Owen—espoused a new

social and economic system in which production and distribution of goods would be planned for the general good of society. Their thought influenced Karl Marx and Friedrich Engels, who in the second half of the nineteenth century, became the most influential formulators and propagators of socialism (see pages 550–554). There were also Christian communitarians who protested the unsettling conditions caused by industrialization and the treatment of the poor; these Christian "socialists" urged believers to share their property and labor and live together in model communities.

Socialists questioned the assumption that society was made up of isolated and self-seeking individuals, and challenged the laws of economics as they were formulated by the laissez-faire economists. They denied that human beings reached the peak of their achievements as individuals, arguing that people achieved more happiness for themselves and for others as a community that worked together and experienced solidarity. Some socialists urged voluntary divorce from the larger society; they proposed communes or model factory towns as places to live the principles of socialism or communitarianism. Some were very perceptive about the nature of industrialization and the future of industrial society; others romantically longed for the past and created schemes that would preserve the values and ethics of village life as it existed before industrialization and urbanization.

Saint-Simon: Technocratic Socialism

Descended from a distinguished French aristocratic family, Henri Comte de Saint-Simon (1760–1825) renounced his title during the French Revolution and enthusiastically preached the opportunity for a new society. He regarded his own society as defective and in need of reorganization: the critical philosophy of the Enlightenment had shattered the old order, but it had not provided a guide for reconstructing society. Saint-Simon believed that he had a mission to set society right by providing an understanding of the new age being shaped by science and industry. Many of the brightest young people in France believed in his mission.

Like the romantics, Saint-Simon saw the importance of religion. He argued that just as Christianity had provided social unity and stability during the Middle Ages, scientific knowledge would bind the society of his time. The scientists, industrialists, bankers, artists, and writers would replace the clergy and the aristocracy as the social elite; Saint-Simon had a romantic love of genius and talent. In the new industrial age, he thought, the control of society must pass to the "industriels"— those who produce or who make it possible to produce. These manufacturers, bankers, engineers, intellectuals, and scientists would harness technology for the betterment of humanity. Saint-Simon's disciples championed efforts to build great railway and canal systems, including the Suez and Panama canals. His vision of a scientifically organized society led by trained experts was a powerful force among intellectuals in the nineteenth century and is very much alive today among those who believe in a technocratic society.

Like the philososphes, Saint-Simon valued science, had confidence in the power of reason to improve society, and believed in the certainty of progress according to laws of social development. Also like the philosophes, he attacked the clergy for clinging to superstition and dogma at the expense of the common people. The essence of Christianity was the Golden Rule—the sublime command that people should treat each other like brothers and sisters. According to Saint-Simon, the traditional clergy, having placed dogma above moral law, had forfeited their right to lead Europe, just as the aristocracy had before the French Revolution forfeited its right to rule. He called for A New Christianity (the title of one of his books) to serve as an antidote to selfish interests and to abjure the narrow nationalism that divided the peoples of Europe.

Fourier: Psychological Socialism

Another early French socialist was Charles Fourier (1772–1837) who believed, as the romantics did, that society conflicted with the natural needs of human beings and that this tension was responsible for human misery. Only the reorganization of society so that it would satisfy people's desire for pleasure and satisfaction would end that misery. Whereas Saint-Simon and his followers had elaborate plans to reorganize society on the grand scale of large industries and giant railway and canal systems, Fourier sought to create small communities to allow men and women to enjoy life's simple pleasures. These communities of about 1,600 people, called *phalansteries*, would be organized according to the unchanging needs of human nature.

Fourier was not greatly concerned about the realities of industrialization, and his ideas reflect the artisan society that still existed in France when he was growing up. In phalansteries, no force would coerce or thwart innocent human drives. Everyone would work at tasks that interested them and would produce things that brought themselves and others pleasure. Like Adam Smith, Fourier understood that specialization bred boredom and alienation from work and life. Unlike Smith, he did not believe that vastly increased productivity compensated for the evils of specialization. In the phalansteries, money and goods would not be equally distributed; those with special skills and responsibilities would be rewarded accordingly. This system of rewards accorded with nature because people have a natural desire to be rewarded.

Both Fourier and the Saint-Simonians supported female equality, placing them among the first social thinkers to do so. Fourier did not define female equality merely in political terms. He thought that marriage distorted the natures of both men and women because monogamy restricted their sexual needs and narrowed their lives' scope to the family alone. Instead, people should think of themselves as part of the family of all humanity.

Because married women had to devote all their strength and time to household and children, they had no time or energy left to enjoy life's pleasures. Fourier did not call for the abolition of the family, but he did hope that it would disappear of its own accord as society adjusted to his theories. Men and women would find new ways of fulfilling themselves sexually and the community would be organized so that it could care for the children. Fourier's ideas found some reception in the United States, where in the 1840s at least twenty-nine communities had been founded on Fourierist principles.

Owen: Industrial Socialism

In 1799, Robert Owen (1771–1858) became part owner and manager of the New Lanark cotton mills in Scotland. Distressed by widespread mistreatment of workers, Owen resolved to improve the lives of his employees and to prove that it was possible to do so without destroying profits. He raised wages, upgraded working conditions, refused to hire children under ten, and provided workers with neat homes, food, and clothing, all at reasonable prices. He set up schools for children and for adults. In every way, he demonstrated his belief that healthier, happier workers produced more than less-fortunate ones. Like Saint-Simon, Owen believed industry and technology could and would enrich humankind, if organized according to the proper principles. Visitors came from all over Europe to see Owen's factories.

Just like many philosophes, Owen also held that the environment was the principal shaper of character—that the ignorance, alcoholism, and crime of the poor derived from bad living conditions. Public education and factory reform, said Owen, would make better citizens of the poor. When parliament balked at reforms, Owen even urged the creation of a grand national trade union of all the workers in England. In the earliest days of industrialization, with very few workers or-

ganized in unions, this dream seemed an impossible one. Owen came to believe that the entire social and economic order must be replaced by a new system based on harmonious group living, rather than on competition. He established a model community at New Harmony, Indiana, but it was short-lived. Even in his factory in England, Owen had some difficulty holding on to workers, many of whom were devout Christians and resented his secular ideas and the dancing taught to their children in his schools.

Nationalism: The Sacredness of the Nation

Nationalism is an awareness shared by a group of people who feel strongly attached to a particular land and who possess a common culture and history marked by shared glories and sufferings. Nationalism is accompanied by a conviction that one's highest loyalty and devotion should be directed toward the nation. Nationalists exhibit great pride in their people's history and traditions and often feel that their nation has been specially chosen by God or history. Like a religion, nationalism provides the individual with a sense of community and with a cause worthy of self-sacrifice.

Thus, in an age when Christianity was in retreat, nationalism became the dominant spiritual force in nineteenth-century European life. Nationalism provided new beliefs, martyrs, and "holy" days that stimulated reverence; it offered membership in a community, which satisfied the overwhelming psychological need of human beings for fellowship and identity. And nationalism gave a mission—the advancement of the nation—to which people could dedicate themselves.

The Emergence of Modern Nationalism

The essential components of nationalism emerged at the time of the French Revolution.

Ferdinand Victor Eugène Delacroix (1799–1863): Massacre at Chios. The Greeks' struggle for liberty against the Ottoman Empire fired the imagination of many romantics. The first Greek letter fraternities in the United States were political clubs sympathetic to the Greek cause. In this painting, Delacroix shows the suffering brought on by the conflict. (*Louvre/Cliché des Musées Nationaux*)

The Revolution asserted the principle that sovereignty derived from the nation, from the people as a whole—the state was not the private possession of the ruler, but the embodiment of the people's will. The nation-state was above king, church, estate, guild, or province; it superseded all other loyalties. The French people must view themselves not as subjects of the king, not as Bretons or Normans, not as nobles or bourgeois, but as citizens of a united fatherland, *la patrie*. These two ideas—that the people possess unlimited sovereignty and that they are united in a nation—were crucial in fashioning a nationalist outlook.

As the Revolution moved from the moderate to the radical stage, French nationalism gained in intensity. In 1793–94, when the Republic was threatened by foreign invasion, the Jacobins created a national army, demanded ever greater allegiance to and sacrifice for the nation, and called for the expansion of France's borders to the Alps and the Rhine. With unprecedented success, the Jacobins used every means—press, schoolroom, rostrum—to instill a love of country.

The Romantic Movement also awakened nationalist feelings. By examining the language, literature, and folkways of their people, romantic thinkers instilled a sense of national pride in their compatriots. Johann Gottfried Herder (1744–1803) conceived the idea of the *Volksgeist*—the soul of the people. For Herder, each people was unique and creative; each expressed its genius in language, literature, monuments, and folk traditions. Herder did not make the theoretical jump from a spiritual or cultural nationalism to political nationalism; he did not call for the formation of states based on nationality. But his emphasis on the unique culture of a people stimulated a national consciousness among Germans and the various Slavic peoples who lived under foreign rule. The Volksgeist led intellectuals to investigate the past of their own people, to rediscover their ancient traditions, and to extol their historic language and culture. From this cultural nationalism it was only a short step to a political nationalism that called for national liberation, unification, and statehood.

The romantics were the earliest apostles of German nationalism. They restored to consciousness memories of the German past, and they emphasized the peculiar qualities of the German folk and the special destiny of the German nation. The romantics glorified medieval Germany and valued hereditary monarchy and aristocracy as vital links to the nation's past. They saw the existence of each individual as inextricably bound up with folk and fatherland, and they found the self-realization for which they yearned by identifying their own egos with the national soul. To these romantics, the national community was a vital force that gave the individual both an identity and a purpose in life. And the nation stood above the individual; the national spirit bound isolated souls into a community of brethren. In unmistakably romantic tones, Ernst Moritz Arndt urged Germans to unite against Napoleon:

German man, feel again God, hear and fear the eternal, and you hear and fear also your Volk *[people], you feel again in God the honor and dignity of your fathers, their glorious history rejuvenates itself in you, their firm and gallant virtue reblossoms in you, the whole German Fatherland stands again before you in the august halo of past centuries. . . .*

No longer Catholics and Protestants, no longer Prussians and Austrians, Saxons and Bavarians, Silesians and Hanoverians, no longer of different faith, different mentality, and different will—be Germans, be one, will to be one by love and loyalty, and no devil will vanquish you.[15]

Most German romantics expressed hostility to the liberal ideals of the French Revolution. They condemned the reforms of the Revolution for trying to reconstruct society by separating individuals from their national past, for treating them as isolated abstractions. They held that the German folk spirit should not be polluted by foreign French ideas.

To the philosophes, the state was a human creation that provided legal safeguards for the individual. To the romantics, the state was something holy, the expression of the divine spirit of a people; it could not be manufactured to order by the intellect. The state's purpose was not the protection of natural rights nor the promotion of economic well-being; rather, the state was a living organism that linked each person to a sacred past, imbued individuals with a profound sense of community, and subordinated the citizen to the nation.

Nationalism and Liberalism

In the early nineteenth century, liberals were the principal leaders and supporters of nationalist movements. They viewed the struggle for national rights—the freedom of a people from foreign rule—as an extension of the struggle for the rights of the individual. There could be no liberty, said nationalists, if people were not free to rule themselves in their own land.

Liberals called for the unification of Germany and Italy, the rebirth of Poland, the liberation of Greece from Turkish rule, and the granting of autonomy to the Hungarians of the Austrian Empire. Liberal nationalists envisioned a Europe of independent states based on nationality and popular sovereignty. Free of foreign domination and tyrant princes, these newly risen states would protect the rights of the individual and strive to create a brotherhood of nationalities in Europe.

In the first half of the nineteenth century, few intellectuals recognized the dangers inherent in nationalism or understood the fundamental conflict between liberalism and nationalism. For the liberal, the idea of universal natural rights transcended all national boundaries. Inheriting the cosmopolitanism of the Enlightenment, liberalism emphasized what all people had in common, called for all individuals to be treated equally under the law, and preached toleration. Nationalists, manifesting the particularist attitude of the in-group and the tribe, regarded the nation as the essential fact of existence. Consequently, they often willingly subverted individual liberty for the sake of national grandeur. Whereas the liberal sought to protect the rights of all within the state, the nationalist often ignored or trampled on the rights of individuals and national minorities. Whereas liberalism grew out of the rational tradition of the West, nationalism derived from the emotions. Because it fulfilled an elemental yearning for community and kinship, nationalism exerted a powerful hold over human hearts. Liberalism demanded objectivity in analyzing tradition, society, and history, but nationalism evoked a mythic and romantic past that often distorted history.

In the last part of the nineteenth century, the irrational and mythic quality of nationalism would intensify. By stressing the unique qualities and history of a particular people, nationalism would promote hatred between nationalities. By kindling deep love for the past, including a longing for ancient borders, glories, and power, nationalism would lead to wars of expansion. By arousing the emotions to a fever pitch, nationalism would shatter rational thinking, drag the mind into a world of fantasy and myth, and introduce extremism into politics. Love of nation would become an overriding passion threatening to extinguish the liberal ideals of reason, freedom, and equality.

Notes

1. Jean Jacques Rousseau, *The Confessions* (New York: Modern Library, 1950), p. 2.

2. Quoted in H. G. Schenk, *The Mind of the European Romantics* (Garden City, N.Y.: Doubleday, 1969), p. 4.

3. William Blake, *Milton,* 40. 34–35.

4. Ibid., 41. 1.

5. Goethe, *Faust,* trans. by Bayard Taylor (New York: Modern Library, 1950), pt. 1, sc. 4.

6. Letter of Keats, November 22, 1817, in Hyder E. Rollins, ed., *The Letters of John Keats* (Cambridge, Mass.: Harvard University Press, 1958), 1: 184–185.

7. Quoted in John Herman Randall, Jr., *The Career of Philosophy* (New York: Columbia University Press, 1965), 2: 80.

8. William Blake, *Milton,* Preface.

9. Quoted in Ernst Cassirer, *An Essay on Man* (New York: Bantam Books, 1970), p. 178.

10. From "The Tables Turned," in *The Complete Poetical Works of Wordsworth,* Andrew J. George, ed., (Boston: Houghton Mifflin, 1904, rev. ed. 1982), p. 83.

11. Horst von Maltitz, *The Evolution of Hitler's Germany* (New York: McGraw-Hill, 1973), p. 217.

12. Edmund Burke, *Reflections on the Revolution in France* (New York: Liberal Arts Press, 1955), pp. 40, 89.

13. Quoted in Frederick B. Artz, *Reaction and Revolution, 1814–1832* (New York: Harper Torchbooks, 1963), p. 73.

14. John Stuart Mill, *On Liberty,* Currin V. Shields, ed. (Indianapolis: Bobbs-Merrill, 1956), ch. 1.

15. Quoted in Hans Kohn, *Prelude to Nation-States* (Princeton, N.J.: D. Van Nostrand, 1967), p. 262.

Suggested Reading

Bullock, Alan, and Maurice Shock, eds., *The Liberal Tradition* (1956). Selections from the works of British liberals, preceded by an essay on the liberal tradition.

de Ruggiero, Guido, *The History of European Liberalism* (1927). A classic study.

Epstein, Klaus, *The Genesis of German Conservatism* (1966). An analysis of German conservative thought as a response to the Enlightenment and the French Revolution.

Fried, Albert, and Ronald Sanders, eds., *Socialist Thought* (1964). Selections from the writings of socialist theorists.

Hayes, Carlton J. H., *Historical Evolution of Modern Nationalism* (1931). A pioneering work in the study of nationalism.

Kohn, Hans, *The Idea of Nationalism* (1961). A comprehensive study of nationalism from the ancient world through the eighteenth century by a leading student of the subject.

———, *Prelude to Nation-States* (1967). The emergence of nationalism in France and Germany.

MacCoby, S., ed., *The English Radical Tradition, 1763–1914* (reprint 1978). Selections from the writings of English radicals.

Markham, F. M. H., ed., *Henri Comte de Saint-Simon* (1952). Selected writings.

Manuel, Frank, *The Prophets of Paris* (1962). Good discussions of Saint-Simon and Fourier.

Poster, Mark, ed., *Harmonian Man* (1971). Selected writings of Fourier.

Schapiro, J. S., *Liberalism: Its Meaning and History* (1958). A useful survey with readings.

Schenk, H. G., *The Mind of the European Romantics* (1966). A comprehensive analysis of the Romantic Movement.

Simon, W. M., *French Liberalism 1789–1848* (1972). Selections from the writings of French liberals.

Shafer, B. C., *Faces of Nationalism* (1972). The evolution of modern nationalism in Europe and the non-European world; contains a good bibliography.

Smith, A. D., *Theories of Nationalism* (1972). The relationship between nationalism and modernization.

Weiss, John, *Conservatism in Europe, 1770–1945* (1977). Conservatism as a reaction to social modernization.

Review Questions

1. The Romantic Movement was a reaction against the dominant ideas of the Enlightenment. Discuss this statement.

2. What was the significance of the Romantic Movement?

3. What were the attitudes of the conservatives toward the philosophes and the French Revolution?

4. "It is with infinite caution that any man ought to venture upon pulling down an edifice which had answered in any tolerable degree for ages the common purposes of society." How does this statement by Burke represent the conservative viewpoint?

5. Why did conservatives reject the philosophy of natural rights?

6. What were the sources of liberalism?

7. The central concern of liberals was the enhancement of individual liberty. Discuss this statement.

8. What was a fundamental difference between French radicals and liberals?

9. What did British radicalism owe to Paine and Bentham?

10. What basic liberal-capitalist doctrines were attacked by early socialists?

11. Why are Saint-Simon, Fourier, and Owen regarded as early socialists? Discuss their ideas.

12. Define nationalism.

13. How did the French Revolution and Romanticism contribute to the rise of modern nationalism?

14. What is the relationship between nationalism and liberalism?

15. Account for nationalism's great appeal.

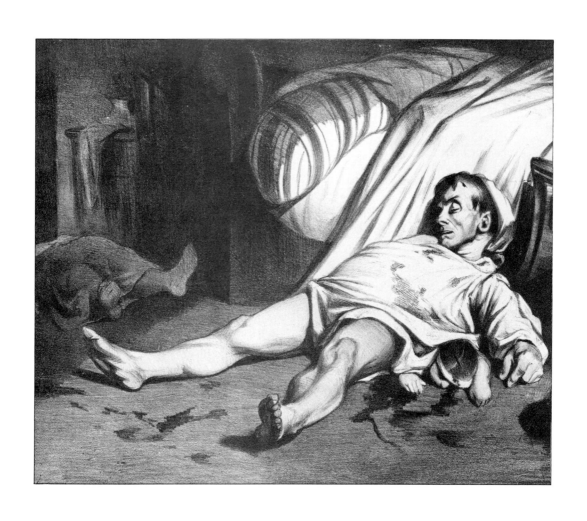

23

*Europe, 1815–1848: Revolution
and Counterrevolution*

The Congress of Vienna
Metternich: Arch-Conservative
Crisis Over Saxony and Poland
The Settlement

Revolutions, 1820–1829

Revolutions, 1830–1832

The Rise of Reform in Britain

The Revolutions of 1848: France
The February Revolution
The June Days: Revolution of the Oppressed

The Revolutions of 1848: Germany, Austria, and Italy
The German States: Liberalism Discredited
Austria: Hapsburg Dominance
Italy: Continued Fragmentation

The Revolutions of 1848: An Assessment

A clash between the forces unleashed by the French Revolution and the traditional outlook of the Old Regime took place during the years 1815 through 1848. The period opened with the Congress of Vienna, which drew up a peace settlement after the defeat of Napoleon, and closed with the revolutions that swept across most of Europe in 1848. Much of the Old Regime outside of France had survived the stormy decades of the French Revolution and Napoleon. Monarchs still held the reins of political power. Aristocrats, particularly in central and eastern Europe, retained their traditional hold over the army and administration, controlled the peasantry and local government, and enjoyed tax exemptions.

The French Revolution had shown that absolutism could be challenged successfully and feudal privileges abolished. Determined to enforce respect for traditional authority and to smother liberal ideals, the conservative ruling elites resorted to censorship, secret police, and armed force. Inspired by the revolutionary principles of liberty, equality, and fraternity, liberals and nationalists continued to engage in revolutionary activity.

The Congress of Vienna

Metternich: Arch-Conservative

After the defeat of Napoleon, a congress of European powers met at Vienna (1814–1815) to draw up a peace settlement. The pivotal figure at the Congress of Vienna was Prince Klemens von Metternich (1773–1859) of Austria, who had organized the coalition that had triumphed over Napoleon. Belonging to the old order of courts and kings, Metternich hated the new forces of nationalism and liberalism. He regarded liberalism as a dangerous disease carried by middle-class malcontents, and believed that domestic order and international stability depended on rule

Congress of Vienna, 1815, by Jean Baptiste Isabey (1767–1855). The delegates to the Congress of Vienna (Metternich is standing before a chair at the left) in 1815 sought to re-establish many features of the Europe that existed before the French Revolution and Napoleon. They can be called shortsighted; nevertheless, the balance of power that they formulated preserved international peace. (*The New York Public Library*)

by monarchy and respect for aristocracy. The misguided liberal belief that society could be reshaped according to the ideals of liberty and equality, said Metternich, had led to twenty-five years of revolution, terror, and war. To restore stability and peace, the old Europe must suppress liberal ideas and quash the first signs of revolution. If the European powers did not destroy the revolutionary spirit, they would be devoured by it.

Metternich also feared the new spirit of nationalism. As a multinational empire, Austria was particularly vulnerable to nationalist unrest. If its ethnic groups—Poles, Czechs, Magyars, Italians, South Slavs, Rumanians—became infected with the nationalist virus, they would shatter the Hapsburg Empire. A highly cultured, multilingual, and cosmopolitan aristocrat, Metternich considered himself the defender of European civilization. He felt that by arousing the masses and setting people against people, nationalism could undermine the foundations of the European civilization that he cherished.

Metternich's critics accuse him of shortsightedness. Instead of harnessing and directing the new forces let loose by the French Revolution, he thought that he could stifle them. Instead of trying to rebuild and remodel, he thought only of propping up dying institutions. Regarding any attempt at reform as opening the door to radicalism and revolution, he refused to make any concessions to liberalism.

Metternich sought to return to power the ruling families deposed by more than two decades of revolutionary warfare, and to restore the balance of power so that no one country could be in a position to dominate the European continent as Napoleon had. Metternich was determined to end the chaos of the Napoleonic period and restore stability to Europe. There must be no more Napoleons who obliterate states, topple kings, and dream of European hegemony. While serving the interests of the Hapsburg monarchy, Metternich also had a sense of responsibility to Europe as a whole. He sought a settlement that would avoid the destructiveness of a general war.

Representing Britain at the Congress of Vienna was Robert Stewart Viscount Castlereagh (1769–1822), the British Foreign Secretary, who was realistic and empirically minded. Although an implacable enemy of Napoleon, Castlereagh demonstrated mature statesmanship in his attitude toward defeated France: "it is not our business to collect trophies, but to try . . . to bring the world back to peaceful habits. I do not believe this to be compatible with any attempt . . . to affect the territorial character of France . . . neither do I think it a clear case . . . that France . . . may not be found a useful rather than a dangerous member of the European system."[1]

Tsar Alexander I (1777–1825) attended the Congress himself. Showing signs of mental instability and steeped in Christian mysticism, the Russian tsar wanted to create a European community based on Christian teachings. Influenced by Baroness von Kruedener, a religious fanatic, Alexander regarded himself as the savior of Europe, an attitude that caused other diplomats to regard him with distrust.

Representing France was Prince Charles Maurice de Talleyrand-Périgord (1754–1838). He had served Napoleon as foreign minister, but when the Emperor's defeat seemed imminent, he worked for the restoration of the Bourbon monarchy. A devoted patriot, Talleyrand sought to remove from France the stigma of the Revolution and Napoleon.

The aging Prince Karl von Hardenberg (1750–1822) represented Prussia. Like Metternich, Castlereagh, and Talleyrand, the Prussian statesman believed that the various European states, in addition to pursuing their own national interests, should concern themselves with the well-being of the European community as a whole.

Crisis over Saxony and Poland

Two interrelated issues threatened to disrupt the conference and enmesh the Great Powers in another war. One was Prussia's intention to annex the German kingdom of Saxony; the other was Russia's demand for Polish territories. The tsar wanted to combine the Polish holdings of Russia, Austria, and Prussia into a new Polish kingdom under Russian control. Both Britain and Austria regarded such an extension of Russia's power into central Europe as a threat to the balance of power. Metternich declared that he had not fought Napoleon to prepare the way for the tsar. Britain agreed that Russia's westward expansion must be checked.

Prince Talleyrand of France suggested that Britain, Austria, and France conclude an alliance to oppose Prussia and Russia. This clever move by Talleyrand restored France to the family of nations. Now France was no longer the hated enemy, but a necessary counterweight to Russia and Prussia. Threatened with war, Russia and Prussia moderated their demands and the crisis ended.

The Settlement

After months of discussion, quarrels, and threats, the delegates to the Congress of Vienna finished their work. Resisting Prussia's demands for a punitive peace, the allies did not punish France severely. They feared that a humiliated France would only prepare for a war of revenge. Moreover, Metternich continued to need France to balance the power of both Prussia and Russia. France had to pay a large indemnity over a five-year period and submit to allied occupation until the obligation was met.

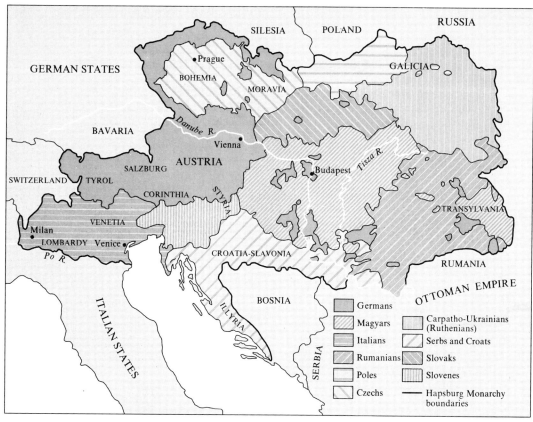

Map 23.1 Peoples of the Hapsburg Monarchy, 1815

The peace settlement changed the borders throughout Europe. Although it lost most of its conquests, France emerged with somewhat more land than it possessed before the Revolution. To guard against a resurgent France, both Prussia and Holland received territories on the French border. Holland obtained the southern Netherlands (Belgium); Prussia gained the Rhineland and part of Saxony, but not as much as the Prussians had desired. Nevertheless, Prussia emerged from the settlement significantly larger and stronger. Russia obtained Finland and a considerable part of the Polish territories, but not as much as the tsar had anticipated; the Congress prevented further Russian expansion into central Europe. The northern Italian province of Lombardy was restored to Austria, which also received adjacent Venetia. England obtained strategic naval bases: Helgoland in the

North Sea, Malta and the Ionian Islands in the Mediterranean, the Cape Colony in South Africa, and Ceylon in the Indian Ocean. Germany was organized into a confederation of thirty-eight (later thirty-nine) states. Norway was given to Sweden. The legitimate rulers, who had been displaced by the Revolution and the wars of Napoleon, were restored to their thrones in France, Spain, Portugal, the Kingdom of the Two Sicilies, the Papal States, and many German states.

The conservative delegates at the Congress of Vienna have often been criticized for ignoring the liberal and nationalist aspirations of the different peoples and turning the clock back to the Old Regime. Critics have castigated the Congress for dealing only with the rights of thrones and not the rights of peoples. But, after the experience of two world wars in the twentieth century, some historians today are impressed with the peacemakers' success in restoring a balance of power that effectively stablized international relations. No one country was strong enough to dominate the Continent; no Great Power was so unhappy that it resorted to war to undo the settlement. Not until the unification of Germany in 1870–1871 was the balance of power upset; not until World War I in 1914 did Europe have another general war of the magnitude of the Napoleonic wars.

Revolutions, 1820–1829

Russia, Austria, Prussia, and Great Britain agreed to act together to preserve the territorial settlement of the Congress of Vienna and the balance of power. After paying its indemnity, France was admitted into this Quadruple Alliance, also known as the *Concert of Europe*. Metternich intended to use the Concert of Europe to maintain harmony between nations and internal stability within nations. Toward this end, conservatives in their respective countries censored books and newspapers, imprisoned liberal activists, and suppressed nationalist uprisings. In 1819, Metternich and representatives from the leading German states met at Karlsbad and drew up several decrees calling for the dissolution of the *Burschenschaft*, a student fraternity that favored German national unity, for the imposition of strict censorship over the press, and for the dismissal of professors who disseminated liberal ideas.

But repression could not contain the liberal and nationalist ideals unleashed by the French Revolution; nothing could halt the transformation of European society. The first revolution during the restorations of legitimate rulers occurred in Spain in 1820. The uprising was essentially a military revolt by infrequently paid and poorly fed soldiers who were being sent to Latin America to win back Spain's colonies, which partly under the inspiration of the American and French Revolutions, had revolted against Spanish rule.

King Ferdinand VII attempted to appease the soldiers by reinstating the liberal constitution of 1812, which had been promulgated during the struggle against Napoleon and revoked two years later. Both Metternich and Tsar Alexander were alarmed. Fearing that the Spanish uprising, with its quasi-liberal overtones, would inspire revolutions in other lands, the Concert of Europe empowered France to intervene. In 1823, 100,000 French troops crushed the revolution. King Ferdinand dismissed the liberal constitution and brutally punished the leaders of the insurrection.

Revolutionary activity in Italy also frightened the Concert of Europe. In 1821 it authorized Austria to extinguish a liberal uprising in the Kingdom of the Two Sicilies. The Austrians also crushed an uprising in Piedmont, in northern Italy (see Chapter 25). Rulers in other Italian states jailed and executed liberal leaders, and several thousand Italians went into exile.

In both instances, Britain strongly opposed the actions of the alliance; it interpreted the alliance differently from the way that Austria, Prussia, and Russia did. The three eastern powers wanted the alliance to smother in the cradle all subversive movements that threatened the old order. To Metternich, the central problem of the age was suppressing revolutions, and he regarded the alliance as a means of preserving the status quo. Britain, however, viewed the alliance solely as a means of guarding against renewed French aggression. It had no desire to intervene in the domestic affairs of other nations.

A revolution also failed in Russia. During the Napoleonic wars and the occupation of France, Russian officers were introduced to French ideas. Contrasting French liberal ideas and ways with Russian autocracy, some officers resolved to change conditions in Russia. Like their Western counterparts, they organized secret societies and disseminated liberal ideas within Russia. When Alexander I died, these liberal officers struck. But representing only a fraction of the aristocracy and with no mass following among the soldiers, they had no chance of success. Their uprising in

Giuseppe Verdi (1813–1901). Verdi and Richard Wagner divide the operatic world of the mid-nineteenth century. Verdi, however, was deeply concerned with the future and fate of Italy. His name became an acronym for explosive sentiment. As the audience cheered, "Viva, Verdi," they cheered for a unified monarchy: <u>V</u>ittorio, <u>E</u>mmanuele, <u>R</u>e <u>D</u>' Italia (Victor Emmanuel, King of Italy). (*The Mansell Collection*)

December 1825 was easily smashed by the new tsar, Nicholas I, and the leaders were severely punished. To prevent Western ideas from infiltrating into his realm, Nicholas imposed rigid censorship and organized the Third Section, a secret police force that spied on suspected subversives. The Decembrists had failed, but their courage would inspire future opponents of tsarist autocracy.

The revolutions in Spain, Italy, and Russia failed, but the Concert of Europe also suffered setbacks. Stimulated by the ideals of the French Revolution, the Greeks revolted against their Turkish rulers in 1821. Although the Turkish sultan was the legitimate ruler, Russia, France, and Britain aided the Greek revolutionaries, for they were Christians, while the Turks were Muslims; moreover,

pro-Greek sentiments were very strong among educated western Europeans who had studied the literature and history of ancient Greece. To them the Greeks were struggling to regain the freedom of their ancient forebears. Not only the pressure of public opinion but fear of Russian motives led Britain to join in intervention. If Russia carried out its intention of aiding the Greeks on its own, no doubt the Russian bear would never release Greece from its hug. Britain could not permit this extension of Russian power in the eastern Mediterranean. Despite Metternich's objections, Britain, France, and Russia took joint action against the Turks.

In 1829, Greece gained its independence. The Metternich system, which aimed to preserve the territorial settlements made at Vienna and to protect traditional and legitimate rulers against liberal and nationalist revolutions, had been breached. The success of the Greeks heartened liberals in other lands.

Revolutions, 1830–1832

After Napoleon's defeat, a Bourbon king, Louis XVIII (1814–1824), ascended the throne of France. Louis XVIII's heart belonged to the Old Regime, but his intellect told him that twenty-five years of revolutionary change could not be undone. Recognizing that the French people would not accept a return to the old order, Louis pursued a moderate course. Although his pseudoconstitution, the Charter, declared that the king's power rested on divine right, it also stipulated that citizens possessed fundamental rights—freedom of thought and religion and equal treatment under the law—and it set up a two-house parliament. But peasants, urban workers, and most bourgeois could not meet the property requirements for voting.

Aided by competent ministers and committed to a policy of moderation, Louis XVIII governed effectively, although he was resisted by diehard aristocrats, called *ultras*. These aristocrats, many of them returned émigrés, wanted to erase the past twenty-five years of French history and restore the power and privileges of church and aristocracy. Their leader was the king's younger brother, the Comte d'Artois, who after Louis' death in 1824 ascended the throne as Charles X (1824–1830).

The new government aroused the hostility of the bourgeoisie by indemnifying the émigrés for the property they had lost during the Revolution, by censoring the press, and by giving the church greater control over education. In the election of 1830, the liberal opposition to Charles X won a decisive victory. Charles responded with the July Ordinances, which dissolved the newly elected chamber; the Ordinances also deprived rich bourgeois of the vote and severely curtailed the press.

The bourgeois, students, and workers rebelled. They engaged in street demonstrations and put up barricades and were joined by army regiments that had deserted Charles. In the fighting that followed, some 2,000 Parisians were killed.

The insurgents hoped to establish a republic, but the wealthy bourgeois who took control of the revolution feared republican radicalism. They offered the throne to the Duc d'Orléans; Charles X abdicated and went into exile in Britain. The new king, Louis Philippe (1830–1848), never forgot that he owed his throne to the rich bourgeois. And the Parisian workers who had fought for a republic and economic reforms to alleviate poverty felt betrayed by the outcome, as did the still-disenfranchised petty bourgeois.

The Revolution of 1830 in France set off shock waves in Belgium, Poland, and Italy. The Congress of Vienna had assigned Catholic Belgium to Protestant Holland; from the outset the Belgians had protested. Stirred by the events in Paris, Belgian patriots proclaimed their independence from Holland. The Dutch could not suppress the insurgents, and the Quadruple Alliance did not act, largely because Russia was tied down by a revolution in Poland. Thus, liberal government was established in Belgium.

Inspired by the uprisings in France and Belgium, Polish students, intellectuals, and army officers took up arms against their Russian overlords. The peasants refused to join the insurrection because the revolutionaries did not promise land reform. The revolutionaries wanted to restore Polish independence, a dream that poets, musicians, and intellectuals had kept alive. Polish courage, however, was no match for Russian might, and Warsaw fell in 1831. The tsar took savage revenge on the revolutionaries; those who failed to escape to the West were executed. Subsequently the tsar's government made strenuous efforts to impose Russian language and culture on Polish students.

In 1831–32, Austrian forces again extinguished a revolution in Italy. Here, too, revolutionary leaders had failed to stir the great peasant masses to the cause of Italian independence and unity.

The Rise of Reform in Britain

Although it was the freest state in Europe in the early decades of the nineteenth century, Britain was far from democratic. A constitutional monarchy, with many limits on the powers of king and state, Britain was nonetheless dominated by aristocrats. Landed aristocrats controlled both the House of Lords and the House of Commons—the House of Lords because they constituted its membership and the House of Commons because they patronized or sponsored men favorable to their interests. The vast majority of people, middle class as well as working class, could not vote. Many towns continued to be governed by corrupt groups. New industrial towns were not allowed to elect representatives to Parliament; often lacking a town organization, they could not even govern themselves effectively. Without a voice in the government, the working classes often resorted to protesting by riot and rampage.

The social separation of noble and commoner was not as rigid in Britain as on the Continent. Younger sons of aristocrats did not inherit titles and were, therefore, obliged to make careers in law, business, the military, and the church. The upper and middle classes mingled much more freely than on the Continent, and the wealthiest merchants tended to buy lands, titles, and husbands for their daughters. Parliament, the courts, local government, the established Anglican church, the monarch—all were a part of a social and political system dominated by aristocratic interests and values. This domination had changed little despite the vast changes in social and economic structure that had taken place in the process of industrialization during the second half of the eighteenth century.

The two political parties in Britain, the Whigs and the Tories, were separated not by class, but by ideas and values and by family connections and patronage. The Whigs saw themselves as champions of civil, political and religious liberties—as defenders of Parliament and the nation against any tyranny of king and state. The Tories saw themselves as defenders of royal authority, the Anglican Church, the empire, and national and imperial glory; they believed that some are born to rule and most to follow. The issues changed with industrialization and with the greatly increased importance of Britain in world affairs, but the general positions did not. Neither party was democratic and at the end of the eighteenth century, during the American and French revolutionary wars, a group of reformers criticized both parties as part of a corrupt oligarchy that deprived the people of ancient liberties and a voice in government.

In 1815, Britain faced depression in industrial areas, and unrest brewed in the rural districts when veterans returning from the Napoleonic wars could find no work. With the war ended, the ruling groups could no longer count on English patriotism to keep out radical ideas simply because they sounded Jacobin; Britons were calling for the right to vote as freeborn Englishmen. Already, during the last years of the Napoleonic wars, there had been an outbreak of rural unrest brought

on by high prices and unemployment and low wages. Some craftsmen and farm workers called Luddites reacted to the introduction of machinery by destroying it. Both the Whigs and the Tories urged strict measures repressing any agitation or violence. The law forbade conspiracies to restrain trade, which included the organization of unions and self-help societies; crimes against property, such as theft, destroying machinery, or poaching (hunting on private property), were severely punished.

Artisans and craftsmen began to agitate for the right to vote. In 1819, at St. Peter's Fields near Manchester, a peaceful crowd of perhaps 50,000 gathered to demand changes in the suffrage law and to listen to radical reformers. The militia charged, killing eleven and wounding hundreds. Nicknamed the "Peterloo Massacre" in derisive comparison to the great victory of Waterloo, the incident provoked increased government repression, which differed little from that used in the autocratic states of Europe to stamp out the ideas of the French Revolution. Many British radicals were imprisoned and some deported. Large meetings were forbidden, seditious libel was severely punished, and many political agitators were hastily tried without due process of law. Newspapers and pamphlets were taxed and homes searched, which violated the English birthright to speak and meet freely, to due process of law, and to the privacy of one's own home.

Some members of parliament urged timely reforms. Two traditions strengthened the reformers. One was the commitment of liberal aristocrats to political, religious, and civil liberty; the other was a pragmatic approach to politics that permitted Whigs, Tories, and radicals to reach compromises and to solve some specific problems without bringing in ideology.

In the 1820s, Robert Peel (1788–1850) made some economic and legal reforms that lowered taxes and stimulated the economy and reduced the number of crimes subject to the death penalty. Reformers also pressed for the end of legal discrimination against Catholics and Nonconformists. The English could worship as they pleased, but the Corporation Act (1661) and the Test Act (1673) required that holders of public office take communion in the Anglican Church. This barred Nonconformists (non-Anglican Protestants) and Catholics from government positions and from the universities. The laws were often ignored, but they still provoked unrest among the lower classes, who were often Nonconformists or, if Irish, Catholics. In 1828 the acts were repealed and public offices were opened to Nonconformists and Catholics. Catholics were still denied seats in Parliament, though, because members of Parliament were required to express opposition to two basic Catholic principles—transubstantiation and the reverence for the Virgin. Liberal Whigs campaigned for "Catholic emancipation." Tories, defenders of the established church, were torn when the Duke of Wellington (the hero of Waterloo) and Robert Peel—both devout Anglicans—decided they must support the removal of the restrictions on Catholics to avoid civil war in Ireland. After 1829, Catholics and Nonconformist Protestants participated in the nation's political life as equals to the Anglicans, although they still suffered from social discrimination.

During the 1830s and 1840s the liberal reform movement continued and accomplished a number of measures, some principled and others pragmatic. In 1833, slavery was abolished within the British Empire (the British slave trade had been abolished earlier). The owners of slaves were compensated for the loss of their property. Humanitarians, pragmatists, and defenders of private property could all champion the reform. The Municipal Corporations Act (1835) granted towns and cities greater authority over their affairs, a first step toward ending corruption and beginning the democratization of town government. The measure created town and city governments which could, if they wished, begin to solve some problems of urbanization and industrialization. These municipal corporations could institute reforms such as sanitation, which Parliament encouraged by passing in 1848 the first Public Health Act.

Jean François Millet (1814–1875): Sheep Shearing. Concentrating mainly on peasant life, Millet expressed the romantic view of the sanctity of humanity's bond with nature. But for the Parisian bourgeoisie of the 1850s, the image of the peasant became a symbol of the discontented lower classes they feared. For social reformers demanding a more equitable distribution of political power and material wealth, this same image was a cry for justice. (*Courtesy, Museum of Fine Arts, Boston*)

Increasingly, reform centered on extension of the suffrage and enfranchisement of the new industrial towns. Middle-class men, and even workers, hoped to gain the right to vote. Because of population shifts, some sparsely populated regions—called rotten boroughs—sent representatives to the House of Commons, while many densely populated factory towns had little or no representation; and in many cases a single important land owner controlled many seats in the Commons. Voting was public which allowed for intimidation, and candidates frequently tried to influence voters with drinks, food and even money.

Intense and bitter feelings built up during the campaign for the Reform Bill of 1832. The very process of passing the Reform Bill created a precedent for party politics and cabinet government for the remainder of the century. The House of Commons, dominated by the Whigs since 1830, passed the bill to extend the suffrage by some 200,000, almost double the number who were then entitled to vote. These new voters would be middle class. The House of Lords, however, refused to pass the bill. There were riots and strikes in many cities, and mass meetings, both of workers and of middle-class people, took place all over the country. King William IV (1830–1837) became convinced, along with many Whig and even some Tory politicians, that the situation was potentially revolutionary. To defuse it, he threatened to increase the number of the bill's supporters in the House of Lords by creating new peers. This threat brought reluctant peers into line and the bill was passed. The Reform Bill of 1832 extended the suffrage to the middle class, and made the House of Commons more representative. The rotten boroughs lost their seats, which were granted to towns. Suffrage did not extend to workers, however, because there were high property qualifications.

Workers did gain some relief, however, when humanitarians pressured Parliament to pass the Factory Act (1833), which legislated that no child under thirteen could work more than nine hours a day and that no one aged thirteen to eighteen could work more than sixty-nine hours a week. The act also provided some inspectors to investigate infractions and to punish offenders. In 1842 an investigation of child labor in the mines shocked the public with graphic descriptions:

A girdle is put round the naked waist, to which a chain from the carriage is hooked and passed between the legs, and the boys crawl on their hands and knees drawing the carriage after them.

The children are well tired at night. . . . Many fall ill. They work from 7 to 5 o'clock.

When the nature of this horrible labour is taken into consideration . . . a picture is presented of deadly physical oppression and systematic slavery.[2]

Parliament responded in the same year by banning children under ten from the mines. The Factory Act of 1847 stipulated that boys under eighteen and women could work no more than ten hours a day in the mines and factories. At first workers resented the prohibition of child labor because it would greatly reduce their family income if their children could not work. Gradually, however, they realized that the humanitarian protection of the children might make their own lives easier and safer, and their wages higher. The ten-hour day for adult male workers would not be enacted until 1874, however.

The Chartist movement—a very diverse and complicated affair—attracted very different kinds of people with widely varying visions of the future. Its adherents came from the ranks of both intellectual radicals and workers. They pressed for political reforms, not for economic ones. During the 1830s and 1840s the Chartists agitated for democratic measures, such as universal manhood suffrage, the secret ballot, salaries and the abolition of property qualifications for members of Parliament, and annual meetings of Parliament. For most of the 1830s these political demands united reformers whose aspirations were in reality very different, and the Chartist platform remained the democratic reform program for the rest of the century, long after the death of Chartism itself at midcentury.

During the "hungry forties," the severe economic hardships added to the numbers of Chartists, but the leaders of the movement split into two groups, one favoring radical and revolutionary action and the other continuing to advocate peaceful tactics. Some Chartists had spent their efforts, allied to middle-class reformers in the Anti-Corn Law League, agitating to remove tariffs on grain in order to lower food prices and strike a blow at the great landowners who dominated British political life. The league succeeded in repealing the Corn Laws in 1846, which effectively established free trade for Britain. Other Chartists who were craftsmen and artisans devoted their efforts to trade unions, cooperatives, and mutual aid societies.

England shared in a general European economic slump from 1846 to 1848. It too suffered from depression and harvest failures, particularly of potatoes blighted by fungus, but there was an upturn in the economy in 1848. The last political effort by the Chartists was led by Feargus O'Connor, a charismatic Irishman, who organized a mass demonstration to present a huge petition of the six demands to Parliament in 1848. The cabinet ignored the great charter, which had signatures of at least two million names. The movement died out just as most of Europe burst into revolution. The working-class leadership of Chartism turned away from political programs to almost exclusively economic activity, such as trade unions that could bring immediate benefits to workers. Others dispersed into other causes.

Unlike the continental states, England avoided revolution. British politicians thought it was because they had made timely reforms in the 1830s and 1840s, and that belief itself became a force in political life. Whenever times were hard there were always political leaders who would say the remedy was reform and that reform would prevent revolution. The political experience of the first half of the nineteenth century laid the foundation for British parliamentary practices, which came to be the model of liberal, progressive, and stable politics. Britain was the symbol for all those who argued for reform rather than revolution. In the rest of Europe in 1848, however, such arguments were meeting with little success.

The Revolutions of 1848: France

Eighteen-forty-eight is often called *the year of revolution,* for throughout Europe, uprisings for political liberty and nationhood took place. The economic crisis of the previous two years intensified political and national unrest. Food riots broke out in many places. The decimation of the potato crop by disease and the grain harvest by drought had caused terrible food shortages. Also, a financial crisis precipitated by overspeculation had caused business failures, unemployment, and reduced wages. The common people blamed their governments for their misery and sought redress. Although economic hardship aggravated discontent with the existing regimes, "it was the absence of liberty," concludes historian Jacques Droz, "which . . . was most deeply resented by the peoples of Europe and led them to take up arms."[3]

The February Revolution

An uprising in Paris set in motion the revolutionary tidal wave that was to engulf much of Europe in 1848. The Revolution of 1830 had broken the back of the ultras in France. There would be no going back to the Old Regime.

But King Louis Philippe and his ministers, moderates by temperament and philosophy, had no intention of going forward to democracy. A new law in 1831 broadened the franchise from fewer than 100,000 voters to 248,000 by 1846. Even so, only about 3 percent of adult males qualified to vote. The government of Louis Philippe was run by a small elite consisting of wealthy bourgeois bankers, merchants, professors, and lawyers, and aristocrats who had abandoned the hope of restoring the Old Regime. This ruling elite championed the revolutionary ideas of equal treatment under the law and of careers open to talent, but feared democracy and blocked efforts to broaden the franchise. When the poorer bourgeoisie protested against the limited franchise, which still excluded professionals and small tradesmen, François Guizot, the leading minister, arrogantly proclaimed: "Get rich, then you can vote." The ruling elite had become a selfish and entrenched oligarchy, unresponsive to the aspirations of the rest of the nation. Articulate intellectuals denounced the government for its narrow political base and voiced strong republican sentiments. To guard against republicanism and as a reaction to repeated attempts to assassinate the king, the government cracked down on radical societies and newspapers.

Radical republicans, or democrats, wanted to abolish monarchy and grant all men the vote. They had fought in the Revolution of 1830, but were disappointed with the results. Patriots and romantics who looked back longingly on the glory days of Napoleon also hated Louis Philippe's government. These French nationalists complained that the king, who dressed like a businessman and pursued a pacifist foreign policy, was not fit to lead a nation of patriots and warriors. Under Louis Philippe, they said, France could not realize its historic mission of liberating oppressed nationalities throughout Europe.

The strongest rumblings of discontent, but barely heeded by the ruling elite, came from the laboring poor. Many French workers, still engaged mainly in pre–Industrial Revolution occupations, were literate and concerned with politics, read the numerous books and newspapers that denounced social injustice and called for social change. Artisans and their families had participated in the great revolutionary outbreaks of 1789 and had defended the barricades in 1830. Like their sans-culotte forebears, they favored a democratic republic that would aid the common people. These people felt betrayed by the regime of Louis Philippe, which had brought them neither political representation nor economic reform.

The few factory workers and the artisans in small workshops were growing attracted to socialist thinkers who attacked capitalism and called for state programs to deal with poverty. Louis Blanc, a particularly popular socialist theorist, denounced capitalist competition and demanded that the government establish cooperative workshops. Owned by the workers themselves, these workshops would assure employment for the jobless.

A poor harvest in 1846 and an international financial crisis in 1847, which drastically curtailed French factory production, aggravated the misery of the laboring poor. Prevented by law from striking, unable to meet the financial requirements for voting, and afflicted with unemployment, the urban workers wanted relief. "I believe that we are at this moment sleeping on a volcano," said Alexis de Tocqueville prophetically.[4]

The government steadfastly refused to pass reforms. Its middle-class opponents sidestepped regulations against political assemblies and demonstrations by gathering at large banquets to protest. When the government foolishly tried to block future banquets, students and workers took to the streets in February 1848, denouncing Guizot and demanding reforms. Barricades began to go up. Attempting to defuse an explosive situation, Louis Philippe dismissed the unpopular Guizot. But the barricades, commanded by republicans, did not come down, and the antigovernment demonstrations continued. When soldiers, confused by a shot that had perhaps gone off accidentally, fired directly into a crowd and killed fifty-two Parisians, the situation got out of hand. Unable to pacify the enraged Parisians, Louis Philippe abdicated. France became a republic, and the people of Paris were jubilant.

Map 23.2 Europe, 1815 ▶

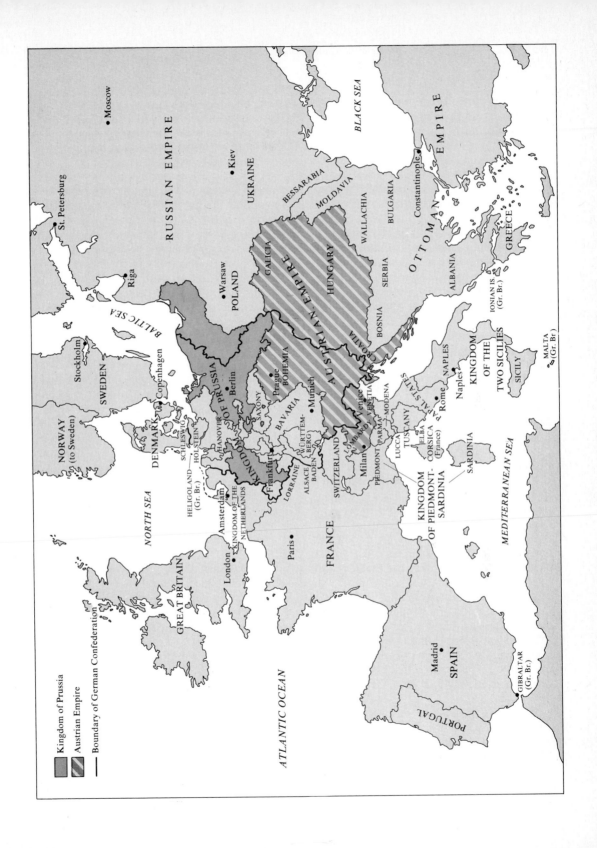

Kingdom of Prussia

Austrian Empire

Boundary of German Confederation

ATLANTIC OCEAN

GREAT BRITAIN

London

NORTH SEA

HELIGOLAND (Gr. Br.)

Amsterdam

KINGDOM OF THE NETHERLANDS

Paris

FRANCE

NORWAY (to Sweden)

Stockholm

SWEDEN

BALTIC SEA

Copenhagen

DENMARK

SCHLESWIG

HOLSTEIN

HANOVER

KINGDOM OF PRUSSIA

Berlin

SAXONY

Frankfurt

Prague

BOHEMIA

Munich

BAVARIA

WÜRTEM-BERG

BADEN

ALSACE

LORRAINE

SWITZERLAND

St. Petersburg

Riga

RUSSIAN EMPIRE

Moscow

Warsaw

POLAND

Kiev

UKRAINE

GALICIA

AUSTRIAN EMPIRE

HUNGARY

BESSARABIA

MOLDAVIA

WALLACHIA

BULGARIA

SERBIA

BOSNIA

CROATIA

Venice

LOMBARDY

VENETIA

Milan

PIEDMONT

PARMA

MODENA

LUCCA

TUSCANY

PAPAL STATES

Rome

Naples

KINGDOM OF THE TWO SICILIES

SICILY

KINGDOM OF PIEDMONT-SARDINIA

CORSICA (France)

ELBA

SARDINIA

BLACK SEA

Constantinople

OTTOMAN EMPIRE

ALBANIA

GREECE

IONIAN IS. (Gr. Br.)

MALTA (Gr. Br.)

MEDITERRANEAN SEA

SPAIN

Madrid

PORTUGAL

GIBRALTAR (Gr. Br.)

The June Days: Revolution of the Oppressed

Except for one workingman, the leadership of the provisional government established in February consisted of bourgeoisie. The new leaders were committed to political democracy but only some, notably the socialist Louis Blanc, favored social reforms. These ministers had little comprehension of or sympathy for the plight of the laboring poor; they regarded socialist ideas as a threat to private property. Although they condemned the inherited privileges of aristocracy, these leaders never questioned the privileges that derived from inherited wealth.

These bourgeois liberals passionately denounced oppressive rulers, but they could not grasp that, to the working class, *they* had become the oppressors. They considered it a sacred duty to fight for the rights of the individual, but they did not include freedom from hunger and poverty among these rights. Meanwhile, workers who could find jobs labored twelve and fourteen hours a day under brutalizing conditions. In some districts, one out of three children died before the age of five, and everywhere in France, beggars, paupers, prostitutes, and criminals were evidence of the struggle to survive.

By occupation and wealth, the middle class considered itself to be apart from the working class. To the bourgeoisie, the workers were dangerous creatures, "the wild ones," "the vile mob." But the inhabitants of the urban slums could no longer be ignored. They felt, as de Tocqueville stated, "that all that is above them is incapable and unworthy of governing them; that the distribution of goods prevalent until now . . . is unjust; that property rests on a foundation which is not an equitable one."[5]

The urban poor were desperate for jobs and bread. Socialist intellectuals, sympathetic to the plight of the worker, proposed that the state organize producer cooperatives run by workers. Some wanted the state to take over insurance companies, railroads, mines, and other key industries. To the property

owners of all classes, such schemes smacked of madness.

The middle-class leaders of the new republic gave all adult males the vote and abolished censorship; however, their attempts to ease the distress of the urban poor were insincere and halfhearted. The government limited the workday to ten hours and legalized labor unions, but it failed to cope effectively with unemployment. Louis Blanc called for the creation of producers' cooperatives in order to guarantee employment for the city poor. The republic responded by establishing national workshops that provided some employment on public works projects. Most workers, however, received wages for doing nothing. Drawn by the promise of work, tens of thousands of laborers left the provinces for Paris, swelling the ranks of the unemployed. The national workshops provided work, food, and medical benefits for some of the unemployed. But to the workers, this was a feeble effort to deal with their monumental distress. To the property-owning peasantry and bourgeoisie, the national workshops were a hateful concession to socialism and a waste of government funds. They viewed the workshops as nests of working-class radicalism, where plans were being hatched to change the economic system and seize their property.

For their participation in the February uprising against Louis Philippe, the workers had obtained meager benefits. When the government closed the workshops, working-class hostility and despair turned to open rebellion. Again barricades went up in the streets of Paris.

The June Revolution in Paris was unlike previous uprisings in France. It was a revolt against poverty and a cry for the redistribution of property; as such, it foreshadowed the great social revolutions of the twentieth century. The workers stood alone. To the rest of the nation, they were barbarians attacking civilized society. Aristocrats, bourgeois, and peasants feared that no one's property would be safe if the revolution succeeded. From hundreds of miles away, Frenchmen flocked to Paris to crush what they considered to be the madness within their midst.

Although they had no leaders, the workers showed remarkable courage. Women and children fought alongside men behind the barricades. After three days of vicious street fighting and atrocities on both sides, the army extinguished the revolt. Some 1,460 lives had been lost, including four generals. The June Days left deep scars on French society. For many years, workers would never forget that the rest of France had united against them; the rest of France would remain terrified of working-class radicalism.

In December 1848, the French people in overwhelming numbers elected Louis Napoleon, nephew of the great emperor, as president of the Second Republic. They were attracted to the magic of Louis Napoleon's name, and they expected him to prevent future working-class disorders. The election, in which all adult males could vote, demonstrated that most Frenchmen were socially conservative; they were unsympathetic to working-class poverty and deeply suspicious of socialist programs.

The Revolutions of 1848: Germany, Austria, and Italy

Like an epidemic, the fever of revolution that broke out in Paris in February raced across the Continent. Liberals, excluded from participation in political life, fought for parliaments and constitutions; many liberals were also nationalists who wanted unity or independence for their nations. Some liberals had a utopian vision of a new Europe of independent and democratic states. In this vision, reactionary rulers would no longer stifle individual liberty; no longer would a people be denied the right of nationhood.

The German States: Liberalism Discredited

After the Congress of Vienna, Germany consisted of a loose confederation of thirty-nine independent states, of which Austria and Prussia were the most powerful. Jealous of their independence and determined to preserve their absolute authority, the ruling princes detested liberal and nationalist ideals. In the southern German states, which had been more influenced by the French Revolution, princes did grant constitutions and establish parliaments to retain the loyalty of their subjects. But even in these states the princes continued to hold the reins of authority.

The German nationalism that had emerged during the French occupation gained in intensity during the restoration (the post-Napoleonic period), as intellectuals, inspired in part by the ideas of the romantics, insisted that Germans, who shared a common language and culture, should also be united politically. During the restoration, the struggle for German unity and liberal reforms continued to be waged primarily by students, professors, writers, lawyers, and other educated people. The great mass of people, knowing only loyalty to their local prince, remained unmoved by appeals for national unity.

The successful revolt against Louis Philippe, hostility against absolute princes, and the general economic crisis combined to produce uprisings in the capital cities of the German states in March 1848. Throughout Germany, liberals clamored for constitutions, parliamentary government, freedom of thought, and an end to police intimidation. Some called for the creation of a unified Germany governed by a national parliament and headed by a constitutional monarch. The poor of town and countryside joined the struggle. The great depression of the 1840s had aggravated the misery of the German peasant and urban masses, and as the pressures of hunger and unemployment worsened, their discontent exploded into revolutionary fervor.

In the spring of 1848, downtrodden artisans, who faced severe competition from the new factories, served as the revolution's shock troops. Unable to compete with the new machines, artisans saw their incomes fall and their opportunities for work decrease. For example, skilled weavers at home earned far less than factory hands did, and some jobless craftsmen were forced to take factory jobs, which they regarded as a terrible loss of status. These craftsmen wanted to restrict the growth of factories, curtail capitalist competition, and restore the power of the guilds that gave them security and status.

Having lost hope that the absolute princes would aid them, craftsmen gave their support to bourgeois liberals, who without their support, could not challenge the throne nor wrest power from the aristocrats. In many German states, the actions of the embittered urban craftsmen determined the successful outcome of the insurrections. (The factory workers in the emerging industries, on the other hand, showed no enthusiasm for revolution, despite the appeals of radical socialists.) Adding to the discomfort of the ruling princes was rioting in the countryside by peasants goaded by crop failure, debt, and oppressive demands from the aristocracy.

Terrified that these disturbances would lead to anarchy, the princes made concessions to the liberals whom they previously had censored, jailed, and exiled. During March and April 1848, the traditional rulers in Baden, Württemberg, Bavaria, Saxony, Hanover, and other states replaced reactionary ministers with liberals, eased censorship, established jury systems, framed constitutions, formed parliaments, and ended peasant obligations to lords.

In Prussia, Frederick William IV was slow to make concessions, and his troops treated the people of Berlin, who had long hated the army quartered in their city, with contempt. On March 18, as tension in Berlin mounted, the king proclaimed reforms. The Berliners gathered in the palace square to applaud Frederick William's decision. But the hostilities between civilians and soldiers led to pushing and the unintentional firing of two shots by two soldiers. The enraged Berliners armed themselves and hurriedly constructed barricades from anything they could find—barrels, pavement stones, fire pumps, bedding, sacks of flour, fruit stalls. Most insurgents

were artisans, but merchants and students also participated in the fighting. Unable to subdue the insurgents, the army urged bombarding the city with artillery. Frederick William opposed the idea and ordered the troops to leave Berlin. The insurgents had won the first round.

The jubilant Berliners paraded the bodies of their fallen fighters in the palace courtyard, demanding that the king come to the window. Frederick William removed his hat and the queen fainted. Recalling that day, the king would later remark: "We all crawled on our stomachs." The Prussian king, like the other German princes, had to agree to the formation of a parliament and the admission of prominent liberals into the government.

But the triumph of the liberals in Prussia and the other German states was not secure. Although reforms liberalized the governments of the German states, the insurrections had not toppled the ruling dynasties. Moreover, the alliance between the bourgeois and the artisans was tenuous. The violence of the artisans frightened the property-owning middle class, which sought only moderate political reforms, preferably through peaceful means. In addition, restoration of the guild system was to the middle class a reactionary economic measure.

Liberals took advantage of their successes in Prussia and other German states to form a national assembly charged with the task of creating a unified and liberal Germany. Representatives from all the German states attended the assembly, which met at Frankfurt. The delegates, including many articulate lawyers and professionals, came predominantly from the educated middle class; only a handful were drawn from the lower classes. After many long debates, the Frankfurt Assembly approved a federation of German states. The German union would have a parliament and would be headed by the Prussian king. Austria, with its many non-German nationalities, would be excluded from the federal union. Some radical democrats wanted to proclaim a German republic, but they were an ineffective minority. Most delegates were

Barricades, Berlin, 1848. During the revolutions of 1848, barricades went up in many European cities. But the revolutionaries ultimately proved no match for the armed forces of conservative rulers. (*Brown Brothers*)

moderate liberals who feared that universal (male) suffrage and the abolition of monarchy would lead to plebeian rule and the destruction of the social order. The deputies selected Frederick William as emperor of the new Germany, but the Prussian king refused; he would never wear a crown given to him by common people during a period of revolutionary agitation.

While the delegates debated, the ruling princes recovered from the first shock of revolution and ordered their armies to crush the revolutionaries. The February Revolution in Paris had shown European liberals that authority could be challenged successfully; the June Days, however, had shown the authorities that revolutionaries could be beaten by professional soldiers. Moreover, the German middle class, frightened by lower-class agitation and unsympathetic to the artisans' demands to restrict capitalism and restore

the authority of the old guilds, was losing enthusiasm for revolution—so, too, were the artisans. The disintegration of the alliance between middle-class liberals and urban artisans deprived the revolutionaries of mass support. A revival of the old order would not face much resistance.

In Prussia, a determined Frederick William ordered his troops to reoccupy Berlin. In March the citizens of Berlin had fought against the king's troops, but in November, no barricades went up in Berlin. Prussian forces also assisted the other German states in crushing the new parliaments. The masses of workers and peasants did not fight to save the liberal governments, which fell one by one. A small minority of democrats resisted, particularly in Baden; many of these revolutionaries died in the fighting or were executed.

German liberalism had failed to unite Germany or to create a constitutional government dominated by the middle class. Liberalism, never securely rooted in Germany, was discredited. In the following decades, many Germans, identifying liberalism with failure, abandoned liberal values and turned to authoritarian Prussia for leadership in the struggle for unification. The fact that authoritarians hostile to the spirit of parliamentary government eventually united Germany had deep implications for future German and European history.

Austria: Hapsburg Dominance

The Hapsburg (Austrian) Empire, the product of dynastic marriage and inheritance, had no common nationality or language; it was held together only by the reigning Hapsburg dynasty, its army, and its bureaucracy. The ethnic composition of the empire was enormously complex. The Germans dominated; concentrated principally in Austria they constituted about 25 percent of the empire's population. The Magyars predominated in the Hungarian lands of the empire. The great bulk of the population consisted of Slavs—Czechs, Poles, Slovaks, Slovenes, Croats, Serbs, Ruthenians. In addition, there were Italians in northern Italy and Rumanians in Transylvania. The Hapsburg dynasty, aided by the army and the German-dominated civil service, prevented the multinational empire from collapsing into anarchy.

Metternich, it is often said, suffered from a "dissolution complex": he understood that the new forces of nationalism and liberalism could break up the Austrian Empire. Liberal ideas could lead Hapsburg subjects to challenge the authority of the emperor, and nationalist feelings could cause the different peoples of the empire to rebel against German domination and Hapsburg rule. To keep these ideas from infecting Austrian subjects, Metternich's police imposed strict censorship, spied on professors, and expelled from the universities students caught reading forbidden books. Despite Metternich's political police,

the universities still remained hotbeds of liberalism.

In 1848, revolutions spread throughout the Austrian Empire, starting in Vienna. Aroused by the abdication of Louis Philippe, Viennese liberals denounced Hapsburg absolutism and demanded a constitution, relaxation of censorship, and restrictions on the police. The government responded with hesitance and limited force to the demonstrations of students and workers, and many parts of Vienna fell to the revolutionaries. The authorities used force that was strong enough to arouse the insurrectionists and create martyrs, but not to subdue them. Confused and intimidated by the revolutionaries, the government allowed freedom of the press, accepted Metternich's resignation, and promised a constitution. The Constitutional Assembly was convened and in August voted the abolition of serfdom. At the same time that the Viennese insurgents were tasting the heady wine of reform, revolts in other parts of the empire—Bohemia, Hungary, and northern Italy—added to the distress of the monarchy.

But the revolutionaries' victory was only temporary, and the defeat of the old order only illusory; the Hapsburg government soon began to recover its balance. The first government victory came with the crushing of the Czechs in Bohemia. In 1848, Czech nationalists wanted the Austrian Empire reconstructed along federal lines that would give the Czechs equal standing with Germans. The Czechs called for a constitution for Bohemia and equal status for the Czech language in all official business. In June, students and destitute workers engaged in violent demonstrations that frightened the middle and upper classes—both Czech and German. General Windischgrätz bombarded Prague, the capital of Bohemia, into submission and re-established Hapsburg authority.

In October 1848, the Hapsburg authorities ordered the army to bombard Vienna. Against the regular army the courageous, but disorganized and divided students and workers had little hope. Imperial troops broke into the city, overcame resistance, and executed several of the revolutionary leaders. In March 1849, the Hapsburg leaders replaced the liberal constitution drafted by the popularly elected Constitutional Assembly with a more conservative one drawn up by its own ministers.

The most serious threat to the Hapsburg realm came from the Magyars in Hungary. Some 12 million people lived in Hungary, 5 million of whom were Magyars. The other nationalities consisted of South Slavs (Croats and Serbs) and Rumanians. The upper class were chiefly Magyar landowners, who enjoyed tax exemptions and other feudal privileges. Drawn to liberal and modern ideas and fearful of peasant uprisings, some Hungarian nobles pressed for an end to serfdom and the tax exemptions of the nobility. Louis Kossuth (1802–1894), a member of the lower nobility, called for both social reform and a deepening of national consciousness. The great landowners, determined to retain their ancient privileges, resisted liberalization.

Led by Kossuth, the Magyars demanded local autonomy for Hungary. Hungary would remain within the Hapsburg Empire, but would have its own constitution and national army and would control its own finances. The Hungarian leadership introduced liberal reforms—suffrage for all males who could speak Magyar and owned some property, freedom of religion, freedom of the press, the termination of serfdom, and the end of the privileges of nobles and church. Within a few weeks, the Hungarian parliament changed Hungary from a feudal to a modern liberal state.

But the Hungarian leaders' nationalist dreams towered above their liberal ideals. The Magyars intended to incorporate lands inhabited by Serbs, Slovaks, and Rumanians into their kingdom and transform these people, whom they regarded as ethnic inferiors, into Hungarians. As historian Hugh Seton-Watson has written,

Kossuth and his friends genuinely believed that they were doing the non-Hungarians a kindness by giving them a chance of becoming absorbed in the superior Hungarian culture. To refuse this

kindness was nationalist fanaticism; to impose it by force was to promote progress. The suggestion that Romanians, Slovaks, or Serbs were nations, with a national culture of their own, was simply ridiculous nonsense.[6]

In the spring of 1849, the Hungarians renounced their allegiance to the Hapsburgs and proclaimed Hungary an independent state with Kossuth as president.

The Hapsburg rulers took advantage of the ethnic animosities inside and outside Hungary. They encouraged Rumanians and South Slavs to resist the new Hungarian government. When Hapsburg forces moved against the Magyars, they were joined by an army of South Slavs whose nationalist aspirations had been flouted by the Hungarians. The recently ascended Hapsburg emperor, Francis Joseph, also appealed to Tsar Nicholas I for help. The tsar complied, fearing that a successful revolt by the Hungarians might lead the Poles to rise up against their Russian overlords. The Hungarians fought with extraordinary courage but were overcome by superior might. Kossuth and other rebel leaders went into exile; about one hundred rebel leaders were executed. Thus, through division and alliance, the Hapsburgs had prevented the disintegration of the empire.

Italy: Continued Fragmentation

Italian nationalists, eager to end the humiliation of Hapsburg occupation and domination and to unite the disparate states into a unified and liberal nation, rose in rebellion in 1848. Revolution broke out in Sicily six weeks before the February Revolution in Paris. Bowing to the revolutionaries' demands, King Ferdinand II of Naples granted a liberal constitution. The Grand Duke of Tuscany, King Charles Albert of Piedmont-Sardinia, and Pope Pius IX, ruler of the Papal States, also felt compelled to introduce liberal reforms.

Then the revolution spread to the Hapsburg lands in the north. The citizens of Milan, in Lombardy, built barricades and stood ready to fight the Austrian oppressor. When the Austrian soldiers attacked, they were fired upon from nearby windows. From rooftops, Italians hurled stones and boiling water. After "Five Glorious Days" (March 18–22) of street fighting, the Austrians withdrew. The people of Milan had liberated their city. On March 22, the citizens of Venice declared their city free of Austria and set up a republic. King Charles Albert, who hoped to acquire Lombardy and Venetia, declared war on Austria. Intimidated by the insurrections, the ruling princes of the Italian states and Hapsburg Austria had lost the first round.

But soon everywhere in Italy the forces of reaction recovered and reasserted their authority. The Austrians defeated the Sardinians and reoccupied Milan, and Ferdinand II crushed the revolutionaries in the south. Revolutionary disorders in Rome had forced Pope Pius IX to flee in November 1848; in February 1849 the revolutionaries proclaimed Rome "a pure democracy with the glorious title of the Roman Republic." Heeding the pope's call for assistance, Louis Napoleon attacked Rome, destroyed the infant republic, and allowed Pope Pius to return. The last city to fall to the reactionaries was Venice, which the Austrians subjected to a merciless bombardment. After six weeks, the Venetians, weakened by starvation and cholera, surrendered. Reactionary princes still ruled in Italy, the Hapsburg occupation persisted in the north; Italy was still a fragmented nation.

The Revolutions of 1848: An Assessment

The revolutions of 1848 began with much promise, but they all ended in defeat. The revolutionaries' initial success was due less to their strength than to the governments' hesitancy to use their superior force. The reactionary leaders of Europe overcame their paralysis, however, and moved decisively to smash the revolutions. The courage of the revolutionaries was no match for regular armies. Thousands were killed and imprisoned; many fled to America.

Class divisions weakened the revolutionaries. The union between middle-class liberals and workers, which brought success in the opening stages of the revolutions, was only temporary. Bourgeois liberals favoring political reforms—constitution, parliament, and protection of basic rights—grew fearful of the laboring poor, who demanded social reforms—jobs and bread. To the bourgeois, the workers were an uneducated mob driven by dark instincts. When the working class engaged in revolutionary action, a terrified middle class deserted the cause of revolution or joined the old elites in subduing the workers.

Intractable nationalist animosities helped to destroy all the revolutionary movements against absolutism in central Europe. In many cases the different nationalities hated each other more than they hated the reactionary rulers. When German liberals at the Frankfurt Convention debated the boundary lines of a united Germany, the problem of Prussia's Polish territories emerged. In 1848, Polish patriots wanted to re-create the Polish nation, but German delegates at the convention by an overwhelming majority opposed returning the Polish lands seized by Prussia in the late eighteenth century. Hungarian revolutionaries dismissed the nationalist yearnings of the Serbs and Rumanians living in Hungary, who in turn helped the Hapsburg dynasty to extinguish the nascent Hungarian state. The Germans of Bohemia resisted Czech demands for self-government and the equality of the Czech language with German.

Before 1848, democratic idealists envisioned the birth of a new Europe of free people and liberated nations. The revolutions in central Europe showed that nationalism and liberalism were not natural allies, that nationalists were often indifferent to the rights of other peoples. Disheartened by these nationalist antagonisms, John Stuart Mill, the English liberal statesman and philosopher, lamented that "the sentiment of nationality so far outweighs the love of liberty that the people are willing to abet their rulers in crushing the

Chronology 23.1 Revolution and Reaction

1819	The Peterloo Massacre; troops fire on English workers
1820	Military revolt in Spain
1821	Austria crushes revolts in Italy
1823	French troops crush revolt in Spain
1825	Uprising in Russia crushed by Nicholas I
1829	Greece gains its independence from Turkey
1830	The July Ordinances in France are followed by a revolution that forces Charles X to abdicate
August 1830	The Belgian revolution
October 1830	Belgians declare their independence from Holland, establishing a liberal government
1831	The Polish revolution fails
1831–1832	Austrian forces crush a revolution in Italy
1832	Reform Bill extends suffrage to the middle class
1848	The year of revolutions
February 1848	Revolution in Paris—Louis Philippe abdicates, and France becomes a republic
March 1848	Uprisings in capital cities of the German states; liberal reforms follow
March 18–22, 1848	"Five Glorious Days" in Milan
March 22, 1848	Citizens of Venice declare their freedom from Austria and establish a republic
June 1848	June Days of Paris—revolutionaries are beaten by professional soldiers
August 1848	The Constitutional Assembly meets in Vienna; serfdom is abolished
December 1848	Louis-Napoleon is elected President of the Second Republic of France
August 1849	The Hungarians' bid for independence is crushed by the Hapsburg forces, aided by Russian troops

liberty and independence of any people not of their race or language."[7]

The liberal and nationalist aims of the revolutionaries were not realized, but liberal gains were not insignificant. All French men obtained the right to vote; the labor services of peasants were abolished in Austria and the German states; parliaments, dominated to be sure by princes and aristocrats, were established in Prussia and other German states. In the decades to come, liberal reforms would become more widespread. These reforms would be introduced peacefully, for the failure of the Revolutions of 1848 convinced many people, including liberals, that popular uprisings were ineffective ways of

changing society. The Age of Revolution initiated by the French Revolution of 1789 had
ended.

Notes

1. Quoted in Henry A. Kissinger, *A World Restored* (New York: Grosset & Dunlap, The Universal Library, 1964), p. 183.

2. From Great Britain, *Parliamentary Papers: Report of the Commissioners: Children's Employment
(Mines)*, session 3 February-12 August, 1842,
15:52, 67, 94.

3. Jacques Droz, *Europe Between Revolutions,
1815–1848* (New York: Harper Torchbooks, 1968),
p. 248.

4. *The Recollections of Alexis de Tocqueville*, trans.
by Alexander Teixeira de Mattos (Cleveland:
Meriden Books, 1969), p. 12.

5. Ibid., pp. 11–12.

6. Hugh Seton-Watson, *Nations and States*
(Boulder, Colo.: Westview Press, 1977), p. 162.

7. Quoted in Hans Kohn, *Nationalism: Its Meaning and History* (Princeton, N.J.: D. Van Nostrand, 1965), pp. 51–52.

Suggested Reading

Droz, Jacques, *Europe Between Revolutions* (1967).
     A fine survey of the period 1815–1848.
Duveau, Georges, *1848: The Making of a Revolution*
     (1967). A valuable history of the two revo-
     lutions in France in 1848.
Fasel, George, *Europe in Upheaval: The Revolutions
     of 1848* (1970). A good introduction.
Fejtö, François, ed., *The Opening of an Era: 1848*
     (1973). Contributions by nineteen eminent
     European historians.
Halévy, Elie, *A History of the English People in
     the Nineteenth Century*, vols. 1–3, rev. ed.
     (1949). A must for anyone who wants to know
     England's experience from 1815 to the 1840s.
Kissinger, Henry A., *A World Restored* (1964).
     A study of the statesmen and their states-
     manship during, and immediately after the
     Congress of Vienna.
Langer, W. L., *Political and Social Upheaval, 1832–
     1852* (1969). Another volume in *The Rise of
     Modern Europe* series by its editor. Rich in
     data and interpretation; contains a valuable
     bibliographical essay.
Robertson, Priscilla, *Revolutions of 1848* (1960).
     Vividly portrays the events and the person-
     alities involved.
Talmon, J. L., *Romanticism and Revolt* (1967).
     The forces shaping European history from
     1815 to 1848.
Thompson, Edward P., *Making of the English
     Working Class* (1966). A very readable, dra-
     matic, enormously influential and contro-
     versial book.
Webb, R. K., *Modern England from the Eighteenth
     Century* (1968). A balanced, well-informed,
     readable book that is up to date on many
     controversial issues.

Review Questions

1. What was Metternich's attitude toward the
French Revolution? What was his attitude toward Napoleon?

2. How did the Congress of Vienna violate the
principle of nationalism? What was the principal
accomplishment of the Congress?

3. Between 1820 and 1832, where were revolutions suppressed, and how? Where were revolutions successful, and why?

4. How did Britain's social structure differ from
the continent's in the period following the French
Revolution?

5. How did Parliament respond to demands for
economic and political reforms during 1815–48?

6. What were the complaints of the urban poor
to the new French government after the February
Revolution in 1848? What was the significance
of the June Days in French history?

7. Why did the Revolutions of 1848 fail in the
German states, the Austrian Empire, and Italy?

8. What were the liberal gains of the Revolutions
of 1848? Why were liberals and nationalists disappointed with the results of the Revolutions
of 1848?

V
An Age of Contradiction: Progress and Breakdown

1848–1914

24

*Thought and Culture in the
Mid-Nineteenth Century:
Realism and Social Criticism*

*T*he second half of the nineteenth century was characterized by great progress in science, a surge in industrialism, and a continuing secularization of life and thought. The principal intellectual currents of the century's middle decades reflected these trends. Realism, positivism, Darwinism, Marxism, and liberalism all reacted against romantic, religious, and metaphysical interpretations of nature and society and focused on the empirical world; adherents of these movements relied on careful observation and strove for scientific accuracy. This emphasis on objective reality helped to stimulate a growing criticism of social ills; for despite unprecedented material progress, reality was often sordid, somber, and depressing. In the last part of the century, reformers motivated by an expansive liberalism, a socially committed Christianity, or both, pressed for the alleviation of social injustice.

Realism and Naturalism

Realism, the dominant movement in art and literature in the mid-nineteenth century, opposed the romantic veneration of the inner life and romantic sentimentality. The romantics exalted passion and intuition, let their imaginations transport them to a presumed idyllic medieval past, and sought subjective solitude amidst nature's wonders. Realists, on the other hand, were preoccupied with the external world, with social conditions and contemporary manners, with the familiar details of everyday life. With clinical detachment and meticulous care, they analyzed how people looked, worked, and behaved.

Like scientists, realist writers and artists carefully investigated the empirical world. For example, Gustave Courbet (1819–1877), who exemplified realism in painting, sought to practice what he called a "living art," painting common people and commonplace scenes—laborers breaking stones, peasants tilling the soil or returning from a fair, a country burial, wrestlers, bathers, family groups. In a matter-of-fact style, without any attempt at glorification, realist artists also depicted floor scrapers, rag pickers, prostitutes, and beggars. Émile de Vogüé, a nineteenth-century French writer, described realism as follows:

They have brought about an art of observation rather than of imagination, one which boasts that it observes life as it is in its wholeness and complexity with the least possible prejudice on the part of the artist. It takes men under ordinary conditions, shows characters in the course of their everyday existence, average and changing. Jealous of the rigour of scientific procedure, the writer proposes to instruct us by a perpetual analysis of feelings and of acts rather than to divert us or move us by intrigue and exhibition of the passions. . . . The new art seeks to imitate nature . . . it expresses the triumph of the group over the individual, of the crowd over the hero.[1]

Romantic writers had written lyrics, for lyric poetry is the language of feeling; the novel, because it lends itself admirably to depicting human behavior and social conditions, was the literary genre used by realist writers. Many realist novels were serialized in the inexpensive newspapers and magazines that the many newly literate common people could read. Thus the commoners' interests helped to shape the content of the novels. Seeking to portray reality as it is, realist writers frequently dealt with social abuses and the sordid aspects of human behavior and social life. Harriet Beecher Stowe's *Uncle Tom's Cabin* (1852) graphically described the horrors of slavery. Ivan Turgenev's *Sketches* (1852) described rural conditions in Russia and expressed compassion for the brutally difficult life of serfs. In *War and Peace* (1863–1869), Leo Tolstoy vividly described the manners and outlook of the Russian nobility and the tragedies that attended Napoleon's invasion of Russia. In *Anna Karenina* (1873–1877), he treated the reality of class divisions and the complexities of marital relationships. Fëdor Dostoevski's *Crime and Punishment* (1866), is a psychological novel that provides penetrating insights into

human behavior. Eugène Sue's serialized novel, *Les Mystères de Paris* (1842–1843) contained harrowing accounts of slum life and crime in Paris. George Sand's *Indiana* (1832), which saw the married woman as a victim, was praised by a reviewer for presenting

a true, living world, which is our world. . . characters and manners just as we can observe them around us, natural conversations, scenes in familiar settings, violent, uncommon passions, but sincerely felt or observed and such as are still aroused in many hearts, under the apparent uniformity and monotonous frivolity of our lives.[2]

Many regard Gustave Flaubert's *Madame Bovary* (1857) as the prototype of the realistic novel; it tells the story of a self-centered wife who shows her hatred for her devoted, hard-working, but dull husband by committing adultery. In *Bleak House* (1853), *Hard Times* (1854), and several other works, Charles Dickens portrayed the squalor of life, the hypocrisy of society, and the drudgery of labor in British industrial cities. In *Mary Barton* (1848) and *North and South* (1855), Elizabeth Gaskell, the wife of a Unitarian minister in Manchester, dealt compassionately with the plight of industrial workers.

Literary realism evolved into naturalism when writers tried to demonstrate that there was a causal relationship between human character and the social environment—that certain conditions of life produced predictable character traits in human beings. This belief that human behavior was governed by a law of cause and effect reflected the immense prestige attached to science in the closing decades of the nineteenth century. Émile Zola, the leading naturalist novelist, had an unreserved confidence in the scientific method; he described the task of the writer in an age of science as follows:

Man is not alone; he lives in society, in a social condition; and consequently, for us novelists, this social condition unceasingly modifies the phenomena. Indeed our great study is just there, in the reciprocal effect of society on the individual and the individual on society. . . . And this is what constitutes the experimental novel: . . . to exhibit man living in social conditions produced by himself, which he modifies daily, and in the heart of which he himself experiences a continual transformation. . . .

I have reached this point: the experimental novel is a consequence of the scientific evolution of the century; it continues and completes physiology, which itself leans for support on chemistry and medicine; it substitutes for the study of the abstract and the metaphysical man the study of the natural man, governed by physical and chemical laws, and modified by the influences of his surroundings; it is in one word the literature of our scientific age, as the classical and romantic literature corresponded to a scholastic and theological age.[3]

In his novels, Zola probed the slums, brothels, mining villages, and cabarets of France, examining how people were conditioned by the squalor of their environment. The Norwegian Henrik Ibsen, the leading naturalist playwright, examined with clinical precision the commercial and professional classes, their personal ambitions and family relationships. In the *Pillars of Society* (1877), Ibsen treated bourgeois social pretensions and hypocrisy; in *A Doll's House* (1879) a woman leaves her husband in search of a more fulfilling life—a theme that shocked a late-nineteenth-century bourgeois audience.

In aiming for a true-to-life portrayal of human behavior and the social environment, realism and naturalism coincided with an attitude of mind shaped by science, industrialism, and secularism. Both movements reasserted the importance of the external world. The same outlook also gave rise to positivism in philosophy.

Head of Balzac by Auguste Rodin (1840–1917). The poem embodied the outlook of Romanticism; the novel, however, satisfied the nineteenth-century concern with social criticism because it could portray the "real" world through careful, empirical observation. Honoré de Balzac wrote nearly 100 novels, novellas, and short stories that explored French life in the late eighteenth and early nineteenth centuries. (*The Metropolitan Museum of Art*)

Positivism

In the nineteenth century, science and technology continued to make astonishing strides, which combined with striking economic advancement, led many Westerners to believe that they were living in an age of such progress that a golden age was on the horizon. Viewing science as the highest achievement of the mind, many intellectuals sought to apply the scientific method to other areas of thought. They believed that this method was a reliable way to approach all problems. They insisted that history could be studied scientifically and society reorganized in accordance with scientific laws of social development. Marxism was one attempt to fashion a science of society; another attempt was positivism.

Positivists held that whereas people's knowledge of nature was vastly expanding, their understanding of society was deficient. This deficiency could be remedied by applying a strict empirical approach to the study of society. The philosopher must proceed like a scientist, carefully assembling and classifying data and formulating general rules that demonstrate regularities in the social experience. Such knowledge based on concrete facts would provide the social planner with useful insights. Positivists rejected metaphysics, which in the tradition of Plato tried to discover ultimate principles through reason alone, rather than through observation of the empirical world. For the positivist, any effort to go beyond the realm of experience to a deeper reality would be a mistaken and fruitless endeavor. The positivist restricted human knowledge only to what could be experienced, and saw the method of science as the only valid approach to knowledge.

A leading figure in the emergence of positivism was Auguste Comte (1798–1857), an engineer with thorough scientific training. Comte served as secretary to Saint-Simon (see page 511) until their association, punctuated by frequent quarrels, ended in 1824. But much of Saint-Simon's thought found its way into Comte's philosophy. Like Saint-Simon (and Marx), Comte called for a purely scientific approach to history and society: only by a proper understanding of the laws governing human affairs could society, which was in a state of intellectual anarchy, be rationally reorganized.

Again like Saint-Simon, Comte held that the Enlightenment and the French Revolution had shattered the Old Regime but had not replaced it with new institutions and a new ideology; this was the pressing need of the age.

Comte called his system *positivism*, because he believed that it rested on knowledge derived from observed facts and was therefore empirically verifiable. Like others of his generation Comte believed that scientific laws underlay human affairs and that they were discoverable through the methods of the geologist and the chemist—that is, through recording and systematizing observable data. "I shall bring factual proof," he said, "that there are just as definite laws for the development of the human race as there are for the fall of a stone."[4]

One of the laws that Comte believed he had discovered was the "law of the three stages." Comte held that the human mind had progressed through three broad historical stages—the theological, the metaphysical, and the scientific. In the theological stage, the most primitive, the mind found a supernatural explanation for the origins and purpose of things, and society was ruled by priests. In the metaphysical stage, which included the Enlightenment, the mind tried to explain things through abstractions—"nature," "equality," "natural rights," "popular sovereignty"—that rested on hope and belief rather than on empirical investigation. The metaphysical stage was a transitional period between the infantile theological stage and the highest stage of society, the scientific or positive stage. In this culminating stage the mind breaks with all illusions inherited from the past, formulates laws based on careful observation of the empirical world, and reconstructs society in accordance with these laws. Peope remove all mystery from nature and base their social legislation on laws of society similar to the laws of nature discovered by Newton. Recognizing that religion is an outlet for human emotional needs, Comte proposed a Religion of Humanity in which the human race, its past and future, would become a divinity replacing the God of Christianity.

Because Comte advocated the scientific study of society, he is regarded as a principal founder of sociology, but he influenced other fields as well. Comte's effort inspired many thinkers to collect and analyze critically all data pertaining to social phenomena. An English historian, Henry T. Buckle (1821–1862), for example, tried to make the study of civilization an exact science. Buckle saw human culture as a product of climate, soil, and food, so that the achievements of western Europe were due to a favorable environment, the backwardness of Russia and Africa to an unfavorable one. Buckle believed that rigorous laws operated in the social world and that they could be uncovered best through statistical studies.

Although Comte attacked the philosophes

for delving into abstractions instead of fashioning laws based on empirical knowledge, he was also influenced by the spirit of eighteenth-century philosophy. Like the philosophes he valued science, criticized supernatural religion, and believed in progress. In this way he accepted the Enlightenment's legacy, including the empirical and anti-theological spirit of Diderot's *Encyclopedia* and Montesquieu's quest for historical laws governing society.

Darwinism

Many contributed to science's steady advance in the nineteenth century. In 1808 John Dalton, an English chemist, formulated the atomic theory. In 1831, another English chemist, Michael Faraday, discovered the principle of electromagnetic induction on which the electric generator and electric motor are based. In 1847 Hermann von Helmholtz, a German physicist, formulated the law of conservation of energy, which states that the total amount of energy in the universe is always the same; energy that is used up is not lost but is converted into heat. In 1887 another German physicist, Heinrich Hertz, discovered electromagnetic waves, which later made possible the invention of radio, television, and radar. In 1869 Dmitri Mendeleev, a Russian chemist, constructed a periodic table for the elements that helped make chemistry more systematic and mathematical. In 1861 Louis Pasteur, a French scientist, proved that diseases were caused by microbes and devised vaccines to prevent them.

Perhaps the most important scientific advance was the theory of evolution formulated by Charles Darwin (1809–1882), an English naturalist. Darwin did for his discipline what Newton had done for physics; he made biology an objective science based on general principles. The Scientific Revolution of the seventeenth century had given people a new conception of space; Darwin radically altered our conception of time.

Charles Darwin with His Eldest Son, William. Darwin's theory of evolution was grounded in empirical observation and sound scientific reasoning. His theory also had a revolutionary impact on religion and social philosophy. (*Courtesy of Down House, Kent*).

Natural Selection

During the eighteenth century, almost all people had adhered to the Biblical account of creation contained in Genesis: God had instantaneously created the universe and the various species of animal and plant life; and he had given every river and mountain and each species of animal and plant a finished and permanent form distinct from every other species. God had designed the bird's wings so that it could fly, the fish's eyes so that it could see under water, and the human legs so that people could walk. All this, it was believed, had occurred some six thousand years ago.

Gradually, this view was questioned. In 1830–1833 Sir Charles Lyell published his three-volume *Principles of Geology*, which showed that the planet had evolved slowly over many ages. In 1794, Erasmus Darwin, the grandfather of Charles Darwin, published *Zoonomia, or the Laws of Organic Life*, which offered evidence that the earth had existed for millions of years before the appearance of people and that animals experienced modifications that they passed on to their offspring.

In December 1831, Darwin sailed as a naturalist on the H.M.S. *Beagle*, which surveyed the shores of South America and some Pacific islands. During the five-year expedition, Darwin collected and examined specimens of plant and animal life; he concluded that many animal species had perished, that new species had emerged, and that there were links between extinct and living species.

Influenced by Lyell's achievement, Darwin sought to interpret distant natural occurrences by means of observable processes still going on today. He could not accept that a fixed number of distinct and separate species had been instantaneously created a mere six thousand years ago. In the *Origin of Species* (1859) and the *Descent of Man* (1871), Darwin used empirical evidence to show that the wide variety of animal species was due to a process of development over many millennia, and he supplied a convincing theory that explained how evolution operates.

Darwin adopted the Malthusian idea (see page 508) that the population reproduces faster than the food supply, causing a struggle for existence. Not all infant organisms grow to adulthood; not all adult organisms live to old age. The principle of *natural selection* determines which members of the species have a better chance for survival. The offspring of a lion, giraffe, or insect are not exact duplications of their parents. A baby lion might have the potential for being slightly faster or stronger than its parents; a baby giraffe might grow up to have a longer neck than its parents; an insect might have a slightly different color. These small variations give the organism a crucial advantage in the struggle for food and against natural enemies. The organism favored by nature is more likely to reach maturity, to mate, and to pass on its superior qualities to its offspring, some of which will acquire the advantageous trait to an even

greater degree than the parent. Over many generations the favorable characteristic becomes more pronounced and more widespread within the species. Over centuries, natural selection causes the death of old species and the creation of new ones. Very few of the species that dwelt on earth ten million years ago still survive today, and many new ones, including human beings, have emerged. People themselves are products of natural selection, evolving from earlier, lower, nonhuman forms of life.

Darwinism and Christianity

Like Newton's law of universal gravitation, Darwin's theory of evolution had revolutionary consequences in areas other than science. Evolution challenged a traditional Christian belief. To some, it undermined the infallibility of Scripture and the conviction that the Bible was indeed the Word of God. Darwin's theory touched off a great religious controversy between fundamentalists who defended a literal interpretation of Genesis and advocates of the new biology. In time, most religious thinkers tried to reconcile evolution with the Christian view that there was a Creation and that it had a purpose. These Christian thinkers held that God was the creator and the director of the evolutionary processes.

Darwinism ultimately helped end the practice of relying on the Bible as an authority in questions of science, completing a trend initiated by Galileo. Darwinism contributed to the waning of religious belief and to a growing secular attitude; the new secularism dismissed or paid scant attention to the Christian view of a universe designed by God and a soul that rises to heaven. For many, the conclusion was inescapable: nature contained no divine design or purpose, and the human species itself was a chance product of impersonal forces. The core idea of Christianity—that people were children of God participating in a drama of salvation—rested more than ever on faith rather than reason. Some even talked openly about the death of

God. The notion that people are sheer accidents of nature was shocking. Copernicus had deprived people of the comforting belief that the earth had been placed in the center of the universe just for them; Darwin deprived people of the privilege of being God's special creation, thereby contributing to the feeling of anxiety that characterizes the twentieth century.

Social Darwinism

Darwin's theories were extended by others beyond the realm in which he had worked. Social thinkers, who recklessly applied Darwin's conclusions to the social order, produced theories that had dangerous consequences for society. Social Darwinists—those who transferred Darwin's scientific theories to social and economic issues—used the terms "struggle for existence" and "survival of the fittest" to buttress economic individualism and political conservatism. Successful businessmen, they said, had demonstrated their fitness to succeed in the competitive world of business. Their success accorded with nature's laws and therefore was beneficial to society; those who lost out in the social-economic struggle had demonstrated their unfitness. Using Darwin's model of organisms evolving and changing slowly over tens of thousands of years, conservatives insisted that society too should experience change at an unhurried pace. Instant reforms conflicted with nature's laws and wisdom and resulted in a deterioration of the social body.

The application of Darwin's biological concepts to the social world where they did not apply also buttressed imperialism, racism, nationalism, and militarism. Social Darwinists insisted nations and races were engaged in a struggle for survival in which only the fittest survive and deserve to survive. Karl Pearson, a British professor of mathematics, wrote in *National Life from the Standpoint of Science* (1905):

History shows me only one way, and one way only in which a higher state of civilization has been produced, namely the struggle of race with race, and the survival of the physically and mentally fitter race. . . . The path of progress is strewn with the wrecks of nations; traces are everywhere to be seen of the hecatombs of inferior races, and of victims who found not the narrow way to perfection. Yet these dead people are, in very truth, the stepping stones on which mankind has arisen to the higher intellectual and deeper emotional life of today.[5]

"We are a conquering race," said U.S. Senator Albert J. Beveridge. "We must obey our blood and occupy new markets, and if necessary, new lands."[6] "War is a biological necessity of the first importance,"[7] exclaimed the Prussian General von Bernhardi in *Germany and the Next War* (1911).

Darwinian biology was used to promote the belief in Anglo-Saxon (British and American) and Teutonic (German) racial superiority. These peoples attributed the growth of the British Empire, the expansion of the United States to the Pacific, and the extension of German power to their racial qualities. The domination of other peoples—American Indians, Africans, Asians, Poles—was regarded as the natural right of the superior race. British naturalist Alfred Russel Wallace, who arrived at the theory of evolution independently of Darwin, wrote in 1864:

The intellectual and moral, as well as the physical qualities of the European are superior; the same power and capacities which have made him rise in a few centuries from the condition of the wandering savage . . . to his present state of culture and advancement . . . enable him when in contact with savage man, to conquer in the struggle for existence and to increase at his expense.[8]

The theory of evolution was a great achievement of the rational mind, but in the hands of the Social Darwinists it served to undermine the Enlightenment tradition. Whereas the philosophes emphasized human equality, Social Darwinists divided humanity into racial superiors and inferiors. Whereas the philosophes believed that states would increasingly submit to the rule of law to reduce violent conflicts, Social Darwinists regarded racial and national conflict as a biological necessity, a law of history and a means to progress. In propagating a tooth-and-claw version of human and international relations, Social Darwinists dispensed with the humanitarian and cosmopolitan sentiments of the philosophes and distorted the image of progress. Their views promoted territorial aggrandizement and military build-up and led many to welcome World War I. The Social Darwinist notion of the struggle of races for survival became a core doctrine of the Nazi party after World War I and provided the "scientific" and "ethical" justification for genocide.

Marxism

Karl Marx (1818–1883) was born of German-Jewish parents (both descendants of prominent rabbis). To save his job as a lawyer, Marx's father converted to Protestantism. Enrolled at a university to study law, Marx switched to philosophy. In 1842, Marx was editing a newspaper that was soon suppressed by the Prussian authorities for its outspoken ideas. Leaving his native Rhineland, Marx went to Paris where he met another German, Friedrich Engels (1820–1895), who was the son of a prosperous textile manufacturer. Marx and Engels entered into a lifelong collaboration and became members of socialist groups. In February 1848 they published the *Communist Manifesto,* which called for a working-class revolution to overthrow the capitalist system. Forced to leave France for his political views in 1849, Marx moved to London where he spent the rest of his life.

Although supported by Engels, Marx was continually short of funds, and at times he and his wife and daughters lived in dreadful poverty. In London, Marx spent years writing *Capital*—a study and critique of the modern capitalistic economic system that he predicted would be destroyed by a socialist revolution.

A Science of History

As did so many thinkers influenced by the Enlightenment, Marx believed that human history, like the operations of nature, was governed by scientific law. Marx was a strict materialist; rejecting all religious and metaphysical interpretations of both nature and history, he sought to fashion an empirical science of society. He viewed religion as a human creation—a product of people's imagination and feelings, a consolation for the oppressed—and the happiness it brought as an illusion. Real happiness would come, said Marx, not by transcending the natural world, but by improving it. Rather than deluding oneself by seeking refuge from life's misfortunes in an imaginary world, one must confront the ills of society and reform them.

The world could be rationally understood and changed, said Marx. People were free to make their own history, but to do so effectively, they must comprehend the inner meaning of history—the laws governing human affairs in the past and operating in the present. To Marx, history was not an assortment of unrelated and disconnected events; rather, like the growth of a plant, it proceeded according to its own inner laws. Marx claimed to have uncovered these laws. He said that economic and technological factors—the way in which goods are produced and wealth is distributed—were the moving forces in history. They accounted for historical change and were the basis of all culture—politics, law, religion, morals and philosophy.

Marx said that material technology—the methods of cultivating land and the tools for manufacturing goods—determined society's social and political arrangements and its intellectual outlooks. For example, the hand mill, the loose yoke, and the wooden plow had given rise to feudal lords, whereas power-driven machines had spawned the industrial capitalists. As material technology expanded, it came into conflict with established economic, social, and political forms, and the resulting tension produced change. Thus, feudal patterns could not endure when power machinery had become the dominant mode of production. Consequently, medieval guilds, communal agriculture, even the domestic production of goods gave way to free labor, private property, and the factory system of manufacturing. As Marx put it, the expansion of technology necessitated and triggered a change from feudal social and economic relationships to capitalist ones. Ultimately, the change in economic-technological conditions would become the cause for great political changes.

This process was most clearly demonstrated by the French Revolution. Radical changes in the economic foundations of society had taken place since the Middle Ages without corresponding political changes. However, the forces of economic change could not be contained in outdated political forms. In France this tension exploded into revolution. Whatever their conscious intentions, said Marx, the bourgeois leaders of the French Revolution had scattered feudal remnants to the wind; they had promoted free competition and commercial expansion and transferred power from the landed aristocracy to the leaders of finance and industry. Not every revolutionary change in history is explosive, according to Marx, but whenever major economic changes take place, political and social changes must follow.

Class Conflict

Throughout history, said Marx, there has been a class struggle between those who own the means of production and those whose labor has been exploited to provide wealth for this upper class. This opposing tension between classes has pushed history forward into higher stages. In the ancient world, when wealth was based on land, the struggle was between master and slave, patrician and plebeian; during the Middle Ages, when land was still the predominant mode of production, the struggle was between lord and serf. In the modern industrial world, two sharply opposed classes were confronting each other— the capitalists owning the factories, mines, banks, and transportation systems, and the exploited wage earners (the proletariat).

The class with economic power also controlled the state, said Marx and Engels. That class used political power to protect and in-

Karl Marx (left) and Friedrich Engels (right) with Marx's Three Daughters, 1860s. Marx saw history solely in terms of economic and social interrelationships, a struggle between laborers and the owners of the means of production. He called for the proletariat to overthrow capitalism and to establish a classless society. (*Culver Pictures*)

crease its property and to hold down the laboring class. "Thus the ancient State was above all the slaveowners' state for holding down the slaves," said Engels, "as a feudal State was the organ of the nobles for holding down the . . . serfs, and the modern representative State is the instrument of the exploitation of wage-labor by capital."[9]

Marx and Engels said, too, that the class that controlled material production also controlled mental production, that is, the ideas held by the ruling class became the dominant ideas of society. These ideas, presented as laws of nature or moral and religious standards, were regarded as the truth by oppressor and oppressed alike. In reality, however, these ideas merely reflected the special economic interests of the ruling class. Thus, said Marx, bourgeois ideologists would insist that natural rights and laissez faire were laws of nature having universal validity. But these "laws" were born of the bourgeoisies' needs in their struggle to wrest power from an obsolete feudal regime and to protect their property from the state. Similarly, nineteenth-century slaveholders convinced themselves that slavery was morally right—that it had God's approval and was good for the slave. Slaveowners and capitalist employers alike may have defended their labor systems by citing universal principles that they thought were true, but in reality their systems rested on a simple economic consideration—slave labor was good for the pocketbook of the slaveowner and wage labor was good in the same way for the capitalist.

The Destruction of Capitalism

Under capitalism, said Marx, the worker knew only poverty. He worked long hours for low wages, suffered from periodic unemployment, and lived in squalid overcrowded apartments. Most monstrous of all, he was forced to send his young children into the factories.

Children of nine or ten years are dragged from their squalid beds at two, three, or four o'clock in the morning and compelled to work for a bare subsistence until ten, eleven, or twelve at night, their limbs wearing away, their frames dwindling, their faces whitening, and their humanity absolutely sinking into a stone-like torpor, utterly horrible to contemplate.[10]

Capitalism also produced another kind of poverty, said Marx—poverty of the human spirit. Under capitalism the factory worker was reduced to a laboring beast, performing tedious and repetitive tasks in a dark, dreary, dirty cave, an altogether inhuman environment that deprived people of their human sensibilities. Unlike the artisans in their own shops, factory workers found no pleasure and took no pride in their work; they did

not have the satisfaction of creating a finished product that expressed their skills. Work, said Marx, should be a source of fulfillment for people. It should enable people to affirm their personalities and develop their potential. Capitalism, by treating people not as human beings, but as cogs in the production process, alienated people from their work, themselves, and one another.

Marx believed that capitalist control of the economy and the government would not endure forever. The capitalist system would perish just as the feudal society of the Middle Ages and the slave society of the ancient world had perished. From the ruins of a dead capitalist society a new economic-social system, socialism, would emerge.

Marx predicted how capitalism would be destroyed. Periodic unemployment would increase the misery of the workers and intensify their hatred of capitalists. Small businessmen and shopkeepers, unable to compete with the great capitalists, would sink into the ranks of the working class, greatly expanding its numbers. Society would become polarized into a small group of immensely wealthy capitalists and a vast proletariat, poor, embittered, and desperate. This monopoly of capital by the few would become a brake on the productive process. Growing increasingly conscious of their misery, the workers—aroused, educated, and organized by communist intellectuals—would revolt. They would smash the government that helped the capitalists maintain their dominance. Then they would confiscate the property of the capitalists, abolish private property, place the means of production in the workers' hands, and organize a new society. The *Communist Manifesto* ends with a ringing call for revolution:

The Communists . . . openly declare that their ends can be attained only by the forcible overthrow of all existing social conditions. Let the ruling classes tremble at a Communist revolution. The proletarians have nothing to lose but their chains. They have a world to win.

Workingmen of all countries, unite![11]

Marx did not say a great deal about the new society that would be ushered in by the socialist revolution. With the destruction of capitalism, the distinction between capitalist and worker would cease and with it the class conflict. No longer would society be divided into haves and have-nots, oppressor and oppressed. Since this classless society would contain no exploiters, there would be no need for a state, which was merely an instrument for maintaining and protecting the power of the exploiting class. Thus, the state would eventually wither away. The production and distribution of goods would be carried out through community planning and communal sharing, replacing the capitalist system of competition. People would work at varied tasks, rather than being confined to one form of employment, just as Fourier had advocated. No longer factory slaves, people would be free to fulfill their human potential, to improve their relationships on a basis of equality with others, and to work together for the common good.

The Influence of Marx

Marxism had immense appeal for both the downtrodden and intellectuals. It promised to end the injustices of industrial society; it claimed the certainty of science; it assured adherents that the triumph of their cause was guaranteed by history. In many ways, Marxism was a secular religion—the proletariat became a chosen class endowed with a mission to achieve worldly salvation for humanity.

Marx's influence grew during the second wave of industrialization in the closing decades of the nineteenth century, when class bitterness between the proletariat and the bourgeoisie seemed to worsen. Many workers thought that liberals and conservatives had no sympathy for their plight and that the only way to improve their lot was through socialist parties. It seemed to Marx's advocates that his predictions would be realized: monopoly capitalist firms in the advanced nations

would swallow small competitors and, for the sake of profit, draw all the world into capitalism. Moreover, severe economic depressions seemed to force more and more people out of farming or small business and into the working class. Others disagreed with this scenario, pointing out that the workers were not getting poorer and that Marx's picture may have been accurate for the mid-century but not for the end of the century, that workers, because of their unions, increased productivity, and the protection by the state had improved their lives considerably (see Chapter 26).

Marx's emphasis on economic forces has immeasurably broadened the perception of historians, who now explore the economic factors in historical developments. This approach has greatly expanded our understanding of Rome's decline, the outbreak of the French Revolution and the American Civil War, and other crucial developments. Marx's theory of class conflict has provided social scientists with a useful tool for analyzing social process. His theory of alienation has been absorbed by sociologists and psychologists. Of particular value to social scientists is Marx's insight that the ideas people hold to be true and the values they consider valid often veil economic interests. On the political level, both the socialist parties of western Europe, which pressed for reform through parliamentary methods, and the communist regimes in Russia and China, which came to power through revolution, claimed to be heirs of Marx.

Critics of Marx

Critics point out serious weaknesses in Marxism. The rigid Marxist who tries to squeeze all historical events into an economic framework is at a disadvantage. Economic forces alone will not explain the triumph of Christianity in the Roman Empire, the fall of Rome, the Crusades, the French Revolution, modern imperialism, World War I, or the rise of Hitler. Economic explanations fall particularly flat in

Dante Gabriel Rossetti (1828–1882): Launcelot in the Queen's Chamber. Pre-Raphaelite artists like Rossetti felt that the dry spirit of utilitarianism stunted the individual. They wanted to save humankind through the power of art. A sweeping Romanticism, with its love of myths and the occult, characterized their works. (*By courtesy of Birmingham Museums and Art Gallery*)

trying to account for the emergence of modern nationalism, whose appeal, resting on deeply ingrained emotional needs, crosses class lines. The great struggles of the twentieth century have not been between classes, but between nations.

Many of Marx's predictions or expectations have not materialized. Workers in Western lands did not become the oppressed and impoverished working class that Marx described in the mid-nineteenth century. Western workers, because of increased productivity and the efforts of labor unions and reform-minded governments, improved their lives considerably, so that they now enjoy the highest standard of living in history. The tremendous growth of a middle class of profes-

sionals, civil service employees, and small-business persons belies Marx's prediction that capitalist society would be polarized into a small group of very rich capitalists and a great mass of destitute workers. Marx believed that socialist revolutions would break out in the advanced industrialized lands. But the socialist revolutions of the twentieth century have occurred in underdeveloped, predominantly agricultural states. The state in communist lands, far from withering away, has grown more centralized, powerful, and oppressive. In no country where communist revolutionaries have seized power have people achieved the liberty that Marx desired. All these failed predictions and expectations seem to contradict Marx's claim that his theories rested on an unassailable scientific foundation.

Anarchism

Anarchism was another radical movement that attacked capitalism. Like Marxists, anarchists protested the exploitation of workers, denounced the coercive authority of government, and envisioned a stateless society. Only by abolishing the state, said anarchists, could the individual live a free and full life. To achieve these ends, a small number of anarchists advocated revolutionary terrorism; others, like the great Russian novelist Leo Tolstoy, rejected all violence. These anarchists sought to destroy the state by refusing to cooperate with it.

Pierre Joseph Proudhon

Anarchists drew inspiration from Pierre Joseph Proudhon (1809–1865), a self-educated French printer and typesetter. Proudhon criticized social theorists who devised elaborate systems that regimented daily life, conflicted with human nature, and deprived people of their personal liberty. He desired a new society that maximized individual freedom. He looked back longingly to preindustrial society, free of exploitation and corruption and of great manufacturers and financiers. He had great respect for the dignity of labor and wanted to liberate it from the exploitation and false values of industrial capitalism. An awakened working class would construct a new moral and social order. Proudhon believed that people would deal justly with each other, respect each other, and develop their full potential in a society of small peasants, shopkeepers, and artisans. Such a society would not require a government; government only fosters privilege and suppresses freedom:

To be governed is to be watched over, inspected, spied on, directed, legislated at, regulated, docketed,
indoctrinated, preached at, controlled . . . censored, ordered about, by men who have neither the right nor the knowledge nor the virtue. To be governed means to be, at each operation, at each transaction, at each movement . . . registered, controlled, taxed . . . hampered, reformed, rebuked, arrested. It is to be, on the pretext of the great interest, taxed, drilled . . . exploited . . . repressed, fined, abused. . . . That's government, that's its justice, that's its morality.[12]

Proudhon was less a theorist than a man who could express passionately the disillusionment and disgust with the new industrial society that was developing in Europe.

Mikhail Bakunin

Anarchism had a particular appeal in Russia, where there was no representative government and no way, other than petitions to the tsar, to legally redress injustice. A repressive regime, economic backwardness, a youth movement passionately committed to improving the lives of the masses, and a magnetic leader, Mikhail Bakunin (1814–1876) all contributed in shaping the Russian anarchist tradition. Bakunin was a man of action who organized and fought for revolution and set an example of revolutionary fervor. The son of a Russian noble, he left the tsar's army to study philosophy in the West, where he was attracted to the ideas of Proudhon and Marx. He was arrested for participating in the German revolution of 1848 and turned over to tsarist officials. He served six years in prison and was then banished to Siberia, from which he escaped in 1861.

Bakunin devoted himself to organizing secret societies that would lead the oppressed in revolt. Whereas Marx held that revolution would occur in the industrial lands through the efforts of a class-conscious proletariat, Bakunin wanted all oppressed people to revolt, including the peasants (the vast majority of the population in central and eastern Europe). Toward this end, he favored secret societies and terrorism. He argued that a single act of terrorism, such as an assassination of a hated official, could spark the revolution.

Marx and Bakunin disagreed on one crucial issue of strategy. Marx wanted to organize the workers into mass political parties, Bakunin, on the other hand, held that revolutions should be fought by secret societies of fanatic insurrectionists. Bakunin feared that after the Marxists overthrew the capitalist regime and seized power, they would become the new masters and exploiters, using the state to enhance their own power. They would, said Bakunin, become a "privileged minority . . . of *ex-workers,* who, once they become rulers or representatives of the people, cease to be workers and begin to look down upon the toiling people. From that time on they represent not the people but themselves and their claims to govern the people."[13] Therefore, said Bakunin, once the workers capture the state, they should destoy it forever. Bakunin's astute prediction that a socialist revolution would lead state power to intensify rather than disappear has been borne out in the twentieth century.

Anarchists engaged in several acts of political terrorism, including the assassination or attempted assassination of heads of state and key ministers, but they never waged a successful revolution. They failed to reverse the trend toward the concentration of power in industry and government that would characterize the twentieth century. But the motives that impelled them to challenge the values and institutions of modern society and to engage in acts of terror express emotional conditions that have not disappeared with the waning of anarchism.

Liberalism in Transition

In the early part of the nineteenth century, European liberals were preoccupied with protecting the rights of the individual against the demands of the state. They championed laissez faire because they feared that state interference in the economy to redress social evils would threaten individual rights and the free market that they thought were essential to personal liberty; they favored property requirements for voting and office holding, because they were certain that the unpropertied and uneducated masses lacked the wisdom and experience to exercise political responsibility.

In the last part of the century, liberals began—not without reservation and qualification—to support extended suffrage and government action to remedy the abuses of unregulated industrialization. This growing concern for the welfare of the laboring poor coincided with and was influenced by an unprecedented proliferaton of humanitarian movements on both sides of the Atlantic. Nurtured by both the Enlightenment and Christian traditions, reform movements called for the prohibition of child labor, schooling for the masses, humane treatment for prisoners and the mentally ill, equality for women, the abolition of slavery, and an end to war. By the beginning of the twentieth century, liberalism had evolved into liberal democracy and laissez faire had been superseded by a reluctant acceptance of social legislation and government regulation. But from beginning to end, the central concern of liberals remained the protection of individual rights.

Alexis de Tocqueville

Few mid-nineteenth century thinkers grasped the growing significance of democracy as did Alexis de Tocqueville, the French aristocrat and statesman. In *Democracy in America* (1835–1840), based on his travels in the United States, de Tocqueville with cool detachment and brilliance analyzed the nature, merits, and weaknesses of his subject. In contrast to France of the Old Regime, said de Tocqueville, American society had no hereditary aristrocracy with special privileges and the avenues to social advancement and political participation were open to all. De Tocqueville held that democracy was more just than aristocratic government, and he predicted that it would be the political system of the future.

But de Tocqueville also recognized and explored a core problem of democracy: in a democratic society people's passion to be equal outweighs their commitment to liberty. Spurred by the ideal of equality, said de Tocqueville, people in a democracy desire the honors and possessions that they think are their due. But since people are not naturally equal in ability, many are frustrated and turn to the state to secure for them those advantages that they cannot obtain by themselves. Consequently, there is an ever-present danger in a democracy that people, driven by a passion for equality, will surrender their liberty to a central state that promises to provide the privileges they seek. To prevent democracy from degenerating into state despotism, de Tocqueville urged strengthening institutions of local government, forming numerous private associations over which the state has no control, protecting the independence of the judiciary, and preserving a free press.

Another danger in a democratic society, said de Tocqueville, is the tendency of the majority to impose its viewpoint over the minority. The majority demands conformity of belief. Its power is so absolute and irresistible, held de Tocqueville, that the minority is fearful to stray from the track which the majority prescribes. De Tocqueville declared: "I think that liberty is endangered when this power [of the majority] is checked by no obstacles which may retard its course, and force it to moderate its own vehemence."[14]

Although recognizing the limitations of democracy, de Tocqueville did not seek to reverse its growth. In this new age that is dawning, he said,

all who shall attempt . . . to base freedom upon aristocratic privilege will fail . . . all who shall attempt to draw and to retain authority within a single class, will fail. . . . All . . . who would establish or secure the independence and the dignity of their fellow-men, must show themselves the friends of equality. . . . Thus the question is not

how to reconstruct aristocratic society, but how to make liberty proceed out of that democratic state of society in which God has placed us.[15]

John Stuart Mill

The transition from laissez-faire liberalism to a more socially conscious and democratic liberalism is seen in the thought of John Stuart Mill, a British philosopher and statesman. Mill's *On Liberty* (1859) is the classic statement of individual freedom—that the government and the majority have no right to interfere with the liberty of another human being whose actions do no injury to others. Mill regarded freedom of thought and expression, the toleration of opposing and unpopular viewpoints, as a necessary precondition for the shaping of a rational, moral, and civilized citizen. Like other liberals, Mill would place limits on the power of government, for in an authoritarian state citizens cannot develop their moral and intellectual potential.

Although he feared the state, Mill also recognized the necessity for state intervention to promote the general good. For example, he maintained that it was permissible for the state to require children to attend school against the wishes of their parents, to regulate hours of labor, to promote public health, and to provide workers' compensation and old age insurance.

In *Considerations on Representative Government* (1861), Mill endorsed the active participation of all citizens, including the lower classes, in the political life of the state. However, he also proposed a system of plural voting in which education and character would determine the number of votes each person was entitled to cast. In this way Mill, a cautious democrat, sought to protect the individual from the tyranny of a politically unprepared majority.

In contrast to most of his contemporaries, Mill felt that differences between the sexes (and between the classes) were due far more to education than to inherited inequalities. Believing that all people—women as well as

John Stuart Mill. Although labeled a utilitarian, John Stuart Mill fits no category exactly. He concerned himself with most of the major issues of industrialization, including the definition of productive and unproductive labor, the distribution of gains from international commerce, and the precise relationship between profits and wages. (*Historical Pictures Service, Chicago*)

men—should be able to develop their talents and intellects as fully as possible, Mill was an early champion of female equality, including the suffrage: In the "Subjection of Women" he wrote:

. . . the principle which regulates the existing social relations between the two sexes—the legal subordination of one sex to the other—is wrong in itself, and now one of the chief hindrances to human improvement: and . . . it ought to be replaced by a principle of perfect equality, admitting no power or privilege on the one side, nor disability on the other.[16]

Thomas Hill Green

Thomas Hill Green, an Oxford University professor, argued that laissez faire protected the interests of the economically powerful class and ignored the welfare of the nation. Accordingly he approved of legislation to promote better conditions of health, labor, and education. Green valued private property but could not see how this principle helped the poor. "A man who possesses nothing but his powers of labor and who has to sell these to a capitalist for bare daily maintenance, might as well . . . be denied rights of property altogether."[17]

For Green, liberalism encompassed more than the protection of individual rights from an oppressive government; a truly liberal society, he said, gives people the opportunity to fulfill their moral potential and human capacities. The liberal state, said Green, has a moral obligation to create social conditions that permit the individual to pursue this self-development. Toward that end, said Green, the state should promote public health, ensure decent housing, and provide for education. An ignorant person, Green held, cannot be a good citizen and cannot be morally self-sufficient. Since many parents will not voluntarily make provisions for the education of their children, it behooves the state to install a system of compulsory education.

Green remained an advocate of capitalism but rejected strict laissez faire which, he said, benefited only a particular class. For Green, the liberal state must concern itself with the common good:

If the ideal of true freedom is the maximum of power for all members of human society alike to make the best of themselves, we are right in refusing to ascribe the glory of freedom to a state in which the apparent elevation of the few is founded on the degradation of the many.[18]

To be sure, many liberals regarded state intervention as a betrayal of the liberal principle of individual freedom and held to the traditional liberal view that the plight of the downtrodden was not a legitimate concern of the state. In *The Man versus the State* (1884) British philosopher Herbert Spencer rejected the idea "that evils of all kinds should be dealt with by the State." The outcome of state intervention, he said, is that "each member of the community as an individual would be a slave to the community as a whole . . . and the slavery will not be mild."[19] Committed to a philosophy of extreme individualism, Spencer never abandoned the view that the state was an evil and oppressive institution.

In general, however, liberals in Britain increasingly acknowledged the need for social legislation in the closing decades of the nineteenth century; the foundations for the British welfare state were being laid. On the continent, too, social welfare laws were enacted. To be sure, the motives behind such legislation were quite diverse and often had little to do with liberal sentiments (see Chapter 26). Nevertheless, in several countries liberalism was expanding into political and social democracy, a trend that would continue in the twentieth century.

Notes

1. Cited in Damian Grant, *Realism* (London: Methuen, 1970), pp. 31–32.

2. Cited in F. W. J. Hemmings, ed., *The Age of Realism* (New Jersey: Humanities Press, 1978), p. 152.

3. Emile Zola, *The Experimental Novel* (New York: Haskell House, 1964), trans. by Belle M. Sherman, pp. 20–21, 23.

4. Quoted in Ernst Cassirer, *The Problem of Knowledge* trans. by William H. Woglom and Charles W. Hendel (New Haven: Yale University Press, 1950), p. 244.

5. Karl Pearson, *National Life from the Standpoint of Science* (London: Adam and Charles Black, 1905), pp. 21, 64.

6. Quoted in H. W. Koch, "Social Darwinism in the 'New Imperialism,' " in H. W. Koch, ed., *The Origins of the First World War* (New York: Taplinger, 1972), p. 341.

7. Ibid., p. 345.

8. Quoted in John C. Greene, *The Death of Adam* (New York: Mentor Books, 1961), p. 313.

9. Friedrich Engels, *The Origin of the Family, Private Property and the State,* in Emile Burns, *A Handbook of Marxism* (New York: Random House, 1935), p. 330.

10. Karl Marx, *Capital* (Chicago: Charles H. Kerr, 1912), 1:268.

11. Karl Marx, *The Communist Manifesto,* trans. by Samuel Moore (Chicago: Henry Regnery, 1954), pp. 81–82.

12. Quoted in James Joll, *The Anarchists* (New York: Grosset and Dunlop, 1964), pp. 78–79.

13. Excerpted in G. P. Maximoff, ed., *The Political Philosophy of Bakunin* (Glencoe, Ill.: The Free Press, 1953), p. 287.

14. Alexis de Tocqueville, *Democracy in America,* trans. by Henry Reeve (New York: Oxford University Press, 1947), p. 162.

15. Ibid., pp. 493–494.

16. John Stuart Mill, *The Subjection of Women* in *On Liberty Etc.* (London: Oxford University Press, 1924), p. 427.

17. Thomas Hill Green, *Lectures on the Principles of Political Obligation* (Ann Arbor, Michigan: The University of Michigan Press, 1967), p. 219.

18. Thomas Hill Green, "Liberal Legislation or Freedom of Contract," a lecture given at Leicester, 1881, excerpted in Alan Bullock and Maurice Shock, eds. *The Liberal Tradition* (London: Adam and Charles Black, 1956), p. 181.

19. Herbert Spencer, *The Man versus the State* (London: Watts, 1940), pp. 34, 49–50.

Suggested Reading

Bullock, Alan and Shock, Maurice, eds., *The Liberal Tradition* (1956). Well chosen selections from the writings of British liberals; the introduction is an excellent survey of liberal thought.

de Ruggiero, G., *The History of European Liberalism* (1927). A good starting point.

Farrington, Benjamin, *What Darwin Really Said* (1966). A brief study of Darwin's work.

Grant, Damian, *Realism* (1970). A good short survey.

Greene, J. C., *The Death of Adam* (1961). The impact of evolution on Western thought.

Hemmings, F. W. J., ed., *The Age of Realism* (1978). A valuable collection of essays and a good bibliography.

Hofstadter, Richard, *Social Darwinism in American Thought* (1955). A classic treatment of the impact of evolution on American conservatism, imperialism, and racism.

Joll, James, *The Anarchists* (1964). A fine treatment of anarchists, their lives, and thought.

McLellan, David, ed., *Karl Marx: Selected Writings* (1977). A balanced selection of Marx's writings.

McLellan, David, *Karl Marx: His Life and Thought* (1977). A highly regarded biography.

Manuel, Frank E., *The Prophets of Paris* (1965). Contains a valuable chapter on Comte.

Richter, Melvin, *The Politics of Conscience* (1964). A study of T. H. Green and his age.

Review Questions

1. How did realism differ from romanticism?

2. Realism and naturalism coincided with an attitude of mind shaped by science, industrialism, and secularism. Discuss this statement.

3. What is the relationship between positivism and science?

4. What was Comte's "law of the three stages"?

5. The theory of evolution had revolutionary consequences in areas other than science. Discuss this statement.

6. Why were Social Darwinist theories so popular?

7. Summarize Marx's philosophy of history?

8. What did Marx have in common with the philosophes of the Enlightenment?

9. Why did Marx think that capitalism was doomed? How would its destruction happen?

10. Why did Proudhon hate government?

11. In what ways did Bakunin and Marx differ?

12. Relate the theories of de Tocqueville, Mill, Green, and Spencer to the evolution of liberalism. Draw relevant comparisons and contrasts regarding their theories.

25

The Surge of Nationalism:
From Liberal to Extreme
Nationalism

*T*he Revolutions of 1848 ended in failure, but nationalist energies were too powerful to contain. In 1867 Hungary gained the autonomy it had sought in 1848, and by 1870, the unification of both Italy and Germany was complete.

The leading architects of Italian and German unification were not liberal idealists or romantic dreamers of the type who had fought in the Revolutions of 1848; they were tough-minded practitioners of *Realpolitik*, "the politics of reality." Shrewd and calculating statesmen, they respected power and knew how to wield it; focusing on the world as it actually is, they dismissed ideals as illusory, noble sentiments that impeded effective action. *Realpolitik* was the political counterpart of realism and positivism. All three outlooks shared the desire to view things coldly and objectively, as they are rather than as idealists would like them to be.

Nationalism, gaining in intensity in the last part of the nineteenth century, was to become the dominant spiritual force in European life. Once Germany was unified, Pan-Germans sought to incorporate Germans living outside the Reich into the new Germany and to build a vast overseas empire. Russian Pan-Slavs dreamed of bringing the Slavs of eastern Europe under the control of "Mother Russia." Growing increasingly resentful of Magyar and German domination, the Slavic minorities of the Hapsburg Empire agitated for recognition of their national rights. In the late nineteenth century, nationalism became increasingly belligerent, intolerant, and irrational, threatening both the peace of Europe and the liberal-humanist tradition of the Enlightenment.

The Unification of Italy

In 1848, liberals had failed to drive the Austrians out of Italy and to unite the Italian nation. By 1870, however, Italian unification had been achieved. But the movement for unification had faced many obstacles.

Map 25.1 Unification of Italy, 1859–1870

The map legend reads:

- Kingdom of Sardinia before 1859
- To Kingdom of Sardinia, 1859
- To Kingdom of Sardinia, 1860
- To Kingdom of Italy, 1866, 1870

Map labels: SWITZERLAND, AUSTRIAN EMPIRE, SAVOY To France 1860, From Austria LOMBARDY, Milan, From Austria VENETIA (1866), Venice, FRANCE, PIEDMONT, Po R., PARMA, MODENA, Bologna, ROMAGNA, OTTOMAN EMPIRE, Genoa, NICE To France 1860, Nice, Florence, Pisa, TUSCANY, THE MARCHES, Tiber R., PAPAL STATES, (1870) Rome, ADRIATIC SEA, CORSICA (France), SARDINIA, Naples, KINGDOM OF THE TWO SICILIES, MEDITERRANEAN SEA, Palermo, SICILY, Straits of Messina

Forces For and Against Unity

In 1815, Italy consisted of several separate states. In the south, a Bourbon king ruled the Kingdom of the Two Sicilies; the pope governed the Papal States in central Italy; Hapsburg Austria ruled Lombardy and Venetia in the north; Hapsburg princes sub-servient to Austria ruled the duchies of Tuscany, Parma, and Modena. Piedmont in the northwest and the island of Sardinia were governed by an Italian dynasty—the House of Savoy.

Besides all these political divisions, Italy was divided economically and culturally. Throughout the peninsula, attachment to the local region was stronger than devotion to national unity. Economic ties between north and south were weak; inhabitants of the northern Italian cities felt little closeness to Sicilian peasants. Except for the middle class, most Italians clung to the values of the Old Regime. Believing that society was ordered by God, they accepted without question rule by prince and pope and rejected the values associated with the French Revolution and the Enlightenment. To these traditionalists, national unity was also hateful. It would deprive the pope of his control over central Italy, introduce liberal ideas that would undermine clerical and aristocratic authority, and depose legitimate princes.

During the wars of the French Revolution, France had occupied Italy. The French eliminated many barriers to trade among the Italian states; they built roads that improved links between the various regions, and they introduced a standard system of law over most of the land. The French had also given the Italian states constitutions, representative assemblies, and the concept of the state as a community of citizens.

The Italian middle class believed that expelling foreign rulers and forging national unity would continue the process of enlightened reform initiated by the French occupation, and that that process would promote economic growth. Merchants and manufacturers wanted to abolish taxes on goods transported from one Italian state to another; they wanted roads and railways built to link the peninsula together; they wanted to do away with the numerous systems of coinage and weights and measures that complicated business transactions. Italians who had served Napoleon as local officials, clerks, and army officers resisted the restoration of clerical and feudal privileges that denied them career opportunities.

An expanding intellectual elite, through novels, poetry, and works of history, awakened interest in Italy's glorious past. They insisted that a people who had built the Roman Empire and had produced the Renaissance must not remain weak and divided,

their land occupied by Austrians. These sentiments appealed particularly to university students and the middle class. But the rural masses, illiterate and preoccupied with the hardships of daily life, had little concern for this struggle for national revival.

Failed Revolutions

Secret societies kept alive the hopes for liberty and independence from foreign rule in the period after 1815. The most important of these societies was the Carbonari, which had clubs in every state in Italy. In 1820 the Carbonari, its members drawn largely from the middle class and the army, enjoyed a few months of triumph in the Kingdom of the Two Sicilies. Supported by the army and militia, they forced King Ferdinand I to grant a constitution and a parliamentary government. But Metternich feared that the germ of revolution would spread to other countries. Supported by Prussia and Russia, Austria suppressed the constitutional government in Naples and another revolution that broke out in Piedmont. In both cases, Austria firmly fixed an absolute ruler on the throne. In 1831–32, the Austrians suppressed another insurrection by the Carbonari in the Papal States. During these uprisings the peasants had given little support; indeed, they seemed to side with the traditional rulers.

After the failure of the Carbonari, a new generation of leaders emerged in Italy. One of them, Giuseppi Mazzini (1805–1872), dedicated his life to the creation of a united and republican Italy—a goal he pursued with extraordinary moral intensity and determination. Mazzini was both a romantic and a liberal. As a liberal, he fought for republican and constitutional government and held that national unity would enhance individual liberty. As a romantic, he sought truth through heightened feeling and intuition and believed that an awakened Italy would lead to the regeneration of humanity. Just as Rome had provided law and unity in the ancient world, and the Roman pope had led Latin Christendom during the Middle Ages, Mazzini believed that a third Rome, a newly united Italy, would usher in a new age of free nations, personal liberty, and equality. This era would represent great progress for humanity: peace, prosperity, and universal happiness would replace conflict, materialism, and self-interest. Given to religious mysticism, Mazzini saw a world of independent states founded on nationality, republicanism, and democracy as the fulfillment of God's plan.

After his release from prison for participating in the insurrection of 1831, Mazzini went into exile and founded a new organization—Young Italy. Consisting of dedicated revolutionaries, many of them students, Young Italy was intended to serve as the instrument for the awakening of Italy and the transformation of Europe into a brotherhood of free peoples. This sacred struggle, said Mazzini, demanded heroism and sacrifice.

Mazzini believed that a successful revolution must come from below—from the people, moved by a profound love for their nation. They must overthrow the Hapsburg princes and create a democratic republic. The Carbonari had failed, he said, because they had staged only local uprisings and had no overall plan for the liberation and unification of Italy. This could be achieved only by a revolution of the masses. Mazzini had great charisma, determination, courage, and eloquence; he was also a prolific writer. His idealism attracted the intelligentsia and youth and kept alive the spirit of national unity. He infused the *Risorgimento,* the movement for Italian unity, with spiritual intensity.

Mazzini's plans for a mass uprising against Austria and the princes failed. In 1834, a band of Mazzini's followers attempted to invade Savoy from bases in Switzerland. But everything went wrong, and the invasion collapsed. Other setbacks were suffered in 1837, 1841, and 1843–44. During the Revolutions of 1848, Italian liberal-nationalists had enjoyed initial successes (see Chapter 23). In Sicily, revolutionaries forced King Ferdinand to grant a liberal constitution. The rulers of Tuscany and Piedmont-Sardinia promised constitu-

tions. After five days of fighting, revolutionaries drove the Austrians out of Milan in Lombardy. The Austrians were also forced to evacuate Venice, where a republic was proclaimed. The pope fled Rome, and Mazzini was elected to an executive office in a new Roman Republic. However, the forces of reaction led by Hapsburg Austria regained their courage and their authority, and one by one, they crushed the revolutionary movements. Louis Napoleon's troops dissolved the infant Roman Republic and restored Pope Pius IX to power. Italy remained divided, and Austria still ruled the north.

Cavour and Victory over Austria

The failure of the Revolution of 1848 contained an obvious lesson: Mazzini's approach—an armed uprising by aroused masses—did not work. The reasons for failure were that the masses were not deeply committed to the nationalist cause, and that the revolutionaries were no match for the Austrian army. Italian nationalists now hoped that the Kingdom of Piedmont-Sardinia, ruled by an Italian dynasty, would expel the Austrians and lead the drive for unity. Count Camillo Benso di Cavour (1810–1861), the Chief Minister of Piedmont-Sardinia, became the architect of Italian unity.

Cavour, unlike Mazzini, was neither a dreamer nor a speechmaker, but a cautious and practical politician who realized that mass uprisings could not succeed against Austrian might. Moreover, mistrusting the common people, he did not approve of Mazzini's goal of a democratic republic. Cavour had no precise blueprint for unifying Italy. His immediate aim was to increase the territory of Piedmont by driving the Austrians from northern Italy and incorporating Lombardy and Venetia into Piedmont-Sardinia. But this expulsion could not be accomplished without allies, for Austria was a great power and Piedmont a small state. To improve Piedmont's image in foreign affairs, Cavour launched a reform program to strengthen the economy. He reorganized the currency, taxes, and the national debt; in addition, he had railways and steamships built, fostered improved agricultural methods, and encouraged new businesses. Within a few years, Piedmont had become a progressive modern state.

In 1855, Piedmont joined England and France in the Crimean War against Russia. Cavour had no quarrel with Russia, but sought the friendship of Britain and France and a chance to be heard in world affairs. At the peace conference, Cavour was granted an opportunity to denounce Austria for occupying Italian lands.

After the peace conference, Cavour continued to encourage anti-Austrian feeling among Italians and to search for foreign support. He found a supporter in Napoleon III (1852–1870), the French emperor, who hoped that a unified northern Italy would become an ally and client of France.

In 1858, Cavour and Napoleon III reached an agreement. If Austria attacked Piedmont, France would aid the Italian state. Piedmont would annex Lombardy and Venetia and parts of the Papal States. For its assistance, France would obtain Nice and Savoy from Piedmont. With this agreement in his pocket, Cavour cleverly maneuvered Austria into declaring war, for it had to appear that Austria was the aggressor.

Supported by French forces and taking advantage of poor Austrian planning, Piedmont conquered Lombardy and occupied Milan. But Napoleon III quickly had second thoughts. If Piedmont took any of the pope's territory, French Catholics would blame their own leader. Even more serious was the fear that Prussia, suspicious of French arms, would aid Austria. For these reasons Napoleon III, without consulting Cavour, signed an armistice with Austria. Piedmont would acquire Lombardy, but no more. An outraged Cavour demanded that his state continue the war until all northern Italy was liberated, but King Victor Emmanuel of Piedmont accepted the Austrian peace terms.

The Piedmont-Sardinian victory, however, proved greater than Cavour had anticipated.

During the conflict, patriots in Parma, Modena, Tuscany, and Romagna (one of the Papal States) had seized power. These new revolutionary governments voted to join with Piedmont. Neither France nor Austria would risk military action to thwart Piedmont's expansion. In return for Napoleon III's acquiescence, Piedmont ceded Nice and Savoy to France.

Garibaldi and Victory in the South

Piedmont's success spurred revolutionary activity in the Kingdom of the Two Sicilies. In the spring of 1860, some one thousand red-shirted adventurers and patriots led by Giuseppe Garibaldi (1807–1882) landed in Sicily. They were determined to liberate the land from its Bourbon ruler, and they succeeded.

An early supporter of Mazzini, Garibaldi had been forced to flee Italy to avoid arrest for his revolutionary activities. He spent thirteen years in South America, where he participated in revolutionary movements. There he learned the skills of the revolutionary's trade and toughened his body and will for the struggle that lay ahead.

Garibaldi held exceptional views for his day. He supported the liberation of all subject nationalities, female emancipation, the right of workers to organize, racial equality, and the abolition of capital punishment. But the cause of Italian national unity was his true religion. Whereas Cavour set his sights primarily on extending Piedmont's control over northern Italy, Garibaldi dedicated himself to the creation of a unified Italy.

Garibaldi returned to Italy just in time to fight in the Revolution of 1848. He was an extraordinary leader who captivated the hearts of the people and won the poor and illiterate to the cause of Italian nationality. A young Italian artist who fought beside Garibaldi in 1849 said of his commander:

I shall never forget that day when I first saw him on his beautiful white horse. He reminded us of . . .

Chronology 25.1 Unification of Italy

1821	Austria suppresses a rebellion by the Carbonari
1831–32	Austria suppresses another insurrection by the Carbonari
1832	Mazzini forms the Young Italy
March 1848	Austrians are forced to withdraw from Milan and Venice
November 1848	Pope forced to flee Rome
1848–49	Austria reasserts its authority in Milan and Venice; Louis Napoleon crushes revolutionaries in Rome
1858	Napoleon III agrees to help Piedmont-Sardinia against Austria
1859	Austro-Sardinian War; Piedmont obtains Lombardy from Austria; Parma, Modena, Tuscany, and Romagna vote to join with Sardinia
1860	Garibaldi invades the Kingdom of Two Sicilies
March 17, 1861	Victor Emmanuel of Piedmont is proclaimed king of Italy
1866	Italy's alliance with Prussia against Austria results in annexation of Venetia by Italy
1870	Rome is incorporated into the Italian state and unity is achieved

our Savior . . . everyone said the same. I could not resist him. I went after him; thousands did likewise. He only had to show himself. We all worshipped him. We could not help it.[1]

After the liberation of Sicily in 1860, Garibaldi invaded the mainland. He occupied Naples without a fight and prepared to advance on Rome. In this particular instance, Garibaldi's success confirmed Mazzini's belief that a popular leader could arouse the masses to heroic action.

Cavour feared that an assault on Rome by Garibaldi would lead to French intervention. Napoleon III had pledged to defend the pope's lands, and a French garrison had been stationed in Rome since 1849. Moreover, Cavour considered Garibaldi too impulsive and rash, too attracted to republican ideals, too popular to lead the struggle for unification.

Cavour persuaded Napoleon III to approve an invasion of the Papal States by Piedmont to head off Garibaldi. A papal force offered only token opposition, and the Papal States of Umbria and the Marches soon voted for union with Piedmont, as did Naples and Sicily. Refusing to trade on his prestige with the masses to fulfill personal ambition, Garibaldi turned over his conquests to the Sardinian king, Victor Emmanuel, who was declared king of Italy in 1861.

Italian Unification Completed

Two regions still remained outside the control of the new Italy: the city of Rome, ruled by the pope and protected by French troops; and Venetia, occupied by Austria. Cavour died in 1861, but the march toward unification continued. During the conflict between Prussia and Austria in 1866, Italy sided with the victorious Prussians and was rewarded with Venetia. During the Franco-Prussian War of 1870, France withdrew its garrisons from Rome; much to the anger of the pope, Italian troops marched in, and Rome was declared the capital of Italy.

The Unification of Germany

In 1848, German liberals and nationalists, believing in the strength of their ideals, had naively underestimated the power of the conservative old order. After the failed revolution, some disenchanted revolutionaries retained only a halfhearted commitment to liberalism or embraced conservatism; others fled the country, weakening the liberal leadership. All liberals came to doubt the effectiveness of revolution as a way to transform Germany into a unified state; all gained a new respect for the realities of power. Abandoning idealism for realism, liberals now thought that German unity would be achieved through Prussian arms, not liberal ideals.

Prussia, Agent of Unification

During the late seventeenth and eighteenth centuries, Prussian kings had fashioned a rigorously trained and disciplined army. The state bureaucracy, often staffed by ex-soldiers, perpetuated the military mentality. As the chief organizations in the state, the army and the bureaucracy drilled into the Prussian people a respect for discipline and authority.

The Prussian throne was supported by the Junkers; these powerful aristocrats, who owned vast estates farmed by serfs, were exempt from most taxes, and dominated local government in their territories. The Junkers' commanding position made them officers in the royal army, diplomats, and leading officials in the state bureaucracy. The Junkers knew that a weakening of the king's power would lead to the loss of their own aristocratic prerogatives.

In late-eighteenth-century France, a powerful and politically conscious middle class had challenged aristocratic privileges. The Prussian monarchy and the Junkers had faced no such challenge, for the Prussian middle class at that time was small and without influence. The idea of the rights of the individual did not deeply penetrate Prussian consciousness nor undermine the Prussian tradition of obedience to military and state authority.

Reforms from Above   The reform movement that began after Napoleon had completely routed the Prussians at Jena arose from distress with the military collapse and the apathy of the Prussian population. High bureaucrats and military men demanded reforms that would draw the people closer to their country and king. These leaders had learned the great lesson of the French Revolution: a devoted citizen army fights more effectively than oppressed serfs. To imbue all classes with civic pride, the reformers abolished hereditary serfdom, gave the urban middle class a greater voice in city government, laid the foundations for universal education, and granted full citizenship to Jews. To improve the army's morale, they eliminated severe punishments and based promotions on performance rather than birth.

But the reformers failed to give Prussia a constitution and parliamentary institutions. The middle class still had no voice in the central government; monarchical power persisted, and the economic, political, and military power of the Junkers remained unbroken. Thus, liberalism had an unpromising beginning in Prussia. In France, the bourgeoisie had instituted reforms based on the principles of liberty and equality; in Prussia, the bureaucracy introduced reforms to strengthen the state, not to promote liberty. A precedent had been established: reform in Prussia would come from conservative rulers, not from the efforts of a middle class aroused by liberal ideals.

In 1834, under Prussian leadership, the German states, with the notable exception of Austria, established the *Zollverein*, a customs union that abolished tariffs between the states. The customs union stimulated economic activity and promoted a desire for greater unity. Businessmen, particularly, felt that having thirty-nine states in Germany was an obstacle to economic progress. The Zollverein provided the economic foundations for the po-

Map 25.2 Unification of Germany, 1866–1871

litical unification of Germany, and it led many Germans to view Prussia, not Austria, as the leader of the unification movement.

Failure of Liberals During the restoration the ideas of legal equality, political liberty, and careers open to talent found favor with the Prussian bourgeoisie. Like the French bourgeois of the Old Regime, Prussian bankers, manufacturers, and lawyers hated a system that denied them social recognition and political influence and rewarded idle sons of

the nobility with the best positions. They also denounced government regulations and taxes that hampered business, and hated the rigorous censorship that stifled free thought. The peasants and artisans—concerned with economic survival, respectful of tradition, and suspicious of new ideas—had little comprehension of nor sympathy for liberal principles.

During the Revolution of 1848, liberals failed to wrest power from the monarchy and aristocracy and to create a unified Germany. Frederick William IV (1840–1861) had refused the crown offered him by the Frankfurt Assembly (see Chapter 23). The Prussian monarch could not stomach a German unity created by a revolution of commoners. But a German union fashioned and headed by a conservative Prussia was different and attractive to Frederick. In 1849, Prussia initiated a diplomatic campaign toward this end. Austria resisted this maneuver because it was determined to retain its pre-eminence in German affairs. Faced with Hapsburg resistance, Prussia renounced its plans for a German union and agreed to the re-establishment of the German confederation. This political humiliation taught Frederick William an obvious lesson: before Prussia could extend its hegemony over the other German states, Austrian influence in German affairs would have to be eliminated.

Bismarck and the Road to Unity

In 1858, Frederick William IV, by then mentally deranged, surrendered control of the government to his brother, who became William I (1861–1888), King of Prussia, when Frederick William died. William also regarded Austria as the principal barrier to the extension of Prussian power in Germany. This was one reason why he called for a drastic reorganization of the Prussian army. But the liberals in the lower chamber of the Prussian parliament blocked passage of the army reforms, for they feared that the reforms would greatly increase the power of the monarchy and the military establishment. Unable to secure passage, William withdrew the reform bill and asked the lower chamber for additional funds to cover government expenses. When parliament granted these funds, he used the money to institute the army reforms. Learning from its mistake, the lower chamber would not approve the new budget in 1862 without an itemized breakdown.

A conflict had arisen between the liberal majority in the lower chamber and the crown. If the liberals won, they would, in effect, establish parliamentary control over the king

and the army. At this critical hour, King William asked Otto von Bismarck (1815–1898) to lead the battle against parliament.

Descended on his father's side from an old aristocratic family, Bismarck was a staunch supporter of the Prussian monarchy and the Junker class and a devout patriot. He yearned to increase the territory and prestige of his beloved Prussia and to protect the authority of the Prussian king who, Bismarck believed, ruled by the grace of God. Liberals were outraged by Bismarck's domineering and authoritarian manner and his determination to preserve monarchical power and the aristocratic order. Set on continuing the reorganization of the army and not to bow to parliamentary pressure, Bismarck ordered the collection of taxes without parliament's approval—an action that would have been unthinkable in Britain or the United States.

When the lower chamber continued to withhold funds, Bismarck took action. He dismissed the chamber, imposed strict censorship on the press, arrested outspoken liberals, and fired liberals from the civil service. The liberals protested against these arbitrary and unconstitutional moves, but they did not use force. Since the army fully supported the government, and there was no significant popular support for challenging the government, an armed uprising would have failed. What led to a resolution of the conflict was Bismarck's extraordinary success in foreign affairs.

Wars with Denmark and Austria To Bismarck a war between Austria and Prussia seemed inevitable, for only by removing Austria from German affairs could Prussia extend its dominion over the other German states. Bismarck's first move, however, was not against Austria but against Denmark. The issue that led to the war in 1864 was enormously complex. Simplified, the issue was that Bismarck (and German nationalists) wanted to free the two duchies from Danish control—both territories, which contained a large number of Germans, had been administered by Denmark, but in 1863 Schleswig was incorporated into the Danish realm. Austria joined as Prussia's ally, because it hoped to prevent Prussia's annexing the territories. After Denmark's defeat, Austria and Prussia tried to decide the ultimate disposition of the territory. What Austria wanted was a joint Austrian and Prussian occupation of the disputed regions. But the negotiations broke down. Bismarck used the dispute to goad Austria into war. The Austrians, on their side, held that Prussia must be defeated for Austria to retain its influence over German affairs.

In 1866, with astonishing speed, Prussia assembled its forces and overran Austrian territory. At the battle of Sadowa (or Königgrätz), Prussia decisively defeated the main Austrian forces and the Seven Weeks' War ended. Prussia took no territory from Austria, but the latter agreed to Prussia's annexation of Schleswig and Holstein and a number of small German states. And Prussia organized a Confederation of North German States from which Austria was excluded. In effect, Austria was removed from German affairs, and Prussia became the dominant power in Germany.

The Triumph of Nationalism and Conservatism over Liberalism The Prussian victory had a profound impact on political life within Prussia. Bismarck was the man of the hour, the great hero who had extended Prussia's power. Most liberals forgave Bismarck for his authoritarian handling of parliament. The liberal press that had previously denounced Bismarck for running roughshod over the constitution embraced him as a hero. Prussians were urged to concentrate on the glorious tasks ahead and to put aside the constitutional struggle, which in contrast appeared petty and insignificant.

Bismarck recognized the great appeal of nationalism and used it to expand Prussia's power over other German states and to strengthen Prussia's voice in European affairs. By heralding his state as the champion of unification, Bismarck gained the support of nationalists throughout Germany. In the past, the nationalist cause had been the property of liberals, but Bismarck appropriated it to

Otto von Bismarck. Between 1862 and 1871, Bismarck worked tirelessly to unite Germany under the Prussian monarchy. Bismarck's wars against Denmark, Austria, and France led to the unification of Germany and earned him the admiration of the German people. He expanded Prussian power and bolstered authoritarianism. (*Brown Brothers*)

promote Prussian expansion and conservative rule.

Prussia's victory over Austria, therefore, was a triumph for conservatism and nationalism and a defeat for liberalism. The liberal struggle for constitutional government in Prussia collapsed. The Prussian monarch retained the right to override parliamentary opposition and act on his own initiative. In 1848, Prussian might had suppressed a liberal revolution; in 1866, liberals beguiled by Bismarck's military triumphs gave up the struggle for responsible parliamentary government.

They had traded political freedom for Prussian military glory and power.

The capitulation of Prussian liberals demonstrated the essential weakness of the German liberal tradition. German liberals displayed a diminishing commitment to the principles of parliamentary government, and a growing fascination with force, military triumph, and territorial expansion. Bismarck's words, written in 1858, turned out to be prophetic: "Exalt his self-esteem toward foreigners and the Prussian forgets whatever bothers him about conditions at home."[2] The liberal dream of a united Germany had been pre-empted by conservatives. Enthralled by Bismarck's achievement, many liberals abandoned liberalism and threw their support behind the authoritarian Prussian state. And Germans of all classes acquired an adoration for Prussian militarism and for the power-state, with its Machiavellian guideline that all means are justified if they result in the expansion of German power. In 1848, German liberals had called for "Unity and Freedom." What Bismarck gave them was unity and authoritarianism.

War with France   Prussia emerged from the war with Austria as the leading power in the North German Confederation; the Prussian king controlled the armies and foreign affairs of the states within the confederation. To complete the unification of Germany, Bismarck would have to draw the South German states into the new German confederation. But the South German states, Catholic and hostile to Prussian authoritarianism, feared being absorbed by Prussia.

Bismarck hoped that a war between Prussia and France would ignite the nationalist feelings of the South Germans, causing them to overlook the differences that separated them from Prussia. If war with France would serve Bismarck's purpose, it was also not unthinkable to Napoleon III, the emperor of France. The creation of a powerful North German Confederation had frightened the French, and the prospect that the South German states might one day add their strength to the new Germany was terrifying. Both France and Prussia had parties who advocated war.

A cause for war arose over the succession to the vacated Spanish throne. Under strong consideration was Prince Leopold of Hohenzollern-Sigmaringen, a distant relative of King William of Prussia. France vehemently opposed the candidacy of Leopold, for his accession might lead to Prussian influence being extended into Spain. William, seeking to preserve the peace, urged Prince Leopold to withdraw his name from consideration.

The French ambassador then demanded that William give formal assurance that no Hohenzollern would ever again be a candidate for the Spanish crown. William refused. In a telegram sent from Ems to Berlin, he informed Bismarck of his conversation with the French ambassador. With the support of high military leaders, Bismarck edited the telegram. The revised version gave the impression that the Prussian king and the French ambassador had insulted each other. Bismarck wanted to inflame French feeling against Prussia and arouse German opinion against France. He succeeded. In both Paris and Berlin, crowds of people, gripped by war fever, demanded satisfaction. When France declared a general mobilization, Prussia followed suit; Bismarck had his war.

With the memory of the great Napoleon still strong, the French expected a quick victory. But the poorly prepared and incompetently led French army could not withstand the powerful Prussian military machine. The South German states, as Bismarck had anticipated, came to the aid of Prussia. Quickly and decisively routing the French forces and capturing Napoleon III, the Prussians went on to besiege Paris. Faced with starvation, Paris surrendered in January 1871. France was compelled to pay a large indemnity and to cede to Germany the border provinces of Alsace and Lorraine—a loss that French patriots could never accept.

The Franco-Prussian War completed the unification of Germany. On January 18, 1871, at Versailles, the German princes granted the title of German Kaiser (emperor) to William

Chronology 25.2 Unification of Germany

1815	Formation of the German Confederation
1834	Establishment of the Zollvere.n under Prussian leadership
1848	Failure of the liberals to unify Germany
1862	Bismarck becomes chancellor of Prussia
1864	Austria and Prussia defeat Denmark in a war over Schleswig-Holstein
1866	Seven Weeks' War between Austria and Prussia; Prussia emerges as the dominant power in Germany
1866	Formation of North German Confederation under Prussian control
1870–71	Franco-Prussian War
January 18, 1871	William I becomes German kaiser

I. A powerful nation had arisen in central Europe. Its people were educated, disciplined, and efficient; its industries and commerce were rapidly expanding; its army was the finest in Europe. Vigorous, confident, and intensely nationalistic, the new German Empire would be eager to play a greater role in world affairs. No nation in Europe was a match for the new Germany. Metternich's fears had been realized—a Germany dominated by Prussia had upset the balance of power. The unification of Germany created fears, tensions, and rivalries that would culminate in world war.

Nationality Problems in the Hapsburg Empire

In Italy and Germany, nationalism had led to the creation of unified states; in Austria, nationalism eventually caused the destruction of the centuries-old Hapsburg dynasty. A mosaic of different nationalities, each with its own history and traditions, the Austrian Empire could not survive in an age of intense nationalism. England and France had succeeded in unifying peoples of different ethnic backgrounds, but they did so during the Middle Ages, when ethnic consciousness was

still rudimentary. The Austrian Empire, on the other hand, had to weld together and reconcile antagonistic nationalities when nationalistic consciousness was high. The empire's collapse in the final stages of World War I marked the end of years of antagonism between its different peoples.

In the first half of the nineteenth century, the Germans, constituting less than one-quarter of the population, were the dominant national group in the empire. But Magyars, Poles, Czechs, Slovaks, Croats, Rumanians, Ruthenians, and Italians were experiencing national self-awareness. Poets and writers who had been educated in Latin, French, and German began to write in their mother tongues and extol their splendor. By searching their past for glorious ancestors and glorious deeds, writers kindled pride in their native history and folklore and aroused anger against past and present injustices.

In 1848–49 the Hapsburg monarchy had extinguished the Magyar bid for independence, the Czech revolution in Prague, and the uprisings in the Italian provinces of Lombardy and Venetia. Gravely frightened by these revolutions, the Austrian power structure resolved to resist pressures for political rights by strengthening autocracy and tightening the central bureaucracy. German and Germanized officials took over administrative and judicial duties formerly handled on a local level. An expanded secret police stifled liberal and nationalist expressions. The various nationalities, of course, resented these efforts at centralizaton and repression.

Magyarization

The defeats by France and Piedmont in 1859 and by Prussia in 1866 cost Austria its two Italian provinces. The defeat by Prussia also forced the Hapsburg monarchy to make concessions to the Magyars, the strongest of the non-German nationalities; for without a loyal Hungary, the Hapsburg monarchy could suffer other humiliations. The Settlement of 1867 split the Hapsburg territories into Austria and Hungary. The two countries retained a common ruler, Francis Joseph (1848–1916), who was emperor of Austria and king of Hungary. Hungary gained complete control over its internal affairs—the administration of justice and education. Foreign and military affairs and common financial concerns were conducted by a ministry consisting of delegates from both lands.

With the Settlement of 1867, Magyars and Germans became the dominant nationalities in the empire. The other nationalities felt that the German-Magyar political, economic, and cultural domination blocked their own national aspirations. Nationality struggles in the half-century following the Settlement of 1867 consumed the energies of the Austrians and Hungarians. In both lands, however, the leaders failed to solve the minority problems, a failure that ultimately led to the dissolution of the empire during the last weeks of World War I.

The nationality problems in Hungary differed substantially from those in Austria. Constituting slightly less than half the population of Hungary, the Magyars were determined to retain their hegemony over the other minorities—Rumanians, Slovaks, Ruthenians, Serbs, Croats, and Jews. In the first phase of their national struggle, the Hungarians had sought to liberate their nation from German domination. In the second phase, after 1867, the landholding aristocracy that ruled Hungary tried to impose the Magyar language and traditions on the other nationalities. Non-Magyars who learned the Magyar language and considered themselves Hungarians could participate as equals in Hungarian society. Those who resisted were viewed as traitors and conspirators and faced severe penalties. Non-Magyars were largely excluded from voting and virtually barred from government jobs, which were reserved for Magyars or those who had adopted Magyar language and culture.

The government tightly controlled the non-Magyar peoples. It suppressed their cultural organizations and newspapers, and the great majority of public schools, even in predominantly non-Magyar regions, carried on instruction largely in Magyar. Because of limited suffrage, the manipulation of districts, and threats of violence, non-Magyars were barely represented in the Hungarian parliament. Protests by the nationalities against this forced Magyarization often led to jail sentences. The repressive measures strengthened the Slavs' and Rumanians' hatred of the regime. At the same time, however, Magyarization brought economic and cultural opportunities. Jews in particular accepted the Magyar government and took advantage of what it offered.

But nationality movements within Hungary constituted less of a threat to the preservation of the Austro-Hungarian Empire than Magyar nationalism itself did. The Independence Party, whose influence grew after 1900, began to demand a complete end to the link with Austria and the "cursed common institutions."

German versus Czech

The Austrian population of the Dual Monarchy was made up of Germans (one-third) and Slavs (two-thirds). Hungary tried to forge a unified state by assimilating the non-Magyars; Austria, on the other hand, made no deliberate effort to Germanize the Slavs.

No attempt was made to make German the official language of the state or to dissociate non-Germans from their native traditions. In Austria, elementary school students were usually taught in their mother tongues. The state acknowledged the equal right of all the country's languages in the schools, in administration, and in public life.

But the nationality problem was aggravated by the haughty attitude of the German Austrians, who considered themselves culturally superior to the Slavic peoples. Neither the Germans nor the Magyars would allow the Czechs and the South Slavs the same control over domestic affairs that had been granted the Magyars in the Settlement of 1867. The Germans believed that they had a historic mission to retain their dominance, an attitude that clashed with the Slavs' growing national consciousness. And the Slavic masses were not only aroused by nationalism but, with the spread of liberal-democratic ideas, were also gaining the vote.

The most serious conflict occurred in Bohemia between the Germans and the Czechs, the largest group of Slavs. The Czechs had the highest literacy rate in the Dual Monarchy, and Bohemia had become the industrial heartland of the empire. The emergence of a Czech university and Czech youth associations and the growth of Czech literature stimulated a national consciousness. Championed by a growing middle class that had made considerable economic and cultural gains, nationalism among the Czechs of Bohemia gained in intensity in the final decades of the nineteenth century. Between the Czechs and the Germans, who constituted one-third of the population of Bohemia, there was great animosity.

Concentrated primarily in the Sudetenland, the German Bohemians regarded themselves as culturally and morally superior to the Czechs and wanted to preserve their predominance in the government's administration. Considering the Czech language fit only for peasants and servants, the Sudeten Germans felt it ridiculous that Czech be placed on an equal level with the German tongue.

The two groups argued over whether street signs and menus should be written in German or Czech. Czech nationalists wanted the same constitutional independence that had been granted to the Hungarians; Sudeten Germans demanded that Austria remain a centralized state governed by a German-dominated bureaucracy. Violent demonstrations, frenzied oratory, and strident editorials fanned the flames of hatred. A growing resentment against the Czechs and a growing admiration for Bismarck's new Germany led some Austrian Germans, particularly the Sudeten Germans, to seek union with Germany. Georg von Schönerer, the leader of the Austrian Pan-German movement, denounced both Slavs and Jews as racial inferiors, and called for the creation of a Greater Germany.

The clash between Czech and German grew uglier when in 1897 a new prime minister, Count Casimir Badeni, required government officials in Bohemia to know both the German and the Czech languages. This requirement was no hardship for Czech officials, since most of them already knew German. Few German officials, however, knew Czech or cared to learn it. Riots broke out in various cities, German and Czech deputies in parliament engaged in fist fights, and the emperor was forced to dismiss Badeni. Eventually the reform was dropped, but Czech-German hostilities remained intense.

South Slavs

The problem of the South Slavs—Serbs, Croats, Slovenes—differed from that of the Czechs. No Czech state served as a magnet for the Czechs living within Austria, whereas in the Kingdom of Serbia (which gained full independence from the Ottoman Turks in 1878), the South Slavs had a foreign power to encourage their nationalist hopes. Serbian nationalists dreamed of extending their rule over their ethnic cousins, the South Slavs of Austria-Hungary. The Hapsburg monarchy viewed this vision of a Greater Serbia as a threat to its existence. This conflict between

A Bohemian Funeral Procession, 1899. The Hapsburg Empire was burdened by conflicts between the different nationalities. In Bohemia, Czechs and Germans often engaged in violent confrontations, as Czechs pressed for recognition of their language and rights. This funeral is for victims of a nationalistic riot. (*Bilderdienst Süddeutscher Verlag*)

Serbia and Austria-Hungary was to trigger World War I.

The awakening of nationalism in the multi-ethnic Austro-Hungarian Empire raised the specter of dissolution. Could the forces of unity—the army, the bureaucracy, and loyalty to the Hapsburg dynasty—contain the centrifugal forces that threatened to shatter the empire into separate parts? A restructuring of the Dual Monarchy into a federated state that would give equality to the Slavs might have eased the pressures within the empire, particularly since only extremists among the minorities were calling for independence. But the leading statesmen resisted the Slavs' demands. At the end of World War I, the empire was fractured into separate states based on nationality.

The Rise of Racial Nationalism

In the first half of the nineteenth century, nationalism and liberalism went hand in hand. Liberals sought both the rights of the individual and national independence and unification. Liberal nationalists believed that a unified state free of foreign subjugation was in harmony with the principle of natural rights, and they insisted that love of country led to love of humanity. "With all my ardent love of my nation," said Francis Palacký, a Czech patriot, "I always esteem more highly the good of mankind and of learning than the good of the nation."[3] Addressing the Slavs, Mazzini declared: "We who have ourselves arisen in the name of our national right, believe in your right, and offer to help you to win it. But the purpose of our mission is the permanent and peaceful organization of Europe."[4]

As nationalism grew more extreme, however, its profound difference from liberalism became more apparent. The extreme nationalism of the late nineteenth and early twentieth centuries was the seed bed of totalitarian nationalism. It contributed to World War I and to the rise of fascism after the war.

Concerned exclusively with the greatness of the nation, extreme nationalists rejected the liberal emphasis on political liberty. They regarded liberty as an obstacle to national power and maintained that authoritarian leadership was needed to meet national emergencies. The needs of the nation, they said, transcended the rights of the individual. Extreme nationalists also rejected the liberal ideal of equality. Placing the nation above everything, nationalists became increasingly intolerant of minorities within the nation's borders and hateful of other peoples. In the name of national power and unity, they persecuted minorities at home and stirred up hatred against other nations. In the pursuit of national power, nationalists increasingly embraced militaristic, imperialistic, and racist doctrines. At the founding of the Nationalist Association in Italy in 1910 one leader declared:

Just as socialism teaches the proletariat the value of class struggle, so we must teach Italy the value of international struggle. But international struggle is war? Well, then, let there be war! And nationalism will arouse the will for a victorious war, . . . the only way to national redemption.[5]

Interpreting politics with the logic of emotions, extreme nationalists insisted that they had a sacred mission to regain lands once held in the Middle Ages, to unite with their kinfolk in other lands, or to rule over peoples considered inferior. They organized patriotic societies, denounced national minorities, particularly Jews, and created a cult of ancestors and a mystique of blood, soil, and a sacred national past. In these ancestral traditions and attachments, the nationalist found a higher reality akin to religious truth. Loyalty to the nation-state was elevated above all other allegiances. The ethnic-state became an object of religious reverence; the spiritual energies that formerly had been dedicated to Christianity were now channeled into the worship of the nation-state.

By the beginning of the twentieth century, conservatives had become the staunchest advocates of nationalism, and the nationalism preached by conservative extremists was stripped of Mazzinian ideals of liberty, equality, and the fellowship of nations. Landholding aristocrats, generals, and clergy, often joined by big industrialists, saw nationalism as a convenient instrument for gaining a mass following in their struggle against democracy and socialism. Championing popular nationalist myths and dreams, and citing Social Darwinist doctrines, a newly radicalized right hoped to harness the instinctual energies of the masses, particularly the peasants and the lower middle class—shopkeepers, civil servants, white collar workers—to conservative causes. Peasants viewed liberalism and socialism as threats to traditional values, while the lower bourgeoisie feared the proletariat. These people were receptive to the rhetoric of ultranationalists who denounced liberalism and socialism as threats to national unity and Jews as aliens who endangered the nation.

Volkish Thought

Extreme nationalism was a general European phenomenon, but it was especially dangerous in Germany. Bismarck's triumphs lured Germans into a dreamworld. Many started to

Richard Wagner (1813–1883), Detail of Portrait by August Friedrich Pecht. Wagner was a crucial figure in the shaping of German romanticism. His operas, glorifying a mythic German past, contributed to the Volkish outlook. (*The Metropolitan Museum of Art; Gift of Frederick Loeser, 1889*)

yearn for the extension of German power throughout the world. The past, they said, belonged to France and Britain; the future, to Germany.

The most ominous expression of German nationalism (and a clear example of mythical thinking) was *Volkish* thought.[6] (*Volk* means folk or people.) German Volkish thinkers sought to bind together the German people through a deep love of their language, traditions, and fatherland. These thinkers felt that Germans were animated by a higher spirit than that found in other peoples. To Volkish thinkers the Enlightenment and parliamentary democracy were foreign ideas that corrupted the pure German spirit. With fanatical devotion, Volkish thinkers embraced all things

German—the medieval past, the German landscape, the simple peasant, the village—and denounced the liberal-humanist tradition of the West as alien to the German soul.

One shaper of the Volkish outlook was Wilhelm von Riehl (1823–1897), a professor at the University of Munich. He contrasted the artificiality of modern city life with the unspoiled existence in the German countryside. Another was Berthold Auerbach (1812–1882), who glorified the peasant as the ideal German. Paul de Lagarde (1827–1891), a professor of oriental languages, called for a German faith, different from Christianity, that would unite the nation; he saw the Jews as enemies of Germany. Julius Langbehn (1851–1907) lauded a mystical and irrational life force as superior to reason and held that the Jews corrupted the German spirit.

Volkish thought attracted Germans frightened by all the complexities of the modern age—industrialization, urbanization, materialism, class conflicts, alienation. Seeing their beloved Germany transformed by these forces of modernity, Volkish thinkers yearned to restore the sense of community that they attributed to the preindustrial age. Only by identifying with their sacred soil and sacred traditions could modern Germans escape from the evils of industrial society. Only then could the different classes band together in an organic unity.

The Volkish movement had little support from the working class, which was concerned chiefly with improving its standard of living. It appealed mainly to farmers and villagers who regarded the industrial city as a threat to native values and a catalyst for foreign ideas; to small artisans and shopkeepers threatened by big business; and to scholars, writers, teachers, and students who saw in Volkish nationalism a cause worthy of their idealism. The schools were leading agents for the dissemination of Volkish ideas.

Volkish thinkers looked back longingly to the Middle Ages, which they viewed as a period of social and spiritual harmony and reverence for national traditions. They also glorified the ancient Germanic tribes that overran the Roman Empire; they contrasted their courageous and vigorous German ancestors with the effete and degenerate Romans. A few tried to harmonize ancient Germanic religious traditions with Christianity.

Such attitudes led Germans to see themselves as a heroic people fundamentally different from and better than the English and French. It also led them to regard German culture as unique—innately superior to and in opposition to the humanist outlook of the Enlightenment. Volkish thinkers, like their romantic predecessors, held that the German people and culture had a special destiny and a unique mission. They pitted the German soul against the Western intellect, feeling and spirit against a drab rationalism. To be sure, the Western humanist tradition still had its supporters in Germany, but the counter-ideology of Volkish thought was becoming increasingly widespread.

Volkish thinkers were especially attracted to racist doctrines. Racist thinkers held that race was the key to history, and that not only physical features, but moral, aesthetic, and intellectual qualities distinguished one race from another. In their view, a race demonstrated its vigor and achieved greatness when it preserved its purity; intermarriage between races was contamination that would result in genetic, cultural, and military decline. Like their Nazi successors, Volkish thinkers claimed that the German race was purer than, and therefore superior to all other races. Its superiority was revealed in such physical characteristics as blond hair, blue eyes, and fair skin—all signs of inner qualities lacking in other races. German racists claimed that Germans were descendants of ancient Aryans.* They held that the Aryans were a superior race and the creators of European civilization and that the Germans had inherited their superior racial qualities.

* The Aryans emerged some 4,000 years ago, probably between the Caspian Sea and the Hindu Kush Mountains. An Aryan tongue became the basis of most European languages. Intermingling with others, the Aryans lost their identity as a people.

Volkish thinkers embraced the ideas of Houston Stewart Chamberlain (1855–1927), an Englishman whose fascination for Germanism led him to adopt German citizenship. In *The Foundations of the Nineteenth Century*, published in 1899, Chamberlain asserted in pseudoscientific fashion that the inner qualities of a people were related to such physical characteristics as the size of the skull. Germans had a superior physical form; consequently they were aesthetically, morally, and intellectually superior and the bearers of a higher culture—in short, members of a master race. Chamberlain's book was enormously popular in Germany; the Kaiser read it aloud to his children.

German racial nationalists insisted that as a superior race, Germans had a national right to dominate other peoples, particularly the "racially inferior" Slavs of the East. The Pan-German Association, whose membership included professors, schoolteachers, journalists, lawyers, and aristocrats, spread racial and nationalist theories and glorified war as an expression of national vitality. The association's philosophy is expressed in the following statement from its journal:

The racial-biological ideology tells us that there are races that lead and races that follow. Political history is nothing but the history of struggles among the leading races. Conquests, above all, are always the work of the leading races. Such men can conquer, may conquer, and shall conquer.[7]

Anti-Semitism

German racial nationalists singled out Jews as the most wicked of races and a deadly enemy of the German people. Anti-Semitism, which was widespread in late-nineteenth-century Europe, provides a striking example of the perennial appeal, power, and danger of mythical thinking. Anti-Semitic organizations and political parties sought to deprive Jews of their civil rights, and anti-Semitic publications proliferated.

Edouard Drumont, a French journalist, held that the Jews, racially inferior and believers in a primitive religion, had gained control of France. Like medieval Christian anti-Semites, Drumont accused Jews of deicide and of using Christian blood for ritual purposes. During the anti-Semitic outbursts accompanying the Dreyfus affair (see page 601), when the French right was shouting "Death to the Jews," Drumont's newspaper (founded with Jesuit funds) blamed all the ills of France on the Jews, called for their expulsion from the country, and predicted that they would be massacred.

Rumania barred most Jews from holding office and from voting, imposed various economic restrictions on them, and restricted their admission into secondary schools and universities. The Rumanian government even financed an international congress of anti-Semites that met in Bucharest in 1886.

Russia placed a quota on the number of Jewish students admitted to secondary schools and higher educational institutions, confined Jews to certain regions of the country, and "to purify the sacred historic capital" expelled some 20,000 Jews from Moscow. The tsarist government permitted and even encouraged *pogroms* (mob violence) against Jews. Between 1903 and 1906, pogroms broke out in 690 towns and villages, most of them in the Ukraine, traditionally a hotbed of anti-Semitism (Ukrainian folk songs and legends glorified centuries-old massacres of Jews). The attackers looted, burned, raped, and murdered, generally with impunity. In Russia, and several other lands, Jews were put on trial for slaughtering Christian children as part of a Passover ritual—a deranged accusation that survived from the Middle Ages.

In Germany and Austria hatred of the Jews developed into a systematic body of beliefs. As historian Hans Kohn says: "Germany became the fatherland of modern anti-Semitism; there the systems were thought out and the slogans coined. German literature was the richest in anti-Jewish writing."[8] Like conservatives in other lands, German conservatives deliberately fanned the flames of anti-Semitism to win the masses over to conservative causes. The Christian Social Workers' Party, founded in 1878 by Adolf Stöcker, a prominent Protestant preacher, engaged in

anti-Semitic agitation in order to recruit the lower bourgeoisie to the cause of the Protestant Church and the Prussian monarchy. In German-speaking Austria, Karl Lueger, a leader of the Christian Socialist party founded by conservative German nationalists, exploited anti-Semitism to win elections in overwhelmingly Catholic Vienna. Georg von Schönerer, founder of the German National Party in Austria, wanted to eliminate Jews from all areas of public life.

Anti-Semitism and the success of the Italians, Germans, Serbians, and others in achieving political independence stirred nationalist feelings among Jews. Jewish nationalism took the form of Zionism—a return to Palestine, the historic homeland of the Jews. A key figure in the emergence of Zionism was Dr. Theodore Herzl (1880–1904), an Austrian journalist, who was horrified by the anti-Semitism he witnessed in Paris during the Dreyfus trial (see page 601). In *The Jewish State* (1896), he argued that the creation of a Jewish state was the best solution to the Jewish question. In 1897 the First Zionist Congress meeting in Switzerland called for the establishment of a Jewish homeland in Palestine, which was then a province of the Turkish empire.

Anti-Semitism had a long and bloodstained history in Europe, stemming both from an irrational fear and hatred of outsiders with noticeably different ways and from the commonly accepted myth that the Jews as a people were collectively and eternally cursed for rejecting Christ. Christians saw Jews as the murderers of Christ—an image that promoted terrible anger and hatred.

During the Middle Ages, people believed and spread incredible tales about Jews. They accused Jews of torturing and crucifying Christian children in order to use their blood for religious ceremonies, of poisoning wells to kill Christians, of worshiping the Devil, and of organizing a secret government that conspired to destroy Christianity. Jews were thought to be physically different from other people—they were said to have tails, horns, and a distinctive odor. Serving to propagate this myth was the decision of the Fourth

Anti-Semitism: Bodies of Jewish Fugitives, Shot While Crossing the Dniester Between the Ukraine and Rumania. In Russia, the government encouraged and supported anti-Semitic outrages. (*Brown Brothers*)

Lateran Council (1215) that required Jews to wear a distinguishing mark on their clothing.

While some medieval popes and bishops condemned these fables and sought to protect Jews from mob violence, the lower clergy and popular preachers spread them to the receptive masses. Periodically mobs humiliated, tortured, and massacred Jews, and rulers expelled them from their kingdoms. Often barred from owning land and excluded from the craft guilds, medieval Jews concentrated in trade and moneylending—occupations that frequently earned them greater hostility. By the sixteenth century, Jews in a number of lands were forced by law to live in separate quarters of the town called *ghettos*. Medieval Christian anti-Semitism, which depicted the Jew as vile and Judaism as repulsive, fertilized the soil for modern anti-Semitism.

In the nineteenth century, under the aegis of the liberal ideals of the Enlightenment and the French Revolution, Jews gained legal equality in most European lands. They could leave the ghetto and participate in many activities that had been closed to them. Traditionally an urban people, the Jews were concentrated in the leading cities of Europe. Taking advantage of this new freedom and opportunity, many Jews achieved striking success as entrepreneurs, bankers, lawyers, journalists, doctors, scientists, scholars, and performers. For example, in 1880 Jews, who constituted about 10 percent of the Viennese population, accounted for 38.6 percent of the medical students and 23.3 percent of the law students in Vienna. Viennese cultural life before World War I was to a large extent shaped by Jewish writers, artists, musicians, critics, and patrons. All but one of the major banking houses were Jewish.

But most European Jews—peasants, pedlars, and laborers—were quite poor. Perhaps 5,000 to 6,000 Jews of Galicia in Austria-Hungary died of starvation annually, and many

Russian Jews fled to the United States to escape from desperate poverty. But the anti-Semites saw only "Jewish influence," "Jewish manipulation," and "Jewish domination." Aggravating anti-Semitism among Germans was the flight of thousands of Russian Jews into Austria and Germany. Poor, speaking a different language (Yiddish), and having noticeably different customs, these Jews offended Germans and triggered primitive fears and hates.

Those Jews who were members of the commercial and professional classes, like other bourgeois, gravitated toward liberalism. Moreover, as victims of persecution, they naturally favored societies that were committed to the liberal ideals of legal equality, toleration, the rule of law, and equality of opportunity. As strong supporters of parliamentary government and the entire system of values associated with the Enlightenment, the Jews became targets for conservatives and Volkish thinkers who repudiated the humanist and cosmopolitan outlook of liberalism. German historian Karl Dietrich Bracher concludes: "Anti-Semitism was a manifestation of a rejection of the 'West' with which the Jews were identified . . . because the Enlightenment and democracy were essential preconditions for their acceptance and progress."[9]

Anti-Semites blamed the Jews for all the social and economic ills caused by the rapid growth of industries and cities and for all the new ideas that were undermining the old order. Their anxieties and fears concentrated on the Jews, to whom they attributed everything that was repellent to them in the modern age, all that threatened the German Volk. The thought of Volkish thinkers demonstrates the mind's extraordinary capacity for mystification. In the mythical world of the Volkish thinkers, the Jews were regarded as evil entrepreneurs and financiers who exploited hardworking and decent Germans, manipulated the stock exchange, and caused depressions; as international socialists who were dragging Germany into class war; as democrats who were trying to impose an alien system of parliamentary democracy on Ger-

many; as intellectuals who undermined traditional German culture; as city people who had no ties to or love for the German soil; as materialists who were totally without German spiritual qualities; as foreign intruders who could never be loyal to the fatherland; as racial inferiors whose genes could infect and weaken the German race; and as international conspirators who were plotting to dominate Germany and the world. This last accusation was a secularized and updated version of the medieval myth that Jews were plotting to destroy Christendom. In an extraordinary display of mythical thinking, Volkish thinkers held that Jews throughout the world were gaining control over political parties, the press, and the economy in order to dominate the planet.

In the Middle Ages, Jews had been persecuted and humiliated primarily for religious reasons, but in the nineteenth century, national-racial considerations were the decisive force behind anti-Semitism. Christian anti-Semites believed that through conversion, Jews could escape the curse of their religion. But to racial anti-Semites, who used the language of Social Darwinism, Jews were indelibly stained and eternally condemned by their genes. Their evil and worthlessness derived not from their religion, but from inherited racial characteristics. As one anti-Semitic deputy stated in a speech before the German Reichstag in 1895:

If one designates the whole of Jewry, one does so in the knowledge that the racial qualities of this people are such that in the long run they cannot harmonize with the racial qualities of the Germanic peoples and that every Jew who at this moment has not done anything bad may nevertheless under the proper conditions do precisely that, because his racial qualities drive him to do it. . . . the Jews . . . operate like parasites . . . the Jews are cholera germs.[10]

The Jewish population of Germany was quite small: in 1900 it was only about 497,000 or 0.95 percent of the total population of 50,626,000. Jews were proud of their many contributions to German economic and intellectual life; they considered themselves patriotic Germans, and regarded Germany as an altogether desirable place to live—a place of refuge in comparison to Russia, where Jews lived in terrible poverty and the government instigated violent attacks against them. German Jews, who felt that they already had a homeland, had little enthusiasm for Zionism.

German anti-Semitic organizations and political parties had failed to get the state to pass anti-Semitic laws, and by the early 1900s these groups had declined in political power and importance. But the mischief had been done. In the minds of many Germans even in respectable circles, the image of the Jew as an evil and dangerous creature had been firmly planted. It was perpetuated by the schools, youth groups, the Pan-German Association, and an array of racist pamphlets and books. Late nineteenth-century racial anti-Semites had constructed an ideological foundation on which Hitler would later build his movement. In words that foreshadowed Hitler, Paul de Lagarde said of the Jews: "One does not have dealings with pests and parasites; one does not rear them and cherish them; one destroys them as speedily and thoroughly as possible."[11]

It is, of course, absurd to believe that a nation of 50 million was threatened by a half million citizens of Jewish birth, or that the 12 million Jews of the world had organized to rule the planet. The Jewish birthrate in Germany was low, the rate of intermarriage high, and the desire for complete assimilation into German life great. Within a few generations the Jewish community in Germany might well have disappeared. Moreover, despite the paranoia of the anti-Semite, the German Jews and the Jews in the rest of Europe were quite powerless. There were scarcely any Jews in the ruling circles of governments, armies, civil services, or heavy industries. As events were to prove, the Jews, with no army or state and dwelling among people who despised them, were the weakest of peoples. But the race mystics, convinced that they were waging a war of self-defense against a Satanic foe, were impervious to ra-

tional argument. Anti-Semites, said Theodor Mommsen, the great nineteenth-century German historian, would not listen to

logical and ethical arguments. . . . They listen only to their own envy and hatred, to the meanest instincts. Nothing else counts for them. They are deaf to reason, right, morals. One cannot influence them. . . . [Anti-Semitism] is a horrible epidemic, like cholera—one can neither explain nor cure it.[12]

Thus racial nationalists attacked and undermined the Enlightenment tradition. They denied equality, scorned toleration and cosmopolitanism, and made myth and superstition vital forces in political life. That many people believed these racial theories was an ominous sign for Western civilization. It showed how tenuous the rational tradition of the Enlightenment is, how receptive the mind is to dangerous myths, and how easily human behavior can degenerate into inhumanity.

Notes

1. Quoted in Christopher Hibbert, *Garibaldi and His Enemies* (Boston: Little, Brown, 1965), p. 45.

2. Otto Pflanze, *Bismarck and the Development of Germany: The Period of Unification* (Princeton, N.J.: Princeton University Press, 1963), p. 232.

3. Hans Kohn, *Pan-Slavism* (Notre Dame, Ind.: University of Notre Dame Press, 1953), pp. 66–67.

4. Ibid., p. 44.

5. Cited in Edward R. Tannenbaum, *1900: The Generation Before the Great War* (Garden City, N.Y.: Doubleday, 1976), p. 337.

6. This discussion is based largely on the works of George L. Mosse, particularly *The Crisis of German Ideology* (New York: Grosset & Dunlap Universal Library, 1964).

7. Cited in Horst von Maltitz, *The Evolution of Hitler's Germany* (New York: McGraw-Hill, 1973), p. 33.

8. Hans Kohn, *Nationalism: Its Meaning and History* (Princeton, N.J.: D. Van Nostrand, Anvil Books, 1965), p. 77.

9. Karl Dietrich Bracher, *The German Dictatorship*, trans. by Jean Steinberg (New York: Praeger, 1970), p. 36.

10. Quoted in Raul Hilberg, *The Destruction of the European Jews* (Chicago: Quadrangle, 1967), pp. 10–11.

11. Quoted in Helmut Krausnick, Hans Buchheim, Martin Broszat, and Hans-Adolf Jacobsen, *Anatomy of the SS State,* trans. by Richard Barry et al. (London: William Collins Sons, 1968), p. 9.

12. Quoted in Peter G. J. Pulzer, *The Rise of Political Anti-Semitism in Germany and Austria* (New York: Wiley, 1964), p. 299.

Suggested Reading

Beales, Derek, *The Risorgimento and the Unification of Italy* (1971). A comprehensive overview followed by documents.

Hamerow, T. S., *Restoration, Revolution, Reaction* (1958). An examination of economics and politics in Germany, 1815–1971, stressing the problems caused by the transition from agrarianism to industrialism.

———, ed., *Otto von Bismarck* (1962). A collection of readings from leading historians.

Hibbert, Christopher, *Garibaldi and His Enemies* (1965). A vivid portrait of the Italian hero.

Jászi, Oscar, *The Dissolution of the Habsburg Monarchy* (1961). Originally published in 1929, this volume examines how nationalist animosities contributed to the dissolution of the Hapsburg monarchy.

Katz, Jacob, *From Prejudice to Destruction* (1980). A survey of modern anti-Semitism; holds that modern anti-Semitism is an outgrowth of traditional Christian anti-Semitism.

Kohn, Hans, *Nationalism: Its Meaning and History* (1955). A concise history of modern nationalism by a leading student of the subject.

Mosse, George L., *Toward the Final Solution* (1978). An analysis of European racism.

———, *The Crisis of German Ideology* (1964). Explores the dark side of German nationalism; excellent study of Volkish thought.

Pauley, B. F., *The Habsburg Legacy, 1867–1939* (1972). A good brief work on a complex subject.

Pflanze, Otto, *Bismarck and the Development of Germany* (1963). An excellent study of the political history of Germany during the period 1815–1871.

Pulzer, Peter G. J., *The Rise of Political Anti-Semitism in Germany and Austria* (1964). Relationship of anti-Semitism to changing socioeconomic conditions; impact of anti-Semitism on politics.

Smith, D. M., ed., *Garibaldi* (1969). A collection of readings; Garibaldi as he saw himself, how his contemporaries saw him, how nineteenth- and twentieth-century historians have viewed him; preceded by a valuable introduction.

Review Questions

1. What forces worked for and against Italian unity?

2. Mazzini was the soul, Cavour the brains, and Garibaldi the sword in the struggle for the unification of Italy. Discuss their participation in and contributions to the struggle.

3. Why is it significant that Prussia served as the agent of German unification, rather than the Frankfurt Assembly in 1848?

4. Prussia's victory over Austria was a triumph for conservatism and a defeat for liberalism. Discuss this statement.

5. What was the significance of the Franco-Prussian War for European history?

6. In the Hapsburg Empire, nationalism was a force for disunity. Discuss this statement.

7. To whom did Volkish thought appeal? Describe why.

8. Why is racial nationalism a repudiation of the Enlightenment tradition and a regression to mythical thinking?

9. What is the relationship between medieval and modern anti-Semitism?

10. Anti-Semites attributed to Jews everything that they found repellent in the modern world. Discuss this statement.

11. Anti-Semitism demonstrates the immense power and appeal of mythical thinking. Discuss this statement.

26

Industrial Europe: The Challenge of Modernization

*I*n the last part of the nineteenth century, European society was transformed by accelerated industrialization. The European nations experienced the process of industrialization differently, depending on their political and social institutions and on the pace at which they industrialized. Every nation had to adjust its traditional preindustrial institutions to the requirements of factories and industrial cities. The old power structures of rural, agrarian, privileged society endured, although perhaps in altered forms, and shaped the political and social institutions of each country during its industrialization. The power of the state grew enormously, although it developed differently in each European nation. Traditional classes and institutions clashed with the massive economic and political transformation brought on by the Industrial Revolution. This interaction created many problems and reshaped each nation.

Industrialization greatly affected international relations. National power was no longer measured by manpower, area, and the size of the army, but by coal and iron production, railways and navies, and the mechanization of industry. Russia's mighty army could not compensate for French, British, or even Belgian, industrial power. Production, trade, and the conquest of foreign markets and empires would alter the European balance of power, changing the positions of France, Russia, and Austria. All the world, not just Europe, appeared vulnerable to the advance of industry and the power of industrialized states in the period from 1850 to 1914.

The Advance of Industry

In 1851 for all the pride and confidence in industrialization that Europeans expressed at the Crystal Palace exhibition of 1851 the industrial revolution was still in its infancy, although everyone knew that the child in the cradle was going to grow to awesome adulthood. Farming was still the major occupation of people everywhere, including Britain, where industrialization was most advanced. Even in Britain there were more domestic servants than factory workers and twice as many agricultural laborers as textile and clothing workers. Large factories were few and crafts still flourished. Electricity was too fragile to power lighting or drive machines and was used only in signaling; steel was so expensive to manufacture that it was treated almost as a precious metal; sailing ships still outnumbered steamships; horses carried more freight than trains; on-the-job training was more common than schooling; and construction and machine making still relied on trial and error rather than architecture or engineering. Within the next sixty years all this would change rapidly and the industrial age would emerge.

The pace of change was so rapid in the second half of the nineteenth century that many historians have called it a second industrial revolution. The great increase in the speed, scale, and scope of change appeared to be a new social and economic development rather than part of the continuous process that had been taking place since the eighteenth century.

After 1850 industrial development can be broken down into at least two periods. First, a midcentury expansion in Europe and America consolidated the accomplishments in production, distribution, transportation, and communications. Between 1850 and the 1870s the shift from hand to machine production began to take firm hold, leading to the concentration of workers in factories and industrial cities and the growth of unions. The real standard of living for most workers rose; invention, legislation, and trade union bargaining relieved the most horrible conditions of early industrialization, and the first regulations of urban development and sanitation began to have some effect. Consumers and investors adjusted to the new industrial world with new patterns of investment and consumption that further influenced industrialization.

Then, following the severe economic depression of 1873, which affected all the major industrial countries, came the development of cartels and monopolies—giant firms able to dominate entire industries nationally and internationally. This phenomenon particularly characterized Germany and the United States, but it affected most of the industrialized countries. From the 1890s to the First World War, there was a marked change in the scale of development: giant firms run by boards of directors, including financiers, operated enormous factories, that were increasingly mechanized and manned by unskilled, low-paid, often seasonal workers. These industrial giants were able to control the output, price, and distribution of commodities; they were able to dominate in the competitive struggle with smaller firms, to finance and control research and development, and to expand far beyond their national frontiers. The owners or managers of these large firms had such extraordinary economic power that they often commanded political power as well; they were, in every sense, the "captains of industry."

Labor responded to these developments by organizing on an industry-wide basis and by voting for candidates who were sympathetic to the plight of labor. In the decade before 1914, the real standard of living for workers in western Europe dropped, as the cost of living rose as much as 10 percent. A wave of strikes, often punctuated by violence, swept through every industrial and industrializing country. Strikes, such as the dock strikes in London and Liverpool, the railroad workers' strike in France, and the miners' strikes in England and France, were suppressed with violence. The railroad workers in France were conscripted and forced to return to work as soldiers. To the eve of the war, the political power of industry so dominated industrial countries that even with the vote, labor had little success in alleviating the sources of its discontent.

Technological Change

Industry developed on a foundation of cheap, rapid distribution of goods and easy access to raw materials. The second industrial revolution was characterized by new forms of business and labor organization, by the rise of the middle class and the decline of traditional groups, and by technological change based on the application of invention and scientific discovery to production.

After midcentury, Europe entered an age of railroads. The metallurgical discoveries of Bessemer and Siemens allowed cheap manufacture of quality steel; the perfection of the steam engine reduced its price and allowed the wider application of steam in the mines and other industries; new forms of capitalization or finance fueled expansion; and the public expressed an overwhelming enthusiasm for railroad building. In the 1840s Britain's railroad "mania" gave it more track mileage than all of Europe. Between 1850 and 1910 the total British mileage rose from 6,600 to 23,400 and the annual number of passengers carried rose from 73 million to 1,307 million. At first in Britain many railroad firms competed, but those firms that could draw in the greatest amounts of capital soon swallowed up their competitors.

In the other nations of Europe, government fostered railroad building. In France, railroads further centralized government and society because all tracks led to and from Paris. In the German states, railroads contributed to unification, just as in Italy, where Cavour sponsored their expansion. The nations most transformed by railways were in North America and Eurasia. In the United States in 1870 there were more miles of railway (176,000) than in Britain and all of Europe combined. The transcontinental railroad offered an avenue into vast unsettled areas. The same story was repeated in Canada. In the 1890s, the Trans-Siberian railroad opened up the tsar's hinterland and carried millions of settlers east from European Russia to the desolate stretches of Central Asia.

The epic expansion of railroads was paralleled in shipping. In 1850, 5 percent of the world's tonnage of ships were steam powered; by 1893 the figure had advanced to half of all tonnage. The shift brought about

changes in marine technology such as the replacement of iron with steel and the substitution of screw-propellers for the paddle-wheels that moved river boats. In 1870, 4½ million tons of goods were shipped by sailing ship and less than a million tons by steamship; by 1881 the tonnage was about equal; by 1885 steam surpassed sail; by 1913 steam carried 11 million tons and sail only 800,000. The whole world had been accessible to Westerners for some time, but by the 1880s, thanks to steamship and railroad transportation, it was also open to the cheap, plentiful goods of European and American manufacturers.

At the turn of the twentieth century, however, the age of steam would begin to come to a close. Two German engineers, Gottfried Daimler and Carl Benz, joined to perfect the internal combustion engine. Together they produced a luxury automobile named for Daimler's daughter Mercedes. The American Henry Ford used mass-production assembly-line techniques to produce his Model T for "the ordinary man"; the automobile age was born. The invention of the diesel engine by another German (Wilhelm Diesel) in 1897 made it possible to use cheaper fuel more efficiently. Diesel engines soon replaced steam engines on giant cargo ships, warships, and luxury liners.

In communications the breakthrough of the telegraph sufficed for industrial expansion for more than a generation. At the time, the undramatic but rapid improvement of postal services was much more important to industrial growth than the spectacular inventions that are so important today—the telephone, invented by Alexander Graham Bell in 1876, and the wireless or radio, invented by Guglielmo Marconi in 1895. It would take twenty to twenty-five years after its invention for either device to be widely used even in industrial countries.

Advances in electronics illustrate a general trend of the second half of the nineteenth century—science and technology joined in inventions that played a greater and more visible role in the industrial expansion than new devices had in the much slower, more cumulative earlier growth. It took more than a half-century after Michael Faraday and James Maxwell discovered the fundamental principles of electricity for inventors like Edison, Bell, and Marconi to turn them to practical use for energy and for communications. Yet by the end of the century electricity would power lights, electric trains for urban and suburban use, and some factory engines.

This same trend is evident in the field of industrial chemistry, which revolutionized the products known to man. In 1850 almost all industrial materials were the same ones people had been using for centuries—wood, stone, cotton, wool, flax, hemp, leather, and the four basic metals and their alloys. Even dyes and drugs were products of plants or animals. However, from midcentury, building on the general framework provided by John Dalton's theory of molecular structure and Dmitri Mendelyev's classification by valence, chemists filled in missing elements (sixty-two were known in 1869 when Mendelyev formulated his periodic table) and perfected combinations. The resulting products included dyes and coal-tar products such as liquid fuel, aspirin and other drugs, saccharin, and disinfectant. By 1900 Germany was the center of applied chemistry—an important segment of that country's industrial expansion.

In medicine, too, the marriage of science and technology produced miraculous progeny. The discovery of anesthetics and antiseptics in the 1850s and the passionate insistence on cleanliness by surgeon Joseph Lister made it possible for most patients to survive surgery and hospitalization. The discovery and isolation of disease-causing bacteria by Louis Pasteur, a French chemist, made it possible to pinpoint the causes of some diseases, to properly isolate or quarantine the diseased, and to immunize or inoculate the healthy against disease. By the end of the century researchers had identified the causes of several killer diseases—typhoid, tuberculosis, cholera, tetanus, diphtheria, and leprosy. Science had exposed poor sanitation and squalor as the breeders of disease. Industrialized countries worked harder and more efficiently than before to ameliorate these conditions. Death rates dropped precipitously, life expectancy grew longer, and population increased. In the more industrialized nations the birth rate declined as the population rose.

Continuing Urbanization

Accelerating industrialization increased the numbers of northwestern Europeans and Americans who lived in cities, which became more numerous, larger, and more populated. London, although not an industrial city, had become a megalopolis of five million people by 1880, but it was home to seven million by 1914. Paris increased from two to three million from midcentury to the First World War. Berlin, a city of only half a million in 1866, reached two million by the First World War. There were only three German cities of more than 100,000 on the eve of unification, but by 1903 there were fifteen, which suggests the relationship between industrialization and unity in Germany.

Urbanization helped to further the breakdown of regional loyalties and the integration of the citizen in political and social activity on the national level. In the cities citizens responded to various influences of education, the press, and patriotic campaigns, becoming conscious of national loyalties and slowly moving away from regional, class, and religious ones. In cities the middle class rose to political, economic, and social prominence, often expressing its new-found importance and prosperity through civic activity. As machinery replaced handcraftsmen, the artisan working class experienced a sharp decline. Reflecting that process, many towns that had been craft centers decayed as artisans moved to larger urban areas in search of employment. Factory workers, their ranks swelled by peasants and artisans, emerged as a numerous and important social group in large urban environments. A city culture developed, although some observers who favored the old regional, religious, and occupational loyalties thought it was no culture at all. Cut off from the regions of their birth, factory-working peasants and artisans shed their old loyalties; in the cities some found a place for themselves in their neighborhoods, some in union and party activities, and some not at all.

Industrialization also created a new "white collar" group of clerks that tried to differentiate itself from factory workers; urban living was the only life this new group had known.

Industrialization and urbanization played a much more important part in national integration than did government campaigns to create homogeneity, like those of Russia or Austria. Often the success of minority cultural resistance to government pressures for integration depended on the relative economic backwardness of the area. As industrialization and urbanization proceeded, maintaining traditional loyalties became more and more difficult. There were exceptions, places where industrialization heightened minority identity—for example, the Czechs and the Basques.

In contrast to northwestern Europe, southern and eastern Europe remained overwhelmingly agricultural until the twentieth century. In Russia, in the Balkans and parts of the Austro-Hungarian Empire, in the Iberian peninsula and in southern Italy peasant discontent undermined the national integration that political leaders sought. In these economically backward areas, peasants who held small pieces of land could not always eke out a living; other peasants without holdings labored on great estates for landlords who paid them little. In eastern Germany, Russia, and Austria-Hungary, the agricultural sector followed the rest of the economy in producing for export rather than for home consumption, which meant that the peasants' standard of living in terms of food and steady employment sometimes actually declined.

Unionization and Worker Politics

Years of prosperity in the middle of the nineteenth century had allowed real wages to rise; factory workers in regular employment lived better than their parents had. Both factory workers and craftsmen joined unions in the 1860s and 1870s, despite the fact that unions were illegal in most countries. There were other legal obstacles to concerted labor activity as well. In addition, as the new forms of business and financial organization took over, new industries required new kinds of labor. Giant enterprises, using the technology of the second wave of industrialization, employed great numbers of unskilled workers who did not fit in the trade or craft unions or syndicates of skilled craftsmen. From the 1880s, skilled craftsmen and trained factory workers watched as machines operated by unskilled workers took their places. The new laborers worked for low pay, usually by the day or the job, if they were lucky enough (or shared enough of their wages with the foreman) to be chosen from a pool of unskilled labor. With pay so low and work so irregular, unions seemed almost impossible to organize and the corporate giants stuck together to defeat attempts at unionization. As a result, conditions were terrible, hours were long, and work remained irregular and low paying.

By the 1890s, however, unskilled workers in England, the United States, France, and Germany began to organize unions that were based not on a single skill or craft, but on an industry. Such organization was difficult, but workers could vote and many people sympathized with their plight. In England, women and girls who worked in match factories, where phosphorus endangered their health, went on strike in 1888. They won the attention of the press and the public, which deplored their miserable conditions and wages. Their strike succeeded because other workers called sympathy strikes; workers began to recognize the importance of solidarity. The next year the impoverished British dock workers struck, but their strike fund was quickly exhausted. Facing defeat, they were rescued when sympathetic Australian and American workers, mainly dock workers who knew how miserable that life was, sent money to help.

In their efforts at organized political activity,

The Twist Factory, Manchester. English cities of the industrial Midlands were dominated by vast factories and the smoke produced by their coal-burning furnaces. (*The Mansell Collection*)

beginning with the trade unions of the 1860s and 1870s and growing with the industrial unions of unskilled labor, workers used the suffrage to pressure government to recognize their unions; to legislate minimum wages, maximum hours, and better working conditions; and to deal with the social consequences of industrialization and urbanization. Governments responded by instituting social legislation: first, in the 1880s Bismarck instituted reforms (see page 604), and then, by 1914, Britain, France, Austria, Italy, Denmark, and Switzerland provided some benefits for sick, injured, and elderly workers. In some countries, such as the United States, workers voted for the same political parties that other classes voted for and the candidates competed with one another for labor's votes. In other countries, such as Britain, workers organized

a separate Labour party that pledged itself to their interests. Elsewhere, as in France, Germany and Italy, workers were attracted to socialist parties or to anarchist parties that called for the end of capitalism.

Over the years from 1850 to 1914, workers' lives did improve as a result of trade union organization, government intervention in the economy, and the general increase in productivity brought on by industrialization. Still, the working class had many reasons to be attracted to socialism and socialist parties. Most workers had to struggle for security for themselves and their families. They lived in overcrowded, bleak tenements, without central heating or running water. They worked long hours—as much as 55 hours a week in trades where governments restricted the length of the work week, and as much as 70 to 75 hours in unregulated trades. Their jobs were exhausting and monotonous. They suffered from malnutrition (the English men and boys who appeared for medical exams to serve in the Boer War were so physically unfit that there was a national crisis of conscience and some reforms were instituted to improve the health and education of the laboring class). They were victims of disease, particularly tuberculosis, and of the lack of medical care. Women died in childbirth from poor treatment and men, particularly miners and dock workers, were maimed and killed by on-the-job accidents that were a regular feature of their trades. Alcoholism was rampant, and temperance campaigns were supported by working-class women and their children, whose lives were frequently ruined by an alcoholic in the family. Middle-class reformers, who thought the workers' misery stemmed from dissipation and improvidence, urged temperance. Working-class union and political leaders thought the economy and the social system were responsible for workers' miserable lives, but they too urged self-discipline through temperance and thrift. These leaders believed that even though workers were not responsible for their impoverishment, they would have to improve themselves, individually and collectively, before they could gain enough freedom to change society.

Socialist parties, which by the 1890s were influenced by Marx's teachings and followers, were divided about tactics for change. Some, who insisted that they were "orthodox" Marxists, believed that socialist-led revolution was the necessary first step. Among the orthodox Marxists were Wilhelm Liebknecht and August Bebel of Germany and Jules Guesde of France. Others, "revisionist" Marxists, argued that Marx's predictions and theory needed revision because industrialization was improving workers' standards of living and because democracy was giving workers political power without revolution. In Germany, revisionists who followed Edouard Bernstein urged socialists to use the political and economic system to build socialism without revolution. In England, where

Marxism had not gained much influence, the Fabians argued the revisionist position along with many members of the Labour party who were socialists. In France the brilliant Jean Jaures was critical of orthodox Marxists.

Great Britain, 1850–1914

Throughout the century despite the extension of the suffrage to the middle class in 1832, "country gentlemen" dominated British politics: two of three members of parliament were landowners, and more than half were related to the inner circle of aristocratic families; cabinets were manned by titled aristocrats, the army and navy were commanded by gentlemen, and the civil service admitted none who were without "good breeding" and fit manners. Only the Indian civil service required written tests, but they emphasized classical languages, eliminating those who did not have a gentleman's education.

Reform and Progress

After the Crimean War and the War of Italian Unification (1859–60) the changes that were taking place in the industrial and commercial world began to modify British politics. Two men emerged as the central political figures of the epoch: William E. Gladstone (1809–1898), a pious, sober man and an orator who could inspire people over issues of taxes and revenues; and Benjamin Disraeli (1804–1881), a flamboyant personality—a novelist and a dreamer who talked of the greatness of empire. Gladstone saw politics as a struggle between the forces of good and evil and believed that God had chosen him to carry out his divine will; Disraeli thought politics was the most fascinating of games and he loved playing the courtier to Queen Victoria. The competition between the two men and their parties in the House of Commons actually stimulated reform.

Such was the case in the passage of the

Reform Bill of 1867. First Gladstone led the Liberals with a measure to extend the suffrage, which failed, forcing his resignation according to the custom of cabinet responsibility. Then Disraeli, trying to go his opponent one better, introduced a bill that would give the vote to the great majority of city workers—far more than Gladstone had envisioned; this measure passed. The Reform Bill of 1867 doubled the electorate, and suddenly the threat of democracy, feared by Liberals and Conservatives alike, became a reality. Disraeli claimed that he was not afraid of the masses. He said the conservatives had a social program that would attract the poor. However, a number of his followers, and many Liberals as well, claimed that in his eagerness to win in the game of passing bills and maintaining majorities, he had been "shooting Niagara" (a reference to the daredevil practice, then a fad, of going over Niagara Falls in a barrel).

The leaders decided it was imperative to educate the masses because the latter now had political power. Controversies over religious education, which had previously blocked educational reform, calmed before the prospect of uneducated workers voting. Parliament passed the Education Act of 1870 to provide elementary education for all. Although real political power remained in the hands of the gentry, the middle classes, and the traditional aristocracy, the Reform Bill of 1867 enfranchised nearly all city workers, bringing democracy nearer. With the Reform Bill of 1884, Gladstone extended the suffrage to country workers, which meant that most English men could vote.

Midcentury Britain's prosperity seemed to envelop all classes to some degree. Complacent members of the gentry thought all Britons shared an ethic of individualism and competition. They maintained that although class divisions and social barriers existed, Britain had not experienced the bitter class conflicts that Continental states had. Indeed, these same people often said that Britain was a deferential society in which the lower orders respected their betters and the upper classes took responsibility for the care of their work-

ers. If that situation ever existed, it ended in 1873 when the Great Depression snuffed out the sense of continuous progress. Many British thinkers questioned the economics of laissez-faire and individual competition. Almost simultaneously, the British realized that their rivals in industry, Germany and the United States, were very keen competitors. And at the very moment that British confidence seemed to be shaken by economic depression, industrial rivalry, and the unresolvable Irish problem, labor armed with the vote became more and more strident in its demands for political and economic reform.

Social and Political Unrest

Irish Troubles   The great famine of 1846–47, in which a million Irish died and another million emigrated, brought unparalleled suffering in Ireland. The English responded to this major catastrophe by callously repressing any expressed discontent. Parliament, justifying its behavior by combining laissez-faire and Malthusian economic principles with prejudice, refused to aid the Irish. As much as Czechs or Italians hated their connections with the Austrians, the Irish hated the union of their nation with England and Scotland (1801). Catholics, who received little in the union, gained the suffrage and the right to elected public office only with Catholic Emancipation (1829), which seemed to be too little reform offered too late. But the bitterness and distrust caused by years of discrimination were mild compared to the national hatred that arose from the great famine.

This national antagonism engendered a revolutionary force—the Fenians—that threatened to disrupt British stability and parliamentary politics. A Republican brotherhood, this group aimed at Irish independence and to that end committed acts of terrorism throughout the 1860s. The Fenians were financed by Irish-Americans and staffed by the unhappy youth of Ireland.

Gladstone staked his reputation and ultimately his party on the Irish question. He

Irish Immigrants Aboard Ship, 1870s. The great famine of 1846–47 opened the floodgates of Irish immigration. The English lacked government machinery, an economic philosophy of intervention when faced with disaster, and sufficient will to ease the suffering of the Irish. The Irish streamed into England and English colonies, as well as to America, in search of a livelihood. The Irish who remained at home demanded Home Rule and then independence. (*Library of Congress*)

launched a series of reforms in the hope of reconciling the Irish to Britain and to parliamentary politics. In 1869 he "disestablished" the Protestant Church of Ireland so that Catholic taxpayers no longer had to financially support a church they did not attend. He also passed a land act that forced landlords to compensate tenant farmers, if they were evicted, for any improvements they had made on the land. This measure was calculated to forestall the steady decrease in Ireland's productivity (renters had no incentive to improve land or farm buildings if they could be evicted without compensation). Despite Gladstone's

reforms, Irish Protestants, who were frequently landlords, still held economic power over Catholics and exercised social privilege.

On the Irish question, Gladstone was making reforms that should have been made in the 1840s and '50s. In the 1880s the issue had become Home Rule. Under the leadership of the anti-English Protestant Charles Stewart Parnell, many Irish in Parliament formed a separate bloc committed to Home Rule. Both the Conservatives and the Liberals had to reckon with Parnell. The Irish used every parliamentary tactic, and some extraparliamentary ones, in their effort to secure a separate legislature and executive for Ireland. When the Fenians engaged in terrorism, Parnell and his supporters were jailed for inciting their followers to violence and intimidation. Parnell denied he had any connection with the Fenians and denounced them. However, although Gladstone urged Home Rule, his party split over the issue, and Parliament enacted extreme measures, suspending trial by jury and many other liberties in Ireland.

At the end of his career, Gladstone knew that he had failed in his most important task—the reconciliation of the Irish. He also knew that two-party parliamentary politics, which he and Disraeli had practiced to perfection, was in danger because militant groups and important issues remained outside the political arena.

Labor Discontent For more than a generation after the failure of the Chartists, British workers devoted their efforts to raising their standard of living and improving their working conditions. They thought the best way to accomplish those goals was though trade unions dealing directly with employers, rather than through political agitation. Worker-supported candidates who were elected to the House of Commons after the Reform Bill of 1867 tended to be loyal to Gladstone and the Liberals; for the most part, they concentrated on domestic politics, on free trade, and on reducing taxes and agricultural prices. However, the Great Depression of 1873 and, in the 1880s, the rise of militant new industrial unions changed labor relations in Britain. At the beginning of the twentieth century, worsening economic and social conditions threatened to undermine the hard-won gains of British workers and drove them to political action to protect their interests.

British workers of the middle decades had never been attracted to the doctrines of socialism, particularly not to Marxism. There was an Owenite socialist current, but there was also a nonconformist, dissenting Christian tradition on which workers could base their protest against injustice. In the 1880s, though, the extensive poverty, the new trends in industry—particularly monopolies and cartels—and the increased competition of foreign workers led some labor leaders to urge more militant practices and to espouse doctrines of an English brand of socialism. The colorful Kier Hardie, who wore a worker's cap and clothes when he took his seat in Commons to represent a poor Welsh mining district, refused to follow the Liberals. He created the Independent Labour party in 1893 to fight for workers' interests. He and other union leaders, sometimes in alliance with middle-class socialist reformers like the Fabians, sometimes with Liberals, hammered out a political and economic program that developed into a platform for a separate Labour party.

The Labour party might never have developed if not for the Taff Vale decision (1901), which awarded damages to an employer picketed by a union. If workers did not pressure for legislation to legalize picketing, they would lose the economic gains of half a century. In the elections of 1906, in which the young Liberal heirs of Gladstone were returned overwhelmingly to the House of Commons, the new Labour party gained twenty-nine members. But high inflation meant a drop in the standard of living for most workers because their wages did not keep up with costs. By 1910 worker discontent generated a wave of labor unrest, which included strikes and violence. The miners, the dock workers, and the railway workers formed an alliance, urging a general strike

for minimum wages. The tactics of the French syndicalists (militant industrial unionists), who advocated the general strike as a method for obtaining substantial political and economic gains, appealed to great numbers of British workers. The traditional trade-union movement and the new unions of unskilled industrial labor pushed each other to greater militancy.

Feminist Agitation Other issues also threatened parliamentary government and British liberal institutions during the years preceding the First World War. Among them, female suffrage was particularly explosive, and the tactics and repression steadily escalated in violence. Women were allowed to vote for and serve as school board members and local government officials; in both arenas they had been very active—in fact, women were the backbone of school boards, and also of the charity organizations that tried to relieve poverty during the period. Their importance in thousands of voluntary activities belied the argument that they did not have the reasoning capacity or the political experience to vote intelligently for members of the House of Commons. But women were denied this suffrage, despite their petitions and their influence with important members of Parliament.

Some feminists (people who urge equality of the sexes) thought that women should concentrate their efforts on improving themselves and making legal efforts to improve their status in society; others thought that approach too slow and proposed radical action to reach equality. Many Liberals and some Labourites favored women's suffrage, but women were advised by the leader of the Liberals "To keep on pestering . . . but exercise the virtue of patience." For those whose patience was running out, a family of feminists— Emmeline Pankhurst and her daughters, Sylvia and Christabel—militantly exercised leadership. They urged demonstrations, invasions of the House of Commons, destruction of property, and hunger strikes. They did not urge these dramatic actions all at once, but when their petitions and demands were ignored, they moved to more and more shocking actions. Suffragettes began a campaign of breaking windows, starting fires in mail boxes, and chaining themselves to the gates at Parliament. As a gesture of protest, one militant threw herself to her death under King Edward VII's horse at the Derby races.

When feminists were arrested for violating the law, they staged hunger strikes. It was an ugly situation, with the police force-feeding the demonstrators and subjecting them to ridicule and rough treatment. Often the police would release half-starved feminists and, when they had recovered their health, reimprison them. A common argument of the time was that the use of such tactics proved women could not participate rationally and maturely in governing the country. Ridiculed, humiliated, and punished—but above all, legally ignored—British feminists refused to accept the passive role that a male-dominated society had assigned them. Their major part on the home front in the First World War changed the minds of the ruling elites and finally, in 1928, brought British women the right to vote on the same terms as men.

Britain on the Eve of War

Between 1906 and 1911 the Liberals introduced a series of important social measures. Spurred on by David Lloyd George (1863–1945) and the then-Liberal Winston Churchill (1874–1965) and aided by the Labour party, they enacted a program of old-age pensions, labor exchanges to help the unemployed find work, unemployment and health insurance (a program deeply influenced by Bismarckian social legislation), and minimum wages for certain industries. Parliament also repealed the Taff Vale decision. In the process of legislating these reforms, however, a constitutional crisis developed between the Liberals with Labour support, and the Conservatives, who dominated the House of Lords.

When Lloyd George introduced the "people's" budget of 1909, the Lords refused to

accept it, although the House of Commons was traditionally responsible for financial measures. The Liberals went to the voters determined to wage an all out struggle with the Lords, many of whom earned the nickname "diehards" and "last ditchers" for their intransigence. Many Lords saw their struggle as the defense of Britain and its empire against the "socialist" campaign of the Liberals, a party of minorities. Social legislation was to be financed by raising the income tax and by levying heavier inheritance taxes ("death duties"), and "unearned" income taxes on rents, investments, and increases in the value of land; all of these taxes were directed toward the wealthy and the privileged.

Following the same procedure used to pass the Reform Bill of 1832, the king threatened to create peers to pass the budget. This course seemed likely to shake the parliamentary system—certainly to destroy the House of Lords. The campaign was a bitter one in which class antagonisms were expressed freely, but the bill was passed. Later, reform eliminated the basis for the crisis; after the Parliament Act of 1911, the Lords could only delay the passage of a bill that Commons wanted, not prevent it.

The class antagonism that came to the surface during the campaign for the people's budget had gone unacknowledged by Britons for a couple of generations. Back and forth across the country, Lloyd George took the issue to the people, and he spoke of the "peers against the people" or of the dukes as "five hundred men, ordinary men, chosen accidentally from among the unemployed." He claimed to speak for the commoners, who he said ought to be the owners of the soil, rather than renters in their own nation.

The continuing bitter struggle for Irish Home Rule made the explosive environment in prewar Britain still more volatile. The House of Lords, dominated by Tory imperialists, used every tactic against Home Rule, but after the Parliament Act of 1911, they could not prevent its passage. The Liberals, sincere disciples of Gladstone, pushed on, but their opponents were so angry about the Irish question that they threatened to violate constitutional practice. They argued that the British Empire was too important to be broken up by party politics, elections, and mere majority rule.

Outside Parliament, militant groups took the law into their own hands. The situation was more violent and revolutionary than it had been in Gladstone's day; Irish Catholic extremist groups, such as the Irish Republican Brotherhood and the Gaelic League, pressed for full independence; and among the Protestant Irish (Ulstermen), the Ulster Volunteers recruited a large private army and openly trained it for revolution in the event that Home Rule was enacted. Gangs smuggled guns, soldiers fired on demonstrators, violence bred violence, and civil war seemed close. Tory leaders threatened mutiny—one going so far as to review 80,000 volunteers in defiance of Parliament and to urge mutiny on the army officers sent to subdue rebellion in Ireland.

At the very moment in 1914 that Great Britain was declaring war in Europe, Ireland was uppermost in British minds. With the onset of war, women and labor suspended their militant campaigns, pledging their loyalty to king and country "for the duration." Many Irish fought for Britain in World War I, but the deferred promise of Home Rule angered many others, who continued their struggle for independence. In 1916, the Easter Rebellion, an Irish insurrection, led by Sir Roger Casement, was suppressed and its leaders were executed for treason. After the war, with ill will on all sides after the repression of civil war, Ireland was divided. The south gained independence and a republican government, and the six counties of Ulster remained part of the United Kingdom. In the Second World War independent Ireland remained neutral.

The bitter differences that beset prewar Britain seemed likely to alter completely the country's image as a stable, liberal, constitutional regime. But parliamentary and liberal government proved itself ready and able to conduct and win gruelling World War I. It survived, but the Liberal party declined in the aftermath, to be replaced by the Labour party.

France, 1848–1914

The Era of Napoleon III

In December 1848, less than a year after the revolution that had dethroned Louis Philippe, Louis Napoleon Bonaparte (1808–1873), nephew of Napoleon I, was elected president of the Second French Republic by an overwhelming majority. Within three years, in a December coup d'état, he had made himself an authoritarian ruler by force, although a plebiscite of the French people ratified the destruction of the Republic. Napoleon III's coup called an abrupt halt to the politics and the reforms of the revolutionary Republic. Thereafter, elections were regularly rigged and opposition controlled. His declaration of the Second Empire signaled a shift to the right and the stabilization of France. Napoleon's actions outraged the liberal and republican forces in France, including some of Europe's most talented minds, such as Alexis de Tocqueville and Victor Hugo. There were some relatively minor uprisings among workers and radicals, but most of the French seemed to accept and perhaps to be proud of their "little Napoleon."

The governments of Prussia, Austria, Russia, and Britain did not immediately see Napoleon as a force for stability. Between 1852 and 1870 the new emperor, descendant of a great military tradition, promised peace but waged two successful wars: one defeated Russia in the Crimea and the other humiliated Austria by helping to unify Italy. In both victories, the forces of progress seemed to triumph over the forces of reaction. Through the wars, Bonaparte made friends with the English, whose enmity had plagued France for more than a century. He also won the support of the Italians and the pope, although he could not call on them as allies simulta-

Map 26.1 European Cities of 100,000 or More, 1800 and 1900

neously because they had different views about the unification of Italy. His foreign adventurism also involved French troops in a dangerous fiasco of imperial expansion in Mexico. He tried unsuccessfully to place the Hapsburg archduke Maximilian on a non-existent throne, but he was able to extricate French troops without too much cost to France. He furthered French imperialism by joining Britain in opening China and by claiming portions of Africa; these moves, however, did not seem likely to upset the balance of power in Europe.

At home, France benefited from the inflation and economic growth that followed the discovery of gold in California and Alaska. The midcentury in France was a period of prosperity, confidence, and political apathy. Certainly during the period from 1851 to 1860, political expression under the authoritarian ruler was impossible; Napoleon kept strict control of the legislature, rarely convening it and always manipulating it. He censored the press and harassed his critics. His support came from property owners, including the mass of peasants, from business and from the Catholic church. They approved of the stability at home and careful expansion abroad and of Napoleon's program of economic development stimulated by railroad construction

and the rebuilding of Paris. It was a period of enormous creativity in France—in the arts the French had no equals, and in the sciences they were major contributors.

In the first years of the Second Empire, Napoleon chose his close personal friends as advisers and administrators; most were legitimate and illegitimate members of his large family, and they seemed to have no particular political position other than loyalty to him. Napoleon claimed that he was a socialist, rather than a Bonapartist (an advocate of rule by a strong man). He did have some ideas about economic progress, which he insisted must be tempered by order. He expressed a sympathy for some of the Saint-Simonian ideas espoused by his supporters—grand schemes of canal and railroad building and of cheap credit from state-sponsored banks. He also talked of the plight of the workers. But few socialists were willing to claim this "Saint-Simonian on horseback" as one of them. The first decade of Napoleon's rule was characterized by careful managing of elections to an impotent chamber of deputies and by a search for people who were willing to accept the new order. It was personal and authoritarian rule by a strong man.

The Italian War of 1859 seemed to mark a turning point in Napoleon's career. Suddenly he was faced with fiascos abroad and critics in government at home. His assistance to the unifiers of Italy, which pleased many liberals, angered Catholics, who insisted that French troops protect the pope in Rome. Even some workers that he himself had subsidized to go to a London exhibition returned filled with the ideas of unionization; they promptly joined in the creation of the First International Workingmen's Association. French businessmen were sorry that they had allowed Napoleon to establish free trade with Britain, because British competition was fierce, despite France's amazing economic progress. The scandals involved in many of Napoleon's building activities became known when greater freedom of the press and of speech in the legislature was allowed in the 1860s. In 1864, strikes were legalized; in 1868, workers were given a limited right to unionize. But these reforms did not win the workers' loyalty for the emperor. When many members of the opposition were elected in 1869, Napoleon accepted a new constitution that reduced his role. The political parties quickly moved to make France a constitutional parliamentary monarchy, with liberal safeguards for individual liberties.

Napoleon III may, after all, have been a sincere liberal who wanted first to establish his power and then give France reforms. But he may also only have succumbed to liberalism because he feared that opposition would lead to revolution. The question of Napoleon's goals still perplexes historians, but whatever his ambitions, his foreign policy drew France into war with Prussia in 1870. Within a year Paris had surrendered.

The Aftermath of the Franco-Prussian War

Defeat in the Franco-Prussian War brought down the empire of Napoleon III. In bitter frustration at the defeat by the invading Prussian armies, the people of Paris rose against the armistice signed by the provisional government—the politicians had replaced the captured Napoleon. The uprising, known as the Paris Commune (1871), began as a patriotic refusal to accept the army's defeat, but it turned into a rejection of the authority of the provisional government as well as that of the corrupt Second Empire. Ultimately, the actions of the Communards (as those who resisted the Prussians and the provisional government were called) challenged property owners. The resistance to the Prussian siege joined together French people of all classes and flared into hostility toward landlords and creditors when the provisional government lifted the moratorium, declared during the war, on rent and debts.

The Parisians held elections, and the revolutionary forces that had been gathering for a generation came to the fore. They differed greatly in their program for the future, but they were republicans. They included the followers of Proudhon, who were very influential among the artisans and small entrepreneurs. The republican and socialist veterans of the Revolution of 1848 reappeared from prisons, from hiding, and from exile. There were also the disciples of Auguste Blanqui, an old insurrectionist who spent most of his life in prison, with brief interludes of glorious freedom when each new revolutionary wave proclaimed him a hero of the people. For two months in the spring of 1871, the revolutionaries ruled Paris, always guided by the heroic precedents of the Jacobins of 1793 and the radicals of June 1848. Then, Adolphe Thiers, head of the provisional government that still governed the rest of France and the man who had accepted Bismarck's peace terms for lifting the Prussian siege, ordered a siege of Paris. French fought French. The fighting was bitter and desperate, with many acts of terrorism and violence. Both sides in this civil war set fires that destroyed large parts of the city they loved. The Communards were defeated and treated as traitors. When apprehended, 20,000 of them were executed without trial; those who were tried received harsh sentences of death, life imprisonment, and transportation to prison colonies.

The Commune became legendary. Across Europe, governing classes were terrified by the hatred that they imagined the revolutionary masses to feel. Most Communards were ardent French patriots, not international revolutionaries; their desperate economic plight had driven them to action, not some ideological commitment to the abolition of private property. Nevertheless, many in the governing elites decided that the people should be ruled with an iron fist.

International revolutionaries, both socialist and anarchist, were encouraged by the radicalization that they thought they saw in the desperate acts of the Communards. However, they also became convinced that just as Thiers had used French troops against French people, the political leaders of other states would use all available means to prevent the peaceful evolution of society toward socialism. The masses, said revolutionaries like Marx, must perfect their organizations for insurrections and violent seizure of power. Workers must learn to be as ruthless as Thiers. Other radicals, appalled by the bloodbath in Paris, argued for the ballot box and the organization of political parties; in their view, the power of the modern state had become too great for insurrection to lead to revolution as it had in the past in 1789, 1830, and 1848.

The Paris Commune and its brutal suppression did not create the social and political differences among Frenchmen, but the events dramatized existing differences and intensified the hatred between social groups. The empire defeated and the Commune suppressed, law and order were re-established under the weight of a harsh Prussian peace treaty. Burdened by an indemnity and the loss of Alsace and part of Lorraine, France pondered how to rebuild and regain its place as a European power.

The Emergence of the Third Republic

No one at the time expected that the government emerging from the next few years of political crises would be a republic—and the longest-lasting one in the history of France (1875–1940). The monarchists were the most numerous and most powerful of the political groups. They seemed to offer stability and order without the dangers of radical or even liberal republicanism. But there were *two* conflicting monarchist parties: the Legitimists and the Orleanists. When the Orleanists agreed to compromise, the Legitimist leader refused to accept the blue, white, and red tricolor, which symbolized the liberties won in the French Revolution, as the state flag.

The disunity among the forces of the right— mainly the monarchists in the first decade after the Franco-Prussian War, but discredited Bonapartists as well—enabled France to become a republic by default. However, the French government did not become wholly republican in the legislative and executive branches of government until 1879. Up to then there were monarchist aspects to the constitution and executive authority was exercised by Marshall MacMahon, but with no king willing to rule, the republicans gained power.

Somewhat in imitation of the British system, the republican government was made up of a powerful bicameral legislature—the Chamber of Deputies, which resembled the House of Commons—and a prime minister who had to have its support. Frenchmen had gained the right to vote in 1848 when the second republic had enacted the most democratic suffrage in Europe. The president was a figurehead, indicating the hope that no new Napoleon would rise to overthrow the regime; the result was an office that no talented politician wanted. Unlike Britain with its two-party system, France had many political parties, which exaggerated the differences between the French, rather than modifying them, and contributed to instability. No one party had sufficient strength within parliament to provide strong leadership. Prime ministers resigned in rapid succession; cabinets rose and fell frequently, giving the impression of a state without direction. Political life seemed to be one of wheeling and dealing. The Republic survived, but not without major crises.

Threats to the Republic

At times during the first generation of the Third Republic, dissatisfaction seemed to unite the right and the left. In the 1880s, scandals—one of which centered on the sale of medals, honors, and influence by the president's son-in-law—threatened to overthrow the Republic. Opposition began to center around a dashing general, Georges Boulanger (1837–1891), whose popularity frightened many French with fresh memories of Napoleon III. It seemed that the history of modern France swung back and forth from anarchy to authoritarianism. But Boulanger was a republican. More important, at the crucial moment of seizing power either his nerve failed him or his personal life undermined him. The whole story never became known, but the man who might have toppled the Third Republic fled to Belgium, where he committed suicide on the grave of his former mistress. The crisis had forced radicals and moderates together in defense of the Republic.

Almost immediately, however, further scandals developed in the effort at financing and building a Panama Canal. Several radical republican deputies were implicated in a giant swindle in which people were sold stocks that constantly diminished in value. The deputies had taken bribes to permit their names to be used in the sale of stocks and bonds and they tried to cover it up. The French were disgusted with the low level of political morality in their republic; many believed that all politics were immoral, and others believed that democratic politics were. Neither attitude helped build a republican morality.

The crisis that tore France in two for over a decade came closely on the heels of the Boulanger affair and the Panama Canal scandals. In 1894, Captain Alfred Dreyfus, an Alsatian-Jewish artillery officer, was wrongly

Edouard Manet (1832–1883): Portrait of Émile Zola. Many intellectuals and students defended an Alsatian Jew, Captain Dreyfus, falsely convicted of treason. France was a battleground of demonstrations and riots over the Dreyfus Affair. Among the Dreyfusards were novelists Émile Zola, Anatole France, Marcel Proust, and Charles Péguy; painter Paul Cézanne; and political figures Georges Clemenceau and Jean Jaurès. (*Brogi/Art Resource*)

accused of treason—of having sold secrets to the Germans; he was condemned to life imprisonment on Devil's Island. Anti-Semitic elements joined with the Republic's opponents to denounce and block every attempt to clear Dreyfus of the charges against him. In the beginning, Dreyfus was defended by very few people and opposed by the vast majority, who felt that the honor of France and of the army was at stake. Then individuals, mainly republicans, came to his defense, including the writers Anatole France and Émile Zola, and Georges Clemenceau (the future radical republican leader), along with university students and other intellectuals. They protested and demonstrated, insisting on a retrial and a revision of the verdict. After many humiliations, Dreyfus was finally cleared in 1906.

The result of the victory of the radical republicans, however, was a fierce campaign to root out those opposing the Republic. The radicals attacked the church, expelled religious orders and confiscated their property, and waged a vigorous campaign to replace the influence of the parish priest with that of the district schoolmaster. Complete separation of church and state was ordered. France became a secular state, and taxes no longer supported the parishes and schools. It was a bitter fight, however, that seemed to cut France in two.

France on the Eve of War

The Dreyfus affair exposed and exaggerated the problems of French society. The struggle for control of education—the secularization of France, as it was called—revealed the vast gulf between the issues that agitated the elite and those that concerned the mass of the people. In England and Germany, the parliaments were beginning at the turn of the twentieth century to make reforms calculated to appeal to the masses. They were providing some rudiments of a state-supported welfare system for working people and were supporting their programs with a fairer tax structure. In France there was no income tax and no national pension scheme until the First World War.

The state of the French economy and the experiences of the French working class led to a history different from that of Britain or Germany. Despite the progress in the middle of the nineteenth century, French economic development lagged. France had fewer and smaller industries than Britain or Germany; more French people lived in rural areas or in small communities; and in general, industry, trade unions, and socialist groups tended to be decentralized rather than national and to be made up of artisans rather than

proletarians. For a generation after the bitter suppression of the Paris Commune, French labor was markedly antipolitical. For a decade, its leadership was broken and dispersed within France or in exile. Labor argued that there could be no cooperation with the Republic or with any bourgeois government.

In the 1880s, however, both trade unionism and political parties with a socialist program began to make headway and to press for social reform through the democratic parliamentary institutions of the republic. Many French socialists thought political action was class collaboration, but Jean Jaures inspired a regenerated democratic socialism. France was very slow to enact social measures such as pensions and regulations governing working conditions, wages, and hours. Such measures, which might have improved the lives of ordinary people, were regarded as socialism by the ruling class and as tokens to buy off workers by many socialists. Radical syndicalism and even anarchism had many supporters among workers and intellectuals. Instead of political action, they preferred to wage economic war against the state through strikes, and a wave of strikes beginning in 1909 ended in the government supression of a national railway strike the following year. Socialists, syndicalists, and anarchists were all suspicious of politics and politicians.

France was a troubled country. The Third Republic was not a popular regime. The church, the army, socialism, and even memories of the monarchy and the empire inspired deeper passions than the Republic, which survived only because the dissension among its enemies allowed it to. France approached the First World War a deeply divided country; at the time, few would have believed that a war would unite the French nation.

Germany, 1870–1914

The German Empire that Bismarck created was, in many ways, exactly the empire that he had desired. Prussia dominated all the

German states; the king of Prussia was emperor and Bismarck was responsible only to the emperor. Most Germans received the act of unification with enormous enthusiasm. Bismarck, the Iron Chancellor, was the man of the hour—not just for conservatives, but for liberals as well.

The Bismarckian Constitution

Bismarck's constitution, however, was hardly liberal. The empire was *kleindeutsch* (little Germany), or Germany without the German-speaking and Catholic Hapsburg lands. The organizational structure was federal. Some powers were reserved for the member states, such as Bavaria, Baden, and Württemberg; other powers, particularly in foreign affairs and defense, were in the hands of the emperor and his appointee, Bismarck. The military, the foreign service, and the top ranks of the bureaucracy were staffed by the aristocracy, which protected its social status by rejecting contact with most of the bourgeoisie and lower bureaucratic ranks. There were no controls over Bismarck, except the ability of the Reichstag, the lower house of the parliament, to refuse to pass the budget. The members of the cabinet did not have to maintain the support of a majority in the Reichstag to keep their offices. The German Empire did not have two-party government or guarantees of civil liberties. If the legislature disapproved of the chancellor, it could not remove him from office. The German Kaiser, unlike the British monarch, had considerable control over lawmaking and foreign affairs and commanded the army and navy. Still, the Reichstag could discuss any issue, and its members were elected by universal male suffrage, which was unusual in the 1870s—only France had such an extensive electorate. Bismarck's constitution gave appearances of liberal and democratic government, but real power was in the chancellor's hands.

Impressed by Bismarck's leadership, German liberals did not struggle enthusiastically for basic political and civil liberties. They tolerated evasions of principle and practices that their liberal British cousins would never have allowed. Germany never developed a truly parliamentary system, and certainly not a liberal society. The civil service was a separate corps with its own special aristocratic spirit—high-minded and honest perhaps, but aloof and incapable of responding to either criticism or the demands of democracy. Bismarck's political practices strengthened illiberal elements, rather than liberal or democratic ones. Bismarck cared little for principle and regarded political parties as mere interest groups to be called on for support; he believed that they were incapable of governing or making policy. As a result of their political experience in Bismarckian Germany, or their lack of it, political parties, with the exception of the Catholics and the Socialists, tended to represent single issues or regional interests.

Bismarck's *Kulturkampf*

In Bismarck's mind, the Catholics and the socialists undermined the unity of his Reich. Almost 40 percent of the German Empire's population was Catholic, despite Austria's exclusion. Taking advantage of a split in the Catholic church over the question of papal infallibility, and of the prejudice stimulated by that doctrine among non-Catholics, Bismarck initiated a systematic persecution of Catholics—the *Kulturkampf* (struggle for culture). Embodied in the May laws of 1873, the Kulturkampf involved an attempt to subject the church to the state. The laws discriminated against the Jesuits and required state supervision of the church and the training of priests in state schools. Catholics were required to be married by the state. Churchmen who refused to accept these laws were imprisoned or exiled.

The long-run effect of the Kulturkampf was exactly the opposite of what Bismarck intended, although not because the liberals defended the civil liberties of Catholics. Persecution strengthened the German Catholics' faith and loyalty, and the Catholic Center party attracted more and more support. Prussian conservatives, Protestant in religion, resented Bismarck's anticlerical policy, which could hurt Lutherans as well as Catholics. With the succession of Leo XIII to the papacy in 1878, Bismarck quietly opened negotiations for peace with the church. Bismarck did in part achieve one of his aims with the Kulturkampf, however, and that was to weaken liberals, who allowed patriotism and anticlericalism to lull them into passivity when they should have defended their principles.

Bismarck versus the Socialists

In the late 1870s, Bismarck turned his attention against the socialists. Ferdinand Lassalle (1825–1864), a charismatic lawyer-reformer whose influence extended from workers and trade unionists to Bismarck himself, had formed a German Workers' Association. He was an ardent German nationalist who was convinced that the government could assist the workers. Marx opposed Lassalle's attempt to join socialism and nationalism. He detested Lassalle's dilettantism, but did not have the lawyer's popularity with the workers or his organization. Other influential socialists, Wilhelm Liebknecht and August Bebel, were Marxists and opposed any courting of the emperor or his Prussian military and bureaucracy. But they joined forces with the Lassalleans in 1875 to create a German socialist party. Courting the emperor made little difference, however, because Bismarck was intent on winning the workers away from their leaders; he wanted to crush the socialists, and the liberals along with them.

Two attempts on the life of William I in 1878 gave Bismarck the excuse that the socialists threatened society and had to be suppressed. In reality, the socialists were not a threat—they were few in number and their immediate practical program was a demand for civil liberties and democracy in Germany. Only the narrowest conservative view could have seen the socialists as dangerous, but many in Germany held such a view. The conservative Junker class, which dominated Prussian political life, would not support the socialists. The liberals, whose principles upheld civil liberties, did not oppose Bismarck's special legislation outlawing subversive organizations and authorizing the police to ban meetings and newspapers. The Social Democratic party, like the Catholic Center party before it, survived the persecution. It grew stronger and better disciplined as the liberals grew weaker, discredited by their unwillingness to act against the Iron Chancellor.

Bismarck tried to win the support of the workers through paternalistic social legislation. He, like many conservatives, was disturbed by the problems of industrialization, which developed in Germany at a rapid pace in the 1850s and 1860s until the worldwide depression of 1873 temporarily slowed growth. Germany was the first state to enact a program of social legislation for the proletariat; it included insurance against sickness, disability, accidents, and old age. Bismarck's laws called for the employer to contribute funding along with the state and the worker. Many people called the Bismarckian social legislation *state socialism*. Like socialists in every other nation, German socialists debated vehemently over whether they should cooperate with the state or try to use the state's power to enact socialism. These debates overstressed the power of the socialists, who were weak until just before the First World War. At that time they became the strongest party in Germany and in the Second International of socialists.

The German working class continued to support the Social Democratic party in elections, and its members belonged to the many socialist political, youth, athletic, and cultural organizations. Nonetheless, great numbers of German workers felt that their government deserved their loyalty. Thus, the revolutionary fervor of French laborers, and the devotion to the trade unions that characterized British workers, were not emotions shared by the Germans.

Germany on the Eve of War

Bismarck was a conservative in economics. Rejecting the liberals' laissez-faire, he placed tariffs on the importation of grain and industrial products, which pleased landowners and industrialists but hurt the workers and the poor. Liberals bitterly opposed his schemes to nationalize the railroads—an unheard of extension of state authority. After the crash of 1873, Germany's economic expansion was steady but moderate, not the rapid growth of midcentury. By the end of the century, Germany and the United States were major industrial powers and serious rivals to Britain. Neither had practiced laissez-faire economics as the British had. Their economies were characterized by the growth of monopolies and cartels that relied on government support.

The German government backed the economic interests of its landowners and industrialists in many ways, including the expansionist colonial policy of the 1880s. At first, Bismarck had claimed Germany was a satiated power and did not need colonies, but increasingly in the 1880s, he responded to groups pressuring for expansion by supporting minor colonial acquisitions in the Pacific and in Africa. Colonialists joined with other pressure groups in urging construction of a powerful navy to support expansion and strengthen German industry. Forces that endangered world peace were set in motion.

In this atmosphere, Kaiser William II (1889–1918) ascended the throne. Germany was changing rapidly. It had the most extensive sector of large-scale and concentrated industrial and corporate capitalism of any Great Power. But its growth was uneven. Although the heavy industries were rapidly developing into giant monopolies or cartels and mining and railroads were state owned and operated, the speed of expansion was more important than the actual percentage of the German economy controlled by such industries. There were many small firms as well and large-scale agriculture was still very powerful. Large unions had arisen to deal with these monopolies, but workers in smaller firms were still predominantly organized by trade. The population rose one-third in the single generation from 1882 to 1902, but the industrial work force increased by 180 percent in that

time, creating an active labor force of 27 million. These people were called directly from the farm to work in heavily concentrated industries in alien urban environments. Only the peasants in Russia or peasant-immigrants to the United States experienced comparable dislocation. The conflicts between traditional sources of political and social power and the new organizations of industry and labor contributed to great social dissatisfaction on the eve of the First World War.

The Kaiser was a brash, outspoken young man who alienated people in other nations. He dismissed Bismarck in 1890, and to gain popularity with the new industrialists and others he shifted to foreign policies that led to the First World War. But before too much disrepute is assigned to William II's behavior, two facts should be remembered: first, Germans were not as horrified by the kaiser's behavior as foreigners were (or as historians have been since); second, Bismarck prepared the way for William II. Bismarck's prestige was so great that he could have withstood the clamor for colonies, but he allowed imperialism to go forward. The alliance system, which played an important part in touching off the declaration of war in 1914, was Bismarck's. The constitution—a peculiar mixture of aristocratic Prussian power in the upper house, democratic universal male suffrage that was manipulated to nonliberal ends, and an unassailable chancellor and military—was Bismarck's creation. Bismarck's opportunistic maneuvers against Catholics, liberals, and socialists undermined the development of a viable parliamentary government. The bureaucracy, the military, and the chancellor remained out of the reach of the voting populace. In 1914 the most highly industrialized and powerful European nation was subject to a political regime that preserved aspects of an absolute monarchy.

Austria-Hungary, 1866–1914

With Austria's domestic Settlement of 1867 following the Austro-Prussian War, Magyars and Germans became the dominant nationalities in the empire (see Chapter 25). The nationality struggles in the half-century following the settlement consumed the Dual Monarchy's energies. However, there were other issues and struggles, too, that were complicated by and obscured by nationality questions.

Social and Economic Development

As in Italy and Russia, government in Austria-Hungary, which needed heavy industries for war and defense, played an important role in industrialization. Government gave tax incentives, tariff protection and direct subsidies to the industries that it favored. The direct interest of the state in industrialization, which in the eighteenth century concentrated on munitions, uniforms, and improvements in transportation and communication, extended in the mid-nineteenth century to many sectors of the economy as the state widened its policy of subsidies, tariffs, and incentives to financiers. Although the defense sectors of the economy remained the largest-scale operations in the Austro-Hungarian Empire, the government showed favoritism and encouraged the tendency to monopolize in many areas.

Other segments of the empire's economic system reflected the economic backwardness of the area. Most industry was consumer oriented—small-scale operations in textiles and food processing. Craftsmen maintained their importance in central and southern Europe in general; but in Austria in particular, of the total of almost a million firms in 1912 more than 75 percent were very small businesses based on agricultural commodities, and this situation continued up to the First World War. On the eve of the war the Austrian provinces still had over 5,000 artisan guilds registered, with membership of a half-million masters and a half-million journeymen, whereas guilds had disappeared more than fifty years before in England, Belgium, and France. Vienna was a large, brilliant, beautiful capital

city of two million inhabitants who earned their livings in much the same way and on the same scale as they had in the previous century.

In Hungary the story was little different, except that an even greater percentage of the population worked in agriculture. About 30 percent of the urban population were independent craftsmen who did not hire any laborers, with another 30 percent employed in small workshops of not more than twenty workers and usually less than ten.

The emergence and concentration of heavy industry in large firms, capitalized by specialist banks, characterized the post-1890s period all over Europe. This tendency was exaggerated in Austria-Hungary (as in Russia and Italy) because late industrialization made the cost of development to compete with advanced countries so great that small entrepreneurs could not meet it. In Austria-Hungary one or two giant enterpreneurs dominated steel, mines, and munitions operations, having absorbed many competitors in a single generation. (In Britain and France, in contrast, the trend toward concentration stretched across several generations.) Such rapid growth caught the imagination of businessmen as well as socialist critics. Few noticed at the time that small business expanded along with big business in central Europe; that is, that the growth of the 1890s and the following decade was general and not limited to monopolies and cartels alone.

The state had extraordinary economic and social power in Austria-Hungary (as in Russia). The court and the old aristocracy of birth were almost totally closed to new ideas and new blood. In Austria, government and society were dominated by three or four hundred aristocratic families whose lives centered on the brilliant Hapsburg court; and the German-speaking, large-landowning leaders of government and society maintained splendid palaces in Vienna and elegant country homes for weekends. Unlike the aristocracies in the rest of Europe, Austria's uppercrust excluded the artistic and intellectual elite as well as the lower-level aristocracy.

The latter were ennobled to lesser ranks (baron, for example) for serving the state in the military, in the bureaucracy, or in other ways. Some very important bankers and industrialists reached this lower level, but the aristocracy's upper rank was closed. Yet the values of the upper rank were accepted by the lower, which meant that the Hapsburgs themselves remained the true source of authority and prestige throughout Austrian society, in much the same fashion as the Romanovs did in Russia.

In Hungary, the entrepreneurial and business classes were even less important than they were in Austria, which reflected the backward state of Hungary's industrial development. The dominant Magyar landed magnates and gentry cared so little for commerce and industry that the field was left open to non-Magyar subjects, in particular Austrians, Germans, Czechs, and Jews. Although the Magyars restricted the national political activities of non-Magyars, the economic development of the overwhelmingly agricultural area was in non-Magyar hands. In this instance, the minorities benefited greatly from Magyar prejudices.

Politics in the Dual Monarchy

There was nothing in the dualist political system that excluded the possibility of representation, or even autonomy, for minority nationalities such as the Czechs, the Poles, or the South Slavs. From 1870–1914 the emperor's advisers, responding to the demands of Magyars and Germans, or to those of Slavic minorities, shifted back and forth between policies of decentralization, to conciliate very real national grievances, and centralization or, at best, dualism. There were times when the two segments of the monarchy pursued very different domestic policies.

In the wake of German unification and the establishment of its own new constitutional forms, Austria tended toward centralization under the control of the Austrian Germans, who were anxious to suppress the Slavs' nationalist aspirations. Centralization was ac-companied by secularization that resembled Bismarck's anticlerical policies. Liberal governments instituted civil marriage and restrictions on the papacy, politically expressing their disapproval of doctrines of papal infallibility promulgated in 1870. Emperor Franz Joseph, a devout Catholic, called a halt to liberal German centralization policies so long as they were tied to anticlericalism, raising the national minorities' hopes for autonomy.

For more than a decade, 1879–1893, a coalition of national minorities, conservatives, and Catholic clerics won concessions to their grievances. In that period, as a result of Austria's increasing industrialization, a labor movement also grew up that was attracted to socialist doctrines. The government chose to follow a Bismarckian policy of suppressing the socialist party while enacting social legislation to protect workers. In the Dual Monarchy, as in Germany, the Socialist party fought for fundamental political rights such as universal manhood suffrage. Socialists argued that the class struggle was the primary issue and that the nationality question was secondary. The universal suffrage measure was overwhelmingly defeated, as virtually every national group decided it was more important to keep their national rivals from voting than to extend the vote among themselves. Rather than advocating universal representation, each group insisted on its special right to political autonomy, like that of the Magyars. It was not until 1907 that universal manhood suffrage passed in the Austrian half of the empire.

Meanwhile, throughout the period from 1867 to the outbreak of World War I, Hungary moved toward greater centralization and demanded even more independence from the Austrians. The hottest issue revolved around the army, where the Magyars insisted on separate Magyar regiments with Magyar, rather than German, as the language of command. The emperor insisted on a unified army and refused to accept the Magyars' demands. The Magyars finally relented, but not until legislative debate on the issue had nearly ended in violence.

Austria-Hungary on the Eve of War

In the decade immediately before the outbreak of the First World War, class conflict in Austria-Hungary became as great an issue as the nationality struggles. In Austria, it was the working class that demanded social change; in Hungary the oppressed peasantry, usually Slavs, challenged all-powerful Magyar landlords whose great wealth was based on agricultural export. In Bohemia, industrialization on a grand scale exacerbated class separation, which intensified the nationality struggle.

The Hapsburg Empire's breakdown in the First World War frequently obscures the facts of its great endurance. The empire had existed for centuries. Even as nationalism burst on the scene in the nineteenth century the Hapsburgs continued to rule. With industrialization, class antagonisms intensified; still the empire survived. But in 1914 the Hapsburg military high command advocated war in the hope of fortifying the emperor and the army—the only remaining institutions of unity.

Italy, 1870–1914

Italian nationalists expected greatness from the unification of their country, so long conquered, plundered, divided, and ruled by absolute princes. But it seemed that in every cause for rejoicing, Italians had to face a nagging doubt as well. The backwardness of the nation and its politicians forestalled economic and political development. The illiterate and impoverished people and their republican leaders expected much of the Italian state, but their expectations would not be fulfilled.

In addition, Italy was split on the religious issue. Many Catholics in the overwhelmingly Catholic country had wanted to see a unified Italy, perhaps even an Italy where the pope played less of a political role. But Pope Pius IX refused to accept this new Italy, whose leaders had confiscated papal territories, closed religious houses, and taken church properties. Also, the liberal and republican leaders wanted to create a secular state, with civil marriage and secular education, which was anathema to the church.

Another divisive factor was Italy's long tradition of separate and often rival states. Some principalities resisted unification under Victor Emmanuel, the Piedmontese king. Many Italians argued for federalism, wherein some government powers—defense, foreign affairs, and perhaps railroad building—would fall to the central government, but many important aspects of life, such as education, would remain in the hands of local governments. To many Italians, no institutions seemed to safeguard local rights to make sure that the central government would deal justly with every area.

Few Italians were able to participate in the constitutional monarchy. Of the 27 million citizens, only about 2 million could vote—even after the reforms of 1881, which tripled the electorate. Liberals could point out that almost every literate male could vote, but this achievement was small consolation to those whose efforts to unite Italy had not required literacy. The government was comprised of ministers responsible to the king (as in Germany), an upper house (appointed members), and a lower house (members elected by the narrow franchise). Italian political parties remained small groups gathered around a few personalities; parties and ideologies did not mean much when an ambitious politician wanted to take office. For example, a man might be elected to the lower house as a member of the left, only to move to the center to gain a cabinet office. To many Italians, parliament seemed to be a place where deals were made and corruption was prevalent.

Among Italian workers, cynicism about the government was so deep that many turned to anarchism and syndicalism, attracted by the rejection of authority and tactics of terrorism, assassination, and the general strike. Such workers shared many of the class feelings that French workers expressed after the Paris Commune. Strong unions, socialist ideals, and a disgust with parliamentary government led the workers to believe that direct action would gain more than elections and parties.

In some rural areas, particularly in the south, the peasants were so isolated from the national political and economic life that traditional patterns of loyalty to the local landowner, now also a political leader, persisted. Catholic, loyal to their landlord, and bitterly unhappy with their economic situation, they saw few signs of the new state other than taxation and conscription. Often their children migrated to the north to work in factories, or moved even farther—to the New World.

The ruling elite brushed aside Italy's difficult social and economic problems and concentrated instead on issues more easily expressed to an inexperienced political nation: nationalism, foreign policy, and military glory. The politicians expressed Italy's ambitions for Great Power status to justify military expenditures beyond the means of such a poor state. They furnished the rationale for Italy's scramble for African and Mediterranean territories: their expansionist foreign policy would provide the solution to all Italy's social ills, they said; the profits from exploiting others would pay for badly needed social reforms, and the raw materials gained would fuel industrialization. None of these promises came true, which deepened the cynicism of a disillusioned people. As a foreign and domestic policy, this pursuit of glory was too costly for the fragile nation.

Politically, on the eve of World War I Italy was deeply divided. A wave of strikes and rural discontent gave sufficient warning to political leaders that they declared neutrality, deciding not to risk the shaky regime by entering the war with Germany and Austria-Hungary. But the appeals of expansionism were too great for them to maintain this policy.

Russia, 1825–1914

Of far greater diversity and territorial sway than even the Hapsburg monarchy, nineteenth-century Russia spread from the Prussian border to the Pacific Ocean, a Eurasian giant. The huge borderlands and the diversity of peoples inhabiting them reaffirmed the autocratic tradition of the Russian state. Russia possessed neither a loyal and intelligent nobility of independent means nor an enterprising and well-to-do middle class; it also lacked the creative competition of free citizens. For several centuries the state itself had taken over the responsibility for mobilizing resources, growing all-powerful while reducing its subjects to pawns. Even in the early nineteenth century, only two classes of people were said to exist in the Russian Empire: the servitors of the tsar—army officers, officials, and the landed nobility from which they sprang—and the serfs who served the servitors. The urban people, merchants and craftsmen who had been forcibly organized into guilds in the late eighteenth century, enjoyed little freedom; they were few in number and generally despised like the common folk by the nobility.

The servitors, Europeanized since the time of Peter the Great, constituted a small privileged minority. They were separated from the mass of the population by barriers of education, culture, and experience that were more profound than any class distinctions in Europe. Like the tsar himself, they lived in fear of popular uprisings. The tsar had additional reasons for fear: the country suffered from external insecurity, especially in its relations with the Great Powers of Europe, which were better armed, more prosperous, and above all, had popular support for their foreign policies.

Russia's fortunes depended on its political order, which centered more than in western Europe on the rulers. The tsarist government, its central institutions reorganized on the lines of Western models in the wake of the French Revolution, took a decidedly conservative turn after Napoleon's defeat, and for good reason. Many returning Russian officers, asking why Russia could not share the civilized life they had seen in western Europe, turned revolutionary. The unsuccessful Decembrist uprising in 1825, during the brief interlude between the death of Alexander I (1801–1825) and the accession of Nicholas I (1825–1855), was the effort of a small group of conspirators demanding a constitution. It determined the character of the reign of Nicholas I and of tsarist governments thereafter.

Aware of the subversive influence of foreign ideas and conditions, Nicholas decreed an ideology of Russian superiority, called *official nationality*. The Russian people were taught to believe that the Orthodox creed of the Russian church, the autocratic rule of the tsar, and Russia's Slavic culture made the Russian Empire superior to the West. To enforce this contrived invincibility, Nicholas I created the Third Section, a secret agency of police spies, and controlled access to his country from Europe, drawing toward the end of his reign a virtual iron curtain to keep out dangerous influences. His ideal was a monolithic country run, like an army, by a vigorous administration centered on the monarch; all Russians were to obey his wise and fatherly commands.

However, in Nicholas's reign, corruption and deceit pervaded the bureaucracy. Society stagnated except for intense intellectual agitation among small circles of students. Yet the tsar also promoted innovation. He ordered a railway built between St. Petersburg and Moscow; he opened schools and universities, hoping in vain to encourage Russian participation in the European advance of knowledge without encouraging subversive comparison with the West.

The Crimean War (1854–1856) deflated Nicholas I's ambition to make Russia victorious in all comparisons with western Europe. Russian threats to the Ottoman Empire and to Anglo-French domination of the eastern Mediterranean led to armed conflict fought on Russian soil. The English and French expeditionary forces defeated the Russian army. During the war, in a mood of profound crisis, a new regime began under Alexander II (1855–1881).

Alexander II was hailed as "tsar liberator," but suffered from an emotional instability that reflected the dilemma of his reign. On one hand, he was determined to preserve autocratic rule; his country lacked all prerequisites for constitutional government. On the other hand, he wanted Russia to achieve what had made western Europe strong—the energetic support and free enterprise of its citizens. Whether stimulating popular initiative was possible without undermining autocracy was the key puzzle for him and for his successors to the end of the tsarist regime.

Alexander's boldest reform was the emancipation of the serfs in 1861. The serfs were liberated from bondage to the nobility and given land of their own, but not individual freedom. They remained tied to their village and to their households, which owned the land collectively. Emancipation did not transform the peasants into enterprising and loyal citizens.

For the nonpeasant minority, a package of other reforms brought new opportunities: limited self-government for selected rural areas and urban settlements, an independent judiciary, and the rule of law. Trial by jury was introduced, as well as a novel profession—lawyers. Military service also underwent reform, so that all male Russians, regardless of status, were drafted into a citizen army granting as much equality as Russian conditions would permit.

Meanwhile, Alexander reopened the borders, allowing closer ties with Europe and westernizing Russian society. The rising class of business people and professional experts looked west and conformed to Western middle-class standards. There was some relaxation in the repression of non-Russian minorities. Railroads were constructed, which facilitated agricultural exports and permitted the import of Western goods and capital. For some years the economy boomed.

More significant in the long run was the flowering of Russian thought and literature. Since the late eighteenth century, the impact of Western culture on Russian life had created an extraordinary intellectual ferment; it came to a climax under Alexander II among a slowly growing group known as the *intelligentsia*. The intelligentsia's members were educated Russians whose minds were shaped by Western schooling and travel, yet who still were prompted by the "Russian soul." Caught

Russians Building the Trans-Siberian Railroad. This scene of railroad building could have been taken in North or South America, in India or China, or in north or south Africa in the nineteenth century. Railroads made vast stretches of land accessible to many settlers. Building the great railroads often brought together laborers from diverse nationalities and races. The Trans-Siberian Railroad, begun in 1891 in the hope that it would usher in an era of heavy industrialization, was completed in 1917, the year of the Bolshevik Revolution. (*BBC Hulton Picture Library/Bettmann Archive*)

between two conflicting cultures, their critical awareness was heightened by alienation. They examined Russian life with Western sensibilities and the West with Russian sensibilities. Members of the privileged classes, they tried to ease their troubled conscience by service to the common people whom they idealized; at their best, they produced a brilliant literature that became a source of intense national pride and exerted a profound influence around the world. Fëdor Dostoevski and Leo Tolstoy wrote their greatest novels in the 1860s and 1870s. The intelligentsia quarreled with fierce sincerity over whether Russia should pursue superiority by imitating the West or by cultivating its own Slavic genius, possibly through a Pan-Slavic movement. Even more than the tsars, the intelligentsia hoped for a glorious Russia that would outshine the West.

Yet tsarist autocracy undercut their hopes. The tsar would not permit open discussion likely to provoke rebellion (in 1863 he faced an uprising in his Polish lands). Liberals advocating gradual change were thwarted by censorship and the police. The 1860s saw the rise of self-righteous fanatics ready to match the chicanery of the police and foment social revolution. By the late 1870s, they organized themselves into a secret terrorist organization. In 1881, they assassinated the tsar. The era of reforms ended.

The next tsar, Alexander III (1881–1894), a firm if unimaginative ruler, returned to the principles of Nicholas I. In defense against the revolutionaries, he perfected the police state, adapting Western methods and even enlisting anti-Semitism in its cause. He updated autocracy and stifled dissent, but he also promoted the economy. Russia had relied too heavily on foreign loans and goods; it had to build up its own resources. It also needed more railroads to bind its huge empire together. So in 1891 the tsar ordered construction of the Trans-Siberian Railroad. Soon afterward, his Minister of Finance, Sergei Witte, used railroad expansion to boost heavy industry and industrialization generally. In 1900, he addressed a far-sighted memorandum to the young Nicholas II (1894–1917), who, hopelessly unprepared and out of tune with the times, had succeeded his father in 1894:

Russia more than any other country needs a proper economic foundation for its national policy and culture. . . . International competition does not wait. If we do not take energetic and decisive measures so that in the course of the next decade our industry will be able to satisfy the needs of Russia and of the Asiatic countries which are— or should be—under our influence, then the rapidly growing foreign industries will . . . establish themselves in our fatherland and the Asiatic countries mentioned above. . . . Our economic backwardness may lead to political and cultural backwardness as well.[1]

Yet forced industrialization also brought perils. It propelled the country into alien and often hated ways of life; it created a discontented new class of workers and it impoverished agriculture; it promoted mobility, literacy, and contact with western Europe, thereby increasing political agitation among the professional classes, intelligentsia, workers, peasants, and subject nationalities. Indispensable for national self-assertion and survival, industrialization strained the country's fragile unity.

The first jolt, the Revolution of 1905, followed Russia's defeat by Japan in the Russo-Japanese War (see Chapter 26). Fortunately for the tsar, his soldiers stayed loyal. The autocracy survived, although now saddled with a parliament called the *Imperial Duma*, a concession to the revolution. The new regime, inwardly rejected by Nicholas II, started auspiciously. Under its freedoms, Russian art and literature flourished and the economy progressed. Agrarian reforms introduced the incentives of private property and individual enterprise into the villages. The supporters of the constitutional experiment hoped for a liberal Russia at last, but the heightened insecurity, as revealed in the pre-1914 international crises, merely prepared the doom of tsarist Russia.

The rulers of Russia between 1825 and 1914 had labored under enormous difficulties in their efforts to match the power and prestige of the great states of Europe. Two of them (Alexander II and Nicholas II) came to violent ends; the other two died in weariness and failure. Although the fear that the tsars inspired was real, their splendor was hollow. Their tragedy was recognized neither by the liberal West nor by their critics among the intelligentsia, with whom they shared the vision of a superior Russia.

A Golden Age?

At the end of the first year of the First World War, the nineteenth century must have seemed a golden era, a period of unparalleled peace and progress full of the promise of all that well-meaning people considered modern—liberal institutions and democratic movements, autonomous nations, scientific progress, and individual human development.

The century seemed one of progress in the production of goods, the alleviation of want, the development of technology and the application of science to industry and medicine. Part of that progress, in most minds, was the extension of constitutional and liberal

Chronology 26.1 Europe in the Age of Industrialization

1846–1847	Great famine in Ireland.
1851	Louis Napoleon Bonaparte overthrows the Second Republic, becoming Emperor Napoleon III
1854–1856	The Crimean War
1860s	Irish movement for republican form of government (the Fenians)
1861	Kingdom of Italy is formed; Alexander II, Russian tsar, emancipates the serfs and institutes reforms
1867	Second Reform Bill doubles the English electorate
1870	The Third French Republic is established
1870–1871	The Franco-Prussian War; the Paris Commune; creation of the German Empire with William I as kaiser and Bismarck as chancellor
1873	The Great Depression
1880s	Charles Stewart Parnell leads the Irish Home Rule movement in the British Parliament
1881	Tsar Alexander II is assassinated
1884	Reform Bill grants suffrage to virtually all English men
1894–1906	The Dreyfus Affair in France
1905	Revolution in Russia—Nicholas II grants the formation of the Imperial Duma
1909	Lloyd George introduces people's budget
1911	Parliament Act

government and the expression of humanitarian concern for others, whether from Christian or secular motives. Serfdom and feudal obligations had been abolished in Europe; so had slavery in the United States and Brazil. Europeans spoke of self-government as a right. The importance of democracy had been acknowledged, and in most of Europe, universal manhood suffrage was in effect before the outbreak of the war.

The world had become smaller, more interdependent and cosmopolitan, better educated, and probably better fed, housed, and clothed. Europe was at the height of its power in the nineteenth century. Its productive ca-

pacities had reached out beyond its frontiers to most of the world. Its culture, whether considered in total as a European culture or, in particular, as German, French, English or Italian culture, was brilliant.

Yet people looking back from the vantage point of 1915 must have realized, too, that something had gone wrong in the nineteenth century. Authoritarian governments persisted in central, eastern and southern Europe. Traditional institutions and groups still exercised their privileges at the expense of others. Doubts had been stirred when the Revolutions of 1848 had failed to reconcile national and class conflicts. Perhaps the bitter reaction to

1848 and the brutal reality of the midcentury wars of unification had perverted the ideals of liberal government and individual freedom. Many had doubted emerging democracy as they saw the passions of the masses manipulated by cynical leadership. Perhaps the ideals of liberal government, individual freedom, national autonomy and economic progress were not equally suited to every situation.

In the last part of the nineteenth century and the first part of the twentieth, liberal-democratic ideals fell prey to authoritarianism, extreme nationalism, imperialism, class conflict, and racism. Yet even through world war, mass destruction, and the manipulation of humanity in the name of nationalist passions, these ideals would survive and spread.

Notes

1. Theodore H. Von Laue, *Sergei Witte and the Industrialization of Russia* (New York: Columbia University Press, 1963), p. 3.

Suggested Reading

Blake, R., *Disraeli* (1967). An excellent one-volume biography.

Chekhov, Anton, *Selected Stories*, especially "The Peasants," "Three Years," and "In Exile."

Dostoevsky, Fyodor, *Notes from the Underground.*

Eyck, Erich, *Bismarck and the German Empire* (1950). A very critical biography; an abridgment of a larger work.

Goldberg, Harvey, *The Life of Jean Jaurès* (1962). The most readily available work on this important man.

Gordon, Craig, *Politics of the Prussian Army* (1955). A very valuable study with important implications for German and European history.

Gorky, Maxim, *My Childhood.*

Holborn, Hajo, *History of Modern Germany, 1840–1945*, 3 vols. (1969). A definitive work.

Jellinek, Frank, *The Paris Commune of 1871* (1937).

Johnson, D., *France and the Dreyfus Affair* (1967). The best of many books on the controversial affair.

Joll, James, *Europe Since 1870* (1973). A valuable general survey, particularly good on socialism in the individual nations.

Kann, Robert, *The Multinational Empire: Nationalism and National Reform in the Hapsburg Monarchy, 1840–1918*, 2 vols. (1950–1964). A definitive text.

Mosse, W. E., *Liberal Europe, 1848–1875* (1974). A comparative history of Europe in the liberal era.

Noland, Aaron, *The Founding of the French Socialist Party, 1893–1905* (1956). A well-informed study of the origins of the socialist party in France.

O'Brien, C. C., *Parnell and His Party, 1880–90* (1957). A good book on this important Irish leader.

Seton-Watson, Christopher, *Italy from Liberalism to Fascism* (1967). Excellent survey of Italian history.

Smith, Dennis Mack, *Italy: A Modern History*, rev. ed. (1969). Excellent survey with emphasis on the theme of the failure of Italy to develop viable liberal institutions or economic solutions.

Taylor, A. J. P., *The Hapsburg Monarchy, 1809–1918* (1965). A well-written, incisive, brief history.

———, *Bismarck: The Man and the Statesman* (1967). A brilliant portrait of a complicated man who dominated the second half of the nineteenth century.

Webb, R. K., *Modern England from the Eighteenth Century to the Present* (1968). A balanced, well-informed, readable book that is up-to-date on controversial issues.

Williams, Roger, *The World of Napoleon III*, rev. ed. (1965). An indispensable fresh look at the "Saint-Simonian on Horseback."

Wright, Gordon, *France in Modern Times*, 2nd ed. (1974). A good survey of the entire period.

Zeldin, Theodore, *France, 1848–1945: Ambition, Love, and Politics*, vol. 1 (1973). An explanation of the forces that held France together.

Review Questions

1. Why was England seen by many as the model liberal nation in the middle decades of the nineteenth century?

2. How did the competition between political parties further reform in Victorian England?

3. How did the Reform Bill of 1867 usher in a new era in British politics?

4. In England, the middle class and the workers often worked together for reform in the period from 1860 to 1914. In France they rarely did. Why?

5. How did Napoleon III's domestic and foreign policies conflict?

6. What was the general crisis of liberalism after 1870?

7. How did the conservatives attempt to win over the masses after 1870?

8. What social problems did unified Italy fail to resolve?

9. Historians disagree about the merits of the Bismarckian legacy to Germany. Discuss evidence for this disagreement.

10. On the eve of the First World War, most of the European states were threatened by a crisis, either political or social. Discuss the threat of revolution or social change among the Great Powers on the eve of the war.

11. What problems did the tsars from Nicholas I to Nicholas II face in ruling Russia? Given the conditions of their country, could they have become constitutional monarchs?

12. How did its social system hold Austria-Hungary together against the disruptive effect of national conflict and government structure?

27

Western Imperialism: Global Dominance

*I*n the last two decades of the nineteenth century, Europeans very rapidly laid claim to Africa, seizing goods, annexing territories and exploiting the weakness of local rulers. They dominated much of East and Southeast Asia, forcing commercial connections on Chinese and Japanese dynasties and carving out empire if local rulers were too weak or too self-interested to prevent it. Often the strongest defense against European rapaciousness was the presence of other Europeans who would not tolerate any monopoly that could be used against them.

From the long perspective, European history has been one of an expansionist society. In the sixteenth century, Europeans had conquered and settled substantial regions of the Americas; in the eighteenth century, Europeans competed with one another in a series of wars for the rights to trade and settle in faraway lands in Asia and the Americas. By the end of the eighteenth century the old slaving stations in Africa had declined, as had the Caribbean sugar trade and the mines of Central and Latin America. Revolutionary wars for independence, beginning with the United States and continuing in Latin America, had seemed to bring an end to colonialism and to usher in a new era of trade and investment without political control. Trade with former colonies was no less profitable, and scarcely less secure, than trade with colonies.

For most of the nineteenth century, Europeans showed little interest in adding to the remnants of the eighteenth-century empires. Free traders argued that commerce, rather than growing with the number of colonies, would go to whichever country could produce the best goods most cheaply. Efforts to add colonies would be better expended in improving industry, they said. Many people thought the days of empire were over—that Europeans had grown too civilized to fight over trade networks. European liberals, in particular, believed that the interdependence of commerce precluded a major war because such a conflict would be too destructive of the livelihoods of too many people.

Nonetheless, European influence over the rest of the world grew in the nineteenth century. Masses of European immigrants made new homes in North and South America, Australia, and New Zealand. As European nations industrialized, world trade expanded greatly, drawing previously untouched peoples into the network of supply and demand of raw materials, finished goods, and capital. Certainly, the expansion of world trade and the spread of Western ideas along with Western technology would continue to take place with or without any extension of political empire. Yet at the end of the century the European presence shifted abruptly from commercial penetration to active conquest, political control, and exploitation of previously unclaimed territories. From about 1880 to 1914, Europeans confronted each other, willing to fight over stretches of desert or rain forest that they could scarcely locate on the map. European control of most of the world persisted until after the Second World War, and the impact of imperialism is felt in our own day. As it progressed, *imperialism* would come to mean the domination by one country of the political, economic, or cultural life of another country or region—a definition much broader than political control alone.

The Emergence of the New Imperialism

The *new imperialism* (so-called to differentiate it from the "old colonialism" of settlement and trade in the sixteenth to eighteenth centuries) began when the Great Powers rather suddenly, from the point of view of contemporaries, announced policies aimed at political control of African territories. A growing expansion of interests was apparent in the mid-1870s, but the special Berlin conference on Congo affairs arranged by Germany and France in 1884–85 became the symbol of the mad race to claim Africa. Between 1880 and 1914 all Africa except Liberia and Ethiopia came under some form of European control.

To explain this burst of expansion after at least half a century in which Europeans more or less tended to their own affairs, some historians suggest the new imperialism was a direct result of industrialization. In their new economic situation, Europeans struggled for raw materials, markets for their commodities, and places to invest their capital. In each large industrial nation, people argued that stiffer competition necessitated control over other areas of the world to avoid national defeat in the economic race. Captains of industry defended the new empires, urging their sometimes reluctant governments to acquire territory and predicting dire consequences if their state did not get its share of world markets.

However, the economic arguments that were advanced for imperial expansion—the need for raw materials, markets, and a place for investment—do not hold up. Most of the areas that were claimed by Europeans and Americans were not profitable sources of raw materials or wealthy enough to be good markets. For Europeans and Americans the primary trading and investment venues were Europe and America. Perhaps individual businesses made colonial profits, but certainly most colonies proved unprofitable for the Western taxpayer. Nor, in general did the colonies attract surplus European population that could contribute to the mother country's far-flung economy; the United States tended to draw most of the European emigration, with Australia, Canada, New Zealand, and South America attracting some as well. Yet, it is important to remember that contemporary national leaders, that is, the makers of imperialist policies, often did embrace the economic rationale for empire. Remembering the period of economic depression around the 1873 crash, they accepted economic necessity as a reason to expand.

Aggressive nationalism, including the struggle for diplomatic and military gains far away from dangerous fields of conflict in Europe, seems to have been one of the strongest forces behind imperial activity. But it is difficult to separate the economic reasons for

A Christian Missionary in Togoland (Ghana).
Throughout the nineteenth century, Christian missionaries had gone to Asia, Africa, and Latin America to preach and to carry on the crusade against slavery. Many of these Christians devoted their lives to accomplish these goals; at the same time, many carried with them the ethnocentric values and judgments of their compatriots who thought that non-Europeans were backward and uncivilized. (*Culver Pictures*)

imperial expansion from the nationalistic ones, because Europeans expressed their economic aims in terms of intense nationalism.

Many historians believe that the antagonisms and power struggles between European states simply extended to Africa and Asia. In this view, the master diplomat Bismarck encouraged the French to expand in Africa, knowing full well that this course would bring them into conflict with the Italians and the English. At first, Bismarck hoped empire would distract the French from Alsace and Lorraine, which Germany had taken from them in 1870. Later, he hoped that imperialism would divide Frenchmen into imperialists and anti-imperialists, creating another rift to weaken France's political system. Germany's own shift to colonialism called for naval expansion; this move, in turn, caused Britain to ally with its rival, France. The British liked to think that they were not aggressively imperialistic, but were merely defending interests and empire already in their possession. They had a way of defining enormous amounts of territory and water as essential to their great subcontinental colony of India. But nations with less extensive or less lucrative empires saw Britain as their primary rival for the spoils of imperialism—for "a place in the sun," as the Germans liked to phrase it. Even in Russia, a small clique of nobles and officers urged expansion with the awareness that imperial activity in Asia and the Middle East would bring Russia into conflict with Britain (and, later, that it would mean confronting the Japanese). Thus, the conflicts between Europeans were played out, for a while, in Asia and Africa, perhaps contributing to the relative peace of Europe itself. But in the long run, the tense atmosphere of imperialism— the militarism and the racism—only contributed to a more hateful war in Europe, and that war engaged the empires as well.

Social Darwinists (see pages 549–550), with their images of national vitality and competition between fit and unfit, vigorously advocated empire. They argued that the strong nations—those successful at expanding industry and empire—would survive, and that others would not. To these elitists, all Europeans were better fit to prevail in the struggle for dominance than non-Europeans, but among Europeans themselves, there were civilizations more fit for the competition. Usually, Social Darwinists thought their own nations the best, which sparked their competitive enthusiasm, but some feared that their people were incapable of the endurance and sacrifice necessary to win. The latter could be imperialistic too, however, and they argued the need for trials of strength to fortify the people and for even greater support from colonies. The arguments were blatantly racist. Social Darwinists even applied racial terms to their own people when expressing class inequality. British imperialists proclaimed the British working class too unfit to serve in the Boer War and urged health and education reforms to improve the British "race" to enable it to rule an empire. In the popular mind, the concepts of evolution justified the exploitation by superior races of "lesser breeds without the law." This language of race and conflict, of superior and inferior people, gave a particularly ominous cast to the extension of the world market and the expansion of European power.

Not all advocates of empire were Social Darwinists, however. Some did not think of themselves as racists. They believed that the extension of empire, law, order, and industrial civilization would raise "backward peoples" up the ladder of evolution and civilization. However, they had little or no sense that other cultures and other peoples had merit and deserved respect. In the nineteenth century Europeans, except for missionaries, rarely adopted the customs or learned the languages of local people when they did business in Asia, Africa, or Latin America. In the seventeenth and eighteenth centuries, in contrast, such adaptation had been common among traders. The European attitude toward and relationship with other civilizations had clearly changed.

Still other Europeans believed it was their duty as Christians to set an example and to educate others. Christian missionaries were the first to meet and learn about many peoples and the first to develop writing for the languages of peoples without written language. Christian missionaries were ardently antislavery, and throughout the century they had gone to regions of Africa unexplored by Westerners to preach against slavery. But to end slavery, many missionaries believed, as did David Livingstone, that Europeans must furnish law, order, and stability. They thought only deeper involvement in the world market economy would offer non-Western peoples alternatives to their ancient occupations of war, pillage, and enslavement of the vanquished.

A legacy of interest in exotic places contributed to the passion for imperialism. The expeditions of the Scot Mungo Park on the Niger River at the turn of the nineteenth century had sparked the romantic imagination. The explorations of Livingstone in the Congo Basin and of Richard Burton and John Speke (who raced with each other and with Livingstone to find the source of the Nile) fascinated many Europeans. In the beginning of the century, expeditions were a matter of adventure and scientific curiosity; they often included explorers from several countries. But after midcentury national prestige was a factor in such forays. Sponsored by national geographic and exploratory societies and encouraged by their nation's military, explorers captured the imagination of Europeans and Americans in much the same way that astronauts do today. Individual personalities, who seemed larger than life to their contemporaries and to themselves, were usually quite devoted to their nations but saw exploration as an escape from the humdrum existence at home.

Individuals and nations competed to find the highest mountain, the longest river, the highest waterfall, the land never before seen by white men. Such superlatives called men and women away from their ordinary lives to adventure—if not to experience it, at least to dream of it. The fiction of English authors Rudyard Kipling (1865–1936), H. Rider Haggard (1856–1925), and many inferior imitators stimulated the passion for faraway places and unknown peoples. Wrote Kipling: "Take up the White Man's Burden—send forth the best ye breed—go bind your sons to exile to serve your captives' need."[1] He also wrote of the Indian Gunga Din, whose faithful service to his white masters, some British soldiers in battle, won him their respect. Writers told of European bravery and sacrifice in the colonies. In books for young people they wrote inspirationally of heroes, adventures, and achievements, shaping the attitudes of the next generation. Until the twentieth century, they rarely wrote of the exploitation, cruelty, and abuses of empire.

A Global Economy

Industrialization did more than create an enormous technological gap between the West and the rest of the world. The Western economy became more international in the nineteenth century and then truly global by the end of the century. New markets, new technology, and overseas trade and investment created a single world market economy. As they industrialized, Western powers, even small ones like Belgium and the Netherlands and backward ones in eastern and southern Europe, exploited the raw materials and markets of the rest of the world.

The underdeveloped areas of the world, in turn, found markets for their crops and were able to buy European commodities. But being part of the world market economy also made these areas subject to the smallest tremor on the European and American stock

exchanges. Participation in the world market could bring wealth for a few people in these areas, but it meant hardship for many, as well as the loss of traditional customs and social relationships.

Increasing crop production to satisfy European and American markets often created problems. Producing for the Western market meant turning land that had grown food for families over to export crops like coffee or indigo, thus reducing the food supply. It often meant consolidation of small peasant holdings in the hands of richer peasants or landlords who could capitalize export commodities; thus market forces drove the poorer peasants off the land, into debt to the landlord or the usurer, and into cities. For most of the nineteenth century the peasants felt bonded to their traditonal masters, but in our century they came to see themselves as enslaved by foreigners who either controlled the government or the world market. The passionate desire to escape this bondage has fueled revolutionary movements in the developing world.

Economic interdependence operated to the great advantage of Europeans and Americans; the world economy enriched and eased the lives of these consumers by the beginning of the twentieth century. Europeans and Americans could be found dressed in Egyptian cotton, Australian wool, Chinese silk, and Argentinian leather, consuming Chinese tea or Colombian coffee in a home or office furnished in hardwoods from Burma, Malaya, or Africa. Westerners could purchase all these goods, and many more, at prices so favorable that many luxury items became available to the nonrich. Europeans and Americans could travel anywhere, using gold or easily available foreign currency exchanged at a rate almost always favorable. They could invest their money in the raw materials or the government debts of virtually any area of the world and expect a good return. They also expected their investments to be secure and their property and person to be protected. Non-Western political authorities who could not guarantee that security, for whatever reason, risked intervention, perhaps even occupation, by European or American forces.

Control and Resistance

In the nineteenth century, changing technology widened the gap between Europe and other areas, making European states for the first time clearly more powerful than the nations of Asia and Africa. This gap in technology gave Europeans much the same advantages that the wheel, firearms, and the horse had given the Spanish over American Indians in the sixteenth century. Europeans could bring to bear the enormous power of industry and of military technology, and the European nation-state could mobilize the support of all its citizens. These factors made it unlikely that a non-European country or people could successfully resist a European state. Yet Ethiopia was able to resist Italy's incursions, north Africans kept the French on the defensive in Algeria and Morocco, and the Chinese and Egyptians discovered that some Westerners would help them resist other Westerners.

Europeans established varying degrees of political control over much of the rest of the world. Control could mean outright annexation and the governing of a territory as a colony. In this way Germany controlled Tanganyika (East Africa) after 1886 and Britain controlled much of India. Or control could mean status as a protectorate, in which the local ruler continued to rule but was directed, or "protected," by a Great Power. In this way the British controlled Egypt after 1882 and maintained authority over their dependent Indian princes. There were also spheres of influence in which a European nation had special trading and legal privileges without any military or political involvement. Persia (Iran today) was divided at the turn of the century between the Russians in the north and the British in the south, each recognizing the other's sphere of influence. Some peoples were so completely dependent on a particular country as a market for their goods or as a

source of bank loans that it seemed they were politically independent only in the most technical sense; they dared take no action that might upset their economic connection.

Nevertheless, many non-Europeans resisted American and European economic penetration and political control in a variety of ways, and the very process of resistance shaped their history and their self-awareness. In many areas, such as the Ottoman Empire, China, and Japan, ruling governments found ways of limiting the political influence of Western trading interests. Some countries tried, as Egypt did, to seek economic independence through modernization. The Turks played Europeans off against one another and maintained control over their lands outside Europe, if not in the Balkans. The Chinese emperor granted trading privileges, even control of cities (spheres of influence) to Europeans, but he kept China under his rule. The Japanese, responding to European and American commercial incursions, drastically changed their economy, their government, even aspects of their social structure; but they continued to control their territory.

Other forms of resistance were not carried on by rulers and governments, but by individuals and groups who held on to traditional ways. These people rejected Western education and secularization, often renewing institutions, particularly religious ones, that were falling into disuse when the Europeans arrived. Such resistance became a statement of both national and individual identity. There are many examples of such resistance: the Sudan Muslims' holy war, led by the Mahdi, against both their Egyptian fellow Muslims, who were regarded as agents of the European nonbelievers, and the Europeans; the Boxer Rebellion in China; and the Sepoy Mutiny in India.

However, in most cases, efforts at resistance only brought non-European peoples more firmly under Western control. When their interests were threatened, the Europeans generally responded by annexing the offending region or establishing a protectorate. Resistance continued; whole peoples in Africa moved from place to place to escape European religion, taxes, and laws; insurgent mountain people in Indochina and Algeria evaded French cultural influence or restricted it to the coastline. In some places the Europeans were never fully secure in their control, but Western domination seemed a relentless global force.

European Domination of Asia

The story of European imperialism in Asia is very complicated. In India, China, and Japan, powerful kingdoms existed when the first Europeans arrived. For several hundred years, trading connections had been established in which the European was usually the weaker party and depended on the good will of the Asian. The Asian kingdoms possessed a sense of cultural unity arising from tradition and from loyalty to Hinduism, Buddhism, Islam, or Confucianism. When in the nineteenth century the Europeans came in much greater numbers and power, the feeling of cultural unity was scarcely a conscious nationalism as Europeans knew it, but animosity toward European domination developed into national feeling that unified many social and religious groups.

India

India was internally torn by religious conflict between Hindus and Muslims, as well as among other religious believers, and by the rivalries of native princes. The subcontinent became the scene of intense European competition in the eighteenth century. By the end of the century, the British had cleared out their rivals one by one. The British East India Company made alliances with princes, carried on trade and collected taxes, and commanded its army of sepoys, native sol-

diers on loan from a subservient prince, until the company controlled much of India. The Parliament in London regulated the chartered monopoly enterprise, but it was not until the Sepoy Mutiny of 1857–58 (the Indians call it the Great Rebellion) that the charter was revoked. The rebellion was a major popular uprising in which Muslim and Hindu soldiers joined with native princes, who finally perceived that the British, rather than neighboring princes, were the real threat to their authority. Peasants, too, who were victims of both their local landlords and market forces, participated in the uprising. Unlike the Chinese and the Japanese, the peoples of India lost all semblance of independence. The British ruled some states through dependent Indian princes, but about two-thirds of the subcontinent was ruled directly by about a thousand British officials.

The British governed India through a civil service. At first, it was entirely British, its officials confident of their superiority to anyone or anything Indian. Later an elite of Indians educated in English and trained in administration became part of the civil service. Indian civil servants, along with soldiers who were recruited from peoples with military traditions such as the Gurkhas and the Punjabis, carried out British policies. The civil service ruled over about 250 million Indians, of almost two hundred languages and several religions, races, and cultures, in territories that today make up India, Pakistan, and Bangladesh. For a time, Burma too was under this administration. The British created a powerful state with a single system of law, administration, and language that showed little regard for the diversity of peoples ruled. (Rule by native princes was a token of respect, but was only allowed to continue so long as they followed British policies.) The peoples of India were so diverse that they might never have joined into a nation without the impact of British imperialism. Ultimately, Britain gave the subcontinent some political unity, an English-educated elite, and focus for discontent—a common resentment of the Britons.

The British built a modern railroad and communications system and developed agriculture and industry to meet the needs of the world market. The railroad, as a link to areas of food surplus, reduced the incidence and impact of local famines, which had plagued India's history. British rule stopped the constant wars and disorder that had been part of the subcontinent's history, but resistance to the British replaced internal wars. Population also increased as a result of Western medicine. Many people believed that the Indian masses did not benefit from economic progress because the increase in population matched the increase in food. Rather than starvation for some, malnutrition for most became the rule. Further aggravating the situation, the British flooded the Indian market with cheap, machine-produced English goods, which drove native hand craftsmen out of competition.

The elitism and racism that excluded the Indian elite from British clubs, hotels, and social gatherings and from the top government positions alienated the leaders that British rule had created. Educated Indians, demanding equality and self-government, created the Hindu Indian National Congress in the 1880s. This organization was not national, being made up only of upper-class Hindus, and not a congress, because it had no representative authority. Despite its narrow membership, this group would free India from the British after World War II. At first the Congress party demanded representation for Indians; later it sought home rule (self-government within the British Empire). But increasingly after Japan's victory in the Russo-Japanese War of 1905 radical nationalists in India, as elsewhere, began to think in terms of independence.

The First World War brought greater solidarity among Indians, who although alike in their opposition to British rule had been far from united. The Muslims had founded their own Muslim League in 1912 to voice the fears and demands of their minority community to the British governors. The Indian elite were able to find grounds for cooperation

among the disparate communities, but the masses continued to be divided by differences of religion, class, and culture, which made Indian self-government seem a distant possibility even to those British who thought it desirable. To undermine opposition, some British governors played on the community differences to divide the groups even further—a policy that left much bitterness. In 1919, partly in response to agitation and partly as a reward for loyal Indian service during the war, the British granted India a Legislative Assembly representing almost 1 million of the 247 million in the subcontinent. An elaborate scheme allotted representation by groups (that is, to non-Muslims, Europeans, Anglo-Indians, and Muslims) and by economic and social functions (that is, to rural, urban, university, landholding, and commercial classes). The British granted some powers to this assembly, but retained most in their own hands.

At the very time when the British granted the legislature, agitation and unrest became most bitter. At Amritsar, in Punjab, a British officer commanded his Gurkha troops to fire into a peaceful demonstration until their ammunition was exhausted. Three hundred seventy-nine Indians died and twelve hundred were wounded; women and children were among the victims. The massacre stung Indians to action, including those who had supported the British and those who had advocated self-government within the British Empire.

Out of this feverish period emerged a gentle but nonetheless determined revolutionary leader—Mohandas K. Gandhi (1869–1948). His doctrine of civil disobedience and nonviolent resistance was based on a belief that the power of love and spiritual purity would ultimately overthrow British rule in India. His was a spiritually uplifting message; it was a shrewd political tactic as well. Gandhi called on the Indian elite to give up the privileges allotted by the British—to resign their

Map 27.1 Asia in 1914 ▶

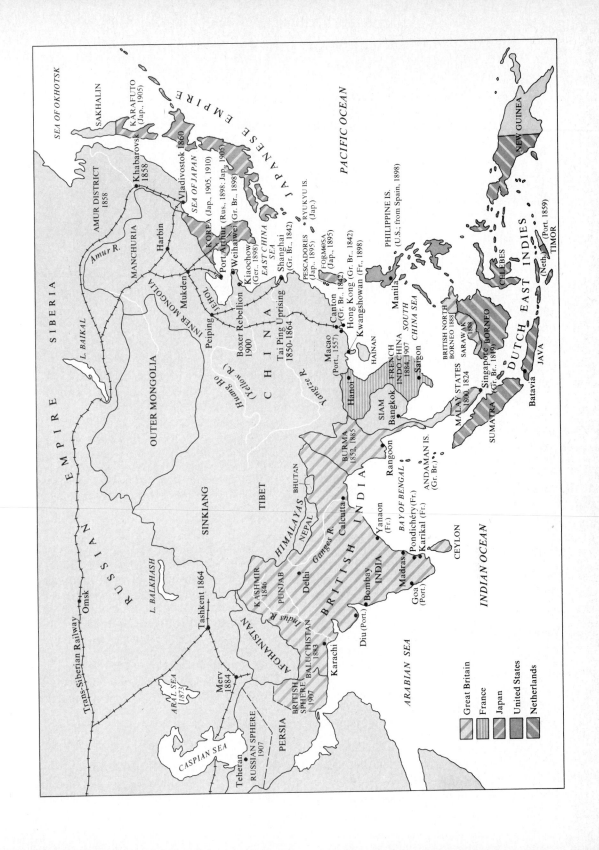

SEA OF OKHOTSK

SAKHALIN

KARAFUTO
(Jap. 1905)

JAPANESE EMPIRE

Khabarovsk
1858

RUSSIAN EMPIRE

SIBERIA

AMUR DISTRICT
1858

Vladivostok 1860

Amur R.

Harbin

MANCHURIA

SEA OF JAPAN

KOREA (Jap. 1905, 1910)

Port Arthur (Rus. 1898; Jap. 1905)

Weihaiwei (Gr. Br. 1898)

EAST CHINA SEA

RYUKYU IS. (Jap.)

PACIFIC OCEAN

L. BAIKAL

OUTER MONGOLIA

INNER MONGOLIA

Mukden

Jehol

Peiping

Kiaochow (Ger. 1898)

Shanghai (Gr. Br. 1842)

PESCADORES (Jap. 1895)

FORMOSA (Jap. 1895)

PHILIPPINE IS.
(U.S. from Spain. 1898)

Trans-Siberian Railway

RUSSIAN EMPIRE

Omsk

L. BALKHASH

SINKIANG

TIBET

C H I N A

Boxer Rebellion 1900

Hoang Ho (Yellow R.)

Tai Ping Uprising 1850–1864

Canton (Gr. Br. 1842)

Macao (Port. 1557)

Hong Kong (Gr. Br. 1842)

Kwangshowan (Fr. 1898)

HAINAN

Manila

SOUTH CHINA SEA

CELEBES

NEW GUINEA

DUTCH EAST INDIES

Tashkent 1864

ARAL SEA (1873)

Merv 1884

AFGHANISTAN

HIMALAYAS

BHUTAN

NEPAL

KASHMIR 1846

PUNJAB

Delhi

Yangtze R.

Ganges R.

Indus R.

BURMA (1852, 1885)

BRITISH INDIA

Calcutta

Yanaon (Fr.)

Rangoon

ANDAMAN IS. (Gr. Br.)

BAY OF BENGAL

Pondichéry (Fr.)

Karikal (Fr.)

SIAM

Bangkok

Hanoi

FRENCH INDO CHINA 1884, 1907

Saigon

MALAY STATES 1800, 1824

BRITISH NORTH BORNEO 1888

SARAWAK 1888

Singapore (Gr. Br. 1819)

BORNEO

SUMATRA

JAVA

Batavia

TIMOR (Neth.) (Port. 1859)

Bombay

Madras

Goa (Port.)

INDIA

CEYLON

INDIAN OCEAN

BALUCHISTAN 1883

BRITISH SPHERE 1907

Karachi

Diu (Port.)

ARABIAN SEA

PERSIA

RUSSIAN SPHERE 1907

Teheran

CASPIAN SEA

Great Britain

France

Japan

United States

Netherlands

A Tiger Hunt in the Raj in the 1870s with the Prince of Wales (later Edward VII). Unity was imposed on the diverse Indian peoples by British imperialism. A handful of British administrators and soldiers with the assistance an of English-educated elite and well-trained regiments of native and British troops, ruled over 300 million Indians. After the Great Rebellion of 1857 (the Sepoy Mutiny), the British lived a separate existence in the subcontinent, widening the distance between themselves and their subjects by their attitude of racial and national superiority. (*BBC Hulton Picture Library/Bettmann Archive*)

positions, to boycott British schools, and finally, to boycott all foreign goods. However, the elite's sacrifice of privilege would not have freed India by itself; mass support was required. Gandhi rallied this support dramatically with "the march to the sea"—a mass refusal to pay taxes on salt. When imprisoned, Gandhi and his followers fasted for spiritual discipline, but their tactic also threatened the British with the possibility that the confined leaders would starve to death, setting off more civil disturbances. Gandhi also emphasized the boycott of foreign goods by spinning cottons and wearing simple native dress. For independence, Gandhi was even willing to sacrifice the higher standard of living that an industrial economy could bring to India.

When independence came after World War II had exhausted British resources and reduced British power, India was partitioned into Muslim Pakistan and predominantly Hindu India. Independence did not require a war between Britain and India, an accomplishment that many credit to the strength of Gandhi's moral leadership. But even his leadership could not prevent conflict between Hindu and Muslim, as bloody massacres at independence so clearly revealed.

China

China in the nineteenth century was hostile to Europeans whether they were Christian missionaries, traders, or soldiers and sailors.

Wanting to preserve their traditional ruling class, economy, and beliefs, the Chinese elite at first resisted Christianity, Western science, and secular ideologies.

However, defeat by the British in the Opium War of 1839–1842 dramatically forced China, ruled by the Manchu Dynasty, open to trade with the West. Any commerce before the war had been severely limited and entirely in the hands of native monopolists granted trading privileges by the emperor. The British aggressively asserted their right to trade opium and demanded compensation for the Indian opium that the Chinese government had destroyed in efforts to end the trade. They seized several trading cities along the coast, including Hong Kong, and the Chinese capitulated. In the Treaty of Nanking (1842), the British insisted that they would determine the tariffs the Chinese might charge them and that their subjects in China would have the right to be tried according to their own law rather than Chinese law (the right of extraterritoriality). Both concessions seriously undermined the emperor's ability to control the foreigners in his country.

Defeat in the Opium War forced the emperor to change, and he did so by drawing on China's traditions and its elite. The mandarins, who were the traditional ruling elite, revitalized the Manchu bureaucracy, cleaning out much of the official corruption that weighed heavily on the poorest taxpayers, and moved to strengthen China against the rapacious Westerners, sometimes hiring Western advisers to train their armies. Nevertheless, widespread economic discontent, hatred of the Manchu, who were regarded as conquerors of China (although the conquest had taken place some two hundred years earlier), and religious mysticism inspired the Taiping rebellion of 1850–1864. The uprising seriously threatened the dynasty, but with Western assistance, the mandarins suppressed the rebels. Western governments took advantage of the situation by extorting additional concessions in exchange for their support. For one thing, they forced the emperor to allow Chinese to emigrate to other lands, such as South Africa or the United States, where they were exploited to build railroads.

For a time the Europeans seemed content with trading rights in coastal towns and preferential treatment for their subjects. But the Sino-Japanese War of 1894–95, in which Japan won an easy victory, encouraged the Europeans to mutilate China. Britain, France, Russia, and Germany all scrambled for concessions, protectorates, and spheres of influence. The domination of China might have followed the same course as that of Africa, but each Western nation, afraid of its rivals, resisted any partition that might possibly give another state an advantage. The United States, which insisted that it be given any trading concession that any other state received, proclaimed an "Open Door" policy that trade should be open to all and that the Great Powers should respect the territorial integrity of China. Some believe the American action may have restrained the Western powers from partitioning China; others see it merely as a way to ensure American interests in China; still others argue that the American policy did little. They see Western capitalism itself as the most powerful threat to China's independent status.

Chinese traditionalists organized secret societies whose aim was to expel foreigners and to punish Chinese who accepted Christianity or in any way fostered westernization. Usually, these societies opposed the Manchu Dynasty, particularly if it tried to make any reforms that would undermine traditional China. In 1900, encouraged by the Empress Tzu-hsi, one of them, the Society of Righteous and Harmonious Fists (called the Boxers by Europeans), attacked foreigners throughout the north of China. An international army of Europeans and Americans suppressed the rebellion, seized Chinese treasures, and forced China to pay an indemnity. They also made China accede to foreign troops stationed on its soil.

Chinese unrest and discontent with the dynasty and the West deepened. When the Japanese defeated the Russians in 1905, many

**"The Real Trouble Will Come with the 'Wake,' "
by Joseph Keppler, 1900.** The Great Powers were
unable to carve up China as they had Africa. The
Europeans were able to wring concessions such as
Hong Kong, trading, and special privileges from the
weak empire. The American late-comers insisted that
China be kept open for the trade of all—the Open
Door policy. With the overthrow of the Manchu Dynasty in 1911, China became a republic, plagued by
civil war and foreign aggression until the end of World
War II. This lithograph from the August 1900 issue
of *Puck* shows the Chinese dragon being fought over
by the Great Powers. (*Library of Congress*)

Chinese argued that the only way to protect
their country was to imitate the West as Japan
had done. There were many signs of growing
nationalism, particularly the widespread
support given a Chinese boycott of American
goods in 1905 to protest America's refusal to
accept Chinese immigrants. In 1911 nationalistic, antiforeign revolutionaries, who were
particularly strong among the soldiers, workers, and students, overthrew the Manchu
Dynasty and established a republic. Sun
Zhongshan (Sun Yat-sen) (1866–1925), who
was in the United States when the revolution
broke out, returned to China to become the
first president of the republic and the head
of the nationalist party.

Espousing the Western ideas of democracy,
nationalism, and social welfare (the three
principles of the people, as Sun Zhongshan
called them), the republic struggled to establish its authority over a China torn by civil
war and ravaged by foreigners. Russia claimed
Mongolia and Britain claimed Tibet. The
northern warlords, who were regional leaders
with private armies, resisted any attempt to
strengthen the republic against foreign imperialists because it might diminish their own
authority. In the south, the republic more or
less maintained control. After Sun Zhongshan's death, the Guomindong (Kuomintang),
under the authoritarian leadership of Jiang
Jieshi (Chiang Kai-shek) (1887–1975), tried to
westernize by using the military power of
the state and introducing segments of a modern economic system. But faced with civil
war, attacked from both the right and the

communist left under Mao Zedong (Mao Tse-tung) (1893–1976), and by the Japanese starting in 1931, the Guomindong made slow progress. A divided China continued to be at the mercy of outside interests until after the Second World War.

Japan

Japan, like China, was opened to the West against its will in the nineteenth century. The Japanese had expelled Europeans in the seventeenth century and had managed to enforce this isolation over the next two centuries. By the 1850s, though, foreign pressure combined with social dissension inside Japan to force the country open to outside trade. The Americans, in particular, refused to accept Japanese prohibitions on commercial and religious contacts with the West, and like China, Japan succumbed to superior technological power. In 1853, Commodore Matthew C. Perry sailed into Tokyo Bay and made an American show of force that gave the Japanese little choice but to make treaties permitting trade with the United States and others. As China had, Japan signed a number of "unequal" treaties that granted Westerners extraterritoriality and control over tariffs.

Forced to reckon with the West, Japan experienced a flood of unrest. The warrior nobility, the *samurai*, who feared for their social status, attacked foreigners and murdered members of their own government. In their minds, trade could only enhance the status of merchants, a social class they despised. In response to samurai belligerence, a fleet of American and European forces attacked and destroyed important Japanese fortresses. However, a group of samurai seized the government, determined to strengthen Japan in order to preserve its independence. This takeover—the Meiji Restoration of 1867—returned power to the emperor, or Meiji, from the feudal military aristocracy that had ruled in his name for almost seven hundred years. Determined to modernize, the new government refused to cling to traditional ways. It

enacted a series of reforms that turned the old feudal regime into a powerful unitary state. Large landowners were persuaded to turn over their estates to the emperor in exchange for compensation and high-level positions in the government. All classes were made equal before the law. The Japanese required universal military service like the French and Germans, which diminished social privilege and helped to imbue Japanese of all classes with nationalistic feelings. The Japanese constitution was modeled on Bismarck's German one: There was a bicameral diet or parliament, but the emperor held the most important authority, which he delegated to his ministers, who did the actual governing of Japan.

In place of the traditional economy, the Meiji regime introduced modern industry and economic competition. Japanese visited factories all over the West and hired Westerners to teach industrial skills. The government, like central and eastern European governments, built defense industries, backed heavy industry and mining, and developed a modern communication system of railroads, roads, and telegraph lines. State capital and government initiative created all this economic development. The government encouraged competitive consumer industries as well. During the 1880s, the government sold factories and mills to wealthy family monopolies, the *zaibatsu*, which came to dominate the Japanese economy. Industry in Japan was based more on cooperation than on competition, and in relations between employer and employee, paternalism set the tone rather than individualism. Westerners regarded the close cooperation of government and powerful families as something peculiar to the Japanese (neither capitalist nor socialist), and within slightly more than a generation of the Meiji Restoration Japan had moved from economic backwardness to a place among the top ten industrial nations. Japan set a pattern of modernization for underdeveloped countries that borrowed in many ways from the West but wedded Western forms to traditonal values and social structure.

Japan's First Railroad, 1872. With the Meiji Restoration of 1868, Japan launched a program of rapid Westernization. In 1895, it demonstrated that it had mastered the imperialists' power politics as well. In that year, Japan successfully waged war with China, to be blocked by the European powers, and in 1905, Japan defeated Russia. This success was a message to the victims of imperialism that Europe was not invincible. (*Historical Pictures Service, Chicago*)

By 1900, Japan had negotiated new treaties with Western nations that ended humiliating foreign restrictions, and had begun to act the part of an imperialist power in the European mold. It went to war with China (1894–95) and won Taiwan and Korea and the same commercial privileges the Chinese granted to Europeans. However, the Great Powers intervened and forced Japan to return some of the spoils of victory; at the same time they grabbed spheres of influence from the defeated and helpless Chinese. The Japanese were infuriated. Finally, in 1904, conflict over influence in Manchuria brought Japan and Russia to war. Japan won, and its victory over a Western power had a tremendous impact on Asian nationalists. If Japan could unite its people and defeat the West with nationalism and strong leadership, other Asians should also be able to do so. The Japanese victory inspired anti-Western and nationalist movements throughout China, Indochina, India, Iran, the Middle East, and even among the South African Indians, who had emigrated from one British colony to another but preserved their national identity.

Japan had earned the respect of imperialists as well as anti-imperialists. The first alliance that Britain negotiated as it moved from a policy of isolation in the early twentieth century was the 1902 naval alliance with Japan. The American president Theodore Roosevelt offered to arbitrate in the Russo-Japanese War. In the First World War, Japan fought on the side of the Allies and emerged as the most powerful Asian state. It took over the former German holdings in the Orient, except for Germany's sphere of influence in China (President Woodrow Wilson blocked that move at the Paris peace conference).

How Japan would exercise its hard-won power was an open question in the post–World War I era. In the 1920s, the prosperous economy fortified the middle class and increased the importance of the working class, strengthening democratic institutions. But Japan's dependence on foreign trade meant that it was hit hard by the Great Depression of 1929, when the major states subjected its trade to tariffs. The depression weakened the elements that contributed to peace, stability, and democracy in Japan. It strengthened the militarist and fascist groups that were determined to remedy Japan's plight by imperial expansion in Manchuria and China. Outwardly in the 1930s, Japan championed racial equality and opposed Western imperialism. Many leaders of nationalist movements in Burma, India, Indochina, and Indonesia were attracted, for a time, by Japan's pose. World War II brought Japanese occupation and exploitation, not freedom and equality for Asians.

Southeast Asia

Southeast Asia was a major venue for European imperialism. The French claimed Indochina in a war with China (1883–1885). The French parliament rejected the government of Jules Ferry for pursuing a war for a faraway and not obviously valuable territory, but France annexed the territory nonetheless. Indochina was a prosperous country, but it traded mostly with Asia and very little with France. Some French individuals profited economically from the colony, and some civil servants, soldiers, priests, and scholars were directly interested in it, but as a whole the country was indifferent to its new acquisition. French expansion might have continued into Siam (Thailand), just as the British might have

expanded there from their base in Burma. But Siam was situated between the colonies of two Great Powers, neither of which, consequently, was willing to let the other take it over. It remained an area of conflict between France and Britain until the Entente Cordiale of 1904 (see page 676), when European politics dominated colonial interest.

British claims to the lands of present-day Malaya and Singapore were recognized by the French in exchange for a province of Siam. But in general, Siam, like Turkey in the Middle East, was able to play the powers off against one another and preserve some territorial integrity. Siam belied the imperialist claim that European rule improved the economies of backward countries. During the nineteenth century independent Siam's prosperity increased much more than that of Burma or the rest of Indochina, both of which were geographically comparable but were colonies.

Elsewhere in Southeast Asia the United States and Germany challenged British and French preeminence. During the Spanish-American War, the Americans seized and annexed the Philippines and Guam. (Although the war was ostensibly fought to free Cuba, its first battle was in Manila Bay.) Once taken, the islands proved difficult to pacify. Germany, the United States, Britain, and France laid claim to various Pacific islands where they built naval stations to symbolize their nations' presence in the East. And throughout the period the Netherlands maintained its holdings in the East Indies (Indonesia)—the remnants of the once great seventeenth-century Dutch empire. Even colonies began to acquire colonies, as New Zealand and Australia pushed claims to Borneo and Tasmania, perhaps for economic reasons but certainly also to assert national identity.

Central Asia

Most of China's border territories fell to the imperialists, bringing the latter into conflict as much with one another as with the weak Chinese dynasty. Central Asia was the scene of conflict between Russia and Britain—a struggle that offers important insights into imperialism as an extension of intense nationalism. Russia expanded in three areas in the last decades of the nineteenth century—southeastern Europe, Central Asia, and East Asia. Russia's eastward expansion threatened territories that had once acknowledged Chinese sovereignty but could not be protected by the declining Manchu Dynasty. In East Asia, the Russians ran up against Japanese interests, leading to the Russo-Japanese War. In Central Asia, Russia and Britain opposed one another. And in southeastern Europe, Russia's push meant conflict with Austria-Hungary and Germany. None of these imperial adventures by the tsarist regime can be said to have been motivated primarily by economic concerns.

The British traditionally had backed the Turks against the Russians in the Near East, although Turkish despots were embarrassing friends. In East Asia, the British found the Japanese more congenial allies than the Russians.

In Central Asia, Russia's moves south into Afghanistan and Persia (Iran), both of which bordered India, alerted the British to a potential threat to their holdings on the subcontinent. The British believed the greatest danger to their position in India was internal rebellion, and a hostile force on the Indian borders might inspire rebellious Indians. After 1889, Britain and Russia vied in loaning the shah of Persia money to build a railroad to Teheran. The Russians were then borrowing money from the French for their own industrialization, but they nonetheless offered capital to create a dependency in Persia. The British moved to stop the Russians, whose aim appeared to be the acquisition of a warm-water port on the Persian Gulf—too close to India for British comfort. The years 1878–1881 and 1884–1885 saw British and Russian troops engaged in Afghanistan, trying to dominate the rim of Asia.

The Russians took advantage of the Boer War (see page 639) to advance into Persia, Tibet, and Afghanistan. In 1904 the British moved on Tibet to prevent the ruling Dalai Lama's tutor from negotiating special trade agreements with the Russians, even though the total volume of trade involved would have been infinitesimally small. In the 1906–1908 negotiations between Russia and Britain, both powers were anxious for a settlement because of European politics, and the Russians agreed to leave the British puppet ruler of Afghanistan alone. Persia would be divided into three zones: one in the north for the Russians; one in the south for the British; and one for the Persians in the middle to keep the two powers separated.

The resolution of Central Asian difficulties made possible the British and Russian alliance in Europe, but it also had tremendous impact on Persia. The Persian shah, backed by the Russians, fought a civil war with nationalists, an elite of his own people, throughout the period from 1905 to 1925. The shah was deposed in 1909 for granting too many favors to the Europeans, particularly the Russians who controlled the north of his country. Torn by the conflicting interests of Britain and Russia, Persia maintained neither independence nor stability under the imperialists. Its situation was further complicated after World War I, because its vast reserves of oil became valuable to the Great Powers. The Pahlavi family, which had gained control of Persia, abolished the special privileges, or capitulations, that had been granted to foreigners. In 1934 the shah granted the U.S. firm Standard Oil the oil concession over the Bahrain Islands. He thought foreigners whose interests seemed to be merely economic might be more easily controlled than foreigners with geopolitical designs. Yet as British power receded in the area during and after World War II, American power moved in to take its place.

The Ottoman Empire

Throughout the nineteenth century, the Ottoman Empire was an arena of combat for

Map 27.2 The Middle East, Post–World War I ▶

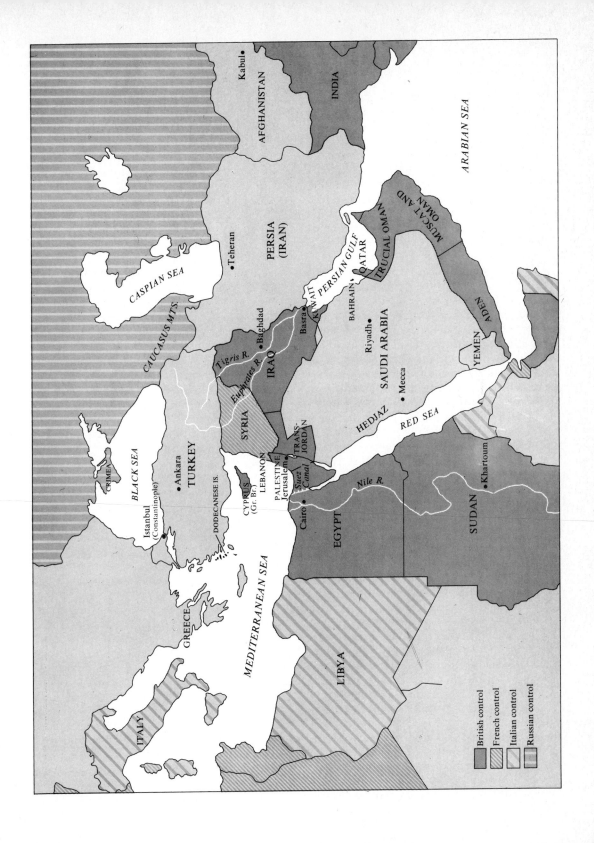

British control

French control

Italian control

Russian control

KABUL •

AFGHANISTAN

INDIA

ARABIAN SEA

PERSIA
(IRAN)

• Teheran

CASPIAN SEA

CAUCASUS MTS.

MUSCAT AND
OMAN

TRUCIAL OMAN

QATAR

PERSIAN GULF

Baghdad •

Tigris R.

IRAQ

Euphrates R.

KUWAIT

Basra

BAHRAIN •

ADEN

Riyadh •

SAUDI ARABIA

YEMEN

SYRIA

Mecca •

HEDJAZ

RED SEA

CRIMEA

BLACK SEA

TURKEY

• Ankara

DODECANESE IS.

CYPRUS
(Gr. Br.)

LEBANON

PALESTINE

Jerusalem •

TRANS-
JORDAN

Suez
Canal

Nile R.

• Khartoum

Istanbul
(Constantinople) •

GREECE

Cairo •

EGYPT

SUDAN

MEDITERRANEAN SEA

ITALY

LIBYA

Europeans. The Russians, who liked to pose as the defenders of Orthodox Christian peoples in Turkish Europe and of the shrines in the Holy Land, pressured the Turks because Russia wanted a warm-water port and access to the Mediterranean. The British supported the Turks because Britain wanted to block Russian access to the Mediterranean, which the British regarded as their special sphere of influence. In 1854, the British and French joined the Turks in the Crimean War to deny Russia its goal.

The development of Slavic nationalism and Austrian interest in the Balkans altered the diplomatic picture. Attempts to reform and westernize the Ottoman Empire and to give some autonomy to Slavic peoples aroused Turkish traditionalism. Abdul Hamid II (1876–1909), who was as harsh and autocratic as any Ottoman ruler before him, made reforms and allowed, even encouraged, harsh treatment of Christian subjects within his empire. In 1876, the Ottomans warred with the Serbs, who laid claim to two provinces of Slavic peoples which were still under Turkish control. The Serbs were defeated, and Abdul Hamid, in an action that shocked all of Europe, ordered the mass murder of some 12,000 Christian Bulgarians because he feared their religion and their nationalism made them doubly unreliable subjects.

British policy shifted abruptly toward intervention, while the Russians declared war and then handed the Turks a treaty (the Treaty of San Stefano) highly favorable to Russia. Austria immediately called a conference of the Great Powers—the Congress of Berlin of 1878—where Bismarck, playing the "honest broker," redressed the balance of power in favor of Austria and Britain to avoid war in Europe. Britain said its true interests were Egypt and the Suez Canal—the route to India—but Disraeli nonetheless left the conference having acquired Cyprus for Britain.

At the turn of the twentieth century, Anglo-Russian rivalry over the "sick man of Europe," as Turkey was called, was overshadowed by Anglo-German rivalry. The origins of the conflict seemed quite innocent, certainly not political. A group of German financiers proposed a railroad from central Turkey to Baghdad on the Tigris River, with a connection down the Euphrates to Basra and the Persian Gulf. A railroad already existed from Berlin through the Balkans to Constantinople and central Turkey. Because the proposed new railroad would further open Turkey and the Ottoman Empire to the world market, the sultan was enthusiastic and offered to subsidize the project by guaranteeing the bonds and profits for the syndicate. The German backers of the railroad offered British and French investment groups a 25-percent share each, with 25-percent control to the Turks; the Germans retained the final quarter for themselves.

The British government, however, refused to allow British citizens to invest. Politics dominated economics; the British were afraid of German ascendancy in an area so close to both India and the Suez Canal. Britain's action, together with German naval expansion, aggravated Anglo-German relations. In World War I the Turks sided with the Germans, partly because of German influence over a generation of the Turkish elite and partly out of fear of the Russian presence in the Caucasus and the Black Sea area.

Throughout World War I the Allies secretly negotiated the division of the Ottoman Empire. Hoping to weaken the Ottoman war effort, Britain sponsored Arab independence movements in the Arabian Peninsula and in the territories that are today Iraq, Syria, Lebanon, Jordan, and Israel. In the Balfour Declaration of 1917, the British also promised the Zionists a Jewish homeland in Palestine.

When the war was over, the Turks, led by Kemal Atatürk, refused to accept the dismemberment of Turkish-speaking territory, although they did accept the loss of Arab lands and some islands off their southwestern coast. The Turks drove the Allies out, declared a republic in 1923 under Atatürk's presidency, and moved the capital to Ankara, far away from the Europeanized city of Constantinople (Istanbul). Turkey, which became a secular state, was no longer the spiritual leader of millions of Muslims. During Atatürk's presidency (1923–1938) the Turkish government ended many ancient customs, such as veils for women, harems, and polygamy. European education and ideas flourished in the new republic. The conflict between modernization and tradition in Turkey was resolved by war and revolution in favor of modern nationalism.

Among the Arabs, several forces around the time of the First World War fostered the desire for national self-determination, particularly the passions and politics of the war. After the war, Britain schemed for a while to establish a puppet Arab ruler, but was rebuffed. The Arab chiefs welcomed British aid against the Turks but deeply resented British intervention in their spiritual and local political affairs. Despite heightened European interest in the area's oil, Arab nationalism, once encouraged against the Turks, could not be controlled when the Turks ceased to be a power. As nationalism developed, it often combined with religion to foment opposition that plagued the imperialists between the two wars.

The Scramble for Africa

The most rapid European expansion took place in Africa. As late as 1880, European nations ruled only a tenth of the continent. By 1914, Europeans had claimed all of Africa except Liberia (a small territory of freed slaves from the United States) and Ethiopia (Abyssinia), which had successfully held off Italian invaders at Adowa in 1896. The only Great Powers that did not play a part in carving up Africa were Russia, Austria-Hungary, and the United States.

European powers had occasionally been involved in Africa early in the century. The French had moved into Algeria in 1830. During the Napoleonic Wars the British had gained Cape Town in South Africa, a useful provisioning place for trading ships bound for India and the East. Dutch cattlemen and

farmers (Boers), who had settled in the Capetown area starting in the mid-seventeenth century, refused to accept the British abolition of slavery in 1834. To get away from the British, they had moved northward on the Great Trek (1835–1837), warring with native tribes along the way. The Boers aggressively asserted their independence from the British and by 1880 they were firmly established in the territory they had taken in the interior.

In general, though, up to the 1870s Great Power interest in Africa seemed marginal and likely to decline even further. Then the astounding activities of Leopold II, king of Belgium, changed the picture. In 1876, as a private entrepreneur, he formed the International Association for the Exploration and Civilization of Central Africa. Leopold sent Henry Stanley (1841–1904) to the Congo River basin to establish trading posts, sign treaties with tribal chiefs, and claim the territory for the association. Stanley was an adventurer and a newspaper reporter who had fought on both sides during the American Civil War. He had earlier led an expedition to central Africa in search of David Livingstone, the popular missionary-explorer. Stanley's "rescue" of Livingstone in 1871 was a human-interest story calculated to delight thousands of readers. For men like Stanley, Leopold's private development efforts promised profit and adventure. For the Africans, they promised brutal exploitation.

The French responded to the news of Leopold's agents' acquisitions by immediately establishing their own protectorate on the north bank of the Congo; in 1881, they took control of Tunisia. The scramble was on. Bismarck and Premier Jules Ferry of France called an international conference in Berlin in 1884 to lay some ground rules for the development of Africa south of the Sahara. Leopold (as an individual rather than as the king of Belgium) was declared the personal ruler of the Congo Free State. The Congo Basin was made a free trade zone for merchants of every nation.

The Berlin Conference established the principle that a European country had to oc-

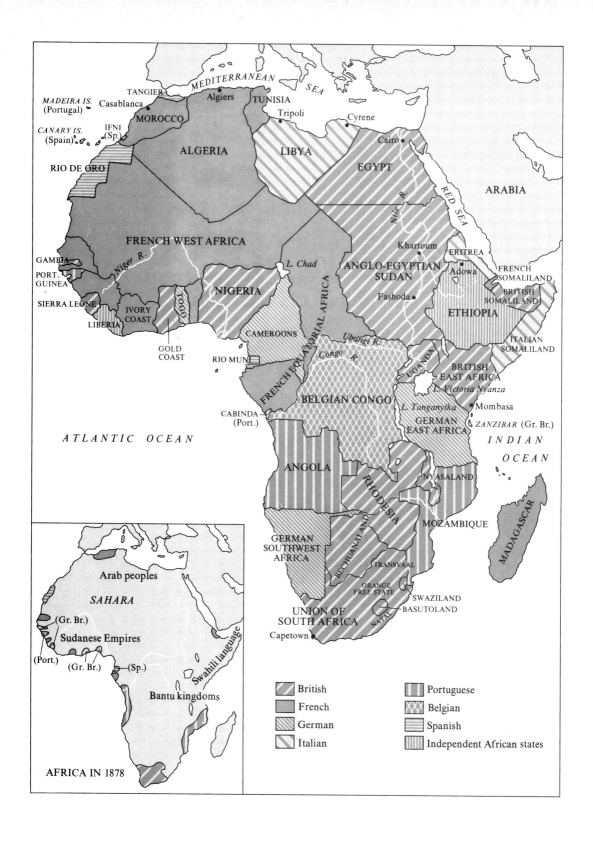

MADEIRA IS.
(Portugal)

TANGIER
Casablanca

CANARY IS.
(Spain)

IFNI
(Sp.)

MOROCCO

RIO DE ORO

MEDITERRANEAN   SEA

Algiers

TUNISIA
Tripoli

Cyrene

ALGERIA

LIBYA

EGYPT

Cairo

ARABIA

FRENCH WEST AFRICA

Niger R.

L. Chad

Khartoum

ANGLO-EGYPTIAN
SUDAN

ERITREA
Adowa

FRENCH
SOMALILAND

BRITISH
SOMALILAND

GAMBIA

PORT.
GUINEA

SIERRA LEONE

LIBERIA

IVORY
COAST

TOGO

NIGERIA

Fashoda

ETHIOPIA

ITALIAN
SOMALILAND

GOLD
COAST

RIO MUNI

CAMEROONS

FRENCH EQUATORIAL AFRICA

Ubangi R.

Congo R.

UGANDA

BRITISH
EAST AFRICA

L. Victoria Nyanza

Mombasa

ATLANTIC   OCEAN

CABINDA
(Port.)

BELGIAN CONGO

L. Tanganyika

GERMAN
EAST AFRICA

ZANZIBAR (Gr. Br.)

INDIAN

OCEAN

ANGOLA

RHODESIA

NYASALAND

MOZAMBIQUE

MADAGASCAR

GERMAN
SOUTHWEST
AFRICA

BECHUANALAND

TRANSVAAL

ORANGE
FREE STATE

SWAZILAND
BASUTOLAND

NATAL

UNION OF
SOUTH AFRICA

Capetown

Arab peoples

SAHARA

(Gr. Br.)

Sudanese Empires

(Port.)

(Gr. Br.)

(Sp.)

Bantu kingdoms

Swahili language

AFRICA IN 1878

British

French

German

Italian

Portuguese

Belgian

Spanish

Independent African states

cupy territory effectively before it could claim it. Explorers and soldiers began a mad race to the interior of Africa. As Europeans rushed to claim territory, they ignored both natural and cultural frontiers. Even today the map of Africa reveals many straight boundary lines that cut across the irregular boundaries of rivers and mountains that had separated culturally distinct tribal groups.

The conference also agreed to stop slavery and the slave trade in Africa. Before long, however, the Congo Association was trying to turn a profit with practices as vicious as those of the slave traders had been. At the turn of the twentieth century, Edward D. Morel, an English humanitarian, and Roger Casement, the Irish nationalist hero who was at the time a British civil servant, waged a vigorous campaign against brutality and murder that were commonly practiced to force blacks to work on the rubber plantations in the Congo. In response to the outcry of public opinion, the Belgian Parliament declared the territory a Belgian colony in 1908, putting an end to Leopold's vicious private enterprise.

Great Britain's activities in Africa exemplify the complicated motives, operations, and results of European imperialism. In the second half of the nineteenth century, Britain maintained only a few outposts along the coast of West Africa; even its hold on South Africa appeared to be loosening. The British navy, from time to time, interfered with slave traders in Africa, but overall British interest there was minimal. In principle, Britain rejected empire. Then, local conditions in Egypt resulted in British occupation.

For a generation (1805–1847) Mehemet Ali, khedive (governor) of Egypt, struggled for his independence from the sultan of the Ottoman Empire. Thereafter strong khedives, with British and French support, had maintained Egypt's autonomy. But foreign investment and influence grew there as successive khedives spent lavishly in attempts to maintain their position and to modernize. The khedives hoped to gain enough power to both resist the Europeans and maintain

◀ **Map 27.3** Africa in 1914

independence from Turkey. Egypt fell deeply into debt to Europeans. Then the building of the Suez Canal (1859–1869), in which the khedive and British and French capitalists were the principal stockholders, brought the country to the verge of bankruptcy. In the long run, the canal promised Egypt trade and contact with the world economy, but it brought immediate disaster. When European creditors demanded cuts in the army to economize so that Egypt could pay debts, the Egyptian soldiers rebelled. The combination of probable national bankruptcy and the khedive's apparent inability to keep law and order was sufficient pretext to bring the British in as "protectors" in 1882.

The canal was important to the British as a waterway to India, but it was only a financial investment to the French. The British invited the French to join their invasion to protect investments, but the latter were unable to for domestic political reasons. The French deeply resented that the British proceeded without them. Patriotic organizations vehemently protested the insult to French national honor and demanded government action.

Prime Minister Gladstone, a "little Englander" (one who opposed empire), promised to withdraw once stability in Egypt was assured. Every day the British remained, Egyptian discontent mounted against them, threatening the stability of markets and investments and even of government. Furthermore, Egyptian opposition took two irreconcilable forms. Some Egyptians wanted to modernize their nation with a strong government and army so that they could throw the British out. Others hated all aspects of westernization because it drew Egypt further away from Islam. As the British became entrenched, resistance became more violent.

Not only did the British not withdraw from Egypt, they also moved further south. In the Sudan, devout Muslims were carrying on a holy war against Egypt because it was under British influence. The British were deeply involved in strengthening the khedive's authority to help him balance his budget so that foreign debts could be paid. In 1883, an

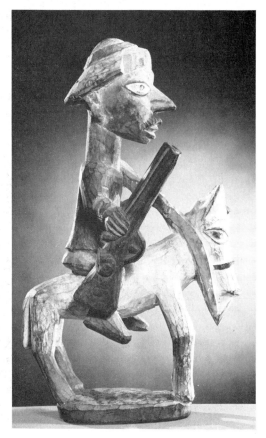

Yoruba Carving of a European. The African artist who carved this figure has captured the spirit of the old colonialism and the new imperialism with the symbols of the European man with a gun and a horse. Aztecs, Chinese, Japanese, and Indian artists also conveyed in their works the sense of the intruder with power. (*The American Museum of Natural History*)

English general commanded 10,000 of the khedive's troops against the Sudanese Muslims, who were led by the Mahdi. The Anglo-Egyptian force was annihilated. English Liberals argued against further support of the khedive in his effort to subdue the Sudan, which Egyptian troops occupied but could not control. Occupation angered the French, and occupation without control angered British financiers.

In 1885, Prime Minister Gladstone sent General Charles "Chinese" Gordon, famous for suppressing the Taiping Rebellion, to the Sudan to see what could be done about the

Mahdi. Uncertain what was expected of him, Gordon tried to restore order without sufficient forces to do so. He was killed at Khartoum, and his head was severed and placed on a pike. A furious public accused Gladstone of martyring the famous hero by forbidding Gordon to wage war and yet sending him to the war zone to take charge. Gladstone held out against demands to annex the Sudan, but in 1898, when the Conservatives were in power, there were further difficulties. General Kitchener was sent to the Sudan, and his men and machine guns mowed down charging Muslims at Omdurman. The casualties were reported to be 11,000 Muslims and 28 Britons, which many Britons felt was appropriate revenge for the death of Gordon.

But the battle of Omdurman was an ominous victory, and 1898 was an ominous year in the history of the British Empire. Immediately after the battle, French and British forces confronted one another at Fashoda in the Sudan. The French, under the command of Captain Marchand, had marched all the way from West Africa to the Sudan in an attempt to lay claim to the territory from West Africa to Somaliland on the Red Sea. The British were moving south from Egypt and north from Kenya into the same territory. In the diplomatic crisis that followed, Britain and France were brought to the brink of war and public passions were inflamed. Too divided by the Dreyfus Affair at home (see Chapter 26) to risk a showdown with Britain, France ordered Marchand's retreat. French statesmen began to negotiate with Britain to reconcile the two nations' ambitions. France did not have the resources to challenge both Germany across the Rhine and Britain in Africa and Asia. The British, too, faced with conflict in the Sudan and mounting troubles in South Africa, realized their limits. They began to see their "splendid isolation" (a policy of avoiding alliances) as a risky policy that might make the whole world their enemy (with the possible exception of the United States, at that moment also isolated by its war with Spain).

Nothing underlined Britain's isolation and

the widespread distrust of British motives more than the Boer War. British relations with the settlers of the Boer territories of the Transvaal and the Orange Free State, had been difficult since the Great Trek. They were aggravated by the discovery of rich deposits of gold and diamonds in Boer territory. Paul Kruger (1825–1904), the Boer, or Afrikaner, president of the Transvaal, tried to gain independence, power, and access to the sea for the Boers and to restrict the foreign prospectors who were flooding into Boer territory by the thousands.

The prime minister of Cape Colony was Cecil Rhodes (1853–1902), a British subject who had made a fortune in diamonds and gold in South Africa. He was responsible for acquiring Rhodesia, a sizable and wealthy territory, for Britain. He dreamed of British red coloring the map of Africa from Cape Town to Cairo, and he built a railroad from the Cape to Rhodesia. In 1895 his close friend, Leander Jameson, led about six hundred armed men into the Transvaal to try to spark an uprising against Kruger, which would give the British a pretext to invade. The raid failed and both men were disgraced for their part in the plot. The scandal reached all the way to Joseph Chamberlain, the imperialist colonial secretary in the British cabinet. Kaiser William II of Germany impetuously sent President Kruger a congratulatory telegram after the Boers had repulsed the Jameson raid. The British took this diplomatic insult as a symbol of their isolation, which it most certainly was.

Everything about the Boer War was unfortunate for the British. The Boers were formidable opponents—farmers by day and commandos by night, armed with the latest French and German rifles. Hatred for the British in the press of other European countries was almost universal. The war was exceptionally costly in both money and lives. It aroused many Britons to a fever pitch of patriotism, but at the same time, antiimperialism gained strength, and the war produced an outcry within Britain at the path that British policy had taken. The British won the major battles, but faced stiff guerrilla resistance.

Humanitarians in London found some British tactics shameful. To deal with their stubborn foe, the British herded, or "concentrated," whole settlements of Boers into compounds surrounded by barbed wire.

The nasty war, which began in 1899, ended in 1902. The British hoped to live together in peace with the Boers and to make a settlement of conciliation rather than revenge. The peace treaty made many concessions to the Afrikaners, including the right to use their own language, Afrikaans (although English remained the official language). Amnesty was offered to any Boer who would swear allegiance to the British king. The Boers almost immediately gained control of government in the states where Afrikaners were most numerous. By 1906, General Louis Botha, who had commanded the Boers, had been elected the prime minister of the Transvaal.

But the settlement that appeared to be generous and just to the belligerents boded ill for other people who were not involved in the war. Justice, equality, and self-government for the Boers and the British did not help the majority black population of South Africa. In fact, Boer autonomy meant that the government in London could do little to protect the rights of black Africans in Boer territories. Few safeguards for blacks were written into the treaty or the constitution of the new Union of South Africa.

The wages of imperialism in Africa seemed hard not only to the British and French, but to other imperialists as well. Defeat by Ethiopians at Adowa (1896) belied Italian dreams of empire and national glory. Bismarck scoffed that the Italians had enormous appetites but very poor teeth. Victory would not have alleviated Italy's economic problems, although it might have reduced political discontent. Germans could take little heart from their African acquisitions—Southwest Africa (Namibia), Southeast Africa (Tanzania, but not Zanzibar, which was British), the Cameroons, and Togo (part of Ghana today). The German colonies were the most efficiently governed (critics said the most ruthlessly), but they yielded few benefits other than pride of ownership and they were costly to govern. And the Belgians obviously gained no prestige from the horrors perpetrated in the Congo. Serious thinkers, contemplating the depths to which Europeans would sink in search of fortune and fame, began to suggest that barbarity characterized the Europeans more than the Africans. The Europeans seemed to be the moral barbarians, as novelist Joseph Conrad and others pointed out. Honor was fleeting and profits illusory, for the most part, in these new African empires.

Yet it appeared that Europeans might go to war with each other for those African lands with few people and fewer resources. Such a war promised to be more deadly that the colonial conflicts between the technologically superior Europeans and the Africans and Asians. Germany expressed its aggressive imperialism in a naval arms race with the British that threatened the latter's power and national self-image. The "Teutonic cousins" eyed each other with deepening suspicion. This tension contributed to the alliances the Great Powers made in the decade before the First World War.

Latin America

Early in the nineteenth century, in the era of democratic revolution that began with the American Revolution in 1776, Latin American colonists rebelled against Spain and gained their independence. They were encouraged by Britain and the young United States, who wanted a free hand for trade; the British minister George Canning and the American president James Monroe both issued warnings against European intervention and colonization in the Americas. During the nineteenth century Argentina, Brazil, Chile, and other countries became primarily immigrant nations. Like the United States, they took in Irish, Germans, Italians, eastern Europeans, and Spaniards. (A few other nations, like Mexico and Peru, resisted the Atlantic mi-

gration; there, native Indian or mestizo cultures dominated.)

Europeans invested heavily in the nineteenth century in both Latin and in North America. During this time, Britain and, to a lesser degree, France were the dominant economic powers in Latin America; they cooperated commercially with local merchants, loaned money, and arranged for treaties favorable to the business interests of their citizens.

Both the Europeans and the local merchants and landowners exploited the lower classes. Brazil relied on African slave labor to produce for European markets; it was the last American nation to abolish slavery. Native Indians were pushed off their lands in Argentina, Brazil, and Chile as ruthlessly as in North America.

Europe dominated the Western Hemisphere culturally. In Latin America a small, wealthy upper class benefited from its connection with Europe and imitated continental culture. At Manaus in the Amazon region, rich South Americans built an ornate opera house, resembling Milan's La Scala, from profits on rubber farms worked by enslaved Indians. Wealthy Americans lived like the British gentry, using profits of cotton or coffee labor. In Buenos Aires, Rio de Janeiro, and Santiago, merchants discussed the latest European intellectual fad. Upper-class Latin and North Americans sent their children to Europe to attend school and to acquire "culture" before they entered business, agriculture, and government in their native lands. In both Latin and North America, some people felt that New World countries must develop their own cultures, not imitate Britain or France. Yet European cultural dominance, including the powerful influence of Christianity, made the Western Hemisphere subject to the intellectual, political, and economic trends that shaped the West.

The wealthy classes in Latin America depended on Europe for trade. They became indebted to Europeans for funds to support their governments and to build their railroads. On their part, the Europeans were content to gain the profits from commerce without

Nitrate Mine in Chile. A world economy began to emerge during the Commercial Revolution. The Age of Imperialism speeded up this process, as more and more resources of the non-European world became developed. (*Historical Pictures Service, Chicago*)

direct colonization. If political dissension threatened to interfere with peaceful trade, Europeans had ways of letting the merchant class know the costs of that dissension. When the rules of free trade were violated, European vessels might blockade harbors or seize customs houses. But unlike the British in Egypt, Europeans in the Americas usually withdrew their troops or ships as soon as they had enforced their will.

An exception to this general policy of non-occupation was Napoleon III's attempt to conquer Mexico and install an Austrian archduke on a bogus throne. The Mexicans, led by Benito Juárez (1806–1872), resisted the French invasion. Napoleon thought better of his dreams of easy glory and abandoned the campaign, which was undertaken to please members of the military more than the business community. The Mexicans captured and executed Maximilian, the archduke-emperor, in 1867, and the experience intensified Mexican nationalism.

Although Latin Americans were sheltered from European imperialism by the business interests of Britain and the United States, they had little protection against the aggressions of the latter. By the end of the nineteenth century, the United States was able to push the British aside and energetically pursue its own interests, first in the Caribbean and Central America and then throughout Latin America. Growing economic power brought the United States into the field of the Great Powers. After the Spanish American War (1898), the Americans occupied Cuba and annexed Puerto Rico and the Philippines; they also restated the Monroe Doctrine, which prohibited colonization of the Americas by foreign nations but did not inhibit U.S. expansionism. In the Roosevelt Corollary (1904), the United States announced that Europeans could not intervene in the Western Hemisphere even to protect their citizens or their business interests. Such intervention was too often the pretext for imperial control of one form or another, which the Americans felt would jeopardize their interests.

Yet Americans continued to interfere freely in Latin American affairs. They engineered the secession of Panama from Colombia in 1903 to obtain the rights to build the Panama Canal on favorable terms. For the next three decades the United States intervened repeatedly in the Caribbean, sending Marines to occupy the Dominican Republic, Haiti, Nicaragua, and the port of Veracruz in Mexico. Seizing customs revenues for payment of debts and threatening Latin American governments, American "gunboat diplomacy" replaced English and French commercial power in northern Latin America. Like the British before them, the Americans used force to maintain their interests while, at the same time, articulating a policy of free competition for trade and commerce—of open doors around the world, including Latin America.

In many ways, American behavior resembled European imperialism. Like the Europeans who acquired bases in China, the Americans took Guantanamo Bay in Cuba, Fonseca in Nicaragua, and the Canal Zone in Panama, which was originally leased to the Americans in perpetuity. The Americans, like the Europeans, invested so heavily in underdeveloped areas that they frequently controlled governments and ruling elites. In 1923, 43 percent of all American foreign investment went to Latin America, 27 percent to Canada, 22 percent to Europe (at a time when Americans were underwriting German recovery from the First World War), and 8 percent to all of Asia and Africa. Foreign investment may have been a mere fraction of total American wealth, but it was significant to important segments of the national economy. The United States practiced "dollar diplomacy" just as Europeans had in Egypt, Persia, Turkey, and China. The United States

put the customs revenues of Haiti (1915) and Santo Domingo (1904, 1916–1924) into receivership, just as the British and French did Egyptian customs. In Central America the Americans controlled the governments as puppet or client states, just as the Europeans directed the governments of the Middle East or Central Asia. And in the early twentieth century, American influence over Mexico under the presidency of Porfirio Diaz (1876–1880, 1884–1911) was very similar to German and British controls over the Turks.

The Latin American response to American imperial actions has been very like responses to European imperialism. The strongest challenge to American interests before World War I came with the Mexican revolution in 1911. Its leaders, Emiliano Zapata, Victoriano Huerta, and Francisco "Pancho" Villa, differed in their motives for the overthrow of Diaz, but together they upset Mexican-American relations. Zapata's goal was to break up great estates and give them to the peasantry; Huerta, who was encouraged by the British, hoped to strengthen industry by increasing foreign investment. In 1916, Villa angered the United States by killing several American engineers and making a raid across the border. Woodrow Wilson ordered American troops into Mexico to pursue Villa.

The troubled relations between the United States and Latin America continued after the First World War, as they do to the present day—a legacy of the distrust that grew out of American imperialism. This legacy is an especially bitter one because the United States, like Great Britain, has paid tribute to human rights and to national self-determination. While Wilson was preaching self-determination for European national groups, sympathetically concerned with the wrongs done to the weak by the strong powers, he was also violating the sovereign state of Mexico, which was torn in pieces by civil war.

American and British arguments for free trade sounded suspiciously like defenses of their industrial and economic superiority, and their policies seemed calculated to maintain Latin American backwardness to ensure a source of raw materials. Some Latin American nations responded to the Great Depression of 1929 much as Italy, Germany, and eastern European states did. Unable to cope with the economic disaster, Argentina and Brazil, for example, experimented with authoritarian nationalist governments like the fascist regimes in Europe. President Roosevelt announced a policy of cooperation with the South Americans—a "good neighbor" policy underlined by the Panamerican Union—in the hope of improving relations and increasing trade between the two continents. Not until the post–World War II era, however, did Latin American states begin to make serious headway in industrialization and economic expansion. Still, for many Latin Americans who wanted to reform social inequality, the enrichment of the few seemed the major result of economic growth, which depended on the United States for capital, for machinery, and for markets.

The Legacy of Imperialism

World War I was a great turning point in relations between mother countries and colonies, although the former seemed scarcely aware of it at the time. Britain and France divided the spoils when they took the German colonies and replaced Turkey as the power in the Middle East. Both empires were at their peak after 1919, and even more than before the war, leaders in both countries regarded their colonies as necessary to the well-being of their nations—for prestige, for manpower, and for trade.

But the origins of decolonization date from the postwar era. Wilson and Lloyd George, who championed national self-determination at the peace conference following World War I, may not have meant the slogans of national self-determination to apply to the colonial world, but many intellectuals both in the colonies and in Europe could not easily draw lines to separate European nationalism from Indian or Chinese patriotism. Liberal dem-

ocrats in the West began to talk of training the colonies for eventual self-government or independence. In France, democrats talked of French citizens of all colors within the empire. In the colonies, forces for independence grew, and intellectuals in the colonies for whom the democrats' timetable for equality or for self-government was too slow found leadership in the anti-imperialist campaign of Lenin and the Bolsheviks.

World War II exhausted the European colonial powers; it depleted their soldiery, their financial resources, and their willingness to wage war against their rebellious colonies. During the war, the Allies had relied on colonies for labor, soldiers, bases, and supplies. Colonies and British Commonwealth states like Australia made giant strides toward industrialization to meet the Allies' demand for supplies. At the very moment that colonies were most important to their mother countries, they were taking steps toward greater economic independence. Furthermore, the Europeans' inability to avoid the slaughter of the war and the racist destruction of the Jews had undercut any moral authority the Westerners might have claimed. For British and French citizens the postwar task was to realize peace, democracy, and social welfare at home. For many, this meant that the colonies, or at least some of them, would have to have self-determination, perhaps even independence. The question was not if, but when, where, and how.

Almost a century after the rapid division of the world among the European and American powers and decades after the decolonization of most of the world, the results of imperialism persist. Western institutions and thought have been spread to people the world over. This Western expansion was religious, social, political, and economic; it affected institutions, customs, and beliefs. Westerners often destroyed local societies and economies. As Europe made demands on non-Europe, confrontation and adaptation were inevitable. For better or for worse, much of the world has been westernized. Non-Europeans, reacting to their contacts with the West, have

Chronology 27.1 Expansion of Western Dominance

1830	The French move into Algeria
1839–1842	British defeat Chinese in Opium War
1853	Commodore Perry with U.S. naval forces opens Japan to trade
1854–1856	The Crimean War
1857	The Sepoy Mutiny—Britain replaces the East India Company and governs India through a viceroy
1867	Mexicans led by Juárez execute Emperor Maximilian; the Meiji Restoration in Japan
1869	The opening of the Suez Canal
1874–1877	Stanley sets up posts in the Congo for Leopold II of Belgium
1878	Congress of Berlin
1878–1881	British and Russian troops occupy Afghanistan
1881	The French take control of Tunisia
1882	Britain occupies Egypt
1883–1885	The French fight the Chinese to claim Indochina
1884–1885	The Berlin Congress on Africa
1886	The British establish a protectorate in Burma; Germany controls East Africa
1894–1895	Sino-Japanese War—the British, Russians, and French intervene to take away Japan's gains
1896	Ethiopians defeat Italian invaders
1898	The Spanish-American War—the United States annexes the Philippines and Puerto Rico and occupies Cuba
1899–1902	The Boer War
1900	The Boxers rebel against foreign presence in China
1904–1905	Russo-Japanese War—the Japanese defeat the Russians
1911	The Mexican Revolution
1911–1912	The Manchu Dynasty is overthrown and a republic formed; Dr. Sun Zhongshan becomes president; civil war breaks out in China
1919	Britain grants a legislative assembly in India; Gandhi's passive resistance movement broadens; the Amritsar Massacre; Kemal Atatürk emerges as the Turkish national leader

developed a sense of nationalism, borrowed the technology of the West, and shaped European ideas and values to their own needs.

Imperialism has left a legacy of deep animosity in countries of Asia, Africa, and Latin America. Although most nations have political independence, Western economic and cultural domination remains today and often influences the policies of autonomous governments. Most of the world is still poor and suffers from a lack of capital, skilled leaders, and stable governments. Parts of the world are in turmoil because they are strategic to the Great Powers or are areas of ideological conflict.

Many people in the non-Western world believe that Lenin's analysis of imperialism explains the poverty of their nations and the rapaciousness of European and American business. On the eve of World War I, Lenin and other socialists argued that the capitalist nations were unable to maintain their economic and social organization because capitalism had become monopolistic in both production and finance. Monopoly capitalism was condemned to periodic depressions for lack of materials, markets, and capital, he said. Unless the governments of capitalist countries were able to ensure high wages and profits for their own people by exploiting colonial peoples, working-class revolutions would break out. Powerful business interests also pushed their governments to the verge of war to safeguard their profits. At the same time, Lenin said, imperialism greatly accelerated the development of capitalism, and opposition to it, among the victims of imperialism in Asia, Africa, and Latin America. Further, Lenin said that the struggle for empire would end in war between the Great Powers, which would draw the colonies into European affairs even faster than the operations of the market.

Imperialism has been a source of great bitterness not only in its economic exploitation, but also in the racism and callous disregard of other cultures that it fostered. In this sense, non-Western nationalism has often had anti-Western elements. Now, Europeans and Americans must deal economically and politically with nations acutely conscious of their nationhood and quick to condemn any policy they perceive as imperialistic.

World War II brought an end to the age of European imperialism. But the world's dependence on European and American industry and technology has not diminished. Out of the Industrial Revolution grew a global economy that has enveloped every part of the world. For food, for manufactured goods, for energy, for technology, all nations and peoples depend on forces beyond the control of any one country. This dependence, complicated by imperialism's legacy of bitterness and distrust, forms the heart of the world order today.

Suggested Reading

Baumgart, Winfried, *Imperialism* (1982). A critical examination of arguments and issues on the subject.

Betts, Raymond, *The False Dawn* (1975).

Brodie, Fawn, *Devil Drives: A Life of Sir Richard Burton* (1967). A fine biography of the great explorer.

Brunschwig, Henri, *French Colonialism: 1871–1914. Myths and Realities* (tr. 1964). His general thesis is similar to Robinson, Gallagher, and Denny; the best book on French imperialism.

Headrick, Daniel, *The Tools of Empire* (1981). Interesting argument for the role of technology in imperialism.

Henderson, W. O., *Studies in German Colonial History* (1963). Several interesting essays on this topic, which is difficult to research in English sources.

Hobson, J. A., *Imperialism: A Study* (1902). This book and those of Luxemburg and Lenin (see below) are highly controversial and influential theoretical analyses.

Jeal, Jim, *Livingstone* (1974). A very readable biography of a fascinating life, with good background on Africa.

Langer, William, *European Alliances and Alignments, 1871–1890* and *Diplomacy of Imperialism, 1890–1902*, 2 vols. (1950). Indispensable sources for information about imperialism with a perspective of diplomatic history.

Lenin, V. I., *Imperialism: The Highest Stage in Capitalism* (1917).

Luxemburg, Rosa, *The Accumulation of Capital* (tr. 1963).

May, Ernest, *Imperial Democracy* (1961). American expansionism discussed more thoroughly and less controversially than is usual.

Porter, Bernard, *The Lion's Share: A Short History of British Imperialism, 1850–1970* (1975). A good survey history.

Robinson, R. E., John Gallagher, and Alice Denny, *Africa and the Victorians: The Official Mind of Imperialism* (1961). An essential book for this fascinating subject; well-written and controversial.

Thornton, A. P., *The Imperial Idea and Its Enemies: A Study in British Power* (1959). An interesting study of the ideas and policies of British imperialism.

Review Questions

1. Why did imperialism grow after 1880? What are the rationalizations for European expansion that were usually offered at the end of the nineteenth century?

2. Why did Bismarck believe Germany to be a satiated power and then change his mind?

3. How did imperialism fit in with the European alliance system? How did it cause it? How did imperialism undermine European stability under the alliance system?

4. What were the specific reasons for expansion of each of the Great Powers: Russia, Britain, France, Germany, and Italy?

5. Why were Japan and China able to withstand imperialist expansion?

6. Why was Africa divided up in such a brief time?

7. How did imperialism threaten world peace in the early twentieth century?

8. Why did England and France (which seemed on the verge of war in 1898) make peace and form an alliance?

9. How was Turkey able to maintain itself in the nineteenth century against the encroachments of Europeans? Why did it fail to do so in the twentieth century?

10. What problems in the Middle East and Central Asia appear to have been resolved because Russia was defeated in World War I?

11. What were the obstacles preventing Indian independence?

28

Modern Consciousness:
New Views of Nature,
Human Nature, and the Arts

*T*he end of the nineteenth and beginning of the twentieth centuries were marked by extraordinary creativity in thought and the arts. Thinkers and scientists achieved revolutionary insights into human nature, the social world, and the physical universe; writers and artists opened up hitherto unimagined possibilities for artistic expression. These developments produced a shift in European consciousness. The mechanical model of the universe that had dominated the Western outlook since Newton had to be altered; the Enlightenment view of human rationality and goodness was questioned; the belief in natural rights and objective standards governing morality was attacked; rules of aesthetics that had governed the arts since the Renaissance were dispensed with. However imaginative and fruitful these changes were for Western intellectual and cultural life, they also helped to create the disoriented, fragmented, and troubled era that is the twentieth century.

Irrationalism

Some late-nineteenth-century thinkers challenged the basic premises of the philosophes and their nineteenth-century heirs. They repudiated the Enlightenment conception of human rationality, stressing instead the irrational side of human behavior. For these thinkers it seemed that reason exercised a very limited influence over human conduct; impulses, drives, instincts—all forces below the surface—determined behavior much more than did logical consciousness. Like the romantics, proponents of the irrational placed more reliance on feeling and intuition than on reason. They belittled the intellect's attempt to comprehend nature and society, praised outbursts of the irrational, and in some instances exalted violence.

Nietzsche

The principal figure in the "dethronement of reason" and the glorification of the irrational was the German philosopher Friedrich Nietzsche (1844–1900). Nietzsche's writings are not systematic treatises but collections of aphorisms, often containing internal contradictions. For this reason his philosophy lends itself to misinterpretation and misapplication, as manifested by Nazi theorists who distorted Nietzsche to justify their theory of the German master race.

Nietzsche attacked the accepted views and convictions of his day as a hindrance to a fuller and richer existence for man. He denounced social reform, parliamentary government, and universal suffrage, ridiculed the vision of progress through science, condemned Christian morality, and mocked the liberal belief in man's essential goodness and rationality. He said that man must understand that life, which is replete with cruelty, injustice, uncertainty, and absurdity, is not governed by rational principles. There exist no absolute standards of good and evil whose truth can be demonstrated by reflective reason.

Modern bourgeois society, said Nietzsche, was decadent and enfeebled—a victim of the excessive development of the rational faculties at the expense of will and instinct. Against the liberal-rationalist stress on the intellect, Nietzsche urged recognition of the dark mysterious world of instinctual desires—the true forces of life. Smother the will with excessive intellectualizing and you destroy that spontaneity that sparks cultural creativity and ignites a zest for living. The critical and theoretical outlook destroyed the creative instincts. For man's manifold potential to be realized, he must forego relying on the intellect and nurture again the instinctual roots of human existence.

Christianity, with all its prohibitions, restrictions, and demands to conform, also crushes the human impulse for life, said Nietzsche. Christian morality must be obliterated, for it is fit only for the weak, the slave. The triumph of Christianity in the ancient world, said Nietzsche, was a revolution of the meek to inherit the earth from the strong. Christian otherworldliness undermined man's will to control the world; Christian teachings saddled man with guilt, preventing him from expressing his instinctual nature.

Although the philosophes had rejected Christian doctrines, they had largely retained Christian ethics. Nietzsche, however, did not attack Christianity because it was contrary to reason, as the philosophes had; he attacked Christianity because he said it gave man a sick soul. It was life-denying; it blocked the free and spontaneous exercise of human instincts and made humility and self-abnegation virtues and pride a vice; in short, Christianity ruined the spark of life in man. This spark of life, this inner yearning which is man's true essence, must again burn.

"God is dead," proclaimed Nietzsche. God is man's own creation; there are no higher worlds. Christian morality is also dead. The death of God and Christian values can mean the liberation of man, insisted Nietzsche. Man can surmount *nihilism* (the belief that moral and social values have no validity); he can create new values and achieve self-mastery. He can overcome the deadening uniformity and mediocrity of modern civilization. He can undo democracy and socialism, which have made masters out of cattlelike masses, and the shopkeeper's spirit, which has made man soft and degenerate. European society is without heroic figures; all belong to a vast herd but there are no shepherds. Europe can only be saved by the emergence of a higher type of man, the *superman* or *overman*, who would not be held back by the egalitarian rubbish preached by democrats and socialists. "It is necessary for *higher* man to declare war upon the masses," said Nietzsche, to end "the dominion of *inferior* men." Europe requires "the annihilation of universal suffrage—this is to say, that system by means of which the lowest natures prescribe themselves as a law for higher natures."[1] Europe needs a new breed of rulers, a true aristocracy of masterful men. The superman is a new kind of man who breaks with accepted morality and sets his own standards. He does not repress his instincts but asserts them. He destroys old values and asserts his prerogative as master. Free of Christian guilt, he proudly affirms his own being; dispensing with Christian "thou shalt not," he instinctively says "I will." He dares to be himself. Because he is not like other people, traditional definitions of good and evil have no meaning for him. He does not allow his individuality to be stifled. He makes his own values, those that flow from his very being. He knows that life is meaningless but lives it laughingly, instinctively, fully. The masses, cowardly and envious, will condemn the superman as evil; this has always been their way.

The German philosopher Arthur Schopenhauer (1788–1860) had declared that beneath the conscious intellect is the will, a striving, demanding, and imperious force that is the real conductor of human behavior. Schopenhauer sought to repress the will. He urged people to stifle desires and retreat into quietude to escape from life's misfortunes. Nietzsche learned from Schopenhauer to appreciate the unconscious strivings that dominate human behavior, but Nietzsche called for the heroic and joyful assertion of the will to redeem life from nothingness.

Supermen are free of all restrictions, rules, and codes of behavior imposed by society. They burst upon the world propelled by that something that urges people to want, take, strike, create, struggle, seek, dominate. Supermen are people of restless energy who enjoy living dangerously, have contempt for meekness and humility, and dismiss humanitarian sentiments. At times Nietzsche declares that supermen, a new breed of nobles, will rule the planet; at other times he states that they will demonstrate their superiority by avoiding public life, ignoring established rules, and refraining from contact with inferiors.

The influence of Nietzsche's philosophy is still a matter of controversy and conjecture. Perhaps better than anyone else, Nietzsche recognized the ills of modern Western civilization and urged confronting them without hypocrisy or compromise. But he had no constructive proposals for dealing with the malaise of modern society. No social policy could be derived from his radical individualism. And his vitriolic attack on European institutions and values, immensely appealing to central European intellectuals, helped to erode the rational foundations of Western civilization. Many young people, attracted to Nietzsche's philosophy, welcomed World War I because they thought that it would clear a path to a new heroic age.

The Nazis regarded themselves as embodiments of Nietzsche's supermen. Nietzsche himself, who detested German nationalism, militarism, and anti-Semitism, would have rejected Hitler; but Nietzsche's extreme and violent denunciation of Western values and his praise of power provided a breeding ground for violence.

Bergson

Another thinker who reflected the growing irrationalism of the age was Henri Bergson (1859–1941), a French philosopher of Jewish background. Originally attracted to positivism, Bergson turned away from the positivistic claim that science could explain everything and fulfill all human needs. Such an emphasis on the intellect, said Bergson, sacrifices spiritual impulses, imagination, and intuition and reduces the soul to a mere mechanism.

The methods of science cannot reveal ultimate reality, Bergson insisted. European civilization must recognize the limitations of scientific rationalism. The method of intuition, whereby the mind strives for an immanent relationship with the object, to become one with it, can tell us more about reality than the method of analysis employed by science. Entering into the object through an intuitive experience is an avenue to truth that is closed to the calculations and measurements of science. Although not based on scientific procedures, Bergson insisted, the method of intuition is a superior avenue to knowledge. The mind is not a collection of atoms operating according to mechanical principles, but an active consciousness with profound intuitive capacities. Bergson's philosophy pointed away from science toward religious mysticism.

Sorel

Nietzsche proclaimed that irrational forces constitute the essence of human nature; Bergson held that a nonrational intuition provided insights unattainable by the scientific mentality. Georges Sorel (1847–1922), who gave up engineering to follow intellectual pursuits, was a French syndicalist philosopher who showed the political potential of the nonrational. Like Nietzsche, Sorel was disillusioned with contemporary bourgeois society, which he considered decadent, soft, and unheroic. Whereas Nietzsche called for the superman to rescue society from decadence and mediocrity, Sorel placed his hopes in the proletariat, whose position made them courageous, virile, and determined.

Sorel wanted the proletariat to destroy the existing order and make the workshop the model of a new society. This overthrow, said Sorel, would be accomplished through a general strike—a universal work stoppage that would bring down the government and give power to the workers.

The general strike had all the appeal of a great myth, said Sorel. What is important is not that the general strike will actually take place, but that its image stirs all the anticapitalist resentments of the workers and inspires them to their revolutionary responsibilities. Sorel understood the extraordinary potency of myths for eliciting total commitment and inciting heroic action. Because they appeal to the imagination and feelings, myths are an effective way of moving the masses to revolt. By believing in the myth of the general strike, workers would soar above the moral decadence of bourgeois society and bear the immense sacrifices that their struggle calls for.

Like Marx, Sorel believed that the goals of the worker could not be achieved through peaceful parliamentary means; he too wanted no reconciliation between bourgeois exploiters and oppressed workers. The only recourse for workers was direct action and violence, which Sorel regarded as ennobling, heroic, and sublime—a means of restoring grandeur to a flabby world.

Sorel's exaltation of violence and mass action, his condemnation of liberal democracy, and his recognition of the power and political utility of fabricated myths would find concrete expression in the fascist movements after World War I. Sorel heralded the age of mass political movements and myths manufactured by propaganda experts.

Freud: A New View of Human Nature

In many ways Sigmund Freud (1856–1939), an Austrian-Jewish doctor who spent most of his adult life in Vienna, was a child of the Enlightenment. Like the philosophes Freud identified civilization with reason and regarded science as the avenue to knowledge. But unlike the philosophes, Freud focused on the massive power and influence of nonrational drives. Whereas Nietzsche glorified the irrational and approached it with a poet's temperament, Freud recognized its potential danger, sought to comprehend it scientifically, and wanted to regulate it in the interests of civilization. Unlike Nietzsche, Freud did not express contempt for the intellect or belittle the rational, but always sought to salvage respect for reason.

Freud held that people are not fundamentally rational; human behavior is governed primarily by powerful inner forces that are hidden from consciousness. These instinctual strivings, rather than rational faculties, constitute the greater part of the mind. Freud's great achievement was to explore the world of the unconscious with the tools and temperament of a scientist. He considered not just the external acts of a person, but also the inner psychic reality that underlies human behavior.

Freud sought to comprehend neuroses—disorders in thinking, feeling, and behavior that interfere with everyday acts of personal and social life. Neuroses can take several forms, including hysteria, anxiety, depression, and so on. To understand neuroses, said Freud, one had to look beyond a patient's symptoms and discover those unconscious factors, generally sexual in nature, that are at the root of the person's distress. The key to the unconscious, he said, was the interpretation of dreams.

The *id*, the subconscious seat of the instincts, constantly demands gratification, said Freud. Unable to endure tension, it demands sexual release, the termination of pain, the cessation of hunger. When the id is denied an outlet for its instinctual energy, people become frustrated, angry, and unhappy. Gratifying the id is our highest pleasure. But the full gratification of instinctual demands is inimicable to civilized life.

Freud postulated a terrible conflict between the relentless strivings of our instinctual nature and the requirements of civilization. Civilization, for Freud, requires the renunciation of instinctual gratification and the mastery of animal instincts, a thesis he developed in *Civilization and Its Discontents* (1930). While Freud's thoughts in this work were no doubt influenced by the great tragedy of World War I, the main theme could be traced back to his earlier writings. Human beings derive their highest pleasure from sexual fulfillment, said Freud, but unrestrained sexuality drains off psychic energy needed for creative artistic and intellectual life. Hence society, through the family, the priest, the teacher, and the police, imposes rules and restrictions on our animal nature. But this is immensely painful. People are caught in a tragic bind. Society's demand for the denial of full instinctual gratification causes terrible frustration; equally distressing, the violation of society's rules under the pressure of in-

stinctual needs evokes terrible feelings of guilt. Either way people suffer; civilized life simply entails too much pain for people. It seems that the price we pay for civilization is neurosis. Most people cannot endure the amount of instinctual renunciation that civilization requires. There are times when our elemental human nature rebels against all the restrictions and "thou shalt nots" demanded by society, against all the misery and torment imposed by civilization.

"Civilization imposes great sacrifices not only on man's sexuality but also on his aggressivity,"[2] said Freud. People are not good by nature as the philosophes had taught; on the contrary, they are "creatures among whose instinctual endowments is to be reckoned a powerful share of aggressiveness." Their first inclination is not to love their neighbor but to "satisfy their aggressiveness on him, to exploit his capacity for work without compensation, to use him sexually without his consent, to seize his possessions, to humiliate him, to cause him pain, to torture and to kill him."[3] Man is wolf to man, concluded Freud. "Who has the courage to dispute it in the face of all the evidence in his own life and in history?"[4] Civilization "has to use its utmost efforts in order to set limits to man's aggressive instincts," but "in spite of every effort these endeavors of civilization have not so far achieved very much."[5] People find it difficult to do without "the satisfaction of this inclination to aggression."[6] When circumstances are favorable, this primitive aggressivness breaks loose and "reveals man as a savage beast to whom consideration towards his own kind is something alien."[7] For Freud, "the inclination to aggression is an original self-subsisting disposition in man . . . that . . . constitutes the greatest impediment to civilization." Civilization attempts "to combine single human individuals and after that families, then races, peoples and nations into one great unity. . . . But man's natural aggressive instinct, the hostility of each against all and of all against each, opposes this program of civilization."[8] Aggressive impulses drive people apart, threatening society with disintegration. For Freud an unalterable core of human nature is ineluctably in opposition to civilized life. To this extent everyone is potentially an enemy of civilization.

Freud's awareness of the irrational and his general pessimism regarding people's ability to regulate it in the interests of civilization did not lead him to break faith with the Enlightenment tradition, for Freud did not celebrate the irrational. He was too aware of its self-destructive nature for that. Civilization is indeed a burden, but people must bear it, for the alternative is far worse. In the tradition of the philosophes Freud sought truth based on a scientific analysis of human nature and believed that reason was the best road to social improvement. Like the philosophes he was critical of religion, regarding it as a pious illusion—a fairy tale in conflict with reason. Freud wanted people to throw away what he believed was the crutch of religion—to break away from childlike dependency and stand alone. Also like the philosophes, Freud was a humanitarian who sought to relieve human misery by making people aware of their true nature, particularly their sexuality. He wanted society to soften its overly restrictive sexual standards because they were injurious to mental health. As a practicing psychiatrist, he tried to assist his patients in dealing with emotional problems. Freud wanted to raise to the level of consciousness hitherto unrecognized inner conflicts that caused emotional distress.

Although Freud undoubtedly was a child of the Enlightenment, in crucial ways he differed from the philosophes. Regarding the Christian doctrine of original sin as myth, the philosophes had believed that people's nature was essentially good. If people took reason as their guide, evil could be eliminated. Freud, however, asserted, in secular and scientific terms, a pessimistic view of human nature. Freud saw evil as rooted in human nature rather than as a product of a faulty environment. Education and better living conditions will not eliminate evil, as the philosophes expected, nor will abolition of private property, as Marx had declared. The philo-

Sigmund Freud with His Fiancée, Martha Bernays, 1885. Freud did not believe that human beings were inherently good and reasonable. Instead he found individuals to be driven by subconscious drives and aggressive tendencies. Freud believed, however, that through psychoanalysis, a scientific study of the subconscious, people could understand and control their behavior. (*The Granger Collection*)

sophes venerated reason; it had enabled Newton to unravel nature's mysteries and would permit people to achieve virtue and reform society. Freud, who wanted reason to prevail, understood that its soft voice had to compete with the thunderous roars of the id. Freud broke with the optimism of the philosophes. His awareness of the immense pressures that civilization places on our fragile egos led him to be generally pessimistic about the future. Unlike Marx, Freud had no vision of utopia.

The Modernist Movement

Breaking with Conventional Modes of Aesthetics

At the same time that Freud was breaking with the Enlightenment view of human nature, artists and writers were rebelling against traditional forms of artistic and literary expression that had governed European cultural life since the Renaissance. Their experimentations produced a great cultural revolution called *modernism*, which still profoundly influences the arts. In some ways, modernism was a continuation of the Romantic Movement that had dominated European culture in the early nineteenth century. Both movements subjected to searching criticism cultural styles that had been formulated during the Renaissance and had roots in ancient Greece.

But even more than romanticism, modernism aspired to an intense introspection—a heightened awareness of self—and saw the intellect as a barrier to the free expression of elemental human emotions. More than their Romantic predecessors, modernist artists and writers abandoned conventional literary and artistic models and experimented with new modes of expression. The consequence of their bold venture, says literary critic and historian Irving Howe, was nothing less than the "breakup of the traditional unity and continuity of Western culture."[9]

Like Freud, modernist artists and writers went beyond surface appearances in search of a more profound reality hidden in the human psyche. Writers like Thomas Mann, Marcel Proust, James Joyce, August Strindberg, D. H. Lawrence, and Franz Kafka explored the inner life of the individual and the psychopathology of human relations; they dealt with the predicament of men and women who rejected the values and customs of their day, and they depicted the anguish of people burdened by guilt, torn by internal conflicts, and driven by an inner self-destructiveness; they showed the overwhelming might of the irrational and the seductive power of the primitive and broke the silence about sex that had prevailed in Victorian literature.

From the Renaissance through the Enlightenment and into the nineteenth century, Western aesthetic standards had been shaped by the conviction that the universe embodied an inherent mathematical order. A corollary of this conception of the outer world as orderly and intelligible was the view that art should imitate reality. From the Renaissance on, says sociologist Daniel Bell, art was seen as "a mirror of nature, a representation of life. Knowledge was a reflection of what was 'out there', . . . a copy of what was seen."[10] Since the Renaissance, artists had deliberately made use of laws of perspective and proportion; musicians had used harmonic chords that brought rhythm and melody into a unified whole; writers had produced works according to a definite pattern that included a beginning, middle, and end.

Modernist culture, however, acknowledged no objective reality of space, motion, and time that means the same to all observers. Rather, reality can be grasped in many ways; a multiplicity of frames of reference apply to nature and human experience. Reality is what the viewer perceives it to be through the prism of the imagination. "There is no outer reality," said the modernist German poet Gottfried Benn, "there is only human consciousness, constantly building, modifying, rebuilding new worlds out of its own creativity."[11] Modernism is concerned less with the object itself than with how the artist experiences it, with the sensations that an object evokes in the artist's very being, with the meaning the artist's imagination imposes on reality. Bell expresses this point in reference to painting:

Modernism . . . denies the primacy of an outside reality, as given. It seeks either to rearrange that reality, or to retreat to the self's interior, to private experience as the source of its concerns and aesthetic preoccupations. . . . There is an emphasis on the self as the touchstone of understanding and on the activity of the knower rather than the character of the object as the source of knowledge. . . . Thus

*one discerns the intentions of modern painting
. . . to break up ordered space. . . . to bridge the
distance between object and spectator, to "thrust"
itself on the viewer and establish itself immediately
by impact.*[12]

Dispensing with conventional forms of aesthetics that stressed structure and coherence, modernism propelled the arts into uncharted seas. Recoiling from a middle-class, industrial civilization that valued rationalism, organization, clarity, stability, and definite norms and values, modernist writers and artists were fascinated by the bizarre, the mysterious, the unpredictable, the primitive, the irrational, the formless. Writers, for example, experimented with new techniques to convey the intense struggle between the conscious and the unconscious, to connote the aberrations and complexities of human personality and the irrationality of human behavior. In particular they devised a new way—the stream of consciousness—to exhibit the mind's every level—both conscious reflection and unconscious strivings—and to capture how thought is punctuated by spontaneous outbursts, disconnected assertions, random memories, hidden desires, and persistent fantasies. Musicians like Igor Stravinsky and Arnold Schoenberg experimented with dissonance and primitive rhythms. When Stravinsky's ballet *The Rite of Spring* was performed in Paris in 1913, the theater audience rioted to protest the composition's break with tonality, its use of primitive jazz-like rhythms, and its theme of ritual sacrifice.

The modernist movement, which began near the end of the nineteenth century, was in full bloom before World War I and would continue to flower in the postwar world. Probably the clearest expression of the modernist viewpoint is found in art.

Modern Art

In the late nineteenth century, artists began to turn away from the standards that had characterized art since the Renaissance. No

Igor Stravinsky (1882–1971), sketched by Picasso. Although Picasso's sketch of Stravinsky is conservative in style, Stravinsky himself introduced revolutionary innovations in music, as Picasso did in art. Stravinsky experimented with dissonance and primitive rhythms. The premiere of his ballet, *Rite of Spring*, was marked by a riot. (*Musée Picasso/© S.P.A.D.E.M., Paris/V.A.G.A., New York*)

longer committed to depicting how an object appears to the eye, they searched for new forms of expression.

The history of modern painting begins with impressionism, which covered the period 1860–1886 and broke with traditional formulas of composition (the arrangement of figures and objects) and treatments of color and light. Impressionism centered in Paris and its leading figures were Edouard Manet, Claude Monet, Camille Pissaro, Edgar Degas, and Pierre Auguste Renoir. Taking Pissaro's advice—"Don't proceed according to rules and principles but paint what you observe and feel"—impressionists tried to give their own immediate and personal impression of an object or an event. They tried to capture how movement, color, and light appeared to the eye at a fleeting instant.

Intrigued by the impact that light has on objects, impressionists left their studios for the countryside, where they painted nature under an open sky. They used bold colors and drew marked contrasts between light and dark to reflect how objects in intense sunlight seem to shimmer against their background.

In addition to landscapes, impressionists painted railways, bridges and boulevards, and people—in dance halls, in cafes, in theaters, in public gardens. Impressionistic painters wanted to portray life, as it was commonly experienced in a rapidly industrializing and urbanizing world. And always they tried to convey their momentary impression of an event or figure.

In the late 1880s and the 1890s several artists went beyond impressionism. Called post-impressionists, they further revolutionized the artist's sense of space and color. Even more than the impressionists, they tried to make art a vivid emotional experience and to produce a personal impression of reality rather than a photographic copy of objects.

Paul Cézanne (1839–1906) was born in the south of France and came to Paris, the center of the Western art world. In 1882, he returned to the region of his birth, where he painted its natural scenery. Cézanne sought to portray his visual perception of an object, not the object itself. In other words, to what is seen, the artist brings a personal apperception, which his or her intelligence organizes into a work of art. When painting objects in a group, Cézanne deliberately distorted perspective, subordinating the appearance of an individual object to the requirements of the total design. Cézanne tried to demonstrate that an object, when placed together with other objects, is seen differently than when it stands alone. His concern with form and design influenced the cubists (see page 658).

No longer bound by classical art forms, artists examined non-Western art, searching for new forms of beauty and new ways of expression. A large number of artifacts and art objects from Asia, Africa, and the Pacific area coming into European capitals as souvenirs of nineteenth-century imperialist ventures and from anthropologists and ethnographers stimulated interest in non-Western art. Paul Gauguin (1848–1903) saw beauty in carvings and fabrics made by such technologically backward people as the Marquesas Islanders. He also discovered that art did not depend on skilled craftsmanship for its power. Very simple, even primitive, means of construction could produce works of great beauty.

A successful Parisian stockbroker, Gauguin abandoned the marketplace for art. He came to view bourgeois civilization as artificial and rotten. By severing human beings from the power of their own feelings, industrial civilization blunted the creative expression of the imagination and prevented people from attaining a true understanding of themselves. For these reasons Gauguin fled to Tahiti. On this picturesque island, which was largely untouched by European ways, he hoped to discover humanity's original nature without the distortion and corruption of modern civilization.

The post-impressionists produced a revolution not only of space but also of color, as exemplified by Vincent van Gogh (1853–1890). The son of a Dutch minister, van Gogh was a lonely, tortured, and impetuous soul. For a short period he served as a lay preacher among desperately poor coal miners. Moving to Paris in 1886, van Gogh came under the influence of the French impressionists. Desiring to use color in a novel way—his own way—van Gogh left Paris for the Mediterranean countryside, where he hoped to experience a new vision of sunlight, sky, and earth. Van Gogh used purer, brighter colors than artists had used before. He also recognized that color, like other formal qualities, could act as a language in and of itself. He believed that the local or "real" color of an object does not necessarily express the artist's experience. Artists, according to van Gogh, should seek to paint things not as they are, but as the artists feel them. In *Public Garden*

Edvard Munch (1863–1944): The Dance of Life. The Norwegian Munch was influenced by Van Gogh's style, in which the naked emotions of the artist dictated the color of his works and the very forms of the shapes he painted. In his work, Munch explored the interior world of psychic pain and sexual terrors. (*Nasjonalgalleriet, Oslo*)

at Arles, the colors of the pathway, the trees, and the sky are all far more intense and pure than the garden's real colors. Thus van Gogh captures the whole experience of walking alone in the stillness of a hot afternoon.

Practically unknown in his lifetime, van Gogh's art became extremely influential soon after his death in 1890. One of the first artists to be affected by his style was the Norwegian artist Edvard Munch (1863–1944), who discovered van Gogh's use of color in Paris. In *The Dance of Life*, Munch used strong, simple lines and intense color to explore the unexpressed sexual stresses and conflicts that Sigmund Freud's studies were bringing to light. In *The Scream*, Munch deliberately distorted the human face and the sky, ground, and water to portray terror.

After the post-impressionists, art moved still further away from reproducing an exact likeness of a physical object or human being.

Increasingly artists sought to penetrate the deepest recesses of the unconscious, which they saw as the wellspring of creativity and the fissured dwelling place of a higher truth. Paul Klee, a prominent twentieth-century artist, described modern art as follows:

Each should follow where the pulse of his own heart leads. . . . Our pounding heart drives us down, deep down to the source of all. What springs from this source, whether it may be called dream, idea or phantasy—must be taken seriously. . . .[13]

In Germany the tendency to use color for its power to express psychological · forces continued in the work of artists known as the German expressionists. In Ernst Ludwig Kirchner's (1880–1938) *Reclining Nude* of 1909, strong, acid yellows and greens evoke feelings of tension, stress, and isolation. Kirchner also used bold, rapid lines to define flat shapes, a technique borrowed from folk art and from non-Western native traditions.

In France, another group of avant-garde artists called the *fauves* (the wild beasts) used color with great freedom to express intense feelings and heightened energy. After examining the works of the fauves, a French critic wrote: "What is presented here . . . has nothing to do with painting; some formless confusion of colors, blue, red, yellow, green, the barbaric and naive spirit of the child who plays with the box of colors he has just got as a Christmas present."[14] Rebelling against new currents in painting, critics failed to recognize the originality and genius of the fauves.

Henri Matisse (1869–1954), the leading fauvist painter, freed color from every restriction. He painted broad areas with stunning pigment unrelated to the real colors of the subject (see Figure 4 following p. 766). His brilliant use of color and design aroused a violent reaction; one New York critic said of a Matisse exhibition: "ugliness that is most appalling . . . artistic degeneration . . . hideousness."[15]

Between 1909 and 1914, a new style called *cubism* was developed by Pablo Picasso (1881–1973) and Georges Braque (1882–1963). They explored the interplay between the flat world of the canvas and the three-dimensional world of visual perception. Like the post-impressionists, they sought to paint a reality deeper than what the eye sees at first glance.

In a typical Renaissance or baroque painting, objects are set inside an imaginary block of space, and they are represented from a single stationary point of view. A cubist work is constructed on a different system, so that it re-creates the experience of seeing in a space of time. One can only know the nature of a volume by seeing it from many angles. Therefore, cubist art presents objects from multiple viewpoints. The numerous fragmentary images of cubist art make one aware of the complex experience of seeing. One art historian describes cubism as follows: "The cubist is not interested in usual representational standards. It is as if he were walking around the object he is analyzing, as one is

free to walk around a piece of sculpture for successive views. But he must represent all these views at once."[16]

The colors used in early cubist art are deliberately banal, and the subjects represented are ordinary objects from everyday life. Picasso and Braque wanted to eliminate eye-catching color and intriguing subject matter so that their audiences would focus on the process of *seeing* itself.

In *Les Demoiselles d'Avignon*, Picasso painted five nudes. In each instance the body is distorted in defiance of classical and Renaissance standards of beauty. The masklike faces show Picasso's debt to African art and together with the angular shapes deprive the subjects of individuality and personality. The head of the squatting figure combines a profile with a full face—Picasso's attempt to present multiple aspects of an object at the same time.

Throughout the period from 1890 to 1914, avant-garde artists were de-emphasizing subject matter and stressing the expressive power of such formal qualities as line, color, and space. It is not surprising that some artists finally began to create work that did not refer to anything seen in the real world. Piet Mondrian (1872–1944), a Dutch artist, came to Paris shortly before World War I. There he saw the cubist art of Picasso and Braque. The cubists had compressed the imaginary depth in their paintings so that all the objects seemed to be contained within a space only a few inches deep. They had also reduced subject matter to insignificance. It seemed to Mondrian that the next step was to get rid of illusionistic space and subject matter entirely. His painting *Broadway Boogie Woogie* (see Figure 6 following page 766), for example, appears flat. Looking at Mondrian's paintings is a kinesthetic experience, as one senses the delicate interplay of balances and counterweights. By eliminating from his painting any reference to the visible world, Mondrian helped to inaugurate abstract art.

Another founder of abstract art was Wassily Kandinsky (1866–1944), a Russian residing in Germany. Kandinsky gradually came to remove all traces of the physical world from his paintings, to create a nonobjective art that bears no resemblance to the natural world. In stating that he "painted . . . subconsciously in a state of strong inner tension,"[17] Kandinsky explicitly expressed a principal quality of modern art.

Just before World War I, a young French artist named Marcel Duchamp (1887–1968) observed that things become art when the artist designates them as such, usually by placing them in an art context. *Art*, in other words, can be defined as a mode of perception. As the cubists had demonstrated, objects are always seen in relation to other objects in the environment. *In Advance of the Broken Arm* is a real snow shovel purchased in a store. If it were seen in a hardware store, one would probably think only of its utility. But when seen in the Yale University Gallery, equipped with stand and label, one thinks of the shovel's sculptural form and notices, as Duchamp intended, that it is not a sensuous sculpture. Its title conjures up scenarios about shoveling snow, preventing broken arms, or having heart attacks. Thus the viewer perceives the shovel in a special way unique to art (see page 767).

The revolution in art that took place near the turn of the twentieth century is reverberating still. After nearly a hundred years, these masters of modern art continue to inspire their audiences with their passion and vision. In breaking with the Renaissance view of the world as inherently orderly and rational, modern artists opened up new possibilities for artistic expression. They all exemplified the growing power and appeal of the nonrational in European life.

Social Thought: Confronting the Irrational and the Complexities of Modern Society

The end of the nineteenth and the beginning of the twentieth centuries mark the great age of sociological thought. The leading socio-logical thinkers of the period all regarded science as the only valid model for correct thinking and all claimed that their thought rested on a scientific foundation. They struggled with some of the crucial problems of modern society. How can society achieve coherence and stability when religion no longer unites people? What are the implications of the nonrational for political life? How can people preserve their individuality in a society that is becoming increasingly regimented?

Durkheim

Emile Durkheim (1858–1917), a French scholar of Jewish background, and heir to Comte's positivism, was an important founder of modern sociology. Like Comte, he considered scientific thought the only valid model for modern society. A crucial element of Durkheim's thought was the effort to show that the essential ingredients of modern times—secularism, rationalism, and individualism—threaten society with disintegration. In traditional society a person's place and function were determined by birth. Modern people, however, captivated by the principle of individualism, will not accept such restraints. They seek to uplift themselves and demand that society allow them the opportunity. In the process, they reject or ignore the social restraints that society so desperately requires, thereby giving rise to a spirit of anarchy.

The weakening of those traditional ties that bind the individual to society constitutes, for Durkheim, the crisis of modern society. Without collective values and common beliefs society is threatened with disintegration and the individual with disorientation. To a Western world intrigued by scientific progress, Durkheim emphasized the spiritual malaise of modern society. Modern people, said Durkheim, suffer from *anomie*—a collapse of values. They do not feel integrated into a collective community and find no purpose in life. In *Suicide* (1897), Durkheim maintained that the pathology of modern society is demonstrated by its high rate of suicide. Modern people are driven to suicide by intense com-

Georges Seurat (1859–1891): Sunday Afternoon on the Island of La Grande Jatte, 1886. In the late 1800s and early 1900s, Newtonian science and the Enlightenment tradition in general were in disarray. Durkheim said that people suffered from *anomie*, a collapse of values. Einstein's theories altered "fixed" rules and emphasized relativity. Seurat's pointillist landscape fragments the real world into thousands of dots of color and seems to capture visually the intellectual fragmentation and scientific exploration of this period. (*Collection of The Art Institute of Chicago*)

petition and the disappointment and dissatisfaction resulting from unfulfilled expectations and lack of commitment to moral principles. People must limit their aspirations and exercise discipline over their desires and passions. They must stop wanting more. Religion once could force people to do these things, but it no longer can.

Durkheim approved of modernity, but he noted that modern ways have not brought happiness or satisfaction to the individual. Modern scientific and industrial society requires a new moral system that will bind together the various classes into a cohesive social order and help to overcome those feelings of restlessness and dissatisfaction that torment people. Like Saint-Simon, Durkheim

called for a rational and secular system of morals to replace Christian dogma, which had lost its power to attract and to bind. If a rational and secular replacement for Christianity is not found, society runs the risk of dispensing with moral beliefs altogether and this vacuum it could not endure. Like the positivists, Durkheim insisted that the new moral beliefs must be discovered through the methods of science.

Durkheim hoped that occupational and professional organizations—updated medieval guilds—would integrate the individual into society and provide the moral force able to restrain the selfish interests of both employer and worker. By curbing egoism, fostering self-discipline, and promoting altruism, these organizations could provide substitutes for religion.

Pareto

Like Comte, Vilfredo Pareto (1848–1923), an Italian economist and sociologist, aimed to construct a system of sociology on the model of the physical sciences. His studies led him to conclude that social behavior does not rest primarily on reason but on nonrational instincts and sentiments. These deeply rooted and essentially changeless feelings are the fundamental elements in human behavior. While society may change, human nature remains essentially the same. Whoever aims to lead and to influence people must appeal not to logic but to elemental feelings. Most human behavior is nonrational; nonlogical considerations also determine the beliefs that people hold. Like Marx and Freud, Pareto believed that we cannot accept a person's word at face value; in human instincts and sentiments we find the real cause of human behavior. People do not act according to carefully thought-out theories; they act first from nonlogical motivations and then construct a rationalization to justify their behavior. Much of Pareto's work was devoted to studying the nonrational elements of human conduct and the various beliefs invented to give the appearance of rationality to behavior that derives from feeling and instinct.

Pareto divided society into two strata—an elite and the masses. In the tradition of Machiavelli, Pareto held that a successful ruling elite must, with cunning, and if necessary violence, exploit the feelings and impulses of the masses to its own advantage. Democratic states, he said, delude themselves in thinking that the masses are really influenced by rational argument. Pareto predicted that new political leaders would emerge who would master the people through propaganda and force, appealing always to sentiment rather than to reason. To this extent, Pareto was an intellectual forerunner of fascism.

Weber

Probably the most prominent social thinker of the age and a leading shaper of modern sociology was Max Weber (1864–1920). To Weber, a German academic, Western civilization, unlike the other civilizations of the globe, had virtually eliminated myth, mystery, and magic from its conception of nature and society. This process of rationalization—the "disenchantment of the world," as Weber called it—was most conspicuous in Western science but it was also evident in politics and economics. Weber considered Western science an attempt to understand and master nature through reason, and Western capitalism an attempt to organize work and production in a rational manner. The Western state has a rational written constitution, rationally formulated law, and a bureaucracy of trained government officials that administers the affairs of state according to rational rules and regulations.

The question of why the West, and not China or India, engaged in this process of rationalization intrigued Weber, and much of his scholarly effort went into answering it. Weber showed how various religious beliefs have influenced people's understanding of nature and their economic behavior. Weber's most famous thesis is that Protestantism produced an outlook that was conducive to the requirements of capitalism (see pages 315–316). Weber also explained how religious values hindered the process of rationalization in China and India.

Weber understood the terrible paradox of reason. Reason accounts for brilliant achievements in science and economic life, but it also despiritualizes life by ruthlessly eliminating centuries-old traditions, denouncing deeply felt religious beliefs as superstition, and regarding human feelings and passions as impediments to clear thinking. The process of disenchantment has given people knowledge, but it has also made people soulless and life meaningless. This is the dilemma of modern individuals, said Weber. Science cannot give people a purpose for living and the burgeoning of bureaucracy in government, business, and education stifles individual autonomy.

It is horrible to think that the world could one day be filled with nothing but those little cogs, little men clinging to little jobs and striving towards bigger ones. . . . This passion for bureaucracy . . . is enough to drive one to despair. . . . That the world should know no men but these: it is in such an evolution that we are already caught up, and the great question is, therefore, not how we can promote and hasten it, but what can we oppose to this machinery in order to keep a portion of mankind free from this parceling-out of the soul, from this supreme mastery of the bureaucratic way of life.[18]

The prospect existed that people would refuse to endure this violation of their spiritual needs and would reverse the process of disenchantment by seeking redemption in the irrational. Weber himself, however, was committed to the ideals of the Enlightenment and to perpetuating the rational scientific tradition, which he felt was threatened by bureaucratic regimentation on the one hand and irrational human impulses on the other.

Like Freud, Weber believed that to safeguard reason, it was necessary to comprehend human irrationality. One expression of the irrational that Weber analyzed in considerable depth was the charismatic leader who attracts people by force of personality. Charismatic leaders may be religious prophets, war heroes, demagogues, or others who possess this extraordinary personality that attracts and dominates others. People yearn for charismatic leadership, particularly during times of crisis. The leader claims a mission—a sacred duty—to lead the people during the crisis; the leader's authority rests on the people's belief in the mission and their faith in the leader's extraordinary abilities. A common allegiance to the charismatic leader unites the community. Weber's analysis of this phenomenon throws light on the popularity of twentieth-century dictators and demagogues.

Modern Physics

Until the closing years of the nineteenth century the view of the universe held by the Western mind rested largely on the classical physics of Newton and included the following principles: (1) Time, space, and matter were objective realities that existed independently of the observer. (2) The universe was a giant machine whose parts obeyed strict laws of cause and effect. (3) The atom, indivisible and solid, was the basic unit of matter. (4) Heated bodies emitted radiation in continuous waves. (5) Through further investigation it would be possible to gain complete knowledge of the physical universe.

Between the 1890s and the 1920s this view of the universe was shattered by a second Scientific Revolution. The discovery of x rays by William Konrad Roentgen in 1895, of radioactivity by Henri Bequerel in 1896, and of the electron by J. J. Thomson in 1897 led science to abandon the conception of the atom as a solid and indivisible particle. Rather than resembling a billiard ball, the atom consisted of a nucleus of tightly packed protons separated from orbiting electrons by empty space.

In 1900 Max Planck, a German physicist, proposed the quantum theory, which holds that a heated body does not radiate energy in a continuous unbroken stream, as had been believed, but in intermittent spurts or jumps called quanta. Planck's theory of discontinuity in energy radiation challenged a cardinal principle of classical physics that action in nature was strictly continuous.

In 1905, Albert Einstein, a German-Swiss physicist of Jewish lineage, substantiated and elaborated on Planck's theory by suggesting that all forms of radiant energy—light, heat, x rays—moved through space in discontinuous packets of energy. Then, in 1913, Niels Bohr, a Danish scientist, applied Planck's theory of energy quanta to the interior of the atom and discovered that the Newtonian laws of motion could not fully explain what happened to electrons orbiting an atomic nucleus.

As physicists explored the behavior of the

atom further, it became apparent that its nature was fundamentally elusive and unpredictable. They soon observed that radioactive atoms threw off particles and transformed themselves from atoms of one element into atoms of an entirely different element. But the transformation of a single atom in a mass of radioactive material could not be predicted according to inexorable laws of cause and effect. For example, it is known that over a period of 1,620 years, half the atoms of the element radium decay and transform themselves into atoms of another element. It is impossible, however, to know when a particular atom in a lump of radium will undergo this transformation. Scientists can only make accurate predictions about the behavior of an aggregate of radium atoms; the transformation of any given radium atom is the result of random chance rather than of any known physical law. That we cannot predict when a particular radioactive atom will decay calls into question the notion of classical physics that physical nature proceeds in an orderly fashion in accordance with strict laws of cause and effect.

Newtonian physics says that given certain conditions, we can predict what will follow. For example, if an airplane is flying north at 400 miles per hour, we can predict its exact position two hours from now, assuming that the plane does not alter its course or speed. Quantum mechanics teaches that in the subatomic realm, we cannot predict with certainty what will take place; we can only say that given certain conditions, it is *probable* that a certain event will follow. This principle of uncertainty was developed in 1927 by German scientist Werner Heisenberg, who showed that it is impossible to determine at one and the same time both an electron's precise speed and its position. Science writer Alan E. Nourse explains:

[*Heisenberg showed*] *that the very act of attempting to examine an electron any more closely in order to be more certain of where it was and what it was doing at a given instant would itself alter* where the electron was and what it was doing at the instant in question. *Heisenberg, in effect, was saying that in dealing with the behavior of electrons and other elementary particles the laws of cause and effect do not and cannot apply, that all we can do is make predictions about them on the basis of probability and not a very high degree of probability at that. . . . the more certain we try to become about a given electron's position at a given instant, the wider the limits of probability we must accept with regard to what its momentum [speed] is at the same time, and vice versa. The more closely either one property of the electron or the other is examined, the more closely we approach certainty with regard to one property or the other, the more wildly uncertain the other property becomes. And since an electron can really only be fully described in terms of both its position and its momentum at any given instant*, it becomes utterly impossible to describe an electron at all *in terms of absolute certainties. We can describe it only in terms of uncertainties or probabilities.*[19]

In the small-scale world of the electron, we enter a universe of uncertainty, probability, and statistical relationships. No improvement in measurement techniques will dispel this element of chance and provide us with complete knowledge of the universe.

Although Einstein could not accept that a complete comprehension of reality was unattainable, his theory of relativity was instrumental in the shaping of modern physics; it altered classical conceptions of space and time. Newtonian physics had viewed space as a distinct physical reality, a stationary and motionless medium through which light traveled and matter moved. Time was viewed as a fixed and rigid framework that was the same for all observers and existed independently of human experience. For Einstein, however, neither space nor time had an independent existence; neither could be divorced from human experience. Once asked to explain briefly the essentials of relativity, Einstein replied: "It was formerly believed that if all material things disappeared out of the universe, time and space would be left.

Albert Einstein. Einstein was a principal architect of modern physics. Forced to flee Nazi Germany before World War II, he became a United States' citizen. He was appointed to the Institute of Advanced Studies at Princeton, N.J. (*Culver Pictures*)

According to the relativity theory, however, time and space disappear together with the things."[20]

Contrary to all previous thinking, relativity theory holds that time differs for two observers traveling at different speeds. Imagine twin brothers involved in space exploration, one as an astronaut, the other as a rocket designer who never leaves earth. The astronaut takes off in the most advanced space ship yet constructed, one that achieves a speed close to the maximum attainable in our universe—the speed of light. After traveling several trillion miles, the space ship turns around and returns to earth. According to the experience of the ship's occupant, the whole trip took about two years. But when the astronaut lands on earth, he finds totally changed conditions. For one thing, his brother has long since died, for according to earth's

calendars some two hundred years have elapsed since the rocket ship set out on its journey. Such illustration seemed to defy all common sense experience, yet experiments supported Einstein's claims.

Motion, too, is relative. The only way we can describe the motion of one body is to compare it with another moving body. This means that there is no motionless, absolute, fixed frame of reference anywhere in the universe. The following illustration by science writer Isaac Asimov illustrates Einstein's theory of the relativity of motion:

Suppose we on the earth were to observe a strange planet ("Planet X"), exactly like our own in size and mass, go whizzing past us at 163,000 miles per second relative to ourselves. If we could measure its dimensions as it shot past, we would find that it was foreshortened by 50 per cent in the direction of its motion. It would be an ellipsoid rather than a sphere and would, on further measurement, seem to have twice the mass of the earth.

Yet to an inhabitant of Planet X, it would seem that he himself and his own planet were motionless. The earth would seem to be moving past him at 163,000 miles per second, and it would appear to have an ellipsoidal shape and twice the mass of his planet.

One is tempted to ask which planet would really be foreshortened and doubled in mass, but the only possible answer is: that depends on the frame of reference.[21]

In his famous equation, $E = mc^2$, Einstein showed that matter and energy are not separate categories but two different expressions of the same physical entity. The source of energy is matter; and the source of matter is energy. Tiny quantities of matter could be transformed into staggering amounts of energy. The atomic age was dawning.

The discoveries of modern physics transformed the world of classical physics. Whereas nature had been regarded as something outside of the individual—an objective reality that existed independently of ourselves—modern physics teaches that our position in space and time determines what we mean by reality and our very presence affects reality itself. When we observe a particle with our measuring instruments, we are interfering with it, knocking it off its course; we are participating in reality. Nor is nature fully knowable, as the classical physics of Newton had presumed; uncertainty, probability, and even mystery are inherent in the universe.

We have not yet felt the full impact of modern physics, but there is no doubt that it has been part of a revolution in human perceptions. Jacob Bronowski, a student of science and culture concludes:

One aim of the physical sciences has been to give an exact picture of the material world. One achievement of physics in the twentieth century has been to prove that that aim is unattainable. . . . There is no absolute knowledge. . . . All information is imperfect. We have to treat it with humility. That is the human condition; and that is what quantum physics says. . . . The Principle of Uncertainty . . . fixed once and for all the realization that all knowledge is limited.[22]

That we cannot fully comprehend nature must inevitably make us less certain about our theories of human nature, government, history, and morality. That scientists must qualify and avoid absolutes has no doubt made us more cautious and tentative in framing conclusions about the individual and society. Like Darwin's theory of human origins, Freud's theory of human nature, and the transformation of classical space by modern artists, the modifications of the Newtonian picture by modern physicists contributed to the sense of uncertainty and disorientation that characterizes the twentieth century.

The Enlightenment Tradition in Disarray

Most nineteenth-century thinkers carried forward the spirit of the Enlightenment, particularly in its emphasis on science and its concern for individual liberty and social reform. In the tradition of the philosophes, nineteenth-century thinkers regarded science as humanity's greatest achievement and believed that through reason society could be reformed. The spread of parliamentary government and the extension of education, along with the many advances in science and technology, seemed to confirm the hopes of the philosophes in humanity's future progress.

But at the same time, the Enlightenment tradition was being undermined. In the early nineteenth century, the romantics revolted against the Enlightenment's rational-scientific spirit. In the closing decades of the century the Enlightenment tradition was challenged by Social Darwinists who glorified violence and saw conflict between individuals and between nations as a law of nature. A number of thinkers, rejecting the Enlightenment view of people as fundamentally rational, held that subconscious drives and impulses govern human behavior more than reason. These thinkers urged celebrating and glorifying the irrational, which they regarded as the true essence of human beings.

Even theorists who studied the individual and society in a scientific way pointed out that below a surface of rationality lies a substratum of irrationality that constitutes a deeper reality. The conviction was growing that reason was a puny instrument in comparison to the volcanic strength of nonrational impulses, that these impulses pushed people toward destructive behavior and made political life precarious, and that the nonrational did not bend very much to education.

At the beginning of the twentieth century the dominant mood remained that of confidence in Europe's future progress and in the values of European civilization. However, certain disquieting trends were evident that would grow to crisis proportions in succeeding decades. Although few people may have realized it, the Enlightenment tradition was in disarray.

The Enlightenment conceived of an orderly, machine-like universe—of natural law and natural rights operating in the social world, of objective rules that gave form and structure to artistic productions, of the essential rationality and goodness of the individual, and of science and technology as instruments of progress. This coherent world-view which had produced an attitude of certainty, security, and optimism, was in the process of dissolution by the early twentieth century. The common-sense Newtonian picture of the physical universe, with its inexorable laws of cause and effect, was altered; the belief in natural rights and objective standards governing morality was attacked; confidence in human rationality and goodness, the efficacy of science and technology, and the inevitability of human progress were being questioned. Rules and modes of expression that were at the very heart of Western aesthetics were dispensed with.

By the early twentieth century the universe no longer seemed an orderly system, an intelligible whole, but something fundamentally inexplicable. Human nature, too, seemed intrinsically unfathomable and problematic. To the question "Who is man?" Greek philosophers, medieval scholastics, Renaissance humanists, and eighteenth-century philosophes had provided a systematic and intelligible answer. By the early twentieth century, Western intellectuals no longer possessed a clear image of the human being; the individual seemed a stranger unto himself or herself, and life seemed devoid of an overriding purpose. This radical, new disorientation led some intellectuals to feel alienated from and even hostile toward Western civilization. At the beginning of the twentieth century, says Jan Romein, "European man, who only half a century earlier had believed he was about to embrace an almost totally safe existence, and paradoxically enough did so in many ways, found himself before the dark gate of uncertainty."[23]

When the new century began, most Europeans were optimistic about the future, some even holding that European civilization was on the threshhold of a golden age. Few suspected that European civilization would soon be gripped by a crisis that threatened its very survival. The powerful forces of irrationalism that had been celebrated by Nietzsche, analyzed by Freud, and creatively expressed in modernist culture would erupt with devastating fury in twentieth-century political life, particularly in the form of extreme nationalism and racism that glorified violence. Disoriented and disillusioned people searching for new certainties and values would turn to political ideologies that openly rejected reason, lauded war, and scorned the inviolability of the human person. These currents began to form at the end of the nineteenth century, but World War I brought them together into a tidal wave.

World War I accentuated the questioning of established norms and the dissolution of Enlightenment certainties and caused many people to regard Western civilization as dying and beyond recovery. The war not only exacerbated the spiritual crisis of the preceding generation, it also shattered Europe's political and social order and gave birth to totalitarian ideologies that nearly obliterated the legacy of the Enlightenment.

Notes

1. Friedrich Nietzsche, *The Will to Power*, trans. by A. M. Ludovici (New York: Russell & Russell, 1964), vol. 2, sec. 861–862, pp. 297–298.

2. Sigmund Freud, *Civilization and Its Discontents* (New York: Norton, 1961), p. 62.

3. Ibid., p. 58.

4. Ibid.

5. Ibid., p. 59.

6. Ibid., p. 61.

7. Ibid., p. 59.

8. Ibid., p. 69.

9. Irving Howe, ed., *The Idea of the Modern in Literature and the Arts* (New York: Horizon Press, 1967), p. 16.

10. Daniel Bell, *The Cultural Contradictions of*

Capitalism (New York: Basic Books, 1976), p. 110.

11. Quoted in Howe, *The Idea of the Modern*, p. 15.

12. Bell, *The Cultural Contradictions of Capitalism*, pp. 110, 112.

13. Paul Klee, *On Modern Art*, trans. Paul Findlay (London: Faber & Faber, 1948), p. 51.

14. Quoted in Alfred H. Barr, Jr., ed., *Masters of Modern Art* (New York: Museum of Modern Art, 1954), p. 46.

15. Quoted in ibid., p. 47.

16. John Canady, *Mainstreams of Modern Art* (New York: Holt, 1961), p. 458.

17. Quoted in G. H. Hamilton, *Painting and Sculpture, 1880–1940* (Baltimore: Penguin Books, 1967), p. 133.

18. Quoted in Robert Nisbet, *The Social Philosophers* (New York: Crowell, 1973), p. 441.

19. Alan Nourse, *Universe, Earth, and Atom* (New York: Harper & Row, 1969), pp. 554–555, 560.

20. Quoted in A. E. E. McKenzie, *The Major Achievements of Science* (New York: Cambridge University Press, 1960), I, 310.

21. Isaac Asimov, *Asimov's Guide to Science* (New York: Basic Books, 1972), pp. 354–355.

22. Jacob Bronowski, *The Ascent of Man* (Boston: Little, Brown, 1973), p. 353.

23. Jan Romein, *The Watershed of Two Eras*, trans. Arnold J. Pomerans (Middletown, Conn.: Wesleyan University Press, 1978), p. 658.

Suggested Reading

Baumer, Franklin, *Modern European Thought* (1977). A well-informed study of modern thought.

Biddiss, Michael D., *The Age of the Masses* (1977). Useful survey of ideas and society in Europe since 1870.

Bradbury, Malcolm, and James McFarlane, eds., *Modernism, 1890–1930* (1974). Essays on various phases of modernism; valuable bibliography.

Coates, W. H., and H. V. White, *The Ordeal of Liberal Humanism*, vol. 2 (1970). A standard survey of intellectual history since the French Revolution.

Cruickshank, John, ed., *Aspects of the Modern European Mind* (1969). A useful collection of sources in modern intellectual history.

Farrington, Benjamin, *What Darwin Really Said* (1966). A brief study of Darwin's work.

Hamilton, G. H., *Painting and Sculpture in Europe, 1880–1940* (1967). An authoritative study.

Hofstadter, Richard, *Social Darwinism in American Thought* (1955). A classic treatment of the impact of evolution on American conservatism, imperialism, and racism.

Hughes, H. Stuart, *Consciousness and Society* (1958). An excellent survey of thought from the 1890s to 1930.

Kaufmann, Walter, *Nietzsche* (1956). An excellent analysis of Nietzsche's thought.

Masur, Gerhard, *Prophets of Yesterday* (1961). Studies in European Culture, 1890–1914.

Monaco, Paul, *Modern European Culture and Consciousness, 1870–1980* (1983). A useful survey.

Nelson, Benjamin, ed., *Freud and the Twentieth Century* (1957). A valuable collection of essays.

Rieff, Philip, *Freud: The Mind of the Moralist* (1961). A well-informed study of Freud's thought and influence.

Roazen, Paul, *Freud's Political and Social Thought* (1968). The wider implications of Freudian psychology.

Stromberg, Roland N., *An Intellectual History of Modern Europe* (1975). A fine text.

Zeitlin, I. M., *Ideology and the Development of Sociological Theory* (1968). Examines in detail the thought of major shapers of sociological theory.

Review Questions

1. What were Nietzsche's attitudes toward Christianity and democracy?

2. What was the significance of Nietzsche's thought?

3. How did Bergson reflect the growing irrationalism of the ages?

4. How did Sorel show the political potential of the nonrational?

5. In what way was Freud a child of the Enlightenment? How did he differ from the Philosophes?

6. What were the standards of aesthetics that had governed Western literature and art since the Renaissance? How did the modernist movement break with these standards?

7. For Durkheim, what constituted the crisis of modern society? How did he attempt to cope with crisis?

8. What do you think of Pareto's judgment that the masses in a democratic state are not really influenced by rational argument?

9. For Weber, what was the terrible paradox of reason?

10. Describe the view of the universe held by Westerners about 1880. How was this view altered by modern physics? What is the significance of this revolution in our perception of the universe?

11. In what ways was the Enlightenment tradition in disarray by the early years of the twentieth century?

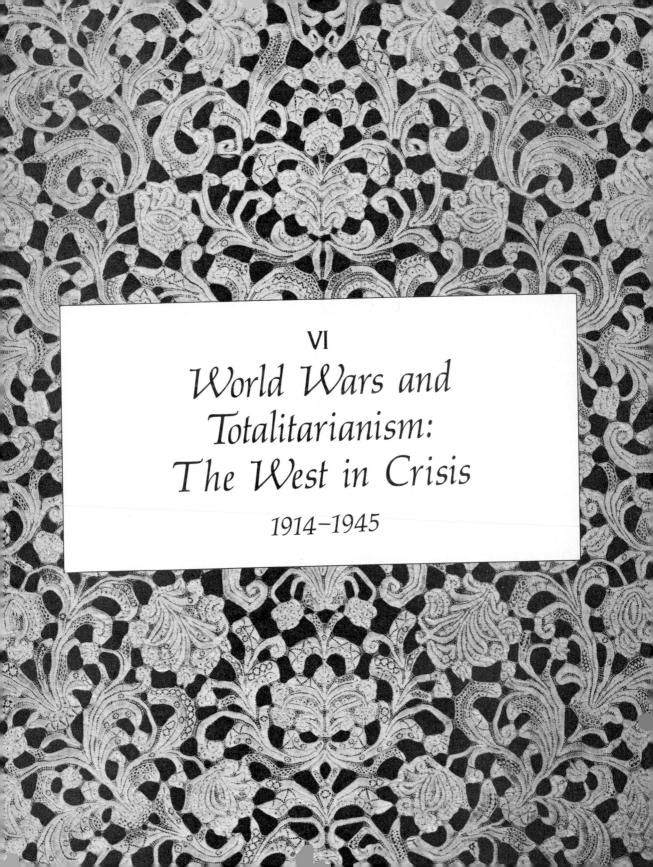

VI

*World Wars and
Totalitarianism:
The West in Crisis*

1914–1945

29

The Road to World War I:
Failure of the European
State System

*P*rior to 1914 the dominant mood in Europe was one of pride in the accomplishments of Western civilization and confidence in its future progress. Advances in science and technology, the rising standard of living, the spread of democratic institutions, the expansion of social reform, the increase in literacy for the masses, Europe's position of power in the world—all contributed to a sense of optimism. Other reasons for optimism were that since the defeat of Napoleon, Europe had avoided a general war, and since the Franco-Prussian War (1870–71), the Great Powers had not fought each other. Reflecting on the world he knew before World War I, Arnold Toynbee recalled that his generation

expected that life throughout the World would become more rational, more humane, and more democratic and that, slowly, but surely, political democracy would produce greater social justice. We had also expected that the progress of science and technology would make mankind richer, and that this increasing wealth would gradually spread from a minority to a majority. We had expected that all this would happen peacefully. In fact we thought that mankind's course was set for an earthly paradise, and that our approach towards this goal was predestined for us by historical necessity.[1]

Few people recognized that the West's outward achievements masked an inner turbulence that was propelling Western civilization toward a cataclysm. The European state system was failing. In the early nineteenth century, liberals had believed that redrawing the political map of Europe on the basis of nationality would promote peaceful relations among states. But quite the reverse occurred. By 1914, national states, answering to no higher power, were fueled by an explosive nationalism and were grouped into alliances that faced each other with ever-mounting hostility. Nationalist passions, overheated by the popular press and expansionist societies, poisoned international relations. Nationalist thinkers propagated pseudoscientific racial and Social Darwinist doctrines that glorified conflict and justified the subjugation of other peoples. Committed to enhancing national power, statesmen lost sight of Europe as a community of nations sharing a common civilization. Caution and restraint gave way to belligerency in foreign relations.

The failure of the European state system was paralleled by a cultural crisis. Some European intellectuals attacked the rational tradition of the Enlightenment and celebrated the primitive, the instinctual, and the irrational. Increasingly, young people grew attracted to philosophies of action that ridiculed liberal bourgeois values and viewed war as a purifying and ennobling experience. Colonial wars, colorfully portrayed in the popular press, ignited the imagination of bored factory workers and daydreaming students and reinforced a sense of duty and an urge for gallantry among soldiers and aristocrats. These "splendid" little colonial wars helped fashion an attitude that made war acceptable, if not laudable. Yearning to break loose from their ordinary lives and to embrace heroic values, many Europeans regarded violent conflict as the highest expression of individual and national life. "Even if we end in ruin it was beautiful," exclaimed General Erich von Falkenhayn, the future Chief of the German General Staff, at the outbreak of World War I.[2] Although technology was making warfare more brutal and dangerous, Europe retained a romantic illusion about combat.

While Europe was seemingly progressing in the art of civilization, the mythic power of nationalism and the primitive appeal of conflict were driving European civilization to the abyss. Few people recognized the potential crisis—certainly not the statesmen whose reckless blundering allowed the Continent to stumble into war.

Aggravated Nationalist Tensions in Austria-Hungary

On June 28, 1914, a young terrorist with the support of The Black Hand, a secret Ser-

bian nationalist society, murdered Archduke Francis Ferdinand, heir to the throne of Austria-Hungary. Six weeks later the armies of Europe were on the march; an incident in the Balkans had sparked a world war. An analysis of why Austria-Hungary felt compelled to attack Serbia, and why the other powers became enmeshed in the conflict, shows how explosive Europe was in 1914. And nowhere were conditions more volatile than in Austria-Hungary, the scene of the assassination.

With its several nationalities, each with its own national history and traditions and often conflicting aspirations, Austria-Hungary stood in opposition to nationalism, the most powerful spiritual force of the age. Perhaps the supranational Austro-Hungarian Empire was obsolete in a world of states based on the principle of nationality. Dominated by Germans and Hungarians, the empire remained unable to either satisfy the grievances or contain the nationalist aims of its minorities, particularly the Czechs and South Slavs (Croats, Slovenes, Serbs).

Austria-Hungary's failure to solve its minority problems had significant repercussions for international relations. The more moderate leaders of the ethnic minorities did not call for secession from the empire. Nevertheless, heightened agitation among the several nationalities, which worsened in the decade before 1914, created terrible anxieties among Austrian leaders. The fear that the empire would be torn apart by rebellion caused Austria to pursue a more forceful policy against any nation that fanned the nationalist feelings of its Slavic minorities. In particular, this policy meant worsening tensions between Austria and small Serbia, which had been independent of the Ottoman Empire since 1878.

Captivated by Western ideas of nationalism, the Serbs sought to create a Greater Serbia by uniting with their racial kin, the South Slavs who dwelt in Austria-Hungary. Since some 7 million South Slavs lived in the Hapsburg Empire, the dream of a Greater Serbia, shrilly expressed by Serbian nationalists, caused nightmares in Austria. Austrian leaders feared that continued Serbian agitation would encourage the South Slavs to press for secession. Regarding Serbia as a grave threat to Austria's existence, such leaders as Foreign Minister Count Leopold von Berchtold and Field Marshal Franz Conrad von Hötzendorf urged the destruction of the Serbian menace.

Another irritant to Austria-Hungary was Russian Pan-Slavism, which called for the solidarity of Russians with their Slavic cousins in eastern Europe—Poles, Czechs, Slovaks, South Slavs, and Bulgarians. Pan-Slavism was based on a mystic conception of the superiority of Slavic civilization to Western civilization and of Russia's special historic mission to liberate its kin from Austrian and Turkish rule. Although Russian Pan-Slavs were few and did not dictate foreign policy, they constituted a significant pressure group. Moreover, their provocative and semireligious proclamations frightened Austria-Hungary, which did not draw a sharp line between Pan-Slavic aspirations and official Russian policy.

The tensions arising out of the multinational character of the Austro-Hungarian Empire in an age of heightened nationalist feeling set off the explosion in 1914. Unable to solve its minority problems and fearful of Pan-Slavism and Pan-Serbism, Austria-Hungary felt itself in a life-or-death situation. This sense of desperation led it to lash out at Serbia after the assassination of Archduke Francis Ferdinand.

The German System of Alliances

The war might have been avoided, however, or might have remained limited to Austria and Serbia had Europe in 1914 not been divided into two hostile alliance systems. Such a situation contains inherent dangers. For example, knowing that it has the support of allies, a country might pursue a more provocative and reckless course and be less conciliatory during a crisis. Second, a conflict

between two states might spark a chain reaction that would draw in the other powers, thereby transforming a limited war into a general war. This course is precisely what followed the assassination. The origins of this dangerous alliance system go back to Bismarck and the Franco-Prussian War.

The New German Nation

The unification of Germany in 1870–71 turned the new state into an international power of the first rank, upsetting the balance of power in Europe. For the first time since the wars of the French Revolution, a nation was in a position to dominate the European continent. How a united and powerful Germany would fit into European life was the crucial problem in the decades following the Franco-Prussian War.

To German nationalists, the unification of Germany was both the fulfillment of a national dream and the starting point for an even more ambitious goal—the extension of German power in Europe and the world. As the nineteenth century drew to a close, German nationalism grew more extreme. Believing that Germany must either grow or die, nationalists pressed the government to build a powerful navy, acquire colonies, gain a much greater share of the world's markets, and expand German interests and influence in Europe. Sometimes these goals were expressed in the language of Social Darwinism—nations are engaged in an eternal struggle for survival and domination.

The Pan-German Association, which included among its members some prominent intellectuals, journalists, and politicians, preached the special destiny of the German race and advocated German expansion in Europe and overseas. Pan-Germans probably had less power than Russian Pan-Slavs. Nevertheless, like their Pan-Slav counterparts, they engaged in shrill propaganda, included people of influence, and frightened observers in other countries. Decisive victories against Austria (1866) and France (1871), the formation of the German Reich, rapid industrialization, and the impressive achievements of German science and scholarship had molded a powerful and dynamic nation. Imbued with great expectations for the future, Germans became increasingly impatient to see the fatherland gain its "rightful" place in world affairs—an attitude that frightened non-Germans.

Bismarck's Goals

Under Bismarck, who did not seek additional territory but wanted only to preserve the recently achieved unification, Germany pursued a moderate and cautious foreign policy. One of Bismarck's principal goals was to keep France isolated and friendless. France suffered deep humiliation as a result of its defeat in the Franco-Prussian War. Prussia's quick and decisive victory shocked the French, who had entered the war brimming with confidence. Compounding French humiliation was the loss of Alsace and Lorraine to Germany. Victor Hugo expressed the "sacred anger" of the French: "France will have but one thought: to reconstitute her forces, gather her energy . . . raise her young generation to form an army of the whole people . . . to become again a great France, the France of 1792, the France of an idea with a sword. Then one day she will be irresistible. Then she will take back Alsace-Lorraine."[3] While French nationalists yearned for a war of revenge against Germany, the government, aware of Germany's strength, was unlikely to initiate such a conflict. Still, the issue of Alsace-Lorraine increased tensions between France and Germany. Germany's annexation of the French provinces proved to be a serious blunder, for it precluded any reconciliation between the two countries.

Bismarck also hoped to prevent a war between Russia and Austria-Hungary, for such a conflict could lead to German involvement, to the breakup of Austria-Hungary, and to Russian expansion in eastern Europe. To maintain peace and Germany's existing borders, Bismarck forged complex alliances. In the decade of the 1880s Bismarck created the Triple Alliance—consisting of Germany, Austria-Hungary, and Italy—and an alliance with Russia.

There was one major weakness to Germany's alliance system: Austria and Russia were potential enemies. Austria feared Russian ambitions in the Balkans and felt threatened by Russian Pan-Slavs. Bismarck knew that an alliance with Austria was essentially incompatible with Germany's treaty obligations to Russia, but he hoped that the arrangement would enable him to exercise a moderating influence over both eastern powers, thereby forestalling a war that would upset the status quo. An additional reason for the treaty with Russia was that it denied France a valuable ally.

Bismarck conducted foreign policy with restraint. He formed alliances not to conquer new lands but to protect Germany from aggression from either France or Russia, not to launch war but to preserve order and stability in Europe. In 1888, a new emperor ascended the German throne; when the young Kaiser William II (1888–1918) clashed with his aging prime minister, Bismarck was forced to resign (1890). Lacking Bismarck's diplomatic skills, his cool restraint, and his determination to keep peace in Europe, the new German leaders would pursue a belligerent and imperialistic foreign policy in the following decades that would frighten other states, particularly Britain. Whereas Bismarck considered Germany a satiated power, these men insisted that Germany must have its place in the sun.

The first act of the new leadership was to permit the treaty with Russia to lapse, thereby allowing Germany to give full support to Austria, which was considered a more reliable ally. Whereas Bismarck had warned Austria to act with moderation and caution in the Balkans, his successors not only failed to hold Austria in check but actually encouraged Austrian aggression. This proved fatal to the peace of Europe.

Map 29.1 Ethnic Groups in Germany, Austria, and the Balkans Before World War I ▶

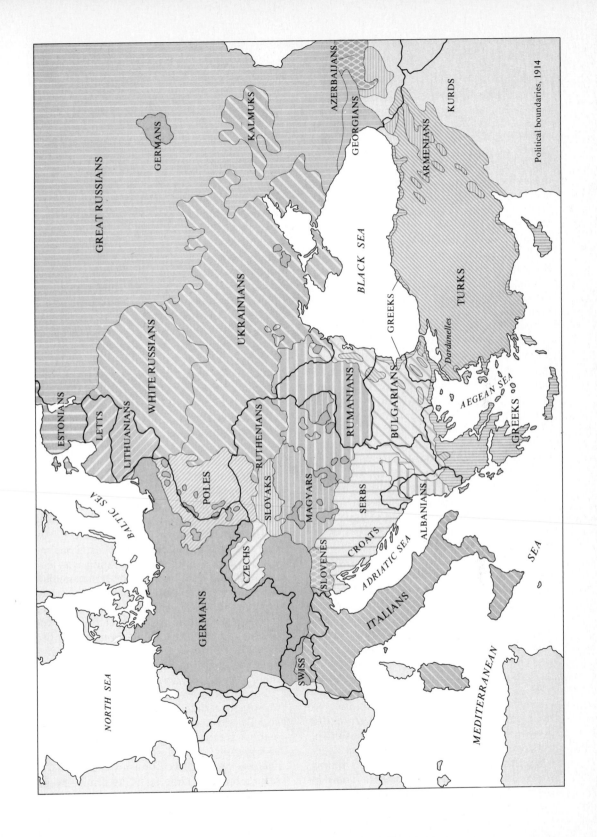

NORTH SEA

BALTIC SEA

GREAT RUSSIANS

GERMANS

KALMUKS

AZERBAIJANS

GEORGIANS

ARMENIANS

KURDS

Political boundaries, 1914

ESTONIANS

LETTS

LITHUANIANS

WHITE RUSSIANS

UKRAINIANS

BLACK SEA

TURKS

POLES

RUTHENIANS

SLOVAKS

MAGYARS

RUMANIANS

BULGARIANS

GREEKS

Dardanelles

AEGEAN SEA

GREEKS

CZECHS

SLOVENES

CROATS

SERBS

ALBANIANS

GERMANS

SWISS

ITALIANS

ADRIATIC SEA

SEA

MEDITERRANEAN

The Triple Entente

Fear of Germany

When Germany broke with Russia in 1890, France was quick to take advantage of the situation. Frightened by Germany's increasing military strength, expanding industries, growing population, and alliance with Austria and Italy, France eagerly coveted Russia as an ally. The French government urged its bankers to invest in Russia, supplied weapons to the tsar, and arranged for the French and Russian fleets to exchange visits. In 1894, France and Russia entered into an alliance; the isolation forced on France by Bismarck had ended.

Like France and Russia, Great Britain was alarmed by Germany's growing military might. Furthermore, because of its spectacular industrial growth, Germany had become a potent trade rival of England. Britain was also distressed by Germany's increased efforts to become a great colonial power—a goal demanded by German nationalists. But most alarming was Germany's decision to build a great navy, for it could interfere with British overseas trade or even blockade the British Isles. Germany's naval program was the single most important reason that Britain moved closer first to France and then to Russia. Germany's naval construction, designed to increase its stature as a Great Power but not really necessary for its security, was one indication that German leaders had abandoned Bismarck's policy of good sense. Eager to add the British as an ally and demonstrating superb diplomatic skill, France moved to end long-standing colonial disputes with Britain. The Entente Cordiale of 1904 accomplished this conciliation. England had emerged from its self-imposed splendid isolation.

The Franco-British understanding increased German anxiety, but Germany also doubted that France and England, who had almost gone to war in 1898 over regions in the Sudan, had overcome their deep animosities. Consequently, Chancellor Bernhard von Bülow (1849–1929) decided to provoke a crisis in Morocco that would test the Anglo-French Entente Cordiale. Von Bülow chose Morocco because earlier the British had resisted French imperialist designs there. He prodded a reluctant Kaiser William II to visit the Moroccan port of Tangier, a sign that Germany would support the Moroccan sultan against France; von Bülow had his crisis. In January 1906, a conference was held in Algeciras, Spain, to resolve it; the outcome was a defeat for Germany, for Britain sided with France, which was given special rights in Morocco. Germany's efforts to disrupt the Anglo-French Entente Cordiale had failed; the two former enemies had demonstrated their solidarity.

Eager to erect a strong alliance to counter Germany's Triple Alliance, French diplomats now sought to ease tensions between their Russian ally and their new British friend. Two events convinced Russia to adopt a more conciliatory attitude toward Britain: a disastrous and unexpected defeat in the Russo-Japanese War of 1904–1905 and a working-class revolution in 1905. Shocked by defeat, its army bordering on disintegration, its workers restive, Russia was now receptive to settling its imperial disputes with Britain over Persia, Tibet, and Afghanistan, a decision encouraged by France. In the Anglo-Russian Entente of 1907, as in the Anglo-French Entente Cordiale of 1904, the former rivals conducted themselves in a conciliatory if not friendly manner. In both instances, what engendered this spirit of cooperation was fear of Germany; both agreements represented a triumph for French diplomacy. The Triple Entente, however, was not a firm alliance, for there was no certainty that Britain, traditionally reluctant to send its troops to the Continent, would give any more than diplomatic support to France and Russia in case there was a showdown with Germany.

Europe was now broken into two hostile camps: the Triple Entente of France, Russia, and Britain and the Triple Alliance of Germany, Austria-Hungary, and Italy. Serving to increase fear and suspicion between the alliances was the costly arms race and the maintenance of large standing armies by all the states except Britain.

German Reactions

Germany denounced the Triple Entente as a hostile anti-German coalition designed to encircle and crush Germany. If Germany were to survive, it must break this ring. In the past, German arms had achieved unification; German military might would also end this threat to the fatherland. Considering Austria-Hungary as its only reliable ally, Germany resolved to preserve the power and dignity of the Hapsburg Empire. If Austria-Hungary fell from the ranks of Great Powers, Germany would have to stand alone against its enemies. At all costs Austria-Hungary must not be weakened.

But this assessment suffered from dangerous miscalculations. First, Germany overstressed the hostile nature of the Triple Entente. In reality, France, Russia, and Britain drew closer together not to wage aggressive war against Germany but to protect themselves against burgeoning German military, industrial, and diplomatic power. Second, by linking German security to Austria, Germany greatly increased the chance of war. Becoming increasingly fearful of Pan-Serbism and Pan-Slavism, Austria might well decide that only a war could prevent its empire from disintegrating. Confident of German support, Austria would be more likely to resort to force; fearful of any diminution of Austrian power, Germany would be more likely to give Austria that support. Unlike Bismarck, the new leadership did not think in terms of restraining Austria but of strengthening it, by war if necessary.

The Drift Toward War

The Bosnian Crisis

After 1908, several crises tested the competing alliances, pushing Europe closer to war. Particularly significant was the Bosnian affair, for it contained many of the ingredients that eventually ignited the war in 1914. The humiliating defeat by Japan in 1905 had dimin-

Nicholas II and His Family. Had he been only head of a family rather than the tsar of Russia, Nicholas and his family might have ended their days peacefully, rather than tragically. Russia's full, rather than partial, military mobilization after the assassination of Archduke Francis Ferdinand helped to turn a limited war between Austria-Hungary and Serbia into a full European war. (*BBC Hulton Picture Library/Bettmann Archive*)

ished Russia's stature as a Great Power, and the abortive revolution in the same year had weakened the government's authority at home. The new Russian foreign minister, Alexander Izvolsky, hoped to gain a diplomatic triumph by compelling Turkey to allow Russian warships to pass through the Dardanelles, fulfilling a centuries-old dream of extending Russian power into the Mediterranean. Izvolsky hoped that England and France, traditional opponents of Russia's Mediterranean ambitions but now Russia's allies, would not block the move. But certainly Austria would regard it as a hostile act.

Like Izvolsky, Baron Lexa von Aehrenthal, the new Austrian foreign minister, sought to restore his country's flagging prestige. The goals of both foreign ministers made an agreement possible. In particular, Aehrenthal desired the annexation of the provinces of Bosnia and Herzegovina. Officially a part of the Ottoman Empire, these provinces had been administered by Austria-Hungary since 1878. The population consisted mainly of ethnic cousins of the Serbs. A formal annexation would certainly infuriate the Serbs, who hoped one day to make the region part of a Greater Serbia. Russia and Austria made a deal. Russia would permit Austrian annexation of Bosnia and Herzegovina, and Austria would support Russia's move to open the Dardanelles. In 1908 Austria proceeded to annex the provinces, but Russia met stiff resistance from England and France when it presented its case for opening the Straits to Russian warships.

Austria had gained a diplomatic victory, while Russia suffered another humiliation. Even more enraged than Russia was Serbia, which threatened to invade Bosnia to liberate its cousins from Austrian oppression. The Serbian press openly declared that Austria-Hungary must perish if the South Slavs were to achieve liberty and unity. A fiery attitude also prevailed in Vienna—Austria-Hungary could not survive unless Serbia was destroyed. One Austrian newspaper that often reflected official thinking declared: "The hour has struck. War is inevitable . . . Our blood throbs in our veins, we strain at the leash. Sire! Give us the signal."

During this period of intense hostility between Austria-Hungary and Serbia, Germany supported its Austrian ally. To keep Austria strong, Germany would even agree to the dismemberment of Serbia and to its incorporation into Austria. As a result of this crisis, Austria and Germany coordinated battle plans in case a conflict between Austria and Serbia involved Russia and France. Unlike Bismarck, who tried to hold Austria in check, German leadership now coolly envisioned an Austrian attack on Serbia, and just as coolly offered German support if Russia intervened.

Balkan Wars

The Bosnian crisis pushed Germany and Austria closer together, brought relations between Austria and Serbia to the breaking point, and inflicted another humiliation on Russia. The first Balkan War (1912) continued these trends. The Balkan states of Montenegro, Serbia, Bulgaria, and Greece attacked a dying Ottoman Empire. In a brief campaign, the Balkan armies captured the Turkish empire's European territory, with the exception of Constantinople. Because it was on the victorious side, landlocked Serbia gained the Albanian coast, which gave it a long-desired outlet to the sea. Austria was determined to keep its enemy from reaping this reward, and Germany, as in the Bosnian crisis, supported its ally. Unable to secure Russian support, an enraged Serbia was forced to surrender the territory, which became the state of Albania.

Thus, during a five-year period, Austria-Hungary inflicted on Serbia two terrible humiliations. Russia shared these humiliations, for it had twice failed to help its small Slavic friend. Incensed Serbian nationalists accelerated their campaign of propaganda and terrorism against Austria. Believing that another humiliation would irreparably damage its prestige, Russia vowed to back Serbia in its next confrontation with Austria. And Austria had reached the end of its patience with Serbia. Emboldened by German encouragement, Austria would end the Serbian threat once and for all. Thus the ingredients for war between Austria and Serbia, a war that might easily draw in Russia and Germany, were present. Another incident might well start a war; it came on June 28, 1914.

Assassination of Francis Ferdinand

Archduke Francis Ferdinand (1863–1914), heir to the throne of Austria, was sympathetic to the grievances of the South Slavs and favored a policy that would place the Slavs on an equal footing with Hungarians and Germans within the Hapsburg Empire. If such a policy succeeded, it could soothe the feelings of the Austrian Slavs and reduce the appeal of a Greater Serbia, the aim of The Black Hand.

On June 28, 1914, Francis Ferdinand was assassinated while making a state visit to Sarajevo, capital of Bosnia. Young Gavrilo Princip, part of a team of Bosnian terrorists, fired two shots at close range into the arch-duke's car. Francis Ferdinand and his wife died within fifteen minutes. The conspiracy was organized by Dragutin Dimitrijevic, chief of intelligence of the Serbian army, who was linked to The Black Hand.* By killing the archduke, the terrorists hoped to bring to a boiling point tensions within the Hapsburg Empire and to prepare the way for revolution.

Feeling that Austria's prestige as a Great Power, and indeed its very survival as a su-pranational empire, were at stake, key offi-cials, led by the foreign minister, Count Leo-pold von Berchtold, decided to use the assassination as a pretext to crush Serbia. For many years leaders of Austria had yearned for war with Serbia in order to end the ag-itation for the union of the South Slavs. Now, they reasoned, the hour had struck. But war with Serbia would require the approval of Germany. Believing that Austria was Ger-many's only reliable ally and that a diminution of Austrian power and prestige threatened German security, German statesmen decided to support Austria. Rather than urging a peaceful settlement of the issue they en-couraged their ally to take up arms against Serbia. Germany and Austria wanted a quick strike to overwhelm Serbia before other countries were drawn in.

Map 29.2 The Balkans, 1914

Germany Encourages Austria

Confident of German backing, on July 23 Austria presented Serbia with an ultimatum and demanded a response within forty-eight hours. The terms of the ultimatum were so harsh that it was next to impossible for Serbia to accept them. This reaction was the one that Austria intended, as it sought a military solution to the crisis rather than a diplomatic one. But Russia would not remain indifferent to an Austro-German effort to liquidate Serbia. Russia feared that an Austrian conquest of Serbia was just the first step in an Austro-German plan to dominate the Balkans. Such an extension of German and Austrian power in a region bordering Russia was unthinkable to the tsar's government. Moreover, after suffering repeated reverses in foreign affairs, Russia would not tolerate another humiliation. As Germany had resolved to back its Austrian ally, Russia determined not to abandon Serbia.

Serbia responded to Austria's ultimatum in a conciliatory manner, agreeing to virtually all Austria's demands. But Serbia would not

---

*Serbia's prime minister, Nikola Pašić, learned of the plot and through the Serbian envoy in Vienna tried to get Austria to cancel Francis Ferdinand's visit. The Austrians, however, were not told of a specific as-sassination attempt for Pašić did not want to admit that such an act of terrorism was being plotted on Serbian soil.

The Assassins of the Archduke Francis Ferdinand and His Wife Being Captured in Sarajevo, June 28, 1914. The assassination of the archduke and his wife was the spark that ignited World War I. The adversaries looked forward to a short, decisive conflict. Emotions ran high with visions of gallantry. Only a few foresaw the collapse of a Western ideal: a world ruled by reason and morality. (*The Granger Collection*)

allow Austrian officials into Serbia to investigate the assassination. Having already decided against a peaceful settlement, Austria insisted that Serbia's failure to accept one provision meant that the entire ultimatum had been rejected and ordered mobilization of the Austrian army.

This was a crucial moment for Germany. Would it continue to support Austria, knowing that an Austrian attack on Serbia would most likely bring Russia into the conflict? Determined not to desert Austria and believing that a showdown with Russia was inevitable anyway, the German war party continued to urge Austrian action against Serbia. They argued that it was better to fight Russia in 1914 than a few years later when the tsar's empire would be stronger. Confident of the superiority of the German army, the war party held that Germany could defeat both Russia and France, that Britain's army was too weak to make a difference, and that,

in any case, Britain might remain neutral. While Germany would have preferred a limited war involving only Austria and Serbia, it was not dismayed by the idea of a general war. Indeed, some military leaders and statesmen were exhilarated by the prospect of a war with Russia and France. The defeat of Germany's enemies would break the ring of encirclement, would increase German territory, and would establish Germany as the foremost power in the world.

On July 24–25 Russia took preliminary steps toward mobilizing against Austria. Russia felt compelled to act immediately because its vast size, inadequate transportation system, and inefficient bureaucracy were major obstacles to effective mobilization. On July 28, 1914, Austria declared war on Serbia; Russia, with the assurance of French support, proclaimed partial mobilization aimed at Austria alone. But the military warned that partial mobilization would throw the slow-moving Russian war machine into total confusion if the order had to be changed suddenly to full mobilization. Moreover, the only plans the Russian general staff had drawn up called for full mobilization, that is, for war against both Austria and Germany. The tsar, pressured by his generals, gave the order for mobilization on July 30. Russian forces would be arrayed against Germany as well as Austria.

Thus the prevailing military theory worked against peace. Germany could not allow Russia the advantage of mobilizing first. Battle plans, worked out years in advance, required the mobilization of huge numbers of soldiers and were geared to tight railroad timetables. Because the country that struck first had the advantage of fighting according to its own plans rather than having to improvise in response to the enemy's attack, generals regarded mobilization by the enemy as an act of war. Therefore, when Russia refused a German warning to halt mobilization, Germany, on August 1, ordered a general mobilization and declared war on Russia. Two days later Germany also declared war on France, believing that France would most likely support its Russian ally. Moreover, German battle plans were based on a war with both Russia and France. Thus a war between Germany and Russia automatically meant a German attack on France.

When Belgium refused to allow German troops to march through Belgian territory into France, Germany invaded the small nation, which brought Britain, pledged to guarantee Belgian neutrality, into the war. Britain could never tolerate German troops directly across the English Channel in any case, nor could it brook German mastery of western Europe. A century before, Britain had fought Napoleon to prevent France from becoming master of Europe. In 1914 it would fight Germany for the same reason. Moreover, British and French military and naval commands had entered into joint planning that linked the two powers closer together. If France were attacked, it would be unlikely that Britain would remain neutral.

Responsibility

The question of whether any one power was mainly responsible for the war has intrigued historians. In assessing blame, historians have been principally concerned with Germany's role. German historian Fritz Fischer argues that Germany's ambition to dominate Europe was the underlying cause of the war. Germany encouraged Austria to strike at Serbia knowing that an attack on Serbia could mean war with Russia and its French ally. Believing that it had the military advantage, Germany was willing to risk such a war. "As Germany willed and coveted the Austro-Serbian war and, in her confidence in her military superiority, deliberately faced the risk of a conflict with Russia and France, her leaders must bear a substantial share of the historical responsibility for the outbreak of general war in 1914."[4]

Attracted by Social Darwinist and militarist doctrines, continues Fischer, Germany aimed to become the foremost economic and political power in Europe and to play a far greater role in world politics; to achieve this goal Germany was willing to go to war. Critics of Fischer point out that other nations, not merely Germany, were enthralled by Social Darwinism and militarism, that this was not a particularly German mode of thinking but part of a general European sickness. They argue further that Germany would have preferred a limited war between Austria and Serbia and in 1914 had no plans to dominate Europe.

The other powers have also come in for a share of the blame. Austria bears responsibility for its determination to crush Serbia and its insistence on avoiding a negotiated settlement. Serbia's responsibility stems from pursuing an aggressive Pan-Serbian policy that set it on a collision course with Austria-Hungary. In 1913 Sir Fairfax Cartwright, the British ambassador to Vienna, warned: "Serbia will some day set Europe by the ears, and bring about a universal war on the Continent. I cannot tell you how exasperated people are getting here at the continual worry which that little country causes to Austria."[5] Russia bears responsibility for instituting general mobilization, thereby turning a limited war between Austria-Hungary and Serbia into a European war; France for failing to restrain Russia and indeed for encouraging its ally to mobilize; and England for failing to make clear that it would support its allies, for had Germany seen plainly that Britain would intervene, it might have been more cautious.

Other historians, dismissing the question of responsibility, regard the war as an obvious sign that European civilization was in deep trouble. Viewed in the broad perspective of European history, the war marked a culmination of dangerous forces in European life: the glorification of power; the fascination for violence; the celebration of the nonrational; the diminishing confidence in the capacity of reason to solve the problems created by the Industrial Revolution; the general dissatisfaction and disillusionment with bourgeois society; the alliance system; and above all, the explosive nationalism.

War as Celebration

When war was certain, an extraordinary phenomenon occurred. Crowds gathered in capital cities and expressed their loyalty to the fatherland and their readiness to fight. Even socialists, whose loyalty was supposed to be given to an international movement, devoted themselves to their respective nations. It seemed as if people wanted violence for its own sake. It was as if war provided an escape from the dull routine of classroom, job, and home; from the emptiness, drabness, mediocrity, and pointlessness of bourgeois society; from "a world grown old and cold and weary," said Rupert Brooke, a young British poet.[6] To some, war was a "beautiful . . . sacred moment" that satisfied an "ethical yearning."[7] But more significantly, the outpouring of patriotic sentiments demonstrated the immense power that nationalism exercised over the European mind. With ex-

traordinary success, nationalism welded millions of people into a collectivity ready to devote body and soul to the nation, especially during its hour of need.

In Paris, men marched down the boulevards singing the stirring words of the French national anthem, the "Marseillaise," while women showered young soldiers with flowers. "Young and old, civilians and military men burned with the same excitement. . . . Beginning the next day, thousands of men eager to fight would jostle one another outside recruiting offices, waiting to join up. . . . The word 'duty' had a meaning for them, and the word 'country' had regained its splendor."[8] Similar scenes occurred in Berlin. "It is a joy to be alive," editorialized one newspaper. "We wished so much for this hour. . . . The sword which has been forced into our hand will not be sheathed until our aims are won and our territory extended as far as necessity demands."[9]

Soldiers bound for battle acted as if they were going off on a great adventure. "My dear ones, be proud that you live in such a time and in such a nation and that you . . . have the privilege of sending those you love into so glorious a battle," wrote a young German law student to his family.[10] The young warriors yearned to do something noble and altruistic, to win glory, and to experience life at its most intense moments.

Many of Europe's most distinguished intellectuals were also captivated by the martial mood, sharing Rupert Brooke's sentiments: "Now God be thanked Who has matched us with His hour,/And caught our youth, and wakened us from sleeping."[11] To the prominent German historian, Friedrich Meinecke, August 1914 was "one of the great moments of my life which suddenly filled my soul with the deepest confidence in our people and the profoundest joy."[12] Besides being gripped by a thirst for excitement and a quest for the heroic, some intellectuals welcomed the war because it unified the nation in a spirit of fraternity and self-sacrifice. It was a return, some felt, to the organic roots of human existence, a way of overcoming a sense of in-

Troops Leaving Berlin, 1914. "The sword has been forced into our hand," said Germans at the outbreak of war. German troops mobilized eagerly and effi- ciently; here a trainload is leaving for the western front. (*Historical Pictures Service, Chicago*)

dividual isolation. To some intellectuals the war would spiritually regenerate European society. It would resurrect glory, nobility, and heroism; it would awaken a spirit of self-sacrifice and give life an overriding purpose; it would rid the nation of wickedness, selfishness, and hypocrisy and cleanse Europe of its spiritual and racial impurities. From the war would emerge a higher civilization, morally reborn.

But it must be emphasized that the soldiers who went off to war singing and the statesmen and generals who welcomed war or did not try hard enough to prevent it expected a short, decisive, gallant conflict. Virtually no one envisioned what the First World War turned out to be—four years of frightful, barbaric, indecisive, senseless bloodletting. But although their gloomy words were drowned out by the cheers of chauvinists and fools, there were prophets who realized that Europe was stumbling into darkness. "The lamps are going out all over Europe," said British Foreign Secretary Edward Grey. "We shall never see them lit again in our lifetime."

Notes

1. Arnold Toynbee, *Surviving the Future* (New York: Oxford University Press, 1971), pp. 106–107.

2. Quoted in James Joll, "The Unspoken Assumptions," in H. W. Koch, ed., *The Origins of the First World War* (New York: Taplinger, 1972), p. 325.

3. Quoted in Barbara Tuchman, *The Guns of August* (New York: Macmillan, 1962), pp. 46–47.

4. Fritz Fischer, *Germany's Aims in the First World War* (New York: W. W. Norton, 1967), p. 88.

5. Quoted in Joachim Remak, *The Origins of World War I* (New York: Holt, 1967), p. 135.

6. From "Peace," in *Collected Poems of Rupert Brooke* (New York: Dodd, Mead, 1941), p. 111.

7. Quoted in Joachim C. Fest, *Hitler* (New York: Harcourt Brace Jovanovich, 1973), p. 66.

8. George A. Panichas, ed., *Promise of Greatness* (New York: John Day, 1968), pp. 14–15.

9. Quoted in Tuchman, *The Guns of August*, p. 145.

10. Quoted in Robert G. L. Waite, *Vanguard of Nazism* (New York: W. W. Norton, 1969), p. 22.

11. From "Peace," in *Collected Poems of Rupert Brooke*, p. 111.

12. Quoted in Koch, *The Origins of the First World War*, p. 318.

Suggested Reading

Berghahn, V. R., *Germany and the Approach of War in 1914* (1975). Relates German foreign policy to domestic problems.

Fay, Sidney, *The Origins of the World War*, 2 vols. (1966). A comprehensive study of the underlying and immediate causes of the war; first published in 1928.

Fischer, Fritz, *Germany's Aims in the First World War* (1967). A controversial work, stressing Germany's responsibility for the war.

Geiss, Imanuel, ed., *July 1914* (1967). Selected documents.

Koch, H. W., ed., *The Origins of the First World War* (1972). Useful essays, particularly those dealing with the glorification of war before 1914.

Lafore, Laurence, *The Long Fuse* (1971). A beautifully written study of the causes of the conflict.

Langer, W. L., *European Alliances and Alignments* (1964). Originally published in 1931, this now-classic work treats the major international issues between 1871 and 1890.

Laqueur, Walter, and George Mosse, eds., *1914* (1966). A valuable collection of essays on the coming of war.

Remak, Joachim, *The Origins of World War I* (1967). A fine introduction.

Stromberg, Roland N., *Redemption by War: The Intellectuals and 1914* (1982). A superb analysis of the reason why so many intellectuals welcomed the war.

Thomson, G. M., *The Twelve Days* (1964). An account of the twelve days preceding the outbreak of war.

Review Questions

1. How did the nationality problems in Austria-Hungary contribute to the outbreak of World War I?

2. What were the principal purposes of Bismarck's system of alliances?

3. What conditions led to the formation of the Triple Entente? How did Germany respond to it?

4. After the assassination of Archduke Francis Ferdinand, what policies were pursued by Austria-Hungary, Germany, Russia?

5. Was World War I inevitable?

6. In assessing responsibility for the war, what arguments have been advanced by historians?

7. Why did many Europeans welcome the war?

30

*World War I: The West
in Despair*

*T*here will be wars as never before on earth," predicted Nietzsche. World War I bore him out. Modern technology enabled the combatants to kill with unprecedented efficiency; modern nationalism infused both civilians and soldiers with the determination to fight until the enemy was totally beaten. The modern state, exercising wide control over its citizens, mobilized its human, material, and spiritual resources to wage total war. As the war hardened into a savage and grueling fight, the statesmen did not press for a compromise peace, but demanded ever more mobilization, ever more escalation, and ever more sacrifices. The Great War profoundly altered the course of Western civilization, deepening the spiritual crisis that had produced the war. How could one speak of the inviolability of the individual when Europe had become a slaughterhouse? Or of the primacy of reason when nations permitted slaughter to go unabated for four years? Now only the naive could believe in continuous progress. Western civilization had entered an age of violence, anxiety, and doubt that still persists.

Stalemate in the West

On August 4, 1914, the German army invaded Belgium. German war plans, drawn up years earlier, principally by General Alfred von Schlieffen, called for the army to swing through Belgium to outflank French border defenses, envelop the French forces, and destroy the enemy by attacking their rear. With the French army smashed and Paris isolated, German railroads would rush the victorious troops to the eastern front to reinforce the small force that had been assigned to hold off the Russians. The German military felt certain that the spirit and skill of the German army would ensure victory over the much larger Russian forces. But everything depended on speed. France must be taken before the Russians could mobilize sufficient numbers to invade Germany. The Germans were confident that they would defeat France in two months or less.

French strategy called for a headlong attack into Alsace and Lorraine. Believing that French strength lay in the spiritual qualities of the French soldier—in the will to victory that had inspired Republican arms in 1792—the French generals completely embraced an offensive strategy. "The French Army returning to its tradition henceforth admits no law but the offensive," began the field regulations drawn up in 1913. Inspired by Napoleon's stress on attack strategy and convinced that French soldiers possessed an unconquerable will and an irresistible nerve, the French army prepared its soldiers only for offensive warfare. The field regulations proclaimed: "Battles are beyond anything else struggles of morale. Defeat is inevitable as soon as the hope of conquering ceases to exist. Success comes not to him who has suffered the least but to him whose will is firmest and morale strongest."[1]

The French doctrine proved an instant failure. Although bayonet charges against machine-gun emplacements demonstrated the valor of French soldiers, they also revealed the incompetence of French generals. Making no effort at concealment or surprise and wearing striking red and blue uniforms, French soldiers were perfect targets. Marching into concentrated fire, they fell like pins. Everywhere the audacious attack was failing, but French generals, beguiled by the mystique of the offensive, would not change their strategy.

German success was not complete, however. Moving faster than anticipated, the Russians invaded East Prussia, which forced General Helmuth von Moltke to transfer troops from the French front, hampering the German advance. By early September the Germans had reached the Marne River, 40 miles from Paris. With their capital at their backs, the regrouped French forces, aided by the British, fought with astounding courage. Meanwhile the Germans were exhausted by

long marches and had outrun their supplies. Moreover, in their rush toward Paris, they had unknowingly exposed their flank, which the French attacked. The British then penetrated a gap that opened up between the German armies, forcing the Germans to retreat. The First Battle of the Marne had saved Paris. Now the war entered a new and unexpected phase—the deadlock of trench warfare.

For 400 miles across northern France, from the Alps to the North Sea, the opposing sides both constructed a vast network of trenches. These trenches had underground dugouts, and barbed wire stretched for yards before the front trenches as a barrier to attack. Behind the front trenches were other lines to which soldiers could retreat and from which support could be sent. Between the opposing armies lay "no man's land," a wasteland of mud, shattered trees, torn earth, and broken bodies. Trench warfare was a battle of nerves, endurance, and courage, waged to the constant thunder of heavy artillery. It was also butchery. As attacking troops climbed over their trenches and advanced bravely across no man's land, they were decimated by heavy artillery and chewed up by machine-gun fire. If they did penetrate the front-line trenches of the enemy, they would soon be thrown back by a counterattack.

Despite a frightful loss of life, little land changed hands. So much heroism, sacrifice, and death achieved nothing. The generals ordered still greater attacks to end the stalemate; this only increased the death toll, for the advantage was always with the defense, which possessed machine guns, magazine rifles, and barbed wire. Tanks could redress the balance, but the generals, committed to old concepts, did not make effective use of them. And whereas the technology of the machine gun had been perfected, the motorized tanks often broke down.

Gains and losses of land were measured in yards, but the lives of Europe's youth were squandered by the hundreds of thousands. In 1915, for example, France launched numerous attacks against German lines but never gained more than three miles in any one place. Yet these small gains cost France 1,430,000 casualties. Against artillery, barbed wire, and machine guns, human courage had no chance; the generals—uncomprehending, unfeeling, and incompetent—persisted in their mass attacks. This futile effort at a breakthrough wasted untold lives to absolutely no purpose.

In 1915, neither side could break the deadlock. Hoping to bleed the French army dry and force its surrender, the Germans in February 1916 attacked the town of Verdun, which was protected by a ring of forts. They chose Verdun because they knew the French could never permit a retreat from this ancient fortress. Compelled to pour more and more troops into battle, France would suffer such a loss of men that it would be unable to continue the war. Verdun was World War I's bloodiest battle. The leadership of General Henri Philippe Pétain, the tenacity of the French infantry, and the well-constructed concrete and steel forts enabled the French to hold on. When the British opened a major offensive on July 1, the Germans had to channel their reserves to the new front, relieving the pressure on Verdun.

France and Germany suffered more than a million casualties at Verdun, which one military historian calls "the greatest battle in world history."[2] No longer was the war a romantic adventure. A young French soldier, shortly before he was killed, expressed the mood of disillusionment that gripped the survivors of trench warfare: "Humanity is mad! It must be mad to do what it is doing. What a massacre! What scenes of horror and carnage. I cannot find words to translate my impressions. Hell cannot be so terrible. Men are mad!"[3]

At the end of June 1916 the British, assisted by the French, attempted a breakthrough at the Somme River. On July 1, after seven days of intense bombardment intended to destroy German defenses, the British climbed out of their trenches and ventured into no man's land. But German positions had not been destroyed. Emerging from their deep dugouts,

German machine gunners fired repeatedly at the British, who had been ordered to advance in rows. Marching into concentrated machine-gun fire, few British troops ever made it across no man's land. Out of 110,000 who attacked, 60,000 fell dead or wounded, "the heaviest loss ever suffered in a single day by a British army or by any army in the First World War," observes British historian A. J. P. Taylor.[4] Some reached the German wire, only to become entangled in it. The Germans killed them with rifle fire and bayonets. For days the wounded lay in no man's land, their shrieks unheeded.

After this initial disaster, common sense and a concern for human life demanded that the attack be called off, but the generals continued to feed soldiers to the German guns. When the battle of the Somme ended in mid-November, Britain and France had lost over 600,000 men; and the military situation remained essentially unchanged. Soldiers in the trenches could see no end to the slaughter. The only victor was the war itself, which was devouring Europe's youth at an incredible rate.

In December 1916, General Robert Nivelle was appointed Commander-in-Chief of the French forces. Having learned little from past French failures to achieve a breakthrough, Nivelle ordered another mass attack for April 1917. The Germans discovered the battle plans on the body of a French officer and withdrew to a shorter line on high ground, constructing the strongest defense network of the war. Knowing that the French had lost the element of surprise and pushing aside the warnings of leading statesmen and military men, Nivelle went ahead with the attack. "The offensive alone gives victory; the defensive gives only defeat and shame," he told the president and the minister of war.[5]

The Nivelle offensive, which began on April 16, was another blood bath. In many places French artillery had not cut the German barbed wire. As the soldiers tried to grope their way through, they were chewed up by German machine-gun fire. Sometimes the fire was so intense that the French could not

War in France. Entrenched Allied troops met the entrenched German army. Stalemate resulted. In 1915, despite many assaults and shockingly high casualty rates, no more than a total of three miles was ever gained in any one place. (*BBC Hulton Picture Library/Bettmann Archive*)

make it out of their own trenches. Although French soldiers fought with courage, the situation was hopeless. Still Nivelle persisted with the attack; after ten days French casualties numbered 187,000.

The soldiers could endure no more. Spontaneous revolts, born of despair and military failure, broke out in rest areas as soldiers refused to return to the slaughter ground. In some instances they shouted "Peace" and "To hell with the War." Mobs of soldiers seized trains to reach Paris and stir up the population against the war. Mutineers took control of barracks and threatened to fire on officers who interfered. The mutiny spread to the front lines as soldiers told their officers they would defend the trenches but not attack. The French army was disintegrating. "The slightest German attack would have sufficed to tumble down our house of cards and bring the enemy to Paris," recalled a French officer.[6]

General Pétain, the hero of Verdun, re-placed the disgraced Nivelle. To restore morale, Pétain granted more leave, improved the quality of food, made the rest areas more comfortable, and ordered officers to demonstrate a personal concern for their men. He visited the troops, listened to their complaints, and told them that France would engage in only limited offensives until the United States, which had just entered the war, reinforced the allies in large numbers. These measures, combined with imprisonments and executions, restored discipline. The Germans, unaware of the full magnitude of the mutiny, had not put pressure on the front; by the time the Germans attacked, Pétain had revitalized the army.

Other Fronts

While the western front hardened into a stalemate, events moved more decisively on the eastern front. In August 1914, according to plan, the bulk of the German army invaded France hoping for a speedy victory, while a small force defended the eastern frontier against Russia. Responding to French requests to put pressure on Germany, the Russians, with insufficient preparation, invaded East Prussia. After some initial successes, which sent a scare into the German general staff, the Russians were soundly defeated at the battle of Tannenberg (August 26–30, 1914) and forced to withdraw from German territory, which remained inviolate for the rest of the war.

Meanwhile Germany's ally Austria was having no success against Serbia and Russia. An invasion of Serbia was thrown back, and an ill-conceived offensive against Russia cost Austria its Galician provinces. Germany had to come to Austria's rescue. In the spring of 1915 the Germans made a breakthrough that forced the Russians to abandon Galicia and most of Poland. Outrunning their supplies, the Germans and Austrians had to slow down their pursuit of the retreating Russians, who were able to build a new line. Germany did not gain the decisive victory it had sought; although badly battered, Russia remained in the war, forcing Germany to fight on two fronts.

In June 1916 the Russians launched an offensive under General Aleksei Brusilov that opened a wide breach in the Austrian lines. Brusilov proved to be a brilliant commander, but he did not get sufficient help from other Russian armies. Hampered by this lack of support and by the inability of the Russian railways to transport his reserves, Brusilov could not maintain the offensive. A German counteroffensive forced a retreat and cost the Russians over a million casualties. After the winding down of the Brusilov offensive, Russia's military position deteriorated and domestic unrest worsened.

In March 1917, food shortages and disgust with the great loss of life exploded into a spontaneous revolution; the tsar was forced to abdicate. The new government, dominated by liberals, opted to continue the war despite the weariness of the Russian masses. In November 1917, a second revolution brought the Bolsheviks or communists, who promised "Peace, Land, Bread," into power. In March 1918, the Bolsheviks signed the punitive Treaty of Brest Litovsk in which Russia surrendered Poland, the Ukraine, Finland, and the Baltic provinces. An insatiable Germany gained 34 percent of Russia's population, 32 percent of its farm land, 54 percent of its industrial enterprises, and 89 percent of its coal mines.

Several countries, which were not belligerents in August 1914, joined the war later. That autumn, the Ottoman Turks entered the conflict as an ally of Germany. Prior to the war, Germany had cultivated the Ottoman Empire's friendship by training the Turkish army; on their part, the Turks wanted German help in case Russia attempted to seize the Dardanelles. To relieve the pressure on Russia, the British planned to seize the Dardanelles and Constantinople. Although the Turks retreated from the Caucasus, Britain persisted with the plan. Its supporters, including Winston Churchill, First Lord of the Admiralty, argued that the opening of another front in the Balkans might compel Germany to withdraw forces from the west. Even more important, the capture of the Dardanelles would enable the Allies to supply Russia and, in turn, to obtain badly needed Russian grain.

In April 1915, a combined force of British, French, Australian, and New Zealander troops stormed the Gallipoli Peninsula on the European side of the Dardanelles. Ignorance of amphibious warfare, poor intelligence, and the fierce resistance of the Turks prevented the Allies from getting off the beaches and taking the heights. Some of the hardest fighting of the war took place on the beaches and cliffs of Gallipoli. The Gallipoli campaign cost the Allies 252,000 casualties, and they had gained nothing.

Although a member of the Triple Alliance, Italy remained neutral when war broke out.

Map 30.1 World War I, 1914–1918 ▶

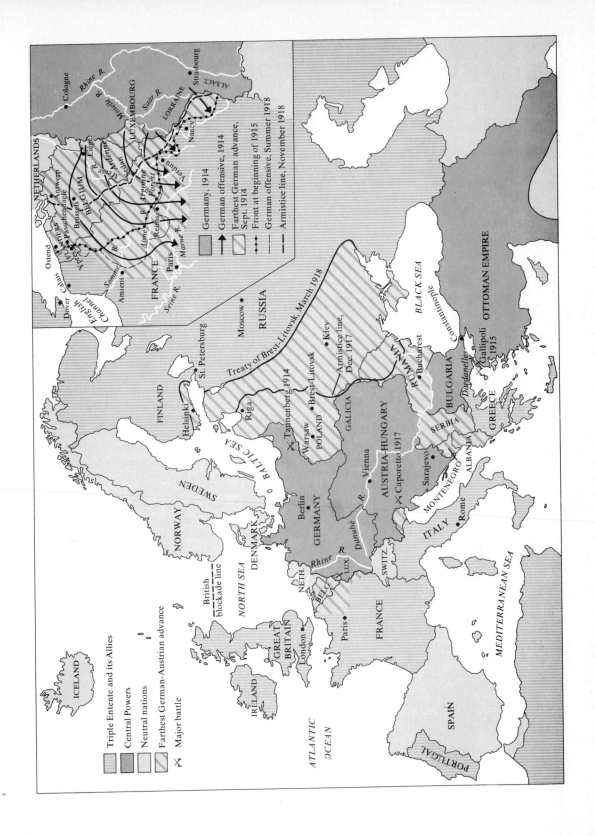

Inset legend:

- Germany, 1914
- German offensive, 1914
- Farthest German advance, Sept. 1914
- Front at beginning of 1915
- German offensive, Summer 1918
- Armistice line, November 1918

Main map legend:

- Triple Entente and its Allies
- Central Powers
- Neutral nations
- Farthest German-Austrian advance
- ✕ Major battle

British blockade line

ICELAND

IRELAND

GREAT BRITAIN · London

ATLANTIC OCEAN

NORTH SEA

NORWAY

SWEDEN

DENMARK

FINLAND · Helsinki

BALTIC SEA

St. Petersburg

Moscow

RUSSIA

Riga

Treaty of Brest-Litovsk, March 1918

Warsaw · POLAND ✕ Tannenberg 1914

Brest-Litovsk

Kiev

Armistice line, Dec. 1917

GALICIA

Berlin · GERMANY

Rhine R.

Danube R.

SWITZ.

Vienna · AUSTRIA-HUNGARY ✕ Caporetto 1917

RUMANIA · Bucharest

Constantinople

BLACK SEA

BULGARIA

SERBIA

GREECE

Dardanelles

Gallipoli 1915

OTTOMAN EMPIRE

Sarajevo

MONTENEGRO

ALBANIA

ITALY · Rome

FRANCE · Paris

SPAIN

PORTUGAL

MEDITERRANEAN SEA

NETH.

BELG.

LUX.

Inset map labels:

Cologne · Rhine R. · Moselle R. · Saar R. · Strasbourg · ALSACE · LORRAINE · LUXEMBOURG · NETHERLANDS · Antwerp · Liège · Brussels · BELGIUM · FLANDERS · Passchendaele · Ostend · Ypres · Calais · Dover · English Channel · Amiens · Somme R. · Seine R. · Paris · FRANCE · Marne R. · Reims · Aisne R. · Argonne Forest · Verdun · Meuse R. · Sedan · Meuse R. · Nancy

In May 1915, on the promise of receiving Austrian territory, Italy entered the war on the side of the Allies. The Austrians repulsed a number of Italian offensives along the frontier and in 1916 took the offensive against Italy. A combined German and Austrian force finally broke through the Italian lines in the fall of 1917 at Caporetto, and the Italians retreated in disorder, leaving behind huge quantities of weapons. Germany and Austria took some 275,000 prisoners.

The Collapse of the Central Powers

American Entry

The year 1917 seemed disastrous for the Allies. The Nivelle offensive had failed, the French army had mutinied, a British attack at Passchendaele did not bring the expected breakthrough and added some 300,000 casualties to the list of butchery, and the Russians, torn by revolution and gripped by war weariness, were close to making a separate peace. But there was one encouraging development for the Allies. In April 1917 the United States had declared war on Germany.

From the outset America's sympathies lay with the Allies. To most Americans, Britain and France were democracies, threatened by an autocratic and militaristic Germany. These sentiments were reinforced by British propaganda that depicted the Germans as cruel "Huns." Since most war news came to the United States from Britain, anti-German feeling gained momentum. What precipitated American entry was the German decision of January 1917 to launch a campaign of unrestricted submarine warfare. The Germans were determined to deprive Britain of war supplies and to starve it into submission. Their resolve meant that German U-boats would torpedo both enemy and neutral ships in the war zone around the British Isles. Since the United States was Britain's principal sup-

plier, American ships became a target of German submarines.

Angered by American loss of life and materiel and by the violation of the doctrine of freedom of the seas, and fearful of a diminution of prestige if the United States took no action, President Woodrow Wilson (1856–1924) pressed for American entry. Also at stake was American security, which would be jeopardized by German domination of western Europe. Leading American statesmen and diplomats feared that such a radical change in the balance of power threatened American national interests. Some argued that a Germany bloated with victory in Europe might one day seek conquests in the Western Hemisphere. As Secretary of State Robert Lansing wrote in a private memorandum just prior to American entry: "The Allies must *not* be beaten. It would mean the triumph of Autocracy over Democracy; the shattering of all our moral standards; and a real, though it may seem remote, peril to our independence and institutions."[7] Not only would a German triumph destroy the balance of power and foment global German expansion, it would also shatter any hopes of building a peaceful and democratic world after the war, which was the idealistic Wilson's principal hope.

In initiating unrestricted submarine warfare, Germany gambled that the United States, even if it became a belligerent, could not intervene in sufficient numbers quickly enough to make a difference. The Germans lost their gamble. The United States broke diplomatic relations with Germany immediately upon learning of the submarine campaign. Three weeks later the British turned over to the Americans a message sent by Berlin to the German ambassador in Mexico City and deciphered by British code experts. Germany proposed that in case of war between Germany and the United States, Mexico should join Germany as an ally; in return Mexico would receive Texas, New Mexico, and Arizona. This fantastic proposal further exacerbated anti-German feeling in the United States. As German submarines continued to attack neutral shipping, President Wilson, on

War in the North Sea. In January 1917, Germany decided to launch a campaign of unrestricted submarine warfare to deprive Britain of war supplies. American ships, as Britain's principal supplier, came under attack by German submarines, as well as by ships and dirigibles like those pictured here. The U.S. Congress declared war on April 6. (*Bildarchiv Preussischer Kulturbesitz*)

April 2, 1917, urged Congress to declare war on Germany, which it did on April 6.

Although the United States may have entered the war to protect its own security, President Wilson told the American people and the world that the United States was fighting "to make the world safe for democracy." With America's entry, the war was transformed into a moral crusade—an ideological conflict between democracy and autocracy. In January 1918, Wilson enunciated American war aims in the Fourteen Points, which called for territorial changes based on nationality and the application of democratic principles to international relations. An association of nations would be established to preserve peace; it would conduct international relations with the same respect for law evidenced in democratic states. In nationalism and democracy, the two great legacies of the nineteenth century, Wilson placed his hope for the future peace of the world.

Germany's Last Offensive

With Russia out of the war, General Erich Ludendorff prepared for a decisive offensive before the Americans could land sufficient troops in France to help the Allies. A war of attrition now favored the Allies, who could count on American supplies and manpower. Without an immediate and decisive victory, Germany could not win the war. Ludendorff hoped to drive the British forces back to the sea, forcing them to withdraw from the Continent. Then he would turn his full might against the French.

On March 21, 1918, the Germans launched the *Kaiserschlacht*—the Emperor's Battle—that was intended to bring victory in the west. Just before dawn, the Germans began bombarding British lines. After hitting the British with artillery, gas, and mortar shells, the Germans climbed out of their trenches and moved across a no man's land enveloped by fog; the attackers could not be seen as they advanced toward the British trenches. They breached the enemy lines, and the British retreated. Expanding their offensive, the Germans now sought to split the British and French forces by capturing Amiens, the major allied communications center, and to drive the British back to the channel ports.

Suddenly the deadlock had been broken; it was now a war of movement. Within two weeks the Germans had taken some 1,250 square miles. But British resistance was astonishing, and the Germans, exhausted and short of ammunition and food, called off the drive. A second offensive against the British in April also had to be called off, as the British contested every foot of ground. Both campaigns depleted German manpower while the Americans were arriving in great numbers to strengthen Allied lines and uplift morale.

At the end of May Ludendorff resumed his offensive against the French. Attacking unexpectedly, the Germans broke through and advanced to within 56 miles of Paris by June 3. General John Pershing, head of the American forces, cabled Washington that "the possibility of losing Paris has become apparent."[8] But the offensive was already winding down as reserves braced the French lines. In the Battle of Belleau Wood (June 6–25, 1918), the Americans checked the Germans. There would be no open road to Paris.

In mid-July the Germans tried again, crossing the Marne River in small boats. Although in one area they advanced 9 miles, the offensive failed against determined American and French opposition. On July 18 the French mounted a mass tank attack against the flank of the advancing Germans and punctured the German lines. The Germans tried to keep the offensive going but were unable to widen the salient and Ludendorff ordered a pullback. By August 3, the Second Battle of the Marne had come to an end. The Germans had thrown everything they had into their spring and summer offensive, but it was not enough. The Allies had bent, but reinforced and encouraged by American arms, they did not break. Now they began to counterattack.

On August 8 the British, assisted by the French and using tanks to great advantage, broke through east of Amiens. Ludendorff said that "August 8th was the black day of the German Army. . . . Our war machine was no longer efficient."[9] And the Kaiser himself declared to his generals: "We have nearly reached the limit of our powers of resistance. The war must be ended."[10] The Allies, their confidence surging, continued to attack with great success in August and September.

Meanwhile German allies, deprived of support from a hard-pressed Germany, were unable to cope. An Allied army of French, Britons, Serbs, and Italians compelled Bulgaria to sign an armistice on September 29. Shortly afterward, British successes in the Middle East compelled Turkey to withdraw from the war. In the streets of Vienna people were shouting "Long Live Peace! Down with the Monarchy!" The Austro-Hungarian Empire was rapidly disintegrating into separate states based on nationality.

At the end of September Ludendorff had concluded: "The enemy had to be asked for peace and an armistice. . . . The military position, which would all too probably get worse, demanded this."[11] By early October the last defensive position of the Germans had crumbled. Fearful that the Allies would invade the fatherland and shatter the reputation of the German army, Ludendorff wanted an immediate armistice. But he needed a way to obtain favorable armistice terms from President Wilson and to shift the blame for the lost war away from the military and the Kaiser to the civilian leadership. Cynically, he urged the creation of a popular parliamentary government in Germany. But events in Germany went further than the general had anticipated. Whereas Ludendorff sought a limited monarchy, the shock of defeat and hunger sparked a revolution that forced the Kaiser to abdicate. On November 11, the new German Republic signed an armistice ending the hostilities. At 11 A.M. the soldiers from both sides walked into no man's land and into the daylight. A newspaper correspondent with the British army in France wrote: "Last night for the first time since August in the first year of the war, there was no light of gunfire in the sky, no sudden stabs of flame through darkness, no spreading glow above black trees where for four years of nights human beings were smashed to death. The Fires of Hell had been put out."[12]

The Peace Conference

Wilson's Hope for a New World

In January 1919, representatives of the Allied Powers assembled in Paris to draw up peace terms; President Wilson was also there. The war-weary masses turned to Wilson as the prophet who would have the nations beat their swords into plowshares. In Paris, two million people lined the streets to cheer Wilson and throw bouquets; his carriage passed under a huge banner proclaiming "Honor to Wilson the Just." In Rome, hysterical crowds called him the god of peace; in Milan, wounded soldiers sought to kiss his clothes; in Poland, university students spoke his name when they shook hands with each other.

For Wilson the war had been fought against autocracy. A peace settlement based on liberal-democratic ideals, he hoped, would sweep away the foundations of war. Wilson proclaimed his message with a spiritual zeal that expressed his Presbyterian background and his faith in American democracy.

None of Wilson's principles seemed more just than the idea of self-determination—the right of a people to have its own state, free of foreign domination. In particular, this goal meant (or was interpreted to mean) the return of Alsace and Lorraine to France, the creation of an independent Poland, a readjustment of the frontiers of Italy to incorporate Austrian lands inhabited by Italians, and an opportunity for Slavs of the Austro-Hungarian Empire to form their own states. While Wilson did not demand the liberation of all colonies, the Fourteen Points did call for "a free, open-minded and absolutely impartial adjustment of all colonial claims," and a territorial settlement "made in the interest and for the benefit of the population concerned."

Aware that a harshly treated Germany might well seek revenge, thereby engulfing the world in another cataclysm, Wilson insisted that there should be a "peace without victory." A just settlement would encourage a defeated Germany to work with the victorious Allies in building a new Europe. But on one point he was adamant: Prussian militarism, which he viewed as a principal cause of the war, must be eliminated.

To preserve peace and to help remake the world, Wilson urged the formation of a League of Nations, an international parliament to settle disputes and discourage aggression. Wilson wanted a peace of justice to preserve Western civilization in its democratic and Christian form.

Obstacles to Wilson's Program

But how could such high-sounding, moralistic proclamations be translated into concrete peace provisions? "Obviously no mortal man this side of the millennium could have hoped to bring about all the things that the world came to expect of Wilson," concludes American historian Thomas A. Bailey. "Wilson's own people were bound to feel disillusioned; the peoples of the neutral and Allied countries were bound to feel deceived; and the peoples of the enemy countries were bound to feel betrayed."[13]

Wilson's negotiating position was undermined by the Republican party's victory in the Congressional elections of November 1918. Before the election, Wilson appealed to the American people to vote for Democrats

Clemenceau, Wilson and Lloyd George Leaving Versailles After Signing the Peace Treaty. Woodrow Wilson was greeted in Europe as the bringer of peace. His presence at the peace conference, where he haggled over points, and the Republican victory in the U.S. congressional election in November 1918 soon tarnished that image. (*Culver Pictures*)

as a vote of confidence in his diplomacy. But Americans elected twenty-five Republicans and fifteen Democrats to the Senate. Whatever the motives of the American people in voting Republican—apparently their decision rested on local and national, not international, issues—the outcome diminished Wilson's prestige at the conference table. To his fellow negotiators, Wilson was trying to preach to Europe when he could not command the support of his own country. Since the Senate must ratify any American treaty, European diplomats had the terrible fear that what Wilson agreed to the Senate might reject—which is precisely what happened.

It has been suggested that Wilson's very presence at the conference table also diminished his prestige. As president of the nation that had rescued the Allies and as initiator of a peace program that held the promise of a new world, Wilson occupied a position of honor from which he could exert considerable influence and authority. But by attending the conference in person and haggling with the other representatives, he was knocked from his lofty pedestal and became all too human. "Messiahs tend to arouse less enthusiasm the more they show themselves," observes Bailey; "the role requires aloofness and the spell of mystery."[14]

Another obstacle to Wilson's peace program was France's demand for security and revenge. Nearly the entire war on the western front had been fought in French territory. Many French industries and farms had been ruined; the country mourned the loss of half its young men. To many in France the Germans were savages, vandals, assassins. The

French people were skeptical of Wilson's idealism. "Let us try out the new order," said a French editorial in the *Echo de Paris,* "but so long as we are not assured of its absolute success . . . let us maintain . . . unsatisfactory though they may be, the pillars of the old order . . . which will seek to maintain peace by the aid of military, political and economic guarantees."[15]

Representing France at the conference table was Georges Clemenceau (1841–1929), nicknamed "the Tiger." Nobody loved France or hated Germany more. Cynical, suspicious of idealism, and not sharing Wilson's hope for a new world or his confidence in the future League of Nations, Clemenceau demanded that Germany be severely punished and its capacity to wage war destroyed. Fearful of Germany's greater population and superior industrial strength, and of its military tradition that would not resign itself to defeat, Clemenceau wanted guarantees that the wars of 1870–1871 and 1914–1918 would not be repeated. The war had shown that without the help of Britain and the United States, France would have been at the mercy of Germany. Because there was no certainty that these states would again aid France, Clemenceau wanted to use his country's present advantage to cripple Germany.

The intermingling of European nationalities was another barrier to Wilson's program. Because in so many regions of central Europe there was a mixture of nationalities, no one could create a Europe completely free of minority problems; some nationalities would always feel that they had been treated shabbily. And the various nationalities were not willing to moderate their demands or lower their aspirations. "To most Europeans," states German-American historian Hajo Holborn, "the satisfaction of their national dreams was an absolute end even when their realization violated the national determination of others."[16] For example, the Fourteen Points called for the creation of an independent Poland with secure access to the sea. But between Poland and the sea lay territory populated by Germans. Giving this land to Poland would

violate German self-determination; denying it to Poland would mean that the new country had little chance of developing a sound economy. No matter what the decision, one people would regard it as unjust. Similarly, to provide the new Czechoslovakia with defensible borders, it would be necessary to give it territory inhabited principally by Germans. This too could be viewed as a denial of German self-determination, but not granting it to Czechoslovakia would mean that the new state would not be able to defend itself against Germany.

Also serving as a barrier to Wilson's program were the secret treaties drawn up by the Allies during the war. These agreements, dividing up German, Austrian, and Ottoman territory, did not square with the principle of self-determination. For example, to entice Italy into entering the war, the Allies had promised it Austrian lands that were inhabited predominantly by Germans and Slavs. Italy was not about to repudiate its prize because of Wilson's principles.

Finally, the war had aroused great bitterness that persisted after the guns had been silenced. Both the masses and their leaders demanded retribution and held exaggerated hopes for territory and reparations. In such an atmosphere of postwar enmity, the spirit of compromise and moderation could not overcome the desire for spoils and punishment. A century earlier, when the monarchs had defeated Napoleon, they sought a peace of reconciliation with France. But democratic statesmen and nations found it harder to set aside their hatreds than had despotic monarchs and aristocratic diplomats.

The Settlement

After months of negotiations, punctuated often by acrimony, the peacemakers hammered out a settlement. Five treaties made up the Peace of Paris—one each with Germany, Austria, Hungary, Bulgaria, and Turkey. Of the five, the Treaty of Versailles, which Germany signed on June 28, 1919, was the most significant. France regained Alsace and Lorraine, lost to Germany in the Franco-Prussian War of 1870–71. The treaty barred Germany from placing fortifications in the Rhineland.

The French military had wanted to take the Rhineland from Germany and break it up into one or more republics under French suzerainty. The Rhine River was a natural defensive border; one had only to destroy the bridges to prevent a German invasion of France. With Germany deprived of this springboard for invasion, French security would be immensely improved. Recognizing that the German people would never permanently submit to the amputation of the Rhineland, which was inhabited by more than 5 million Germans and contained key industries, Wilson and British Prime Minister David Lloyd George (1863–1945) resisted these French demands. They did not want to create an Alsace-Lorraine in reverse by awarding France a region that was overwhelmingly German. Nor could Wilson ever agree to such a glaring violation of the principle of self-determination.

But Clemenceau did not willingly agree to give up France's demand for control of the Rhineland. The confrontation between Wilson and Clemenceau was so bitter that the president made plans to return to the United States, threatening to disrupt the conference. Faced with the opposition of Wilson and Lloyd George, Clemenceau backed down and agreed instead to Allied occupation of the Rhineland for fifteen years, the demilitarization of the region, and an Anglo-American promise of assistance if Germany attacked France in the future. This last point, considered vital by France, proved useless. The alliance only went into effect if both the United States and Britain ratified it. Since the Security Treaty did not get past the United States Senate, Britain also refused to sign it. France had made a great concession on the Rhineland issue but received nothing in exchange; the French people felt that they had been duped and wronged.

A related issue concerned French demands for annexation of the coal-rich Saar Basin, which adjoined Lorraine. By obtaining this region, France would weaken Germany's military potential and strengthen its own. France argued that this would be just compensation for the deliberate destruction of the French coal mines by the retreating German army at the end of the war. But here too France was disappointed. The final compromise called for a League of Nations commission to govern the Saar Basin for fifteen years, after which the inhabitants would decide whether their territory would be ceded to France or returned to Germany.

In eastern Germany, in certain districts of Silesia that had a large Polish population, a plebiscite determined the future of the region. As a result, part of Upper Silesia was ceded to Poland. The settlement also gave Poland a corridor cut through West Prussia and terminating in the Baltic port of Danzig, and Danzig itself was declared an international city to be administered by a League of Nations commission. The Germans would never resign themselves to this loss of territory that separated East Prussia from the rest of Germany, especially since it was awarded to the Poles, whom many Germans viewed as cultural and racial inferiors.

Regarding the Germans as unfit to care for colonial peoples, Wilson supported stripping Germany of its overseas possessions, all of which had been seized by the Allies during the war. The disposition of Ottoman colonies was also at issue. But instead of the outright annexation of colonies by the victorious powers, Wilson proposed the mandate system, whereby small nations would be entrusted with the administration of the colonies under the guidance of the League of Nations. Such an arrangement would accord with the spirit of the Fourteen Points. Here too, Wilson's proposal conflicted with secret agreements made by Britain with its dominions—the Union of South Africa, Australia, New Zealand—and with Japan.

Map 30.2 Post–World War I: Broken Empires and Changed Boundaries ▶

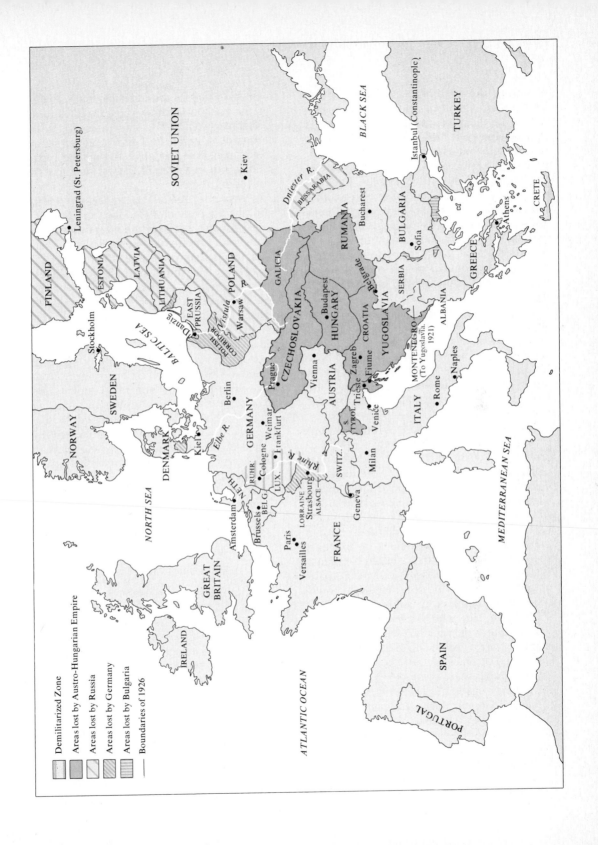

Demilitarized Zone

Areas lost by Austro-Hungarian Empire

Areas lost by Russia

Areas lost by Germany

Areas lost by Bulgaria

Boundaries of 1926

FINLAND

Leningrad (St. Petersburg)

SOVIET UNION

Kiev

BLACK SEA

TURKEY

Istanbul (Constantinople)

ESTONIA

LATVIA

LITHUANIA

Dniester R.

BESSARABIA

RUMANIA

Bucharest

BULGARIA

Sofia

GREECE

CRETE

Athens

Stockholm

BALTIC SEA

EAST PRUSSIA

POLISH CORRIDOR

Danzig

Vistula R.

Warsaw

POLAND

GALICIA

CZECHOSLOVAKIA

Prague

Budapest

HUNGARY

CROATIA

Zagreb

Fiume

SERBIA

Belgrade

YUGOSLAVIA

MONTENEGRO
(To Yugoslavia, 1921)

ALBANIA

SWEDEN

NORWAY

DENMARK

Kiel

Berlin

Elbe R.

GERMANY

RUHR

Cologne

Weimar

Frankfurt

Rhine R.

Vienna

AUSTRIA

Trieste

S. TYROL

Venice

Milan

ITALY

Rome

Naples

NORTH SEA

NETH.

Amsterdam

Brussels

BELG.

LUX.

LORRAINE

Strasbourg

ALSACE

SWITZ.

Geneva

FRANCE

Paris

Versailles

GREAT BRITAIN

IRELAND

ATLANTIC OCEAN

SPAIN

PORTUGAL

MEDITERRANEAN SEA

Backing down from his position on the German and Ottoman colonies, Wilson permitted the victorious nations to be awarded control. However, these nations held colonies not outright but as mandates under the supervision of the League, which would protect the interests of the native peoples. Thus the division of Ottoman and German colonies represented a compromise between traditional imperialism and Wilsonian idealism. The mandate system implied the ultimate end of colonialism, for it clearly opposed the exploitation of colonial peoples and asserted independence as the rightful goal for subject nations.

To prevent a resurgence of militarism, the settlement abolished the German general staff and forbade military conscription in Germany. The German army was limited to 100,000 volunteers and deprived of heavy artillery, tanks, and warplanes. The German navy was limited to a token force that did not include submarines.

The issue of reparations (compensation) aroused terrible bitterness between Wilson and his French and British adversaries. Goaded by public opinion and enticed by Germany's helplessness, Lloyd George and Clemenceau sought to make Germany pay the total costs of the war. While Wilson resisted such an impossible demand, he did make considerable concessions on exacting vast reparations from the defeated Germans. Wilson agreed that the costs of pensions paid to Allied veterans and their families should be borne by Germany, an inclusion that nearly tripled the bill. The American delegation wanted the treaty to fix a reasonable sum that Germany would have to pay and specify the period of years allotted for payment. But no such items were included; they were left for future consideration. The Treaty of Versailles left Germany with an open-ended bill that would probably take generations to pay. The Allies had not considered Germany's capacity to pay, and Wilson had lost on the issue of reasonable reparations.

Moreover, Article 231, which preceded the reparation clauses, placed sole responsibility for the war on Germany and its allies. The Germans responded to this accusation with contempt. Clearly the German government would feel little incentive to pay the reparations and considerable moral justification in evading them.

In separate treaties the conference dealt with the dissolution of the Hapsburg Empire. In the closing weeks of the war, the Austro-Hungarian Empire had crumbled as the various nationalities proclaimed their independence from Hapsburg rule. In most cases, the peacemakers ratified with treaties what the nationalities had already accomplished in fact. Serbia joined with Austrian lands inhabited by Croats and Slovenes to become Yugoslavia. Czechoslovakia arose from the predominantly Czech and Slovak regions of Austria. Hungary, which broke away from Austria to become a separate country, had to concede considerable land to Rumania and Yugoslavia. Austria had to turn over to Italy the South Tyrol, which was inhabited by 200,000 Austrian Germans. This clear violation of the principle of self-determination greatly offended liberal opinion. Deprived of its vast territories and prohibited from union with Germany, the new Austria was a third-rate power.

Assessment and Problems

The Germans unanimously denounced the Treaty of Versailles, for in their minds the war had ended not in German defeat but in a stalemate. They regarded the armistice as the prelude to a negotiated settlement among equals based on Wilson's call for a peace of justice. Instead the Germans were barred from participating in the negotiations. And they viewed the terms of the treaty as humiliating and vindictive—designed to keep Germany militarily and economically weak. What standard of justice, they asked, allowed the Allies to take the German colonies for themselves, to reduce the German military to a pitiful size without themselves disarming, to ban Germany from the League of Nations, to saddle Germany with impossible reparations, to take away approximately one-eighth of German territory and deprive it of one-tenth of its population, to blame the war on Germany alone, to provide for the self-determination of Poles while precluding the union of German-speaking Austria with Germany, to hand over to Italy some 200,000 Austrian Germans, to place Germans under Polish rule and declare the German port of Danzig a free city?

The Germans protested that when the United States entered the war, Wilson had stated that the enemy was not the German people, but their government. Surely, the Germans now argued, the new German democracy should not be punished for the sins of the monarchy and the military. To the Germans, the Treaty of Versailles was not the dawning of the new world that Wilson had promised, but an abomination—a vile crime.

War weary, torn by revolutionary unrest, desperately short of food, its economy in disarray, and with the Allies poised to invade, the new German Republic had no choice but to sign the treaty. However, the sentiments of the German people were clearly and prophetically expressed by the Berlin *Vorwärts*, the influential Social Democratic newspaper. "We must never forget it is only a scrap of paper. Treaties based on violence can keep their validity only so long as force exists. Do not lose hope. The resurrection day comes."[17]

Critics in other lands also condemned the treaty as a punitive settlement in flagrant violation of Wilsonian idealism. The peacemakers, they argued, should have set aside past hatreds and, in cooperation with the new democratic German Republic, forged a just settlement that would serve as the foundation of a new world. Instead they burdened the fledgling German democracy with reparations that were impossible to pay, insulted it with the accusation of war guilt, and deprived it of territory in violation of the principle of self-determination. All these provi-

sions, said the critics, would only exacerbate old hatreds and fan the flames of German nationalism. This was a poor beginning for democracy in Germany and for Wilson's new world.

Defenders of the peace settlement insisted that had Germany won the war it would have imposed a far harsher settlement on the Allies. They pointed to German war aims, which called for the annexation of parts of France and Poland, the reduction of Belgium and Rumania to satellites, and German expansion in central Africa. They pointed also to the treaty of Brest-Litovsk (see page 715), which Germany compelled Russia to sign in 1918, as an example of Germany's ruthless appetite. Moreover, they insisted that the peace settlement was by no means a repudiation of Wilson's principles. The new map of Europe was the closest approximation of the ethnic distribution of its peoples that Europe had ever known.

What is most significant about the Treaty of Versailles is that it did not solve the German problem. Germany was left weak but unbroken—its industrial and military power only temporarily contained, its nationalist fervor undimmed. The real danger in Europe was German unwillingness to accept defeat or surrender the dream of expansion.

Would France, Britain, and the United States enforce the treaty against a resurgent Germany? The war had demonstrated that an Allied victory depended on American intervention. But in 1920 the U.S. Senate, angry that Wilson had not taken Republicans with him to Paris and fearing that membership in the League of Nations would involve America in future wars, refused to ratify the Treaty of Versailles. Britain, feeling guilty over the treatment of Germany, lacked the will for enforcement and even came to favor treaty revision. The responsibility for preserving the settlement therefore rested primarily with France, which was not encouraging. The Paris peace settlement left Germany resentful but potentially powerful, and to the east lay small and weak states, some of them with sizable

German minorities, that could not check a rearmed Germany.

The War and European Consciousness

World War I was a great turning point in the history of the West. The war left many with the gnawing feeling that Western civilization had lost its vitality and was caught in a rhythm of breakdown and disintegration. It seemed that Western civilization was fragile and perishable, that Western people, despite their extraordinary accomplishments, were never more than a step or two away from barbarism. Surely any civilization that could allow such senseless slaughter to last four years had entered its decline and could look forward to only the darkest of futures.

European intellectuals were demoralized and disillusioned. The orderly, peaceful, rational world of their youth had been destroyed. The Enlightenment world-view, weakened in the nineteenth century by the assault of romantics, Social Darwinists, extreme nationalists, race mystics, and glorifiers of the irrational, was now disintegrating. The enormity of the war had shattered faith in the capacities of reason to deal with crucial social and political questions. It appeared that civilization was fighting an unending and seemingly hopeless battle against the irrational elements in human nature and that war would be a continuous phenomenon in the twentieth century.

Confidence in the future gave way to doubt. The old beliefs in the perfectibility of humanity, the blessings of science, and ongoing progress now seemed an expression of naive optimism. A. J. P. Taylor concludes:

The First World War was difficult to fit into the picture of a rational civilization advancing by ordered stages. The civilized men of the twentieth century had outdone in savagery the barbarians of all preceding ages, and their civilized virtues— organization, mechanical skill, self-sacrifice—had made war's savagery all the more terrible. Modern man had developed powers which he was not fit to use. European civilization had been weighed in the balance and found wanting.[18]

Western civilization had lost its spiritual center. The French writer Paul Valéry summed up the mood of a troubled generation for whom the sun seemed to be setting on the Enlightenment.

The storm has died away, and still we are restless, uneasy as if the storm were about to break. Almost all the affairs of men remain in a terrible uncertainty. We think of what has disappeared, and we are almost destroyed by what has been destroyed; we do not know what will be born, and we fear the future, not without reason. We hope vaguely, we dread precisely; our fears are infinitely more precise than our hopes; we confess that the charm of life is behind us. There is no thinking man . . . who can hope to dominate this anxiety, to escape from this impression of darkness. . . . But among all these injured things is the Mind. The Mind has indeed been cruelly wounded; its complaint is heard in the hearts of intellectual men; it passes a mournful judgment on itself. It doubts itself profoundly.[19]

This disillusionment heralded a loss of faith in liberal-democratic values that contributed to the widespread popularity of fascist ideologies in the postwar world. Having lost confidence in the power of reason to solve the problems of the human community, in liberal doctrines of individual freedom, and in the institutions of parliamentary democracy, many people turned to fascism as a simple saving faith. Far from making the world safe for democracy as Wilson and other liberals had hoped, World War I gave rise to totalitarian movements that would nearly destroy democracy.

The war produced a generation of young people who had reached their maturity in combat. Violence had become a way of life for millions of soldiers hardened by battle and for millions of civilians aroused by four years of propaganda. The astronomical cas-

Käthe Kollwitz: The Survivors. With an estimated 10 million dead and 21 million wounded, World War I shattered the hope that western Europe had been making continuous progress toward universal peace and a rational and enlightened civilization. (*National Gallery of Art, Washington; Rosenwald Collection*)

ualty figures—some 10 million dead and 21 million wounded—had a brutalizing effect. Violence, cruelty, suffering, and even wholesale death seemed to be natural and acceptable components of human existence; the sanctity of the individual seemed to be liberal and Christian claptrap.

The fascination for violence and contempt for life lived on in the postwar world. Many returned veterans yearned for the excitement of battle and the fellowship of the trenches. The brutalizing effect of the war is seen in the following statement by a German soldier for whom the war never ended:

People told us that the War was over. That made us laugh. We ourselves are the War. Its flame burns strongly in us. It envelops our whole being and fascinates us with the enticing urge to destroy. We . . . marched onto the battlefields of the postwar world just as we had gone into battle on the Western Front: singing, reckless, and filled with the joy of adventure as we marched to the attack; silent, deadly, remorseless in battle.[20]

The Great War's veterans made ideal recruits for extremist political movements that glorified action and promised to rescue society from a decadent liberalism.

Both Hitler and Mussolini, themselves ex-soldiers imbued with the ferocity of the front, knew how to appeal to veterans. The lovers of violence and the harbingers of hate who became the leaders of fascist parties would come within a hairsbreadth of destroying Western civilization. The intensified nation-

Chronology 30.1 World War I

June 28, 1914	Archduke Ferdinand of Austria is assassinated at Sarajevo
August 4, 1914	The Germans invade Belgium
August–September 1914	The Russians invade East Prussia; the battle of Tannenberg (Russians are defeated by the Germans)
September 1914	The battle of the Marne (Germans retreat)
April 1915	The Allies storm Gallipoli Peninsula, withdrawing after 252,000 casualties are suffered
May 1915	Italy enters the war on the Allies' side
1915	Germany forces Russia to abandon Galicia and most of Poland
February 1916	General Pétain leads French forces at Verdun (Germans fail to capture the fortress town)
June 1916	General Brusilov leads a Russian offensive against Austrian lines with a million casualties
July–November 1916	The battle of the Somme—Allies suffer 600,000 casualties
January 1917	Germany resumes unrestricted submarine warfare
April 6, 1917	The United States declares war on Germany
May 1917	General Pétain restores morale and discipline

alist hatreds following World War I also helped to fuel the fires of World War II. The Germans swore to regain lands lost to the Poles; some Germans dreamed of a war of revenge. Italy, too, felt aggrieved because it had not received more territory from the dismembered Austro-Hungarian Empire.

However, while the experience of the trenches led some veterans to embrace an aggressive militarism, others were determined that the horror should never be repeated. Tortured by the memory of the Great War, European intellectuals wrote pacifist plays and novels and signed pacifist declarations. In the 1930s, an attitude of "peace at any price" discouraged resistance to Nazi Germany in its bid to dominate Europe.

World War I was total war—it encompassed the entire nation and was without limits. States demanded total victory and total commitment from their citizens. They regulated industrial production, developed sophisticated propaganda techniques to strengthen morale, and exercised ever greater control over the lives of their people, organizing and disciplining them like soldiers. This total mobilization of nations' human and material resources provided a model for future dictators. With ever greater effectiveness and ruthlessness, dictators would centralize power and manipulate thinking. The first indication that the world would never be the same again, and perhaps the most important consequence of the war, was the Russian Revolution in 1917 and the Bolshevik seizure of power.

Notes

1. Quoted in Barbara Tuchman, *The Guns of August* (New York: Macmillan, 1962), p. 51.

Chronology 30.1 continued

July–November 1917	Britain is defeated at Passchendaele
Fall 1917	The Italians are defeated at Caporetto
November 1917	The Bolsheviks take power in Russia
January 1918	U.S. President Woodrow Wilson announces his Fourteen Points
March 1918	Russia signs Treaty of Brest-Litovsk, losing territory to Germany and withdrawing from the war.
March 21, 1918	Germans launch great offensive to end war.
June 3, 1918	Germans advance to within 56 miles of Paris.
August 8, 1918	The Black Day for Germany as British win Battle of Amiens
October 1918	Turkey is forced to withdraw from the war after several British successes
November 3, 1918	Austria-Hungary signs an armistice with the Allies
November 11, 1918	Germany signs an armistice with the Allies, ending World War I
January 1919	Paris Peace Conference
June 28, 1919	Germany signs the Treaty of Versailles

2. S. L. A. Marshall, *The American Heritage History of World War I* (New York: Dell, 1966), p. 215.

3. Quoted in Alistair Horne, *The Price of Glory* (New York: Harper, 1967), p. 240.

4. A. J. P. Taylor, *A History of the First World War* (New York: Berkley, 1966), p. 84.

5. Quoted in Richard M. Watt, *Dare Call It Treason* (New York: Simon & Schuster, 1963), p. 169.

6. Quoted in ibid., p. 215.

7. Quoted in Daniel M. Smith, *The Great Departure* (New York: Wiley, 1965), p. 20.

8. Quoted in Marshall, *The American Heritage History of World War I*, p. 334.

9. Erich Ludendorff, *My War Memories* (London: Hutchinson, 1919), p. 679.

10. Quoted in John Terraine, *To Win a War:*

1918, the Year of Victory (Garden City, N.Y.: Doubleday, 1981), p. 102.

11. Ibid., p. 141.

12. Excerpted in Louis L. Snyder, ed., *Historic Documents of World War I* (Princeton: D. Van Nostrand, 1958), p. 183.

13. Thomas A. Bailey, *Woodrow Wilson and the Lost Peace* (Chicago: Quadrangle Books, 1963), p. 29.

14. Ibid., p. 209.

15. Quoted in *The Nation*, 108 (January 18, 1919): 86.

16. Hajo Holborn, *The Political Collapse of Europe* (New York: Alfred A. Knopf, 1966), p. 102.

17. Quoted in Bailey, *Woodrow Wilson and the Lost Peace*, p. 303.

18. A. J. P. Taylor, *From Sarajevo to Potsdam* (New York: Harcourt, Brace and World, 1966), pp. 55–56.

19. Paul Valéry, *Variety* (New York: Harcourt, Brace, 1927), pp. 27–28.

20. Quoted in Robert G. L. Waite, *Vanguard of Nazism* (New York: W. W. Norton, 1969), p. 42.

Suggested Reading

Albrecht-Carrie, René, *The Meaning of the First World War* (1965). How the war upset the delicate equilibrium of Europe.

Bailey, Thomas, *Woodrow Wilson and the Lost Peace* (1963). A critical interpretation of the role of the United States at the peace conference.

Essame, H., *The Battle for Europe, 1918* (1972). The last campaign.

Falls, Cyril, *The Great War* (1961). A good narrative of the war.

Fussell, Paul, *The Great War and Modern Memory* (1977). The influence of the Great War on British writers.

Horne, Alistair, *The Price of Glory* (1967). Brilliantly recaptures the Battle of Verdun.

Marshall, S. L. A., *The American Heritage History of World War I* (1966). Probably the best account available.

Panichas, George A., ed. *Promise of Greatness* (1968). Recollections of the war by people of prominence.

Remarque, Erich Maria, *All Quiet on the Western Front* (1969). A novel that has become a classic.

Terraine, John, *To Win a War: 1918, The Year of Victory* (1981). The final campaign; contains numerous passages from primary sources.

Tuchman, Barbara, *The Guns of August* (1962). A beautifully written account of the opening weeks of the Great War.

Watt, R. M., *Dare Call It Treason* (1963). A brilliant study of the French Army mutinies of 1917.

Williams, John, *The Other Battleground* (1972). A comparison of the home fronts in Britain, France, and Germany.

Review Questions

1. What battle plans did Germany and France implement in 1914? What prevented Germany from reaching Paris in 1914?

2. Describe trench warfare.

3. Identify and explain the historical significance of the battles of Verdun, the Somme, and Gallipoli.

4. Why did the United States enter the war?

5. Why did General Ludendorff seek an armistice?

6. What was Wilson's peace program? What obstacles did he face?

7. What were the provisions of the Treaty of Versailles regarding Germany? How was Austria-Hungary affected by the war? What was the German reaction to the treaty?

8. Why was World War I a great turning point in the history of the West?

31

The Soviet Union: Modernization and Totalitarianism

A fateful consequence of World War I, even before its final battles were fought, was the Russian Revolution of 1917. The revolution occurred in two stages. In March, the tsarist regime was overthrown. The March revolution ushered in a period of liberal government and freedom, which soon led to a complete breakdown of law and order. Taking advantage of the chaos, the Bolsheviks, in a second stage of the revolution, seized power in November and established a communist dictatorship.*

These events were fateful not only for Russia, but also for Europe and the world; they foreshadowed basic trends of the twentieth century. More than ever, the victory of the Western powers in the war carried Western institutions and values beyond the territorial base of Western civilization. In Asia and Africa, as in many parts of Europe, indigenous tradition did not fit the Western heritage; democracy, industrialism, and social justice were alien imports that undermined the bonds holding society together. How could unprepared peoples run their society in the Western manner? How could their governments hold their unruly subjects together and build up their skills for survival in times of social change and worldwide competition for power? The Russian Revolution of 1917 highlighted the problems caused by the expansion of Western civilization and Western power into the non-Western world.

The overthrow of the tsar showed that governments without a base of support among the mass of their people could not survive. The collapse of Russian liberalism in the first stage of the revolution demonstrated the difficulty of establishing Western liberal-democratic forms of government in countries lacking a sense of unity, a strong middle class, and a tradition of responsible participation in public affairs. After World

*Until March 1918, events in Russia were dated by the Julian calendar, 13 days behind the Gregorian calendar used in the West.

War I, the weaknesses of liberal government became more glaring. In one country after another in central, eastern, and southern Europe liberal government was replaced by an authoritarian regime. European—and later non-Western—dictators copied the Russian communists who pioneered the first experiment of trying to match the accomplishments of Western civilization, including its power, with the culturally unprepared human resources at their disposal.

The Russian Revolution of 1917

The Collapse of Autocracy

Fears of revolution had long troubled foresighted Russians. In the opening years of the twentieth century they sat, as some of them put it, on a volcano ready to explode. Their country, a huge multinational empire held together by force, was in mortal crisis. The mass of the people were peasants; the peasants provided the workers for food production as well as for factories. Illiterate and resentful of the controls foisted upon them by the tsars in the past, workers and peasants had shown their hatred in the revolution of 1905. They also disliked the Westernized minority that dominated the country's finance, industry, and professions; those comfortable people were the agents of the tsars. The educated elite, sharply splintered in its own ranks and dreading the "dark" masses, likewise opposed the tsar; it called for constitutional government and freedom. Most non-Russian nationalities in the empire felt imprisoned and demanded freedom too. Increased contact with "the West," as Russians called Europe, raised expectations and deepened dissatisfaction among all classes, as did the spread of ideas promoted by rising literacy and the freer movement offered by the new railways. It seemed that only the tsar could be responsible for the country's poverty and backwardness. Threatened by rising dissatisfaction, the tsarist

regime had turned into a police state—not very effectively, as the events of 1905 showed.

Russian backwardness and disaffection undermined Russian power in the world at large. The country lacked the industries needed for modern war; it also lacked the necessary political unity. Defeat by Japan, followed by the revolution of 1905, raised an ominous spectre: external humiliation aggravated by internal revolution might destroy the empire. In 1905 the army remained intact; loyal soldiers quelled the revolution. But what about the next crisis?

After the outbreak of war in 1914, the volcano came to life. On the German front, the Russian armies—ill-equipped, poorly led, and suffering huge losses—were soon defeated and, never regaining the initiative, began a long retreat to the east. The German government prepared plans for dismembering the Russian Empire. By 1916, the home front began to fall apart. Shops were empty, money valueless, and hunger and cold stalked the working quarters of cities and towns. But Tsar Nicholas II (1868–1918), who was determined to preserve autocracy, resisted any suggestion that he liberalize the regime for the sake of the war effort.

The people of Russia had initially responded to the war with a show of patriotic fervor. But by January 1917, virtually all Russians, and foremost the soldiers, despaired of autocracy: it had failed to protect the country from the enemy and economic conditions had deteriorated. Autocracy was ready to collapse at the slightest adversity. In early March (February 23 by the calendar then in use) a strike, riots in the food lines, and street demonstrations in Petrograd, as the capital was then called, flared into sudden unpremeditated revolution. The soldiers, who in 1905 had stood by the tsar, now rushed to support the striking workers. The Romanov dynasty, after three hundred years of rule (1613–1917), came to a petty and inglorious end a month before the United States entered the war "to make the world safe for democracy."

Even before the tsar had abdicated, two rival centers of government sprang up in Petrograd: first a council of soldiers and workers called the Petrograd *Soviet (council),* representing those who had fought in the street and risked their lives; and soon thereafter a committee of various liberals afraid of revolution and the soviet. The latter claimed office as the Provisional Government—provisional until a representative Constituent Assembly (to be elected as soon as possible) could establish a permanent regime. Both the Petrograd Soviet and the Provisional Government agreed that henceforth all Russians should enjoy full freedom.

Thus, at the height of a disastrous war, mounting shocks mobilized the unresolved social and political tensions of many centuries; the long dreaded volcano exploded. Liberty came, hot and furious, to an utterly unprepared Russia that soon reduced it to hopeless anarchy. Liberal democrats in Western countries had never suffered conditions like those now emerging in Russia.

The Problems of the Provisional Government

The collapse of autocracy was followed by what supporters in Russia and the West hoped would be a liberal-democratic regime pledged to give Russia a constitution. In reality, however, the course of events from March to November 1917 resembled a free-for-all, no-holds-barred fight for the succession to autocracy, with only the fittest surviving. Events also demonstrated, under conditions of exceptional popular agitation and mobility, the desperate state of the Russian Empire, its internal disunity, and the furies of the accumulated resentments. Both Germany and national minorities in Russia took advantage of the anarchy to dismember the country.

Among the potential successors to the tsars, the liberals of various shades seemed at first to enjoy the best chances. They represented the educated and forward-looking elements in Russian society that had arisen after the reforms of the 1860s—lawyers, doctors, professional people of all kinds, intellectuals,

businesspeople and industrialists, many landowners, and even some bureaucrats. Liberals had opposed autocracy and earned a reputation for leadership. Their strength lay in the Party of Popular Freedom, generally known by its previous name of Constitutional Democrats (or Cadets). The liberals had joined the March revolution only reluctantly, for they were afraid of the masses and the violence of the streets; they dreaded social revolution that could result in the seizure of factories, dispossession of landowners, and tampering with property rights. Although most leaders of the Provisional Government had only modest means, they were "capitalists," believing in private enterprise as the source of economic progress. Their ideal was a constitutional monarchy, its leadership entrusted to the educated and propertied elite familiar with the essentials of statecraft. For them, freedom meant rule by the educated minority.

Unfortunately, the liberals deceived themselves about the mood of the people. Looking to the Western democracies—including, after April 1917, the United States—for political and financial support, they were eager to continue the war on the side of the Allies, which discredited them among the war-weary masses. The liberals also antagonized the peasants by not giving them landlords' lands free of charge. As nationalists, the liberals also opposed the self-determination sought by national minorities; their Russia was to remain whole and undivided.

In all their plans, the liberals acted as if conditions were normal and Russia still had a chance of winning the war. The aims of the liberals were not shared by the people. In fact, not enough steel was produced to supply both the railroads with rails and the army with artillery shells. Almost 2 million soldiers had deserted, "voting for peace with their legs," as Lenin, leader of the opposition Bolsheviks, said; more were to be demobilized for lack of food.

Because of the talents it commanded and the moderation still prevailing in the first months, the Provisional Government's legislative achievement was considerable. It could not, however, create an administrative network capable of taking the place of the tsarist bureaucracy. Consequently the Russian Empire ceased to function as a state. More soviets of workers and soldiers sprang up; some villages even declared themselves independent. In the face of the rising chaos, many liberals gave up all hope for a free Russia; said one of them in early May: ". . . on the day of the revolution Russia received more liberty than she could take, and the revolution has destroyed Russia. Those who made it will be cursed. . . ."[1]

To workers, soldiers, and peasants—all classified as peasants before 1917—freedom meant for once speaking their own untrained minds and having their own kind of government. The government created by the soldiers and workers after their own liking was the Petrograd Soviet. Representing the city's garrison of peasant soldiers even more than the workers, and self-consciously excluding all nonpeasant elements except for a few socialist intellectuals, the Petrograd Soviet spoke for the Russian masses. Feeling incapable with their untrained constituency to take the lead, they tolerated the Provisional Government as long as it respected the sentiments of the Soviet. Some Soviet leaders eventually joined the Provisional Government in a series of coalitions between "capitalists" and "socialists." In July, Aleksandr Kerensky (1881–1970), a radical lawyer of great eloquence who from the start had belonged to both camps, became the leader of the Provisional Government, the symbol of a liberal-democratic Russia determined to continue the war. The coalitions, however, did not halt the drift toward soviet democracy.

That drift, swelling to a mighty tide of spontaneous social revolution in midsummer, was fed from many sources. The war brought further disasters; the army disintegrated, sending its deserters into the countryside as armed agitators. The peasants began to divide the landlords' land among themselves, which encouraged more soldiers to desert in order to claim a share of the land. The breakdown of the railways stopped factory production; enraged workers ousted factory managers and owners. Consumer goods grew scarce and prices soared, and the peasants could see no reason to sell their crops if they could buy nothing in return. Thus the specter of famine in the cities arose. Hardships, and anger, mounted.

The suffering of the people was blamed on the *burzhui*. The *burzhui* (bourgeoisie) was taken to mean all the "capitalists," all those who had been associated with the Europeanized elite—anybody with clean fingernails and soft hands. The popular mood turned ugly; now at last it was time to settle age-old scores. Among the groups carried away by the tide were the non-Russian nationalities—Finns, Ukrainians, Georgians, and others. Sometimes supported by German money, they demanded self-determination and even secession. Freedom obviously was not leading to a grand upsurge of patriotic resolve to drive out the enemy, as had happened in the course of the French Revolution, but rather to dissolution and chaos.

By July 1917, it had become clear that law and order could be upheld only by brute force. In late August and early September, a conspiracy led by an energetic young general, Lavr Kornilov, aimed at setting up a military dictatorship. Kornilov had the support not only of the officer corps and the tsarist officials, but also of many liberals fed up with anarchy. What stopped the general was not Kerensky's government (which had no troops), but the workers of Petrograd. Their agitators demoralized the soldiers sent to suppress the Soviet, thereby proving that a dictatorship of the right had no mass support. The workers also repudiated Kerensky and the Provisional Government as well as their own moderate leaders; henceforth they voted for the Bolsheviks.

In this setting the Bolsheviks, under Lenin, were ready to attempt their solution for Russia's supreme crisis: a dictatorship of the left exclusively based on the soviets, with mass support from the peasants in uniform, the peasants at the factory, and to some extent, even from the peasants in the villages. Thus entered the Bolsheviks—communists as they soon called themselves—a small band of unknown but surprisingly well-prepared political soldiers.

The Bolshevik Revolution

Lenin and the Rise of Bolshevism

By the fall of 1917, revolutionary Bolshevism had a long history. Rooted in the Russian revolutionary tradition, it harked back to the early nineteenth century when educated Russians began to compare their country unfavorably with western Europe. They too wanted constitutional liberty, the rights to free speech and political agitation, in order to make their country modern. Prohibited from speaking out in public, the critics went underground, giving up their original liberalism as too pacifist and narrow for their ends. Revolutionary socialism, with its idealistic vision and compassion for the multitude, was a better ideology in the harsh struggle with the police. By the 1870s many socialists had evolved into austere and self-denying professional revolutionaries who, in the service of the cause, had no moral scruples, just as the police had no scruples in the defense of the tsars. Bank robbery, murder, assassination, treachery, and terror were not immoral if they served the revolutionary cause.

In the 1880s and 1890s, the most alert of these hardened revolutionaries learned industrial economics and sociology from Marx; from Marxism they also acquired a vision of a universal and inevitable progression toward socialism and communism, which satisfied their semireligious craving for salvation in this world, not the next. Marxism also allied them with socialist movements in other lands, giving them an internationalist outlook. History, they believed, was on their side, as it was for all the proletarians and oppressed peoples in the world.

By 1900 a number of able young Russians had rallied to revolutionary Marxism, almost all of them from privileged families or favored by education. The most promising was Vladimir Ilyich Ulyanov, known as Lenin (1870–1924), the son of a teacher and school administrator who had attained the rank of a nobleman. Lenin was trained as a lawyer, but he practiced revolution instead. His first contribution to the revolution lay in adapting Marxism to Russian conditions, taking considerable liberties with the master's teaching. His second followed from the first: outlining the organization of an underground party capable of surviving against the tsarist police. It was to be a tightly knit conspiratorial elite of professional revolutionaries; its headquarters would be safely located abroad, and it would have close ties to the masses, that is, to the workers and other potentially revolutionary elements. To protect against police infiltration, Lenin rejected the formal democracy within the party practiced by Western Marxist parties. He trusted that an informal give-and-take among comrades would occur, never admitting that the lack of checks and balances promoted abuses of personal power.

Two prominent Marxists close to Lenin were Leon Trotsky (1879–1940) and Joseph Stalin (1879–1953). Trotsky, whose original name was Lev Bronstein, was the son of a prosperous Jewish farmer from southern Russia and was soon known for his brilliant pen. Stalin (the man of steel), was originally named Iosif Dzhugashvili; he was from Georgia, beyond the Caucasus mountains. Bright enough to be sent to the best school in the area, he dropped out for a revolutionary career. While they were still young, Lenin, Trotsky, and Stalin were all hardened by arrest, lengthy imprisonments, and exile to Siberia. Lenin and Trotsky later lived abroad, while Stalin, following a harsher course, stayed in Russia; for four years before 1917 he was banished to bleakest northern Siberia, conditioned to ruthlessness for life.

In 1903, the Russian Marxists had split into two factions, the moderate Mensheviks, so named after finding themselves in a minority (*menshinstvo*) at a rather unrepresentative vote at the Second Party Congress, and the extrem-

Lenin with Stalin, 1922. The Russian architect of the revolution, Lenin is shown two years before his death with his successor. Lenin was a visionary with intelligence, discipline, and dedication to his goals. Stalin, however, though often idealized in patriotic posters, was ruthless. He was determined to reshape the Soviet people's consciousness through the revolution of totalitarianism, and his purges laid the foundation for Russia's emergence as a superpower. (*The Mansell Collection*)

ist Bolsheviks, who at that moment were in the majority (*bolshinstvo*). They might more accurately have been called the "softs" and the "hards." The "softs" (Mensheviks) preserved basic moral scruples; they would not stoop to crime or undemocratic methods for the sake of political success. For that the "hards" (Bolsheviks) ridiculed them, noting that a dead, imprisoned, or unsuccessful revolutionary was of little use.

Meanwhile, Lenin perfected Bolshevik revolutionary theory. He violated Marxist tradition by paying close attention to the revolutionary potential of peasants (thereby anticipating Mao Zedong). Lenin also looked closely at the numerous peoples in Asia who had recently fallen under Western imperialist domination. These people, he sensed, constituted a potential revolutionary force. In alliance with the Western—and Russian—proletariat, they might overthrow the world-wide capitalist order. Imperialism, he said, was caused by the giant monopolies of the Great Powers. Driven by their rivalry for profits, they had pushed their countries into colonial expansion and now into suicidal war. Lenin overlooked that the financing of colonial ventures was but a minute part of capitalist enterprise and that the international monopolies, handling business in many different states, were bound to suffer by war. He did, however, anticipate the anti-Western groundswell that arose from the great outpouring of European power and culture in the decades before the war; he saw that that tide might rise to a mighty world revolution. The Bolsheviks, the most militant of all revolutionary socialists, were ready to assist in that gigantic struggle.

Lenin's Opportunity

On April 16, 1917, Lenin, with German help, arrived in Petrograd from exile in Switzerland. Of all Russian political leaders, Lenin possessed the clearest insight into his country's condition. Russia was, he said, the freest country in the world, but the Provisional Government could not possibly preserve Russia from disintegration. The bulk of the soldiers, workers, and peasants would repudiate the Provisional Government's cautious liberalism in favor of a regime expressing their demand for peace and land. Nothing would stop them from avenging themselves for centuries of oppression. Lenin also felt that only complete state control of the economy could rescue the country from disaster. The sole way out, he insisted, was the "dictatorship of the proletariat" backed by the soviets of soldiers, workers, and peasants, particularly the poorer peasants.

Lenin was a Russian nationalist as well as a socialist internationalist; he stepped forward with a vision of a modern and powerful Russian state destined to be a model in world affairs. As he boasted in October 1917: "The [March] revolution has resulted in Russia catching up with the advanced countries in a few months, as far as her political system is concerned. But that is not enough. The war is inexorable; it puts the alternative with ruthless severity; either perish or overtake and outstrip the advanced countries *economically* as well."[2] Russian communism was thus nationalist communism; the Bolsheviks saw the abolition of income-producing property by the dictatorship of the proletariat as the most effective way of mobilizing the country's resources. Yet in twentieth-century style, the Bolshevik mission was also internationalist. The Russian Revolution was to set off a world

revolution, liberating all oppressed classes and peoples around the world, thereby achieving a higher stage of civilization.

With arguments like these, Lenin prepared his party for the second stage of the revolution of 1917—the seizure of power by the Bolsheviks. Conditions favored him, as he had predicted. The Bolsheviks obtained majorities in the soviets everywhere. The peasants were in active revolt, seizing the land themselves. The Provisional Government lost all control over the course of events.

The planning and execution of the Bolshevik coup was entrusted to Trotsky, who gloried in his role as a revolutionary leader. As a Marxist theorist, he made the overthrow of the Provisional Government into a universal model for proletarian revolutions. The coup's details were subsequently dramatized in Soviet literature and art as the grand opening of a new era. Thus dressed up it has also impressed people in the West. At the time, however, the Bolshevik coup was a minor event. On November 6 and 7 (October 24 and 25 by the old calendar), the Bolsheviks hardly seized power; it rather fell into their laps.

In the name of the Second All-Russian Congress of Soviets that was just assembling in Petrograd, the Bolsheviks quickly organized a government proclaiming "soviet democracy," but they were determined to establish a dictatorship. Only a dictatorship of the left, they said, had a chance of restoring government authority. The rest of the world, preoccupied with war, paid little attention. *The New York Times* on November 10 called the Bolsheviks "political children, without the slightest understanding of the vast forces they are playing with." Thus began a novel political experiment destined to change the world. Its ultimate aim was nothing less than to raise the poor and helpless peoples of backward lands to the power and wealth of Western countries.

Its immediate necessity, however, was merely to survive. The Bolshevik seizure of power in Petrograd was another step toward civil war—the real test of power for all forces eager to take the place of the tsars. The credit for Bolshevik survival belongs to Lenin.

The Bolsheviks Survive

Lenin as Leader

Lenin is most commonly remembered in Soviet Russia from the ever-present, eye-catching posters framed with slogans addressed to the masses. The posters show Lenin in a dark business suit and sport cap, addressing a spellbound audience of workers and soldiers. His sweeping gestures, right arm outstretched as if to drive home his point, show him not commanding like Peter the Great, but pleading, persuading, cajoling, and sometimes threatening—a symbol to idolize. Lenin looked like a source of inexhaustible energy and confidence—he alone had grasped the opportunity for a socialist revolution; he had sustained a wavering, uncertain party and had led the advance into a totally unknown and risky future.

Lenin pleaded that he was guiding the Russian proletariat and all humanity toward a higher social order, symbolizing—in Russia and much of the world—the rebellion of the disadvantaged against Western (or "capitalist") superiority. That is why, in 1918, he changed the name of his party from Bolshevik to Communist. For Lenin, as for Marx, a world without exploitation was humanity's noblest ideal. Under this creed he matched his mission against that of Woodrow Wilson, who wanted to make the world safe for democracy. There were now two ideals of democracy—soviet style and American style. If individuals can be taken as symbols of historic turning points, Lenin counted among the greatest in the twentieth century.

Dismemberment, Civil War, and Foreign Intervention

Staggering adversity confronted Lenin after his seizure of power. In the prevailing anarchy, Russia lay open to the German armies.

Invoking the plea for national self-determination, the German government was quick to demand the liberation of territories held by Russia for its own benefit. Under the Treaty of Brest-Litovsk, signed in March 1918, the lowest point in Russian history for over two hundred years, Russia lost Finland, Poland, the Baltic provinces—regions inhabited largely by non-Russians—plus the rebellious Ukraine, its chief industrial base and breadbasket. Yet Lenin had no choice but to accept the humiliating terms.

After the Treaty of Brest-Litovsk was signed, the civil war that had been brewing since the summer of 1917 broke out in full. In the winter of 1917–1918, tsarist officers had been gathering troops in the south, counting on the loyalty of the Cossacks; other anticommunist centers rose in Siberia, still others in the extreme north and along the Baltic coast. The political orientation of these anticommunist groups, generally called Whites in contrast to the Communist Reds, combined all shades of opinion from moderate socialist to reactionary, the latter usually predominating. All received support from foreign governments that freely intervened in Russia's agony. The Germans, until their own revolution in November 1918, occupied much of southern Russia. England, France, and the United States sent troops to points in northern and southern European Russia; England, Japan, and the United States also sent troops to Siberia. At first they hoped to offset German expansion, later to overthrow the communist regime. In May and June 1918, Czech prisoners of war, about to be evacuated, precipitated anticommunist uprisings along the Siberian railway, bringing the civil war to fever pitch.

In July 1918, Nicholas II and his entire family were murdered by communists. In August, a noncommunist socialist nearly assassinated Lenin, while the White forces in the south moved to cut off central Russia from its food supply. In response, the communists speeded the buildup of their own Red Army. Recruited from the remnants of the tsarist army and its officer corps, the Red Army was reinforced

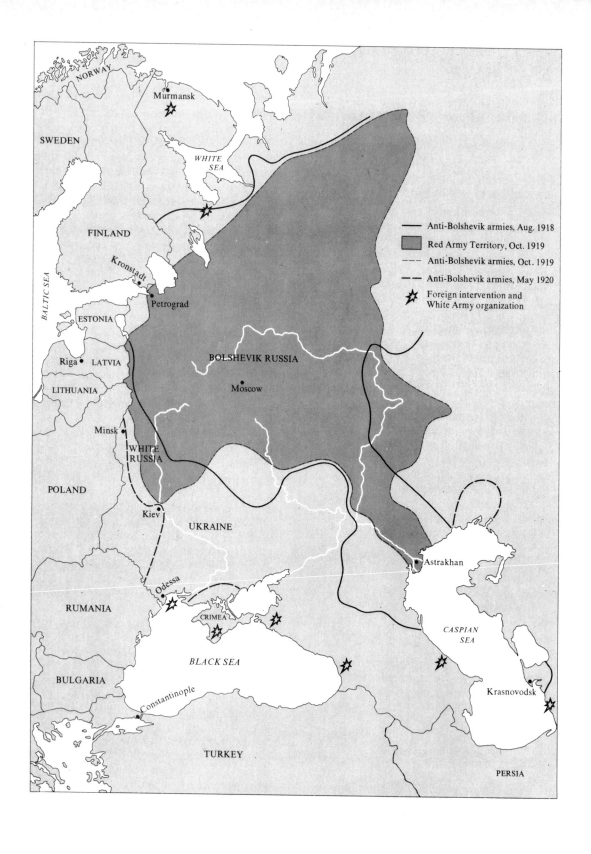

NORWAY

SWEDEN

Murmansk

WHITE
SEA

FINLAND

BALTIC SEA

Kronstadt

Petrograd

ESTONIA

Riga • LATVIA

LITHUANIA

Minsk

WHITE
RUSSIA

POLAND

Kiev

UKRAINE

RUMANIA

Odessa

CRIMEA

BULGARIA

BLACK SEA

Constantinople

TURKEY

BOLSHEVIK RUSSIA

Moscow

Astrakhan

CASPIAN
SEA

Krasnovodsk

PERSIA

—————— Anti-Bolshevik armies, Aug. 1918

Red Army Territory, Oct. 1919

– – – – Anti-Bolshevik armies, Oct. 1919

– – – – Anti-Bolshevik armies, May 1920

✦ Foreign intervention and
White Army organization

by compulsory military service and strict discipline; Trotsky reintroduced the death penalty, which had been outlawed by the provisional government. Patriotism prompted many tsarist officers to continue serving their country, even though their loyalty was often severely strained. As a check on them, Trotsky appointed political commissars to be responsible for the political reliability and morale of the troops. Despite these measures, the Red Army, like the armies of the Whites, lacked discipline. In the civil war, soldiers butchered their own comrades as well as civilians. Their leaders, among both Whites and Reds, spared no lives to maintain control. Only the most ruthless commanders, including Trotsky and Stalin, prevailed.

In 1919, thanks to the Allied victory and the American contribution to it, the German menace ended. Yet foreign intervention stepped up in response to the formation of the Communist International (Comintern), an organization founded by Lenin to guide the international revolutionary movement that he expected to issue from the World War. Lenin sought revolutionary support from abroad for strengthening his hand at home; his enemies reached into Russia to defeat at its source the revolution that they feared in their own countries. At the same time the civil war rose to its climax.

In the spring of 1919, the White forces in Siberia marched west. Too late to prevent their defeat, other White units advanced from the south toward Moscow, where Lenin had moved his capital in early 1918. Meanwhile, on the Baltic coast, still other White troops came within thirty miles of Petrograd. Yet having the advantage of interior communications and greater popular support, the Red Army gradually prevailed over its enemies. The last White forces, entrenched on the Crimean peninsula, were evacuated with British help in November 1920. At the same time, foreign interventionists called off their efforts. War-weariness and communist propaganda undermined the morale of Allied soldiers, and public opinion demanded their return.

◀ **Map 31.1** Russian Civil War, 1918–1920

Before winning the civil war, the communists faced a sudden invasion from Poland. After initial victories, the Red Army was routed and Lenin was forced to accept a new Polish-Russian boundary running deep inside Russian territory. By 1921, Soviet Russia had been virtually ejected from eastern Europe, yet the major parts of Russia had at last been brought under communist control. Faced with the utter exhaustion of the country, Lenin called for a retreat from the impetuous revolutionary advance he had advocated in 1917.

Hardpressed as Lenin's party had been, it had prevailed. Its enemies were divided among themselves and discredited by their association with the tsarist regime; they lacked their opponents' political skills and experience with terror. But the communist victory in the civil war had exacted a staggering price. Reds and Whites alike had carried the tsarist tradition of political violence to a new pitch of horror (some of it described in famous novels by Pasternak and Sholokhov). The entire population, including the Communist Party and its leaders, suffered in the war, which was followed in 1921–22 by a famine that took still more millions of lives.

Yet the communists prevailed not by terror alone. Lenin succeeded in establishing a dictatorial regime because he could rely on a disciplined party as the core of Soviet power.

The Communist Party

Numbering about 500,000 in 1921, the Communist Party was indeed remarkable. It was controlled by a small, close-knit core of professional political leaders, the best of them unusually disciplined in personal dedication. This new elite's organizational skills permitted them to preserve their original revolutionary drive in the face of both failure and success. From the start, those who did not pull their weight were purged. The Communist Party was more adaptable, energetic, and effective than the tsarist bureaucracy.

For most Russians the onerous duties of good communists were not easy. They had

Starving Children in a Famine Region of Russia, 1921. The privations suffered by the Russian people in the years immediately following World War I and the Bolshevik Revolution are incalculable. The first four years of the new Communist regime 1917–1921 were marked by civil war and foreign invasion. Cities faced starvation and food was taken from peasants at gunpoint. Several million lives were lost. (*Historical Pictures Service, Chicago*)

to be political activists well versed in Marxism-Leninism, observing strict party discipline, toeing the party line, and setting a model of communist dedication in every job they held. Reality, however, was somewhat different. Especially in the lower ranks, sloppiness, corruption, an abuse of authority spoiled the high ideals.

The top leaders, however, were superior to tsarist officials. They combined a long experience of working with the masses and a fierce patriotic ambition to rescue their country from defeat and backwardness. They were inexperienced in statecraft, but they were ready to learn and explosively energetic.

Under its constitution, the "Russian Com-munist Party (Bolshevik)," as its formal title read, was a democratic body. Its members elected delegates to periodic party congresses, which in turn elected the membership of the central committee, where leadership originally centered. However, power soon shifted to a smaller and more intimate group—the *politburo* (political bureau). There the key leaders, Lenin, Trotsky, Stalin, and a few others, determined policy, assigned tasks, and appointed key officials. Ideally, their leadership was democratic in the sense that the flow of decisions from the top down was matched by an upward flow of information and opinion—a system called "democratic centralism." In the face of continuing crises, however, individual leaders like Lenin, or later Stalin, dominated their associates. And as the party grew, so did the need for centralization and bureaucratic organization; the higher echelons controlled the lower; there was never time for consensus-building consultation.

Thus the conditions favoring the one-party dictatorship in Russia also shaped the Communist Party. To guarantee the unity of the country, the party had to be monolithic itself. For that reason, the politburo assumed a dictatorial role. Impatient with unending disputes among righteous and strong-willed old revolutionaries, Lenin, in agreement with other top leaders, demanded unconditional submission to his decisions. He even ordered that dissidents be disciplined; no price was too high for the sake of unity.

The party dominated all public agencies; its key leaders held the chief positions in government. No other political parties were tolerated, and trade unions became agents of the regime. Never before had the people of Russia come to depend so abjectly on their government.

The One-Party Dictatorship

It was with the help of the Communist Party, then, that Lenin from the start imposed a ruthless but effective dictatorship. Almost immediately after the seizure of power, the communists, in a temporary coalition with radical peasant-oriented socialists, outlawed all other political parties and suppressed their newspapers. In January 1918, the communists dispersed the Constituent Assembly, the last vestige of the Provisional Government. Then, losing their peasant-socialist partners after the Treaty of Brest-Litovsk, they established a full-blown one-party state. Already in November, they had set up a commission (called the *Cheka*) to ferret out all counterrevolutionary activity. Staffed with hardened revolutionaries, the Cheka soon became a dreaded secret police.

As former victims of tsarist repression, the communists felt no moral objection to the use of force or even of stark terror. As Lenin admonished his followers: "cleanse the land of Russia of all sorts of harmful insects, of crook-fleas, and bedbugs," by which he meant "the rich, the rogues, and the idlers." He even suggested that "one out of every ten idlers be shot on the spot."[3] Those not shot found themselves, with Lenin's blessings, in forced-labor camps directed by the Cheka.

The communists also made sure of continued popular support. Caught between Red and White, most of the people tended to favor the Reds because they offered more. Out of respect for the ideal of self-determination among the non-Russian nationalities (and in violation of their Marxist belief in centralization), the communists adopted a federal constitution, granting at least cultural and administrative autonomy to non-Russian areas. At the same time, they pleased Russian nationalists by forcibly bringing back most of those nationalities that had tried to escape from the empire. By warding off foreign intervention, the communists also claimed credit for defending Mother Russia.

More important, the communists gave land to the peasants, although with reservations about the peasants' capitalist instincts. They reluctantly allowed workers to control factories, gradually strengthening the more enlightened authority of the trade unions. They also abolished the power of the Orthodox Church, the traditional ally of tsarism and the enemy of innovation. They were militant atheists, believing with Marx that religion was "opium for the people"; God had no place in their vision for a better society. Yet the Orthodox Church and other religions survived, much reduced in influence and closely watched, an enduring target for atheist propaganda.

The communists also simplified the alphabet, changed the calendar to the Gregorian system prevailing in the capitalist West, and brought theater and all arts, hitherto reserved for the elite, to the masses. Above all, they wiped out—by expropriation of property and discrimination, expulsion, and execution —the educated upper class of bureaucrats, landowners, professional people, and industrialists.

The Russia of the communists was "Soviet" Russia. It was the first regime in Russian history to derive its power and legitimacy from below—from the toiling masses—and it spoke their rough language and expressed their crude sense of social justice. The communists' constituency, significantly, was both men and women. The party promised "to liberate woman from all the burdens of antiquated methods of housekeeping, by replacing them by house-communes, public kitchens, central laundries, nurseries, etc."[4] Traditional values, particularly in the Asian parts of the Soviet Union, hardly favored equality between the sexes, especially in political work. The practical necessity of combining work with family responsibility, moreover, tended to keep women out of managerial positions in the party and the organizations of the state, but the ideal remained alive.

The Bolsheviks derived much acclaim from their emphasis on redistributing housing, food, and clothing and making education available to the masses. They were not opposed to some private property; they allowed items for personal use, provided they were in keeping with the standards of the common people. But they outlawed income-producing private property that enabled capitalists to employ (or exploit, as the communists said) others for their own profit. With the disappearance of private enterprise, the state gradually became the sole employer, thereby forcefully integrating the individual into the reconstruction of the country. Socialism promised a far more intense mobilization of the country than a system based on private property. The Bolsheviks never ceased to stress that they worked strenuously for the welfare of the vast majority of the population.

The latter point, unfortunately, was not easily proved, for Lenin's views of the country's needs differed sharply from common opinion. The working people wanted democracy, by which they meant governing themselves in their own customary ways. Lenin, on the other hand, wanted socialism, reeducating the masses to a higher standard of individual conduct and economic productivity that would be superior even to capitalism. In the spring of 1918, he argued that the Russian workers had not yet matched capitalist performance: "The Russian worker is a bad worker compared with the workers of the advanced, i.e., western countries." To overcome this fatal handicap, Lenin urged competition—socialist competition—and relentlessly hammered home the need for "iron discipline at work" and "unquestioning obedience" to a single will—that of the Communist Party. There was no alternative: "Large-scale machinery calls for absolute and strict unity of will, which directs the joint labors of hundreds and thousands and tens of thousands of people. A thousand wills are subordinated to one will. . . ."[5]

In these words lay the essence of subsequent Soviet industrialization. The entire economy was to be monolithic, rationally planned in its complex interdependence, and pursuing a single goal: overcoming the weaknesses of Russia so disastrously demonstrated in the war. Leaving the workers to their own spontaneity, Lenin realized, would merely perpetuate Russian backwardness. Instead he called for a new "consciousness," a hard-driving work ethic expressed in the Russian Marxist revolutionary vocabulary.

Lenin's words showed that the Bolshevik Revolution had a double—and contradictory—objective. Its first aim was to overthrow the Europeanized elite by an uprising from below, making the ordinary folk of Russia feel more in control of their country. In that respect the Bolshevik Revolution resembled the French Revolution. Its second objective, however, ran against the grain of the first. In attempting to transform their Soviet Russia into a modern industrialized state that would serve as a model for the world, the Bolsheviks imposed a new autocracy even more authoritarian than the old. Russia must be rebuilt on an uncongenial design adapted from the West—against the people's will, if necessary.

The second objective recreated, with twentieth-century refinements, the service state of Peter the Great. It was led by a revolutionary party in close touch with the masses. Yet it also worked for their long-range betterment in terms that they could not grasp and that required a discipline they resented. In the view of the party leaders, the masses always needed firm guidance.

The minds of the people, therefore, also came under extreme control. Through education from kindergarten through the university, in press and radio, in literature and the arts, the Communist Party fashioned people's thoughts to create the proper "consciousness." It made Marxism-Leninism the sole source of inspiration, eliminating as best it could all rival creeds, whether religious, political, or philosophical. Minds were to be as reliably uniform as machine processes and totally committed to the party. Moreover, they were to be protected against all subversive capitalist influences. Soviet Russia, so the party boasted, had risen to a superior plane of social existence; it would attract other soviet socialist states to its federal union, until eventually it covered the entire world. Lest Soviet citizens doubt their new superiority, the party prohibited all uncontrolled comparison with other countries.

An Ideology for World Revolution

In one respect, Lenin was far bolder than any tsar: he turned Russian state ambition into an international revolutionary force.

The Russian Revolution deeply touched hitherto suppressed nationalistic ambitions for political self-determination and cultural self-assertion among a growing number of peoples around the world, especially in Asia. It appealed particularly to intellectuals educated in the West (or in Westernized schools) yet identifying themselves with their downtrodden compatriots. Taught to worship the ideals of the French Revolution—liberty, equality, and fraternity—they noted that the Europeans (or white people everywhere) did not apply these ideals to people of different cultures and colors (if indeed they applied them among themselves). These intellectuals were determined to turn these ideals to their own advantage, if necessary by revolution. Like Lenin, they were of a double mind: they spoke for their own countries and cultures, but they also were eager to make their countries modern, that is, to reshape them in some form after the model of Western power. These patriots included moderates like Gandhi and Nehru in India, who soon repudiated Lenin, and radicals like Ho Chi Minh in Vietnam, and Zhou En-lai and Mao Zedong (Mao Tse-tung) in China, who became his disciples. Lenin made himself the spokesman for the rising tide of anti-Westernism, soliciting support for the common aim of unhinging the capitalist world order based on Western superiority.

As a political tool for this purpose, Lenin used the Communist—or Third—International (Comintern). The most radical successor to earlier socialist international associations, it helped to create small communist parties in western Europe which, in time, became dependable, although rather powerless, agents of Soviet Russia. In Asia, where no proletariat existed, Lenin tried to work closely with incipient nationalist movements and even envisaged setting up peasant soviets. He also held out the possibility that backward countries might skip the hated capitalist phase altogether, provided they allied themselves with the "leading socialist country," namely the Soviet Union.* It was soon clear that the anti-Western agitation of the twentieth century would not follow the path of world revolution as predicted by Lenin. Yet Lenin and the Bolshevik Revolution had inspired admiration and instinctive loyalty among the colonial and semi-colonial peoples in what would come to be called *the Third World*.

Unwittingly, Lenin also contributed to a novel division in the world. In the uncertain times following the First World War, the specter of world revolution created extravagant hopes and fears. Some people believed in the communist vision; others were thrown into a panic by it. The spread of communism was more than matched in western and central Europe, and in the Americas as well, by a vigorous anticommunism which, in turn, contributed to the rise of right-wing or fascist movements. Propertied and patriotic men and women had good reason to be scared; world revolution threatened their sense of security, their religion, their very sanity. World opinion became polarized: fear of communism became an obsession in the West, as did the fear of capitalism in Russia and many poor countries around the world.

World revolution, however, was never a realistic prospect. The tide of Western ascendancy was still running strong. Moreover, the Comintern was never a truly international force; it remained a tool of the Russian Communist Party. Yet the fear it aroused served

---

*Western Marxists believed that in the progression from feudalism to capitalism, and from capitalism to socialism and communism, no stage could be omitted. A country could start on a higher stage of development only if it had acquired all the social and technical skills of the preceding stage. Having argued, in contrast, that Russia could advance to socialism even though it had not matched the achievements of capitalism, Lenin advocated an even quicker shortcut for underdeveloped countries under Soviet leadership. He argued this case in his "Theses on the National and Colonial Question" (1920).

Lenin well: it made Soviet Russia appear strong when in fact the country was exhausted. At very little cost, the Comintern put prestige-conscious Russia back on the map of world politics. Capturing the attention of the world, Soviet Russia now stood out as the communist alternative to the capitalist West.

The Stalin Revolution

Stalin's Rise to Power

Secure after the end of the civil war, the communist service state gradually embarked on the daring experiment of social engineering envisaged in November 1917. Having set forth a master plan, Lenin was not destined to see it carried into action. He himself called for a retreat from his ambitious vision. In 1921 the country's exhaustion showed, and an uprising of sailors at the Kronstadt naval base and of workers in nearby Petrograd indicated the need for a sharp change of course. In March 1921 the people who in 1917 had been ready to give their lives for the revolution now rose against the repression that had been introduced during the civil war; they called for a restoration of soviet democracy. Trotsky ruthlessly suppressed that uprising, but the lesson was clear: the communist regime had to grant some measure of freedom; normal life had to resume.

In 1921 the Communist Party adopted the New Economic Policy, generally called NEP, which lasted until 1928. Under a system that Lenin characterized as "state socialism," the government retained control of finance, industry, and transportation—"the commanding heights" of the economy—but allowed the rest of the economy to return to private enterprise. The peasants, after giving part of their crops to the government, were free to sell the rest in the open market; traders could buy and sell as they pleased. With the resumption of small-scale capitalism, an air of prewar freedom returned, making the NEP

era a paradoxical mixture of the old and the new in Russia.

Lenin himself, incapacitated by strokes soon after the NEP was adopted, relinquished control of the party. In the leisure of his sickroom, Lenin began to realize how little his backward country was prepared for building a superior society. His last words urged patient hard work in learning from capitalism.

The task of achieving the goal that Lenin had set in his impatient prime was taken up by Stalin. The man of steel was crude and vulgar, toughened by the revolutionary underground and tsarist prisons and by the roughest aspects of Russian life. Nobody in 1917 would have foreseen this high-ranking Bolshevik as the successor to the university-trained, cosmopolitan Lenin. Relentlessly energetic, but relatively inconspicuous among the more temperamental and intellectual key Bolsheviks, Stalin was given, in 1922, the unwanted and seemingly routine task of general secretary of the party. It became his responsibility, in the chaotic aftermath of the Revolution and the civil war, to give reality to the Leninist vision of the monolithic party. He did so to his own advantage, building up a reliable party cadre—apparatus men, or *apparatchiki*, as they came to be called—and dominating the party as not even Lenin had. When in the protracted struggles for the succession to Lenin he was challenged, particularly by Trotsky and his associates, it was too late to unseat him. None of Stalin's rivals could rally the necessary majorities at the party congresses. Although equally ruthless, none could match Stalin's skill in party infighting or in making rough and anarchic people into docile members of the Communist Party apparatus.

Stalin, like Lenin, is best known from his poster image. Soviet citizens saw him as an energetic man clad in a simple military tunic, devoid of show or pomp, a fatherly figure, a good conciliatory chairman signifying a mood of bureaucratic control suitable to the industrial era. Yet the image was a façade. Behind it lay a coarse, vindictive, impatient temperament cast in preindustrial times, surcharged with the furies of a raw and brutal society rebelling against authority and yet wanting to survive in power and glory. The real Stalin was an appalling mixture of good and evil, each raised to superhuman proportions by his office as the dictator of Soviet Russia. To this day he is a fiercely controversial figure; but nobody has ever suggested that he took his tasks lightly.

Modernizing Russia: Industrialization and Collectivization

To Stalin, Russia's most pressing need was not world revolution but the fastest possible buildup of Soviet power through industrialization. The country could not afford another near-annihilation as it had suffered in the war and the civil war that followed. Bolshevik pride dictated that the country be made strong as much as possible by Russian efforts. Stalin's slogan was "socialism in one country," which signified that Soviet Russia by itself possessed all the necessary resources for "surpassing and overtaking" capitalism in the shortest time possible. It was a staggering job.

Stalin decided on all-out industrialization at the expense of the toiling masses. Peasants and workers, already poor, would be required to make tremendous sacrifices of body and spirit to overcome the nation's weaknesses. The Bolshevik Revolution had cleared the way for decisive action. Dependent as never before on their government, the Russian people could offer little resistance.

Stalin decided to end the NEP and decreed a series of Five-Year Plans, the first and most experimental one commencing in 1928. The industrialization drive was heralded as a vast economic and social revolution, undertaken by the state on a rational plan. The emphasis lay on heavy industry, the construction of railroads, power plants, steel mills, and military hardware like tanks and warplanes. Production of consumer goods was cut down to the minimum. All small-scale private trading, revived under the NEP, came to an end;

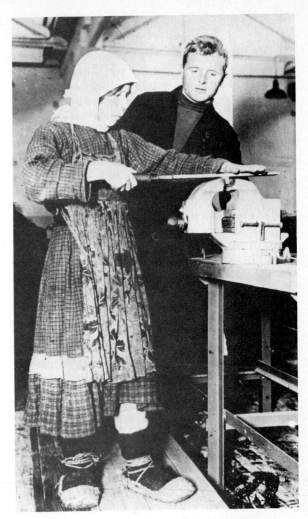

Foreman Teaching a Young Peasant Girl at the Gorki Auto Works, 1931. The task of industrializing the Soviet Union was staggering. The subsequent hardships endured by its people during the 1920s and 1930s are hard to imagine. For decades, the working masses were rewarded with nothing more than hope for a vague future success. (*Tass from Sovfoto*)

the state shops and cooperatives were bare, the service in them poor. Russians who had just come within sight of their pre-1914 standard of living now found their expectations dashed for decades to come.

Thus a new grim age began with drastic material hardships and profound mental anguish. Few Soviet citizens understood the necessities for the Five-Year Plan, but in the early years, young people particularly were fired to heroic exertions. They were proud to sacrifice themselves for the building of a superior society. When the Great Depression in the capitalist countries put millions out of work, no Soviet citizen suffered from unemployment; gloom pervaded the West, but confidence and hope, artificially fostered by the party, buoyed up Soviet Russia. The first Five-Year Plan had to be scrapped before running its course. Subsequent Five-Year Plans, however, gradually improved the quality of planning as well as of production. At no time, though, did the planning produce Western-style industrial efficiency.

Meanwhile, a second and far more brutal revolution overtook Soviet agriculture, for the peasants had to be forcibly integrated into the planned economy through collectivization. Agriculture—the peasants, their animals, their fields—had to submit to the same rational control as industry. Collectivization meant the pooling of farmlands, animals, and equipment for the sake of more efficient large-scale production. The Bolshevik solution for the backwardness of Russian agriculture had long been that the peasants should become like workers. But knowing the peasants' distaste for the factory, their attachment to their own land, and their stubbornness, the party had hesitated to carry out its ambition. In 1929, however, Stalin realized that for the sake of industrialization he had no choice. If the Five-Year Plan were to succeed, the government had to receive planned crops of planned size and quality at planned times. With collectivization, the ascendancy of the party over the people of Russia became almost complete.

For the peasants, the price was horrible. Stalin declared war on the Russian countryside. The kulaks (the most enterprising and well-to-do peasants) were sent to forced labor camps or killed outright. Their poorer and less efficient neighbors were herded onto collective farms at the point of a bayonet. The peasants struck back, sometimes in pitched battles. The horror of forced collectivization broke the spirit even of hardened officials.

"I am an old Bolshevik," sobbed a secret police colonel to a fellow passenger on a train; "I worked in the underground against the Tsar and then I fought in the civil war. Did I do all that in order that I should now surround villages with machine-guns and order my men to fire indiscriminately into crowds of peasants? Oh, no, no!"[6]

Defeated but unwilling to surrender their livestock, the peasants slaughtered their animals, gorging themselves in drunken orgies against the days of inevitable famine. The country's cattle herds declined to one-half, inflicting irreparable secondary losses as well. The number of horses, crucial for rural transport and farm work, fell by one-third. Crops were not planted or not harvested, the Five-Year Plan was disrupted, and in 1931–1933 millions starved to death. Yet Stalin rejoiced: the kulaks had been wiped out as a class; the peasants had been cowed into submission.

By 1935, practically all farming in Russia was collectivized. In theory, the collective farms were run democratically, under an elected chairman; in practice, they followed, as best they could, the directives handed down from the nearest party office. People grumbled about the rise of a new serfdom; agricultural development had been stifled.

Total Control

To quash resistance and mold a new type of suitably motivated and disciplined citizen, Stalin unleashed a third revolution, the revolution of totalitarianism. It aimed at a total reconstruction of state and society down to the innermost recesses of human consciousness. It called for "a new man" suited to the needs of Soviet industrialism. Society was reshaped for the utmost productivity. The hallowed revolutionary ideal of equality was denounced as petty bourgeois.

Soviet citizens had to work as hard as they could, with the rewards going to those who made special contributions toward plan fulfillment, to engineers, scientists, managers, and certain heroes of labor, like the famous

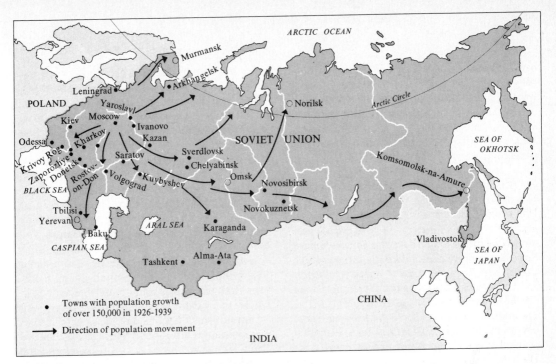

Map 31.2 Soviet Population Growth and Movement, 1926–1939.

miner Stakhanov, who set records of output. Workers were paid piece wages; the trade unions henceforth became tools of the state, enforcing work discipline. A new elite of party-trained industrial managers rose. In addition, family discipline and sexual mores, exceedingly lax after the Revolution, were tightened by decree into a new work-oriented ethic.

In 1935 Stalin, summing up these changes, officially declared socialism achieved in the Soviet Union. The Soviet Constitution of 1936 set forth major institutions and principles guiding the new society; it left no doubt as to what was expected of Soviet citizens. They must "abide by the Constitution, observe the laws, maintain labor discipline, honestly perform public duties, respect the rules of socialist intercourse, and safeguard and strengthen public property" (theft of state property was a widespread practice). All offenders were called "enemies of the people" and threatened with dire punishment. The list of duties ended with the words "treason is the most heinous of crimes. The defense of the Fatherland

is the most sacred duty of every citizen"— ominous words indeed.

The revolution of totalitarianism extended even further. All media of communications— literature, the arts, music, the stage—were forced into subservience to the Five-Year Plan. In literature, as in all art, an official style was promulgated called *Socialist Realism.* It was to give human detail to the abstract goals of the planned economy.

Novels in the Socialist Realist manner told how the romances of tractor drivers and milkmaids, or of lathe operators and office secretaries, led to new victories of production under the Five-Year Plan. Composers found their music examined for remnants of bourgeois spirit; they were to write simple tunes suitable for heroic times. Everywhere, huge high-color posters showed men and women hard at work with radiant faces calling others to join them; often Stalin, the wise father and leader, was shown taking the salute among them. In this manner artistic creativity was locked into a dull, utilitarian straitjacket of official cheerfulness; creativity was allowed only to boost industrial productivity. Behind the scenes, all artists were disciplined to conform to the will of the party or be crushed.

Education, from nursery school to university, was likewise harnessed to train dutiful and loyal citizens. Said one text on Soviet pedagogy:

We must cultivate in our children the realization that the Union of Soviet Socialist Republics is a land where a socialist society is being constructed for the first time in history. We must develop in them a feeling of pride in the most revolutionary class, the working class, and in its vanguard, the Communist Party. This party, the party of Lenin and Stalin, was able to organize the toiling masses for the construction of a new communist society. Through the victories of the Stalin five-year plans, our land was transformed into a mighty industrial country, the most advanced and most cultured. We must make every school child aware of the grandeur of our struggle and our victories; we must show him the cost of these great successes in labor and blood; we must tell him how the great people of our epoch—Lenin, Stalin, and their companions in arms—organized the workers in the struggle for a new and happy life.[7]

But still the Russian masses resisted the enforced change to the large-scale, rigidly restrictive cooperation of modern industrialism. Against that stubborn resistance, Stalin unleashed raw terror to break stubborn wills and compel conformity. Terror had been used as a tool of government ever since the Revolution (and the tsars had also used it, moderately and intermittently). After the start of the first Five-Year Plan, show trials were staged that denounced as saboteurs the engineers who found Stalin's tempo counterproductive. The terror used to herd the peasants onto collective farms was of a larger scale. Stalin also used terror to crush opposition and to instill an abject fear not only in the ranks of the party, but also in Russian society at large.

Purges had long been used to rid the party of weaklings. After 1934, however, they became an instrument of Stalin's drive for un-

challenged personal power. A party congress in that year had expressed doubts about Stalin's brutality in dealing with the peasants; it advanced a potential rival, Sergei Kirov. Soon thereafter, Kirov was murdered at Stalin's request. In 1936 Stalin's vindictive terror broke into the open. The first batch of victims, including many founders of the Communist Party, was accused of conspiring with the exiled Trotsky to set up a "terrorist center" and of scheming to terrorize the party; they were blamed for the murder of Kirov. The world watched the great show trials with amazement and horror as Stalin intimidated his people. After being sentenced to death, the first group was immediately executed. In 1937 the next group, including prominent communists of Lenin's day, was charged with cooperating with foreign intelligence agencies and wrecking "socialist reconstruction," the term for Stalin's revolution; they too were executed. Shortly afterward, a secret purge wiped out the military high command, leaving the Soviet army without leadership for years.

In 1938 the last and biggest show trial advanced the most monstrous accusation of all: sabotage, espionage, and attempting to dismember the Soviet Union and kill all its leaders (including Lenin in 1918). In the public hearings some defendants refuted the public prosecutor, but in the end all confessed before being executed. Western observers were aghast at the cynical charges and the tortures used to obtain the confessions.

The great trials, however, involved only a small minority of Stalin's victims; many more perished in silence. The terror hit first of all members of the party, especially the Old Bolsheviks, who had joined before the Revolution; they were the most independent-minded members and therefore the most dangerous to Stalin. But Stalin also diminished the cultural elite that had survived the Lenin revolution. Thousands of engineers, scientists, industrial managers, scholars, and artists disappeared; they were shot or sent to forced-labor camps where most of them perished. No one was safe. To frighten the common people in all walks of life, men, women, and even children were dragged into the net of Stalin's secret police—a soul-killing reminder to the survivors: submit or else.

The toll of the purges is reckoned in the tens of millions; it included Trotsky, who in 1940 was murdered in Mexico. The bloodletting was ghastly, as Stalin's purge officials themselves followed each other into death and ignominy.

The human price that Soviet Russia paid for Stalin's effort to wipe out his country's inferiority has been documented by the great Russian writer Aleksandr Solzhenitsyn in his work *The Gulag Archipelago*. Yet by Solzhenitsyn's own testimony, the responsibility for the atrocities was not Stalin's alone; the "wolfishness" of the terror flowed from Russian life itself. Speaking of the torturers, the "Blue Caps" who interrogated and often killed innocent victims of the terror, Solzhenitsyn asks: "Where did this wolf-tribe appear from among our people? Does it really stem from our own roots? Our own blood?" Devastatingly he answers: "It is our own."[8]

Stalin, who had passed through the hands of the tsarist police and had participated in the carnage of the civil war, certainly was untroubled by the repulsive waste of life. In his eyes new talent was readily available; he provided opportunities for spectacular careers. And he got results: productivity, especially of armaments, increased.

In foreign even more than in internal affairs, Stalin's policy was marked by fear; the danger of war was always uppermost in his mind. It was to Soviet advantage to make a show of strength, but underneath this façade Stalin pursued a conservative policy, husbanding Russia's resources for internal reconstruction and hoping that the capitalist states would fall out among themselves, allowing him to play the happy bystander, entering the fray only for the kill. Stalin did not follow up Lenin's teaching about world revolution. He realized that the key to the future of Soviet communism lay in the power of the Soviet Union and that its power was never sufficient amid the dangers it confronted in the world. His personal sense of insecurity reflected the persistent insecurity of his country. By the end of the 1930s, after the Stalin revolution, yet another era of profound and cruel perils began for his country—the Second World War and the battle with Nazi Germany, followed by the cold war.

Soviet Communism in Perspective

The fateful events in Russia from the end of World War I to the late 1930s profoundly excited opinion everywhere. Some Marxists saw their ideals realized; others felt that Stalin had betrayed the cause of socialism. Some disillusioned Western liberals agreed with the American visitor to the Soviet Union who said that he "had seen the future and it worked."[9] But most Westerners were appalled by Soviet theory and practice, although for profit or political expediency some cooperated with the Soviet regime. In the face of the Great Depression and Japanese expansion, for instance, the United States officially recognized the Soviet Union in 1933. The purges disenchanted many early communist sympathizers, including George Orwell, who in revulsion wrote *Animal Farm* and *1984*. In the countries of Asia, on the other hand, the progress of the Five-Year Plans was watched with envy and admiration: if Russia could raise itself by its bootstraps, why could others not follow its example?

In retrospect, Nikita Khrushchev's attack (see page 833) on "the cult of personality" (as the glorification of Stalin came to be called after his death) and the works of Solzhenitsyn have driven home Stalin's inhumanity. At the same time, hindsight makes clearer the continuity from Lenin to Stalin and their places in both the course of Russian history and the contexts of their times. Both men, but Stalin especially, fitted into the tradition of cruel and overbearing state-building tsars like Peter the Great.

Stalin left no doubt about the ultimate jus-

Chronology 31.1 The Rise of the Soviet Union

March 1917	The Bolsheviks take power, led by Lenin
1917–1920	Civil War
January 1918	The communists disband the Constituent Assembly
May–June 1918	Nicholas II and his family are executed
1919	Lenin moves the capital to Moscow; Lenin forms the Comintern
March 1919	The Treaty of Brest-Litovsk
April 1920	Russia loses eastern European territory to Poland
November 1920	The last remnants of the White Army's forces evacuate from the Crimean Peninsula
1921–1928	The New Economic Policy is implemented
1922	Stalin becomes General Secretary of the Communist Party
1928	Stalin's first Five-Year Plan begins
1936	Stalin's purges begin
1940	Trotsky is murdered in Mexico

tification for such policy. In 1931, bluntly disregarding Marxist-Leninist jargon and forgetting about Russian expansion into Asia, he said:

Those who fall behind get beaten. But we do not want to be beaten. No, we refuse to be beaten. One feature of the history of old Russia was the continual beatings she suffered for falling behind, for her backwardness. All beat her—for her backwardness, for military backwardness, cultural backwardness, political backwardness, for industrial backwardness, for agricultural backwardness. She was beaten because to do so was profitable and could be done with impunity. . . . You are backward, you are weak—therefore you are wrong, hence you can be beaten and enslaved. You are mighty, therefore you are right, hence we must be wary of you. Such is the law of the exploiters. . . . That is why we must no longer lag behind.[10]

He set forth the stark reckoning of Russian history: the cost of foreign enslavement against the costs of a terror-driven mobilization.

Westernizing an unprepared Russia was bound to be a wasteful and cruel experiment. It was made more cruel yet by the tradition of violence in both Russian statecraft and the revolutionary movement, by the battles of World War I, the excitements of revolution, and the passion of civil war. In his own part of that experiment, Stalin worked with unsuitable human resources to make his country conform to essential aspects of the Western heritage. Marxism-Leninism adapted Western models to the conditions of the Russia empire. The Stalin constitution imitated Western constitutional language. Soviet industrialization took its lead from Western urban-industrial society. And above all, Soviet international political ambition was patterned after the fullness of Western power around the world. In these essentials Stalin westernized his country and laid the foundations for the rise of Soviet Russia into a superpower, more secure and respected in the world than any previous Russian regime. For this historic success he could claim the same moral justification by which Western statesmen had sent millions of people to their deaths in World War I. Monstrous indeed are the stakes of twentieth-century power politics, but it is in this perspective that Stalin must be understood.

Notes

1. V. A. Maklakov, quoted in *The Russian Provisional Government 1917*, III, documents selected and edited by Robert Paul Browder and Alexander F. Kerensky (Stanford, California: Stanford University Press, 1961), p. 1276.

2. V. I. Lenin, "The Impending Catastrophe and How to Combat It," *Lenin on Politics and Revolution*, selected writings, ed., James E. Connor (New York: Pegasus, 1968), p. 183.

3. V. I. Lenin, "On Revolutionary Violence and Terror," *The Lenin Anthology*, ed., R. C. Tucker (New York: Norton, 1975), p. 432.

4. All-Russian Communist Party (Bolsheviks), 1919, in *Soviet Communism: Programs and Rules. Officials Texts of 1919, 1952, (1956), 1961*, ed. Jan F. Triska (San Francisco: Chandler, 1962), p. 23.

5. V. I. Lenin, "The Immediate Tasks of the Soviet Government," *The Lenin Anthology*, pp. 448ff.

6. Quoted in Isaac Deutscher, *Stalin. A Political Biography* (New York, Oxford University Press, 1966), p. 325.

7. *"I Want to Be Like Stalin,"* from the Russian Text on Pedagogy by B. P. Yesipov and N. K. Goncharov, trans. by George S. Counts and Nucia P. Lodge, with an introduction by George S. Counts (New York: John Day, 1947), pp. 36–37.

8. Aleksandr I. Solzhenitsyn, *The Gulag Archipelago*. Vol. I (New York: Harper and Row, 1974), p. 160.

9. Lincoln Steffens, "I have been over into the future, and it works." In *Autobiography* (New York: Harcourt, Brace, 1931), p. 799.

10. J. V. Stalin, "Speech to Business Executives" (1931), in *A Documentary History of Communism*

from Lenin to Mao, ed. Robert V. Daniels (New York: Random House, 1960), 2:22.

Suggested Reading

Antonov-Ovseenko, Anton, *The Time of Stalin. Portrait of a Tyranny* (1981). A recent anti-Stalinist treatment by a Soviet author.

Carr, E. H., *The Russian Revolution from Lenin to Stalin* (1970). A brief summary based on the author's multivolume study of the years 1917–1929.

Cohen, Stephen, *Bukharin and the Bolshevik Revolution* (1971–1980). Argues that there existed more moderate alternatives to Stalin's policies.

Deutscher, Isaac, *Trotsky: 1879–1940*, 3 vols., *The Prophet Armed* (1954), *The Prophet Unarmed* (1959), *The Prophet Outcast* (1963). The classic work on Trotsky.

Ginzburg, Eugenia, *Journey into the Whirlwind* (1967). A woman's experiences under the Terror.

Koestler, Arthur, *Darkness at Noon* (1941). A revealing novel about the fate of an Old Bolshevik in the terror purge.

Lewin, Moshe, *Russian Peasants and Soviet Power* (1968). A thoughtful analysis by a French scholar.

Mandelshtam, Nadezhda, *Hope Against Hope: A Memoir* (1976). A poet's wife comments on the Soviet scene.

Nove, Alec, *Stalinism and After* (1975). An excellent short work from an economist's perspective.

Pasternak, Boris, *Doctor Zhivago* (1958). The tragedies of Russian life from Nicholas II to Stalin as seen through the eyes of a superbly sensitive and observant poet.

Scott, John, *Behind the Urals, An American Worker in Russia's City of Steel* (1942, reprint 1973). A firsthand account of life under the first Five-Year Plan.

Sholokhov, Mikhail, *And Quiet Flows the Don; The Don Flows Home to the Sea*, 2 vols. (1934–1940). A Nobel Prize-winning novel on the brutalizing effects of war, revolution, and civil war.

Solzhenitsyn, Aleksandr I., *One Day in the Life of Ivan Denisovich* (1963). The first account of life in one of Stalin's forced labor camps to reach the public.

———, *The Gulag Archipelago* (3 vols., 1973–1975). The classic account of Stalin's terror, especially vol. I.

———, *The First Circle* (1968). The life of privileged victims of the terror.

Trotsky, Leon, *The Russian Revolution: The Overthrow of Tsarism and the Triumph of the Soviets* (1932). A classic account of the Bolshevik Revolution by its chief organizer. Read especially the chapters entitled "Five Days" and "The Seizure of the Winter Palace."

Tucker, Robert C., *Stalin as a Revolutionary* (1973). A psychological study of the young Stalin.

———, *The Lenin Anthology* (1975). For those who want a taste of Lenin's writings.

Ulam, Adam B., *The Bolsheviks: The Intellectual and Political History of the Triumph of Communism in Russia* (1965). A full account built around Lenin.

———, *Stalin: The Man and His Era* (1973). The best biography to date.

Von Laue, Theodore H., *Why Lenin? Why Stalin?* (1970). A readable survey emphasizing the global contexts.

Review Questions

1. Why did the Provisional Government and liberal democracy fail in 1917?

2. Why, by contrast, were the Bolsheviks successful in seizing and holding power from 1917 to 1921?

3. By what institutions and methods did Lenin build the Soviet state? What innovations did he introduce after the collapse of the tsarist regime and the failure of the provisional government?

4. How did the peasants fare through war, revolution, and the rise of the Soviet state? Why did Stalin collectivize agriculture?

5. How did the Soviet leaders view the position of Russia in the world? What were their aims and ambitions? How did their goals compare with those of other states?

6. What were Stalin's motives and justifications for the terror purge?

7. How do you explain the fact that the communist regime was far more ruthless in its methods of government than the tsarist regime? Which regime accomplished more for the power of Russia?

8. Compare and contrast the treatment of religion in American life with its treatment under Soviet rule. How do you account for the differences? Likewise, compare and contrast the organization of agriculture and industry in the United States with the organization of their counterparts under Soviet rule. Again, how do you account for the differences?

9. How would you define the differences between the conditions shaping American history and the conditions shaping Russian history in the years covered by this chapter? Can you see any of the conditions that shaped the Soviet regime at work in American society and government? Or, to put the question differently, to what extent do you think American ways of thinking are applicable to the conditions prevailing in Russia?

32

The Rise of Fascism:
The Attack on Democracy

*L*iberals viewed the Great War as a conflict between freedom and autocracy and expected an Allied victory to accelerate the spread of democracy throughout Europe. In the immediate aftermath of the war it seemed that liberalism would continue to advance as it had in the nineteenth century. The collapse of the autocratic German and Austrian empires had led to the formation of parliamentary governments throughout eastern and central Europe. Yet within two decades, in an extraordinary turn of events, democracy seemed in its death throes. In Spain, Portugal, Italy, and Germany, and in all the newly created states of central and eastern Europe except Czechoslovakia, democracy collapsed and various forms of authoritarian governments emerged. The defeat of democracy and the surge of authoritarianism was best exemplified by the triumph of totalitarian fascist movements in Italy and Germany.

The emergence of fascist movements in more than twenty European lands after World War I was a sign that liberal society was in a state of disorientation and dissolution. Fascism was a response to a postwar society afflicted by spiritual disintegration, economic dislocation, political instability, and thwarted nationalist hopes. It was an expression of fear that the Bolshevik Revolution would spread westward. It was also an expression of hostility to democratic values and a reaction to the failure of liberal institutions to solve crushing problems of modern industrial society. To fascists and their sympathizers, democracy seemed an ineffective, spiritless, and enfeebled old regime ready to topple.

In their struggle to bring down the liberal state, fascist leaders aroused primitive impulses, resurrected ancient folkways and tribal loyalties, and made use of myths and rituals to mobilize and manipulate the masses. Organizing propaganda campaigns with the thoroughness of a military operation, fascists aroused and dominated the masses and confused and undermined their democratic opposition, breaking its will to resist. Fascists were most successful in countries with weak democratic traditions. When parliamentary government faltered, it had few staunch defenders and many who yearned to dance at its death.

The proliferation of fascist movements demonstrated that the habits of democracy are not quickly learned or easily retained. Particularly during times of crisis, people lose patience with parliamentary discussion and constitutional procedures, sink into nonrational modes of thought and behavior, and are easily manipulated by unscrupulous politicians. For the sake of economic or emotional security and national grandeur, they will often willingly sacrifice political freedom. Fascism starkly manifested the immense power of the irrational; it humbled liberals, making them permanently aware of the limitations of reason and the fragility of freedom.

The fascist goal of maximum centralization of power was furthered by developments during World War I—the expansion of bureaucracy, the concentration of industry into giant monopolies, and the close cooperation between industry and the state. The instruments of modern technology—radio, motion pictures, public address systems, telephone, teletype—made it possible for the state to indoctrinate, manipulate, and dominate its subjects.

Elements of Fascism

Fascist movements were marked by an extreme nationalism and a determination to eradicate liberalism and Marxism—to undo the legacy of the French Revolution of 1789 and the Bolshevik Revolution of 1917. Fascists believed that theirs was a spiritual revolution, that they were initiating a new era in history, that they were building a new civilization on the ruins of liberal democracy. "We stand for a new principle in the world," said Mussolini. "We stand for sheer categorical, definitive, antithesis to the world of democracy . . . to the world which still abides by the fundamental principles laid down in 1789."[1] The chief principle of Nazism, said Hitler, "is to abolish the liberal concept of the individual and the Marxist concept of

humanity, and to substitute for them the *Volk* community, rooted in the soil and united by the bond of its common blood."[2]

Fascists accused liberal society of despiritualizing human beings, of transforming them into materialistic creatures who knew no higher ideal than profit—whose souls were deadened to noble causes, heroic deeds, and self-sacrifice. Idealistic youth and intellectuals rejoiced in fascism's activism; they saw it as a revolt against the mediocrity of mass society, as a reaffirmation of the highest human spiritual qualities, as an answer to despair.

Fascists regarded Marxism as another enemy, for class conflict divided the nation. To fascists, the Marxist call for workers of the world to unite meant the death of the national community. Fascism, in contrast, would reintegrate the proletariat into the nation and end class hostilities that divide and weaken the state and its people. By making people of all classes feel that they were a needed part of the nation, fascism offered a solution to the problem of insecurity and isolation in modern industrial society.

In contrast to liberalism and Marxism, fascism attacked the rational tradition of the Enlightenment and exalted will, blood, feeling, and instinct. Intellectual discussion and critical analysis, said fascists, cause national divisiveness; reason promotes doubt, enfeebles the will, and hinders instinctive, aggressive action. Glorifying action for its own sake, fascists aroused and manipulated brutal and primitive impulses and carried into politics the combative spirit of the trenches. They formed private armies that attracted veterans—many of them rootless, brutal, and maladjusted men who sought to preserve the loyalty, camaraderie, and violence of the front.

Fascism exalted the leader, who intuitively grasped what was best for the nation, and called for rule by an elite of dedicated party members. The leader and the party would relieve the individual of the need to make decisions. Holding that the liberal stress on individual freedom promoted competition and conflict that shattered national unity, fascists pressed for monolithic unity—one leader, one party, and one national will.

Fascism drew its mass support from the lower middle class—small merchants, artisans, white-collar workers, civil servants, peasants of moderate means—who were frightened by both big capitalism and socialism. They hoped that fascism would protect them from the competition of big business and prevent the hated working class from establishing a Marxist state that would threaten their property. The lower middle class saw in fascism a noncommunist way of overcoming economic crises and restoring traditional respect for family, native soil, and nation. Many of these people also saw in fascism a way of attacking the existing social order, which denied them opportunities for economic advancement and social prestige. Having no patience for parliamentary procedures or sympathy for democratic principles they were drawn to demagogues who exuded confidence and promised direct action.

While a radicalized middle class gave fascist movements their mass support, the fascists could not have captured the state without the aid of existing ruling elites—landed aristocrats, industrialists, and army leaders. In Russia, the Bolsheviks had to fight their way into power; in Italy and Germany the old ruling order virtually handed power to the fascists. In both countries fascist leaders succeeded in reassuring the conservative elite that they would not institute widespread social reforms or interfere with private property and would protect the nation from communism. The old elite abhorred the violent activism and demagoguery of fascism and had contempt for fascist leaders, who were often brutal men without breeding or culture. Yet to protect their interests, the old ruling class entered into an alliance with the fascists.

The Rise of Fascism in Italy

Postwar Unrest

Although Italy had been on the winning side in World War I, it had the appearance of a defeated nation. Food shortages, rising prices, massive unemployment, violent strikes, workers occupying factories, and peasants squatting on the uncultivated periphery of large estates created a climate of crisis. These dismal conditions contrasted sharply with the vision of a postwar world painted by politicians during the war. Italy required effective leadership and a reform program, but the liberal government was paralyzed by party disputes; with several competing parties, the liberals could not organize a solid majority that could cope with the domestic crisis.

The middle class was severely stressed. To meet its accelerating expenses, the government had increased taxes, but the burden fell unevenly on small landowners, small-businessowners, civil-service workers, and professionals. Moreover, the value of war bonds, purchased primarily by the middle class, had declined considerably because of inflation. Instead of finding a return to the good days and their former status once the war ended, these solid citizens found their economic position continuing to deteriorate.

Large landowners and industrialists feared that their nation was on the verge of a Bolshevik-style revolution. They took seriously the proclamations of the socialists: "The proletariat must be incited to the violent seizure of political and economic power and this must be handed over entirely and exclusively to the Workers' and Peasants' Councils."[3] In truth, Italian socialists had no master plan to seize power. Peasant squatters and urban strikers were responding to the distress in their own regions and did not significantly coordinate their efforts with those in other localities. Moreover, when the workers realized that they could not keep the factories operating, their revolutionary zeal waned and they started to abandon the plants. The workers' and peasants' poorly led and futile struggles did not portend a Red Revolution. Nevertheless the industrialists and landlords, with the Bolshevik Revolution still vivid in their minds, were taking no chances.

Adding to the unrest was national outrage at the terms of the peace settlement. Italians felt that despite their sacrifices—500,000 dead and one million wounded—they had been robbed of the fruits of victory. While Italy

Mussolini at Rome, Celebrating the Tenth Anniversary of the Fascist Gathering in Milan for the March on Rome. Initially Mussolini was able to bluff his way to power because an indecisive liberal regime did not counter force with force. Although Mussolini established a one-party state and manipulated mass organizations and the mass media, he was less successful than Hitler or Stalin in creating a totalitarian regime. (*AP/Wide World Photos*)

had received the Brenner Pass and Trieste, it had been denied the Dalmatian coast, the Adriatic port of Fiume, and territory in Africa and the Middle East. Nationalists blamed the liberal government for what they called a "mutilated victory." In 1919, a force of war veterans led by the poet and adventurer Gabriele D'Annunzio (1863–1938) seized Fiume, to the delirious joy of Italian nationalists and the embarrassment of the government. D'Annunzio's occupation of the port lasted more than a year, adding fuel to the flames of Italian nationalism and demonstrating the weakness of the liberal regime in imposing its authority on rightist opponents.

Mussolini's Seizure of Power

Benito Mussolini (1883–1945) was born in a small village in east central Italy. Proud, quarrelsome, violent, and resentful of the humiliation he suffered for being poor, the young Mussolini was a troublemaker and was often brought before school authorities. But he was also intelligent, ranking first on final examinations in four subjects. After graduation, Mussolini taught in an elementary school, but this did not suit his passionate temperament. From 1902 to 1904 he lived in Switzerland, where he broadened his reading, lectured, and wrote. He also came under the influence of anarchists and socialist revolutionaries. Returning to Italy, he was labeled a dangerous revolutionary by the police. As a reward for his zeal and political agitation, which led to five months in prison for inciting riots, Mussolini in 1912 was made editor of *Avanti*, the principal socialist newspaper. During the early days of World War I he was expelled from the Socialist party for advocating Italian intervention in the war. After

Italy entered the war, Mussolini served at the front and suffered a serious wound during firing practice, for which he was hospitalized.

In 1919 Mussolini organized the Fascist party to realize his immense will to power; this quest for power, more than a set of coherent doctrines, characterized the young movement. A supreme opportunist rather than an ideologist, Mussolini exploited the unrest in postwar Italy in order to capture control of the state. He attracted converts from the discontented, disillusioned, and uprooted. Many Italians, particularly the educated bourgeoisie who had been inspired by the unification movement of the nineteenth century, viewed Mussolini as the leader who would gain Fiume, Dalmatia, and colonies and win Italy's rightful place of honor in international affairs. Hardened battle veterans joined the Fascist movement to escape the boredom and idleness of civilian life. They welcomed an opportunity to wear the uniforms of the Fascist militia (Black Shirts), parade in the streets, and do battle with socialist and labor-union opponents. Squads of Fascist Black Shirts (*squadristi*) raided socialist and trade-union offices, destroying property and beating the occupants. It soon appeared that Italy was drifting toward civil war as socialist Red Shirts responded in kind.

Industrialists and landowners, hoping that Mussolini would rescue Italy from Bolshevism, contributed large sums to the Fascist party. The lower middle class, fearful that the growing power of labor unions and the Socialist party threatened their property and social prestige, viewed Mussolini as a protector. Middle-class university students, searching for adventure and an ideal, and army officers, dreaming of an Italian empire and hateful of parliamentary government, also were receptive to Mussolini's party. Intellectuals disenchanted with liberal politics and parliamentary democracy were intrigued by Mussolini's philosophy of action. Mussolini's nationalism, activism, and anticommunism gradually seduced elements of the power structure—capitalists, aristocrats, army officers, the royal family, the church. Regarding

liberalism as bankrupt and parliamentary government as futile, many of these people yearned for a military dictatorship.

In 1922 Mussolini made his bid for power. Speaking at a giant rally of his followers in late October, he declared: "Either they will give us the government or we shall take it by descending on Rome. It is now a matter of days, perhaps hours." A few days later thousands of Fascists began the March on Rome. Some members of parliament demanded that the army defend the government against a Fascist coup. It would have been a relatively simple matter to crush the 20,000 Fascist marchers armed with little more than pistols and rifles, but King Victor Emmanuel III (1869–1947) refused to act. The king's advisers, some of them sympathetic to Mussolini, exaggerated the strength of the Fascists. Believing that he was rescuing Italy from terrible violence, the king appointed Mussolini prime minister.

Mussolini had bluffed his way into power. Fascism had triumphed not because of its own strength—the Fascists had only 35 of 535 seats in parliament—but because the liberal regime, irresolute and indecisive, did not counter force with force. In the past, the liberal state had not challenged Fascist acts of terror; now it feebly surrendered to Fascist blustering and threats. No doubt liberals hoped that once in power, the Fascists would forsake terror, pursue moderate aims, and act within the constitution. But the liberals were wrong; they had completely misjudged the antidemocratic character of Fascism.

The Fascist State in Italy

Consolidation of Power

In October 1922, when the liberal regime in Italy capitulated, the Fascists by no means held total power. Anti-Fascists still sat in parliament and only four of fourteen ministers in Mussolini's cabinet were Fascists. Cautious and shrewd, Mussolini resisted the extremists in his party who demanded a second revolution—the immediate and preferably violent destruction of the old order. In this early stage of Fascist rule, when his position was still tenuous, Mussolini sought to maintain an image of respectability and moderation. He tried to convince the power structure that he intended to operate within the constitution, that he did not seek dictatorial power. At the same time he gradually secured his position and turned Italy into a one-party state. In 1923, an electoral law, approved by both chambers of the parliament, decreed that the party with the most votes in a national election (provided that the figure was not less than 25 percent of the total votes cast) would be granted two-thirds of the seats in the Chamber of Deputies. In the elections of 1924, marred by Fascist terrorism, Mussolini's supporters received 65 percent of the vote. Even without the new electoral law, the opponents of Fascism would have been enfeebled; Mussolini had consolidated his power.

When socialist leader Giacomo Matteotti protested Fascist terror tactics, Fascist thugs killed him (in 1924). Although Mussolini had not ordered Matteotti's murder, his vicious attacks against his socialist opponent inspired the assassins. Repelled by the murder, some sincere democrats withdrew from the Chamber of Deputies in protest and some influential Italians called for Mussolini's dismissal. But the majority of liberals, including the leadership, continued to support Mussolini. And the king, the papacy, the army, large landowners, and industrialists, still regarding Mussolini as the best defense against internal disorder and socialism, did not lend their support to an anti-Fascist movement.

Pressed by the radicals within the Fascist party, Mussolini moved to establish a dictatorship. In 1925–26 he eliminated non-Fascists from his cabinet, dissolved opposition parties, smashed the independent trade unions, suppressed opposition newspapers, replaced local mayors with Fascist officials, and organized a secret police to round up troublemakers. Many anti-Fascists fled the country or were deported.

Mussolini then turned on the extremist Fascists, the local chieftains (*ras*) who had led squadristi in the early days of the movement. Lauding violence, daring deeds, and the dangerous life, the ras were indispensable during the party's formative stage. But Mussolini feared that the radical adventurism of the ras posed a threat to his personal rule. And their desire to replace the traditional power structure with people drawn from their own ranks could block his efforts to cooperate with the established elite—industrialists, aristocratic landowners, and army leaders. Mussolini therefore expelled some squadristi leaders from the party and gave others positions in the bureaucracy to tame them.

Mussolini was less successful than Hitler and Stalin in fashioning a totalitarian state. The industrialists, the large landowners, the church, and to some extent even the army, never fell under the complete domination of the party. Nor did the regime possess the mind of its subjects with the same thoroughness as the Nazis did in Germany. Life in Italy was less regimented and the individual less fearful than in Nazi Germany or Communist Russia. The Italian people might cheer Mussolini, but few were willing to die for him.

Control of the Masses

Like Communist Russia and Nazi Germany, Fascist Italy used mass organizations and mass media to control minds and regulate behavior. As in the Soviet Union and the Third Reich, the Fascist regime created a cult of the leader. "Mussolini goes forward with confidence, in a halo of myth, almost chosen by God, indefatigable and infallible, the instrument employed by Providence for the creation of a new civilization," wrote the philosopher Giovanni Gentile.[4] To convey the image of a virile leader, Mussolini had himself photographed barechested or in a uniform with a steel helmet. Other photographs showed him riding horses, driving fast cars, flying planes, and playing with lion cubs. Mussolini frequently addressed huge throngs of admirers from his balcony. His tenor voice, grandiloquent phrases, and posturing—jaw thrust out, hands on hips—captivated audiences; idolatry from the masses, in turn, intensified Mussolini's feelings of grandeur. Elementary school textbooks depicted Mussolini as the savior of the nation, a modern-day Julius Caesar.

Fascist propaganda inculcated habits of discipline and obedience: "Mussolini is always right." "Believe! Obey! Fight!" Propaganda also glorified war: "A minute on the battlefield is worth a lifetime of peace." The press, radio, and cinema idealized life under Fascism, implying that Fascism had eradicated crime, poverty, and social tensions. Schoolteachers and university professors were compelled to swear allegiance to the Fascist government and to propagate Fascist ideals, while students were urged to criticize instructors who harbored liberal attitudes. Millions of youths belonged to Fascist organizations in which they participated in patriotic ceremonies and social functions, sang Fascist hymns, and wore Fascist uniforms. They submerged their own identities into the group.

Economic Policies

Fascists denounced economic liberalism for promoting individual self-interest, and socialism for instigating conflicts between workers and capitalists that divided and weakened the nation. The Fascist way of resolving tensions between workers and employers was to abolish independent labor unions, prohibit strikes, and establish associations or corporations that included both the workers and employers within a given industry. In theory, representatives of labor and capital would cooperatively solve labor problems in a particular industry. In practice the representatives of labor turned out to be Fascists who protected the interests of the industrialists. Although the Fascists lauded the corporative system as a creative approach to modern economic problems, in reality it

played a minor role in Italian economic life. Big business continued to make its own decisions, paying scant attention to the corporations.

Nor did the Fascist government solve Italy's long-standing economic problems. To curtail the export of capital and to reduce the nation's dependency on imports in case of war, Mussolini sought to make Italy self-sufficient. To win the "battle of grain," the Fascist regime brought marginal lands under cultivation and urged farmers to concentrate on wheat rather than other crops. While wheat production increased substantially, total agricultural output declined because wheat had been planted on land more suited to animal husbandry and fruit cultivation. To make Italy industrially self-sufficient, the regime limited imports of foreign goods, with the result that Italian consumers paid higher prices for Italian-manufactured goods. Mussolini posed as the protector of the little people, but under his regime the power and profits of big business grew and the standard of living of small farmers and urban workers declined. Government attempts to grapple with the Depression were half-hearted. Aside from providing family allowances—an increase in income with the birth of each child—the Fascist regime did little in the way of social welfare.

The Church and the Fascist Regime

Although anticlerical since his youth, Mussolini was also expedient. He recognized that coming to terms with the church would improve his image with Catholic public opinion. The Vatican regarded Mussolini's regime as a barrier against communism and as less hostile to church interests and more amenable to church direction than a liberal government. Pope Pius XI (1922–1939) was an ultraconservative whose hatred of liberalism and secularism led him to believe that the Fascists would increase the influence of the church in the nation.

In 1929 the Lateran Accords recognized the

independence of Vatican City, repealed many of the anticlerical laws passed under the liberal government, and made religious instruction compulsory in all secondary schools. The papal state, Vatican City, became a small enclave within Rome over which the Italian government had no authority. Relations between the Vatican and the Fascist government remained fairly good throughout the decade of the 1930s. One crisis arose in 1931 when Mussolini, pushed by militant anticlericals within his party, dissolved certain Catholic youth groups as rivals to Fascist youth associations, but a compromise that permitted the Catholic organizations to function within certain limits eased tensions. When Mussolini invaded Ethiopia and intervened in the Spanish Civil War, the church supported him. Although the papacy criticized Mussolini for drawing closer to Hitler and introducing anti-Jewish legislation, it never broke with the Fascist regime.

The New German Republic

In the last days of World War I, a revolution brought down the German imperial government and led to the creation of a democratic republic. In October 1918 the German admirals had ordered the German navy to engage the British in the English Channel, but the sailors, anticipating peace and resentful of their officers (who commonly resorted to cruel discipline), refused to obey. Joined by sympathetic soldiers, the mutineers raised the Red Flag of revolution. The revolt soon spread, as military men and workers demonstrated for peace and reform and in some regions seized authority. Reluctant to fire on their comrades and also fed up with the war, German troops did not move to crush the revolutionaries. On November 9, 1918, the leaders of the government announced the end of the monarchy and Kaiser William II fled to Holland. Two days later, the new German Republic, headed by Chancellor Friedrich Ebert (1871–1925), a Social Democrat, signed an

armistice agreement ending the war. In the eyes of many Germans, the new democratic leadership was responsible for the defeat.

In February 1919 the recently elected National Assembly met at Weimar and proceeded to draw up a constitution for the new state. The Weimar Republic—born in revolution, which most Germans detested, and military defeat, which many attributed to the new government—faced an uncertain future.

Threats from Left and Right

The infant republic, dominated by moderate socialists, faced internal threats from both the radical left and the radical right. In January 1919 the newly established German Communist party, or Spartacists, disregarding the advice of their leaders Rosa Luxemburg and Karl Liebknecht, took to the streets of Berlin and declared the government of Ebert deposed. To crush the revolution, Ebert turned to the Free Corps—volunteer brigades of ex-soldiers and adventurers, led by officers loyal to the emperor, who had been fighting to protect the eastern borders from encroachments by the new states of Poland, Estonia, and Latvia. The men of the Free Corps relished action and despised Bolshevism. They suppressed the revolution and murdered Luxemburg and Liebknecht on January 15. In May 1919 the Free Corps also marched into Munich to overthrow the Soviet Republic set up there by communists a few weeks earlier.

The Spartacist revolt and the short-lived Soviet Republic in Munich (and others in Baden and Brunswick) had profound effects on the German psyche. The communists had been easily subdued, but fear of a communist insurrection remained deeply embedded in the middle and upper classes, a fear that drove many of them into the ranks of the Weimar Republic's right-wing opponents.

The Spartacist revolt was an attempt by the radical left to overthrow the republic; in March 1920, the republic was threatened by the radical right. Refusing to disband as the government ordered, detachments of the right-wing Free Corps marched into Berlin and declared a new government headed by Wolfgang von Kapp, a staunch nationalist. President Ebert and most members of the cabinet and National Assembly fled to Stuttgart. Insisting that it could not fire on fellow soldiers, the German army, the Reichswehr, made no move to defend the republic. A general strike called by the labor unions prevented Kapp from governing and the coup collapsed. However, the Kapp Putsch demonstrated that the loyalty of the army to the republic was doubtful.

Economic Crisis

In addition to uprisings by the left and right, the republic was burdened by economic crisis. During the war, Germany financed its military expenditures not by increasing taxation but through short-term loans, thereby accumulating a huge debt that now had to be paid. A trade deficit and enormous reparation payments worsened the nation's economic plight. Unable to meet the deficit in the national budget, the government simply printed more money, causing the value of the German mark to decline precipitously. In 1914, the mark stood at 4.2 to the dollar; in 1919, 8.9 to the dollar; in early 1923, 18,000 to the dollar. In August 1923 a dollar could be exchanged for 4.6 million marks, and in November for 4 billion marks! Bank savings, war bonds, and pensions, representing years of toil and thrift, became worthless. Blaming the government for this disaster, the ruined middle class became more receptive to rightist movements that aimed to bring down the republic.

With the economy in shambles, the republic defaulted on reparation payments. Premier Raymond Poincaré (1860–1934) of France took a hard line and in January 1923 ordered French troops into the Ruhr—the nerve center of German industry. Responding to the republic's call for passive resistance, factory workers, miners, and railroad workers in the Ruhr refused to work for the French. To provide strike benefits for the Ruhr workers, the gov-

ernment printed yet more money, making inflation even worse.

In August 1923, Gustav Stresemann became chancellor. The new government lasted only until November 1923, but during those one hundred days Stresemann skillfully placed the republic on the path to recovery. Warned by German industrialists that the economy was at the breaking point, Stresemann abandoned the policy of passive resistance in the Ruhr and declared Germany's willingness to make reparation payments. Stresemann issued a new currency backed by a mortgage on German real estate. To reduce public expenditures that contributed to inflation, the government fired some civil-service workers and lowered salaries; to get additional funds, it raised taxes; to protect the value of the new currency, it did not print another issue. Inflation receded and confidence was restored.

A new arrangement regarding reparations also contributed to the economic recovery. Recognizing that in its present economic straits Germany could not meet its obligations to the Allies or secure the investment of foreign capitalists, Britain and the United States pressured France to allow a reparation commission to make new proposals. In 1924 the parties accepted the Dawes Plan, which reduced reparations and based them on Germany's economic capacity. During the negotiations, France agreed to withdraw its troops from the Ruhr, another step toward easing tensions for the republic.

From 1924 to 1929 economic conditions improved. Foreign capitalists, particularly Americans, were attracted by high interest rates and the low cost of labor. Their investments in German businesses stimulated the economy. By 1929 iron, steel, coal, and chemical production exceeded prewar levels. The value of German exports also surpassed that of 1913. This spectacular boom was due in part to more effective methods of production and management and the concentration of related industries in giant trusts. Real wages were higher than before the war, and improved unemployment benefits also made life better for the workers. It appeared that Germany had also achieved political stability, as threats from the extremist parties of the left and the right subsided. Given time and economic stability, democracy might have taken firmer root in Germany. But then came the Great Depression (see page 746). The global economic crisis that began in October 1929 starkly revealed how weak the Weimar Republic was.

Fundamental Weaknesses of the Weimar Republic

German political experience provided poor soil for transplanting an Anglo-Saxon democratic parliamentary system. Imperial Germany had been a semiautocratic state ruled by an emperor who commanded the armed forces, controlled foreign policy, appointed the chancellor, and called and dismissed parliament. This authoritarian system blocked the German people from acquiring democratic habits and attitudes; still accustomed to rule from above, still adoring the power-state, many Germans sought the destruction of the Weimar Republic.

Traditional conservatives—the upper echelons of the civil service, judges, industrialists, large landowners, army leaders—were contemptuous of democracy and were avowed enemies of the republic. They wanted to restore a pre-1914 Prussian-type government that would fight liberal ideals and protect the fatherland from Bolshevism. Nor did the middle class feel a commitment to the liberal-democratic principles on which the republic rested. The traditionally nationalistic middle class identified the republic with the defeat in war and the humiliation of the Versailles Treaty; rabidly antisocialist, this class saw the leaders of the republic as Marxists who would impose on Germany a working-class state. Right-wing intellectuals often attacked democracy as a barrier to the true unity of the German nation. In the tradition of nineteenth-century Volkish thinkers, they had contempt for reason and political freedom and glorified instincts, blood, and action. In doing so, they turned many Germans against the republic, thereby eroding the popular support on which democracy depends. German historian Kurt Sontheimer concludes:

Nothing is more dangerous in political life than the abandonment of reason. The intellect must remain the controlling, regulating force in human affairs. The anti-democratic intellectuals of the Weimar period betrayed the intellect to "Life." They despised reason and found more truth in myth or in the blood surging in their veins. . . . Had they a little more reason and enlightenment, these intellectuals might have seen better where their zeal was leading them and their country.[5]

The Weimar Republic also showed the weaknesses of the multiparty system. With the vote spread over a number of parties, no one party held a majority of seats in the parliament (Reichstag), so the republic was governed by a coalition of several parties. But because of ideological differences, the coalition was always unstable and in danger of failing to function. This is precisely what happened during the Great Depression. When effective leadership was imperative, the government could not act. Political deadlock caused Germans to lose what little confidence they had in the democratic system. Support for the parties that wanted to preserve democracy dwindled, and extremist parties that aimed to topple the republic gained strength. Supporting the republic were Social Democrats, Catholic Centrists, and German Democrats; a coalition of these parties governed the republic during the 1920s.* Seeking to bring

---

* The Social Democrats hoped one day to transform Germany into a Marxist society, but they had abandoned revolutionary means and pursued a policy of moderate social reform. The largest party until the closing months of the Weimar Republic, the Social Democrats were committed to democratic principles and parliamentary government. The Catholic Center party opposed socialism and protected Catholic interests, but like the Social Democrats supported the republic. The German Democratic party consisted of middle-class liberals who also opposed socialism and supported the republic. Although the right-wing German People's party was more monarchist than republican, on occasion it joined the coalition of parties that sought to preserve the republic.

down the republic were the Communists, on the left, and two rightist parties—the Nationalists and the National Socialist German Workers party led by Adolf Hitler.

The Rise of Hitler

The Early Years

Adolf Hitler (1889–1945) was born in the town of Braunau am Inn, Austria, on April 20, 1889, the fourth child of a minor civil servant. Much of his youth was spent in Linz, a major city in Upper Austria. A poor student at secondary school, although by no means unintelligent, Hitler left high school and lived idly for more than two years. In 1907 the Vienna Academy of Arts rejected his application for admission. With the death of his mother in December 1907, the nineteen-year-old orphan (his father had died in 1903) drifted around Vienna viewing himself as an art student. Contrary to his later description of these years, Hitler did not suffer great poverty, for he received an orphan's allowance from the state and an inheritance from his mother and an aunt. When the Vienna Academy again refused him admission in 1908, he did not seek to learn a trade or to work steadily, but earned some money by painting picture postcards.

Hitler was a loner, often given to brooding and self-pity. He found some solace by regularly attending Wagnerian operas, by fantasizing about great architectural projects that he would someday initiate, and by reading. He read a lot, especially in art, history, and military affairs. He also read the racial, nationalist, anti-Semitic, and Pan-German literature that abounded in multinational Vienna. This literature introduced Hitler to a bizarre racial mythology: a heroic race of blond, blue-eyed Aryans battling for survival against inferior races. The racist treatises preached the danger posed by mixing races, called for the liquidation of racial inferiors, and marked the Jew as the embodiment of evil and the source of all misfortune.

In Vienna, Hitler came into contact with Georg von Schönerer's Pan-German movement. For Schönerer, the Jews were evil not because of their religion, not because they rejected Christ, but because they possessed evil racial qualities. Schönerer's followers wore watch chains etched with pictures of hanged Jews. Hitler was particularly impressed with Karl Lueger, the mayor of Vienna, a clever demagogue who skillfully manipulated the anti-Semitic feelings of the Viennese for his own political advantage. In Vienna, Hitler also acquired a hatred for Marxism and democracy and the conviction that the struggle for existence and the survival of the fittest are the essential facts of the social world. His years in Vienna emptied Hitler of all compassion and scruples and filled him with a fierce resentment of the social order that he felt ignored him, cheated him, and condemned him to a wretched existence.

When World War I began, Hitler was in Munich. He welcomed the war as a relief from his daily life, which had been devoid of purpose and excitement. Volunteering for the German army, Hitler found battle exhilarating and he fought bravely, twice receiving the Iron Cross.

The experience of battle taught Hitler to value discipline, regimentation, leadership, authority, struggle, ruthlessness—values that he carried with him into the politics of the postwar world. The shock of Germany's defeat and revolution intensified his commitment to racial nationalism. To lead Germany to total victory over its racial enemies became his obsession. Like many returning soldiers, he required vindicating explanations for lost victories. His own explanation was simple and demagogic: Germany's shame was due to the creators of the republic—the "November criminals"; and behind them was a Jewish-Bolshevik world conspiracy.

The Nazi Party

In 1919, Hitler joined the German Workers' Party, a small right-wing group and one of the more than seventy extremist military-political-Volkish organizations that sprang up in postwar Germany. Displaying fantastic energy and extraordinary ability as a demagogic orator, propagandist, and organizer, Hitler quickly became the leader of the party, whose name was changed to National Socialist German Workers' party (commonly called *Nazi*). As leader, Hitler insisted on absolute authority and total allegiance—a demand that coincided with the postwar longing for a strong leader who would set right a shattered nation. Without Hitler, the National Socialist German Workers' party would have remained an insignificant group of discontents and outcasts. Demonstrating a Machiavellian cunning for politics, Hitler tightened the party organization and perfected the techniques of mass propaganda.

Like Mussolini, Hitler incorporated military attitudes and techniques into politics. Uniforms, salutes, emblems, flags, and other symbols infused party members with a sense of solidarity and camaraderie. At mass meetings, Hitler was a spellbinder who gave stunning performances. His pounding fists, throbbing body, wild gesticulations, hypnotic eyes, rage-swollen face, and repeated, frenzied denunciations of the Versailles Treaty, Marxism, the republic, and Jews inflamed and mesmerized the audience, transforming it into a single mass. Hitler's torrent of words, impassioned conviction, and extraordinary self-confidence swept away all doubt, all rational judgment, all critical faculties. Hitler instinctively grasped the innermost feelings of his audience—its resentments and its longings. "The intense will of the man, the passion of his sincerity seemed to flow from him into me. I experienced an exaltation that could be likened only to religious conversion," said one early admirer.[6]

In November 1923, Hitler attempted to seize power (the Munich or "Beer Hall" Putsch) in the state of Bavaria as a prelude to toppling the republic. The putsch failed and the Nazis made a poor showing—they quickly scattered when the Bavarian police opened fire. Ironically, however, Hitler's prestige increased, for when he was put on trial, he used it as an opportunity to denounce the republic and the Versailles Treaty and to proclaim his philosophy of racial nationalism. His impassioned speeches, publicized by the press, earned Hitler a nationwide reputation and a light sentence—five years' imprisonment with the promise of quick parole. While in prison, Hitler dictated *Mein Kampf*, a rambling and turgid work that contained the essence of his world-view.

The unsuccessful Munich Putsch taught Hitler a valuable lesson: armed insurrection against superior might fails. He would gain power not by force, but by exploiting the instruments of democracy—elections and party politics. He would use apparently legal means to destroy the Weimar Republic and impose a dictatorship. As Nazi propaganda expert Joseph Goebbels would later express it: "We have openly declared that we use democratic methods only to gain power and that once we had it we would ruthlessly deny our opponents all those chances we had been granted when we were in the opposition."[7]

Hitler's World-View

Some historians view Hitler as an unprincipled opportunist and a brilliant tactician who believed in nothing, but cleverly manufactured and manipulated ideas that were politically useful in his drive for power. To be sure, Hitler was not concerned with the objective truth of an idea but with its potential political usefulness. He was not a systematic thinker like Marx. Whereas communism claimed the certainty of science and held that it would reform the world in accordance with rational principles, Hitler proclaimed the higher validity of blood, instinct, and will and regarded the intellect as an enemy of the soul. Hitler nevertheless possessed a remarkably consistent ideology, as Hajo Holborn concludes:

Hitler was a great opportunist and tactician, but it would be quite wrong to think that ideology was for him a mere instrumentality for gaining power. On the contrary, Hitler was a doctrinaire of the first order. Throughout his political career he was guided by an ideology . . . which from 1926 onward [did] not show any change whatsoever.[8]

Hitler's thought comprised a patchwork of nineteenth-century anti-Semitic, Volkish, Social Darwinist, antidemocratic, and anti-Marxist ideas. From these ideas, many of which enjoyed wide popularity, Hitler constructed a world-view rooted in myth and ritual. Given to excessive daydreaming and never managing to "overcome his youth with its dreams, injuries, and resentments,"[9] Hitler sought to make the world accord with his fantasies—struggles to the death between races, a vast empire ruled by a master race, a thousand-year Reich.

Racial Nationalism   Nazism rejected both the Judeo-Christian and the Enlightenment traditions and sought to found a new world order based on racial nationalism. For Hitler, race was the key to understanding world history. He believed that Western civilization was at a critical juncture. Liberalism was dying, and Marxism, that "Jewish invention," as he called it, would inherit the future unless it was opposed by an even more powerful world-view. "With the conception of race National Socialism will carry its revolution and recast the world," said Hitler.[10] As the German barbarians had overwhelmed a disintegrating Roman Empire, a reawakened, racially united Germany, led by men of iron will, would carve out a vast European empire and would deal a decadent liberal civilization its deathblow. It would conquer Russia, eradicate communism, and reduce to serfdom the subhuman Slavs, "a mass of born slaves who feel the need of a master."[11]

In the tradition of Volkish thinkers, Hitler divided the world into superior and inferior races and pitted them against each other in a struggle for survival. This fight for life was a law of nature and of history. The Germans, descendants of ancient Aryans, possessed superior racial characteristics; a nation degenerates and perishes if it allows its blood to be contaminated by intermingling with lower races. Conflict between races was desirable, for it strengthened and hardened racial superiors; it made them ruthless—a necessary quality in this Darwinian world. As a higher race, the Germans were entitled to conquer and subjugate other races. Germany must acquire *Lebensraum* ("living space") by expanding eastward at the expense of the racially inferior Slavs.

The Jew as Devil   An obsessive and virulent anti-Semitism dominated Hitler's mental outlook (see pp. 579–583 on anti-Semitism). In waging war against the Jews, Hitler believed that he was defending Germany from its worst enemy. In Hitler's mental picture the Aryan was the originator and carrier of civilization. As descendants of the Aryans, the Germans embodied creativity, bravery, and loyalty. As the counterpart of the Aryan, the Jew was stained with the vilest qualities. "Two worlds face one another," said Hitler, "the men of God and the men of Satan! The Jew is the anti-man, the creature of another god. He must have come from another root of the human race. I set the Aryan and the Jew over and against each other."[12] Everything Hitler despised—liberalism, intellectualism, pacifism, parliamentarism, internationalism, communism, modern art, individualism—he attributed to the Jew.

For Hitler, the Jew was the mortal enemy of racial nationalism. The moral outlook of the ancient Hebrew prophets, which affirmed individual worth and made individuals morally responsible for their actions, was totally in opposition to Hitler's morality, which subordinated the individual to the national community. He once called conscience a Jewish invention. The prophetic vision of the unity of humanity under God, equality, justice, and peace were also in opposition to Hitler's belief that all history is a pitiless struggle between races and that only the strongest and most ruthless deserve to survive.

Hitler's anti-Semitism also served a functional purpose. By concentrating all evil in one enemy, "the conspirator and demonic" Jew, Hitler provided the masses with a simple, consistent, and emotionally satisfying explanation for all their misery. By defining themselves as the racial and spiritual opposites of Jews, Germans of all classes felt joined together in a Volkish union. By seeing themselves engaged in a heroic battle against a single enemy who embodied evil, their will was strengthened. Even failures and misfits gained self-respect. Anti-Semitism provided insecure and hostile people with powerless but recognizable targets on whom to focus their antisocial feelings.

The surrender to myth served also to disorient the German intellect. When the mind accepts an image such as Hitler's image of Jews as vermin, germs, and satanic conspirators, it has lost all sense of balance and objectivity. Such a disoriented mind is ready to believe and to obey, to be manipulated and led; it is ready to brutalize and to tolerate brutality.

The Importance of Propaganda Hitler understood that in an age of political parties, universal suffrage, and a popular press—the legacies of the French and Industrial revolutions—the successful leader must win the support of the masses. To do this, Hitler consciously applied and perfected elements of circus showmanship, church pageantry, American advertising, and the techniques of propaganda that the Allies had effectively used to stir their civilian populations during the war. To be effective, said Hitler, propaganda must be aimed principally at the emotions. The masses are not moved by scientific ideas or by objective and abstract knowledge, but by primitive feelings, terror, force, discipline. Propaganda must reduce everything to simple slogans incessantly repeated and must concentrate on one enemy. The masses are aroused by the spoken, not

The Flagbearer. Hitler knew the value of propaganda. In this poster, he appears as a knight from medieval myth and bears the flag of the nation against all enemies. (*U.S. Army*)

the written word—by a storm of hot passion erupting from the speaker "which like hammer blows can open the gates to the heart of the people."[13]

The most effective means of stirring the masses and strengthening them for the struggle ahead, said Hitler, is the mass meeting. Surrounded by tens of thousands of people, individuals lose their sense of individuality and no longer see themselves as isolated. They become members of a community bound together by an esprit de corps reminiscent of the trenches during the Great War. Bombarded by the cheers of thousands of voices, by marching units, by banners, by explosive oratory, individuals become convinced of the truth of the party's message and the determination of the movement. Their intellects overwhelmed, their resistance lowered, they lose their previous beliefs and are carried along on a wave of enthusiasm. "The man who enters such a meeting doubting and wavering leaves it inwardly reinforced; he has become a link to the community."[14]

Hitler Gains Power

When Hitler left prison in December 1924, after serving nine months, he proceeded to tighten his hold over the Nazi party. He relentlessly used his genius for propaganda and organization to strengthen the loyalty of his cadres and to instill in them a sense of mission. In 1925, the Nazi party counted about 27,000 members; in 1929, it had grown to 178,000 with units throughout Germany. But its prospects seemed dim, for since 1925 economic conditions had improved and the republic seemed politically stable. In 1928 the National Socialists (NSDAP) received only 2.6 percent of the vote. Nevertheless, Hitler never lost faith in his own capacities or his destiny; he continued to build his party and waited for a crisis that would rock the republic and make his movement a force in national politics.

The Great Depression, which began in the United States at the end of 1929, provided that crisis. As Germany's economic plight worsened, the Nazis tirelessly expanded their efforts. Everywhere they staged mass rallies, plastered walls with posters, distributed leaflets, and engaged in street battles with their opponents of the left. Hitler promised all things to all groups, avoided debates, provided simple explanations for Germany's misfortunes, and insisted that only the Nazis could rescue Germany. Nazi propaganda attacked the communists, the "November criminals," the democratic system, the Versailles Treaty, reparations, and, above all, the Jews. It depicted Hitler as a savior. Hitler would rescue Germany from chaos; he understood the real needs of the Volk; he was sent by destiny to lead Germany in its hour of greatest need. These propaganda techniques worked. The Nazi party went from 810,000 votes in 1928 to 6,400,000 in 1930, and its representation in the Reichstag soared from 12 to 107.

The Social Democrats (SPD), the principal defenders of democracy, could draw support only from the working class; to the middle class, the SPD were hated Marxists. Moreover, in the eyes of many Germans the SPD were identified with the status quo, that is, with economic misery and national humiliation. The SPD simply had no program that could attract the middle class or arouse their hope for a better future.

To the lower middle class the Nazis promised effective leadership and a solution to the economic crisis. To them the Great Depression was the last straw, final evidence that the republic had failed and should be supplanted by a different kind of regime. They craved order, authority, and leadership and abhorred the disputes of political parties that provided neither. They wanted Hitler to protect Germany from the communists and organized labor. The traumatic experience of the Great Depression caused many bourgeois—hitherto apathetic about voting, politically immature, impatient, and easily excitable—to cast ballots. The depression was also severe in England and the United States, but the liberal foundations of these countries were strong; in Germany they were not, because the middle class had not committed itself to democracy nor indeed had any liking for it. Democracy endured in Britain and the United States; in Germany it collapsed.

But Nazism was more than a class movement. It appealed to the discontented and disillusioned from all segments of the population—embittered veterans; romantic nationalists; idealistic intellectuals; industrialists and large landowners frightened by communism and social democracy; rootless and resentful people who felt they had no place in the existing society; the unemployed; lovers of violence; and newly enfranchised youth yearning for a cause. The Social Democrats spoke the rational language of European democracy. The Communists addressed themselves to only a part of the nation, the proletariat, and were linked to a foreign country, the Soviet Union. The Nazis reached a wider spectrum of the population and touched deeper feelings.

And always there was the immense attraction of Hitler. Many Germans were won over by his fanatic sincerity, his iron will, and his conviction that he was chosen by fate to rescue Germany. Many others, no doubt, voted for Hitler not because they approved of him or his ideas, but because he was a strong opponent of the Weimar Republic. What these people wanted, above all, was the end of the republic they hated.

Meanwhile the parliamentary regime failed to function effectively. According to Article 48 of the constitution, during times of emergency the president was empowered to govern by decree, that is, without parliament. When President Paul von Hindenburg (1847–1934), the aging field marshall, exercised this emergency power, in effect the responsibility for governing Germany was transferred from the political parties and parliament to the president and chancellor. Rule by the president, instead of by parliament, meant for one thing that Germany had already taken a giant step away from parliamentary government in the direction of authoritarianism.

In the election of July 31, 1932, the Nazis received 37.3 percent of the vote and won 230 seats, far more than any other party but still not a majority. Determined to become chancellor, Hitler refused to take a subordinate position in a coalition government. Meanwhile, the recently resigned chancellor Franz von Papen persuaded Hindenburg, whose judgment was distorted by old age, to appoint Hitler chancellor. In this decision Papen had the support of German industrialists, aristocratic landowners, and the Nationalist party.

As in Italy, the members of the ruling elite were frightened by internal violence, unrest, and the specter of communism. They thought Hitler a vulgar man and abhorred his demagogic incitement of the masses. But they regarded him as a useful instrument to fight communism, block social reform, break the backs of organized labor, and rebuild the armament industry. Hitler had cleverly reassured these traditional conservatives that the Nazis would protect private property and business and go slow with social reform. Like the Italian upper class, which had assisted Mussolini in his rise to power, the old conservative ruling elite intrigued to put Hitler

in power. Ironically, this decision was made when Nazi strength at the polls was beginning to ebb. Expecting to control Hitler, conservatives calculated badly, for Hitler could not be tamed. They had underestimated his skill as a politician, his ruthlessness, and his obsession with racial nationalism. Hitler had not sought power to restore the old order but to fashion a new one. The new leadership would be drawn not from the traditional ruling segments, but from the most dedicated Nazis, regardless of their social background.

When Hitler became chancellor on January 30, 1933, the army, fearing that the country was heading for civil war, did not offer any resistance. Nor did the Social Democratic and trade-union leaders rally the working class against the Nazis. Never intending to rule within the spirit of the constitution, Hitler quickly moved to assume dictatorial powers. In February 1933 a Dutch drifter with communist leanings set a fire in the Reichstag. Hitler persuaded Hindenburg to sign an emergency decree suspending civil rights on the pretext that the state was threatened by internal subversion. The chancellor then used these emergency powers to arrest, without due process, Communist and Social Democratic deputies.

In the elections of March 1933, Nazi thugs broke up Communist party meetings and Hitler called for a Nazi victory at the polls to save Europe from Bolshevism. Intimidated by street violence and captivated by Nazi mass demonstrations and relentless propaganda, the German people elected 288 Nazi deputies in a Reichstag of 647 seats. With the support of 52 deputies of the Nationalist party and in the absence of Communist deputies who were under arrest, the Nazis now had a secure majority. Hitler then bullied the Reichstag into passing the Enabling Act (in March 1933), which permitted the chancellor to enact legislation independently of the Reichstag. With astonishing passivity, the political parties had allowed the Nazis to dismantle the government and make Hitler a dictator with unlimited power. Hitler had used the instruments of democracy to destroy the republic and create a dictatorship. And he did it far more thoroughly and quickly than Mussolini had.

Nazi Germany

Mussolini's Fascism exhibited much bluster and bragging, but Fascist Italy did not have the industrial and military strength or the total commitment of the people necessary to threaten the peace of Europe. Nazism, on the other hand, demonstrated a demonic quality that nearly destroyed Western civilization. The impact of Hitler's sinister, fanatic, and obsessive personality was far greater on the German movement than was Mussolini's character on Italian Fascism. Also contributing to the demonic radicalism of Nazism were certain deeply rooted German traditions that were absent in Italy—Prussian militarism, adoration of the power-state, and belief in the special destiny of the German Volk. These traditions made the German people's attachment to Hitler and Nazi ideology much stronger than the Italian people's devotion to Mussolini and his party.

The Leader-State

The Nazis moved to subjugate all political and economic institutions and all culture to the will of the party. There could be no separation between the private life and politics; ideology must pervade every phase of daily life; all organizations must come under party control; there could be no rights of the individual that must be respected by the state. The party became the state, its teachings the soul of the German nation.

Unlike absolute monarchies of the past, a totalitarian regime requires more than outward obedience to its commands; it seeks to control the inner person, to shape thoughts, feelings, and attitudes in accordance with the party ideology. It demands total allegiance and submission. An anonymous Nazi poet succinctly expressed the totalitarian goal:

We have captured all the positions
And on the heights we have planted
The banners of our revolution.
You had imagined that that was all that we
    wanted
We want more
We want all
Your hearts are our goal,
It is your souls we want.[15]

The Third Reich was organized as a leader-state in which Hitler, the *Fuehrer* (leader), embodied and expressed the real will of the German people, commanded the supreme loyalty of the nation, and held omnipotent power. As a Nazi political theorist stated: "The authority of the Fuehrer is total and all-embracing . . . it embraces all members of the German community. . . . The Fuehrer's authority is subject to no checks or controls; it is circumscribed by no . . . individual rights; it is . . . overriding and unfettered."[16] To the Fuehrer the German people owed complete loyalty.

To strengthen the power of the central government and coordinate the nation under Nazism, the regime abolished legislatures in the various German states and appointed governors who made certain that Nazi directives were carried out throughout the country. The Nazis took over the civil service and used its machinery to enforce Nazi decrees. In this process of *Gleichschaltung* (coordination), the Nazis encountered little opposition. The political parties and the trade unions collapsed without a struggle.

In June 1933, the Social Democratic party was outlawed, and within a few weeks the other political parties simply disbanded on their own. In May 1933, the Nazis seized the property of the trade unions, arrested the leaders, and ended collective bargaining and strikes. The newly established German Labor Front, an instrument of the party, became the official organization of the working class. While there is evidence that the working class in 1933 would have resisted the Nazis, the leadership never mobilized proletarian organizations. With surprising ease the Nazis had imposed their will over the nation.

Hitler made strategic but temporary concessions to the traditional ruling elite. On June 30, 1934, Nazi executioners swiftly murdered the leaders of the SA (the storm troopers who had battled political opponents) to eliminate any potential opposition to Hitler from within the party. With this move, Hitler also relieved the anxieties of industrialists and landowners, who feared that Ernst Röhm, the leader of the SA, would persuade Hitler to remove them from positions of power and to implement a program of radical social reform that would threaten their property.

The execution of the SA leaders (including Röhm) was also approved by the generals, for they regarded the SA as a rival to the army. In August, all German soldiers swore an oath of unconditional allegiance to the Fuehrer, cementing the alliance between the army and National Socialism. The army tied itself to the Nazi regime because it valued the resurgence of militaristic values and applauded the death of the Weimar Republic. German historian Karl Dietrich Bracher concludes: "Without the assistance of the Army, at first through its toleration and later through its active cooperation, the country's rapid and final restructuring into the total leader state could not have come about."[17]

Economic Life

Hitler had not sought power to improve the living standards of the masses but to convert Germany into a powerful war machine. Economic problems held little interest for this dreamer in whose mind danced images of a vast German empire. For him the "socialism" in National Socialism meant not a comprehensive program of social welfare but the elimination of the class antagonisms that divided and weakened the fatherland. Radicals within the party wanted to deprive the industrialists and landowners of power and social dignity and expropriate their property. The more pragmatic Hitler wanted only to deprive them of freedom of action; they were to serve, not control, the state. Germany remained capitalist, but the state had unlimited power to intervene in the economy. Unlike the Bolsheviks, the Nazis did not destroy the upper classes of the Old Regime. Hitler made no war against the industrialists. From them he wanted loyalty, obedience, and a war machine. German businessmen prospered but exercised no influence on political decisions. The profits of industry rose, but the real wages of German workers did not improve, although rearmament did end the unemployment crisis.

Nazism and the Churches

Nazism conflicted with the core values of Christianity. "The heaviest blow that ever struck humanity was the coming of Christianity," said Hitler to intimates during World War II.[18] Had Germany won World War II, the Nazis would no doubt have tried to root Christianity out of German life. In 1937 the bishop of Berlin defined the essential conflict between Christianity and Nazism:

The question at stake is whether there is an authority that stands above all earthly power, the authority of God, Whose commandments are valid independent of space and time, country and race. The question at stake is whether individual man possesses personal rights that no community and no state may take from him; whether the free exercise of his conscience may be prevented and forbidden by the state.[19]

Nazism could tolerate no other faith alongside itself. Recognizing that Christianity was a rival claimant for the German soul, the Nazis moved to repress the Protestant and Catholic churches. In the public schools, religious instruction was cut back and the syllabus changed to omit the Jewish origins of Christianity. Christ was depicted not as a Jew, heir to the prophetic tradition of Hebrew monotheism, but as an Aryan hero. The *Gestapo* (secret state police) censored church newspapers, scrutinized sermons and church activities, forbade some clergymen to preach, dismissed the opponents of Nazism from theological schools, and arrested some clerical critics of the regime.

The clergy are well represented among those Germans who resisted Nazism; some were sent to concentration camps or were executed. But these courageous clergy were not representatives of the German churches which, as organized institutions, capitulated to and cooperated with the Nazi regime. Both the German Evangelical and German Catholic churches demanded that their faithful render loyalty to Hitler; both turned a blind eye to Nazi persecution of Jews; both condemned resistance and found much in the Third Reich to admire; both supported Hitler's war. When Germany attacked Poland, starting World War II, the Catholic bishops declared: "In this decisive hour we encourage and admonish our Catholic soldiers, in obedience to the Fuehrer, to do their duty and to be ready to sacrifice their whole existence."[20] Both churches urged their faithful to fight for fatherland and Fuehrer, pressured conscientious objectors to serve, and celebrated Nazi victories.

Varied reasons explain why the German churches, which preached Christ's message of humanity, failed to take a stand against Nazi inhumanity. Many German church leaders feared that resistance would lead to even more severe measures against their churches. Traditionally the German churches had bowed to state authority and detested revolution. Church leaders also found some Nazi ideas appealing. Intensely nationalistic, antiliberal, antirepublican, and anti-Semitic, many members of the clergy were filled with hope when Hitler came to power. The prominent Lutheran theologian who "welcomed that change that came to Germany in 1933 as a divine gift and miracle,"[21] voiced the sentiments of many members of the clergy. Such feelings encouraged prolonged moral myopia, not a revolt of Christian conscience. When the war ended the German Evangelical church leaders lamented:

. . . we know ourselves to be one with our people in a great company of suffering and in a great solidarity of guilt. With great pain do we say: Through us endless suffering has been brought to many people and countries. . . . We accuse our-

selves for not witnessing more courageously, for not praying more faithfully, for not loving more ardently.[22]

Shaping the "New Man"

Propaganda had helped the Nazis come to power. Now it would be used to consolidate their hold on the German nation and to shape a "new man" committed to Hitler, race, and Volk. Hitler was a radical revolutionary who desired not only the outward form of power but also control over the inner person—over the individual's thoughts and feelings. Nazi propaganda conditioned the mind to revere the Fuehrer and to obey the new regime. It intended to deprive individuals of their capacity for independent thought. By concentrating on the myth of the race and the infallibility of the Fuehrer, Nazi propaganda disoriented the rational mind and gave the individual new standards to believe in and obey. Propaganda aimed to mold the entire nation to think and respond as the leader-state directed. Even science had to conform to Nazi racial ideology. Thus Johannes Stark, a Nobel Prize winner, held that scientific thought is a function of race:

. . . natural science is overwhelmingly a creation of the Nordic-Germanic blood component of the Aryan peoples. . . . The Jewish spirit is wholly different in its orientation. . . . True, Heinrich Hertz made the great discovery of electromagnetic waves, but he was not a full-blooded Jew. He had a German mother, from whose side his spiritual endowment may well have been conditioned.[23]

The Ministry of Popular Enlightenment, headed by Dr. Joseph Goebbels (1897–1945), controlled the press, book publishing, the radio, the theater, and the cinema. Goebbels, holder of a doctoral degree in the humanities, was intelligent and a master in the art of propaganda; he was also vain, cynical, and contemptuous of the very masses he manipulated. But the German people were not merely passive victims of clever and ruthless leaders. "The effective spread of propaganda and the rapid regimentation of cultural life," says Bracher, "would not have been possible without the invaluable help eagerly tendered by writers and artists, professors and churchmen." And the manipulation of the minds of the German people "would not have been effective had it not been for profound historically conditioned relations based . . . on a pseudoreligious exaggerated nationalism and on the idea of the German mission."[24] While some intellectuals showed their abhorrence of the Nazi regime by emigrating, the great majority gave their support, often with overt enthusiasm. While some individuals rejected Nazi propaganda, the masses of German people came to regard Nazism as the fulfillment of their nationalist longings.

The Nazis kept the emotions in a state of permanent mobilization, for Hitler understood that the emotionally aroused are most amenable to manipulation. Goose-stepping SA and SS (elite military and police) battalions paraded in the streets; martial music quickened the pulsebeat; Nazi flags decorated public buildings; loud-speakers installed in offices and factories blared the Nazi message, and all work stopped for important broadcasts. Citizens were ordered to greet each other with "Heil Hitler," a potent sign of reverence and submission. The regime made a special effort to reach young people. All youths between the ages of ten and eighteen were required to join the Hitler Youth, and all other youth organizations were dissolved. At camps and rallies, young people paraded, sang, saluted, and chanted: "we were slaves; we were outsiders in our own country. So were we before Hitler united us. Now we would fight against Hell itself for our leader."[25]

Nazification of Education   The schools, long breeding grounds of nationalism, militarism, antiliberalism, and anti-Semitism, now indoctrinated the young in Nazi ideology. The Nazis instructed teachers how certain subjects were to be taught; and to insure obedience, members of the Hitler Youth were asked to report suspicious teachers. Portraits of Hitler and Nazi banners were displayed in classrooms. War stories, adventures of the Hitler Youth, and ancient Nordic legends replaced fairy tales and animal stories in reading material for the young. The curriculum upgraded physical training and sports, curtailed religious instruction, and introduced many courses in "racial science." Decidedly anti-intellectual, the Nazis stressed character building over book learning. They intended to train young people to serve the leader and the racial community, to imbue them with a sense of fellowship for their Volkish kin, that sense of camaraderie found on the battlefield. Expressions of individualism and independence must be checked.

The universities quickly abandoned freedom of the mind, scientific objectivity, and humanist values. "We repudiate international science, we repudiate the international community of scholars, we repudiate research for the sake of research. Sieg Heil!"[26] declared one historian. Even before the Nazi takeover, many university students and professors had embraced Volkish nationalism and right-wing radicalism. Two years before Hitler came to power, for example, 60 percent of all undergraduates supported the Nazi student organization and anti-Semitic riots broke out at several universities.

For seventy years or more, the professors had preached aggressive nationalism, the German destiny of power, hero worship, irrational political Romanticism, and so forth, and had increasingly deemphasized, if not eliminated, the teachings of ethical and humanist principles. . . . Essentially neither [professors nor students] wanted to have anything to do with democracy. In the Weimar Republic . . . both groups, on the whole, seemed equally determined to tear down that Republic. The professors did their part by fiery lectures, speeches, and writings; the students did theirs in noisy demonstrations, torch-light parades, vandalism, and physical violence. . . . When Hitler came to power, both professors and students fell all over themselves to demonstrate their allegiance.[27]

In May 1933, professors and students proudly burned books considered a threat to Nazi ideology. Many academics praised Hitler and the new regime. Some 10 percent of the university faculty, principally Jews, Social Democrats, and liberals, were dismissed, and their colleagues often approved. "From now on it will not be your job to determine whether something is true but whether it is in the spirit of the National Socialist revolution," the new minister of culture told university professors.[28] Numerous courses on racial science and Nazi ideology were introduced into the curriculum.

Giant Rallies Symbolic of the Nazi regime were the monster rallies staged at Nuremberg. Scores of thousands roared, marched, and worshiped at their leader's feet. In a delirium of ordered emotion, ungoverned by thought, they celebrated Hitler's achievements and demonstrated their loyalty to their savior. Everything was brilliantly orchestrated to impress Germans and the world with the irresistible power, determination, and unity of the Nazi movement and the greatness of the Fuehrer. Armies of youths waving flags, storm troopers bearing weapons, and workers shouldering long-handled spades paraded past Hitler, who stood at attention, his arm extended in the Nazi salute. The endless columns of marchers, the stirring martial music played by huge bands, the forest of flags, the chanting and cheering of spectators, and the burning torches and beaming spotlights united the participants into a racial community. "Wherever Hitler leads we follow," thundered thousands of Germans in a giant chorus. The Nuremberg rallies were among the greatest theatrical performances of the twentieth century.

Terror Terror was another means of insuring compliance and obedience. The instrument of terror was the SS, which was organized in 1925 to protect Hitler and other party leaders and to stand guard at party meetings. Under the leadership of Heinrich Himmler (1900–1945), a fanatic believer in Hitler's racial theories, the SS was molded into an elite force of disciplined, dedicated, and utterly ruthless men. Myopic, narrow chested, and sexually prudish, Himmler contrived a cult of manliness. He envisioned the SS, who were specially selected for their racial purity and physical fitness, as a new breed of knights—Nietzschean supermen who would lead the new Gemany.

The SS staffed the concentration camps established to deal with political prisoners. Through systematic terror and torture, the SS sought to deprive the inmates of their human dignity and to harden themselves for the struggles that lay ahead. Knowledge that these camps existed and that some prisoners were never heard from again was a strong inducement for Germans to remain obedient.

Anti-Semitic Legislation

The Nazis instituted many anti-Jewish measures designed to make outcasts of the Jews. Thousands of Jewish doctors, lawyers, musicians, artists, and professors were barred from practicing their professions, and Jewish members of the civil service were dismissed. A series of laws tightened the screws of humiliation and persecution. Marriage or sexual encounters between Germans and Jews were forbidden. Universities, schools, restaurants, pharmacies, hospitals, theaters, museums, and athletic fields were gradually closed to Jews.

In November 1938, using the assassination of a German diplomat by a Jewish youth as a pretext, the Nazis organized an extensive pogrom. Nazi gangs murdered scores of Jews and burned and looted thousands of Jewish homes and synagogues. The Reich then imposed on the Jewish community a fine of one billion marks. These measures were a mere prelude, however; the physical extermination of European Jewry became a cardinal Nazi objective during World War II.

Mass Support

The Nazi regime became a police state symbolized by mass arrests, the persecution of Jews, and concentration camps that institu-

Jews Being Rounded up to Enter Concentration Camps. As Germans overran Europe, Hitler broadened his campaign against the Jews; it was no longer confined to Germany. He sought the "final solution of the Jewish problem" through genocide. (*Collection Viollet*)

tionalized terror. The Nazis skillfully established the totalitarian state without upsetting the daily life of the great majority of the population. Moreover Hitler, like Mussolini, was careful to maintain the appearance of legality. By not abolishing parliament or repealing the constitution, he could claim that his was a legitimate government. By consolidating power in stages and retaining the institutions of the republic, the Nazis lulled both Germans and people in other countries into believing that legitimate statesmen, not gangsters, governed Germany.

To people concerned with little but family, job, and friends—and this includes most people in any country—life in the first few years of the Third Reich seemed quite satisfying. People believed that the new government was trying to solve Germany's problems in a vigorous and sensible manner, in contrast to the ineffective Weimar leadership. Hitler's rearmament program had virtually eliminated unemployment and restored German might. It seemed to most Germans that Hitler had awakened a sense of self-sacrifice and national dedication among a people dispirited by defeat and depression. He had united a country torn by class antagonisms and social distinctions and given the little people a sense of pride. Workers had jobs, businessmen profits, and generals troops—what could be wrong?

Many intellectuals, viewing Hitlerism as the victory of idealism over materialism and of community over selfish individualism, lent their talents to the regime and endorsed the burning of books and the suppression of freedom. To them, Hitler was a visionary who had shown Germany and the world a new way of life—a new creed.

Hitler's spectacular foreign policy successes made the world take notice of the new Germany. Having regained confidence in themselves and their nation, Germans rejoiced in Hitler's leadership, regretted not at all the loss of political freedom, and remained indifferent to the plight of the persecuted, particularly Jews. Hitler's popularity and mass support rested on something far stronger than propaganda and terror. The simple truth is that he had won the hearts of a sizable proportion of the German people. To many Germans, Hitler was exactly as Nazi propaganda had depicted him: "He stands like a statue grown beyond the measure of earthly man."[29]

There was some opposition and resistance to the Hitler regime. Social Democrats and communists, in particular, organized small cells. Some conservatives who considered Hitler a threat to traditional German values, and some clergy who saw Nazism as a pagan religion also formed small opposition groups. But only resistance from the army could have toppled Hitler. Some generals, even before World War II, urged such resistance, but the overwhelming majority of German officers either preferred the new regime, were too concerned about their careers to do anything, or considered it dishonorable to break their oath of loyalty to Hitler. These officers would remain loyal until the bitter end. Very few Germans realized that their country was passing through a long night of barbarism, and still fewer considered resistance.

Liberalism and Authoritarianism in Other Lands

The Spread of Authoritarianism

After World War I, in country after country, parliamentary democracy collapsed and authoritarian leaders came to power. In most of these countries, liberal ideals had not penetrated deeply; liberalism met resistance from conservative elites.

Spain and Portugal In both Spain and Portugal, parliamentary regimes faced strong opposition from the church, the army, and large landowners. In 1926, army officers overthrew the Portuguese Republic that had been created in 1910, and gradually Antonio de Oliveira Salazar (1889–1970), a professor of economics, emerged as dictator. In Spain, after antimonarchist forces won the election of 1931, King Alfonso XIII (1902–1931) left the country and Spain was proclaimed a republic. But the new government, led by socialists and liberals, faced the determined opposition of the ruling elite. The reforms introduced by the republic—expropriation of large estates, reduction of the number of army officers, dissolution of the Jesuit order, and the closing of church schools—only intensified the old order's hatred.

The difficulties of the Spanish Republic mounted: workers, near starvation, rioted and engaged in violent strikes; the military attempted a coup; Catalonia, with its long tradition of separatism, tried to establish its autonomy. Imitating the example of France (see page 757), the parties of the left, including the communists, united in the Popular Front, which came to power in February 1936. In July 1936, General Francisco Franco (1892–1975), stationed in Spanish Morocco, led a revolt against the republic. He was supported by army leaders, the church, monarchists, landlords, industrialists, and the Falange, a newly formed fascist party. Spain was torn by a bloody civil war. Aided by Fascist Italy and Nazi Germany (see pages 786–787), Franco won in 1939 and established a dictatorship.

Eastern and Central Europe Parliamentary government in eastern Europe rested on weak foundations. Predominantly rural, these countries lacked the sizable professional and commercial classes that had promoted liberalism in western Europe. Only Czechoslovakia had a substantial native middle class with a strong liberal tradition. The rural masses of eastern Europe, traditionally subjected to monarchical and aristocratic authority, were not used to political thinking or civic responsibility. Students and intellectuals, often gripped by a romantic nationalism, were drawn to antidemocratic movements. Right-wing leaders also played on the fear of communism. When parliamentary government failed to solve internal problems, the opponents of the liberal state seized the helm. Fascist movements, however, had little success in eastern Europe. It was authoritarian regimes headed by traditional ruling elites—army leaders or kings—that put an end to democracy there.

With the dissolution of the Hapsburg Empire at the end of World War I, Austria became a democratic republic. From the start, it suffered from severe economic problems. The Hapsburg Empire had been a huge free-trade area, permitting food and raw materials to circulate unimpeded throughout the empire. The new Austria lacked sufficient food to feed the population of Vienna and needed raw materials for its industries. Worsening its plight was the erection of tariff barriers by each of the states that had formerly been part of the Hapsburg Empire. Between 1922 and 1926, the League of Nations had to rescue Austria from bankruptcy. The Great Depression aggravated Austria's economic position. Many Austrians believed that only an *Anschluss* (union) with Germany could solve Austria's problems.

Austria was also burdened by a conflict between the industrial region, including Vienna, and the agricultural provinces. Factory workers were generally socialist and anticlerical; the peasants were strongly Catholic and antisocialist. The Social Democrats controlled Vienna, but the rural population gave its support to the Christian Socialist party. Each party had its own private army: the workers had the *Schutzbund* and the provincials the *Heimwehr*. During the Great Depression, Chancellor Engelbert Dollfuss (1892–1934) sought to turn the country into a one-party state. In February 1934, police

and Heimwehr contingents raided Social Democratic headquarters. When the Social Democrats called a general strike, Dollfuss bombarded a workers' housing project, killing 193 civilians, and suppressed the Social Democratic party. Austria had joined the ranks of authoritarian states.

When Hitler came to power in Germany, Austrian Nazis pressed for Anschluss. In July 1934, a band of them assassinated Dollfuss, but a Nazi plot to capture the government failed. Four years later, however, Hitler would march into Austria, bringing about the Anschluss desired by many.

The new Hungary that emerged at the end of World War I faced an uprising by communists inspired by the success of the Bolsheviks in Russia. Béla Kun (1885–1937), supported by Russian money, established a Soviet regime in Budapest in March 1919. But Kun could not win the support of the peasants and was opposed by the Allies, who helped Rumania crush the revolutionary government. In 1920 power passed to Admiral Miklós Horthy (1868–1957), who instituted a white terror that exceeded the red terror of the Kun regime. During the Great Depression, the Horthy government, which favored the large landholders, was challenged by the radical right, which preached racial nationalism, anti-Semitism, and anticapitalism and sought to win mass support through land reform. Its leader, Gyula Gömbös (1886–1936), who served as prime minister from 1932 to 1936, sought to align Hungary with Nazi Germany. Seeking to regain territories lost in World War I and aware of Hitler's growing might, Hungary drew closer to Germany in the late 1930s.

Poland, Greece, Bulgaria, and Rumania became either royal or military dictatorships. The new state of Czechoslovakia, guided by President Tomáš Masaryk (1850–1937) and Foreign Minister Eduard Beneš (1884–1948), who were both committed to the liberal-humanist tradition of the West, preserved parliamentary democracy. Its most serious problem came from the 3.1 million Germans living within its borders, primarily in the Sudetenland (see page 575). The German minority founded the Sudetenland German party, which modeled itself after Hitler's Nazi party. Hitler later exploited the issue of the Sudetenland Germans to dismember Czechoslovakia.

The Western Democracies

While liberal governments were everywhere failing, the great Western democracies—the United States, Britain, and France—continued to preserve democratic institutions. In Britain and the United States, fascist movements were no more than a nuisance. In France, fascism was more of a threat, because it exploited a deeply ingrained hostility in some quarters to the liberal ideals of the French Revolution.

The United States   The central problem faced by the Western democracies was the Great Depression, which started in the United States. In the 1920s, hundreds of thousands of Americans had bought stock on credit; this buying spree sent stock prices soaring well beyond what the stocks were actually worth. In late October 1929, the stock market was hit by a wave of panic selling; prices plummeted. Within a few weeks, the value of stocks listed on the New York Stock Exchange fell by some 26 billion dollars. A terrible chain reaction followed over the next few years. Businesses cut production and unemployment soared; farmers unable to meet mortgage payments lost their land; banks that had made poor investments closed down. American investors withdrew the capital they had invested in Europe, causing European banks and businesses to fail. Throughout the world, trade declined and unemployment rose.

When President Franklin Delano Roosevelt (1882–1945) took office in 1933, over 13 million Americans—one-quarter of the labor force—were out of work. Hunger and despair showed on the faces of the American people. Moving away from laissez faire, Roosevelt instituted a comprehensive program of national planning, economic experimentation,

and reform known as the New Deal. Although the American political and economic system faced a severe test, few Americans turned to fascism or communism, and the government, while engaging in national planning, did not break with democratic values and procedures.

Britain   Even before the Great Depression, Britain faced severe economic problems. Loss of markets to foreign competitors hurt British manufacturing, mining, and shipbuilding; rapid development of water and oil power reduced the demand for British coal, and outdated mining equipment put Britain in a poor competitive position. To reduce costs, mine owners in 1926 called for salary cuts; the coal miners countered with a strike and were joined by workers in other industries. To many Britons, the workers were leftist radicals trying to overthrow the government. Many wanted the state to break the strike. After nine days, industrial workers called it off, but the miners held out for another six months; they returned to work with longer hours and lower pay. Although the General Strike had failed, it did improve relations between the classes, for the workers had not called for revolution and they refrained from violence. The fear that British workers would follow the Bolshevik path abated.

The Great Depression cast a pall of gloom over Britain. The Conservative party leadership tried to stimulate exports by devaluing the pound and to encourage industry by providing loans at lower interest rates, but in the main, it left the task of recovery to industry itself. Not until Britain began to rearm did unemployment decline significantly. Despite the economic slump of the 1920s and the Great Depression, Britain remained politically stable, a testament to the strength of its parliamentary tradition. Neither the communists nor the newly formed British Fascist party gained mass support.

France   In the early 1920s, France was concerned with restoring villages, railroads, mines, and forests that had been ruined by the war. From 1926 to 1929 France was relatively prosperous; industrial and agricultural production expanded, tourism increased, and the currency was stable. Although France did not feel the Great Depression as painfully as did the United States and Germany, the nation was hurt by the decline in trade and production and the rise in unemployment.

The political instability that had beset the Third Republic virtually since its inception continued, and hostility to the republic mounted. As the leading parties failed to solve the nation's problems, a number of fascist-type groups gained strength. On February 6, 1934, right-wing gangs threatened to invade the Chamber of Deputies. What brought on the crisis was the exposure of the shady dealings of Alexander Stavisky, a financial manipulator with high government connections. The resultant violence left hundreds wounded and several dead. The whole affair was too poorly organized to constitute a serious threat to the government. But to the parties of the left—socialists, communists, and radicals—the events of February 6–7 constituted a rightist attempt to establish a fascist regime.

Fear of growing fascist strength at home and in Italy and Germany led the parties of the left to form the Popular Front. In 1936 Léon Blum (1872–1950), a socialist and a Jew, became premier. Blum's Popular Front government instituted more reforms than any other ministry in the history of the Third Republic. To end a wave of strikes that tied up production, Blum gave workers a forty-hour week and holidays with pay and guaranteed them the right to collective bargaining. He took steps to nationalize the armaments and aircraft industries. To reduce the influence of the wealthiest families, he put the Bank of France under government control. By raising prices and buying wheat, he aided farmers. Conservatives and fascists denounced Blum as a Jewish socialist who was converting the fatherland into a communist state. "Better Hitler than Blum," grumbled French rightists.

Despite significant reforms, the Popular Front could not revitalize the economy. In 1937 the Blum ministry was overthrown and the Popular Front, always a tenuous alliance, fell apart. Through democratic means the Blum government had tried to give France its own New Deal, but the social reforms passed by the Popular Front only intensified hatred between the working classes and the rest of the nation. France had preserved democracy against the onslaught of domestic fascists, but it was a demoralized and divided nation that confronted a united and dynamic Nazi Germany.

Notes

1. Quoted in Zeev Sternhill, "Fascist Ideology," in Walter Laqueur, *Fascism: A Reader's Guide* (Berkeley: University of California Press, 1976), p. 338.

2. Quoted in John Weiss, *The Fascist Tradition* (New York: Harper & Row, 1967), p. 9.

3. F. L. Carsten, *The Rise of Fascism* (Berkeley: University of California Press, 1969), p. 53.

4. Quoted in Max Gallo, *Mussolini's Italy* (New York: Macmillan, 1973), p. 218.

5. Kurt Sontheimer, "Anti-Democratic Thought in the Weimar Republic," in *The Path to Dictatorship 1918–1933*, trans. John Conway with an introduction by Fritz Stern (Garden City, N.Y.: Doubleday Anchor Books, 1966), pp. 48–49.

6. Quoted in Joachim C. Fest, *Hitler*, trans. Richard and Clara Winston (New York: Harcourt Brace Jovanovich, 1974), p. 162.

7. Quoted in Karl J. Newman, *European Democracy between the Wars* (Notre Dame, Ind.: University of Notre Dame Press, 1971), p. 276.

8. Hajo Holborn, *Germany and Europe* (Garden City, N.Y.: Doubleday, Anchor Books, 1971), p. 215.

9. Fest, *Hitler*, p. 548.

10. Quoted in Alan Bullock, *Hitler: A Study in Tyranny* (New York: Harper Torchbooks, 1964), p. 400.

11. *Hitler's Secret Conversations, 1941–1944*, with an introductory essay by H. R. Trevor Roper

(New York: Farrar, Straus & Young, 1953), p. 28.

12. Quoted in Lucy S. Dawidowicz, *The War Against the Jews 1933–1945* (New York: Holt, Rinehart and Winston, 1975), p. 21.

13. Adolf Hitler, *Mein Kampf* (Boston: Houghton Mifflin, 1962), p. 107.

14. Ibid., p. 479.

15. Quoted in J. S. Conway, *The Nazi Persecution of the Churches* (New York: Basic Books, 1968), p. 202.

16. Quoted in Helmut Krausnick, Hans Buchheim, Martin Broszart, and Hans-Adolf Jacobsen, *Anatomy of the SS State* (London: Collins, 1968), p. 128.

17. Karl Dietrich Bracher, *The German Dictatorship*, trans. Jean Steinberg (New York: Praeger, 1970), p. 243.

18. *Hitler's Secret Conversations*, p. 6.

19. Quoted in Hans Rothfels, "Resistance Begins," in *The Path to Dictatorship*, pp. 160–161.

20. Quoted in Guenter Lewy, *The Catholic Church and Nazi Germany* (New York: McGraw-Hill, 1965), p. 226.

21. Quoted in Hermann Graml, et al., *The German Resistance to Hitler* (Berkeley: University of California Press, 1970), p. 206.

22. Quoted in Conway, *The Nazi Persecution of the Churches*, p. 332.

23. Excerpted in George L. Mosse, ed., *Nazi Culture* (New York: Grosset & Dunlap, 1966), pp. 206–207.

24. Bracher, *The German Dictatorship*, pp. 248, 251.

25. Quoted in T. L. Jarman, *The Rise and Fall of Nazi Germany* (New York: New York University Press, 1956), p. 182.

26. Quoted in Horst von Maltitz, *The Evolution of Hitler's Germany* (New York: McGraw-Hill, 1973), pp. 433–434.

27. Ibid., pp. 438–439.

28. Quoted in Bracher, *The German Dictatorship*, p. 268.

29. Quoted in Fest, *Hitler*, p. 532.

Suggested Reading

Allen, William Sheridan, *The Nazi Seizure of Power* (1965). An illuminating study of how the people of a small German town reacted to Nazism during the years 1930–1935.

Bracher, Karl Dietrich, *The German Dictatorship* (1970). A highly regarded analysis of all phases of the Nazi state.

Bucheim, Heim, *Totalitarian Rule* (1968). Nature and characteristics of totalitarianism, by a German scholar.

Bullock, Alan, *Hitler: A Study in Tyranny* (1964). An excellent biography.

Cassels, Alan, *Fascist Italy* (1968). A clearly written introduction.

Conway, J. S., *The Nazi Persecution of the Churches* (1968). Nazi persecution of the churches and the capitulation of the clergy.

Fest, Joachim C., *Hitler* (1974). An excellent biography.

Haffner, Sebastian, *The Meaning of Hitler* (1979). A German journalist's inquiry into Hitler's successes and failures.

Jackel, Eberhard, *Hitler's Weltanschauung* (1972). An analysis of Hitler's world-view.

Kirkpatrick, Ivone, *Mussolini: A Study in Power* (1964). A solid biography.

Laqueur, Walter, ed., *Fascism: A Reader's Guide* (1976). A superb collection of essays.

Maltitz, Horst von, *The Evolution of Hitler's Germany* (1973). In trying to explain how it was possible, the author discusses the German roots of Nazism.

Mayer, Milton, *They Thought They Were Free* (1955). The lives of ordinary citizens who became Nazis.

Mosse, George L., *Nazi Culture* (1966). A representative collection of Nazi writings with a fine introduction.

Paxton, Robert O., *Europe in the Twentieth Century* (1975). A first-rate text with an excellent bibliography.

Rogger, Hans, and Eugen Weber, eds., *The European Right* (1966). A valuable collection of essays on right-wing movements in various European countries.

Smith, Denis Mack, *Mussolini* (1982). By America's leading historian of modern Italy.

Turner, Henry A., ed., *Reappraisals of Fascism.* Collection of useful essays.

Review Questions

1. How did fascist principles "stand for the sheer, categorical, definitive antithesis to the world of democracy and the world which still abides by the fundamental principles laid down in 1789"?

2. Why did some Italians support Mussolini?

3. How did Mussolini bluff his way to power?

4. How did Mussolini try to extend his control over Italy?

5. What were Mussolini's policies toward the church? The economy?

6. In what ways was Mussolini less effective than Hitler in establishing a totalitarian state?

7. How was Hitler's outlook shaped by his experiences in Vienna?

8. What was the significance of the Munich Putsch of 1923?

9. What were Hitler's attitudes toward democracy, the masses, war, the Jews?

10. Why did Hitler's views prove attractive to Germans?

11. How was Hitler able to gain power?

12. How did the Nazis extend their control over Germany?

13. How did Nazism conflict with the core values of Christianity? What was the general policy of the Nazis toward the churches? Why did the German churches generally fail to take a stand against the Nazi regime?

14. What was the purpose of the giant rallies?

15. By 1939, most Germans were enthusiastic about the Nazi regime. Explain this statement.

16. What lessons might democratic societies draw from the experience of fascist totalitarianism?

17. After World War I, in country after country, parliamentary democracy collapsed and authoritarian leaders came to power. Explain.

18. How did the United States, Britain, and France try to cope with the Great Depression?

33

Thought and Culture in an Era of World Wars: Disorientation, Doubt, and Commitment

*T*he modern mentality may be said to have passed through two broad phases—an early modernity and a late modernity. Formulated during the era of the Scientific Revolution and the Enlightenment, the outlook of early modernity stressed confidence in reason, science, human goodness, and humanity's capacity to improve society for human betterment. In the late nineteenth and early twentieth centuries, a new outlook took shape. It broke with standards of aesthetics that had been established during the Renaissance, altered the view of nature shaped during the Scientific Revolution, and rejected the Enlightenment attitude toward reason and progress. Shattering old beliefs, late modernity left Europeans without landmarks, without generally accepted cultural standards or agreed upon conceptions of the human person and life's meaning. The presuppositions of early modernity, already eroding in the decades prior to the Great War, seemed near collapse after 1918—another casualty of trench warfare. Westerners no longer possessed a frame of reference, a common outlook for understanding nature, themselves, their times, or the past. The triumph of Bolshevism in Russia, the emergence of fascism—both directly linked to the Great War—and the Depression also profoundly disoriented the European mind.

There were a variety of responses to this crisis of consciousness. Some intellectuals retreated into despair or found escape in their art. Others sought a new hope in the Soviet experiment or in fascism; still others reaffirmed the rational-humanist tradition of the Enlightenment. Christian thinkers, repelled by the secularism, materialism, and rootlessness of the modern age, urged Westerners to find renewed meaning and purpose in their ancestral religion. A philosophical movement, called existentialism, aspired to make life authentic in a world stripped of universal values.

Intellectuals and Artists in Troubled Times

Postwar Pessimism

After the Great War, Europeans looked at themselves and their civilization differently. It seemed that in science and technology Europeans had unleashed powers they could not control and that belief in the stability and security of European civilization was an illusion. Also illusory was the expectation that reason would banish surviving signs of darkness, ignorance, and injustice and usher in an age of continual progress. European intellectuals felt that they were living in a "broken world." In an age of heightened brutality and mobilized irrationality, the values of old Europe seemed beyond recovery. "All the great words," wrote D. H. Lawrence, "were cancelled out for that generation."[1] The fissures discernible in European civilization prior to 1914 had grown wider and deeper. To be sure, Europe also had its optimists—those who found reason for hope in the League of Nations and in the easing of international tensions and improved economic conditions in the mid-1920s. However, the Great Depression and the triumph of totalitarianism intensified feelings of doubt and disillusionment.

The somber mood that gripped European intellectuals in the immediate postwar period had been anticipated by Freud in 1915, when he wrote:

We cannot but feel that no event has ever destroyed so much that is precious in the common possessions of humanity, confused so many of the clearest intelligences or so thoroughly debased what is highest. . . . the war in which we had refused to believe broke out, and it brought—disillusionment. . . . It tramples in blind fury on all that comes in its way, as though there were to be no future and no peace among men after it is over. It cuts all the common bonds between the contending peoples, and threatens to leave a legacy of embitterment that will make any renewal of these bonds impossible for a long time to come.[2]

A pessimistic outlook also pervaded Freud's *Civilization and Its Discontents* (1930), in which he held that civilized life was forever threatened by the antisocial and irrational elements of human nature (see page 652). Other expressions of pessimism abounded. In 1919, Paul Valéry stated: "We modern civilizations have learned to recognize that we are mortal like the others. We feel that a civilization is as fragile as life."[3] "We are living today under the sign of the collapse of civilization,"[4] declared humanitarian Albert Schweitzer in 1923. "There is a growing awareness of imminent ruin tantamount to a dread of the approaching end of all that makes life worthwhile,"[5] said German philosopher Karl Jaspers in 1932. The novels of Aldous Huxley rejected belief in progress and expressed a disenchantment with the modern world. Ernest Hemingway's *The Sun Also Rises* (1926) described a lost postwar generation. In Erich Maria Remarque's *All Quiet on the Western Front* (1929), a German soldier ponders the war's impact on youth.

I am twenty years old; yet I know nothing of life but despair, death, fear, and fatuous superficiality cast over an abyss of sorrow. I see how peoples are set against one another, and in silence, unknowingly, foolishly, obediently, innocently slay one another. I see that the keenest brains of the world invent weapons and words to make it yet more refined and enduring. . . . all my generation is experiencing these things with me. . . . What do they expect of us if a time ever comes when the war is over? Through the years our business has been killing. . . . Our knowledge of life is limited to death. What will happen afterwards?[6]

In the "Second Coming" (1919), William Butler Yeats conveyed this sense of dark times:

Mere anarchy is loosed upon the world,
The blood-dimmed tide is loosed, and everywhere
The Ceremony of innocence is drowned;
The best lack all conviction, while the worst
Are full of passionate intensity.
Surely some revelation is at hand
Surely the Second Coming is at hand.[7]

T. S. Eliot's "The Waste Land" (1922) is pervaded by the image of a collapsing European civilization. Eliot creates a macabre scenario. Hooded hordes, modern-day barbarians, swarm over plains and lay waste cities. Jerusalem, Athens, Alexandria, Vienna, and London—each once a great spiritual or cultural center—are now "falling towers." Amid this destruction, one hears "high in the air/Murmur of maternal lamentation."[8]

Carl Gustav Jung, a Swiss psychologist who broke with Freud, said in *Modern Man in Search of a Soul* (1933):

I believe I am not exaggerating when I say that modern man has suffered an almost fatal shock, psychologically speaking, and as a result has fallen into profound uncertainty. . . . The revolution in our conscious outlook, brought about by the catastrophic results of the World War, shows itself in our inner life by the shattering of our faith in ourselves and our own worth. . . . I realize only too well that I am losing my faith in the possibility of a rational organization of the world, the old dream of the millennium, in which peace and harmony should rule, has grown pale.[9]

In 1936, Dutch historian Johan Huizinga wrote in a chapter entitled "Apprehension of Doom":

We are living in a demented world. And we know it. . . . Everywhere there are doubts as to the solidity of our social structure, vague fears of the imminent future, a feeling that our civilization is on the way to ruin. . . . almost all things which once seemed sacred and immutable have now become unsettled, truth and humanity, justice and reason. . . . The sense of living in the midst of a violent crisis of civilization, threatening complete collapse, has spread far and wide.[10]

The most influential expression of pessimism was Oswald Spengler's *The Decline of the West*. The first volume was published in July 1918 as the Great War was drawing to a close, and the second volume in 1922. The work achieved instant notoriety, particularly in Spengler's native Germany, shattered by

defeat. Spengler viewed history as an assemblage of many different cultures which, like living organisms, experience birth, youth, maturity, and death. What contemporaries pondered most was Spengler's insistence that Western civilization had entered its final stage and that its death could not be averted.

Spengler defined a culture as a spiritual orientation that pervades a people's literature, art, religion, philosophy, politics, and economics; each culture has a distinctive style that distinguishes it from another culture. The ancient Greeks, said Spengler, viewed themselves as living in a clearly defined and finite world. Hence classical sculpture was characterized by the life-sized nude statue, architecture by the temple with small columns, and political life by the small city-state rather than by a kingdom or an empire. Modern Westerners have a different cultural orientation, said Spengler; they exude a Faustian urge to expand, to reach out. Thus Europeans developed perspectival art that permits distance to be depicted on a canvas; they sailed the oceans, conquered vast regions of the globe, and communicated over great distances by telephone and telegraph.

Spengler maintained that cultures, like biological organisms, pass through necessary stages—a heroic youth, a creative maturity, and a decadent old age. In its youth, during the Renaissance, said Spengler, Western culture experienced the triumphs of Michelangelo, Shakespeare, and Galileo; in its maturity, during the eighteenth century, Western culture reached its creative height in the music of Mozart, the poetry of Goethe, and the philosophy of Kant. But now, Faustian culture, entering old age, shows signs of decay— a growing materialism and skepticism, a disenchanted proletariat, rampant warfare and competition for empire, decadent art forms. "Of great painting or great music there can no longer be, for Western people, any question,"[11] concluded Spengler.

To an already troubled Western world, Spengler offered no solace. The West, like other cultures and like any living organism, is destined to die; its decline is irreversible, its death inevitable, and the symptoms of degeneration are already evident. Spengler's gloomy prognostication buttressed the fascists, who claimed that they were creating a new civilization on the ruins of a dying European civilization.

Literature and Art: Innovation, Disillusionment, and Social Commentary

Postwar pessimism did not prevent writers and artists from perpetuating the cultural innovations initiated before the war. In the works of D. H. Lawrence, Marcel Proust, André Gide, James Joyce, Franz Kafka, T. S. Eliot, and Thomas Mann the modernist movement achieved a brilliant flowering. Often these writers gave expression to the troubles and uncertainties of the postwar period.

Franz Kafka (1883–1924), whose major novels, *The Trial* and *The Castle*, were published after his death, did not receive recognition until after World War II. Yet perhaps better than any other novelist of his generation, Kafka grasped the dilemma of the modern age. In Kafka's world, human beings strive to make sense out of life, but everywhere ordinary occurrences thwart them. They are caught in a bureaucratic web that they cannot control; they live in a nightmare society dominated by oppressive, cruel, and corrupt officials and amoral torturers—a world where power is exercised without limits and traditional values and ordinary logic do not operate. In *The Trial*, for example, the hero is arrested and eventually executed without knowing why. In these observations, Kafka proved a prophet of the emerging totalitarian state. (Kafka's three sisters perished in the Holocaust.)

Kafka was a German-speaking Jew in the alien Slav environment of Czechoslovakia, was intimidated by a tyrannical father, and contracted tuberculosis, from which he died at an early age. In giving expression to his own deep anxieties, he expressed the feelings of alienation and isolation that characterize the modern individual; he explored life's dreads and absurdities, offering no solutions or consolation. In Kafka's works people are defeated and unable to comprehend the irrational forces that contribute to their destruction. The mind yearns for coherence but, Kafka tells us, uncertainty, if not chaos, governs human relationships. We can neither be certain of our own identities or of the world we encounter, for human beings are the playthings of forces too unfathomable to comprehend, too irrational to master.

Before World War I, German writer Thomas Mann (1875–1955) had earned a reputation for his short stories and novels, particularly *Buddenbrooks* (1901), which portrayed the decline of a prosperous bourgeois family. At the outbreak of the war, Mann was a staunch conservative who disliked democracy; after the war he drew closer to the values of the Western liberal-humanist tradition, supporting the Weimar Republic and attacking the Nazi cult of irrationalism. After Hitler's seizure of power, Mann went to Switzerland and eventually to the United States, where he remained a staunch foe of totalitarianism.

In the *Magic Mountain* (1924), Mann reflected on the decomposition of bourgeois European civilization. The setting for the story is a Swiss sanitarium, whose patients, drawn from several European lands, suffer from tuberculosis. The sanitarium symbolizes Europe, and it is the European psyche that is diseased.

One patient, the Italian Ludovico Settembrini, stands for the humanist ideals of the Enlightenment—reason, individual liberty, and progress. While Mann is sympathetic to these ideals, he also indicts Settembrini for his naive faith in progress, his shallow view of human nature, which gives little significance to the will, and his lofty rhetoric. Seeing the human being as purely rational, Settembrini foolishly believes that people will mend their ways once they are enlightened by reason's sweet voice. Thus, he even claims that merely by looking at a sick person "rationally," he cured him.

Pitted against Settembrini is Leo Naphta, a Spanish-trained Jesuit of Jewish-Polish descent who rejects completely the Italian's liberal-humanist values. He is an authoritarian who insists that people do not need freedom, but authority, whether it be the state or God; he is a fanatic who subscribes to torture and terror. Believing that the dictatorship of the proletariat is the means of salvation demanded by the age, Naphta embraces Marxism. Borrowing from medieval mysticism, Nietzschean irrationalism, and Marxist militancy, he attacks every facet of the existing order.

Mynheer Peeperkorn, a wealthy Dutch planter from Java, is nonintellectual, illogical, and inarticulate, but he radiates pure vitality and emotional intensity. This charismatic personality dwarfs the humanist and the authoritarian and dominates the patients, who find him irresistible.

The *Magic Mountain* raised, but did not resolve, crucial questions. Was the epoch of rational-humanist culture drawing to a close? Did Europeans welcome their spiritual illness in the same way that some of the patients in the sanitarium had a will-to-illness? How could Europe rescue itself from decadence?

D. H. Lawrence (1885–1930), the son of an illiterate British coal miner, was saddened and angered by the consequences of industrial society—the deterioration of nature, tedious work divorced from personal satisfaction, a life-denying quest for wealth and possessions. He looked back longingly on preindustrial England and wanted people to reorient their thinking away from money making and suppression of the instincts. In *Lady Chatterley's Lover* (1928) and other works he dealt with the clash between industrial civilization and the needs of human nature, between regimentation and passion.

Like nineteenth-century romantics, Lawrence found a higher truth in deep-seated passion than in reason; this led him to rail against Christianity for stifling human sexuality. Like Nietzsche, he believed that excessive intellectualizing destroyed the life-affirming, instinctual part of human nature. In 1913 he wrote:

Thomas Mann (1875–1955) at the Danubian Congress, New York, 1938. In his novel *Buddenbrooks* (1901), Mann chronicled the decay of a prosperous commercial family. In *The Magic Mountain* (1924), he probed the minds of patients in a tuberculosis sanatorium. These people were symbols of an equally diseased Europe. (*AP/Wide World Photos*)

My great religion is a belief in the blood, the flesh, as being wiser than the intellect. We can go wrong in our minds. But what our blood feels and believes and says is always true. The intellect is only a bit and a bridle. What do I care about knowledge. All I want is to answer to my blood without fribbling intervention of mind, or moral, or what not. . . . We have got so ridiculously mindful, that we never know that we ourselves are anything.[12]

Many writers, shattered by World War I, disgusted by fascism's growing strength, and moved by the terrible suffering of the Depression, became committed to social and political causes. Erich Maria Remarque's *All Quiet on the Western Front* (1929) was one of many antiwar novels. In *The Grapes of Wrath* (1939), John Steinbeck captured the suffering of American farmers driven from their land by the Dust Bowl and foreclosure during the Depression. George Orwell's *Road to Wigan Pier* (1937) recorded the bleak lives of English coal miners. Few issues stirred the conscience of intellectuals as did the Spanish Civil War, and many of them volunteered to fight with the Spanish Republicans against the fascists. Ernest Hemingway's *For Whom the Bell Tolls* (1940) expressed the sentiments of these thinkers. In *Mario and the Magician* (1930), Thomas Mann explicitly attacked fascism, and implied that it would have to be resisted by arms.

The new directions taken in art before World War I—abstractionism and expressionism—continued in the postwar decades. Picasso, Mondrian, Kandinsky, Matisse, Roualt, Braque, Modigliani, and other masters continued to refine their styles. In addition, new art trends emerged that mirrored the trauma of a generation that had experienced the war and lost its faith in Europe's moral and intellectual values.

In 1915 in Zurich, artists and writers founded a movement called Dada to express their revulsion against the war and the civilization that spawned it. From neutral Switzerland, the movement spread to Germany and Paris. Dada shared in the postwar mood of disorientation and despair. Dadaists viewed life as essentially absurd (Dada is a nonsense term) and cultivated indifference. "The acts of life have no beginning or end. Everything happens in a completely idiotic way,"[13] declared the poet Tristan Tzara, one of Dada's founders and its chief spokesman. Dadaists expressed contempt for artistic and literary standards and rejected both God and reason. "Through reason man becomes a tragic and ugly figure," said one Dadaist; "beauty is dead," said another. Tzara declared:

What good did the theories of the philosophers do us? Did they help us to take a single step forward or backward? . . . We have had enough of the intelligent movements that have stretched beyond

measure our credulity in the benefits of science. What we want now is spontaneity because everything that issues freely from ourselves, without the intervention of speculative ideas represents us.[14]

For Dadaists the world was nonsensical and reality disordered; hence they offered no solutions to anything. "Like everything in life, Dada is useless,"[15] said Tzara.

Dadaists showed their contempt for art (one art historian calls Dada "the first anti-art movement on record"[16]) by deliberately producing works devoid of artistic value. Marcel Duchamp's shovel is an example, as is his Mona Lisa with a mustache. Despite the Dadaists' nihilistic aims and "calculated irrationality," says art historian H. W. Janson, "there was also liberation, a voyage into unknown provinces of the creative mind." Thus Duchamp's painting with the nonsense title *Tu m'* was "dazzlingly inventive [and] far ahead of its time."[17]

Dada ended as a formal movement in 1924 and was succeeded by surrealism. Surrealists inherited from Dada a contempt for reason; they stressed fantasy and made use of Freudian insights and symbols in their art to reproduce the raw state of the unconscious and to arrive at truths beyond reason's grasp. To penetrate the interior of the mind, said André Breton, a French surrealist poet, the writer should "write quickly without any previously chosen subject, quickly enough not to dwell on and not to be tempted to read over what you have written."[18] Writing should not be dictated by the intellect, but should flow automatically from the unconscious. Surrealists tried to portray the world of fantasy and hallucination, the marvelous and the spontaneous. Breton urged artists to live their dreams, even if it meant seeing "a horse galloping on a tomato." In their attempt to break through the constraints of rationality in order to reach a higher reality—that is, a "Surreality"—leading surrealists like Max Ernst (1891–1976), Salvador Dali (1904–), and Joan Miró (1893–1983) produced works of undeniable artistic merit.

The Emergence of Modern Art

Figure 1 Le Corbusier: Notre-Dame-du-Haut, from the Southeast, 1950–1955. Ronchamp, France. (© *Ph. Charliat/Rapho*)

Figure 2 Paul Gauguin: *Soyez Amoureuses, Vous Serez Heureuses*. Painted wood sculpture. (*Museum of Fine Arts, Boston*)

Figure 3 Paul Cézanne: *Still Life with Apples*, 1885–1898. Oil on canvas. H. 27 in. W. 36 1/2 in. (*Collection, The Museum of Modern Art, New York. Lillie P. Bliss Collection*)

Toward the end of the nineteenth century, obscure groups of artists working in France and Germany began to re-evaluate the meaning and function of art. By the 1890s the tumultuous changes of the preceding century had profoundly altered the world-view of many intellectuals. To some artists the cool, orderly figure style and calm compositions of the Renaissance, based on Greco-Roman models, and the more elaborate baroque and neoclassical styles of the seventeenth and eighteenth centuries no longer seemed appropriate forms of artistic expression.

Freed from the grip of classical values, artists began to recognize the power and eloquence of non-Western art. Like many others of his time, France's Paul Gauguin (1848–1903) was attracted to the art of "primitive" people because they seemed uncorrupted by industrial society, closer to the earth, and more in tune with nature. The elemental force of nature, respect for non-European traditions, and the simple, "primitive" technique of wood-carving all appear in Gauguin's *Soyez Amoureuses* (Figure 2).

During the 1880s, Vincent van Gogh (1853–1890) of the Netherlands and Gauguin recognized that color, like other formal elements, could act as a language in and of itself. The local or "real" color of an object does not necessarily express the artist's experience. Artists, according to van Gogh and Gauguin, should seek to paint things not as they appear to the eye, but as they are felt. (See van Gogh's painting opening Chapter 28.)

In pre–World War I Germany, the Expres-

Figure 4 Henri Matisse: *The Red Studio*, 1911. Oil on canvas. H. 71 1/4 in. W. 7 ft. 2 1/4 in. (*Collection, The Museum of Modern Art, New York, Mrs. Simon Guggenheim Fund*)

sionists developed some of these ideas, often using bold, flat color to convey psychological forces that Sigmund Freud had explored. For example, the *Convalescent Woman* of Erich Heckel (1883–1970) is depicted with colors that evoke feelings of tension, stress, and isolation (Figure 7). In France, on the other hand, the bold color and line of Henri Matisse (1869–1954) produced paintings of extroverted, joyous vitality. The single continuous area of color in the *Red Studio* is unrelated to the real color of his workshop, yet it expresses the artist's perception of the place (Figure 4). Further, the red area can be interpreted both as surface color and as the imaginary space of the interior.

Alongside the revolution in color, another was occurring in the use of space. From about 1880 on, Paul Cézanne (1839–1906) developed a new way of expressing the experience of seeing. He sought to create paintings with perfectly designed compositions, true both to the subject matter and to his own perceptions. He also wanted to subsume and build upon the Western artistic tradition.

Cézanne's *Still Life with Apples* (Figure 3) has the solidity, monumentality, and balanced composition of a classical French painting from the seventeenth century. The space of the painting, however, is not treated as a block viewed from a stationary position. Instead, it is compressed, and the fruit, tabletop, and drapery are each seen from a slightly different angle. The fluid viewpoint helps to convey time and movement, which are part of the visual experience. In looking at the painting,

Figure 5 *Above:* Walter Gropius: Bauhaus, Dessau, 1925–1926. (*Leonard/Bauhaus-Archiv, Berlin*)

Figure 6 *Right:* Piet Mondrian: *Broadway Boogie Woogie,* 1942–1943. Oil on canvas. H. 50 in. W. 50 in. (*Collection, The Museum of Modern Art, New York*)

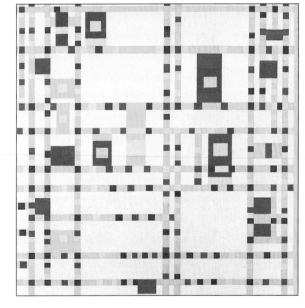

one is struck with its breadth, its order, and the intense concentration of Cézanne's vision.

Between 1909 and 1914 in Paris, Pablo Picasso (1881–1973) and Georges Braque (1882–1963) worked together to develop a new style that is called cubism. Cubist space is even more shallow and compressed than the space of Cézanne. The idea of multiple views is extended so that the shifts of viewpoint are more numerous and more extreme. Several objects in Picasso's *Interior with a Girl Drawing* (Figure 9) are represented this way. Cubist artists explored the interdependence of art and life in other areas besides the depiction of space. In this case the model is an artist herself; her subject might be Picasso painting.

Throughout the period from 1890 to 1914, avant-garde artists were de-emphasizing subject matter and stressing the expressive power of such formal qualities as line, color, and space. It is not surprising that some artists

Figure 7 Erich Heckel: *Convalescent Woman*, 1913. Central panel of triptych. Entire work 38 3/4 in. by 95 3/4 in. (*Courtesy of the Harvard University Art Museums, Busch Reisinger Museum Purchase—Mrs. Busch Greenough Fund*)

Figure 8 Henry Moore: *Family Group*, 1948–1949. Bronze, cast 1950. 59 1/4 in. by 46 1/4 in., at base 45 × 29 7/8 in. (*Collection, The Museum of Modern Art, New York, A. Conger Goodyear Fund*)

finally began to create work that did not refer to anything seen in the real world. Piet Mondrian (1872–1944), a Dutch artist, saw the cubist art of Picasso and Braque just before World War I. The cubists had compressed the space of their paintings and reduced subject matter to insignificance. For Mondrian the next step was to eliminate illusionistic space and subject matter. His *Broadway Boogie-Woogie*, for example, seems entirely flat (Figure 6). Its effect is musical. Moving from colored rectangles to black bands, from tiny squares to broad, syncopated blocks of color, one feels the visual rhythm of the painting.

Geometric abstraction has been a major theme in many fields of twentieth-century art. Mondrian's work was a great inspiration, not only for painters, but for architects and graphics designers as well, because he envisioned the complete integration of art and the human environment. The Bauhaus, an institute established in Germany in 1919, fostered the creation of high quality art, design, and architecture that could be made available to people of all socio-economic levels. The building designed by Walter Gropius (1883–1970) (Figure 5) exemplifies the Bauhaus ideal in its simplicity and directness. Gropius avoids

Figure 9 Pablo Picasso: *Interior with a Girl Drawing*, February 12, 1935. Oil on canvas. 51 1/4 by 76 5/8 in. (*Collection, The Museum of Modern Art, New York, Nelson A. Rockefeller Bequest*)

monotony and sterility by arranging rectangular voids and solids in a rhythmic, dynamic way, very much akin to Mondrian's painting.

Notre-Dame-du-Haut (Figure 1), a chapel designed by Swiss architect Le Corbusier (1887–1965), represents another trend in modern architecture, one that might be called "primitivist." For this sanctuary on a mountain top, Le Corbusier used reinforced concrete to create great walls and overhangs; these and the concealed doors to the sacred interior evoke prehistoric and ancient religious constructions.

Twentieth-century artists have devised new definitions for art, invented new ways of treating color, space, and drawing, explored new media, and developed abstract, nonreferential styles. At the same time, however, some very gifted artists, such as Henry Moore (b. 1898), have used traditional media (bronze) to continue the Western tradition of monumental figure sculpture. Within that tradition, Moore treats universal human concerns, such as the dangers of war and the bonds of family and children (Figure 8). His figure style recapitulates the theme of timeless values by recalling associations with Neolithic fertility images.

—KATHERINE CRUM

Artists, like writers, expressed a social conscience. George Grosz combined a Dadaist sense of life's meaninglessness with a new realism to depict the moral degeneration of middle-class German society. In *After the Questioning* (1935), Grosz, then living in the United States, dramatized Nazi brutality; in *The End of the World* (1936) he expressed his fear of another impending world war. Still another German artist, Käthe Kollwitz, showed a deep compassion for the sufferer—the unemployed, the hungry, the ill, the politically oppressed.

In a series of paintings, *The Passion of Sacco and Vanzetti* (1931–1932), American artist Ben Shahn showed his outrage at the execution of two radicals. William Gropper's *Migration* (1932) dramatized the suffering of the same dispossessed farmers described in Steinbeck's novel *The Grapes of Wrath*. Philip Evergood, in *Don't Cry Mother* (1938–1944), portrayed the apathy of starving children and their mother's terrible helplessness.

In his etchings of maimed, dying, and dead soldiers, German artist Otto Dix produced a powerful visual indictment of the Great War's cruelty and suffering. In *Guernica* (1937), Picasso memorialized the Spanish village decimated by saturation bombing during the Spanish Civil War. In the *White Crucifixion* (1938), Marc Chagall, a Russian-born Jew who had settled in Paris, depicted the terror and flight of Jews in Nazi Germany.

Communism: "The God That Failed"

The economic misery of the Depression and the rise of fascist barbarism led many intellectuals to find a new hope, even a secular faith, in communism. They praised the Soviet Union for supplanting capitalist greed with socialist cooperation, for replacing a haphazard economic system marred by repeated depressions with one based on planned production, and for providing employment for everyone when joblessness was endemic in capitalist lands. American literary critic Edmund Wilson said that in the Soviet Union,

Marcel Duchamp (1887–1968): In Advance of the Broken Arm. Duchamp was a founder of the Dada movement in art. He observed that things became art when the artist designates them as such. Dadaists looked at the aftermath of World War I and were appalled. To them, life was disordered and nonsensical. Their art reflects this chaos, and explores a new world of total irrationality. (*Yale University Art Gallery, Gift of Katherine S. Dreier for the Collection Société Anonyme*)

one felt at the "moral top of the world where the light never really goes out."[19] British political theorists Sidney and Beatrice Webb declared that there was no other country "in which there is actually so much widespread public criticism and such incessant reevaluation of its shortcomings as in the USSR."[20] To these intellectuals, it seemed that in the Soviet Union a vigorous and healthy civilization was emerging and that only communism could stem the tide of fascism. For many, however, the attraction was short-lived. Sickened by Stalin's purges and terror, the denial of individual freedom, and the suppression of truth, they came to view the Soviet Union as another totalitarian state and communism as another "god that failed."

One such intellectual was Arthur Koestler. Born in Budapest of Jewish ancestry and educated in Vienna, Koestler worked as a correspondent for a leading Berlin newspaper chain. He joined the Communist party at the very end of 1931 because he "lived in a disintegrating society thirsting for faith," was sensitized by the Depression, and saw communism as the "only force capable of resisting the onrush of the primitive [Nazi] horde."[21] Koestler visited the Soviet Union in 1933, experiencing firsthand both the starvation brought on by forced collectivization and the propaganda that grotesquely misrepresented life in Western lands. While his faith was shaken, he did not break with the party until 1938 in response to Stalin's liquidations.

In *Darkness at Noon* (1941), Koestler explored the attitudes of the Old Bolsheviks who were imprisoned, tortured, and executed by Stalin. These dedicated communists had served the party faithfully, but Stalin, fearful of opposition, hateful of intellectuals, and driven by megalomania, denounced them as enemies of the people. In *Darkness at Noon*, the leading character, the imprisoned Rubashov, is a composite of the Old Bolsheviks. Although innocent, and without being tortured, Rubashov publicly confesses to political crimes that he never committed.

Rubashov is aware of the suffering that the party has brought to the Russian people:

. . . in the interests of a just distribution of land we deliberately let die of starvation about five million farmers and their families in one year. . . . [to liberate] human beings from the shackles of industrial exploitation . . . we sent about ten million people to do forced labour in the Arctic regions and the jungles of the East, under conditions similar to those of antique galley slaves. . . . to settle a

difference of opinion, we know only one argument: death. . . . Our poets settle discussions on questions of style by denunciations to the secret police. . . . The people's standard of life is lower than it was before the Revolution, the labour conditions are harder, the discipline is more inhuman. . . . Our Press and our schools cultivate Chauvinism, militarism, dogmatism, conformism and ignorance. The arbitrary power of the Government is unlimited, and unexampled in history; freedom of the Press, of opinion and of movement are as thoroughly exterminated as though the proclamation of the Rights of Man had never been. We have built up the most gigantic police apparatus, with informers made a national institution, and with the most refined scientific system of physical and mental torture. We whip the groaning masses of the country towards a theoretical future happiness, which only we can see.[22]

Nevertheless Rubashov remains the party's faithful servant; true believers do not easily break with their faith. By confessing, Rubashov performs his last service for the revolution: for the true believer, everything—truth, justice, and the sanctity of the indivdual—are properly sacrificed to the party.

Reaffirming the Christian Philosophy of History

By calling into question core liberal beliefs—the essential goodness of human nature, the primacy of reason, the efficacy of science, and the inevitability of progress—the Great War led thinkers to find in Christianity an alternative view of the human experience and the crisis of the twentieth century. Christian thinkers, including Karl Barth, Paul Tillich, Reinhold Niebuhr, and T. S. Eliot, asserted the reality of evil in human nature and assailed liberals and Marxists for postulating a purely rational and secular philosophy of history and for anticipating an ideal society within the realm of historical time. In the Christian conception of history as a clash between human will and God's precepts, these thinkers found an intelligible explanation for the tragedies of the twentieth century. In 1933, Christopher Dawson, an English Catholic thinker, wrote:

If our civilization is to recover its vitality, or even to survive, it must cease to neglect its spiritual roots and must realize that religion is not a matter of personal sentiment which has nothing to do with the objective realities of society, but is, on the contrary, the very heart of social life and the root of every living culture.[23]

In 1934 British historian Arnold Toynbee published the first three volumes of his monumental *A Study of History,* in which he tried to account for the rise, growth, breakdown, and disintegration of civilization. Underlying Toynbee's philosophy of history was a religious orientation, for he saw religious prophets as humanity's greatest figures and higher religions as humanity's greatest achievement. Toynbee attributed the problems of Western civilization to its breaking away from Christianity and embracing of "false idols," particularly the national state which, he said, had become the object of Westerners' highest reverence.

Toynbee regarded nationalism as a primitive religion that induces people to revere the national community rather than God. This deification of the parochial—tribal or local—community, he said, intensifies the brutal side of human nature and provokes wars among people sharing a common civilization. To Toynbee, Nazism was the culmination of the worst elements in modern European nationalism, "the consummation . . . of a politico-religious movement, the pagan deification and worship of parochial human communities which had been gradually gaining ground for more than four centuries in the Western world at large."[24] The moral catastrophe of Nazism, he said, demonstrates the inadequacy of liberal humanism, for the Enlightenment tradition proved a feeble barrier to Nazism's rise and spread. The secular values of the Enlightenment, divorced from Christianity, are insufficient to restrain human nature's basest impulses. For the West to save itself, said Toynbee, it must abide by the spiritual values of its religious prophets.

Reaffirming the Ideals of Reason and Freedom

Several thinkers tried to reaffirm the ideals of rationality and freedom that had been trampled on by totalitarian movements. In *The Treason of the Intellectuals* (1927), Julien Benda, a French cultural critic of Jewish background, castigated intellectuals for intensifying hatred between nations, classes, and political factions. "Our age is indeed the age of the *intellectual organization of political hatreds,*"[25] he wrote. These intellectuals, said Benda, do not pursue justice or truth, but proclaim that "even if our country is wrong, we must think of it in the right."[26] They scorn outsiders, extol harshness and action, and proclaim the superiority of instinct and will to intelligence; or they "assert that the intelligence to be venerated is that which limits its activities within the bounds of national interest."[27] The logical end of this xenophobia, said Benda, "is the organized slaughter of nations and classes."[28]

José Ortega y Gasset, descendant of a noble Spanish family and a professor of philosophy, gained international recognition with the publication of *Revolt of the Masses* (1930). Ortega held that European civilization, the product of a creative elite, was degenerating into barbarism because of the growing power of the masses, who lack the mental discipline and commitment to reason to preserve Europe's intellectual and cultural traditions. Ortega did not equate the masses with the working class and the elite with the nobility; it was an attitude of mind, not a class affiliation, that distinguished the "mass-man" from the elite. The mass-man, said Ortega, has a commonplace mind and does not set high standards for himself. He is inert until driven by an external compulsion. Faced with a problem, he "is satisfied with thinking the first thing he finds in his head," and "crushes . . . everything that is different, everything that is excellent, individual, qualified, and select. Anybody who is not like everybody, who does not think like everybody, runs the risk of being eliminated."[29] Such intellectually vulgar people, declared Ortega, cannot control the processes of civilization. The fascists exemplify this revolt of the masses:

Under fascism there appears for the first time in Europe a type of man who does not want to give reasons or to be right, but simply shows himself resolved to impose his opinions. This is the new thing: the right not to be reasonable, the "reason of unreason." Hence I see the most palpable manifestation of the new mentality of the masses, due to their having decided to rule society without the capacity for doing so.[30]

The mass-man, said Ortega, does not respect the tradition of reason; he does not enter into rational dialogue with others or defend his opinions logically.

[Because his thoughts are] nothing more than appetites in words. . . . the mass-man would feel himself lost if he accepted discussion. . . . Hence the "new thing" in Europe is to have done with discussions, and detestation is expressed for all forms of intercommunion which implies acceptance of objective standards, ranging from conversation to Parliament, and taking in science. This means that there is a renunciation of the common life based on culture which is subject to standards, and a return to the common life of barbarism.[31]

The mass-man rejects reason and glorifies violence—the ultimate expression of barbarism. If European civilization is to be rescued from fascism and communism, said Ortega, the elite must sustain civilized values and provide leadership for the masses.

Ernst Cassirer, a German philosopher of Jewish lineage, emigrated after Hitler came to power, eventually settling in the United States. A staunch defender of the Enlightenment tradition, Cassirer in 1932, just prior to Hitler's triumph, wrote:

More than ever before, it seems to me, the time is again ripe for applying . . . self-criticism to the present age, for holding up to it that bright clear mirror fashioned by the Enlightenment. . . . The age which venerated reason and science as man's highest faculty cannot and must not be lost even for us. We must find a way not only to see that age in its own shape but to release again those original forces which brought forth and molded this shape.[32]

In his last work, *The Myth of the State* (1946), Cassirer described Nazism as the triumph of mythical thinking over reason. The Nazis, said Cassirer, cleverly manufactured myths— of the race, the leader, the party, the state— that disoriented the intellect. Germans who embraced these myths surrendered their capacity for independent judgment, leaving themselves vulnerable to manipulation by the Nazi leadership. Cassirer warned:

In politics we are always living on volcanic soil. We must be prepared for convulsions and eruptions. In all critical moments of man's social life, the rational forces that resist the rise of old mythical conceptions are no longer sure of themselves. In these moments the time of myth has come again. For myth has not been really vanquished and subjugated. It is always there, lurking in the dark and waiting for its hour and opportunity. This hour comes as soon as the other binding forces of man's social life . . . lose their strength and are no longer able to combat the demonic mythical powers.[33]

To contain the destructive powers of political myths, Cassirer urged strengthening the rational-humanist tradition, and called for the critical study of political myths, for "in order to fight an enemy you must know him. . . . We should carefully study the origin, the structure, the methods, and the technique of the political myths. We should see the adversary face to face in order to know how to combat him."[34]

Like Cassirer, and many other German-

Jewish intellectuals, Erich Fromm, a social theorist and psychoanalyst, settled in the United States after the Nazi seizure of power. In *Escape from Freedom* (1941), Fromm sought to explain the triumph of Nazism within the larger context of European history. With the end of the Middle Ages, he said, the individual grew increasingly independent of external authority and experienced new possibilities for personal development. The individual's role in the social order was no longer rigorously determined by birth; increasingly the world was explained in natural terms, freeing people from magic, mystery, and authority; and the possibility for the full development of human potential here on earth was proclaimed. In the political sphere, this new orientation culminated in the democratic state. However, while Westerners were becoming more "independent, self-reliant, and critical," they also became "more isolated, alone, and afraid."[35]

During the Middle Ages, said Fromm, the individual derived a sense of security from a structured social system that clearly defined the role of clergy, lords, serfs, and guildsmen and from the Christian world-view that made life and death purposeful. Modern Westerners have lost this sense of security, said Fromm. Dwelling in vast cities, threatened by economic crises, no longer comforted by the medieval conception of life's purpose, they often are tormented by doubts and overwhelmed by feelings of aloneness and insignificance. People try to overcome this "burden of freedom" by surrendering themselves to a person or power that they view "as being overwhelmingly strong"; they trade freedom for security by entering into "a symbiotic relationship that overcomes . . . aloneness."[36]

Because modern industrial society has made the individual feel powerless and insignificant, concluded Fromm, fascism is a constant threat. Fromm would meet the challenge of fascism by creating social conditions that lead the individual to be free and yet not alone, to be critical and yet not filled with doubts,

to be independent and yet feel an integral part of humankind.

Existentialism

Intellectual Background

The philosophic movement that best exemplified the anxiety and uncertainty of Europe in an era of world wars was existentialism. Like writers and artists, existentialist philosophers were responding to a European civilization that seemed to be in the throes of dissolution.

By the early twentieth century, the attitude of Westerners toward reason had undergone a radical transformation. Some thinkers who placed their hopes in the rational tradition of the Enlightenment were distressed by reason's inability to resolve the tensions and conflicts of modern industrial society. Moreover, the growing recognition of the nonrational—of human actions determined by hidden impulses—led people to doubt that reason plays the dominant role in human behavior. Other thinkers viewed the problem of reason differently. They reviled an attitude of mind that found no room for Christianity because its teachings did not pass the test of reason and science. Or they attacked reason for fashioning a technological and bureaucratic society that devalued and crushed human passions and stifled individuality; these thinkers insisted that human beings cannot fulfill their potential, cannot live wholly, if their feelings are denied.

For some thinkers the crucial problem was the great change in the European understanding of truth. Since the rise of philosophy in ancient Greece, Western thinkers had believed in the existence of objective, universal truths—truths that were inherent in nature and applied to all peoples at all times. (Christianity, of course, also taught the reality of truth as revealed by God.)

It was held that such truths—the natural

rights of the individual, for example—could be apprehended by the intellect and could serve as a standard for individual aspirations and social life. The recognition of these universal principles, it was believed, compels people to measure the world of the here and now in the light of rational and universal norms and to institute appropriate reforms. It was the task of philosophy to reconcile human existence with the objective order.

During the nineteenth century, the existence of universal truth came into doubt. A growing historical consciousness led some thinkers to maintain that what people considered truth was merely a reflection of their culture at a given stage in history, their perception of things at a specific point in the evolution of human consciousness. These thinkers, called historicists, held that universal truths were not woven into the fabric of nature. There are no natural rights of life, liberty, and property that constitute the individual's birthright; there are no standards of justice or equality that are inherent in nature and ascertainable by reason. It was people, said historicists, who elevated the beliefs and values of an age to the status of objective truth. This radical break with the traditional attitude toward truth contributed substantially to the crisis of European consciousness that marked the first half of the twentieth century. Traditional values and beliefs, either those inherited from the Enlightenment or those taught by Christianity, no longer gave Europeans a sense of certainty and security; people were left without a normative order to serve as a guide to living.

What route should people take in a world where old values and certainties had dissolved, where universal truth was rejected and God's existence was denied? How could people cope in a society where they were menaced by technology, manipulated by impersonal bureaucracies, and overwhelmed by feelings of anxiety? If the universe is devoid of any overarching meaning, what meaning could one give to one's own life? These questions were at the crux of existentialist philosophy.

Basic Principles

Existentialism does not lend itself to a single definition, for its principal theorists did not adhere to a common body of doctrines. For example, some existentialists were atheists, like Jean Paul Sartre, or omitted God from their thought, like Martin Heidegger; others, like Karl Jaspers, believed in God but not in Christian doctrines; still others, like Gabriel Marcel and Nikolai Berdyaev, were Christians, and Martin Buber was a believing Jew. Perhaps the essence of existentialism appears in the following principles, although not all existentialists would subscribe to each point or agree with the way it is expressed.

1. Reality defies ultimate comprehension; there are no timeless truths that exist independently of and prior to the individual human being.

2. Reason alone is an inadequate guide to living, for people are more than thinking subjects who approach the world through critical analysis. They are also feeling and willing beings who must participate fully in life, who must experience existence directly, actively, passionately. Only in this way does one live wholly and authentically.

3. Thought must not merely be abstract speculation, but must have a bearing on life; it must be translated into deeds.

4. Human nature is problematic and paradoxical, not fixed or constant; each person is like no other. Self-realization comes when one affirms one's own uniqueness; one becomes less than human when one permits one's life to be determined by a mental outlook—a set of rules and values—imposed by others.

5. We are alone. The universe is indifferent to our expectations and needs, and death is ever stalking us.

6. We are free. It is in the act of choosing freely from among different possibilities that the individual shapes an authentic existence. There is a dynamic quality to human existence; the individual has the potential to become more than he or she is.

Nineteenth-Century Forerunners

Three nineteenth-century thinkers—Sören Kierkegaard (1813–1855), Fëdor Dostoevski (1821–1881), and Friedrich Nietzsche (see Chapter 28)—were the principal forerunners of existentialism. Their views of reason, will, truth, and existence greatly influenced twentieth-century existentialists.

Kierkegaard Sören Kierkegaard, a Danish religious philosopher and Lutheran pastor, held that self-realization as a human being comes when the individual takes full responsibility for his or her life; the individual does this by choosing one way of life over another. In making choices, said Kierkegaard, the individual overcomes the agonizing feeling that life in its deepest sense is nothingness.

For Kierkegaard, the highest truth is that human beings are God's creatures. However, God's existence cannot be demonstrated by reason; the crucial questions of human existence can never be resolved in a logical and systematic way. For Kierkegaard, the individual does not know God through disinterested reflection, but by making a passionate commitment to him. In contrast to Christian apologists who sought to demonstrate that Christian teachings did not conflict with reason, Kierkegaard denied that Christian doctrines were objectively valid; for him, Christian beliefs were absurd and irrational and could not be harmonized with reason. The true Christian, said Kierkegaard, commits himself to beliefs that are unintelligible; with confidence, he plunges into the absurd.

Twentieth-century existentialists took from Kierkegaard the idea that an all-consuming dread is the price of existence. Dread can cause us to flee from life and to find comfort in delusions, but it can also spark courage, for it is an opportunity to make a commitment. For both Kierkegaard and twentieth-century existentialists, the true philosophical quest is a subjective experience—the isolated individual, alone and without help, choosing a way of life, struggling with his or her own being to make a commitment. Only in this

way does the individual become a whole person. Kierkegaard's dictum that "it is impossible to exist without passion"—that our actions matter to us—is at the heart of existentialism.

Dostoevski Fëdor Dostoevski, a Russian novelist and essayist, wrote some masterpieces of world literature, including *Crime and Punishment* (1866), *The Idiot* (1868), and *The Brothers Karamazov* (1879–1880). In 1849, Dostoevski and several other members of a secret socialist society were sentenced to death for publishing articles deemed treasonous by the tsarist regime. As the bound and blindfolded victims stood before the firing squad, a message from the tsar arrived commuting the death sentence to imprisonment. This harrowing encounter with death greatly influenced Dostoevski's outlook on life, as did his four years of anguish and deprivation in a Siberian prison. Abandoning his attraction to socialism and reform, Dostoevski became a staunch advocate of tsarist autocracy, the Russian orthodox faith, and Russian nationalism.

While existentialist themes pervade several of Dostoevski's works, it is in *Notes from the Underground* (1864) that he treats explicitly the individual's quest for personal freedom, self-identity, and meaning and the individual's revolt against established norms. In this work, the narrator, the Underground Man, rebels against the efforts of rational humanists to define human nature and to reform society so as to promote greater happiness. He rebels against science and reason—against the entire liberal and socialist vision; and he does so in the name of human subjectivity—the uncontainable, irrepressible, whimsical, and foolish human will. For the Underground Man, there are no absolute and timeless truths that precede the individual and to which the individual should conform. There is only a terrifying world of naked wills vying with each other; and equally terrifying, the individual has the freedom of will to take on self-inflicted suffering and pain ("even in a toothache there is enjoyment"). This is the way it should be, says Dostoevski, for by following irrational impulses and engaging in irrational acts, human beings assert their individuality; they prove that they are individually free. To the rationalist who aims to eliminate suffering and deprivation, Dostoevski replies that some people freely choose suffering and depravity, because it gratifies them, and are repelled by wealth, peace, security, and happiness. They do not want to be robots in a stringently regulated social order that creates a slot for everything, and they consider excessive intellectualizing—"over-acute consciousness"—a disease that keeps the individual from living fully.

> . . . it seems that something that is dearer to almost every man than his greatest advantages must really exist, . . . for which, if necessary, a man is ready to act in opposition to all laws, that is, in opposition to reason, honor, peace, prosperity. . . . One's own free unfettered choice, one's own fancy, however wild it may be, one's own fancy worked up at times to frenzy—why that is that very "most advantageous advantage" which we have overlooked, which comes under no classification and through which all systems and theories are continually being sent to the devil. . . . What man needs is simply independent choice, whatever that independence may cost and wherever it may lead.[37]

The Underground Man struggles to define his own existence according to his own needs, rather than in accordance with standards and values created by others. He regards freedom of choice as a human being's most priceless possession and holds that choice derives not from the intellect, but from impulses and feelings that account for our essential individuality. These themes are crucial to the outlook of twentieth-century existentialists.

Nietzsche For several reasons Friedrich Nietzsche was an important forerunner of existentialism. Nietzsche said that philosophical systems are merely expressions of an individual's own being and do not constitute an objective representation of reality;

there is no realm of being that is the source of values. Nor does religion provide truth, for God is dead. And, asked Nietzsche, is not this godless world absurd? Nietzsche held that modern Westerners had lost all their traditional supports.

> *Disintegration characterizes this time, and thus uncertainty: nothing stands firmly on its feet or on a hard faith in itself; one lives for tomorrow as the day after tomorrow is dubious. Everything on our way is slippery and dangerous, and the ice that still supports us has become thin: all of us feel the warm, uncanny breath of the thawing wind; where we still walk, soon no one will be able to walk.[38]*

To overcome nothingness, said Nietzsche, individuals must define life for themselves and celebrate it fully, instinctively, heroically. Nietzsche's insistence that the individual confront existence squarely, without hypocrisy, and give meaning to it—his own meaning—was vital to the shaping of existentialism.

Twentieth-Century Existentialists*

Heidegger German philosopher Martin Heidegger (1889–1976), generally regarded as the central figure in the development of twentieth-century existentialist thought, presents a problem to students of philosophy. First, Heidegger rejected being classified as an existentialist. Second, he wrote in a nearly incomprehensible style that obscured his intent. Third, in 1933 Heidegger, recently appointed as rector of the University of Freiburg by Hitler's government, joined the National Socialist party and publicly praised Hitler and the Nazi regime. The following year he resigned as rector and gave no further support to the Third Reich. However, Heidegger's brief dalliance with Nazism caused some

---

* The following discussions are based on works written before 1946.

thinkers either to dismiss him or to minimize his importance as a philosopher.

Heidegger's principal book, *Being and Time* (1927), is a path-breaking work in twentieth-century philosophy. In it Heidegger asked: what does it mean to be, to say I am? Most people shun this question, said Heidegger; consequently they live inauthentically, merely accepting a way of life set by others. Such people, he said, have "fallen from being"; they do not reflect on their existence or recognize the various possibilities and choices that life offers. Rather, they flee from their own selves and accept without reflection society's values. Neither their actions nor their goals are their own; they have forfeited a human being's most distinctive qualities—freedom and creativity.

To live authentically, declared Heidegger, the individual has to face explicitly the problem of Being; that is, one has to determine one's own existence, create one's own possibilities, and make choices and commitments. Choosing, said Heidegger, is not just a matter of disengaged thought, for the human creature is more than a conscious knower. The authentic life encompasses the feelings as well as the intellect; it is a genuine expression of a person's whole being.

Coming to grips with death, said Heidegger, provides us with the opportunity for an authentic life. The trauma of our mortality and finiteness, the image of the endless void in which Being passes into non-Being, overwhelms us with dread; we come face to face with the insignificance of human existence, with the directionless lives that we pursue. To escape this dread, said Heidegger, some people simply immerse themselves in life's petty details or adopt the values prescribed by others. But dread of death is also an opportunity. It can put us in touch with our own uniqueness, our own Being, permitting us to take hold of our own existence and to make life truly our own.

The authentic life requires, said Heidegger, that we see ourselves within the context of historical time, for we cannot escape that our lives are bound by conditions and outlooks inherited from the past. Human beings are thrown into a world that is not of their own making, said Heidegger; they dwell in a particular society that carries with it the weight of the past and the tensions and conflicts of the present. Without knowledge of these conditions, he declared, events and things will always impose themselves on us and we will not have the courage to reject conventions that are not of our own making.

Jaspers Karl Jaspers (1883–1969), a German psychiatrist turned philosopher, was a leading figure in the existentialist movement. Jaspers came into disfavor with the Nazi regime (he advocated liberal-humanist values and his wife was Jewish) and lost his position as professor of philosophy at Heidelberg University. Like Kierkegaard, Jaspers held that philosophy and science cannot provide certainty. Also like Kierkegaard, he sought to discover the genuine self through an encounter with life. Like Heidegger, he held that while death makes us aware of our finitude, thereby promoting anxiety, it also goads us to focus on what is truly important and to do so immediately. Jaspers insisted that the individual has the power to choose; to be aware of this freedom and to use it is the essence of being human. He declared in 1930:

Man is always something more than what he knows of himself. He is not what he is simply once for all, but is a process; he is . . . endowed with possibilities through the freedom he possesses to make of himself what he will by the activities on which he decides.[39]

Feelings of guilt and anxiety inevitably accompany free will, said Jaspers; nevertheless, we must have the courage to make a choice, for it is in the act of choosing that the individual shapes his or her true self.

Jaspers rejected revealed religion, dogma, and the authority of churches, but he did postulate what he called "philosophical faith." He thought of human existence as an encounter with Transcendence—"the eternal, indestructible, the immutable, the source

[that] . . . can be neither visualized nor grasped in thought."[40] Jaspers did not equate Transcendence with God in the conventional sense, but the concept is laden with theistic qualities. Although not a traditional Christian, Jaspers was no atheist.

Sartre The outlook of several French existentialists—Jean Paul Sartre (1905–1980), Maurice Merleau-Ponty (1908–1961), Albert Camus (1913–1960), and Simone de Beauvoir (1908–)—was shaped by their involvement in the resistance to Nazi occupation during World War II. Sartre, the leading French existentialist, said their confrontation with terror and torture taught them "to take evil seriously." Evil is not the effect of ignorance that might be remedied by knowledge or of passions that might be controlled, said Sartre; rather, it is a central fact of human existence and is unredeemable. Facing capture and death, the members of the Resistance understood what it is to be a solitary individual in a hostile universe. Living on the cutting edge of life, they rediscovered the essence of human freedom: they could make authentic choices. By saying no to the Nazis and resisting them, they confronted existence squarely.

Sartre served in the French army at the outbreak of World War II and was captured by the Germans. Released after the French surrender, he taught philosophy while serving in the Resistance. In addition to his philosophic writings, Sartre, after World War II, gained international acclaim for his novels and plays, many of them written from an existentialist point of view.

The individual is self-defined said Sartre. "Not only is man what he conceives himself to be, but he is also only what he wills himself to be. . . . Man is nothing else but what he makes of himself. . . . existentialism's first move is to make every man aware of what he is and to make full responsibility of his existence rest on him."[41]

In contrast to Kierkegaard and Jaspers, Sartre defined himself as an atheist and saw existentialism as a means of facing the consequences of a godless universe. Atheistic existentialism, he said, begins with the person and not with God, a preestablished ethic, or a uniform conception of human nature. The individual has nothing to cling to but is thrown into the world "with no support and no aid."[42] It is the first principle of existentialism, said Sartre, that we must each choose our own ethics, define ourselves, and create ourselves through involvement with others and the world. In this way the individual gives life meaning. We are what we do, said Sartre; each individual is "nothing else than the ensemble of his acts, nothing else than his life. . . . man's destiny is within himself."[43]

Religious Existentialism Several thinkers are classified as religious existentialists, among them Nikolai Berdyaev (1874–1948), an exile from communist Russia, Martin Buber (1878–1965), a Jew who fled Nazi Germany, and Gabriel Marcel (1889–1973). During World War I, Marcel served with the French Red Cross accounting for soldiers missing in battle. This shattering experience brought the sensitive thinker face to face with the tragedy of human existence. A growing concern with the spiritual life led him to convert to Catholicism in 1929.

The modern individual, said Marcel in 1933, "tends to appear to himself and to others as an agglomeration of functions." A person is viewed as an entrepreneur, a laborer, a consumer, a citizen. The hospital serves as a repair shop and death "becomes, objectively and functionally, the scrapping of what has ceased to be of use and must be written off as a total loss."[44] In such a functional world, maintained Marcel, people are valued for what they produce and possess. If they do not succeed as merchants, bookkeepers, or ticket-takers, people judge them and they judge themselves as personal failures. Such an outlook suffocates spirituality and deprives the individual of the joy of existence. It produces an "intolerable unease" in the individual "who is reduced to living as though he were in fact submerged by his function. . . . Life in a world centered on function is liable to de-

Jean Paul Sartre and Simone de Beauvoir, 1956. The major philosophical movement in the twentieth century is existentialism. Sartre and de Beauvoir were two of its first exponents. (*AP/Wide World Photos*)

spair because in reality this world is *empty, it rings hollow.*"[45]

Marcel wanted people to surpass a functional and mechanical view of life and to explore the mystery of existence—to penetrate to a higher level of reality. Marcel held that one penetrates ultimate reality when one overcomes egocentricity and exists for others, when one loves and is loved by others. When we exist through and for others, when we treat another person not as an object performing a function but as a "thou" who matters to us, we soar to a higher level of existence. When we are actively engaged with others in concrete human situations, we fulfill ourselves as human beings; when we actively express love and fidelity toward others, life attains a higher meaning. Such involvement with others, said Marcel, provides us with a glimpse of a transcendent reality and is a testimony to God's existence. Marcel maintained that faith in God overcomes anxiety and despair, which characterize the modern predicament. It also improves the quality of human relationships, for if we believe that all people matter to God, they are more likely to matter to us.

The Modern Predicament

The process of fragmentation that had showed itself in European thought and the arts at the end of the nineteenth century accelerated after World War I. Increasingly, philosophers, writers, and artists expressed disillusionment with the rational-humanist tradition of the Enlightenment; they no longer shared the Enlightenment's confidence in either reason's capabilities or human goodness, and they viewed perpetual progress as an illusion.

While many thinkers focused on reason's limitations, others, particularly existentialists, pointed out that reason was a double-edged sword; it could demean as well as ennoble the individual. These thinkers attacked all theories that subordinated the individual to a rigid system. They denounced positivism for reducing human personality to psychological laws, and Marxism for making social class a higher reality than the individual. They rebelled against political collectivization that regulated individual existence to the needs of the corporate state, and they assailed modern technology and bureaucracy, creations of the rational mind, for fashioning a social order that devalued and depersonalized the individual, denying people an opportunity for independent growth and a richer existence. These thinkers held that modern industrial society, in its drive for efficiency and uniformity, deprived people of their uniqueness and reduced flesh and blood human beings to cogs in a mechanical system.

In the decades shaped by world wars and totalitarianism, intellectuals raised questions that went to the heart of the dilemma of modern life. How can civilized life be safeguarded against human irrationality, particularly when it is channeled into political ideologies that idolize the state, the leader, the party, or the race? How can individual human personality be rescued from a relentless rationalism that reduces human nature and society to mechanical systems and seeks to regulate and organize the individual as it would any material object? Do the values associated with the Enlightenment provide a sound basis around which to integrate society? Can the individual find meaning in what many now regarded as a meaningless

universe? World War II gave these questions a special poignancy.

Notes

1. Quoted in Barbara Tuchman, *The Guns of August* (New York: Macmillan, 1962), p. 440.

2. Sigmund Freud, "Thought for the Times on War and Death," in the *Standard Edition of the Complete Psychological Works of Freud,* James Strachey, ed. (London: Hogarth Press, 1957), pp. 275, 278.

3. Quoted in Hans Kohn, "The Crisis in European Thought and Culture," in Jack J. Roth, ed., *World War I: A Turning Point in Modern History* (New York: Knopf, 1967), p. 28.

4. Quoted in Franklin L. Baumer, "Twentieth-Century Version of the Apocalypse," *Cahiers d'Histoire Mondiale (Journal of World History),* 1, no. 3 (January 1954), 624.

5. Ibid.

6. Erich Maria Remarque, *All Quiet on the Western Front,* trans. A. W. Wheen (Boston: Little, Brown, 1929), p. 224.

7. W. B. Yeats, "The Second Coming," *Collected Poems of W. B. Yeats* (New York: Macmillan, 1956), pp. 184–185.

8. T. S. Eliot, "The Wasteland," *Collected Poems, 1909–1962* (New York: Harcourt, 1970), p. 67.

9. Carl Gustav Jung, *Modern Man in Search of a Soul,* trans. W. S. Dell and Cary F. Baynes (New York: Harcourt, Brace, 1933), pp. 231, 234–235.

10. Johan Huizinga, *In the Shadow of To-morrow* (London: Heinemann, 1936), pp. 1–3.

11. Oswald Spengler, *The Decline of the West,* trans. Charles F. Atkinson (London: Allen & Unwin, 1926), p. 40.

12. Harry T. Moore, ed., *The Collected Letters of D. H. Lawrence* (New York: Viking, 1962), I, p. 180.

13. Tristan Tzara, "Lecture on Dada (1922)," trans. Ralph Mannheim, in Robert Motherwell,

ed., *The Dada Painters and Poets* (New York: Witterborn, Schultz, 1951), p. 250.

14. Ibid., p. 248.

15. Ibid., p. 251.

16. Edward Lucie-Smith, in Donald Carrol and Edward Lucie-Smith, *Movements in Modern Art* (New York: Horizon Press, 1973), p. 49.

17. H. W. Janson, *History of Art*, 2nd ed. (Englewood Cliffs, N.J.: Prentice-Hall, 1977), p. 661.

18. André Breton, *What Is Surrealism?* trans. David Gascoyne (London: Faber & Faber, 1936), p. 62.

19. Quoted in David Caute, *The Fellow Travellers* (New York: Macmillan, 1973), p. 64.

20. Ibid., p. 92.

21. Richard Crossman, ed., *The God That Failed* (New York: Bantam Books, 1951), pp. 15, 21.

22. Arthur Koestler, *Darkness at Noon* (New York: Macmillan, 1941), pp. 158–159.

23. Quoted in C. T. McIntire, ed., *God, History, and Historians* (New York: Oxford University Press, 1977), p. 9.

24. Arnold J. Toynbee, *Survey of International Affairs, 1933* (London: Oxford University Press, 1934), p. 111.

25. Julien Benda, *The Betrayal of the Intellectuals*, trans. Richard Aldington (Boston: Beacon Press, 1955), p. 21.

26. Ibid., p. 38.

27. Ibid., p. 122.

28. Ibid., p. 162.

29. José Ortega y Gasset, *The Revolt of the Masses* (New York: W. W. Norton, 1957), pp. 63, 18.

30. Ibid., p. 73.

31. Ibid., pp. 73–74.

32. Ernst Cassirer, *The Philosophy of the Enlightenment*, trans. Fritz C. A. Koelln and James P. Pettegrove (Boston: Beacon Press, 1955), pp. xi–xii.

33. Ernst Cassirer, *The Myth of the State* (New Haven: Yale University Press, 1946), p. 280.

34. Ibid., p. 296.

35. Erich Fromm, *Escape from Freedom* (New York: Avon Books, 1965), p. 124.

36. Ibid., pp. 173, 246.

37. Fyodor Dostoevsky, *Notes from the Underground* and *The Grand Inquisitor*, trans. Ralph E. Matlaw (New York: E. P. Dutton, 1960), pp. 20, 23.

38. Friedrich Nietzsche, *The Will to Power*, trans. Walter Kaufmann and R. J. Hollingdale (New York: Vintage Books, 1967), sec. 57, p. 40.

39. Karl Jaspers, *Man in the Modern Age*, trans. Eden and Cedar Paul (Garden City, N.Y.: Doubleday Anchor Books, 1951), p. 159.

40. Quoted in John Macquarrie, *Existentialsm* (Baltimore: Penguin Books, 1973), p. 246.

41. Jean-Paul Sartre, *Existentialism*, trans. Bernard Frechtman (New York: Philosophical Library, 1947), pp. 18–19.

42. Ibid., p. 28.

43. Ibid., pp. 38, 42.

44. Gabriel Marcel, "On the Ontological Mystery," in *The Philosophy of Existentialism*, trans. Manya Harari (Secaucus, N.J.: Citadel Press, 1980), p. 10.

45. Ibid., p. 12.

Suggested Reading

See also the books suggested for reading at the end of Chapter 28.

Barrett, William, *Irrational Man* (1958). Especially good on the intellectual and cultural roots of existentialism.

Blackham, H. J., *Six Existentialist Thinkers* (1952). Useful analyses of Kierkegaard, Nietzsche, Jaspers, Marcel, Heidegger, and Jean-Paul Sartre.

——, ed., *Reality, Man and Existence* (1965). Essential works of existentialism.

Cain, Seymour, *Gabriel Marcel* (1963). Brief, informative survey.

Cruickshank, John, ed., *Aspects of the Modern*

European Mind (1969). A useful collection of sources in modern intellectual history.

Jaspers, Karl, *Man in the Modern Age* (1930). A discussion of modern problems, particularly the impact of technology as seen from a half-century ago.

Kaufmann, Walter, ed., *Existentialism from Dostoevsky to Sartre* (1956). The basic writings of existentialist thinkers.

McIntire, C. T., ed., *God, History, and Historians* (1977). Selections from Christian thinkers; many deal with the crises of the twentieth century.

Macquarrie, John, *Existentialism* (1972). A lucid discussion of existentialism.

Pawel, Ernst, *The Nightmare of Reason* (1984). A recent biography of Kafka.

Perry, Marvin, *Arnold Toynbee and the Crisis of the West* (1982). Toynbee's understanding of the nature, meaning, and destiny of Western civilization.

Wagar, W. Warren, ed., *European Thought Since 1914* (1968). A valuable collection of sources.

Review Questions

1. What factors contributed to a mood of pessimism in the period after World War I?

2. What signs of decay did Spengler see in Western civilization?

3. Better than any other novelist of his time, Kafka grasped the dilemma of the modern age. Discuss this statement. Do his insights still apply today?

4. In *The Magic Mountain,* Mann reflected on the decomposition of bourgeois European civilization. Discuss this statement.

5. What was D. H. Lawrence's attitude toward the industrial revolution? Do you agree with him?

6. In what ways were both Dada and surrealism an expression of the times?

7. How did art and literature express a social conscience during the 1920s and 1930s?

8. Why were many intellectuals attracted to communism in the 1930s?

9. What is the theme of *Darkness at Noon*?

10. How did Toynbee interpret nationalism and Nazism?

11. What did Ortega mean by the "mass-man"? What dangers were presented by the mass-man?

12. Why did Benda entitle his book: *The Treason of the Intellectuals*?

13. What was Cassirer's attitude toward the Enlightenment? How did he interpret Nazism?

14. How did Fromm explain the rise of Nazism?

15. What were some of the conditions that gave rise to existentialism? What are the basic principles of existentialism?

16. Why are each of the following considered forerunners of existentialism: Dostoevski, Kierkegaard, and Nietzsche?

17. Why are each of the following considered to be existentialists: Heidegger, Jaspers, Sartre, and Marcel?

18. What do you like, or dislike, about existentialism?

34

World War II: Western Civilization in the Balance

———

The Aftermath of World War I

The Road to War
Hitler's Foreign Policy Aims
Breakdown of Peace
Czechoslovakia: The Apex of
Appeasement
Poland: The Final Crisis

The Nazi Blitzkrieg
The Fall of France
The Battle of Britain
Invasion of Russia

The New Order
Exploitation and Terror
Extermination
Resistance

The Turn of the Tide
The Japanese Offensive
Defeat of the Axis Powers

The Legacy of World War II

———

*F*rom the early days of his political career, Hitler dreamed of forging a vast German empire in central and eastern Europe. He believed that only by waging a war of conquest against Russia could the German nation gain the living space and security it required and, as a superior race, deserved. War was an essential component of National Socialist ideology, and it accorded with Hitler's temperament. For the former corporal from the trenches, the Great War had never ended. Hitler aspired to political power because he wanted to mobilize the material and human resources of the German nation for war and conquest. Although historians may debate the question of responsibility for World War I, few would deny that World War II was Hitler's war:

It appears to be an almost incontrovertible fact that the Second World War was brought on by the actions of the Hitler government, that these actions were the expression of a policy laid down well in advance in Mein Kampf, *and that this war could have been averted up until the last moment if the German government had so wished.*[1]

Western statesmen had sufficient warnings that Hitler was a threat to peace and the essential values of Western civilization, but they failed to rally their people and take a stand until Germany had greatly increased its capacity to wage aggressive war.

The Aftermath of World War I

World War I had shown that Germany was the strongest power on the Continent. In the east, the German army had triumphed over Russia; in the west, Britain and France could have hoped for no more than a deadlock without the aid of the United States. The Treaty of Versailles had weakened Germany, but had not permanently crippled it.

In the decade after the war, responsibility for preserving the peace settlement rested essentially with France. The United States had rejected the treaty and withdrawn from European affairs; Soviet Russia was consolidating its revolution; Britain, burdened with severe economic problems, disarmed, and traditionally hostile to Continental alliances, did not want to join with France in holding Germany down. France sought to contain Germany by forging alliances with the new states of eastern Europe, which the French hoped would serve as a substitute for alliance with a now untrustworthy communist Russia. France entered into alliances with Poland, Czechoslovakia, Rumania, and Yugoslavia during the 1920s. But no combination of small eastern European states could replace Russia as a counterweight to Germany. Against Hitler's Germany, the French alliance system would prove useless.

A feeling of general hope prevailed during the 1920s. The newly created League of Nations provided a supranational authority to which nations could submit their quarrels. At the Washington Naval Conference (1921–1922), the leading naval powers—the United States, Britain, France, Italy, and Japan—agreed not to construct new battleships or heavy cruisers for a ten-year period and established a ratio of capital ships between them. It was hoped that avoiding a naval arms race would promote international peace.

In the Locarno Pact (1925), Germany, France, and Belgium agreed not to change their existing borders, which meant, in effect, that Germany had accepted both the loss of Alsace and Lorraine to France and the demilitarization of the Rhineland—two provisions of the Versailles Treaty. The Locarno Pact held the promise of a détente between France and Germany. But it was only an illusion of peace, for Germany gave no such assurances for its eastern border with Czechoslovakia and Poland, France's allies.

Other gestures that promoted reconciliation followed. In 1926, Germany was admitted to the League of Nations, and in 1928 the Kellogg-Briand Pact renouncing war was signed by most nations. The signatories condemned war as a solution for international disputes and agreed to settle quarrels through peaceful means. Ordinary people welcomed the Kellogg-Briand Pact as the dawning of a new era of peace, but because the pact contained no clauses for its enforcement, the agreement only fostered the illusion of peace.

Nevertheless, between 1925 and 1930, hopes for reconciliation and peace were high. Recovery from the war and increased prosperity coincided with the easing of international tensions. As evidence of the new spirit of conciliation, France and Britain withdrew their forces from the Rhineland in 1930, four years ahead of the time prescribed by the Versailles Treaty.

The Road to War

Hitler's Foreign Policy Aims

After consolidating his power and mobilizing the nation's will, Hitler moved to implement his foreign-policy objectives—the destruction of the Versailles Treaty, the conquest and colonization of eastern Europe, and the domination and exploitation of racial inferiors. In some respects, Hitler's foreign policy aims accorded with the goals of Germany's traditional rulers. Like them, Hitler sought to make Germany the pre-eminent power in Europe. During World War I, German statesmen and generals had sought to conquer extensive regions of eastern Europe, and in the Treaty of Brest-Litovsk, Germany took Poland, the Ukraine, and the Baltic states from Russia. But Hitler's racial nationalism—the subjugation and annihilation of inferior races by a master German race—marked a break with the outlook of the old governing class. Germany's traditional conservative leaders had never restricted the civil rights of German Jews and had sought to Germanize, not enslave, the Poles living under the German flag.

In foreign affairs, Hitler demonstrated that same blend of opportunism and singleness of purpose that had brought him to power. He behaved like a man possessed, driven by a fanatical belief that his personal destiny was tied to Germany's future. Here, too, he made use of propaganda to undermine his opponents' will to resist. The Nazi propaganda machine, which had effectively won the minds of the German people, became an instrument of foreign policy. Nazi propaganda tried to win the support of the 27 million Germans living outside the borders of the Reich proper; to promote social and political disorientation in other lands, the Nazis propagated anti-Semitism on a worldwide basis; Nazi propagandists tried to draw international support for Hitler as Europe's best defense against the Soviet Union and Bolshevism. The Nazi anticommunist campaign "convinced many Europeans that Hitler's dictatorship was more acceptable than Stalin's and that Germany—'the bulwark against Bolshevism'—should be allowed to grow from strength to strength."[2]

As Hitler anticipated, the British and the French backed down when faced with his violations of the Versailles Treaty and threats of war. Haunted by the memory of World War I, Britain and France went to great lengths to avoid another catastrophe—a policy that had the overwhelming support of public opinion. Moreover, Britain suffered from a bad conscience regarding the Versailles Treaty. Believing that Germany had been treated too severely, and woefully unprepared for war from 1933 to 1939, Britain was amenable to making concessions to Hitler. Although France had the strongest army on the Continent, it was prepared to fight only a defensive war—the reverse of its World War I strategy. France built immense fortifications, called the *Maginot Line,* to protect its borders from a German invasion, but it lacked a mobile striking force that could punish an aggressive Germany. The United States, concerned with the problems of the Great Depression and standing aloof from Europe's troubles, did nothing to strengthen the resolve of France and Britain. Since both France and Britain feared and mistrusted the Soviet Union, the grand alliance of World War I was not renewed. There was an added factor: suffering from a failure of leadership and political and economic unrest that eroded national unity, France was experiencing a decline in morale and a loss of nerve. It consistently turned to Britain for direction.

British statesmen championed a policy of appeasement—giving in to Germany in the hope that a satisfied Hitler would not drag Europe through another world war. British policy rested on the disastrous illusion that Hitler, like his Weimar predecessors, sought peaceful revision of the Versailles Treaty, and that he could be contained through concessions. This perception was as misguided as the expectation of Weimar conservatives that the responsibility of power would compel Hitler to abandon his National Socialist radicalism. Some British appeasers, accepting the view that Nazi propaganda cleverly propagated and exploited, also regarded Hitler as a defender of European civilization and the capitalist economic order against Soviet communism.

In *Mein Kampf,* Hitler had explicitly laid out his philosophy of racial nationalism and *Lebensraum* (living space), and as dictator, he had established a one-party state, confined political opponents to concentration camps, and persecuted Jews. But the proponents of appeasement did not properly assess these signs. They still believed that Hitler could be reasoned with. Appeasement, which in the end was capitulation to blackmail, failed. Germany grew stronger and the German people more devoted to the Fuehrer. Hitler did not moderate his ambitions, and the appeasers did not avert war.

Breakdown of Peace

To realize his foreign-policy aims, Hitler required a formidable military machine; Germany had to rearm. The Treaty of Versailles

Map 34.1 German and Italian Aggressions, 1935–1939 ▶

ICELAND

Germany and Italy
Italian possessions in Africa before 1935
German aggressions, 1935-1939
Italian aggressions, 1935-1939

NORWAY

SWEDEN

FINLAND

ESTONIA
LATVIA
Moscow •

DENMARK

NORTH SEA

BALTIC SEA

Memel • LITHUANIA

SOVIET UNION

IRELAND

GREAT BRITAIN
• London

NETHERLANDS

Danzig • EAST PRUSSIA

Berlin •

POLISH CORRIDOR

• Warsaw

POLAND

Brussels •
BELGIUM

GERMANY

RHINELAND 1936

SUDETENLAND 1938

ATLANTIC OCEAN

Paris •
LUXEMBOURG

Weimar •

• Prague
CZECHOSLOVAKIA 1939

Nuremberg •
Munich •

FRANCE

SWITZERLAND

Vienna •
AUSTRIA 1938

HUNGARY

RUMANIA

BLACK SEA

YUGOSLAVIA

BULGARIA

PORTUGAL

• Madrid
SPAIN
(Civil War, 1936-1939)

• Barcelona

ITALY

• Rome

ALBANIA 1939

GREECE

TURKEY

MEDITERRANEAN SEA

AFRICA

LIBYA

ERITREA

ETHIOPIA 1935-1936

IT. SOMALILAND

A F R I C A

had limited the size of the German army to 100,000 volunteers; restricted the navy's size; forbidden the production of military aircraft, heavy artillery, and tanks; and disbanded the general staff. Throughout the 1920s, Germany had evaded these provisions, even entering into a secret arrangement with the Soviet Union to establish training schools for German pilots and tank corpsmen on Russian soil.

In March 1935, Hitler declared that Germany was no longer bound by the Versailles Treaty. Germany would restore conscription, build an air force (which it had been doing secretly), and strengthen its navy. The German people were ecstatic over Hitler's boldness. France protested, but offered no resistance; and Britain negotiated a naval agreement with Germany, thus tacitly accepting Hitler's rearmament.

A decisive event in the breakdown of peace was Italy's invasion of Ethiopia in October 1935. Mussolini sought colonial expansion and revenge for a defeat the African kingdom had inflicted on Italian troops in 1896. The League of Nations called for economic sanctions against Italy, and most League members restricted trade with the aggressor. But Italy continued to receive oil, particularly from American suppliers. Believing that the conquest of Ethiopia did not affect their vital interests and hoping to keep the Italians friendly in the event of a clash with Germany, neither Britain nor France sought to restrain Italy, despite its act of aggression against another member of the League of Nations.

Mussolini's subjugation of Ethiopia discredited the League of Nations, which had already been weakened by its failure to deal effectively with Japan's invasion of the mineral-rich Chinese province of Manchuria in 1931. At that time the League formed a commission of inquiry and urged nonrecognition of the puppet state of Manchukuo created by the Japanese, but the member states did not restrain Japan. Ethiopia, like Manchuria, showed that the League was reluctant to use force to resist aggression.

On March 7, 1936, Hitler marched troops into the Rhineland, violating both the Ver-

sailles Treaty and the Locarno Pact. German generals had cautioned Hitler that such a move would provoke a French invasion of Germany and reoccupation of the Rhineland, which the German army, still in the first stages of rearmament, could not repulse. But Hitler gambled that France and Britain, lacking the will to fight, would take no action.

Hitler had correctly assessed the Anglo-French mood. Britain was not greatly alarmed by the remilitarization of the Rhineland. Hitler, after all, was not expanding the borders of Germany, but was only sending soldiers to Germany's frontier. Such a move, reasoned British officials, did not warrant risking a war. France regarded the remilitarization of the Rhineland as a grave threat. It deprived France of the one tangible advantage that it had obtained from the Treaty of Versailles—a buffer area. Now German forces could concentrate in strength on the French frontier, either to invade France or to discourage a French assault if Germany attacked Czechoslovakia or Poland, France's eastern allies. France lost the advantages of being able to retaliate by invading a demilitarized zone.

Three factors explain why France did not try to expel the 22,000 German troops that occupied the zone. First, France would not act alone, and Britain could not be persuaded to use force. Second, the French general staff overestimated German military strength and thought only of defending French soil from a German attack, not of initiating a strike against Germany. Third, French public opinion showed no enthusiasm for a confrontation with Hitler.

The Spanish Civil War of 1936–1939 was another victory for fascism. Nazi Germany and Fascist Italy aided Franco; the Soviet Union supplied the Spanish Republic. The republic appealed to France for help, but the French government feared that the civil war would expand into a European war. With Britain's approval, France proposed the Nonintervention Agreement. Italy, Germany, and the Soviet Union signed the agreement, but continued to supply the warring parties. By October 1937, some 60,000 Italian "volun-

Pablo Picasso (1881–1973): Guernica (Mural), 1937. Eager to test their military might, the Germans leveled the town of Guernica in an air raid. These strikes foretold the blitzkrieg of World War II. Picasso's *Guernica* (11′ 6″ × 25′ 8″) captures the barbarism of all wars. The Spanish Civil War was another defeat for democracy. Aided by Hitler and Mussolini, Franco overcame the forces of the Republic. (*Museo del Prado*/© *S.P.A.D.E.M., Paris/V.A.G.A., New York*)

teers" were fighting in Spain. Hitler sent from 5,000 to 6,000 men and hundreds of planes, which proved decisive. By comparison, the Soviet Union's aid was meager.

Without considerable help from France, the Spanish Republic was doomed, but Prime Minister Léon Blum continued to support nonintervention. He feared that French intervention would cause Germany and Italy to escalate their involvement, bringing Europe to the edge of a general war. Moreover, supplying the republic would have dangerous consequences at home, because French rightists were sympathetic to Franco's conservative-clerical authoritarianism.

In 1939, the republic fell, and Franco established a dictatorship. The Spanish Civil War provided Germany with an opportunity to test weapons and pilots and demonstrated again that France and Britain lacked the determination to fight fascism. It also widened the breach between Italy and Britain and France that had opened when Italy invaded Ethiopia and drew Mussolini and Hitler closer together. In October 1936, Mussolini sent his foreign minister to visit with Hitler in Berlin. The discussions bore fruit and on November 1 Mussolini proclaimed that a Rome-Berlin "Axis" had been created.

One of Hitler's aims was incorporation of Austria into the Third Reich. The Treaty of Versailles had expressly prohibited the union of the two countries. But in *Mein Kampf*, Hitler had insisted that an Anschluss was necessary for German Lebensraum. In February 1938, under intense pressure from Hitler, Austrian Chancellor Kurt von Schuschnigg promised to accept Austrian Nazis in his cabinet and agreed to closer relations with Germany. Austrian independence was slipping away, and increasingly, Austrian Nazis undermined Schuschnigg's authority. Seeking to gain the support of his people, Schuschnigg made plans for a plebiscite on the issue of preserving Austrian independence. An enraged Hitler ordered his generals to draw up plans for an invasion of Austria. Hitler then demanded Schuschnigg's resignation and the formation of a new government headed by Arthur Seyss-Inquart, an Austrian Nazi.

Believing that Austria was not worth a war, Britain and France informed the embattled chancellor that they would not help in the event of a German invasion. Schuschnigg then resigned, and Austrian Nazis began to take control of the government. Under the pretext of preventing violence, Hitler ordered his troops to cross into Austria, and on March 13, 1938, Austrian leaders declared that Austria was a province of the German Reich. The Austrians celebrated by ringing church bells, waving swastika banners, and attacking Jews and looting their property.

Czechoslovakia: The Apex of Appeasement

Hitler had obtained Austria merely by threatening force. Another threat would give him the Sudetenland of Czechoslovakia. Of the 3.5 million people living in the Sudetenland, some 2.8 million were ethnic Germans. The Sudetenland contained key industries and strong fortifications; since it bordered Germany, it was also vital to Czech security. Deprived of the Sudetenland, Czechoslovakia could not defend itself against a German attack. Encouraged and instructed by Germany, the Sudeten Germans, led by Konrad Henlein, shrilly denounced the Czech government for "persecuting" its German minority and depriving it of its right to self-determination. The Sudeten Germans agitated for local autonomy and the right to profess the National Socialist ideology. Behind this demand was the goal of German annexation of the Sudetenland.

While negotiations between the Sudeten Germans and the Czech government proceeded, Hitler's propaganda machine accused the Czechs of hideous crimes against the German minority and warned of retribution. Hitler also ordered his generals to prepare for an invasion of Czechoslovakia and to

complete the fortifications on the French border. Fighting between Czechs and Sudeten Germans heightened the tensions. Seeking to preserve peace, Prime Minister Neville Chamberlain (1869–1940) of Britain offered to confer with Hitler, who then extended an invitation.

Britain and France held somewhat different positions toward Czechoslovakia—the only democracy in eastern Europe. In 1924, France and Czechoslovakia had concluded an agreement of mutual assistance in the event either was attacked by Germany. Czechoslovakia had a similar agreement with Russia, but with the provision that Russian assistance depended on France's first fulfilling the terms of its agreement. Britain had no commitment to Czechoslovakia. Some of the British officials, swallowing Hitler's propaganda, believed that the Sudeten Germans were indeed a suppressed minority entitled to self-determination, and that the Sudetenland, like Austria, was not worth a war that could destroy Western civilization. Hitler, they said, only wanted to incorporate Germans living outside of Germany; he was only carrying the principle of self-determination to its logical conclusion. Once these Germans lived under the German flag, argued these British officials, Hitler would be satisfied. In any case, Britain's failure to rearm between 1933 and 1938 weakened its position. The British chiefs of staff believed that the nation was not prepared to fight, that it was necessary to sacrifice Czechoslovakia to buy time.

Czechoslovakia's fate was decided at the Munich Conference (September 1938) attended by Chamberlain, Hitler, Mussolini, and Prime Minister Édouard Daladier (1884–1970) of France. The Munich Agreement called for the immediate evacuation of Czech troops from the Sudetenland and its occupation by German forces. Britain and France then promised to guarantee the territorial integrity of the truncated Czechoslovakia. Both Chamberlain and Daladier were showered with praise by the people of Britain and France for keeping the peace.

Critics of Chamberlain have insisted that the Munich Agreement was an enormous blunder and tragedy. Chamberlain, they say, was a fool to believe that Hitler, who sought domination over Europe, could be bought off with the Sudetenland. Hitler regarded concessions by Britain and France as signs of weakness; they only increased his appetite for more territory. Second, argue the critics, it would have been better to fight Hitler in 1938 than a year later when war actually did break out. To be sure, in the year following the Munich Agreement, Britain increased its military arsenal, but so did Germany, which built submarines and heavy tanks, strengthened western border defenses, and trained more pilots.

Had Britain and France resisted Hitler at Munich, it is likely that the Fuehrer would have attacked Czechoslovakia. But Czechoslovakia would not have lain down and died. The Czech border defenses, which had been built on the model of the French Maginot line, were formidable. The Czechs had a sizable number of good tanks and the Czech people were willing to fight to preserve their nation's territorial integrity. By itself the Czech army could not have defeated Germany. But while the main elements of the German army were battling the Czechs, the French, who could mobilize a hundred divisions, could have broken through the German West Wall, which was defended by only five regular and four reserve divisions, invaded the Rhineland, and devastated German industrial centers in the Ruhr. (Such a scenario, of course, depended upon the French overcoming their psychological reluctance to take the offensive.) And there was always the possibility that the Soviet Union would have come to Czechoslovakia's aid in fulfillment of its agreement.

After the annexation of the Sudetenland, the Fuehrer plotted to extinguish Czechoslovakia's existence. He encouraged the Slovak minority in Czechoslovakia, led by a fascist priest, Josef Tiso, to demand complete separation. On the pretext of protecting the Slovak people's right of self-determination, Hitler ordered his troops to enter Prague. In March 1939, Czech independence came to an end.

The destruction of Czechoslovakia was of a different character from the remilitarization of the Rhineland, the Anschluss with Austria, and the annexation of the Sudetenland. In all these previous cases, Hitler could claim the right of self-determination, Woodrow Wilson's grand principle. The occupation of Prague and the end of Czech independence, though, showed that Hitler really sought European hegemony. Outraged statesmen now demanded that the Fuehrer be deterred from further aggression.

Poland: The Final Crisis

After Czechoslovakia, Hitler turned to Poland, demanding that the free city of Danzig be returned to Germany and that railways and roads, over which Germans would enjoy extraterritorial rights, be built across the Polish Corridor, linking East Prussia with the rest of Germany. Poland refused to restore the port of Danzig, which was vital to its economy. The Poles would allow a German highway through the Polish Corridor but would not permit German extraterritorial rights. France informed the German government that it would fulfill its treaty obligations to aid Poland. Chamberlain also warned that Britain would assist Poland.

On May 22, 1939, Hitler and Mussolini entered into the Pact of Steel, promising mutual aid in the event of war. The following day, Hitler told his officers that Germany's real goal was the destruction of Poland. "Danzig is not the objective. It is a matter of expanding our living space in the east, of making our food supplies secure. . . . There is therefore no question of sparing Poland, and the decision remains to attack Poland at the first suitable opportunity."[3] In the middle of June, the army presented Hitler with battle plans for an invasion of Poland.

Britain, France, and the Soviet Union had been engaged in negotiations since April. The

Chronology 34.1 Road to World War II

1931	Japan invades Manchuria
March 1935	Hitler announces German rearmament
October 1935	Italy invades Ethiopia
1936–1939	The Spanish Civil War
March 7, 1936	Germany reoccupies the Rhineland
October 1936	Berlin-Rome Axis is formed
November 1936	German-Japanese anticommunist pact
July 1937	Japan invades China
March 13, 1938	Austria becomes a German province
September 1938	Munich Agreement—Germany's annexation of Sudetenland is approved by Britain and France
1939	Franco establishes a dictatorship in Spain
March 1939	Germany invades Czechoslovakia
April 1939	Italy invades Albania
May 22, 1939	Pact of Steel between Hitler and Mussolini
August 23, 1939	Nonaggression pact between Germany and Russia
September 1 & 3, 1939	Germany invades Poland; Britain and France declare war

Soviet Union wanted a mutual-assistance pact including joint military planning, and demanded bases in Poland and Rumania in preparation for a German attack. Britain was reluctant to endorse these demands, fearing that a mutual assistance pact with Russia might cause Hitler to embark on a mad adventure that would drag Britain into war. Moreover, Poland would not allow Russian troops on its soil, fearing Russian expansion.

At the same time, Russia was conducting secret talks with Nazi Germany. Unlike the Allies, Hitler could tempt Stalin with territory that would serve as a buffer between Germany and Russia. Moreover, a treaty with Germany would give Russia time to strengthen its armed forces. On August 23, 1939, the two totalitarian states signed a nonaggression pact that stunned the world. A secret section of the pact called for the partition of Poland between the two parties and Russian control over Latvia and Estonia. By signing such an agreement with his enemy, Hitler had pulled off an extraordinary diplomatic coup: he blocked the Soviet Union, Britain, and France from duplicating their World War I grand alliance against Germany. The Nazi-Soviet Pact was the green light for an invasion of Poland, and at dawn on September 1, 1939, German troops crossed the frontier. When

Germany did not respond to their demand for a halt to the invasion, Britain and France declared war.

The Nazi Blitzkrieg

Germany struck at Poland with speed and power. The German air force, the Luftwaffe, destroyed Polish planes on the ground, attacked tanks, pounded defense networks, and bombed Warsaw, terrorizing the population. Tanks opened up breaches in the Polish defenses, and mechanized columns overran the foot-marching Polish army, trapping large numbers of soldiers. The Polish high command could not cope with the incredible speed and coordination of German air and ground attacks. By September 8, the Germans had advanced to the outskirts of Warsaw. On September 17, Soviet troops invaded Poland from the east. On September 27, Poland surrendered. In less than a month the Nazi *blitzkrieg* (lightning war) had vanquished Poland.

The Fall of France

For Hitler the conquest of Poland was only the prelude to a German empire stretching from the Atlantic to the Urals. When weather conditions were right, he would unleash a great offensive in the west. Meanwhile, the six-month period following the defeat of Poland was nicknamed the "phony war," for the fighting on land consisted only of a few skirmishes on the French-German border. Then, in early April 1940, the Germans struck at Denmark and Norway. Hitler wanted to ensure that Swedish iron ore would continue to reach Germany through Norwegian territorial waters. He knew that Britain and France had plans to occupy the mining region and the key Swedish and Norwegian ports. In addition, Hitler expected to establish naval bases on the Norwegian coast from which to wage submarine warfare against Britain.

Denmark surrendered within hours. A British-French force tried to assist the Norwegians, but the landings, badly coordinated and lacking in air support, failed. The Germans won the battle of Norway. But the Norwegian campaign produced two positive results for the Allies: Norwegian merchant ships escaped to Britain to be put into service; and Winston Churchill (1874–1965), who had opposed appeasement, replaced Chamberlain as British prime minister. (The German victory in Norway eroded Chamberlain's support in the House of Commons and he was forced to give up the helm.) Dynamic, courageous, and eloquent, Churchill had the capacity to stir and lead his people in the struggle against Nazism.

On May 10, 1940, Hitler launched his offensive in the west with an invasion of neutral Belgium, Holland, and Luxembourg. While armored forces penetrated Dutch frontier defenses, airborne units seized strategic airfields and bridges. On May 14, after the Luftwaffe bombed Rotterdam, destroying the center of the city and killing many people, the Dutch surrendered.

A daring attack by glider-borne troops gave Germany possession of two crucial Belgian bridges, opening the plains of Belgium to German *Panzer* (tank) divisions. Believing that this was the main German attack, French troops rushed to Belgium to prevent a German breakthrough, but the greater menace lay to the south on the French frontier. Meeting almost no resistance, German Panzer divisions had moved through the narrow mountain passes of Luxembourg and the dense Forest of Ardennes in southern Belgium. On May 12, German units were on French soil near Sedan. Thinking that the Forest of Ardennes could not be penetrated by a major German force, the French had only lightly fortified the western extension of the Maginot Line; the failure to counterattack swiftly was a second mistake. The best elements of the Anglo-French forces were in Belgium, but the Ger-

The Fall of France. French civilians of Marseilles show the shock of defeat in 1940. Hitler's army accomplished what the German generals of World War I had planned but not brought about: the capture of Paris and the fall of France. The might of motorized warfare had prevailed over the French army and its outmoded World War I methods. (*UPI/Bettmann Archive*)

mans were racing across northern France to the sea, which they reached on May 20, cutting the Anglo-French forces in two.

The Germans now sought to surround and annihilate the Allied forces converging on the French seaport of Dunkirk, the last port of escape. But inexplicably Hitler called off his tanks just as they prepared to take Dunkirk; instead he ordered the Luftwaffe to finish off the Allied troops, but fog and rain prevented German planes from operating at full strength. Taking advantage of this breathing space, the Allies tightened their defenses and prepared for a massive evacuation. While the Luftwaffe bombed the beaches, some 338,000 British and French troops were ferried across the English Channel by destroyers, merchant ships, motorboats, fishing boats, tugboats,

and private yachts. The British left all their equipment on the beaches but saved their armies to fight another day. Hitler's personal decision to hold back his tanks made the miracle of Dunkirk possible.

Meanwhile the battle for France was turning into an even worse disaster for the French. Whole divisions were cut off or in retreat and millions of refugees in cars and carts and on motorcycles and bicycles fled south to escape the advancing Germans. On June 10, Mussolini also declared war on France. With authority breaking down, demoralization spreading, and resistance dying, the French cabinet appealed for an armistice, which was signed on June 22 in the same railway car in which Germany had agreed to the armistice ending World War I.

How can the collapse of France be explained? Neither French military leaders, who experienced the debacle, nor historians are in agreement as to the relative strength of the French and German air forces. It is likely that the Germans and the French (including the British planes based in France) had some 3,000 planes each. But many French planes—in what still remains a mystery—remained on the airfields; the planes were there, but the high command either did not use them or did not deploy them properly. Unlike the Germans, the French did not comprehend or appreciate the use of aviation in modern warfare. The French had as many tanks as the Germans, and some were superior in quality. Nor was German manpower overwhelming. France met disaster largely because its military leaders, unlike the German command, had not mastered the psychology and technology of motorized warfare. "The French commanders, trained in the slow-motion methods of 1918, were mentally unfitted to cope with panzer pace, and it produced a spreading paralysis among them," says British military expert Sir Basil Liddell Hart.[4] One senses also a loss of will among the French people— a product of internal political disputes that divided the nation, poor leadership, the years of appeasement and lost opportunities, and German propaganda, which depicted Nazism as irresistible and the Fuehrer as a man of destiny. It was France's darkest hour. According to the terms of the armistice, Germany occupied northern France and the coast. The French military was demobilized, and the French government, now located at Vichy in the south and headed by Marshal Pétain, the hero of World War I, would collaborate with the German authorities in occupied France. Refusing to recognize defeat, General Charles de Gaulle (1890–1970) escaped to London and organized the Free French forces. The Germans gloried in their revenge; the French wept in their humiliation; the British gathered their courage, for they now stood alone.

The Battle of Britain

Hitler expected that after his stunning victories in the west, Britain would make peace. The British, however, continued to reject Hitler's peace overtures, for they envisioned only a bleak future if Hitler dominated the Continent. "The Battle of Britain is about to begin," Churchill told the people of Britain. "Upon this battle depends the survival of Christian civilization. . . . if we fail, then . . . all we have known and cared for will sink into the abyss of a new Dark Age."[5]

With Britain unwilling to come to terms, Hitler proceeded in earnest with invasion plans. But a successful crossing of the English Channel and the establishment of beachheads on the English coast depended on control of the skies. Marshal Hermann Goering assured Hitler that his *Luftwaffe* (air force) could destroy the British Royal Air Force (RAF), and in early August 1940 the Luftwaffe began massive attacks on British air and naval installations. Virtually every day during the "Battle of Britain," weather permitting, hundreds of planes battled in the sky above Britain. "Never in the field of human conflict was so much owed by so many to so few," said Churchill of the British pilots, who rose to the challenge. On September 15 the RAF shot down sixty aircraft, convincing Hitler that Goering could not fulfill his promise to

destroy British air defenses, and on September 17 the Fuehrer postponed the invasion of Britain "until further notice." The development of radar by British scientists, the skill and courage of British fighter pilots, and the inability of Germany to make up its losses in planes saved Britain in its struggle for survival. With the invasion of Britain called off, the Luftwaffe concentrated on bombing English cities, industrial centers, and ports. Every night for months, the inhabitants of London sought shelter in subways and cellars to escape German bombs, while British planes rose time after time to make the Luftwaffe pay the price. British morale never broke during the "Blitz."

Invasion of Russia

The obliteration of Bolshevism and the conquest, exploitation, and colonization of Russia were cardinal elements of Hitler's ideology. In Russia the Nazi empire would take control of wheat, oil, manganese, and other raw materials, and the fertile Russian plains would be settled by the master race. German expansion in the east could not wait for the final defeat of Britain. In July 1940, Hitler instructed his generals to formulate plans for an invasion of Russia. On December 18, Hitler set May 15, 1941, for the beginning of Operation Barbarossa, the code name assigned for the blitzkrieg against the Soviet Union. But events in the Balkans forced Hitler to postpone the date to the latter part of June.

Seeking to make Italy a Mediterranean power and to win glory for himself, Mussolini had ordered an invasion of Greece. In late October 1940, Italian troops stationed in Albania—which Italy had occupied in 1939— crossed into Greece. The poorly planned operation was an instant failure; within a week, the counterattacking Greeks advanced into Albania. Hitler feared that Britain, which was encouraging and aiding the Greeks, would use Greece to attack the oil fields of Rumania, which were vital to the German war effort, and to interfere with the forthcoming invasion of Russia. Another problem emerged when a military coup overthrew the government of Prince Paul in Yugoslavia, which two days earlier had signed a pact with Germany and Italy. Hitler feared that the new Yugoslav government might gravitate toward Britain. To prevent any interference with Operation Barbarossa, the Balkan flank had to be secured. On April 6, 1941, the Germans struck at both Greece and Yugoslavia. Yugoslavia was quickly overrun and Greece, although aided by 50,000 British, New Zealand, and Australian troops, fell at the end of April.

For the war against Russia, Hitler had assembled a massive force—some 4 million men, 3,300 tanks, and 5,000 planes. In the early hours of June 22, 1941, the Germans launched their offensive over a wide front. Raiding Russian airfields, the Luftwaffe destroyed 1,200 aircraft on the first day. The Germans drove deeply into Russia, cutting up and surrounding the disorganized and unprepared Russian forces. The Russians suffered terrible losses. In a little more than three months, 2.5 million Russian soldiers had been killed, wounded, or captured and 14,000 tanks destroyed. Describing the war as a crusade to save Europe from "Jewish Bolshevism," German propaganda claimed that victory had been assured.

But there were also disquieting signs for the Nazi invaders. The Russians, who had a proven capacity to endure hardships, fought doggedly and courageously, and the government would not consider capitulation. Russian reserve strength was far greater than the Germans had estimated. The Wehrmacht (German army), far from its supply lines, was running short of fuel, and trucks and cars had to contend with primitive roads that turned into seas of mud when the autumn rains came. One German general described the ordeal: "The infantryman slithers in the mud, while many teams of horses are needed to drag each gun forward. All wheeled vehicles sink up to their axles in the slime. Even tractors can only move with great difficulty. A large portion of our heavy artillery was soon stuck fast. . . . The strain that all this

caused our already exhausted troops can perhaps be imagined."[6] Conditions no longer favored the blitzkrieg.

Early and bitter cold weather hampered the German attempt to capture Moscow. Without warm uniforms, tens of thousands of Germans suffered from frostbite; without antifreeze, guns did not fire. The Germans advanced to within twenty miles of Moscow, but on December 6 a Red Army counterattack forced them to postpone the assault on the Russian capital. The Germans were also denied Leningrad, which since September had been almost completely surrounded and under constant bombardment. During this epic siege, the citizens of Leningrad displayed extraordinary courage in the face of famine, disease, and shelling that cost nearly one million lives.

By the end of 1941, Germany had conquered vast regions of Russia but had failed to bring the country to its knees. There would be no repetition of the collapse of France. The Russian campaign demonstrated that the Russian people would make incredible sacrifices for their land and that the Nazis were not invincible.

The New Order

By 1942, Germany ruled virtually all of Europe from the Atlantic to deep into Russia. Some conquered terrritory was annexed outright; other lands were administered by German officials; in still other countries, the Germans ruled through local officials sympathetic to Nazism or willing to collaborate with the Germans. Over this vast empire, Hitler and his henchmen imposed a New Order.

Exploitation and Terror

"The real profiteers of this war are ourselves, and out of it we shall come bursting with

Map 34.2 World War II: The European Theater ▶

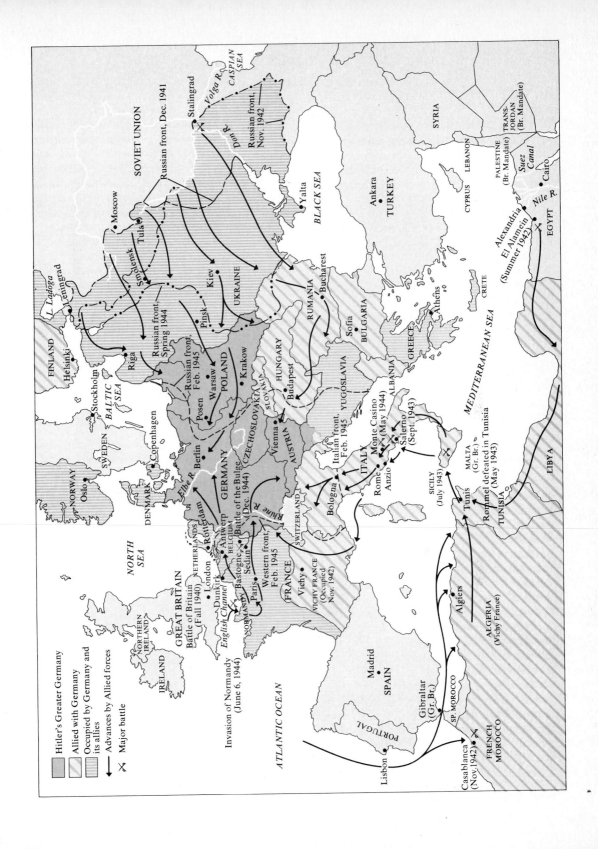

Hitler's Greater Germany

Allied with Germany

Occupied by Germany and its allies

Advances by Allied forces

Major battle

ATLANTIC OCEAN

IRELAND

NORTHERN IRELAND

GREAT BRITAIN

Battle of Britain (Fall 1940)

London

Dunkirk

English Channel

NORMANDY

Invasion of Normandy (June 6, 1944)

Paris

Sedan

Bastogne

Battle of the Bulge (Dec. 1944)

Antwerp

Rotterdam

NETHERLANDS

BELGIUM

FRANCE

Western front, Feb. 1945

Rhine R.

SWITZERLAND

Vichy

VICHY FRANCE (Occupied Nov. 1942)

NORTH SEA

Oslo

NORWAY

SWEDEN

Stockholm

DENMARK

Copenhagen

BALTIC SEA

FINLAND

Helsinki

L. Ladoga

Leningrad

Riga

Russian front, Spring 1944

Smolensk

Tula

Moscow

SOVIET UNION

Russian front, Dec. 1941

Volga R.

Stalingrad

Don R.

Russian front, Nov. 1942

CASPIAN SEA

Berlin

Elbe R.

GERMANY

Posen

Warsaw

POLAND

Krakow

Russian front, Feb. 1945

CZECHOSLOVAKIA

Vienna

AUSTRIA

SLOVAKIA

HUNGARY

Budapest

YUGOSLAVIA

Italian front, Feb. 1945

Bologna

Rome

Monte Casino (May 1944)

Anzio

ITALY

Salerno (Sept. 1943)

ALBANIA

MALTA (Gr. Br.)

SICILY (July 1943)

RUMANIA

Bucharest

Kiev

Pinsk

UKRAINE

BLACK SEA

Yalta

BULGARIA

Sofia

GREECE

Athens

CRETE

TURKEY

Ankara

MEDITERRANEAN SEA

CYPRUS

SYRIA

LEBANON

PALESTINE (Br. Mandate)

TRANS-JORDAN (Br. Mandate)

Suez Canal

Cairo

Alexandria

El Alamein (Summer 1942)

EGYPT

Nile R.

LIBYA

Tunis

TUNISIA

Rommel defeated in Tunisia (May 1943)

Algiers

ALGERIA (Vichy France)

SP. MOROCCO

FRENCH MOROCCO

Casablanca (Nov. 1942)

Gibraltar (Gr. Br.)

SPAIN

Madrid

PORTUGAL

Lisbon

fat," said Hitler. "We will give back nothing and will take everything we can make use of."[7] The Germans systematically looted the lands they conquered, taking gold, art treasures, machinery, and food supplies back to Germany and exploiting the industrial and agricultural potential of non-German lands to aid the German war economy. Some foreign businesses and factories were confiscated by the German Reich; others produced what the Germans demanded. Germany also requisitioned food from the conquered regions, significantly reducing the quantity available for local civilian comsumption. German soldiers were fed with food harvested in occupied France and Russia; they fought with weapons produced in Czech factories. German tanks ran on oil delivered by Rumania, Germany's satellite. The Nazis also made slave laborers of conquered peoples. Some 7 million people from all over Europe were wrested from their homes and transported to Germany. These forced laborers, particularly the Russians and Poles whom Nazi ideology classified as subhumans, lived in wretched, unheated barracks and were poorly fed and overworked; many died of disease, hunger, and exhaustion.

The Nazis ruled by force and terror. The prison cell, the torture chamber, the firing squad, and the concentration camp symbolized the New Order. In the Polish province annexed to Germany, the Nazis jailed and executed intellectuals and priests, closed all schools and most churches, and forbade Poles from holding professional positions. In the region of Poland administered by German officials, most schools above the fourth grade were shut down. Himmler insisted that it was sufficient for Polish children to learn "simple arithmetic up to five hundred at the most; writing of one's name; a doctrine that it is a divine law to obey the Germans and to be honest, industrious, and good."[8] The Germans were particularly ruthless toward the Russians, whom they regarded as an especially low form of humanity. Soviet political officials were immediately executed; many prisoners of war were herded into camps and deliberately starved to death. In all, the Germans took some 5.5 million Russian prisoners, of whom more than 3.5 million perished.

Extermination

Against the Jews of Europe, the Germans waged a war of extermination. The task of imposing the "Final Solution of the Jewish Problem" was given to Himmler's SS; Himmler fulfilled his grisly duties with fanaticism and bureaucratic efficiency. Seized by a mass psychosis akin to the witchcraft hysteria of the sixteenth century, Himmler and the SS believed that they had a holy mission to rid the world of the lowest species of humanity—a satanic foe that was plotting to destroy Germany. Regarding themselves as idealists who were writing a glorious chapter in the history of Germany, the SS tortured and murdered with immense dedication. The mind of the SS was dominated by the mythical world-view of Nazism, as the following tract issued by SS headquarters reveals:

Just as night rises up against the day, just as light and darkness are eternal enemies, so the greatest enemy of world-dominating man is man himself. The sub-man—that creature which looks as though biologically it were of absolutely the same kind, endowed by Nature with hands, feet and a sort of brain, with eyes and mouth—is nevertheless a totally different, a fearful creature, is only an attempt at a human being, with a quasi-human face, yet in mind and spirit lower than any animal. Inside this being a cruel chaos of wild, unchecked passions: a nameless will to destruction, the most primitive lusts, the most undisguised vileness. A sub-man—nothing else! . . . Never has the sub-man granted peace, never has he permitted rest. . . . To preserve himself he needed mud, he needed hell, but not the sun. And this underworld of sub-men found its leader: the eternal Jew![9]

Special squads of SS—the *Einsatzgruppen*, trained for mass murder—followed on the heels of the German army into Russia. Entering captured villages and cities, they rounded up Jewish men, women, and children, herded them to execution grounds, and slaughtered them with machine gun and rifle fire. Aided by Ukrainian, Lithuanian, and Latvian auxiliaries, the Einsatzgruppen massacred some two million Russian Jews.

To speed up the Final Solution, concentration camps, originally established for political prisoners, were transformed into killing centers and new ones were built for that purpose. Jews from all over Europe were rounded up—for "resettlement," they were told. The victims dismissed rumors that the Germans were engaged in genocide. They simply could not believe that any nation in the twentieth century was capable of such evil. "Why did we not fight back? . . . I know why. Because we had faith in humanity. Because we did not really think that human beings were capable of committing such crimes," declared one survivor.[10] Jammed into sealed cattle cars, eighty or ninety to a car, the victims traveled, sometimes for days, without food or water, choking from the stench of vomit and excrement, and shattered by the crying of children. Disgorged at the concentration camps, they entered another planet.

Corpses were strewn all over the road; bodies were hanging from the barbed-wire fence; the sound of shots rang in the air continuously. Blazing flames shot into the sky; a giant smoke cloud ascended about them. Starving, emaciated human skeletons stumbled forward toward us, uttering incoherent sounds. They fell down right in front of our eyes gasping out their last breath.

Here and there a hand tried to reach up, but when this happened an SS man came right away and stepped on it. Those who were merely exhausted were simply thrown on the dead pile. . . . Every night a truck came by, and all of them, dead or not, were thrown on it and taken to the crematory.[11]

SS doctors quickly inspected the new arrivals, "the freight," as they referred to them. Rudolf Hoess, commandant of Auschwitz—the most notorious of the murder factories—described the procedure:

[I] estimate that at least 2,500,000 victims were executed and exterminated [at Auschwitz] by gassing and burning, and at least another half million succumbed to starvation and disease, making a total dead of about 3,000,000. This figure represents about 70 per cent or 80 per cent of all persons sent to Auschwitz as prisoners, the remainder having been selected and used for slave labor in the concentration camp industries. . . .

The "final solution" of the Jewish question meant the complete extermination of all Jews in Europe. I was ordered to establish extermination facilities at Auschwitz in June, 1941. . . . It took from three to fifteen minutes to kill people in the death chamber, depending upon climatic conditions. We knew when the people were dead because their screaming stopped. We usually waited about one-half hour before we opened the doors and removed the bodies. After the bodies were removed our special commandos took off the rings and extracted the gold from the teeth of the corpses. . . .

The way we selected our victims was as follows . . . Those who were fit to work were sent into the camp. Others were sent immediately to the extermination plants. Children of tender years were invariably exterminated since by reason of their youth they were unable to work. . . . We endeavored to fool the victims into thinking that they were to go through a delousing process. Of course, frequently they realized our true intentions, and we sometimes had riots and difficulties due to that fact. Very frequently women would hide their children under clothes, but of course when we found them we would send the children in to be exterminated.[12]

The naked bodies, covered with blood and excrement and intertwined with each other, were piled high to the ceiling. To make way for the next group, a squad of Jewish prisoners emptied the gas chambers of the corpses and removed the gold teeth, which along with the victims' hair, eyeglasses, and clothing, were carefully collected and catalogued for the war effort. Later, the bodies were burned in crematoria specially constructed by I. A. Topf and Sons, of Erfurt. The chimneys vomited black smoke and the stench of burning flesh permeated the entire region.

Auschwitz was more than a murder factory. It also provided the German industrial giant, I. G. Farben, which operated a factory adjoining the camp, with slave laborers, both Jews and non-Jews. The working pace at the factory and the ill treatment by guards was so brutal, reported a physician and inmate, that "while working many prisoners suddenly stretched out flat, turned blue, gasped for breath, and died like beasts."[13]

Auschwitz also allowed the SS, the elite of the master race, to shape and harden themselves according to the National Socialist creed. A survivor recalls seeing SS men and women amuse themselves with pregnant inmates. The unfortunate women were "beaten with clubs and whips, torn by dogs, dragged by the hair, and kicked in the stomach with heavy German boots. Then, when they collapsed, they were thrown into the crematory—alive."[14] By systematically overworking, beating, terrorizing, and degrading the inmates, by making them live in filth and sleep sprawled all over each other in tiny cubicles, the SS deliberately sought to strip prisoners of all human dignity, to make them appear, behave, and believe that they were indeed "sub-man," as National Socialist ideology viewed them. When prisoners, exhausted, starved, diseased, and beaten, became unfit for work, generally within a few months, they were sent to the gas chambers. Many went mad or committed suicide; some struggled desperately, defiantly, and heroically to maintain their humanity. Nazi extermination camps, perhaps the vilest assault on human dignity ever conceived, were the true legacy of National Socialism and the SS the true end product of National Socialist indoctrination and idealism.

The Holocaust—the systematic extermination of European Jewry—was the terrible fulfillment of Nazi racial theories. Believing that they were cleansing Europe of a lower and dangerous race that threatened the German people, Nazi executioners performed their evil work with dedication and resourcefulness, with precision and moral indifference—a terrible testament to the power of mythical thinking. Using the technology and bureaucracy of a modern state, the Germans killed approximately 6 million Jews—*two-thirds* of the Jewish population of Europe. Some 1.5 million of the murdered were children. Tens of thousands of entire families were wiped out without a trace. Centuries-old Jewish community life vanished, never to be restored. Burned into the soul of the Jewish people was a wound that could never entirely heal. Written into the history of Western civilization was an episode that would forever cast doubt on the Enlightenment conception of human goodness, rationality, and the progress of civilization.

Resistance

Each occupied country had its collaborators who welcomed the demise of democracy, saw Hitler as Europe's best defense against communism, and profited from the sale of war material. Each country also produced a resistance movement that grew stronger as Nazi barbarism became more visible and prospects of a German defeat more likely. The Nazis retaliated by torturing and executing captured resistance fighters and killing hostages—generally fifty for every German killed.

In western Europe the resistance rescued downed Allied airmen, radioed military intelligence to Britain, and sabotaged German installations. Norwegians blew up the German stock of heavy water needed for atomic research. The Danish underground sabotaged railways and smuggled into neutral Sweden almost all of Denmark's 8,000 Jews just before they were to be deported to the death camps. The Greek resistance blew up a vital viaduct, interrupting the movement of supplies to German troops in North Africa. After the Allies landed on the coast of France in June 1944, the French resistance delayed the movement of German reinforcements and liberated sections of the country. Belgian resistance fighters captured the vital port of Antwerp.

The Polish resistance, numbering some

300,000 at its height, reported on German troop movements and interfered with supplies destined for the eastern front. In August 1944, with Soviet forces approaching Warsaw, the Poles staged a full-scale revolt against the German occupiers. The Poles appealed to the Soviets, camped ten miles away, for help. Thinking about a future Russian-dominated Poland, the Soviets did not move. After sixty-three days of street fighting, remnants of the Polish underground surrendered and the Germans destroyed what was left of Warsaw.

Russian partisans numbered several hundred thousand men and women. Operating behind the German lines, they sabotaged railways, destroyed trucks, and killed scores of thousands of German soldiers in hit-and-run attacks.

The mountains and forests of Yugoslavia provided excellent terrain for guerrilla warfare. The leading Yugoslav resistance army was headed by Josip Broz (1892–1980), better known as Tito. Moscow-trained, intelligent, and courageous, Tito organized the partisans into a disciplined fighting force that tied down a huge German army and ultimately liberated the country from German rule.

Jews participated in the resistance movements in all countries and were particularly prominent in the French resistance. Specifically Jewish resistance organizations emerged in eastern Europe, but they suffered from shattering handicaps. Poles, Ukrainians, Lithuanians, and other East European peoples with a long history of anti-Semitism gave little or no support to Jewish resisters and, at times, even denounced them to the Nazis. For centuries, European Jews had dealt with persecution by complying with their oppressors and had unlearned the habit of armed resistance that their ancestors had demonstrated against the Romans. Nevertheless, revolts did take place in the ghettos and concentration camps. In the spring of 1943 the surviving Jews of the Warsaw ghetto, armed only with a few guns and homemade bombs, fought the Germans for several weeks.

Italy and Germany also had resistance movements. After the Allies landed in Italy in 1943, bands of Italian partisans helped to liberate Italy from Fascism and the German occupation. In Germany, army officers plotted to assassinate the Fuehrer. On July 20, 1944, Colonel Claus von Stauffenberg planted a bomb at a staff conference attended by Hitler, but the Fuehrer escaped serious injury. In retaliation, some 5,000 suspected anti-Nazis were tortured and executed in exceptionally barbarous fashion.

The Turn of the Tide

The Japanese Offensive

At the same time that Germany was subduing Europe, its ally, Japan, was extending its dominion over areas of Asia. Seeking raw materials and secure markets for Japanese goods, and driven by a xenophobic nationalism, Japan in 1931 had attacked Manchuria in northern China. Quickly overrunning the province, the Japanese established the puppet state of Manchukuo in 1932. After a period of truce, the war against China was renewed in July 1937. Japan captured leading cities, including China's principal seaports, and inflicted heavy casualties on the poorly organized Chinese forces, forcing the government of Chiang Kai-shek (1887–1975) to withdraw to Chungking in the interior.

In 1940, after the defeat of France and with Britain standing alone against Nazi Germany, Japan eyed southeast Asia—French Indochina, British Burma and Malaya, and the Dutch East Indies. From these lands Japan planned to obtain the oil, rubber, and tin vitally needed by Japanese industry and enough rice to feed the nation. Japan hoped that a quick strike against the American fleet in the Pacific would give it time to enlarge and consolidate its empire. On December 7, 1941, the Japanese struck with carrier-based planes at Pearl Harbor in Hawaii. Taken by surprise, the Americans suffered a total defeat: the attackers sank seventeen ships, including seven of eight battleships; destroyed 188 air-

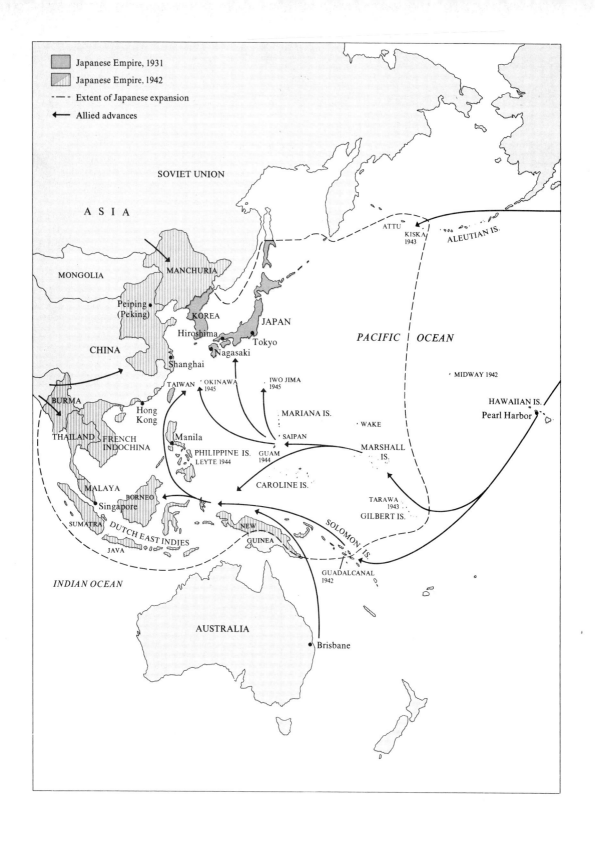

Japanese Empire, 1931
Japanese Empire, 1942
Extent of Japanese expansion
Allied advances

SOVIET UNION

ASIA

MONGOLIA

MANCHURIA

Peiping
(Peking)

KOREA

Hiroshima

JAPAN

CHINA

Nagasaki

Tokyo

Shanghai

TAIWAN

OKINAWA
1945

IWO JIMA
1945

Hong
Kong

BURMA

THAILAND

FRENCH
INDOCHINA

Manila

PHILIPPINE IS.
LEYTE 1944

MARIANA IS.

SAIPAN

GUAM
1944

MALAYA

Singapore

BORNEO

SUMATRA

DUTCH EAST INDIES

JAVA

NEW
GUINEA

CAROLINE IS.

SOLOMON IS.

GUADALCANAL
1942

INDIAN OCEAN

AUSTRALIA

Brisbane

PACIFIC   OCEAN

ATTU

KISKA
1943

ALEUTIAN IS.

MIDWAY 1942

HAWAIIAN IS.
Pearl Harbor

WAKE

MARSHALL
IS.

TARAWA
1943
GILBERT IS.

planes and damaged 159 others; and killed 2,403 men. The Japanese lost only 29 planes. After the attack on Pearl Harbor, Germany declared war on the United States. Now the immense American industrial capacity could be put to work against the Axis powers—Germany, Italy, and Japan.

By the spring of 1942, the Axis powers held the upper hand. The Japanese empire included the coast of China, Indochina, Thailand, Burma, Malaya, the Dutch East Indies, the Philippines, and other islands in the Pacific. Germany controlled Europe almost to Moscow. When the year ended, however, the Allies seemed assured of victory. Three decisive battles—Midway, Stalingrad, and El Alamein—reversed the tide of war.

At Pearl Harbor the Japanese had destroyed much of the American fleet. Assembling a mighty flotilla (8 aircraft carriers, 11 battleships, 22 cruisers, and 65 destroyers), Japan now sought to annihilate the rest of the United States Pacific fleet. In June 1942, the main body of the Japanese fleet headed for Midway, 1,100 miles northwest of Pearl Harbor; another section sailed toward the Aleutian Islands in an attempt to divide the American fleet. But the Americans had broken the Japanese naval code and were aware of the Japanese plan. On June 4, 1942, the two navies fought a strange naval battle; it was waged entirely by carrier-based planes, for the two fleets were too far from each other to use their big guns. Demonstrating marked superiority over their opponents and extraordinary courage, American pilots destroyed 4 aircraft carriers and downed 322 Japanese planes. The battle of Midway cost Japan the initiative. With American industrial production accelerating, the opportunity for a Japanese victory had passed.

Defeat of the Axis Powers

After being stymied at the outskirts of Moscow in December 1941, the Germans renewed their offensive in the spring and summer of 1942.

◄ **Map 34.3** World War II: The Pacific Theater

Hitler's goal was Stalingrad, the great industrial center located on the Volga River; control of Stalingrad would give Germany command of vital rail transportation. The battle of Stalingrad was an epic struggle in which Russian soldiers and civilians contested for every building and street of the city. So brutal was the fighting that at night half-crazed dogs sought to escape the city by swimming across the river. A Russian counterattack in November caught the Germans in a trap. Exhausted and short of food, medical supplies, weapons, and ammunition, Friedrich Paulus, Commander of the Sixth Army, urged Hitler to order a withdrawal before the Russians closed the ring. The Fuehrer refused. After suffering tens of thousands of additonal casualties, their position hopeless, the remnants of the Sixth Army surrendered on February 2, 1943. Some 260,000 German soldiers had perished in the battle of Stalingrad and another 110,000 were taken prisoner.

In January 1941, the British were routing the Italians in northern Africa. Hitler assigned General Erwin Rommel (1891–1944) to halt the British advance. Rommel drove the British out of Libya and with strong reinforcements might have taken Egypt and the Suez Canal. But Hitler's concern was with seizing Yugoslavia and Greece and preparing for the invasion of Russia. In the beginning of 1942, Rommel resumed his advance, intending to conquer Egypt. The British Eighth Army, commanded by General Bernard L. Montgomery, stopped him at the battle of El Alamein in October 1942. The victory of El Alamein was followed by an Anglo-American invasion of northwest Africa in November 1942. By May 1943, the Germans and Italians were defeated in North Africa.

After securing North Africa, the Allies, seeking complete control of the Mediterranean, invaded Sicily in July 1943 and quickly conquered the island. Mussolini's fellow fascist leaders turned against the Duce and the king dismissed him as prime minister. In September, the new government surrendered to the Allies and in the following month Italy declared war on Germany.

Italian partisans, whose number would

Kamikaze Attack on the *Hornet*, Painted from Combat Experience by Lt. Dwight C. Chepler, U.S.N.R. With the bombing of Pearl Harbor, Japan had destroyed much of the American fleet and expected a quick, easy victory. The U.S. triumph at the Battle of Midway on June 4, 1942, however, broke Japan's initiative. (*Popperfoto*)

grow to 300,000, resisted the Germans, who were determined to hold on to central and northern Italy. At the same time, the Allies fought their way up the peninsula. The fighting in Italy would last until the very end of the war. Captured by partisans, Mussolini was executed (April 28, 1945) and his dead body, hanging upside-down, was publicly displayed.

On June 6, 1944—D-Day—the Allies landed on the beaches of Normandy in France. They had assembled a massive force for the invasion—2 million men and 5,000 vessels. Although suspecting an imminent landing, the Germans did not think that it would occur in Normandy and they dismissed June 6 because weather conditions were unfavorable. The success of D-Day depended on securing the beaches and marching inland, which the Allies did despite stubborn German resistance on some beaches. By the end of July, the Allies had built up their strength in France to a million and a half. In the middle of August, Paris rose up against the German occupiers and was soon liberated.

As winter approached, the situation looked hopeless for Germany. Brussels and Antwerp fell to the Allies; Allied bombers were striking German factories and mass-bombing German cities in terror raids that took a terrible toll of life; the desperate Hitler made one last gamble. In mid-December 1944 he launched an offensive to split the Allied forces and regain the vital port of Antwerp. The Allies were taken by surprise in the Battle of the Bulge, but a heroic defense by the Americans at Bastogne stopped the German offensive.

While their allies were advancing in the

west, the Russians were continuing their drive in the east, advancing into the Baltic states, Poland, and Hungary. By February 1945, they stood within one hundred miles of Berlin.

Also in February the Allies in the west were battling the Germans in the Rhineland, and on March 7, 1945, American soldiers, seizing a bridge that the Germans had failed to destroy, crossed the Rhine into the interior of Germany. By April 1945, British, American, and Russian troops were penetrating into Germany from east and west. From his underground bunker near the chancellery in Berlin Hitler, physically exhausted and emotionally unhinged, engaged in wild fantasies about new German victories. On April 30, 1945, with the Russians only blocks away, the Fuehrer took his own life. In his last will and testament, Hitler insisted: "It is not true that I or anybody else in Germany wanted war in 1939. It was wanted and provoked exclusively by those international statesmen who either were of Jewish origin or worked for Jewish interests."[15] On May 7, 1945, a demoralized and devastated Germany surrendered unconditionally.

After the victory at Midway in June 1942, American forces attacked strategic islands held by Japan. American troops had to battle their way up beaches and through jungles tenaciously defended by Japanese soldiers, who believed that death was preferable to the disgrace of surrender. In March 1945, 21,000 Japanese perished on Iwo Jima; another 100,000 died on Okinawa in April 1945 as they contested for every inch of the island. On August 6, 1945, the United States dropped an atomic bomb on Hiroshima, killing more than 78,000 people and demolishing 60 percent of the city. President Truman said that he ordered the atomic attack to avoid an American invasion of the Japanese homeland that would have cost hundreds of thousands of lives. Truman's decision has aroused considerable debate. Some analysts say that dropping the bomb was unnecessary, that Japan, deprived of oil, rice, and other essentials by an American naval blockade and defenseless against unrelenting aerial bombardments, was close to surrender and had

Two Inmates of Changi Prison Camp After Release, 1945. World War II in the Pacific Theater continued three months after the Allied victory in Europe on May 7, 1945. After the United States dropped a second atomic bomb on Japan at Nagasaki on August 9, Japan surrendered and the prisoners who survived their ordeal in Japanese camps like Changi were released. (*Popperfoto*)

indicated as such. It has been suggested that with the Soviet Union about to enter the conflict against Japan, Truman wanted to end the war immediately, thereby depriving the USSR of an opportunity to extend its influence in East Asia. On August 8, Russia entered the war against Japan, invading Manchuria. After a second atomic bomb was dropped on Nagasaki on August 9, the Japanese asked for peace.

The Legacy of World War II

World War II was the most destructive war in history. Estimates of the number of dead range as high as 50 million, including 20 million Russians, who sacrificed more than the other participants in both population and material resources. The war produced a vast migration of peoples unparalleled in modern European history. The Soviet Union annexed the Baltic lands of Latvia, Lithuania, and Estonia, forcibly deporting many of the native inhabitants into central Russia. The bulk of East Prussia was taken over by Poland, and Russia annexed the eastern portion. Millions of Germans fled or were forced out of Prussia and regions of Czechoslovakia, Rumania, Yugoslavia, and Hungary, places where their ancestors had lived for centuries. Material costs were staggering. Everywhere cities were in rubble; bridges, railway systems, waterways, and harbors destroyed; farmlands laid waste; livestock killed; coal mines wrecked. Homeless and hungry people wandered the streets and roads. Europe faced the gigantic task of rebuilding. Yet Europe did recover from this material blight, and with astonishing speed.

World War II produced a shift in power arrangements. The United States and the Soviet Union emerged as the two most powerful states in the world; the traditional Great Powers—Britain, France, Germany—were now dwarfed by these *superpowers*. The United States had the atomic bomb and immense industrial might; the Soviet Union had the largest army in the world and was extending its dominion over eastern Europe. With Germany prostrate and occupied, the principal incentive for Soviet-American cooperation had evaporated.

Whereas World War I was followed by an intensification of nationalist passions, after World War II western Europeans progressed toward cooperation and unity. The Hitler years had convinced many Europeans of the dangers inherent in extreme nationalism, and fear of the Soviet Union fortified the need for greater cooperation.

World War II accelerated the disintegration of Europe's overseas empires. The European states could hardly justify ruling over Africans and Asians after they had fought to liberate European lands from German imperialism. Nor could they ask their peoples, exhausted by the Hitler years and concentrating all their energies on reconstruction, to fight new wars against Africans and Asians pressing for independence. In the years just after the war, Great Britain surrendered India, France lost Lebanon and Syria, and the Dutch departed from Indonesia. In the 1950s and 1960s, virtually every colonial territory gained independence. In those instances where the colonial power resisted independence for the colony, the price was bloodshed.

The consciousness of Europe, already profoundly damaged by World War I, was again grievously wounded. Nazi racial theories showed that in an age of sophisticated science, the mind remains attracted to irrational beliefs and mythical imagery; Nazi atrocities demonstrated that people will torture and kill with religious zeal and machinelike indifference. The Nazi assault on reason and freedom demonstrated anew the precariousness of Western civilization. Both the Christian and Enlightenment traditions had failed the West. Some intellectuals, shocked by the irrationality and horrors of the Hitler era, drifted into despair. To these thinkers, life was absurd, without meaning; human beings could neither comprehend nor control it. In 1945 only the naive could have faith in continuous progress or believe in the essential goodness of the individual. The future envisioned by the philosophes seemed further away than ever.

World War II ushered in the atomic age. At the end of the war, only the United States had the atomic bomb, but soon the Soviet Union and other states acquired an arsenal of atomic weapons. That people now possess the weapons to destroy themselves and their planet is the ever-present, ever-terrifying, and ultimately most significant legacy of World War II.

Notes

1. Pierre Renouvin, *World War II and Its Origins* (New York: Harper & Row, 1969), p. 167.

Chronology 34.2 World War II

September 27, 1939	Poland surrenders
November 1939	Russia invades Finland
April 1940	Germany attacks Denmark and Norway
May 10, 1940	Germany invades Belgium, Holland, and Luxembourg
May 14, 1940	The Dutch surrender
May 27–June 4, 1940	British forces are evacuated from Dunkirk
June 22, 1940	France surrenders
August–September 1940	The Battle of Britain
September 1940	Japan begins conquest of Southeast Asia
October 1940	Italian troops cross into Greece
April 6, 1941	Germany attacks Greece and Yugoslavia
June 22, 1941	Germany launches offensive against Russia
December 7, 1941	Japan attacks Pearl Harbor; United States enters the war against Japan and Germany
1942	The tide of battle turns in the Allies' favor: Midway (Pacific), Stalingrad (Soviet Union), and El Alamein (North Africa)
April–May 1943	Uprising of Jews in Warsaw ghetto
September 1943	Italy surrenders to Allies, following invasion
June 6, 1944	D-Day—Allies land in Normandy, France
August 1944	Paris is liberated; Poles revolt against German occupiers
January 1945	Soviet troops invade Germany
March–April 1945	Allies penetrate Germany
May 7, 1945	Germany surrenders unconditionally
August 1945	United States drops atomic bombs on Hiroshima and Nagasaki; Soviet Union invades Manchuria; Japan surrenders

2. Z. A. B. Zeman, *Nazi Propaganda* (New York: Oxford University Press, 1973), p. 109.

3. *Documents on German Foreign Policy, 1918–1945*, vol. VI (London: Her Majesty's Stationery Office, 1956), series D, no. 433.

4. Basil H. Liddell Hart, *History of the Second World War* (New York: G. P. Putnam's Sons, 1970), pp. 73–74.

5. Winston S. Churchill, *The Second World War: Their Finest Hour* (Boston: Houghton Mifflin, 1949), 2:225–226.

6. Quoted in William L. Shirer, *The Rise and Fall of the Third Reich* (New York: Simon & Schuster, 1960), p. 860.

7. *Hitler's Secret Conversations, 1941–1944*, with an introductory essay by H. R. Trevor Roper (New York: Farrar, Straus, Young, 1953), p. 508.

8. Quoted in Gordon Wright, *The Ordeal of Total War* (New York: Harper Torchbooks, 1968), p. 124.

9. Quoted in Norman Cohn, *Warrant for Genocide* (New York: Harper Torchbooks, 1969), p. 188.

10. Gerda Weissman Klein, *All But My Life* (New York: Hill & Wang, 1957), p. 89.

11. Judith Sternberg Newman, *In the Hell of Auschwitz* (New York: Exposition, 1964), p. 18.

12. *Nazi Conspiracy and Aggression* VI (Washington, D.C.: United States Government Printing Office, 1946), pp. 787–789.

13. Quoted in Joseph Borkin, *The Crime and Punishment of I. G. Farben* (New York: The Free Press, 1978), p. 143.

14. Gisella Perl, *I Was a Doctor in Auschwitz* (New York: International Universities Press, 1948), p. 80.

15. Excerpted in George H. Stein, *Hitler* (Englewood Cliffs, N.J.: Prentice-Hall, 1968), p. 84.

Suggested Reading

Bauer, Yehuda, *A History of the Holocaust* (1982). An authoritative study.

Baumont, Maurice, *The Origins of the Second World War* (1978). A brief work by a distinguished French scholar.

Calvocoressi, Peter, and Wint, Guy, *Total War* (1972). A good account of World War II.

Cohn, Norman, *Warrant for Genocide* (1966). An astute analysis of the mythical components of modern anti-Semitism.

Des Pres, Terrence, *The Survivors* (1976). A sensitive analysis of life in the death camp.

Eubank, Keith, *The Origins of World War II* (1969). A brief introduction, with a good bibliographical essay.

Gilbert, Martin, and Gott, Martin, *The Appeasers* (1963). A study of British weakness in the face of Hitler's threats.

Hilberg, Raul, *The Destruction of the European Jews* (1967). A monumental study of the Holocaust.

Hildebrand, Klaus, *The Foreign Policy of the Third Reich* (1973). A brief assessment of Nazi foreign policy.

Marks, Sally, *The Illusion of Peace* (1976). The failure to establish peace in the period 1918–1933.

Michel, Henri, *The Shadow War* (1972). An analysis of the European resistance movement, 1939–1945.

———, *The Second World War*, 2 vols. (1975). Translation of an important study by a prominent French historian.

Remak, Joachim, *The Origins of the Second World War* (1976). A useful essay followed by documents.

Wiesel, Elie, *Night* (1960). A moving personal record of the Holocaust.

Review Questions

1. What efforts promoted reconciliation during the 1920s? How did these efforts only foster the illusion of peace?

2. What were Hitler's foreign-policy aims?

3. Why did Britain and France practice a policy of appeasement?

4. Discuss the significance of each of the following: Italy's invasion of Ethiopia (1935); Germany's remilitarization of the Rhineland (1936); the Spanish Civil War (1936–1939); Germany's union with Austria (1938); the occupation of Prague (1939); and the Nazi-Soviet Pact (1939).

5. What factors made possible the quick fall of France?

6. What problems did the German army face in Russia?

7. Describe the New Order the Nazis established in Europe. What meaning does the Holocaust contain?

8. Discuss the significance of each of the following battles: Midway (1942); Stalingrad (1942–1943); El Alamein (1942); and D-Day (1944).

9. What was the legacy of World War II?

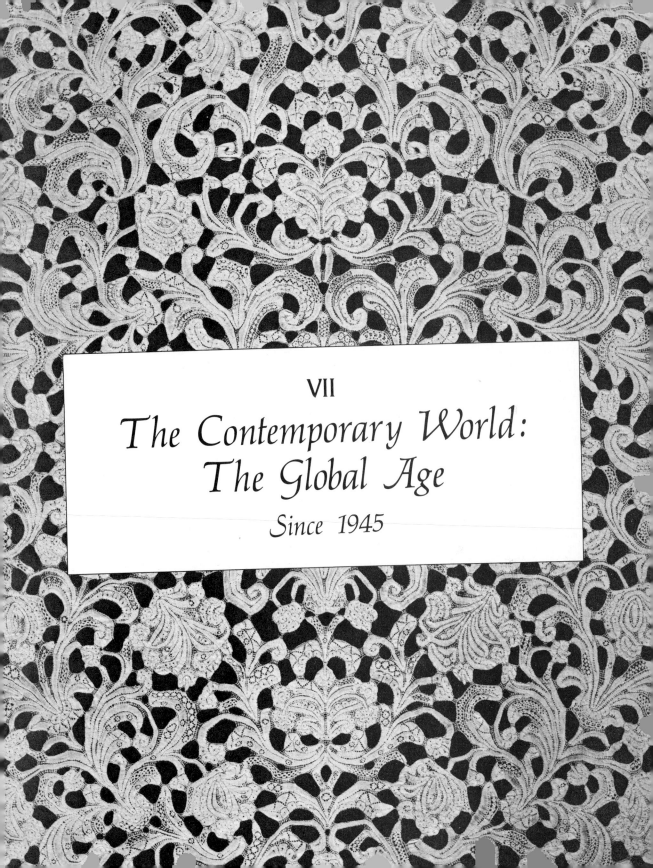

VII
The Contemporary World:
The Global Age

Since 1945

35

Western Europe Since 1945:
Recovery and Realignment

The Cold War

Western Europe Since 1949
European Unity
Economic Developments
Political Developments
Problems and Tensions

The Leading Western European States
France
West Germany
Great Britain
Italy

Western Europe and the World

$\mathcal{A}$t the end of World War II, Winston Churchill lamented: "What is Europe now? A rubble heap, a charnel house, a breeding ground for pestilence and hate."[1] Everywhere the survivors counted their dead. War casualties had been relatively light in western Europe. England and the Commonwealth suffered 460,000 casualties; France, 570,000; and Italy, 450,000. War casualties were heavier in the east—5 million people in Germany, one in every five persons in the total population of Poland (largely because of the extermination of 3 million Polish Jews), one in every ten in Yugoslavia, and over 20 million in the Soviet Union. The material destruction had been unprecedentedly heavy in the battle zones of northwestern Europe, northern Italy, and Germany, growing worse farther east, where Hitler's and Stalin's armies had fought without mercy to people, animals, or the environment. Industry, transportation, and communication had come to a virtual standstill; bridges, canals, dikes, and farmlands were ruined. Ragged, worn people picked among the rubble and bartered their valuables for food, while strangers straggled by. Members of families looked for each other; prisoners of war made their way home; Jews from extermination camps or from hiding places returned to open life; displaced persons by the millions sought refuge.

An estimated 40 to 50 million people in central and eastern Europe (as much as the entire population of France) were driven from their homes as part of the boundary changes imposed by the Red Army or fled to escape from Stalin's terror. They included Finns, Estonians, Latvians, Lithuanians, Poles, Czechs, Rumanians, Ukrainians, and above all Germans. These refugees made up an enforced *Völkerwanderung* ("migration of nations") of people too exhausted to complain, their suffering on a scale with the human sacrifices of the war itself. In France, some collaborators were lynched before courts could be set up. In western Germany, citizens were paraded past piles of skeletonlike corpses from concentration camps.

The Cold War

Among the heavy anxieties of those days one stood out: what was to be the future order of Europe? Having escaped from German tyranny, would Europe now be swallowed up by Soviet communism? One great conflict having just ended, another one, called the *cold war* (in a phrase coined in 1947 by American financier Bernard Baruch), immediately took its place. The prospect loomed that the contest between the United States and the Soviet Union, the two superpowers, might erupt into still another world war.

The evolution of the cold war—how it began and why it quickly snowballed into the dominating force in world politics—is a subject of some dispute among American historians. It is fair to say, however, that its causes were embedded in the divergent historical experiences and the incompatible universal aims of the United States and the Soviet Union, which clashed head-on as a new global order took shape. Hitler's empire in Europe had collapsed and left a vacuum: which superpower was to fill it? In the world at large the overseas empires of Britain, France, and other western European nations were dissolving: which superpower was to become the predominant influence around the world?

During the war the incompatibility of basic aims had been glossed over. Western self-interest had dictated giving the utmost support to the Red Army—the more powerful it was, the easier the western onslaught against Hitler would be. Stalin, however, had never shed his Bolshevik fear of capitalist superiority; nor had western leaders, Churchill foremost, given up their anticommunism. Once the common danger receded, the differences between political institutions and ideologies pushed again to the fore, aggravated by the flush of victory and postwar opportunity. The whole world was in a state of flux. America was proudly inheriting the pre-eminence once claimed by the Europeans. American leaders, their country untouched by the ravages of war and stronger than ever (especially after the explosion of the first

atomic bomb in July 1945), were determined not to lose the initiative in world affairs, having followed, already during the war, a course that would extend American influence around the world. Stalin, too, was unwilling to forego the advantages derived from Germany's defeat. Like his American rivals, he sought to increase his country's power and prestige. Thus hostility escalated between the superpowers, propelled by mutual fear, aggressive self-protection, raised ambitions, and collective pride—by all the complexities and confusions of modern statecraft. After 1945 the grim logic of irreconcilable political rivalry took its course.

The incompatibility of objectives became clear even before the armistice. As the Red Army moved west, the fate of the peoples of Eastern Europe hung in the balance. Would the promise of self-determination and democratic freedom espoused by the Western allies be applied to them? Or would Stalin treat them as conquered peoples, knowing that left to their own devices they would return to their traditional anti-Soviet orientation?

Attention first focused on Poland. In January 1945, Roosevelt, Churchill, and Stalin held a summit conference at Yalta on the Crimean peninsula to plan the final stages of the war. At the time, Soviet troops were approaching Berlin, while the American and British armies were stalled west of the Rhine; in addition, American generals still counted on Soviet help for the invasion of Japan. For these reasons the Western allies were in no position to stop Stalin from doing as he wished in Poland. As the Red Army occupied the country, he installed a pro-Soviet regime. In other countries of Eastern Europe, as well, the Americans had no way of keeping Soviet troops out. Whatever Stalin's ultimate plans for the area, the Soviet occupation of Eastern Europe was considered a dire calamity by the local populations and their sympathizers in Western Europe and the United States.

The fate of Germany became an even more crucial bone of contention. The division of Germany into zones of occupation had been agreed to in 1944. The capital, Berlin, located

Map 35.1 Western Europe After 1945

Legend:
- Territory lost by Germany
- Communist countries
- "Iron Curtain" after 1950
- NATO members
- Nonallied Western countries
- □ Original Common Market members
- △ Subsequent Common Market members

deep within the Soviet zone, was to be the seat of the joint Allied Control Commission. A permanent partition of Germany was ruled out at the Potsdam Conference in July–August 1945, and joint reparations were imposed in principle. Yet from the start the Soviets proceeded on their own, removing from their zone all portable resources and taking them to their own ravaged territories, and bringing in a planeload of docile German communists

under Walter Ulbricht (1893–1973) to take charge of political reconstruction. The Soviets also kept out observers from the other occupying powers—the United States, Britain, and later France—which meanwhile had put their political imprint on their own zones.

The foreign ministers of the four occupying powers kept trying—in Paris, Moscow, and London—to arrive at common conditions for a peace treaty with Germany, but each time they drifted further apart. In 1947 England, France, and the United States joined their zones, and in 1949 the West German Federal Republic was established and Berlin divided. Stalin matched the Western powers' every step by formally consolidating communist rule in his zone, thus adding anguish over the partition of Germany to the mounting fear of oppression in Eastern Europe.

Meanwhile, the United States and the Soviet Union had collided also in Western Europe as it tried to recover from the war. Communists had been prominent in the anti-Nazi resistance movements of Italy and France; they now claimed their share in the postwar reconstruction of their countries. Fearing that they were Stalin's agents, Americans by overt and covert means drove them from all positions of influence; the new democratic governments were solidly anticommunist; in response the pro-Soviet regimes in Eastern Europe were compelled to become more Stalinist. Further afield, in the eastern Mediterranean, Stalin was blamed, unjustly it seemed, for the Greek Civil War of 1946; he was also accused of claiming for his country not only the Straits of Constantinople but also the former Italian colony of Libya and of unduly prolonging the wartime Soviet occupation of northern Iran.

To Russians the territorial extension of Soviet rule, however, seemed limited compared with the worldwide expansion of the American presence. After 1945, the United States dominated the Pacific Ocean, occupying Japan, the Philippines, and South Korea. A string of military bases linked American forces in the Far East with American troops stationed in West Germany, with an outpost in Soviet-surrounded Berlin. For the time being, Americans also held a monopoly of the atomic bomb as a subtle threat against Soviet expansionism. In peaceful pursuits, they took the initiative in rebuilding the world economy and in launching the United Nations as a potential instrument of worldwide, Western-influenced cooperation.

Thus, a sharp change took place in American foreign policy; prewar isolationism gave way to worldwide vigilance against any Soviet

effort at expansion. Swayed by wartime compassion for the Soviet Union, American opinion had at first favored "bringing the boys home" as soon as the war was over. In 1946, however, it seemed better to continue occupying Germany as long as the Soviets did. At the same time, Churchill warned of the "iron curtain" that Stalin had drawn from the Baltic Sea to the Adriatic, cutting Europe in half. In March 1947, alarmed by the threat of Soviet penetration into the eastern Mediterranean and by British weakness in that area, President Truman proclaimed the Truman Doctrine: "it must be the policy of the United States to support free people who are resisting attempted subjugation by armed minorities or by outside pressures." The Truman Doctrine was the centerpiece of the new policy of "containment," of holding Soviet power within its then-current boundaries. American military and economic support soon went to Greece and Turkey.

In June 1947 the American government took a further step toward strengthening the West. Secretary of State George Marshall announced an impressive scheme of economic aid to Europe (the European Recovery Program) for rebuilding prosperity and stability. By December 1959, the Marshall Plan had supplied Europe with a total of over 74 billion dollars, a modest pump-priming for the subsequent record upswing in American, European, and even global prosperity. Western Europe recovered and the United States gained economically strong allies.

These measures were accompanied by a massive ideological mobilization of American opinion against communism and a new apprehension about national security, both of which rivaled Soviet paranoia. The foundations were laid for what, years later, President Eisenhower called the military-industrial complex, allied with the government through the National Security Council and the Central Intelligence Agency (both established in 1947). American intelligence agents soon locked horns with their Soviet counterparts, copying Soviet methods, even using Nazi war criminals for their purposes.

In 1948, finally, the Vandenberg Resolution

Berlin Airlift: U.S. Army Transport Planes Unloading at Templehof Airfield, 1948. Only four years after the end of World War II, Europe was divided into a Soviet-dominated, communist eastern half and an American-oriented, western half. Both superpowers clashed over divided Berlin, an "island" in communist East Germany. The U.S.S.R. attempted to shut off West Berlin entirely from June 1948 to May 1949, but the United States helped restore Berlin's lifeline to the west through the airlift. (*Popperfoto*)

sanctioned the stationing of American troops abroad wherever necessary.

These American measures met with a quick Soviet response. Stalin intensified ideological and political controls not only in his own country but also in Eastern Europe. In February 1948, with couplike suddenness, he replaced the mildly procommunist coalition government of Czechoslovakia with an outright Stalinist clique. Stalin also promoted a Communist Information Bureau (Cominform) to enforce tighter obedience among communist parties in Eastern and Western Europe. By these and similar actions he profoundly alarmed Western Europeans who, three years after the end of the war, redoubled their search for military security.

The most spectacular test between the two superpowers took place from June 1948 to May 1949 when the Soviet authorities severed all overland access to the western sectors of Berlin (occupied by French, British, and American troops). The Soviets aimed to starve into submission a half-city of about 2 million inhabitants who, because of their freedom, were "a bone in the communist throat" (as Khrushchev later put it). West Berlin was saved by an impressive airlift, as under American direction, the French, British, and Americans heroically flew in supplies around the clock in all kinds of weather. During the anxious days of the airlift the outline of the present European order became visible.

By 1949, Europe was divided into a Soviet-dominated communist eastern half and an American-oriented western half under democratic governments (except for Spain and Portugal which retained dictatorships into the 1970s). The division of Europe was marked at the center by the division of Germany, and the division of Germany by the division of Berlin. Few Europeans at the time were reconciled to the unnatural severance of historic ties between Western and Eastern Europe; few accept it even now. The partition of Germany, however, caused little regret among non-Germans.

The separate halves of Europe were quickly organized into rival military alliances. Already in 1948, the leading countries of Western Europe—Great Britain, France, and the Benelux countries (Belgium, the Netherlands, and Luxembourg)—had drawn up a military alliance called the Brussels Pact. In 1949, aware of their continued military weakness, they joined the United States, Canada, Portugal, Norway, Iceland, Denmark, and Italy (with Greece and Turkey soon added) in the North Atlantic Treaty Organization (NATO). Under American leadership, NATO offered the security needed to let political and economic life in Western Europe return to normal. A parallel consolidation took place in Eastern Europe. Stalin's satellites, called *people's democracies*, were tied to the Soviet Union by a treaty for mutual economic assistance and, in 1955, by a military alliance called the Warsaw Pact. When West Germany joined NATO in 1956, the partition of Europe into two hostile camps was complete. The only neutral countries were Sweden, Finland, Switzerland, and Austria, which are commonly considered part of Western Europe.

As Western Europe became reluctantly dependent upon the United States, the center of gravity for what was left of the Western tradition shifted toward that country. In this shift the Western heritage became subject to the dynamics of American life and politics and, perhaps more significantly, to the disorienting openness of an increasingly competitive and interdependent world. Seen from the American perspective, "Europe" now meant a client "Western Europe"—a collection of states that had entrusted its defense to the United States. While the hostility and the arms race between the superpowers grew ever more ominous, Western European states still tried to preserve a measure of independence and even to achieve a new solidarity for their own protection.

Western Europe Since 1949

European Unity

Although Europeans share a common cultural heritage, the diversity of their history and national temperaments has burdened them in the past with incessant warfare. After two ruinous world wars, many people at last began to feel that the price of violent conflict had become excessive; war no longer served any national interest. In addition, the extension of Soviet power made some form of unity imperative for all states not under Soviet domination. The first call for a united Europe was sounded by Winston Churchill who, reviving a project first launched in the seventeenth century, declared in 1946: "We must build a kind of United States of Europe."[2]

Despite such hopes, the major governments of Western Europe and their peoples were unprepared suddenly to submerge their separate national traditions under a common government empowered to regulate their internal affairs. Political unity was not forthcoming, but in the field of economics the movement for unity made headway.

Western European economic cooperation began rather modestly with the creation of the European Coal and Steel Community (ECSC) in 1951. It drew together the chief Continental consumers and producers of coal and steel, the two items most essential for the rebuilding of Western Europe. Its members were France, West Germany, the three Benelux countries, and Italy; these six countries thus became the core countries of Western European unity. Their design was to put the Ruhr industrial complex, the heart of German industrial power, under international control, thereby promoting cooperation and reconciliation as well as economic strength. Their project was endorsed by Konrad Adenauer, who expected it to restore confidence in Germany. West Germany has stood in the forefront of European integration since then.

Emboldened by the success of the ECSC, the Six soon pressed forward. "In order to maintain Europe's place in the world, to restore her influence and prestige, and to ensure a continuous rise in the living standards of her people," their foreign ministers, led by Belgium's Paul-Henri Spaak, prepared two treaties, signed in Rome in March 1957. One treaty created a European Atomic Energy Community (called Euratom) for joint research on nuclear energy, and the other established the European Economic Community, also known as the Common Market. The EEC, which eventually absorbed Euratom, became the focus of the European search for unity, prosperity, and power.

Minimally, the EEC was to be a customs union, creating a free market among the Six, with a common external tariff for protection from the rest of the world, yet pledged to participate in the worldwide reduction of trade barriers. At the same time the EEC aimed higher: it was to improve living conditions among the people, help reduce the differences existing between the various regions and countries, and mitigate "the backwardness of the less favored" among member countries. It also promised to confirm "the solidarity which binds together Europe and overseas countries" in the spirit of the United Nations. Finally, it called on the other states of Europe to join the Six "in an ever closer union."[3] Toward the outside world the EEC was empowered to act as agent for its members in all commercial transactions. It has negotiated a great variety of special agreements with an ever-widening circle of Western European states and Third World countries.

It was clear from the outset that free trade within the EEC called for increasing uniformity among all the factors affecting the marketplace. The free movement of goods and people encouraged standardization and cooperation in every aspect of the economy. For that reason, the "Eurocrats" in Brussels, the headquarters of the European Economic Community, were forever eager to extend their authority. They and the governments of the Six also worked hard to make the Common Market more inclusive. In 1973 the original Six were joined by three new members—Great Britain, Ireland, and Denmark.

The Nine, sometimes calling themselves simply the European Community (EC), began to work for greater political integration. By 1979 three more states had applied for membership: Spain, Portugal, and Greece. Greece was admitted in 1981, while negotiations with the other two continued, thus far unsuccessfully. The inclusion of less well-off states presents the EC with profound challenges. Apart from working with governments only recently turned democratic, it must harmonize competition among Western European farmers who raise similar crops.

Meanwhile political integration among the Nine has made some progress. In June 1979 direct elections were held for delegates to the European Parliament sitting at Strasbourg. Although possessing only advisory power, the Strasbourg Assembly provides the first transnational representative forum for the discussion of common concerns. The Nine also have aimed at cooperation in their foreign policy. Their foreign ministers meet for regular consultation, trying to head off any conflicts among themselves or with outside powers. To negotiate effectively with the Soviet Union, the EC ministers presented a common front in 1973–1975 at the Helsinki Conference on Security and Cooperation in Europe—the larger Europe that includes the Soviet Union and its Eastern European satellites. Favoring relaxation of tension between the superpowers and welcoming negotiations for arms limitation, they joined the United States in signing the Helsinki Agreement, thereby accepting as permanent the division of Europe produced by World War II.

The hopes of 1975 were not fulfilled, however. The unity achieved during the good years could hardly be preserved under economic and political adversity, and efforts at integration began to flag. By the early 1980s the vision of European unity was fading, beset by differences of economic condition and national policy, disillusioned public opinion, and rising hostility between the superpowers.

Within this shifting framework of European cooperation, economic, political, and cultural developments took their course.

Economic Developments

The most striking fact of recent history in the West, as in the world generally, is the unprecedented economic advance. Between the early 1950s and the late 1970s production in Western Europe and the United States, as elsewhere, surpassed all previous records. The ascent was marred by a few temporary slowdowns; by the late 1960s it had begun to level off. By the time the economic advance came to an end, it had created a new world economic order requiring adjustments in Western Europe, the United States, and around the world. In Western Europe the standard of living increased dramatically. Health service, housing, and educational opportunities were provided for nearly everyone. Never in all history have the world's peoples multiplied so rapidly and increased their material fortunes so markedly as in the years since the end of World War II.

The miraculous economic recovery of Western Europe is sometimes reckoned as a triumph of capitalism. But the term "capitalism" is an oversimplification. The Western European economy has always been the product of a fluctuating interaction between diverse public and private interests. The state has always been present, prodding, controlling, and directing, with an eye to the survival of the country as a whole.

In the immediate aftermath of the war the necessities of reconstruction demanded the fullest use of state authority. Following long-standing tradition, most European governments extended their control over essential economic functions. Nearly everywhere, the biggest banks were nationalized, together with key industries and public utilities; nationwide economic planning was harnessed to the same purpose. Social welfare programs were also extended. With the arrival of Marshall Plan aid and under American prodding the trend swung back toward private initiative working together with public authority. All national economies in Western Europe thus became "mixed" economies, combining public and private enterprises in complex interlocking arrangements.

However, the increase in the public sector everywhere has been offset in recent years in the private sector. Private-sector influence has been enhanced by mergers, consolidations, and the rise of large holding corporations, often with monopoly or near-monopoly status. Stimulated by the expansion of American business into Western Europe and by the opportunities offered by the European Economic Community, many European companies have become multinational and grown bigger than any nationalized industry. The Western European economy is now dominated by gigantic private and public enterprises that are tied to other parts of the world and subject to a growing volume of transnational regulation and guidance. It is also participating in the immense technological upsurge of the age. In science and technology, in research and development, Western Europeans are determined to stand up to American and Japanese competition for leadership.

While industrial development took the lead, agriculture in the key areas of Western Europe held its own. Admittedly, as in all industrialized societies, the agricultural population has continued to shrink, yet without loss of agricultural productivity. On the contrary, Western European farms, modernized after the war and highly subsidized by the European Economic Community, are producing embarrassing surpluses in meat, dairy products, and wines. Western Europe is almost self-sufficient in foodstuffs and determined to protect its farmers from cheap American imports.

The economic advance of Western Europe (as of the world generally) was not destined to last forever. It had been fed by abundant and exceptionally cheap supplies of oil, but after 1973 the Organization of Petroleum Exporting Countries (OPEC) drastically raised the price of that essential source of energy. OPEC's action aggravated adverse worldwide economic trends that had been evident since the late 1960s (and were caused in part by the American war in Vietnam). Inflation, unemployment, falling productivity, competition, from Japan especially, in automobiles

Final Assembly Line at the Volkswagen Plant in Wolfsburg, Germany. Despite the fact that European cities and industry lay in a heap of rubble in 1945, recovery was astonishingly quick, aided by the Marshall Plan, especially in Germany. In 1946, Churchill had called for a "United States of Europe." By 1975 the European Economic Community, a group of nine countries, worked toward political integration; in the 1980s, those goals have disappeared, with renewed nationalistic policies. (*Edo König/Black Star*)

and electronics, and by 1980, a worldwide economic recession plagued all governments of Western Europe. Economic slippage frustrated the extravagant expectations of material wealth aroused by the good years; people began to feel insecure, putting state, society, and the European Economic Community under new strains. However, the expansion of social services by virtually all governments there has held social and political costs of austerity to a minimum in Western Europe.

Political Developments

Boosted until recently by rising standards of living, the overall trend of political life in the West since World War II has been toward constitutional democracy. Although Spain and Portugal retained their prewar dictatorships until the mid-1970s and Greece for a time wavered between democracy and dictator-ship, by the late 1970s even these countries had conformed to the common pattern. Membership in the European Economic Community requires democratic government; with its expansion, the Common Market has confirmed the liberal-democratic tradition.

Popular political allegiance remained scattered among parties spread over the spectrum of political creeds (yet somewhat to the left by American standards). Communists and various factions of socialism constituted the left. The center claimed the largest support. Lacking clear formulations, the center relied on traditional convictions and proceeded pragmatically, steering a cautious course between state control and free enterprise. Depending on circumstances, it might ally itself with the moderate left or the moderate right, with socialists or conservatives. On the right, the conservatives generally adhered to nineteenth-century liberalism and to laissez-faire economics. Authoritarian or protofascist right-wing movements periodically rose and waned; they never had a serious chance; nor did the terrorists, who came to the fore in the early 1970s. Depending on local circumstances, terrorism stood to the left of communism or to the extreme right; militant regionalism also spawned terrorism.

Political power essentially lay with the center parties which, recovering from the destruction of constitutional regimes before and during the war, reconstituted their political platforms around the established traditions of Western Europe: Christianity and liberal democracy. In continental Western Europe the political and economic reconstruction after the war was largely the work of Christian Democratic parties: in France known as Mouvement Républicain Populaire (MRP)—rather shortlived under the conditions of French politics; in West Germany as Christian Democratic Union (CDU), which has lasted to the present; and in Italy as Christian Democrats, also lasting to the present. Great Britain, whose constitution remained intact throughout the great wars, retained its traditional two-party system. But here, too, the winning majorities for both parties came from center votes shifting toward either the Conservative or the Labour party.

It was a sign of the times that ideologically oriented moderate socialist parties did poorly at the polls. Strong immediately after the war, they lost support the longer they adhered to their doctrines. The new social awareness in private enterprise, the rise of the welfare state, and the complexity of modern life reduced their appeal. Dogmatic socialists quarreled, splintered, and declined in power, or else they turned pragmatist, creating reformist mass parties slightly left of center. For example, both the West German Social Democratic party (SPD) and the British Labour party supported a number of mildly socialist policies but avoided a socialist program.

The major communist parties of Western Europe, especially those of Italy and France, could not escape the temper of the times. Dropped in 1947, in response to American pressure, from the government coalitions in their countries, communists steadily held their own in the next three decades; in France they polled between one-fifth and one-fourth of the total vote, and in Italy up to one-third. Yet in national politics, communists were condemned to play the role of frustrating ineffectual opposition, even in Italy. Barred from national leadership, communists have been effective in local government, especially in Italy, where they run the administration of most communities, including large cities.

Yet patriotism, prosperity, the brutality of the Soviet system, and the complexity of all things modern somewhat eroded the dogmatism of Western European communists. By the mid-1970s a new variety of communism called *Eurocommunism* emerged. Strongest in Italy, this movement still cherished the memory of prewar communist militancy (thereby keeping alive traditional anticommunism); but Eurocommunism was determined to prove itself under the established democratic ground rules as a mass movement dedicated to better government, without rigid ideological commitment to the Soviet party line. Although critical of the Soviet Union, it could not, however, free itself from association with it.

Problems and Tensions

Western Europe did not escape serious problems and tensions. With the rise of the public sector and the increase in social services, government and bureaucracy grew huge and more impersonal. Individuals felt dwarfed by the state and lost in a complex interdependent society.

Youths especially were in ferment, tending to repudiate the new affluence and the complexity on which it was based. They also emphasized its drawbacks: stark inequality in the world, social callousness at home, the breakdown of human intimacy and community, and the mounting strain on human energy and integrity. In their protest, the young sided with a romantic and ostensibly antimodern counterculture which, paradoxically, was ultramodern in its disdain for traditional middle-class restraints, above all in sex, and also in its sense of solidarity with all oppressed peoples around the world. On the whole, the protest was nonpolitical, a part of the new "youth culture" that in an illustration of the new complexity, had split off from the dominant culture of adult society.

In 1968 youthful frustration for a time broke into politics—angrily and sometimes destructively—foremost in France and slightly less drastically throughout Western Europe (as it did, more mildly, in the anti–Vietnam War agitation in the United States). During May 1968 a spontaneous and embittered demonstration of students and workers in Paris set off a massive general strike such as France had not seen since 1936. Yet no revolution followed, no sudden social change, only a conservative backlash at the next national election. The majority of the French people, like their contemporaries elsewhere, realized that they cannot escape the vast size and complexity that burdens contemporary state and society. The events of 1968, however, made them more aware of the need for the human touch in all official business.

Some impatient young protesters, meanwhile, turned to outright terrorism, especially in West Germany and Italy. In their eyes, the entire system of state and society was inhumane and deserved destruction by any means available. The targets of their attacks were leading representatives of "the system": politicians, industrialists, judges, and the police. After a few spectacular assassinations, public opinion began to favor more effective countermeasures, thus curtailing terrorist violence, at least in West Germany.

Tensions in the body politic were also reflected in the rise of separatist and nationalist movements within well-established nation-states. Great Britain was troubled by nationalist movements in Wales and Scotland, and especially in Northern Ireland, where Catholics and Protestants, driven by long-standing political and religious differences, continued to murder and maim each other; the violence occasionally spilled over into England. France suffered from separatist movements in the northwest and southwest. In Belgium, Walloons and Flemings strained their country's unity. In Spain, the restoration of constitu-

tional government after the death of General Franco in 1975 was marred by the terrorism of Basque extremists hoping to create a Basque state. Terrorists of all kinds established links with their counterparts in other troubled areas of the world, creating a sort of international terrorist movement. Although raw violence provided no answer to the intricate problems of modern society, it did offer young idealists the opportunity for politically aware and self-denying heroism that is sadly lacking in contemporary life.

Since the early 1980s the nuclear arms race provided a new and more peaceful outlet for pent-up idealism, the peace movement. Throughout Western Europe men and women, including many young mothers, gathered in massed demonstrations calling attention to the threat of nuclear war. The demonstrations reached a peak in the fall of 1983 when the United States began a program of placing intermediate-range missiles close to the Soviet Union. Aware that no protection exists against nuclear weapons (short of preventing war altogether), the members of the peace movement feared that their countries would be destroyed if war broke out. At the time, their protests proved ineffectual because of widespread fear of Soviet expansionism. Yet amidst the ever-increasing hostility among the superpowers, the determination behind the peace movement was bound to grow.

Meanwhile the massive spurt of affluence had an unsettling effect on European culture. Although prosperity provided more people with more material goods, it also encouraged a hedonistic self-indulgence that ran contrary to the ascetic strain in Western tradition. Material security and abundance undermined the bourgeois work ethic; life became too easy. An influx of alien people, goods, and human values both stimulated and fragmented intellectual and artistic life. One particular group of newcomers, called *guest workers*, caused special tension. Attracted by economic opportunity, they came from southern Europe, the countries of North Africa, Greece, Turkey, and elsewhere. Even after the onset of recession, many of them remained, raising families and claiming citizenship while retaining their culture or religion; they have posed a profound challenge to the cohesion of European society and have been an object of discrimination and a source of political tension and occasional violence. In its wealth and immense diversity of stimuli, Western Europe has been increasingly caught up in the ferment of the new globalism.

The guardians of traditional religion were among the chief victims of cultural diversity and the easy life. The Catholic church passed through much collective soul-searching during the great council of Vatican II (1962–1965), asking how traditional dogma and pastoral care could be reconciled with modern conditions. Earnestly searching for answers, the council infused new vitality into the worldwide church. Among Protestants, whether in the established state churches (as in West Germany, the Scandinavian countries, and Great Britain) or in free churches, confusion also reigned. Church membership generally declined, especially among established churches; some fundamentalist churches and sects like Jehovah's Witnesses gained members, as did non-Western world religions like Bahai.

Underneath their outward conformity and ready acceptance of the material boons of contemporary society, many Western Europeans live in spiritual doubt, their inner lives out of tune with their outward existence. Tied to global interdependence, suspended among troubled national economies and half-hearted economic integration under the European Economic Community, and caught in the tensions between the two superpowers, the peoples of Western Europe face an uncertain future—in their material conditions and in all aspects of their lives.

The Leading Western European States

France

After 1945 France quickly laid the foundation for its subsequent rapid economic advance.

Under the leadership of Jean Monnet, an able group of economists and planners mapped out strategies and institutions that have become models of state guidance in a mixed economy of public and private enterprise. During the 1950s the French economy grew at a very respectable rate. In national politics the sense of common purpose was less evident. In 1946 a new constitution created the Fourth Republic, following the pattern of the Third.

The twenty-six short-lived governments of the Fourth Republic valiantly coped with a number of grave problems, putting down communist-led strikes in 1947 and 1948, assisting in the organization of Western European defense, laying the groundwork for the European Economic Community, and promoting political reconciliation with Germany.

The biggest problem France faced was decolonization. In two areas, the French army fought colonial liberation movements to the bitter end. In Indochina the French army suffered a resounding defeat in 1954. In Algeria, administratively a part of France proper, French settlers and soldiers were determined to thwart demands for independence.

The long and bloody Algerian conflict had serious repercussions for French political life. In 1958 the insubordination of army leaders brought down the Fourth Republic with a resounding call for the return of General de Gaulle. De Gaulle then wrote the constitution of the Fifth Republic, largely to suit his own style as president. Elections were held regularly, reinforced by referendums, but they were manipulated to give support to the president; in emergencies the president could even claim dictatorial powers. Although De Gaulle thought that he embodied France's greatness and therefore stood above all political parties, his political instincts remained moderate.

De Gaulle's grand design was simple enough: to restore France to its rightful place in Europe and the world. At home this meant that France had to modernize its economy, encourage science and technology, and regain a common will. Abroad it had to assert its presence by all means available—cultural, economic, political, and even military. De Gaulle insisted that France have its own nuclear force, and he pulled France out of the NATO high command. He increased French prestige among Third World Countries, consenting to Algerian independence over the protest of the army and retaining the good will of the new African states formerly under French rule. But his France, a mere middle-size state in the global world, was too small for De Gaulle's ambition; his grand style in foreign policy did not survive him. His successors, Georges Pompidou (1969–1974) and Valéry Giscard D'Estaing (1974–1981), did emphasize, however, that France was "the third nuclear power" after the United States and the Soviet Union and was determined to assert its independence.

After De Gaulle's death, France produced no leader of equal stature. President Pompidou avoided his predecessor's flamboyant style but was unable to mend the country's political disunity. Giscard D'Estaing—aristocratic, increasingly aloof, and tainted with scandal—was even more troubled by lack of mass support. He took a more centrist line than the followers of the Gaullist tradition, trying to make France "an advanced liberal society," which led to endless friction in the center-right coalition on which he depended for legislative action.

On the left, meanwhile, communists and socialists (the latter led by François Mitterrand) competed for working-class and peasant votes. Their feuds prevented the emergence of a left-of-center government until 1981, when the communists reluctantly agreed to a coalition dominated by Mitterrand. As a result of that year's election Mitterrand, an experienced politician and noted intellectual, replaced Giscard D'Estaing. The new president shifted course sharply to the left with a program to nationalize industries and banks and increase government jobs. But even more than his predecessor, he was plagued by the adversities besetting the country's economy. The liberal measures enacted under Giscard D'Estaing had failed to prevent mounting inflation, unemployment, public frustration,

and political fragmentation. Yet the socialist remedies applied by Mitterrand failed even worse, forcing the government into a course of highly unpopular austerity and further heightening the country's internal tensions.

Whether governed under a center-right or socialist-left course, the Fifth Republic has been held back by the forces of tradition. The French distrust their government as well as impersonal large-scale industrial or commercial organizations. Many French peasants have failed to become efficient farmers, and still more have left the land altogether. Society is localized and divided by social status. The political parties on which the government relies are unstable and shifting, often centered more on personalities than on issues. Deeply patriotic, the French fear that becoming modern means becoming less French.

West Germany

In 1945, its cities in ruins, Germany had been defeated, occupied, and branded as a moral outcast for the horrors that Nazi rule had brought to Europe. Divided among four occupying powers, the German nation was politically extinct. The state of Prussia was declared dissolved; extensive eastern lands were handed to Poland and the Soviet Union; and some territory also was lost to France. The dream of national glory that had provided the chief momentum in German life for more than a century was over.

By 1949, two new and chastened Germanies had emerged. The Federal Republic of Germany, formed from the three Western zones of occupation, faced a hostile, Soviet-dominated German Democratic Republic in the East. The partition of Germany signified not only the destruction of Germany's traditional political identity, but also a personal tragedy for almost all Germans: families were split as the division interrupted communication between the two Germanies. The national trauma reached a peak in August 1961 when the East German government suddenly threw up a wall dividing the city of Berlin and for years tightly sealing off East from West Germany.

The cold war proved a boon to West Germany; feared and despised though they were, the West Germans were needed. Located next door to the Red Army, they were in a strategic position for the defense of Western Europe. Even more important, German industry and expertise were indispensable for the success of the Marshall Plan. Finally, a democratic West Germany would aid the course of Western European unity.

On this basis, the Federal Republic of Germany (far larger than its communist counterpart in the East and the most populous of all Western European countries) began to build a political identity of its own. The new West Germany was a demilitarized and decentralized federal state consisting of ten member states (plus West Berlin, which continued to exist under a special status). The executive power was held by the chancellor, who was checked by both a democratically elected parliament and the representatives of the member states.

Because of constitutional precautions against the proliferation of parties, only three emerged: two dominant parties—the Christian-Democratic Union (CDU) and the Socialist Party of Germany (SPD); and a minor one—the Free Democratic Party (FPD). The latter enjoyed the advantage of being indispensable to either of the major parties for a parliamentary majority. The CDU was the dominant party under the long chancellorship of Konrad Adenauer (1949–1963).

Adenauer was the founding hero of the Federal Republic of Germany. A vigorous old-timer (he was seventy-five when appointed Chancellor), known as a courageous anti-Nazi in the Hitler years, he represented the pro-Western, liberal-democratic tradition of the Weimar Republic. His aim was simple: restore respect for Germany in cooperation with the United States and the leading states of Western Europe. Never giving up hope for the reunification of Germany, he worked foremost for the integration of West Germany into the emerging Western European community. Yet while boycotting all relations with the communist German Democratic Republic, Ad-

enauer also promoted normal relations with Moscow. As a patriot, he rebuilt a cautious continuity with the German past, courageously shouldering responsibility for the crimes of the Nazi regime.

Adenauer's chancellorship proved popular, for it provided the stability and order required for West Germany's spectacular economic advance. Adenauer's economic policy was conducted by Minister of Finance Ludwig Erhard, who preferred private enterprise in a liberal market economy safeguarded from monopolies and made socially responsible through the extensive participation of labor unions. Given the opportunity, West Germans threw themselves into rebuilding their economy and their country, quickly creating a citadel of economic strength. Their exports grew famous throughout the world and their currency became the soundest in Western Europe. The whole world admired the West German "economic miracle."

Adenauer's policy paid off within a few years; West Germany regained its sovereignty. In 1955, a cautiously remilitarized West Germany became a member of NATO, and in 1957 the country was a founding member of the European Economic Community, of which it soon became the linchpin. Subsequent West German governments have generally followed the course set by Adenauer, completing Germany's rehabilitation when, in 1972, both West and East Germany were admitted to the United Nations.

After Adenauer's death, German voters gradually shifted from center-right to center-left. In 1966 the CDU entered into a "grand coalition" with the SPD, its arch-opponent. The coalition did not last, however, and in 1969 the SPD emerged as the leading party. Under Chancellors Willy Brandt (1969–1974) and his more pragmatic successor Helmut Schmidt (1974–1982), it ruled in coalition with the small FDP, guiding German politics with remarkable stability. Willy Brandt expanded Adenauer's foreign policy (as well as opportunities for the West German economy) through better cooperation with the German Democratic Republic and countries of the Soviet bloc. His initiative for the "opening toward the East" contributed to the temporary relaxation of tension—the brief era of "détente" in the early 1970s—in relations between the superpowers. During these years neither political extremists nor terrorists managed to shake public confidence in the constitution.

German minds, however, were hardly at peace. The Nazi era remained a moral embarrassment. After the war, the Nuremberg trials of the major war criminals had been followed by de-Nazification under West German courts. Members of Nazi elite organizations were barred from public office and higher education. Many people guilty of atrocities were prosecuted; others went into hiding in Germany or abroad; Jews themselves tracked down some notable fugitives, like Adolf Eichmann, and brought them to justice (Eichmann was tried in Jerusalem in 1961). The search and the trials still continue, the West German Parliament having consistently refused to enact a statute of limitations on crimes committed under the Nazis. In an effort at restitution, the goverment also has paid damages to Israel and to survivors among Nazi victims and their kin.

Most older Germans tried to forget the past and ask no hard questions. Even young people were undecided, caught between the democratic values introduced after the war and the national heritage; the schools often sidetracked discussion. Since the 1960s, however, the major aspects of Nazi rule have been openly aired; Nazi anti-Semitism has even been dramatized by the showing on German television of an American program called *Holocaust*.

While older Germans are still troubled by the Nazi years, the generation now growing up feels less burdened by the catastrophes of a rapidly receding past. Its concern is over the physical environment, threatened by industrial pollution and nuclear power, as well as by war. Loosely organized in a party called "the Greens," young people express a romantic alienation from contemporary society and politics. All the same, they have carried their agitation into parliamentary elections,

at the expense largely of the Social Democrats, a party increasingly splintered under the impact of economic recession. The young people have also frightened their uneasy elders, who in the face of recession and rising hostility to the Soviet Union, have turned more conservative. In 1982 Helmut Schmidt was replaced by Helmut Kohl, the leader of the CDU, who has governed with the help of the indispensable FDP and with public support, as demonstrated by his strong victory in the 1983 election.

Even under a right-center government Germans are uneasy, confronted with major challenges testing the unity of the country. On the left, "the Greens," because of their concern for the environment, have gained ground. Repudiating the organizational discipline of a political party, thereby limiting their effectiveness, they nevertheless have strong support among the young generation worried about the future. The economy, although strong, must adjust to greater worldwide competitiveness; there will be continued unemployment and austerity and bitter controversy over the rapid decay of the country's forests. Furthermore, the country has become more dependent on OPEC, the European Economic Community, the United States, and the world economy at large. Although caught in the rising hostility between the United States and the Soviet Union, it is determined, even under a conservative government, to advance the unity of West and East Germany and to maintain its economic ties to the members of the Soviet bloc.

Great Britain

In 1945 Britain was a member of the victorious alliance. It had escaped foreign occupation and suffered less physical damage than any other European belligerent; its political institutions were intact, its prestige and democratic convictions riding high. Yet after this moment of glory it passed through a steady decline, requiring of its people a drastic reassessment of their place in the world, without the happy ending of an economic boom.

World War II compounded Britain's long-standing economic woes, leaving the country impoverished and highly vulnerable in its dependence on imported food and raw materials. The British Empire was gradually and peaceably dismantled. Unlike the French, the English fought no last-ditch wars for retaining colonial control. British sea power waned, replaced by the American navy and air force. Confronted with the choice between maintaining a global military presence and building a welfare state at home, the British people clearly preferred the latter. Although still enjoying a special relationship with the United States, the British were thrown back on themselves and their neighbors in continental Europe. Among themselves they quarreled over autonomy for Scotland and Wales. In the late 1960s the ever-simmering conflict in Northern Ireland between Protestants and the large Catholic minority broke into unending and often vicious violence.

In their association with Western Europe, the British also fared poorly. Their first application for membership to the EEC, made in 1961, was vetoed by De Gaulle; they were not admitted until twelve years later in 1973. But it soon became apparent that Britain not only constituted an economic liability rather than an asset to the other members, it also gained no immediate benefit for itself. Poor, insular, and hesitant about merging its fortune with Western Europe, the United Kingdom still glories in the traditions of empire, although by current standards of power and productivity it has become a second-rate state.

Under these circumstances, successive British governments have done well in holding the ship of state together. A Labour government under Clement Attlee (1883–1967), elected immediately after the war, carried out the wartime promises of increased social services. Health care for the British people, traditionally deficient by Western European standards, was particularly improved. For better control over the national economy, the Labour government also nationalized the Bank of England, public transport, and the coal mines; eventually even the iron and steel industries came under government ownership.

The Labour government, which lost the 1951 election largely because it seemed to have prolonged the postwar austerity unnecessarily, was succeeded by the Conservatives. With Winston Churchill as prime minister, they rode the postwar tide of prosperity. In 1959, under Harold Macmillan, the Conservatives successfully campaigned for re-election under the slogan "You've never had it so good." They favored private enterprise but continued the extension of the welfare state, most notably by an ambitious public construction program that greatly improved British housing.

Economic setbacks, scandal, failure in foreign policy, and indifferent leadership among the Conservatives brought the Labour party back into power from 1964 to 1970; their promise was to boost the ailing economy. That, however, proved an impossible task. British industry had not modernized itself as rapidly as its chief competitors. It was hampered by poor management and frequent strikes, many of them caused by disputes among rival labor unions. British exports were lagging while imports soared; the value of the pound continued to decline. Costly imports and pressures for higher wages and welfare benefits contributed to high inflation.

Behind the economic ills lay a political problem: how to restrain the demands of British labor for a higher income and how to counter the strikes by which the workers backed up their demands. On this ground, the Labour party was weak, since it depended on worker support. Under the strain its leader, Harold Wilson, could hardly keep peace between the pragmatic majority and the socialist left wing. Yet when the Conservatives returned to power in 1970, they were equally helpless to restrain the unions. In 1974 Prime Minister Edward Heath called a general election over the question: Who rules Britain, the government or the unions? The voters preferred the Labour party, by a small margin. Reversing themselves in 1979, the voters elected a Conservative government under

Mahatma Gandhi with Lord and Lady Mountbatten, 1947. For over two decades, Gandhi had been India's spiritual and political guide toward independence, gained in 1947. He saw his nation finally become autonomous after more than a century of British rule—Lord Mountbatten was the last viceroy and first governor general of India. (*The Photo Source*)

Margaret Thatcher, the first British woman prime minister.

"Maggie" Thatcher, appealing to traditional virtues, soon proved herself an "Iron Lady." A vigorous partisan of private enterprise, she favored the return of nationalized industries to private hands. Despite continued high unemployment she fought inflation with rigorous austerity (although she never tried to eliminate unemployment benefits and other essentials of the welfare state); she prefers to let adversity bestir British employers and workers into efficiency and innovation. She also electrified the raw nerve of patriotism, long dulled by the decline of imperial fortune, when British forces drove an Argentine occupying force out of the distant Falkland Islands, one of Britain's remaining possessions. Against Thatcher's popularity the opposition has been powerless. The Labour party, torn by factionalism and deserted by many workers, is in decline. Many of its former supporters have moved toward the old Liberal party allied with a new Social Democratic party. However, this loose coalition has yet to prove itself a viable political force.

Beset by adversity, the British people face many doubts. For now they seem content to live with their membership in the European Economic Community, their uncertain place in the competitive global economy, and their dependence on the United States in the conflict between the superpowers.

Italy

A country half the size of France yet with a population larger by several million, Italy has

Prime Minister Margaret Thatcher. Elected in 1979, Margaret Thatcher became Britain's first woman prime minister. Mrs. Thatcher appeals to traditional virtues and stirs patriotism; she encourages the English to meet challenges and overcome them. Under her leadership, private enterprise has been favored over the welfare state. (*Philippe Achache/Gamma/Liaison*)

always occupied an ambiguous position in Europe. It has been respected, even revered, for its illustrious Roman past. It has also been condemned or even ridiculed for its backwardness in modern times, for its shaky or dubious liberal democracy, for its penchant for living beyond its means, and for its me-too desire for power culminating in Mussolini's theatrical bid for empire. The victory of the Anglo-American countries allied with the Soviet Union had a sobering effect. Fascism was refuted, its chief henchman punished. In 1946 even the monarchy, discredited by its subservience to Mussolini, was rejected. Italy was humbled and ravaged by war.

After the war, Italy was a democratic republic that even the communists were pledged to uphold. The constitution, approved in 1947, resembled that of the French Fourth Republic, which meant that Italy would suffer from weak and unstable government. The average span of Italian cabinets to the present has been less than a year.

Hopeful for the future, the new republic could not escape the past. Italy has always been divided by internal rifts, the chief of which is the contrast between north and south, each worlds apart from the other. A lively localism impeded national unity; so did an anarchical individualism. Far from forming an organic whole, the state and the individual were in continuous tension and conflict. The political parties, scattered over a wide spectrum of opinion from communism to neofascism, likewise enjoyed little internal cohesion, except for the communists. The socialists were ceaselessly in agitation among themselves, without, however, losing their following. The Christian Democrats were the leading party, closely associated with the Catholic church. Despite continuing corruption they have contributed continuity to Italian politics, supplying (until 1983) the prime ministers and forming and reforming coalitions with lesser parties. From 1976 to 1978 they even enjoyed the tacit support of the communists. But the Christian Democrats were only a loose alliance of Catholics split into right, center, and left; in 1983 their support shrank to about a third of the popular vote. As a result, a socialist (Bettino Craxi) became the prime minister, heading an unsteady coalition. The parties as well as the national temperament have accentuated the weakness of the constitution.

Spurred by the new postwar opportunities, Italian enterprise produced a striking economic advance. Its rate of growth, culminating in the years 1958–1962, propelled it into the ranks of the ten leading industrial nations of the world. Private corporations (like Fiat) and industries under large government holding companies led the way in introducing an efficiency that unfortunately had no parallel in the civil service or the government. The boom was aided by cheap and abundant labor, by high profits reinvested in innovation, and by the timely discovery of natural gas and some oil in the Po Valley. As a result, personal incomes, particularly in northern Italy, came to resemble those of the richer European countries. Italy seemed to have caught up.

The sudden spurt of industrialization inevitably aggravated the traditional weaknesses in Italian society. The economic advance remained incomplete, merely superimposing a layer of progressive prosperity on a backward and divided country. In their eagerness to catch up, most Italians preferred to live well for the moment rather than save for the future. The contradiction led to a deterioration in Italy's position in the European Economic Community and to widespread apathy in the face of mounting corruption in the government and terrorist violence. Terrorists (not counting the criminal elements) have come from the extremes at both ends of the political spectrum. The neo-fascists, however, have been less active than the left-wing Red Brigades. Trying to create conditions favoring the overthrow of the ineffectual democratic constitution, the terrorists have resorted to bombings, kidnapings, maimings, and political murders, including that in 1978 of the much-respected Aldo Moro, leader of the Christian Democratic party.

What form of government can provide better leadership? Some have suggested a presidential republic like De Gaulle's. A "historic compromise" between the communists and the Christian Democrats was once advocated by Enrico Berlinguer, the secretary of the Italian Communist party and a leading Eurocommunist. A neo-fascist regime supported by the army is the solution proposed by some. Given the strong democratic pull exerted by the European Economic Community and NATO, extreme solutions are unlikely. Yet the question remains whether the Italians can undertake the personal sacrifices and self-discipline necessary to build a vigorous ad-

ministration and an economy capable of mastering the uncertainties of the future.

Western Europe and the World

Western Europe now is a vital but complex and divided center in a polycentric interdependent world. It struggles, however half-heartedly, to achieve greater economic and political cohesion, aware that only unity can enhance its role in world affairs. It is knitted into the world economy separately, by countries, and jointly through the Economic Community, and it participates in all agencies of the United Nations. Considered fully developed, it plays a significant part in assisting the developing countries. It also furnishes the headquarters for the Organization for Economic Cooperation and Development (OECD), which serves the most highly industrialized countries in Europe, North America, and the Far East. In the struggle between the superpowers it tries to follow a middle course; unwilling (or unable) to pay for its own defense, it remains dependent on the United States. It shares with its trans-Atlantic ally a deep fear of the Soviet Union; it cautiously favors greater independence for the Soviet satellites—anxious, for its own prosperity, to maintain good economic relations with the entire Soviet bloc. Europeans know there is nothing to gain in military confrontation, of which they would be the first victims. They distrust American policy that escalates hostility; they—and the West Germans foremost—are divided over stationing American nuclear weapons on the Continent. In the United States, Western Europe appears to be a troublesome ally (in economic affairs as well), while from the Western European perspective, the United States seems unduly self-centered and excessively confident in military power. As Europeans know from the effect of two world wars, war brings questionable results even with conventional weapons. The next war, they expect, will be fought with nuclear weapons.

Notes

1. Quoted in Walter Laqueur, *Europe Since Hitler* (Baltimore: Penguin Books, 1970), p. 118.

2. Quoted in Roger Morton, *West European Politics Since 1945* (London: P. T. Botsford, 1972), p. 91.

3. Preamble to Treaty of Rome, 1958, in ibid., pp. 132–133.

Suggested Reading

Barzini, Luigi, *The Italians* (1977). A superb, far-ranging introduction to contemporary Italy.

Becker, Jillian, *Hitler's Children: The Story of the Baader-Meinhof Terrorist Gang* (1977). Good insights into the terrorist state of mind.

Böll, Heinrich, *Group Portrait with Lady* (1973). The foremost West German novelist looks back at the last years of the Nazi regime.

Craig, Gordon, *The Germans* (1982). Key aspects of postwar 1945 Germany in historical perspective.

De Gaulle, Charles, *Memoirs of Hope, Renewal and Endeavor* (1971). An autobiographical account of his work after 1958, reflecting the grandeur of the man.

Dornberg, John, *The New Germans, Thirty Years After* (1975). A German-born American journalist looks at the many faces of contemporary Germany.

Periodicals providing current analyses of European developments. *Europe, Magazine of the European Community* (Washington, D.C.); *Current History* (Philadelphia), and *Foreign Affairs* (New York).

Sampson, Anthony, *The Changing Anatomy of Britain* (1982). A perceptive and well-informed British journalist analyzes contemporary Britain; an excellent survey.

Servan-Schreiber, Jean-Jacques, *The American Challenge* (1969). A famous treatise on European reaction to American influence.

Wiskeman, Elizabeth, *Italy since 1945* (1971). A brief survey by an English specialist on Italian history.

Wylie, Lawrence, *Village in the Vaucluse* (1974). A well-written glimpse of French peasant life through the eyes of an American anthropologist.

Yergin, Daniel, *The Shattered Peace* (1977). The most balanced and readable of the analyses of the cold war.

Review Questions

1. How did the cold war affect the reorganization of Europe from 1945 to 1958?

2. Trace the evolution of the European Economic Community. What information about its current activities do you find in the current news?

3. Which of the major peoples of Western Europe faced the greatest adjustments after World War II? What reasons do you give for your choice?

4. France and Italy are often compared because of their common Latin heritage. Do you see any similarities in their histories after 1945?

5. What have been the major problems of government in Great Britain since 1945? What has been the recent news about Britain?

6. How, after the partition of Germany in 1945, did West Germany rise to its present pre-eminence in the European Community and in world affairs?

7. How do you account for the rise of terrorism in postwar Europe? What about European terrorists in the recent news?

8. What have been the major aspects of Western Europe's relations with the United States since 1945? What is the current state of American relations with the countries of Western Europe?

9. The possibility of the collapse of NATO has been raised. The reasons for this include the stationing of American missiles in Europe, U.S. policy in Central America, and excessive American hostility to the Soviet Union. What do you think about European distrust of American policy? What do you think American policy should be?

36

Eastern Europe Since 1945:
Extension of Soviet Power

*F*our trends dominated the evolution of the Soviet Union after 1945: the continuing increase in Soviet military power matched by caution in foreign policy; the gradual relaxation of the extreme measures of national mobilization designed by Stalin; the marked improvement in the material condition of the people; and the routinization of party rule—government action became more predictable. With these trends the Soviet Union further adapted to essential aspects of the Western style of achievement.

Until Stalin's death in 1953, Stalinism grew more burdensome and rigid. Yet it laid the groundwork for the production of atomic weapons and space rockets. Stalinism also consolidated communist rule in the postwar period within the Soviet Union and among the countries conquered by the Red Army. Stalin's successors continued to build up Soviet power, achieving parity with the United States in nuclear weapons and space exploration by the mid-1970s. They also improved the material well-being of their peoples; Soviet Russia shared in the worldwide economic upswing of the postwar decades.

Feeling more secure, the Soviet rulers relaxed the extreme controls of the Stalin era without endangering the pre-eminence of the Communist party or weakening the country's unity. They changed the form of government from the "dictatorship of the proletariat" to "the state of all the people," sponsoring controlled public participation in running the country. They also eased their hold over their Eastern European satellites, allowing them a higher standard of living than that of the Soviet people without reconciling them to Soviet domination. Poland, the largest of the satellite countries, proved particularly troublesome.

Contrary to expectations abroad, the problem of succession in the Communist dictatorship was handled smoothly. Within two years of Stalin's death, Nikita Khrushchev peacefully emerged as leader, boldly revealing the excesses of Stalinism but erratic in remedying them. Quietly retiring him in 1964, his more practical successors—among whom Leonid Brezhnev gradually rose to pre-eminence—introduced a sense of orderliness and routine that the country had lacked since 1914. In the mid-seventies the Soviet Union claimed a role in world affairs unprecedented in Russian history. After Brezhnev's death in 1982, Yurii Andropov quickly took command. Aging himself, he soon fell victim to a prolonged illness and died early in 1984. In another smooth and rapid transition, Konstantin Chernenko came to power. He faced a host of unresolved problems left him by his enfeebled predecessors; he and his country face an uncertain future.

Stalin's Last Years

In Soviet experience, World War II was but another cruel landmark in the long succession of wars, revolutions, and crises that had started in 1914; nothing basically changed even after its end. The liberation from terror and dictatorship, which many soldiers had hoped for as a reward for their heroism, never occurred. Stalin viewed the postwar scene in the light of his life's lessons. He had helped Lenin seize power and fight the cruel civil war in fear and hatred of the capitalist world. As Lenin's successor, he had demanded unprecedentedly brutal efforts from his people to strengthen Soviet Russia against its enemies. The epic struggle against the Nazi invaders had further hardened the man of steel. Sixty-six years old in 1945, corrupted by unlimited power and unrestrained adulation, Stalin displayed in his last years an unrelenting ruthlessness and a suspiciousness raised to the pitch of paranoia.

Stalin's assessment of Soviet Russia's condition at the end of the war was consistent with his previous thinking. He saw no ground for relaxing control. The country still had immense problems: the large anti-Soviet populations in Eastern Europe; the lack of atomic weapons; the traditional poverty and

additional destruction wrought by the war; the political unreliability of returning soldiers and prisoners of war; and the overwhelming strength of the United States. Wherever he looked, Stalin saw cause for concern. The government, the party, communist ideology, the economy—all were in disarray. The generals were riding high, threatening his own supremacy and that of the party. Ideological control had slackened during the war. The exhausted people were in danger of falling into a postwar slump, yearning for greater freedom in their personal lives. Tired and hungry as they were, how could they be goaded to work for the speedy reconstruction of their country? How could the party be reinvigorated? Communist parties in other lands not directly under his thumb were to be trusted even less. Against these threats, Stalin had to exercise full Bolshevik vigilance. His indomitable ambition, undiminished by age, was to build up Soviet power in his lifetime, whatever the human cost. More Five-Year Plans, more terror were needed.

On this familiar note the Soviet Union slid from war into peace, staggering through the hardships and hunger of the war's aftermath, mourning its dead soldiers, desperately short of men. As before, the peasants were squeezed to the utmost to furnish the state with food without receiving more than the barest minimum in return. The urban-industrial population fared slightly better. With planning, much selfless hard work, manpower released from the army, and resources requisitioned from all occupied territories, industrial production was back to prewar levels within three years—no mean achievement.

With the return to Five-Year Plans came a deliberate tightening of ideological control. The party boss of Leningrad, Andrei Zhdanov (1896–1948), lashed out against well-known literary figures for their "escapist, unorthodox, and un-Soviet" thinking. His target was any form of Western influence and personal withdrawal from the tasks set by the party. Thus thousands of returning soldiers and prisoners of war, who had seen too much in the West, were sent to forced-labor camps; the Soviet intelligentsia was again terrorized into compliance with the party line.

A shrill, dogmatic superpatriotism became mandatory for all Soviet citizens. This patriotism extolled Russia's achievements past and present over those of the West. Even scientists had to submit, at a fearful cost to research (except in nuclear physics). Zhdanov singled out the most famous composers, Dmitri Shostakovich and Sergei Prokofiev, whom he accused of "bourgeois formalism," a derogatory term for refined artistic standards. *Zhdanovism*, as the anti-intellectual campaign was called, was accompanied by renewed political terror, again centered on Leningrad. In 1948 the chief leaders of the heroic struggle against the Nazi siege were arrested and shot.

The cold war drove Stalin to further exertions, some of them ill-considered. Eastern Europe had to be brought under a tight rein. In 1948 he set an example by overthrowing the moderately procommunist democracy of Czechoslovakia and instituting cruel purges. In the same year he tried to oust Marshal Tito of Yugoslavia, but he misjudged Tito's determination. Tito stayed in power and proclaimed a rival communist creed, thus breaking the unity of world communism under Soviet leadership. In 1949 Stalin had to accept, although he did not welcome it, the victory of the Chinese communists. The "fraternal" relations between the Russian and Chinese communist parties were decidedly cool. Mao's China diminished rather than enhanced Stalin's power and was destined to establish a third variant of communist ideology. In 1950 the North Korean communists, possibly with Stalin's approval, attacked South Korea, which further intensified the cold war.

In his last years Stalin withdrew into virtual isolation, surrounded by a few fawning and fearful subordinates, and his sickly suspicion worsened. Before he died, he "recognized" a plot among the doctors who treated him and personally issued orders for their torture (which killed one of them). When on March 5, 1953, the failing dictator died of a stroke, his advisers sighed with relief, but many

people wept: to them Stalin was the godlike leader and savior of the nation.

One of the most remarkable people of the twentieth century, Stalin was a towering figure in the Russian mold of Ivan the Terrible or Peter the Great. Like them, he had stirred popular imagination at the deepest layers of human consciousness. For those who had trembled for their lives in his shadow his death was a cosmic event. The human costs of his labor had been immense, but of his achievements in raising Soviet power there can be no doubt. By 1949, sooner than expected, Soviet Russia possessed the atomic bomb. By 1953, at the same time as the United States, it had the hydrogen bomb as well. Stalin also helped lay the foundation for *Sputnik I* (see page 834), the first artificial satellite to orbit the earth.

More important perhaps, Stalin also bequeathed to his successors a tamed and even cowed population, more malleable and cooperative than any previous generation. Stalin himself was the last of the self-willed, self-centered revolutionaries. His successors were masterful organization men ruling over obedient and hard-driven subjects; the party could now count on a growing number of people with a personal stake in the regime and its institutions.

The Khrushchev Years

The chief question after Stalin's death was: who would succeed him and in what manner? The succession struggles of the 1920s and their bloody aftermath in the terror purges were still on everybody's mind. How would the issues be settled this time? Would the new leadership be able to cope with Russia's difficult problems? Above all, how were the new leaders to deal with Stalin, whose body was now resting next to Lenin's in the mausoleum on Red Square?

The most hated among Stalin's potential heirs was Lavrenti Beria, the head of the secret police and the vast empire of forced labor camps. In December 1953 he was suddenly executed, together with his chief henchmen, for having been a "foreign spy." These cynical accusations and violent deaths were the last gasp of Stalinism; ever since, the rivals for supreme leadership have died of natural causes.

Gradually leadership was assumed by a team headed by Nikita Khrushchev (1894–1971). Although a long-time associate of Stalin, he breathed fresh air into Soviet life. Khrushchev was the driving force behind the "thaw" that emptied the forced-labor camps and allowed the return to their native regions of most nationalities that had been forcibly resettled during the war. Khrushchev also relaxed censorship, although he repressed religion, which during and after the war had enjoyed a limited freedom. And Khrushchev dared to attack Stalin himself.

After 1953, Stalin had been cautiously downgraded and even denounced under the cover of charges against "the cult of personality." In a speech at the Twentieth Party Congress in February 1956, Khrushchev brought the issue to a sudden head. His audience gasped with horror as he recited the facts: "Of the 139 members and candidates of the Party Central Committee who were elected at the 17th congress, 98 persons, i.e., 70%, were arrested . . . and shot. . . ." In this vein, Khrushchev cited example after example of Stalin's terror, summing up with the charge that "the accusations were wild, absurd, and contrary to common sense" and the tortures used to extract confessions "barbaric, cruel, and inhuman." He also enumerated Stalin's mistakes, as for instance in not sufficiently preparing for Hitler's attack in 1941. Throughout, he revealed, Stalin had "discarded the Leninist methods of convincing and educating" and "abandoned the method of ideological struggle for that of administrative violence, mass repression, and terror. . . ."[1] Three years after Stalin's death these were potent and unsettling revelations; yet they were needed. They acknowledged and rejected the excesses of Stalinism. In so doing, they lifted from Soviet politics—and from people's consciences—an intolerable

burden of crime and complicity, restoring a modicum of honesty and humaneness.

Khrushchev's revelations created a profound stir around the world and promoted defection from communist ranks everywhere. Among the Soviet satellite countries, Poland in 1956 was on the brink of rebellion; a workers' uprising forced a change of leadership. In Hungary in 1956 the entire communist regime was overthrown before the Red Army reoccupied the country. Only Mao objected to the downgrading of Stalinism.

After the stormy events of 1956 Khrushchev's standing temporarily declined; in June 1957 his opponents in the politburo even forced a showdown. Yet only a year later he had reached the height of his power and occupied, as Stalin had, the leading posts in both the party and the state administration.

Personable and approachable, ever admonishing officials high and low and pushing his rapidly changing projects, Khrushchev talked to all and sundry in a folksy, unceremonious manner that occasionally bordered on bad taste. He was excitable and carried away by visions of Soviet superiority, particularly after the launching of *Sputnik I* in early October 1957. *Sputnik I*—meaning "fellow traveler" (of the Earth)—opened the space age and boosted Khrushchev's pride beyond bounds. In 1957 he boasted to visiting Americans, "We will bury you," meaning that the Soviet Union would soon outproduce the United States in all essentials of life and would take America's place as the model for the world.

Eager to prod his country toward a higher level in Marxist-Leninist ideology, Khrushchev presented a new party program and impatiently pressed for reforms in industry, agriculture, and party organization. An idealist of sorts, he called for wider public participation in the administration of the country, extending freedom of public discussion and encouraging individual initiative. Khrushchev also allowed the publication of Aleksandr Solzhenitsyn's short novel, *One Day in the Life of Ivan Denisovich,* which offered a first public glimpse into life at a forced-labor camp.

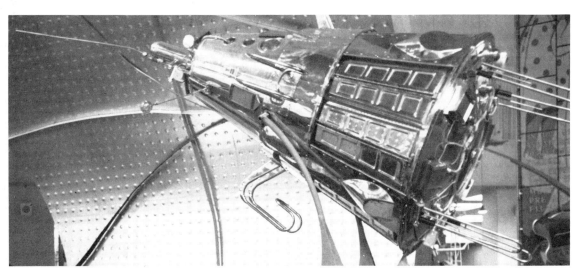

Sputnik. In early October 1957, the Soviet Union launched the world's first artificial satellite into space. It was the high point of Khrushchev's visions, which led him to boast to Americans, "We will bury you." He saw the U.S.S.R. as a model for the world in all industrial and scientific production. With Sputnik's success, the space race between the superpowers began. (*UPI/Bettmann Archive*)

He permitted the public showing of abstract art. He tried to curb the privileges of the well-entrenched upper layers of bureaucrats and went so far as to declare that the dictatorship of the proletariat had ended, to be replaced by "the state of all the people." In 1961 he moved Stalin from Lenin's tomb to a less distinguished spot on the Kremlin wall. However, the people responded to Khrushchev's programs with increased restlessness.

In foreign policy, Khrushchev professed to promote peace, although he also made some provocative moves by threatening Western access to West Berlin and placing missiles in Cuba; American pressure forced him to withdraw in both cases. Not wishing to help communist China build atomic weapons, he withdrew, after mutual recrimination, all Soviet advisers in 1960, causing a break between two communist nations. Mao then charged him with "revisionism" as well as imperialism.

In whatever he undertook, Khrushchev could not escape his Stalinist training; arbitrariness and impetuosity counteracted his good intentions. His ceaseless reorganizations and impatient manner antagonized wide sections of state and party administration. In October 1964, while he was on vacation, his comrades on the politburo unceremoniously ousted him for "ill health" or, as they later added, his "hare-brained schemes." He was retired and allowed to live out his years in peace, leaving to his successors the task of finding a steadier middle course between Stalinist tradition and creative innovation.

Khrushchev's years in power marked basic changes in Soviet and even in Russian history. The Soviet regime proved that it could settle the succession from one leader to another in a peaceful manner, without the benefit of written constitutional procedure. Infinitely more important, Soviet Russia acquired protection from foreign attack as never before in Russian history.

The Brezhnev Years

Khrushchev was succeeded, as was Stalin, by a group of leaders acting in common:

Nikolai V. Podgorny (1903–1977), the official president of the Soviet Union (the least significant office); Aleksei Kosygin (1904–1980) as prime minister heading the state organization; and Leonid Brezhnev (1906–1982) directing the party. While they reversed some of Khrushchev's hasty reforms, they undertook no notable changes of policy or personnel. Raised within the party and associated with the key industries of space and defense, the new leaders were pragmatic bureaucrats—cautious, aware of the need for smooth cooperation among the many interlacing administrative agencies of the party and the government, and mellowed by age and experience.

Among these old men, Leonid Brezhnev gradually rose to the fore. He was a versatile administrator who with prodigious energy and dedication had advanced to key responsibilities under Stalin and Khrushchev. Frequently sick after 1975, he eventually held the top positions in the party and the government, like Stalin and Khrushchev before him. Under his leadership the government of the U.S.S.R. turned from a personal dictatorship into an oligarchy—the collective rule of a privileged minority. Brezhnev's style stressed reasoned agreement rather than command; he respected security of office, status, and autonomy among the rank and file. Soviet officials breathed more easily, feeling grateful toward their boss. Soviet society grew less restless—and more corrupt, finding unofficial ways to make the Soviet system more humane.

Domestic Policies

In internal affairs the long-range trend was toward cautiously reducing traditional restrictions; by the mid-1970s, for instance, Soviet young people were allowed access to Western styles of music and dress. More issues of state policy were opened to public debate and more latitude granted to artistic expression. The lifeless stereotypes of socialist realism gave way to more candid treatment of human reality and even of tragedy; art moved closer to actual experience, although still in a running battle with censorship. Interest in religion revived. More significantly, Russian nationalism, anti-Western and even anti-Marxist, reappeared from the pre-Soviet past. In part it responded to the marked increase in the non-Russian population of the Soviet Union; in part it replaced Marxist-Leninist ideology, which as one communist admitted, had turned into "stale bread." Even the party seemed sympathetic to the new nationalism.

Dissent, furthermore, was treated with greater circumspection; it seemed less dangerous because the country was no longer poor and weak. Protest literature, ranging from anti-regime Leninism to fascist racism, received wide attention even abroad. Born of the "thaw" under Khrushchev, the protest enlisted a tiny, splintered, but heroic nucleus of the literary, artistic, and scientific elite; some people called it *the democratic movement.* Dissenters distributed a variety of protest writings, known by their mode of production as *samizdat* (self-published) and sometimes of high artistic or scholarly quality.

Some dissenters, including Andrei Sakharov, who helped to develop the Soviet H-bomb, were treated leniently, partly because of the attention their cases received abroad and partly because of the moral authority they enjoyed at home. The most adamant critics, like Aleksandr Solzhenitsyn or Andrei Amalrik, were expelled (or allowed to emigrate), rather than shot or worked to death. Other critics, who stayed, were declared insane and confined in mental hospitals, following a practice begun under Nicholas I. The secret police (KGB) remained as powerful as ever, its head a member of the politburo. It practiced greater discretion and less open terror, closely watching the trends of Soviet opinion and the impact of external hostility, ever ready to resume overt repression. Forced labor camps still existed. While the regime tolerated a greater diversity of opinion, it continued to effectively suppress anti-Soviet dissent.

Under Brezhnev, the life of the Soviet elite became more abundant and secure; Soviet power also was more visible and respected in the world. Technicians, scientists, and managers, the country's most crucial asset, felt committed out of self-interest to order and continuity. Imperial Russia had rendered few if any services to the majority of its subjects. In contrast, Soviet Russia had become a full-fledged welfare state. While living conditions did not match those of Western Europe, unemployment was, and remains, rare. Job security became both a boon to the population and a source of gross economic inefficiency.

The party under Brezhnev stepped up its policy of providing more consumer goods, falling in with the worldwide trend toward affluence. Soviet citizens now could obtain household appliances and television sets. Housing improved. The greatest concession to consumerism was the production of automobiles for private use, at least among the privileged, although services and road facilities remained limited. Today, Soviet consumers still do not compare with their Western European contemporaries, but they know that their standard of living has risen.

The party under Brezhnev also continued to devote much attention to agriculture, channeling heavy investments into fertilizers, farm machinery, and farm welfare, yet it could not raise output enough to achieve self-sufficiency. Soviet agriculture was, and remains, the least productive sector of the economy. The motivation of collective farmers continues to be poor. Private plots, which often produce a good income, are allowed to them on their collective farms, and they still prefer raising their own produce to working in the collective work brigades. The young people drift to the cities, which offer more amenities. Bad harvests through the 1970s forced the government to import large quantities of grain (mostly from the United States), thereby increasing Soviet dependence on capitalist countries.

Brezhnev continued to give top priority to heavy industry and capital construction. Roads, bridges, railways, pipelines for gas and oil, mines and oilwells, steel mills and power plants are necessary to give the huge country an adequate infrastructure. The U.S.S.R. forged ahead of the smaller and better-equipped United States in the production of iron, steel, coal, and cement; it took advantage of its ample reserves of fossil fuels. The center of industrial activity began to shift gradually eastward, into western Siberia, with careful planning of newly integrated industrial regions. Soviet planners continued to pay special attention to the defense and space industries, both crucial to the country's prestige in the world.

Apart from a small sector limited to farm products and to a thriving black market (or "underground capitalism"), all economic activity remained subject to vigorous central planning. Planning grew to an unimagined complexity that belies the claim of rational control. Regulations designed to increase output reduced it instead. Secure in their jobs, workers lacked incentives. Today, the huge regimented economy continues to suffer from a counterproductive inflexibility. Soviet planners have tried to keep up with the demands made on them by introducing new management procedures, better computer systems, and tighter techniques of control. But they have been unable to overcome the inherent conservatism of huge, interdependent bureaucracies. Inventors have been known to land in jail rather than earn promotions—innovation upsets too many routines.

Yet, although Brezhnev is gone, the call for planning never ceases. Facing a growing labor shortage and rising costs of production, Soviet leaders, like industrialists elsewhere, must pay closer attention to making more with less. They can look back with pride over the fast growth of their economy in the recent past. By comparison with the United States, though, the Soviet Union is still poor. In Brezhnev's declining years the economy stagnated. Major changes are needed for giving it a new vigor.

In their efforts to increase productivity, Soviet leaders in the Brezhnev era did not hesitate to establish closer economic ties with capitalist countries around the world. The

Soviet Union, like every other nation, lives in an age of global interdependence.

Foreign Policy

In the interdependent world, Soviet foreign policy under Brezhnev was shaped by the need for domestic consolidation and by a cautious self-assurance derived from economic growth and military might. While avoiding dangerous confrontations, the Soviet Union wanted to make its presence felt around the world, as the United States was doing. Its leaders advocated *détente* (the diplomatic term for the relaxation of tensions) because it promised the best results for their aims.

One result of détente was the Strategic Arms Limitation Treaty with the United States signed in 1972, which was to limit the mutual buildup of nuclear weapons. Of greater benefit were the Helsinki Agreements on Security and Cooperation, signed in 1975, in which the NATO powers recognized the boundaries established in 1945. In return, the governments of the Soviet bloc promised to relax internal controls for the sake of better cultural relations with the West; the promise included easier emigration from the U.S.S.R. for Jews. Because of the danger to their regimes resulting from greater contact with the West, however, the governments of the Soviet bloc have not lived up to the expectations aroused among the noncommunist nations that signed the Helsinki Agreement.

Despite these gains, and despite continuing Strategic Arms Limitation Talks leading to SALT II, détente did not add to Soviet security. Soviet leaders still feared the awesome power of the United States. They were also afraid of communist China, a potential ally of the United States and a troublemaker in communist ranks. The pressure of the Chinese population on their eastern territories made the Soviets feel vulnerable in East Asia.

They also felt vulnerable in central Asia. In 1979, a crisis broke out in neighboring Afghanistan. In the past the Soviet Union, like the United States, had assisted in the modernization of that country, which was then governed by a mildly pro-Soviet regime. However, that regime collapsed in an anti-modern revolt by Islamic tribesmen echoing the one that had recently toppled the Shah in neighboring Iran. Brezhnev decided that he could not risk letting a hostile Afghan regime take power that might stir unrest among the Soviet Union's own Islamic minorities. In late 1979 the Soviet army occupied the key centers of the country, while the tribesmen, now fighting as guerrillas, struck back. Viewed as another case of communist expansionism, the Soviet move drew worldwide criticism contributing to the revival of cold war hostility and the escalation of the arms race. SALT II was never ratified by the U.S. Senate. Meanwhile the Afghan war continued inconclusively.

In the wider world, Soviet Russia pressed its self-appointed role as leader of all anti-imperialist forces—with uncertain results. After initial successes in the mideast, for example, the Soviets saw their influence in the area drastically decline again. Soviet Russia remains the main source of support, directly or indirectly through its satellites (especially Cuba), for indigenous challengers of white supremacy in southern Africa. But the long-range effects are uncertain, for Africans are not interested in exchanging Western for Soviet domination. Soviet aid to developing countries is decidedly meager, the bulk going to countries nearest the U.S.S.R., like India, and the rest to others, Cuba foremost, which loudly subscribe to Marxist ideology. In no case, except possibly for Cuba, has Soviet economic or military assistance created a dependable ally anywhere in the world. International communism, once firmly under Kremlin control, has been fragmented by nationalism and has lost its compelling ideological force. It remains, however, the most effective ally for all peoples or governments resisting American influence or power. Local conflicts, whether in Central America or the Middle East, are thus drawn into the Super Power confrontation.

Although the Soviet Union has steadily in-

Afghan Resistance Fighter in Panjshir, 1983. In 1979 an anti-modern revolt by Islamic tribesmen topped a pro-Soviet regime in Afghanistan. To support the former regime, the Soviet army moved in. The tribes- men adopted guerrilla tactics to fight the invaders and their modern weapons. The cold war revived, and there was an escalation of the arms race. (*Jean-Patrick Voudenay/Gamma*)

creased its naval presence on the high seas, the center of Soviet power continues to lie in the country's capacity to sustain the nuclear-arms race. Although Soviet military power now equals that of the United States, in other respects the country is still weak. It cannot count on loyalty and dedication to efficiency among its peoples. Nor can it count on effective leadership.

After Brezhnev

Brezhnev was seventy-four years old when he died in 1982; his illnesses had long stifled initiative for badly needed reforms. His successor, KGB chief Yuri Andropov, who took command quickly, was sixty-eight and not in good health either. He died in early 1984, replaced by Konstantin Chernenko, a member of Brezhnev's generation. Meanwhile a younger set of officials, better educated and further removed from Stalinism, but inexperienced, is waiting to cope with the problems of the future: improving agriculture, stimulating creativity in the economy, limiting corruption and disillusionment with Soviet ideals, raising the standard of living, and matching American influence around the world. The new leadership will have to work with a shrinking, increasingly non-Russian labor force and must channel vital resources into the arms race. And they must struggle to retain Soviet control over their Eastern European satellites.

The Satellite Countries

Soviet Russia's power is closely tied to its relations with its *satellite* countries (nations that it dominates politically) within the Soviet bloc in eastern and southeastern Europe.

Eastern Europe (Poland, East Germany, Czechoslovakia, and Hungary) and south-eastern Europe (the Balkan countries: Yugoslavia, Albania, Bulgaria, and Rumania) have been a long-standing concern of Russian and Soviet leaders. When in 1944 and 1945 the Red Armies poured into these lands on their way to Germany, Stalin was faced with a historically unique opportunity—Soviet Russia now controlled the entire area, and if it could continue its domination in peacetime, it would have a huge territorial buffer against invasion from the West. Conditions both favored and opposed Soviet rule. Most inhabitants of Eastern Europe (the Baltic peoples, the Hungarians, and Rumanians excepted) were fellow Slavs. Many Eastern Europeans belonged to the Eastern Orthodox church, another tie, at least to traditional Russia. At the same time, they shared a common suspicion or even hostility toward the giant to the east. Some among them, Poles and Czechs foremost, saw themselves as representatives of the superior culture of the West and wanted to strengthen ties with Western Europe rather than Russia. All, remembering centuries of foreign domination, were passionately nationalist. The majority, moreover, being of peasant stock, opposed collectivization and socialism. Under any regime, the peoples of these countries (now numbering about 100 million) would have been difficult to govern. They were split into innumerable groups, many of them fostering their own separatist movements, although they intermingled in the same territory with others. Most of them were stubborn, suspicious of government, and prone to violence. National independence between the First and Second World Wars had not been peaceful.

The Stalinization of Eastern Europe

Whatever the prospects for domination, Stalin seized the opportunity. As the Red Armies fought their way west, Eastern European communists, trained in the Soviet Union, followed behind them. The Baltic States (Lithuania, Latvia, Estonia), seized after the Nazi-Soviet Pact of 1939 and then lost to Hitler, were reincorporated into the Soviet Union as "soviet socialist republics." Elsewhere Stalin respected, outwardly at least, the national sovereignty of the occupied countries by ruling through returning native communists and whatever sympathizers he could find.

By the end of 1948, however, the countries of eastern and southeastern Europe had emerged as "people's democracies," distinct both from the "bourgeois democracies" of the West and from the "soviet socialist republics" of the U.S.S.R.; eventual incorporation into the Union of Soviet Socialist Republics remained a theoretical possibility. In any case, the Soviet Union continued to claim the right, based on conquest, of intervening at will in the internal affairs of its satellites.

Thus the pall of Stalinism hung over wartorn and impoverished Eastern Europe. The puppet regimes leveled the formerly privileged classes and drove out the scattered German minorities. Private enterprise was curtailed or abolished. The economy was socialized and rigid and hasty plans were implemented for industrialization and the collectivization of agriculture. Religion and the churches were repressed and political liberty and free speech stamped out. Even the "proletarian masses" derived few benefits from the artificial revolution engineered from Moscow, because Stalin drained Eastern Europe of its resources for the sake of rebuilding the Soviet Union. All contact with Western Europe or the United States was banned. Each satellite existed in isolation, surrounded by borders fortified with barbed wire and watch towers set along mined corridors cut through the landscape. Fear and terror reached deep into every house and individual soul as little Stalins copied their mentor's style in East Berlin, Warsaw, Prague, Budapest, Sofia, and Bucharest.

Two exceptions to this trend emerged: Albania and Yugoslavia, located on the flanks of the Soviet westward surge. During the war, indigenous communist parties had conducted successful guerrilla war in these countries; the parties rose to power when the Germans withdrew, each under the lead-

German territory to Poland
Acquired by Soviet Union, 1939-1945
Soviet satellites
Communist, nonsatellite nation
"Iron Curtain" after 1950

NORWAY
SWEDEN
FINLAND
Helsinki
Leningrad
G. of Finland
Stockholm
ESTONIA
Moscow
DENMARK
LATVIA
Copenhagen
BALTIC SEA
LITHUANIA
SOVIET UNION
Hamburg
Gdansk (Danzig)
NETHERLANDS
Elbe R.
Berlin
Vistula R.
Warsaw
WHITE RUSSIA
EAST GERMANY
POLAND
WEST GERMANY
Bonn
Prague
Kiev
Rhine R.
CZECHOSLOVAKIA
UKRAINE
Dnieper R.
Munich
Dniester R.
Vienna
AUSTRIA
Budapest
Bessarabia
SWITZERLAND
HUNGARY
CRIMEA
Po R.
RUMANIA
BLACK SEA
Belgrade
Bucharest
ITALY
YUGOSLAVIA
Danube R.
CORSICA
Rome
BULGARIA
Sofia
Istanbul
ADRIATIC SEA
Tirane
Ankara
SARDINIA
ALBANIA
TURKEY
GREECE
AEGEAN SEA
Athens
SICILY
CYPRUS
MEDITERRANEAN SEA

ership of a strong man: Enver Hoxha in Albania, and Josip Broz, known as Marshal Tito, in Yugoslavia. A Stalinist even after Stalin's death, Hoxha turned against Moscow in 1961, making Albania a satellite of Mao's China. Tito (1892–1980), in contrast, became a symbol of defiance to Stalin. The child of Croatian peasants, Tito showed his mettle in a tough succession of careers. Starting as a mechanic, Tito became a sergeant in the Austro-Hungarian army. As a prisoner of war in Russia during World War I, Tito learned his communism from the Bolshevik Revolution and the Russian Civil War. After his return to Yugoslavia, he became a communist organizer and was soon condemned to spend many years in jail. In 1937 Stalin chose him to reorganize the Yugoslav Communist party. During World War II he led the Yugoslav resistance movement against Nazi occupation. A convinced and hardened communist, Tito was also a Yugoslav patriot committed to rebuilding and unifying his country.

Yugoslavia escaped Soviet occupation, but Stalin did not ignore it. Arrogant Soviet advisers descended on Belgrade, determined to bend Tito's policies to Stalin's bidding. In June 1948 Stalin tried to get rid of Tito. His words, recalled by Khrushchev, were: "I will shake my little finger and there will be no more Tito; he will fall."

To Stalin's dismay, Tito did not fall. On the contrary, backed by his party and his people Tito pioneered, with increasing confidence, his own brand of communism. He accused Stalin of betraying true Marxism-Leninism by establishing an imperialist and bureaucratic dictatorship. He also boldly attempted a more democratic communist regime based on workers' participation in industry. Tito's communism has served as a model of socialist ownership of production combined with workers' control and, more broadly, with extensive popular participation in the administration of the entire state. Stalin ruthlessly purged all potential Titos in other communist parties, everywhere suspecting "bourgeois nationalism," his pet phrase for Titoism.

◀ **Map 36.1** Eastern Europe After 1945

The other satellite countries bore the marks of Soviet control. All communist parties (by whatever name) were guided by Moscow; Soviet troops remained strategically stationed in the area. Economic life was regulated by the Council of Mutual Economic Assistance (sometimes called Comecon), planned in 1949 as a move to counter the Marshall Plan. In 1955 a further bond was created in the Warsaw Pact or Warsaw Treaty Organization (WTO). It coordinated the armies of the satellite countries with the Red Army as a military instrument for preserving the ideological and political unity of the bloc and for counterbalancing NATO.

A New Era of Permissiveness and Reprisals

Stalin's successors, realizing that continued repression among the satellites would provoke trouble, began to relax their controls. A new era began for eastern and southeastern Europe. The Soviet satellites began to move toward greater national self-determination, searching for their own forms of industrialization, collectivizaton of agriculture, and communist dictatorship. The history of the region since 1953 was thus a series of experiments to determine what deviations from Soviet practice in domestic politics and what measure of self-assertion in foreign policy the Kremlin would tolerate.

No event proved more crucial than Khrushchev's attack on Stalin in 1956. It set off a political earthquake throughout the bloc, discrediting Stalinists and encouraging moderates in the parties, reviving cautious discussion among intellectuals, and even arousing visions of national self-determination. The first tremors of protest rumbled in June 1956 in Poland—the largest and most troublesome of the satellite countries. Workers took to the streets to protest low wages and high prices. Their anger forced a change of leadership; the new government joined in the anti-Russian agitation while preserving the ascendancy of the Communist party. The crisis came to a head in October: would Poland revolt, inviting invasion by the Red Army, or would Khrushchev ease Soviet control? The Soviet boss yielded in return for a Polish pledge of continued loyalty to the Soviet Union. Thereafter, Poland breathed more freely, clinging to its Catholic faith as a cornerstone of its national identity.

The Hungarian Uprising of 1956 Although "the Polish October" ended peacefully, events moved to a brutal showdown in Hungary. The Stalinists had suppressed national pride in Hungary for too long. On October 20, 1956, an uprising in Budapest raised anti-Soviet feeling to a fever pitch and forced Soviet troops to withdraw from the country. Next, a moderate communist government, eager to capture popular sentiment, called for Western-style political democracy and Hungary's withdrawal from the Warsaw Pact with the aim of gaining neutral status like Finland's. Thoroughly alarmed, and with the backing of Mao and even Tito, the Soviet leaders struck back. On November 4, 1956, Soviet troops re-entered the country and crushed all opposition. Yet the bold uprising had left its mark.

The new communist leader of Hungary, János Kádár (born 1912), was a moderate who with Khrushchev's approval, built a pragmatic regime of consumer-oriented "goulash communism" that granted considerable opportunity to private enterprise. Kádár's regime also allowed noncommunists to participate extensively in public affairs. Relaxation and decentralization of planning made possible in the 1970s a remarkable increase in popular prosperity and individual freedom; the Hungarian experiment became the envy of all other Soviet-bloc countries and invited imitation even in the Soviet Union itself. In return for this moderate self-determination, the Hungarians resumed their membership in the Warsaw Pact and demonstrated loyalty to the Soviet leadership.

After 1956, Soviet leaders grew more circumspect in their approach to the satellite countries' internal affairs, allowing increasing diversity of political development. No country

went further in asserting its identity than Rumania, which was given special leeway by the Kremlin because it was surrounded on all sides by other Soviet-bloc countries and preserved a tight dictatorship of its own. Yet the new permissiveness was never without risks, even under the milder regime of Brezhnev.

The Czech Revolt of 1968 In 1968, it was Czechoslovakia's turn to face the consequences of liberating innovation. A new group of communist leaders sought to liberalize their regime to include noncommunists, allow greater freedom of speech, and rid the economy of the rigidities that for so long had prevented prosperity. Their goal was a "humanist democratic socialism" or "socialism with a human face"—a communist party supported by public good will rather than by the secret police.

Their program enjoyed the full support of the Czech and Slovak communists as well as of Tito, but it panicked the governments of East Germany, Poland, and the Soviet Union. On August 21 East German, Polish, Hungarian, and Soviet troops, under the provisions of the Warsaw Pact, carried out a swift and well-prepared occupation of Czechoslovakia but failed to break the rebellious will of its communists. While Soviet tanks rumbled through Prague, an extraordinary Czechoslovak party congress secretly met in choked fury. Never had the Soviet leaders encountered such united resistance by a communist party! Yet before the year was out, the revolt had ended in failure. The party was purged; all reforms were cancelled; and the country was reduced to abject hopelessness. But the Soviet Union had paid a high price: a cry of moral outrage resounded around the world; protests were heard even in Moscow.

In the Brezhnev years, on the whole, caution and moderation prevailed. Soviet leaders could point to the positive results of their control over eastern and southeastern Europe. They had promoted industrialization in predominantly agrarian and comparatively backward countries; they had reduced the gap between rich and poor, substantially advancing education and cultural opportunity. They had also muted the instability and violence so evident in the region in the past. Yet Moscow's efforts to integrate its satellites' economies into its own even less advanced economy never succeeded. One by one, the satellite governments resumed ties with capitalist states, incurring considerable indebtedness in the process. More significantly, Soviet control had not won popular allegiance, as was most obvious in the case of Poland.

Poland Since 1970   Even after 1956, Poland had never been quiet. Industrial workers, presumably the real masters in communist regimes, embarrassed their government by taking the lead in pressing for freedom. In 1970, Polish troops shot some workers who were protesting a sharp increase in consumer prices; yet the protesters' martyrdom forced a change in communist leadership. Agitation continued when the economy declined (in part because of low morale in industry and the regime's opposition to private farming); Soviet assistance and massive loans from Western European countries brought no relief. The slightest relaxation of Soviet control only encouraged Polish nationalism which, for lack of other outlets, had long found expression in the Roman Catholic Church.

When Karol Woityla, a Polish cardinal, became Pope John Paul II in 1978, patriotism surged, fired even more by his visit the next year. In 1980, workers under the leadership of an electrician named Lech Walesa succeeded, with the blessing of the church, in forming an independent labor union called Solidarity. Pressured by relentless strikes, the government, just reorganized under a new leader, recognized the union despite threats of Soviet intervention. In 1981, matters came to a head: some of Solidarity's more radical members spoke of bringing free elections to Poland. The country was straining against the Soviet yoke. Would the Red Army, poised on the border, drown the revolt in blood as it had done earlier in Hungary? In December, after the mounting tension reached into Western Europe and the United States, a military dictatorship, suddenly formed under General Wojciech Jaruzelski, imposed martial law. Walesa and other leaders of Solidarity were arrested; the new regime crushed freedom of speech and assembly and dispersed protesting workers by force. Significantly, however, tight communist control was reestablished by a Polish general, rather than by the Soviet army. Martial law, lasting a year and a half, restored a sense of reality. When a second visit by the pope in 1983 proved that in Polish hearts Solidarity was still alive, both church and state—and even Andropov in Moscow—recognized that some compromise had to be reached for the sake of peace in the country and relations in Europe as well. Yet a durable domination in which subject Poles can peacefully coexist with Russians will be difficult to ensure.

East Germany   The Poles receive little sympathy in their troubles from their western neighbor, the German Democratic Republic (East Germany), Moscow's most reliable satellite. Established simultaneously with the Federal Republic of Germany (West Germany), it controls the parts of the old Germany assigned at the end of the war to Soviet occupation, minus the territories ceded to Poland. The Soviet Union's western-most outpost and indispensable for its contribution to the economy of the entire Soviet bloc, East Germany is closely watched by the politburo.

Under the leadership of German communists who had spent the Nazi years in the Soviet Union and therefore felt no responsibility for Nazi atrocities, the German Democratic Republic at first shared the fate of all Soviet satellites. Industry was nationalized, agriculture collectivized, and the people were regimented under the Communist party (here called Socialist Unity Party). Because of its close historical association with West Germany, however, it soon developed its own distinctive character.

Protests against Stalinism appeared earlier than elsewhere. In June 1953 the workers of Berlin staged an uprising, gaining some

Pope John Paul II in Poland. Poland has always been an unwilling communist satellite. There were uprisings in 1956 and 1970. The 1978 election of John Paul as the first Polish pope fired patriotism. In 1980 with the blessing of the Roman Catholic Church, Solidarity, an independent labor party, was formed. (*Chuck Fishman/Woodfin Camp & Associates*)

concessions. Then followed a steady exodus of skilled manpower to West Germany, mostly via West Berlin. More than three million people escaped before the East German government, in August 1961, suddenly threw up a wall—the famous "Berlin Wall"—and built equally deadly barriers along the entire border with West Germany. For a time all contact between the two Germanies ceased.

With increased control over their people, the communist leaders—first Walter Ulbricht and, since the early 1970s, Erich Honecker—concentrated on advancing the economy, with marked success. Their people, numbering less than a quarter of the West German population, enjoy the highest standard of living in the entire Soviet bloc. The East German standard of living is higher even than England's, and although the East Germans lack the freedom of the English, they do not feel that they live in a police state, despite the presence of Soviet troops.

In 1972 détente led to the establishment of diplomatic relations between the two Germanies and to closer economic ties, which made East Germany virtually a beneficiary of the European Economic Community. Welcoming close economic relations with West Germany for their own good, the Soviet masters raised no objections. They are opposed, however, to any speculation about German reunification. The leaders of the Democratic Republic consider their country a separate "socialist" Germany, drawing on the best elements in the German past, including Martin Luther's Reformation and Prussian efficiency. They can rely on their subjects' resigned acceptance of their rule. East Germans are aware of their privileged position within the Soviet bloc; they recognize the futility of revolt and work hard at their jobs. Secretly they may hope to escape someday to the West, to which they have access through West German television.

Their leaders meanwhile pursue a difficult course. Dependent on the Soviet Union and knowing their subjects' secret desires, they need good relations with West Germany. The Bonn government contributes in many ways to East Germany's high standard of living. It is also a partner with East Germany in the attempt to reduce the hostility between the superpowers and thus to assure peace for the peoples of central Europe.

The Soviet Union in an Age of Globalism

A measure of troubled security has come at last to Russia in the late twentieth century, partly because of the exertions and sacrifices exacted by the Stalin revolution in the 1930s and by the Great Fatherland War (1941–1945), and partly because of accidental factors. Soviet Russia moved into the political vacuum created in eastern and central Europe by the German defeat; its landlocked empire held together while the overseas empires of Western Europe fell apart. It now possesses nuclear weapons equal to those of the United States. As long as the balance of terror prevents a nuclear war, the Soviet Russian empire is militarily more secure than ever before in the country's entire history.

The Soviet Union makes its presence felt over the entire world, strengthening its borders, seeking out its opportunities, tightly holding on to its gains, and with imposing moral righteousness advertising its achievements as examples for all. It follows its long-range goal, hoping, like the United States, to reshape the world in its own interest. National liberation movements directed against Western nations find a willing ally in Moscow. Still feeling humiliated by Western superiority, Moscow tries to outdo the West on its own

terms, whether in space exploration and other spectacular technological feats, in setting up bases around the world, or in the ultimate promise of the best society.

In world affairs the Leninist dream of world revolution has faded. The Kremlin now conducts its foreign relations pragmatically, guided by a sober sense of self-interest. Trying to expand its power at the expense of the other superpower, it is also dependent on the Western world in the widening network of global interdependence. Soviet Russia still needs to draw on Western know-how (along with Japan's), to satisfy the material wishes of its subjects (whom it cannot entirely insulate from the outside).

Underneath their show of strength and self-confidence, Soviet leaders still have reason to be afraid. They rule over an empire whose subjects crave freedom yet lack the knowledge and heritage of self-discipline necessary for managing a prosperous and powerful society by peaceful cooperation. Their peoples are made powerful and modern by an artificially imposed system of national endeavor, with the help of elaborate compulsions backed, if necessary, by "reeducation" in forced labor camps. Soviet authority at home and Soviet prestige in the world depend on deliberate manipulation and violence rather than on peaceful persuasion. The Soviet Union is still only the second superpower, negotiating with the first from weakness, rather than strength, in everything but nuclear weapons.

Notes

1. Nikita S. Khrushchev's speech (in translation) in *The Crimes of the Stalin Era: Special Report to the 20th Congress of the Communist Party of the Soviet Union*, annotated by Boris I. Nicolaevsky, *The New Leader* (New York), 1956.

Suggested Reading

Amalrik, Andrei, *Notes of a Revolutionary* (1982). A noted dissident on the fate of dissidents under Brezhnev.

Ascherson, Neal, *The Polish August: The Self-Limiting Revolution* (1982). A good insight into the rise and fall of Solidarity.

Berliner, Joseph S., *Innovation Decision in Soviet Industry* (1976). A scholarly study of the vital question: how innovative is the Soviet planned economy?

Davies, Norman, *God's Playground: A History of Poland* (1982). A much-praised survey, introducing the reader to Poland's history.

Fetjo, Francois, *A History of the People's Democracies: Eastern Europe Since Stalin* (1971). A good survey of Eastern Europe after World War II.

Hough, Jerry F., and Merle Fainsod, *How the Soviet Union Is Governed* (1979). The updated version of a classic study of the Soviet system.

Khrushchev, Nikita S., *Khrushchev Remembers* (1974). Although its authenticity has been questioned, this autobiography is alive with his personality.

Periodicals specializing in Soviet and Soviet-related subjects: *Problems of Communism* (Washington, D.C.), a journal of East and West studies (London); and the *Current Digest of the Soviet Press* (Columbus, Ohio), which provides weekly translations from the most significant latest items in the Soviet press.

Pond, Elizabeth, *From the Yaroslavsky Station: Russia Perceived* (1981). A sensitive American correspondent takes the train from Moscow to Vladivostok and describes her experiences.

Smith, Hedrick, *The Russians* (1976). The best account by an American journalist in recent years of everyday life in the Soviet Union.

Solzhenitsyn, Aleksandr, *Cancer Ward* (1968). A novel about readjustment after release from Stalin's Gulag, based on the author's own experience.

Ulam, Adam B., *The Rivals: America and Russia Since World War II* (1972). A stimulating essay on American-Soviet relations to the beginning of détente.

———, *Dangerous Relations: The Soviet Union in World Politics, 1970–1982* (1983). Soviet foreign relations under Brezhnev.

Werth, Alexander, *Russia: The Post-War Years* (1972). A firsthand account by an experienced journalist who had watched the Soviet Union throughout the war.

Review Questions

1. What problems in the Soviet Union did Stalin face after the end of World War II? How did he try to cope with them?

2. What happened to Stalinism after Stalin's death? What was Khrushchev's role? What was the role of Khrushchev's successors?

3. Imagine that you are a member of the politburo. What would be your major anxieties? What would be your sources of pride?

4. How do Soviet leaders view their Eastern European satellites? How do these satellite countries view the Soviet Union?

5. How has the Soviet system of government handled the problem of succession in the top leadership? How does the Soviet system of choosing political leaders compare with the American system?

6. What are the aims of Soviet foreign policy? How do Soviet foreign-policy aims compare with those of the United States?

37

Globalism: The Stresses of Interdependency

*A*t this point in its long history, Western civilization has entered the age of globalism, an age of its own making. For better or worse, the peoples of Europe and of European descent took the initiative in creating the single, irreversibly interdependent world with which the present and all future generations of humanity must cope. No other civilization in human history has managed to so universalize itself by imposing its achievements and its spirit on all others. Penetrating into all lands, the West has transformed a fragmented world of villages, loosely structured political communities, and a few effective nation-states into a "global city." Never before have so many human beings from so many different cultural backgrounds been brought into such close association. And never before has there existed such sharp disagreement about the realities that human beings face in the present and the future.

The New Globalism

The appalling human toll of World War II helped raise awareness of the realities of global interdependence. The worldwide war against Germany and Japan had pulled many peoples in America, Europe, Asia, and Africa out of their traditional isolation. Chastened by suffering, they were ready to redefine their self-interest in broader perspectives. Thus World War II opened a new chapter in human history—the age of global interdependence.

International Agencies

At the end of the war, American initiative helped to establish an array of international agencies designed to promote peaceful cooperation for the new globalism. Foremost among these agencies stood the United Nations, founded in April 1945 at San Francisco. Its charter grandly expressed the idealism generated at the end of the war: "We the peoples of the United Nations," it said, are determined "to save succeeding generations from the scourge of wars, . . . to reaffirm faith in fundamental human rights, . . . to establish justice and respect for treaties and other sources of international law, . . . and to employ international machinery for the promotion of the economic and social advancement of all peoples. . . ." The signatories to these noble promises included all countries that had fought against Germany and Japan. Subsequently other countries joined, including, in due time, the former enemies. The UN now numbers over 160 members large and small.

The key members—the United States, the Soviet Union, and Great Britain*—were permanently established in the Security Council. Despite their pledges of cooperation, they made sure that their national interests were respected. Each key member retained the right to veto all UN decisions and would not accept a majority vote in the UN's General Assembly that ran counter to its interests. The United Nations clearly was not meant to be a world government; its success depended on the willingness of its key members to work together. That willingness soon faded; the United Nations never became a forum for settling major issues of war and peace around the world. The postwar years witnessed ever more armed conflict and outright wars; violence escalated.

Still, the United Nations stood as a symbol of peace and justice, its ideals spelled out more fully in 1948 under the Universal Declaration of Human Rights, which upheld the right to individual privacy, to work, to education, to free mobility between countries, and to other goals of Western liberal democracy. Yet as with political cooperation, so with universal human rights, reality differed ever more drastically from the ideals.

While virtually all governments signed the declaration, they used or abused its principles as it suited their interests. A high universal standard, the declaration is flagrantly violated in practice.

A touch of the original inspiration of the United Nations remained alive in the many agencies created for promoting "the economic and social advancement of all peoples." To mention a few of them: the World Health Organization (WHO) looks after worldwide medical problems; the Food and Agricultural Organization (FAO) is concerned with improving food supply; the United Nations Educational, Scientific, and Cultural Organization (UNESCO) promotes the common interests listed in its title. The United Nations also organizes innumerable world conferences on urgent issues of common concern, including population, food, and environmental control. In conflicts between minor countries, it supports peace-keeping forces supplied by neutral member states. For managing all these activities, the United Nations maintains a large, cumbersome bureaucracy of international civil servants at its headquarters in New York City.

As the Security Council became deadlocked by the veto right of its key members, the United Nation's center of political activity shifted to the General Assembly. In that body all states, large and small, are represented with equal votes. The majority is composed of newcomers to global politics—the countries created in the process of decolonization (see pages 852–854). Although speaking for the majority of humanity, they nevertheless wield little influence. The General Assembly has passed hundreds of resolutions that have been ignored by the superpowers and their allies. Nevertheless, it continues to serve as a worldwide forum, occasionally addressed by important heads of state.

Trade and Economic Development

In another basic respect, however, the postwar spirit of globalism has succeeded more

* China, then ruled by the Kuomintang regime of General Xian Kaishek, was also included on the mistaken assumption that it would play a major role in world affairs; France joined later.

fully, largely because of American backing: there has been a vast promotion of worldwide trade and economic development for the benefit, most immediately, of the advanced countries. Economic planning for the postwar world economy under American auspices began in 1944. It created a Bank for International Trade and Development (the World Bank) and the International Monetary Fund (IMF); both assisted in the phenomenal increase in world prosperity during the 1950s and 1960s. Regular world conferences and "summit" meetings of heads of state from the leading industrial nations have encouraged the flow of goods and services for the common benefit—with less success, however, as prosperity waned in the 1970s and political pressures for protectionism rose.

The new globalism is manifest also in the work of hundreds of multinational corporations doing business, in good years and bad, over the entire world and creating what one observer has called "the global factory." Its products are "world products" designed for use over the entire world, made up of parts produced and assembled locally yet designed in the United States, Japan, or Western Europe. In this manner self-contained national economies have come to an end. Economic interdependence is an inescapable fact of life. It throws people out of work in some countries and provides new opportunities in others, as in developing countries that offer low-cost labor or cheap sources of energy.

The world economy is the subject of deep concern all around and has given rise to a variety of specialized global bodies. The industrial giants in North America, Western Europe, and Japan participate in the Organization for Economic Cooperation and Development (OECD). A more notorious agency of transnational cooperation is the Organization of Petroleum Exporting Countries (OPEC), which regulates the flow and price of oil. Founded in 1960, it suddenly rose to prominence in 1973 when it began to take advantage of its control over that essential energy source, increasing its price sixfold in the next decade. Because of OPEC's pricing

policies, oil consumers around the world helplessly acknowledged a new facet of interdependence.

The Politics of Modernization

Politically, the new globalism has engendered large-scale organizations transcending nation-states. The North Atlantic Treaty Organization (NATO) and its Soviet counterpart, the Warsaw Pact, enforce military cooperation among member states. The Organization of African Unity (OAU) tries to maintain order in Africa and to represent that continent in world affairs; the Organization of American States (OAS) pursues somewhat similar objectives in the Western Hemisphere. The Association of South East Asian Nations (ASEAN) promotes political cooperation among noncommunist states in that corner of the world.

There is no end, in economics or politics, to new alliances, all of them operating in the confusing combinations of collaboration and rivalry typical of global interdependence. But these cooperative ventures conduct their business far above the heads of ordinary folk who barely make ends meet on the ground-floor of life in their local communities. Local and national parochialism imposes sharp limitations on the effectiveness of transnational bodies and strengthens the hands of isolation-minded governments.

However impressive the volume of international cooperation, effective power in the world still lies with self-centered nation-states. But even the most powerful are inescapably enmeshed in the pressures of global interdependence. In their rivalry, the two superpowers proudly demonstrate their superiority around the world, while lesser states play powerful roles in regional systems like the Middle East or Africa; even the smallest countries must watch the global scene if only for their public image. The competition for status is exceedingly keen: under the new globalism the world has come to be perceived as a pyramid of prestige and power. At the top stand the "advanced" countries, repre-

Iraqi Attack on an Oil Tanker in the Persian Gulf, 1984. Countries still jockey for positions of prestige and power. However, where instant telecommunication links countries closely together, this global outlook often intensifies the ramifications of national conflicts; this is especially true regarding conflict associated with oil. (*ITC/Gamma-Liaison*)

senting essentially the states of Western Europe and North America; they have been joined since the 1960s by Japan. The rest of humanity occupies the lower levels—the "Second World" of the Soviet bloc ranks above the "Third World," where the "less developed" rank above the "least developed" countries.

"Backwardness," in any form and by any name, represents humiliation to be escaped as fast as possible by "development"—by catching up to the "advanced" countries. "Development" aims at raising the standard of living, at industrialization, at participation in scientific and technological progress, and foremost, at prestige in the world. In this sense the struggle for development among non-Western peoples represents the culmination of westernization. All humanity strives to "modernize"—to master institutions and economic values originally developed by the West.

Unfortunately, the newcomers to modern statehood—the great majority of humanity—are entirely unprepared for managing the large-scale organizations required for statehood and global competition. Although anti-Western by political instinct and determined to preserve their inherited cultural identity, they are compelled to abide by the rules of power laid down by the West and enforced by the new globalism. Trying to assert their independence, they must nevertheless copy, for the sake of being counted in the world, the Western nation-state and its style of economic competition and achievement. To do so requires institutions and attitudes that parallel those in the West. What is needed are not only the visible aspects of Western accomplishment like statehood or industrialism, but also the invisible social discipline derived from Judaeo-Christian asceticism. These prerequisites, however, frequently fail to mesh with the habits and desires, or even the moral values, of non-Western peoples, causing disorientation and resistance. In addition, what the non-Westerners observe in their contacts with Westerners are not the invisible restraints but the externals of power, including flagrant luxury and self-indulgence. The West sets a tempting model but at the same time, in its present affluence, undermines the ascetic dedication needed to match it. The transfer of the visible aspects of a culture, including its stated ideals, does not unfortunately include the host of implicit assumptions that make institutions and ideals work in their original setting. Nothing in Western experience ever matched the magnitude of the problems faced by new non-Western states.

Decolonization and Worldwide Westernization

After the Second World War a new phase in the relationship between the West and non-Western peoples began. It gave vent to the accumulated resentment of previous generations. The rising militancy of Western-trained anti-Western nationalist movements bloomed amidst the declining resources of the colonial empires. The political agitation of the war, in which many colonial soldiers loyally fought, fired the desire for political independence; after all, freedom and self-determination had been prominent Allied war slogans. France and Holland had been overrun by Nazi Germany, their Asian colonies by the Japanese; they had no strength left for colonial rule. Great Britain, exhausted by the war, also was ready to let its colonies go as soon as it could responsibly do so. Equally important, the United States, in its new superpower role, took a decidedly anti-imperialist stand. The Soviet Union, although it tightened control

over its Asian subject nationalities and reacted to its geographic insecurity in Eurasia, also affirmed its customary moral support for all oppressed peoples. Too weak to provide aid, the Soviet Union nevertheless furnished a heroic model of rapid mobilization for ambitious leaders in non-Western countries (see Chapter 31). In this setting, a mighty groundswell of decolonization after 1946 abolished all overseas empires and propelled their former subjects into independent statehood. At best, the colonial powers, under the threat of violence, relinquished their control quietly. At worst, they were driven out by bitter wars of liberation. Sometimes independence was followed by civil war. Whatever the course of events, decolonization profoundly altered the political landscape of the world, giving the non-Western states a worldwide numerical superiority over their former masters and ending for good the unquestioned ascendancy of the West. Great was the jubilation in Asia and Africa.

Decolonization began when in 1946 the United States granted independence to the Philippines. In 1947 India and Pakistan attained sovereign statehood. In 1948 Burma and Ceylon (later renamed Sri Lanka) emerged. In 1949 it was the turn of the Dutch possessions in Indonesia. In 1954 the French quit Laos, Cambodia, and Vietnam (leaving the Americans to defend South Vietnam against the communist revolutionaries of North Vietnam until 1973). In 1956 France freed its northern African colonies, Morocco and Tunisia (but not Algeria, which attained independence in 1962 after a cruel revolutionary war).

To the cheers of black people everywhere, Ghana in 1957 declared its independence, the first sub-Saharan African country to do so. After 1959 virtually all French and English possessions in Africa were decolonized. In 1960 the Belgians reluctantly left the Congo (now called Zaire), which started independence amidst a civil war. By 1975 even the

Map 37.1 New States in Africa and Asia ▶

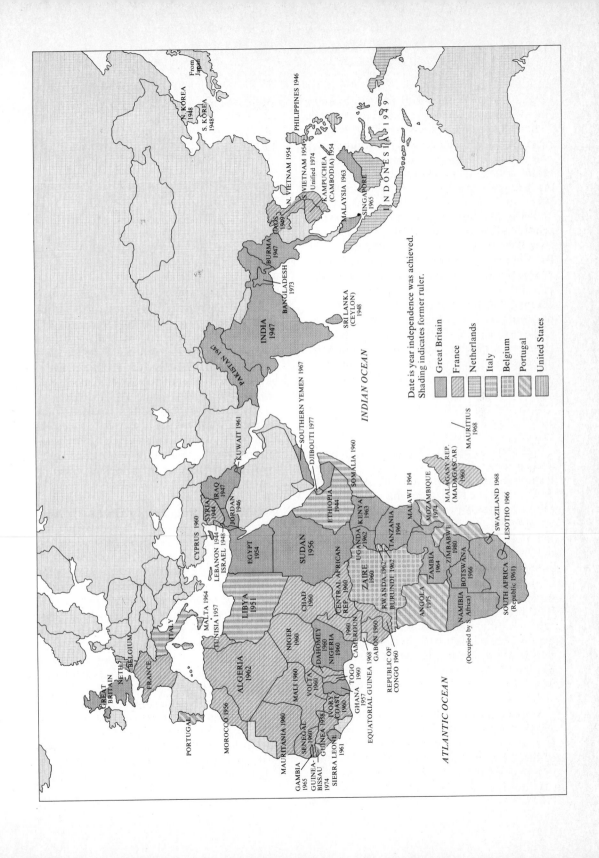

Date is year independence was achieved.
Shading indicates former ruler.

Great Britain
France
Netherlands
Italy
Belgium
Portugal
United States

INDIAN OCEAN

ATLANTIC OCEAN

N. KOREA 1948
S. KOREA 1948
From Japan
PHILIPPINES 1946
N. VIETNAM 1954
Unified 1974
KAMPUCHEA (CAMBODIA) 1954
MALAYSIA 1963
SINGAPORE 1965
INDONESIA 1949
LAOS 1949
BURMA 1947
BANGLADESH 1973
INDIA 1947
PAKISTAN 1947
SRI LANKA (CEYLON) 1948
SOUTHERN YEMEN 1967
DJIBOUTI 1977
KUWAIT 1961
IRAQ 1947
SYRIA 1944
JORDAN 1946
LEBANON 1944
ISRAEL 1948
CYPRUS 1960
MALTA 1964
TUNISIA 1957
EGYPT 1954
LIBYA 1951
ALGERIA 1962
MOROCCO 1956
PORTUGAL
GREAT BRITAIN
NETH.
BELGIUM
FRANCE
ITALY
MAURITANIA 1960
GAMBIA 1965
SENEGAL 1960
GUINEA-BISSAU 1974
GUINEA 1958
SIERRA LEONE 1961
MALI 1960
NIGER 1960
VOLTA 1960
DAHOMEY 1960
IVORY COAST 1960
GHANA 1957
TOGO 1960
NIGERIA 1960
EQUATORIAL GUINEA 1968
CAMEROUN 1960
GABON 1960
REPUBLIC OF CONGO 1960
CHAD 1960
SUDAN 1956
CENTRAL AFRICAN REP. 1960
ETHIOPIA 1944
UGANDA 1962
KENYA 1963
SOMALIA 1960
ZAIRE 1960
RWANDA 1962
BURUNDI 1962
TANZANIA 1964
MALAWI 1964
MOZAMBIQUE 1974
MALAGASY REP. (MADAGASCAR) 1960
MAURITIUS 1968
ANGOLA 1975
ZAMBIA 1964
ZIMBABWE 1980
BOTSWANA 1966
NAMIBIA (Occupied by S. Africa)
SWAZILAND 1968
LESOTHO 1966
SOUTH AFRICA (Republic 1961)

Portuguese, determined to the last to keep their African colonies, were driven out. In 1980, white-ruled Rhodesia became the African state of Zimbabwe. Only in South Africa and Southwest Africa (renamed Namibia) did white settlers, including the long-established Afrikaners, continue to defy black majority rule.

In the Mideast, Egypt and Saudi Arabia, which had become independent before World War II, were joined between 1951 and 1971 by other free Arab states. By the mid-1970s Western colonialism had formally come to an end. But the accumulated resentments of colonial rule and the struggle for independence remained a potent political legacy.

For a time, expectations ran high that the days of humiliation had ended and that non-Western peoples could build societies free of exploitation and inhumanity, yet still following the pattern of the European nation-state. While often fiercely anti-Western, the new states adopted both the ambition and the trappings of European rule.

National anthems, flags, armies, navies, and air forces all proclaimed national power. Putting forth the most advanced ideals of democracy, socialism, and the welfare state, the new constitutions were paper models of enlightened governments. Moreover, they put the most Westernized and cosmopolitan elements in the population into the seats of power, where they had so long yearned to be. But disillusionment arrived swiftly. After independence, the new masters discovered that their countries were unprepared for achieving the global respectability that they craved—often excruciatingly poor, composed of quarreling ethnic groups that felt no attachment to the new nation, and crowded with illiterate, disease-ridden, stubborn peasants.

Thus began an endless round of political, social, economic, and cultural experimentation in search of wealth and power. The highlights of these efforts offer a panorama of a world in transition and range from remarkable success to brutal failure.

Experiments in Modernization

In the effort to mobilize its people by the use of Western or Western-derived cultural skills, each non-Western country conducted its own experiments, limited by its own history and resources.

Asia

Japan   The most spectacular model of triumphant modernization was Japan, which enjoyed the benefit of a headstart. Starting in 1867 under the Meiji emperor (see page 629), the Japanese government, with the full support of leading elements of Japanese society, had deliberately copied those aspects of Western civilization that lay behind superior military power, including Western forms of government, law, education, science, and technology. At the same time Japan kept its own spiritual traditions—Christianity made few converts. Unlike any of the other non-Western peoples, the Japanese succeeded in fusing their own cultural strand with that of the West. A unique case, they contributed from their own history the essentials of modern power: a high level of technical competence, an ascetic self-discipline needed for civic cooperation, and a tradition of readily absorbing foreign cultures into their own.

The fusion of Western and Japanese culture was not complete, however. In the 1930s the Japanese warrior heritage gained the upper hand; it encouraged an anti-Western orientation that led to war—and disaster. Defeated and utterly exhausted, Japan had to make a new start, laboring for seven years under American occupation. The Americans imposed a Western democratic constitution and, while preserving the role of the emperor, abolished the traditional strongholds of power. Thus began Japan's miraculous rise to the position of economic superpower, rivaling and, in some respects, even outpacing the United States.

This miracle was possible, first of all, because the country started with a clean slate. Its own industrial capacity destroyed, it began reconstruction by humbly taking the best and the latest advances in technology and industrial science from the United States and Western Europe, gradually learning to improve the imported techniques and concentrating on long-range goals. Second, undaunted by their misery after the war, the Japanese people were willing to work hard and live austerely, putting the welfare of the country ahead of their individual gain. Third, the tradition of selfless civic cooperation, unbroken by defeat and foreign occupation, permeated the political, economic, and social life of the country; little time was lost in social conflict, strikes, or work stoppages. Finally, national pride ran high, spurred by the desire to escape the humiliation of 1945, by the marked successes in industrial technology, and by the world's respect for the superior quality of Japanese products. In the 1970s Japanese steel, ships, cameras, automobiles, and computers were rated among the best—if not *the* best—in the world; Japanese firms dominated world trade, entering into partnership with firms in the United States and other countries. Correspondingly, the Japanese standard of living rose, although not to where it matched the American level.

Admittedly, Japan was aided by the fact that, under American military protection, it could concentrate entirely on peacefully advancing its economy in the expanding world market. It manifested no political ambition except to maintain the worldwide stability necessary for its economic security; more than any other country it depended for its prosperity on the secure flow of imports and exports. By necessity, therefore, Japan became the most globally minded country, leading the way, some observers suggest, into the twenty-first century. Yet questions remain: In the global competition can an economic superpower survive over the long haul without wielding corresponding political clout? Can the fusion of Western and Japanese ways withstand the strains of increased partici-

Japanese Microchip Industry. After World War II, Japan rebuilt its industry using the latest techniques and the newest machinery. The Japanese character, hardworking and civically oriented, complemented the superior technology. Japanese automobiles, ships, steel, and computers vie with the world's best. (*Chuck O'Rear/Woodfin Camp & Associates*)

pation in world politics? Can the Japanese maintain their unique civic-mindedness despite their involvement with other countries and cultures? In any case, at the end of the twentieth century Japan is the envy of non-Western countries in which indigenous tradition and Western ways forever refuse to mesh.

China   While Japan rose from ashes to economic glory, events next door in China took a different and infinitely more tragic course. The Chinese experiment in modernization after World War II is known as Maoism, for the name of its leader, Mao Zedong (1898–1976), chairman of the Chinese Communist Party (founded in 1921). The Chinese experiment came after a long series of failures in preparing the once glorious empire for wealth and power in a Western-dominated world—failures caused in part by the lack of mass support. Mao's regime combined the elitism of the Chinese Communist Party with close support from the peasants. Coming from a peasant family somewhat better off than most, Mao became a student of Western learning; he went into politics with the Chinese Communist Party, risking his life and living under extreme hardships as he was pursued by the forces of Xian Kaishek. He tried to win the peasants over to the demanding routines of guerrilla warfare, political agitation, and more efficient agriculture. His success came because he stayed close to the people and, unlike other rulers of China, showed genuine concern for their needs.

In Mao's mind Chinese tradition mixed uneasily with the teachings of Marx, Lenin, and Stalin. His close comrade, Chou En-lai (1898–1976), who had studied in France, was more open to Western ideas than Mao, who had never left China. Both men espoused a Marxism that was less doctrinaire and rigid than Lenin's or Stalin's. They put pragmatic experience (Chinese experience) before theory. Ardent patriots, the Chinese communists fought the Japanese invaders more vigorously than did Xian's forces. In the civil war following World War II the communists defeated Xian's Kuomintang, and in 1949, with superior organization and purpose, as well as with peasant support, they became masters of a New China, reunited and liberated at last from foreign domination.

The communist victory was dearly bought. The Chinese people had suffered terribly in the conflict with Japan and the civil war. Nor was the communist victory the end of their trials. Although poor, internally disorganized and externally weak, communist China was ambitious—by virtue of both its Maoist Marxism and the imperial heritage of Old China—to be a leader in human progress. Chairman Mao thought of his work as a continuing cultural revolution that would carry China to the glory of full communism. It proved to be an endless and discouraging ascent.

To move the huge population in his vast country, Mao had to develop his own ap-

proach. For quick results, he could adopt the Stalinist model and put the mobilization of China into the hands of a dictatorial bureaucracy of administrators and experts. The flaw in the Stalinist approach was that it would condemn the Chinese masses to the sullen passivity that had ruined the empire; it would restore the same type of elitism that had undermined the imperial regime. Or, deviating from Stalinism, Mao could take the slow road of liberating the creative energies of the peasants—at the price of letting China fall further behind in acquiring the latest methods of economic productivity. By temperament, Mao inclined toward the latter solution. He hated the presumption of bureaucrats and experts and trusted that the creativity of the masses, once liberated, would conquer all obstacles. Yet many of his ablest comrades remained unconvinced.

Mao also oversimplified the complexities of industrial society. This trait showed up disastrously when in 1958 he staked his leadership on a campaign to create giant communes engaged in agriculture, industry, education, defense, and administration. As his Soviet critics had predicted, this Great Leap Forward into communism proved a catastrophe; Mao for a while retired from the limelight. At the same time the Chinese communists, angered by Soviet arrogance and traditionally suspicious of Russian territorial ambition at China's expense, broke away from Moscow's leadership. The Sino-Soviet rift inflicted a serious blow to the unity of world communism.

China's isolation was greatest in 1965, when Mao, with the help of the army, staged the Great Proletarian Cultural Revolution. It was directed at entrenched and autocratic bureaucrats and experts, and at any lingering veneration of the Chinese past or foreign models. The agents of this new revolution were young zealots carrying a little red book of *Quotations from Chairman Mao*. In these years Chairman Mao was God; never was the cult of personality and revolutionary zeal carried to greater extremes. The revolution closed universities and institutes of scientific research for many years and carried the country to the verge of economic and civic chaos; it unleashed a wave of violence as brutal as Stalin's terror, discrediting in its aftermath the integrity of revolutionary idealism. The only experts spared were the scientists working on nuclear weapons, the most prestigious instruments of national security. Four years later Mao, having purged potential rivals, returned to a calmer course. Yet he laid down no firm guidelines for governing the country with continuity. At his death in 1976, at the age of eighty-three, it was clear that China was still unstable.

Yet Mao stands out as one of the greatest political leaders of the twentieth century. He had, at a heroic personal risk and a high price for his people, restored unity and a common purpose to China. If the political experiments he undertook to make China a worldwide model proved inconclusive, the flaw did not lie in his lack of ingenuity or daring, but in the magnitude and novelty of the task: recasting an ancient and deeply rooted culture of one billion people into an alien modern mold.

Mao left to his successors a troubled country. Admitting that he had made mistakes, they cautiously reversed his policies, reinstating the victims of the Great Proletarian Cultural Revolution and setting a new course toward the "Four Modernizations"—in science and technology, in industry, in agriculture and in national defense. Under the leadership of Deng Xiaoping they allowed a measure of private enterprise and, more important, opened the country to the outside world. Still fearing the subversion of their Chinese ways and communist dedication, they were eager to attract foreign enterprise from Europe, the United States, Japan and even overseas Chinese, to help them accomplish their goals. In a short time they had made their country more self-assured and prosperous. Yet the pressure of a huge and still growing population upon the country's limited resources remains a baffling problem.

In contrast with the experiment on the mainland, the Chinese offshore island of Tai-wan, where the survivors of the Kuomintang had fled, proved a remarkable success under far more favorable circumstances. Firmly ruled by a dictatorial regime under American military protection, working with a small population open to the outside world, and benefitting from heavy American investment. Prosperous Taiwan has been held up by Western traditionalists as proof that free enterprise is superior to Marxist collectivism as practiced on mainland China. Smallness combined with easy access to the world market and American help obviously facilitated economic modernization.

India Yet another experiment was started in India which, with its 700 million people, is the most populous nation in the world after China. British political tradition and the diversity of people helped to preserve a pluralist democratic order, protected by a federal constitution. Under the leadership of Jawaharlal Nehru (1889–1964), the country started its independence with high hopes and Five Year plans; industrialization was considered essential for overcoming poverty and unemployment. Yet, as Nehru observed, "We are not only industrializing the country through democratic processes, but also, at the same time, trying to maintain the unique features in Indian philosophy and way of life and the individuality of India. Thus we believe we shall serve the Indian people best and perhaps the rest of the world also."[1] India too wanted to be a global model.

Reality took a less promising course. Admittedly, the country's industry and agriculture made remarkable progress, with assistance from Western countries and the Soviet Union; India did manage to feed itself. But modernization created two Indias existing side by side in stark contrast. Westernized India is capable even of exporting industrial equipment; it lives in reasonable comfort. Yet the other India persists—poor, traditional, caste-ridden, violent, and with little hope for improvement. Ancient customs long suppressed by the British, like widow-burning or banditry, have stealthily reemerged. Ten-

Makeshift Street Living in Bombay, India. For all the prosperity of Europe and the successful Westernization of parts of Asian and African countries, about half of the world's population lack adequate food, clean water, and medical facilities. (*Bhupendra Karia/Magnum*)

sions run high between the westernized and traditional Indias; Nehru's hope for an organic combination of the best in Indian tradition with industrial modernism has not materialized. The country is burdened also by fear of its neighbor, Islamic Pakistan, against which it has developed its own nuclear weapons. India was the first non-Western state to join the nuclear elite, despite Gandhi's pacifist teaching. All in all, the Indian experiment has been inconclusive.

Southeast Asia Further east, meanwhile, the greatest catastrophes in the collision between traditional cultures and the realities of modern

life took place in French Indo-China, now called Vietnam and Cambodia (Kampuchea). Little touched by Western ways until the 1940s, these countries thereafter were plunged, utterly unprepared, into the vortex of world politics. In Vietnam a liberation movement under Ho Chi Minh (1890–1969) ousted the French colonialists in 1954; following the Chinese model, it set up a communist regime in North Vietnam and began fighting to reunite the country.

South Vietnam, meanwhile, had come under American protection and was defended

Map 37.2 Southeast Asia ▶

against North Vietnam in a murderous war employing the latest weapons short of nuclear bombs. This war, which lasted twelve years, brought experimentation in imposing Western culture to a new level of irrationality. The most modern and powerful country in the world ever more recklessly poured its resources into a small and tradition-ridden non-Western country, trying to produce a viable Western-oriented state capable of holding its own against determined indigenous communists eager to drive out all capitalists.

The experiment failed disastrously. The South Vietnamese rulers propped up by the Americans could think of little besides their own personal profit. The war brought utter destruction and poverty to the country. Virtually all South Vietnamese saw members of their families killed or maimed, their farms and livelihood ruined for decades to come. Unable to prevail among alien people in a tropical climate and prodded by American opinion outraged over the war's futility, the Americans withdrew in 1973 as the communists swept aside the inept South Vietnamese army. Yet the unified communist Vietnam made no progress subsequently in living up to its Marxist promise of peace and well-being; it embarked instead on expansion into strife-torn neighboring Cambodia.

In the wake of the American withdrawal, Cambodian communists, called the Khmer Rouge, seized power under their leader Pol Pot, an enraged patriot radicalized in Left-Bank Paris and fanatically determined to avenge the brutalities committed in his country by both Vietnamese and Americans. He drove over 2 million people from the capital city of Phnom Penh and tried to establish a new order based on ideologically regimented rural communes. Hundreds of thousands of people died in the evacuation and more died later in the countryside. In 1979 the blood-stained and starving country was occupied by Vietnamese troops, visiting further catastrophe on its people. Meanwhile the communist government of Vietnam, resuming an age-old hostility toward China, began to eject Chinese residents of Vietnam, putting them out to sea without a place to land—a shocking reminder that nationalist passion outbids communist solidarity and human decency.

The Middle East

Another and hardly less bloody experiment in modernization took place in Iran. The shah of Iran, Mohammed Riza Pahlavi (1919–1980), was the son of an uneducated army sergeant who had risen to be Iran's ruler for a time. In 1941, Riza Pahlavi succeeded his father after the latter's abdication, but it was not until 1953 that he consolidated his power with American help. Relying on traditional forms and symbols artificially but grandly updated, he pressed a precipitous revolution of westernization from above. With the help of his country's oil riches, Western investments, and American weapons, the shah attempted to build a modern state and economy, disregarding his country's religious leaders and savagely repressing all resistance. Yet the forces of tradition, threatened with extinction, struck back. Deeply stirred, Shiite Muslim fundamentalists, basing their creed on the Koran and moving the mass of people to acts of bravery and martyrdom, staged a revolution that drove out the shah in early 1979.

Then began a new experiment, as extreme as that of the shah, under Ayatollah (the highest rank of religious leader) Ruholla Khomeini (born 1902). An aged, unbending and puritanical Muslim, he decries all Western influences, trying to make his Iran—half modern and half traditional—conform to the simple teachings of the prophet Muhammad. Yet Khomeini and his supporters cannot escape modernity. They proclaimed a constitution and held elections. They must collect taxes to run the government and buy weapons to fight secessionist Kurds and wage war against Iraq. They must satisfy the expectations of their people for a better life, give

Map 37.3 The Middle East. (Libya, west of Egypt, is also an OPEC member.) ▶

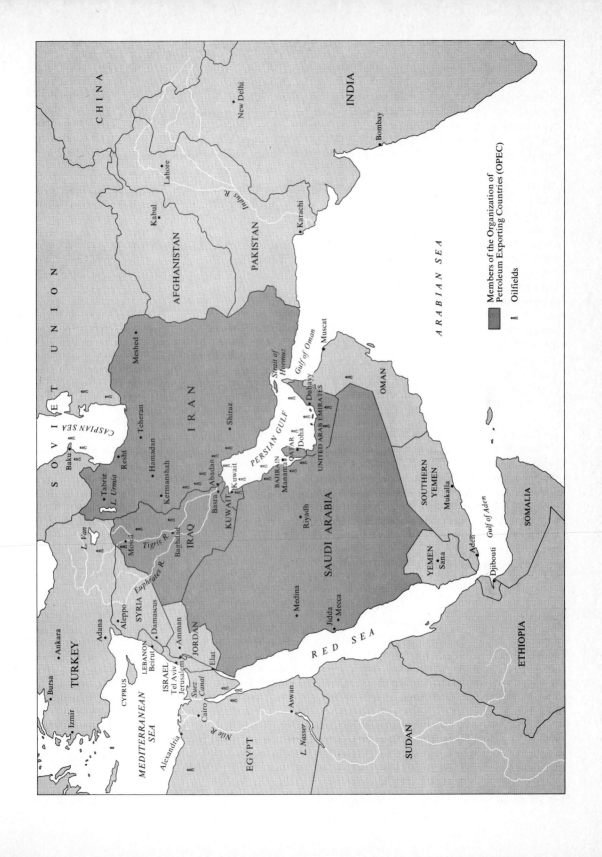

Members of the Organization of Petroleum Exporting Countries (OPEC)

Oilfields

jobs to the unemployed, conduct foreign relations, import food, and sell oil. Although they denounce the materialist immorality of the West and rage against the United States for its support of the shah, they must come to terms with the complex Western instruments of power if their revolution is to survive.

No experiment in modernization or in protest against it has yet proved conclusive. Experimentation continues in the Arab states near the Persian Gulf where immense oil wealth, suddenly descending on ancient desert kingdoms, calls for equally immense adjustments. Here, too, the Koran is the guide to life. Yet is the spiritual ascendance and the social and political order built under the inspiration of the Koran compatible with oil money?

Can the Koran bring peace to the Middle East? The Arab world is sharply divided politically. Iraq, at war with Iran (a non-Arabic country), is also at odds with neighboring Syria, which in turn is distrusted by next door Jordan and feared by Israel. Egypt, having made peace with Israel, tries to be a source of peace, like Saudi Arabia, with little success. Palestinians, craving a homeland, live scattered throughout the area, their leaders driven out of Lebanon, all unwilling to recognize the existence of Israel. And Lebanon, splintered into many warring factions, is caught in apparently endless civil war exacerbated by the Israeli invasion of 1983. Behind the regional tensions looms the conflict between the superpowers, each furnishing military and political support to its local allies. Modernization has come to the Middle East mostly through war.

War also has helped to shape Israel, where another experiment is under way. Israel is a tiny state starting afresh after long centuries of exile and bringing together Jews from many lands, under embittered conflict with its Arab neighbors. Israel has great assets. Bound together by a common religion and living under daily threat of war, it can count on the loyalty of its citizens. It also has free access to Western capital and knowledge. In its democratic government and guarantee of civil liberties, it is part of the West; yet it also is a hazardous long-range experiment, set into the worldwide superpower conflict. Can it fuse together its heterogeneous Jewish peoples, many from non-Western countries? Can it evolve a constructive relationship with its Arab neighbors, above all the Palestinians, many of whom were displaced from their homesteads? Can it harmonize the demands of religious tradition with the requirements of a modern state?

Africa

The African experience of decolonization is well illustrated by the example of Ghana. The hero of African liberation was Kwame Nkrumah (1909–1972), who transformed the small but comparatively advanced British colony of the Gold Coast into the independent country of Ghana, named after a fabled medieval empire in the western Sahel region of central Africa. From Ghana, Nkrumah hoped to advance the ideal of a powerful united Africa. As the spokesman for a distinct African personality he symbolized the promise of the new Africa. After living in the United States for ten years he emerged after World War II in England as a prominent West African nationalist with Pan-African aspirations. Back in the Gold Coast in 1947, he soon became the charismatic leader of the most westernized elements among the population and was eventually jailed for incitement to violence. From jail he stepped directly into the top post in the government created by the colonial administration in preparation for full self-government. He joyfully presided over the celebration of independence in 1957.

Democratic at the outset, Nkrumah's regime turned into a personal dictatorship, and his one-party state became an instrument for the personal enrichment of his lieutenants, despite its increasingly socialist ideology. Nkrumah took Ghana out of the British Commonwealth, spent the financial reserves left from British rule on hasty and overambitious ventures of economic development, and antagonized the leaders of other newly independent African states. He soon lost the confidence of even his own people. Exiled in 1966 by a military coup, he died a spokesman for a Soviet-oriented scientific socialism that allowed little room for the glorification of African tradition. His successors—military, civilian, and military again—have failed to restore the promise or even the prosperity with which Ghanaian independence began. Unable to understand the causes of their subsequent misery, Ghanaians remember Nkrumah with renewed affection.

The tribulations of Ghana were shared by most of the other newly created African states. Starting with democratic constitutions, they changed into one-party states, military dictatorships, or personal regimes. Some of them were benevolent, like those of Jomo Kenyatta of Kenya or Julius Nyerere of Tanzania. All had to try desperately to hold their multiethnic states together, while also paying lip service to African unity. Throughout sub-Saharan Africa, loyalty still centers on family, lineage, and ethnic groups. Only the most uprooted foreign-educated Africans put their country first.

Unity often was preserved by compulsion and repression, sometimes degenerating into genocidal violence. In a few lands time-honored African forms of government were perverted by the demands of statehood into unbridled personal rule, rendered murderous by imported Western techniques, as in the case of Idi Amin Dada of Uganda. Some lands, like the formerly French Colonies of Senegal and the Ivory Coast, remained closely associated with their ex-masters; there economic conditions improved and governments remained stable. Among the former English colonies, Nigeria was rent by a destructive civil war and barely prevented secession of a large section of the country. By 1979 the most powerful of the sub-Saharan states, its economy buoyed by large exports of oil, Nigeria changed from a military to a civilian regime, beginning a short-lived experiment of democratic rule. Immediately after the first election in early 1984, the army again took over.

As for economic conditions, the testimony (in 1979) of the Executive Secretary of the United Nations Economic Commission for Africa, a Nigerian, speaks for itself. The UN secretary found Africa "basically undeveloped," with low per-capita incomes, a high percentage of the population in subsistence farming, a narrow industrial base, insufficient enterprise, and low productivity in all branches of the economy, whose most modern sectors are dominated by foreigners. He concluded that "the very strategies of development which African governments have been pursuing . . . have come from outside." But how are Africans going to help themselves when the sources of capital, knowledge, and technology and the markets for African goods continue to lie in the developed industrial countries?

Latin America

Africa's problems were familiar also to the countries of Latin America, whose cultural evolution had lagged after they attained independence in the wake of the American Revolution. With their often sizable Indian (and sometimes black) populations, they failed to escape their poverty, their helplessness toward foreign (especially American) business, their political instability, and their sense of frustration. Brazil proved the most successful in industrializing its economy; Mexico and Venezuela capitalized on their oil. A spectacular experiment in revolutionary mobilization was carried out in Cuba by Fidel Castro (born 1927), who with the help of the Soviet Union made his country a force among anti-Western nations, especially in Africa.

Dictatorship, open or disguised, rather than democracy was the rule, with revolution or counter-revolution a constant danger for all governments; stark social inequality prevented economic and political stability. In Central America the opponents in civil war invited support by powerful outsiders, the United

States or Cuba, drawing Latin America into the conflict between the superpowers.

Development: Which Way?

As the foregoing cases show, the experiments of westernization and modernization, of adjustment to an interdependent competitive world, have exacted an excruciating human toll from societies culturally unprepared for drastic changes. Unwilling and unable to break with their cultural heritage yet eager to reap the benefits of modernity, people still wonder: which way should they go, the Western or "capitalist" way, or the socialist way?

In both cases Western democracy had little or no chance. Sooner or later the disunity resulting from rapid change amid incompatible Western and non-Western ways produced authoritarian governments. But regimes that recognized free enterprise allowed their subjects considerable leeway for their own experiments in adjustment; amidst appalling inequality and corruption, some people learned to sharpen their wits for coping with innovation. Under socialist systems, in contrast, people were compelled to conform to the official experiment, also amid appalling inequality and corruption. Neither model has helped to advance equality, peace, or human rights in the world.

Nor did the efforts of the United Nations bring the desired results. The General Assembly, dominated by developing countries, passed resolutions and issued an elaborate blueprint for a New International Economic Order. But the dialogue between the advanced and the developing countries has made no headway. The rich tell the poor to help themselves by changing their ways; the poor protest that without help from the rich they do not have even the tools for learning how to change. Meanwhile the elites among the poor countries splurge scarce money on luxuries in order to imitate the splendor of the global leaders. The hard fact is that cultural adjustment to the competition of global coexistence is a challenge still beyond the comprehension of the bulk of humanity.

The basic question is this: Can the ascetic self-discipline built into Western civilization—and indispensable for all large-scale human organization—be transferred to people in other cultures lacking this tradition? Can that social discipline be expanded to make possible the peaceful management of global interdependence?

Concluding Reflections: Optimism or Pessimism?

The world is inhabited by four and one-half billion human beings; the figure is expected to be around six billion by the year 2000. Helping to sustain them are a vast array of originally Western achievements: the nation-state, industrialism, science and modern technology, and world-spanning organizations for business and international cooperation. Non-Western peoples are now matching Western accomplishments; keeping up with the latest innovations has become an ardent desire—or even an outright necessity—among all people, no matter how attached to their past they feel. Survival depends on mastery of the skills of modernity—Western skills—in economic productivity, in scientific and technological progress, and in the development of the most advanced weapons; these capabilities are the keys that command power and prestige in the world. Thus, through westernization and economic interdependence, a new globalism has become an irresistible worldwide reality, and it has ominously accelerated the pace of change. Has the transformation been for the better or worse?

Westerners naturally dwell on the positive aspects. Global interdependence, they argue, has vastly increased worldwide cooperation. For the first time in all human experience,

Map 37.4 World Population Densities ▶

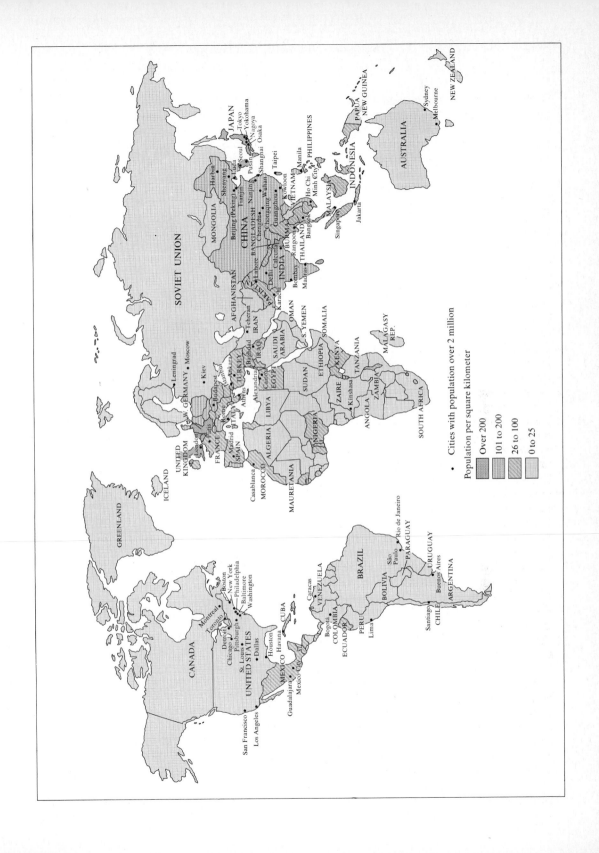

Cities with population over 2 million

Population per square kilometer

Over 200
101 to 200
26 to 100
0 to 25

people from the entire world have a chance to work together for the common good. Look at the impressive results. The volume of world trade has tripled, providing new material security for human life—and resulting in a rapid increase in the world's population. People hitherto isolated have been brought into worldwide circulation, with new opportunities for personal development; they have become mobile in their search to improve their lot.

Global interdependence, furthermore, has stimulated minds over the entire world, recruiting talent from many countries. The advances in all fields of learning have been astounding. Science and technology, more closely linked than ever, have increased human control over nature beyond the wildest dreams of earlier ages. Physicists have explored the atom down to the smallest components of matter; biologists have laid bare the genetic structures of animate matter. At the opposite end of the scale, human beings have set foot on the moon. Rockets with sophisticated equipment have been sent deep into the solar system. Advances in electronics have brought the whole world to remote villages in Asia and Africa through radio and television. Computers, indispensable to scientists and engineers, have invaded everyday life in finance and business, even in ordinary households.

In the arts and literature the interaction of cultural influences from all parts of the world has been a creative stimulus. Even more significantly, concern for human dignity has spread. However spurned in practice, the United Nations Universal Declaration of Human Rights sets a worldwide standard as a guide for the future. Agencies like Amnesty International keep track of human rights violations; others send relief in case of famine, epidemic, or natural catastrophe. These developments have created a mood of optimism for some people who perceive a chance for enlightened control of human destiny over the entire world. Postwar prosperity brought with it an international effort at cooperation to bring natural resources and world population into a steady equilibrium, to provide greater equality around the world, and to

avoid devastating world wars. That mood is still alive in some quarters.

At the same time, however, there is a contrary mood of pessimism. In reality, the bulk of humanity is still miserable; more people means more poverty. Of the world's 4.5 billion human beings, 600 million are unemployed or underemployed; 800 million adults are illiterate, 250 million children attend no school whatever. Inadequate supplies of food, clean water, or medical help diminish the opportunities of about half the world's population. Underfed, diseased, and untrained people perpetuate or even increase the already widespread poverty.

The richest and the poorest in the world now live virtually side by side, thanks to modern means of communication. It is no wonder that the anger of the poor is rising. In the past thirty years all well-meant efforts to bridge the gap between rich and poor have failed; in fact the gap has widened. And more, the good life among the well-to-do in the metropolitan centers of the world constantly raises the expectations of the poor. Yet the resources of their own societies cannot possibly meet those expectations. The poor can hardly improve themselves when they have no money for even the most basic necessities. Meanwhile the military expenditures of developed countries have risen to record heights; in 1982 their arms budgets were seventeen times higher than their aid to underdeveloped countries.

Disabled by poverty, non-Western lands also have to struggle with cultural disorientation. In most non-Western parts of the world, traditional cultures have been subverted by Western influence. A generally Western-educated elite follows a Western life style—sometimes with irresponsible extravagance—while still tied to native tradition. The bulk of the population is caught between tradition and Western ways, far closer to the parochial past than to the global present. The old ways, with their moral obligations justified by tradition and religion, are discredited by the influx of modernity from the West which, however, teaches no effective alternative morality. The moral vacuum encourages corruption, violence, and all-too-often utter in-humanity. Under these conditions stable governments have little chance to emerge, and without stable governments, effective self-help seems impossible. The historical record of the past thirty years shows a rising level of violence within the new states created after World War II and in the rest of the world as well. The faster the population increases, it seems, the greater the human toll of anger and violence. The brutal communist and fascist regimes before World War II have their imitators in many parts of today's world. Terrorism born of desperation and fanaticisim is rising around the world; the suppression of terrorism requires further violence.

Consider also the rising scarcity of the basic resources—arable land, water, and fuel—needed to support ever-larger populations. The new globalism has raised, for the first time in human existence, alarm over the limited physical resources of Planet Earth. Anxiety also has risen over the migration of the poor from villages to the ever-expanding cities, and from overcrowded lands to richer opportunities in Western Europe or North America. Such migration has already heightened racial, religious, and cultural tensions.

In other ways, too, the countries of the West themselves are no longer immune to the troubles they have created around the world. They are caught in headlong change. They suffer from the economic competition of newly industrialized countries, Japan foremost. More importantly, their self-confidence has been challenged, raising doubts about the universal benefits of their way of life. The widespread preoccupation with technology, for instance, has not refined human sensibilities; the improvement of human relations has not kept pace with technological innovation. As a result, the quality of life has suffered. The former sense of common purpose, moreover, has been undermined also by the free influx of foreign ways, which threatens the cultural security of Western countries, as does military belligerence around the world. Pushed on the defensive, they have built up their security forces as never before, thereby undermining their antimili-

tarist traditions. Indeed, they have created an "ultimate" weapon that can wipe out the human race altogether. Given the rising tide of hostility around the world, is it possible, outraged critics ask, to prevent these weapons from being used? Will the nuclear holocaust, killing all non-Westerners as well, be the culmination of Western civilization?

Optimists and pessimists, as well as pro-Western and anti-Western voices, clash furiously in the contemporary world. In the growing confusion, powerful groups of fundamentalists want to go back to the preglobal past, to the old creeds, and not only in the West. Many western-trained intellectuals in non-western countries cultivate ancient traditions. Others want to reorder the world according to universal prescriptions such as socialism or communism, which hold the past in contempt. Americans advertise their own experience as a prescription for global peace and happiness. Meanwhile many people, confused by the diverse views and data that impinge upon them, tend to shrink into themselves, concentrating on the work before them and seeking their own pleasures. They thereby aggravate the fragmentation and promote violence in a world that can serve its inhabitants only by raising their sights and improving their capacity for peaceful worldwide cooperation.

How now are individuals to find their way in this discordant world? How can they help? Will the culmination of Western civilization in the unification of the world be for the better or for the worse, for the advantage or ruin of humanity? In the disorientation and moral indifference prevailing at the end of the twentieth century, it is a sign of hope that millions of people everywhere work hard to make the best qualities of Western civilization available to all humanity.

Notes

1. Jawaharlal Nehru, Foreword to Jean Filliozat, *India* (1962).

Suggested Reading

Achebe, Chinua, *Man of the People* (1966). A great Nigerian novelist describes the ways of Nigerian politics after independence.

———, *No Longer at Ease* (1982). A novel describing the trials of a Nigerian returning home after being educated in England.

Barnet, Richard J., *The Lean Years: Politics in the Age of Scarcity* (1980). A useful survey of the relationship between population and world resources, with an eye to the politics involved.

Liang Heng and Judith Shapiro, *Son of the Revolution* (1983). A personal account of life in Mao's China.

Naipaul, V. S., *A Bend in the River* (1977). Insights into culture conflict in central Africa.

———, *India: A Wounded Civilization* (1978). An account of India in the clash of cultures by one of the world's foremost contemporary writers, himself the product of several cultures.

———, *Among the Believers: Islamic Journey* (1982). An account of culture change in Islamic society from Iran to Indonesia.

Nkrumah, Kwame, *Ghana: The Autobiography of Kwame Nkrumah* (1977). An excellent insight into the man who took the lead in bringing independence to Africa.

North-South: A Program for Survival. The Report of the Independent Commission on International Development Issues under the Chairmanship of Willy Brandt (1980). A significant document on the needs for peace, justice, and jobs in the Third World.

Schell, Jonathan, *The Fate of the Earth* (1982). The book everybody must read about the prospects of nuclear war.

Van Dusen, Henry P., *Dag Hammarskjöld: The Statesman and His Faith* (1967). An introduction to the work of the United Nations as reflected in the life of its most prominent official.

Vogel, Ezra, *Japan Number One* (1980). A challenging view of Japan's rapid advance.

Wilson, Dick, ed., *Mao Tse Tung in the Scale of History* (1977). A series of essays by experts on various aspects of Mao's work.

Review Questions

1. Do you consider the United Nations a useful institution? If so, in what respects is it useful?

2. What experience do you have of a non-Western country? Do you think American society is sufficiently well informed about non-Western cultures?

3. Suppose you were a member of the Chinese government. What problems do you see for your country's development? How would you try to solve these problems? Do you think that giving the Chinese people the same freedoms Americans enjoy would solve their problems?

4. Do you consider yourself an optimist or a pessimist? Which reaction do you think would make one a better citizen?

Index